D0138519

COGNITION, BRAIN, AND CONSCIOUSNESS

COGNITION, BRAIN, AND CONSCIOUSNESS

Introduction to Cognitive Neuroscience

Edited by

BERNARD J. BAARS

NICOLE M. GAGE

AMSTERDAM • BOSTON • HEIDELBERG • LONDON • NEW YORK • OXFORD
PARIS • SAN DIEGO • SAN FRANCISCO • SINGAPORE • SYDNEY • TOKYO

Academic Press is an imprint of Elsevier

Academic Press is an imprint of Elsevier
84 Theobald's Road, London WC1X 8RR, UK
30 Corporate Drive, Suite 400, Burlington, MA 01803, USA
525 B Street, Suite 1900, San Diego, California 92101-4495, USA

First edition 2007

Copyright © 2007 Elsevier Ltd. All rights reserved

No part of this publication may be reproduced, stored in a retrieval system
or transmitted in any form or by any means electronic, mechanical, photocopying,
recording or otherwise without the prior written permission of the publisher

Permissions may be sought directly from Elsevier's Science & Technology Rights
Department in Oxford, UK: phone (+44) (0) 1865 843830; fax (+44) (0) 1865 853333;
email: permissions@elsevier.com. Alternatively you can submit your request online by
visiting the Elsevier web site at http://elsevier.com/locate/permissions, and selecting
Obtaining permission to use Elsevier material

Notice
No responsibility is assumed by the publisher for any injury and/or damage to persons
or property as a matter of products liability, negligence or otherwise, or from any use
or operation of any methods, products, instructions or ideas contained in the material
herein. Because of rapid advances in the medical sciences, in particular, independent
verification of diagnoses and drug dosages should be made

British Library Cataloguing in Publication Data
A catalogue record for this book is available from the British Library

Library of Congress Cataloging in Publication Data
A catalog record for this book is available from the Library of Congress

ISBN: 978-0-12-373677-2

For information on all Academic Press publications
visit our web site at http://books.elsevier.com

Typeset by Charon Tec Ltd (A Macmillan Company), Chennai, India
www.charontec.com
Printed and bound in Hong Kong

07 08 09 10 11   10 9 8 7 6 5 4 3 2 1

Front cover: For centuries, epileptic episodes have been known to evoke striking visual experiences. The
outside cover art shows an acrylic painting by artist Craig Getzlaff, called Brainstorms #20. The artist writes,
"In these paintings, I am trying to communicate to the public and to myself what an immense experience an
epileptic seizure really is" (p. 27). The painting comes from a collection called *Visions: Artists living with
epilepsy* (*Source:* Schachter, 2003, with kind permission).

**Working together to grow
libraries in developing countries**

www.elsevier.com | www.bookaid.org | www.sabre.org

ELSEVIER   BOOK AID
International   Sabre Foundation

Contents

Chapter 4 The tools: Imaging the living brain
Bernard J. Baars and Thomas Ramsøy

Chapter 5 The brain
Bernard J. Baars

Chapter 6 Vision
Frank Tong and Joel Pearson

Chapter 12 Goals, executive control, and action
Elkhonon M. Goldberg and Dmitri H. Bougakov

Chapter 13 Emotion
Katharine McGovern

Chapter 14 Social cognition: Perceiving the mental states of others
Katharine McGovern

Preface

Keeping up to date with cognitive neuroscience is much like surfing the Big Wave at Waikiki Beach. New findings keep rolling in and maintaining a stable balance is a big challenge. It is exciting, fun and, at times, a little bit scary. But we keep climbing back on our mental surfboards, to catch the coming rollers of advancing science. This book aims to provide an overview of the emerging science of mind and brain in a way that is accessible to students and interested readers at all levels.

As Christopher Frith, Michael Posner and others have written, we are seeing a marriage of the cognitive and brain sciences, building on historic advances over the last few decades. Cognitive and perceptual mechanisms that were inferred from behavior can now be observed more directly in the brain, using a variety of novel brain imaging methods. For the first time, we can observe the living brain in real time, doing what it has evolved to do over hundreds of millions of years. The result is astonishingly rich, combining psychology and biology, medicine, biochemistry and physics. Yet most scientific studies use well-established psychological concepts and methods. As a result, we are now seeing how psychology and brain science complement each other in surprising and gratifying ways. The field of *cognitive neuroscience* is becoming a basic educational requirement in psychology, biology, education and medicine.

Cognitive neuroscience has been difficult to cover in a single course. Many instructors discover that they spend most of the term explaining the brain, with little time left for integrative topics. While understanding the brain is vital, an exclusive focus on anatomy can defeat the instructors' objectives.

This text approaches that challenge in several ways. First, the body of the text follows the gentlest learning curve possible, running along familiar lines: sensory perception in vision and audition, working memory, attention and consciousness, memory, executive functions, language and imagery, problem-solving, emotion, social cognition and development. The brain is introduced step by step, with gradually increasing sophistication. To make sense of the material we use a *functional framework* throughout the book. This widely accepted set of ideas allows us to see our major topics in a single schematic diagram, which grows in depth and detail over the course of the book. The functional framework can be seen from different perspectives. For example, memory stores may be viewed from an active working memory perspective; or perception, cognition and control may be seen as playing upon permanently stored information in the brain (Chapter 2). The framework helps either way.

A website for teachers and students is available at http://textbooks.elsevier.com via a free registration. Supportive materials for teachers include all figures and captions from the book in powerpoint format, as well as instructional video and multimedia files. Student materials include chapter reviews, quizzes, figures, and videos. The support site will be dynamic. Materials will be added and changed as warranted by new advances, and the authors are happy to consider additional ideas and suggestions for new supportive materials.

Instructors may present the chapters in any order that suits their goals. For advanced students, Chapters 4 and 5 on brain imaging and anatomy may be covered lightly. For introductory courses those chapters are essential and may be supplemented with the more challenging Appendix B (by Thomas Ramsøy and colleagues). The Appendices can also be used as convenient reference sources.

Neural networks have become increasingly important in cognitive psychology and neuroscience. A tutorial on modern neurocomputation is provided in Appendix A, written by a prominent expert, Igor Aleksander of Imperial College, London. It presents the material in the simplest possible way and, in courses that wish to emphasize neurocomputation, Appendix A can be read after Chapter 3, the introduction to neuronal processes and models.

A full range of brain disorders are covered, from HM and the case of Clive Wearing (Chapters 2 and 9), to blindsight, visual neglect, face blindness and other visual deficits. Chapter 11 on executive function covers disorders of undercontrol and overcontrol. In certain disorders, motor and cognitive control is not directly impaired at all; it seems as if patients are just not willing to act. At the other pole, patients sometimes spontaneously imitate another person's actions as if they cannot stop themselves. Such patients may stand up impulsively when the examining physician stands up. Disorders of overcontrol and undercontrol reveal basic aspects of human executive functioning.

Some disorders have close psychological analogs. Professional musicians, like pianist Van Cliburn, are sometimes unable to inhibit their tendency to sing along with instrumental playing. Highly trained experts can lose some executive control over automatic behaviors, especially if they are working under mental workload. On the opposite side, a classic symptom of severe depression is that patients seem unable to initiate and pursue actions. Brain regions involved in such 'purely psychological' deficits are often implicated in similar organic disorders. We see another striking simplification of the evidence, giving readers a chance to understand unifying principles rather than scattered facts.

Psychological topics are often simplified by brain evidence. For example, the verbal part of classical working memory – the capacity mentally to rehearse numbers and words – is now thought to be a part of our normal language capacity. Baddeley (2003) has emphasized the discovery that silent rehearsal activates the well-known speech regions of cortex. Thus the 'phonological loop' of traditional working memory is no longer seen as a separate cognitive feature, but rather as a silent way of using speech cortex. Similarly, Kosslyn and others have shown that visual imagery makes use of a subset of the cortical areas involved in normal visual perception (2004). Even more surprising, visual attention appears to be closely related to eye movement control. Athletes and musicians use the sensorimotor brain to engage in silent mental practice. Thus 'inner' and 'outer' processes seem to involve overlapping regions of the brain, a major simplification of the evidence.

While cognitive neuroscience does not always simplify things, it does so often enough to allow us to organize this text along recurring themes. This makes the material easier to teach and understand. It allows us to explore a wide range of basic topics, including emotion, social cognition and development.

The companion materials are designed to enrich student learning by way of vivid classroom demonstrations, images and learning points, using Powerpoint presentations and movie clips. A number of phenomena in the text can be best illustrated by way of experiments and movie clips. For example, a patient is shown with locked-in syndrome, able to communicate only by means of eye movements directed at a keyboard display. For comparison, we show patients who look superficially the same, but who are suffering from true coma.

At the end of each chapter, review questions and brain drawing exercises are designed to help students learn interactively. We particularly emphasize drawing and coloring exercises as a way to grasp the knotty three-dimensional organization of the brain.

This text covers some frontier topics in the ever-changing vista of cognitive neuroscience. One popular topic is the relationship of 'the mind' as we experience it and 'the brain' as we observe it: i.e. the historic topic of consciousness and its brain correlates. Alan Baddeley recently noted that, 'Perhaps the greatest change over the last twenty years within cognitive psychology and cognitive science . . . has been the acceptance of consciousness as a legitimate and tractable scientific problem'.

The renewed acceptance of consciousness has changed research in perception, memory and attention, as seen in pioneering work by Endel Tulving, Daniel Shachter, Gerald Edelman, Francis Crick, Christof Koch and numerous others. While some textbooks have added chapters on consciousness, we believe that the topic has now become so pervasive that it needs to be addressed throughout. As *Science* journal recently noted in its 125th anniversary issue, consciousness is now thought to be one of the major unsolved problems in biological science. While much remains to be learned, psychologists have long studied conscious processes under such headings as 'explicit cognition' and 'focal attention'. Those constructs are all assessed by the behavioral index of accurate report, which has been taken to signal conscious events since the beginning of psychophysics, some two centuries ago. Thus 'consciousness' can be seen as an umbrella label, much like 'memory' and 'perception', with a number of subtopics like subliminal perception, autobiographical memory and focal attention.

Voluntary control is also back on the forefront of research, sometimes under the rubric of 'strategic control' and 'executive functions'. In the brain, voluntary and non-voluntary functions can be clearly distinguished anatomically and physiologically. Robust differences also appear in functional brain imaging and behavior. Finally, the notion of executive control appears to be moving toward new insights on the 'self' of everyday life, as studied in social and personality psychology.

All these topics show a striking convergence of behavioral and brain evidence.

The brain basis of emotion and social relationships is developing as well. 'Mirror neurons' are involved with the ability to perceive intentions in others; unconscious 'threat faces' can stimulate the amygdala; and conflicting aspects of self-control are apparently played out in competing impulses in prefrontal cortex.

Cognitive neuroscience is challenging; it is also one of the most important frontiers in science. Students will be rewarded with a new depth of understanding of human nature, one that has never been quite as clear and convincing as it is today.

The editors are especially grateful to Dr Johannes Menzel, the Neurosciences Editor for Elsevier Publishers. We appreciate his consistent kindness, advice and support throughout a very challenging project. Indeed, the current text would have been impossible without the vast archival resources of Elsevier.

The first editor is particularly grateful to Dr Gerald Edelman and his colleagues at the Neurosciences Institute in San Diego, as a unique source of insight and collegial guidance on many topics in neuroscience. He is also indebted to the Mind Science Foundation of San Antonio, Texas, for supporting pioneering explorations in the cognitive neuroscience of consciousness. MSF's Board and Executive Director, Joseph Dial, have been especially active in working to unify behavioral and brain approaches to conscious experience (http://www.mindscience.org).

A number of colleagues and friends have helped us to gain a deeper understanding of mind and brain. There are too many to list here, but we want them to know of our gratitude. Among recent colleagues, Stan Franklin, Walter Freeman, William P Banks, E R John, Christof Koch, Francis Crick, Karl Pribram, Dan Dennett, Patricia Churchland, Patrick Wilken, Geraint Rees, Chris Frith, Stan Dehaene, Bjorn Merker, Jaak Panksepp, Stu Hameroff, Thomas Ramsøy, Antti Revonsuo, Henry Montandon, Murray Shanahan and many others have helped us to think through the issues. We have not always agreed, but we have always felt grateful for their constantly interesting and important ideas.

We have been fortunate to have the help of outstanding co-authors for this book. Their contributions are acknowledged in the Contents. This book would be poorer without their depth of knowledge and desire to communicate.

In a broader but very real sense, this book owes everything to the community of scholars and scientists who are cited in its pages.

In more personal terms, the first editor would like to acknowledge his loved ones for putting up with him during this daunting project. His parents, now deceased, are still a constant source of inspiration and guidance. He would also like to express his gratitude to Dr Barbara Colton for constant feedback and support, which have made the book much more readable and the editor far more sensible.

Ms A Lisette Isenberg was invaluable in helping to put this book through its final stages. Mr Shawn Fu provided a number of beautiful brain illustrations.

The second editor is particularly grateful to the first editor for sharing his concept and passion for this project. Our collaboration on this text began a few years ago during a 3-hour layover in Chicago and has blossomed into this full-blown project, along with a strong friendship. She is also indebted to many colleagues and friends with whom she has learned about how language gets wired up in the brain. There are too many to include here, but she is indebted to them all. She is particularly grateful to Greg Hickok, David Poeppel, Tim Roberts, Bruce Berg, Norm Weinberger, Bryna Siegal, Anne Spence and Kourosh Saberi for good conversations, on-going debates and thoughtful discussions through the years.

The second editor would like to acknowledge her family for their constant support during this project. Last, she is indebted to Kim for his insight and love.

List of contributors

Igor Aleksander
Imperial College of Science, Technology and
Medicine, London, UK

Bernard J. Baars
The Neurosciences Institute, La Jolla, California, USA

Daniela Balslev
Danish Research Centre for Magnetic Resonance,
Hvidovre Hospital, Denmark

Dmitri Bougakov
Department of Neurology, New York University
School of Medicine, New York, New York, USA

Jason M. Chein
Psychology Department, Temple University,
Philadelphia, Pennsylvania, USA

Melanie Cohn
Department of Psychology, University of Toronto,
Ontario, Canada

Nicole M. Gage
Department of Cognitive Sciences, University of
California Irvine, Irvine, California, USA

Elkhonon Goldberg
Department of Neurology, New York University
School of Medicine, New York, New York, USA

Mark H. Johnson
Center of Brain and Cognitive Development, School
of Psychology, Birkbeck College, London, UK

Katharine McGovern
California Institute for Integrative Studies,
San Francisco, California, USA

Morris Moscovitch
Department of Psychology, University of Toronto,
Toronto, and Baycrest Center for Geriatric Care,
Rotman Research Institute, North York, Ontario,
Canada

Olaf Paulson
Danish Research Centre for Magnetic Resonance,
Hvidovre Hospital, Denmark

Joel Pearson
Department of Psychology, Vanderbilt University,
South Nashville, Tennessee, USA

Thomas Ramsøy
Danish Research Centre for Magnetic Resonance,
Hvidovre Hospital, Denmark

Deborah Talmi
Department of Psychology, University of Toronto,
Toronto, Ontario, Canada

Frank Tong
Department of Psychology, Vanderbilt University,
South Nashville, Tennessee, USA

. . . from the brain, and from the brain alone, arise our pleasures, joys, laughter and jokes, as well as our sorrows, pains, griefs and tears. Through it, in particular, we think, see, hear, and distinguish the ugly from the beautiful, the bad from the good, the pleasant from the unpleasant. . . all the time the brain is quiet, a man can think properly.

Attributed to Hippocrates, 5th century BCE
(quoted by Kandel *et al.*, 1991).

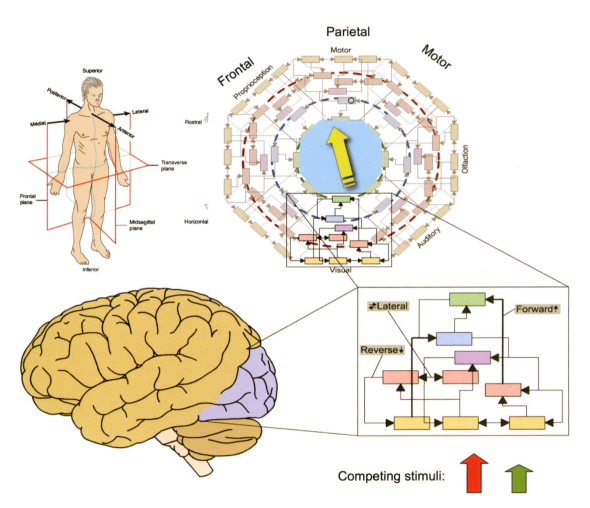

Upper left: The human body and its basic orientation planes. *Lower left*: a standard view of the brain from the left side. The left hemisphere is 'looking' left. The light blue region in the back of the brain is the occipital lobe. The diagram on the lower right shows a 'neural hierarchy,' a simplified way of showing neural connections in the cortex, and on the upper right we see the entire cortex as a 'circle of hierarchies.' The yellow arrow in the center depicts a common view of the role of perceptual consciousness in the brain. *Source*: Drake, 2004.

CHAPTER

1

Mind and brain

Bernard J. Baars

1.0 INTRODUCTION

This chapter gives an overview of cognitive neuroscience, the combined study of mind and brain. The brain is said to be the most complex structure in the known universe – with tens of billions of neurons, connected by trillions of transmission points. It can be changed by taking in molecules, as in drinking a glass of wine, and by external stimulation, like listening to exciting news. Some neuronal events happen over a thousandth of a second, while others take decades. In spite of this vast range of working conditions, we know many facts about the mind-brain that are basic and fairly simple. This book aims to let those facts stand out.

2.0 AN INVITATION TO MIND-BRAIN SCIENCE

It is hard to talk about the last dozen years in cognitive neuroscience without using words like 'remarkable' and 'revolutionary'. In a sense, a century of behavioral and brain science has received resounding confirmation with the new technology of brain imaging, the ability to observe the living brain in real time. That does not

Cognition, Brain, and Consciousness, edited by B. J. Baars and N. M. Gage
ISBN: 978-0-12-373677-2

Copyright 2007, Elsevier Ltd. All rights reserved.

FIGURE 1.1 Rembrandt, The Anatomy Lesson of Dr Tulp. This historic painting by Rembrandt shows the excitement of the first revolution in scientific thinking about the human brain and body. Dr Tulp, on the right, is demonstrating how the muscles of the forearm control hand movements. The systematic dissection of human cadavers signaled a rebirth of careful empirical observation which still guides us today. *Source*: Masquelet, 2005.

mean, of course, that we have merely confirmed what we thought we knew. Rather, the ability to record from the living brain has proved to be fruitful in bringing out new evidence, raising new ideas and stirring new questions. Many scientists have a sense that a great barrier – between the study of mind and brain – is being bridged. Historically tangled questions continue to yield quite beautiful insights.

Along with this feeling of progress has come a great expansion. Just ten years ago, behavioral scientists might not have seen a connection between human cognition and the genetic revolution, with brain molecules, or with the mathematics of networks. Today, those topics are all part of a connected island chain of knowledge. Previously avoided topics are now anchored in plausible brain correlates – topics like conscious experience, unconscious processes, mental imagery, voluntary control, intuitions, emotions and even the self. Some puzzles seem bigger than before – the nature of the permanent memory trace, for example. There seem to be more continuities than ever before between psychological and brain studies of perception, memory and language.

In some cases, brain evidence helps to resolve puzzles that psychologists have wrestled with for decades. For example, in the study of attention a debate has raged between 'early' and 'late selection' of attended information. People may pay attention to a coffee cup based on low-level visual features like color, texture and location. Alternatively, they might focus on the coffee cup

based on higher-level properties like 'usefulness for drinking hot liquids'. Evidence can be found for both. After decades of debate, brain studies have now shown that attentional selection can affect neurons at almost *any* level of the visual system. The answer therefore seems to be that there can be *both* early and late selection, as many psychologists have also argued. In many cases like this we find surprising convergence between brain and behavioral evidence.

3.0 SOME STARTING POINTS

3.1 Distance: seven orders of magnitude

To understand the mind-brain, it helps to have an idea of its orders of magnitude, the powers of ten that tell us the basic units of interest. From front to back, a brain is perhaps a seventh of a meter long. If you take one step, the length of your stride is about one meter (a little more than a yard). If you raise that length to the next order of magnitude, 10 meters, you might obtain the rough length of a classroom. One hundred meters is a standard sprinting distance, and a thousand meters or one kilometer is a reasonable length for a city street. By the time we raise the exponent to 10^7 meters, or $10\,000\,km$, we are already at 6000 miles, the distance from coast to coast in North America, or from Paris to the equator in Europe and Africa. That is ten million steps. In order to understand

TABLE 1.1 Distance from 10^{-7} m to one meter

1 If you drink alcohol your brain will change. Alcohol molecules are about 10^{-7} meters in size (Figure 1.2) (0.0000001).
2 If you swallow a tranquillizer, the chemical concentration that flows across some of your synapses will be changed, at 10^{-6} m for the width of a synapse (one-millionth of a meter, or one micron).
3 The cell bodies of neurons are about a hundred times larger than synapses, around 10^{-4}.
4 However, neurons do not act alone; they are grouped with others in small networks, perhaps ten times larger than single neurons. Small cortical columns are about 10^{-3} m or one millimeter in diameter. We have now reached one-thousandth of a meter, which we can see with the naked eye.
5 Brain maps, such as those in the visual system, can be quite large. The first cortical map of the light array is called area V1, the first visual region of cortex. It is about the size of a credit card, several square centimeters in size, or 10^{-2} m^2.
6 Visual maps don't work in isolation. They are part of brain wide activation networks that interact in constantly changing patterns. Such widespread networks operate at an order of magnitude of ten centimeters (10^{-1}), well inside the visible range if you could see brain activity through the scalp. Indeed, some current methods observe the brain's constantly varying activity by simply shining a laser through the shaved scalp of rats or other small mammals. One can watch the flow of blood to brain surfaces that are active, just as we can see increased blood flow to the skin when people have been running hard.

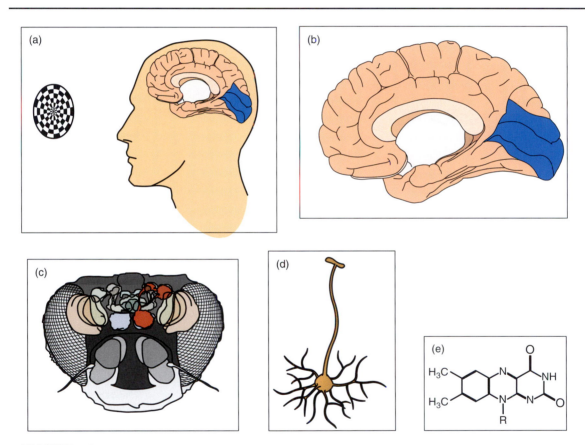

FIGURE 1.2 Spatial powers of ten. (a) A brain image of a subject looking at a rotating black and white stimulus, so that his visual cortex (in the rear of the brain) is intensely stimulated. (b) A midline view of the cortex, with area V1 marked – the first place where the visual pathway reaches cortex. V1 is about the size of a credit card. (c) The head of a fruit fly. The fruit fly brain has about 1 000 000 neurons. A single neuron is shown in (d). Neurons vary in size, but they are extraordinarily small; we have tens of billions in our brains. (e) A dopamine molecule. Dopamine plays an essential role in working memory, in the experience of pleasure, and in the control of muscles. Parkinson's disease is one result of a decline of the dopamine system. From (a) to (e), the range of sizes involves about seven orders of magnitude.

the most important magnitudes of the brain we can simply imagine going the other way, seven orders of magnitude from one meter to 10^{-7} (Table 1.1). Considered this way, it is an awesome prospect in size and complexity.

Visible behavior takes place anywhere from a centimeter and up. A finger striking a keyboard moves only a few centimeters. When we speak, our tongue moves only a centimeter or two. A single walking step is about a meter long. Most people are a little less than

FIGURE 1.3 Small molecules can change the brain. Some of the smallest molecules like nitrous oxide (N_2O) can change specific brain functions. That came as a big surprise to Western medical doctors around 1800, like the ones above, shown in a drawing by a medical student in 1808. However, such facts continue to surprise us. Nitric oxide (NO), which is toxic when breathed, is produced in tiny quantities as a crucial neurotransmitter. The erectile drug, Viagra, promotes NO transmission in penile blood vessels. *Source*: Adelman and Smith, 2004.

two meters in height, and the longest neurons in the human body may be about 1 meter.

3.1.1 A note about neurochemicals: the smallest level

Neurotransmitters range in size, and diffuse across gaps between neurons – the synapses – which vary between 25 nanometers to 100 micrometers (Iversen, 2004). Most brain-changing chemicals promote or block molecular communication between nerve cells. The list of everyday chemicals that change the brain includes nicotine, alcohol, oxygen (in the air), toxic gases like carbon monoxide, glucose from the liver and sucrose from foods, chocolate, coffee, nerve toxins like lead, and a long list of medications (Figure 1.3). It is hard to overstate the importance of such molecules in everyday life.

Molecular messengers in the brain can be divided into two large groups. The first group, the neuromodulators, are 'sprayed' throughout large parts of the forebrain from small fountain-like clumps of cell bodies at the base of the brain. These are informally called 'spritzers', because they secrete neurochemicals from widely dispersed axons, to modulate large parts of the brain. However, neuromodulators can have local effects if they lock into specific types of local receptors. For example, while dopamine is spread very widely, the D1/D2 dopamine receptors are believed to have local effects in

the frontal cortex related to working memory (Gibbs and D'Esposito, 2006). Thus, a very wide-spread neuromodulator, dopamine, can have more local effects when it locks into receptors in a specific region of the brain.

The second major group of neurotransmitters have much more localized actions. They are mostly peptides, i.e. small subunits of proteins, which are secreted directly into synaptic gaps. More than 40 types of neuropeptides have now been found throughout the brain. The two best-known examples are *glutamate*, the most widespread excitatory neurotransmitter in the cortex, and *GABA*, the most common inhibitory neurotransmitter.

Scientific advances often follow our ability to observe at different magnitudes. The wave of discoveries we are seeing today results from our new ability to observe the living brain. The ability to observe over some seven orders of spatial magnitude makes mind-brain science possible.

3.2 Time: ten orders of magnitude

Human beings function over a great range of time scales (Table 1.2). Behaviorally, one-tenth of a second (100 ms) is an important unit to keep in mind. The fastest (simple) reaction time to a stimulus is about 100 milliseconds, and the time it takes for a sensory stimulus to become conscious is typically a few hundred milliseconds. This makes sense in the environment in which human

TABLE 1.2   Time: ten orders of magnitude, from years to milliseconds

1   When you listen to a high musical note, your auditory nerve is firing as fast as the sound waves that vibrate your ear drum, up to 1000 times per second, or one wave per millisecond (ms). (Reminder: cycles per second = Hertz = Hz).

2   Neurons can fire as fast as 1000 Hz, although the average neuron in the cortex fires about ten times per second.

3   The auditory nerve is a bundle of nerve axons, each of which fires slower than 1000 cycles per second, but together they can respond at millisecond speed. Some sensory events are even faster. In a remarkable feat, our brain can distinguish differences between sounds arriving at the two ears, down to several *microseconds*, or millionths of a second. That is 1000 times faster than the fastest firing rate of a neuron (see Chapter 7). However, for our purposes, milliseconds are the most useful unit at the small end of the time scale.

4   By comparison, if you count to yourself from one to ten, your counting takes place on the order of seconds, or tens of seconds. If you study this chapter carefully, it will take you an hour or more – more than three thousand seconds (sorry about that!).

5   Going back down the scale again, if the sound track of a movie is delayed by a fraction of a second behind the video, you will notice a disconnect between the sounds and the movements of an actor's mouth. The break-up of audio-visual synchrony occurs after about 100 milliseconds (ms) lag, or one-tenth of a second. This is another reason to think of one-tenth of a second as a special order of magnitude.

6   One hundred milliseconds is also about the fastest we can react to an event that we know will come soon, as in starting a car at a traffic light (*simple reaction time*). One-tenth of a second is also about the rate of individual alpha and theta waves in the brain. (Alpha waves range between 8–12 Hz, and theta between 5–7 Hz.) It is also the order of magnitude required to become conscious of a sensory stimulus.

beings evolved. If you took several seconds to react to a hungry predator, you will soon provide it with a tasty protein snack. Biologically, you would not get a chance to reproduce. On the other hand, if you tried to react as fast as 10 milliseconds – one-hundredth of a second – you would be driving your brain faster than it could combine the sights and sounds of a running tiger. It would be hard to tell what direction a predator might be coming from. So the 100 ms range gives a useful middle ground.

Brain events at different time and spatial scales go on at the same time, like the elements of a symphony – notes, phrases and whole musical movements. When you listen to a song, you are conscious of only a few notes at any time, but the notes you hear fit into a larger cognitive structure which makes it possible to appreciate how the entire song is developing. Movie frames are shown at 24 images per second, or about 40 milliseconds per frame, to show smooth movement. (That's why they call them movies!) Slower rates than 24 Hz start to look jerky, like the early silent movies. However, the plot of a movie takes place over minutes and hours. In a mystery film, if you cannot remember the crime at the beginning, the fact that the perpetrator is found at the end will not make sense. Thus, understanding movie plots requires cognitive integration over many minutes. All these time scales must somehow be combined. Each kind has a structure and a typical time range. The brain keeps track of all simultaneously.

At the longer end of the time scale, it can take years to learn a difficult skill, like skiing or playing guitar. Infants learn their first language over several years, while adults tend to keep their basic personality structure over decades. Such long-term processes depend upon the same brain as 100-millisecond events. In the time domain, therefore, we need to understand about ten orders of magnitude, from one-thousandth of a second (a millisecond) for a single neuron to fire, to more than 100 000 seconds per day, and tens of millions of seconds per year.

3.3   The need to make inferences – going beyond the raw observations

Science depends on a constant process of inference, going from raw observations to explanatory concepts. Thousands of years ago, when human beings began to wonder about lights in the sky like the sun, the moon, and the stars, they noticed that some were predictable and some were not. The 'wanderers' in the night sky were called *planete* by the Greeks, and we call them 'planets' in English. These wandering lights became a source of fascination. It was not until the 17th century that their paths were understood and predicted. The solution to the wandering lights puzzle was to realize that the planets were giant earth-like spheres revolving in orbit around the biggest object of them all, the sun. It took centuries of argument and observation to settle on that solution. Isaac Newton had to invent the infinitesimal calculus to bring the debate down to a simple equation: planetary orbits can be predicted from the simple fact that gravitational force equals the mass of the orbiting planet times its acceleration (or squared velocity). Notice that all those words – 'sun', 'planet', 'force', and 'gravity' – are *inferred concepts*. They are far removed from the first observations of lights in the sky (Figure 1.4), yet they explain those raw observations: they are explanatory inferences.

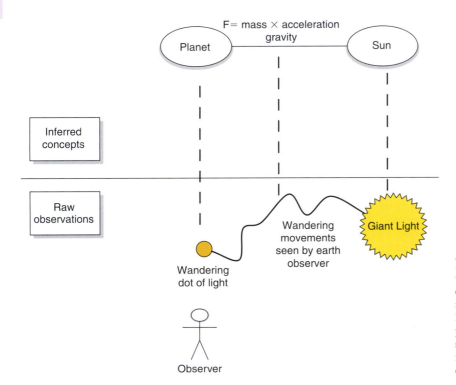

F= mass × acceleration

FIGURE 1.4 Making inferences about lights in the night sky. To an earthbound observer the planets look like wandering lights in the night sky. After many years of careful astronomical observations, Isaac Newton and others determined that the complex wandering path of the planets reflects a very simple reality. The leap from raw observation to inferred concepts and explanations is a crucial part of science.

All science depends upon careful observations and conceptual inferences. The resulting explanatory framework has been called a 'nomological network' – that is, a network of labeled concepts and relationships, which together provide us a sense of understanding. Along the way, successful science allows us to make more accurate predictions, and to apply the resulting knowledge in ways that sometimes transform life. It all begins with exact observations and plausible inferences.

These basic ideas have a direct bearing on cognitive neuroscience. When we talk about cognition – language, learning, or vision – we also use *inferred concepts*, which must be firmly anchored in reliable observations. For example, the capacity of immediate memory – the kind we can mentally rehearse – is about seven plus or minus two items, as George A. Miller famously noted in a paper called 'The magical number seven plus or minus two' (1956). That number seems to apply to many kinds of randomly selected items: colors, numbers, short words, musical notes, steps on a rating scale, and so on. The recent consensus is that the actual capacity of immediate memory is even less than seven, about four different items (Cowan, 2001). But the most important point is the remarkable consistency in the data. Try to remember ten different foods on your shopping list, for example, and you will find that only about seven are remembered – and if you are busy thinking about other things, that number

drops to four. It is an amazingly narrow limit for a giant brain.

There are only a few basic conditions for obtaining the size of working memory. One is that each item must be attended for only a brief time – perhaps several seconds – so that it cannot be memorized well enough to enter permanent memory. A second condition is that the items must be *unpredictable* from existing knowledge. If we ask people to remember a regular number series like 0, 5, 10, 15, 20, 25 . . . they only need to remember the rule, and it will seem that their working memory capacity is endless. Cognitive concepts like 'working memory' are the product of decades of experimental observations which finally become so solid that we can summarize the evidence in one basic concept (Figure 1.5).

Ideas like working memory have turned out to be useful, but it is quite possible that we will find a more attractive way to think about them tomorrow. All inferred concepts are somewhat tentative. Newton's idea of gravity dominated physics for three centuries, then Einstein found another way to look at the evidence. Scientific concepts are not metaphysical certainties. They are always subject to revision.

Cognitive neuroscience is also based on inferences from raw observations. Because brain scans have the appearance of physical objects that we can see and touch,

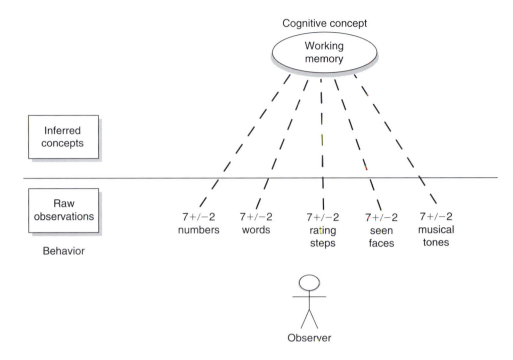

Cognitive concept

Working memory

Inferred concepts

Raw observations

Behavior

7+/−2 numbers   7+/−2 words   7+/−2 rating steps   7+/−2 seen faces   7+/−2 musical tones

Observer

FIGURE 1.5 Cognitive concepts are based on consistent behavioral observations. Concepts like 'working memory' are not given in nature. They emerge after many years of testing, when a large body of evidence seems to be explained by an inferred concept. Working memory was proposed in 1974 after two decades of study of immediate memory. Today it has expanded in scope, so that visual, verbal, and other temporary buffers are called working memories.

BOX 1.1   Imaging the living brain

The very idea of observing the living brain in action was unimaginable a decade or two ago. Methods from physics and molecular biology have been applied to the formidable problem of recording brain activity. A perfect method would be able to follow tens of billions of neurons, and sample each one a thousand times per second. It should then be possible to track the constantly shifting interplay between smaller and larger groups of neurons, involving trillions of possible connections. By analogy, a perfect spy satellite in orbit around the earth would be able to see every single human being, as well as the changing relationships between individuals and groups, from families to entire nations.

Such a perfect method does not exist. Our understanding of the brain is a kind of collage of many fragments of the puzzle, glued together to make a reasonable picture of the whole. But thinking about a perfect observation method gives us the parameters we might aim for.

Brain imaging has been a breakthrough technology for cognitive neuroscience, adding new evidence to decades of cognitive psychology, behavioral conditioning methods, psychophysics and fundamental brain science. Before these techniques matured, our knowledge came from animal studies and from the haphazard injuries incurred by

human beings. But brain injuries are extremely imprecise, and even to describe the damage, neurologists often had to rely on post-mortem examination of patients' brains. The brain can often compensate for injuries, and lesions change over time as cells die and adaptation occurs, so that post-mortems do not necessarily reflect the injury at the time of diagnosis. Animal studies relied on presumed homologies – i.e. similarities across species – which were often not persuasive to everybody. No other animals besides humans have language and other distinctive human specializations. It was therefore very difficult to understand brain functions.

Many of those problems were resolved when it became possible to observe the living human brain, first by electroencephalography (EEG), then by X rays, then computer tomography (the study of slices – from the Greek word for 'slice,' *tomos* – based on X-rays). Today, we have more than a dozen techniques that are rapidly evolving toward greater precision and a broader range of application. The most widely used methods are EEG, positron emission tomography (PET), magnetic resonance imaging (MRI), functional MRI, and magnetoencephalography (MEG). See Chapter 4 for a detailed description of these and other new techniques for investigating the dynamic human brain.

---

we are tempted to think that we are seeing 'raw reality' in brain scans. But that is a seductive fallacy. Electroencephalography (EEG) is an inferential measurement of brain activity, as is functional magnetic resonance imaging (fMRI), positron emission tomography (PET),

and all the other advanced tools we have today (Box 1.1). Even recording from neurons only gives us a tiny sample of single cell firing among tens of billions of cells. Neurons make perhaps ten thousand connections, and there is evidence that even the input branches of a single

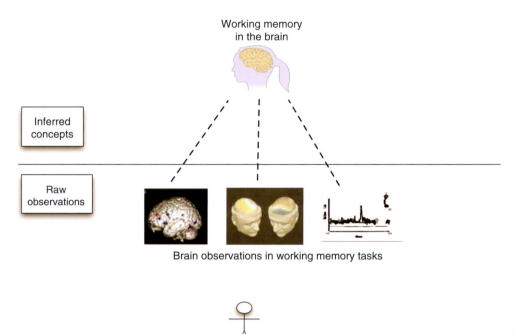

Working memory
in the brain

Inferred
concepts

Raw
observations

Brain observations in working memory tasks

Observer

FIGURE 1.6 Brain measures of working memory are also inferential. Working memory functions in the brain have been studied using behavioral measures, but also with fMRI, EEG, and single-neuron recordings. Each of these measures has its pros and cons, but none of them is the 'ultimate measure' of working memory. Overall, brain indices of working memory converge well with behavioral measures. Cognitive neuroscience is based on the study of such combined sources of evidence, but we must be prepared to find that our current concepts may be interpreted in a different way.

neuron (the dendrites) may compute information (Alle and Geiger, 2006). Therefore, measuring the electrical activity of single neurons is only a tiny sample of a very complex dance of molecules and electromagnetic fluxes. Recent imaging techniques are extraordinarily useful, but they still involve inferences about the working brain.

Yet we must make *some* simplifying assumptions – that is how science develops. It is just important to keep in mind what the assumptions are, and to be prepared to change them if necessary. Figure 1.6 illustrates this point. In cognitive neuroscience we make inferences based on behavioral and brain observations. We don't *observe* 'attention' or 'working memory' directly. For that reason, it is essential to understand the nature of the evidence that we use to make those inferences.

3.4 The importance of convergent measures

When that mythical first cave dweller pointed to a star at night, we can imagine that nobody else in the clan believed him or her. What lights in the sky? The sky was the abode of the gods; everybody knew that. That kind of skepticism is the norm. When Galileo first used a crude telescope to look at the moons of Venus, some critics refused to look through the telescope, since they held that only the unaided eye could tell the truth.

Skepticism is still the norm, and science always makes use of *converging measures* to verify observations. Today, any major hypothesis in cognitive neuroscience is tested over and over again, using single-neuron recordings, animal studies, EEG, fMRI, MEG, and behavioral measures such as verbal reports and reaction time. No single study settles a hypothesis. Every major claim requires multiple sources of support.

Part of the debate is focused on exactly what it is that is being measured. Every new method of observation is met with that kind of question. The most popular method today is functional magnetic resonance imaging (fMRI). But as we will see, there is ongoing debate about what it is that fMRI measures. The same is true of behavioral measures of working memory, single cell recordings, EEG, and all the rest.

3.5 Major landmarks of the brain

How does brain activity relate to cognition? We will present functional brain images to guide you in interpreting the studies presented in this text. But brain function is always grounded in anatomy, and we will cover the basic geography of the brain for that reason. Figure 1.7 (top) shows the outside view of the left hemisphere, also called the *lateral view*. Below it is the *medial view* of the right hemisphere, also called the

Medial (midline) view

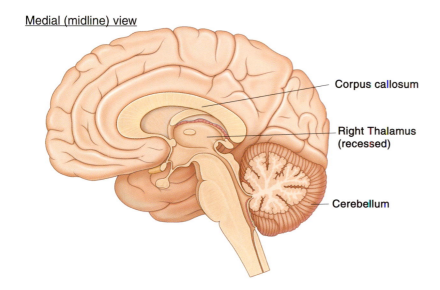

Corpus callosum

Right Thalamus (recessed)

Cerebellum

Lateral (side) view

Central sulcus (separates posterior and frontal cortex)

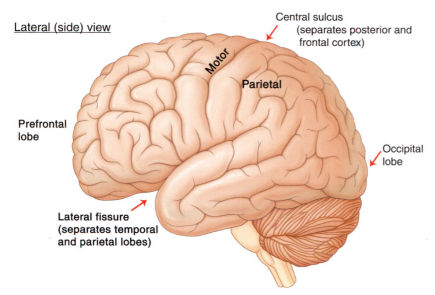

Motor

Parietal

Prefrontal lobe

Occipital lobe

Lateral fissure (separates temporal and parietal lobes)

FIGURE 1.7 The brain: lateral and medial views. Top panel shows a view of the left hemisphere from a lateral (outside) viewpoint. The front of the brain is on the left side of the figure and the back of the brain is on the right side. The four lobes and the cerebellum are labeled. The lower panel shows a medial view of the right hemisphere with major structures highlighted. This view is also called the mid-sagittal section of the brain. *Source*: Drake *et al.*, 2005.

mid-sagittal section of the brain. It is a slice through the midline, from the nose to the back of the head. Every other slice that runs parallel to it is called *sagittal* (see Figure 1.8).

It is important to learn the major landmarks in the brain. Some of the most important ones are the big folds or valleys in the cortex, the outer structure of the brain. The largest valley runs along the midline between the right and left hemispheres and is called the *longitudinal fissure*. A second large fold runs forward at a slant along the side of the brain, and is called the *lateral sulcus* (from the word for the 'ditch' or 'furrow'). The lateral sulcus divides the 'arm' of the temporal lobe from the 'body' of the main cortex. Since the temporal lobe always 'points'

in the direction of the eyes, identifying it is the easiest way to tell which way the brain is facing. Spotting the temporal lobe is one of the first things to do when looking at a brain picture.

The *corpus callosum*, another major landmark, is a great fiber bridge flowing between the right and left hemispheres. It is visible on the lower portion of Figure 1.7 as a curved section that begins behind the frontal lobe and loops up and to the back, ending just in front of the cerebellum. When the corpus callosum is cut, it looks white to the naked eye because it consists of white matter (i.e. nerve axons covered by white myelin cells, filled with fat-like lipid molecules). The corpus callosum was called the 'calloused (or tough) body',

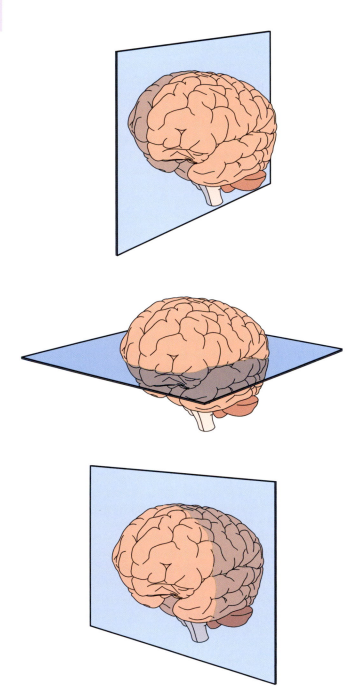

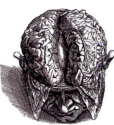

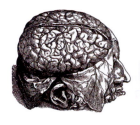

FIGURE 1.8 The major planes of section (cuts). The three main slices or sections of the brain. Top panel shows a vertical section of the brain, called *sagittal*, from the front of the brain to the back. When the slice is exactly through the midline, between the two hemispheres, it is called *mid-sagittal*. The center panel shows a *horizontal* slice through the brain. The lower panel shows a *coronal* section (named for its crown shape) like a sliced sausage. (These terms have synonyms that are explained in Chapter 5.)

FIGURE 1.9 Andreas Vesalius, showing a dissected arm and hand. (Top) Andreas Vesalius was a Belgian physician (1514–1564) who overturned the traditional teaching of anatomy by performing post-mortem dissections of human bodies. He is shown here displaying the exposed hand and arm. The arm and hand were important to Vesalius as evidence for the divine hand in worldly affairs. Until Vesalius, it was widely believed that women had one less rib than men, based on the Biblical story of Adam and Eve. Real dissections of human bodies were not performed, and accurate drawings were rare. Vesalius's published his new anatomy, called *On the Fabric of the Human Body* in 1543, the same year as Copernicus' *On the revolution of the celestial spheres*, the revolutionary book about the solar system. Both works became famous and hotly debated. They are milestones in the history of science. *Source*: Masquelet, 1986. (Bottom) These remarkable ink drawings of the exposed brain are attributed to the great painter Titian, who illustrated Vesalius' classic anatomy, which was a true work of art as well as science. Notice that the two cortical hemispheres on the right have been separated to show the corpus callosum, the great fiber bridge running between the two halves, with some 100 million neuronal axons. To the early anatomists it appeared to be a tough or calloused tissue, and was therefore called the 'calloused body', *corpus callosum* in Latin. *Source*: Squire *et al.*, 2003.

because that is how it appeared to early anatomists who named these structures. It was discovered early on, because it can be exposed simply by gently separating the two great hemispheres. In Figure 1.9, the corpus callosum is shown beautifully in a classic drawing by the great Renaissance painter Titian, drawn for the first detailed book of anatomy by Antonio Vesalius.

A final landmark is the central sulcus, which divides the rear half of the brain (the posterior half) from the frontal lobe. The posterior cortex is predominantly sensory, with visual, spatial, auditory and body-sense regions, while the frontal lobe is motor and cognitive. The central sulcus is a clear dividing line between the input and output-related areas of cortex.

Locating these three major folds is the first step in orienting yourself.

The cortical lobes flow over to the inside of each half cortex, as we will see. Because it is not easy to understand a knotty three-dimensional object from all perspectives, it helps to use your own hands (in the orientations shown in Figure 1.8) to remind yourself. It is essential to know the major lobes and other major brain divisions, just as it is to know the names of the continents in earth geography. Throughout this text, we will be presenting brain studies and relating their findings to our understanding of human cognition. These basic brain figures will serve as a guide for interpreting the data of neuroimaging studies that are provided throughout this text.

4.0 SOME HISTORY, AND ONGOING DEBATES

The idea of the brain as the source of our experiences goes back many centuries, as shown by the quotation at the beginning of this chapter (attributed to Hippocrates some 2500 years ago). But careful, cumulative study of the brain really began with the Renaissance. The Antwerp anatomist, Andreas Vesalius, was the first to publish a detailed atlas of the human body, including the brain, in 1543. Before that time, religious and legal prohibitions made it a crime to dissect human cadavers. A century later, a famous Rembrandt painting called 'The Anatomy Lesson of Dr Tulp' shows the sense of wonder felt by physicians actually to be able to see the human body in detail (see Figure 1.1). Leonardo da Vinci made sketches of the human skull and body at about the same time (1490–1510). The Renaissance was interested in everything human, and the effort to understand the brain grew as part of that broad sense of curiosity.

Today's research is deeply rooted in the history of science. The behavioral sciences date their beginnings to the 19th century. But careful brain studies go to the very beginnings of modern science in the European Renaissance, the time of Galileo, Copernicus, Newton, and Descartes. Color perception really began to be studied with Newton's prism experiments in 1665. The greatest work on brain anatomy since antiquity was compiled by Andreas Vesalius, an Antwerp physician, in the year 1543, the same year that Copernicus' book on the revolution of the planets appeared. The invention of the light microscope by Leeuwenhoek and others in the 1600s leads straight to discoveries about nerve cells and their properties by Santiago Ramon y Cajal in the 19th and 20th centuries.

One pattern in the history of science is that the more we learn, the more we can see simple and general patterns in the evidence. We will bring out these simplifying principles throughout the book.

The Renaissance origins of brain science are clearly apparent even today. Brain terminology is based on Latin, the international language of science for many centuries. We still talk about the *occipital, temporal, parietal*, and *frontal lobes* of the *cortex*, all Latin words. Because early studies were done with the naked eye or with simple microscopes, most were named for the way they looked visually. Thus, the *thalamus* means the 'bridal chamber', the *amygdala* is the 'almond', *cortex* means 'outer bark', and so on. Practically all brain terms use everyday Latin words. That fact will simplify your understanding of anatomical terms, and we will mention the origins of each term when it is introduced.

The human brain evolved over some 200 million years from early mammalian origins. It is very complex, even the parts that can be seen with the naked eye. Generations of scholars have contributed to its study. For example, Rene Descartes (Figure 1.10) is known today mostly as a mathematician and philosopher. But he was also a careful student of the brain. In one famous observation he obtained the eye of an ox, scraped off the tissue from the back of the eyeball to expose its tough white outer shell, the *sclera*, and showed that light images coming through the lens of the eye were projected onto the white sclera like a screen, so that one could see projected images by pointing the eyeball at a well-lit object. It astonished many people that the visual stimulus was projected *upside-down* on the back of the eye. Descartes was able to show that this is a direct result of the optics of the lens[1].

4.1 The mind and the brain

Descartes is often considered to be the originator of modern mind/body philosophy. The basic question seems simple: is the world basically mental or physical?

---

[1]It still baffles many people that we do not experience the visual world upside-down, since that is how the image is projected on the retina. What do you think is the answer?

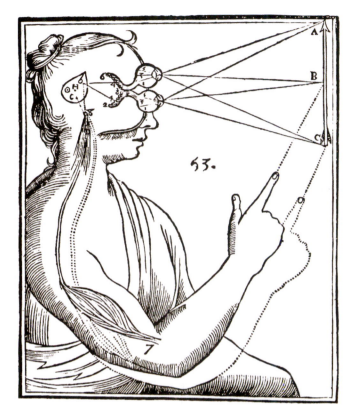

FIGURE 1.10 Descartes: philosopher, mathematician, brain explorer. Rene Descartes (left) and his figure showing the optics of the eyes (right). Because Descartes was convinced that the soul or psyche was a unified whole, he rejected the idea that paired structures of the brain could support the soul. But almost all of the brain *looks* doubled to the naked eye: two hemispheres, two eyes and ears, two subcortical halves, and two sides of the cerebellum. Descartes therefore decided that the tiny pineal gland, which looks like a tiny dot to the naked eye, must be the point of connection between the divine soul and the earthly body. Unfortunately for Descartes, microscopic studies after the 17th century showed that the pineal gland also has bilateral symmetry, just like the rest of the brain. *Source*: Bennett, 1999.

Or, in today's language, can your conscious experience be explained by neurons? Perhaps nerve cells themselves are just ideas in the minds of scientists. The brain basis of consciousness has now become mainstream in cognitive neuroscience (Edelman, 1989; Palmer, 1999; Koch, 1996; Tulving, 2002; Baars *et al.*, 2003a). Numerous articles have appeared in the last fifteen years. In July of 2005, *Science* magazine listed 'the biological basis of consciousness' as one of the top questions in science today. Nobel-winning scientists like Francis Crick, Gerald Edelman and Herbert Simon have devoted years of effort to the question.

In everyday language we constantly switch back and forth between the language of mind and brain. We take a *physical* aspirin for a *mental* headache. We walk to the *physical* refrigerator because we experience a *mental* craving for ice cream. Do conscious experiences 'cause' physical actions, or vice versa? Common sense doesn't care. It just jumps back and forth between the discourse of mind and body. But things get complicated when we try to think more carefully. In the physical realm of aspirins and refrigerators, ordinary causality explains how things happen. Ice cream melts in the sun and aspirins dissolve in water. They follow the laws of physics and chemistry. But mental events are affected by *goals*, *emotions* and *thoughts*, which seem to follow different laws. Ice cream does not melt because it *wants* to – but humans eat ice cream because they want to. Human language has thousands of words to describe desires and experiences, but those words do not apply to physical objects.

As we will see, for the first time, we have a large body of empirical evidence that has a direct bearing on the question of conscious cognition. Some brain regions, like the 'ventral visual stream', are widely believed to support conscious contents, the visual events that people can easily report. There is good evidence, however, that not all brain regions support conscious, reportable events. For example, the dorsal visual stream enables hand-eye coordination in reaching for an object, but there is good evidence that by themselves, these brain areas do not support conscious contents (Goodale *et al.*, 1991). Similarly, it is believed that brain regions like the cerebellum do not support conscious experiences. There is growing agreement that the relationship of mind to brain is an empirical, testable question.

4.2 Biology shapes cognition and emotion

Human emotions turn out to have deep biological roots in the mammalian brain, regulated by more recent layers of the neocortex. As a result, the evolutionary history of the human brain, going back some two hundred million years to early mammals, is relevant to a host of important questions. Maternal love and infant attachment now seem to be rooted in an ancient mammalian structure called the peri-aqueductal gray matter or PAG. Vocalizations of distress and attachment seem to have an evolutionary connection to the emergence of speech prosody – the sing-song of language – and even to music. Thus, biology turns out to have relevance in many different ways.

More than anyone else, Charles Darwin helped to establish the biological context of the human species. Darwin made numerous observations about emotional expressions in animals and humans (Figure 1.11). For hundreds of years people must have noticed the similarities, but in Europe and other regions it was essentially taboo to point out those similarities. There is now good evidence about the emotional brain regions that humans share with other mammals (Panksepp, 2005). In Darwin's time that idea was very controversial. Today, Darwin's book *The Expression of Emotions in Animals and Man* is considered a classic (Ekman, 2003).

Darwin would never deny the importance of culture and environment. Humans are the most adaptable species we know, the one most capable of learning new things by way of cultural transmission. The 'nature-nurture' controversy is not really a divisive debate any more. Most scientists see human behavior as combining biology, culture and environment (see Chapter 15).

Helmoltz was a great sensory physiologist and psychologist in the 19th century, whose works on vision and audition are still read (Figure 1.12). But his biggest claim

FIGURE 1.11 Charles Darwin and the biology of mind. Many people in the centuries after Rene Descartes were fascinated by the conscious mind and its relation to the brain. Charles Darwin, for example, wrote a book called *The Expression of Emotions in Man and Animals*. Darwin thought about human emotions as biologically based – which was not meant to minimize our vast cultural and individual influences, of course. The picture shows Darwin as a young man, around the time of his historic voyage to the Pacific Ocean on *The Beagle*. *Source:* Finkelstein, 2000.

to fame is the physical law of conservation of energy, which he demonstrated using electrical stimulation of dissected frog's legs. The insight that electricity was part of nervous activity led to the discovery of nerve potentials and the electrical activity of the brain in the early 20th century. Today, the electromagnetic activity of the brain gives us a whole set of imaging methods: EEG, evoked potentials, single-neuron recording, MEG, and even TMS, magnetic stimulation of the brain (Chapter 4). Indeed, all brain-imaging tools make use of fundamental physics and chemistry.

In Helmholtz' time it was well known that an electrical pulse would cause a pair of frog's legs to contract, as if the frog were jumping. The idea that the brain and body are pervaded with electricity caught the popular fancy, leading to cult ideas like 'animal magnetism'. Helmholtz' conservation of energy experiment in frogs'

FIGURE 1.12 Hermann von Helmholtz was an amateur who ended up making historic contributions to science. Helmholtz was one of the first to propose that the visual system makes 'unconscious inferences' that go far beyond the raw input from the eyes. That idea was so controversial that he was forced to withdraw it, but it is a standard notion in sensory science today.
Source: Bennett, 1999.

legs was a major step towards a naturalistic conception of the brain and body (Figure 1.13).

4.3 Cajal's neuron doctrine: the working assumption of brain science

Santiago Ramon y Cajal (Figure 1.14) is credited with the *neuron doctrine*, one of the founding assumptions of brain science, stating that 'the nervous system consists of numerous nerve units (neurons), anatomically and genetically independent'. It is important to realize that the idea that the body is composed of cells dates back only to 1839, with the use of light microscopes and tissue-staining techniques that showed the details of living cells for the first time in human history.

It became thereby possible to prove that all body tissues consisted of cells, *except* for nervous tissue. The reason was that neurons are immensely branched, and their axons and dendrites spread so thickly, and make such close contact with other nerve cells that it was impossible to tell whether they actually touched or not. Thus a controversy arose over the nature of the nervous system — whether it consisted of billions of cells, or whether it was essentially one great continuous network.

In Madrid, Santiago Ramon y Cajal used the Golgi stain, which brought out a small sample of neurons in a slice of tissue in such a way that the shape of the cells could be seen (Figure 1.15). Cajal was also able to prove that axons end in free terminals, and must therefore be separate cells.

The nerve impulse – the electrochemical 'spike' that travels down the axon to its terminals – was first demonstrated in the giant axon of the squid. Because nerve cells are found in all animals, and their basic properties appear to be conserved among many species, the squid axon is an important test-bed for other classes of neurons. That discovery was made in 1939, a century after the cell doctrine was proposed. Ten years later it was found that sodium and potassium ions ($Na+$ and $K+$) rapidly move in and out of nerve axons to propagate the axonal spike and, in 1952, Hodgkin and Huxley (1952) constructed the model of the action potential that we use today (Figure 1.16). About the same time, it became possible to observe the even tinier synapse through the use of electron microscopes, down to several hundred micrometers.

There is an ironic ending to the Cajal story, however. The great controversy about whether neurons are separate continues today. Cajal seemed to have settled the question forever when he showed that axons had free nerve endings. However, recent evidence shows that many points of transmission between nerve cells are not chemical synapses but electrically continuous tissue called *gap junctions*. Some neurons are nestled against each other, without the classical synaptic gaps. It is, therefore, possible that some neurons do form a continuous structure, though there is no question that chemical synapses exist in the trillions. Like so many other scientific controversies, the debate goes on at ever more refined levels.

4.4 Pierre-Paul Broca and the localization of speech production

Medical observations are also relevant to the mind and brain sciences. It was the French physician, Pierre-Paul

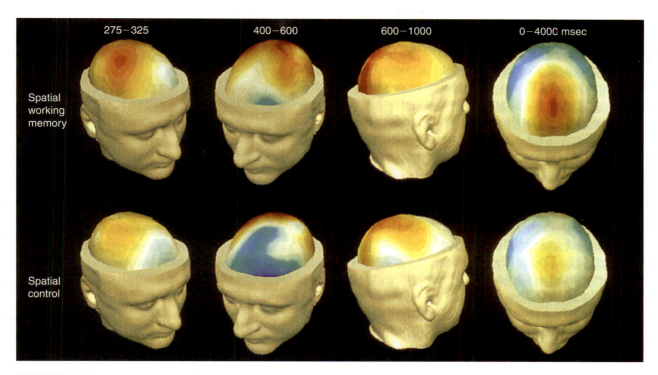

FIGURE 1.13 Electricity and nerves: mapping brain activity. This high-resolution EEG shows the time course (in milliseconds) of spatial working memory – the ability to remember the spatial location of a stimulus for about ten seconds – compared to a spatial control task. This method is an advanced development of the historic idea that electrical activity was a normal part of nervous system function. In this image, the red and yellow colors signify higher voltages in the surface layers of the brain. Notice how quickly the distribution of electrical voltages flows from place to place during the first four seconds after the memory stimulus is presented. *Source*: Gevins *et al.*, 1995.

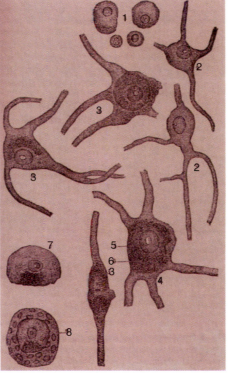

FIGURE 1.14 *Left*: Santiago Ramon y Cajal, founder of brain science. Golgi color stains were used by Santiago Ramon y Cajal, perhaps the most important early pioneer in neuroscience, to bring out basic facts about nerve cells under the light microscope. Cajal showed the microanatomy of neurons. His beautiful illustrations of his microscopic observations are shown on the right. Today's methods for studying neuronal microstructure are advanced versions of the Golgi-Cajal approach (see Figure 1.16) *Source*: DeFelipe, 2002.

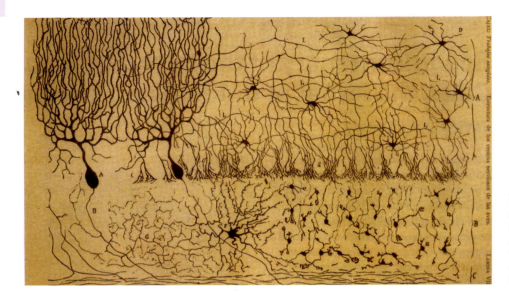

FIGURE 1.15 Cajal's first drawing of a microscopic slice of nerve tissue, from the cerebellum of a hen. Cajal made use of the *Golgi staining method*, which caused small numbers of nerve cells to stand out from the surrounding tissue. *Source*: DeFelipe, 2002.

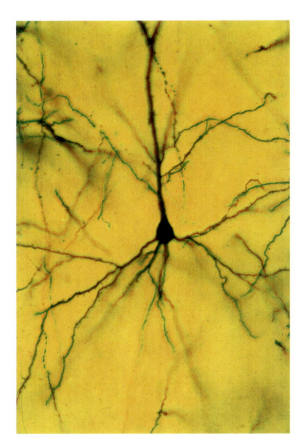

FIGURE 1.16 A modern version of Cajal's figure. Neurons in a modern X-ray micrograph using a chemical stain. *Source*: Standring, 2005.

FIGURE 1.17 Pierre-Paul Broca, who defined expressive aphasia. He was the first to make a convincing case for a single, highly specialized function in a specific location in cortex. *Source*: Aminoff and Daroff, 2003.

Broca (Figure 1.17), who first discovered a region of the left hemisphere that was unquestionably tied to language production, a higher mental function. The 'speaking' region of the left hemisphere is therefore called Broca's area.

Controversy has raged over the question of brain localization – whether specific regions of the brain serve very specific functions. Broca was the first to establish firmly a specialized region of the higher brain in 1861, based on a patient who suffered from epilepsy.

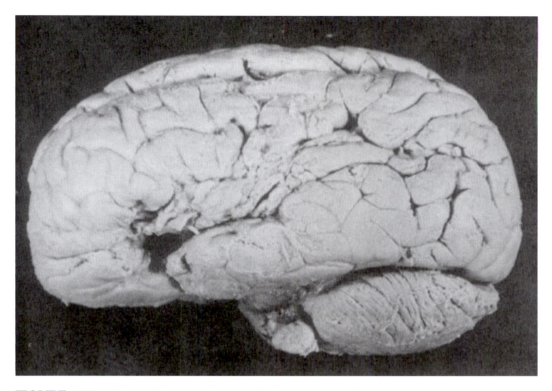

FIGURE 1.18   The brain of Broca's early patient has been preserved. If you look at the frontal region of the left hemisphere you can see a large hole in 'Broca's area'. *Source*: Ramachandran, 2002.

Broca's patient had lost all ability to speak except the single word 'tan'. After the patient died, Broca was able to perform an autopsy, finding 'damage to the posterior part of the third frontal convolution in the left hemisphere' (Figure 1.18). He concluded that this part of the frontal lobe was indispensable for speech production. Six months later, Broca presented a similar case, again with damage to this part of the left frontal lobe. Despite criticisms that other areas of the brain were involved in his cases and that some patients with similar disorders did not have frontal lobe lesions, Broca's observations came to be accepted because the weight of subsequent evidence. Today, Broca's area in the left frontal lobe is widely recognized as a critical component of the language region (Aminoff and Daroff, 2003).

Much of what we know about the human brain was first discovered from very careful study of specific deficits. That effort continues today. Another important finding for language was made by Carl Wernicke (Figure 1.19), who published a monograph in 1874 describing a model for language based on his work in human pathology that remains a key aspect of cognitive neuroscience today. Today, Wernicke's area in the left upper part of the temporal lobe is widely recognized as

an important brain area for receptive language. Patients with brain damage in this region and deficits in speech comprehension are still called 'Wernicke's aphasics'. However, with better techniques of brain imaging, these areas are turning out to be more complex and flexible than they were thought to be.

The brain of Broca's patient has been preserved and you can see the location of the damage in the frontal region of the left hemisphere in Figure 1.18.

Here is a speech sample from a modern patient (FL) with receptive aphasia, due to damage in or near Wernicke's area (Dronkers and Ogar, 2003):

Examiner: Tell me what you think your problem is.
FL: Ah, where do I start the tesseinemen from? They tell me that my brain, physically, my brain is perfect, the attitudes and everything is fine, but the silence now, that I have to reeh-learn through edgit again, physically nothing wrong with it. It's perfect the doctors tell me. They have attitude. Physically I have loozing absolute nothing on my head, but now I have to go through these new attitudes to looalize how, some, how can I say to? Some what that I can reeh-learn again so I can estep my knowledges, so th'you kyou again, what how can I say that y. . .

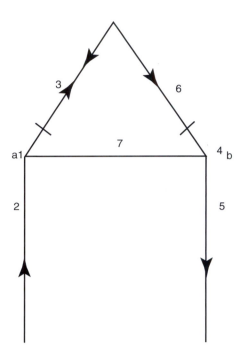

FIGURE 1.19 Wernicke and the comprehension of speech. Some years after Broca's work on speech *output*, the German physician Carl Wernicke (left panel) discovered a part of the brain involved in speech *input* – perception and comprehension. Wernicke studied a variety of aphasic patients (a-phasia, meaning 'not speech'), and concluded that damage in different cortical locations led to different disorders. He distinguished between *semantic* aphasias and *receptive* and *productive* types. The right panel shows a sophisticated theory of the different language areas from the 19th century. *Source*: Wernicke and Koehler, 2003.

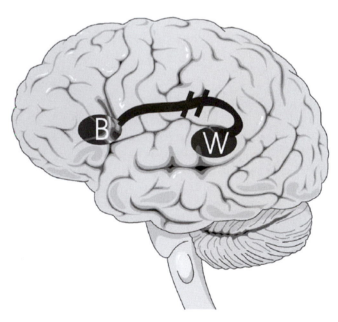

FIGURE 1.20 Conduction aphasia. Careful anatomical dissections showed a fiber bundle connecting Broca's and Wernicke's areas of the left hemisphere. Based on this evidence, Wernicke was able to predict a new language deficit in 1874 called *disconnection aphasia*. If the fiber bundle between Broca's and Wernicke's areas were damaged, he thought, patients should have difficulty transferring information from the receptive area to the production region. That prediction was borne out and this type of deficit is called conduction aphasia. *Source*: Dronkers and Ogar, 2003.

Notice that this patient is much more fluent than Broca's classic patient of 1861 who could only pronounce one syllable. However, this patient's ability both to produce and comprehend meaningful speech is impaired. Using brain imaging, the location of focal damage is routinely determined today, so that diagnosis is no longer dependent only on neurological inferences and autopsies.

It was well known in the 19th century that most of the mass of the cortex is *white matter*, consisting of billions of axons emerging from the gray cell bodies in the surface layers of the cortex. Those axons are wrapped in the white protective and supportive myelin cells, filled with fat-like lipid molecules. They therefore look white to the naked eye. Most of the white matter therefore consists of great fiber bundles, connecting every region of cortex to every other, like some great highway system. Careful anatomical dissections showed a fiber bundle connecting Broca's and Wernicke's areas in the left hemisphere. These fiber bundles are known as *arcuate fasciculi*, Latin for 'arched little bundles'. (Again, an everyday Latin term has become a long and complicated-sounding word to our ears.)

Based on this evidence, Wernicke was able to predict a new language deficit in 1874 called *disconnection aphasia*. If the fibers between Broca's and Wernicke's areas were

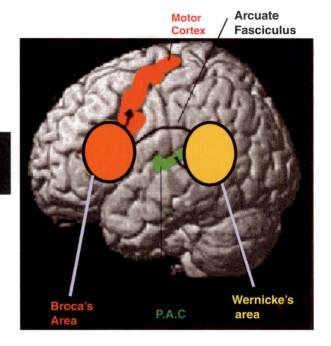

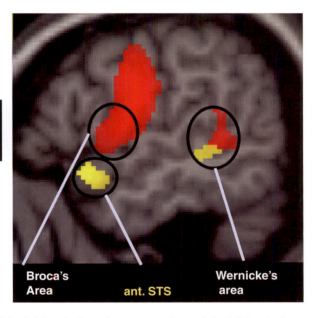

FIGURE 1.21 Language regions of the left hemisphere. Language regions of the left hemisphere, studied by fMRI (functional magnetic resonance imaging). Red areas are involved in speech *production*, while yellow ones show up in speech *perception* and *comprehension*. The classic Broca's and Wernicke's areas are marked by circles. Notice the close similarity between the modern understanding of language regions and the 19th century account. (PAC = Primary Auditory Cortex, the initial region in the cortex for second processing; ant. STS = anterior superior temporal sulcus, the front part of the upper fold of the temporal lobe.) *Source*: Frackowiak, 2004.

damaged, he thought, patients should have difficulty *repeating* speech sounds – transferring information from the receptive area (Wernicke's) to the production region (Broca's). That prediction was borne out (see Figure 1.20). It is believed that there are a number of such disconnection syndromes, with somewhat different

symptoms from lesions that involve damage to the outer cell bodies of cortex. A number of other types of aphasia are thought to exist.

Notice that these language areas usually exist in the left hemisphere (Figure 1.21). Modern evidence shows that the right side of the brain does comprehend

FIGURE 1.22 William James taught brain anatomy. While William James is best known today as a psychologist and philosopher, he also trained to be a physician and artist. James was first hired at Harvard University to teach brain anatomy, and his 1890 description of the brain is in good agreement with our understanding today. *Source*: Courtesy of the National Library of Medicine.

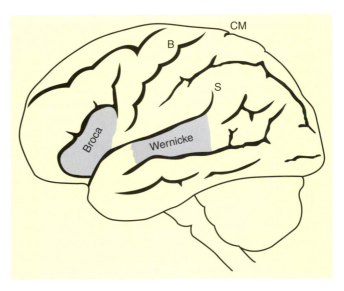

FIGURE 1.23   James showed Broca's and Wernicke's areas based on the medical evidence from brain damage. *Source*: James, 1890.

process language, but it does not control vocal output. The right side is believed to be sensitive to the emotional content of language, such as humor and irony. Left-side dominance seems to apply to about 90 per cent of the population. About 10 per cent of normal people have right hemisphere dominance for language.

William James (Figure 1.22) is best known today as a psychologist and philosopher, however, he also trained to be a physician and painter. James was first hired at Harvard University to teach brain anatomy, and his 1890 description of the brain is in good agreement with our understanding today. Note his drawing showed Broca's and Wernicke's areas based on the medical evidence from aphasias (Figure 1.23).

James' *Principles of Psychology* is often considered the best summary of 19th century psychology and brain science in the English language. Among many other points, James discussed the brain studies of a Dr Mosso, who observed that the blood supply to active brain regions increased (Figure 1.24). That finding is the basis of modern brain imaging methods based on *hemodynamics* (the flow of blood), including PET scans and MRI (Figure 1.25).

[In Mosso's experiments] the subject to be observed lay on a delicately balanced table which could tip downward either at the head or at the foot if the weight of either end were increased. The moment emotional or intellectual activity began in the subject, down went the balance at the head-end, in consequence of the

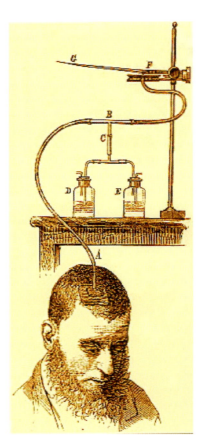

FIGURE 1.24   William James (1890) described the research of Dr Mosso, who found a way to measure blood pressure during demanding mental tasks. Mosso's work anticipated current measures of brain blood flow like fMRI. *Source*: James, 1890.

redistribution of blood in his system. (William James, *Principles of Psychology* (1890))

Thus, 19th century scientists discovered localized brain functions for language. They were not only concerned with the classic psychological aspects of the mind, but also with their relation to the brain.

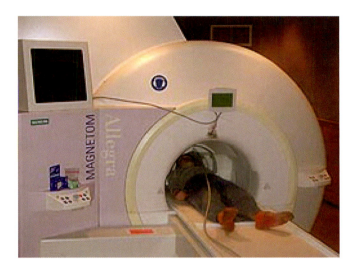

FIGURE 1.25 Functional MRI measures local blood flow changes in the brain. Contemporary fMRI experiments are based on blood flow changes in the brain whenever some brain regions require more oxygen and glucose. It is a modern version of Dr Mosso's 19th century discovery. *Source*: Thomas Ramsøy.

4.5 The conscious and unconscious mind

Nineteenth century physicians believed that human conscious experience depended on the cortex, the outer layer of the brain. James wrote:

But is the consciousness which accompanies the activity of the cortex the only consciousness that man has? or are his lower centres conscious as well?. . . the cortex is the sole organ of consciousness in man.

Contemporary neuroimaging evidence tends to support James' claim, although some scientists believe that subcortical regions are also involved (see Chapters 2 and 8). The question of conscious perception and cognition has again become a major focus of research, as we will see.

Nineteenth century scientists were profoundly interested in the question of consciousness. Ramon y Cajal proposed the idea of a 'psychic neuron' in the cortex, a type of neuron that would support conscious experiences. The beginning of psychophysics in the early 19th century was very much inspired by an effort to solve the mind-body puzzle, and the pioneering psychophysicist, Gustav Fechner, claimed that he had found the answer by showing a mathematically exact relationship between subjective sensory intensity and physical stimulus intensity. At the end of the 19th century, William James proclaimed that 'Psychology is the science of mental life', by which he meant *conscious* mental life (James, 1890/1983, p. 15). James was not alone.

About that time, some began to disagree. Scientists like Helmholtz, Loeb and Pavlov advocated a more physicalistic view of mental life. After 1900, Pavlov became famous for his experiments on classical conditioning in dogs. This helped to convince many psychologists that ultimately all of behavior could be explained in terms of simple behavioral units, based on reflexes (Figure 1.26). In the USA, John B. Watson was the first person to make radical behaviorism famous, arguing that any reference to consciousness was improper, since

FIGURE 1.26 Radical behaviorism: Pavlov, Watson and Skinner. Although Pavlov was a sophisticated physiologist, his proposal that conditional reflexes are the basic unit of all human learning is no longer generally believed. However, Pavlovian conditioning is widely used in research and is relevant to clinical issues like anxiety disorders and the treatment of phobias. *Source*: http://www.sruweb.com/~walsh/intro_unit_four.html.

we can only publicly observe physical behavior and the physical brain. Watson's famous slogan was that 'consciousness is nothing but the soul of theology', and therefore unscientific. For much of the 20th century, human consciousness was avoided by scientists. Some saw it as too burdened with philosophical questions, too difficult to test experimentally, or too subjective to be studied scientifically.

There were some practical reasons for this. It is difficult in many cases to be sure about someone else's experience, so that it can be hard to repeat experiments in the way reliable science requires.

5.0 THE RETURN OF CONSCIOUSNESS IN THE SCIENCES

In the 1970s, many psychologists became dissatisfied with behaviorism and began to pursue a different path. While using behavioral measures in the laboratory, cognitive psychologists were interested in making inferences from those observations. We will see one prominent example in this chapter, the idea of working memory. There are many others. Cognitive psychologists have brought back visual imagery, various types of memory, unconscious (implicit) cognition, and many other terms. However, these concepts are always studied behaviorally in the laboratory under very closely controlled conditions. The concepts of working memory, imagery, and so on, are inferred from behavioral observations. They are theoretical explanations, much as electrons are in physics. No one has ever seen an electron, but the concept of an electron explains many different kinds of observable phenomena (Baars, 1986).

Perhaps the greatest change over the last twenty years within cognitive psychology and cognitive science more generally, has been the acceptance of consciousness as a legitimate and tractable scientific problem. During much of the twentieth century the field was enmeshed in the philosophical tangles of the body-mind problem, and stifled by the empirical limitations of introspectionism. More recently, it has gradually become clear that neither of these represent the sort of fundamental obstacle that was originally feared. Furthermore, the need to account for phenomena such as blindsight and implicit memory, in which perception and recall were clearly proceeding in ways that were at variance with the conscious experience of the perceiver or the rememberer, argued strongly for the need to bring back the study of conscious awareness into the empirical psychological fold. (Baddeley, personal communication)

In recent years, the reluctance to study consciousness has begun to fade. Many cognitive psychologists study both explicit (conscious) and implicit (unconscious) processes. As we will see, there is now a large body of evidence that our perception of the world around us is partly unconscious, although the *result* of the perceptual process is conscious. Many aspects of memory are unconscious, while episodic memory involves the record of conscious events in the past. With the advent of functional imaging technology, it has become possible to make careful comparisons between brain events involving conscious versus unconscious cognition. Currently, about 5000 articles per year refer to consciousness and its many synonyms. The synonyms include 'awareness', 'explicit cognition', 'episodic recall', and 'focal attention'. Those terms are defined experimentally by measures of 'accurate report'. We simply ask people if they perceived or recalled an event, and then try to check the accuracy of their reports. In that sense, the different synonyms for conscious events are assessed in the same way, and therefore seem to have a basic similarity. We will call them 'conscious', but also use the technical terms (see Baars *et al.*, 2003).

In the 19th century, figures like Sigmund Freud and William James were deeply interested in understanding the relationship between mind and brain. Freud began his medical career in neurology, and even developed an early neural network model. Early in his career he discovered a new chemical stain – gold chloride – which allowed certain neurons to stand out clearly under the microscope. The first such stain was discovered by the Camillo Golgi in 1873, and revolutionized the ability to observe nerve cells under the light microscope (see http://nobelprize.org/medicine/articles/golgi/).

5.1 How conscious and unconscious brain events are studied today

Psychologists and neuroscientists have devised a very wide range of methods for studying conscious and unconscious processes in the brain. Table 1.3 shows a subset of all the methods currently available. They all have pros and cons, of course. Some have implications for episodic memory (memory for conscious events), while others show that visually guided reaching for objects is largely unconscious. There are many unresolved questions, whether 'conscious' cognition is the best terminology, whether selective attention must precede conscious experiences, and much more. All these debates are healthy and normal. The most important advance is that we now have a number of reliable

BOX 1.2   The mind-brain debate today

Philosophers continue to debate whether conscious experiences can be understood in terms of the brain. However, many scientists today believe that it has become a productive scientific question again. Patricia Churchland has been among the leading philosophers coming back to a naturalistic approach to the mind and brain. She recently said that 'neuroscientific data are relevant to long-standing, traditional problems in philosophy: the nature of consciousness, the self, free will, knowledge, ethics and learning'.

Psychologists have studied sensory processes since the early 1800s. We experience our world through our senses: we have the feeling that our mind-brain is intricately involved with the interplay between our physical world and our brain. We readily get help for our perceptual abilities by obtaining eyeglasses at optometrists, hearing aids at the audiologists. And we spend time tuning the objects that provide us with some of our sensory inputs, such car speakers and audio equipment. Yet the correspondence between our visual and auditory perception of the world and the physical properties of that world is still not entirely known. Clearly, the mind and brain have a sense of sights and sounds within our environment, yet mapping the path between the physical and the perceived remains a mystery.

It seems that words like 'mind' and 'brain' represent different *sources* of information. If we look out at the world from within our brains (as we are always doing), things seem different than if we look at our brains from the outside, in a brain scanner, for example.

When a computer shows us how much memory it has, no one thinks that it has just discovered a new realm of existence. When people tell us about their sensory experiences, they have not done so either. But they have told us something valuable. Philosophical journals are still filled with mind/body debates, but scientists must define questions in empirical terms. Today, we are increasingly confident about the evidence from both mental and brain perspectives, and we are beginning to see how the two points of view converge when we study them carefully.

FIGURE 1.27   Patricia Churchland has been among the leading philosophers coming back to a naturalistic approach to the mind and brain. *Source*: Patricia Churchland, UCSD.

TABLE 1.3   Commonly studied conscious and unconscious brain events

Conscious	Unconscious
1 Explicit cognition	Implicit cognition
2 Immediate memory	Longer term memory
3 Novel informative and significant events	Routine, predictable and non-significant events
4 Attended information	Unattended information
5 Focal contents	Fringe contents (e.g. familiarity)
6 Declarative memory (facts etc.)	Procedural memory (skills etc.)
7 Supraliminal stimulation	Subliminal stimulation
8 Effortful tasks	Spontaneous/automatic tasks
9 Remembering (recall)	Knowing (recognition)
10 Available memories	Unavailable memories
11 Strategic control	Automatic control
12 Grammatical strings	Implicit underlying grammars
13 Intact reticular formation and bilateral intralaminar thalamic nuclei	Lessened reticular formation or bilateral intralaminar nuclei
14 Rehearsed items in working memory	Unrehearsed items
15 Wakefulness and dreams (cortical arousal)	Deep sleep, coma, sedation (cortical slow waves)
16 Explicit inferences	Automatic inferences
17 Episodic memory (autobiographical)	Semantic memory (conceptual knowledge)
18 Automatic memory	Noetic memory
19 Intentional learning	Incidental learning
20 Normal vision	Blindsight (cortical blindness)

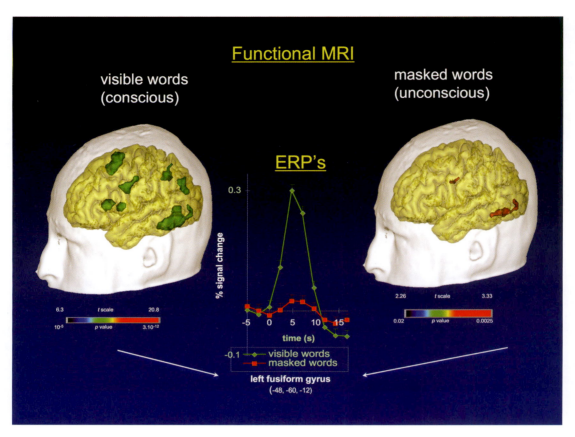

FIGURE 1.28 Unconscious versus conscious vision. A recent wave of experiments compares conscious and unconscious phenomena in the same study. For example, a method called visual backward masking allows us to compare fMRI activity in the same person for conscious and unconscious visual words. This figure from Dehaene et al. (2001) shows that unconscious words trigger local activity in visual cortex, but matched conscious words *also* evoke strong forward activity in the cortex, in the parietal and frontal lobes. In both experimental conditions the same physical stimulus reaches the retina, so that the difference must be higher up in the brain. This pattern of results has now been found a number of times. Evidence like this has convinced a number of scientists that conscious cognition can be studied with the proper kinds of experimental designs. *Source*: Baars *et al.*, 2003.

methods for studying both conscious and unconscious brain events (Figure 1.28). We can contrast brain activation patterns for imagined versus actual events, as well as for stimuli that are not consciously perceived, see Table 1.3.

The most important point is that, from a scientific point of view, conscious cognition is much like working memory or attention. It is a *construct inferred from behavioral observations* (Mandler, 2003). Fortunately, it also corresponds usually to our own personal experience. In the study of perception, for example, you can report the type-face of *these words*, or even your memory of this morning's breakfast. This topic has been emerging in a number of fields within cognitive neuroscience such as memory, vision, and lesion studies, as we will see in later chapters.

5.2 History hasn't stopped

Practically all the historical debates are still alive today, often appearing in a new guise (see Table 1.4). The practical applications of cognitive neuroscience continue to grow. Modern neurology makes extensive use of brain

TABLE 1.4   Ongoing debates today

Local versus widespread functions in the brain
The neuron doctrine
The question of consciousness
Unconscious inferences in vision
Capacity limits in the brain
Short-term and long-term memory: are they separate?
The biological bases of emotions
Nature *versus* nurture, genes *versus* environment

BOX 1.3   Adaptation or representation?

There is another debate that continues today: should brains be viewed as adaptive or representational? This debate concerns how we think about cognitive processes and the way in which to map them onto brain systems. Here is some background.

As you read this sentence, you are engaging in a *symbolic interpretation* of a string of black squiggles on a colored background. Linguists and psychologists think about language in terms of symbols: phonemes, letters, morphemes, words, phrases and sentences. Those symbolic units are combined by the regularities of grammar and usage. Educated speakers of English understand about 100 000 words, often with more than one meaning – roughly the number of words in a good dictionary. At a higher level, we think in terms of sentences that encode abstract concepts and propositions, and these can be combined into even larger-scale discourse structures, like expository paragraphs, conversations and stories. Even the expressive function of language – the emotional singsong of a phrase, or a verbal statement of anger or love – can be described symbolically: human languages have many words for emotions. In sum, we are remarkably skilled in the use of symbols. They are essential in cultural developments like science, mathematics and logic, but also in literature, music and the visual arts. Even computer programs are symbolic systems that perform useful work. Symbols are all around us, and it is therefore natural to think about the brain as a symbolic processor.

Yet the physical brain only contains neurons, connected to each other in a variety of ways. Should we think about the mind-brain as a symbol processor, or as a hyper-complex web of neurons? Each approach has pros and cons. Symbols allow us to explore questions of meaning and purpose fairly easily. Symbolic flow diagrams, like the 'functional framework' of Chapter 2, help to clarify questions that can be tested in the laboratory.

On the other hand, artificial neuronal network models (ANNs) can simulate simple learning tasks better than symbolic systems (see Chapter 2 and Appendix A). We therefore have a range of tools – flow diagrams, artificial neural networks, semantic networks, tree diagrams, and models – that combine symbols and neurons. In fact, if you look closely, even neural networks have nodes and connections with symbolic names.

Scientists are constantly debating these questions. Cognitive neuroscience is a discipline in ferment, with waves of new evidence and theory constantly challenging our ability to understand. It is an exciting and fun enterprise, and we hope that in the coming chapters you will catch a glimpse of what keeps us fascinated with a flow of new insights into human minds and brains.

imaging and cognitive techniques to assess subtle kinds of damage that are not visible in scans. New research has shown unsuspected deficits, for example, such as emotional blindness and the inability to use certain nouns and verbs. These subtle signs can point to serious brain damage that is not otherwise detectable.

6.0 SUMMARY

In this first chapter, we explored some of the questions we try to understand in cognitive neuroscience. They encompass some ancient issues such as the mind versus the body, as well as some that arise from very recent experiments. The scientific exploration of the relationship between the mind and the brain is a central issue addressed by this text. The advent of imaging techniques has brought many of these questions back to life.

Cognitive neuroscience combines psychology, neuroscience, and biology. The historical roots of the discipline go back to some of the earliest writings in Eastern and Western traditions. Questions that were out of bounds a few years ago are now being explored. For students, new careers are opening up. Practical applications are emerging in education, medicine, and psychotherapy. Major challenges remain, but there is a sense of excitement in the air. New findings are coming faster than ever before.

The goal of this chapter has been to give you an overview of the combined study of mind and brain. We now have brain imaging studies of vision and hearing, learning and memory, conscious and unconscious processes, visual imagery and inner speech. It is an extraordinary scientific time. Most imaging experiments use standard cognitive tasks, so there is a growing integration of the behavioral and brain evidence. The implications for brain functioning in health and disease are immense.

The field of cognitive neuroscience aims to make sense of the flow of new evidence. This chapter presented a first broad overview. Our goal is to show you how mind and brain evidence often fit together in a surprising and satisfying way.

BOX 1.4   How to study in this course

We highly recommend drawing and coloring as a way of learning the geography of the brain. As you know, learning requires active involvement. That is especially true in a course like this. There is no substitute for careful reading, thinking, asking questions and exploring answers. It can be helpful to study with another person who is also focused on learning. But because the brain is a 'hypercomplex surface', drawing is especially valuable. Most chapters in this book will present drawing and coloring exercises at the end.

The traditional way to learn the brain is by dissecting sheep and frogs. That is effective because the student is constantly interacting with the physical brain. We will ask you to study this text and its graphics just as if it were a living brain, but without having to harm any creature. Our figures are designed to show the many levels of anatomy and to illustrate the most important experiments.

Because the brain is a vast, three-dimensional structure squeezed over millions of years of evolution into a very small space, learning its ins and outs is much like getting to know a city, to drive or walk around it, to memorize the major landmarks, and to visit some of the back alleys and individual houses. This book will be your tour guide, pointing out landmarks and the customs of the inhabitants.

For major learning points in the text there will be a demonstration, a graphic image, or experimental evidence. In the coming chapters will see case histories of people who have suffered brain injuries, and explore some of the limits of normal brains as well.

Finally, it is important to break down the technical terms into their parts. Anatomical studies of the brain began four centuries ago, when the international language of science was Latin. Many brain terms are therefore still compounds of Latin and Greek. For that reason it is important to recognize *cognates* – words that are similar to English. For example, in this chapter we saw the cortex from one side (the *lateral* view), from the midline (the *medial* view), the bottom (*inferior* view) and the top (*superior* view). Those four words – *lateral, medial, inferior* and *superior* – have obvious English analogs. Fortunately, much of our English vocabulary comes from Latin-based languages, so that you will often be able to spot connections with familiar words.

It will help you to do *elaborative learning*, rather than just repeating new words to yourself. The top of the brain is often called the dorsal part, because *dorsum* means 'back' in Latin, and if you look at dogs or cats walking, the top of their brain is an extension of their backs. As we just mentioned, the side is called lateral; therefore structures that are on top *and* to the side are called *dorsolateral*. We will explain those subunits as each new word is introduced.

Anatomy students often use memory techniques. You may want to explore them to see which ones work best for you. Medical students traditionally draw the brain and color its parts. But any kind of active association will help – rhyming the words, making up visual images, or thinking of analogies. You might visualize the brain as an automobile, and associate different brain structures with the tires or the hood. Don't worry if the associations seem silly, so long as you get a clear mental connection between what you are learning and what you already know. Just as there are no bad questions, there are no silly memory techniques. Just ones that work for you, or don't.

Finally, *self-testing* is an essential ingredient of learning, just as it is for playing an instrument. Otherwise we tend to overestimate what we know. Remember that just being able to *recognize* a word does not mean that you'll be able to *recall* it when you need it. If you expect a recall test, it helps to practice recall.

It may help you to browse the web for different ways of looking at cognitive experiments and brain images. If you feel ambitious, the National Library of Medicine has a free web database with tens of millions of scientific abstracts. *PubMed* will answer all kinds of scientific and medical questions (search for *Entrez PubMed*). There are outstanding brain anatomy sites, and many excellent websites that demonstrate basic cognitive and perceptual phenomena.

7.0 END OF CHAPTER EXERCISES

7.1 Study questions

1 Name three small-scale spatial events in the brain, with their order of magnitude.
2 Name three small-scale temporal events in the brain, with their order of magnitude.
3 What was the dominant viewpoint about the nature of psychology in the 19th century? In the early 20th?
4 What is a major difference between behavioral and cognitive psychology?
5 What influence did physiologists like Pavlov have on psychology?
6 Explain some ways in which psychology and brain science interact.
7 What are some difficulties in studying brain damage scientifically?
8 What is the relationship between the 'mental' point of view and 'physical' perspective? What is philosophical naturalism?
9 In everyday life, are you aware of using inner speech? Visual imagery? If so, in what situations? If not, what everyday situations might show that kind of process? (Note that there are considerable

individual differences in visual imagery; not everybody reports having spontaneous images.)

7.2 Drawing exercise

We highly recommend drawing and coloring to help you remember the physical layout of the brain.

Here is a model brain for your use. It is very helpful to draw or color the following areas. Many people find it useful to make a habit of coloring brain parts in consistent colors, to help to associate brain regions by color. All kinds of memory aids can help.

1 The major lobes (seen from the outside view, both right and left).
2 What are the names of the major lobes?
3 Where is Broca's area? Wernicke's? What are their traditional functions?
4 What anatomical structure connects these two areas?
5 Draw the brain from the left side, labeling the major lobes.
6 Which area is associated with vision? With speech? With executive control?

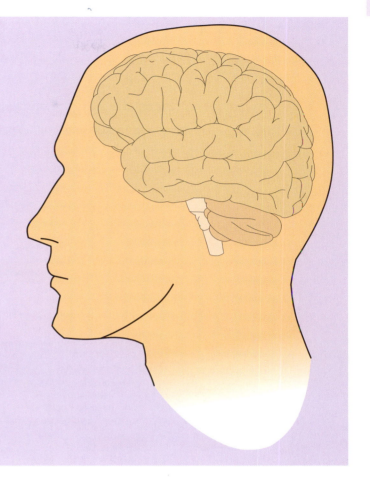

It seems that the human mind has first to construct forms independently before we can find them in things . . . Knowledge cannot spring from experience alone, but only from a comparison of the inventions of the intellect with observed fact.

Albert Einstein (1949)

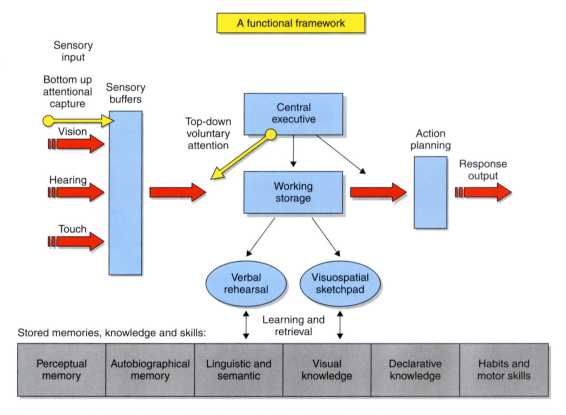

This functional framework, used throughout this book, combines two classical models of cognition (Baddeley and Hitch, 1974; Atkinson and Shiffrin, 1968). Two yellow arrows symbolize voluntary (top-down) and spontaneous (bottom-up) attention. Long-term memories, knowledge and skills are shown in the row of gray boxes at the bottom. In Chapter 8 we add "conscious cognition" for reportable brain events, such as your conscious perception of the page in front of you (Baddeley, 2002). While the diagram is only an outline, it has the advantage of simplicity and wide acceptance. It should be taken as a first sketch of mind and brain functions. A recent version of Baddeley's Working Memory model is shown in the center.

A framework

Bernard J. Baars

1.0 INTRODUCTION

In this chapter, we introduce a framework that will help to organize a good deal of cognitive neuroscience. While not all of the details are settled, it combines a large body of brain and psychological evidence into a single diagram. Because cognitive neuroscience can be complicated, an organizing framework will help you learn.

The figure on page 32 shows our framework schematically, and Figure 2.1 shows some associated regions of the cortex. As we will see, there is both behavioral and brain evidence for all the components. But we will hold this organization lightly, as just one way to understand the evidence. When there are debates about how to interpret the facts, we will explore their pros and cons.

In this chapter, we will briefly touch on each aspect of the functional framework. Each 'box' is expanded in later chapters.

The left side of the figure on page 30 begins with the sensory systems. The senses all begin from receptor

Cognition, Brain, and Consciousness, edited by B. J. Baars and N. M. Gage
ISBN: 978-0-12-373677-2

Copyright 2007, Elsevier Ltd. All rights reserved.

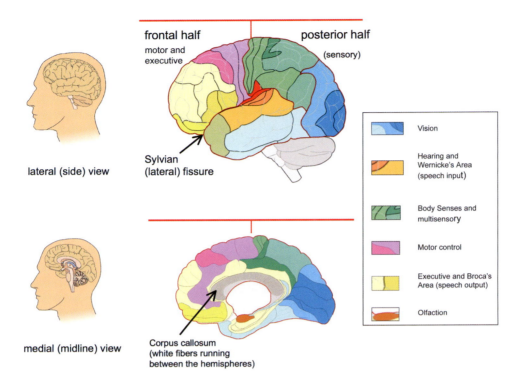

frontal half
motor and
executive

posterior half

(sensory)

Sylvian
(lateral) fissure

lateral (side) view

Vision

Hearing and
Wernicke's Area
(speech input)

Body Senses and
multisensory

Motor control

Executive and Broca's
Area (speech output)

Olfaction

medial (midline) view

Corpus callosum
(white fibers running
between the hemispheres)

FIGURE 2.1   Some major functions of the human cortex. The lateral (side) and medial (midline) views of cortex are colored to show major functional regions. The colored regions should be memorized to make it easier to understand the rest of the book. On the right of both figures are the sensory halves of cortex, the posterior cortex, including the occipital cortex for vision and part of the upper temporal cortex for hearing. The body senses are represented just behind the central sulcus (light green). On the left side of the central sulcus are motor regions (light purple), and in front of the motor cortex, the prefrontal cortex for executive functions. Thus we can conveniently divide the cortex into input regions in the posterior half and output regions in the front half, at least as a first approximation. (This figure does not show subcortical regions or input-output pathways.) (See Chapter 5.) *Source*: Drawn by Shawn Fu.

surfaces containing millions of receptors, like the retina at the back of the eye. All sensory pathways terminate in the rear half of the cortex, as shown in Figure 2.1. Each of the classical senses is believed to have a brief storage ability called a *sensory buffer*. Vision and audition have been studied for more than two centuries and a great deal is known about them. The body senses, like touch, pain and proprioception, are also well understood. However, even though the smell and touch senses were the earliest to evolve, they are not as well understood as the others. New sensory abilities are still being discovered, including those involved in circadian rhythms, digestion, and even for sexual and reproductive functions.

Sensory activities are flexibly enhanced by *selective attention*, shown by the two yellow arrows in the figure on page 30. As the diagram shows, attention has a 'bottom up' component, to reflect the times when our sensory experience is captured by a flash or a bang, or more subtly by the sight of someone's face. We can also pay attention to a range of events voluntarily, in a 'top down' fashion. That is how we normally call each other's

attention to something interesting. While there continues to be debate about brain regions involved in selective attention, recent evidence shows that cortical regions for visual attention show marked overlap with eye movement control (see Chapter 8).

While this diagram has no symbol for conscious experience, we will see in Chapter 8 that there is an intimate relationship between selective attention and perceptual consciousness.

2.0 CLASSICAL WORKING MEMORY

In the middle column of boxes we have the classical components of working memory (Baddeley and Hitch, 1974; Baddeley, 2002). These components have been studied in great depth over three decades.

Starting from the top, working memory includes the *central executive*, which is the subject of much current research. The central executive was first studied in learning tasks. However, as the frontal lobes have become better understood, executive functions have expanded to include supervisory control over all voluntary activities (e.g. Luria, 1976, Goldberg, 2001; see Chapters 8 and 11). It is often described by the metaphor of a chief executive officer of an organization. For example, Mateer *et al.* write:

> Imagine the role of the executive of a large company, who has overriding control over the company's actions. This person sets goals, plans and organizes company activity to meet those goals, and decides when to start to do something, when to stop doing it, when to do something else, and when to do nothing at all.
>
> The executive is *future directed* and *goal oriented* and, to be effective, must be *flexible* and adaptive. At a basic level, this is what the prefrontal cortex does for humans. Mateer *et al.*, 2005; italics added)

The word 'prefrontal' means the forward part of the frontal lobes. The prefrontal executive regions are located in front of the purple motor regions of the brain (see Figure 2.1). They are marked in light beige and yellow colors, on both the outside and inside views of the hemispheres. Notice that Broca's area, first discovered in the 19th century, is technically a part of the prefrontal cortex. However, the light purple motor regions (on both sides of each hemisphere) also have some executive functions, though typically more local ones compared to the classical prefrontal cortex. These boundaries are not absolute, but they are convenient as a first approximation. Later chapters explore executive functions in more detail (see Chapter 12).

Just below the central executive box in the figure on page 30, the diagram shows a *working storage* element. In the brain, working storage is believed to involve the medial temporal cortex and prefrontal regions (see Figures 2.4 and 2.5). Working storage is dynamic – i.e. it involves active populations of neurons called *cell assemblies*, which can 'crystallize' into permanent memories. Because working storage is dynamic, it is more vulnerable to disruption than are permanent memories.

2.1 The 'inner senses'

Another step down in the diagram are two of the 'inner senses', labeled *verbal rehearsal* and the *visuospatial sketchpad*. Notice that they interact constantly with the gray boxes along the bottom, the long-term stores. Verbal rehearsal is now thought to be another term for inner speech, the fact that human beings seem to spend most of their waking hours talking to themselves (Luria, 1976; Morin, 1993). Inner speech is not just for rehearsing and memorizing information; rather, it keeps a running

commentary on our 'current concerns', while the vocal tract is inhibited, so that we do not express our inner speech out loud (Singer, 1993). Because it involves the sophisticated human language capacity, inner speech is closely tied to the *linguistic and semantic* component of the long-term stores, shown at the bottom of the diagram.

It is easy to demonstrate basic features of verbal rehearsal by means of immediate memory tasks, like trying to remember a telephone number or a shopping list. In the brain, Broca's and Wernicke's areas are involved in inner speech, as you might expect from Chapter 1 (see the bright yellow and orange regions in Figure 2.1). However, language-related areas extend far beyond the traditional Broca-Wernicke cortex. As we will see, semantics, the representation of abstract concepts, also engages temporal and frontal lobes.

The visuospatial sketchpad refers to our ability temporarily to hold visual and spatial information, such as the location of a parked car, or the route from home to a grocery store. Visual imagery is easy to demonstrate, for example by asking people to visualize their front door, and then asking them on which side the doorknob is located. Even people who do not consider themselves to be vivid imagers usually report 'seeing' their doorknob on the right or left side of their imagined front door. Kosslyn and others have found many brain and behavioral similarities between visual imagery and visual perception (e.g. Kozhevnikov *et al.*, 2005). In general, these authors believe that visual imagery makes use of a subset of visual perception areas. Thus the blue areas of the brain figures might participate in visual imagery.

However, the visuospatial sketchpad also involves more abstract and *cross-modal* (involving more than one sense or 'mode') spatial information. For example, we can close our eyes and identify objects by touch, even though we may never have touched them before. There must therefore be cross-modal transfer between vision and touch. Such cross-modal flow of information is associated with parietal cortex, sometimes called the 'Where stream' (see Figure 2.1), as opposed to the 'What stream' of the lower visual areas. The auditory sense also has a spatial component – we can locate sounds quite accurately with our eyes closed, especially if they have fast, high-pitched transients, like the chirps of a sparrow. Thus, all the sensory systems begin as domain-specific visual, auditory or touch perception, but are quickly interpreted as part of a common multimodal space that surrounds our bodies.

The visuospatial sketchpad and the verbal rehearsal component of the functional framework involve mental capacities that we use to remember new words, new faces, spatial information, such as whether to turn right at a specific street corner, and so on. These everyday capacities have an evolutionary basis in language and the spatial senses. It seems likely that there are also 'inner senses' involved with smell and taste, body sensations, pain and pleasure, and the like. It has been shown, for example, that expected pain activates brain regions that overlap with those that become active for real pain. However, it is the verbal and visuospatial 'inner senses' that have been studied the most. We will focus on them.

Long-term stores are represented by the horizontal row of boxes along the bottom of the figure on page 30. These are the brain stores for autobiographical episodes, various kinds of knowledge, and practiced expertise. Once these memory types are stored, they are not conscious. However, they interact constantly with active functions.

All parts of the system work with the others – and they may occasionally compete against some of them as well. For example, visual and auditory stimuli tend to compete if they cannot be integrated into a unified experience. A good example is a movie in which the sound and visual tracks are out of sync. When they are desynchronized by more than about one-tenth of a second, they tend to interfere with each other. When they are synchronized, they tend to unite perceptually (McGurk and MacDonald, 1976). We perceive the speech as coming from the person whose mouth is moving in just the right way at the same moment.

2.2 Output functions

On the right hand side of our diagram are the output components. These include the *central executive*, *action planning*, and *motor output*. The best example here is voluntary motor functions, notably the ones that control our skeletal muscles – the muscles of the torso, head and face. We have no voluntary control over the smooth muscle systems of digestion and blood flow, or over the vital hormonal system. Because these physiological systems have long been known to be autonomous from voluntary control, they were called the *autonomic nervous system*. The autonomic nervous system is anatomically separate from the voluntary motor system, which is under frontal control.

Humans also have voluntary control over some mental functions. A good example is verbal rehearsal and mental rotation of a visual image. If you can visualize a kitchen chair, you may be able to rotate it upside-down mentally. This kind of imagery task activates motor, spatial (parietal) and visual cortex. Because it is voluntary, it is presumably controlled by prefrontal regions.

To see how the functional framework can be used, we will consider a tragic type of brain damage, the case of a man who lost his ability to translate his moment-to-moment experiences into lasting memories.

2.3 Only a fleeting moment . . .

One day in 1985, a rising young musician in Britain realized that he could not remember his wife's name. That same evening, Clive Wearing tried to remember the names of his two children and failed (Figure 2.2).

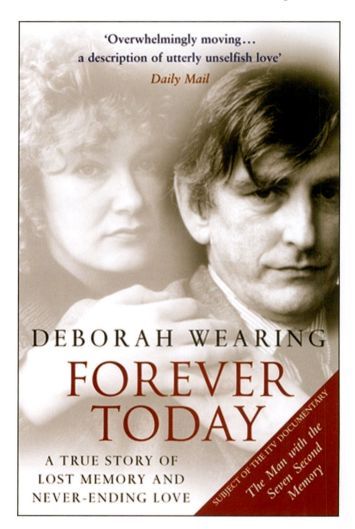

FIGURE 2.2 Clive Wearing (with his wife Deborah Wearing) on the cover of Deborah Wearing's book. After losing both hippocampi (plus some damage to frontal regions), Clive Wearing was still able to play piano and conduct musical pieces that he knew before the injury. However, he could not learn new episodic (conscious) events. Wearing could retain conscious experiences for perhaps ten or twenty seconds, suggesting that aspects of his immediate memory were intact. However, he was catastrophically impaired for episodic learning, i.e. for transferring conscious information into long-term episodic memory. *Source*: Wearing, 2005.

Deborah and Clive Wearing had been married shortly before the onset of his condition, but he could not recollect the wedding. His condition, which was permanent, came on without warning after two days of severe headaches and fever. That was long enough for a viral infection to destroy regions in Clive Wearing's brain that are needed for new memories to form. Wearing was stricken with chronic, dense amnesia of unusual severity, including both *episodic* memory loss – he could not remember any past experiences – as well as a partial loss of *semantic* memory – an inability to understand some domains of meaning (Wilson *et al.*, 1995). Most crucially, he was unable to learn new information. His life, as his wife Deborah later said, was suddenly narrowed to 'a single, blinkered moment', without past or future.

Clive Wearing has been the subject of twenty years of news stories, studies and television documentaries. His case is particularly dramatic because he seems unchanged as a person. He is fully conscious of the immediate world around him, can read and write, and carry on a conversation in the present moment. Wearing can even conduct his small chorus in a classical music piece, provided he already knows the music. He is an emotionally intense person, perhaps even more than before his injury, particularly in expressing his feelings for his wife Deborah.

Clive Wearing lives in an eternal present. For the first eight years, he spent every day in his hospital room writing in his diary, trying to recapture what he called his consciousness. Every few minutes he wrote down the time of day, followed by the exclamation, 'I am now conscious for the first time!!' A few minutes later, he would cross out the previous entry, believing that he had not really been conscious at all, because he could not recall that moment. The same routine was repeated thousands of times, filling numerous diaries. But when his wife or friends came to visit, he greeted them as if he had never seen them before: they were familiar, but not identifiable. If they left for a few moments, Clive Wearing could no longer remember their visit. Even today, whenever Clive Wearing sees his wife Deborah he believes he has not seen her for a long time. Read more about the story of Clive and Deborah in Deborah's own words (Wearing, 2005).

We know more about Clive Wearing's personal life than about others with similar damage. However, by far the most scientific studies have been conducted with a patient we know only as HM, who was first studied by Brenda Milner and Herbert Scoville (Scoville and Milner, 1957). In the 1950s, there were few drug treatments for epileptic seizures. A treatment of last resort for severe, untreatable epilepsy was the surgical removal of part of the temporal lobe. In the case of HM, the two hippocampi and some surrounding regions in the middle temporal lobes were removed on both sides (Figure 2.3). Careful studies over decades showed that HM was unable to store new autobiographical episodes – defined as memories of his conscious life experiences. However, HM was able to learn new sensorimotor skills, called procedural memories. Like Clive Wearing, HM's ability to understand of the meaning of language and of basic events was largely spared. Thus, his *semantic memory* – his ability to understand the meaning of things – was not seriously impaired.

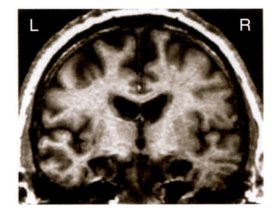 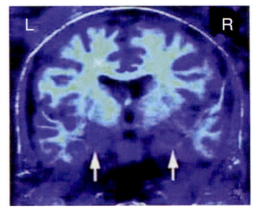

FIGURE 2.3   HM's hippocampal damage. Left: a coronal (i.e. crown-shaped) view of HM's brain, a vertical section from ear to ear. Notice how it compares to the normal brain section on the right. The two arrows on the right side show where the hippocampi are located. In HM's brain we can only see black areas where surgeons removed the extended hippocampal regions. Those cavities have filled with fluid, and appear dark on the brain scan. The two hippocampi are difficult to visualize in these cross-sections, since they are looped and hidden inside of each temporal lobe. (See Figure 2.4.) *Source*: Hodges and Graham, 2001.

The idea of basic differences between autobiographical (episodic), procedural and semantic memory emerged over many years of study, including human patients, animal lesions, and people with healthy brains. In addition to these memory types, our brains have large *perceptual memory capacities*, long-lasting changes in our ability to perceive the world. For example, learning to hear musical instruments in a new song may involve new perceptual memory capacities. As children grow, their ability to perceive the sounds of speech, the constancy of visual objects, to see faces and identify voices, all become part of their permanent perceptual memories. In the case of Clive Wearing, it seems that his trained capacity to perceive and enjoy music is not impaired. (Experienced musicians can perceive more aspects of a musical piece than novices; i.e. their perceptual memories for music are highly developed.)

There are other long-term capacities. Humans have a vast amount of knowledge about their native language, their culture and the surrounding world. Educated speakers of English can understand some 100 000 words, and each word involves a network of associated knowledge. We have expert skills in processing grammar, discourse, and the interpersonal world. Most of this knowledge is unconscious at any given time (Bargh *et al.*, 2006). As far as we know, Clive Wearing's linguistic and semantic knowledge is unchanged, even with his severe brain damage.

Humans live in a rich visual world that we know a lot about. For example, we know that an egg can fall from a table and break, but a table does not usually fall from an egg and break. The oddity of the second idea reflects our vast amount of unconscious knowledge about the visual world. We have no reason to believe that Clive Wearing's and HM's visual knowledge is impaired.

Finally, *declarative knowledge* is commonly defined as our ability to recall facts and beliefs. It is the things we learn in school, which can be 'declared' as propositions. 'China is a large country', 'Whales are marine mammals', and so on. Again, there is no indication that hippocampal damage impairs previously established declarative knowledge. It seems that *existing* knowledge and memory is largely spared with hippocampal patients like HM and Clive Wearing. And yet, according to Deborah Wearing, her husband's life was devastated. His greatest loss was in his capacity to store and retrieve his everyday experiences from memory.

While debate continues about the exact role of the hippocampus itself, there is no doubt about the significance of the hippocampal region, located in the medial temporal lobe (MTL) (Figures 2.4 and 2.5). For that reason, it has become common to refer to the 'medial

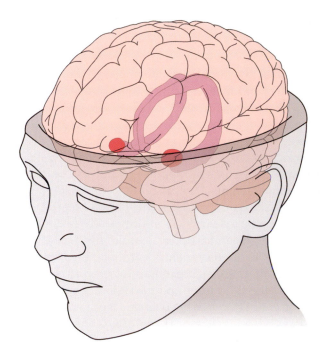

FIGURE 2.4 The two hippocampi. A see-through image of the cortex with the hippocampi nestled inside the temporal lobes. The red bulbs near the tips are the amygdalas, which play a fundamental role in emotion. Surrounding areas of the medial temporal lobe (MTL) also play important roles in memory. (See Figure 2.5.)

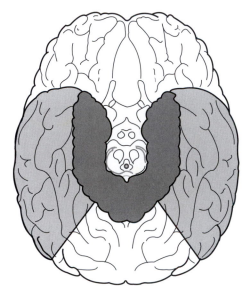

FIGURE 2.5 A bottom view of the brain shows regions removed by surgery in HM. Because more than just the hippocampi are believed to be needed for immediate memory storage, it is now usual to refer to the entire medial temporal lobe (MTL), which is marked. The term 'medial' refers to the midline of the brain, running from front to back. Notice the important landmarks for orientation: the eyeballs, the optic tract, olfactory bulbs, and the temporal lobes.

temporal lobe' or the 'hippocampal complex' as a whole. Notice that the hippocampi are complex spatial structures, a double loop inside each of the temporal lobes but joining across the midline of the brain.

It is easiest to see the medial temporal lobe from the bottom of the brain, which is another important viewpoint of the brain to be able to recognize. The brain is a massively complex organ, evolved over hundreds of millions of years, but packed into a very small space. For that reason, it is often important to recognize a structure like the hippocampal region from two or three points of view (Figure 2.5).

HM is one of the classic patient cases in the history of science, much like Broca's speech-impaired patient in the 1860s. He has been the subject of more than a hundred scientific publications. While HM and others have been enormously important scientifically, the case of Clive Wearing gives us a richer human context. Deborah Wearing has worked for many years to communicate the nature of hippocampal damage to the larger world (Wearing, 2005). Through their personal tragedies, such patients teach us crucial facts about mind and brain.

The two hippocampi – one in each hemisphere – are elongated loops, nestled in the middle of each temporal lobe. The hippocampi and their neighboring structures in the medial temporal lobe cannot be seen from the outside, but they are crucial to our ability to store, work with and retrieve experiences from memory.

2.4 Understanding Clive Wearing in the functional framework

HM and Clive Wearing have lost the ability to move information from their everyday experiences into memory. One hypothesis about this kind of damage is shown in our framework diagram (Figure 2.6). First, consider all the functions that are *not* impaired in hippocampal damage in both hemispheres. Clive Wearing seems to be quite healthy in his sensory functions, including his ability to appreciate music; his conscious experiences and executive control seem normal; so does motor control (though Wearing has some motor difficulties that seem unrelated to hippocampal damage); as we pointed out, some types of long-term memory seem to be unimpaired, except for his

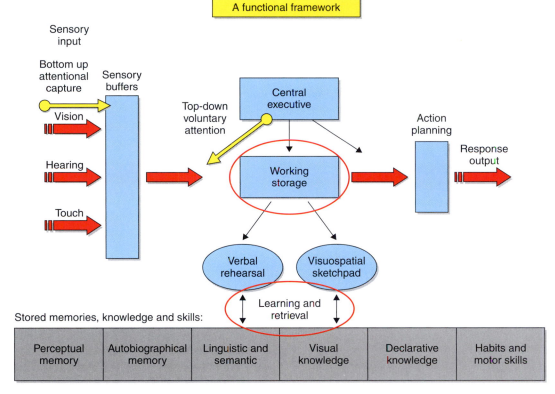

FIGURE 2.6 How medial temporal lobe (MTL) damage can be viewed in the functional framework. Notice that most cognitive functions are spared in classic cases of medial temporal lobe damage in both hemispheres. However, these patients have lost the ability to encode and retrieve conscious experiences – to transfer the present moment to lasting memories and recall them again.

critical inability to store and retrieve his autobiographical experiences; and even his immediate memory persists for perhaps ten seconds. Wearing speaks and understands language at a high level of proficiency. In most tests of intelligence Wearing may score well, except where learning and autobiographical recall are concerned.

Clive Wearing is intensely upset about his condition, showing that he has an understanding that there is something profoundly wrong. His personal relationships with other people are also intensely emotional. It is Clive Wearing's very normality that makes his condition both remarkable and extremely frustrating.

Clive Wearing's crucial loss, therefore, is not in most of the boxes of the functional diagram. It seems that his deficit is primarily limited to the transfer between immediate memory and long-term memory, in both directions:

between encoding conscious experiences and retrieving them (Figure 2.6).

2.5 The importance of immediate memory

Immediate memory is needed even for the simplest activities. If you cannot remember the beginning of this sentence you cannot understand its ending. Because a sentence takes several seconds to read, you must be holding information for that length of time. Similarly, if your brain cannot store information from one visual fixation while scanning the rest of your visual field, you cannot put together the separate elements of the scene in front of your eyes (Figure 2.7). Finally, if you need to eat but you cannot keep your goal in mind long enough do something about it, you may end up going hungry. Research over the last fifty years supports the

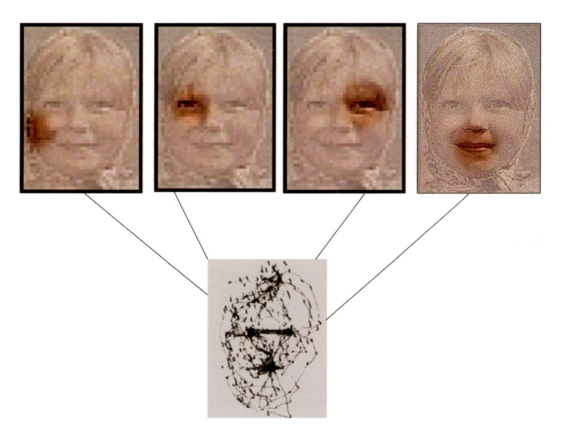

FIGURE 2.7 Immediate memory is needed to integrate small foveal fixations into a single conscious scene. Immediate memory is needed for virtually all cognitive functions. Long eye movements (saccades) jump from one point to another in a visual scene, stopping for only a fraction of a second in the most important parts of the field. At each fixation point the high-resolution part of the retina (the fovea) only picks up a small patch of information, shown by this classic picture from Yarbus (1967); modified by Mark Dubin, used here with permission). The pattern of saccadic movements and momentary fixations are shown by lines superimposed on the girl's face, below. It is believed that the brain stores each foveal snapshot, plans the next saccade, and integrates all the small 'snapshots' into a single coherent visual representation. For that reason an immediate visual buffer memory is needed to integrate many fragmentary records into a coherent conscious scene. *Source*: Adapted from M. Dubin, with permission.

idea that all sensory, motor and cognitive functions require some immediate memory component[1].

Clive Wearing and HM have taught us a great deal. The hippocampal neighborhood continues to be an active topic of research. Because the medial temporal lobe is part of the ancient olfactory brain, which constitutes a large part of the early reptilian and mammalian brain, it has many different functions. (Note that the two olfactory bulbs point upward in Figure 2.5. They terminate in each temporal lobe.) The medial temporal lobe is also an area of great convergence between different sense modalities.

Long-term stores may be located in many places, as we will see. These may include the entire cortex, and even subcortical structures like the basal ganglia and cerebellum (see below). But almost everything we can see in Figure 2.1 is the evolutionarily more recent cortex, called the *neocortex* (i.e. the new cortex, as opposed to the ancient cortex of reptiles and early mammals). Neocortex expanded greatly over mammalian evolution, accelerating during primate and hominid evolution of the last three million years. The hippocampal regions themselves are called *paleocortex*, or 'old cortex'. While neocortex has six distinct cellular layers, paleocortex has four or five. In humans and other mammals, the hippocampal region is constantly interacting with the neocortex, to encode, maintain and retrieve memories when needed.

The role of the hippocampal complex is one example of the constant interplay between limited-capacity and large-capacity abilities in the brain. 'Limited capacity processes' include conscious cognition, selective attention, immediate memory, and voluntary control. 'Large-capacity functions' include long-term memories, highly practiced skills, and our language vocabulary. We will explore this theme next.

3.0 LIMITED AND LARGE-CAPACITY FUNCTIONS

Even though human brains have tens of billions of neurons, in some ways they have very narrow capacity limits. The limits of short-term memory – the kind we can mentally rehearse – is about 'seven plus or minus two' separate items, as George A. Miller famously described in 1956. That number seems to apply to many kind of unrelated items – colors, numbers, short words, musical notes, steps on a rating scale, and so on. There are only a few conditions. One is that each item must be consciously noticed for only a brief time; if it is made consciously available many times, it becomes part of long-term memory. Second, the items must be *unpredictable* from previous knowledge. If we simply ask people to remember a rule, like the number series 1, 5, 10, 15, 20, 25 . . . (etc.), they can keep much more information in immediate memory because they only have to remember the rule. When we are prevented from mentally rehearsing items in immediate memory, the capacity of immediate memory drops from about seven to less than four separate items (Cowan, 2001).

Selective attention is another limited capacity function. It was initially studied by Donald Broadbent and others, using the dichotic listening paradigm (Figure 2.8). In this method, subjects wear headphones with two separate speech channels, often one into each ear. Because they are asked to 'shadow' one of the two channels (i.e. to repeat the incoming speech with minimum lag time), subjects can hear only one channel. It is easy to demonstrate this by listening to two radio news broadcasts at the same time, for example. Under these conditions people can only understand one channel, though they can pick up the voice quality in the unattended channel.

For a gigantic brain, these capacity limits are tiny. Compared to a digital computer, for example, they are astonishingly small. But surprising limits are found beyond immediate memory and selective attention. Table 2.1 shows a dozen other phenomena that show similar, narrow capacity limits.

3.1 Dual task limits

Personal technology has made it possible for us to try to study, listen to favorite music, and talk on a cellphone at the same time. Sadly, our efficiency in multitasking goes down rapidly the more different things we try to do at the same time. We cannot generally do even two conscious things at a time, such as carrying on a complicated conversation and driving in rush hour traffic. If we don't need to think much about talking, we can drive at the same time, and vice versa, but the more conscious involvement is needed for each task the more they will compete. For that reason, dual-task methods are often used to study how much of our limited capacity

---

[1] There is also evidence for an *intermediate* memory capacity lasting hours or days, but not longer – to remember where we left a bicycle, what food to buy for dinner, how to navigate a new environment, or recent interpersonal events (Delaney *et al.*, 2004).

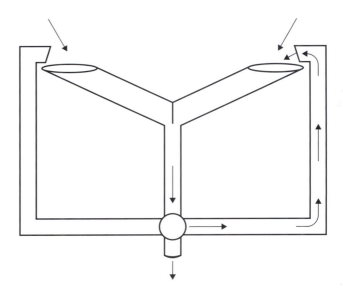

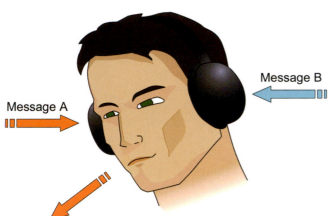

Message A

Message B

FIGURE 2.8 Donald Broadbent and selective attention. Renewed interest in selective attention emerged in the 1950s with an influential experimental program started by Donald A. Broadbent. The upper image shows Broadbent's 'funnel' image of limited capacity functions, which dramatizes the fact that our large brains have narrow limits for selective attention, conscious perception, and voluntary control. Broadbent's selective listening task, in which two messages are sent simultaneously to the two ears, is a classical dual task method for studying limited capacity functions. *Photograph Source*: From Broadbent, with permission.

TABLE 2.1   Limited capacity tasks

1   Dual-input limits. Some fifty years of research shows that people cannot consciously understand two incompatible streams of information at the same moment.
   a Selective listening: receiving two streams of auditory input at the same time.
   b Inattentional blindness: tracking two competing visual streams on a single screen.
   c Binocular rivalry and its variants: receiving different visual input to the two eyes.
2   Immediate memory limits, including the capacity to hold recalled memories.
3   Ambiguous stimuli and meanings, such as the Necker cube, ambiguous words, and many other cases where input can be interpreted in more than one way.
4   Competition between different features of the same object, such as the Stroop color-naming effect (see Chapter 3).
5   Conjoined feature search: for example, searching for both color and shape in a complex display.
6   Effortful tasks compete against each other. The more difficult two tasks are perceived to be, the more they tend to interfere. There may even be an upper bound on the number of effortful tasks one can accomplish per day (Muraven and Baumeister, 2000).
7   Response competition. Two different output plans or actions tend to compete against each other (Pashler, 1989)
8   Limits on temporal integration:
   a Attentional blink: in a rapid series of visual letters, a 'blind' period may occur some 200–500 milliseconds after a target letter.
   b Change blindness: the difference between two visual scenes may go unnoticed if a brief white flash interrupts them. This may be a limit on the construction of coherent temporal events.

(Continued)

TABLE 2.1   (Continued)

9	Long-term memory search may be limited, as in the case of word retrieval difficulties.
10	Conceptual incompatibility and functional fixedness. It may be difficult or impossible for people to understand an 'obvious' problem from an unexpected point of view.
11	Domain-specific limits. Specific input and output modalities may have local limitations. One example is the very small size of high resolution vision, using the fovea. Another is our difficulty in doing certain bimanual actions, such as patting one's head and rubbing one's stomach at the same time.

TABLE 2.2   Very large-capacity functions

Some brain features show massive capacity.
1 The various kinds of long-term memory.
  a Episodic and autobiographical memory has been estimated to be 1 000 000 000 bits (Landauer, 1986). Using recognition memory, one can retrieve old movie scenes, childhood landmarks, the faces of fellow students, and the like, dating back five decades or longer.
  b Semantic memory for facts and concepts is very large.
  c Procedural memory for highly practiced skills.
2 The language vocabulary: educated speakers of English can recognize about 100 000 words, each of which involves a complex network of related ideas, sounds, and written words.
3 The great complexity of sensory and motor processes.
4 The vast number of neurons, connections, and functional networks in the brain.

is taken up by a task. As the cognitive demands of one task rise, the efficiency of the second task will go down correspondingly. Dual-task methods have therefore been immensely important in the development of cognitive neuroscience.

How do we cope in the face of capacity limits? There are at least two ways. One is *chunking*, the ability to condense a vast amount of information into a single, organized unit. The words of human languages are often chunks: imagine the amount of information we can access using words like 'mother', 'school', 'love', and so on. We have many other ways of condensing information into single chunks. In studying this chapter, chances are that you will condense it into main points. That is a good chunking strategy, because you can summarize thousands of words into a few dozen sentences.

We can also get around capacity limits by practice. In general, humans are much better with practiced tasks than with novel ones. The brain seems to solve novel problems rather slowly; it makes many errors, and tends to sequence even things that might be done at the same time. Conscious access drops when skills become more practiced and efficient (Raaijmakers and Shiffrin, 1992; Chein and Schneider, 2005). Thus a skilled video gamer may be able to talk at the same time as playing the game, while a novice must concentrate on the game. Practice is a way of lowering the limited capacity cost of doing a task.

However, there is another side to the capacity story. Some cognitive capacities are very large indeed (Table 2.2).

3.2 Some very large brain capacities

At the level of the cells, a structure like the cerebral cortex is immense – a vast, looming starship unto itself, containing, by recent estimates, between 10 and 100 billion neurons. Seen from the outside, it is an elaborately folded structure with many hills and valleys, neatly tucked into the upper half of the cranial cavity. If we could carefully unfold the great cortical mantle we would see a sheet about three feet square (1 m^2), with six layers, each composed of myriads of bushy neurons surrounded by supportive cells. This layered sandwich can be parsed into millions of vertical columns, so that we can imagine a vast six-layered array in three dimensions. Each layer seems to specialize in input, output, or internal connections in the cortex (see Chapters 3 and 5).

Cortical neurons are connected by vast tracts of *axonal fibers*, wrapped in white sheathing cells called *myelin*. If we simply slice through cortex we see mostly white matter, an indication of how many connective fibers there are. To the naked eye, cortex looks like a double fruit covered with a thin skin of cell bodies, the gray matter that we see from the outside. But the white matter contains miles of tiny axons that descend from the gray cell bodies and end up coming back to cortex on the opposite side of the brain. Current estimates for the left-to-right fibers that cross through the corpus callosum – the large fiber bridge between the hemispheres – is on the order of 200 million. Each of these fibers sends an electrochemical message about ten times per second, making for message traffic of about 2 billion events per second.

An equally large number of axon bundles loops beneath the cortex and comes back up on the *same* side. Thus, there is an immense amount of traffic between the two hemispheres, and within them as well.

The outermost layer of the six-layered sandwich, Layer I, is so densely woven horizontally that it has been called a *feltwork*, a large skin of tight webbing on top of the sandwich. While most long-distance communication in cortex seems to run through long vertical output fibers (axons), the top layer is so tightly interconnected horizontally that many brain scientists believe there is also a great deal of spreading activity within it.

Cortical neurons do more than connect with other cortical neurons. They also project in vast elegant fiber bundles to the neural organs nestled tightly under the cortex, like small bird eggs in a nest. Among the bird eggs, the *thalamus* serves as a great traffic hub, the way station for almost all sensory messages going to the cortex, and therefore a strategic control point. An equally large mass of fibers goes from cortex to the basal ganglia and cerebellum, both necessary for normal movement.

When we become conscious in the morning the brain is globally activated, every part showing faster and more widely connected neural traffic. It is as if suddenly all the neurons jumped into their cars and decided to go places. As a novel or surprising event catches our attention, a vast electrical tidal wave rushes all over the brain, a few tenths of a second after the triggering event. This is the called the 'event-related potential', discussed in Chapter 4 and Appendix B.

There is good evidence that anatomical regions in the brain can serve very specialized functions (e.g. Luria, 1976; Geschwind, 1979a). A number of scientists have interpreted the organization of the cerebral cortex in terms of distributed 'unit modules' (Mountcastle, 1978; Edelman and Mountcastle, 1978). Rozin (1976) viewed the evolution of intelligence as an increase in the ability to apply these specialized functions to life situations. Your ability to read, for example, is not something human beings are born with. Unlike heard and spoken speech, babies do not spontaneously learn to read. It takes years of training. But we can learn to use our visual system astonishingly well to take in language by eye rather than ear, and to express language by writing instead of our vocal apparatus. The ability to learn sign language and read in Braille tells the same story. Reading seems to ride on biological preadaptations.

Rozin and others suggest that brain capacities tend to evolve as specialized adaptations. But in the human lifetime, he suggests, specialized functions can become available for new adaptive purposes.

3.3 Why are there such narrow capacity limits?

It would be nice to be able to do half a dozen things at the same time. Why do some functions seem to be so limited in a brain with tens of billion of neurons? It isn't just that we have a limited capacity to *do* things – only one mouth to speak with and two hands to hold things with. Capacity limits also operate in perception, the *input* system, so the limitations of hands and mouth are not the only reason. Ambiguous figures, like the famous Necker Cube, are very limited: we can only perceive one interpretation of an ambiguous stimulus at any given moment.

So the problem isn't just the fact that we can only do one thing at a time in the motor system. And it is not that the brain lacks sheer processing capacity – its ability to store and transform information is beyond our current ability to describe. Some scientists have argued that capacity limits are due to the role of consciousness in combining numerous components of a very large brain into an integrated whole (Baars, 1988, 2002b; Edelman, 1989; Llinas and Pare, 1991). Limited functions are closely associated with conscious experience, while very large capacity functions are generally unconscious (see Tables 2.1 and 2.2). However, it is not clear at this time why that should be so.

3.4 Measuring working memory

The middle column in the figure on page 30 corresponds to classical working memory (Baddeley and Hitch, 1974; Burgess and Hitch, 1999; Baddeley, 2000). Working memory emerged in cognitive psychology several decades ago when scientists began to understand how important immediate memory capacities are. It provides a useful way of thinking about the cognitive brain. More than ten thousand studies have been published on the topic, and working memory is often used to provide a perspective or other functions as well – including mental imagery, language, inner speech and executive control. The amount of psychological evidence about working memory is immense and, in the last ten years, our understanding of their brain basis has expanded very rapidly. Working memory therefore offers a convenient and widely understood way of approaching the complexity of the mind and brain.

According to Cowan *et al.* (2005), 'Working Memory is the set of mental processes holding limited information in a temporarily accessible state in service of cognition'. This broad definition will prove useful. Working memory has come to stand for the many things we can keep temporarily accessible. Its meaning has broadened considerably since the concept was first proposed in somewhat different words by Atkinson and Shiffrin (1968) and by Baddeley and Hitch (1974). But, in a general sense, the working memory framework has remained quite consistent.

Notice that Cowan's definition is broad enough to allow for expansion to other domains, not just verbal rehearsal and the visuospatial sketchpad. For example, we can imagine mentally humming a song. If we do that successfully, and we can verify it empirically, we could consider adding a working memory component of 'inner music'. Experienced musicians seem to have a number of ways of manipulating notes and melodies in their heads. Athletes can mentally practice sports, and their actual performance improves as a result. Scientists are currently considering different types of working memory for eye movements and emotional processes, perhaps even for dreams and daydreams. Working memory in this very general sense can use a number of

different modalities. A great deal of brain and behavioral evidence supports a wider application of these basic ideas.

Once sensory information is attentionally selected, it is often said to become available to working memory. By Cowan's definition (above), that means that an odor or a taste could be 'in a temporarily accessible state in service of cognition'. If you dwell on that definition for ten seconds or so, you are holding your thoughts in working memory. As you can tell, your ability to think about it is vulnerable to distracting events, including your own thoughts and feelings – and reading this sentence. Your ability to think about any topic is therefore capacity-limited. Thus, we might talk about 'thinking working memory', or 'conceptual working memory', as well as visual or verbal working memory.

Measurement is crucial in science, and working memory is typically assessed in several different ways. Figure 2.9 shows one way in which visual working memory may be assessed, simply by presenting visual shapes, in a series of slides over specific time periods, often measured in hundreds of milliseconds. Any stimulus may be presented and re-tested some seconds later, either asking for recall or presenting the original stimulus for recognition. Behaviorally, one can assess working memory by accuracy of recall or recognition, and by the speed of responding (*reaction time*).

These simple but powerful methods allow for numerous variations. One popular method is *delayed match to*

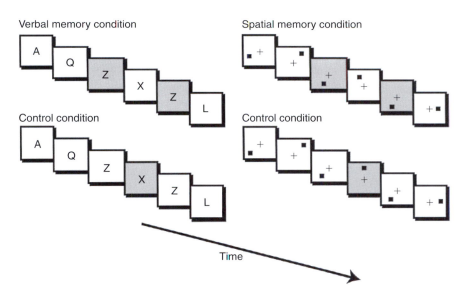

FIGURE 2.9 This figure shows one way in which visual working memory may be assessed, simply by presenting visual shapes, in a series of slides over specific time periods, often measured in hundreds of milliseconds. Any stimulus may be presented and re-tested some seconds later, either asking for recall or presenting the original stimulus for recognition.

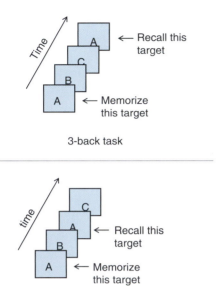

3-back task

2-back task

FIGURE 2.10 A difficult continuous memory task: in the *n*-back Working Memory tasks, subjects are asked to recall the item presented one, two or three slides before. This is a very demanding task. When *n*-back tasks are compared on fMRI, cortical activity increases markedly as *n* goes from 1 to 4. (See Figure 2.12).

sample (DMTS), in which subjects are asked to respond when they see a match with their recent memory. This method can be used for animals and infants as well as adults.

What about brain assessment of working memory? Figure 2.10 shows an '*n*-back task', an important variant of the simple WM task. N-back tasks allow us to vary the degree of mental workload, a variable that has major brain effects. The concept is fiendish but simple. In any series of stimuli, your job as a subject is to remember the last one you saw – that is fairly easy. But now you are asked to remember the second word you saw *before* the current slide, then the third before, and so on. To do this, subjects must rehearse the last *n* stimuli and not confuse the *n*-back stimulus with the others that have to be kept in working memory.

This is subjectively harder and harder to do as *n* grows from one to three or four, and the brain shows consistently wider activation. For example, Figure 2.11 shows blood-oxygen changes at the bottom of the brain, using functional magnetic resonance imaging (fMRI) (see Chapter 4). The bottom of the temporal lobe contains many neurons specialized in visual object perception. In addition, it is adjacent to the medial temporal lobe, which contains the two hippocampi. Because this is a demanding executive task – the cognitive equivalent of

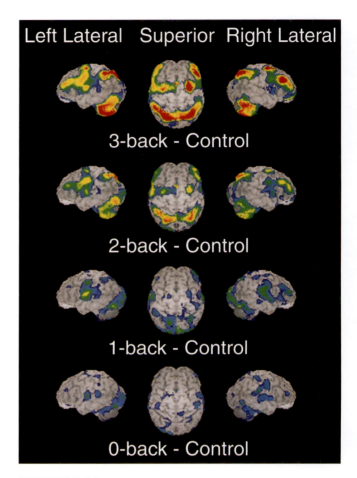

FIGURE 2.11 Brain activity increases with the Working Memory load. Brain imaging using fMRI shows dramatic increases in the amount of cortex involved in the *n*-back task, as *n* rises from 0 to 3. In the 0-back condition, subjects only need to name the visible slide. On these brain images, brighter colors signal higher levels of activity.

juggling half a dozen balls at the same time – we also see increased activity in prefrontal regions.

4.0 THE INNER AND OUTER SENSES

There is now good evidence that *endogenous* (internally generated) events imitate the outer senses to some degree (Figure 2.12). To see the similarity between them you should recall that the posterior half of the cortex is mainly sensory. Even though our eyes, ears, nose and mouth point forward – the direction we usually move – all sensory pathways terminate in the back of the cortex, where sensory stimuli are analyzed at the highest level.

Each sensory pathway reaches cortex in its own *primary projection area*. It is easiest to remember the primary cortices as V1 (for the primary visual projection area), A1 (for primary auditory), and S1 (for primary

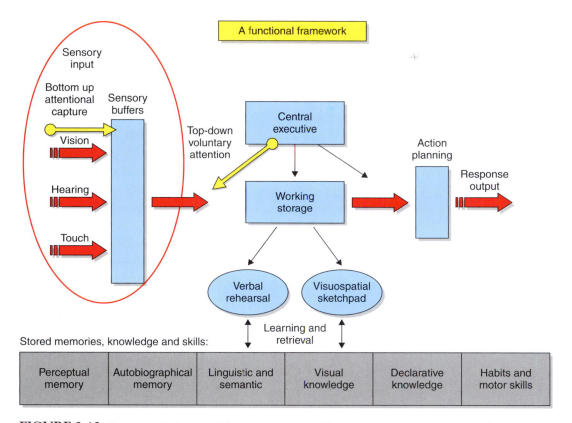

FIGURE 2.12   Framework diagram with sensory emphasis. The sensory systems receive input from arrays of receptors which transform physical energy patterns into neuronal firing. Sensory cortex in vision and the body senses is mapped to the stimulus array in a topographical fashion.

FIGURE 2.13   Occipital activation for visual stimulation. This brain scan shows activation in the occipital cortex, which is mapped point to point to the retinal light input. *Source*: Singh *et al.*, 2000.

somatosensory cortex, the body map). V1 is an accurate map of the retinal input. It projects in its turn to V2, V3, and so on, each higher visual area representing the visual array in more and more abstract ways (see Chapter 6). As the visual signal traffic flows into parietal cortex, it becomes integrated with hearing, touch, body space and motor control.

4.1 The mind's eye, ear and voice

In the 4th century BC, Aristotle suggested that visual images were 'faint copies' of visual sensations, i.e. he thought that imagery was a kind of vague internal perception. In the last few decades, a mounting body of evidence seems to show he was right. The American

PERCEPTION   IMAGERY   PERCEPTION – IMAGERY

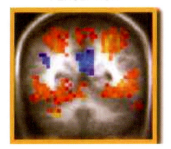 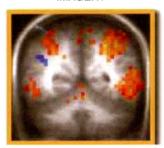 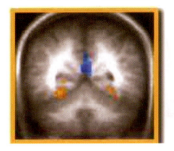 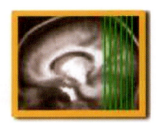

FIGURE 2.14   Visual imagery may activate parts of visual cortex. In these brain scans from Ganis *et al.* (2004), activity for perception and imagery are so similar that they can be subtracted from each other, yielding very little difference. As the right-most figure shows, these virtual slices were selected from the occipital and parietal region. Note that Perception – Imagery means perception *minus* imagery effects. *Source*: Ganis *et al.*, 2004.

psychologist, C.W. Perky, demonstrated this elegantly early in the 20th century when she showed that people can confuse faint visual pictures with their own mental images (Perky, 1910).

Psychologists have devised a number of methods to test visual imagery. Stephen Kosslyn has demonstrated that 'the mind's eye' is a surprisingly realistic figure of speech. The human visual field has a characteristic size and shape, which is easy to demonstrate. Simply look at an object in the room in which you are reading this, allowing your eyes to fixate on a point without moving your head. Now bring your hands in from the sides of your visual field until you can barely see them; the horizontal limits of the active visual field will be on the order of 120 degrees of visual arc. Do the same for the vertical limits, and it will turn out to be less than half of that. The *working* visual field seems to be a flat oval, perhaps 45 visual degrees in height by 120 degrees wide.

If you now close one eye and fix the open eye on a single target, like a single letter in this sentence, the field will shrink dramatically to only a few degrees of visual arc, corresponding to *foveal* vision. The fovea is a small, central patch of each retina that has very high density of visual receptors, hence the highest visual resolution. It is the keyhole-size 'sight' that we aim at the world to get high-resolution snapshots. The fovea subtends about four degrees of visual arc.

You can measure your inner field of your 'mind's eye' in much the way you did with your visual field – naturally, by using your imaginary hands. Closing your eyes, move your virtual hands to the sides of your 'mind's eye', and write down the horizontal extent of your field. Now do the same in the vertical dimension. People generally will come up with somewhat less than 120 degrees of horizontal arc, and about 45 degrees

vertical. A variety of such experiments shows a remarkable resemblance between the physical visual field and its mental double. Over the last several years, research has begun to reveal the reason for this resemblance. Kosslyn, Martha Farah and others have shown that visual imagery elicits activity in parts of the visual cortex. Ganis *et al.* (2004) write that, 'Visual imagery and visual perception draw on most of the same neural machinery'.

However, there are many ways of seeing the world, and many ways to use one's visuospatial imagery. Depending upon experimental conditions, different patterns of activity may be found in visual cortex. By using conditions designed to match visual perception and visual imagery as much as possible, Ganis *et al.* showed that brain activity from visual imagery can be nearly identical to visual perception. Figure 2.14 shows that the two activity patterns can be subtracted from each other, point by point, leaving few visible differences. This is a striking result.

Kosslyn (1994) points out that imagery, 'is not a unitary ability, but consists instead of a host of specialized abilities'. The famous mental rotation task devised by Shephard and Cooper (1982), for example, seems to require visual, spatial, motor *and* executive regions (Figure 2.15). Because V1 has point-to-point mapping to the retina, Kosslyn wrote, 'It is possible that (V1) is activated only by tasks that require high resolution images'.

4.2 The imagery sketchpad may use visual regions of cortex

Can you remember the first time you saw this book? If you can, do any visual images come to mind? Can you bring to mind the place and the way the book looked to you? Did you see it lying flat, or propped up? Was it right side up or upside down? People vary in the

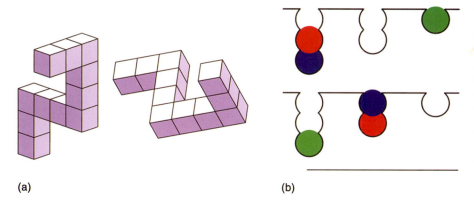

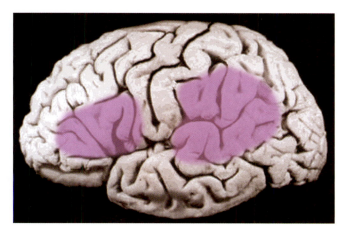

(a)   (b)

FIGURE 2.15 Different imagery tasks. (a) The classic mental rotation stimuli from Shephard and Cooper (1982). The subject is asked to report whether the two arbitrary shapes are the same or different. To answer the question, subjects mentally rotate one shape to see if it matches the other. (b) A classic 'tower' task, which can be thought of as rolling colored balls from one pocket to another. How can you transform the upper picture into the lower? Here again, subjects appear to use visual imagery, but the task is quite different from mental rotation, or from the task shown in Figure 2.15. *Source*: Heslow, 2002.

FIGURE 2.16 Approximate location of Broca's and Wernicke's areas. Although 19th century physicians were not equipped with sophisticated brain recording instruments, their conclusions converge well with modern imaging studies. *Source*: Squire *et al.*, 2003.

vividness of their spontaneous mental imagery, but most people can do these tasks. Where does this happen in the brain? Figure 2.14 suggests similar brain regions are active when seeing versus imagining.

Notice how well cognitive and brain findings converge in these examples. Vision involves occipital, temporal and parietal cortex, and so does 'mental vision' or visual imagery, under carefully controlled conditions.

4.3 Is inner speech like outer speech?

Most human beings go around the world talking to themselves. People are often quite willing to tell us about their private monologue. Simply by asking them to write down clear internal speech as soon as it occurs, a body of useful evidence has been gathered. If we include *inner speech* in the inner senses, we can find similarities between inner and outer articulation of words.

The psycholinguist Gary Dell has shown that internal tongue-twisters create errors very similar to overt tongue-twisters (Dell and Sullivan, 2004). For example, try repeating, 'Peter piper picked a peck of pickled peppers' in your inner speech, as quickly as you can. Do you notice any inner pronunciation errors? But you have no inner tongue to twist – or do you? Imaginary practice can be effective – which makes a lot of sense if we use the same brain tissue for mental and physical practice.

Given what we know about Broca's and Wernicke's areas from Chapter 1 (see also Figure 2.16), where would you predict activation for silent verbal rehearsal?

Mentally rehearsing numbers to ourselves may sound like a vague kind of speech. Scientists have speculated for many years that we actually speak to ourselves silently, and there has been indirect evidence for that hypothesis. It has now been supported by functional brain imaging (see Figure 2.17).

In later chapters, we will see things become a little more complicated, because there are many ways of speaking and listening, and many ways of seeing and visualizing. Yet this is the big picture: it does seem that the 'outer senses' have corresponding 'inner senses', like visual imagery and internal speech (see Figure 2.18).

4.4 Is there only one working memory?

We have used the term 'working memory' as if it were a single thing, but that is a hotly debated question. As we will see, there is evidence for both 'domain specific' and 'non-specific' temporary holding memories (see Chapter 8). Some researchers talk about working memories for concepts, for space, and for semantics, as well as vision and speech. Current evidence favors a combination of the two hypotheses: there seem to be both domain-specific and non-specific working memory capacities.

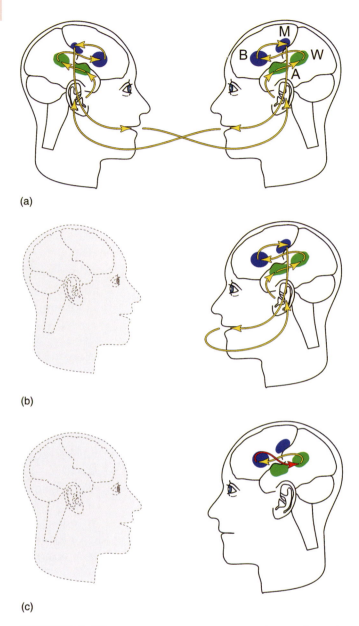

(a)

(b)

(c)

FIGURE 2.17 Inner speech can be considered normal speech (a) with the vocal organs inhibited ('covert'). Covert speech uses the classical speech areas of the left hemisphere. A summary brain figure showing some areas activated in an inner speech task. (B = Broca's area; W = Wernicke's area; M = motor cortex; A = auditory cortex). *Source*: Heslow, 2002.

5.0 THE CENTRAL EXECUTIVE

As mentioned before, the prefrontal lobes play an important executive role in the brain. They are needed for voluntary control over actions. Prefrontal regions also support emotional processes and seem to be necessary to control one's own unwanted impulses.

The neurologist Oliver Sacks writes (in Goldberg, 2001b):

> The frontal lobes are the latest achievements of the nervous system; it is only in human beings (and great apes, to some extent) that they reach so great a development. . . . they lack the simple and easily identifiable functions of the more primitive parts of the cerebral cortex, the sensory and motor areas. . . but they are overwhelmingly important. They are crucial for all higher-order purposeful behavior – identifying the objective, projecting the goal, forging plans to reach it, organizing the means by which such plans can be carried out, monitoring and judging the consequences to see that all is accomplished as intended. . . . Without the great development of the frontal lobes in the human brain (coupled with the development of the language areas) civilization could never have arisen.

> Thus in the famous case of Phineas Gage – a railway foreman who, while setting an explosive charge in 1848, had a two-foot tamping iron blown through his frontal lobes when the charge backfired – while there was preservation of Gage's intelligence as well as his ability to move and talk and see, there were other, profound changes in him. He became reckless and improvident, impulsive, profane; he could no longer plan or think of the future; and for those who had known him before, 'he was no longer Gage'. He had lost himself, the most central part of his being, and (as is the case with all patients with severe damage to the frontal lobes), he did not know it.

The Stroop Color-naming Task is commonly used to test for frontal lobe damage. In the Stroop Task a conflict is set up between reading a word and naming its color. By using printed color names we can present the word 'blue' in a green color, and ask people to name only the colors as quickly as possible (Figure 2.20). Since educated people are highly practiced readers, their automatic tendency is to *read* the word rather than name its color. The task instructions therefore ask them to do the opposite of what they have practiced doing for many years. In people with healthy brains, the Stroop task sets up a conflict involving prefrontal cortex, but it can usually be resolved. Response times are slowed compared to a control condition, and people sometimes make errors. But, in frontal lobe patients, the effects of the conflict is more debilitating, leading to more errors, longer response times, and a greater sense of subjective difficulty and frustration. The Stroop Test is useful to probe for subtle frontal lobe damage that may be missed by brain scans.

Over playing   Covert playing

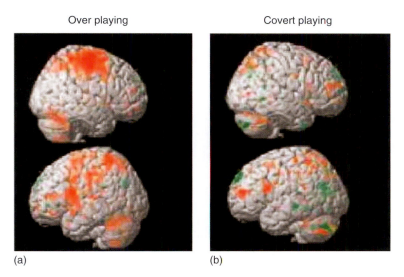

(a)   (b)

FIGURE 2.18   An inner musician? The 'inner senses' are not limited to verbal and visuospatial abilities. We may have 'inner musicians' and 'inner athletes' as well. These brain scans compare overt and covert instrumental playing by amateur musicians. While overt play shows higher activation in motor and somatosensory areas, generally similar regions of the brain show activity in both conditions. *Source*: Lotze *et al.*, 2000.

5.1 Executive effort and automaticity

A remarkable finding from brain scanning experiments is that many different tasks involving executive effort all 'light up' two crucial regions of the frontal brain. On the *sides* of the frontal lobes, this involves the *dorsolateral prefrontal cortex* (DL-PFC)[2]. Along the *midline* of each hemisphere, an important executive region is the front of the cingulate cortex, the *anterior cingulate cortex* (ACC). These areas also show high activity in the Stroop Task, which involves a conflict between highly practiced skills like word reading, and a novel task like color naming (Duncan and Owen, 2000; Frackowiak, 2004).

Voluntary actions become automatic with practice (Shiffrin and Schneider, 1977). As they do so, we also tend to lose some executive control over them (e.g. Langer and Imber, 1979). Our loss of control over highly practiced and predictable habits seems to go along with a loss of conscious access to their details (Schneider,

1995). In brain scans, we see a dramatic reduction of cortical activity when a predictable voluntary action is practiced to the point of automaticity. There is evidence that routinized voluntary actions may be taken over in part by subcortical regions of the brain, notably the basal ganglia and cerebellum.

However, we should not make an all-or-none distinction between voluntary and automatic actions. Automatic actions can come under voluntary control again when predictable aspects of the action become unpredictable, as when we break a leg and try to walk in our usual way (Sacks, 1984). Most everyday activities are a mixture between voluntary and automatic control. The most highly practiced components of our habitual actions tend to be automatic, while the most novel and unpredictable ones tend to remain under voluntary control. Thus, we may be able to make voluntary decisions about which way to walk at a new street intersection, but

[2] Terms like 'dorsolateral prefrontal' sound intimidating, but are actually quite simple. They are much like the compass terminology 'North, South, East, West, North-West, etc.' 'Dorsal' means 'upper' in the human brain, lateral means 'side', while 'medial' is along the midline. 'Inferior, superior and middle' are what you might expect. We therefore get compound names, such as dorsolateral, meaning the upper part of the side of the cortex, and 'ventromedial', the lower half of the midline of the brain. If that is hard to visualize, it is an excellent idea to draw these directional terms on some visual object, like a picture of a shoe or car. Some students prefer to think of a pair of shoes, to represent the left and right halves of cortex. These objects are useful because they have a clearly defined front, back, left and right side. If you then simply translate the Latin-based vocabulary into words like 'front, back, upper, lower, middle, and sides' you will find it easy to cope with this terminology. We will use a hyphen to separate the directional part from the brain part. Prefrontal cortex is abbreviated as PFC. The upper side part of the PFC is therefore 'DL-PFC'. When in doubt, be sure to decompose the long words into their subunits.

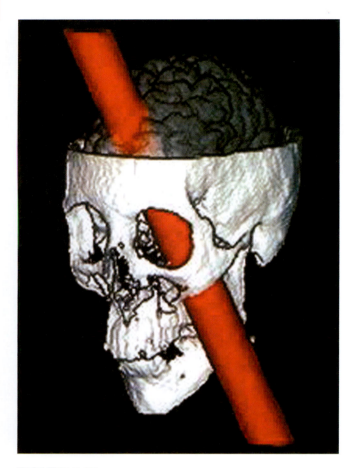

FIGURE 2.19 Hannah Damasio's computerized reconstruction of the brain damage suffered by Phineas Gage in 1848, based on his death mask (Damasio *et al.*, 1994). At the time, most people would have died from an infection of the wound, if not from brain damage and blood loss. Gage was fortunate to survive and recover most of his abilities, but he could no longer pursue his old life goals or control impulsive actions. These changes were so profound as to signal a change in personality. Similar phenomena are observed in other cases of frontal lobe injury (see Chapter 12). *Source*: Caplan and Gould in Squire *et al.*, 2003.

BLUE   GREEN   YELLOW

PINK   RED   ORANGE

GREY   BLACK   PURPLE

TAN   WHITE   BROWN

TAN   WHITE   BROWN

GREY   BLACK   PURPLE

PINK   RED   ORANGE

BLUE   GREEN   YELLOW

FIGURE 2.20 The Stroop Color-naming Task reflects executive functions. Try to name the colors on top, and you are likely to find it difficult. When the words are unreadable, color naming is easier, faster, and more accurate (bottom half). *Source*: Miller and Wallis in Squire *et al.*, 2003.

once we decide to turn right we are rarely conscious of each step we take. The same general point applies to speaking, reading, eye movement control, and much more. Automatic and voluntary control work hand in hand.

An interesting point is the existence of dual-control systems in the brain. For example, we can smile voluntarily or spontaneously (Figure 2.21). These similar muscle actions are triggered by different regions, the voluntary one being more cortical, using the frontal lobes.

Likewise, we can take a deep breath 'at will', but we normally breathe in a spontaneous and automatic rhythm. Large eye movements can also be controlled voluntarily as well as automatically. For smiling, breathing and eye movements, automatic control is much more common than voluntary, cortical control. As we will see, selective attention also has dual control, both voluntary (executive) attention and spontaneous attentional selection.

Such dual control is a common strategy of the brain, but it does not apply to vital functions, like the control of heart rate. For obvious reasons, heart rate control is automatic; it would be disastrous to try to stop or start it at will. The same is true for other autonomic functions. Brain injuries can sometimes dissociate voluntary and automatic control centers from each other, as happens in disorders that impair only voluntary smiles, but not spontaneous ones (see Figure 2.21). There are also brain lesions that work the other way: damage to the brainstem can cause automatic control to be disabled while voluntary control is spared.

There is a debate whether voluntary actions are equivalent to consciously decided ones (Shiffrin, 1995; Schneider, 1995). This is a difficult issue to settle. However, there is little disagreement that voluntary control

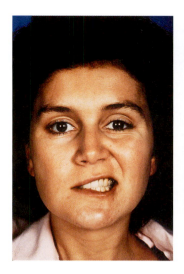

FIGURE 2.21 Selective damage to voluntary but not spontaneous smiles. On the left, this patient cannot make a symmetrical
smile, while on the right her smile looks quite normal. On the left,
she is trying to smile voluntarily, while in the right photo she is smiling spontaneously. The damage to her frontal lobe motor regions
does not affect her (subcortical) facial expressions. Other patients
show the opposite damage, impairing spontaneous smiles but not
voluntary ones. The ability to show that two brain functions can be
damaged independently of each other is called a double dissociation
Source: Paxinos and Mai, 2004.

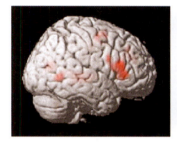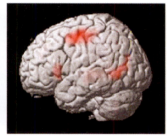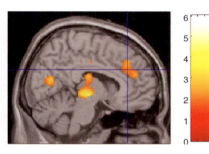

FIGURE 2.22 Posner's model of executive attention. Selective attention is part of the working framework. It can
be defined as the ability to select among two or more alternative events. The figure shows the executive attentional
network proposed by Posner and coauthors (Fan *et al.*, 2005). Notice that two lobes show most activation, the prefrontal and the parietal cortex. Attentional selection can change activity in many regions of the brain. *Source*: Holstege
et al., 2004.

and conscious cognition are strongly associated with
each other.

Recent evidence also suggests that the executive system corresponds to the 'self' of everyday life (Vogeley
et al., 1999; Baars, 2002b). We will explore this question
in later chapters on executive function and emotion.

5.2 Executive and spontaneous attention

You can decide to pay attention to a single word in this
sentence, or the same word could be flashed on and
off, so that it tends to compel your attention without
executive control. Michael Posner has shown that the
executive attention system in the brain involves prefrontal regions, as well as parietal ones, when spatial
selection is concerned (Figure 2.22).

The visual 'pop-out' effect is a common example of
spontaneous attention (Figure 2.23). Some stimuli come
to mind without voluntarily controlled visual search.
When the same stimuli are embedded in field of similar

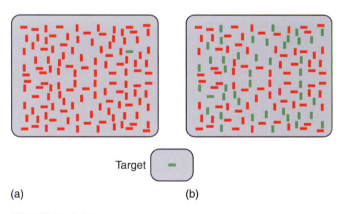

(a)   (b)

FIGURE 2.23 Spontaneous attentional capture. The task on
both sides is to search for the horizontal green bar. On the left side,
the green bar appears to 'pop out' spontaneously, with little effort.
On the right hand side, finding the green target bar requires effortful
search, which is thought to involve executive regions of the brain.
Visual 'pop-out' also applies to salient stimuli – ones that are biologically or personally significant, like faces or human bodies, or those
that are physically intense. Thus, we have two different kinds of
selective attention: voluntary, goal-directed executive attention, and
spontaneous, bottom-up attentional 'capture' by salient stimuli.
Source: Squire *et al.*, 2003.

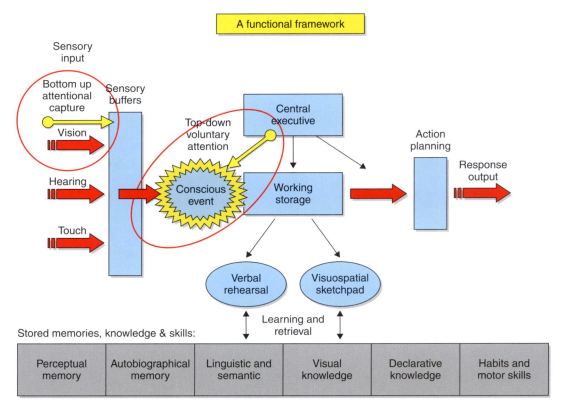

FIGURE 2.24   In practice, conscious events are defined as events that people can report accurately. The functional diagram showing a hypothesized relationship between selective attention and conscious events. A number of scientists believe that selective attention may be needed for conscious sensory experiences. However, there are some contrary findings. A new experimental literature has now grown to explore such questions.

stimuli, the pop-out effect disappears and voluntary search becomes necessary.

Attention is often thought to be required for conscious experiences. We can represent this hypothesis in the functional diagram (Figure 2.24). As we will see in Chapter 8, this hypothesis is not always true, but in normal life conditions, attentional selection appears to lead to conscious experiences more often than not. The role of consciousness in human cognition has become a hot research topic, and we now have a good deal of evidence that helps to clarify the issue (see Chapter 8). Obviously, there is still a great deal that we do not know about consciousness, but it appears to be a productive topic for scientific research.

6.0 ACTION

The last elements of the functional diagram involve output: control of voluntary actions. There are some

striking parallels between perception and action. Fuster (2003) points out that both input and output levels can be viewed as processing hierarchies. The visual hierarchy begins with retinal 'pixels' in cortical area V1, the primary visual cortex, and proceeds to areas specialized for color, motion, and object recognition. On the output side, the motor hierarchy begins with general goals, influenced by emotional and motivational input from limbic regions. The most general goals are represented in more prefrontal areas and proceed down the motor hierarchy to supplementary and premotor regions which may trigger intentions and the urge to act (e.g. Penfield and Roberts, 1959). The primary cortical motor region (M1) directly triggers movement of skeletal muscles.

Figure 2.25 shows brain regions that become active in pushing a button with the right hand. The lower right panel shows a time scale marked in seconds, and anticipatory brain activity begins several seconds before the finger press. Notice that motor cortex is active on the *left* side, opposite to the hand that is

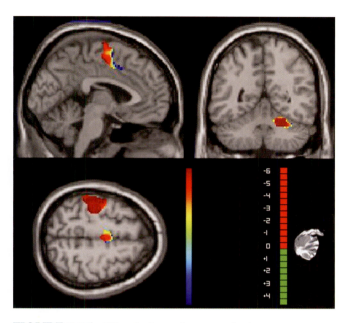

FIGURE 2.25 What the brain does to push a button. Hulsmann *et al.* (2003) has shown how the voluntary goal of pressing a button rises over seconds before a spontaneous action. This snapshot shows the target time (time zero), when the finger press occurs (lower right). The two scans on the left show activation in motor regions of the *left* hemisphere, which controls the right hand. However, the upper right image shows activation on the *right* side of the cerebellum, which is required for fine motor movements like finger presses. This crossover activity is consistent with the known anatomy of motor control. (Note that these brain images do not show other regions known to be involved in action control, including the basal ganglia and motor pathways.) *Source*: Hulsmann *et al.*, 2003.

commanded to move (this is called the *contralateral* side). However, motor cortex activates cerebellar activity on the *same* side as the moving hand (*ipsilateral*) until finally the finger press occurs at the zero point in the time scale.

7.0 CONSOLIDATION OF SHORT-TERM EVENTS INTO LONG-TERM MEMORY

Clive Wearing was able to experience the present moment, but he could no longer store that experience in long-term autobiographical memory. Long-term stores are shown in the functional diagram along the bottom, ranging from perceptual memory to highly practiced habits (Figure 2.26).

The question of long-term storage continues to be one of the mysteries. However, there is a great deal of indirect evidence for the *consolidation hypothesis*, suggesting that memory is stored in the same areas that support active moment-to-moment brain functions. Working memory changes quickly and is vulnerable to interference because it depends on dynamic electrochemical activities in large populations of neurons and synapses. After enough rehearsal, however,

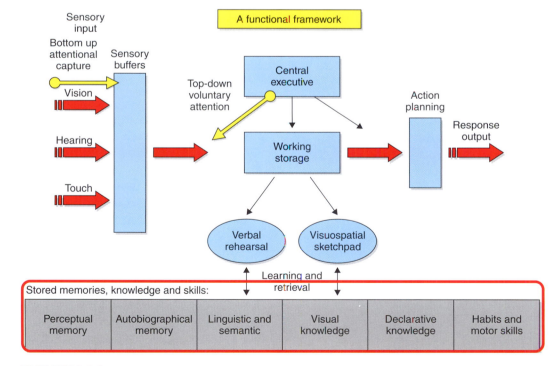

FIGURE 2.26 Long-term stores are shown in the functional diagram along the bottom, ranging from perceptual memory to highly practiced habits. When memory stores are not activated, their contents are unconscious.

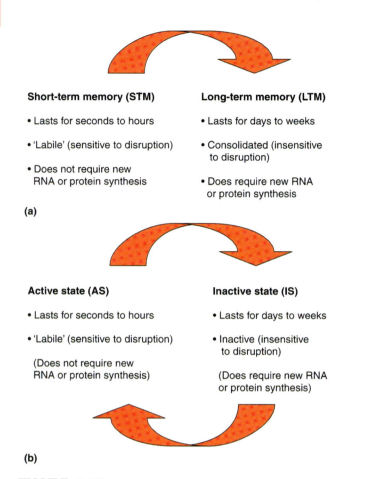

(a)

Short-term memory (STM)	Long-term memory (LTM)
• Lasts for seconds to hours	• Lasts for days to weeks
• 'Labile' (sensitive to disruption)	• Consolidated (insensitive to disruption)
• Does not require new RNA or protein synthesis	• Does require new RNA or protein synthesis

(a)

Active state (AS)	Inactive state (IS)
• Lasts for seconds to hours	• Lasts for days to weeks
• 'Labile' (sensitive to disruption)	• Inactive (insensitive to disruption)
(Does not require new RNA or protein synthesis)	(Does require new RNA or protein synthesis)

(b)

FIGURE 2.27 Transient memories become consolidated over time. Short-term memories are subject to interference, probably because they involve active neuronal circuits in the brain. If information is retained over a period of seconds to hours it may become permanent or 'consolidated'. A good night's sleep is now known to facilitate memory consolidation. Long-term memories are believed to require protein synthesis, which increases the efficiency of synaptic connections. *Source*: Nader, 2003.

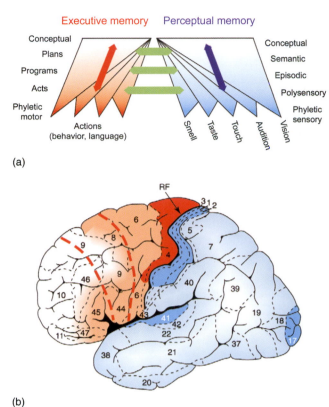

(a)

(b)

FIGURE 2.28 If the consolidation hypothesis is true, memory may be stored in many different regions of the brain by means of long-lasting synaptic connections. Fuster (2003) suggests, therefore, that the rear (posterior) half of cortex can be thought of as involving sensory memory systems, and the frontal half may involve executive and motor memories. In addition, the hippocampal neighborhood is certainly involved with episodic memory (memory for conscious experiences), while subcortical areas like the basal ganglia and cerebellum play a role in motor learning. Fuster's hypothesis provides a useful way to think about the brain basis of long-term memory. *Source*: Fuster, 2003.

the synaptic connections needed to store memories are thought to become more efficient and longer lasting. Figure 2.27 suggests that dynamic synaptic contacts are converted to more permanent connections, using protein synthesis and RNA. The traditional slogan for the consolidation hypothesis is: 'Neurons that fire together, wire together' (see Chapter 3).

A number of memory theorists propose that long-term memory traces may be stored in the same areas of the brain that are involved in their active forms. Figure 2.28 by Joaquin Fuster illustrates this point about the cortex. The figure shows the posterior half of cortex (shades light blue) is mostly involved with sensory functions, and is thought also to store sensory and perceptual memories. As mentioned above, the frontal half involves executive functions, motor control, Broca's area and other cognitive functions, and may therefore be involved in consolidating memory for those functions (see Chapter 5).

The consolidation hypothesis provides a useful simplification of much evidence. Long-term memory is covered in detail in Chapter 9.

7.1 Is working memory just re-activated permanent memory?

The consolidation hypothesis raises an interesting question: is it possible that immediate memory just activates long-term traces encoded in the brain? We can look at this question from both long-term and short-term

TABLE 2.3   Some brain hypotheses for the functional framework

Sensory input and sensory stores	Sensory cortex (posterior half of cortex), as well as sensory pathways and thalamic relay nuclei
Voluntary selective attention	Prefrontal and parietal regions may modulate sensory cortex to select some input signals over others
Spontaneous selective attention	Sensory regions may trigger orienting and selective signal processing
Verbal WM	Extended Broca and Wernicke's areas, prefrontal cortex, and medial temporal lobe
Visuospatial sketchpad	Visual cortex, including the parietal lobe and prefrontal regions
Response output	Prefrontal and motor cortex, basal ganglia, cerebellum and motor pathways
Transient storage of WM	Medial temporal lobe interacting with neocortex
Long-term memory systems	Lasting changes in cortical connectivity

memory perspectives. At this point, you may want to keep this possibility in mind – just to remind yourself that all of today's ideas in cognitive neuroscience may be seen from more than one point of view. It is important to stay open until the evidence is beyond dispute.

Table 2.3 suggests some possible brain regions for the cognitive framework. Later chapters will explore these hypotheses in greater detail.

8.0 SUMMARY

This chapter has explored a broad functional framework for cognitive neuroscience, based on widely accepted ideas. We have also shown some brain correlates of the functional framework.

Chapter 1 summarized some history about Broca's and Wernicke's studies of the speaking hemisphere, and this chapter shows how those regions seem to be involved in internal speech (verbal rehearsal). Similarly, visual imagery seems to make use of visual cortex, and even 'inner music' may involve brain areas involved in overt music listening and playing. As a simplifying hypothesis, we can therefore look for similarities between overt and covert cognitive functions. This tentative hypothesis will aid in understanding later chapters.

Immediate memory seems to depend on the medial temporal lobe, including the two hippocampi and their surrounding regions. Damage to those regions impairs the ability to transfer information from the present moment to long-term storage. The consolidation hypothesis suggests that long-term memory may be a permanent strengthening of the active connections established by current experiences held in working memory.

The rear half of cortex is involved in sensory processes, and probably also in sensory-perceptual memory.

The front half of cortex is involved with motor and executive functions, and probably also with long-term memory needed for those processes. Indeed, immediate memory can be looked at the other way, in terms of long-term capacities that are evoked by current input.

Selective attention has been studied for some fifty years and, in the last 15 years, the traditional question of conscious experience has again come to the fore. As we will see, it has been studied using many different experimental methods. Conscious cognition complements the other features of the functional diagram.

It is important to hold these ideas lightly as a way of thinking about cognitive neuroscience. They will be tested in more detail in later chapters.

There is ongoing debate about the meaning of terms like 'working memory', 'attention' and 'conscious experiences'. Such debates are common in science. We have a reasonable working consensus today, however, about empirical definitions – the kind of evidence that is believed to tell us about these concepts. In practice, 'working memory' has come to mean any brief memory phenomenon, on the order of tens of seconds, that allows us to retain and manipulate information. Simply remembering a telephone number while reaching for the phone fits this definition. So does mental arithmetic, and thinking about the best route to take in walking from one place to another. Working memory was first explored by giving people lists of unrelated words or numbers, and asking them to recall them ten to thirty seconds later. Another popular approach is 'delayed match to sample', in which people are given a stimulus to remember and are asked to respond 'yes' or 'no' when they see it.

Delayed match to sample (DMTS) is commonly used in animal studies, since we cannot ask rats or monkeys to report their experiences. Perhaps we can think of successful matching to a past event as a kind of reporting. Animal studies have been an important source of evidence. For example, they helped confirm the role of the hippocampus in learning. In practice, the defining feature of 'working memory' is the ability to hold an item in memory for several seconds. This reasoning has been applied to working memory for odors and even planned eye movements.

There has been a wealth of new knowledge learned about human cognition and the brain. It is an intricate business to tease apart these aspects of human thought and action experimentally. While the field has made progress in understanding how these areas of cognition interact, we have far to go before we will have a clear understanding of the dynamic integrative and interactive processes that underlie the human condition.

9.0 STUDY QUESTIONS AND DRAWING PRACTICE

9.1 Study questions

1 What have the cases of Clive Wearing and HM taught us about memory?
2 What brain areas are believed to be involved in working memory and long-term memory? In visual imagery and spatial planning?
3 What is inner speech and how does it relate to everyday cognition?

4 Which brain landmarks could you use to tell where the eyes are looking? Where is the back of the head? The left side? The right side?
5 What is a useful definition for working memory? For selective attention? For the different types of long-term stores?

9.2 Drawing exercises

1 Label the Framework in Figure 2.29.
2 Label the colored functional regions in the brain diagram in Figure 2.30.

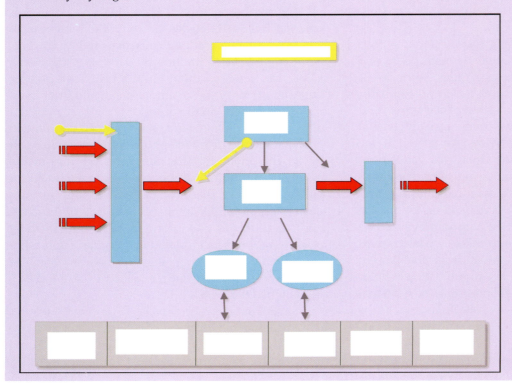

FIGURE 2.29

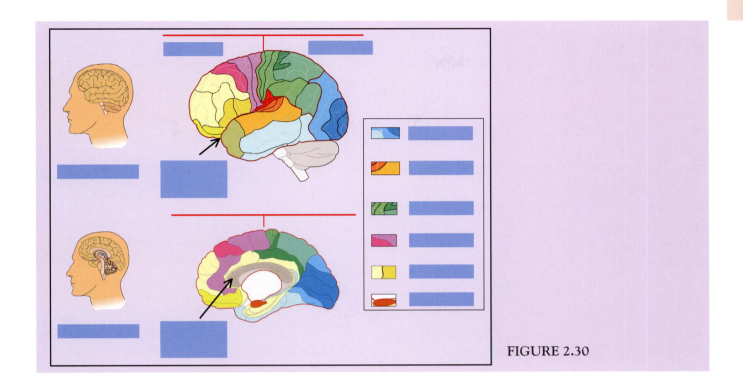

FIGURE 2.30

There is no more important quest in the whole of science probably than the attempt to understand those very particular events in evolution by which brains worked out that special trick that enabled them to add to the scheme of things: color, sound, pain, pleasure, and all the facets of mental experience.

Roger Sperry (1976)

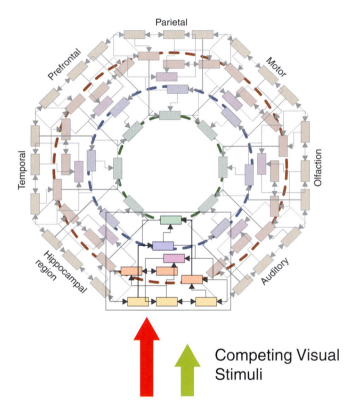

How neurons are often organized. It is helpful to think of neurons in the cortex (and many other structures) as layered hierarchies. In the cortex, signals can flow in any direction. The figure shows a circle of such layered hierarchies, allowing communication between auditory, visual and other regions. *Source*: Modified from Friston, 2003.

CHAPTER

3

Neurons and their connections

Bernard J. Baars

1.0 INTRODUCTION

Chapter 2 gave a first overview of brain functions like perception, working memory, attention and executive control. These have become easier to study since the discovery of brain imaging methods. But what do we know at the level of the neuron? Can we tell a plausible story at a more detailed biological level?

We begin with some basic ideas about neurons and their connections. In Chapter 1, we pointed out that science always makes inferences that go *beyond* raw observations, using abstract concepts that 'make a

believable story'. Neurons have been studied for two centuries, and the simplifications we will use here are well based in evidence. But, like any other simplified story, this one may encounter surprises. If it does, we must change it accordingly.

Brains are made of signaling cells – neurons – which are highly conserved over evolution. That is, they have remained relatively stable over hundreds of millions of years, as suggested by the fact that very different animal species have similar kinds of neurons. In most respects, neurons are like other body cells, but they are highly specialized for electrochemical signaling: they accept

Cognition, Brain, and Consciousness, edited by B. J. Baars and N. M. Gage
ISBN: 978-0-12-373677-2

Copyright 2007, Elsevier Ltd. All rights reserved.

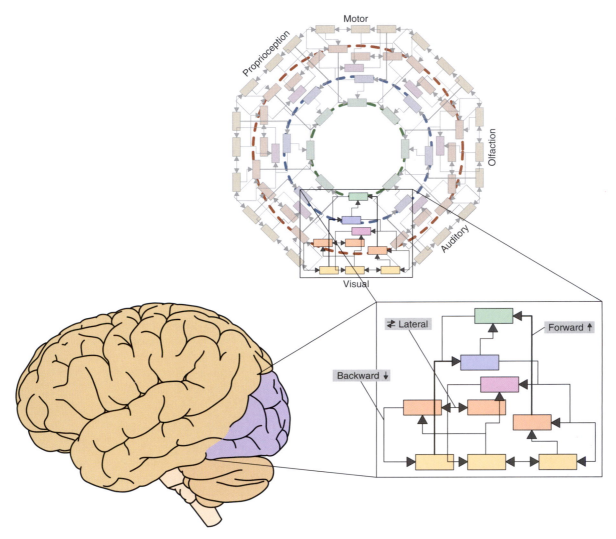

FIGURE 3.1   Neurons, networks, and the brain. Three levels of description, from neurons to large 'nets of nets'. Sensory and motor cortex are often viewed as processing hierarchies (Friston, 2003). In this example, visual maps in the occipital lobe go from simple (V1) to complex representations of the visual world, flowing deeply into the temporal and parietal lobes. The upper circle of hierarchies represents the overall architecture of the cortex. *Source*: Friston, 2003.

input at their dendrites from other cells, and send an electrochemical signal along an output branch, the axon. The entire brain can be viewed as a hypercomplex surface of neurons and their connections (Figure 3.1).

Dendrites and *axons* are thin micron-level tubes extruding from the cell body; an average neuron may have ten thousand input branches, and one or more output fibers (Figures 3.2, 3.3). Nerve cells fire their spikes much more slowly than the electronic arrays that run computers, but they still do some things far better than current computers. Computers do not reach human performance at this time in terms of perception, language, semantic memory, action control or artistic creativity.

1.1   Real and idealized neurons

The brain is a kind of Amazon rain forest with many undiscovered species of trees, plants and animals. To begin we will focus only on one prototypical tree, but this is only a convenient fiction. The great diversity of the neurons in the brain is suggested by Figure 3.4 – there are many classes of neurons, neurochemicals, and potential mechanisms of information processing. Our first simplification, therefore, is to focus only on an *integrate and fire neuron* (see Figure 3.3). This classical neuron accepts input from other nerve cells in its dendritic branches with graded membrane potentials; i.e. the voltages across the membranes can have continuous

Axon

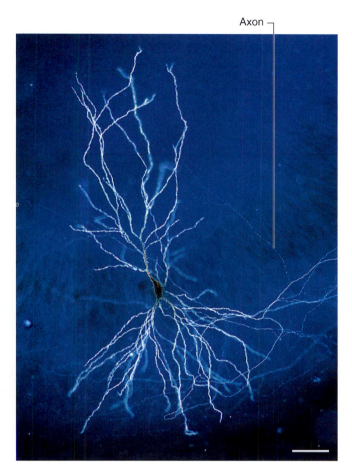

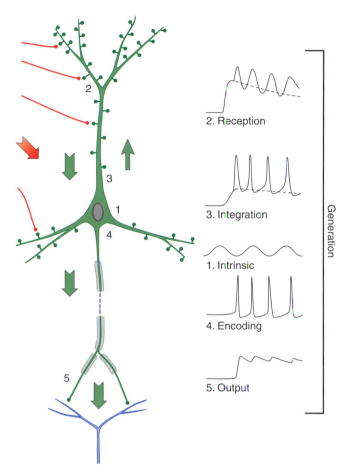

FIGURE 3.2   A single neuron. A spectacular recent photomicrograph of a single bipolar neuron. Cortical neurons may have ten thousand dendrites (input fibers) and one or more axons (output fibers). All fibers have smaller spines tipped with synapses connecting to neighboring neurons. The photo does not show the three-dimensional bushy shape of the neuron. *Source*: Standring, 2005.

FIGURE 3.3   An idealized neuron. A simplified neuron with its dendrites on top, showing their spines as tiny knobs. Dendrites receive synaptic inputs that evoke graded membrane potentials (labeled Reception). When dendritic potentials rise above threshold in a very brief time interval (Integration), and are added to the Intrinsic membrane potentials, they can trigger a fast depolarization of the axonal membrane – an all-or-none spike (Encoding). Spikes cause the release of neurochemicals at the axon terminals, which repeat the whole process, by evoking graded potentials in the next cell (Output). *Source*: Byrne and Roberts, 2004.

values. The graded dendritic potentials add up and, if the total voltage over a brief time interval exceeds about −50 mV, they trigger a fast traveling spike or action potential in the axon of the nerve cell (see Figures 3.3 and 3.5). (See Appendix C for more details.)

The classical neuron is thought to send its signal by firing spikes – sending *action potentials* from the cell body down the axon to the terminal buttons. At the terminals, a neurochemical messenger is released to diffuse across a very small synaptic gap. It then triggers a postsynaptic potential in the neighboring neuron. Figures 3.3 to 3.5 shows an abstract version of this process. In cognitive neuroscience, we usually focus on the ways neurons connect and interact in networks. The prototypical neuron is a useful starting point.

Given the complexity of the brain, our ideas for understanding it are basically simple. But simple units combine to make up massive nervous systems. There are many ways to use nerve cells for a host of different receptors, pathways, circuits, networks, and effectors.

1.2   Excitation and inhibition

Classical neurons are connected by way of synapses, which can be *excitatory* or *inhibitory*. Thus, the probability that the next neuron will fire a spike can be either increased or decreased. A neuron in cortex may have

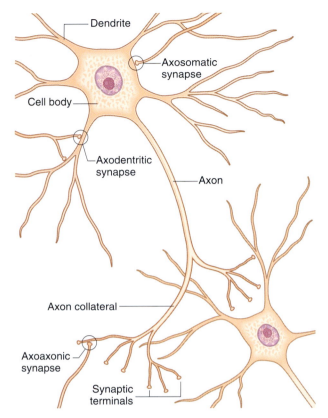

FIGURE 3.4 Two neurons connect across a synpase. Note that some synapses feed back on the original neuron. *Source*: Byrne and Roberts, 2004.

some ten thousand input synapses, and a dozen output synapses terminating on other neurons. Dozens of other factors determine the activities of neurons – the sleep-waking cycle, the availability of chemicals for making neurotransmitters, and more. These factors all affect the likelihood of a signal going between two neurons, and they can be summarized as synaptic *weights*, which represent the chances that one neuron will cause the next one to fire. Thus, the great variety of neurons is often simplified into an idealized neuron, the integrate-and-fire unit; and the many ways in which neurons can trigger each other is simplified into connection probabilities between neurons.

Neurons have a great variety of shapes, branching patterns, and synapses. There are at least half a dozen major *neurotransmitters*, with at least thirty 'minor' ones, the neuropeptides (see Appendix C). It is now known that electrical synapses, which use no neurotransmitter at all, are much more common than was previously believed. Even the dendrites of a single nerve cell may be able to compute useful information. There is evidence that neuroglia, the support cells for neurons, may also have an information processing function. Other surprises keep coming. For example, for more than a century it was believed that unlike other body cells, new neurons were not produced after birth. However, it is now known that stem cells – new,

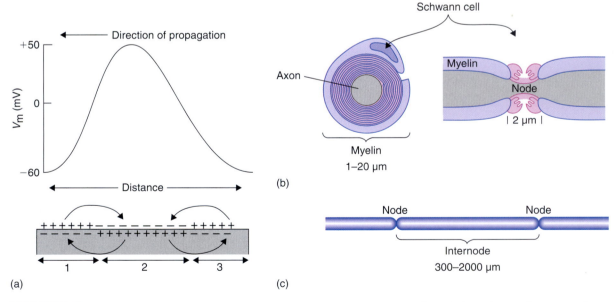

FIGURE 3.5 Signals traveling along the axon. (a) Neuronal signals travel along axons through the exchange of positive and negative ions in adjacent regions of membrane. In the axon, region 2 is undergoing depolarization, while region 3 has already generated the action potential and is now hyperpolarized. The action potential or spike will propagate further by depolarizing region 1. (b) Myelinated axons are wrapped in specialized Schwann cells. The axon is only exposed at the nodes of Ranvier. (c) Action potentials in myelinated fibers are regenerated at the nodes. Myelinated fibers have higher conduction velocity than bare axons. *Source*: Ramachandran, 2002.

undifferentiated progenitor cells for neurons – are born in some parts of the adult brain. Synapses are known to grow throughout the adult lifetime, and small dendritic spines can grow in minutes to support new synapses. Thus, the standard neuron is only part of the whole picture. New evidence is bound to keep coming in for years to come.

As Shepherd writes (2004):

> The idea of the nerve cell as an independent cellular unit . . . continues to be one of the foundations of our concepts of nervous function. However, it has become clear that the whole neuron represents only one level in the organization of neural circuits and systems. We now recognize that nervous function arises out of many levels of organization, some of them within the neuron, some of them involving multineuronal interactions. . .

1.3 Neural computation

What justifies studying these simplified neurons? Perhaps more than anything else, it is the success of neural network models that have used simplified neurons in the last few decades. *Artificial neural nets* (ANNs) have been used to model many of the functions the brain performs – to recognize patterns, to plan actions in robots, learn new information, and use feedback to improve performance. Most ANN simulations are relatively small-scale and limited. None of them come close to the massive complexity of a living brain. But, for some jobs, ANNs have been more successful in doing human-like tasks than computer programs that use logic and standard mathematics. It is important to remember that ANNs *are* artificial. They are not the real thing, but they give us a greater understanding of the ways neural computation might work.

In the history of science, new mathematical techniques often help to understand new questions. Neural computation similarly helps to understand nervous systems. A great deal of progress has occurred on the basic mathematics of neural networks. There seems to be a small number of basic architectures – i.e. arrangements of simple units – with similarities to the networks found in the brain. A tutorial on neural networks is presented in Appendix A, authored by a distinguished expert, Professor Igor Aleksander (Aleksander *et al.*, 1998; Aleksander, 2005). Here we will cover some basics.

Cognitive neuroscientists commonly focus on *biologically plausible* neural net models, those that are based on the known properties of a specific set of neurons and their connections. However, artificial neural nets often provide useful approximations to the reality.

In addition to the simplified neuron of Figure 3.3, we will also use simplified synapses. As mentioned above, we will assume there are only two kinds of synaptic connections, excitatory ones (which increase the chance of triggering the next neuron), and inhibitory ones (which decrease that chance). *Glutamate*, the most common neurotransmitter in the brain, is known to be excitatory. *GABA* (gamma-amino butyric acid) is the most common inhibitory neurotransmitter. So our simplification is a part of neural reality.

2.0 WORKING ASSUMPTIONS

We have discussed using simple and idealized neurons in order to describe the basics of neural firing and connectivity. We will use these basic ideas already laid out as working assumptions as we continue our discussion of neurons and their connections. To summarize our working assumptions, they are:

1 The *integrate-and-fire neuron*. We will assume that neurons work by adding graded voltage inputs until the total membrane voltage on the target neuron goes past a threshold value (approximately -50 mV in real neurons). If it does, an all-or-none spike fires down the output branch, the axon.

2 Connections are either *excitatory* or *inhibitory*. We can therefore assign a single number to the probability that neuron A will trigger neuron B. That number is called the *weight* of the connection. As probabilities, connection weights have numbers between -1 and $+1$. Plus 1 means a 100 per cent certainty of triggering the next neuronal spike, and -1 is 100 per cent certainty of stopping the next neuron from firing. Weighting schemes can be more complex, but this is a useful first approximation. The vastly complicated neurochemistry can be reduced to just one number for the probability of transmission, the 'weight' of each connection.

3 A second reason for the simplified neuron and synapse is that the basic mathematics of networks appears to be very successful in simulating cognitive functions. *Neural nets* can simulate the kind of pattern recognition that sensory systems perform, although our models are much simpler than any brain mechanism known today. Neural nets can learn and store information in much the way real neurons are believed to. Since the basic types of artificial neural nets (ANNs) were worked out in detail over the last several decades, they have been applied to many practical uses, from computer-based

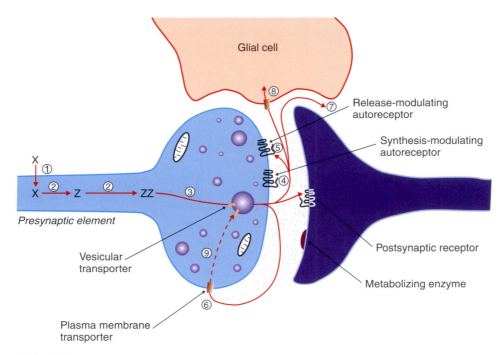

FIGURE 3.6　A basic synapse. Two cells in contact are labeled *presynaptic* (the lighter blue) and *postsynaptic* (darker blue). A spike in the presynaptic cell triggers release of a chemical neurotransmitter that diffuses across the synapse, and lowers the membrane potential of the postsynaptic cell. Some of the neurochemical machinery of this extraordinarily complex biological system is shown here. *Source*: Standring, 2005.

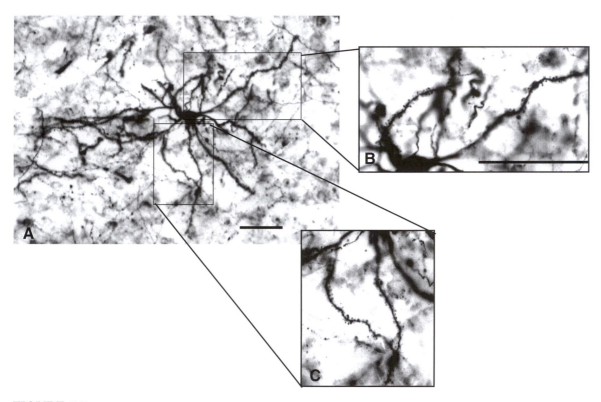

FIGURE 3.7　An actual photomicrograph of a single neuron in the basal ganglia. Notice the dendritic spines – tiny protrusions on the dendrites, often containing end buttons for synapses. The horizontal bars mark 50 micrometers. *Source*: Paxinos, 2004.

face recognition to predicting the stock market. That is also scientifically important, because it shows that we understand enough about networks to begin to see how the brain might do those things. As always, we must be prepared to see the limits of our knowledge; but we have a basis for departure.

4 Neurons can form one-way pathways, such as the optic nerve to the visual thalamus (the lateral geniculate nucleus). However, one-way pathways are quite rare. More likely, neurons run in two directions, forming two-directional pathways and networks, in which activity at point A triggers activity at point B, and vice versa. This is often called *re-entrant connectivity* (Edelman, 1989).

5 As we will see, the nervous system loves *arrays* of neurons, often called *maps*. The cerebral cortex is a massive six-layer array, with an estimated ten billion cells and trillions of synaptic connections between them. The retina at the back of the eye is another array, this time with three layers (see Chapter 6). In fact, *all* sensory surfaces are arrays of receptors and their closely linked layers of relay and processing cells. Other arrays are found in the sensory thalamic nuclei, in the superior colliculi (which control eye movements), and in arrays of cells that control muscles. The brain's liking for arrays and maps, with dense connections between them, is another useful working assumption.

6 *Hebbian cell assemblies*: when neurons combine by triggering other neurons, the resulting pattern of activity may be stable or unstable. Unstable patterns tend to die out, while stable patterns remain for some period of time. Such stable patterns are often called *cell assemblies*, and the term 'cell assembly' is often attributed to Donald O. Hebb (Hebb, 1949). Hebbian cell assemblies may involve neighboring cells, or they may involve cells that are far away from each other. Cell assemblies that combine both excitatory and inhibitory connections tend to be more stable and lasting, as we will see. In the brain, transient connections are thought to be mainly electrochemical, while more lasting ones are thought to require protein synthesis.

2.1 Starting simple: receptors, pathways and circuits

While reflex circuits can be triggered by outside stimuli, they are normally integrated seamlessly into voluntary, goal-directed activities. For example, you can turn your head from side to side while reading this

sentence. That is, you can follow a voluntary goal (stated in the previous sentence), and your oculomotor system will still keep your eyes focused on the moving window of the words you are reading at this instant in time. It is a remarkable achievement of sensorimotor adaptation, and most of the time it is quite unconscious and automatic. Oculomotor coordination is not just a simple reflex arc.

Voluntary brain mechanisms, guided by explicit goals, are associated with cortex in humans. Very sophisticated subcortical circuitry is also engaged in planning and executing actions. Spinal centers may carry out commands from higher centers using sensorimotor reflexes, but they also return feedback signals to the brain. All these levels of control have *endogenous* (internal) as well as *exogenous* (sensory) input, both conscious and unconscious (Goodale and Milner, 1992). Thus, while there are certainly some simple reflex circuits like the famous knee-jerk reflex in Figure 3.8, reflexes rarely work in isolation. They normally work in the service of cortical goals.

Reflexes are innate circuits. They emerge during normal development and some disappear after some time, like a baby's innate grasping reflex, which allows

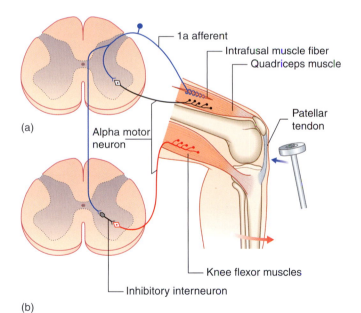

FIGURE 3.8   A simple reflex circuit. If you drape one leg over the other and tap just below the kneecap, your lower leg will jump out. This is the famous knee-jerk reflex, technically called the patellar tendon reflex. It is a classical example of a spinal reflex, controlled by a simple circuit. Sensory neurons pick up the mechanical tap, and transform it into a neural signal which is sent to the spinal cord. There, an interneuron links the sensory impulses to motor neurons, which contract the muscles in the upper thigh, making the lower leg jump outward. *Source*: Standring, 2005.

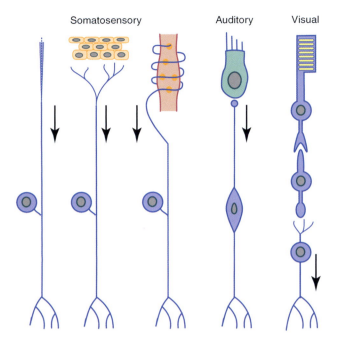

Somatosensory   Auditory   Visual

FIGURE 3.9 Receptors transform external energy patterns into neuronal activity. Although these receptors belong to different sensory systems, they are similar in structure and function. All convert physical energy from the environment into neural signals. *Source*: Hendry *et al.* in Squire *et al.*, 2003.

it to take strong hold of an adult's finger. But *learned* non-voluntary processes are not reflexes. They are complex, interactive routines called *automatic processes* – highly practiced skills and habits. For example, as a skilled reader you automatically process the difference between the letters 'b' and 'p', even though they may look similar to non-readers. In speaking and typing, your muscle control is very fast, highly organized and mostly unconscious. Humans use numerous automatic processes to carry out normal actions. Such learned automatisms are typically unconscious, effortless, and not under detailed voluntary guidance. They should not be confused with reflexes. Automatic skills start out under cortical control, but after sufficient practice they tend to come under subcortical control (Haier *et al.*, 1992; Chein and Schneider, 2005).

Each sensory nerve may actually contain parallel channels, conveying somewhat different features of the world. Thus, vision has a color pathway called magnocellular (because it has somewhat larger cells), and a separate bundle of 'black and white' neurons called parvocellular (meaning small cells). Similarly, the somatosensory pathway combines parallel channels for light touch, for heat, pain, and so on.

Most sensory nerves stop off at the thalamus, where they contact synaptic relays on their way to cortex (Figures 3.10 and 3.11). These thalamic nuclei provide point-to-point connections. Vision and touch are *topographically* organized, projecting receptor maps into higher level maps, well into the cortex. Audition tends to be more *tonotopically* organized, with neuron arrays corresponding to sound frequencies.

Most sensory and motor pathways split and cross over the midline of the body on their way from the periphery to cortex. The evolutionary reason for crossover is still mysterious, but it is a pervasive feature in humans and other mammals.

While we tend to think of input-output pathways as carrying one-way signal traffic, this is actually rare. Most pathways run in both directions. For example, while there is a one-way flow of signals from the retina to the visual thalamus, the next stage goes in both directions. Thus going from thalamus to V1, about 90 per cent of the neurons are running the wrong way (i.e. from V1 *downward* to the visual thalamus)! In the auditory system, the downward flow of neural signals goes to the very receptors themselves (see Chapter 5).

This two-way signal traffic means that much of the central nervous system should be viewed not as simple traffic arteries, but as re-entrant loops – equivalent to neural networks with two or more layers (Figure 3.11). Edelman (1989) and colleagues have particularly emphasized re-entrant processing as a basic feature of the brain. From this point of view the brain is a vast collection of mutually echoing maps and arrays.

2.1.1 Receptive fields and lateral interactions

Lateral inhibition was first proposed as a hypothesis by Ernst Mach, a German physicist in the 1860s, based on the tendency of continuous visual gradients to be perceived as discontinuous. It was a brilliant hypothesis that has since been confirmed by directed testing (Figure 3.16). Lateral inhibition seems to be used in many places in the brain. In the retina, neighboring cells can inhibit each other, so that a tiny point of light on one cell will tend to stand out in contrast to the adjacent ones. In touch neighboring cells in the skin also use lateral inhibition. At higher levels in the brain, similar semantic concepts may have the effect of inhibiting each other, so that 'astronomy' and 'astrology' might not be confused. Like the other neural strategies discussed in this chapter, the brain often borrows successful tricks and tips from an earlier evolutionary form and may translate it into later adaptations.

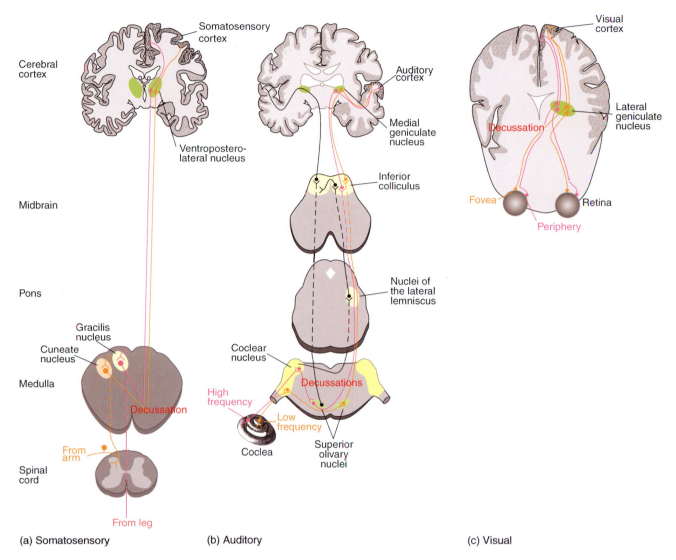

FIGURE 3.10 Similarities between sensory pathways: body senses, hearing, and vision. All the senses begin with arrays of receptors, like the layers of touch receptors of the skin and the array of light receptors of the eye. After local processing, sensory information is condensed into a single nerve pathway, a compact bundle of neurons, which carries sensory signals to cortex. Note that these three sensory pathways stop off in thalamic relay nuclei, marked in green. All three pathways also split and cross over to the opposite side on their way to the cortex, called *decussation*. *Source*: Hendry *et al.* in Squire *et al.*, 2003, Elsevier.

3.0 ARRAYS AND MAPS

As we have pointed out, neuronal *arrays* are widely found in the brain. When arrays represent a spatial pattern, they are often called *maps*. Spatial maps are a form of spatial coding in neurons. The brain performs temporal as well as spatial coding, and may have a number of other ways of representing and processing information. Nevertheless, spatial maps are the most obvious kind of neural code (Figure 3.12).

The retina itself can be thought of as a three-layered map of light receptors and their neighboring neurons, including ganglion cells, which send their axons from the retina to the visual relay cells of the thalamus (the lateral geniculate nucleus) (see Chapter 6). The thalamic visual cells then project their fibers to the first visual area of the cortex, area V1 of the occipital lobe. V1 also looks like a detailed map of the visual input, with different quadrants of the visual field projected to different parts of this region. From area V1, most of the

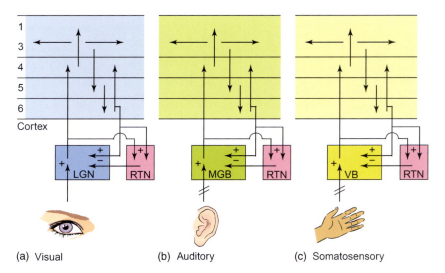

(a) Visual   (b) Auditory   (c) Somatosensory

FIGURE 3.11   Sensory regions interact with thalamic nuclei. The thalamus is often called the 'hub' of the brain. It is not the only hub, but perhaps the most important. Notice that vision, hearing and touch pathways all stop off in the thalamus on their way to their cortical projection regions. However, information is constantly bounced back from the cortex to various thalamic nuclei, so that there is a constant flow of signaling between all parts of cortex and thalamic nuclei. In some cases, the thalamus amplifies cortical activity, while in others it blocks or inhibits it. Note the striking similarities between cortical input and output layers in these three senses. *Source*: Alitto and Ursey, 2003.

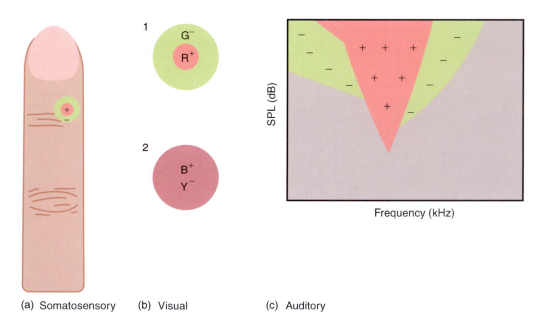

(a) Somatosensory   (b) Visual   (c) Auditory

FIGURE 3.12   Receptive fields: cells in sensory cortex respond to specific stimuli. A classic experiment on visual cells in the cortex of the cat. A microelectrode is inserted into the first region of the visual cortex, area V1. There it picks up the axonal spikes of single neurons that are sensitive to visual line orientation. The electrical activity is amplified and displayed on a screen, where it appears as short peaks, corresponding to the firing of the cell. Notice that this cell is most responsive to a slanted line and becomes progressively less responsive the more the visual stimulus deviates from its preferred input. Area V1 contains many millions of cells that pick up low-level visual features like dots and lines (or contrast edges). *Source*: Rodman *et al.* in Squire *et al.*, 2003.

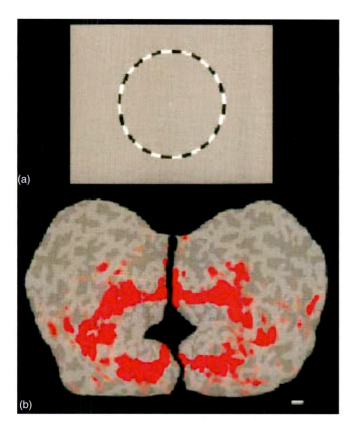

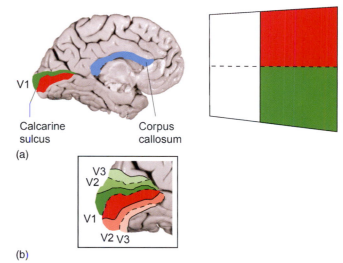

FIGURE 3.14 Visual quadrants map to cortical quadrants. Notice that the first visual projection area V1 represents different visual quadrants in different regions of cortex. The bottom right quadrant projects into V1 in the left hemisphere, in the upper half of V1. The early visual areas are folded tightly into the occipital cortex, around a fold called the calcarine sulcus. *Source*: Zeki, 2003.

FIGURE 3.13 The visual input projects to cortical areas. In a classic experiment, Tootell *et al.* (1996) showed that a circle around the center of visual fixation evokes corresponding activity in the first visual projection area, Area V1. The authors made use of the fact that V1 expresses a topographical visual input, and that circles are symmetrical around the fixation point. *Source*: Tootell *et al.*, 1996.

visual information projects to other 'maps' in the cortex, some of them in the visual cortex itself, but also beyond it. While the resolution of spatial details tends to blur after V1, higher-level visual maps respond to more complex and abstract stimuli, like faces, objects, visual scenes, attentional, emotional, and perhaps even decision-making networks, as they work their way forward in the cortex. Thus vision involves what looks like a large and widespread set of maps of the light input to the eyes. While this view is undoubtedly too simple, it captures a good deal of evidence.

The body senses, like touch and pain perception, also project to map-like regions of cortex. Other senses like hearing, smell and taste are less spatial in nature, but the auditory cortex has map-like regions organized by pitch, like the strings of a harp. Thus, even the non-spatial senses show regular neuronal arrays and map-like regions. Finally, information from specific sensory systems is combined in the parietal cortex, using spatial arrays that combine auditory, visual, touch information

into map-like regions. These include a body-centered map (called egocentric) and an object-centered spatial array (called allocentric). It seems as if our brains like to organize a vast amount of incoming information in arrays that mirror the layout of the spatial surroundings. And motor cortex, as you might guess, looks much like a distorted map of the output systems, the skeletal muscles of the body (see Chapter 5).

It is tempting to think that with the sensory half of cortex (the posterior half) using so many maps, there must be a little person inside looking at the maps. But this is the 'homunculus fallacy', as philosophers call it. The trouble with this idea is that it explains nothing, but merely moves the question to another level: Does the homunculus have its own brain, with its own spatial maps, and another, even tinier homunculus sitting inside?

The question for scientists is therefore how to make sense of the great number of spatial and other neuronal arrays in the brain without resorting to the fallacy of supposing that we all have a little creature inside, looking at all the neuronal maps. Neural network models provide one set of answers today, as we will see.

3.1 Maps flow into other maps

The nervous system often uses layers of neurons in giant arrays; indeed, the entire cortex is a massive

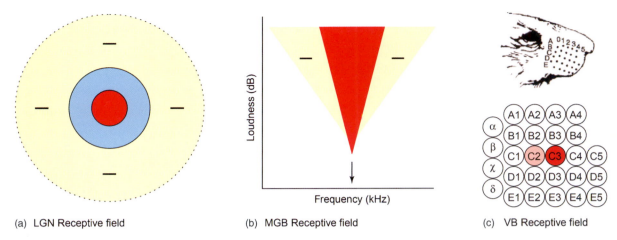

(a) LGN Receptive field   (b) MGB Receptive field   (c) VB Receptive field

FIGURE 3.15 Lateral interactions. The brain often uses the same strategy in many different places. On the left is a 'center surround' cell of the visual thalamus (the lateral geniculate nucleus). Light falls on the red circle in the middle but no light falls in the surrounding ring. Neurons pick up both light input and the absence of surrounding light, and enhance the contrast by mutual inhibition in the same layer, called lateral inhibition. The same mechanism is used in the center image, and even in the barrel cortex of the rat, the place in cortex where its whiskers project their neurons in a very simple, one-to-one fashion. Barrel cortex is often used to study cortical processing for this reason. Adjacent whiskers also show lateral inhibition, which is also found in touch, hearing, and even attentional control in the human brain. *Source*: Alitto and Ursey, 2003.

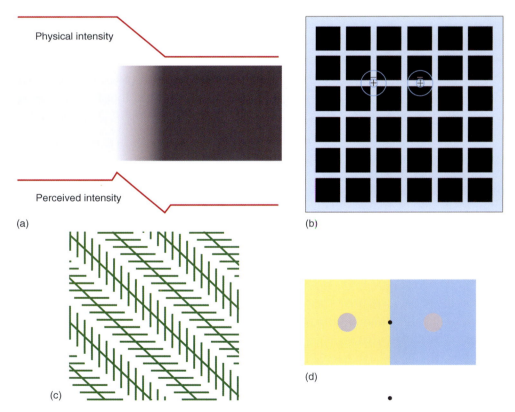

FIGURE 3.16 Visual demonstrations of lateral inhibition. Lateral inhibition was first proposed as a hypothesis by Ernst Mach, a German physicist in the 1860s, based on the tendency of continuous visual gradients to be perceived as discontinuous. It was a brilliant hypothesis that has since been confirmed by directed testing. Notice that lateral inhibition also applies to adjacent black squares, to color perception between opponent colors, and even to the perception of 'train tracks stimuli' which signal spatial depth to the brain. *Source*: Eagleman, 2001.

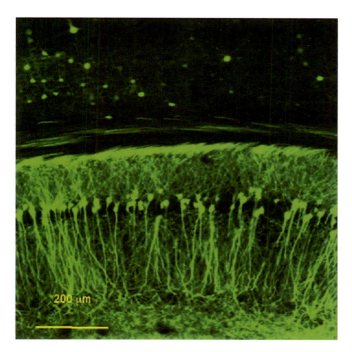

FIGURE 3.17 Neurons commonly organize in layers. A state-of-the-art fluorescent micrograph of pyramidal neurons in the hippocampus of the cat. Pyramidal neurons have pyramid-shaped cell bodies (on top), and long axons (the vertical stalks). Notice the beautiful array of neurons, all lined up in a single layer. Also note the 200 micrometer resolution. *Source*: Mizhari *et al.*, 2003

six-layered array containing about ten billion nerve cells. Neuronal hierarchies are stacked arrays of nerve cells.

3.2 Neuronal arrays usually have two-way connections

There is one very important surprise in this tidy picture of maps flowing into higher-level maps of the visual input: after the thalamic nucleus, most axons run *downward* from cortex to the thalamus. Some 90 per cent of the axons between LGN (lateral geniculate nucleus) and V1 send spikes downward to LGN, rather than upward to V3. Higher up, there is always two-way traffic of signals between V1 and V2, V2 and V3, and onward. This might seem pretty odd for a simple transmission idea of the visual pathway. But we will see that bi-directional flow of spikes is the norm in the brain, not the exception. There are very few one-way streets in cortex. This is a very important point, which compels us to think of neuronal signals in a richer way. We will explore two-way transmission in more detail below. Receptive fields of sensory neurons become larger and more complex as we go up in the visual hierarchy.

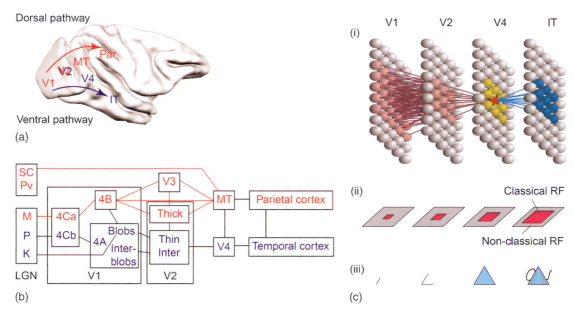

FIGURE 3.18 Visual maps in the macaque. The rhesus macaque monkey's visual brain is often studied because of its similarities to the human visual brain. On the left are the major visual pathways in the macaque cortex. Each one flows from topographical map to topographical map. Starting with area V1, the information flows to later 'V' areas while preserving the topography of the input. The upper pathway is sensitive to location, and is therefore called the 'Where' pathway. The lower pathway is sensitive to color, shape, contrast, and object identity, and is called the 'What' pathway. It is believed that activity in the 'What' pathway is directly involved in conscious visual experiences, perhaps beginning in the object recognition area (IT). The 'Where' pathway may provide spatial frameworks for the 'What' pathway. It may not be directly conscious, but it shapes the perceived location of objects. (RF = receptive field.) *Source*: Lamme and Roelfsma, 2000.

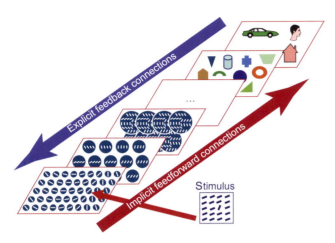

FIGURE 3.19   Two-way traffic between arrays. Two-way traffic is the norm in the brain. For that reason, it makes more sense to think of the arrays of visual regions as layers of a two-way network, rather than one-way paths from point to point. Notice that lower maps are sensitive to simpler stimuli, while higher ones show faces and cars. However, there is constant predictive flow of information from higher to lower maps, to make it easier to identify all levels of description. *Source*: Ahissar and Hochstein, 2004.

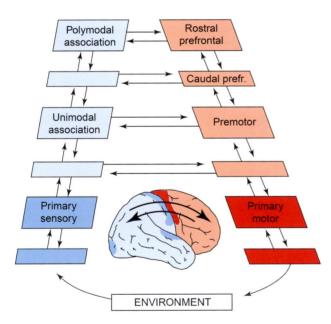

FIGURE 3.20   Sensory and motor hierarchies are themselves arranged in hierarchies. Fuster (2004) suggests that all of cortex can be seen in terms of cycling sensory and motor hierarchies, with information flowing between the posterior (sensory) regions and the frontal (motor and planning) areas. Early sensory cortex flows into unimodal association areas, which interact with premotor cortex, which is believed to encode the 'urge' to perform an action. Higher up the sensory hierarchy, polymodal association areas combine hearing, touch and vision, and interact with the forward part of the prefrontal cortex. Notice that there is constant exchange of information through the environment as well. Thus, we can hear ourselves speaking, and we can see a flow of visual vistas when we walk. *Source*: Fuster, 2004.

FIGURE 3.21   A step pyramid as a hierarchy. One useful image for a brain hierarchy is a step pyramid, like the Inca city of Machu Pichu. While the levels are stacked on top of each other, signaling can take place through many different pathways in the hierarchy. Thus, the people exploring the step pyramid can walk up, down, or sideways.

3.3 Sensory and motor systems work together

Finally, while there are very clear anatomical divisions between sensory and motor pathways, they are constantly interacting. When we speak, we also hear ourselves speak. When we walk, an array of visual information streams across our retina. Video games that simulate the flow of optical vistas really given a sense of motion, even though they are only visual. The brain is constantly updating its motor systems by means of sensory input, and telling the sensory systems what to expect by way of motor signals. Fuster's classical diagram of the cortex makes this point emphatically (Figure 3.20). Functionally, the nervous system is always cycling information between input and output channels, to keep the sensory and motor world in synchrony (Fuster, 2004; Kandel *et al.*, 2004).

Fuster (2004) suggests that both front and back can be viewed as massive hierarchies of local hierarchies,

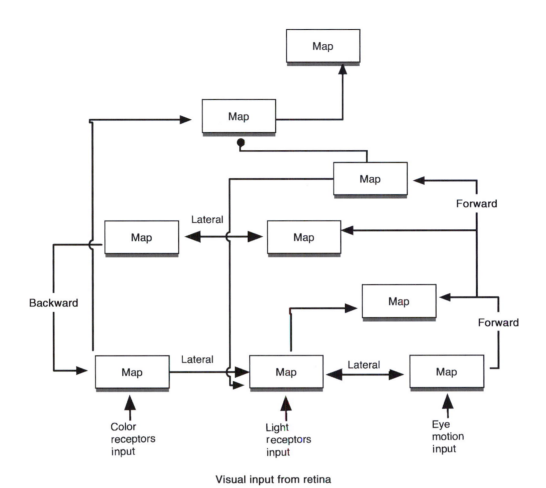

FIGURE 3.22 An abstract hierarchy. Notice that like the step pyramid above, this hierarchy allows information to flow in all directions. This is a typical layout for sensory and motor hierarchies. *Source*: Friston, 2003, redrawn.

starting from sensory receptors, and becoming more and more general as information flows upward in the sensory hierarchy (see Figure 3.20). The motor hierarchy can be viewed as going in the opposite direction, ending up at motor neurons. However, as the diagram indicates, more and more information is exchanged between the two hierarchies in an ongoing perception-action cycle, from a low level (as in listening to one's own voice speaking) to a very high level of planning, thinking, and anticipating the future.

Friston (2003) has published a useful diagram for a processing hierarchy (Figure 3.22), which we will adopt here. Each neuronal array is called a 'map' in this version, and while maps exist at different levels, signals may travel up, down, and laterally. We will see some examples in later chapters.

Notice that neural net models sometimes use different directional names to refer to the same idea. 'Bottom up' is the same as 'feedforward'. 'Top-down' flow is often

called 'feedback'. We can simply flip the hierarchy on its right side to make 'bottom up' look like 'feedforward'.

3.4 Temporal codes: spiking patterns and brain rhythms

Arrays, maps and hierarchies support *spatial* coding in neurons. But the brain makes use of *temporal* coding as well. Figure 3.23 shows an example of a single neuron in the thalamus which shows two different spiking patterns. Neurons like this may serve as pacemakers for large populations of cortical neurons during delta sleep, for example (Figure 3.24). Another hypothesis suggests that fast firing of thalamic neurons may trigger waking when the sound of a loud noise or a crying baby is detected, or some other significant stimulus. Arboreal primates, for example, need to respond very quickly if a tree branch breaks.

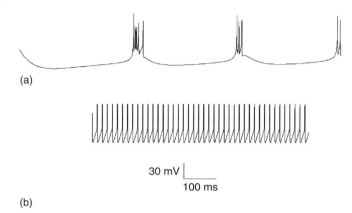

(a)

(b)

30 mV

100 ms

FIGURE 3.23 Neurons have different spiking codes. While it is easy to visualize the map-like spatial coding in the brain, neurons also code information over time. The two electrical traces show the voltages of simulated thalamic neurons. These neurons have two different spiking codes (McCormack and Huguenard, 1992). *Source*: White, 2002 in Ramachandran, 2002.

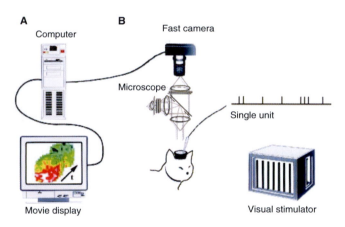

FIGURE 3.24 How single neurons are recorded in living animals. The needle electrode causes no pain, since the brain itself has no pain receptors. It is implanted using a scalp attachment that allows the cat to move comfortably. The electrode picks up 'spikes' from a single neuron, which are amplified and shown on the upper right. Trials over time are shown on the colored screen. *Source*: Tsodyks *et al.*, 1999.

Individual neurons also exhibit *spiking codes*. For example, the auditory nerve performs frequency coding (see Chapter 5). Every time the eardrum vibrates, three tiny bones in the inner ear transfer mechanical ripples to a fluid, which in turn moves hair cells on the basilar membrane. The hair cells are the auditory receptors, which fire whenever they are mechanically stimulated. Together their axons make up the auditory nerve and, so long as the incoming sound frequency is fairly low, the firing rate of the auditory nerve follows the movements of the eardrum. The auditory nerve therefore shows a simple one-to-one frequency code. It is a temporal code rather than a spatial map of input (see Section 3.5).

When we look at the electrical activity of tens of billions of neurons, the entire brain seems more like an orchestra than like a single piccolo. After hundreds of millions of years of evolution, it seems likely that the brain has evolved neurons with many kinds of temporal and spatial codes.

3.5 Choice-points in the flow of information

If the brain had only straight highways it would be easy to understand. Instead, it has pathways with many choice-points, in which traffic can flow right or left, or jump a whole level forward or backward. That is the point of the step pyramid in Figure 3.21: it looks like a staircase, but hikers can go up or down, laterally, or in more complex interactive dance patterns (see Figure 3.39).

How do we know there are choice points in neuronal traffic flow? The anatomical connections indicate as much, but the fact that humans and animals constantly deal with *ambiguities* is an important source of evidence as well. Most words in natural language have more than one meaning (a fact we rarely notice consciously, but a glance at a good dictionary will show it). Dictionaries understate the degree of ambiguity in language because they are used by skilled native speakers who bring a great deal of contextual knowledge to their reading of verbal definitions. There is much that a dictionary writer can simply take for granted – but the nervous system cannot.

In the visual world we also encounter constant ambiguities that we do not bother to make conscious. Daylight changes color at sunset. When we walk through woods the light is filtered through green leaves. Wearing sunglasses filters colors, and even glass windows create reflectance patterns that change the visual world. Those differences rarely become conscious, because the visual system tends to maintain color constancy, sometimes from memory. But in the brain, those differences must be processed, and separated from color signals that we need to notice. Animals cannot afford to miss a predator stalking through the tall grass just because it's sunset, or because there are shadows from surrounding trees, or because there is an early morning mist. We need excellent visual brains to survive.

The famous Necker cube is shown in Figure 3.25(b). Figure 3.25(a) shows the two 'kissing faces' of the well-known face-vase illusion.

One might object that the visual ambiguities in the figures are so artificial that they would never occur in

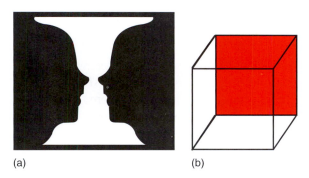

(a)   (b)

FIGURE 3.25 Ambiguous stimuli pose choices for interpretation. Two famous ambiguous figures: (a) the 'face-vase illusion' and (b) the Necker cube. The corners of a rectangular room will flip back and forth if they are seen through a tube that blocks out the visual surroundings. *Source*: Kim and Blake, 2005.

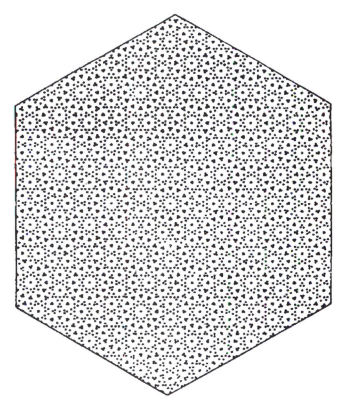

FIGURE 3.26 An ambiguous object: What is it? Shapes are sometimes hard to identify, even under natural conditions, as you can tell by trying to see objects in a bush or wooded area, watching birds during a morning mist, or looking at oncoming cars when the sun is in your eyes. *Source*: Feldman, 2003.

the natural world, but that would not be accurate. In any room with rectangular walls, the corners make up parts of a Necker cube. (To demonstrate this, just roll up a piece of paper into a tube, and look at the corners of a room. You should be able to flip it visually from an inside corner to an outside one.)

A cat stalking prey may look around a tree with only one eye, while the other eye just receives input from the tree: that leads to binocular rivalry, competition between the input to the two eyes. An animal walking through tall grass constantly receives different input to the two eyes, and some animals, like rabbits and deer, do not have overlapping visual fields at all, so that fused visual input is quite rare.

Faces are biologically important for humans and other primates. Mother-infant bonding occurs face to face in our species, for example, as do competitive confrontations, mating interactions and the like. But faces also show ambiguities. Which way is Humphrey Bogart facing in the white-on-black photo (Figure 3.27)? What emotion does his face express? Which picture looks more skeptical or suspicious?

3.6 Top-down or expectation-driven processing

The brain constantly generates expectations about the world it encounters. Walking downstairs in the dark, we have expectations about every step we take. In dealing with ambiguities like the figures shown here, we constantly make predictions about which of two perceptual interpretations is the best one. Most words in English are ambiguous, so that even as you are reading this sentence you are resolving ambiguities. The brain is driven by more than just input; it has many ways of

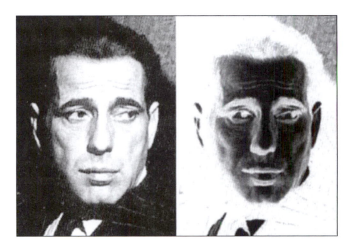

FIGURE 3.27 Which way is Humphrey Bogart looking? Human faces are among the most important objects in our environment. Being able to tell gaze direction and facial expression is a basic social skill. *Source*: Wexler, 2001.

biasing choice-points by means of *predictions* and *expectations*. *Lateral* processing is also important, as we have seen, to sharpen differences between neighboring stimuli in the visual array. As we will see later, selective attention allows us dynamically to adjust our sensory biases (see Chapter 8), and long-term memory strengthens synapses that are associated with accurate perception.

Maps and layers are not the only functional units. Many cortical regions are massively interconnected with each other, so that activity in one part of the cortex quickly spreads to other regions. A number of scientists believe, therefore, that the entire cortex, together with satellite regions like the thalamus, should be considered as a functional unit. This is often called the thalamo-cortical system. But to understand how those massive systems work, we will study their smaller components in some detail.

4.0 HOW NEURAL ARRAYS ADAPT AND LEARN

Learning has been studied very intensively in layered arrays of simulated neurons. After a slow start (see Appendix A), the study of 'neural nets' took off in the 1980s (Rumelhart and McClelland, 1986a, b). *Connectionism* has been the theoretical framework for much of this movement. Much of this chapter reflects lessons learned from the connectionist movement (see also Neural Darwinism, below). While neural nets were first explored in the 1950s, the early efforts encountered difficulties in doing useful processing. By the 1980s, it became clear that adding an additional (hidden) layer would solve many of those problems, and that feedback also helped. These insights helped to launch the connectionist movement.

4.1 Hebbian learning: 'Neurons that fire together, wire together'

Donald Hebb proposed, in 1949, that assemblies of spiking cells could learn an input pattern by strengthening the connections between cells that fire at the same time. This idea is encoded in the slogan that 'neurons that fire together, wire together'. It is a very useful learning method for neural networks, and there is some direct evidence for *Hebbian learning* in the nervous system.

The key idea in Hebbian learning is that more efficient synaptic connections are the physical substrate of learning and memory. As Figure 3.29 points out, however,

FIGURE 3.28   Donald R. Hebb: cell assemblies that learn. Donald R. Hebb was one of the most influential theorists for cognitive science and neuroscience. He clarified the notion of a 'cell assembly', and proposed the best-known learning rule for neural networks, summarized by the slogan 'neurons that fire together, wire together'. *Source*: Brown and Milner, 2003.

there are a number of ways in which synaptic transmission could become more efficient. Two neighboring neurons can gain more synapses, the synapses may be supplied with more nutrients that lead to more neurotransmitter chemicals, the receptors for those neurotransmitters could become more efficient, and so on.

Two kinds of synaptic changes are believed to be involved in learning; they can be considered strengthened excitation and strengthened inhibition. Long-term increases in excitation from one neuron to another are called *long-term potentiation* (LTP). Long-term decreases are called *long-term depression* (LTD). There is some evidence for both in the hippocampus.

It is always important to remember how long the brain took to develop – the mammalian brain is some 200 million years old and, prior to that time, even earlier vertebrate brains were able to develop high degrees of sophistication for their ecological niches. For that reason, while there is solid evidence for learning mechanisms like Hebbian learning, it is believed that there may be other mechanisms as well.

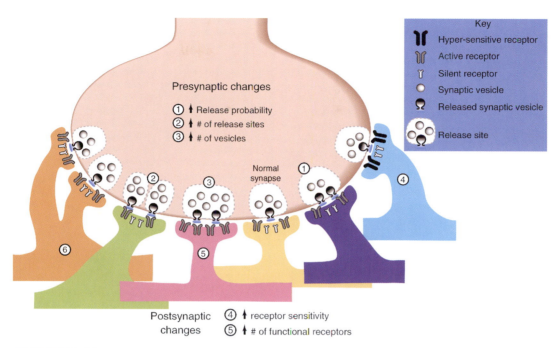

FIGURE 3.29 Hebbian synapses and long-term potentiation. There may be several ways to increase the efficiency of synaptic connections. *Source*: Byrne in Squire *et al.*, 2003.

Hebbian learning can be shown visually as a thickening of lines between the nodes of a network, like the simple cell assemblies of Figure 3.30. In this case, a visual circle is activating corresponding cells in a model of early visual cortex. The nodes in this circle represent points or small regions in the visual field, and they are being strengthened by correlated firing. That is the theory. Figure 3.31 shows a remarkable set of findings that seems to confirm the model, with actual strengthening of connection probabilities ('weights') in the hippocampus of the cat. The brain is a large place, of course, so that finding apparent Hebbian learning in one location does not prove its existence everywhere. Nevertheless, this is an encouraging result, and suggests that the overall direction is productive.

In Figure 3.32 a simple network may be used for classifying input patterns. In this case, there are two-way connections vertically, with lateral inhibition in each layer of the network. This is sometimes called a 'local' network, because it does not involve learned strengthening of connection weights. It is nevertheless useful for explaining some basic cognitive phenomena (Rumelhart and McClelland, 1986b).

Figure 3.33 shows a breakthrough in network modeling. Early models were devised in the 1950s by Rosenblatt (1962) and others. These were one or two-layer models, and were found to have logical limits when it came to basic brain functions like learning and

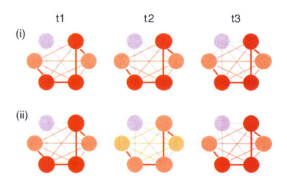

FIGURE 3.30 Hebbian learning in cell assemblies. Neurons are represented by circles and their connections by lines. Redder colors represent more active units and thicker lines indicate stronger connection weights between units. At time t1, the cell assembly encodes input in its connections weights. In this example, memory is retained at times t2 and t3. More realistic models may show forgetting over time, and permanent memories may need to be strengthened by repeated exposures to the same stimulus. *Source*: Abraham and Robins, 2005.

recognizing patterns. For some time neural models went into decline, until some twenty years later, when it was realized that adding a layer of 'hidden units' and allowing the network to adjust its connection weights could solve the earlier difficulties. Figure 3.33 shows a classical three-layer feedforward network with a hidden layer and adjustable weights. This network can learn efficiently when its output is compared to a wanted output

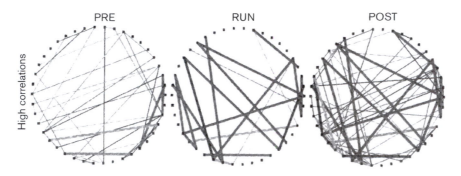

FIGURE 3.31 Observed Hebbian learning. Strengthening of neuronal connections has been observed directly in hippocampal neurons in the cat. *Source*: Sutherland and McNaughton, 2000.

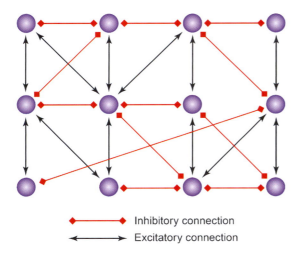

Inhibitory connection
Excitatory connection

FIGURE 3.32 A simple network. Notice the combination of excitatory and inhibitory connections. *Source*: Palmer-Brown *et al.*, 2002.

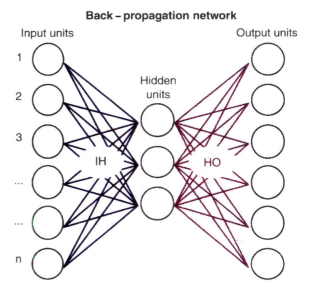

FIGURE 3.33 A classical three-layer network. The hidden layer makes the network much more flexible. Back-propagation allows network output to be compared to a teaching source, and changes network weights to match the source. Thus, the network can learn from feedback to approach its goal. *Source*: Abraham and Robins, 2005.

pattern, and the network weights are systematically adjusted to come closer and closer to the set goal. This process is called 'back-propagation', and is much like a negative feedback loop, the kind that we find in thermostats. This kind of network is used most often today, though mathematical and empirical studies continue to advance the understanding of brain-like information processing.

Figure 3.34 shows a self-organizing auto-association net, in which the output is led to match the input. That is a useful strategy for recognizing patterns like the sound of a familiar voice. Self-organizing systems arise in nature in many situations. Biological organisms can be viewed as self-organizing systems, and perhaps nervous systems are a refinement based on biological cells. However, a marker of human culture is the immense amount of teaching that takes place. From birth onward, we learn from other people. Thus, culture may go a few steps beyond self-organizing

learning systems, and develop knowledge and skills that can be taught, more like the network shown in Figure 3.33.

Figure 3.35 shows how a self-organizing network may be applied to the fundamental human problem of face recognition. Babies learn to respond to normal faces (but not scrambled faces) early in their lives, and soon can tell familiar from unfamiliar ones. This example is much simpler than the task that babies solve so effortlessly, because it involves only a line drawing. The network learns to predict a mouth at the bottom of the picture, and two eyes on top. But it could not function under more subtle three-dimensional visual conditions, in changing light conditions, moving mouths, eyes and heads, and so on. Nevertheless, the face

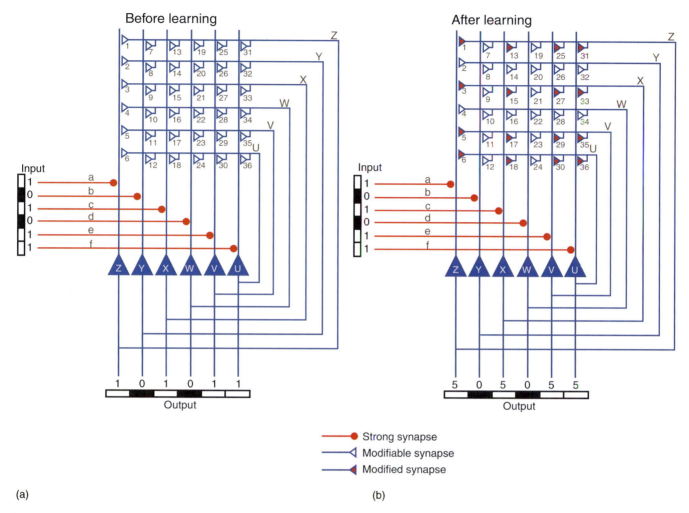

FIGURE 3.34 A pattern recognition net. An auto-associative network matches its output with its input, a feature that is useful for recognizing patterns, like faces or cars. *Source*: Byrne in Squire *et al.*, 2003.

recognition network in Figure 3.35 gives us a way to try to understand how the brain performs a basic life task (see Chapter 6).

4.2 Neural Darwinism: survival of the fittest cells and synapses

The neuroscientist Gerald Edelman has proposed that the brain is a massive *selectionist* organ. Edelman's theory is called *Neural Darwinism*, since it suggests that neurons develop and make connections following Darwinian principles. In biological evolution, species adapt by *reproduction*, by *mutations* leading to diverse forms, and *selection* among the resulting repertoire of slightly different organisms. Over long stretches of time this weeding process yields species that are very well adapted to their niches. A similar process occurs in the immune system, where millions of immune cells

adapt to invading toxins. Cells that can successfully match the invaders multiply, while unsuccessful ones dwindle in number. The immune system can therefore learn to recognize and combat even novel invaders from the environment. *Selectionism* therefore leads to very flexible adaptation.

According to Edelman (1989), the brain has two stages of selectionist adaptation. The first begins soon after conception, when the first neurons are born, multiply, differentiate, and are selected if they fit their local niches. The outcome of this stage is a collection of neurons that looks like a brain. The second, overlapping stage, begins when neuronal connections are made. Adaptive connections tend to survive while others die out. A kind of Darwinian selection therefore operates both developmentally and as a result of learning (Figure 3.36). Two-way connections between neuronal maps allow for re-entrant (two-directional) processing.

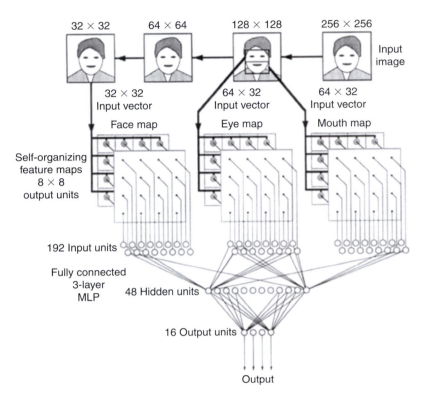

FIGURE 3.35 A face recognition network. Recognizing faces is a basic problem for the visual system. With simple line drawings face-recognition can be done. But when real faces are seen under natural lighting conditions the job becomes far more complex and variable. *Source*: Luckman *et al.*, 1995.

If a re-entrant process is stable, it will tend to survive among all the other transitory waves of activation in the brain. If not, it will simply fade away.

If we add the Hebbian principle that 'neurons that fire together, wire together', a stable cell assembly will tend to make stronger connections between its units. Thus, the Darwinian process would lead to longer-lasting neuronal 'species', cell assemblies that enable the tasks of adaptation, learning, pattern recognition, and the like.

These ideas have been refined by brain studies and computer simulations. The Darwin series of robots has employed selectionist principles to simulate how regions like the hippocampus seem to work. In Figure 3.37a, a neural Darwinist 'rat' simulates the behavior of a rat in a Morris water maze, in which the animal needs to find a platform hidden under the surface of the water, which allows it to rest. In Figure 3.37b, a selectionist robot is learning to play soccer. While these tasks are very different, they are learned using the same principles.

4.3 Symbolic processing and neural nets

Standard computer programs use symbols. That is, they employ logical and mathematical expressions. Neural nets can be expressed in mathematical terms, but they tend to be more *parallel* (with many different computations happening at the same time), and *distributed* (able to process information in different places, using different memories, and so on). That is to say, neural nets are closer to biological information processing than to standard algebra and logic.

However, humans created mathematics and logic, and natural language makes us very good at understanding symbolic expressions. Most of the words we use are symbols referring to some class of events in the world. Furthermore, neural nets are easily translated into mathematical expressions.

How can these two different computational philosophies be reconciled? One method suggested by McClelland and Rogers (2003) is shown in Figure 3.38, where a neural network was designed to express symbols (like 'sunfish', and 'grow') and their logical relations (like 'has a property'). For a human mind, this is a complicated way of expressing a simple idea like 'sunfish can grow'. But for massive neural networks with many millions of units and trillions of connections – such as our brains – the McClelland and Rogers version is more compatible with the wiring of the brain.

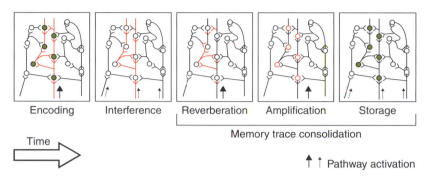

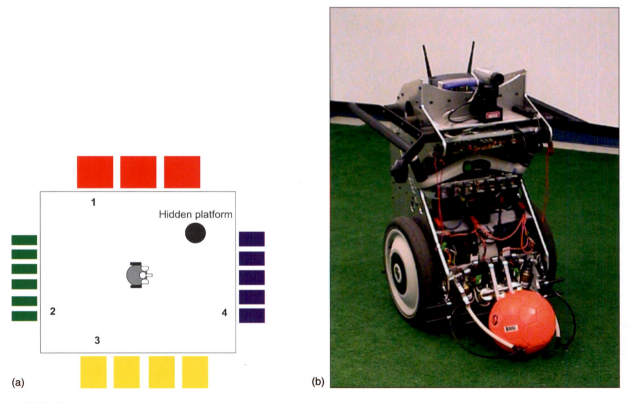

FIGURE 3.36 An example of Neural Darwinism in learning. This figure shows stages of encoding a neural activation pattern until dynamic synaptic activity allows permanent connections to be strengthened, thereby enabling memories to be stored in the same locations where the original connections were made. *Source*: Ribeiro *et al.*, 2006.

FIGURE 3.37 (a) This figure simulates a rat in a Morris water maze, swimming until it finds a platform to stand on. The brain-inspired simulation creates a neural map of the water maze, so that the simulation learns to find the platform. (b) A robot uses a Neural Darwinist brain model to learn to play soccer. *Source*: Neurosciences Institute, Krichmar, with permission.

In sum, it seems that neural nets can be translated into symbolic form, and symbols can be converted into neural nets. Thus, the debate over symbolic versus neural net expressions is not either-or. The scientific question therefore would seem to be which theoretical language is more useful for any given problem. If we want to understand brains at the level of neurons, networks are quite natural. If we want to understand the grammar of English, symbols might be better. It all depends on the question we want to explore.

Adaptation and *representation* are two complementary ways of thinking about the brain. We will see evidence that brains are specialized for knowing the world. There is also evidence that brains behave in adaptive ways, adjusting constantly to changing conditions. Both of these ideas seem to be fundamental. Some findings may

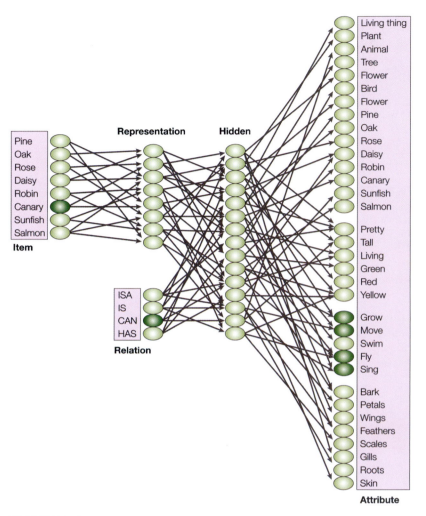

FIGURE 3.38   Neural nets can handle symbolic expressions. In this example, a network represents a large set of propositions such as 'a robin is a bird' and 'a rose has petals'. *Source*: McClelland and Rogers, 2003.

seem more adaptational, others more representational. We will find both perspectives useful.

5.0 COORDINATING NEURAL NETS

The brain is often called a massively parallel organ, because neurons appear to be working quite independently of each other. There is no central command post that tells all neurons exactly what to do.

There are a number of ways in which neurons can be coordinated, however. One way is for large-scale rhythms to pace populations of neurons, much like the conductor of a symphony orchestra. When many neurons fire in unison, their activity adds up, just as a large crowd of people sounds louder when they are chanting in unison. There is a limit to this, however. Epileptic seizures have long been believed to be caused by neural scar tissue, called the epileptic focus, which sends out intense, slow, and regular slow waves that recruit other brain regions, so that spreading populations of neurons begin to chant the same song. The result is a loss of consciousness and physical seizure activity.

Obviously, the brain must balance the degree of pacing and coordination against the need for local neurons and their neighbors to work on local functions. There must be a balance between *integration* and *differentiation* (Edelman and Tononi, 2000).

Figure 3.39 shows averaged correlations between visual regions while the subject was watching a movie. As you can see, similar regions in both hemispheres, symbolized by (l) and (r), tend to become active at the same time, as indicated by the red and yellow lines. Since both sides receive basically the same input from the two eyes, this result makes good sense. In addition, within each hemisphere strong correlations show up

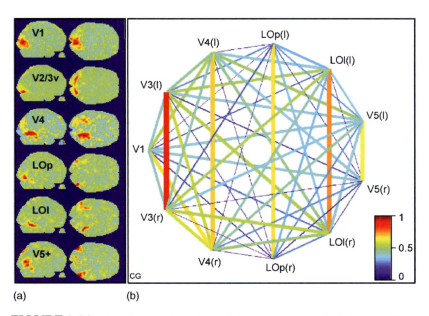

(a)   (b)

FIGURE 3.39 Correlated brain regions while watching a movie. A dramatic illustration of correlated activation in the visual cortex while the subject was watching a movie. The upper half of the large panel is in the left hemisphere, the lower half in the right hemisphere. V areas with the same number correspond to the left and right sides, which are usually connected across the midline. 'Hotter colors' and thicker lines indicate higher correlations between visual areas. Notice that the strongest correlations are between corresponding regions of left and right hemispheres. Lop = posterior part of the lateral occipital complex; LOI = lateral part of the lateral occipital complex; (l) = left hemisphere; (r) = right hemisphere. On the left are local fMRI activations. *Source*: Bartels and Zeki, 2005.

between early visual analysis and the area for visual object perception (LO). However, because this study used functional magnetic resonance imaging (fMRI) and averaged over long periods of time, we are not seeing fast correlated activity. This is a limitation of the specific methodology, which scientists are currently working to overcome. A number of recent results show much faster gamma and theta correlation, for example, at the frequencies at which the brain seems to do much of its work (Fries, 2005).

Regular EEG rhythms are now believed to signal distinct, coordinated processes. For example, a high density of gamma rhythms has been related to conscious visual perception, and to the process of discovering a solution to a simple word problem. Alpha rhythms are traditionally associated with an absence of focused attentional tasks, but theta rhythms are now believed to coordinate the hippocampal region and the frontal cortex during the retrieval of memories. And delta rhythms, the traditional signal of deep sleep, are believed to group fast neuronal activity in order to facilitate the consolidation of learned events (Kemp *et al.*, 2004).

Figure 3.40 shows a very simple and reasonable hypothesis about how regular brain rhythms may coordinate the firing of millions of separate cells.

Neurons that fire at the peak of the alpha wave (for example) add a tiny amount of electrochemical activity to the whole chorus. Neurons that fire during the trough of the regular rhythm subtract their activity. Thus, neurons that fire in sync with the dominant rhythm are strengthened by feedback from the millions of other neurons that are keeping up the alpha rhythm, while those that are out of sync are weakened. Such a mechanism would tend to reinforce rhythmic firing.

As we have already pointed out, however, simple synchronized firing is not enough. Different coalitions of firing neurons must be able to generate different input representations, which can compete against other coalitions to recruit new members. Such a model is shown in Figure 3.36, where it supports a kind of Neural Darwinian competition between different populations of nerve cells.

5.1 Functional redundancy

When engineers build airplanes, they always introduce *functional redundancy* into their designs, so that there is a backup for critical functions that could go wrong. If one jet engine fails, most aircraft are designed to fly

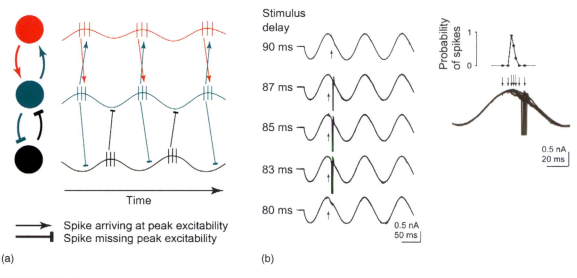

(a)   (b)

FIGURE 3.40 Neural nets can represent symbolic concepts. Symbolic concepts and relationships can be represented by neural networks. *Source*: McClelland and Rogers, 2003.

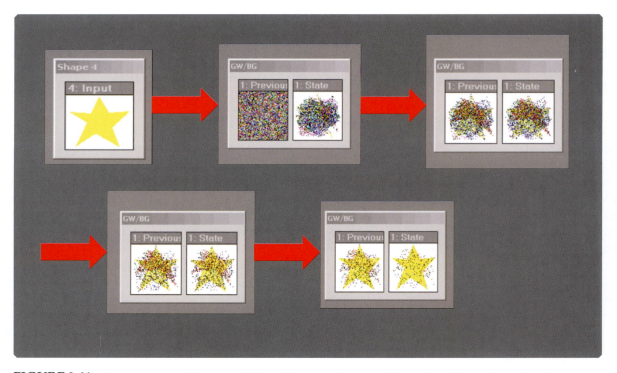

FIGURE 3.41 A pattern-recognition network. The yellow star in the upper left panel provides an input shape into a neural network. Later panels give the current state of the network, shown in an array of colored dots. Notice that the yellow star emerges slowly, as the network learns about the input, and eliminates alternative possibilities. *Source:* M. Shanahan, Imperial College London, with kind permission.

using the remaining ones. Humans and animals also evolved with functional redundancy in all their organ systems – we have two lungs, two sides of the heart, and so on. The brain is no exception. Even the loss of the speaking half of cortex can be overcome, if it occurs early in childhood. The brain can often keep working, even in the face of some damage.

6.0 SUMMARY

The most basic question in cognitive neuroscience is how nerve cells can combine to perform complex cognitive functions, like perception, memory and action. That problem has not been solved in all its richness, but significant progress has been made. The integrate-and-fire neuron has been well studied, and is understood in considerable detail. However, there are a great many kinds of neurons, types of transmission between them, and neurochemicals that play crucial roles. We take the integrate-and-fire neuron to be our prototype, because it is well established and can be simplified, so that its action can be understood by detailed modeling. Both artificial neural networks (ANN) and biologically inspired networks are useful for this purpose.

Neurons sometimes make up simple circuits, like the knee-jerk reflex. More often, however, they organize themselves into large two-dimensional arrays, which link higher and lower level arrays into hierarchies. All the sensory and motor systems can be viewed as such complex hierarchies. In vision, touch, and motor control, arrays of neurons are topographically arranged as 'maps' of the spatial surroundings. The visual system, for example, can be viewed as a hierarchy of topographical maps.

Hierarchies are not rigid, one-way pathways. They allow signals to flow upward, downward, and laterally. A major function of downward flow of information in the sensory systems is the need to resolve ambiguities in the input. Ambiguities are common in visual scenes,

but also in language and the other senses. In motor systems, upward (bottom-up) flow of information is similarly useful to help make choices in output plans and motor commands.

Lateral inhibition is a widely used biological strategy for emphasizing differences between inputs, like two patches of light and dark in a visual scene. Cells in the sensory systems have receptive fields that are attuned to specific types of input, such as line orientation, color, movement, shape, and object identity. As the visual maps go deeper into cortex, their spatial resolution becomes less, but their ability to integrate large amounts of information goes up. While we study the sensory and motor systems separately, the brain is a giant sensorimotor engine, which allows constant interaction of input and output at all higher levels.

Spatial arrays of neurons support spatial coding of information, but there is temporal coding as well. The major regular rhythms of EEG are believed to correspond to massive coordinated activities among large populations of neurons. Recent research suggests that gamma activity may be involved in such processes as sensory integration into conscious percepts, and theta has been associated with retrieval from long-term memory.

7.0 STUDY QUESTIONS AND DRAWING EXERCISES

7.1 Study questions

1 Describe the basic function of an integrate-and-fire neuron.
2 What is lateral inhibition and how does it relate to perception?
3 Explain how sensory and motor regions can be viewed as hierarchies.
4 Describe the role that re-entrant (two-way) connections play in brain function.
5 What is Neural Darwinism and what aspects of brain processes does it relate to?
6 List three or more common features of sensory systems.

7.2 Drawing exercises

1 Label the parts in Figure 3.42.
2 Draw Hebbian learning of cell assemblies for a visual circle. What slogan describes Hebbian learning?

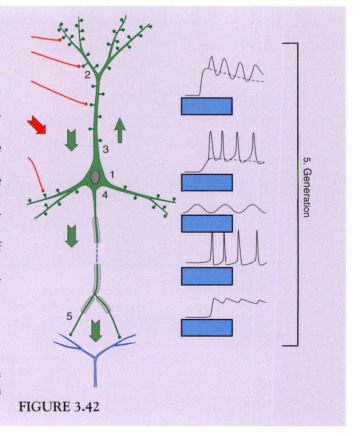

FIGURE 3.42

I believe that the study of neuroimaging has supported localization of mental operations within the human brain.

Michael I. Posner (2003)

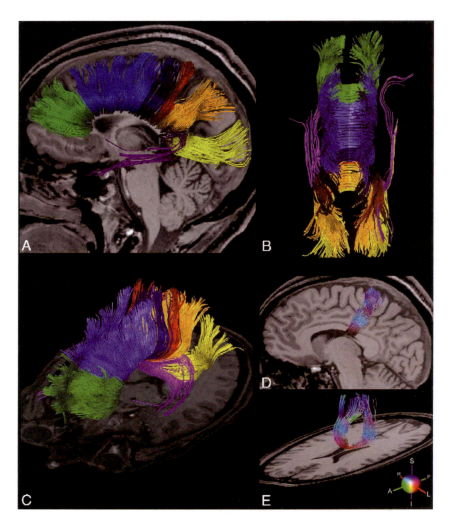

Different views of the 'internal highway system' of the cortex – fiber tracts running through the inner brain, using a method called Diffusion Tractography. All fibers in these images are running crosswise across the corpus callosum, and then arch upward like fountains on either side. (A) is a side view, showing fibers sweeping upward in the left side of the hemisphere. Green fibers are in front (prefrontal), light blue begin and end in premotor cortex, dark blue fibers are coming from the specific motor cortex, orange ones are parietal, and yellow fibers flow from the occipital cortex on one side of the brain to the other. The violet fibers along the side run between the temporal lobes on each side of the brain. (B) shows just the fiber bundles alone, on both sides of the brain, viewed from back (yellow) to front (green). On the bottom right, note the orientation compass: A, anterior; I, inferior; L, left; P, posterior; R, right; S, superior. *Source:* Hofer and Frahm, 2006.

4

The tools: Imaging the living brain

Bernard J. Baars and Thomas Ramsøy

1.0 INTRODUCTION

This chapter presents the tools of brain recording from the viewpoint of an intelligent user, trying to understand how the brain works. Appendix B presents the tools in more detail.

A perfect observer of the mind-brain would be able to follow tens of billions of neurons and sample each one a thousand times per second. The perfect observer should then be able to track the constantly shifting interplay between smaller and larger groups of neurons, making trillions of possible connections. By analogy, a perfect spy satellite in space would be able to see every single human being, as well as the changing relationships between individuals and groups, from families to whole nations.

Such a perfect observer does not exist. Our understanding of the brain is a kind of collage of many fragments of the puzzle, glued together to make a reasonable picture of the whole. But thinking about a perfect observer gives us the parameters we can aim for.

Brain imaging has been a breakthrough technology for cognitive neuroscience, building on decades of cognitive psychology, behavioral conditioning, psychophysics and brain science. Before imaging techniques matured, our knowledge came from animal studies and the haphazard injuries incurred by human beings. But brain injuries are extremely imprecise, and even to locate the

Cognition, Brain, and Consciousness, edited by B. J. Baars and N. M. Gage
ISBN: 978-0-12-373677-2

Copyright 2007, Elsevier Ltd. All rights reserved.

damage, neurologists often had to rely on post-mortem examination of the patients' brains – as in the case of Broca's and Wernicke's patients discussed in Chapter 1. The brain can often compensate for damage, so that lesions change over time, as cells die and adaptation occurs. Therefore, post-mortem examinations do not necessarily reflect the injury at the time of diagnosis. Animal studies depend on presumed homologies – similarities across species – that were often not convincing to everybody. No other animals have language, and other distinctively human specializations. It was therefore very difficult to understand how brain functions in animals mapped onto human cognition.

Many of these problems were resolved when it became possible to observe the living brain, first by electroencephalography (EEG), then by X rays, then computer *tomography* (the study of slices – from the Greek word for 'slice,' *tomos*) based on X-rays, positron emission tomography (PET), magnetic resonance imaging (MRI), etc.). Today, we have perhaps a dozen techniques that are rapidly becoming more precise. Medical needs often drive this very expensive technology because it applies to many organs in the body. As a result, we now have ways to study the distribution of billions of neurochemical receptors in the brain, the thickness of cortex,

the great highway system of white fiber bundles, and most important for cognitive neuroscience, the *functional* activity of the brain – the basis of its adaptive capacities. New advances are allowing scientists to investigate not only functional activity located in specific brain regions, but also to measure the dynamic pattern of connectivity between them. Some of the massive 'wiring' of the brain is shown in Figures 4.2 and 4.3, but like the world wide web, the wiring is only part of the story: there are ever-changing dynamic connections made between neural populations that can alter in a fraction of a second.

1.1 Brain recording: more and less direct measurements

Some neuroimaging methods pick up neuronal activity more directly than others. If we place an electrode next to (or inside) a neuron we can record its electrical activity, typically its axonal spikes. This single-electrode measurement can be seen as a direct measure of the electrical activity of the neuron. As we have seen in Chapter 3, however, neurons do more than fire spikes. The input branches of a neuron, the dendrites, also

FIGURE 4.1 A structural head and brain scan. A structural MRI (magnetic resonance image) of a head and cutout view of the brain. Notice the horizontal, sagittal (from nose to back), and coronal (from ear to ear) sections. Structural MRI does not show dynamic brain activity, but gives the locations where functional brain activity can be shown. *Source*: Mark Dow, U Oregon, with permission.

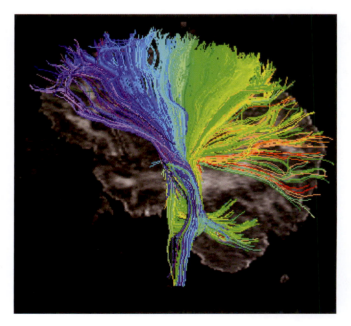

FIGURE 4.2 A fountain-like image of the white fiber tracts. This beautiful spray of neuronal tracts results from a magnetic imaging technique called diffusion tractography, which allows us to view the white (myelinated) fiber tracts. These are the vertical traffic arteries that flow from the cortex (especially frontal ones, in blue) down into the spinal cord; and upward from the spinal cortex to the rear half of cortex (in yellow and green). Most of the volume of cortex is taken up by these massive fiber tracts. *Source*: Maria Lazar, with permission.

engage in important activity. By recording different parts of a neuron we get somewhat different measures of its activities.

This is nicely illustrated in a recent study by Quiroga and colleagues at Caltech (Quiroga *et al.*, 2005) (Figure 4.4). These researchers found that a single neuron in the medial temporal cortex was selectively activated by pictures of actress Jennifer Aniston. It was not activated by pictures of other actresses, or actors, or by other kinds of images such as houses, scenery and objects. The researchers also found other cells that were highly selectively activated, including a neuron that was sensitive to pictures of actress Halle Berry and one for the Sydney Opera House. It is important to keep in mind, of course, that we are sampling just some out of billions of neurons. In all probability, there is a complex

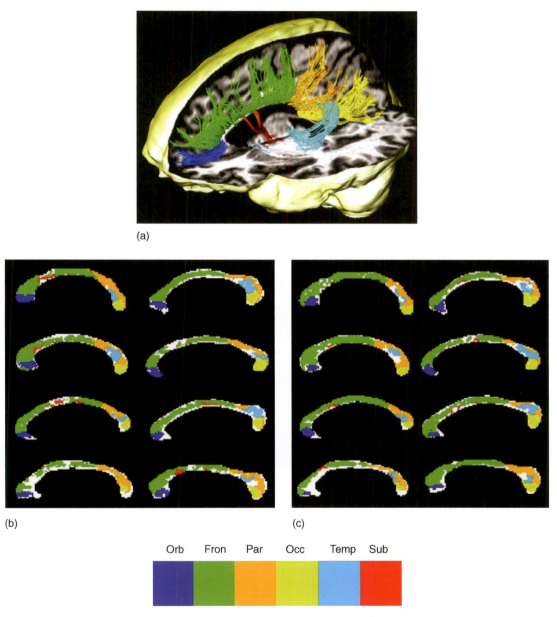

(a)

(b)   (c)

Orb   Fron   Par   Occ   Temp   Sub

FIGURE 4.3 Diffusion tractography brings out the corpus callosum and other large fiber tracts. Notice that we are looking at a cutaway image of the brain, in which the right hemisphere is intact. We can see the green-marked fibers projecting upward in front, and yellow-marked ones projecting toward the rear. Different artificial colors are assigned by computer to different directions of travel of the fiber highways. The c-shaped structures are the corpus callosum (the 'calloused body'), which looks white to the naked eye. The corpus callosum contains about 100 million fibers, running sideways from one hemisphere to the other. Millions of cells in the left hemisphere connect to a corresponding point in the right hemisphere. *Source*: Huang *et al.*, 2005.

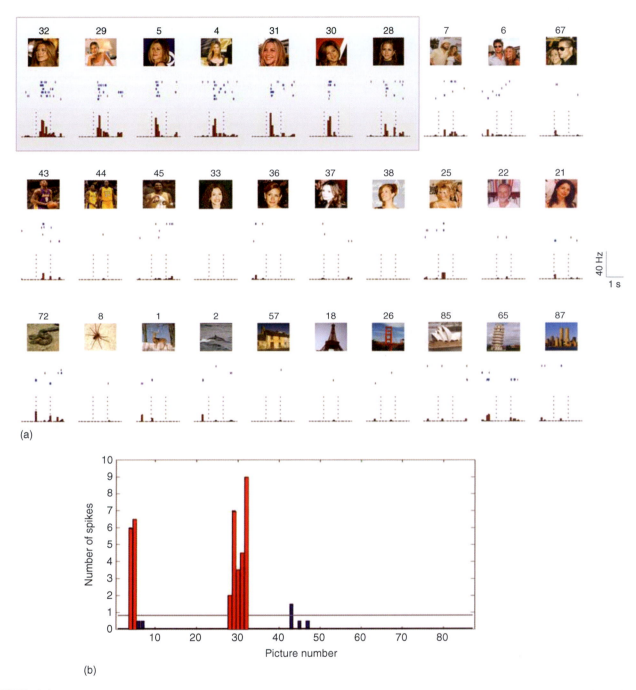

(a)

(b)

FIGURE 4.4 The Jennifer Aniston neuron. Quiroga and colleagues (2005) found a neuron in the left hippocampus that selectively responded to different views of the actress Jennifer Aniston. Responses in 30 of a total of 87 images are shown ((b) the responses to images of Jennifer Aniston). Numbers indicate the image number; graph indicates number of neural spikes recorded. Single neurons are likely to represent large networks with different sensitivities and preferences.

network of related neurons, and a lucky hit will reveal a Jennifer Aniston or Sydney Opera House fan.

The researchers used the axonal firing rate of single neurons as the measure of their activity. Would this mean that this single neuron 'knows' about Jennifer Aniston? Not at all. We should rather think of the activity of this cell as a representative for a large and widely distributed network of neurons that are sensitive to one particular face. If this neuron were lost, the person would still be able to recognize Jennifer Aniston. The brain as a whole would not show a detectable change.

Single cell recordings are only rarely possible in human subjects. It is ethically allowable in patients with medically untreatable epilepsy or brain tumor, where the

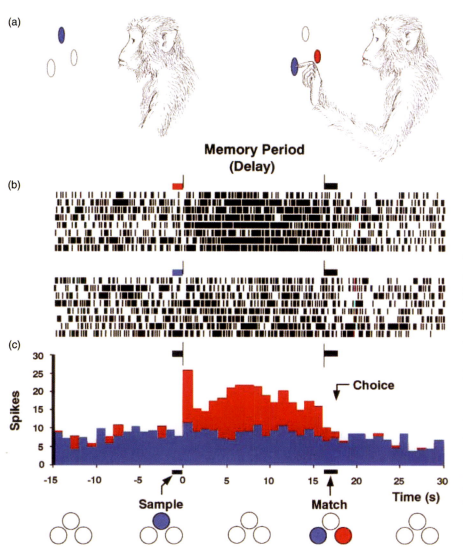

FIGURE 4.5 Working memory activity in single neurons. The macaque monkey is performing a working memory task called Delayed Match to Sample (DMTS). The 'sample stimulus' in this case is the blue dot in the display (A). Note that the monkey successfully presses the blue disk about 20 seconds later. Thus the animal can 'match to sample' even after the original stimulus is gone, implying that it must be kept in memory for a brief period of time. (B) shows a single-neuron electrode picking up neuronal firing in the temporal lobe of the monkey brain. (C) shows the firing of the neuron. This particular neuron has a background firing rate shown in blue, of 5-10 Hz, typical for cortical cells. However, between the sample stimulus and the successful matching choice, the neuron doubles its firing rate, shown in red. Such neurons are believed to be involved in the temporary stage of Working Memory contents. They often occur in the temporal and prefrontal lobes. *Source:* Fuster, 1997.

only treatment is surgical removal of the affected region. Depth electrodes are inserted to identify vital cognitive areas such as the language areas. If such a surgical procedure is required, scientists may be allowed a brief time to test a subject while the electrodes are in place.

In many countries deep electrode recordings are allowed in primates, such as the macaque monkey, under suitable ethical constraints. The macaque brain has some striking similarities to human brains. Single-neuron recording in the macaque prefrontal cortex may show working memory phenomena. In a typical experiment, a macaque is trained to fixate visually on a cross on a computer screen, and to perform a delayed response to a visual stimulus. The animal is trained to wait for a moment before looking in the direction where a stimulus appears; or alternatively, to look in the opposite direction. We can then record the activity of a single prefrontal neuron in the three phases: (1) the presentation of a visual stimulus; (2) the period when the monkey keeps the location of the visual stimulus in working memory; and (3) the response of looking in the direction of the stimulus after it disappears, or in the opposite direction. This is illustrated in Figure 4.5.

1.2 The time-space tradeoff

Today's most popular methods are shown in Figure 4.6. Notice that they do not yet have the space or time resolution needed to track single neurons, or even small clusters of neurons, like the columns of the cortex. They are gaining ground, however. Techniques like fMRI, which record physiological changes like blood oxygenation, are typically thought to have good spatial resolution

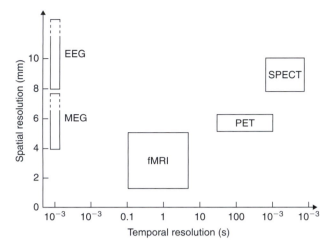

and relatively poor temporal resolution. fMRI has a response time of about six seconds, because changes in local blood supply take some time – too slow for tracking neurons and neuron populations directly. However, some recent studies show fMRI signal reflects neuronal firing six seconds before.

fMRI has very good spatial specificity compared to EEG and magnetoencephalography (MEG), which use electrical and magnetic signals respectively. Thus, fMRI is often used to localize brain functions. But EEG and MEG have excellent temporal resolution – almost instantaneous – and relatively poor spatial precision. They can track cell populations firing and fading over tens and hundreds of milliseconds, but it is hard to know *which* set of neurons is causing the signal. Some studies therefore combine EEG with fMRI to obtain the best temporal *and* spatial precision. A great deal has been learned with combined recording techniques.

Here we present some MRI images to demonstrate the ability they provide to map out brain regions (Figure 4.7). Differing views can be taken on brain anatomy using different slices, such as coronal (Figure 4.8), horizontal (Figure 4.9), or mid-sagittal (Figure 4.10).

FIGURE 4.6 Temporal versus spatial resolution. Different brain recording methods have pros and cons in accuracy. Notice that single-cell recording gives us the highest resolution in space and time. Single cells do not represent the tens of billions of other cells in the brain, of course. MEG and EEG have an almost instantaneous temporal resolution, but poor spatial resolution. PET and fMRI have better spatial resolution but poorer temporal accuracy. Different methods also pick up different aspects of neural activity. Some detect signals from input to neurons (dendrites), while others pick up action potentials. Not shown are methods that show the distribution of neurochemicals. *Source*: Laureys *et al.*, 2002.

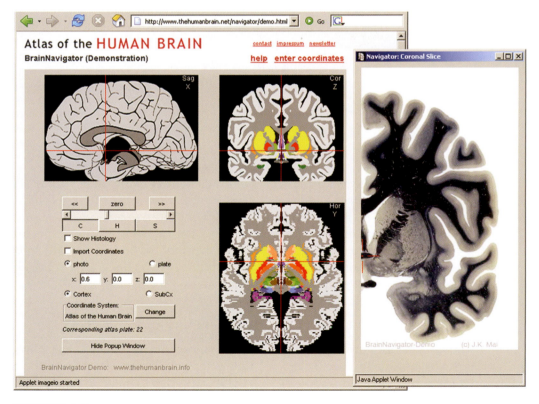

FIGURE 4.7 A brain navigation program. Brain navigation software allows the user to translate precise locations (in x,y,z coordinates) into brain locations. Notice the orientation of the standard slices. The x,y,z coordinates are known as the Talairach system (Talairach and Tournoux, 1988). Anatomical landmarks like the corpus callosum can be seen in the upper left display. *Source*: Mai and Thomas, 2006, with kind permission.

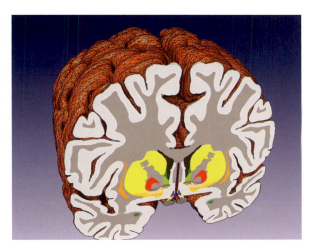

FIGURE 4.8 A coronal 'sausage slice'. A close-up in three dimensions from the Brain Navigator software. Notice that different 'sausage slices' (coronal sections) provide very different views of inside of the brain. *Source*: Mai & Thomas, 2006, with permission.

2.0 A RANGE OF USEFUL TOOLS – MEASURING ELECTRIC AND MAGNETIC SIGNALS

2.1 Single-unit recording

Our most precise recording method today is single-neuron or 'unit' recording, using deep needle electrodes, sometimes implanted in the brain (Figure 4.11). Unit recording is often done so as to sample a dozen or even a few hundred neurons in a single study. Needle electrodes typically pick up axonal spikes, which are believed to be crucial in information processing and transmission. But unit recording has a sampling problem – how do we know that local spikes represent a whole region of the brain? It also matters whether cells are *excitatory* (making others fire more) or *inhibitory* (making others fire less). In addition, inserting a needle into the brain is invasive

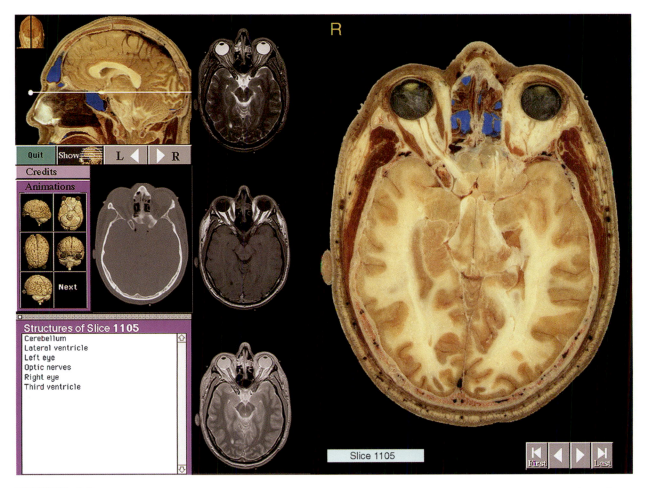

FIGURE 4.9 A horizontal slice seen from above. This display shows a detailed horizontal brain section, seen from above, through the eyeballs at the top of the image. Notice the white matter on the inside of the cortex, and the gray outer layer (shown in brown). A side view of the horizontal cut is shown on the upper left, just below the corpus callosum. This horizontal plane defines the zero point of the vertical dimension. (The horizontal section is also called axial, since it follows the neural axis.) *Source*: nlm.nih.gov.

and potentially harmful – it requires surgery. It is therefore done only in experimental animals or in humans with medical conditions such as untreatable epilepsy, where exploratory surgery is required. We will see examples of each kind.

We can, in fact, record from single neurons that do important things, ever since Hubel and Wiesel (1962)

were able to record single feature-sensitive cells in the visual cortex of the cat, an achievement for which they received a Nobel Prize in 1981. More recent work has recorded in medial temporal lobes (Figure 4.12). Like every method, electrical recording of axonal firing has its limitations, but it continues to be a major source of information. Neurons fire a maximum of 1000 Hz, but

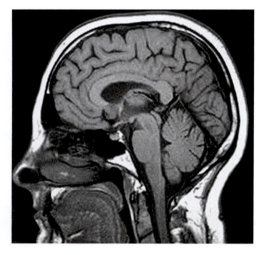

FIGURE 4.10 A midline view of the brain: mid-sagittal. A classic view of the midline section, called mid-sagittal. How many anatomical features can you name? *Source*: Standring, 2005.

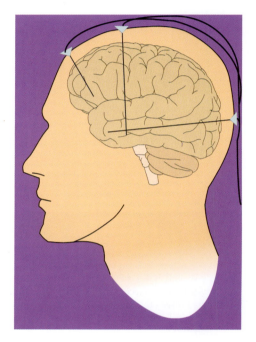

FIGURE 4.11 Single neuron recording deep in the brain. Intracellular and extracellular recording of single cells. Notice also the ability to stimulate single neurons, using the same electrodes. Single unit recording comes close to the desirable level of temporal and spatial resolution for brain recordings. It works very well in tracing circuits of neurons. However, this method does not allow us to track large-scale populations of neurons.

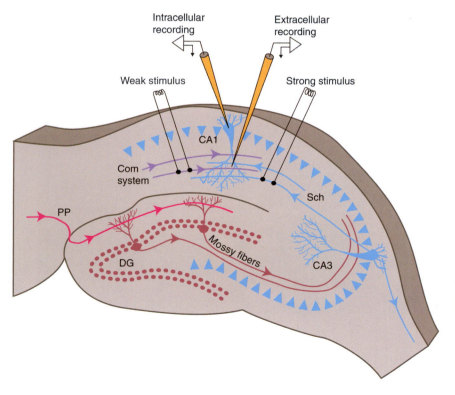

FIGURE 4.12 Unit recording in the hippocampus. Microscopic needles can be inserted into single neurons, or they can record extracellular electrical field potentials. The same electrodes can then be used to stimulate specific cells. The hippocampus contains regular arrays of neurons with distinct functions. *Source*: Squire *et al.*, 2003.

cortical neurons average about 10 Hz. We have no 'universal census' of cortical neurons, so we do not know with certainty how representative the small samples we can observe really are.

Depth electrodes have been used in humans. Typically, these electrodes are implanted before surgery in a patient who has otherwise untreatable epilepsy. The implants can determine where epileptic foci begin at the onset of a seizure, and where critical regions of the brain are located that must not be lesioned (Figure 4.13).

How does recording in a single neuron relate to human perception? While a single cell cannot tell us much about human cognition, a recent experiment provided some intriguing results regarding conscious and unconscious visual perception (Figure 4.14).

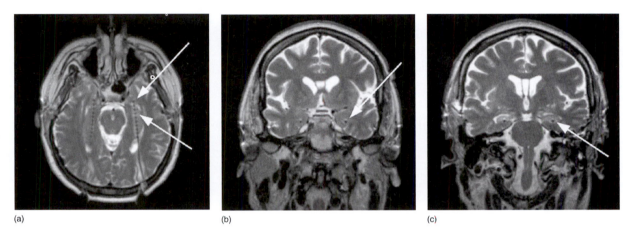

FIGURE 4.13 Depth electrodes in humans. While most single-cell recording is done in animals, human studies have been done when depth electrode recording is medically necessary. The arrows point to electrode placements in the temporal lobe. If you look carefully at the left MRI scan (a), you can see the electrode tracks, and the small holes in the rear of the scalp through which they were inserted. Neurosurgery like this is generally safe and pain-free, because the brain itself does not contain pain-sensing neurons. *Source*: Dietl *et al.*, 2005.

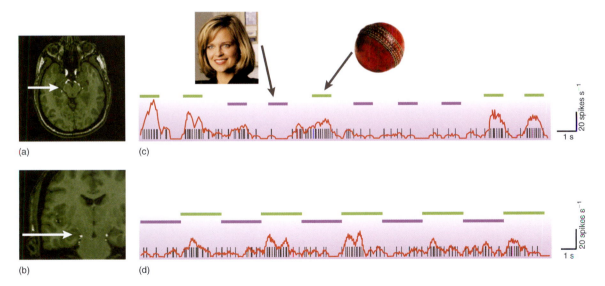

FIGURE 4.14 Human single cell recording and conscious perception. A remarkable experiment in which both conscious and unconscious stimuli were shown simultaneously to the two different eyes, using a variant of binocular rivalry (see Chapter 6). In the upper row (c), the woman's face is conscious but the soccer ball is not; in the lower row (d), this is reversed. Neurons that respond mainly to the conscious visual input, but not unconscious input, are shown by green horizontal bars. The brain seems to determine which of the two simultaneous stimuli will become conscious when the signal reaches object recognition cortex. The electrode locations are shown on the brain scans on the left. *Source*: Rees *et al.*, 2002.

While the spiking neuron is a plausible unit of brain activity, there are important alternative views. Some scientists believe that graded dendritic currents in each neuron may do useful information processing; some argue for subcellular processes inside the cell; others point to non-classical cells and synapses, which are known to be much more common than previously thought; others believe that glial cells participate in information processing; and many scientists believe that real brain processes only take place at the level of *populations* of neurons. Therefore, recording axonal spikes is important, but it may not be the only important thing going on. Obviously, it's a risky business to jump from a single neuron to more than 10 billion in the vast forest of the brain.

2.2 Animal and human studies cast light on each other

Non-human primates, such as macaque monkeys, have been extensively studied using single and multiple unit recordings. Much of what we know about vision, memory, attention and executive functions comes from studies of the macaque (Figure 4.15).

How do brain regions in macaque correspond to human brain regions? While there are clearly some major anatomical differences, especially in frontal and parietal lobe regions, there remain some strong similarities between macaque and human brains (Figure 4.16).

Single unit studies in macaque do not just map sensory and perceptual features, they may also involve more cognitive aspects such as attention. (See Figure 4.17 for a study of visual attention in macaque.)

Single unit studies have provided us with a wealth of information regarding the encoding properties of neurons across cortical regions. However, neurons respond as ensembles, with complex networks of cells in multiple locations. How can we capture this type of dynamic brain response? An early technique for doing just that is presented in the next section: electroencephalography.

2.3 Electroencephalography (EEG)

The brain's large-scale electrical activity can be recorded through the scalp or on the surface of the cortex. Rather than picking up electrical activity direct from neurons, which are essentially tiny batteries, the electroencephalogram picks up the electrical field. The resulting brain record is referred to as an *electroencephalogram* (EEG) or electrical brain record. The EEG was discovered in 1929 by Hans Berger. Because electromagnetic waves

FIGURE 4.15 Monkeys have striking similarities to humans. Macaque monkeys are extensively studied because of apparent brain homologies (biological similarities) to humans. The macaque visual brain has been our best guide to the human visual cortex until very recently, when it became possible to study the human cortex more directly. Macaques also have emotional similarities to humans, close infant-mother bonding, and even prefrontal regions that resemble the human prefrontal cortex. Obviously, they do not have language and other species-specific human traits.

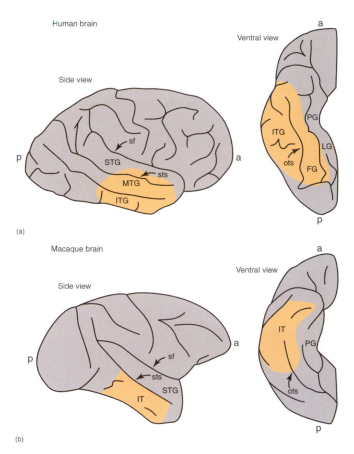

FIGURE 4.16 Brain homologies between humans and macaques. Upper, the human brain, and below, the macaque brain. The yellow areas are specialized in visual object recognition in both species. The right-hand figures show the bottom of the right hemispheres, facing upward.

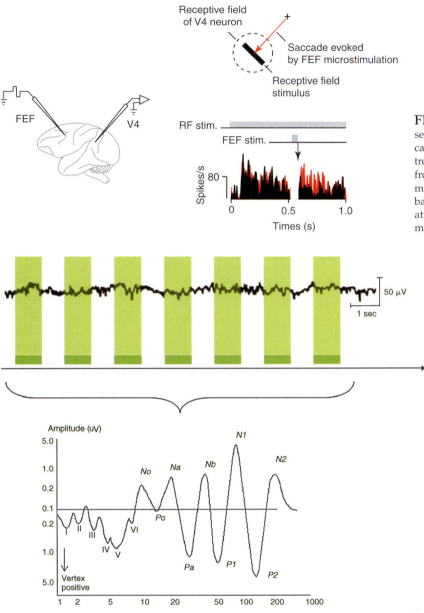

FIGURE 4.17 Single neurons show the effects of selective attention. Attentional neurons in the macaque can be recorded and also stimulated by the same electrodes. In this example, electrodes are placed in the frontal eye field (FEF), which controls voluntary eye movements, and in area V4, which detects the diagonal bar in its receptive field (RF) when the monkey pays attention to that stimulus. The firing rate of neurons is measured in spikes per second. *Source:* Awh *et al.*, 2006.

FIGURE 4.18 Evoked potentials (EPs). Beautifully regular curves are obtained when a strong or salient stimulus is repeated, and EEG is averaged over repetitions, much as the sound of a crowd in a football stadium can be heard when it chants a simultaneous cheer. Averaging periods are defined as one second after the stimulus, such as a loud click or visual flash (green regions). The EPs are highly stereotyped, and are therefore labeled with numbers and letters. N = negative waveform; P = positive waveform. Note that the Negative waves point upward, an arbitrary convention. *Source:* Hobson and Stickgold, 1995.

propagate essentially instantaneously, EEG is highly sensitive temporally. However, EEG is quite selective, being more sensitive to neurons near the surface than to deeper neurons. EEG is picked up through layers of moist tissue, so that the original electrical activity is attenuated and distorted by the shape and conductive properties of the intervening cells. Some researchers believe that EEG is largely sensitive to the first layer of the cortex, which mainly consists of a tightly woven 'feltwork' of cortical dendrites (Freeman, 2004).

It is easiest to record EEG from the scalp, though it is sometimes recorded from electrodes placed directly on the cortical surface. Like unit electrodes, EEG is a relatively direct measure of the brain's electrical activity. But with tens of billions of cortical neurons firing about 10 Hz, we have several trillion electrical events per second. The raw EEG is therefore difficult to understand, and it was difficult to interpret before the advent of powerful computerized analysis.

However, when the EEG is averaged over a number of experimental trials and 'locked' to a specific zero point, like the onset of a stimulus, the averaged electrical activity yields elegant and regular waveforms. This event-related potential (ERP) is sensitive to large neuronal population activity that characterizes visual, auditory and even semantic processes (Figure 4.18).

2.3.1   Sampling populations of neurons

The activity of large-scale populations and networks is another important level of analysis (Freeman, 2004; John, 2004). Spontaneous EEG shows different patterns of activation. The brain can operate with many different levels of interactivity. For example, during deep sleep, the raw EEG shows large, slow waves. This indicates that large groups of neurons are synchronized on a very large scale throughout the brain. When the subject wakes up, this slow pattern is replaced by small, rapid electrical waves, indicative of rapid and flexible information patterns of interaction in the brain. It is currently believed that cortical neurons do not fire at different rates during deep sleep compared to waking, but rather that waking EEG allows a far greater amount of interactive processing. Sleep is not a passive state, therefore, but a different operating mode of the brain,

with its own functions. One of these is believed to be the consolidation of memories based on waking experiences (Hobson and Stickgold, 1995).

The 'raw' (unprocessed) EEG shows visibly different waveforms like alpha, beta-gamma, theta and delta. However, raw EEG is believed to be a combination of many different kinds of activity. Using mathematical analysis, we can decompose these complex and noisy waveforms into frequencies components. This is not unlike taking noisy radio static and decomposing it into frequency bands – which is exactly what we do by tuning to a specific radio station. The analyzed EEG shows that certain tasks may show a specific rhythm, such as alpha or gamma, in specific regions of the brain. This is illustrated in Figure 4.19.

Some of these typical frequency bands are shown in Table 4.1.

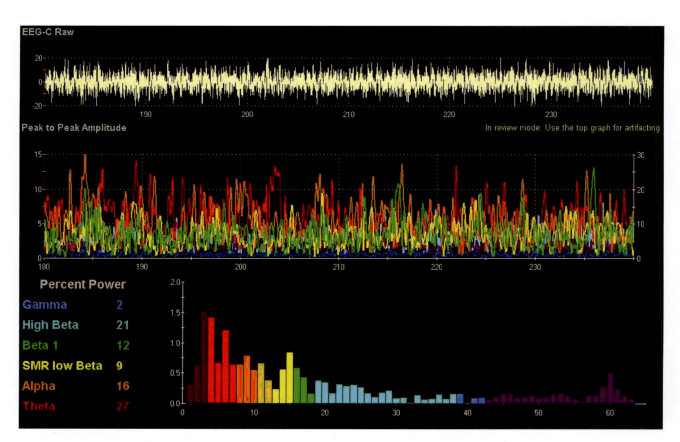

FIGURE 4.19 Regular rhythms in different parts of the brain. A method called Fourier analysis allows us to decompose the density (or power) of regular wave forms that are buried in noisy EEG (see Table 4.1). The graphs show the resulting power curves. According to this source, the greatest alpha density is found over the occipital cortex, while the greatest theta density is over the frontal cortex. Theta is thought to involve hippocampal-frontal interactions during long-term memory retrieval. Gamma is found widely through the brain, and is believed to reflect functional interactions between different regions during the conscious state. The colors correspond to different frequency ranges. *Source*: From Zoran Josipovich, with permission.

TABLE 4.1   EEG frequencies and their associated functions

NAME AND EXAMPLE	DESCRIPTION
Delta	Delta is thought to be the lowest frequency. They are less than 4 Hz and occur in deep sleep and in certain abnormal brain states such as coma and vegetative state. It is therefore thought to reflect the brain of an unconscious person. The Delta frequency tends to be the highest in amplitude and the slowest waves. Delta waves increase in relation to our decreasing awareness of the physical world.
Theta 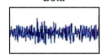	Theta activity has a frequency of 3.5 to 7.5 Hz. Theta waves are thought to involve many neurons firing synchronously. Theta rhythms are observed during some sleep states, and in states of quiet focus, for example meditation. They are also manifested during some short term memory tasks, and during memory retrieval. The origins and function of theta rhythms are currently unclear. However, it is likely that human sources of theta rhythm are similar, and that cholinergic projection from the basal forebrain to throughout the cerebral cortex drive the theta rhythm seen in human EEG patterns, Similarly, they show hippocampal theta rhythms that are probably mediated by inputs from the medial septum.
Alpha 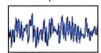	Alpha waves are those between 7.5 and 13 Hz that arise from synchronous and coherent (in phase) electrical activity of large groups of neurons in the human brain. They are also called Berger's waves in memory of the founder of EEG. Alpha waves are predominantly found to originate from the occipital lobe during periods of relaxation, with eyes closed but still awake. Conversely alpha waves are attenuated with open eyes as well as by drowsiness and sleep.
Beta 	Beta activity is 'fast' irregular activity, at low voltage. Beta waves are usually associated with normal waking consciousness, often active, busy or anxious thinking and active concentration. Rhythmic beta with a dominant set of frequencies may be associated with various pathologies and drug effects. Beta is usually seen on both sides in symmetrical distribution and is most evident frontally. It may be absent or reduced in areas of cortical damage.
Gamma	Gamma generally ranges between 26 and 70 Hz, centered around 40 Hz. Gamma waves are thought to signal active exchange of information between cortical and subcortical regions. It is seen during the conscious waking state and in REM dreams (Rapid Eye Movement sleep). Note that gamma and beta activity may overlap.

The classical EEG waveforms can be picked up directly, from the 'raw' or unanalyzed EEG. Notice especially the widespread, low-amplitude beta and gamma activity typical of waking conscious states. The opposite state occurs in deep sleep, when the EEG is slow, high in amplitude and much more regular. Other unconscious states show similarities (Baars *et al.*, 2004). Alpha activity may be seen over the occipital cortex when subjects are in a relaxed but alert state.

As mentioned, while EEG has a millisecond time resolution, its spatial resolution is rather poor. It is very difficult to locate the electrical source of the EEG signal. It helps to increase the number of electrodes and to use sophisticated analytical methods (Figure 4.20). However, EEG gives us little information about brain regions deep beneath the cortex. Since subcortical regions like the thalamus are very important, EEG seems to have inherent limits.

Early uses of EEG were to evaluate brain responses during sleep and dreaming states (Figure 4.21).

New improvements using high-density arrays of electrodes have enabled scientists to make better, more detailed measurements of brain responses (Figure 4.22).

An important aspect of EEG recording is to measure the evoked potential (ERP) that occurs in response to specific stimuli. To improve the signal to noise, these responses are averaged over many trials (Figure 4.23).

For example, visual ERPs have been measured to investigate the time course of visual processing

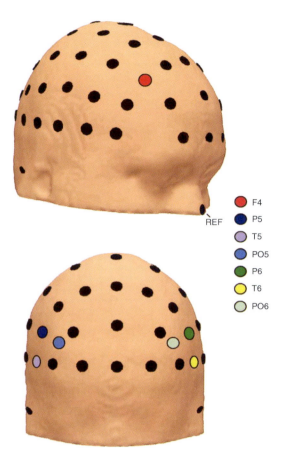

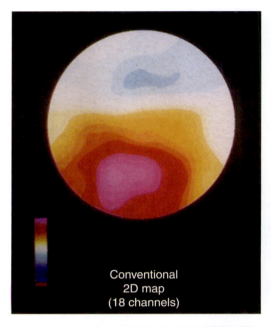

Conventional
2D map
(18 channels)

FIGURE 4.20 Scalp electrodes record EEG. A high-density array of EEG electrodes is placed on the scalp, in precisely determined locations. (*Top*: Frontal view; *Bottom*: Rear view). Electrode labels: F = frontal; P = parietal; T = temporal; PO = parieto-occipital boundary; REF = reference electrode (is placed on the nose or ear). EEG picks up an electrical field with major contributions believed to come from dendrites in the outside layers of cortex. While it is hard to localize the sources of EEG signals, their temporal resolution is excellent. *Source*: Doniger *et al.*, 2001.

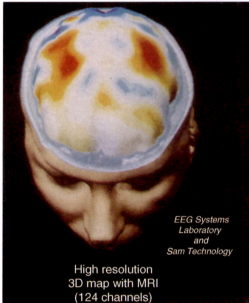

EEG Systems
Laboratory
and
Sam Technology

High resolution
3D map with MRI
(124 channels)

FIGURE 4.21 The first EEG. This historic EEG signal was recorded by Hans Berger in 1929, using a single pair of electrodes, on the scalp. Above, an EEG signal recorded on Berger's son, showing alpha activity (the regular sine wave in the upper trace). The lower trace is an electrical timing wave of 10 Hz. *Source*: Gottesmann, 1999.

FIGURE 4.22 High resolution EEG with many electrodes. *Top*, standard EEG of the entire scalp. Note the fuzzy resolution. *Bottom*, high-resolution EEG, using many more electrodes and sophisticated signal analysis. Red and yellow colors indicated increased electrical power (density) of the signal. *Source: Gevins et al.*, 1995.

(Figure 4.24). The ERP is sensitive to many factors that are important in human cognition, such as hearing your own name (Figure 4.25) or listening to music (Figure 4.26).

The standard method for analyzing highly complex EEG is Fourier analysis, named after the French mathematician Pierre Fourier, who showed that any complex signal can be decomposed into sine waves with differing amounts of power (density) in each frequency range (Figure 4.19).

EEG reveals brain patterns during sleep and waking, abnormalities during diseases like epilepsy, and even the brain areas that respond to music. A more recent

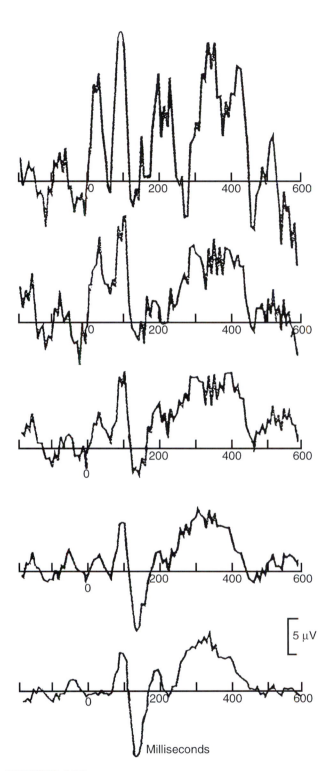

FIGURE 4.23 The evoked potential: signal emerging from noise. From the top to the bottom traces, more signals are averaged in, and the curves become more and more regular. Standard EEG is so complex that when it is averaged over time, the result is a flat line. However, when EEG is averaged over short stretches that are time-locked to a stimulus, an elegant waveform appears, called the evoked or event-related potential (EP or ERP). The peaks and valleys of the EP are believed to reflect waves of activity in large populations of neurons involved in analyzing the stimulus. (See Figure 4.18). *Source*: Squire *et al.*, 2003.

technique, magnetoencephalography (MEG), is highly related to EEG and has provided new ways to image the human brain.

2.4 Magnetoencephalography

Magnetoencephalography (magnetic brain recording) measures the magnetic field produced by electrical activity in the brain. Its spatial resolution at parts of the cortical surface is now approaching a few millimeters, while its temporal resolution is in milliseconds (Figures 4.28–4.30).

Because of the physics of magnetism, MEG is highly sensitive to dendritic flow at right angles to the walls of the sulci (the cortical folds), but much less sensitive to the bottom. MEG has excellent temporal resolution and somewhat better spatial accuracy than EEG.

Like any other method that measures brain activity, MEG results must be superimposed upon a structural image of the living brain. MEG uses a process called *magnetic source imaging* (MSI) to co-register the magnetic sources of brain activity onto anatomical pictures provided by MRI. In this way, MSI combines the high spatial resolution of MRI with the high temporal resolution of MEG. MSI techniques are used before brain surgery, to pinpoint brain regions with vital functions that must be protected during surgery.

MEG has the advantage of being entirely silent and non-invasive. As we will see, MRI is quite noisy, and of course depth electrodes require surgery. Thus, MEG is attractive for use with children and vulnerable people (Figure 4.31).

2.5 Zapping the brain

We have discussed techniques for non-invasive recording of brain signals, but what if you could evoke neural activity in a safe fashion? Such a method would be especially useful to test causal relationships between evoked neural activity and cognitive functions.

Early work on direct electrical brain stimulation began with Wilder Penfield, a neurosurgeon at the Montreal Neurological Institute (Figures 4.32 and 4.33). Penfield and his colleagues treated patients with intractable epilepsy. In open brain surgery, patients can remain awake and responsive, since only local anesthetic is needed at the site. There are no pain receptors in the brain itself, so that the cortex brain can be stimulated and operated upon without general anesthesia. This is a vital part of the operation, because surgeons need to map out brain regions that are needed for normal

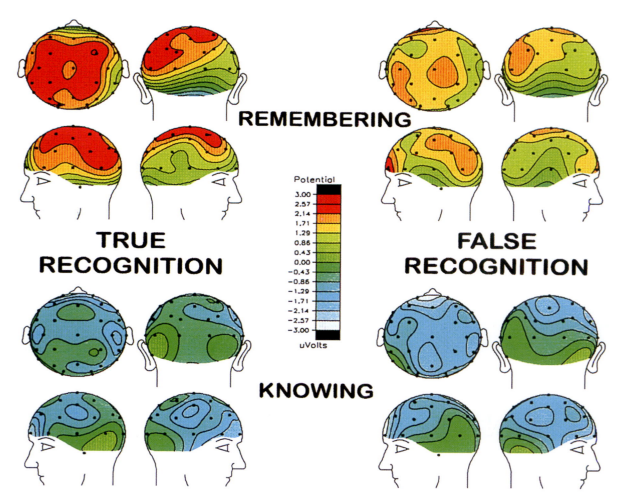

FIGURE 4.24 Evoked potentials are often shown by topographical maps of averaged voltages across the scalp. Redder colors are higher voltages. In this case, explicit remembering of conscious memories evokes much higher ERPs than the 'feeling of knowing' for the same memories. Brain activity is not as well localized with ERPs as it would be with PET or fMRI. *Source:* Düzel *et al.*, 1997.

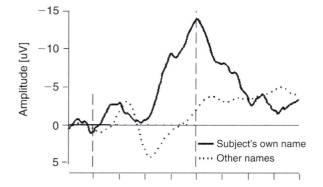

FIGURE 4.25 The evoked potential is highly sensitive to cognitive factors. The solid line shows the averaged evoked potential to the subject's own name, while the dotted line shows the response to someone else's name. Thus, personal significance of a spoken word makes a big difference. *Source:* Muller and Kutas, 1996.

functions. Epileptic foci, which trigger major seizures, can then be cut out with minimal side effects.

2.5.1 A safe way of interfering with brain function: transcranial magnetic stimulation (TMS)

It is now possible to simulate brain lesions in healthy subjects. Without cutting a person's brain, we can alter the brain's level of activity very locally. Brief magnetic pulses over the scalp either inhibit or excite a small region of cortex. For example, if you stimulate the hand area of the motor cortex, the subject's hand will suddenly move and twist. Applying an inhibitory pulse over the same area will cause subjects to have

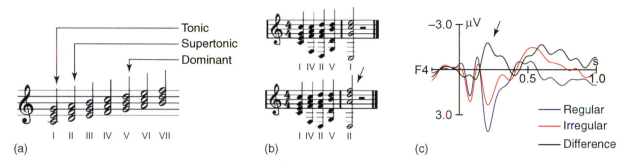

FIGURE 4.26 Evoked potentials to musical meaning. Regular musical sequences are perceived as more pleasant, and show a larger evoked potential (see the arrow in the graph). Irregular musical sequences evoked a very different brain response. *Source*: Koelsch and Siebel, 2005.

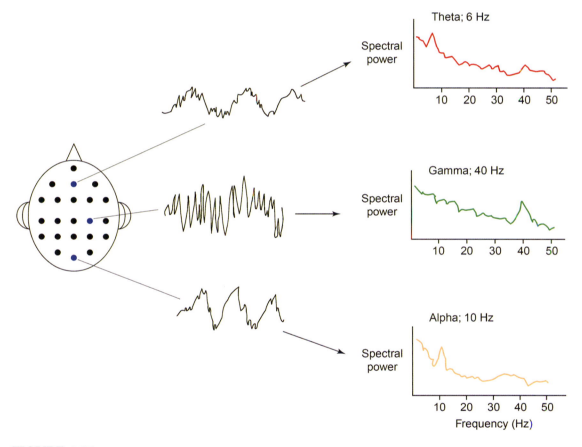

FIGURE 4.27 Regular waveforms from different brain regions. Three waveforms with important cognitive functions are alpha, classically associated with relaxed and alert states, and often found over the occipital cortex. Frontal theta is now believed to reflect interactions between the hippocampus and cortex. Finally, gamma activity is often thought to reflect transient large-scale assemblies of neurons associated with conscious percepts and other cognitive processes. *Source*: Ward, 2002.

difficulty moving their hands. This is called *transcranial magnetic stimulation* (TMS) or, as one leading researcher has called it, 'zapping the brain' (Cowey and Walsh, 2001). TMS (Figures 4.34 and 4.35) appears to be generally safe. By applying TMS, we can now test causal hypotheses about the contribution of specific brain regions to complex cognitive processes. Since the TMS works at the millisecond scale, it is also possible to study how rapid waves of processing develop.

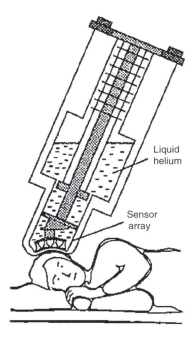

Liquid
helium

Sensor
array

FIGURE 4.28 An MEG scanner. The MEG scanner consists of a large number of individual detectors that record millisecond fluctuations in the magnetic field surrounding the brain. Using multiple detectors we can reconstruct the spatial origin of the signal. MEG's millisecond temporal resolution makes it possible to detect rapid changes in activity (Hari *et al.*, 2004). MEG has advantages but also limitations. Because of the direction of the magnetic field produced by cortical neurons, MEG is strongly affected by the hills and valleys of the cortex, the sulci and gyri. This is illustrated in Figures 4.30 and 4.31. The signals recorded by MEG tend to miss the bottom of the sulci. And, like EEG, MEG does not pick up subcortical activity (see Figure 4.29).

Overgaard *et al.* (2004) used TMS to explore visual consciousness. Subjects were given simple geometric shapes, like triangles, squares and circles, in three different colors (red, green and blue). The stimuli were presented in one of three locations on the screen. All the shapes were shown long enough to be seen by all subjects. The researchers then applied a TMS inhibitory pulse to the mid-temporal region in both hemispheres, roughly just in front of each ear. If the pulse was applied about 120 milliseconds after the stimulus was shown,

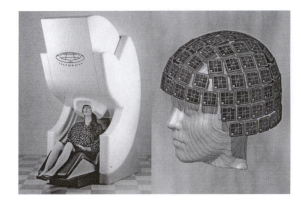

FIGURE 4.29 Magnetic recording of brain activity. Electrical and magnetic fields are two aspects of the same physical event. Above, a modern MEG scanner, consisting of highly sensitive magnetic coils cooled to superconductive temperatures. *Source*: Jousmaki, 2000.

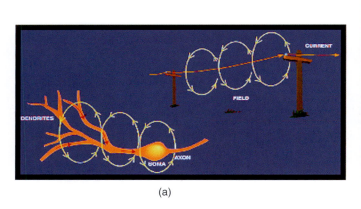

(a)

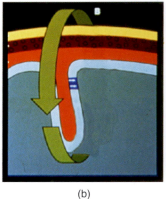

(b)

(c)

FIGURE 4.30 The neural basis for the MEG signal. (a) In the same way that an electrical wire produces a measurable magnetic field, the neuron produces a small magnetic field along its axis. (b) MEG is insensitive to the magnetic fields of neurons at the top and bottom of the sulci (valleys) of the cortex. Electromagnetic activity in the walls of the sulci are better measurable. (c) However, MEG can measure the magnetic field properties of large ensembles of cortical neurons. *Source*: 4-D Neuroimaging, reproduced with permission.

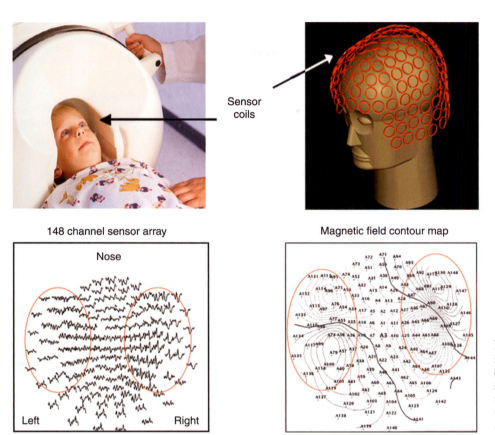

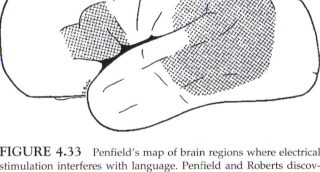

148 channel sensor array

Nose

Left   Right

Magnetic field contour map

FIGURE 4.31 MEG is silent and non-invasive. MEG is silent and easy for young children to tolerate, as long as they can stay relatively still. The pictures at the bottom of the figure show the vector fields of the MEG over the head of the subject. *Source*: 4D Neuroimaging, San Diego.

FIGURE 4.32 Wilder Penfield. Penfield and colleagues devised open-brain neurosurgery for untreatable epilepsy in the 1950s. *Source*: Adelman and Smith, 2004.

FIGURE 4.33 Penfield's map of brain regions where electrical stimulation interferes with language. Penfield and Roberts discovered that electrical stimulation in the indicated regions interfere with language production or perception. Notice how closely these regions correspond to the classical Broca's and Wernicke's patients studied a century before. *Source*: Adelman and Smith, 2004.

there was a dramatic drop in subjects' awareness of the stimuli. They no longer had a clear perception of the figures, but either a vague impression that something had been shown, or none at all.

Interestingly, when subjects were asked to guess the stimuli, they all showed normal performance. Yet they did not report being conscious of the stimuli. The stimuli must still have been detected (unconsciously) to permit accurate detection. Yet no subjective experience of the words was reported.

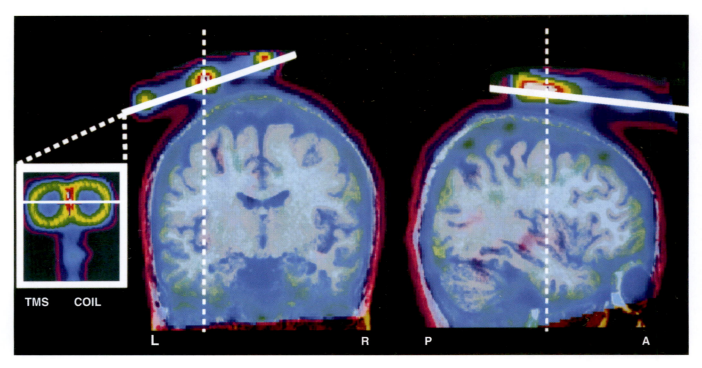

FIGURE 4.34 'Zapping' the brain with Transcranial Magnetic Stimulation (TMS). How an electromagnetic coil induces electrical activity across the scalp inside of the brain. The flat coil is positioned over the brain as shown. The upper left brain scan shows L (left) and R (right), and the upper right one shows the brain from P (posterior) to (A) anterior. *Source: Paus et al., 1997.*

Now let's turn to methods for investigating the brain that use spatial mapping techniques to explore both brain anatomy and function.

3.0 fMRI AND PET: INDIRECT SIGNALS FOR NEURAL ACTIVITY

EEG and MEG measure brain activity fairly directly. Other neuroimaging measures use indirect measures, such as blood flow or regional oxygen level. Currently, the most popular method is fMRI (functional magnetic resonance imaging), and especially the kind that measures the oxygen level of the local blood circulation (called BOLD, for blood-oxygen level dependent activity, see pages 108–113).

When neurons fire they consume oxygen and glucose and secrete metabolic waste products. An active brain region consumes its local blood oxygen supply, and as oxygen is consumed we can see as a small drop in the BOLD signal. In a fraction of a second the loss of regional oxygen triggers a new influx of oxygen-rich blood to that region. Here, we see a recovery of the signal. However, as the compensatory mechanism overshoots, flooding more oxygenated blood into the area than is needed, we also see that the signal rises high above the baseline. Finally, as unused oxygen-rich blood flushes out of the region, we can see a drop in the BOLD signal, back to the baseline.

Thus, as the oxygen content of blood produces changes in the BOLD signal, we can measure neural activation indirectly. The BOLD signal comes about six seconds after the onset of neuronal firing. The relationship between neural activation and the BOLD fMRI signal is shown in Figures 4.36 and 4.37.

3.1 Pros and cons of PET and fMRI

Positron emission tomography (PET) was developed much earlier than MRI or fMRI, and provides a measure of metabolic brain activity (Figure 4.39). PET is used less often for research today, because it is very expensive, requiring a cyclotron. It also requires subjects to be injected with a radioactive tracer. For non-medical investigations, MRI and fMRI have largely taken over the research field. However, PET is still important,

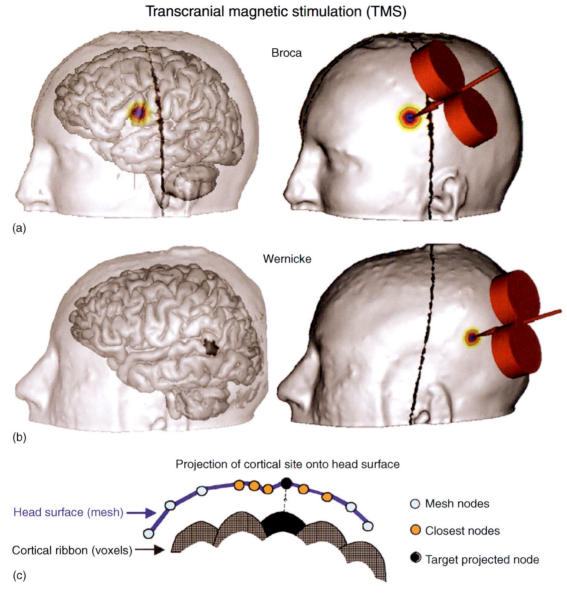

Transcranial magnetic stimulation (TMS)

Broca

(a)

Wernicke

(b)

Projection of cortical site onto head surface

Head surface (mesh) →

Cortical ribbon (voxels) →

○ Mesh nodes

● Closest nodes

● Target projected node

(c)

FIGURE 4.35   Magnetic brain stimulation is not surgically invasive. Brain stimulation can be applied without surgery. In this example, it is being applied over Broca's and Wernicke's areas in the left hemisphere of the subject. TMS appears to be safe at mild levels of intensity and frequency. It allows causal hypotheses to be tested in brain experiments, a major methodological advance. *Source*: Andoh *et al.*, 2006.

because different tracers can be linked to different molecules. The distribution of neurochemicals in receptors can therefore be determined.

Today, it is not possible to have high spatial and high temporal resolution at the same time using the same recording device. There is a tradeoff. Methods like fMRI and PET tell us *where* in the brain something is happening. EEG, MEG and single cell recordings show millisecond changes in the brain. In any study, it is important ask

is why the authors chose a particular method, and what they observed – or might have missed – by the choices they made. In the best cases we can see different methods showing convergent results.

3.2 Regions of interest

Finding your way around the brain is not easy. An even harder task is to figure out which areas play which

Blood Oxygenation Level Dependent (BOLD) effect

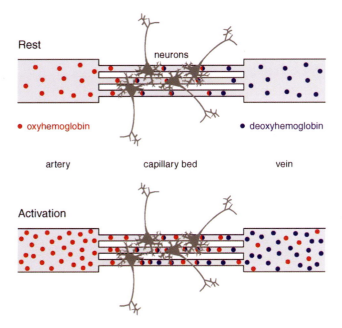

FIGURE 4.36 The basis of functional MRI (fMRI). The most popular brain imaging method today is probably fMRI, which is less expensive than PET, and provides a good localization of brain activity. fMRI is an indirect measure of neuronal regional activity, as shown here. Neuronal activation increases the oxygen demand of neurons and related cells, leading to additional blow flow carrying oxygen molecules to the region. This can be measured using BOLD – Blood Oxygen Level Dependent activity. Since neurons start firing several seconds before additional BOLD activity starts, there is a built-in lag time in fMRI. *Source: Dogil et al., 2002.*

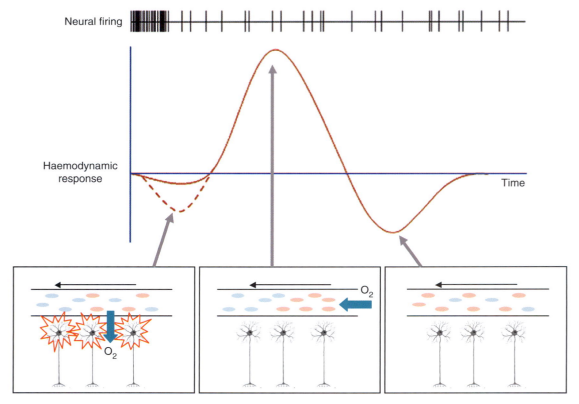

FIGURE 4.37 A typical BOLD response to a neural population. The top line shows a burst of activity in a population of neurons somewhere in the brain. In a few seconds, the active brain region has used up its immediate supply of nutrients – oxygen and glucose. The BOLD curve therefore dips to reflect the loss of oxygen. Next, an upward sweep of the BOLD curve reflects a wave of new, blood-carried nutrients to the active region to keep it going. This wave of oxygen is used up again by energy-thirsty neurons, and the curve dips down again. Eventually, the nutrient supply comes to equilibrium with the neural demand, and the curve goes back to baseline. The BOLD response is called 'hemodynamic' because it reflects fast and precise changes in the blood supply.

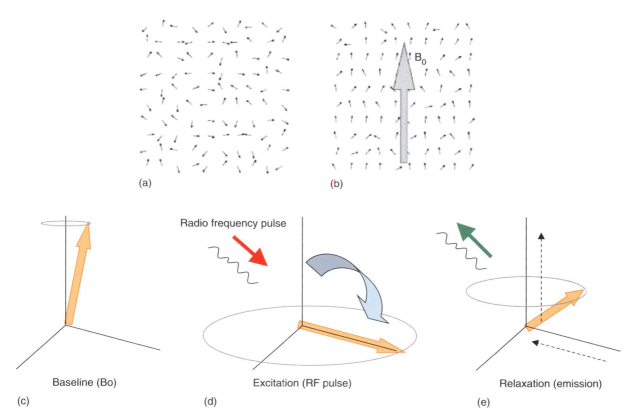

Radio frequency pulse

Baseline (Bo)   Excitation (RF pulse)   Relaxation (emission)

(a)   (b)

(c)   (d)   (e)

FIGURE 4.38 A little bit of fMRI physics. Magnetic resonance imaging depends upon the basic physical property of magnetic spin resonance in vast numbers of atoms. In the case of the BOLD fMRI, blood oxygen can be picked up by stimulating oxygen atoms with high-intensity magnetic fields, so that all atomic spin values line up. When the field is turned off, the lined-up nuclear spin 'relaxes', so that it returns to a more normal, random state of individual spin for each particle. Relaxation of nuclear spin is picked up as a signal by sensitive coils surrounding the subject's head, and can be localized in three dimensions. *Source*: van Essen, 2005.

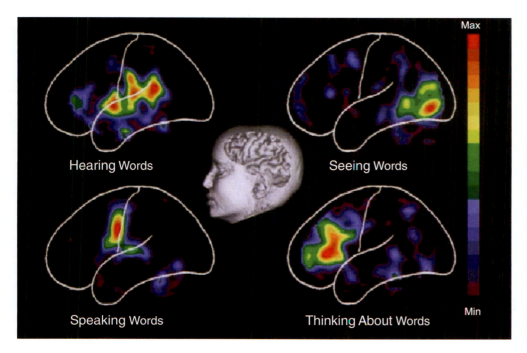

FIGURE 4.39 A classical PET finding: visual versus auditory brain activity. Early PET scans showing different speaking, seeing, hearing, and internally generating words (Posner and Raichle, 1994). Notice that visual, auditory, somatosensory regions appear to be activated. However, the surrounding brain outline (white lines) is only approximate. In more recent brain images, the functional activity would be superimposed upon a structural MRI of the same subject's brain. *Source*: Posner and Raichle, 1994.

fMRI SHOWS THE ACTIVITY OF THE BRAIN

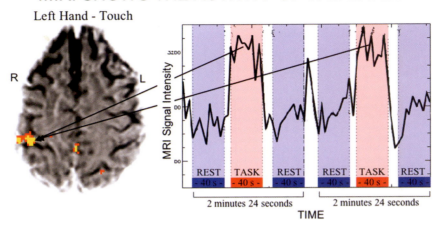

FIGURE 4.40 How the BOLD signal cycles on and off. The basic physics of BOLD requires a high magnetic field to be turned on and off frequently to detect the radio frequency changes due to spin changes in oxygen atoms. Because cognitive tasks occur over seconds and fractions of seconds, a common method is to alternate Task and Rest conditions every half minute or so (in this case, 40 seconds per phase). This allows for excellent within-subject control. On the left, the functional signal (i.e. BOLD) is superimposed on a structural brain scan (using MRI). All brain images superimpose the task-related activity upon brain structure, and average out background activity. *Source*: Robinson, 2004.

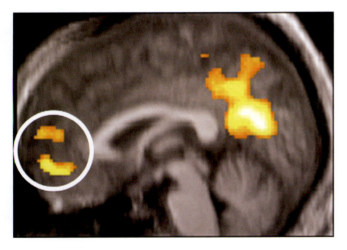

FIGURE 4.41 The BOLD fMRI signal for pain on the left side of the body. By stimulating the left hand to produce mild pain, a BOLD signal emerges in the right-side body map (somatosensory cortex, not shown), and also in these areas along the midline of the right hemisphere. The pain pathways are well known, and mild pain perception is an easy way to test the fidelity of a brain imaging technique. *Source:* Valet *et al.*, 2004.

roles in major cognitive processes such as language, attention and vision. One way is to define regions of interest (ROIs) ahead of the research study, and to make predictions about expected activity in ROIs.

3.2.1 Co-registration of functional activity on a structural scan

The first step is to define the living brain anatomically, to make out different areas, connections and layers of organization. Structural MRI gives us a tool to map out brain structure, including the axonal (white matter) connections between brain regions. MRI shows structure but not function.

On the right side of Figure 4.41, we see an image with two yellow 'hot spots', reflecting increased fMRI activity. The color is arbitrarily chosen to indicate the degree of activity. In order to pin down the location of the yellow hot spots, we need to superimpose the functional image on the structural MRI, which has a better spatial resolution. In a process called *co-registration*, the functional and structural images are aligned to each other. Co-registration ensures that the two images end up in the same space using the same metric. With higher spatial resolution we can ask questions that are anatomically specific.

Another approach is to mark regions of interest (ROI) on the structural image alone, to constrain the statistical analysis.

Newer MRI machines (Figure 4.43) with higher magnetic field strength now make it possible to look at the cellular organization of the living brain, and to compare

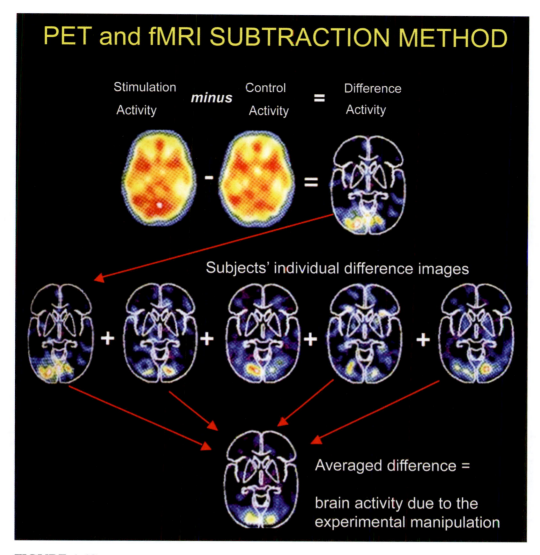

FIGURE 4.42   The subtraction method for PET and fMRI. The brain has constant dynamic background activity. To remove background activity, the BOLD or PET signal for an experimental task is subtracted, point by point, from a closely-matched control task. Individual scans of the differences are then averaged, and produce the group average. *Source: Posner and Raichle, 1997.*

brains between groups of people (e.g. people with schizophrenia and healthy subjects). Different layers of cortex have either local or distant connectivity, so that layer information is useful to find out how cortical regions interact.

Because the brain is remarkably active at all times, it is still a challenge to isolate fleeting, task-related activity. One common method is *subtraction* between fMRI conditions: for example, the brain's response to the task of interpreting Arabic numerals (1,2,3, . . .) is compared to its response to the same numbers when they are spelled out in printed words (one, two, three, . . .) (Figure 4.42). Subtraction is used because it tends to remove most of the 'irrelevant' brain activity, which would otherwise drown out the signal of interest. It is

much like comparing a choppy sea before and after a whale swims by. If you want to see the waves generated by the whale alone, you might subtract a record of the waves alone. It is the *difference* between the two conditions that matters.

Subtracting conditions can have unwanted consequences. There might be important things going on in both conditions. (See Section 3.3 and Figure 4.46). In addition, the variance of experimental and comparison conditions might be different, there might be interactions between independent variables, and so on. Another approach therefore is *parametric variation*, in which the variance for each main variable and their interactions, can be separated statistically. For example, if you study working memory (WM), instead of subtracting brain

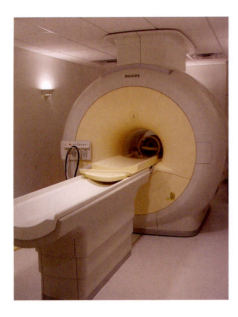

FIGURE 4.43 How the MRI equipment looks to the subject. Most fMRIs are taken with the subject lying down. Today's MRIs are still very noisy, as the electromagnetic coil is switched on and off. Small visual displays may be used to present stimuli, or headphones for auditory stimuli. Because the machine generates high-intensity magnetic fields, no metal objects like pens or even paperclips can be taken into the experimental room. *Source:* Sharma and Sharma, 2004.

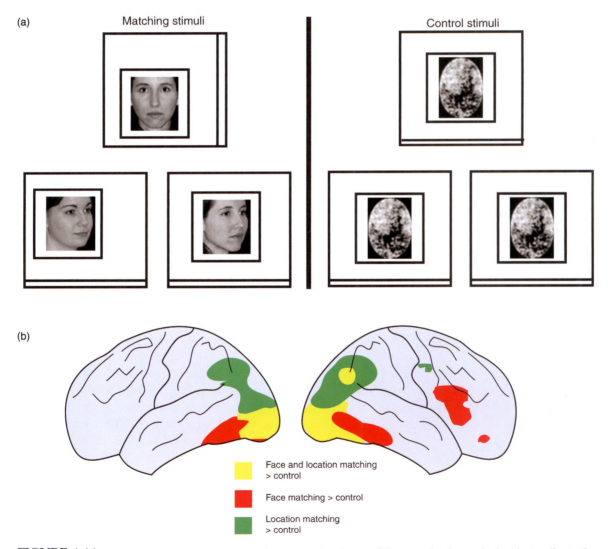

(a) Matching stimuli | Control stimuli

(b)

- Yellow: Face and location matching > control
- Red: Face matching > control
- Green: Location matching > control

FIGURE 4.44 A typical visual experiment using fMRI. Note that the visual faces are closely matched with visually similar stimuli. The face stimuli are compared to nonface objects in the same spatial orientation. Subjects need to pay attention, so a matching task is used, in which they press a button when the matching stimulus appears. The results show higher BOLD signals for faces in red areas, higher for location in the green areas, and higher face+location in the green-shaded parts of the brain. *Source:* Squire *et al.*, 2003.

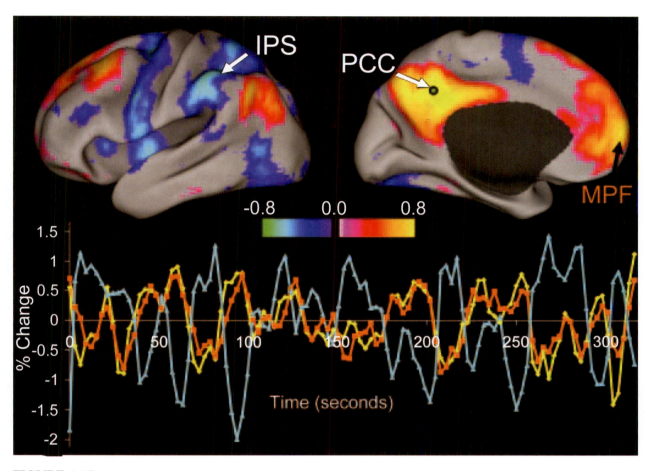

FIGURE 4.45 The brain is an active place. This fMRI shows background brain activity in both the left hemisphere (left) and the right hemisphere (midline view, right). The bottom shows these activities over 300 seconds. While such 'task-unrelated' activity is different from typical experimental tasks, we know that humans are constantly thinking, imagining, feeling, anticipating, remembering, and talking to themselves, even without being given a specific task to do. *Source:* Fox *et al.*, 2005.

activity during working memory from activity without it, one can study how gradually increasing the WM load leads to changes in neural activation. Since statistical testing must be done for every point of interest in the scan, over every unit of time, this is a large data set.

3.3 The resting brain is not silent

As neuroimagers began to study different cognitive functions, the main approach was to use a contrastive, subtractive approach. Here, the neural activation during a given cognitive function, such as speech production, was compared to a period where subjects were instructed to relax and 'do nothing'. Such active-versus-rest comparisons showed powerful main effects. Hundreds of comparison studies have been conducted to map the brain regions for cognitive functions.

Yet there is a hidden assumption in these studies. If you are asked just to lie still and 'rest' what will you do? Will your mind be a blank screen? A great deal of

evidence shows that people just go back to their everyday thoughts, images, and feelings. You might be thinking about something that happened the day before; or that you need to do later, or even daydream a bit. You are likely to have inner speech, visual imagery, episodic memories coming to mind and so forth. For the brain, that is not 'rest'. Instead, the experimental comparison is really between two active states of the brain. One is driven by experimental task demands, while the other reflects our own thoughts, hopes, feelings, images, inner speech, and the like. In some ways, spontaneous activity may tell us more about the natural conditions of human cognitive activity than specific experimental tasks. Both are obviously important.

An important literature has now sprung up to study the cognitive 'rest' condition, i.e. a condition under which subjects are not asked to do anything in particular.

The use of MRI to produce both precise anatomical images and to provide functional maps of brain areas has literally revolutionized the field of cognitive

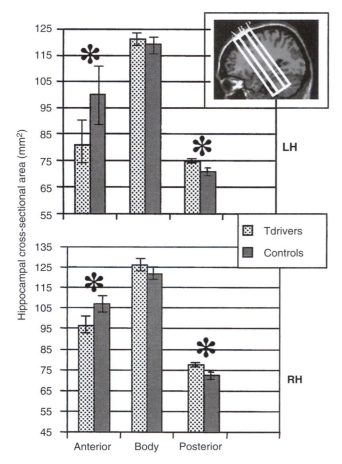

FIGURE 4.46 Hippocampal size in London taxi drivers. London taxi drivers showed substantial differences in the size of a spatial region of the brain, the hippocampus. *Source*: Maguire *et al.*, 2000.

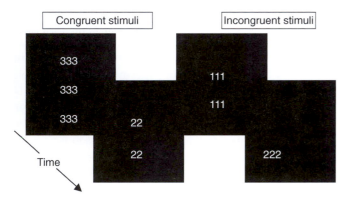

FIGURE 4.47 The Counting Stroop task. Count how many words are presented in each box as quickly as you can. Note that there can be a *mismatch* between your count and the figures you are counting. For most subjects, counting incongruent number words is more effortful than counting non-number words. People tend to make more errors, and reaction times tend to be slower. *Source*: Matthews *et al.*, 2004.

neuroscience. New and better ways to use fMRI are presented in the following section.

3.4 Empirically defining cognitive functions: the creative key

The best science is done by combining imaging techniques with genuine creativity. A lot of creativity goes into the selection of functional variables. What is the best way to understand vision? Selective attention and conscious cognition? A great deal of ingenuity has been devoted to those questions.

Here are a few examples. For example, taxi drivers are well known for their ability to know their way around a city. They know not only how to get from A to B, but also the most efficient way to get there. Such ability to navigate through a complex road system depends on our spatial ability. Studies have shown that the hippocampus, a part of the medial temporal lobe, plays an important part in the navigation and memory of places and routes. Rats with lesions to the hippocampus have been known for decades to perform disastrously on spatial tests. Birds and other animals that bury or hide their food at multiple places have larger hippocampi than non-storing animals. Therefore, one question that arises when we think about taxi drivers is, are the brain regions responsible for spatial navigation more developed in taxi drivers than other people? Indeed, it has been found that part of the hippocampi of taxi drivers was larger than the same region in a group of people with a different background (see Figure 4.46). OK, you might question, but what if people with large hippocampi choose to be taxi drivers, and not vice versa? Here, the study showed that the size of the hippocampus depended on how long people had been working as taxi drivers. In other words, the longer you work as a taxi driver (and use your spatial navigation ability) the bigger your relevant part of the hippocampus will become.

Notice how imaginative the taxi driver study was. It is usually easier randomly to select human subjects (usually undergraduate students!) to stand for the entire human population. But the fact is that there are differences of age, particular abilities and talents, and other cognitive capacities between 'average' subjects. London taxi drivers are highly experienced experts (they are required to pass tests on the geography of the city), and they can be compared to a plausible control group. One important implication is that the sheer size of brain structures may change with specific experiences (Maguire *et al.*, 2000). That claim has now been supported for other brain regions as well. The taxi driver study is therefore an excellent example of creative selection of comparison conditions, leading to new insights.

4.0 CONSCIOUS VERSUS UNCONSCIOUS BRAIN EVENTS

Conscious cognition is a new direction in cognitive neuroscience. It involves trying to understand the difference between conscious and unconscious brain events. In the last decade or two, scientists have made use of many experimental paradigms to compare the two. One major example is binocular rivalry, presenting a stream of two different visual stimuli to the two eyes, so that only one stream of input is conscious at any given time. Behaviorally, humans can only report one stream (see Chapter 6). Binocular rivalry works in macaque monkeys much the way it does in humans (Logothetis, 1998), and the wave of current interest in visual consciousness may be dated to a classic series of binocular rivalry studies in macaques, using single neuron recording at different levels of the visual hierarchy (Sheinberg and Logothetis, 1997); see also the discussion of binocular vivalry in Chapter 6.

5.0 CORRELATION AND CAUSATION

We typically combine brain and behavioral observations. We can present visual images on a screen, have the subject read aloud or meditate. Thus, we typically observe a *correlation* between behavior and brain activity. In methods with high spatial resolution, such as fMRI, different tasks show local increases or decreases in the BOLD signal, indicating that the brain works more in some regions than others (see Figure 4.47).

We can take the example of the 'Counting Stroop Task', in which subjects are asked simply to count the number of words shown on a computer screen. On some occasions a word like 'dog' is shown three times. The subject should say 'three', which is not difficult. However, we can introduce a conflict between the words shown and the number of words. If we show the word 'one' four times, there is an automatic tendency for expert readers (like college students) to say the word 'one'. But the correct answer is 'four'. This is very much like the Color-naming Stroop Task (see Chapter 2). Subjects take longer to answer correctly, since they must inhibit their automatic tendency just to read the words on the screen.

You can try this yourself. How many words are shown in Figure 4.47?

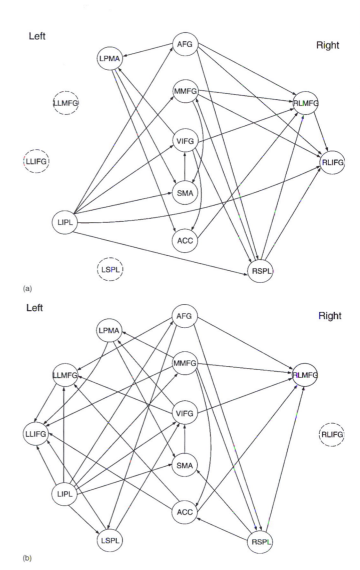

FIGURE 4.48 Causal relationships between brain activities during the Stroop task. Brain activity during simple counting with no interference is shown at the top (a), and the activation during counting with interference is shown at the bottom (b). Each circle represents a region of the brain. As can be seen, interference (b) leads to the engagement of a more widespread network than the control condition (a). This change in causal coupling between brain areas is seen in spite of the fact that many of the same areas are active in both conditions. Note also that some of the connections are lost between the control and the interference condition. (Adapted from Zheng and Rajapakse, 2006.)

Zheng and Rajapakse (2006) reported the BOLD activity during the two versions of word counting (Figure 4.48). While many brain regions show activation during both conditions, frontal parts of the brain were more active during the conflict condition. This kind of result has now been found many times for conflictual tasks. One of the major roles of prefrontal cortex is

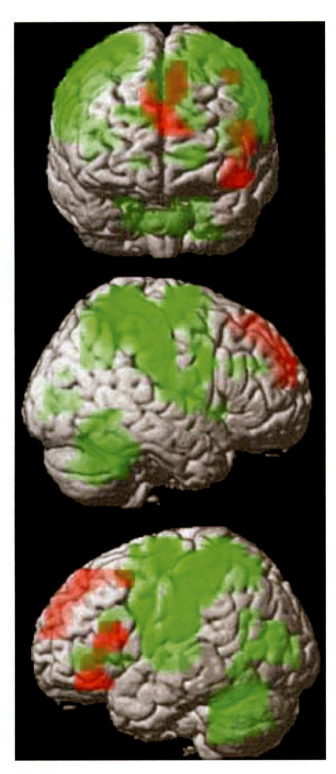

FIGURE 4.49   Are these the truthful and the deceptive areas of the cortex? fMRI differences between brain regions that had greater BOLD activity when people were telling the truth (green) and cortical areas when they were made to tell a lie (red). Is this the truth-telling cortex (green) and the lying cortex (red)? Why or why not? *Source: Davatzikos et al., 2005.*

to resolve conflicting tendencies, like the automatic tendency just to read words, against the tendency to follow the experimental instructions. Thus, we have a correlation between (a) frontal activation, (b) longer reaction times, (c) a sense of subjective effort, (d) a greater number of errors in the conflict condition. These are significant results, since there are many real-life conditions where conflicting tendencies need to be regulated.

However, so far we have no way to test causal hypotheses. For example, we know that the task requires visual word recognition, response preparation, choosing between two possible answers, perhaps detecting conflict, stopping the wrong answer from being said, selecting the right answer instead, and so on. An approach called *dynamic causal modeling* (DCM) is one to analyze for causal relationships. Zheng and Rajapakse (2006) performed DCM on the brain activation they found in both word counting tasks. As you can see in Figure 4.48, DCM suggested that each task had a different activation pattern. Although many of the same regions of the brain are active during both tasks, their relative connectivity and contribution was altered. Interestingly, the analysis also showed that the interference condition recruits wider activity than the control condition. This is another common finding for mentally effortful conditions (Duncan and Owen, 2000).

5.1 Why we need multiple tests of brain function

According to some media headlines, brain scientists recently discovered the parts of the brain used for deception and lying. This kind of headline comes from studies like the one shown in Figure 4.49. It shows fMRI differences between brain regions that had greater BOLD activity when people were telling the truth (green) and cortical areas when they were made to tell a lie. Such experiments often use playing cards, and ask a group of subjects to 'lie' by reporting a different card than the one they actually see.

One major purpose of cognitive neuroscience is to identify function with structure, i.e. to see whether specific brain locations do specific things for us. In that process, however, we must be very clear about the kinds of inferences that we can make from the evidence. The popular media may not be quite as careful as scientists need to be. Do you believe that the green areas in Figure 4.49 are really the "truth telling" areas of the brain?

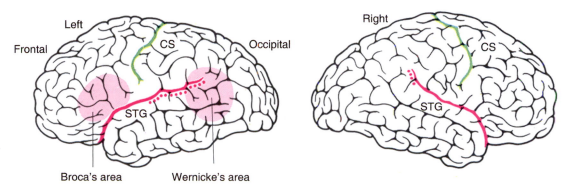

FIGURE 4.50 Language area lesions. Lesions to either Broca's or Wernicke's areas produce very different effects on language. Notice that the right hemisphere has no Broca's and Wernicke's areas, traditionally, even though it is involved in the comprehension of speech and language. *Source*: Standring *et al.*, 2005.

5.2 Brain damage and causal inferences

Brain injuries can provide evidence areas that are necessary for certain cognitive functions. Historically, Paul Broca discovered patients who were unable to speak and also showed damage to the left frontal lobe. However, their ability to comprehend language was relatively spared. About the same time, Carl Wernicke made the discovery that damage to different regions of the left hemisphere was associated with the ability to understand language, while their ability to speak was intact. Today, we call this complementary pair of facts a *double dissociation*.

Brain damage is correlational, since we cannot produce it and test its results in humans. Nevertheless, after a great deal of debate and controversy, there is no serious doubt today that one important function of Broca's area is the production of speech, and likewise, that one important function for Wernicke's region is speech comprehension (Figure 4.50). Lesions near Broca's area can lead to *dysarthria*, a condition where the control of mouth and tongue movement is disrupted, but language production is still intact. Thus, we have three lesions that lead to three different speech problems: one seems to be important for language comprehension; another is vital for language production; and a third region is important for the motor commands to produce vocal expressions.

Brain injuries in humans happen for a host of reasons, ranging from car accidents to strokes. Accidental lesions do not neatly follow the borders between brain regions. To test brain-mind hypotheses it is preferable to be much more precise about exactly where in the brain deficits occur. In order to do this, studies have been conducted in experimental animals, typically rats and monkeys. However, language is a species-specific function for humans, and we have no direct parallels in other species. (However, as mentioned above, there is now a way to produce safe interference in specific brain areas, using TMS.)

Very precise lesions have been studied in monkeys and rats for many years, with significant results. For example, Buckley and Gaffan (2006) made precise lesions in different areas of the medial temporal lobe (MTL) in macaque monkeys. Very specific damage to the *perirhinal* cortex (meaning 'near the smell cortex') caused monkeys to make more errors on a visual object discrimination task. Lesions to surrounding areas did not produce this deficit. The harder the discrimination task became – the more alike the visual objects were – the more errors were made by the lesioned monkeys. Yet the monkeys performed normally in simple visual discriminations between different colors, shapes and orientations. This suggests that the perirhinal cortex may have a specific *causal* role in processing complex visual objects like faces. A variety of human studies now support this finding. Animal studies have often played this pioneering role, allowing us to pick up leads that are later tested and often verified in humans.

Comparing damaged and healthy brains is a powerful source of evidence for understanding basic neural processes.

6.0 SUMMARY

Brain techniques measure single neurons to large cortical regions, brain structure, dynamic brain activity, and connectivity. The advent of brain imaging has transformed the study of human cognition. New and more refined methods are constantly being produced. One recent advance is to use multiple methods in the same study, so as to optimize the tradeoffs between electromagnetic and indirect measures of brain activity.

7.0 CHAPTER REVIEW

7.1 Drawing exercises and study questions

1. Label the differences between the brain scans in Figure 4.51, and describe the reasoning of the subtraction method for each image.

2. Define the BOLD response. What does the abbreviation BOLD mean?
3. What is the time lag between neural activity and a BOLD response? Between neural activity and an EEG response?

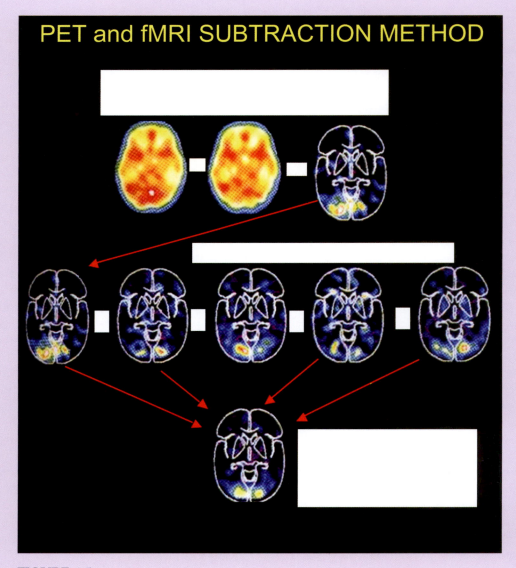

FIGURE 4.51

4. What are the pros and cons of single-cell recording in the brain?
5. What problem might arise when brain activity in a cognitive task is compared to a resting baseline?
6. What does Figure 4.49 tell us about lying and the cortex?

7. Judging by diffusion tractography, how much tissue is devoted to connections between cortical neurons (approximately)?
8. Describe four common brain electrical rhythms. What functions are they often associated with (see Table 4.1)?

The brain, is contained within the cranium, and constitutes the upper, greatly expanded part of the central nervous system.

Henry Gray (1821–1865) Anatomy of the Human Body, 1918

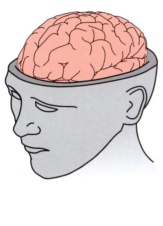

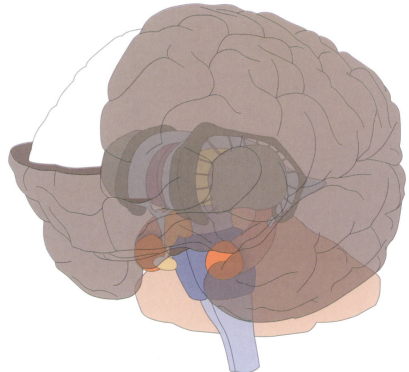

Looking through the gray outer layer of the cortex, you can see a mass of white matter. At the center is a cluster of large nuclei, including the basal ganglia, the hippocampi, the amygdalae, and two egg-shaped structures at the very center, barely visible in this figure, the thalami. The thalami rest on the lower brainstem (dark and light blue). You can also see the pituitary gland in front (beige), and the cerebellum at the rear of the brain (pink). In this chapter we will take these structures apart and re-build them from the bottom up.

C H A P T E R

5

The brain

Bernard J. Baars

1.0 INTRODUCTION

Our brains give us our biggest evolutionary edge. Other large mammals have bigger muscles and greater speed, but humans have an exceptionally big and flexible brain, specialized for excellent vision and hearing, language and social relationships, and for manual control and flexible executive control. Human brains make culture and technology possible.

In this chapter, we look at the structure of the brain, while in the coming chapters we will cover its functions – how it is believed to work. It is important to understand that brain anatomy is not a static and settled field; new and important facts are constantly being discovered. On the microscopic and nanoscopic levels, whole new classes of neurons, synapses, connection patterns, and transmitter molecules have been found.

While knowledge of the brain is constantly expanding, we will focus on the basics.

Cognitive neuroscience inevitably focuses on the cortex, often considered to involve the 'highest level' of processing. The cortex is only the outer and visible portion of an enormous brain, one that has developed over hundreds of millions of years of evolution. The word 'cortex' means *bark*, since that was how it appeared to early anatomists. While the cortex is vital for cognitive functions, it interacts constantly with major 'satellite' organs, notably the thalamus, basal ganglia, cerebellum, hippocampus and limbic regions, among others. The closest connections are between the cortex and thalamus, which is often called the *thalamo-cortical system* for that reason. In this core system of the brain, signal traffic can flow flexibly back and forth, like air traffic across the earth.

Cognition, Brain, and Consciousness, edited by B. J. Baars and N. M. Gage
ISBN: 978-0-12-373677-2

Copyright 2007, Elsevier Ltd. All rights reserved.

The major lobes of cortex are comparable to the earth's continents, each with its population centers, natural resources, and trade relations with other regions. While cortical regions are often specialized, they are also densely integrated with other regions, using web-like connections that spread throughout the cortex and its associated organs. This outer sheet is called the *gray matter* from the way it looks to the naked eye. It is the outer 'skin' of the *white matter* of cortex which appears to fill the large cortical hemispheres, like the flesh of a fruit. However, this is only appearance. In fact, the gray matter contains the cell bodies of tens of billions of neurons that send even larger numbers of axons in all directions, covered by supportive myelin cells that are filled with white lipid molecules. These white myelin sheaths of cortical neurons are so pervasive that they make the connections between cortical neurons look white to the naked eye.

1.1 The nervous system

The brain is part of the nervous system which pervades the human body. The two main parts are the central nervous system (CNS), which includes the brain and the spinal cord, and the peripheral nervous system (PNS), which contains the autonomic and peripheral sensory and motor system (Figure 5.1).

Together the CNS and PNS provide a dynamic and massive communication system throughout all parts of the body, with a hub at the brain that is accessed through the spinal cord. We will focus in this chapter on one part of the CNS, the brain (Figure 5.2).

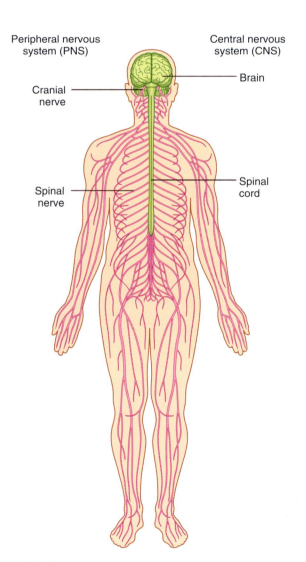

FIGURE 5.1 The central and peripheral nervous systems. *Source*: Standring, 2005.

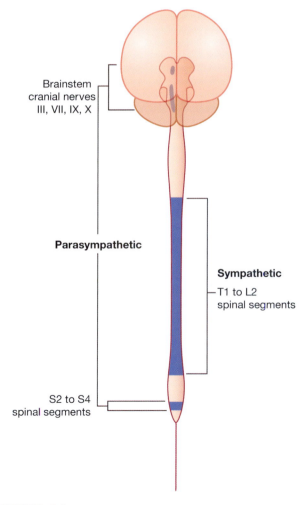

FIGURE 5.2 Parts of the central nervous system include the spinal cord and the brain. *Source*: Standring, 2005.

In this chapter, we will focus on two sensory input systems within the brain, vision and hearing. Although there are other sensory input systems, such as olfaction (smell) and somatosensory (touch), vision and hearing have been most studied in the human brain. We will focus on two output systems, speech and hand-arm control, again because they have been the target of much study. Throughout this chapter on the brain, we will describe the anatomy of the brain and brain regions and we will also highlight the function they serve. We will begin with discussing the many levels of analysis that we can take in describing the brain – from large-scale regions such as cerebral hemispheres and cortical lobes, to finer-scale classifications, such as cortical layer topography.

1.2 The geography of the brain

Let's begin with the large-scale brain areas and work our way down to a finer analysis. First, to state the rather obvious, the brain is located in the human head, as depicted in Figure 5.3.

We can look at the brain at different geographical levels – from continents to countries, states and cities. Thus, we have several levels of detail. The first distinct geographical regions are the two cerebral hemispheres, which are entirely separate, joined through a complex connective region called the corpus callosum. We will discuss the hemispheres in more detail later in the chapter: the question of why we have two separate hemispheres in the brain has long intrigued scientists and philosophers alike.

Next, we have the cortical lobes (Figure 5.4): there are four lobes in each hemisphere. Beginning at the

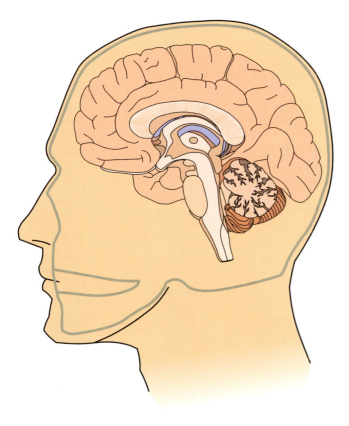

FIGURE 5.3 The location of the brain in the head, showing a mid-sagittal view of the right hemisphere.

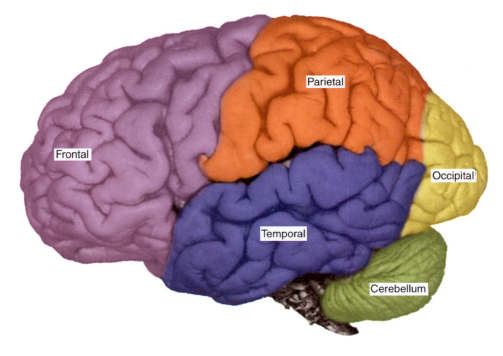

FIGURE 5.4 The four major lobes of the cortex are visible from a lateral view of the brain. Here we show a view of the left hemisphere with the frontal lobe (purple) at the anterior of the brain, the parietal lobe (orange) posterior to the frontal lobe at the superior aspect of the brain, the temporal lobe (blue) posterior to the frontal lobe and inferior to the parietal lobe, and the occipital lobe (yellow) posterior to both the parietal and temporal lobes. Just below the occipital is the cerebellum (green), which is not part of the cortex but is visible from most aspects of the brain. *Source*: Squire *et al.*, 2003.

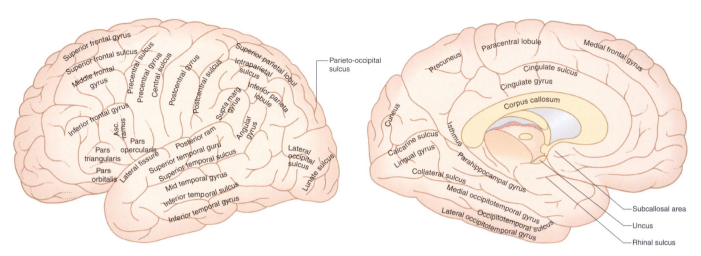

FIGURE 5.5   Some important landmarks of the brain in the left hemisphere from a lateral perspective (left panel) and a mid-sagittal perspective (right panel). *Source*: Standring, 2005.

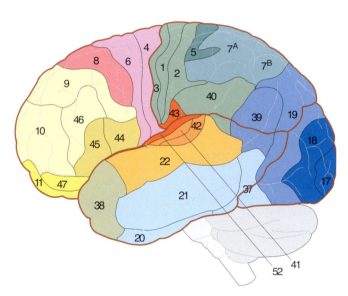

FIGURE 5.6   The Brodmann classification of regions in the left hemisphere, shown in a lateral view. Areas 41 and 42 are indicated by lines. Some areas, like the insula and auditory region, are tucked away behind the temporal lobe.

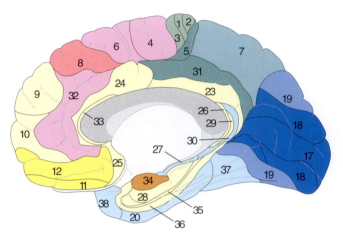

FIGURE 5.7   The Brodmann classification of regions in the right hemisphere, shown in a mid-sagittal view.

front or anterior part of the brain (shown on the left side of Figure 5.4), we see the *frontal lobe*. Immediately behind the frontal lobe, at the top or superior part of the brain, we find the *parietal lobe*. Below, or inferior to, the parietal lobe and adjacent to the frontal lobe, we find the *temporal lobe*. At the back or posterior part of the brain, we find the *occipital lobe*. We will discuss the anatomical features and cognitive function of these lobes later in the chapter.

We can see the major lobes with the naked eye, along with their hills and valleys, the gyri and sulci. Some of these are so important that we will call them landmarks – we need to know them to understand everything else. In Figure 5.5, we show some of the major landmarks that brain scientists have long used to identify regions in the brain. These landmarks are widely used today when discussing the results of neuroimaging studies.

At a more microscopic level of description, we have the *Brodmann areas*, the numbered postal codes of the cortex. When the surface layers of cortex are carefully studied under a microscope, small regional differences can be seen in the appearance of cells in the layers and

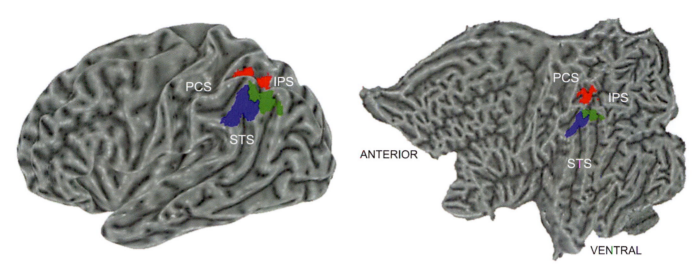

FIGURE 5.8   The cortex is a flat sheet, folded many times to fit into the narrow space of the cranium. All cell bodies (the gray matter) are in the outer sheet, making six layers about one millimeter thick. Spread out, the sheet of cortex is about two feet square ($0.6 \, m^2$). The fibers coming from the gray cell bodies are the 'white matter' – the color of myelinated axons and dendrites, which make up the fiber tracts. These white fiber tracts fill the visible brain. *Source*: Wheeler and Buckner, 2004.

their connections. Those subtle differences were first described by Korbinian Brodmann in 1909, and are therefore known as Brodmann areas, each with its own unique number (Figure 5.6 shows a lateral view of Brodmann areas in the left hemisphere, and Figure 5.7 a medial (mid-sagittal) view of the Brodmann areas in the right hemisphere). About 100 Brodmann areas are now recognized, and it is therefore convenient to take this as a rough estimate of the number of specialized regions of the cortex. The Brodmann areas correspond well to different specialized functions of the cortex, such as the visual and auditory areas, motor cortex, and areas involved in language and cognition. They are essentially the postal codes of the brain. They range in size from a few square inches – the primary visual cortex, for example, is about the size of a credit card – to the small patch of Brodmann area 5 at the top of the somatosensory cortex.

Notice that in Figure 5.6, with the brain facing left, neighboring Brodmann areas are colored to show their major functions including vision, hearing, olfaction, motor control, Broca's area (speech output), and Wernicke's area (speech perception and comprehension). This figure will be a used as a reference map throughout this book.

We can focus even more specifically by observing hypercolumns, columns, and single neurons. At this fine level of resolution the current standard is the *Talairach coordinates* (Talairach and Tournoux, 1988), which is used in functional brain imaging (Figure 5.8). The Talairach system can be compared to the map coordinates of the world, as shown on a GPS locator. They indicate the street addresses of the brain.

The fine red lines show the axes of a three-dimensional coordinate system. On the upper left, we see the medial view of the right hemisphere, looking to the left (see the small head inset for orientation). In this image, the horizontal red line always runs between the pineal body (not visible), and the small cross-section of the *anterior commissure* – one of the tiny white fiber bridges that run between the two sides of the brain. The three-dimensional zero point $(0, 0, 0)$ of the coordinate system is always at the front of these two points. This allows all three dimensions to be defined with good reliability. Notice the three standard perspectives on the brain: the medial view (mid-sagittal), the horizontal or axial, and the coronal (crown-shaped) cross-slice. This software display allows any point in the brain to be specified precisely, by entering numbers for the points in three dimensions. While human brains vary a great deal, much as human faces do, the Talairach system allows different brains to be mathematically 'squeezed into a shoebox', so that different brains can be compared in a single framework.

Let's continue our description of the geography of the brain with a look at the fine structure of the cortex. The visible outer brain consists of a large thin sheet only six cellular layers thick, called the cortex (meaning 'bark', like the outside bark of a tree). This sheet is called the gray matter from the way it looks to the naked eye. Not all cortex has six layers; only the giant mammalian cortex does, and is therefore sometimes called 'neocortex'. (That is, the new cortex, because it only emerged 200 million years ago!). Older regions of cortex are also found in reptiles, like salamanders, for example, such as the limbic cortex, which we will discuss later in this chapter. This region has five cortical layers and is sometimes referred to as 'paleocortex'.

The six horizontal layers of cortex are organized in *cortical columns*, vertical barrel-shaped slices. These often contain closely related neurons, such as visual cells that respond to different orientations of a single light edge in just one part of the visual field. Columns may be clustered into hypercolumns, which may be part of an even larger cluster. Thus, cortex has both a horizontal organization into six layers, and a vertical one, into columns, hypercolumns, and eventually entire specialized regions. The visual cortex of the macaque monkey is often used as an animal model to study vision. Human visual cortex looks quite similar. Note that there are six layers, with numbering (in Roman numerals) beginning at the top with layer I and progressing down to layer VI.

The geography analogy is useful, but the brain, like the world, is a dynamic place. New streets are built and old ones move or are rebuilt. Houses and their residents appear and disappear. Until about a decade ago, it was believed that neurons did not change in the adult brain, but we now know of a number of ways in which neurons continue to grow, migrate, connect, disconnect and die, even in the healthy mature brain. The brain is never frozen into a static rock-like state.

These dynamic aspects of the brain can be seen even at the level of the six layers of cortex. Let's take another look at the six layers of the cortex, this time using a schematic drawing of the layers and their inputs and outputs (Figure 5.9). Notice that some cortical neurons send their axons to the thalamus, while others receive input from thalamic neurons. Millions of cortical nerve cells go to the opposite hemisphere (the contralateral hemisphere), while many others project their axons to the same hemisphere (the ipsilateral side). However, the densest connections are to neighboring neurons. Cortical layer I consists largely of dendrites (input fibers) that are so densely packed and interconnected that this layer is sometimes called a 'feltwork', a woven sheet of dendrites. The neurons in

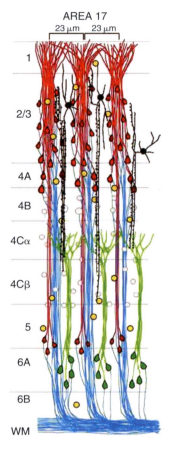

FIGURE 5.9 The six major layers of cortex in cross section. The figure shows three columns in Area 17, also called V1, the first visual projection area to the cortex. *Source*: Squire *et al.*, 2003.

this drawing are called 'pyramidal' because their bodies look like microscopic pyramids. They are embedded in a matrix of glial cells, which are not shown here. These connection patterns in cortex undergo major change in human development and throughout the lifespan (see Chapter 14 for more discussion of this).

2.0 GROWING A BRAIN FROM THE BOTTOM UP

2.1 Evolution and personal history are expressed in the brain

We usually see the brain from the outside, so that the cortex is the most visible structure. But the brain grew and evolved from the inside out, very much like a tree,

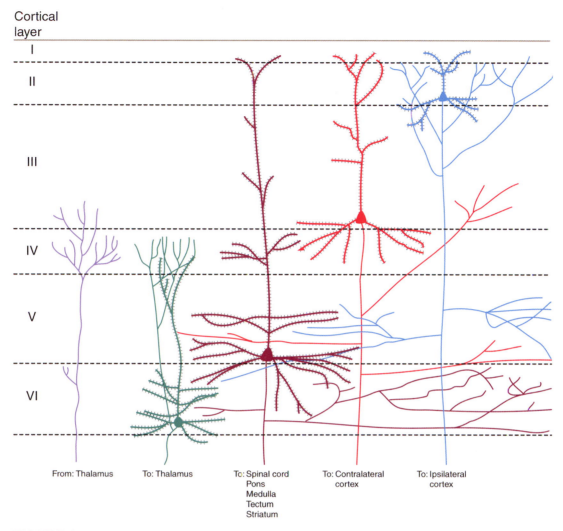

Cortical layer

I

II

III

IV

V

VI

From: Thalamus   To: Thalamus   To: Spinal cord   To: Contralateral   To: Ipsilateral
                                   Pons   cortex   cortex
                                   Medulla
                                   Tectum
                                   Striatum

FIGURE 5.10   A schematic drawing of the six layers of cortex, the gray matter. Note that some cortical neurons send their axons to the thalamus, while others receive input from thalamic neurons. Ipsilateral = same side of the cortex; Contralateral = opposite side.

beginning from a single seed, then turning into a thin shoot, and then mushrooming in three directions: upward, forward and outward from the axis of growth. That point applies both to phylogenesis – how species evolved – and ontogenesis – how the human brain grows from the fetus onward (Figure 5.11).

The mature brain reveals that pattern of growth and evolution. It means, for example, that lower regions like the brainstem are generally more ancient than higher regions, such as the frontal cortex. Basic survival functions like breathing are controlled by neural centers in the lower brainstem, while the large prefrontal cortex in humans is a late addition to the basic

mammalian brain plan. It is located the farthest upward and forward in the neural axis (Figure 5.12). Thus, local damage to prefrontal cortex has little impact on basic survival functions, but it can impair sophisticated abilities like decision-making, self-control, and even personality.

2.2 Building a brain from bottom to top

Because the brain involves hundreds of millions of years of evolutionary layering on top of older layers, the more recent levels hide the older ones. That is particularly true for the fast-ballooning neocortex in primates and

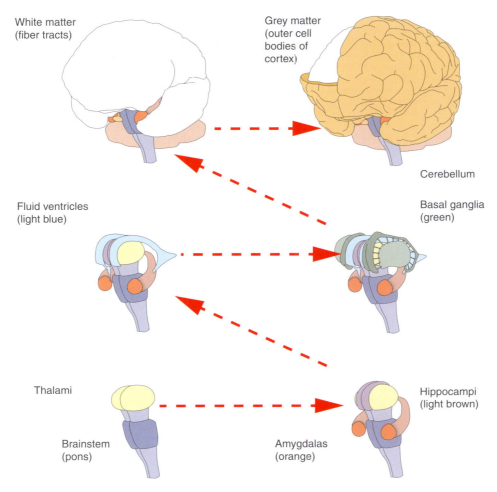

White matter (fiber tracts)

Grey matter (outer cell bodies of cortex)

Cerebellum

Fluid ventricles (light blue)

Basal ganglia (green)

Thalami

Hippocampi (light brown)

Brainstem (pons)

Amygdalas (orange)

FIGURE 5.11 Growing the brain from the bottom up. If you can memorize these basic shapes, you will have a solid framework for understanding the brain. Notice how the brain builds on the brainstem, with the thalami on top as major input hub. The hippocampi and amygdalas are actually nestled inside each of the temporal lobes. The light blue fluid ventricles have no neurons, but provide the brain's own circulatory system. The basal ganglia can be thought of as the output hub of the system. A great deal of traffic flows back to the cortex as well.

humans, called the 'new cortex' because it is more recent, and has six layers rather than the four or five layers of the reptilian and early mammalian brain. The brain therefore grows a little bit like a mushroom over the course of evolutionary time. The neuraxis – the spinal cord and brain – grows from tiny cellular clumps, then forward into a slender cylindrical shoot, and then thickening centrifugally to form the spinal cord, covered by an approximate mushroom shape. In the womb, the embryonic brain develops into an S shape, and then the neocortex covers the older regions.

We can follow the brain from bottom to top to show structures that are normally hidden by the head of the

mushroom. We encourage you to draw these successive levels of the great tower of the brain.

Unlike most other mammals, humans stand upright, and therefore bend their eyes and cortices at a right angle forward. That is why the upper direction of the human brain is both called 'dorsal', meaning 'toward the back' and also 'superior', meaning upward. The other directions are called 'ventral', 'toward the belly', and also 'inferior', meaning downward. We have a double vocabulary for the human brain, an important point to understand in order to avoid getting confused.

In this section, we will 'grow' a brain, beginning at the bottom with the older regions of the brain and

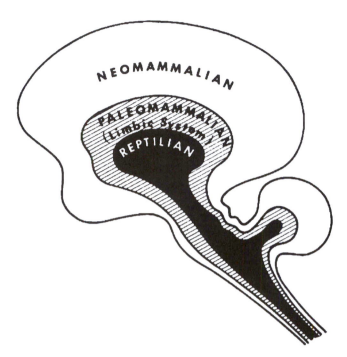

FIGURE 5.12 Diagram of the evolution of the mammalian brain. The forebrain evolves and expands along the lines of the three basic neural assemblies that anatomically and biochemically reflect ancestral commonalities with reptiles, early mammals, and late mammals. *Source*: Adapted from MacLean, 1967, with kind permission.

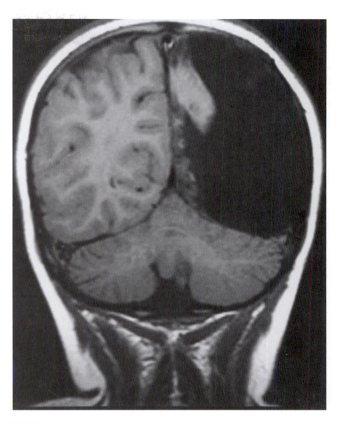

FIGURE 5.13 Do you really need a cortex? A structural brain scan (MRI) from a 7-year-old girl who had a surgical removal of her left hemisphere at age 3 for Rasmussen's Encephalitis. Such surgeries can save children's lives if they are performed early enough. Because the brain is highly flexible at this age, the language capacity has shifted to the right hemisphere. Notice, however, that her brainstem and thalami are intact. The brainstem is crucial to life functions, and cannot be removed. She is able to play and talk, and has mild right side motor impairment. *Source*: Borgstein and Grotendorst, 2002.

layering on until we come to the newest part of the brain, the neocortex. We begin with the *brainstem* and *pons* (Figure 5.13) which are at the bottom or 'oldest' section of the brain.

The brainstem (Figure 5.14) is continuous with the spinal cord. Its upper section, the pons, has nerve fibers that connect the two halves of the cerebellum. The brainstem and pons form a major route from the spinal cord to the brain. Some basic functions such as control of breathing and heart rate are controlled here.

Next, we have the *thalamus* – actually, they are the thalami, because there are two of them, one in each hemisphere (Figure 5.15). The two egg-shaped thalami form the upper end of the brainstem. The thalami are the great traffic hubs of the brain. They are also intimately connected with each great hemisphere.

Immediately below and in front of each thalamus is a cluster of nuclei called the *hypothalamus*. It is connected with the pituitary gland, often called the 'master gland' of the body (Figure 5.16). Together, the hypothalamus and pituitary are an extraordinarily important neurohormonal complex. Many types of physiological

homeostasis are monitored by the hypothalamus. When hypothalamic neurons detect a deviation from the proper blood level of oxygen, they trigger increased breathing – such as the sigh you might make after reading intensively in a cramped position. The hypothalamus also has crucial emotional functions.

Seated on top of the thalami like a rider on a horse are the two *hippocampi*, one on each side (Figure 5.17). Each hippocampus is nestled inside of a temporal lobe on each side, as we will see later on. But it is important to see the doubled structure of two hippocampi. As we have seen, the hippocampus plays a major role in transferring experiential information to longer-term memory, and in retrieving episodic memories as well. It is also involved in spatial navigation.

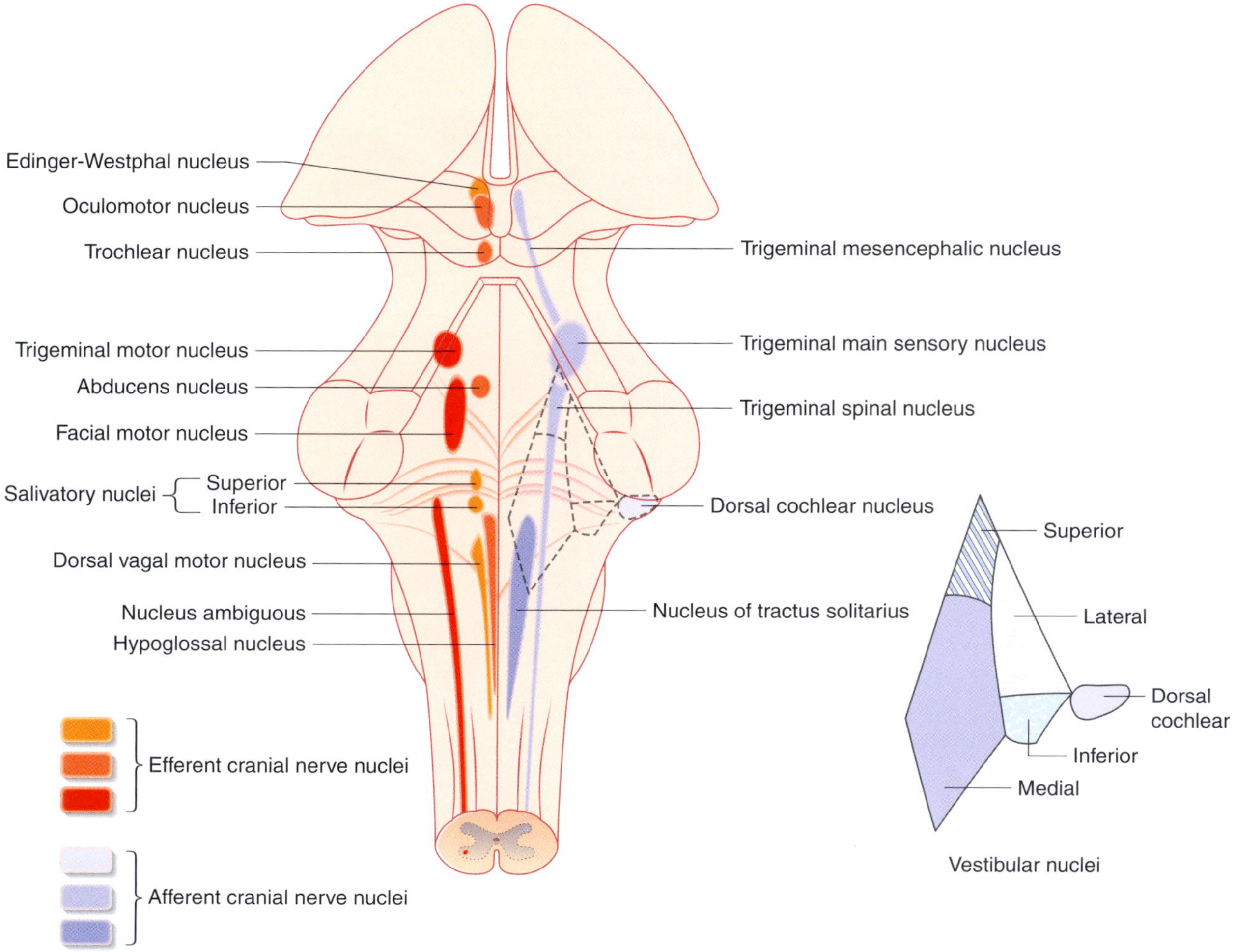
Edinger-Westphal nucleus
Oculomotor nucleus
Trochlear nucleus
Trigeminal mesencephalic nucleus
Trigeminal motor nucleus
Abducens nucleus
Facial motor nucleus
Trigeminal main sensory nucleus
Trigeminal spinal nucleus
Salivatory nuclei
Superior
Inferior
Dorsal cochlear nucleus
Dorsal vagal motor nucleus
Nucleus ambiguous
Hypoglossal nucleus
Nucleus of tractus solitarius
Superior
Lateral
Dorsal
cochlear
Inferior
Medial
Vestibular nuclei
Efferent cranial nerve nuclei
Afferent cranial nerve nuclei

FIGURE 5.14 Detailed anatomy of the brainstem and pons. Notice that all the major input-output pathways of the brain emerge here, either flowing down the spinal cord, or out through narrow openings in the cranium. Vision, hearing, olfaction and taste use cranial nerves as major pathways. Touch and pain perception in the head do the same. The brainstem also controls vital functions like breathing and heart rate. (Afferent = input to cortex; efferent = output from cortex). *Source*: Standring, 2005.

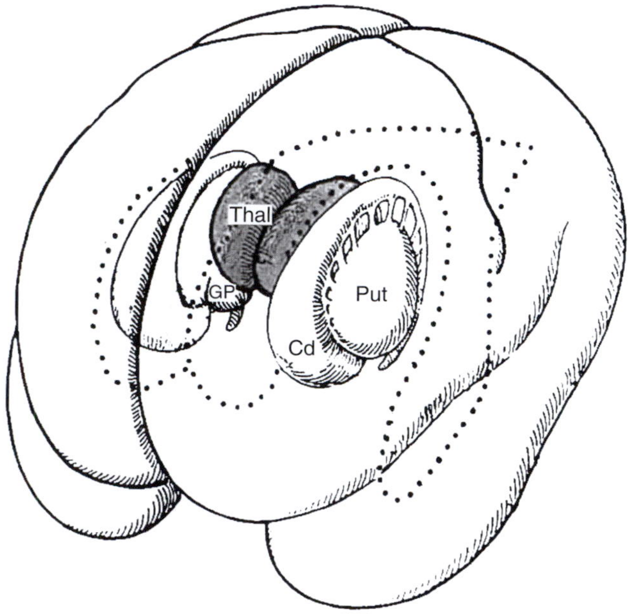
Thal
GP
Put
Cd

FIGURE 5.15 Transparent overview of the thalamus in the center of each hemisphere, and the basal ganglia looking like a 'shield and loop' on the outer side of each thalamus. *Source*: Ohye, 2002.

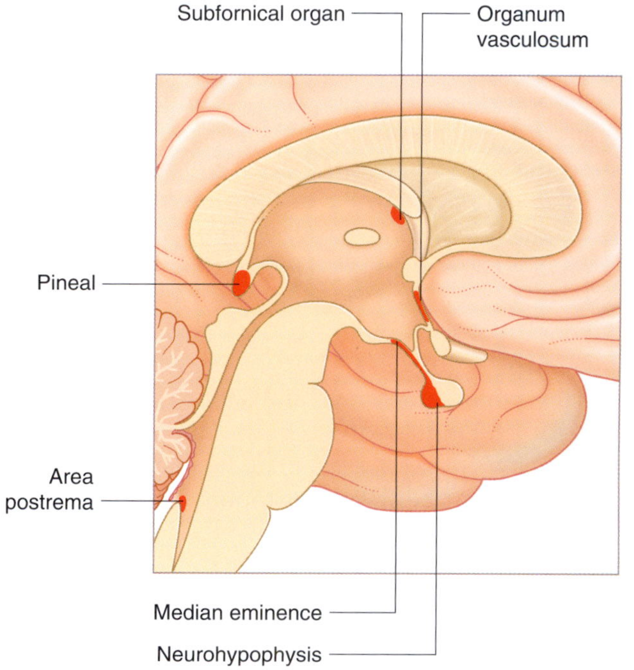
Subfornical organ
Organum
vasculosum
Pineal
Area
postrema
Median eminence
Neurohypophysis

FIGURE 5.16 Midline view of the hypothalamus and surrounding regions. *Source*: Standring, 2005.

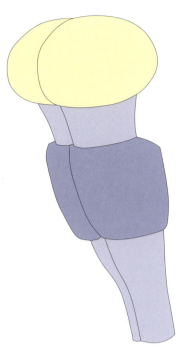

FIGURE 5.17 We begin 'growing' the brain with the brainstem and pons.

FIGURE 5.18 Schematic drawing of the hippocampi.

Near the tip of each hippocampal loop is an almond-shaped structure called the *amygdala*, which plays a starring role in emotions and emotional association (Figure 5.18).

The next level up is deceiving (Figure 5.19). It looks like a neural structure but is not. It is the *four ventricles*, of which you can see the right and left one. The ventricles are small cavities containing a circulating fluid that is separate from the bloodstream. This brain-dedicated circulatory system descends into the spinal cord through a tiny tube called the aqueduct, and the fluid of the ventricular system is therefore called the cerebrospinal fluid. The ventricular walls have recently been found to be sites for neural stem cells, much to the surprise of many scientists. It was long believed that neurons could not be replaced during life, but certain regions like the hippocampus and olfactory surface replace their cells, just as the rest of the body does. The ventricular stem cells are believed to be a source of these new neurons.

Next up are the *basal ganglia*, literally, the clumps at the bottom of the brain (Figure 5.20). There is one outside of each thalamus. The elegant shield-like structure with outward radiating tubes is called the putamen. Looping over each is another artistic structure called the caudate nucleus. This 'shield and loop' structure is fundamentally important for control of movement and cognition. Notice that the basal ganglia are located outside of the thalami.

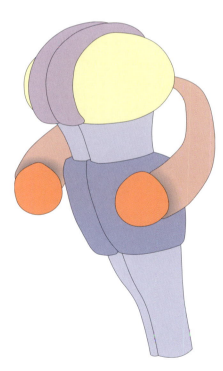

FIGURE 5.19 The amygdalas are situated just in front of the tip of each hippocampus.

Finally, we can mount the two hemispheres on top of the lower levels of the brainstem, thalami, hippocampi and amygdala, ventricles and basal ganglia (Figure 5.21). So you should not be surprised when you carve

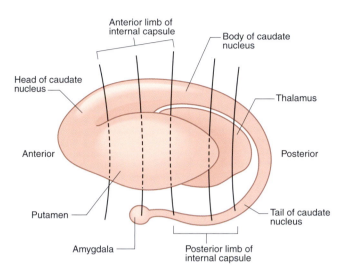

FIGURE 5.20 Side view of the basal ganglia, with the 'shield and loop' formed by the putamen and caudate nucleus respectively. *Source*: Standring, 2005.

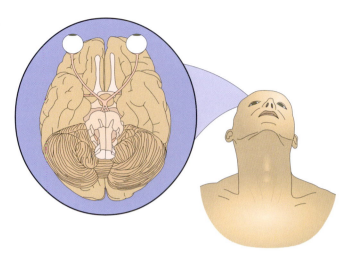

FIGURE 5.22 A view of the brain from below showing the medial temporal lobe and optic tracts.

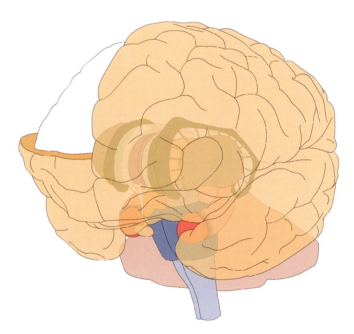

FIGURE 5.21 The cerebral hemispheres are shown mounted above the brainstem and other subcortical bodies.

away the cortex to see deeply buried, more ancient brain structures appear in the excavation.

One final note on 'growing' the brain: we present a bottom view of the brain in order to show you some brain regions that are difficult to see otherwise (Figure 5.22). You will notice the optic nerve linking the eyes, for example, to the cortex.

So there you have the brain, shown 'growing' from ancient areas to the neocortex in the two hemispheres. Now let's take a look at the functional significance of

these brain areas in human cognition. In this discussion, we will proceed in a 'top down' fashion, beginning with the two hemispheres, moving through the major lobes, and then on to the subcortical 'satellites' of the brain.

3.0 FROM 'WHERE' TO 'WHAT': THE FUNCTIONAL ROLES OF BRAIN REGIONS

We have discussed the many levels of analysis with which to understand brain structure and shown where the major brain areas are located. Let's work through the brain now, beginning with the neocortex and ending with the brainstem, and discuss the functional roles they play in human cognition.

3.1 The cerebral hemispheres: the left-right division

The two mirror-image halves of the cortex have puzzled people for centuries. Why are there two hemispheres? If we have but one mind, why do we have two hemispheres? Sir Charles Sherrington (1947) wrote:

> This self is a unity . . . it regards itself as one, others treat it as one. It is addressed as one, by a name to which it answers. The Law and the State schedule it as one. It and they identify it with a body which is considered by it and them to belong to it integrally. In short, unchallenged and unargued conviction assumes it to be one.

The logic of grammar endorses this by a pronoun in the singular. All its diversity is merged in oneness.

The philosopher Rene Descartes, for example, was dumbfounded by the doubled nature of the brain. Because he believed that the soul must be a unitary whole, he looked for at least one brain structure that was not doubled, and finally decided on the small pineal gland at the back of the brainstem. There he believed the soul resided – roughly what we mean by subjective experience. Unfortunately for Descartes, when microscopes became powerful enough to examine the tiny pineal gland in detail, it also turned out to have two symmetrical halves, roughly mirror images of each other.

How do the two hemispheres 'talk' to each other? The answer lies in the fiber tract that runs from the front to the back of the brain, linking the two hemispheres.

3.1.1 The corpus callosum

The hemispheres are completely separate, divided by the longitudinal fissure that runs between the two hemispheres from the anterior (front) to the posterior (back) part of the brain. The link between the hemispheres is provided by the *corpus callosum*, a large arch of white matter (Figure 5.23). The number of axons traveling between the two hemispheres is estimated at more than 100 million. The corpus callosum has fibers

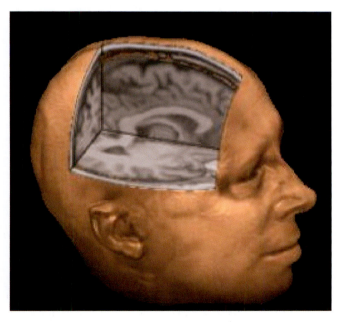

FIGURE 5.23 A cut-away of a three-dimensional magnetic resonance image showing the location of the corpus callosum – a white fiber arch extending horizontally from the anterior of the brain to the posterior, forming a fiber link between the two hemisphere.

that project between the hemispheres in an orderly way, with regions in the anterior portion connecting similar brain areas in the frontal lobes and regions in the posterior portion connecting similar brain areas in the occipital lobe.

The role of the two hemispheres in human cognition and the mind-brain has been the subject of extensive study, and we are still unfolding the subtle and not so subtle differences in the roles that the mirror-image hemispheres play in perception, language, thought, and consciousness. There are some hemispheric differences that are fairly well understood, such as crossover wiring. Many aspects of sensory and motor processing entail the crossing over of input (sensory) or output (motor) information from the left side to the right, and vice versa (Figure 5.24).

For example, each optic nerve coming from the retina is split into a nasal half (on each side of the nose), which crosses over to the opposite side of the brain, and a lateral half, which proceeds to the same side (ipsilaterally). Only the olfactory nerve, which is a very ancient sensory system, stays on the same side of the brain on its way to cortex. The cortical output control of the hands is also crossed over, with the left hemisphere controlling the right hand, and the right controlling the left hand (Figure 5.25). While the left and right hemisphere have some different functions, the corpus callosum has some 100 million fibers, constantly trafficking back and forth, which serves to integrate information from both sides. The time lag between the two hemispheres working on the same task may be as short as 10 ms, or one-hundredth of a second (Handy *et al.*, 2003). Therefore, when the great information highway of the corpus callosum is intact, the differences between the hemispheres are not very obvious. But when it is cut, and the proper experimental controls are used to separate the input of the right and left half of each eye's visual field, suddenly major hemispheric differences become observable.

The question of the perceived unity of the world continues to interest scientists. The most spectacular finding in that respect has been the discovery that the corpus callosum can be cut in humans, without changing the perceived unity of the world and of the self. Indeed, for many years such callosectomies (separation or cutting the corpus callosum) were performed to improve uncontrollable epilepsy (Figure 5.26). A complete slicing of the corpus callosum is called a callosotomy; more common, today, is a partial cut of only the regions of the two hemispheres that spread epileptic seizure activity. This partial cut is called a callosectomy. Doctors and their patients believed that cutting some

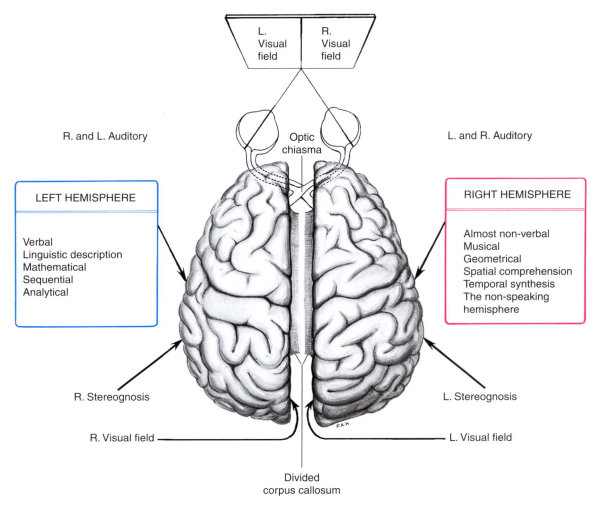

FIGURE 5.24 A top view of the two hemispheres. Schematic drawing of the two halves of the cerebral cortex, showing some major functions of the right and left hemispheres. Note the massive bridge of the corpus callosum connecting the two sides. The eyes on top focus on converging lines in order to enable stereoscopic depth perception. *Source:* Standring, 2005.

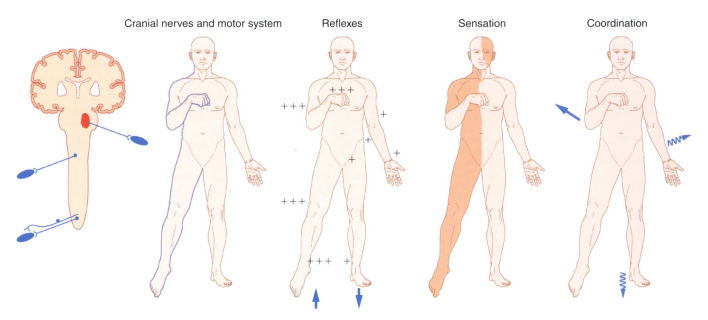

FIGURE 5.25 The pattern of cortical control over regions of the body. Notice that sensation and cortical motor control pathways cross over in the brain. Simple reflexes do not cross over, and coordination involves interaction between both sides. *Source:* Standring, 2005.

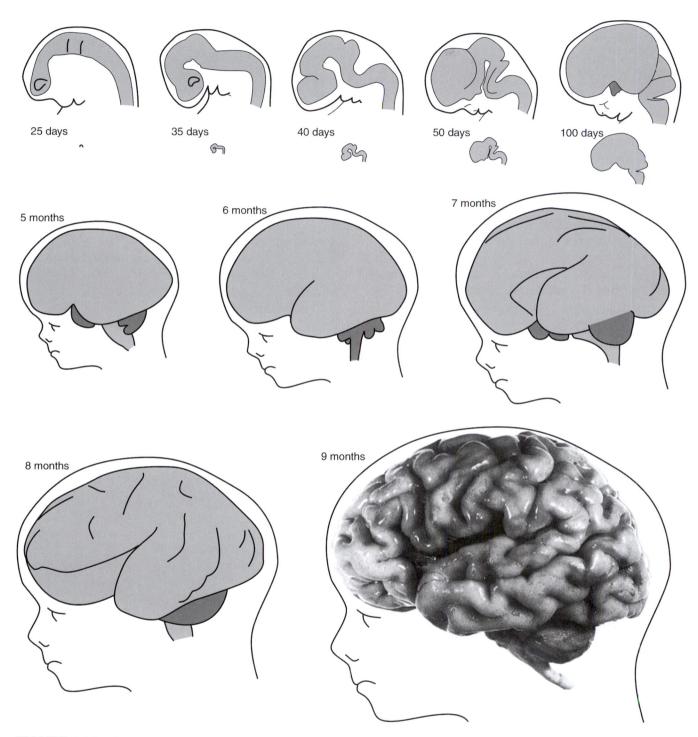

FIGURE 5.26   The development of the human brain, showing the progression from the first days of life to birth. *Source*: Squire *et al.*, 2003.

100 million fibers in the corpus callosum had no noticeable effect at all! It is a dramatic illustration of the capacity of the brain to adapt to quite severe damage – to fill in the missing details of the experienced world by means of eye movements, for example. More careful study, however, has provided evidence that a complete slicing, a callosotomy does have subtle but long-lasting effects and so a partial resection, or callosectomy, is preferred.

3.2 Output and input: the front-back division

The cortex is a folded sheet of gray matter that would measure roughly 2 feet by 2 feet (60 cm by 60 cm) if it were unfolded. To fit within the skull, the cortex is folded into hills (gyri) and valleys (sulci). The cortex contains four lobes that are visible from the outside and two large regions that are not visible. Before we discuss the functions of these regions, let's take a look at another major division of the brain: the front-back division of the cerebral cortex. In order to understand this division, you will need to be able to locate some landmarks in the brain. In Figure 5.27, see if you can locate the *central sulcus* that runs vertically between the frontal lobe and the parietal lobe. To locate it, look for the region labeled 'primary somatosensory'. The central sulcus is just in front of, or anterior to, this region. The second landmark to look for is the *Sylvian fissure*. It runs more or less horizontally from the frontal lobe posterior, separating the temporal lobe from the parietal and frontal lobes.

The sensory – or input – regions of the cortex are located posterior to the central sulcus and the Sylvian fissure, in the parietal, temporal, and occipital lobes. These lobes contain the visual cortex, auditory cortex, and somatosensory cortex, where information coming from the eyes, ears, and body is processed. The visual cortex, for example, begins in the occipital lobe but extends to the parietal and temporal lobes. The auditory cortex is located in the temporal lobe but also extends to the parietal lobe. Somatosensory areas are located in the parietal lobe. Taste and smell regions are located at the bottom of the temporal lobes. This 'back of the brain' large region, encompassing three cortical lobes, is not simply a site for processing sensory information. It is also the region of cortex for associative processes, where information from the various senses is 'bound together' for higher order processing. Think about watching a movie – these association areas will help you understand how to relate what you are hearing to what you are seeing on the screen. Much of this type of processing occurs in the parietal lobe, and we will discuss this important lobe in more detail in the next section. These association regions are largest in primates and largest of all in humans.

The motor – or output – regions of the cortex are located in the frontal lobe, anterior to the central sulcus and the Sylvian fissure. Look again at Figure 5.27 and locate the region labeled 'primary somatosensory', just posterior to the central sulcus. Although it is not labeled on this figure, the primary motor region is in the frontal lobe, just across the central sulcus and anterior to the somatosensory regions in the parietal lobe. The close physical connection between the somatosensory cortex and the motor cortex allows for a tight coupling between the senses of touch, pressure, and pain and the action or motor system. In fact, there is an intricate

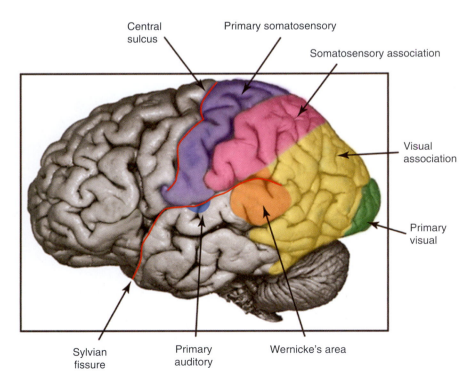

FIGURE 5.27　A view of functional areas in some of the sensory regions of the cortex. The central sulcus is seen separating the frontal lobe from the parietal lobe. Immediately posterior to the central sulcus is the primary somatosensory area. The Sylvian fissure is also called the lateral fissure.

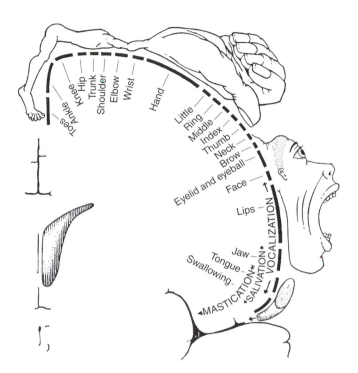

FIGURE 5.28 Drawing of the somatosensory homunculus, showing the representation of body areas in the cortex. Note that some body areas, such as the face, have a disproportionately larger representation than other areas, such as the trunk. *Source*: Standring, 2005.

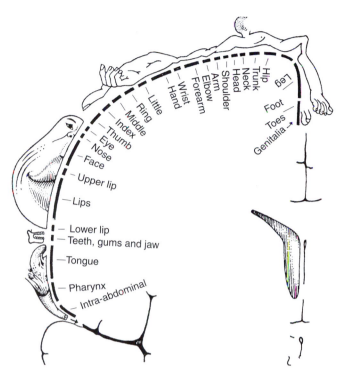

FIGURE 5.29 Drawing of the motor homunculus, showing the representation of body areas in motor cortex. Note that some body areas, such as the face, have a disproportionately larger representation than other areas, such as the trunk. *Source*: Standring, 2005.

mapping of the body that is reflected in similar ways in the somatosensory region located just posterior to the central sulcus and its corresponding motor region located just anterior. This intricate mapping is a representation of areas of the body: the different regions of the body are not equally represented in these cortical regions, some areas such as the face and hands have quite a disproportionately large representation and other regions, such as the center of the back, have a disproportionately small representation. Consider how much more sensitive your fingertips are to touch, pressure, and pain than, say, the small of your back. The representational map in cortex reflects this differing sensitivity. There are two maps of the body: one is in the somatosensory cortex and a very similar one is in motor cortex (Figures 5.28 and 5.29).

These two body maps or homunculi ('little men') were first discovered by the pioneer neurosurgeon Wilder Penfield at the University of Montreal in the 1950s and 1960s. Penfield's team was the first to stimulate the cortex of awake patients, which is possible because the cortical surface contains no pain receptors. Therefore, local anesthetic applied to the incision was enough to dull the pain of the removal of the scalp, and

surgeons could electrically stimulate the exposed cortical surface and ask their awake patients about their experiences as a result. Their discoveries have largely stood the test of time. Exploration by electrical stimulation was medically necessary in order to know where to operate in the brain, while minimizing damage to functional regions in patients. In the case of the sensory homunculus (somatosensory), local stimulation would evoke feelings of touch in the corresponding part of the body. Stimulation of the motor homunculus would evoke specific body movements, but interestingly, patients would deny a sense of ownership of those movements. When Penfield would ask, 'Are you moving your hand?' when stimulating the hand region, a patient might say, 'No, doctor, you're moving my hand'. If, however, the surgeon moved perhaps a centimeter forward to the pre-motor strip, stimulation would evoke a reported intention to move one's body, without a sense of being externally controlled. It is a fundamental distinction, which we will return to later.

The essential point here is that the central sulcus is an important landmark to know. Not only does it separate the sensory and motor homunculi but, more broadly, the central sulcus separates the more sensory half of cortex (posterior), from the frontal half (anterior). Posterior cortex contains the projection regions of the major sense organs – vision, hearing, touch, smell, taste. In contrast, frontal cortex is involved in action control, planning, some working memory functions, language production, and the like. In a sense, the posterior half deals with the perceptual present, while anterior half tries to predict and control the future.

3.3 The major lobes: visible and hidden

We have used the analogy of the geography of the brain. In this setting, the major lobes can be viewed as large continents in brain geography. While each is separate from the other and has its own local functions and anatomical features, each is part of the whole, the brain, and thus is united and intimately linked to total brain function. The four 'continents' of the brain are shown in Figure 5.30 and include the frontal, parietal, temporal, and occipital lobes. In this section, we will discuss their functional roles in cognition. Two other major regions, not visible from the exterior view of the brain, play important roles in cognition and we will describe those as well.

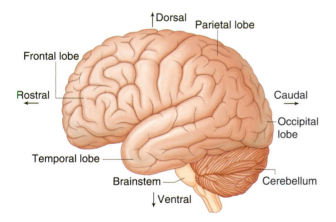

FIGURE 5.30 Basic brain directions. Because the human brain is rotated 90 degrees forward from the spinal cord (unlike most mammals and reptiles), it has two sets of labels. The dorsal direction is also called superior, the ventral is also called inferior, and rostral is roughly the same as frontal and caudal is sometimes called posterior. To simplify, just use plain language, like front, back, upper and lower.

3.3.1 Frontal lobe

The massive frontal lobe is the site for motor planning and motor output. As we mentioned, the motor areas are tightly connected to the somatosensory regions with similar homunculus maps representing body areas. These motor functions that are present in the human brain are present in most mammalian brains in a similar way. But the frontal lobe in humans is far larger than in non-human primates or any other creature. What other functions does the frontal lobe perform and how is its role unique in humans?

The frontal lobe has been termed the 'organ of civilization' (Luria, 1966). The regions of the frontal lobe that have earned this term are primarily in the prefrontal cortex. The prefrontal cortex is located on the medial, lateral, and orbital surfaces of the most anterior portion of the frontal lobe (Figure 5.31).

The prefrontal cortex is the non-motor part of frontal cortex. Notice that prefrontal cortex is the most forward part of the frontal cortex. The term 'prefrontal' is somewhat confusing, but it means 'at the front of the frontal cortex'. There are no obvious boundary markers for prefrontal cortex, which is defined instead by a set of projections from the thalamus. Nevertheless, prefrontal cortex is perhaps the most distinctively 'cognitive' part of the brain. The prefrontal cortex is a large cortical region, taking up an estimated one-third of the entire area of cortex. What is the prefrontal cortex specialized for and why is it so uniquely a human region?

The prefrontal cortex is specifically needed for:

- initiating activities
- planning
- holding critical information ready to use (an aspect of working memory)
- changing mental set from one line of thinking to another
- monitoring the effectiveness of one's actions
- detecting and resolving conflicting plans for action
- inhibiting plans and actions that are ineffective or self-defeating.

This list shows how important the prefrontal cortex is to human cognition. Many anatomists believe that prefrontal cortex is largest in humans, and distinguishes our species from other primates. In addition, the prefrontal cortex has regions for emotional and personality processes as well as social cognition – knowing 'how to behave' for example. On the lateral convexity, interposed between the dorsolateral prefrontal and the ventral portion of premotor cortex, is Broca's area. This area is involved in the abstract mediation of the verbal expression of language, a uniquely human function.

The frontal lobe, then, is far larger in humans than other primates and has developed many new functions and processes for dealing with human activities such as language, thought, and executive control of higher

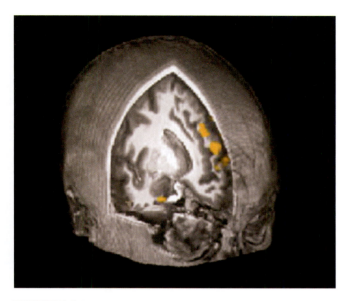 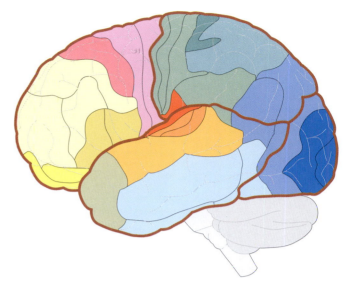

FIGURE 5.31 *Left:* an activation map rendered on a three-dimensional magnetic resonance image showing regions in the medial prefrontal cortex. *Right:* how to find the prefrontal cortex. The entire frontal cortex is in front of the central sulcus, the vertical fold that runs from the top of the cortex down to the temporal lobe. Locate the central sulcus in this figure. The two purple gyri (hills) immediately in front of the central sulcus are called the motor and premotor cortex. The reddish-purple patch in front of that is called the supplementary motor cortex. However, the three shades of yellow in the frontal third of the whole cortex is prefrontal cortex, often considered the most 'cognitive' part of the brain. *Source*: Harenski and Hamann, 2006.

order processes. A second lobe that has also evolved to be much larger in humans is the parietal lobe and we will see what functions it performs in the next section.

3.3.2 Parietal lobe

As we noted earlier, the anterior region of the parietal lobe holds the somatosensory cortex. However, the parietal lobe is not just a somatosensory region in humans, much as the frontal lobe is not just a motor region. One important function of the parietal lobe is multiple maps of body space. What does 'body space' mean exactly? Think about sitting in a chair at a table and looking down at your hands. Your eyes bring sensory input to your brain about where your hands are in respect to your body, but there are other inputs telling you where you hands are as well (which is why you know where your hands are even if your eyes are closed). Your imagined hand position will be from your own perspective, or the egocentric perspective. Now imagine a friend sitting across the table from you and conjure up where your hands are from his perspective. How do you do this? It is easy to accomplish and regions in the parietal lobe are where this type of processing take place (Figure 5.32).

Posterior and inferior to the somatosensory region is an area termed the inferior parietal lobe or IPL. The functional significance of this region is still being elucidated,

however, it is thought to be the site for multisensory integration.

3.3.3 Temporal lobe

The temporal lobe is the region where sound is processed and, not surprisingly, it is also a region where auditory language and speech comprehension systems are located. The auditory cortex is located on the upper banks of the temporal lobe and within the Sylvian fissure. Just posterior to the auditory cortex is Wernicke's area for speech comprehension. But the temporal lobe is not only a sound and language processing region. The middle sections of the temporal lobe are thought to contain conceptual representations for semantic knowledge. More inferior and posterior temporal lobe areas are more finely tuned for representing visual objects and include the fusiform face area.

3.3.4 Occipital lobe

The occipital lobe, at the very posterior region of cortex, is home to visual cortex. Most of visual cortex is hidden within the calcarine fissure. The visual system occupies a large area within the occipital lobe that extends anterior to the parietal and temporal lobes. New techniques provide the ability to 'inflate' these cortical regions to remove the folds and allow us to see the functional visual

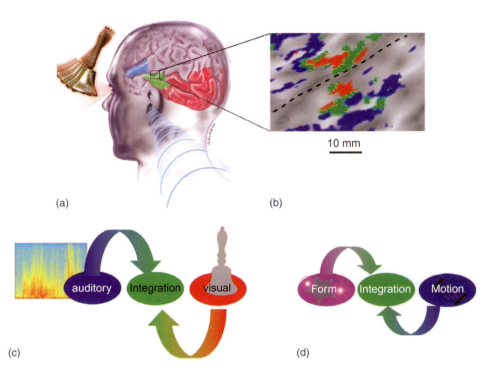

(a)   (b)

(c)   (d)

FIGURE 5.32   Schematic of some of the multisensory functions of the parietal lobe. The sight and sound of the bell are combined by neurons in the parietal cortex, using a 'map' of the space surrounding the body (egocentric space). *Source*: Beauchamp, 2005.

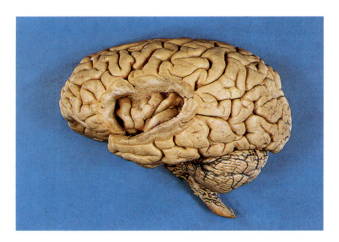

FIGURE 5.33   An actual human brain, showing the insula just above and hidden behind the temporal lobe. *Source*: Standring, 2005.

regions that are normally tucked into the calcarine fissure and difficult to see on a brain scan.

3.3.5 The insula and Sylvian fissure

Like a large tree, the cortex has grown to cover up large parts of itself, as we can see by inflating the cortex mathematically and spreading it into a flat sheet. Two

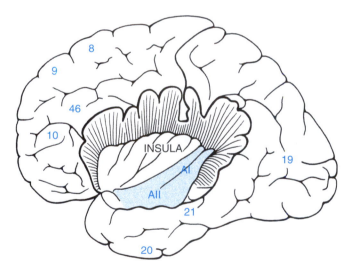

FIGURE 5.34   A cut-away view of the left hemisphere revealing the insula, which is not visible from a lateral view. 'Insula' means 'island' because of this appearance when the brain is dissected. *Source*: Standring, 2005.

of the areas that are hidden by the expanding cortex are especially important: the *insula* and the Sylvian fissure. When the temporal lobe is gently pulled away from the rest of cortex, a new hidden world appears. This region is called the 'insula', or 'island', because it appears like a separate island of cortex (Figures 5.33 and 5.34). The

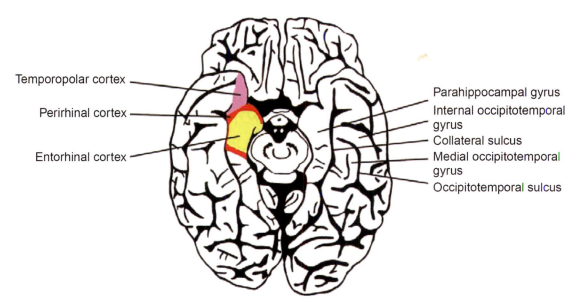

Temporopolar cortex

Perirhinal cortex

Entorhinal cortex

Parahippocampal gyrus

Internal occipitotemporal gyrus

Collateral sulcus

Medial occipitotemporal gyrus

Occipitotemporal sulcus

FIGURE 5.35 The Medial Temporal Lobe (MTL) – the midline regions seen from the bottom. This is the ancient 'smell brain' which is now surmounted by a massive 'new' cortex in higher mammals. It is therefore difficult to see from the outside, but it still retains many essential functions, including encoding conscious events into memories (episodic memories).

insula is not often seen in popular accounts of the brain, but it involves hundreds of millions of neurons and quite a wide expanse of cortical surface. Neurological evidence suggests that it may be involved in 'gut feelings' like the conscious sense of nausea and disgust. But the insula is so large that it probably has multiple functions. There does seem to be good convergent evidence that interoception – feelings of one's inner organs – may be one of the major roles of the secret island of cortex.

One researcher suggests that: 'In humans, . . . the right anterior insula, . . . seems to provide the basis for the subjective image of the material self as a feeling (sentient) entity, that is, emotional awareness' (Craig, 2005).

The Sylvian fissure is a very large sulcus that runs in a roughly horizontal direction from the frontal lobe, between the parietal and temporal lobes, ending near the junction of the parietal, temporal, and occipital lobes. The anatomy of the fissure differs widely across individuals and also between hemispheres. Tucked inside the Sylvian fissure, on the upper banks of the superior temporal gyrus, is the *supratemporal plane*. This region is called a plane because is it a somewhat flat bank of cortex extending from the lateral surface into the medial regions. The supratemporal plane is home to primary and secondary auditory cortex as well as parts of Wernicke's area for speech comprehension. The upper bank of the Sylvian fissure, adjacent to the parietal lobe and opposite the supratemporal plane, is home to

somatosensory cortex that wraps around and under the top section of the fissure.

3.3.6 *The medial temporal lobe*

The *medial temporal lobe* (MTL) is actually part of the temporal lobe, but its function and anatomy differ strikingly and it is typically referred to as a separate structure. The MTL is home to the hippocampi and related regions that are associated with memory functions (Figure 5.35). There are many regions in the MTL, as you see in the figure. Notice in Figure 5.35, on the left side, an area referred to as emotional cortex. This is the *limbic* area. The word 'limbus' means 'boundary', and true to its name, there is a great deal of debate about the proper boundaries of this region. You will occasionally see the entire complex of hippocampus, amygdala, and limbic cortex being called the 'limbic system'. All these terms have their uses, and it is just important to be aware of what is intended.

The upper arc (Figure 5.36) is called the cingulate gyrus ('cingulum' means belt or sash as in 'cinch'). The front half of this region generally lights up in brain scans during tasks that involve conflicting stimuli or responses, a very important aspect of executive function. In the classical Stroop effect, for example, there is a conflict between the color of words and the meaning of the same words. The front half of the cingulate is

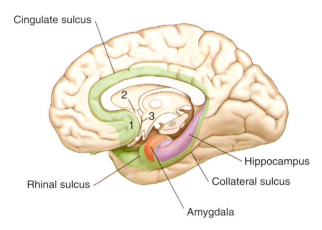

FIGURE 5.36 The Medial Temporal Lobe and cingulate gyrus (green upper loop), seen from the midline section of the brain. The hippocampus is colored purple and amygdala orange. They are actually embedded inside of the temporal lobe. *Source*: Heimer and Van Hoesen, 2006.

somehow involved in detecting or resolving such conflicting signals.

The lower arc of the limbic lobe is originally a part of the smell brain, the rhinal cortex and is therefore called the perirhinal cortex ('peri-' means 'around' and 'rhinal' means 'nose'). Recall that we stated earlier that not all cortex has six layers; only the giant mammalian cortex does, which is why it is called 'neocortex' (new cortex, because it only emerged 200 million years ago). Older regions of cortex are also found in reptiles, like salamanders, for example, such as the limbic cortex, shown in Figure 5.36. This region has five cortical layers and is sometimes referred to as 'paleocortex'. It is often associated with emotion and memory and, in the case of the upper arc of the limbic region, with decision-making and the resolution of competing impulses. In addition, the limbic cortex flows continuously into the hippocampus and amygdala, which are hidden inside the temporal lobe, and therefore invisible from the medial perspective. Recent research shows very close interaction between these ancient regions of cortex and episodic memory, i.e. memory for conscious experiences. This is the ancient reptilian brain, which is, however, still a vital center of activity in humans and other mammals.

3.4 The massive interconnectivity of the cortex and thalamus

While the lobes may be thought of as the continents of the brain, their processes are nonetheless intricately intertwined not only with each other, but also with the satellites of the subcortex in the massively interconnected brain.

Sprouting from the cells in the grayish layers of cortex are billions of axons, the output fibers from nerve cells, and dendrites, which provide electrical input to each cell. When white support cells, called the myelin, wrap around those fibers, they look like a white mass to the naked eye, and are therefore called the white matter. The whole giant structure of the cortex is shaped much like a superdome stadium, with two giant halves, each filled with billions of cables going in all directions, centered on a thalamic hub nestled in the middle of each hemisphere (Figure 5.37). The two cortical half-domes, with a thalamic traffic hub on each side, create an extraordinary biological structure. In primates and humans it becomes so large that it must fold many times to fit into the limited space of the cranium, the upper half of the head.

Think of the thalamus as a relay station: almost all input stops off at the thalamus on the way to cortex; almost all output also stops off at the thalamus, going out to the muscles and glands.

Fibers emanating from cortical cells spread in every direction, flowing horizontally to neighboring cells, hanging in great bundles on their way to distant regions of cortex, and converging downward on the great traffic hub, the thalamus, of each half of the cortex. In addition, hundreds of millions of axons flow crosswise, from one hemisphere to the other, creating white axon bridges called commissures (Figure 5.38). The largest crosswise fiber bridge is called the corpus callosum, or 'calloused body'. When the brain is sliced straight through the midline, you can see the corpus callosum as a curved white bow shape. The white color, again, comes from the myelin surrounding the cortical axons that form the great bridge connecting the two hemispheres.

Finally, cortical sensory and motor pathways make up the incoming and outgoing highways of the brain (Figure 5.39). All of these pathways flow from the bottom of the brain. The sensory and motor pathways can be divided into two sets. One set of pathways emerge through small holes in the cranium, the upper skull, and are therefore called the cranial nerves. These include the optic nerve from the back of the eyes, the auditory, olfactory, and taste nerves, as well as the feelings of touch and pain from the face and oral cavity; on the motor side, our facial expressions, vocal apparatus, and mouth, tongue, and so on are also controlled by cranial nerves. The second set of pathways flows into the spinal cord, and controls all our bodily functions,

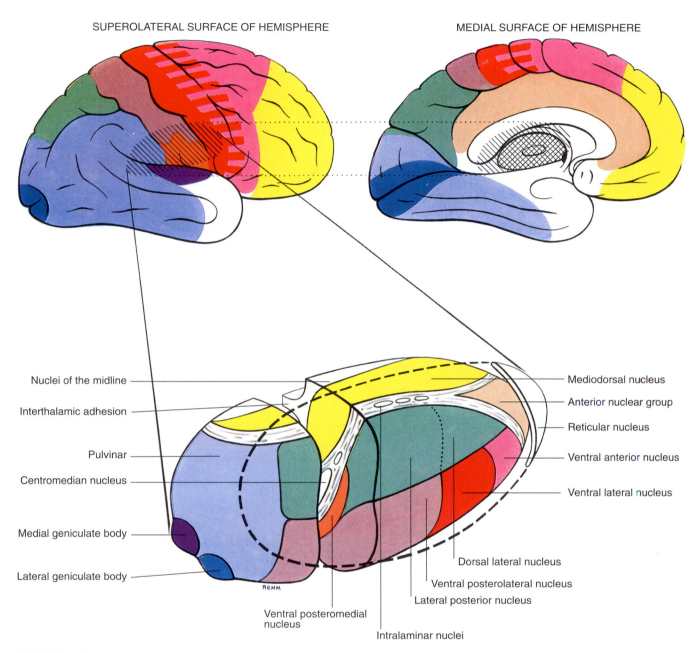

SUPEROLATERAL SURFACE OF HEMISPHERE

MEDIAL SURFACE OF HEMISPHERE

Nuclei of the midline

Interthalamic adhesion

Pulvinar

Centromedian nucleus

Medial geniculate body

Lateral geniculate body

Mediodorsal nucleus

Anterior nuclear group

Reticular nucleus

Ventral anterior nucleus

Ventral lateral nucleus

Dorsal lateral nucleus

Ventral posterolateral nucleus

Lateral posterior nucleus

Ventral posteromedial nucleus

Intralaminar nuclei

FIGURE 5.37 Cortex and thalamus: a single unified system. A schematic drawing showing a color-coded mapping of connections from the thalamus to cortical regions. *Source*: Standring, 2005.

both voluntary – like movements of the torso, arms and legs – and vegetative (autonomic), like blood pressure and sweating. On the input side, sensory nerves from the body give us all the information, both conscious and unconscious, that we receive from the body. While these pathways are complex in detail, the overview is straightforward.

It is conventional to put an '-o-' between the names of brain regions that are connected, so that we can speak of the thalam-o-cortical' connections. Signal flow from cortex to thalamus is called corticothalamic, and, believe it or not, neuronal traffic can even be cortico-thalamo-cortical. It's a little less complicated if you think about it as the traffic flow in a city, or even as the

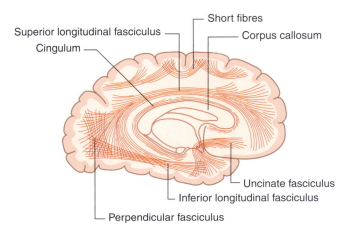

Superior longitudinal fasciculus —
Cingulum —
Short fibres
Corpus callosum
Uncinate fasciculus
Inferior longitudinal fasciculus
Perpendicular fasciculus

FIGURE 5.38 Schematic drawing of the connectivity of the brain, showing major fiber patterns. *Source*: Standring, 2005.

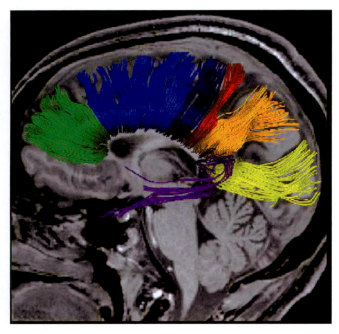

FIGURE 5.39 White bundles of myelinated axons run in all directions through the cortical domes. *Source*: Mario Lazar, with kind permission.

world-wide web, connecting millions of computers by way of major hubs and pathways.)

3.5 The satellites of the subcortex

Because the human cortex is so large, it covers important subcortical organs, which act as satellites to the cortex,

constantly interacting with it. These subcortical structures don't look like the popular idea of a brain at all – they are giant clusters of neurons often called 'ganglia' or 'nuclei'. Subcortical organs often have remarkably elegant shapes, like loops, horns and egg-like ovals.

The satellite regions are especially important in cognitive neuroscience. The thalamus, often called the gateway to cortex, was described above; the two thalami reside at the very center of the brain, on both sides of the midline (so you can't actually see them in the medial view). The thalami also connect differing cortical regions, so there are important cortico-thalamo-cortical circuits that have been shown to play a role in attentional processing and other higher order cognition functions. The thalami are nestled above the brainstem and just below cortex, a perfect location to serve their role as the relay station for the brain.

The *hippocampal complex* (see Figure 5.17) is critical to remembering conscious experiences, and appears as two small sausages embedded in each temporal cortex. However, it is now known that areas adjacent to the 'sausage' of hippocampus are also needed for episodic (experiential) memory. For that reason we will talk about the entire hippocampal complex, rather than just the hippocampus alone.

At the very front tip of each hippocampus is the *amygdala*, Latin for 'almond' (see Figure 5.18). It has a small spherical nut-like shape, profoundly important for emotions like fear and anger, as well as learning processes that involve those emotions. Finally, the *basal ganglia* (see Figure 5.20) are complex disk-and-loop structures just outside of each thalamus, and the *cerebellum* (or little brain) rides on the back of the entire upper brainstem and thalami. The basal ganglia have been implicated in action planning and unconscious cognitive operations. New evidence, however, has linked the basal ganglia to higher order cognitive functions, such as decoding the grammar, or syntax, of language.

The cerebellum is seated on the rear of the lower brainstem. It is itself a very large structure. In many mammals, the cerebellum has as many neurons as the cortex itself, though they have shorter axons. Most cerebellar neurons are connected locally, in small clusters. Historically, the cerebellum was thought to be mainly involved in controlling fine motor movements, like the finger movements of a typist or musician. It is now also known to be necessary for cognitive functions as well. Indeed, functional imaging shows the cerebellum to 'light up' in almost any cognitive task. The reason for this is not completely understood.

Finally, a number of tiny nuclei of the brainstem and basal forebrain send cell fibers widely through the upper brain. These neuromodulating nuclei are sometimes informally called 'spritzers', because they spray neurochemicals from their axon terminals so that those chemicals are widely dispersed. Spritzers may contain only a few thousand neurons, but they are crucial to a healthy brain. Major disorders like Parkinson's disease, characterized by disabling motor tremor, result from defects of such neuromodulators. They also control the daily sleep-waking cycle.

We end this section with a description of the reticular formation, located at a central point in the brain (Figure 5.40). This is a particularly intriguing area of the brain in terms of its role in human conscious experience. The reticular formation is called 'reticular' (i.e. network-like) because the neuronal axons in this system are usually very short, suggesting a great amount of interaction between adjacent neurons. Further, it receives input from all sensory and motor systems, as well as from other major structures in the brain. Through its connections with the thalamus, it can send information to, and receive it from, all areas of the cortex.

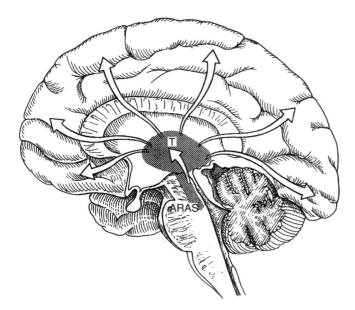

FIGURE 5.40 The Ascending Reticular Activating System (ARAS) is found in the brainstem and thalamus, and sends projections throughout cortex. The ARAS is thought to be required for the normal conscious waking state. *Source*: Filley, 2002.

What does this suggest about the role of the reticular formation in conscious experience? There is neurophysiological evidence that specialist systems in the brain can cooperate and compete for access to a central integrative 'blackboard'. There is reason to think that the *extended reticular-thalamic system* (ERTAS) corresponds to this 'blackboard'.

This is not a new notion; Aristotle's 'common sense' was supposed to be a domain of integration between the different senses. In fact, anatomists who have studied the reticular formation have pointed to its resemblance to Aristotle's concept. Scheibel and Scheibel (1965) point out that: 'Anatomical studies of Kohnstamm and Quensel, which suggested pooling of a number of afferent and efferent systems upon the reticular core, led them to propose this area as a "centrum receptorium 2" or "sensorium commune" – a common sensory pool for the neuraxis'.

Moreover, these authors note that: '. . . the reticular core mediates specific delimitation of the focus of consciousness with concordant suppression of those sensory inputs that have been temporarily relegated to a sensory role' (p. 579). Along similar lines, Gastaut (1958) describes the brainstem reticular formation as an area of: 'convergence . . . where signals are concentrated before being redistributed in a divergent way to the cortex'. Thus, different sensory contents can suppress each other, as we would indeed expect of input to a global workspace. This suggests that different specialized processors can compete for access to the ERTAS.

How does this 'blackboard' concept actually work in terms of neural processes and how are messages broadcast? In one possible scenario, one sensory projection area of the cortex provides input to the ERTAS. If this input prevails over competing inputs, it becomes a global message which is widely distributed to other areas of the brain, including the rest of the cortex. Thus, one selected input to the ERTAS is amplified and broadcast at the expense of others. Thus, in this way, the ERTAS underlies the 'global broadcasting' function of consciousness, while a selected perceptual 'processor' in the cortex supplies the particular contents of consciousness which are to be broadcast.

What is the role of the ERTAS in conscious thought? It may be the case that any cortical activity must trigger ERTAS 'support' in a circulating flow of information, before it can be broadcast globally and become conscious (e.g. Scheibel and Scheibel, 1965; Shevrin and Dickman, 1980). Dixon (1971) has also argued that a circulating flow of information between the reticular formation and the sensory areas of the cortex is required before sensory input becomes conscious.

The possible role of the ERTAS in conscious experience is an intriguing one! It makes intuitive sense that there must be some kind of broadcast system in the brain that allows for all modes of sensory processing – sight, hearing, touch – to combine with conscious thought and experience in order to focus on some inputs and suppress others. Clearly, the ERTAS does not work in isolation in these types of brain functions. The thalami and regions in the prefrontal cortex are likely closely intertwined with ERTAS-like processes. Nevertheless, ERTAS seems to play a key role in human conscious experience.

4.0 SUMMARY

It is a difficult task indeed to attempt to describe a dynamic and complex biological structure such as the brain in a few short pages. Our aim in this chapter was to provide you with the basic structures and regions of the brain and their function in human cognition. Some important points to remember are that the brain has developed and changed through time and so some areas of the brain are 'older' than others. The cortex or neocortex represents recent brain developments in the

human and the frontal and parietal lobes have expanded their neural territory tremendously as compared to non-human primates. While there are separable regions and parts of the brain, such as the two hemispheres and the four major lobes, nonetheless, the brain is highly interconnected with an extensive fiber pathway system that connects the hemispheres, the lobes, and provides circuits to subcortical regions.

Some important questions about human brain structure and function remain a puzzle to us. Why do we see so much evidence of duality in the brain, with two hemispheres, two thalami, for example, when we have one mind? What role does the mirror image regions of the brain play in human cognition? While some 'newer' regions of the brain, such as the prefrontal cortex and the inferior parietal lobe, seem to be the site for higher order associative cognition, there are also some ancient regions, such as the reticular formation, that seem to play a key role in consciousness. New and ancient, the many regions of the brain come together to form a dynamic and intricate biological structure that holds many more puzzles for scientist to unravel.

5.0 CHAPTER REVIEW

5.1 Study questions

1 Why is the cortex sometimes referred to as the 'neocortex'?
2 What are the four major lobes of the brain and what are some of their key functions in human cognition?
3 Where is the medial temporal lobe located? What are its key structures?
4 Briefly describe the role of the thalami in brain processing.
5 How are the hemispheres linked? Are there any differences in how they function?
6 What is the reticular formation and what role may it play in conscious thought?

5.2 Drawing exercises

Show the locations and names of the major brain landmarks, using Figure 5.41, opposite.

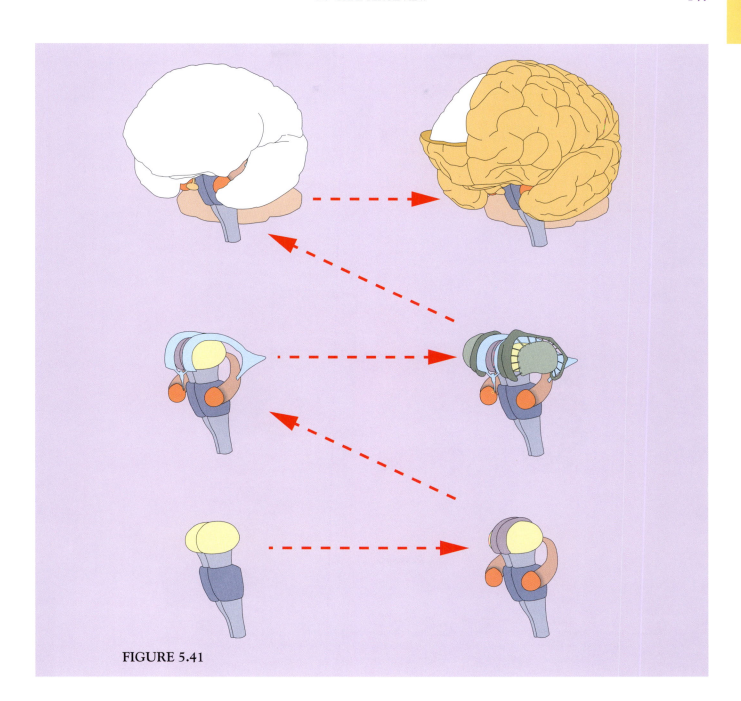

FIGURE 5.41

The question is not what you look at, but what you see.

Henry David Thoreau

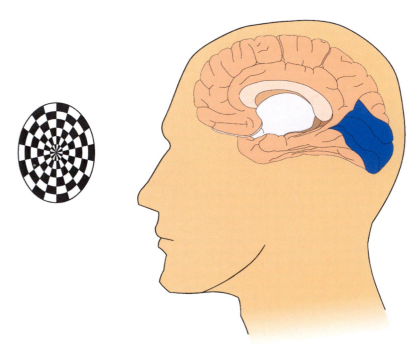

An abstract figure showing a rotating checkerboard stimulus, which highly activates the early visual areas located in the occipital lobe (in blue). Notice that we are looking at a medial view of the right hemisphere.

6

Vision

Frank Tong and Joel Pearson

1.0 INTRODUCTION

1.1 The mystery of visual experience

Think back to the last time you stood aloft a high lookout, looking down at the world below. Perhaps you were at the top of a summit and could see the wide expanse of the horizon cut by repeating mountaintops, forests, valleys, and rivers below, or perhaps you were at the top of a tall building as the bustling swirling colors of rush-hour traffic, cars, and people flowed through the streets. It's worth pausing for a moment to think about how such vivid and powerful impressions can be the simple result of a collection of neurons firing

Cognition, Brain, and Consciousness, edited by B. J. Baars and N. M. Gage
ISBN: 978-0-12-373677-2

Copyright 2007, Elsevier Ltd. All rights reserved.

inside your brain. How can the collective electrical activity of billions of neurons be responsible for everything you are seeing and experiencing at this very moment? These are some of the perplexing but fascinating questions that arise when we consider the relationship between brain activity and subjective visual experience.

Most people intuitively think that human vision works much like a camera (Figure 6.1(a)). As we go about our daily activities, it is easy to believe that we see our entire world in crisp full resolution color – much like a high-resolution photograph. However, as it turns out, this is far from the case. Due partly to the structure of our eyes (which we will revisit shortly), our visual perception is in full color and high resolution only at the center of gaze. This may seem hard to believe, as you dart your eyes around the room now; the illusion that you are experiencing the whole visual scene in full color and clarity seems convincing. However, if you fix your gaze at a particular point in space – say the corner of the window sill or this word on the page – and get someone to hold up some fingers out at the edge of your field of view, you will find that without moving your eyes it is extremely hard to count the number of fingers they hold up. Also, you may notice that your experience of color is somehow dull and lacking in richness.

There are several reasons why it makes sense to restrict high resolution vision to only a small portion of our visual space – this is just one of the many strategies that the brain uses to help represent the specific features and objects we see in the most efficient and effective way possible. It is a testament to the brain's ability seamlessly to represent the outside world that we normally remain oblivious to this striking fact.

1.2 The purpose of vision: *knowing what is where*

For most people, vision may be the most important of the five senses for getting around in everyday life and getting things done. What is the purpose of vision? David Marr, an early vision scientist and computer expert, made the deceptively simple comment that the goal of vision is *'to know what is where'*. For example, if you are walking or driving to the university to find a class in a new building, it is important to know: *where are the other cars and pedestrians, is the light red or green, which way is that car going, how fast is it approaching, do I turn at this street corner, is this the building I'm looking for?*

Considering the goal of vision, it becomes clear that visual perception is far more complicated than simply taking a picture with a digital camera (Figure 6.1(a)). A digital camera can capture the image projected from the environment and store it in an array of pixels. However, the camera doesn't really do anything with this image and doesn't have any knowledge about what is stored in the image, such as what objects are in the photo or

(a)

(b)

FIGURE 6.1 Visual experiences. (a) Just one of millions of images you can experience with your visual system. Unlike the camera, you actually experience the image, you know what it is you are looking at. (Image courtesy of the Tong lab.) (b) Another example of the detailed, multifeature capabilities of your visual system. You can differentiate many different orientations, colors and shapes.

where they are. The easiest way to figure out what is in the picture is to have someone look at the picture and interpret it with his or her brain. Visual perception is what happens *after* the picture reaches the eyes – the image forms a pattern of activity on the array of receptors in the eye, and the detailed pattern is analyzed by the visual centers of the brain, thereby revealing what is where.

1.3 Knowing what: *perceiving features, groups and objects*

How does the brain perceive what something is? Studies of human visual perception and neuroscience suggest that there are many levels of perception. At the most basic level, the human brain appears to process basic *visual features* such as *color, orientation, motion, texture,* and *stereoscopic depth*. For example, when looking at the picture of the flower shown in Figure 6.1(b), we may perceive that the center of the flower is yellow, the leaf just below is green, and the two stems are each at different angles. We are very good at perceiving small differences in orientation (1–2 degrees of angular tilt), subtle differences in color (e.g. the red of a rose or the red of a strawberry), and very faint traces of motion.

As we will see in the next section, most neurons in early visual areas of the brain are highly tuned to specific features – some may fire very strongly to a line shown at a particular angle, to a particular color, or to a particular motion direction. These neurons respond to a very small region of the visual field (i.e. your current field of view), ranging from just a fraction of a degree to a few degrees of visual angle. (If you hold your thumb at arm's length, the width of your thumb is probably about two degrees of visual angle (O'Shea, 1991). The moon, when viewed from Earth, is about 0.5 degrees in diameter.)

If the activity of each of these neurons represents only a small part of the visual field, such as whether a small patch of the visual field contains vertical or horizontal, red or blue, motion or something stationary, then how is the brain able to combine this information across many neurons? Somehow, the brain is able to organize these basic feature elements into organized *perceptual groups*. The *Gestalt* psychologists proposed that perception could not be understood by simply studying the basic elements of perception (Wertheimer, 1912; Koffka, 1935). The German word, *Gestalt*, is difficult to translate directly, but expresses the idea that *the whole is greater than the sum of the parts*. These psychologists proposed the *Gestalt laws of perceptual grouping*, such as the laws

of *similarity, proximity, good continuation, common fate,* and so forth (Figure 6.2). These laws suggest that elements more similar in color or shape are more likely to be perceived as a group. Likewise, if a set of elements is arranged in a way that they are more closely spaced in rows or columns, this will determine whether they are perceived as rows or columns.

Why is perceptual grouping so important? It helps us perceive which features belong to a possible object, and

Grouping by similarity

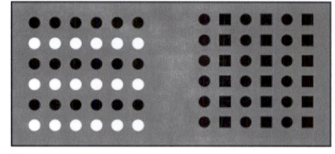

(a)

Grouping by proximity

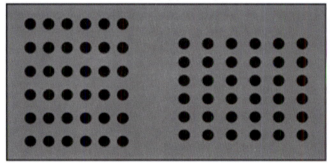

(b)

Grouping by good continuation

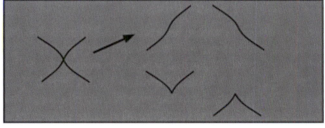

(c)

FIGURE 6.2 Gestalt grouping. (a) Grouping by similarity, the white dots are grouped with other white dots. On the right, the squares group with squares. The objects with similar features tend to group together. (b) Here, even though all the objects are circles, due to their grouped locations or proximity to each other, we perceive two separate groups of dots. (c) Grouping by good continuation. On the left, we perceive one object. On the right, the exact same lines are drawn but separated so that there is no continuation across the entire object. In all these cases, the collections of objects form groups or larger global objects, which are greater than the simple sum of the parts.

helps us distinguish an object from the background. For example, imagine seeing a golden retriever lying in tall grass. Grouping by similarity may help us see that the dog is separate from the grass, and the neighboring wagging tail might be recognized as part of the dog, even though only the end of the tail can be seen. If the dog starts to run towards a bush, barking furiously, the cat hidden behind the bush may be invisible until it starts to move, because the cat's motion leads to grouping by common fate, which may evoke a vivid impression of the complete shape of the animal rather than bits and fragments of fur separated by branches and leaves.

Finally, we can perceive the shape of entire *objects*, and match these shape representations to the objects we know from previous experience. To perceive an object, the brain has to go through many stages of visual processing, from processing the feature elements of the object, putting the elements together into coherent groups, and finally figuring out how those elements form a coherent organized shape. This representation of the object's shape must then be matched to the correct object representation stored in memory. Given that there are thousands of objects and that the two-dimensional image of any object projected onto the back of the eye can vary from changes in viewpoint, lighting or viewing conditions, this makes the problem of object recognition especially challenging. Somehow, the brain must abstract the stable or invariant properties of an object while disregarding all the superficial ways in which the 2D image of an object can vary.

Later in this chapter, we will discuss how the brain processes different types of visual features and objects.

1.4 Knowing where things are

How do we know where objects are located in the world? When we look at the world, the image that strikes the back of our eye is essentially two-dimensional, similar to the image that would be taken by a camera. This two-dimensional map of the world projected onto the eye is preserved in the early visual areas of the cerebral cortex, which provides a map of where objects are located relative to the center of gaze. The brain is also able to figure out the missing third dimension and estimate how far away objects are in space. Whereas early visual areas represent the positions of objects relative to the center of gaze, higher brain areas in the parietal, temporal or frontal lobe are more likely to represent the position of objects in a more abstract (less visual) manner, relative to the person's body position or relative to the global environment.

2.0 FUNCTIONAL ORGANIZATION OF THE VISUAL SYSTEM

When the light coming from an object reaches our eyes, it triggers a cascade of neural events as this visual pattern is converted into neural impulses that travel up the visual system, from one brain area to the next. Through a series of neural processes in many brain areas, the activity of neurons in numerous brain areas somehow leads to the visual experience and recognition of the object and its many component features. Let's trace the sequence of events to understand how the brain processes visual information at each stage of visual processing. This will help us understand how different visual areas of the brain contribute to visual perception.

2.1 The retina

There are two types of photoreceptors: *cones* and *rods* (Figure 6.3). Cones are color-selective, less sensitive to dim light than rods, and important for detailed color vision in daylight. Each cone contains one of three kinds of *photopigment*, specialized proteins that are sensitive to different wavelengths of light. These wavelengths roughly correspond to our ability to distinguish red, green and blue. When light strikes a photopigment molecule, the light energy is absorbed and the molecule then changes shape in a way that modifies the flow of electrical current in that photoreceptor neuron. Cones are densely packed into the *fovea*, the central part of the retina that we use to look directly at objects to perceive their fine details. In the periphery, cones are more spread out and scattered, which is why objects in the periphery appear blurrier and their colors are less vivid.

Rods contain a different photopigment that is much more sensitive to low levels of light. Rods are important for *night vision* – we rely on seeing with our rods once our eyes have adapted to the darkness (*dark adaptation*). Curiously, there are no rods in the fovea, only cones, and the proportion of rods increases in the periphery. This is why you may have noticed when gazing at the night sky that a very faint star may be easier to see if you look slightly off to one side.

The signals from photoreceptors are processed by a collection of intermediary neurons, *bipolar cells, horizontal cells* and *amacrine cells*, before they reach the *ganglion cells*, the final processing stage in the retina before signals leave the eye. The actual cell bodies of ganglion cells are located in the retina, but these cells have long axons that leave the retina at the *blind spot* and form the *optic nerve*. Each ganglion cell receives excitatory

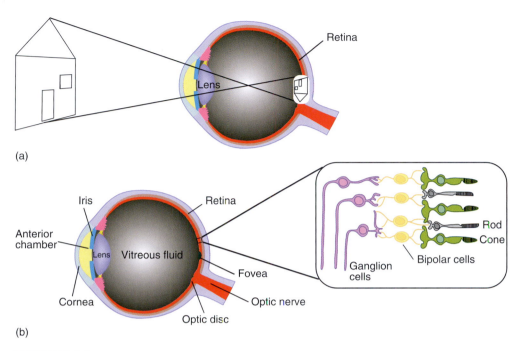

(a)

(b)

FIGURE 6.3 The eye. (a) Illustration showing how objects in the environment are physically projected to the back of the eye – the retina. (b) The eye and a cross-section of the retina. The cross-section of the eye shows where the photoreceptors are located in the retina. Both the rods and cones are shown. They respond to different types of light. The neural signal then travels via bipolar cells and then to the ganglion cells. The axons of the ganglion cells take the neural information out of the eye and backward toward the cortex. *Source*: Squire *et al.*, 2003.

inputs from a collection of rods and cones – this distillation of information forms a *receptive field* – a concept we will revisit shortly. Ganglion cells at the fovea receive information from only a small number of cones, while ganglion cells in the periphery receive inputs from many rods (sometimes thousands). With so many rods providing converging input to a single ganglion cell, if any one of these rods is activated by photons of light, this may activate the cell, which increases the likelihood of being able to detect dim scattered light. However, this increase in sensitivity to dim light is achieved at the cost of poorer resolution – rods provide more sensitivity, but also a more 'blurry' picture than the sharp daytime image provided by cone vision.

Retinal ganglion cells receive both excitatory and inhibitory inputs from bipolar neurons, and the spatial pattern of these inputs determines the cell's *receptive field* (Figure 6.4(a)). A neuron's receptive field refers to the portion of the visual field that can activate or strongly inhibit the response of that cell. Retinal ganglion neurons have center-surround receptive fields. For example, a cell with an *on-center off-surround* receptive field will respond strongly if a spot of light is presented at the center of the receptive field. As that spot of light is enlarged, responses will increase up to the point

where light begins to spread beyond the boundaries of the on-center region. After that, the response of the ganglion cell starts to decline as the spot of light gets bigger and stimulates more and more of the surrounding off-region. (A cell with an off-center on-surround receptive field will respond best to a dark spot presented in the center of the receptive field.)

How can the behavior of retinal ganglion cells be understood? A key concept is that of *lateral inhibition* (Kuffler, 1953). Lateral inhibition means that the activity of a neuron may be inhibited by inputs coming from neurons that respond to neighboring regions of the visual field. For example, the retinal ganglion cell in Figure 6.4(b) receives excitatory inputs from cells corresponding to the on-center region, and inhibitory inputs from the off-center region. The strength of these excitatory and inhibitory inputs are usually balanced, so that if uniform light is presented across both on- and off-regions, the neuron will not respond to uniform illumination.

Why are center-surround receptive fields and lateral inhibition so important? Lateral inhibition is important for enhancing the neural representation of *edges*, regions of an image where the light intensity sharply changes. These sudden changes indicate the presence of possible contours, features, shapes or objects in any visual scene,

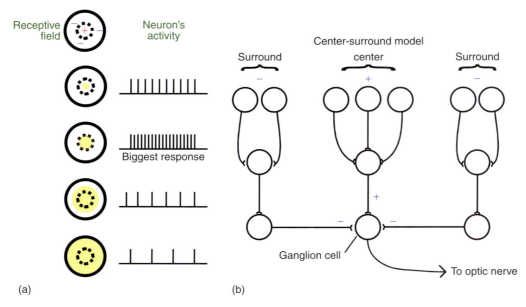

FIGURE 6.4 Center-surround receptive fields. (a) Schematic example of a center-surround cell's response to different-sized patches of light. Notice that the biggest spiking response (shown by the lines on the right) occurs for the intermediate-sized center light patch. The spot of light has to be just the right size to get the maximum response out of that particular neuron. (b) A model of how a center-surround receptive field might be achieved by the collaboration and competition between different connective neurons in the retina.

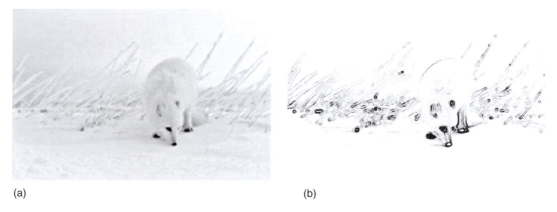

FIGURE 6.5 The edges hold most information. An example of how most of the information in the picture comes from the edges of objects. Figure on the left is the original, on the right is information from the edges only – taken from the image using a computer algorithm.

whereas uniform parts of a picture are not particularly informative or interesting. Figure 6.5 shows a picture of the fox in original form and after using a computer to filter out just the edges (right picture), so that the regions in black show where ganglion cells would respond most strongly to the image. Lateral inhibition also leads to more efficient neural representation, because only the neurons corresponding to the edge of a stimulus will fire strongly; other neurons with receptive fields that lie in a uniform region do not. Because the firing of neurons takes of a lot of *metabolic energy*, this is much more efficient. This is an example of *efficient neural*

coding – only a small number of neurons need to be active at any time to represent a particular visual stimulus.

Lateral inhibition also helps ensure that the brain responds in a similar way to an object or a visual scene on a dim gray day and on a bright day. Changes in the absolute level of brightness won't affect the pattern of activity on the retina very much at all; it is the relative brightness of objects that matters most. Finally, lateral inhibition at multiple levels of visual processing, including the retina, lateral geniculate nucleus (LGN), and visual cortex, may lead to interesting visual illusions such as the Hermann grid illusion (Figure 6.6).

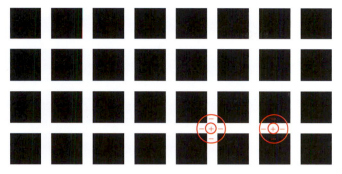

2.2 Lateral geniculate nucleus (LGN)

From the eye, retinal ganglion cells send their axons to a structure in the thalamus called the *lateral geniculate nucleus* (LGN). Specifically, the left half of each retina projects to the left LGN; the right half of the retina projects to the right LGN. For this to happen, the inputs from the nasal portion of each retina must cross at the *optic chiasm* to project to the opposite LGN (Figure 6.7). The result is that the left LGN receives input from the right visual field, and the right LGN receives input from the left visual field, so that each LGN serves to represent the *contralateral* (i.e. opposite) visual field. Note that the inputs from each eye go to separate monocular layers of the LGN, so signals from the two eyes remain separate until they reach the *primary visual cortex* where these signals are combined.

What do the receptive fields in the LGN look like? Well, they share the same shape and basic properties of the retinal ganglion cells, with center-surround receptive fields. The thalamus is often considered a way station

FIGURE 6.6 Hermann grid illusion. Take a careful look at the collection of black squares in the figure. Do you notice anything unusual? Do you have the impression of seeing small dark circles in between the black squares in the periphery? Don't be alarmed, this is completely normal. This is a great example of receptive fields with lateral inhibition at work (Herman, 1870). In the rightmost matrix of squares, some possible receptive fields are shown. A receptive field that falls between the corners of four dark squares will have more of its inhibitory surround stimulated by the white parts of the grid than a receptive field that lies between just two of the dark squares. As a result, neurons with receptive fields positioned between four dark squares will fire more weakly, leading to the impression of small dark patches at these cross points. At the fovea, receptive fields are much smaller so the illusion is only seen in the periphery.

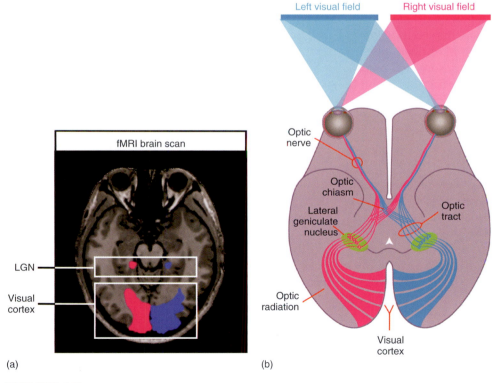

(a)   (b)

FIGURE 6.7 The visual pathways from retina to cortex. (a) Example of a brain slice from a functional magnetic resonance imaging (fMRI) scan, showing the lateral geniculate nucleus (LGN) and primary visual areas at the back of the brain (the occipital cortex). The two different colors denote the two hemispheres of the brain. (b) Schematic illustration showing the visual pathways from the retina in the eyes to the primary visual cortex at the back of the brain. You can see here that the neural information from the nasal or inner sides of the eyes crosses over at the optic chiasm, to be processed in the contralateral side of the brain. The left visual field, in blue, is processed by the right visual cortex (also blue). The LGN, displayed in green, relays the visual information to the primary visual areas of the cortex. *Source*: Squire *et al.*, 2003.

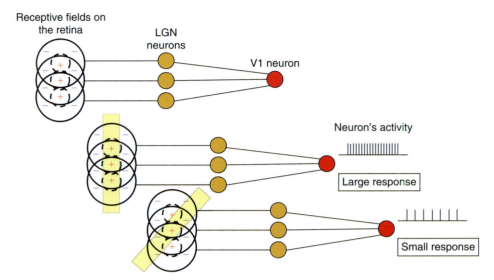

Receptive fields on the retina
LGN neurons
V1 neuron
Neuron's activity
Large response
Small response

FIGURE 6.8 Orientation selectivity in V1. An example of how a collection of center-surround receptive fields could lead to orientation selectivity in V1 neurons. The overlapping circles on the left show center-surround receptive fields. When the bar of light lays vertically it triggers all the on-centers (+) of each receptive field, whereas when its orientation changes (the bar tilts) fewer centers and more surrounds are activated resulting in a smaller neural response (fewer spike bars in the graph). Hence the vertical bar gives a larger neural response, when the stimulus is oriented the magnitude of the V1 response is reduced. This constitutes orientation selectivity – only observed in the cortex.

for signals finally to reach the cerebral cortex, where the neurons start to respond in very different ways.

So how would LGN neurons or retinal ganglion cells respond to the simple outline of the house, as is illustrated in Figure 6.10? Cells with on-center receptive fields positioned on any of the contours of the house would fire strongly. Note though, these cells will fire just as strongly for a vertical, horizontal or tilted line. Although a small portion of the inhibitory surround is stimulated by these lines, the entire proportion of the on-center region is being stimulated, leading to greater excitation than inhibition, and therefore a steady level of firing.

2.3 Primary visual cortex (V1)

From the LGN, neurons send their signals to the primary visual cortex, sometimes called *V1* because this region is the first cortical visual area. About 90 per cent of the outputs from the retina project first to the LGN and then onward to V1. The left LGN projects to V1 in the left hemisphere; the right LGN projects to right V1 (Figure 6.7). In V1, the spatial layout of inputs from the retina is still preserved. Left V1 receives an orderly set of inputs from the left half of both retinas, via the thalamus. The foveal part of the visual field is represented in the posterior part of the occipital lobe, near the occipital pole and the more peripheral parts of the visual field are represented more anteriorly. Left V1 therefore contains a *retinotopic map* of the entire right visual field, while right V1 contains a map of the entire left visual field. This retinotopic organization is very prevalent in early visual areas (V1 through V4), where neurons have small receptive fields, but becomes weaker and less orderly in higher visual areas outside of the occipital lobe.

Neurons in V1 are sensitive to a whole host of visual features, not seen in the LGN. One of the most important visual features is *orientation* (Hubel and Wiesel, 1962, 1968). Some V1 neurons respond best to vertical lines, some to 20-degree tilted lines, others to horizontal lines and so forth. How do these neurons attain these new properties or receptive fields? Figure 6.8 shows an example of a model for V1 orientation selectivity. If a V1 neuron receives excitatory input from three LGN neurons with aligned center-surround receptive fields, then the V1 neuron will respond best to a matching oriented line. For example, if a vertical bar is presented, the neuron shown in the figure will respond at its strongest, because the entire excitatory region will be stimulated, whereas the inhibitory surround will not be stimulated. If the bar is tilted somewhat away from vertical, the neuron will respond more weakly because part of the inhibitory surround will now be stimulated and part of the excitatory center will not. Finally, if a horizontal bar is presented, the neuron may not fire at all, because equal proportions of the center and the surround regions will be receiving stimulation, leading to a balance in the strength of incoming excitatory and inhibitory inputs. This configuration of center-surround receptive fields can explain the orientation selectivity of V1 neurons.

V1 neurons are also sensitive to many other *visual features* besides orientation (Hubel and Wiesel, 1998). Some neurons respond best to a particular *direction of motion*, such as upward motion, leftward motion or downward motion. Other neurons respond best to particular colors or color differences (e.g. red versus green, yellow versus blue), though some basic types of color-sensitive neurons can also be found in the retina and LGN. Finally, some neurons respond best to particular

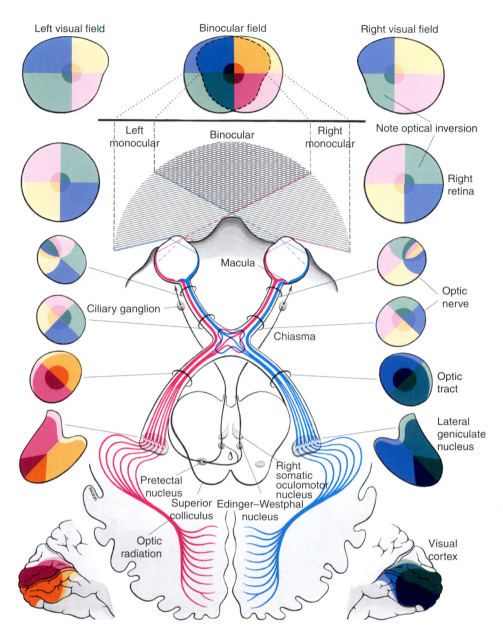

FIGURE 6.9 Pathways in the visual system: from the eye to V1. A schematic drawing of the pathways in binocular vision, showing the visual input from left and right visual fields (top of figure) through the optic nerve and optic tract (center of figure), continuing on through the LGN and onto V1 in cortex (bottom of the figure). *Source*: Standring, 2005.

binocular disparities (Barlow *et al.*, 1967; Cumming, 2002), which refer to the degree of alignment between images in the two eyes. Small displacements between images in the two eyes are what allow us to perceive stereo-depth when we look at objects with both eyes open. (Try closing one eye, extending your arms to full length and try quickly to move your two index fingers to meet one another. Now try this again with both eyes open. If you have normal binocular vision, this should be much easier to do with both eyes open because you can better judge the distance of your two fingers.) See Figure 6.9 for a schematic view of pathways in the binocular vision system.

So how will V1 neurons respond to the outline of the house? A V1 neuron that is tuned to 45-degree tilted lines and has its receptive field in the position along the roof may fire strongly to the angled roof. A V1 neuron that responds best to vertical will help signal the presence of the vertical wall and a horizontal neuron will respond to the ceiling or floor of the house. In this sense, it can be readily seen that V1 neurons do much more than respond to simple spots of light, as the LGN does. V1 neurons provide a *neural representation* of the orientation of visual features that comprise the contours and shapes of objects. Figure 6.10 provides a summary of the hierarchy of visual processing. From the LGN, V1,

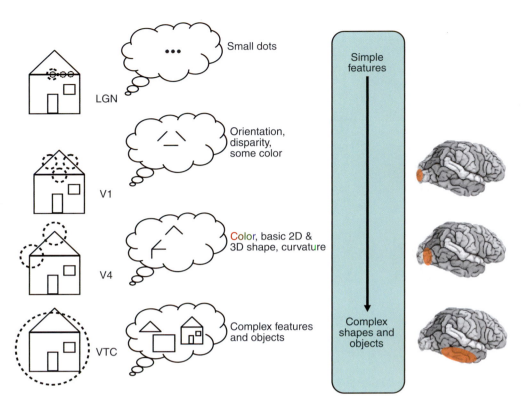

FIGURE 6.10 The hierarchy of visual processing. A demonstration of the hierarchical response properties of the visual system to simple and complex stimuli. The leftmost column shows our house stimulus and what receptive fields of each visual area we would see in the balloons. Not only do the receptive field sizes increase in each visual area, but also the complexity of the shapes they respond to. The rightmost column shows an estimate of where each area is in the brain. You can see that early visual areas respond to simple features and, as we move along the processing stream, areas respond to more complex shapes and objects. This is a well-established theme of the visual system.

V4 to the ventral temporal cortex, you can see that neurons gradually respond to more complex stimuli from one area to the next.

So, to summarize, V1 is important in analyzing the visual features at a fine level of detail. These neurons have small receptive fields that are sensitive to orientation, color, motion or binocular disparity. After visual signals are analyzed in V1, they are sent to higher visual areas for further processing.

2.4 Extrastriate visual areas – outside of V1

V1 sends *feedforward* signals to many higher visual areas, including areas such as V2, V3, V4 and *motion-sensitive area MT*, to name a few (Figure 6.11) (Felleman and Van Essen, 1991). *Area V4* is known to be especially important for the *perception of color* (Zeki, 1977) and some neurons in this area respond well to more complex features or combinations of features (Pasupathy and Connor, 2002). For example, some V4 neurons are sensitive to curvature or to two lines that meet at a specific angle. These neurons might signal the presence of a curving contour

or a corner. From our example of the house, a V4 neuron might respond best to the meeting of the two lines forming the point of the roof or to another corner of the house.

How then are these various bits and parts of the house, as represented by simple line orientations and corners, eventually represented as an entire object? Area V4 sends many outputs to higher visual areas in the *ventral visual pathway*, which is important for object recognition (Ungerleider and Mishkin, 1982). The anterior part of the ventral visual pathway consists of the ventral temporal cortex, which is especially important for object recognition.

2.5 Area MT

The middle-temporal area, or what is commonly called area MT (see Figure 6.11), is important for motion perception. Almost all of the neurons in area MT are direction-selective, meaning that they respond selectively to a certain range of motion directions and do not respond to directions beyond that range (Zeki, 1974; Albright, 1984). Moreover, some of these neurons respond well to

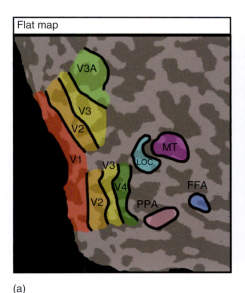

(a)

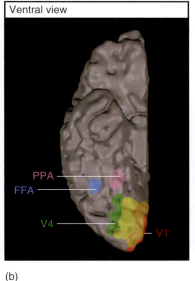

(b)

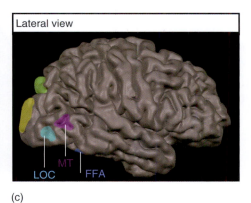

(c)

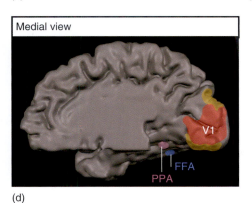

(d)

FIGURE 6.11 Visual areas of the brain. Functionally defined visual areas of the human brain, shown on a reconstruction from anatomical brain scans. (a) A flattened cortical representation of the human visual system. The flat map was created by unfolding the convoluted surface of the cerebral cortex, applying a cut through the calcarine sulcus, which divides area V1 into dorsal and ventral halves, and flattening the cortical sheet using computerized methods. This allows one to see all the visual areas of one hemisphere, including those buried in the sulci, in a single image. The upper half shows dorsal portions of visual areas V1, V2 and V3, as well as V3A. The lower half shows ventral visual areas V1, V2, V3 and V4, as well as the parahippocampal place area (PPA) and fusiform face area (FFA). Areas LOC and MT are also shown. (b) A ventral view of one hemisphere, showing the location of these areas in the cortex. (c) Lateral view of the same hemisphere, showing the positions of the different visual areas. (d) A medial view of the hemisphere showing mainly V1. *Source*: Squire *et al.*, 2003.

patterns of motion (Albright, 1992), meaning that these neurons can integrate many different motion directions and calculate what the overall direction of an object might be. As we will see, the activity in this region seems to be closely related to motion perception and, when activity in this region is disrupted, motion perception may be severely impaired.

2.6 The ventral and dorsal pathways: knowing *what* and *where*

The projections from V1 to higher areas in the cortex can be roughly divided according to two major parallel pathways: a *ventral pathway* leading from V1 to the *temporal lobe* that is important for representing *'what'* objects are and a *dorsal pathway* leading from V1 to the *parietal lobe* that is important for representing *'where'* objects are located (Figure 6.12).

This distinction between the ventral and dorsal pathways, sometimes referred to as the *what* and *where*

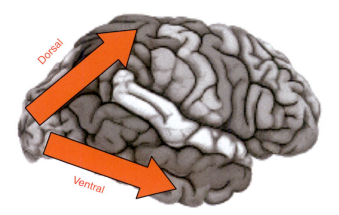

FIGURE 6.12 What and where pathways. The 'where' pathway is typically called the dorsal pathway because it includes dorsal areas like MT and the parietal cortex, that are along the top of the brain. The 'what' pathway includes ventral areas like V4, LOC and IT, hence it is known as the ventral processing pathway. These two pathways form a nice way of visualizing the flow of different cortical information. *Source*: Squire *et al.*, 2003.

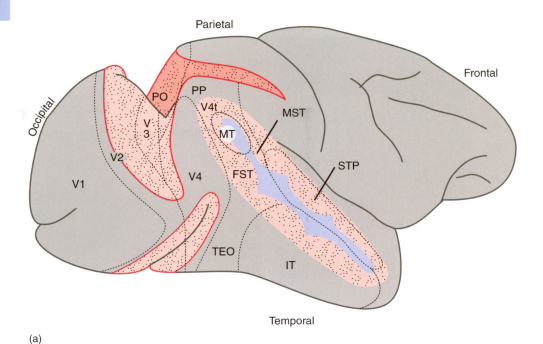

(a)

(b)

FIGURE 6.13 Dorsal and ventral visual pathways. From the pioneering work of Ungerleider and Mishkin (1982), a schematic drawing of the dorsal and ventral pathways based on studies in monkey. (a) A lateral view of monkey brain, showing the location of primary vision cortex (V1), extra-striate cortex (V2–V4) and other key vision areas such as MT. (b) A schematic showing visual areas involved in dorsal and ventral processing streams. *Source*: Squire *et al.*, 2003.

pathways respectively, is an important organizational principle of the visual system proposed by Ungerleider and Mishkin (1982).

Support for this distinction comes from what has been discovered about the anatomical connections between visual areas in these two pathways, the response properties of visual areas in each pathway and the visual deficits that can result from damage to the parietal or temporal lobe.

In the dorsal pathway, signals from V1 travel to dorsal extrastriate areas, such as area MT and V3A, which then send major projections to many regions of the parietal lobe. The dorsal pathway is important for representing the *locations* of objects, so that the visual system can guide actions towards those objects (Goodale and Humphrey, 1998). Consider what is involved in reaching for any object, such as a coffee mug sitting on a table; this type of vision requires detailed information about the precise location, size and orientation of the object. Without such detailed information, you might

reach towards the wrong location, your grasp might not match the size of the handle of the mug, or your hand might not be angled properly for gripping the handle. Areas MT and V3A are important for processing visual motion and stereo-depth, while specific regions in the parietal lobe are specialized for guiding eye movements or hand movements to specific locations in visual space.

In the ventral pathway, many signals from V1 travel to ventral extrastriate areas V2, V3 and V4 and onward to many areas of the temporal lobe. The ventral or 'what' pathway is important for processing information about the color, shape and identity of visual objects, processing which emphasizes the stable, *invariant* properties of objects. For example, the ventral pathway is less concerned about the exact size, orientation and position of the coffee mug; instead, its goal is to be able to identify such an object anywhere in the visual field and to be able to tell it apart from other similar objects (e.g. cups, bowls, teapots). We will be talking about the properties of the ventral pathway in much greater detail, especially different regions of the temporal lobe.

While this dorsal-ventral pathway distinction is useful for grouping areas of the brain and understanding how much of the information flows back and forth between visual areas, it should not be taken as an absolute distinction. There is plenty of cross talk between the two pathways. Also, the parietal and temporal lobes send projections to some common regions in the *prefrontal cortex*, where information from each pathway can also be reunited.

2.7 Areas involved in object recognition

Single-unit recordings in monkeys have revealed that many neurons in the ventral temporal cortex respond best to contours, simple shapes, or complex objects. For example, some neurons in this region may respond best to square or round shapes, others to triangles and others still to even more complex figures, such as the outline of a house (see Figure 6.10), which looks like a triangle lying on top of a square. Some neurons in this region are highly selective and respond to only a particular kind of object, such as a hand, a face shown from a particular viewpoint, a particular animal, a familiar toy or an object that the monkey has learned to recognize and so forth (Desimone *et al.*, 1984; Gross, 1992; Logothetis *et al.*, 1995; Tanaka, 1996).

Human neuroimaging studies have revealed many brain areas involved in processing objects. These object-sensitive areas, which lie just anterior to early visual areas V1–V4, respond more strongly to coherent

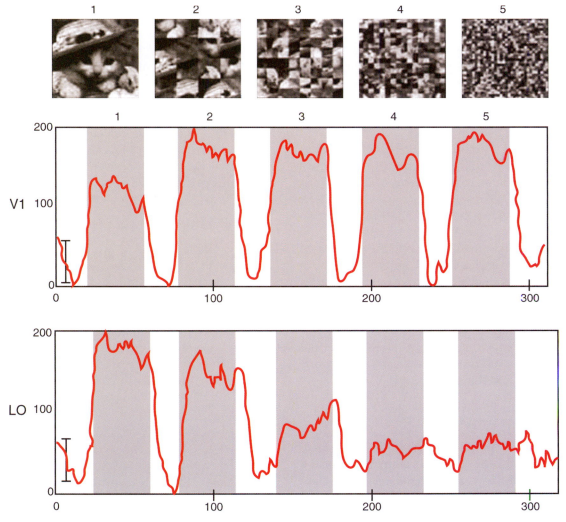

FIGURE 6.14   Neural response from low and high level areas. The response of primary visual cortex (V1) and lateral occipital (LOC) to a picture of a kitten at different coherencies. As the picture is scrambled V1 continues to respond – in fact, it actually increases its response once the image is scrambled. This demonstrates that it is not the image of the kitten which is driving responses in V1, but local patches of luminance and orientation. Conversely, the activity in lateral occipital cortex shows a large response to the kitten but, as the picture is scrambled, the activity in LOC drops down dramatically. This demonstrates that unlike V1, the activity in LOC is in response to the kitten.

shapes and objects, as compared to scrambled, meaningless stimuli. In this chapter, we will focus on three such brain areas (see Figure 6.10). The *lateral occipital complex* (LOC) lies on the lateral surface of the occipital lobe, just posterior to area MT. Because this region is strongly involved in object recognition, we will consider it as part of the ventral pathway, even though its position is quite dorsal when compared to other object areas. The *fusiform face area* lies on the fusiform gyrus, on the ventral surface of the posterior temporal lobe. The *parahippocampal place area* lies on the parahippocampal gyrus, which lies just medial to the fusiform gyrus on the ventral surface of the temporal lobe.

2.8 Lateral occipital complex (LOC)

The lateral occipital complex seems to have a general role in object recognition and responds strongly to a variety of shapes and objects (Malach *et al.*, 1995). Figure 6.14 shows an example of the neural activity in LOC compared to V1. As the picture becomes more and more scrambled, V1 continues to respond and even gives a larger response, whereas activity in LOC declines. This shows that LOC prefers intact shapes and objects more than scrambled visual features.

This region seems to represent the particular shapes of objects. Presumably, different neurons in this region respond best to different kinds of objects. Because human brain imaging lacks the resolution to measure the object preferences of individual neurons, another method to test for object selectivity is to measure *neural adaptation* to a particular shape. This involves presenting two objects in a row – if the same object shape is presented twice in a row, then a region with object-selective neurons should adapt to the repeated shape and respond more weakly the second time around. This is exactly what LOC does, even when the repeated object is presented in a new location or in a different format so that retinotopic visual areas (V1–V4) won't adapt to the image (Grill-Spector *et al.*, 1999; Kourtzi and Kanwisher, 2001).

2.9 Fusiform face area (FFA)

Neurophysiological studies have shown that face-selective neurons can be found in many parts of the temporal lobe of monkeys. Some of these *face cells* show remarkable precision in what they respond to and might respond best to a face of a particular identity, facial expression, or to a particular viewpoint of a face (e.g. right profile). Usually, these face cells can be found intermixed with neurons that respond to different types of objects, which led scientists to believe that there

might not be a part of the brain that is dedicated to processing faces.

However, human neuroimaging studies have shown that there is a region in the fusiform gyrus, called the *fusiform face area* (FFA) that responds more strongly to faces than to just about any other category of objects (Kanwisher *et al.*, 1997). This region responds more to human, animal and cartoon faces than to a variety of non-face stimuli, including hands, bodies, eyes shown alone, back views of heads, flowers, buildings and inanimate objects (Kanwisher *et al.*, 1997; McCarthy *et al.*, 1997; Tong *et al.*, 2000; Schwarzlose *et al.*, 2005). In a recent study, researchers tried scanning the brains of monkeys to see if they might also have a face-selective area in the ventral temporal cortex and it turns out that they do too (Tsao *et al.*, 2006). The researchers could then record the activity of single neurons in this face area and discovered that 97 per cent of the neurons in this region responded more to faces than to other kinds of objects. Moreover, these neurons were very good at telling apart different identities of faces but poor at telling apart different identities of objects, suggesting they may have an important role in recognizing and telling apart different faces. Because this region is very small, this highly face-selective region that consists almost entirely of face cells was never discovered before. As we will see, this region seems to be important for the conscious perception of faces.

2.10 Parahippocampal place area (PPA)

The parahippocampal place area (PPA) is another strongly category-selective region that responds best to houses, landmarks, indoor and outdoor scenes (Epstein and Kanwisher, 1998). In comparison, this brain area responds more weakly to other types of stimuli, such as faces, bodies or inanimate objects. Because this region responds to very different stimuli than the fusiform face area, many studies have taken advantage of the different response properties of the FFA and PPA to study the neural correlates of visual awareness, as we will see later.

3.0 THEORIES OF VISUAL CONSCIOUSNESS: WHERE DOES IT HAPPEN?

So is it possible to say where along this cascade of neural activity consciousness is really happening? Is it possible to point to a particular set of neurons or a particular brain area and say, *There it is . . . , there is the place in my brain where I am experiencing the visual world in my mind*?

It turns out that the answer is not so simple, but scientists are gathering important clues. Even if a person's eyes are closed or a person can no longer see because of damage to the eyes or to the LGN, it is still possible for a person to 'experience seeing' if electrical stimulation is applied to their primary visual cortex. In other words, it is possible to bypass stimulation of the retina and the LGN and induce visual experiences by directly stimulating area V1.

Is it possible to bypass the primary visual cortex and induce a clear visual experience? We don't know the definite answer yet but, so far, the answer seems to be 'no'. Primary visual cortex seems to be important for our ability consciously to perceive any visual feature, while higher visual areas may have a more specialized role in perceiving certain visual features or objects (Tong, 2003). As we will see in the remainder of this chapter, different cortical visual areas seem to play different roles in our conscious visual experience. An emerging view is that many of the same brain areas and neurons involved in processing specific kinds of visual stimuli, such as orientation, motion, faces or objects, are also involved in representing these types of stimuli in consciousness. Many neurons are more active when a person is conscious of seeing a stimulus than when the stimulus is shown but fails to reach consciousness. So far, there doesn't seem to be any single area in the brain that is solely responsible for consciousness. Instead, many brain areas seem to work together to achieve this remarkable feat. Brain areas involved in attentional processing are also important for ability to perceive and respond to visual and other sensory inputs, a topic that will be covered in Chapter 8.

3.1 Hierarchical and interactive theories of vision

According to one theory of visual consciousness, called the *hierarchical theory* (Crick and Koch, 1995; Rees *et al.*, 2002), consciousness is organized in a hierarchical fashion with increasingly higher visual areas being more closely related to our internal conscious experience (Figure 6.15a). This theory is consistent with the notion that higher visual areas respond to more complex stimuli, such as entire objects and can integrate information about many visual features, which are processed in early visual areas. However, if this is the case, how is it that we can be aware of specific visual features or very fine spatial details, information that is best represented in early visual areas such as V1?

The *interactive theory* of visual consciousness emphasizes a different idea. It turns out that the signals entering the brain do not simply travel up the visual hierarchy: higher visual areas send feedback signals back down to early visual areas, especially to area V1 (Bullier, 2001). There are as many *feedback projections* in the visual system, neurons projecting from higher visual areas to lower visual areas, as there are *feedforward projections*. According to the interactive theory, once a stimulus is presented, feedforward signals travel up the visual hierarchy, activating many neurons in its path, but this feedforward activity is not enough for consciousness. Instead, high-level areas must send feedback signals back to lower-level areas where the feedforward signals came from, so that neural activity returns full circle, forming a neural circuit (Figure 6.15b) (Pollen, 1999; Lamme and Roelfsema, 2000). Why might this combination of feedforward-feedback signals be important for awareness? This may be because higher areas need to check the sig-

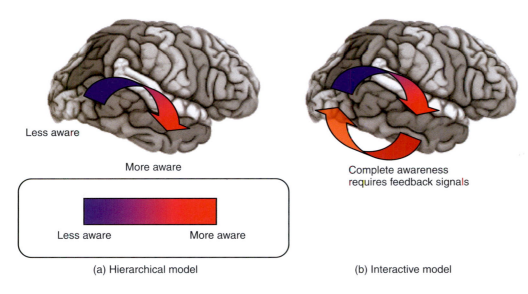

Less aware

More aware

Less aware   More aware

(a) Hierarchical model

Complete awareness
requires feedback signals

(b) Interactive model

FIGURE 6.15 Hierarchical and interactive models of visual awareness. (a) In the hierarchical model, with each step further in visual processing, awareness is more likely to result from that processing. (b) In the interactive model, feedback signals from later processing areas to earlier processing areas are needed to attain awareness. At present, it is not clear which of the two models best describes the way brain activity results in visual awareness.

nals in early areas and confirm if they are getting the right message, or perhaps to link neural representations of an object to the specific features that make up the object.

So far, it is not clear which theory will prove true and odds are that both theories capture some parts of the bigger picture. An emerging view is that our conscious experience may reflect the distributed pattern of brain activity involving many visual areas, a kind of dialogue between neurons in early visual areas, including V1, and high-level areas such as those in the ventral temporal cortex and the parietal lobe. That said, the contribution of each brain area may be somewhat different or in some cases, unique. The next parts of this chapter will describe the highlights of this story.

4.0 BRAIN AREAS NECESSARY FOR VISUAL AWARENESS: LESION STUDIES

In the previous section, we learned about how the neurons in different visual areas respond best to certain visual features, objects, or spatial information. Such findings from single-neuron recordings or human neuroimaging may indicate that a particular brain area has a role in processing a certain type of stimulus, but cannot reveal whether that brain area is actually *necessary* for perceiving that stimulus. Perhaps that brain area could be removed without causing any troubles with perception. For example, if multiple brain areas are involved in processing a particular visual feature (e.g. motion), then damage to any single brain area might not impair the ability to perceive that feature because other intact brain areas would be able to compensate for the loss.

Brain lesion studies are important for understanding what brain areas may be necessary for certain kinds of visual awareness – awareness of color, motion, faces, objects, or the capacity to be aware of seeing anything at all! Brain lesions may be performed experimentally, in animal studies, or may be investigated in humans who have suffered from unfortunate injury to certain parts of the brain, which may result from strokes, tumors, trauma, or neurodegenerative diseases. Visual deficits resulting from damage to certain parts of the visual system can be very debilitating. However, by studying these patients, it may be possible to understand the neural causes of their impairment, which may inform scientists about brain function and eventually lead to new ways to help treat such impairments.

4.1 Consequences of damage to early visual areas

Different visual deficits can result from neural damage at different levels of the visual processing hierarchy. Damage to the retina or optic nerve of one eye can result in monocular blindness – the loss of sight from one eye. Damage to the LGN, the optic radiations that travel to V1, or V1 itself, can lead to loss of vision in the contralateral visual field (see Figure 6.7). Damage to a small part of V1 can lead to a clearly defined scotoma, a region of the visual field where perception is lost. The first retinotopic maps of V1 were actually constructed by mapping the trajectory of bullet wounds of soldiers injured in the Russo-Japanese war and World War I; there was a clear relationship between the location of each case of scotoma and the part of V1 that was injured (Inouye, 1909; Holmes, 1918).

4.1.1 V1 and blindsight

Do lesions to V1 lead to a complete loss of visual function? In 1965, researchers investigated this question in a rhesus monkey named Helen, after the majority of visual cortex was removed. For the initial 19 months, Helen displayed behavior that suggested she was completely blind. Gradually however, it seemed that her vision was returning. In time, she could navigate among objects in a crowded room and even reach out to catch a passing fly. Initially, she would only look at and reach for objects when they moved. Then, as time passed, she responded to flashing lights, then a stationary light source and, finally, a stationary dark object against a light background (Humphrey and Weiskrantz, 1967; Humphrey, 1974). This is an excellent example of how *recovery of function* can occur after brain injury. Helen was able to locate salient objects, but seemed unable to recognize them.

Was Helen aware of what she saw, or was she able to perform visually guided actions despite a lack of visual awareness? It is difficult to ask an animal if it is conscious of something or not, but a recent study of monkeys with unilateral V1 lesions suggests that they might not be aware of what they see. In this study, monkeys were able to report the locations of objects in their 'blind' hemifield accurately if they were forced to make a choice between two options. However, if they were given the choice of reporting whether an object was presented or not and an object was sometimes presented in the good hemifield, in the blind hemifield, or not at all, they would fail to report objects presented in the blind hemifield (Cowey and Stoerig, 1995; Stoerig *et al.*, 2002). It is as if these objects were not 'seen'.

Interestingly, humans with V1 lesions may show similar above-chance performance, even though they report a lack of visual experience in their blind hemifield. Patient DB suffered extreme migraines because of a venous tumor lodged in his right calcarine cortex (V1). Surgical removal of the tumor led to the loss of his right primary visual cortex. As you might expect, this procedure left him practically blind in his left visual field. Interestingly, however, when he was systematically tested in his blind hemifield, his performance suggested otherwise.

Weiskrantz et al. (1974) reported that when DB was asked to point to a target in his blind visual field, DB claimed he could see nothing at all, yet he could point quite accurately to the location of the light source. He could also accurately report whether a stick was angled vertically or horizontally. This ability to perform visual tasks at above-chance levels, despite the patient's reports of lacking any visual impressions, is known as *blindsight*. In different experiments, his task was to discriminate between Xs and Os. His performance was quite accurate and improved as a function of the size and duration of the stimuli. During all these experiments DB insisted that he saw nothing. Interestingly, when pressed, he reported sometimes having the feeling of 'smoothness' or 'jaggedness' in discriminating the Xs and Os, but denied that these feelings were associated with any visual experience. So how is this possible? How can DB point to or discriminate visual stimuli without being able to see them?

These findings suggest that there can be dissociations between visual processing in the brain and a person's subjective awareness – sufficient information is reaching DB's visual system to allow him to make forced-choice discriminations, but this information is not sufficient to support awareness (Weiskrantz, 1986). However, one concern is whether visual awareness is completely absent in blindsight. Patients might be reluctant to report weak visual impressions that are nonetheless sufficient for making forced-choice discriminations. Similar effects can occur in normal subjects under near-threshold conditions. Some blindsight patients report residual impressions of salient moving stimuli, which they describe as 'black moving on black', but normally they report seeing nothing when shown static stimuli. Vision in blindsight is severely degraded, but not always completely absent.

Intact extrastriate cortex may be crucial for blindsight, as patients who have had an entire hemisphere removed show little evidence of residual visual abilities (Faubert et al., 1999). Although the pathway from retina to LGN to V1 provides the vast majority of visual input to cortex, several alternative *subcortical* pathways project to extrastriate areas, bypassing V1. Single-unit recordings in monkeys indicate that visual information can still reach extrastriate areas after V1 has been lesioned. Although firing rates are reduced, a substantial proportion of neurons in motion area MT and V3 remain selectively responsive to visual stimuli (Rodman et al., 1989; Girard et al., 1991). Recent neuroimaging studies show that unperceived stimuli presented to the blind hemifield still evoke robust fMRI responses from motion-sensitive area MT, color-sensitive area V4 and regions involved in object perception (Goebel et al., 2001). Thus, considerable stimulus selectivity is maintained in extrastriate cortex, yet this activity appears insufficient to support awareness in the absence of V1. This is consistent with the predictions of *interactive models*. However, it remains possible that extrastriate signals are too weak or degraded to support conscious perception but sufficient to support forced-choice discrimination.

4.2 Extrastriate lesions – damage outside area V1

Lesions to V1 can eliminate almost all visual awareness in the corresponding areas of visual space, even though sufficient visual information seems to be reaching extrastriate areas to support blindsight behavior. This in itself informs us as to the role of V1 in the mediation of visual awareness. So what happens when extrastriate areas are damaged?

4.2.1 Motion blindness

Perhaps because we are so sensitive to seeing motion, it is very rare for brain damage to lead to a complete loss of motion perception. However, there is a striking example of one patient who can no longer perceive motion after suffering strokes leading to large bilateral lesions that encompassed area MT and extensive surrounding areas. For this patient, the world appeared to be a series of still snapshots, like living in a strobe-lit world. Simple tasks like crossing the street became dangerous, because she could not tell how fast the cars were approaching (Figure 6.16a). Even pouring a cup of coffee became a challenge, since she couldn't tell how fast the liquid was rising, so the cup would overflow.

Other studies have found that smaller lesions just to area MT usually lead to more moderate deficits in the ability to perceive motion and both patients and animals may also show considerable recovery over time (Plant et al., 1993; Pasternak and Merigan, 1994). So it seems

(a)

(b)

FIGURE 6.16   Color and motion blindness. (a) Damage to motion area MT in both hemispheres can lead to a loss of motion perception: *akinotopsia*. Patients describe seeing multiple still frames instead of smooth motion. This can make simple tasks like crossing the road challenging and dangerous. (b) Damage to color areas in only one hemisphere of the cortex can result in a loss of color perception to one side of visual space. Cortical color blindness is called *achromotopsia*.

that area MT is very important for motion perception, but other visual areas can contribute to motion perception even when MT is damaged.

4.2.2 Cortical color blindness

Damage to ventral area V4 can lead to cortical color blindness or what is sometimes called *achromotopsia* (Meadows, 1974a; Bouvier and Engel, 2006). Patients report that the world appears to be drained of color, almost like shades of gray, perhaps like the illustration in Figure 6.16b. These patients can still perceive the boundaries between colors, but have difficulty with identifying the colors themselves. Achromotopsia is typically associated with lesions that include area V4 and possibly regions just anterior to area V4. Damage to one hemisphere can even lead to selective loss of color perception in the contralateral visual field.

4.3 Damage to ventral object areas

4.3.1 Visual agnosia

Patients with *visual agnosia* have difficulties with recognizing objects because of impairments in basic perceptual processing or higher-level recognition processes. Such patients can still recognize objects by using other senses such as touch, hearing or smell, so the loss of function is strictly visual. The word, agnosia, can be translated from Greek as meaning, 'to lack knowledge of', so visual agnosia implies a loss of visual knowledge.

Here, we will discuss three types of visual agnosia: apperceptive agnosia, associative agnosia, and prosopagnosia. Patients with *apperceptive agnosia* can still detect the appearance of visually presented items, but they

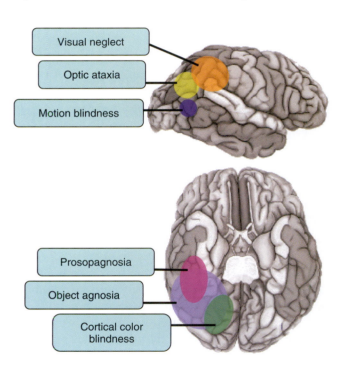

FIGURE 6.17   Visual deficits and brain areas. The areas of the brain in which damage can result in the associated visual deficit. Here, the areas are only shown on one hemisphere, although for some deficits like motion blindness damage to both hemispheres is required.

have difficulty perceiving their shape and cannot recognize or name them. These patients usually fail at shape-copying tests and may have difficulty copying very simple shapes, such as a circle, square, or perhaps even a single tilted line. Carbon monoxide poisoning is a frequent cause of apperceptive agnosia, as this can lead to profuse damage throughout the occipital lobe.

Remarkably, some apperceptive agnosics show evidence of unconscious visual processing of visual features

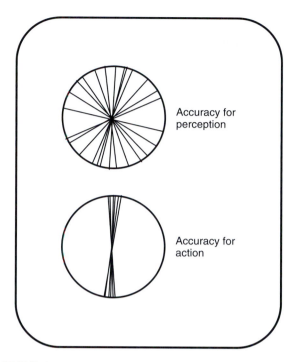

FIGURE 6.18 She can do it, but can't report it. Results from subject DF. Each line represents one of DF's attempts at either matching the orientation of a mail slot or actually posting a letter into it. The top panel shows DF's attempts at matching the orientation of the slot to the card (no execution of action). Here, the lines are distributed around the circle suggesting that DF had trouble in perceiving the orientations. However, the lower panel shows DF's accuracy in posting the card into the oriented slot, adjusted so that each correct orientation is vertical. Because the lines are all grouped around vertical this suggests that DF is accurate when executing the action of posting. Patient DF can post the letters with no problem; her hand knows what to do. But when asked to match the orientation of the slot, DF performs very badly.

they cannot consciously perceive. Goodale *et al.* (1991) tested an apperceptive agnosic patient, DF, who had difficulty reporting the orientation of simple lines or real objects. When asked to report the orientation of a narrow slot cut into the face of a drum, she was unable to report the angle of the slot and made many errors (Figure 6.18, top panel; the drum was rotated to a new orientation on each trial). However, when asked to post a card through the slot, she could do so with remarkable accuracy (Figure 6.18, lower panel) and was even surprised by her own ability to do so. Surprisingly, when she was asked just to hold the letter by her side and rotate it to match the angle of the slot, her performance was poor once again and she reported that the slot seemed 'less clear' than when she was allowed to post the card. What can account for this behavioral dissociation between DF's ability to report the angle of the slot and to perform a visually guided action?

Patient DF provides strong evidence to suggest that there are separate pathways for processing 'what' an object is and 'where' it is with respect to performing a visually guided action. According to Goodale and Milner, patient DF has damage to the ventral visual pathway but intact processing in the dorsal pathway, a claim that has recently been supported by brain imaging studies (James *et al.*, 2003). They propose that the dorsal system is not only responsible for processing 'where' objects are, but also 'how' actions can be performed towards a particular object, such as pointing or reaching for that object. Apparently, visual processing in the dorsal system is not accessible to consciousness – the patient can't report the orientation of the slot – yet the dorsal system can guide the right action. Complementary studies of patients with *optic ataxia* have revealed the opposite pattern of visual deficits, indicating a *double dissociation* between conscious visual perception and visually guided action. Optic ataxia typically results from damage to the parietal lobe, which is part of the dorsal pathway. These patients can perceive visual orientations and recognize objects well, but have great difficulty performing visually guided actions.

Associative agnosia refers to the inability to recognize objects, despite apparently intact perception of the object. For example, when asked to copy a simple picture, patients with associative agnosia manage to do a reasonable job, especially if given enough time. In comparison, this task would almost be impossible for an apperceptive agnosic.

Dr Oliver Sacks described a patient who, as a result of brain injury, 'mistook his wife for a hat'. The patient had great difficulty identifying objects, even though his vision was otherwise normal and he could describe the features of what he saw. When presented with a rose from Dr Sacks' lapel, the patient described it as 'a convoluted red form with a linear green attachment', but only upon smelling it did he realize that it was a rose. When his wife came to meet him at the doctor's office, he accidentally reached for her head when he wanted to retrieve his hat from the coat rack (Sacks, 1985).

Associative agnosia usually results from damage to the ventral temporal cortex. Typically, associative agnosics will have difficulty recognizing a variety of objects, especially objects that are all from a single category, such as faces. However, as we will see below, this is often but not always the case.

Although most patients with visual agnosia will have difficulty with recognizing both faces and objects, there are some remarkable exceptions that have been reported. Patients with *prosopagnosia* are still able to recognize objects well, but have great difficulty recognizing or telling apart faces (Bodamer, 1947; Meadows, 1974b). Deficits can be severe; some prosopagnosic patients can no longer recognize close family members or friends and, instead, must rely on other cues such as the person's voice or clothing to recognize that person. Some patients can no longer recognize their own face in photos or even in the mirror.

Is prosopagnosia really due to a specific impairment in face recognition? Maybe face recognition is just more difficult than other forms of object recognition. After all, faces are very visually similar to one another – every face has the same basic shape and configuration of features, whereas objects are much more distinct from one another (see Box 6.1 for discussion).

Studies have revealed a few patients who can discriminate between subtle differences in objects but can no longer distinguish between faces. For example, a prosopagnosic farmer became very poor at recognizing human faces but could still recognize the different sheep in his flock (McNeil and Warrington, 1993). Another patient could no longer recognize upright faces accurately and was actually better at recognizing upside-down faces, which is just the opposite of normal subject performance (Farah *et al.*, 1995). What might be the reason for this? According to one theory, the brain may have specialized mechanisms for processing upright faces, whereas upside-down faces are processed by a general object recognition system (see the face inversion demonstration in Figure 6.19). So, if the face recognition system is damaged in a prosopagnosic patient, then this system might lead to automatic errors when the patient is presented with an upright face. However, upside-down faces would not be automatically processed by this system, thereby allowing the object recognition system to take over the task.

Perhaps the strongest evidence for some separation between face and object recognition systems comes from a study of a very unusual object agnosic patient, CK, who was very impaired at recognizing objects but could recognize upright faces just as well as normal subjects (Moscovitch *et al.*, 1997). Remarkably, if the faces were turned upside-down, CK became severely impaired, performing six times worse than normal participants under these conditions. Apparently, CK has an intact system for processing upright faces, but the system responsible for processing objects and upside-down faces is badly damaged. Taken together, evidence from patient CK and prosopagnosic patients provide evidence of a double dissociation between the visual processing of upright faces as compared to objects and upside-down faces.

What type of brain damage leads to prosopagnosia? Prosopagnosia can result from bilateral damage around the regions of the lateral occipital cortex, inferior temporal cortex and the fusiform gyrus (Meadows, 1974b; Bouvier and Engel, 2006). In some cases, unilateral damage to the right hemisphere may lead to this impairment. Because lesions are usually quite large and might damage fiber tracts leading to a critical brain region, it is difficult to identify a precise site. Nonetheless, the brain lesion sites associated with prosopagnosia appear to encompass the fusiform face area and extend much more posteriorly.

4.4 Damage to dorsal parietal areas

Damage to the posterior parietal lobe (or superior temporal gyrus) can lead to a striking global modulation of visual awareness called *neglect*, in which a patient completely ignores or does not respond to objects in the contralateral hemifield (Driver and Mattingley, 1998). Patients with right parietal damage may ignore the left half of the visual field, eat just half of the food on their plate or apply make-up to just half of their face. They may also ignore sounds or touches coming from their left.

This syndrome can resemble a disorder of visual perception. However, neglect happens in the absence of damage to the visual system and can involve multimodal deficits, including motor and tactile deficits. Moreover, when patients are instructed to attend to the neglected field they can sometimes respond to these stimuli (Posner, 1980). So this syndrome, rather than an inability to perceive stimuli is more a deficit of *attention*. Without specific cuing, patients find it difficult to perceive objects in their neglected field. We will not spend much time delving into the many interesting facets of visual attention as an entire chapter is dedicated to it (see Chapter 8).

Bilateral lesions to parietal areas can lead to a much more profound deficit called *Balint's syndrome*, which is primarily a disruption of spatial attention. It can be characterized by three main deficits: (1) *optic ataxia*, the inability to point to a target; (2) *ocular apraxia*, the inability voluntarily to shift gaze; and (3) *simultanagnosia*, the inability to perceive more than one object in the visual field simultaneously, even when the objects occupy a common region of space. People with Balint's syndrome can often appear blind because, in fact, they can only focus on one region of visual space or one object at a time and find it hard voluntarily to shift their attention to different locations. These results again highlight the importance of attention-related brain areas in supporting visual awareness.

BOX 6.1   How are faces and objects represented in the brain?

There are two primary theories about how the visual system manages to process and recognize objects and faces. The brain could either do it in a *modular* fashion, with distinct modules for processing faces, or the processing could be done in a *distributed* way across multiple areas of the ventral temporal cortex. According to the modular view, object perception is broken down into neural modules, specific areas of the brain that specialize in processing a particular object category. Research suggests that the fusiform face area (FFA) might be a specialized module for the processing and recognition of upright faces (Kanwisher *et al.*, 1997; Tsao *et al.*, 2006). In addition, an area that responds to the presentation of places (e.g. a house) seems also to be a specialized module (Epstein and Kanwisher, 1998). This area has become known as the parahippocampal place area (PPA). This trend for modular representation of objects does not span every object, in fact it is primarily observed only in the two above-mentioned cases. For example, there is not a banana or shoe area in the human brain.

An interesting twist on the modular hypothesis is the *expertise hypothesis*, which proposes that the so-called fusiform face area is actually specialized for expert object recognition (Gauthier *et al.*, 2000). We probably spend more time looking at faces than at any other object (especially if

you include watching faces on TV). Just stop a moment and think about how much information you can get from all the subtle changes in someone's face when you're talking to them and you soon realize you are indeed a face expert. It has been proposed that the FFA is responsible for the recognition process of any object we are 'experts' at. Research shows that, while looking at pictures of birds, bird experts show somewhat stronger activity in the FFA than do nonbird experts (Gauthier *et al.*, 2000). Whether the FFA is specific for face recognition or any object of expertise, both cases involved a specialized structure that is distinct from regions of the ventral temporal cortex involved in object processing. Look at the two faces in Figure 6.19 – do you notice anything strange? Now turn the book upside down and look again – now do you see it? This is an example of the face inversion effect. When faces are upside down we are really bad at identifying them. This is an example of how specialized we are at face perception.

The other hypothesis is that the brain processes faces and objects in a distributed way across multiple areas in the ventral pathway. A study by Haxby and colleagues demonstrated that regions outside of the FFA still show differential responses to faces, as compared to other types of stimuli (Haxby *et al.*, 2001). Even if the response difference

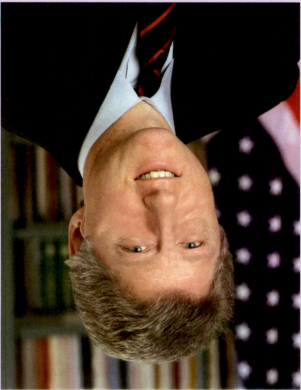

FIGURE 6.19   The face inversion effect. Demonstration of how bad we are at recognizing upside down faces. Look at the two pictures of Bill Clinton, do you notice anything strange? Now turn the page upside down and look again. Now you should see that one of the pictures has been severely distorted. This effect called the face inversion effect, demonstrates just how specialized our visual system is for processing upright faces.

(Continued)

between faces and different objects is quite small in many of these areas, there is enough information across all of these regions outside of the FFA to tell the difference between faces and objects. However, neuropsychological evidence of double dissociations between face recognition and object recognition are difficult to explain according to this account. One possible resolution is that the activity of highly face-selective neurons in regions such as the FFA may be important for telling apart subtle differences between individual faces, but that more distributed activity patterns outside of these highly face-selective regions are enough for telling apart basic differences between faces and objects and perhaps more obvious differences between faces (e.g. male versus female, young versus old).

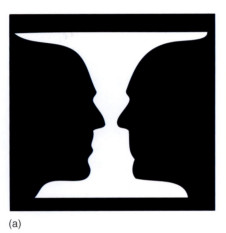
(a)

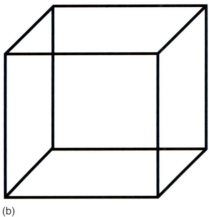
(b)

FIGURE 6.20 Bistable figures. (a) After looking at this figure for a while you will notice that there are two interpretations. One is a central vase, the second one silhouettes of two faces looking in at each other. This image is bistable: while you look at it your perception will alternate between the vase and the faces. (b) This wire-frame cube, typically know as the Necker cube, has two equally likely spatial interpretations. Perception tends to alternate between the config-uration of the closest side projecting upwards and the closest side projecting downwards. Like the vase and silhouettes above, this is bistable. This bistability allows a dissociation of low level stimulation and awareness. The physical pattern does not change, but your awareness of it does!

5.0 LINKING BRAIN ACTIVITY AND VISUAL EXPERIENCE

At any given moment, millions of neurons are firing in the visual part of your brain. The activity of some of these neurons is probably closely linked to what you are consciously perceiving here and now, while the activity of other neurons may be far removed from immediate experience. If scientists could somehow iso-late the neurons that closely reflect a person's conscious experience, would this reveal which neurons or brain areas are central to consciousness and which are not? This search is for the neurons that *correlate* with changes in perceptual awareness or consciousness, hence it has been called the search for the *neural correlates of con-sciousness* or the NCC for short (Crick and Koch, 1995).

The first challenge involves telling apart *stimulus-driven activity* from activity linked to awareness. Not all visual responses are conscious, as can be told from the fact that many visual areas respond well to stimuli even when an animal is anesthetized.

How then is it possible to measure awareness-related activity and separate this from any possible unconscious activity that is driven by the visual stimulus itself? There are many tools scientists can use for this purpose. The next section will discuss some of the most popular and useful methods for isolating neurons whose activity correlates with changes in visual awareness.

5.1 Multistable perception

Have you ever been in the dark, perhaps lying in bed, staring at some strange shape across the room? At one moment it might look like a person, then like some strange static animal, then like a rock statue. After racking your brain to identify this mysterious object, you finally hit the light switch and lo and behold it's only the dim light catching your jacket on the chair. In this example, when vision was difficult and *ambiguous*, perception did something uncommon – it faltered or alternated between different things. This is an example of *multi-stable perception*: the jacket on the chair (the physical stimulus) did not change while your perception of it did! This kind of situation is a valuable tool, as it enables scientists to study changes in visual awareness independ-ent of any changes in the visual stimulus.

There are many examples of *multistable patterns* or ambiguous figures that scientists can use to investigate these neural correlates of consciousness. Patterns that primarily have only two primary interpretations are called *bistable patterns* (Figure 6.20). Try to see if you can perceive both interpretations of each ambiguous figure, the face and the vase and the two views of the Necker cube. Bistable perception can still occur if you keep your eyes fixed on a single point in the middle of the stimulus. In this case, the image on your retinas – and hence the stimulus-driven activity – is pretty much constant over time, while your perception fluctuates.

By looking for brain areas that show activity changes correlated with perceptual changes, scientists can identify the neural correlates of consciousness.

5.2 Binocular rivalry: *what you see is what you get activated*

One of the most powerful and best-studied examples of bistable perception is a phenomenon called *binocular rivalry*. When two very different patterns are shown, one to each eye, because they are so different the brain cannot fuse them together like it would normally do. What then happens is quite striking: awareness of one pattern lasts for a few seconds, then the other pattern seems magically to appear and wipe away the previously visible pattern. It is like the two patterns are fighting it out in the brain for your perceptual awareness! If you can get your hands on a pair of red-green filter glasses then you can experience binocular rivalry by viewing Figure 6.21a. Otherwise try cross-fusing the two patterns in Figure 6.21b. (To cross-fuse, try letting your eyes cross so the two patterns appear one on top of the other. The dots in the center and surrounding square should fuse.

If these demos work for you, you should see one pattern, while the other is completely invisible, almost like closing one eye and then the other.)

What happens in the brain during binocular rivalry? Tong *et al.* (1998) tackled this problem by focusing on two category-selective areas in the ventral temporal lobes, the FFA and the PPA. They used red-green filter glasses to present a face to one eye and house to the other eye while measuring fMRI activity from these brain areas (Figure 6.21c). In this study, participants might first perceive the house, then flip to the face and then back again – as is typical of binocular rivalry (Figure 6.22a). Remarkably, the FFA was active only when subjects reported that they saw the face. Likewise, the PPA was active only when the participants reported that they saw the picture of the house (Figure 6.22b). Next, the researchers tested physical alternations between two the pictures, switching one picture on while switching the other off. The resulting stimulus-driven responses in the FFA and PPA were about the same strength as those measured during binocular rivalry and, surprisingly, no stronger. It seems that the activity in these brain areas closely mirrors what the observer perceives

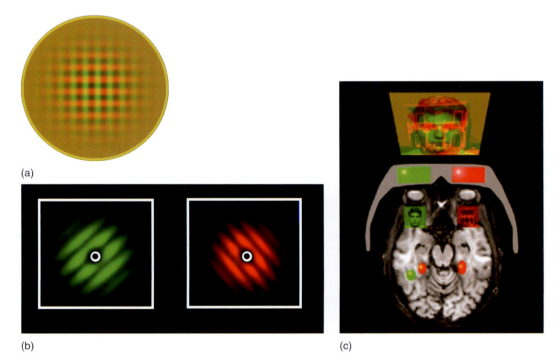

(a)

(b)   (c)

FIGURE 6.21   Binocular rivalry. (a) If you have a pair of red-green filter glasses, this image should produce binocular rivalry. Your awareness should alternate back and forth between vertical and horizontal striped patterns. (b) If you don't have a pair of red-green glasses, try cross-fusing these two patterns. To cross-fuse, you need to cross your eyes so the two patterns line up and appear to be on top of one another. The surrounding squares can help you do this. Line up the square outline and the bullseye dot in the middle. (c) Schematic of how Tong *et al.* (1998) used red-green glasses to attain binocular rivalry in the fMRI scanner and the FFA and PPA where they found activity that correlated with awareness.

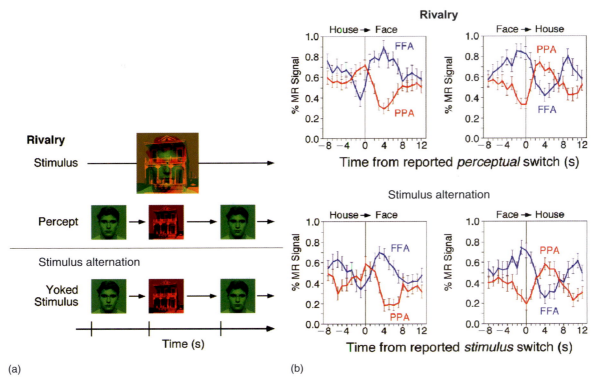

FIGURE 6.22   The stimuli and data from Tong *et al.* (1998). (a) Top panel shows the binocular rivalry condition. Subjects experienced first the face, then the house, then the face etc. Lower panel shows a control condition with no binocular rivalry; the images were switched on and off the screen. (b) Top panel shows the fluctuations in activity in both the FFA (blue) and PPA (red) during binocular rivalry. When each image became perceptually dominant, activity in the corresponding area increased. Lower panel shows the neural response in the same areas to the control condition with no binocular rivalry. The alternations in activity in both conditions were around the same size. *Source*: Tong *et al.*, 1998.

during rivalry and doesn't reflect the temporarily suppressed stimulus that is still activating the retina.

Other brain imaging studies have found that activity at earlier stages of visual processing is closely linked to what the observer perceives during binocular rivalry. For example, strong awareness-related modulations have been found in human V1 (Polonsky *et al.*, 2000; Tong and Engel, 2001), and even in the lateral geniculate nucleus (Haynes *et al.*, 2005; Wunderlich *et al.*, 2005). These results favor the notion that activity in early visual areas may be important for awareness, as is suggested by the *interactive model*. However, scientists are still trying to discover whether the interactive model or hierarchical model of awareness is a better description of the way the brain works.

Another approach is to train monkeys to report which of two patterns is dominant during binocular rivalry (Figure 6.23). This takes some training but can be done by providing fruit juice rewards for the monkey. Then, while the monkeys report their perception during rivalry, researchers can measure the activity of single neurons in different parts of the brain. These studies find strong modulations in the ventral temporal cortex that match the monkey's reported perception during rivalry (Sheinberg and Logothetis, 1997). In fact, around 85 per cent of the neurons recorded in the temporal lobe showed these modulations. Although related studies have found weaker effects of rivalry in the early visual areas of monkeys (Leopold and Logothetis, 1996), the studies described above reveal that it is indeed possible to study the neural correlates of consciousness in both monkeys and humans.

5.3   Visual detection: *did you see it?*

Another way to separate physical stimulation and perceptual awareness is to get people to do a *visual detection* task. Here, a subject has to detect and say when they see a particular pattern. The researcher makes the pattern harder and harder to see, so on different instances the pattern might be easy to see while at others times almost impossible and sometimes it won't even be there. Because this task gets difficult, people will get it wrong sometimes. There will be occasions when someone

FIGURE 6.23 Monkeys and binocular rivalry. Illustration of monkey doing a perceptual binocular rivalry task, while researchers record from neurons in the monkey's brain, as in Sheinberg and Logothetis, (1997). *Source*: Blake and Logothetis, 2002.

reports seeing the pattern when it wasn't even presented and other times when they will miss the pattern and report seeing nothing. When this kind of experiment is done in the fMRI scanner and the pattern is presented to subjects, we can see the pattern of brain activity corresponding to the visual pattern. Also, when no pattern is displayed and subjects report that they don't see the pattern (*true negative*), we don't see that type of brain activity for the pattern. However, what do you think happens when someone gets it wrong? This is the case when no pattern is actually presented but the subject thinks they saw something and so reports 'yes the pattern was there' (*false positive*). Interestingly, activity in areas V1, V2 and V3 closely follows what we think we saw. In other words, on trials where a faint stimulus is presented but the subject fails to detect it, activity is much weaker in these areas (Ress and Heeger, 2003). However, if no stimulus is presented but the subject mistakenly thinks that a faint stimulus was presented, it turns out that activity is greater in V1, V2 and V3 on these trials.

What accounts for these fluctuations in activity level from trial to trial? This has been attributed to trial-to-trial variability in neural activity or *neural noise* in the system. Your memory of the pattern could 'shape' the random neural activity present in sensory areas, tipping the balance and making you think you saw the pattern. This is another example of how the brain's activity may closely reflect the phenomenal experience of seeing something, even when nothing was actually presented. This is interesting because it demonstrates that it doesn't matter what physical pattern is presented to a person, what does matter is what is happening in their brain!

5.4 Constructive perception: *more to vision than meets the eye . . .*

If you drive a car then you probably know what a blind spot is – for the driver it's the area behind the car that cannot be seen in the side or rear view mirrors. Our eyes also have a *blind spot*, at the back of the retina where the axons of the retinal ganglion cells meet to form the optic nerve as it exits the eye (see Figure 6.3b). There are no photoreceptors in the blind spot and hence we are blind in that area.

It is easy to demonstrate the blind spot. Look at the diagram in Figure 6.24a. Close your left eye, look directly at the cross with your right eye and move the textbook close to your nose, then move it slowly away from your face, while keeping your eye fixed on the cross. At the right distance, which should be around 12 inches (30 cm) away from the page, you should notice the dot vanish. As the image of the dot on your retina moves into the blind spot, it disappears!

Hopefully this demonstration worked on you, and perhaps you are thinking. . . . wait a minute, if there is a blind spot in my vision all the time then why don't I see a hole in my vision when I look around at things with one eye covered? Well, the brain does something remarkable, it actually *fills in* perception of the blind spot. The brain uses the visual information from around the blind spot to infer what should be in the blind spot and it constructs awareness of what it 'thinks' should be there. Filling-in at the blind spot is an example of *constructive perception* or *perceptual filling-in*.

Another way to demonstrate the filling-in can be seen by viewing Figure 6.24b. Move the page around until the gap between the lines is in the blind spot. When each group of lines is abutting the blind spot, what you will see are continuous long lines. The red dot should be replaced by one continuous set of lines. The brain fills in the path of the lines so you don't see the red dot in the gap anymore. This is a case of perceptual filling-in; the brain actively creates the perception

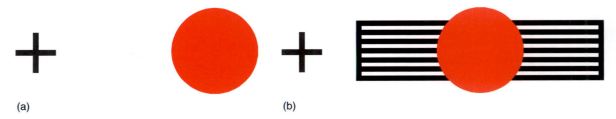

(a)   (b)

FIGURE 6.24 Demonstrations of the blind spot. (a) Close your left eye, look directly at the cross with your right eye and move the page up close to your nose, then move it slowly away from your face, while keeping your eye fixed on the cross. At the right distance, which should be around 12 inches (30 cm) away from the page, you should notice the red dot vanish. As the image of the dot on your retina moves into the blind spot, which has no photoreceptors, it disappears! (b) Likewise, notice how the black stripes now fill-in; they become joined and the red dot vanishes.

of a complete object from the separate segments that lie on either side of the blind spot.

Perceptual filling-in not only happens in the blind spot, but also occurs in other parts of the visual field. Notice how the area between the colored lines in Figure 6.25a somehow appears colored. However, careful inspection reveals that this background area is actually just white – no color at all. This illusion is called *neon color spreading* and the experience of color here seems to come from constructive filling-in mechanisms at work in the visual cortex. Recent brain imaging studies have found that activity in V1 is greater in corresponding regions where subjects perceive neon color spreading (Sasaki and Watanabe, 2004). This suggests that neurons as early as V1 may be important for perceptual filling-in and our experience of color, even illusory colors.

During another type of filling-in known as *visual phantoms* (Figure 6.25b), our visual system can also fill in gaps between two patterns. In Figure 6.25b, you may have the impression of dark bands continuing across the blank gap, even though there is no stimulus being presented there at all. Using moving stimuli can further enhance the visual phantom illusion. When we experience this type of filling in, cortical areas V1 and V2 respond as if a real pattern were being presented in the gap (Meng *et al.*, 2005).

Not only can the brain fill in color and patterns, but also motion. If you flash a spot of light in one location, then follow it by a similar flash at a different location at the appropriate time, observers experience the illusion of movement – *apparent motion*. This kind of trick is used all the time in overhead shop signs and it's the basis for why motion films look so smooth and real. If you look at the actual film running through the projector you will find that they are a series of stills that are flashed onto the screen one after another, the experience of smooth motion is simply an illusion. Recent studies have found that the perceived path of apparent motion is represented by neural activity in V1 (Jancke *et al.*, 2004; Muckli *et al.*, 2005). As with the previous examples

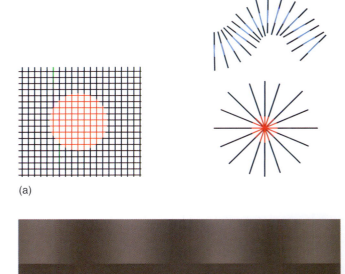

(a)

(b)

FIGURE 6.25 Demonstrations of perceptual filling-in. (a) In these three examples the background is white – it has no color. However, you might notice that the red and the blue tend to fill-in, coloring the white background. (b) The light patches and dark patches in the top and bottom panels tend to give the impression of light and dark sectors along the center strip, even though the center strip is a uniform gray. This illusion works much better when moving.

of color and pattern, the brain seems to fill-in apparent motion both perceptually and neurally, even when there is no physical motion occurring.

From the above examples, it should be clear that the brain can actively construct perceptual representations, even when there is no physical stimulus presented in a particular region of the visual field. Filling-in appears

FIGURE 6.26 These images are called Mooney faces. They are originally made from photos of real faces. Because these face images can be hard to recognize they are useful in studying object recognition. When people do finally recognize the face, you see an increase in neural activity in the fusiform face area.

to occur in early visual areas, as early as V1, suggestive that early visual areas may provide the basis for constructive visual experiences.

5.5 Neural correlates of object recognition

What brain areas are important for object recognition? As we saw in the study of binocular rivalry, activity in the fusiform face area and parahippocampal place area is closely linked to the observer's awareness of faces and houses. Similarly, if subjects are presented with ambiguous figures such as those shown in Figure 6.20a, regions of the ventral temporal cortex show greater activity when recognition switches to the other interpretation. For example, when viewing Rubin's face-vase display, switches to the face percept lead to increases in activity in the fusiform face area.

Other studies have investigated awareness of visually masked objects, which are so briefly presented that they can just barely be recognized. When observers are able successfully to recognize a briefly flashed object, activity is greater in many regions of the ventral temporal cortex than when recognition is unsuccessful (Grill-Spector et al., 2000; Bar et al., 2001). Also, if observers are shown an ambiguous black and white image, like a Mooney face shown in Figure 6.26, right panel, which when shown at different orientations is hard to recognize, activity is much greater in ventral temporal areas when subjects become aware of the hidden object (Dolan et al., 1997; McKeeff and Tong, 2006). Interestingly, in most of these studies, early visual areas don't show a difference between conditions in which observers perceive the object or not. Perhaps what is even more remarkable, when subjects are simply asked to imagine

a face, this can lead to activation of the fusiform face area (O'Craven and Kanwisher, 2000). Likewise, imagining a place or landmark can activate the parahippocampal place area. These studies suggest that simply retrieving a visual memory of a particular object can activate these object areas.

6.0 MANIPULATIONS OF VISUAL AWARENESS

In the previous section, we discussed *correlational methods* of studying conscious perception that relied on finding the neural correlates of consciousness. Knowing that activity in area A correlates with perception B (e.g. seeing leftward motion) provides *correlational evidence* that area A is involved in representing perception B. However, something can be correlated with a particular function without being causal. For example, the engine of a car roars whenever it is working hard, but the roaring sound of the engine isn't what makes the wheels turn. Dampening the sound of the engine won't stop the car from moving, but disrupting the pistons from moving will.

To provide further evidence of the role of a brain area in consciousness, we need to provide *causal evidence* showing that manipulating the activity in area A can *produce* or *disrupt* perception B. There are many causal methods in neuroscience, which involve inducing or disrupting activity in a certain brain area, either temporarily or permanently (e.g. lesion studies). This next section will highlight some of the findings from manipulations of neural activity and visual awareness.

Electrical stimulation of the occipital lobe can elicit subjective visual sensations or what are called *phosphenes*. For example, blind patients who had electrical implants in primary visual cortex reported having their first visual experience in years when this area was stimulated. When small regions were stimulated, the subjects reported seeing phosphenes that looked like 'small grains of rice held at arm's length'.

This seems obvious if we remember that the language of the brain is really electrical. Neurons communicate via weak electrical currents, hence when a current is applied to a collection of neurons it is not surprising that the person experiences some sensation. There are many ways to do this: during a surgical operation neurons can be electrically stimulated or, on a larger scale, an electrical current can be passed through the skull. However, a more recent and less invasive method is transcranial magnetic stimulation (TMS).

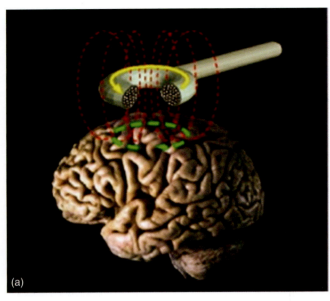

(a)

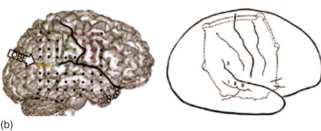

(b)

FIGURE 6.27 Stimulating the brain. (a) A transcranial magnetic stimulation (TMS) coil over the brain. The dashed lines show the magnetic field and the area tissue that is primarily affected. TMS is a valuable research tool to investigate the cause-effect relationship between brain activity and visual awareness. (b) When a collection of these electrodes were stimulated the patient reported the experience of looking down at her own body – an 'out of body experience'. *Source*: Blake and Logothetis, 2002.

6.1 Transcranial magnetic stimulation

Transcranial magnetic stimulation, or TMS, involves rapidly generating a magnetic field outside of the head to induce electrical activity on the cortical surface (Walsh and Cowey, 2000). This is usually done using a handheld TMS coil that can be placed on the surface of the scalp. When the electrical current is switched on the magnetic field is activated – triggering neural activity on the cortical surface (Figure 6.27a). This induced activity can either act as a type of 'visual stimulus' itself, or disrupt ongoing visual activity.

6.1.1 Phosphenes and V1 stimulation

When TMS is applied over early visual areas, there are two primary perceptual consequences. One, when people have their eyes closed they tend to experience a

weak flash of light, a phosphene. As mentioned above, this is attributed to the activation of visual neurons. The second consequence is that you can experience a visual hole or momentary blind spot – a transient *scotoma* in visual stimulation just after the TMS (Kamitani and Shimojo, 1999).

What is interesting is that the type of phosphene people experience corresponds to the area of cortical tissue stimulated with TMS. For example when V1 is stimulated, people report smallish static phosphenes. When area MT (the motion area) is stimulated individuals report moving phosphenes (Pascual-Leone and Walsh, 2001)!

These findings taken alone could be viewed as evidence that these areas are responsible for processing of the corresponding visual features (objects, motion etc.). However, we know that most parts of the brain are joined to most other parts and neural activity can travel very quickly from one location to another, hence it might be the case that when you stimulate one area activity travels out to multiple other areas. So what if you used TMS stimulation at multiple locations at different times? Might this inform us about neural transmission and neural feedback?

6.1.2 TMS and cortical feedback

A recent study provided new evidence to support the role of feedback connections in visual awareness (Pascual-Leone and Walsh, 2001). Motion phosphenes were reliably elicited by applying TMS to area MT/V5 (motion areas) and a second TMS pulse was applied to either V1 or MT at various times before or after the first pulse. Perception of the motion phosphene was selectively impaired when V1 stimulation occurred shortly after MT stimulation (10–40 ms later), but not beforehand. In other words, researchers would first pulse MT, which is higher in the processing hierarchy. Then, at a given time later, they would pulse V1, which is earlier in the stream of processing. When this was done at the right time interval, subjects no longer perceived the phosphenes. This suggests that feedback projections from MT to V1 might be necessary for conscious perception of the phosphenes. The authors concluded that MT activity *alone* might be insufficient to support awareness of motion and that feedback activity to V1 may be necessary for visual awareness. These findings provide support for the interactive theory of visual awareness.

A TMS study of a blindsight patient, GY, (remember that patients with blindsight typically have a large section of V1 damaged) provides some evidence in favor of the feedback re-entrant model of visual awareness

(Cowey and Walsh, 2000). In GY, stimulation of MT elicited motion phosphenes only when applied to the hemisphere housing the intact V1, but not on the side with damaged V1 cortex. So even though area MT was perfectly fine in both cortical hemispheres, stimulating MT on the same side of the head as the damaged V1 did not lead to the perception of phosphenes. In contrast, motion phosphenes were successfully elicited in all normal subjects tested as well as in a retinally blind patient. Further tests of the interactive model should pursue whether direct cortical stimulation of extrastriate areas can elicit phosphenes in patients with V1 damage.

Another fascinating example of the modulation of visual awareness comes from a study in which researchers directly stimulated neurons in a monkey's brain (Salzman *et al.*, 1990). As we mentioned earlier, neurons in cortical area MT respond selectively to particular directions of motion and neurons that prefer similar directions tend to be clustered in cortical columns. In other words, a select bunch of neurons in MT might only be vigorously active when a monkey is presented with rightward motion. In this experiment, researchers directly stimulated some of these direction-selective neurons in the monkey's area MT. They did this while the animal was viewing ambiguous dots moving in many possible directions, while performing a motion discrimination task. This microstimulation biased the animal's judgments toward the direction of motion that the stimulated neurons typically respond to. In other words, it was as if stimulating these neurons led to a stronger perception of that particular motion direction, enough to shift the monkey's impression of motion a fair bit, if the motion in the stimulus was quite ambiguous.

Much more complex perceptual experiences may be triggered by neural stimulation, even what might be called *out-of-body experiences*. An epilepsy patient who (due to the severity of her condition) had electrodes temporarily implanted in her brain reported such experiences. When two specific electrodes were stimulated over the temporal parietal junction (see Figure 6.27b), she reported the novel sensation of falling or floating (Blanke *et al.*, 2002). She described the sensation as 'falling from a height'. Stronger stimulation led to a report of an apparent out-of-body experience. That's right, she claimed actually to experience seeing her body from above, lying in bed. However, she did not see her own face, only from her trunk downwards. This finding is important because the angle she reported seeing her body from was different from what she normally experienced. So, this suggests that familiar experiences (her normal body view) can be combined to form novel experiences of seeing her own body from different angles. This concept has exciting implications for the study of perceptual experience, because it suggests that experiences of an internal origin do not simply have to be a repeat of previous perceptual phenomena.

Stimulation studies allow scientists to pin down the cause-effect relationships between neural activity and perceptual experiences and can therefore reveal what brain areas are responsible for what we see. In essence, it is like taking control of the brain. By directly stimulating the cortex and bypassing sensory organs, such as the retina, it may be possible to identify which brain areas are more directly linked to perceptual experience.

6.2 Unconscious perception

How can something be both unconscious and still be called perception? Wouldn't the fact that you're not aware of something suggest that your brain was unable to process or identify that stimulus? In the current context, we use the term *unconscious perception* to refer to situations when subjects report not seeing a given stimulus, but their behavior or brain activity suggests that specific information about the unperceived stimulus was indeed processed by the brain. Neural activity does not always lead to awareness. Neurons may fire in a stimulus-specific way at many levels of the brain, but this activity may not be strong enough, last long enough, or involve enough neurons or brain areas to lead to awareness. One of the best examples of this comes from neural recordings in animals under anesthesia; visual neurons in many brain areas still show strong stimulus-selective responses. In this section, we will learn that even when a person is fully awake and alert, unconscious visual processing can also occur in many situations.

In a previous section, you learned about how 'what you see is what you get activated' during binocular rivalry. In other words, if you become conscious of a particular stimulus, then neurons in your brain that represent that pattern will become highly active. However, here we will learn that the opposite is not necessarily true. If you have some activity in a given brain area, this does not mean you will necessarily perceive the stimulus. Without *enough* activity in the *right* brain areas, awareness may simply fail: the result is unconscious perception.

When two different stimuli are flashed briefly enough in quick succession, the visual system can no longer separate the two stimuli. Instead, what people perceive is a mix, or a fused blend of the two images. For example, if we were to expose you to a red square, then quickly follow it with a green square, what you might

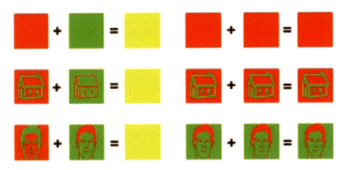

FIGURE 6.28   Red + green = yellow. The red and green combine to form the yellow square of color. Hence, the images of the house and face become invisible when briefly shown one to each eye. However, the brain still responds to these unseen patterns. *Source*: Moutoussis and Zeki, 2002.

experience is a combination of the two – a yellow square. This method can be used to present invisible patterns, such as a face or a house, by flashing red contours on a green background to one eye and the opposite colors to the other eye (Figure 6.28). When subjects were presented with such images in the fMRI scanner, the fusiform face area responded more strongly to faces and the parahippocampal place area responded more to houses, even though subjects were no longer aware of the images (Moutoussis and Zeki, 2002). This is an example of unconscious perception. The activity in ventral temporal parts of the brain could differentiate, to some degree, whether a face or house was presented, even though the subject could not verbally report a difference. So just because an area is somewhat active does not mean we will be aware of what that brain area represents. Perhaps this level of activity is just not enough. Stronger responses were found in these brain areas when just a single red-green pattern was shown so it was clearly visible.

Area MT, a brain area specialized for processing motion, also responds to unperceived motion. When a moving stimulus is presented far out in the periphery of the visual field and is crowded by other stimuli, area MT still responds to motion – even when subjects are not aware of the motion (Moutoussis and Zeki, 2006). In this experiment, the motion stimulus was flanked on two sides by flickering stimuli, making the visual space so busy and cluttered that subjects could not see the motion in the display. Although MT responded somewhat to the perceived motion stimulus, it responded much more strongly when the surrounding flickering stimuli were removed and the motion stimulus was clearly perceived.

In other studies, researchers used binocular rivalry (which we discussed in an earlier section) to render pictures of fearful faces invisible (Figure 6.29a). The expressions of the faces carried emotional content, although the subjects were never aware of seeing the faces. The amygdala, a brain region in the medial temporal lobe that normally responds to emotional stimuli, also responded to the invisible fearful faces (Pasley *et al.*, 2004). Figure 6.29b is a plot of the activity in the amygdala; the red line represents the response of the amygdala to the emotional face images.

It is clear that many brain areas may continue to show stimuli-specific activity despite the fact that we are unaware of that stimulus. One thing this suggests is that even if a brain area is processing a stimulus, this doesn't mean we will *perceive* that stimulus. If neural activity in a given area is not enough to result in awareness, then what is? In most of these studies, greater activity was found when subjects were aware of a stimulus than when they were not, suggesting that a minimum level of activity may be needed to make the difference between no awareness and awareness. A low level of neural activity below a specific *threshold* might not be adequate to result in being aware of a stimulus.

This idea of a neural threshold for visual awareness fits nicely into both the hierarchical and interactive models of visual awareness we discussed earlier. For the hierarchical model, an adequate level of neural activity would have to be maintained in high-level visual areas for awareness to occur. For the interactive model, feedback signals might act to boost neural activity at each level of processing, leading to activity that surpasses the threshold for visual awareness in multiple brain areas. In sum, we can conclude that at least two things are needed for visual awareness: (1) activity in the right neurons or brain areas and (2) activity that exceeds a critical threshold. Further research may show which of these models best describes the brain basis of visual awareness.

7.0 SUMMARY

Vision is perhaps our most important sense modality. It is certainly the one that has seen the most research. Over the last decade or so, scientists have learned a great deal about the neural correlates of conscious and unconscious perception and how the disruption of different brain areas can disrupt specific aspects of visual consciousness. A consistent finding is that primary visual cortex seems to be important for the ability to perceive any visual feature at all, while higher brain

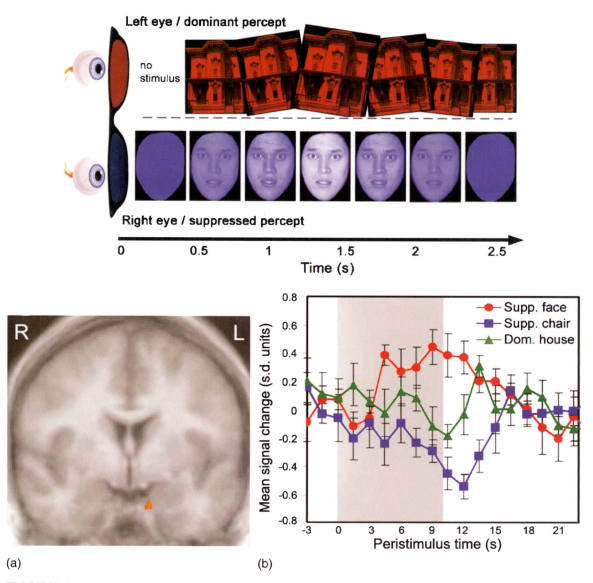

FIGURE 6.29 The emotion is still perceived but not the face. (a) Schematic of the stimulus used in the Pasley *et al.* (2004) study. The red building presented to the left eye suppresses the face in the right eye out of awareness, as in binocular rivalry. The faces have emotional expressions. (b) This graph shows the activity in the amygdala (an emotional response area of the brain). The red plot shows that the activity in the amygdala increases when emotional faces are presented, even though they are out of awareness. The brain cannot see the face, but it can detect the emotion. *Source*: Pasley *et al.*, 2004.

areas may be important for perceiving *particular* visual features or objects. Current evidence provides support for both hierarchical and interactive theories of visual awareness. Future studies will improve our understanding of how the brain gives rise to our subjective visual experiences.

In this chapter, we traced the functional properties of neurons as visual signals travel up from the retina to the primary visual cortex and onward to higher areas in the dorsal and ventral visual pathways. Progressing up the visual pathway, receptive fields gradually become

larger and respond to more complex stimuli, following the hierarchical organization of the visual system.

V1 is selective for many visual features, including orientation, motion and binocular disparity. Damage to V1 can severely impair or eliminate conscious vision, although remaining activity in extrastriate areas may support the ability to detect visual events even without being visually conscious, the condition called blindsight. Extrastriate visual areas (the ones outside of V1) seem to be important for perceiving specific visual features: area V4 is important for color perception and area MT for motion perception. Damage to these areas may lead to selective impairment in the perception of these higher-level features of the visual world.

According to the hierarchical theory, higher extrastriate areas are closely linked to visual awareness whereas V1 is not. In contrast, the interactive theory emphasizes that feedback signals to V1 may be important for awareness. Current evidence provides support for both theories.

Damage to the dorsal pathway can lead to *optic ataxia* (impairments in visually guided actions) or *visual neglect*. Damage to the ventral temporal cortex can lead to impairments in visual perception, object recognition or face recognition. Patients with brain injuries in the ventral and dorsal pathways reveal a dissociation between the conscious perception of basic shapes and orientations and the ability to perform visually guided actions.

In the ventral temporal cortex, some brain regions, such as area LOC, seem to have a general role in object recognition, while other areas, such as the fusiform face area and parahippocampal place area, appear to have more specialized roles. Many studies show that activity in these areas is strongly associated with the conscious perception of objects. Nonetheless, evidence of unconscious processing can be found in many brain areas, including high-level object areas.

8.0 STUDY QUESTIONS AND DRAWING EXERCISES

1   For the brain drawing in Figure 6.30:
    a   Copy the brain figure. Which way is it facing?
    b   Identify the visual regions (labeled) and some of the things they do.
    c   Can you color in the dorsal and ventral streams? What is the difference between their functions?

2   In Figure 6.31, can you describe what is happening in your own words? What is the cat seeing? Which visual areas are likely to be involved? What kind of neural mechanisms improve the ability of the cat to perceive contrasts and boundaries?

3   For Figure 6.32
    a   Draw each figure in color.
    b   What can we learn from (a)? What parts of the visual cortex are likely to be involved?
    c   How about (b)? Are different parts of the visual cortex likely to be involved than in (a)?
    d   For the third image in the figure, what does the subject in the experiment perceive? Why do the colors look mixed together? What is the purpose of this experiment and what are the results?

4   A question to think about: how can we compare conscious and unconscious visual stimuli?

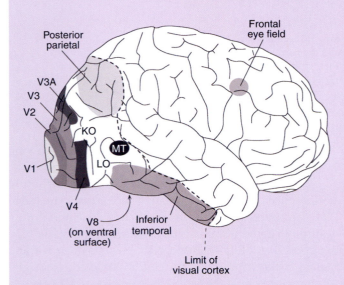

FIGURE 6.30   Visual areas of the human cortex. *Source*: Rosa, 2002.

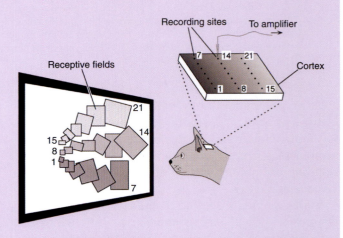

FIGURE 6.31   Recording from the brain of a cat. *Source*: Rosa, 2002.

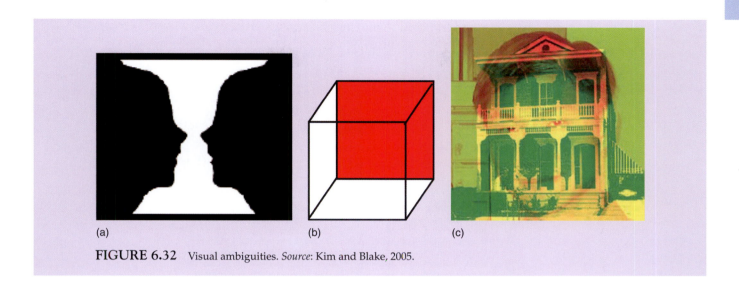

(a)

(b)

(c)

FIGURE 6.32   Visual ambiguities. *Source*: Kim and Blake, 2005.

It was very fortunate that, even in Helmholtz's time, the great anatomical discoveries by Corti (and others) had already made it clear that the vibrating tissue most important for hearing is the basilar membrane of the inner ear, because the cells on which the nerve endings terminate are seated on this membrane. . . . the problem of how we hear was reduced largely to a mechanical question: how does the basilar membrane vibrate when the eardrum is exposed to a sinusoidal sound pressure?

Bekesy, Nobel Prize Lecture (online)

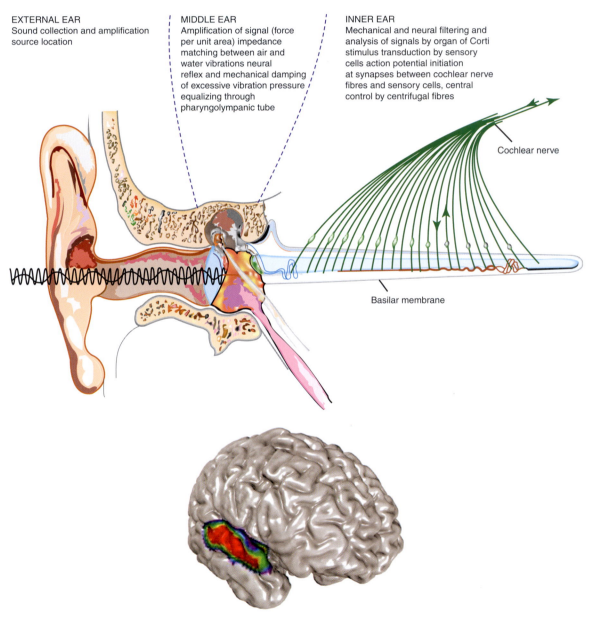

EXTERNAL EAR
Sound collection and amplification
source location

MIDDLE EAR
Amplification of signal (force
per unit area) impedance
matching between air and
water vibrations neural
reflex and mechanical damping
of excessive vibration pressure
equalizing through
pharyngolympanic tube

INNER EAR
Mechanical and neural filtering and
analysis of signals by organ of Corti
stimulus transduction by sensory
cells action potential initiation
at synapses between cochlear nerve
fibres and sensory cells, central
control by centrifugal fibres

Cochlear nerve

Basilar membrane

The auditory system really starts deep inside the ear canal at the ear drum. Air vibrations, which are fast compressions and expansions of the air, vibrate the ear drum, which transmits mechanical vibrations that end up triggering receptors (hair cells) located on the basilar membrane. Axons from the receptor cells combine to make up the auditory nerve, which goes through several stages of processing before reaching cortex. The auditory system is extraordinarily sensitive, able to pick up even the sound of air molecules in very quiet environments. *Sources: Top*, Standring, 2005; *Bottom*, Ramachandran, 2002.

Hearing and speech

Nicole M. Gage

1.0 INTRODUCTION

This chapter provides an overview of how we hear – from simple sounds, to complex speech, to symphonies. We begin with basic information about how we process sounds: from the ear, through the ascending auditory pathways, to auditory cortex. Next, we discuss specific types of sound processing such as speech and music perception. As you can imagine, sound perception

changes throughout life, for example as we acquire speech and language as infants and young children. You might have an intuition – and you would be correct! – that the neural systems underlying sound processing may be set up somewhat differently for people who are skilled musicians or for linguists who speak several languages fluently. Therefore, we will discuss the effects of learning and expertise on brain systems for sound processing and how they differ throughout life and

Cognition, Brain, and Consciousness, edited by B. J. Baars and N. M. Gage
ISBN: 978-0-12-373677-2

Copyright 2007, Elsevier Ltd. All rights reserved.

across individuals. But sound processing does not happen in isolation – what we hear combines with what we see and touch, as well as with our stored memories and experiences.

1.1 A model for sound processing

Our environment is frequently quite noisy with many types of sounds reaching our ears at the same time. Think about a large college classroom before a lecture begins: there are the sounds of students' voices, chairs scraping, doors opening and closing, backpacks being unzipped, books being dropped onto desktops. All of these sounds hit our ears at the same time and yet we have little difficulty in perceiving them as separate events or auditory 'objects'. This process is called *auditory scene analysis* and forms the basis for understanding how the auditory system decodes a complex listening environment (Bregman, 1990). In this chapter, we will discuss how the auditory system decodes this type of auditory scene. We will begin, however, with a functional

framework with which to understand the processes of the auditory system and how they interact with other subcortical and cortical systems.

1.1.1 A working framework for sound perception

In Chapter 2, we discussed a modal model for understanding brain processing. The same general concepts hold for auditory processing: sensory (sound) inputs enter the system and there is a very brief storage (echoic memory) for these inputs (Figure 7.1). Selective attention allows the system to direct its attention to a subset of the inputs for further processing. At this stage, there are complex interactions between the new inputs and existing memory and experiences, as well as with other sensory systems. The ultimate goal or 'action' to be performed is important as well and will affect how information is encoded and stored. It is important to note that this model for auditory processing is not a one-way process, with sounds being decoded, understood, and then stored into long-term memory. There are interactions

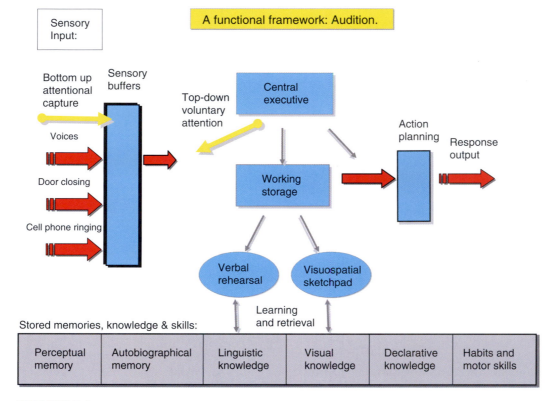

FIGURE 7.1   A functional framework for auditory processing, adapted from the general functional framework presented in Chapter 2. Sensory inputs, such as the sound of someone's voice or a cell phone ring, enter the system (see red arrows on the left side of the figure). There are early influences from bottom up and top down attentional processes (yellow arrows). These inputs make contact with working storage, long-term knowledge, and action systems. It is important to keep in mind that the processes underlying auditory function are highly interactive, with feedforward, feedback and integrative processes.

that occur throughout the encoding of sounds, both within the auditory system itself and across other sensory, cognitive, memory, and motor systems. The anatomy and connectivity of the auditory system reflects this complexity, with multiple stages of processing and neural pathways, including the ascending pathways from the ear to the brain, descending pathways that carry information back to the peripheral system, and many parallel pathways within brain regions and across the two hemispheres.

1.1.2 Limited and large capacity

As we discussed in Chapter 1, brain processes have both limited and large capacity aspects: this is the case for the auditory system. There are some specific limitations in decoding sound inputs. For example, if you present speech through headphones, it is easy to attend to each word uttered. However, if two different speech streams are presented to the two ears, it becomes a very difficult task to try to attend to each stream. In fact, we selectively listen to one stream or the other (Broadbent, 1982). Thus, there are some limits to the capacity for decoding complex sounds entering the auditory system and a role for central executive function in directing attention selectively to some of the sounds in a complex listening environment. On the other hand, our capacity for learning new sounds or auditory objects (such as spoken words) continues throughout life and appears to be virtually unlimited in capacity. In fact, an average adult's vocabulary is estimated at more than 100 000 words. The same is true for recognizing new melodies and the voices of new friends and acquaintances. Therefore, while some capacity limits exist in attending to sounds during perception and encoding, once learned there appear to be virtually no limits regarding the capacity to remember new sound-based items.

1.1.3 Orders of magnitude and levels of analysis

As in other brain systems, auditory processing contains processing units that comprise many orders of magnitude from individual hair cells at the periphery, to single neurons in auditory cortex, to large-scale neural networks in the auditory language system. The auditory system has been studied at each of these levels of analysis in both human and in animal. In this chapter, we will include information that we have learned at each of these levels of analysis. However, a large focus of the evidence presented in this chapter will be on what we have learned about auditory processing at the system level from neuroimaging – positron emission tomography

(PET), magnetic resonance imaging (MRI), functional MRI (fMRI), magnetoencephalography (MEG) and electroencephalography (EEG) – studies. The advent of non-invasive measures to investigate cortical processing has revolutionized the field of cognitive neuroscience and psychology in general. Previously, we relied on data from animal studies, made inferences from behavioral and psychophysical studies with healthy individuals, or investigated sound and language processing in humans who had suffered brain damage due to injury, disease, or stroke. The capability of investigating brain processes in healthy individuals has provided us with a wealth of new information about sound and language processing. It has also provided us with the ability to investigate brainwide processes in large-scale systems that span across multiple brain regions, such as the language system.

1.1.4 Time

Time is a critical aspect of auditory processing: the auditory system differs from the visual system in that all sound processing occurs over time. Nothing 'stands still' in sound processing. Speech, the most complex signal that the auditory system must decode, has differences in speech sounds (phonemes) such as /b/ and /p/ that occur on a scale of 20–30 thousandths of a second (milliseconds), and yet our speech perceptual processes decode these transient differences with ease, even in relatively noisy environments (Gage et al., 1998, 2002).

Thus, the speech decoding system has a high temporal resolution of fine-grained and transient changes at the level of the phoneme. However, the speech system also needs to decode information that changes over a longer time span than those contained within phonemes: syllabic stress (such as the different pronunciation of 'melody' and 'melodic') is an important speech cue and occurs in a time window of approximately 200 ms. Other key information occurs over 1–2 seconds (1000–2000 ms) at the level of a sentence, such as the rising intonation that is associated with asking a question. Thus, each of these time windows – 20, 200, 2000 ms – is critical to the accurate decoding of speech and information extracted from each of these decoding processes must be available for integration in the complex processes underlying the mapping of sound onto meaning (Figure 7.2).

Before we begin our discussion of how the brain processes complicated listening environments, with human voices, complex environmental sounds, music, we need to discuss some basic principles of sound and hearing. We will begin with the physical features of sounds and how these features correspond to psychological aspects of sounds. Next, we will step through the processes and stages of peripheral hearing and subcortical feature extraction.

20 ms   **200 ms**

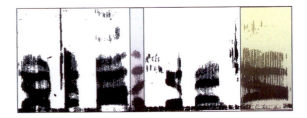

0   1000 ms   2000 ms

FIGURE 7.2   A spectrogram is a picture of the sound-based features in speech. Time is represented on the x-axis and frequency is represented on the y-axis. The darker shading represents higher intensity. Speech contains harmonic content (formants) at specific regions in the spectral (frequency based) aspect of the spectrogram. Here we show a spectrogram showing 3 time scales critical for decoding speech. Upper left: detail of the transients at the onset of a consonant, with transitions that occur on a time scale of ~20 ms. Upper right: detail of the formants in a syllable which occurs on a time of ~200 ms. Bottom: a sentence that occurs on a time scale of ~2000 ms.

1.2 Sound and hearing basics

1.2.1 Physical features of sounds

How does the human auditory system transform sounds into comprehensible speech or recognizable melodies?

Let's begin with how we encode simple sounds at the level of the ear. A physical definition of sound is the vibration that occurs when an object moves in space, producing an audible sound. What we hear is not the vibration itself but the effects of vibration in sound waves that move, or propagate, through space and make contact with our ears. The sinusoid (Figure 7.3) is a basic building block of sound that has three main physical aspects: frequency, intensity and time. The frequency of a sound is the rate of sound wave vibration and is measured as cycles completed per second, or *hertz* (Hz). A sinusoid with 1000 cycles per second has the frequency of 1000 Hz. The human auditory system can detect sounds across a wide range of frequencies, estimated at 20 to 20 000 Hz.

The intensity of a sinusoid reflects the amplitude (or displacement) of the wave within its cycle and over time. In Figure 7.3 (left panel), we show a 1000 Hz sinusoidal tone in the time domain, with time on the x-axis and intensity on the y-axis. On the right panel of Figure 7.3, we show the same tone in the frequency domain, with the frequency (Hz, or cycles per second) on the y-axis and time on the x-axis. Note that the spectral energy of a sinusoidal tone is limited to a single narrow band, so a 1000 Hz tone has energy centered only at 1000 Hz. This is why a sinusoidal tone is frequently referred to as a 'pure' tone.

Of course, most sounds that we hear are more complex than a pure tone. A piano chord, a car horn honking, a person's voice, all have complicated structures. How do we describe these complex sounds in terms of the three physical parameters, frequency, intensity, and time? Joseph Fourier (1768–1830), a Frenchman who lived in the Napoleon I era, developed a series of theorems that describe how even complex signals can be separated into a series of simpler constituent parts through what

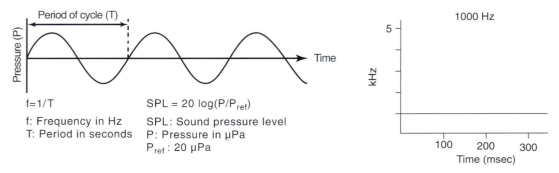

FIGURE 7.3   Left panel shows a sinusoidal tone. Time is represented on the x-axis, amplitude is shown on the y-axis. The frequency of the sinusoid is based upon the number of cycles per second, thus a 1000 Hz tone has 1000 cycles per second. Right panel shows the same sinusoidal tone with its frequency focused on 1000 Hz. Sinusoidal tones have a single frequency, which is why they are referred to as 'pure' tones. Most sounds we hear are spread over multiple frequency bands. *Sources*: *left*: Brown, 2003, *right*: Boatman, 2006.

is now called a *Fourier analysis* (Fourier, 1822). The work of Fourier was advanced by Georg Ohm (1789–1854), who proposed that the separation of complex sounds into simpler sinusoids occurred at the ear in hearing.

While we have mentioned the frequency, intensity, and time of a sound as comprising the basic physical features, sounds have other qualitative aspects. For example, if you heard someone play Middle C (261 Hz) on a piano while at the same time an oboist played Middle C, could you tell these sounds apart in spite of the fact that they are of identical frequency? Of course you could easily do so, suggesting that there must be many more dimensions in sound quality than just frequency. In this example, the *timbre* or quality of the note helps us distinguish between musical instruments, even when the notes they produce are identical in frequency. Timbre also allows us to distinguish human voices.

1.2.2 A scale for sound intensity

The dynamic range of the human hearing system is extremely broad: we can hear barely perceptible sounds of very low intensity and very loud sounds that actually cause pain. This range has been calculated as ranging from 1 unit of intensity to 1 000 000 000 000 000 (10^{15}) units. This range is so large that it is difficult to deal with using normal numbering schemes. We typically use a logarithmic scale in order to deal more easily with the huge range in units of intensity, the *decibel* (dB) system. The dB scale is a relative (not absolute) scale and is based upon the ratio of two quantities: the relative intensity of a sound based on either the sound pressure level (SPL) in the air where hearing is occurring, or based upon the hearing threshold or sensation level (SL) of an individual. (Note: there are many other ratios used in describing hearing, we use SPL and SL here because they are common ratios used to describe sound intensity.) Human hearing ranges from ~1 (threshold) to 150 dB SPL (Figure 7.4).

1.2.3 Psychological aspects of sounds

While sounds have physical parameters (frequency, intensity, time) that can be measured with a fine degree of accuracy, how do we know how they are perceived? The physical parameter of frequency, or cycles per second, corresponds to the psychological or perceptual quality of *pitch*. Pitch is a subjective perception, usually

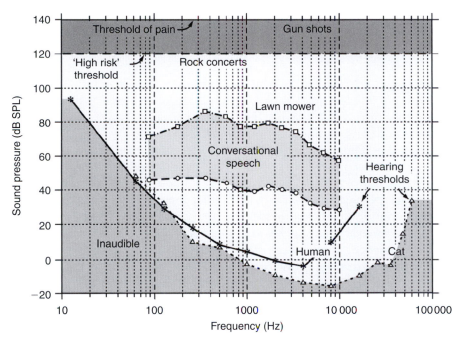

FIGURE 7.4 Hearing threshold and range of hearing for human listeners. Shown also are the ranges of frequency and sound pressure level of common environmental sounds, including human speech. The most intense sounds are capable of damaging the inner ear receptor organ. The hearing sensitivity of the cat, a laboratory animal commonly used in studies of the peripheral and central auditory system, is illustrated as well. *Source*: Adapted with permission from Brugge and Howard, 2002.

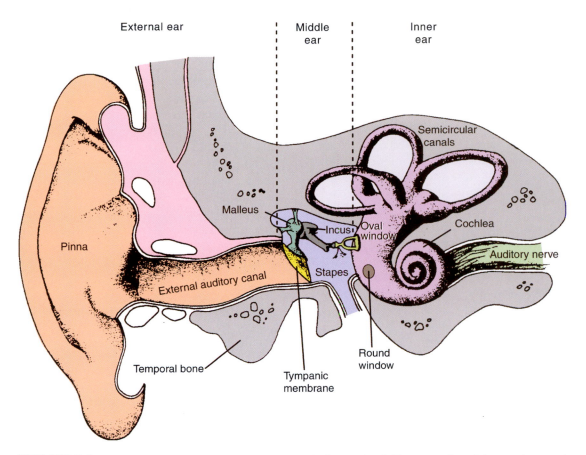

FIGURE 7.5 Drawing of the auditory periphery within the human head. The external ear (pinna and external auditory canal) and the middle ear (tympanic membrane or eardrum, and the three middle ear ossicles: malleus, incus, and stapes) are indicated. Also shown is the inner ear, which includes the cochlea of the auditory system and the semicircular canals of the vestibular system. There are two cochlear windows: oval and round. The oval window is the window through which the stapes conveys sound vibrations to the inner ear fluids. *Source*: Brown, 2003.

described as the 'highness' or 'lowness' of a sound, for example, the pitch of a person's voice or of a note on a piano. We use the physical and psychological terms differently when discussing sound perception. Here's why: while we may know the frequency of a sound because we have measured the cycles per second, we do not know the precise pitch that an individual experiences. A highly trained opera singer, for example, may have a very different sense of the differences in pitch between closely matched sounds than an untrained individual, even though both have normal hearing. This is also the case for the physical parameter of intensity, which corresponds to the subjective perception of *loudness*. Individual listeners have a wide variety in how they perceive the loudness of sounds, depending on many factors ranging from hearing loss to personal preference. Therefore, it is important when describing sounds to be aware if you are describing the *measured* physical parameters or the *subjective* psychological features.

1.2.4 From the eardrum to the auditory nerve

As we mentioned above, we will step through the stages of hearing and subcortical feature extraction processes as sounds are transmitted to auditory cortex. You will see that there are complex mechanisms at work, even in decoding relatively simple sounds in a quiet environment. Let's begin with how sounds proceed from vibrations at the eardrum, through the fluid of the inner ear, to innervate fibers at the auditory brainstem on their way to auditory cortex.

Vibrating objects cause sound waves to move through air. When these sound waves reach the tympanic membrane, or eardrum, they propagate through the middle ear through the mechanical action of the three bones of the middle ear: the hammer, anvil, and stirrup, to the cochlea, the organ of hearing in the inner ear (Figure 7.5) (for more on hearing fundamentals, see Moore, 1995).

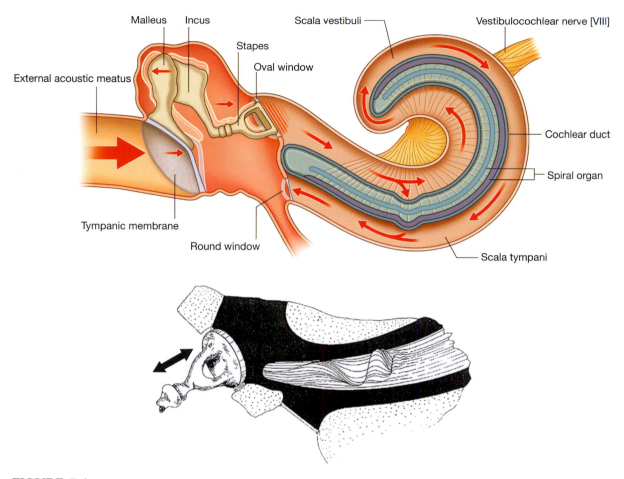

FIGURE 7.6 *Upper* panel depicts the transmission of sound, with a perspective view of the cochlea showing the basilar membrane. Note that the red arrows depict sound transmission and are bi-directional. *Lower* panel depicts a traveling of sound as it crosses the basilar membrane. The wave is shown as frozen in time and somewhat exaggerated in order to illustrate the movement across the basilar membrane by sound. *Sources: upper,* Drake, 2005; *lower,* Javel, 2003.

At the stage of the *cochlea*, in the inner ear, the physical aspects of the sounds are encoded. (See Figure 7.6, upper panel, for a perspective of the cochlea showing the shape of the *basilar membrane*.) The traveling wave of sound moves across the basilar membrane from the base to the apex (Figure 7.6, lower panel). The basilar membrane is topographically organized in a frequency-specific manner, called *tonotopy*, with higher frequencies encoded at the base and lower frequencies encoded at the apex.

How is the traveling wave converted to a neural code and transmitted to the brain? Within the cochlea, there are approximately 16 000 sensory receptors called the *hair cells*. The motion of the traveling wave along the basilar membrane sets the tiny hair cells into motion. The peak amplitude of the traveling wave causes maximal bending of the hair cells located in specific regions or places of the basilar membrane, thus encoding the

frequency of sounds. This is called the *place principle* of hearing and is based on the theory that the brain decodes the frequencies heard based upon which hair cells along the basilar membrane are activated.

At this stage of processing, the movement of the hair cells produced by the traveling wave of sound is transformed or transduced into electrical responses in fibers of the *auditory nerve* (Kelly *et al.*, 1996). Specific hair cells map onto to specific fibers in the auditory nerve and these fibers have a *characteristic frequency* to which they are most sensitive.

The fine mapping of hair cells onto auditory nerve fibers preserves the frequency information in the sound as it is converted from vibration at the eardrum, to mechanical movement in the middle ear, to traveling wave at the cochlea, to neural coding at the auditory nerve. A schematic of the pathways at the auditory brainstem is shown in Figure 7.7, top panel, with fibers

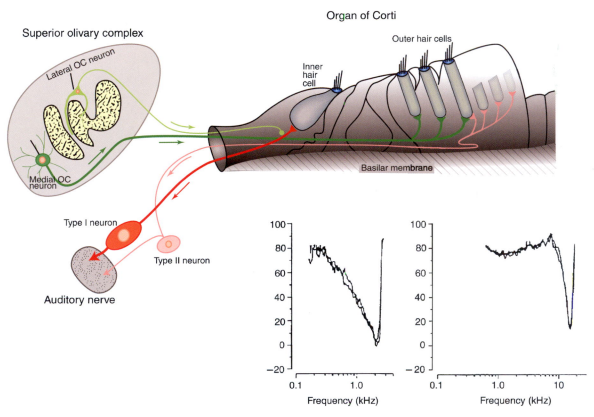

FIGURE 7.7   Top panel depicts innervation patterns of afferent and efferent neurons in the organ of Corti. Afferent inner-vation is provided by ganglion cells of the spiral ganglion in the cochlea, which have central axons that form the auditory nerve. There are two types of afferent neurons: (1) type I neurons, which receive synapses from inner hair cells, and (2) type II neurons, which receive synapses from outer hair cells. The central axons of these ganglion cells form the auditory nerve. Efferent inner-vation is provided by a subgroup of neurons in the superior olivary complex that send axons to the cochlea and are hence called the olivocochlear (OC) neurons. There are two types of OC neurons: (1) lateral OC neurons, which innervate type I dendrites near inner hair cells, and (2) medial OC neurons, which innervate outer hair cells. Lateral OC neurons are distributed mainly ipsilateral to the innervated cochlea, whereas medial OC neurons are distributed bilaterally to the innervated cochlea, with approximately two-thirds from the contralateral (not illustrated) and one-third from the ipsilateral side of the brain. Bottom panel depicts auditory nerve fiber tuning curves, with a fiber tuned to 2000 Hz (left curve) and 15 000 Hz (right curve), fre-quency is shown on the x-axis. The y-axis is threshold in decibels sound pressure level. *Sources: top*, Brown, 2003; *bottom*, Javel, 2003.

that show a 'best' or center frequency response in the bottom panel.

Thus, in this manner, sounds travel from the external ear canal, through the middle and inner ears, and on to the auditory brainstem. At this stage, the information in sounds is transduced through fibers on its way to auditory cortex. You may have noticed that long before the information in sound reaches cortex, there are many recoding and transforms that occur. These trans-formations of sound inputs are key to understanding how the brain decodes the multiple complexities of an everyday listening environment, such as the college classroom example described early in this chapter.

2.0 THE CENTRAL AUDITORY SYSTEM

The information in sound undergoes many transforma-tions as it ascends to auditory cortex. In this section, we will review the major aspects of the anatomy and neuro-physiology of the central auditory system. The auditory system is comprised of many stages and pathways that range from the ear, to the brainstem, to subcortical nuclei, and to cortex. The three main divisions of the auditory system are the peripheral system, which we have already discussed, the pathways (ascending to cortex, descend-ing from cortex, and parallel pathways across cortical

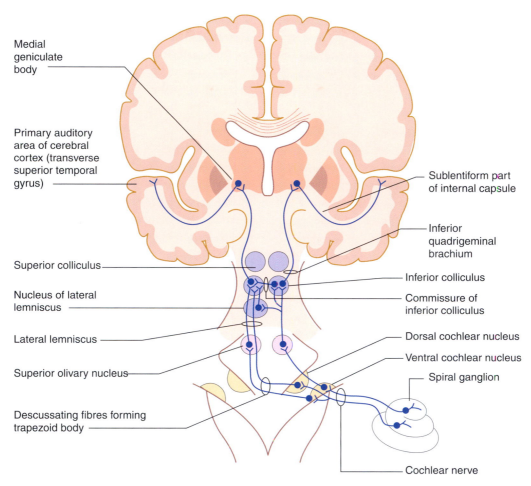

Medial geniculate body

Primary auditory area of cerebral cortex (transverse superior temporal gyrus)

Superior colliculus

Nucleus of lateral lemniscus

Lateral lemniscus

Superior olivary nucleus

Descussating fibres forming trapezoid body

Sublentiform part of internal capsule

Inferior quadrigeminal brachium

Inferior colliculus

Commissure of inferior colliculus

Dorsal cochlear nucleus

Ventral cochlear nucleus

Spiral ganglion

Cochlear nerve

FIGURE 7.8 Illustration of the human auditory system showing pathways and subcortical nuclei in the ascending and descending pathways. *Source*: Standring, 2005.

sites), and the central (cortical) system. While each stage and pathway have functional significance in the decoding of sounds, it is important to consider the auditory system as a whole because of the complex interactions across and within its constituent parts.

2.1 Auditory pathways

As we mentioned earlier, all sound processing occurs over time. The hallmark of the auditory system is its exquisite temporal resolution for decoding intricate information in sounds (Gage and Roberts, 2000; Gage *et al.*, 2006). One important aspect of the high temporal resolution of the auditory system is the fast and accurate transmission of sound information along and throughout its many pathways. Not only do transient features in complex sounds – such as the harmonic structure of consonants in speech or musical phrases – need to be conveyed rapidly from eardrum to cortex, but the

information from the two ears needs to combined and integrated in a meaningful way en route. Let's discuss how and where this happens in sound processing.

The *ascending* (afferent) pathways transmit information about sounds from the periphery to cortex. There are many stages of computation along the way: this pathway is not a simple delivery system but entails a significant amount of encoding and recoding of information in the sounds. The neural signal travels from the auditory nerve to the lower (ventral) *cochlear nucleus*. The cochlear nucleus is tonotopically organized. From the cochlear nucleus, the signal continues along the ascending pathway through the lateral lemniscus, inferior colliculus, thalamus, to auditory cortex (Figure 7.8). This is not a single pathway, but is complex and includes many computational stages as well as the combination of sound inputs from the two ears. A key function of the ascending pathway is to evaluate the information from the two ears in order to localize sounds in space – and we will discuss this in more depth later in the chapter.

The *descending* (efferent) pathways from regions in the cortical and subcortical auditory system cortex to the periphery are under direct or indirect cortical control. Recent research indicates that this control extends all the way to the hair cells in the cochlea! One important function of the descending pathway is to provide 'top down' information that aids in selective attention processes and in perceiving sounds in a noisy environment. The precise way in which the descending pathways function in sound processing is not well understood in humans, however, here is an example of some aspects of listening in which the descending pathways play a role. Imagine that you are having a very important conversation with a close friend as you stand outside a college classroom. You are focusing on the conversation, but meanwhile a motorcycle starts up in an adjacent parking lot, a helicopter passes overhead, and a gardener mows the nearby lawn with a power mower. You struggle to hear your friend, but manage to tune out most of these competing sounds. Suddenly the doors of the classroom open and scores of students erupt from the classroom, chatting and laughing. This may put an end to your conversation for a few moments, however, throughout the process of listening to your friend's voice during this noisy scene, your auditory pathways have been at work helping you both to focus your attention specifically to your friend and in extracting your friend's voice out of the competing noises coming at you from all directions.

The auditory pathways are not just ascending to or descending from cortex, there are many important connections between the auditory cortices in the left and right hemispheres via the corpus callosum. These connections between the hemispheres are tonotopically organized. There are also cortico-cortical pathways that provide integration of auditory processes with other sensory systems, as well as with working and long-term memory processes, and stored memories and knowledge. Together with the ascending and descending pathways, the cortical pathways represent complex connectivity patterns that are critical, not only for processing sound, but also for integrating information to other regions in the brain.

2.2 Auditory cortex

At last we have arrived at auditory cortex and, in this section, we will discuss the anatomy of brain areas in auditory cortex as well as the neurophysiological features of these regions of cortex. Auditory cortex is the region within cortex specialized for sound processing. It is located in each hemisphere within the Sylvian fissure on the surface of the supratemporal plane and the upper banks of the superior temporal gyrus (Figure 7.9).

As we have discussed, information in sounds is transmitted from the ear to auditory cortex via the ascending auditory pathways. Along the way, the signal is transformed and recomputed in many ways. Auditory cortex is not the end-stage of this pathway, but serves as a hub or nexus for sound processing, interacting dynamically with other systems within cortex, across the hemispheres, and back down the descending pathways to the cochlea. These dynamic processes provide a wide range of perceptual acuity and allow us to perform complex perceptual tasks such as selectively listen to one person's voice in a crowded and noisy room or recognize a melody even though it is played in another key or at a different tempo. These perceptual tasks are so complex that we do not totally understand how the auditory system performs them, however, we do them every day with little or no conscious effort on our part.

Auditory cortex is not a unitary brain area but is comprised of several structural (anatomical) areas that differ in their role in decoding sound. Early descriptions of these areas within auditory cortex were made based on the structure, such as a gyrus within this cortical region, and by underlying neurophysiological features, such as the cytoarchitectonic classification. Although we do not fully understand the role of each area within human auditory cortex, work is in progress to map out regions within auditory cortex and their corresponding role in perception. We discuss our current knowledge about human auditory cortex below, with a description of the structure or anatomy followed by details regarding the cellular organization and response properties, or neurophysiology.

2.2.1 Auditory cortical anatomy

Much of what we know about auditory cortical anatomy comes from work in non-human primates (Galaburda and Pandya, 1983). In macaque monkeys, the major regions of auditory cortex are the core, belt, and parabelt regions (Figure 7.10, left panel). These distinct regions are distinguished by their cytoarchitectural, physiological, and connective properties. The core receives inputs from the thalamus and in turn projects to regions in the lateral belt areas (Kaas *et al.*, 1999). This anatomical and connective structure has led scientists to suggest that there is a hierarchical organization in auditory cortex, with subcortical projections to the core or primary auditory (A1) region. A1 is thought to decode basic properties or

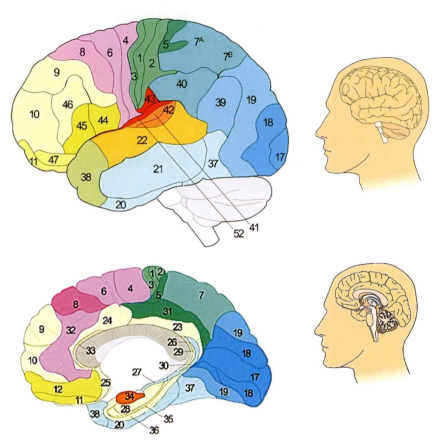

FIGURE 7.9 Top panel shows an illustration of the human brain from a lateral view, bottom panel from a medial view. Colored brain regions are adapted from Brodmann, 1909. Auditory and receptive language cortical regions include Brodmann 22, 41, 42, and 52.

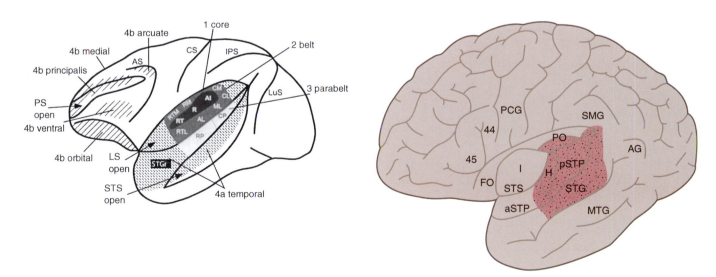

FIGURE 7.10 Left panel depicts levels and regions of auditory cortical processing in the macaque monkey. The areas shown are located on the superior temporal gyrus and in the depths of the superior temporal sulcus, which has been opened to show the extension of auditory-related cortex into this sulcus. Right panel depicts similar regions in the human, with the Sylvian fissure opened to show regions of auditory cortex on the supratemporal plane. (Adapted with permission from Zatorre, 2002.) *Source*: Caplan and Gould, 2003.

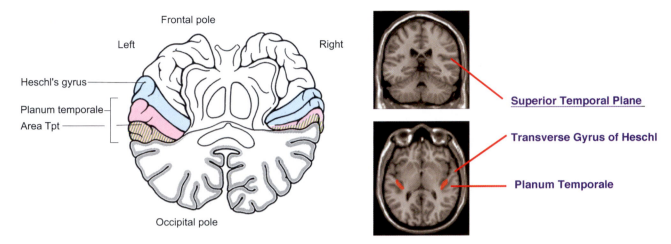

FIGURE 7.11   Left panel illustrates regions within auditory cortex, showing typical pattern of asymmetries in the left and right hemispheres. Right panel shows an MRI depiction of localizations of sound processing in the same regions. *Sources: left*, Standring, 2003; *right*, Frakowiak, 2004.

features in sounds. From A1, there are projections to the belt regions where more complex feature extraction processes occur (Kaas *et al.*, 1999). The belt and parabelt regions surrounding A1 are specialized for sound processing and thus are unimodal auditory cortex. Human auditory cortex (see Figure 7.10, right panel) shows similar regions, with the Sylvian fissure opened to show regions of auditory cortex that correspond to the regions presented for the macaque in Figure 7.10 left panel.

In humans, primary auditory cortex is located within *Heschl's gyrus* (Figure 7.11 left panel) and is roughly analogous to core regions described in non-human primates. Heschl's gyrus corresponds to Brodmann's area 41 (Brodmann, 1909). Typically, primary auditory cortex comprises only a portion (one to two thirds) of the medial aspect of Heschl's gyrus. There is significant variability in the anatomy of Heschl's gyrus both in the two hemispheres and across individuals: Heschl's gyrus is typically located somewhat anterior (~6 mm) in the right hemisphere than in the left, and some individuals have more than one Heschl's gyrus. This structural variability in Heschl's gyrus has important implications when interpreting functional neuroimaging findings, since the actual size and location of Heschl's gyrus varies so much across individuals (Figure 7.11, right panel; Frakowiak, 2004).

Auditory cortex extends from Heschl's gyrus in the anterior-inferior direction and the posterior-superior direction along the supratemporal plane and the upper bank of the superior temporal gyrus. A second important anatomical region in human auditory cortex is the *planum temporale*, located just posterior to Heschl's gyrus. There are both hemispheric and individual differences in

the planum temporale, however, unlike Heschl's gyrus, the differences fall into a general pattern: the *planum temporale* is typically much larger in the left hemisphere than in the right. In fact, the left planum temporale can be up to ten times larger in the left hemisphere in right-handed individuals (Figure 7.11, left panel). Planum temporale asymmetries were reported in a series of anatomical studies by Geschwind and colleagues (Geschwind and Galaburda, 1985a, b, c). These scientists noted that language function tends to be lateralized to the left hemisphere. They suggested that the larger left hemisphere planum temporale reflects its role in decoding auditory language. More recent neuroimaging studies, however, have provided a method specifically to test this hypothesis and provide differing views of the role of the planum temporale in sound processing. Just anterior to Heschl's gyrus is the planum polare. This region has not been the focus of much study in humans, and little is known about its role in auditory perception. Posterior to the planum temporale and other unimodal auditory areas is Brodmann area 22. This is the area that Carl Wernicke hypothesized played an important role in speech comprehension (Wernicke, 1874/1977). According to Wernicke, this region was not an auditory region per se, but formed the language area for speech comprehension processes that were closely related (physically and functionally) to auditory processes. This region is typically referred to as Wernicke's area.

2.2.2 Neurophysiology

Several guiding principles of auditory cortical organization have been established in studies of cats and

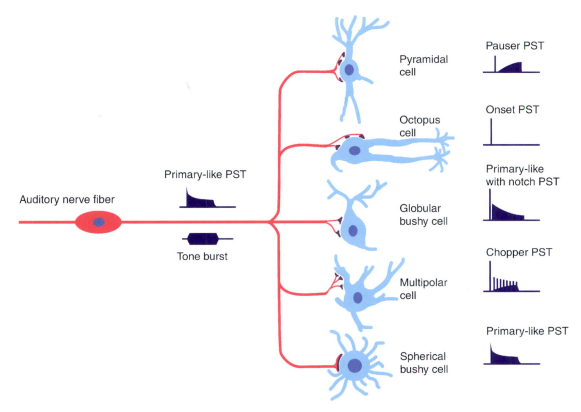

Auditory nerve fiber

Primary-like PST

Tone burst

Pyramidal cell

Octopus cell

Globular bushy cell

Multipolar cell

Spherical bushy cell

Pauser PST

Onset PST

Primary-like with notch PST

Chopper PST

Primary-like PST

FIGURE 7.12 Schematic of the main anatomical cell types of the cochlear nucleus and their corresponding post-stimulus time (PST) histograms. Left: an auditory nerve fiber is shown with its typical response, a primary-like PST. Center: the auditory nerve fiber divides to innervate the main cochlear nucleus cell types. Right: PST histograms corresponding to these cell types are shown. In their PST histograms, pauser units fire an initial spike and then have a distinct pause before a slow resumption of activity. Onset units fire mainly at the tone burst onsets. Primary-like units get their name from the similarity of their PSTs to those of primary auditory nerve fibers, but the primary-like with notch type additionally has a brief notch following the initial spike. Chopper units have regular interspike intervals that result in regular peaks in the PST. Most of these patterns are very different from the primary-like PST and irregular interspike intervals of the auditory nerve fiber. For histograms, the sound stimulus is typically a 25 ms tone burst with frequency at the center frequency of the neuron and sound level at 30 dB above threshold. *Source*: From Brown, 2003.

non-human primates. The basic units of organization in auditory cortex, as in other cortical sensory areas, are neurons, cortical columns, and neural networks. There are several differing types of neurons in the auditory system (Figure 7.12). These neurons have different response properties for coding frequency, intensity, and timing information in sounds as well as for encoding spatial information in processes for localizing sounds in space. Most cortical neurons respond to binaural inputs (inputs from both ears), demonstrating the importance of cortical processes for decoding binaural information for sound localization and other complex hearing processes. Together, these differing types of neurons form a dynamic network that encodes transient features in sounds. Far less is known about the types of neurons in human auditory cortex, however, the large pyramidal cells that are distributed along the

supratemporal plane likely play a key role in sound processing.

Mapping receptive field properties of neurons in auditory cortex has been the focus of many animal studies. A large proportion of auditory cortical neurons have inputs from both ears, however, the two ears are not represented in the same way within each hemisphere. In auditory cortex in the left hemisphere, the right ear, the *contralateral* ear, has a much larger or stronger representation than the left ear, the *ipsilateral* ear. A similar and opposite pattern is observed in the right auditory cortex, with a stronger representation of the left ear versus the right. This general asymmetry for the representation of the two ears in binaural hearing holds true for humans as well (Woldorff *et al.*, 1999).

One important aspect of decoding features in sounds is determining where the sound is in relation to the

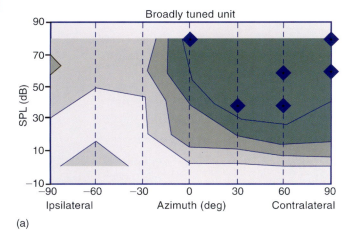

(a)

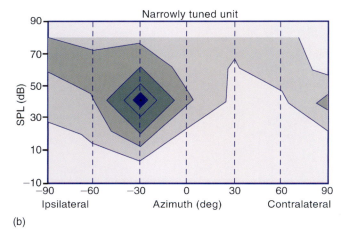

(b)

FIGURE 7.13 Receptive fields of two auditory cortex neurons plotted as a function of sound pressure level and azimuth in the frontal hemifield. Noise bursts were used as stimuli. Small diamonds show points of maximal response, and progressively lighter shading shows regions of progressively smaller response. Zero degrees azimuth refers to directly ahead, and positive azimuths refer to points in the contralateral hemifield. *Source*: Brown, 2003.

listener. In Figure 7.13, we show receptive field properties of two auditory cortical neurons as a function of where the sound is located in space relative to the head (the x-axis), and of how loud the sound is (the y-axis). The receptive field of the neuron presented in the top panel shows a large shaded region across sounds coming from the contralateral ear and across a lot of sound intensities. These receptive field properties indicate that this neuron is *broadly tuned* to sound information across loudness levels from the contralateral ear. In the lower panel, the neuron shows a sensitivity that is much more narrowly focused, in this case to sounds that are presented at 30–60 dB and coming from the ipsilateral ear. This neuron is *narrowly tuned*. Broadly and narrowly tuned neurons play differing roles in

sound processing. A broadly tuned neuron may not provide detailed information regarding just where a sound is located in space or precisely how loud it is, however, this neuron will be highly sensitive to detecting any sound within a large loudness scale coming from the contralateral ear. Thus, this neuron may be important for the *detection* of the presence of a new sound and provides general information about which ear the sound is coming from. A narrowly tuned neuron will provide more specific information regarding where a sound is, not just which ear but where in space on that side of the head, as well as more specific information about how loud the sound is. Thus, this neuron may be important for the *discrimination* of finer details about a sound.

As in other cortical sensory regions, auditory cortex has a *columnar organization*, meaning that neurons are organized into columns that span across all six cortical layers (see Chapter 3). Within an individual column, neurons show similar response properties. A general scheme for the columnar organization in auditory cortex is that neurons that respond to binaural inputs are organized into alternating columns that have differing roles in sound processing, either causing an excitatory (summation) or inhibitory (suppression) effect on information coming from the two ears (Brugge and Merzenich, 1973). These complex interactions of summing or suppressing the information coming from the two ears likely underlie perceptual functions, such as selectively attending to information coming from one ear.

A central guiding principle for non-human auditory cortex is the *tonotopic* organization. Within the core in cat auditory cortex, for example, receptive fields of neurons reflect a tonotopic organization in primary (A1) regions that has a mirror image in adjacent (anterior and posterior) core regions (Figure 7.14).

While the basic aspects of neurophysiology are likely similar for humans, the uniqueness of human speech, language, and music perception, as well as the substantially larger regions of cortex devoted to auditory cortex in humans, probably mean that there are neurons and networks that are specialized for these complex processes and specific to human auditory cortex. For example, although many auditory cortical regions in non-human primates reflect a tonotopic organization, evidence for tonotopy has been less robust in human studies and may be limited to primary auditory cortex and not represent the basic organizational principle in non-primary auditory areas (Wessinger *et al.*, 2001). The investigation of the organizational principles of human auditory cortex is work in progress, much aided by the

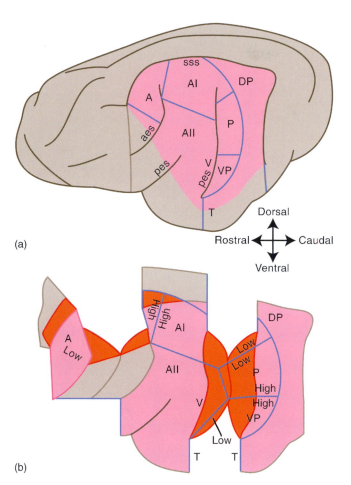

(a)

(b)

FIGURE 7.14 Auditory cortical fields in the temporal cortex of the cat. (a) Lateral view. (b) Lateral view that is 'unfolded' to show the part of the fields that are normally hidden within the sulci (orange shading), as well as the high- and low-frequency limits of the tonotopic fields. The four tonotopic fields are the anterior (A), primary (AI), posterior (P), and ventroposterior (VP). Positions of the lowest and highest center frequencies in these fields are indicated in (b). Note that at the boundaries of the tonotopic fields, the direction of tonotopy is reversed so that adjacent fields have 'mirror-image' tonotopy. Other cortical fields have less rigidly organized tonotopy or little tonotopy. These fields are secondary (AII), ventral (V), temporal (T), and dorsoposterior (DP). Also indicated are suprasylvian sulcus (sss) and anterior and posterior ectosylvian (aes, pes). *Source*: Brown, 2003.

advent of new techniques for its study, such as transcranial magnetic stimulation (TMS) and fMRI.

3.0 FUNCTIONAL MAPPING OF AUDITORY PROCESSING

Within auditory cortex, are there sub-regions that are specialized for decoding different types of sounds such as tones versus speech versus music? Or are all areas of

auditory cortex involved in all sound processing, regardless of the class of stimulus? Are sounds processed identically in the left and right hemispheres or are there subtle differences? Auditory scientists are still unraveling these puzzles. The advent of neuroimaging techniques has provided us with new ways to investigate brain areas for sound processing. Much of this work has been motivated by the investigation of brain regions that may be specialized for decoding speech and language. While neuropsychological studies of patients with brain damage have provided a wealth of information regarding specific language deficits and their correspondence to brain areas, neuroimaging allows the investigation of speech and language processes in healthy individuals. Neuroimaging also provides a way to investigate aspects of auditory function that have not been able to be addressed before, such as what brain areas are involved in imagining a sound versus hearing a sound? And what happens in auditory cortex while we sleep?

3.1 Primary auditory cortex

We have discussed a hierarchical model for sound processing, developed in animal studies, with neurons in primary auditory cortex tuned to extract basic physical features in sounds while neurons in non-primary auditory cortex are tuned for extracting more complex features. Recent studies in humans have provided evidence that this hierarchy is present in human auditory function, with basic features in sounds encoded in primary auditory cortex and more complex information in sounds encoded in the planum temporale (Wessinger *et al.*, 2001). This area of investigation is still in its early stages, and so we must treat these initial findings with a bit of caution until we have learned more. Thus, the investigation of the functional role of human primary auditory cortex is still unfolding, and it is likely that human auditory areas serve somewhat differing functions from those found for non-human species.

3.2 The role of the planum temporale in sound decoding

Early anatomical studies provided evidence for an important asymmetry in human auditory cortex: the planum temporale (PT) was much larger in the left hemisphere for right handed individuals (Geschwind and Levitsky, 1968). The prevalence of this asymmetry and its location in auditory areas close to Wernicke's area for speech comprehension motivated the hypothesis that PT was the site for auditory speech and language

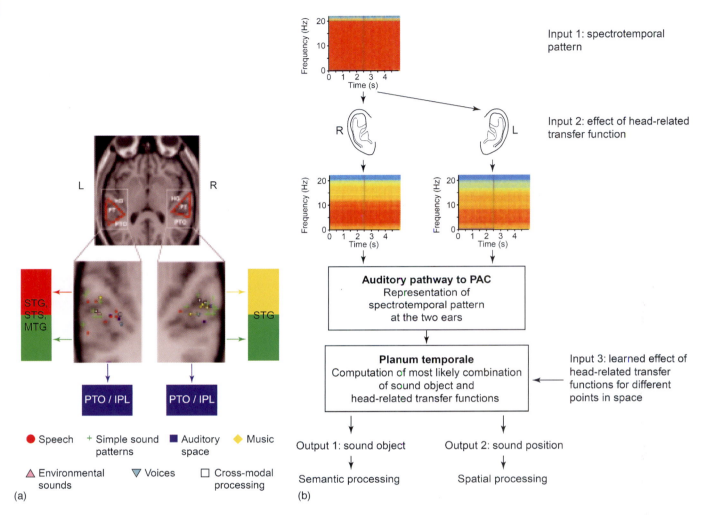

FIGURE 7.15   Left panel shows the planum temporale (PT) as an anatomical and functional hub. (a) Tilted axial section through the superior temporal plane of the human brain. The PT lies posterior to Heschl's gyrus (HG), the site of the primary auditory cortex. Ninety-five per cent probability maps for the boundaries of left and right PT in humans are outlined in red. (b) Insets centered on left and right PT showing functional activation peaks within PT associated with different types of complex sound processing. Abbreviations are IPL, inferior parietal lobe; MTG, middle temporal gyrus; PTO, parieto-temporal operculum; STG, lateral superior temporal gyrus; STS, superior temporal sulcus. Right panel shows the PT as a computational hub in action: auditory spatial analysis. The spectrotemporal pattern at the two ears results from convolution of the acoustic signal in space (in this example, a square-wave amplitude modulated noise, similar to the sound of a helicopter) with the head-related transfer function (HRTF) at the two ears (in this example, corresponding to a location above the subject, to the right). Initial processing of spectrotemporal patterns, including comparison between ears, occurs in the ascending pathway to the primary auditory cortex (PAC). *Source*: Adapted from Griffiths and Warren, 2002.

processing. This idea has been supported by neuroimaging studies investigating the functional role of PT in speech perception. However, neuroimaging studies of PT response to different classes of speech and non-speech sounds provide evidence that the functional role of PT is not limited to speech sounds. These findings have resulted in a new assessment of the role of PT in sound processing. A recent model proposes that PT performs as a computational hub for auditory scene analysis (Griffiths and Warren, 2002). Recall that Bregman (1990) provided a model for how the auditory system analyzes

a complex auditory scene, proposing grouping principles for scene segmentation into streams. Griffiths and Warren propose that the PT is the site of these analytic functions, decoding sensory inputs and comparing them to stored memories and experiences in order to segment the auditory scene (Figure 7.15, left panel).

Griffiths and Warren further theorize that the PT has a role in directing further cortical processing into streams for decoding spatial location and auditory object identification information. Subcortical sound localization computations are further analyzed in the PT, with the output transmitted to cortical spatial processing systems. Similarly, auditory object features are analyzed in the PT, with the output transmitted to cortical semantic processing systems (Figure 7.15, right panel). While the model proposed by Griffiths and Warren makes intuitive sense based on our current knowledge of human auditory function, it is important to note that it is a hypothetical model. Much more investigative work is needed in order to provide a thorough account of the role of functional areas in human auditory cortex, such as the planum temporale.

3.3 Cortical auditory 'what' and 'where' systems

The central role of the auditory perception system is to extract information from the listening environment in order to determine what is happening around us. Consider again the large college classroom where doors are opening and closing, students are talking, backpacks are being unzipped, books are being dropped on desktops. All of these sound events are happening at the same time and are overlapping in frequency and intensity. How does the auditory system decode the individual auditory 'objects' such as a friend's voice, a door shutting, a cell phone ringing? To accomplish this, the auditory system must keep track of many aspects of the complex auditory scene: *where* sounds are occurring in space, *when* sounds occur – are they simultaneous or does one sound precede another? – to determine *what* the sound represents in terms of known auditory objects such as speech or music or new auditory objects to be learned. Of course, these perceptual tasks are not limited to the auditory system but make contact with other sensory systems as your brain integrates what you hear with what you see, feel, and smell. These tasks also interact with your memories and learned information already stored regarding auditory objects that have taken a lifetime to develop. Let's begin with some auditory perceptual processes within the framework of the auditory system.

3.3.1 'Where' system: sound localization

An important aspect of auditory scene segmentation is to know where a sound is coming from. Imagine a busy airport baggage area where you are waiting for a friend to arrive. The area is full of people talking, there are frequent public address announcements: this is a complex auditory scene! Eventually your friend spies you and calls out: 'I'm over here!' This is not extremely helpful to you because you don't know where 'over here' actually is, calling out, 'I am 10 feet (3 m) behind you and slightly to the right!', would seem to be somewhat more useful (although it actually is not: sound localization computations are much faster than speech comprehension). Despite the limited information in 'over here', you will likely spin around and make visual contact quickly. This is your auditory system doing what it does best: localizing sound even in complex listening environments with many competing sounds.

Sound localization is a fundamental process for the auditory system. Knowing where a particular sound is coming from is quite useful in decoding the auditory scene, but of course, it is also critical for survival – allowing us to jump out of the way of an oncoming car or to duck when we hear a loud noise. How does the brain locate sounds in space? You may have an intuition that this is a much more difficult process in some ways than the way the visual system maps the visual scene in space (see Chapter 6). Sounds are always changing in time and the mapping of auditory space is a complex one. Here is how it works: when a sound occurs, it will likely be off to one side or the other of you. It could also be behind you. In order to determine where the sound is in relation to you, your auditory system must make a very quick determination of the sound's arrival at the two ears. Two basic types of cues are used when our system localizes sound. The first is the *interaural (between ear) time difference*: the difference in time between a sound reaching your left ear versus your right. A second important cue for localizing sounds is the *interaural level difference*. This is the small difference in loudness that occurs when a sound travels towards the head from an angle. The head produces a 'sound shadow', so that sounds reaching the far ear are somewhat quieter than the near ear and the absolute level differences depend on the frequency of the sound. (See Figure 7.16 for a schematic of sound localization processes.)

Thus, sound localization processes rely on the basic notion is that if a sound occurs to the left of you, it will make contact with the eardrum of the left ear slightly before the right ear and it will be slightly louder in the left ear than in the right. The actual computations that produce sound localization functions involve complex algorithms called *head-related transfer functions* to calculate the location of sounds in auditory space. The neural computations that underlie sound localization are not well understood. One central 'problem' that these computations must address is the fact that the human head changes size rather dramatically throughout childhood. The neural code for the head-related transfer

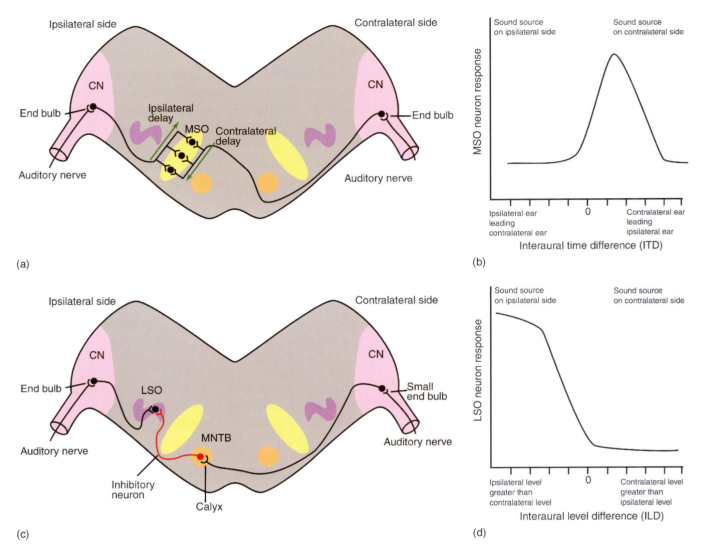

FIGURE 7.16   Innervation schematics and responses of two circuits in the lower brainstem that are important in binaural sound location. Neuronal cell bodies are shown as dots, and fiber pathways are shown as lines; positions of large synaptic terminals (end bulbs and calyces) are indicated. (a) Circuit of the medial superior olive (MSO), which is sensitive to interaural time differences (ITD). Input to the cochlear nucleus (CN) from the auditory nerve terminates at the large end bulbs of Held that synapse onto spherical bushy cells. Bushy cells project bilaterally such that a single MSO receives input from both sides. Bushy cell inputs form delay lines such that ITD is mapped along the MSO. Data suggest that the delay line is oriented rostrocaudally and that only contralateral inputs are delayed. (b) Response of an MSO neuron as a function of ITD. Neurons within the MSO respond when spikes from their two inputs arrive at the same time. The response plotted is of a neuron in the lower part of the MSO drawn in (a); there is a large response when the ipsilateral input lags so that early contralateral input has time to proceed down the axonal delay line to reach the neuron at the same time as the lagging ipsilateral input. This type of lagging ipsilateral input would be produced by a sound source located on the contralateral side. (c) Circuit of the lateral superior olive (LSO), which is sensitive to interaural level differences (ILD). Excitatory input arises from the ipsilateral CN. Inhibitory input (red line) from the contralateral side is through the medial nucleus of the trapezoid body (MNTB), a nucleus of inhibitory neurons. There is a large response when sound is of high level on the ipsilateral side and no response when sound is of higher level on the contralateral side. Thus a response is produced by a sound source located on the ipsilateral side. *Source:* Brown, 2003.

functions must be able to take into account a changing head size.

Recent investigations show that these computations are performed both in subcortical and cortical auditory regions, however, there remains some debate as to how these regions interact. For example, in a series of MEG studies to evaluate the cortical dynamics of spatial processing, Tiitinen and colleagues (Tiitinen *et al.*, 2006) have reported that while both left and right auditory areas appear to be involved in decoding spatial information, the right hemisphere response is more prominent (Figure 7.17). Does this mean that the right hemisphere is specialized for decoding sound localization information? Probably not: while there may be a

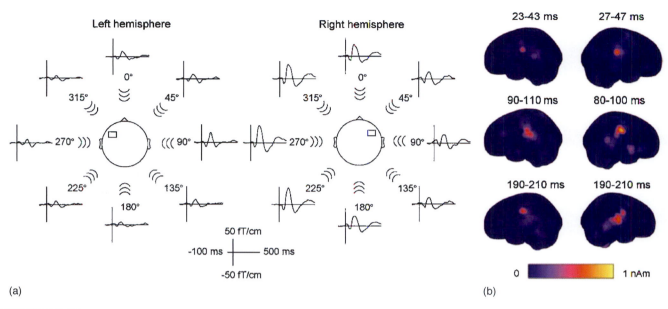

(a)   (b)

FIGURE 7.17 The P1m, N1m, and P2m responses as indicators of the cortical processing of sound source direction. Realistic spatial sound was presented from eight equally spaced source directions in the azimuth plane. (a) Grand-averaged MEG responses. Sounds from each source direction elicited a response complex comprising the P1m, N1m, and P2m. The right-hemisphere P1m and N1m peaked earlier for sound sources contralateral to the hemisphere. The amplitude of the P1m and N1m in both hemispheres and the right-hemispheric P2m varied according to the sound source direction. Overall, sound sources in the contralateral hemisphere resulted in larger peak amplitudes, and the right-hemispheric responses were larger in amplitude than the left-hemispheric ones. (b) Grand-averaged minimum current estimates (MCE) obtained at the latencies of the P1m, N1m, and P2m to the 3D sound from the direction angle of 90 degrees. Activation restricted to the vicinity of the auditory cortex was observed at each latency. *Source*: Adapted with permission from Tiitinen *et al.*, 2006.

subtle bias in the right hemisphere for processing spatial information, more studies are required in order to map out how complex and time-varying spatial information is decoded in auditory cortex.

There is, however, general agreement that the interaural time and level differences for sound localization are minuscule (fractions of a millisecond) and demand a system that can decode tiny differences in sounds with amazing precision. In fact, the encoding systems for localizing sound form the basis of complex hearing and likely form the neural underpinnings of speech and music perception in humans.

A 'where' system for spatial attention

While most auditory cortical neurons respond to inputs from both ears, the response is asymmetric, with a stronger representation of information from the contralateral ear compared to the ipsilateral ear. Is there a similar effect for attending to different sides of auditory space? Early investigations by Hillyard and colleagues provided evidence that there is. Using event-related potentials (ERPs), Hillyard reported a predominant N1 larger response for the attended ear in contralateral cortex (Hillyard *et al.*, 1973). More recent neuroimaging

studies have also provided a way to investigate the effects of selectively attending to auditory space, confirming the earlier findings by Hillyard with different methodology (Tzourio *et al.*, 1997; Woldorff *et al.*, 1999). In a PET study, higher levels of activation in right auditory cortex were found when subjects attended to the left, and higher levels of activation in left auditory was found when subjects attended to the right (Figure 7.18) (Tzourio *et al.*, 1997).

This study is an example of 'top down' processing: rather than presenting sounds to the left or right side of the subject, the investigators merely instructed the subject to attend to the left or the right side of auditory space. These results demonstrate the powerful role of attention in the auditory system. And, since the hemisphere differences are due to the subject's attention being focused in differing auditory spatial locations, it also demonstrates the importance of careful experimental design when using neuroimaging techniques to investigate auditory cortical processing. For example, if you were investigating hemisphere differences for vocal music versus instrumental music, it would be important to make sure your subjects were not attending to just the left or just right side of auditory space while listening!

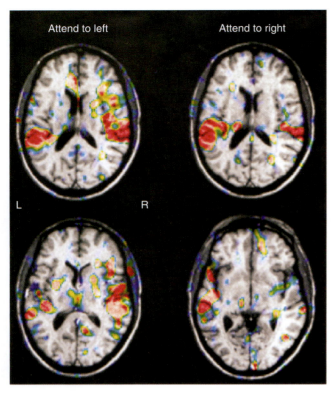

FIGURE 7.18 Example of individual PET activation images obtained at the Heschl's gyrus level (top) and through the superior temporal gyrus (bottom) in one subject. Left column, attend to the left deviant sounds versus rest; right column, attend to the right deviants versus rest. *Source*: Adapted from Tzourio *et al.*, 1997.

Expertise in spatial attention networks

While the role of attention in processing spatial information has been studied for many years, we are still unraveling some of the mysteries of how our brains accomplish the complexities involved in these processes. One focus of recent study is investigating individual differences in how individuals use attentional processes in decoding spatial cues. While this area of study is still in early stages, we highlight a recent study by Munte and colleagues (Munte *et al.*, 2001) where musical conductors' use of spatial attention was contrasted with other musical individuals (pianists) and a control group of non-musicians. The underlying notion was that a conductor must be able to attend to many spatial locations at once as he or she is leading a large number of musicians in playing a musical score. Munte and colleagues reported that conductors showed a higher sensitivity for sounds presented in peripheral listening regions than either of the other groups (Figure 7.19).

While these findings are intriguing, more studies must take place before we may understand the types of individual differences that occur in spatial attention processes.

3.3.2 'What' system: auditory object recognition and scene analysis

Our knowledge about sounds and what they mean begins before birth (see Chapter 15) and continues throughout life as we experience complex auditory scenes. You can imagine that the neural processes for decoding the college classroom example that we have used throughout this chapter did not get established overnight, but are the outcomes of years of experience. In this section, we will discuss the learning processes associated with forming mental representations of auditory objects as well as those for decoding complicated listening environments. Let's begin with auditory objects.

Auditory object recognition

Knowing *where* a sound is coming from is an important aspect of auditory scene analysis and critical for survival. The next step is to understand *what* you are hearing. To accomplish this, the auditory system must decode sounds 'online' as they occur in order to form a percept of a sound event or auditory object. These objects are learned over time as we grow from infant, to child, to adult, and they change with experience throughout our lifetime. Auditory objects can take many shapes, similar to visual objects, and vary widely in complexity from a simple computer alert chime, to the slamming of a car door, to a friend's voice, to a symphony. It seems that the brain has a nearly limitless capacity for storing and retrieving auditory objects. Auditory objects are organized into categories, such as human voices, musical instruments, animal sounds, that aid us in decoding learned objects as well as learning new ones. Over time, associations are formed between learned auditory objects and coinciding inputs from other sensory systems and these different sensory memories become integrated in the conceptual representation system. Early work on describing how these sensory inputs are experienced and combined to form conceptual knowledge was provided by Carl Wernicke, who proposed that with experience, when you hear the sound of a bell, you will recognize it as such and the sound of the bell will also bring to mind (activate) the visual features of a bell, the feel of a bell, etc. (Wernicke, 1874/1977).

Because language is uniquely human, it is probably not surprising that there have been many investigations into how the brain decodes speech. We will

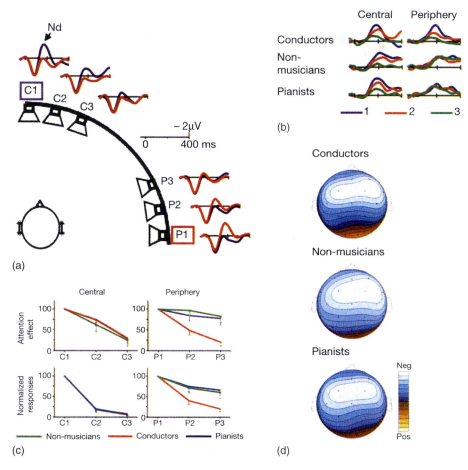

FIGURE 7.19 Effects of auditory attention in conductors, pianists, and controls. (a) Experimental set-up; speakers are spaced 6 degrees apart. Group-average event-related potentials (ERPs; frontal midline site) recorded from the conductors and invoked by frequent standards stimuli are represented by blue lines that indicate response to stimuli from a particular speaker when attending to loudspeaker C1; red lines represent ERPs in response to the same stimuli when attending to speaker P1. Attended stimuli give rise to an enhanced negativity starting at 60 ms. ERPs associated with adjacent speakers show a similar declining gradient. (b) Difference waves obtained by subtracting unattended-direction from attended-direction responses. All subject groups showed a gradient ERP for central locations, for peripheral sounds, a gradient is evident only for the conductors. (c) Top row, electrophysiological attention effect (frontal midline electrode, mean amplitude, 180–220 ms; C1/P1 set to 100%). No differences between groups were found for central locations. Conductors show steeper gradient in the periphery. Bottom row, button presses in response to infrequent stimuli. For peripheral sounds, conductors show a decreased false alarm rate for adjacent locations. (d) Spine-interpolated scalp maps of the attention effect for the centermost speaker (time window, 180–220 ms) show a similar topography across groups. *Source*: Adapted from Munte *et al.*, 2001.

discuss these later in this chapter. For now, let's focus on how the brain decodes non-speech sounds such as environmental sounds. Here we highlight a recent study by Binder and colleagues (Lewis *et al.*, 2004) who investigated brain areas for recognizing environmental sounds (for example, the sounds of a doorbell, a hammer pounding a nail). Results are presented in Figure 7.20: the key finding was that auditory areas in the superior temporal

gyrus were activated by both recognized and unrecognized (reversed) environmental sounds, however, recognized sounds also activated regions in the superior temporal sulcus and the middle temporal gyrus (MTG) in both hemispheres. These results are interesting in light of previous investigations of the functional processes of the MTG: the regions identified in this study partially overlap with semantic systems and with areas that

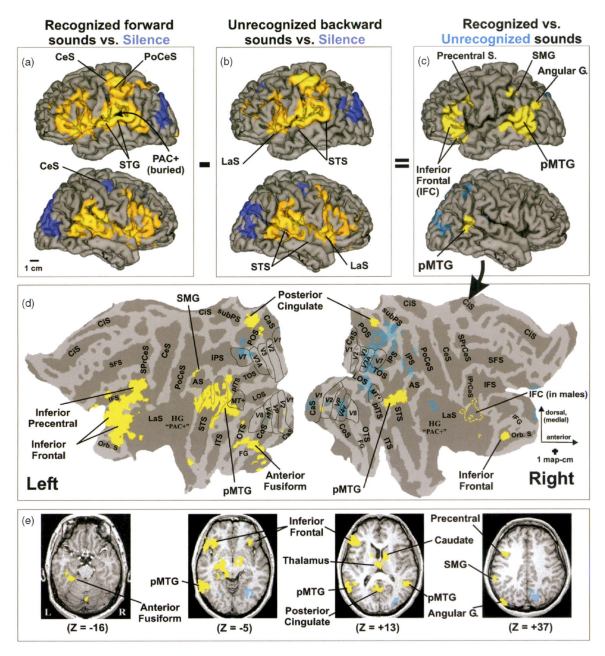

FIGURE 7.20 Brain regions involved in environmental sound recognition. Yellow hues show group-averaged activated regions and dark blue shows relative decreases evoked by (a) recognizable, forward sounds relative to silence or (b) the corresponding unrecognizable, backwards sounds relative to silence. (c) Data from (b) subtracted from (a), revealing regions preferentially involved in recognizing sounds (yellow) versus not recognizing the corresponding backward-played sounds (light blue), both relative to silence. (d) Flat maps showing data from (c). The left superior temporal sulcus is outlined in gray for clarity. (e) Axial sections of data from (c) displayed on the brain of one subject. *Source*: Lewis *et al.*, 2004.

have been reported as important for recognition of visual objects such as tools. During the process of learning an environmental sound, it is likely that the sound of a hammer will be heard at the same time movement of the hammer is seen. Thus, the sound and the sight of hammering are likely to be linked during the process

of learning. Binder and colleagues propose that this is the case and that the MTG region is a likely candidate for the brain region for this type of object recognition processing.

The results of the study by Binder and colleagues (Lewis *et al.*, 2004) are in good accord with earlier studies of individuals with brain lesions who suffered from auditory agnosia, the inability to recognize auditory objects. Cases where the patient suffers from a specific ('pure') deficit for recognizing environmental sounds, while leaving speech recognition intact, are rare. The investigations of the cases that do exist have reported a complex location of lesions, with reports of left hemisphere damage, right hemisphere damage, or in some cases bilateral damage (see Clarke *et al.*, 2002). The results of Binder and colleagues, showing auditory object recognition related activity in several areas in both hemispheres, provides evidence that the neural substrates of auditory environmental object perception are likely complex and include multiple regions in both hemispheres. This work is an example of how the results of lesion studies inform scientists using neuroimaging techniques to investigate complex cortical processes.

The cocktail party effect

We have described how a sound is decoded by the auditory system to be recognized or learned as an auditory object. This process seems relatively straightforward when you consider a situation where a single sound event occurs in a quiet environment. But how is this perceptual task accomplished in noisy environments, with complex sounds that occur simultaneously in time, with overlapping frequencies, and possibly coming from the same spatial location? How does the auditory system distinguish them as separate sound events? This perceptual task – the 'cocktail party problem' (Cherry, 1953) – has been the subject of many investigations of auditory perception from a theoretical perspective to understand how the auditory system extracts information from complex signals as well as a practical perspective in designing speech recognition systems. Bregman (1990) provided a model to describe how the auditory system segregates the many different signals in a noisy environment. The four elements in this model are:

1   the source
2   the stream
3   grouping
4   stream segregation.

The *source* is the sound signal itself. The *stream* is the percept related to the sound. This distinction between the physical signal and the related perception is analogous to the relationship we described earlier in this chapter between the frequency (in Hz) of a sound and the pitch perceived by the listener: the source represents the physical features of the signal which can be well described in terms of its frequency, intensity, spatial location, etc., while the stream represents the psychological aspects which may vary widely across individuals.

Grouping refers to how the signals are perceptually combined to identify and maintain attention to some aspects of the auditory scene (such as listening to one friend's voice in a crowd of people). Perceptual grouping processes create the stream. There are two basic types of grouping: *simultaneous grouping*, where if two or more sounds have common onsets and offsets, they may be grouped together. Think of a choir or an orchestra: you will not typically hear each individual voice or instrument, but will group them into a single stream due to the beginning and ending of their music together as well as their shared spatial location. (On the other hand, if you pay particular attention, you can attend to a single voice or instrument: this is the dynamic auditory system at work!) *Sequential grouping* refers to the process in which features or properties are shared across sounds that occur over time. An example of this grouping process is if you are listening to a professor lecture and someone in front of you coughs. The stream coming from the professor is interrupted by the cough but you will likely not notice an effect in hearing what is being said. This is your auditory system recognizing that the professor's voice represents a single stream despite the brief interruption produced by the cough.

Stream segregation uses the grouping processes to segregate separate auditory objects or events into streams. Here are the basic grouping principles that Bregman developed in his model:

1   Proximity: sounds that occur close together in time and share common features or properties may be grouped together
2   Closure: sounds that share belongingness will be grouped, such as the example of the cough during a lecture – the cough does not 'belong' to the stream produced by the lecture and is not grouped into that stream
3   Good continuation: sounds that have smooth transitions are likely to be grouped together (this is similar to the proximity principle)
4   Common fate: sounds that come from the same location or coincide in time may be grouped together (such as the orchestra example)
5   Exclusive allocation: this is an important principle for speech perception and states that one may attend to (or allocate neural resources for) one stream or another but not both at one time. This aspect of auditory processing is frequently referred to as selective listening. If one speaker's voice is presented to your

two ears in headphones, you have no difficulty in understanding what is being said. If, however, two different speakers' voices are presented simultaneously to your left and right ears, you will only be able to attend to one stream at a time, although you may switch back and forth.

How does the brain perform auditory scene analysis? Investigations of the neural substrates of perceptual organization have led to the formation of several theories of how and where perceptual streaming is decoded. One view holds that auditory stream segregation involves primary auditory cortex and that the underlying mechanisms for this segregation involve neural suppression of information not contained within an auditory stream (Fishman *et al.*, 2001). A second view holds that auditory stream segmentation exploits cortical change detector mechanisms in detecting aspects of the auditory scene that are not part of a single stream (Sussman, 2005). According to this view, an individual auditory stream is detected based on the acoustic aspects of the auditory sound, such as its frequency and location in space. Once these characteristics are formed into a neural representation of the stream, inputs that do not match this stream are detected using auditory cortical change detection

mechanisms. A third view is that the perceptual organization processes take place in an area of cortex that is thought to underlie binding processes for visual and somatosensory input, the intraparietal sulcus (Cusack, 2005). In this view, the perceptual organization of multiple auditory streams occurs external to auditory cortex in neural territory that is implicated in multimodal cortex (Figure 7.21).

The segmentation of an auditory scene into its constituent parts, or streams, is a complex 'problem' for the auditory system to resolve and likely has an equally complex neural basis. Thus, it is not surprising that the neural substrates for auditory scene analysis are still being elucidated in the relatively new field of cognitive neuroscience.

3.3.3 'What' and 'where' processing streams

We have discussed important aspects of auditory perception, including decoding binaural cues to determine *where* a sound is in space and extracting spectral and temporal features to determine *what* that sound is. 'What' and 'where' processing streams have been the topic of many invasive investigations in non-human primates in both the visual and auditory modalities. Converging evidence from these investigations provides evidence of distinct and separable streams for processing 'what' and 'where' information (Figure 7.22).

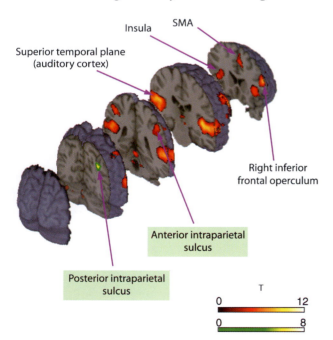

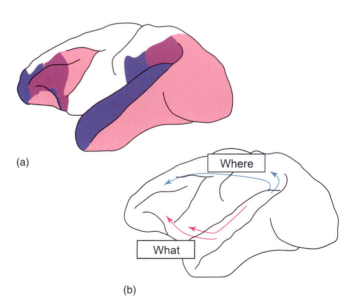

FIGURE 7.21 Cortical areas for auditory stream analysis: region (shown in light green) in the intraparietal sulcus (IPS) when two auditory streams are perceived versus 1. The IPS has been implicated as a region for perceptual organization (binding) of multimodal (vision, touch, sound) information. *Source*: Adapted from Cusack, 2005.

FIGURE 7.22 Auditory regions and streams in the primate brain. (a) The lateral surface of a macaque brain showing regions of visual (pink) and auditory (blue) responsivity. Multimodal responsivity is shown in purple. (b) Two broad 'streams' of processing within the auditory system. *Source*: Adapted from Scott, 2005.

There is a large and growing body of evidence that cortical networks for decoding what and where information in sound are processed in separate (but highly interactive) processing streams in the human brain. The planum temporale has been suggested to serve as a hub in early auditory cortical processing (see Figure 7.15), making contact with two differing streams of processing for decoding spatial location and auditory object identification (Griffiths and Warren, 2002), however, the role of the planum temporale in sound processing is continuing to be elucidated.

Recent neuroimaging studies have investigated processing of where and what information and have shown differing patterns of activity for decoding this information. In a recent review article, Scott (2005) provides a summary of findings to date and provides hypothesized brain regions for 'what', 'where' and 'how' processing streams in the human brain (Figure 7.23), however, the functional mapping of cortical auditory processing streams remains an ongoing investigation.

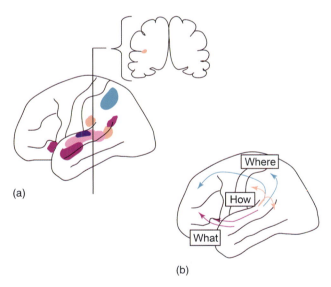

FIGURE 7.23 Functional responses to speech and candidate stream of processing in the human brain. (a) The lateral surface of the human brain: the colored regions indicate broadly to which type of acoustic signal each temporal region (and associated parietal and frontal region) responds. Regions in blue show a specific response to language-specific phonological structure. Regions in lilac respond to stimuli with the phonetic cues and features of speech, whereas those in purple respond to intelligible speech. Regions in pink respond to verbal short-term memory and articulatory representations of speech. Regions in green respond to auditory spatial tasks. (b) The putative directions of the 'what', 'where', and 'how' streams of processing in the human brain. *Source*: Adapted from Scott, 2005.

4.0 SPEECH PERCEPTION

Now let's turn to an important area of investigation in the topic of human auditory function: the decoding of speech sounds. Since language is a uniquely human function, it may well be the case that the auditory system in humans differs sharply from those in non-human primates. Let's begin our discussion of how we decode human speech with a brief discussion of the units of analysis in speech.

The basic task of the speech system is to map sounds onto meaning. This seems to be a relatively straightforward process: when a speech sound, such as 'd', is heard, the physical sound is mapped onto an abstract representation of that sound, the *phoneme*. The two main types of phonemes are consonants (such as 'd') and vowels (such as 'i'). Individual phonemes are stored in echoic memory while an entire word is being spoken, for example 'dig'. In order to decode the spoken word 'dig', you might imagine that the neural representations for 'd', 'i', and 'g' are decoded individually and sequentially, and combined to map onto a sound representation of the word 'dig'. The result is that the word 'dig' is activated in the semantic/conceptual knowledge system. Unfortunately, this description makes perfect sense but it is not how the speech system actually works. In fact, there is little agreement in the field of speech perception regarding the basic 'building blocks' of speech: is an individual phoneme the smallest unit of analysis for speech systems? Or is the syllable the appropriate unit? We will return to this question later in the chapter. For now, consider that the speech system must not only decode the individual phonemes in speech to map the sound information to meaning, but it must also decode 'who' information in order to know who is speaking and 'when' in order to understand the temporal order of speech phonemes, syllables, words, and sentences. As mentioned earlier in the chapter, the speech signal must be evaluated across multiple time scales (20, 200, 2000 ms, see Figure 7.2). This information must be decoded accurately regardless of the differences in human speech: whether we hear a high-pitched voice of a child or a low-pitched voice of a man, whether we are speaking very loudly or whispering, or whether we are speaking quickly or slowly. Obviously, the speech system is doing a lot more than a simple mapping of sound onto meaning and it cannot rely solely on the physical aspects of speech since they vary so widely both within and across speakers. Despite the intricacies of speech perceptual processes, they occur with little attention or apparent effort on our part. Let's begin with a little history of speech science.

4.1 Background and history

Research into how speech is decoded is a relatively young area of investigation. While scientists have long studied language in the brain and investigations of the physical properties of sound date back to the early 19th century, the specific study of how acoustic signals map onto meaning is relatively new. Speech perception investigations began during the pre-World War II era. Several events combined to move the study of speech perception into the forefront. First, prior to and during World War II, there was a need for developing speech recognition systems for covert war-related communications. Next, two inventions changed the way we thought about and studied human speech. First, the *vocoder* (voice + coder) developed by Homer Dudley of Bell Telephone Laboratories (Dudley, 1936). The vocoder provided a method to transmit speech signals over long telephone circuits by analyzing and recoding speech into simpler signals that contained far less information than natural human speech. The outcome was a far simpler speech signal that was, nonetheless, quite understandable, providing evidence that the speech signal contained many redundant features. These findings launched experiments to determine what was the minimal information required to comprehend speech.

BOX 7.1   From Vocoder to bionic hearing

The technology underlying early vocoders remains in active use today and forms the basis for the way in which cochlear implants stimulate the auditory system to provide hearing for individuals with certain kinds of hearing loss (see Figure 7.24).

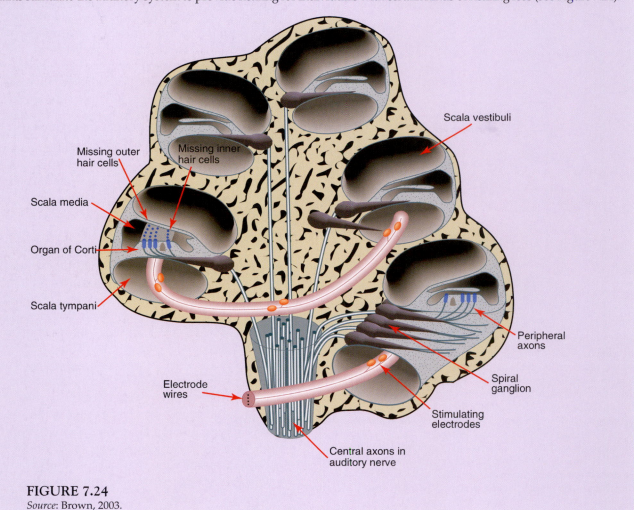

FIGURE 7.24
Source: Brown, 2003.

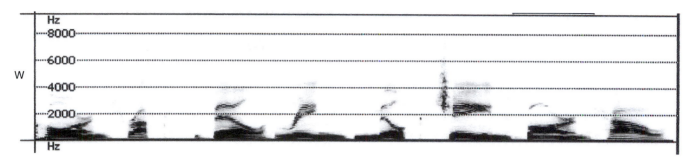

FIGURE 7.25 Spectrograms of individual spoken words. Time is depicted on the x-axis and frequency is depicted on the y-axis. Darker shadings indicate higher amplitude, mostly contained in the formants within each speech sound. *Source:* Adapted with permission from Binder *et al.*, 2000.

A second invention was actually developed during World War II but kept secret until after the war ended: the *spectrograph*. The spectrograph was also developed by scientists at Bell Labs and was based on some of the principles Dudley developed during the making of the vocoder. The spectrograph analyzed the sound signals and produced a picture called a *spectrogram* (Figure 7.25) or visible speech (Potter *et al.*, 1947). In a spectrogram, frequency of the speech signal is presented on the y-axis and time on the x-axis. The shading of the speech signal represents a third dimension, intensity (or energy). Intensity is presented in two ways: across time (x-axis) and within frequency (y-axis). In this way, the amount of intensity or energy can be represented both as a function of time during a sentence and as a function of frequency band within a spoken syllable or word. No shading (white areas) in regions of the spectrogram along the x-axis indicates silence at those points in time. No shading in regions up and down the y-axis, within each speech sound, indicates no energy at that frequency. Similarly, darker shading along the y-axis indicates more energy at that frequency band. You will note that each speech sound presented in Figure 7.25 has regions of darker shading at fairly narrow frequency bands: these are the *formants* that occur in human speech. Formants occur at fairly regular intervals and are produced by air that oscillates as it ascends through the vocal tract. The formants or harmonics differ by individual, based on the size of their vocal tract. The spectrograph radically changed how speech perception was investigated and provided a method for scientists to evaluate substructural elements of the speech signal in a way never before possible.

There were two important outcomes of early investigations of speech using spectrograms: first, spectrograms of sentences showed that gaps or silences within sentences did not map onto word boundaries, but occurred within words in many cases; and second,

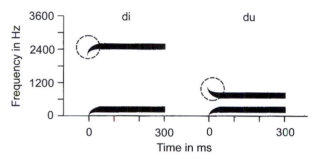

FIGURE 7.26 Schematic illustration of the direction and frequency of formant onsets in the syllables /di/ and /du/, demonstrating that, although the percepts of the two syllables beginning with the sound 'd' will map onto a single phoneme /d/, the physical instantiations of the initial /d/ are quite different. *Source:* Carroll, 1999, originally from Liberman, 1970.

inspection of the detailed information for individual phonemes showed that the formant structure for phonemes, such as /d/, differed sharply depending on the following vowel (Figure 7.26).

These two findings had important ramifications on models describing how the brain decodes speech. First, gaps or silences in the speech stream do not provide the speech decoding system with information about when a word begins or ends. Clearly, the speech system needed to use other cues for word recognition. Second, individual phonemes in speech were physically quite different depending on the phonemes that occurred just before and after them. This *lack of invariance* implied that there were no simple sound templates in the brain that mapped in a one-for-one basis to phoneme identities.

Despite these complexities regarding how speech is decoded, spectrograms enabled speech scientists to describe pictorially important features in phonemes, such as where in the speech articulation system they are produced (place of articulation) and the duration of the onset of vocal cord vibration (voice onset time).

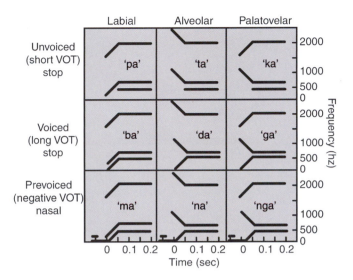

FIGURE 7.27 Schematic illustrations of the formant patterns for distinctive features in classes of speech sounds. *Source*: Brown, 2003.

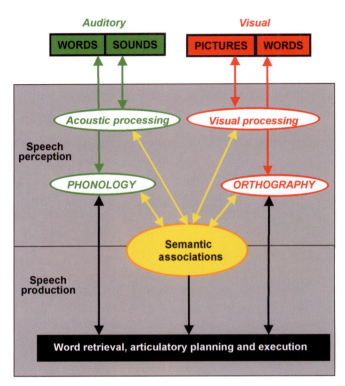

FIGURE 7.28 A process model for word comprehension. *Source*: Adapted from Frackowiak, 2004.

Consonants could now be categorized according to these *distinctive features* (Figure 7.27).

4.2 Early theories of speech perception

An important outcome of early speech science was the realization that the physical features in individual speech sounds or phonemes did not provide invariant information for their decoding. Recall that the work of Fourier and Ohm provided a basis for deconstructing complex sounds into simpler sinusoidal parts. The findings of lack of invariance in speech sounds indicated that speech decoding systems must be quite different than those for decoding other types of sound. That is, if speech perception did not entail an analysis of the sum of the physical parts, and it clearly could not because the physical parts vary widely for a single phoneme, then how was it performed? One theory was that the neural systems for speech decoding were specialized and not part of the general auditory system. A strong view of this theory that 'speech was special' held that the special systems for speech decoding occurred as early as the ear (Liberman *et al.*, 1967). The lack of invariance finding led Liberman and colleagues to develop the *motor theory of speech perception* (for a review, see Liberman and Mattingly, 1985). This theory suggested that speech perception was tightly coupled to speech production, specifically the motor articulation processes or gestures used in producing speech. While the acoustics of phonemes lack invariance, the motor theory held that the articulatory gestures used

to produce them were invariant and the neural representations of these gestures were accessed in speech perception. Other theories for speech perception have been developed since the motor theory, and this work is ongoing in speech science, with the underlying notion that the speech system must have a way to maintain a perceptual constancy across a wide variety of physical features in phonemes and words.

A central debate in speech perception science has raged since the work of Liberman and colleagues during the 1950s and 1960s: the 'speech is special' view holds that speech and language processes are encapsulated within a specific language system, i.e. they are *domain-specific* (where the domain is language). An alternative view is that speech and language processes exploit brain systems in use in general cognition, i.e. they are *domain-general*. For speech perception, early work by Tallal and colleagues provided evidence that left lateralized language processing was not due to domain-specific language organization in that hemisphere but, rather, was due to a domain-general auditory processing bias in the left hemisphere for decoding rapidly changing temporal features in sounds, such as those contained in speech (for a review, see Tallal, 2001). These two opposing viewpoints are still the topic of ongoing discussion and have not yet been resolved, however, it is likely that the neural systems for decoding speech have a combination of domain-specific and domain-general processing.

4.2.1 Units of analysis – the building blocks for the speech system

What are the basic elements or units for decoding speech? Is it the phoneme? The syllable? The early findings of a lack of invariance in phonemes provide evidence against the phoneme as the best unit of analysis for speech perception, although phonemes are clearly critical elements in speech perception. Speech contains multiple cues, however, and so it is perhaps not surprising that a simple one-to-one mapping of phonemes to words does not provide a full description of the processes underlying speech perception (see Scott and Wise, 2004, for a review). Recall that the auditory system is not a uni-directional system, but has complex feedback systems that extend all the way to the cochlea as well as parallel interactive systems across cortical regions within auditory cortex, across the hemispheres, and extending to other sensory and memory systems.

These complex processing pathways clearly aid in decoding the speech signal. The syllable as a basic unit of speech makes some intuitive sense because of the lack of invariance issue as well as the importance of decoding syllabic stress when mapping sound onto meaning. For example, the words 'melody' and 'melodic' are very similar in terms of the sequence of the phonemes, however, the syllabic stress differences in the two words lend an important cue to understanding their meanings. Nevertheless, the field of speech science has not agreed upon an answer to the question of what is the best unit of analysis for understanding speech and this issue must remain unresolved here.

4.2.2 Minimal information for decoding speech

Since the speech signal is so complex with many overlapping cues, perhaps a better way to understand how speech is encoded is to investigate what is the minimal information required to comprehend speech? This approach was taken by Shannon and colleagues (Shannon *et al.*, 1998) with the central idea that the 'shape' of the speech signal, i.e. the rising and falling fluctuations over time or *temporal envelope*, carries the minimal information required for decoding speech. Shannon presented degraded speech that had no frequency information but differing levels of temporal information. Listeners were able to decode continuous speech with remarkable accuracy, indicating that while frequency information is obviously important in

decoding speech, it is not necessary. Shannon's work provided evidence that the temporal envelope of speech might carry more relevant information for its decoding than the fine-grained features found in phonemes.

The lack of general agreement regarding the basic building blocks of speech in the field of speech science makes the investigation of the neural bases of speech perception somewhat more difficult! Nevertheless, there have been many studies of how speech and other classes of sounds are decoded in the brain and we highlight some of these here for you in the following section.

4.3 Functional mapping of speech-specific processes

Early neuroimaging studies by Binder and colleagues (for a review, see Binder, 1997) investigated stimulus-based differences in auditory cortex by comparing brain activation in response to speech sounds (words) versus tones or noise. A general finding was more widespread activation in superior temporal gyrus and the superior temporal sulcus for words as compared to the tones or noise. Although these results could be interpreted as representing speech-specific processing in those auditory regions, they were difficult to interpret, however, because words and the non-speech sounds (tones, noise) differed not only in terms of representing speech versus non-speech classes of sounds, but also in their complexity. Therefore, different brain activation patterns might reflect speech versus non-speech functional areas, but might also reflect areas that differ in terms of decoding complex features in sounds.

A recent investigation addressed these issues with the presentation of many classes of sounds, including noise bursts, tones, words, pseudowords (pronounceable non-words, such as 'hig', and reversed speech (Binder *et al.*, 2000). The aims of this study were to investigate auditory cortical regions that were activated for speech versus non-speech, and compare regions that were activated for words versus pseudowords versus reversed speech (Figure 7.29).

The major findings were that Heschl's gryus and the planum temporale were activated similarly for all sound stimuli. This result supports the notion that sound is processed in a hierarchical fashion, with Heschl's gyrus showing activation for all classes of sounds and likely representing an early sensory analysis. Speech sounds activated a larger region of auditory cortex than the non-speech sounds, extending into the posterior superior temporal gyrus and the superior temporal sulcus. Interestingly, the activation did not differ for words, pseudowords, and reversed speech. These findings

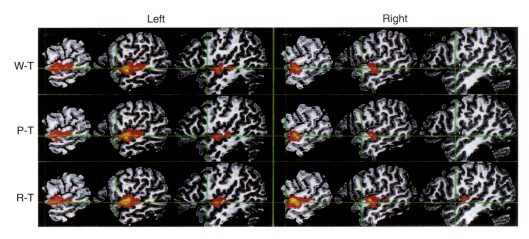

FIGURE 7.29 Comparison between three speech-Tones contrasts (Word-Tones (W-T), Pseudowords-Tones (P-T) and Reversed-Tones (R-T)). Areas responding more to speech than to Tones are very similar for all contrasts. *Source*: Adapted from Binder *et al.*, 2000.

indicate that speech activates a larger-scale network of auditory cortex than the simpler noise bursts and tones. Because there were no differences between the words, pseudowords, and reserved speech conditions, Binder and colleagues concluded that these regions likely do not reflect semantic processing of the word meaning, but reflect phonological processing of the speech sounds.

There are many active lines of investigation into the neural mechanisms and regions employed in decoding human speech and this work is ongoing. Let's move ahead to a discussion of the relationship between 'hearing' and 'saying': speech perception versus production.

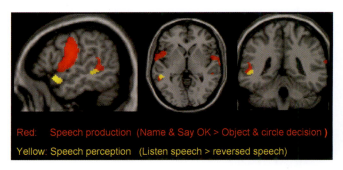

FIGURE 7.30 Red shaded areas show activation for speech production while yellow shaded areas show activation for listening to speech. *Source*: Adapted from Frackowiak, 2004.

4.4 The link between speech perception and production

Early neuroimaging studies investigated brain activation for hearing versus producing speech. One important finding that has been reproduced many times is that auditory cortex is activated during speech production tasks as well as during the perception of speech (Figure 7.30).

Why is auditory cortex active during speech production? Is it simply the case that while producing speech, we hear our own voice? Or does the auditory system play a role in speech production? There is evidence from neuroimaging studies, as well as from lesion studies with patients with aphasia, that speech perception and production systems are tightly coupled. From infancy, as speech and language are acquired, there are complex interactions between heard language and spoken language which guide the development of language. In fact, Carl Wernicke proposed a model for language

processing in the late 19th century that included a pathway from auditory speech perception areas to motor speech production areas and proposed that the sound images of words would serve to constrain the output when producing words. This model remains in use today, and while we know more about dynamic brain processes now than during Wernicke's time, the model has provided an important theoretical framework for studying human language systems.

4.4.1 Inner speech

What about brain areas for speech production when actual speech is not actually produced, when we talk to ourselves? The investigation of brain areas involving inner speech provides an intriguing way in which to study our own consciousness. In a recent article, Hesslow (2002) addressed this issue and proposed a simplified

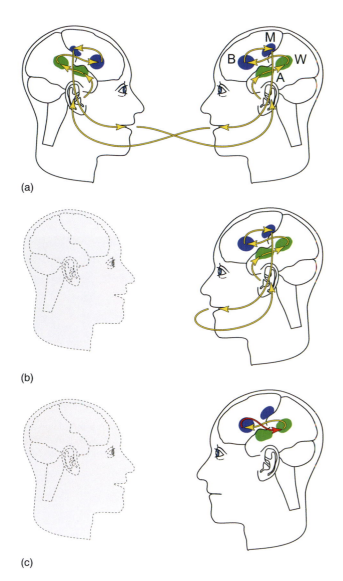

(a)

(b)

(c)

FIGURE 7.31 Internal simulation of conversation. (a) We can respond to a question without being conscious of our behavior. The verbal signal enters the primary auditory cortex (A) and then Wernicke's are (WA). This will elicit formation of a reply in Broca's area (B) and the primary motor cortex (M). (b) We can also listen and respond to our own talk using the same brain regions. (c) If the preparation of the verbal response can be fed directly (red arrow) into auditory cortex or Wernicke's area, we can also speak silently to ourselves using essentially the same mechanisms. *Source*: Adapted from Hesslow, 2002.

model of brain areas that may be employed for inner speech (Figure 7.31).

There is some empirical support for Hesslow's notion, from a neuroimaging study of brain areas active during silent inner speech (Figure 7.32).

While there are clearly complex interactions between brain areas for decoding speech and producing speech, theorized in early motor theories of speech perception

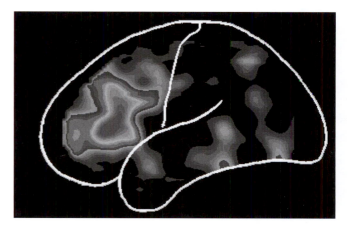

FIGURE 7.32 Left hemisphere brain areas active during inner (silent) speech. *Source*: Adapted from Frackowiak, 2004.

and realized in later brain studies, the exact nature of the integrative processes and neural territory that are shared during listening versus producing speech are still being elucidated in the field of human language research.

4.5 Damage to speech perceptual systems

Prior to the advent of neuroimaging, much of what we learned about brain systems for decoding speech came from investigations with individuals who had brain damage, typically due to a stroke since they produce damage that is more limited in brain area than, for example, a closed-head injury. Strokes, nevertheless, can vary widely in the amount of brain area affected. The result of the stroke is a blockage of blood flow, which causes neuronal death and produces a lesion. The lesion in the area affected by the stroke, in turn, produces behavioral symptoms due to the brain damage. When a stroke patient has impaired language function it is called *aphasia*. Patients with aphasia have widely varying symptoms depending on the location and the size of their lesion. Two basic classifications of aphasia come from 19th century neuroanatomical investigations of brain areas for language: Paul Broca discovered a region in the inferior frontal lobe that was important for speech production, and Carl Wernicke discovered a region in the temporal lobe that was important for speech perception. Damage to these regions would produce aphasia with symptoms that differed depending on which area was affected: an individual whose major symptoms are impaired speech production is classified as a *Broca's aphasic*, an individual whose major symptoms are impaired speech comprehension is classified as a Wernicke's aphasic (Figure 7.33).

Blumstein and colleagues (for a review, see Blumstein, 1997) used careful testing to determine which aspects of speech comprehension were affected in aphasia. One series of experiments was designed to determine if speech comprehension problems were due to damage to speech perceptual processes for mapping the acoustic sound onto abstract phoneme representations (*phonemic deficit*) or if they were due to word recognition processes for mapping the phonemes onto meaning (*semantic deficit*). Blumstein used an auditory word-to-picture matching task to test the aphasic patients. In this task, the patient hears a word and must point to the picture that matches the word. The picture choices include a picture of the word that was heard (the target) and three incorrect choices (foils): one foil is similar in its sound (phonemic), one is similar in meaning (semantic), and one is unrelated to the target word in either sound or meaning. In Figure 7.34, we recreate this experiment: the left panel shows examples of target words 'keys' and 'peas' which differ in the place of articulation of the initial consonant but otherwise share distinctive features (voicing: they are both voiceless, manner: they are both stop consonants). The right panel shows representational picture choices, with a semantic foil (carrots) on the top left, an unrelated picture on the top right, a phonemic foil (keys) on the bottom right, and the correct choice, peas, on the bottom left.

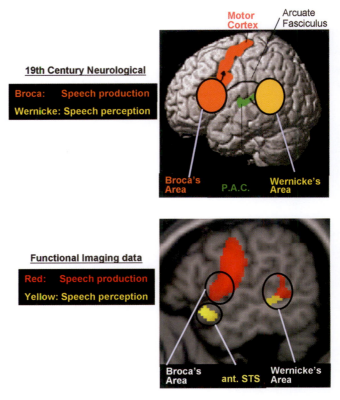

FIGURE 7.33 Upper panel shows classical language areas adapted from 19th century neuroanatomists. Lower panel shows contemporary view of the classical models. *Source*: Adapted from Frackowiak, 2004.

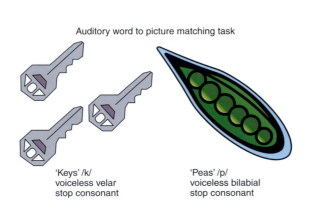
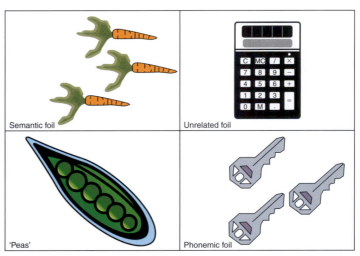

FIGURE 7.34 Left panel illustrates the minimal pairs of words that have initial consonants that differ in a single distinctive feature. In this case, the initial /k/ and /p/ differ in place of articulation (velar versus bilabial) but are matched for voicing (voiceless) and manner (stop consonant). Right panel depicts the stimuli used for a single trial in an auditory-word-to-picture naming task. The subject hears a word, in this case 'peas' and is asked to point to the picture that matches the word. Upper left panel shows a meaning-based (semantic) foil, upper right panel shows an unrelated foil, lower left panel shows the correct (target) response, and the lower right panel shows a sound-based (phonemic) foil.

The pattern of errors (pointing to the incorrect picture) made by the patient provides information about which decoding processes are damaged. If the patient makes mostly phonemic or sound-based errors, then the inference is that processes underlying the mapping of acoustic sound onto phonemes are impaired. On the other hand, if the patient makes mostly semantic errors, the inference is that sound mapping processes are intact and the speech recognition problems are due to impairments in systems for mapping phonemes onto meaning. Two important results of these investigations are that the pattern of errors made by patients did not correspond in a meaningful way to their aphasia classification: for example, one might suppose that Wernicke's aphasics would make many more phonemic errors, due to damage in speech comprehension brain areas, than Broca's aphasics. This was not the case however. The second important result was that all aphasics – Broca's and Wernicke's – did quite well on this task. The conclusion drawn was that speech perception, the ability to map the acoustic features of a sound onto representational phonemes, is largely intact in aphasia. The deficits in comprehending speech, therefore, are not due to sound based impairments. These and other investigations of brain areas that subserve speech perception provide evidence that, while language function tends to be lateralized to the left hemisphere in most right-handed individuals, speech perceptual processes may be organized bilaterally, i.e. in both hemispheres.

Subsequent studies have provided further evidence to support this conclusion: in order for an individual to show severe speech perception impairment (called 'pure word deafness'), brain damage must include lesions in both hemispheres or lesions in the left hemisphere that include damage to the corpus callosum, prohibiting right hemisphere information flow to the left (see Poeppel, 2001 for a review).

4.6 A working model for speech perception in the brain

For most right-handed individuals, language is lateralized to the left hemisphere. The language system is not unitary, however, and includes many computational stages from decoding the speech sounds to form an abstract representation, to making contact with semantic and grammatical systems, to producing speech. A recent model of the auditory language system proposes that early speech decoding processes are organized bilaterally in left and right auditory fields while later semantic/

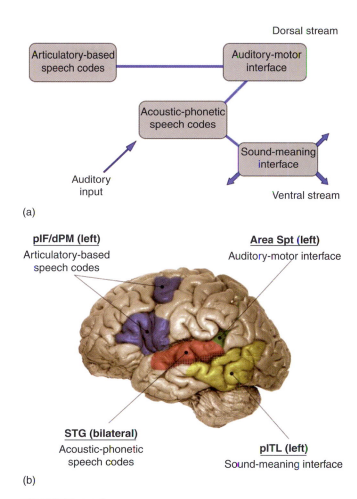

(a)

(b)

FIGURE 7.35 (a) Shows a schematic for the model of auditory language processing proposed by Hickok and Poeppel, 2004. (b) Shows brain regions proposed to reflect stages of the model. Note that early speech perceptual systems for mapping the acoustic-phonetic information in sounds onto meaning are proposed to be mediated bilaterally in left and right hemispheres while later processes are proposed to be mediated by left hemisphere regions. *Source*: Adapted from Hickok and Poeppel, 2004.

syntactic processes are organized in the left hemisphere (Figure 7.35) (Hickok and Poeppel, 2004).

While we have learned a lot about how speech is processed in the brain, through neuroimaging studies with healthy individuals and neuropsychological studies of individuals with brain damage, our understanding of how speech is perceived is still an ongoing investigation. Perhaps this is not surprising since speech perception scientists have not agreed upon the basic units of analysis for speech perception! New techniques, such as TMS, and innovative experimental designs are providing new data for understanding how we decode speech and where in the brain these systems are located.

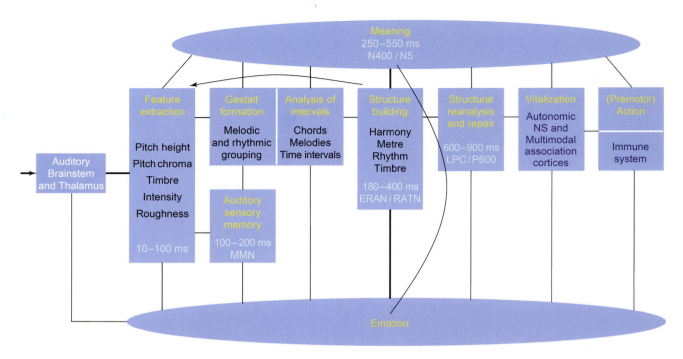

FIGURE 7.36   A processing model for music perception. *Source*: Adapted from Koelsch and Siebel, 2005.

5.0 MUSIC PERCEPTION

Like speech perception, music perception is uniquely human. There are many similarities in speech and music perception: music has complex phrase structures and its perception involves the mapping of sound onto meaning (and emotion). Music perception allows for the recognition of melodies despite differences in instruments, keys, and tempos, thus it cannot be a system built on absolutes but must have relative representations. Thus, music perception systems must have the ability to maintain a perceptual constancy in music representation. A central difference between speech and music perception is that all typically developing humans master speech perception. We are not only good at speech perception, we are masters! This is not the case in music perception: there is tremendously more variability in music perception abilities and significantly more explicit learning that goes along with musical acuity. The variability in music perception abilities combined with the many levels of musical training and skill has made the study of music perception difficult because of these inherent individual differences. These difficulties, however, provide a unique opportunity in that they provide an opportunity to understand the effects of learning and plasticity in the brain areas that decode music.

5.1 Stages of music processing

The perception of features in music involves many stages of processing within the auditory system as well as across brain regions (Figure 7.36). This processing must include feedback as well as feedforward systems as well as making contact with stored memories and experiences as well as emotional systems. Music perception is quite different than speech perception in that many musical signals do not contain any lyrics. Thus, the music perception processes likely have a more abstract (non-linguistic) representational basis.

While the music signal is complex, like all sound, music has basic physical elements: frequency, intensity and time. The psychological aspects of frequency and time in music correspond to pitch (melody) and temporal structure (rhythm). Traditionally, melodic and temporal aspects of music have been investigated as separate features of music perception, however, they likely are not completely independent. Just as some speech scientists propose that speech may be processed in brain areas specialized just for speech, music scientists have theorized that there may be neural systems specialized for music. Evidence in support of music-specific systems in the brain has been provided in neuropsychological studies with patients who have suffered brain damage. Peretz and colleagues have provided a series of investigations

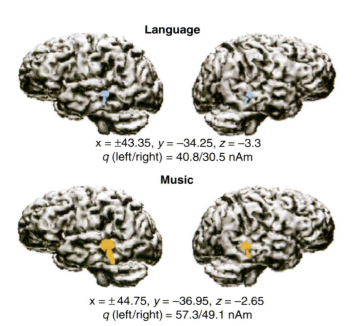

Language

$x = \pm 43.35$, $y = -34.25$, $z = -3.3$
q (left/right) = 40.8/30.5 nAm

Music

$x = \pm 44.75$, $y = -36.95$, $z = -2.65$
q (left/right) = 57.3/49.1 nAm

FIGURE 7.37 Top panel shows brain areas active for language. Bottom panel shows brain areas active for music. *Source*: Adapted from Koelsch, 2005.

with brain damaged individuals showing that, in some individuals, pitch or melody perception may be selectively damaged, leaving temporal structure perception intact, while in other individuals temporal perception may be damaged while pitch perception is intact. These findings have led to the development of a model for the brain organization for music perception (Peretz and Zatorre, 2005), where melodic features in music are processed preferentially in the right hemisphere and can be selectively impaired with right hemisphere brain damage, whereas temporal structure in music is decoded in a larger network of brain areas in both hemispheres.

5.2 A separate system for music perception?

Is music perception a separable aspect of auditory processing? While the work of Peretz and colleagues provides compelling evidence that this is the case, a recent review (Koelsch, 2005) of neuroimaging studies of music perception describes a growing body of evidence in support of the view that some aspects of music perception, notably the musical structure or syntax and the musical meaning or semantics, share neural territory with brain areas for language processing (Figure 7.37).

While there is ample evidence from the work of Peretz and colleagues (see Peretz and Zatorre, 2005, for a

review) that music perception may be selectively – and differentially – damaged with lesions in left or right hemispheres, the studies reviewed by Koelsch (2005) provide compelling evidence for at least some shared systems in music and language processing. Language and music are both uniquely human and highly structured signals, with multiple dimensions along spectral and temporal axes for understanding their basic and complex structures. Perhaps there is no unitary brain region for either language or music: it may be the case that language and music systems have some neural territory that is specific for their processing and some neural territory that is shared. Complicating an already complicated issue are the differing amounts of musical training and levels of expertise among humans, musicians and non-musicians.

6.0 LEARNING AND PLASTICITY

A central theme in the study of human cognition has been the investigation of how new information is encoded in the brain during *learning* and how the brain adapts and reorganizes to new situations or following damage, *plasticity*. These issues are of theoretical value in understanding brain function but also have important practical relevance. One key question is how the auditory cortex responds to deprivation of sensory input due to acquired hearing loss, neural damage, or deafness. For example, if a child is born profoundly deaf and is fitted with a cochlear implant at age 2, will his auditory cortex be receptive to sound and will he hear normally? Or will the 2 years of no exposure to sound limit the effectiveness of the implant? These and other questions regarding cortical plasticity are under intense investigation by auditory scientists.

6.1 Plasticity due to deprivation

Much of what we have learned about the plasticity of the auditory system due to deprivation comes from animal studies. Recall that the cochlea and brainstem are organized tonotopically and that this organization is also present in auditory cortex. In animal studies of neural plasticity after deprivation, specific areas within the cochlea or in the brainstem are lesioned so that a range of frequencies will no longer be encoded and transmitted to auditory cortex. Following lesioning, the organization of auditory cortex is studied to determine if there are frequency specific changes, reflecting neural plasticity. Irvine and colleagues have conducted many studies using this general approach and reported evidence that the cortical frequency maps do indeed undergo changes following the lesioning (Rajan *et al.*, 1993). We cannot ethically lesion human cochlea or brainstems and so our studies of plasticity following deprivation in humans must be accomplished in a non-invasive manner. While these studies are still in early stages, there is evidence that adults with sudden onset high frequency hearing loss have some changes in neural population response in auditory cortex, implying that cortical organizational changes occur following hearing loss in humans in a manner similar to findings in animal studies (Dietrich *et al.*, 2001). However, these adults had sudden onset hearing loss and far less is known about slow onset hearing loss that may occur over many years or about more subtle forms of hearing loss.

What about children who are born with partial or complete deafness? When they are fitted with hearing aids or implanted with cochlear implants, will they develop normal hearing? Eggermont and colleagues have investigated the responses in auditory cortex in typically developing children and children with hearing loss who had cochlear implants (Ponton *et al.*, 1996a,b). The implanted children showed some maturational lag compared to the controls, however, following implantation their auditory system continued to mature in a typical fashion, showing evidence for plasticity in the implanted children. These results are heartening in that they show that auditory cortex may develop in a typical way even if there is deprivation early in life.

6.2 Plasticity due to learning

Our auditory system is constantly exposed to novel sensory inputs that must be decoded in order for us to interpret our listening environment. New voices, musical melodies, and environmental sounds are learned every day. What are the brain mechanisms for learning new sounds? How are these new sensory memories formed and where are they located in the brain? These questions have been the topic of years of investigation by scientists using animal models for understanding learning and plasticity in the auditory system. While some scientists hold that sensory-based memories are formed and stored in central memory systems, others suggest that these sensory-specific memories are formed and stored within the sensory area in which they were learned. For example, Weinberger and colleagues (see Rutkowski and Weinberger, 2005, for a recent review) have developed a model for auditory learning that holds that the changes in neural tuning for new and relevant sounds happen almost immediately, within a few trials of training, and occur in primary auditory (A1) cortex. According to this view, the neural tuning of neurons in A1 changes to reflect the features in sounds that are behaviorally relevant. Using classical conditioning experimental paradigms, Weinberger and colleagues presented tones paired with mild electrical shock. After conditioning, the representational maps of A1 reflected a reorganization, with more neural area devoted to encoding the frequency of the paired tone (Figure 7.38).

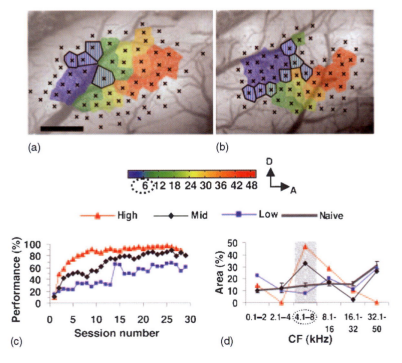

FIGURE 7.38 Examples of the effects of training on representational area. Organization of center frequencies (CFs) in A1 (primary auditory cortex) for a representative untrained naïve (a) and a trained experimental (b) rat. Each 'x' indicates an electrode penetration, with colored polygons indicating the estimated AI are representing the CF according to the color bar shown below the maps; D, dorsal, A, anterior. Cortical area representing CFs within the conditioned stimulus (CS) octave band, i.e. 4.1–8 kHz, is highlighted by outlined polygons and vertical hatching. (c) Learning curves for three animals showing low (blue squares), mid (black diamonds), and high (red triangles) levels of motivation level. (d) Corresponding distributions of relative representational area (per cent of total A1 area) for each animal, together with mean naïve areas (gray line), are shown. Vertical bars on naïve area distribution indicate +/− SEM; dashed circle and light gray box highlight the CS bin. *Source*: Adapted from Rutkowski and Weinberger, 2005.

6.3 Plasticity due to expertise

Non-invasive behavioral studies show similar patterns for learning in humans in that learning changes occur fairly rapidly and are relatively long lasting. One aspect of learning that has intrigued scientists is whether highly trained musicians have a different kind of brain than unskilled individuals. Certainly, the musicians have spent more time and effort on musical training – does this change the way their auditory cortex is tuned? The work of Rupp and colleagues provide evidence that it does (Schneider *et al.*, 2002) (Figure 7.39).

The notion of brain changes due to situation-specific experiences such as hearing loss or deprivation, learning, and expertise is an intriguing one and there are many studies ongoing to investigate the correspondence between experience and mechanism, mind and brain.

7.0 AUDITORY AWARENESS AND IMAGERY

We can close our eyes and shut out visual images but we cannot close our ears to shut out auditory events. What is the effect on the auditory system? The auditory system is the last sensory system to fall asleep (or become unconscious with sedation) and the first to awaken. In this section, we highlight some recent studies of auditory awareness during less-than-conscious states, such as sleep or sedation. We also highlight studies of auditory activation for imagined-not-heard sounds. These aspects of auditory processing are in their infancy, however, brought about by the advent of neuroimaging techniques to measure brain responses that are not easily accessed using other techniques, and so much more work must be done before we can state definitively how auditory awareness and imagery are instantiated in the brain.

7.1 Auditory awareness during sleep and sedation

Think about the best way to wake up a sleepy friend – call his name! A neuroimaging study investigated brain responses in sleep and in wakefulness in two conditions: neutral, where the sound was a simple beep, and significant: where the sound was the subject's own name (Portas *et al.*, 2000). Two main results of that study were that beeps and names activated auditory cortex both when the subject was awake and when the subject was sleeping, indicating that auditory cortex processes sounds even during sleep (Figure 7.40). A second key finding was that auditory cortex response for the neutral tone versus the subject's name did not differ during sleep, indicating that auditory processing during sleep encodes the presence of sounds but did not differentiate between these very different sounds.

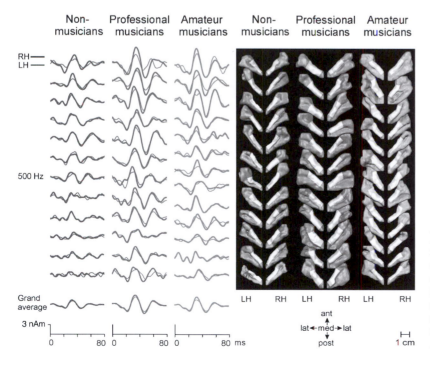

FIGURE 7.39 The neurophysiological and anatomical data show a large increase in professional musicians and a smaller increase in amateur musicians. Left, dipole strength of the primary cortical response at 500 Hz. Sources in the right (thick lines) and left (thin lines) hemispheres are superimposed. Right, highlighted areas show the Heschl's gyrus for each subject, aligned in the same order as the primary evoked responses. *Source*: Adapted from Schneider *et al.*, 2002.

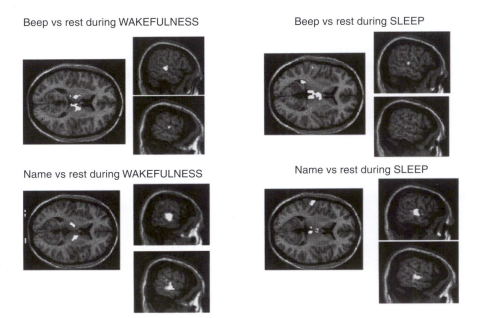

Beep vs rest during WAKEFULNESS

Beep vs rest during SLEEP

Name vs rest during WAKEFULNESS

Name vs rest during SLEEP

FIGURE 7.40   Upper panel: brain areas active for beep versus rest during recorded during wakefulness and sleep. Lower panel: brain areas for name versus rest recorded during wakefulness and sleep. *Source*: Adapted from Portas *et al.*, 2000.

Brain activation patterns for names versus tones did differ, however, in middle temporal gyrus and frontal lobe regions. There were also areas in the amgydala that were more active during the presentation of the subject's own name during sleep than when awake. Do these brain areas represent a circuit in the brain that alerts us to wake us up when we hear our own name? More investigations are needed to support this theory, however, these findings provide intriguing evidence for how the auditory system 'wakes itself up'.

A related finding was recently reported by Zatorre and colleagues (Plourde *et al.*, 2006) in a study investigating the effects of anesthesia on surgical patients. Many recent studies have investigated the level of auditory awareness in surgical patients who are anesthetized, with the primary motivation of ensuring that anesthetized patients do not hear sounds in the operating room that may be upsetting to them. Results of the study by Zatorre and colleagues are similar to those reported by Portas and colleagues: auditory cortex was activated by simple and complex sounds during anesthesia and response patterns did not differ for speech versus non-speech sounds (Figure 7.41).

The authors interpreted these findings to indicate that while auditory cortex responds to the presence of sounds, even during sedation, the response is non-specific. This is a similar finding to the results for beeps and names during sleep and wakefulness. However, in

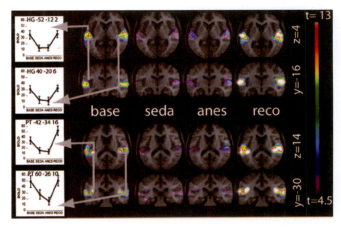

FIGURE 7.41   Group average responses for all sounds-silence. Activation maps overlaid over average anatomical images. The right side of the images corresponds to the right hemisphere. Line diagrams show the mean signal amplitude (difference in effect size between the two conditions, i.e. sound versus silence). *Source*: Adapted from Plourde *et al.*, 2006.

the anesthesia study, the authors suggested that their findings of no differences across types of sounds meant that complex (semantic, emotional) processes engaged during conscious states were not activated during sedation. Which study is right? More investigations with similar stimuli and experimental designs must be conducted in order to determine if there are brain areas that are active during sleep or anesthesia and that might reflect the brain's monitoring of auditory events.

7.2 Auditory imagery

'Sounds not heard' are playing in our heads all day. Some sounds are uncalled for, they just seem to happen: a melody that spins around in your head, your inner voice talking to yourself. Other sounds not heard aloud are planned: practicing lines for a school play or rehearsing a phone number before dialing. Where are these sounds processed in the brain? We are aware that we actually seem to 'hear' these inner sounds, does that mean that auditory cortex is activated when they are playing despite the fact that there is no actual sound? Halpern and colleagues (Halpern *et al.*, 2004) have investigated this question using neuroimaging techniques to measure brain activation for imagined sounds versus heard sounds. Results (shown in Figure 7.42) show that non-primary auditory cortex is indeed active during imagined – and not heard – sounds.

A related finding was reported by Jancke and colleagues (Bunzeck *et al.*, 2005). These investigators wanted to study auditory imagery for environmental sounds. Using fMRI, they recorded neural responses to subjects perceiving sounds and imagining those sounds. Results are presented in Figure 7.43: primary and secondary auditory cortex in both hemispheres is active

when perceiving sounds (left panel), while secondary (and not primary) auditory cortex is active when imagining those same sounds (right panel).

These findings provide compelling evidence that imagined sounds activate similar neural regions in auditory cortex that are activated when sounds are heard. Recall the learning data from Weinberger and colleagues showing that sound-based memory and learning occurred in auditory cortex. The findings presented here, while representing only a small proportion of the ongoing investigation of auditory imagery, indicate that

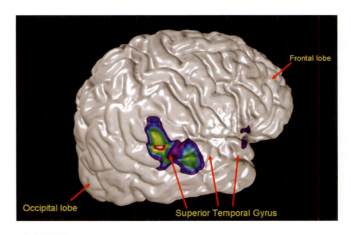

FIGURE 7.42 Illustration of brain areas active for imagined sounds. *Source*: Adapted from Zatorre and Halpern 2006.

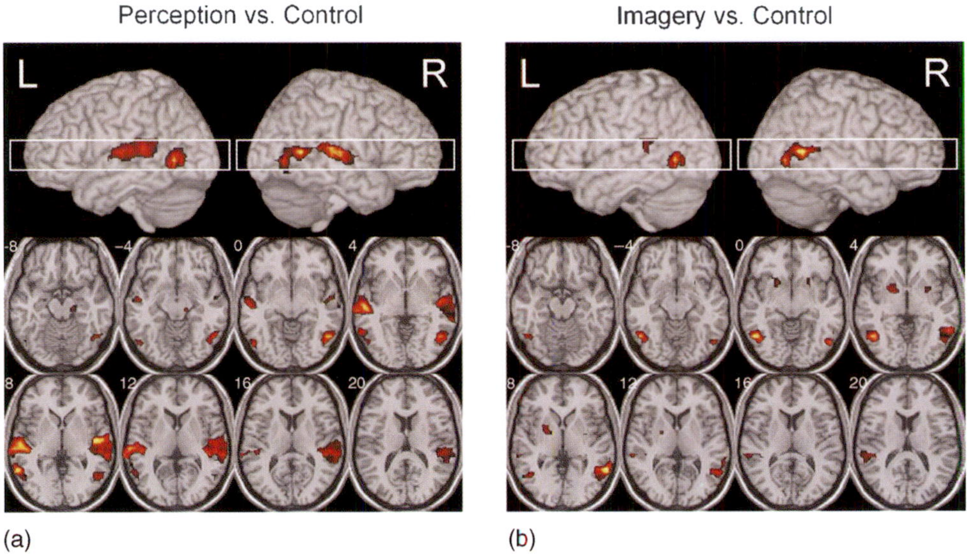

FIGURE 7.43 fMRI study of perceived sounds versus imagined sounds. The sounds used in this study were neither language nor music, in order to determine the localization of imagined non-linguistic or musical sounds. Primary auditory cortex was active during the perception phase of the experiment but not during the imagery phase. *Source*: Adapted from Bunzeck *et al.*, 2005.

similar processes occur in humans as well, with imagining and perceiving sounds sharing neural territory.

8.0 SUMMARY

In this chapter, we presented an overview of the complex auditory system, from hearing basics to music perception to auditory imagery. The advent of neuroimaging techniques has provided a wealth of new data for understanding the cortical auditory system and how it interfaces with other cortical regions. While we have made major inroads on understanding the puzzle of auditory perception, there is still much work to be done. For example, teasing apart neural systems that underlie music and speech perception is still in early phases. There are many other key questions that are being addressed in the field of auditory brain science. For example, what are the differing roles of the left and right hemispheres in speech and music perception?

There is fruitful work in the investigations of processing streams in the auditory system and in the brain. And while the work in non-human primates has informed us greatly about the existence of 'where' and 'what' processing streams, these streams may be established differently for humans due to the unique and important roles of speech and music perception in the evolution and development of the human brain. The next time an uncalled melody plays inside your head, consider the areas that might be activated in your brain as you 'hear' your silent song!

9.0 CHAPTER REVIEW

9.1 Study questions

1 What are the basic physical features and psychological aspects of sound?
2 What are the main parts of the auditory system and what are their roles in perception?
3 Briefly describe some differences between the 'what' and 'where' processing streams.
4 What are the basic units of analysis for speech perception?
5 What have new brain imaging techniques provided us in terms of investigating auditory function?

9.2 Drawing exercise

We highly recommend drawing and coloring to help you remember the physical layout of the brain.

1 Top panel of Figure 7.74: identify auditory cortical areas that are visible on the lateral aspect of the brain.
2 Bottom panel of Figure 7.74: identify the auditory cortical regions denoted by blue, pink, and brown shading.

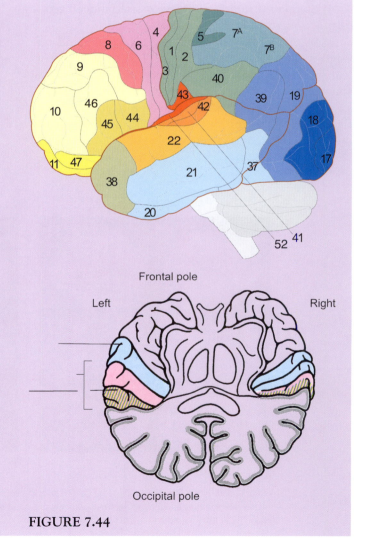

FIGURE 7.44

9.3 Exploring more

Suggested reading and web sources.

Blumstein, S. E. (1997). A perspective on the neurobiology of language. *Brain Lang*, **60**(3), 335–46.

Hickok, G., Poeppel, D. (2004). Dorsal and ventral streams: a framework for understanding aspects of the functional anatomy for language. *Cognition*, **92**, 67–99.

Moore, B. C. (2002). Psychoacoustics of normal and impaired hearing. *BrMed Bull*, **63**, 121–134.

Peretz, I., Zatorre, R. J. (2005). Brain organization for music processing. *Annu Rev Psychol*, **56**, 89–114.

NIH website on the auditory cortex http://www.ncbi.nlm.nih.gov/books/bv.fcgi?rid=neurosci.section.919

NIH website for searching the literature on auditory processes Entrez Pubmed – http://www.ncbi.nlm.nih.gov/entrez/

You can enter names of scientists mentioned in this chapter into a search engine like Google. Many have laboratory websites that are interesting to explore. http://www.google.com

Millions of items . . . are present to my senses which never properly enter into my experience. Why? Because they have no interest for me. My experience is what I agree to attend to. . . . each of us literally chooses, by his ways of attending to things, what sort of a universe he shall appear to himself to inhabit.

William James (1890), *Principles of Psychology*, Ch. XI

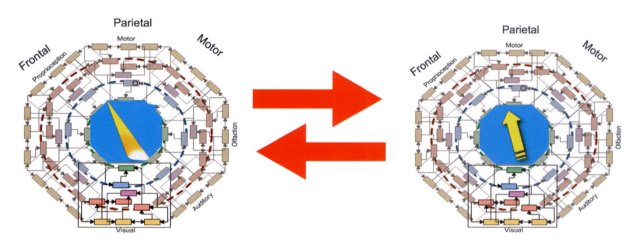

Attention is often thought of as a spotlight, aiming to select some part of the world for conscious access. The 'spotlight of attention' is often thought to involve frontal and parietal cortex as well as subcortical regions. Recent evidence suggests that perceptual consciousness may operate in the opposite direction, beginning from primary sensory cortex and activating frontoparietal regions. Thus we can think of two streams of countervailing information, one selective (selective attention), and the other distributive in its effects (perceptual consciousness).

C H A P T E R

8

Attention and consciousness

Bernard J. Baars

1.0 INTRODUCTION

Attention and consciousness are often thought of in terms of *selection* and *integration*. Attention involves the brain's ability to focus on and select information, as you are doing now; and then to integrate that information – as you are also doing – by perceiving and understanding this sentence, and using it to think, memorize, recall, feel, plan and act in the world. In everyday life, selection and integration work together inseparably. But, by means of careful experiments, it is possible to tease out

selective attention and to distinguish it quite clearly from the *conscious experiences*, which can be reported with accuracy (Baars, 1988, 2002b; Edelman, 1989; Crick and Koch, 1995; Dehaene, 2001; Rees *et al.*, 2002).

2.0 A DISTINCTION BETWEEN ATTENTION AND CONSCIOUSNESS

Common sense makes a distinction between *attention* and *consciousness*. In English, we can ask someone to

Cognition, Brain, and Consciousness, edited by B. J. Baars and N. M. Gage
ISBN: 978-0-12-373677-2

Copyright 2007, Elsevier Ltd. All rights reserved.

'please pay attention' to something, but not to 'please be conscious' of it. But of course, when people pay attention to something they generally do become conscious of it. Likewise, we can 'call' someone's attention by prodding the person or shouting; as soon as we succeed, he or she becomes conscious of us.

The common sense distinction between attention and consciousness suggests that there are *attentional control mechanisms* that often determine what will or will not become conscious. This belief is backed by good evidence. We can obviously control what we will be conscious of in a number of voluntary ways: we can decide whether or not to continue reading this book, whether to turn on the television, whether to stop thinking some unpleasant thought, and so on. Many scientists suggest there are also unconscious or automatic ways for things to come to consciousness – if stimuli are intense, dynamic or personally important, for example (Moray, 1959; Hahn *et al.*, 2006). Music videos are perhaps the ultimate example of bottom-up attention. They are designed to capture attention by intense sound and sights, fast cross-cutting of video shots, rapid zooms, and emotionally provocative scenes.

While there is debate about the scientific meaning of 'consciousness' and 'attention', in actual practice these terms are clear enough. 'Attention' implies *selecting* one event over another, while *conscious* events are those that humans can report accurately. Attentional selection often leads to conscious results, in much the way that your eye movements lead to the conscious experience of a coffee cup on the table in front of you.

The contents of consciousness[1] include the immediate perceptual world; inner speech and visual imagery; the fleeting present and its fading traces in immediate memory; bodily feelings like pleasure, pain, and excitement; autobiographical memories when they are remembered; clear and immediate intentions, expectations and actions; explicit beliefs about oneself and the world; and concepts that are abstract but focal. Obviously, we are conscious of much more than we report at any given time, but humans can answer questions about a remarkable range of conscious events – the sight of a single star on a dark night, the difference between the sounds 'ba' and 'pa', and the goal of studying for an exam. All sensory systems do a great deal of unconscious processing, leading to conscious, reportable sights, sounds, and feelings.

Recalling an autobiographical memory also results in conscious experiences, like your memory of seeing this book for the first time. Inner speech and imagery have conscious aspects. Asking someone to rehearse a list of words usually results in conscious inner speech. People vary in the vividness of their visual images, but dreams, for example, are classically reported to have vivid imagery (Stickgold *et al.*, 2001). Finally, action planning can have conscious components, especially when we have to make choices about our actions (Lau *et al.*, 2004a,b). Normally, we may not have to think much about the action of walking, but if we break a leg, even standing up and walking can become a consciously planned process (Sacks, 1984).

There is good evidence that we have a spontaneous inner flow of conscious contents which constantly compete against the perceptual world (Singer, 1994; Mazoyer *et al.*, 2001; Fox *et al.*, 2005). In sum, in everyday life, there is ongoing competition between inner and outer events, between perceiving and responding, and between simultaneous input streams. Attentional selection seems to operate every moment of the waking day.

2.1 Cortical *selection* and *integration*

If we go back to our view of the brain as a set of processing hierarchies – sensory, motor, interpretive, cognitive, executive – we can see a need to make the whole system work coherently, but without having it become rigid and inflexible. Figure 8.1 shows how selective attention can be viewed in our overview figure from Chapter 1, p. 2. A large amount of evidence indicates that attention is controlled by a network of frontal and parietal regions, as we will see.

Interestingly, there is now a substantial literature showing that conscious sensory stimuli activate frontal and parietal regions as well (see Figure 8.4). By comparison, unconscious stimuli seem to evoke only local activity in visual areas (Dehaene, 2001; Baars, 2002b; Rees *et al.*, 2002).

It is not known at present whether the same areas in frontoparietal cortex are involved in both consciousness and attention, but there is likely to be some overlap. Attention and consciousness may be two sides of the same coin, with attention selectively biasing some sensory inputs. When selected information becomes conscious, it may activate some of the original frontoparietal loci that selected it in the first place, thus creating a self-sustaining feedback loop for some period of time. That is surely too simple, but it may be part of the picture.

The spotlight metaphor is useful for thinking about selective attention, especially in separating the guidance of the attentional 'spotlight' and its target. These aspects have clear brain correlates, since guidance is

---

[1] In this chapter we use 'awareness' as a synonym for consciousness.

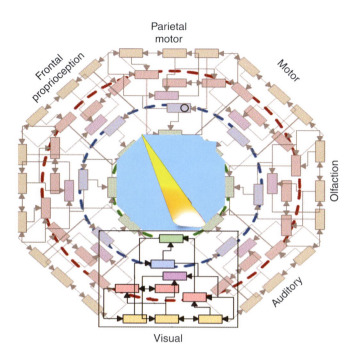

FIGURE 8.1 An attentional spotlight selects among competing inputs. Cortex can be seen as a large array of processing hierarchies for sensory, motor, and cognitive tasks (see Chapter 3). Notice the spotlight icon in the middle of the Friston circle of brain hierarchies. The spotlight is guided by frontal and parietal regions, but it shines on visual cortex to increase signal clarity in visual regions, in this case. *Source*: After Friston, 2003.

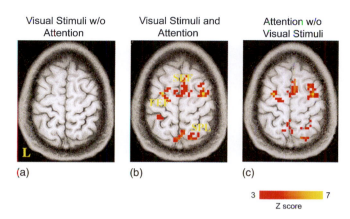

FIGURE 8.2 Visual attention is guided by frontal and parietal cortex, as shown in (b) and (c), but the selected *target* of attention is in visual cortex. *Source*: Kastner and Ungerleider, 2001.

accomplished by a specialized network of brain regions outside of sensory cortex, while the target of sensory attention are the sensory cortices. The spotlight metaphor is widely used (e.g. Treisman and Gelade, 1980; Posner *et al.*, 1982), but like any scientific metaphor, it must be treated with care.

Experiments designed to tease apart attentional selection and visual processes have shown separate activations in sensory and attentional events (Figure 8.2). Attentional selection, directed by prefrontal cortex, 'highlights' visual regions.

Current concepts of conscious cognition suggest that it involves widespread *integration* driven by conscious contents – i.e. the information that is highlighted by selective attention. This might look like Figure 8.3. Consciously-driven integrative processes are critical for learning, decision-making, memory, problem-solving, adapting emotionally and motivationally, and dealing with conflicting inputs: in short, with making sense of the world, and behaving accordingly.

These ideas define the basic story of this chapter. As we will see, it is useful to think of selective attention as a way by which one part of the brain can 'highlight'

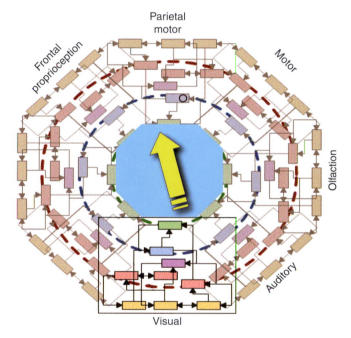

FIGURE 8.3 Sensory consciousness evokes frontoparietal activity. One way of thinking of a conscious visual event, spreading from visual cortex to other regions of the brain. As we will see, a number of imaging studies appear to show this phenomenon, which may be part of the way conscious events lead to wide brain integration. *Source*: After Friston, 2003.

another, like the visual cortex, to bring out selective visual contents. Conscious cognition is often thought to be a result of selection. As we will see, there is reason to think that conscious events may be integrated into other brain functions, including memory, interpretive semantic capacities, and targets for the motor system. That evidence is explored below.

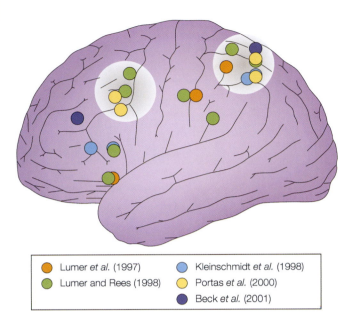

●	Lumer et al. (1997)	●	Kleinschmidt et al. (1998)
●	Lumer and Rees (1998)	●	Portas et al. (2000)
		●	Beck et al. (2001)

FIGURE 8.4 Frontal and parietal correlates of consciousness. Dozens of studies implicate frontal and parietal activation for conscious events, ranging from visual to auditory and even pain perception (Baars, 2002b). This brain drawing summarizes five studies comparing conscious and unconscious sensory events. *Source*: Rees et al., 2002.

2.2 Selective attention: voluntary and automatic

The term attention is used most intuitively when there is a clear voluntary or executive aspect. We ask people to pay attention to things – which implies they can choose to do so, or not, depending upon some executive, decision-making processes. The easiest concept of attention therefore is *voluntary selection* of information. In human experiments we invariably ask participants to pay attention to the stimulus conditions of the experiment. Voluntary attention is the kind that is studied most often, and as one might guess from the other chapters, it is likely to use prefrontal cortex in humans (see Chapter 12).

Corbetta *et al.* (2002) recently wrote that voluntary attention, 'is involved in preparing and applying goal-directed (top-down) selection for stimuli and responses'. Automatic attention, on the other hand, 'is not involved in top-down selection. Instead, this system is specialized for the detection of behaviorally relevant stimuli, particularly when they are salient or unexpected'. While the two systems overlap, they provide a useful first take on the brain basis of selective attention.

However, when we hear a sudden loud noise, our attention is 'captured' even without executive guidance. *Attentional capture* is an important topic, as we will see in the next section on stimulus-driven attention. As you might expect, visual attention can be captured by

human faces, emotional expressions, and bodies, when compared to other objects. Intense or sudden stimuli, or unexpected events in general, generate larger brain responses than control stimuli. Thus, we can talk about *bottom up* capture of selective attention, driven by stimuli, as well as *top down* goal-driven attention, under executive guidance.

In the real world, voluntary and automatic attention are generally mixed. We can train ourselves to pay attention to the sound of the telephone ringing. When it rings and we suddenly pay attention to it, is that voluntary or automatic? Well, it began being more voluntary and becomes more automatic. The dimension of voluntary versus automatic attention is therefore a continuum. Perhaps the strongest case of voluntary is the one where we must exert intense mental effort over a period of time (Chapter 10). A clear example of the opposite pole of the continuum might be a case of a loud sound, or a biologically important event like a crying baby, which is hard not to pay attention to. Figure 8.5 shows a careful study of the *balance* between active and passive viewing, showing increasing top-down effects as attention becomes more active or voluntary.

In sum, attention is defined here as the ability to select information for cognitive purposes. Selection may be shaped by emotion, motivation, and salience, and is at least partly under executive control. Thus, selective attention works closely with all the other components of our framework diagram (Figure 8.6).

Without flexible, voluntary access control, human beings could not deal with unexpected emergencies or opportunities. We would be unable to resist automatic tendencies when they became outdated, or change attentional habits to take advantage of new opportunities. On the other hand, without stimulus-driven attention, we would be slow in selecting significant events. We need both voluntary and automatic attention.

As we have seen before, specific regions of the brain support functions like sensory perception, working memory, language and long-term memory. The same is true of selective attention. As techniques have focused on smaller brain areas working at faster speeds, we have learned more about attentional networks and how they select specific kinds of sensory information. Many lines of evidence now agree on some basic facts.

3.0 EXPERIMENTS ON ATTENTION

How can we study the roles of voluntary and automatic attention in human perception? We mentioned previously that a central facet of attentional processes is

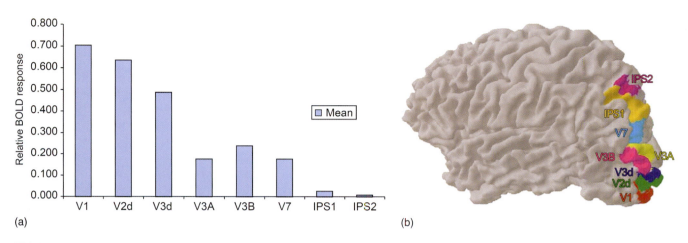

(a)

(b)

FIGURE 8.5 Voluntary versus stimulus-driven attention. Visual brain activity with passive and active viewing. (a) The ratio between top-down and bottom-up activity in visual areas, showing that top-down attention has increasing effects in higher visual areas. (b) The visual cortex seen from the back of the brain for one subject. Notice that some parietal areas are included in visual cortex. *Source*: Serences and Yantis, 2006.

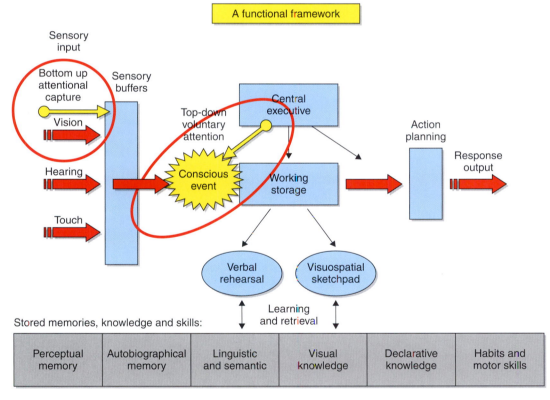

FIGURE 8.6 Selective attention selects different sensory and cognitive processes, as if the yellow arrow can point to any part of the diagram. Conscious cognition is often the result of attentional selection. Currently influential theories suggest that conscious events recruit large-scale activity in frontal and parietal regions.

the presence of competing stimuli. Typically, attention experiments present two or more stimuli to a subject and observe the brain mechanisms by which only one is selected. A great deal has been learned from five decades of such experiments (Itti *et al.*, 2005). For example, we can show a brain difference between *executive attention*, involving voluntary stimulus selection, and *stimulus-driven attention*, in which attention is *captured* by salient stimuli, like the flashing red light on a police car (Hahn *et al.*, 2006). Voluntary or 'top down' attention appears to be initiated in the left frontal lobes, while stimulus-driven or 'bottom up' attention may be enabled by sensory and parietal regions. While we have mentioned some stimulus-driven attentional capture stimuli, such as a loud alarm or a flashing light, other features in stimuli that are not as obviously 'capturing' as loud noises or bright lights can capture our attention. For example, recently, Downing *et al.* (2004) found that pictures of human bodies captured attention even when nothing specific was expected.

3.1 Methods for studying selective attention

3.1.1 Selective listening

Early investigations of selective attention were done by Broadbent (1957) and Cherry (1953). These investigators studied the way we can selectively listen to competing sound inputs. In these classic experiments, Broadbent and Cherry presented their subjects with two streams of speech, one to each ear. Subjects were instructed to repeat each word out loud as soon as they heard it, a task called *shadowing*. They found that people only reported hearing one of the two different speech streams. In other words, they could selectively listen to just a single speech stream at a time, although they could switch between the two (Figure 8.7).

3.1.2 Visual attention

The flanker task (Posner *et al.*, 1984) is an important tool for studying visual attention. The basic method is to present a fixation point to the subject, and then to present stimuli that 'flank' the fixation point, just outside of the foveal region of maximum visual resolution (Figure 8.8). Notice that these tasks do not allow eye movements, but

rely on covert shifts of visual attention. One reason is that eye movements involve large electrical potentials that interfere with brain measurements. Another is that at the beginning of research on this topic, one major question was to avoid confusing eye movement control with attention. As we will see, however, current evidence suggests that visual attention is inseparable from the control systems for eye movements, and may have arisen in evolution from those systems.

Because the flanker task is the most common method for studying visual attention, we will go through it in

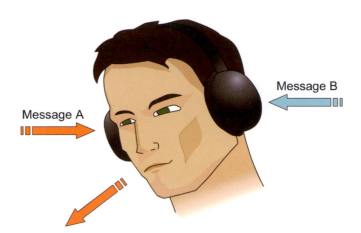

FIGURE 8.7 Selective listening. In a classic series of experiments, Broadbent and Cherry presented subjects with two streams of speech, one to each ear (Cherry, 1953; Broadbent, 1957). Subjects were told to say each word out loud as soon as they heard it, a task called shadowing. In a result that has been repeated thousands of times, they found that people only reported hearing one of the two different speech streams. Linguistic meaning, syntax and words are typically well separated, but vocal quality can be heard on both sides.

A peripheral cue appears (illumination of the left box)   The target appears at the cue location

FIGURE 8.8 The flanker task. The flanker paradigm is used to study visual selective attention and its brain basis. The subject looks at the '+' symbol and peripheral cues draw attention to left or right flanker cues. Accuracy and response speed indicate changes in attentional efficiency. *Source*: Reynolds *et al.*, 2003.

detail. The flanker task is simple, it is effective in triggering separable brain networks, and it is very adaptable. For example, the target stimuli can easily be emotional faces, allowing us to explore how the brain pays attention to emotional events (Posner and Petersen, 1990; Fan *et al.*, 2002).

Here is how the flanker task works:

1 Subjects keep their gaze fixed on the fixation point (+). They look at it from a precise distance, so that the degree of visual arc subtended by the plus sign (+) is constant. The fixation point fills the fovea (the highest-density region of the retina). Outside of the fovea, which covers only 2–4 degrees of arc, the retina loses resolution, and is sensitive only to light and dark edges. (It follows that our normal sense of a rich and colorful visual world is a construction of the visual brain, not a literal record of the input into the retina.)

2 When flanking stimuli appear on either side of the fixation point, they can only be detected using *implicit* attention, because the eyes are fixed on the crosshairs. Posner and Petersen (1990) discovered that people can selectively increase the attentional processing efficiency of retinal inputs that are a few degrees off the fovea (see Chapter 6).

3 Subjects are cued whether to expect a target to flash briefly to the right or left of the crosshairs. In Figure 8.8, a momentary brightening of the left flanker box tells the subject that the target will soon flash on the left side, with 80 per cent probability.

4 In the figure, the target is flashed in the expected location for a fraction of a second. Subjects respond as quickly as possible. Because their expectation is correct in this case, their reaction time and accuracy are optimal.

5 However, the target might also be flashed to the right of the crosshairs, in the unexpected location. This unexpected event imposes a cost in reaction time and accuracy.

Thus, attention has both benefits and costs. An increase in speed and accuracy at the expected location compared to an un-cued neutral condition is considered to be a *benefit* of attention. A loss of speed and accuracy of the unexpected stimulus is considered to be the *cost* of the absence of attention to that event. The flanker task therefore permits quantitative assessment of the cost-benefit tradeoffs for speed and accuracy.

The attention network task (ANT)

The ANT task (Fan *et al.*, 2002) is a generalization of the flanker task, to allow testing of three separable aspects of attention: *alerting* before an expected signal, *orienting* to a specific location in space where the target is expected to appear, and *executive attention* to act against expectations set up by the task.

For example, consider a college student in a large lecture hall. In order to cope with the complex environment with many sensory inputs competing for his attention, he must first be ready and in an *alert* state. Next, he must be flexible in changing his attentional focus to *orient* to new sensory inputs, for example, or to re-orient to relevant information when required. Last, he must have a means for *controlling* these attentional resources.

In adults, brain areas for alerting processes are located in frontal and parietal regions in the right hemisphere (Witte and Marrocco, 1997). Brain areas for orienting are located in right hemisphere temporoparietal junction and the inferior frontal gyrus (Corbetta *et al.*, 2000). Brain areas for executive attention include the anterior cingulate and lateral prefrontal cortex (Marrocco and Davidson, 1998). The last kind is most important for us here.

Visual search paradigms

A well-known case of stimulus-driven attention comes from Anne Treisman's visual search paradigm (Treisman and Gelade, 1980). In the panel on the left in Figure 8.9, the red vertical bar seems to 'pop out' immediately. The same red vertical bar is fairly easy to see in the second panel, but it requires more voluntary effort in the rightmost panel. Treisman and others have suggested that rapid *popout* occurs because of *parallel*

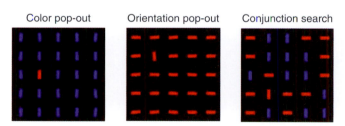

FIGURE 8.9 'Popout' in attentional search. A classical experiment on visual 'popout' for basic features like color and object orientation (Treisman and Gelade, 1980). Notice that the vertical red bar in the left panel tends to come to mind immediately. Reaction time is fast and independent of the number of similar stimuli, called distractors. The identical stimulus in the middle panel is detected somewhat more slowly, and on the right panel we may have to search carefully for the target. In the right-hand panel, where subjects must do voluntary 'conjunction search' for color *and* orientation, search time rises with the number of distractors. These results are interpreted to mean that conjunction search is a serial process, while popout is parallel. *Source*: Treisman and Gelade, 1980.

search, in which all candidate stimuli are available at the same time. The identical red vertical bar on the right-hand panel seems to require *serial search* – a lot of possible candidates are tested before we hit on the right one. As the display becomes more crowded, we can also expect that more voluntary attentional control and eye movements will be needed. Current studies suggest that visual attention can be either parallel or serial, depending on task conditions (Wolfe, 2003).

Other stimuli that drive attention involuntarily include unexpected sounds, abrupt visual stimuli, meaningful words, one's own name, and emotional stimuli like threatening faces (Mack *et al.*, 2002). As we will see, stimulus-driven attention depends on sensory cortex, emotional areas, and some parietal regions.

On the other hand, voluntary attention makes use of executive brain regions, the frontal lobes. In the case of spatial orienting, parietal cortex also becomes part of the voluntary attention network (Posner and Desimone, 1998; Kastner and Ungerleider, 2000).

The Stroop test (Box 8.1) has become a very popular way to test executive attention. It is important to try this for yourself. Look for three things: your own sense of effort in the color-name competition; your reaction time (you can ask somebody else to time you); and your error rate. All three tend to go together.

The Stroop phenomenon generalizes easily to related tasks, as long as different features of the same visual event have different degrees of practice and automaticity. Naming the color of a word is unusual for us, so we require some guided attention to do it. But saying color names is something we've practiced since we learned to read English. The color-naming task therefore creates a conflict between a novel and a well-practiced skill. To resolve that conflict, executive attention is needed. The Stroop test is remarkably effective in evoking activity in executive regions of the brain, as we will see. (See also Chapters 9–11.)

BOX 8.1   Stroop color-naming and executive attention

1	2	3	4
red	blue	xxx	green
green	green	mmmmmm	blue
yellow	red	hhhh	yellow
red	blue	sssss	green
blue	yellow	hhhh	red
green	blue	xxx	blue
blue	green	sssss	yellow
red	red	xxx	xxx
yellow	yellow	mmmmmm	green
blue	green	sssss	red
yellow	yellow	mmmmmm	blue
green	red	hhhh	yellow

Time ____   ____   ____   ____

Fig. 1. The Stroop task.

Equipped with a stopwatch and Fig. 1, you can easily replicate Stroop's original demonstration (Ref. a). For columns 1 and 2, the task is to read each list of words aloud as fast as possible, ignoring their print color. Begin by covering all of the columns except column 1. Start the timer when you say the first word and stop it when you say the last word. Record your time. Now cover all columns except column 2 and read the words aloud again. For columns 3 and 4, the task is changed to naming the print colors aloud as fast as possible, ignoring the letters or words. Do this for the rows of colored letters in column 3 and then for the rows of colored words in column 4.

Stroop observed three primary results. First, reading words was faster than naming colors. This is consistent with word reading being more practised and hence more automatic than color naming (Refs b,c). Second, there was little

Source: Box adopted from Botnnick *et al.*, 2004.

difference in reading the words in columns 1 and 2 (Stroop's Experiment 1): mismatched ink colors did not produce interference in reading the words. Third, in sharp contrast, switching from nonwords to words in color naming made a very large difference between columns 3 and 4 (Stroop's Experiment 2): naming the colors of incompatible color words showed dramatic interference. Apparently, the greater automaticity of word reading leads to the words being read even though they should not be, producing conflicting responses to each stimulus. This both slows down color naming responses and makes errors – reading words instead of naming colors – more likely.

Modern versions of the Stroop task are typically computer-controlled displays of a single word in color, rather than multiple items on a card, permitting more control and more precise measurement of individual item and sequence effects. Also, although Stroop did not include a congruent condition (RED printed in red; say 'red'), modern versions of the task often do. Both of these modifications were introduced by Dalrymple-Alford and Budayr (Ref. d).

References

a Stroop, J.R. (1935) Studies of interference in serial verbal reactions. *J. Exp. Psychol.* 18, 643–662 [Reprinted in *J. Exp. Psychol, Gen.* 121, 15–23]

b Cattell, J.M. (1886) The time it takes to see and name objects. *Mind* 11, 63–65

c Fraisse. P. (1969) Why is naming longer than reading? *Acta Psychol.* 30, 96–103

d Dalrymple-Alford, E.C. and Budayr, B. (1966) Examination of Some aspects of the Stroop color-word test. *Percept. Mot. Skills* 23, 1211–1214

4.0 THE BRAIN BASIS OF ATTENTION

William James wrote, in 1890, that attention helps to:

1 perceive
2 conceive
3 distinguish
4 remember
and
5 shorten reaction-time.

A range of experiments suggests that James was right. Pessoa *et al.* (2003) write:

> What we perceive depends critically on where we direct our attention. For example, attention to a location dramatically improves the accuracy and speed of detecting a target at that location. Attention has been shown not only to increase perceptual sensitivity for target discrimination but also to reduce the interference caused by nearby distracters. Moreover, attention is highly flexible and can be deployed in a manner that best serves the organism's momentary behavioral goals: to locations, to visual features, or to objects. Attention can also be based on internal goals (e.g. finding a familiar face in the crowd) or depend on the external environment (e.g. as when a loud alarm sounds).

4.1 Attention as biased competition among neuron populations

In our busy world, our brain must constantly select among many sensory inputs. Competing inputs may involve spoken words, printed words, songs, or the audio track of a movie that lags a fraction of a second behind the video track. Selective attention may involve a stream of overlapping red and green pictures; it may use binocular rivalry, in which two different pictures are presented to the two eyes. Or it may show a basketball game on top of a football video (Neisser and Becklen, 1975). *Any two sources of input that cannot be integrated and consciously perceived as a whole tend to compete against each other.*

As we discussed in Chapter 1, visual imagery seems to make use of visual cortex, inner speech uses the existing brain regions for outer speech and so on. Interestingly, attention has its own pre-existing analog: visual attention, at least, seems to be closely related to visual eye movements.

We will discuss the evidence for this proposal a little later. But the general point is worth emphasizing: eye movements are *selective* – they are orienting movements of one of our major receptor arrays. They result in a greater focus on one part of a visual scene, while shutting out other parts. That is precisely what selective attention

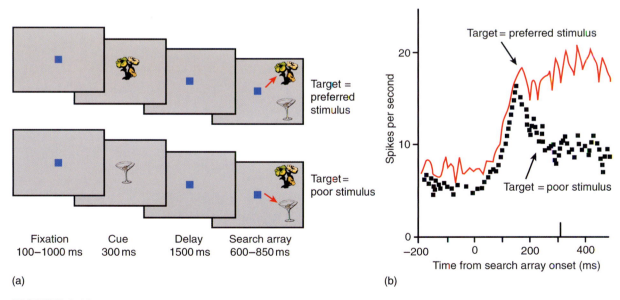

(a)

(b)

FIGURE 8.10 Higher neuronal firing to an attended stimulus. A classic example of an attentional increase in sensitivity at the level of single neurons. The recorded neurons are located in area IT (inferotemporal cortex, the object recognition area), and therefore respond better to some visual objects than others. In this example the flower is the preferred stimulus. This study showed that the neuron begins firing in anticipation of the preferred stimulus at a higher level than for the non-preferred stimulus. *Source*: Reynolds *et al.*, 2003.

does in a more abstract and general fashion. It's attractive to think, therefore, that there may be a relationship between the two. After all, the most visible sign of selective attention in humans and animals is *orienting* one's receptors toward an object: looking, sniffing, listening, and exploring by touch. However, in flanker visual attention experiments, keep in mind that the eyes are not allowed to move.

It is quite remarkable that voluntary attention to a visual stimulus can increase the activity of neurons from V1 to the object-sensitive cells of the lower temporal lobe. Figure 8.11 shows an example from Reynolds and Desimone (2003) in the macaque. This figure shows the effect of training the monkey to attend to horizontal and vertical gratings called Gabor jets, which are known to evoke activity in V8. The graphs show the mean response of only 19 neurons. The researchers began by empirically defining the specific receptive fields of the monitored neurons, by moving the stimuli until they evoked maximum firing from the neurons being recorded. Thus receptive fields were defined for each neuron (see Chapter 6 for a description).

4.2 Guiding the spotlight

One of the uses of a spotlight metaphor of attention is to distinguish between the *brain effects* of selective attention, and the *sources* that guide what is being selected (see Figure 8.1). If we think of attention as a spotlight, we must also ask the question what is guiding it. In the case presented in Figure 8.12, brain areas like the prefrontal cortex are suggested as sources of control for voluntary attention, and the result is improvement of efficiency in the visual cortex.

4.3 Salience maps help guide attentional selection

What determines what object the attentional system selects? Ultimately, attention cannot be understood without emotion, motivation, and salience. Recent evidence indicates that salience maps, which are sensitive to the prominence of an event, exist in many different regions. In the visual system there is now evidence that

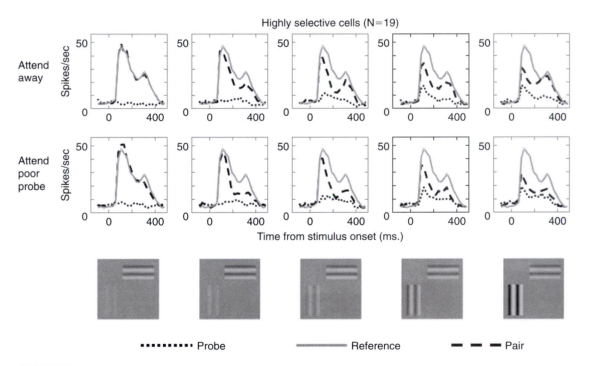

FIGURE 8.11 Input competition within visual receptive fields. Single neurons show a diminished response when a competing input activates the same receptive field. A consistent finding is that while attention normally increases firing rates in visual cortex, that is no longer true when two stimuli compete against each other in the same receptive field. In that case, the attended stimulus actually decreases. This suggests that attention may involve competing populations of both sensory and higher-level neurons. *Source*: Reynolds and Desimone, 2003.

salience may be encoded all the way down to area V1, the first cortical map of the primary visual pathway. In later chapters we will see how emotion and motivation constantly interact with selective attention.

In selective listening experiments, Moray (1959) showed that subjects listening to two different streams of speech could hear their own names 'break through'

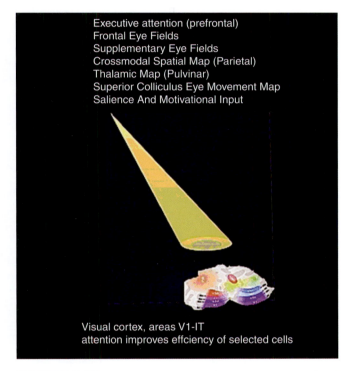

Executive attention (prefrontal)
Frontal Eye Fields
Supplementary Eye Fields
Crossmodal Spatial Map (Parietal)
Thalamic Map (Pulvinar)
Superior Colliculus Eye Movement Map
Salience And Motivational Input

Visual cortex, areas V1-IT
attention improves effciency of selected cells

FIGURE 8.12 A spotlight metaphor for attention – control and selection. One of the uses of a spotlight metaphor is to distinguish between the brain effects of selective attention, and the sources that control what is being selected. In this case, brain areas like the prefrontal cortex are suggested as sources of control for voluntary attention, and the result is improvement of efficiency in the visual cortex. (The visual maps are flattened MRI maps of early visual regions shown in artificial colors.) *Source*: Van Essen, 2005.

from the unattended auditory channel. Salience in attentional capture has been studied in non-human primates, with pictures of expressive (threat) faces attracting or 'capturing' attention (Figure 8.13).

Multiple salience maps have been proposed for humans, with brain arrays that encode different types of information in a visual scene (Figure 8.14). For example, posterior parietal cortex has been hypothesized to have a visual salience map, while prefrontal cortex has been hypothesized to have a map for encoding top-down, task-relevant information, and the superior colliculus may store attentional guidance system for controlling the focus of attention.

4.4 Executive (voluntary) attention

Listening to a ringing telephone may be automatic for most adults, since they have trained themselves to answer phones over a period of years. Children may not bother to listen to a ringing phone. For adults, it may in fact take more voluntary control *not* to pay attention to the telephone. The idea that more executive or voluntary attentional control may be needed to go *against* our existing tendencies is the basis of the executive attention task in Figure 8.15. It is a version of the flanker task described above. In this case, the task is to override the tendency covertly to attend to the cued stimulus. Instead, the subject must pay attention in the opposite direction. Interestingly, the brain network involved in this very slight behavioral change is quite different from the one that guides visual attention to an expected stimulus. Executive attention involves more prefrontal and parietal regions (Figure 8.16). An example of executive response to override a conflicting response, such as in a Stroop task, is shown in Figure 8.17. A schematic diagram of the executive system is presented in Figure 8.18.

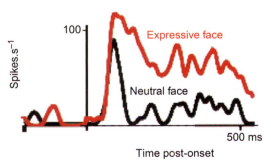

100

Spikes.s⁻¹

Expressive face

Neutral face

500 ms

Time post-onset

FIGURE 8.13 A monkey's threat face draws attention. Biologically significant stimuli draw attention. Monkeys can be quite dangerous, even to adult humans and certainly to children and to other primates. Baring the teeth is a widespread mammalian threat gesture that predicts attack, and attentional systems are attuned to such threats. Thus face recognition neurons in the lower temporal lobe respond very actively to threat faces compared to neutral facial expressions. *Source*: Vuilleumier, 2005.

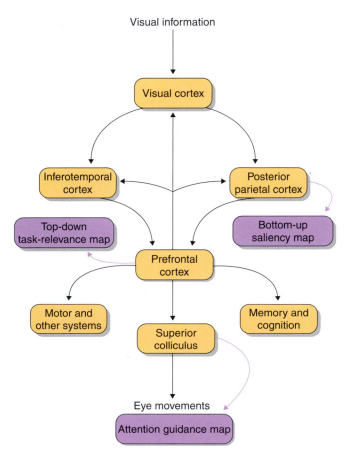

FIGURE 8.14 Multiple salience maps (in purple). Attention selects what is most important for survival and reproduction, including learned sources of salience. It is therefore proposed that the brain must contain salience maps, which keep track of significant events. Such maps have been found in the superior colliculus, frontal eye fields, and even early visual cortex. They are influenced by emotional and motivational regions of the brain. *Source*: Navalpakkam and Itti, 2005.

4.5 Visual attention may have evolved from eye movement control

As we discussed in Chapter 1, visual imagery seems to make use of visual cortex, inner speech uses the existing brain regions for outer speech and so on. The general principle seems to be that the brain builds on its existing adaptations. Interestingly, attention has its own pre-existing analog: visual attention, at least, seems to be closely related to visual eye movements.

We will discuss the evidence for this proposal a little later. But the general point is worth emphasizing: eye movements are also *selective* – they are orienting movements of our major distance sense, vision. They result in a greater focus on one part of a visual scene, while shutting out other parts. That is precisely what

selective attention does in a more abstract and general fashion. It is attractive to think therefore that there may be a relationship between the two. After all, the most visible sign of selective attention in humans and animals is *orienting* one's sensory receptors toward an object: looking, sniffing, listening, and exploring by touch.

Visual selective attention overlaps the brain regions for eye movement control (Corbetta *et al.*, 1998). That makes good sense if we consider eye movements as highly evolved selectional skills; selective attention may be an additional layer of evolutionary sophistication (Figure 8.19). Eye movements are a fundamentally important source of information in cognitive neuroscience. The sizable laboratory apparatus needed to track eye movements has now been reduced to a simple backpack, so that visual selection can be studied in the natural world (Figure 8.20).

Thus, subcortical regions are also part of attentional selection, especially the thalamus (its pulvinar nucleus) and the visual nucleus that controls eye movements (the superior colliculus). All these brain areas contain visuospatial maps, which may synchronize with each other to focus attention on some visual event. There is increasing evidence that the visuospatial maps of the brain may be synchronized with gamma-band rhythms, centered about 40 Hz.

4.6 Maintaining attention against distraction

If you've ever tried to study while your roommate was playing loud music, you have experienced the effort of keeping your limited capacity focused on whatever you select voluntarily. Mental effort is often needed to stay focused in this kind of situation, and with persistent distractions we need to renew our effort to focus over and over again (Duncan and Owen, 2000). Shutting out distracting events can load our limited processing capacity.

On the other hand, you might find it easy to shut out distractions if you are listening to your favorite music. Lavie (2005) has suggested an answer to this apparent paradox: that it is often easy to shut out distractions to perceptually interesting streams of information (like music), while it may be quite hard to stay focused on a more cognitive task that requires executive attention in the face of distraction.

Lavie suggests there is a crucial difference. She writes that:

> The ability to remain focused on goal-relevant stimuli in the presence of potentially interfering distractors is crucial for any coherent cognitive function. However, simply

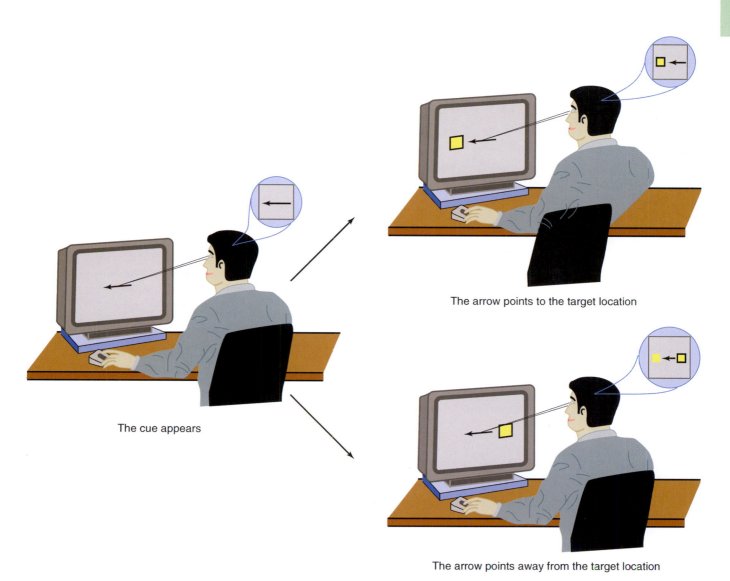

The arrow points to the target location

The cue appears

The arrow points away from the target location

FIGURE 8.15 Executive attention – going against expected targets. The flanker method can be used to study attentional shifts that override the subject's initial expectation, a common executive task (Chapter 12). In this example the subject is led to expect a stimulus in the left location. In the first case (above), his expected location is confirmed. Below, it is disconfirmed, and he must override his previous expectation. *Source*: Gore and Roberts in Squire *et al.*, 2003.

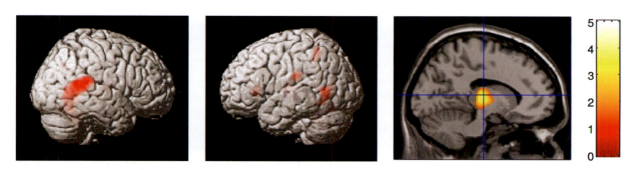

FIGURE 8.16 Executive attention in the flanker task. Regions involved in executive (or voluntary) attention: the extra executive involvement evokes activity in prefrontal and parietal regions. *Source*: Fan *et al.*, 2005.

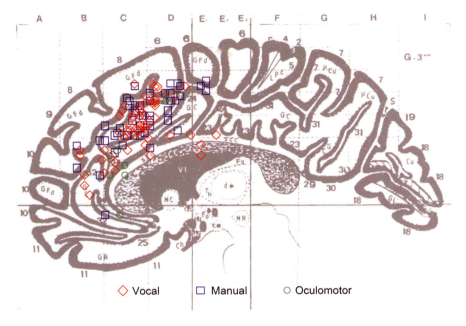

FIGURE 8.17 Executive attention in Stroop conflict. Although the experimental methodology is very different, executive attention in the Stroop color-naming task activates the anterior cingulate region of the medial prefrontal cortex. Other parts of the prefrontal cortex also show high activity. *Source*: Botvinick *et al.*, 2004.

◇ Vocal   □ Manual   ○ Oculomotor

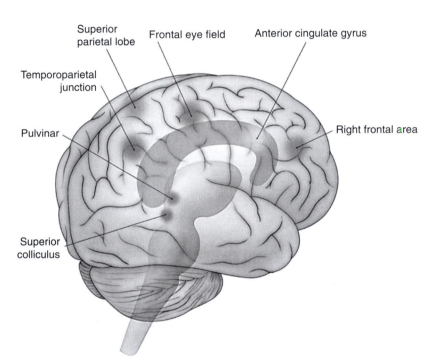

FIGURE 8.18 A brain summary of selective attention. Attention is critical to survival and reproduction, and a sophisticated biological brain network has evolved to guide it. Cortical regions of attentional guidance include the frontal areas such as the frontal eye fields, involved in voluntary control of eye movements. The anterior cingulate plays a major role in detecting and resolving conflicting information, such as overriding the expected eye movement in Figure 8.15. Right frontal and parietal regions are especially important for spatial guidance toward attentional targets. Two subcortical areas are also important, the pulvinar nucleus of the thalamus, which connects the cortical areas, and the superior colliculus, a 'hub' for eye movement control. Visual attention rides on the biologically prior eye movement control system. Notice that sensory cortex is not shown in this figure, but that attentional guidance has major effects on sensory neurons. *Source*: Posner, 2003.

instructing people to ignore goal-irrelevant stimuli is not sufficient for preventing their processing. . . . Whereas high perceptual load can eliminate distractor processing, high load on 'frontal' cognitive control processes increases distractor processing.

'Mental effort' involves voluntary control against competition. Every child knows how it feels to have homework when s/he really wants to go outside and play.

This involves decision-making, but the decision is not in the first instance about doing something – it is about paying attention to something. That is, it is a struggle whose first outcome is purely mental. The act of paying attention to homework is more novel and effortful and less pleasant, and hence requires more conscious involvement, than the routine and pleasant act of thinking about playing. But once the issue is decided, one may become absorbed in the chosen path. Then the experience of

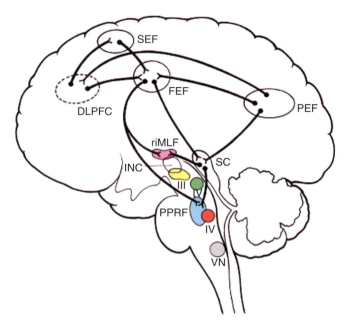

FIGURE 8.19 Eye movements and attentional guidance. Humans are highly specialized for eye movement control, since vision is our most developed distance sense. Eye movement has both cortical and subcortical parts. The cortical ones include the frontal eye fields near the frontal lobe, and the parietal eye fields. Both can be guided by explicit goals – we can deliberately move our eyes upon request, for example. That capacity is believed to require a prefrontal region on the upper lateral cortex, the dorsolateral-prefrontal cortex (DL-PFC). This area has many executive functions. Subcortically, the superior colliculus (SC) is a hub for the very sophisticated eye movement guidance system. *Source*: Standring, 2005.

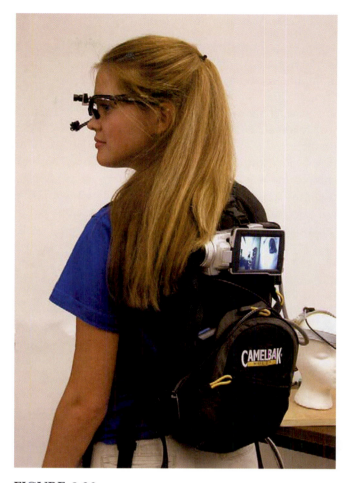

FIGURE 8.20 Tracking eye movements in the real world. Eye movements are a fundamentally important source of information in cognitive neuroscience. The sizable laboratory apparatus needed to track eye movements has now been reduced in size to a simple backpack, so that visual selection can be studied in the natural world. *Source*: Hayhoe and Ballard, 2005.

struggle and effort may disappear, even for tasks that were first seen as onerous and boring.

Thus, mental effort may come from a struggle between voluntary and automatic attention. Presumably the conscious goal of having to do homework serves to recruit neural networks that may be able to inhibit the automatic attentional tendency promising fun and adventure by playing outside. This voluntary decision may have to be repeated more than once at natural choice-points in a difficult task. After taking a break from homework, the same struggle may have to be repeated. At each decision point, the intention to think about playing outside will tend to come up automatically, while the intention to continue with homework will have to be raised voluntarily, perhaps with the aid of a powerful motivating goal.

Each decision point can be viewed as a case of neuronal competition, but one that is metacognitive – i.e. it concerns one's own cognitive processes. Metacognition is closely associated with executive attention (Posner and Rothbart, 2005). Obviously, some of the recruited neural populations may be more significant than others.

If some basic goal is recruited to support doing homework – such as the promise of quick approval by a loving parent, or the threat of ridicule by an older sibling – the relevant deeper goals can move the vote in one direction or another. During the decision struggle, conscious thoughts related to these deeper goals may aid one or the other side in the process.

We can see this struggle for control especially in vigilance tasks, in which people are asked to monitor a blip on a radar screen, or some similar perceptual event in an otherwise boring situation. Attentional control drops quite rapidly under these circumstances (Mackworth and Bruner, 1970). But variation in attentional focus is quite normal even in interesting tasks. In all of these cases, one may enter a period of conflict between the voluntary tendency to continue attending, and a spontaneous tendency to allow one's attention to wander.

4.7 Attention and consciousness

There is an intimate connection between attention and consciousness. Most of the time, the things we try to pay attention to tend to become conscious. In reading this sentence, for example, your eye movements are guided mostly unconsciously. One way to observe that is just to watch someone's eyes while they are reading. You may be surprised to see their eyes jumping from one fixation to the next, even if they have the subjective sense of smooth movement. Eyes normally jump from point to point in large ballistic movements called *saccades*. These are generally planned and guided unconsciously. We *can* move our eyes voluntarily, but normally we leave it to a sophisticated unconscious brain system to do the work. As G.A. Miller (1962) pointed out, 'we are generally conscious of the *results* of a mental process but not of the process itself'.

In human experiments, we ask subjects to direct their attention – to select one event from many. We test people on their adherence to the experimental protocol by asking them about the selected stimulus – i.e. we test whether they are conscious of the experimental conditions. Conscious events, as indexed by accurate report, are therefore a basic condition of almost all experiments.

As we will see, both attention and consciousness recruit very widespread brain activity. These phenomena are not limited to one or two boxes in our functional framework.

Historically, however, the idea of 'consciousness' has been controversial in the sciences, for both philosophical and practical reasons (e.g. Baars, 1986; Baars *et al.*, 2003a). In recent years, scientific reservations about the topic have faded, in response to a number of methodological and theoretical advances. A flow of scientifically rigorous studies has begun to show steady progress. In 2004, the journal *Science* listed 'the biological basis of consciousness' as one of the top unsolved problems in the sciences, reflecting greater confidence that we can learn more about one of the most enduring philosophical questions.

5.0 THE BRAIN BASIS OF CONSCIOUS EXPERIENCE

We began this chapter by drawing a distinction between attention and consciousness. Attention is most often seen as selective capacity, an ability to focus on one thing and not another. We study it by giving subjects two different sources of information, and observing what brain networks may be involved in selecting and processing both competing sources.

Conscious cognition is closely related, but not identical. We are usually conscious of the results of attentional selection, but not necessarily of selection itself. Over recent decades, scientists have come to study consciousness by comparing closely matched conscious and unconscious events, in order to study the difference between them. Conscious events can be reported accurately, unconscious ones cannot. A theory of conscious cognition would tell us how the brain deals with them differently. An emerging research literature is beginning to do exactly that.

To tease out the effects of consciousness experimentally we need to treat consciousness as a variable, just as we can treat the selectivity of attention as a variable in the experiments discussed above. For that reason, a different kind of experiment has been devised to test conscious cognition. These experiments compare conscious versus unconscious conditions in the same experiment, and using the same stimuli. By using both behavioral and brain measures, the effort is made to ensure that the conscious and unconscious comparisons are as similar to each other as possible, so that the critical brain differences can be isolated.

Just as the flanker task and the Stroop effect have become standard methods to study attention, useful experimental methods have emerged to study conscious perception and memory. These include:

- Inattentional blindness
- Visual backward masking
- Change blindness
- Attentional blink
- Automaticity due to practice
- Remembering versus knowing
- Conscious versus unconscious word priming.

We will describe some of these below.

5.1 Conscious cognition

At this instant, you are conscious of some aspects of the act of reading *these letters* against the white texture of the page, and the inner sound of *these words*. But you are probably not aware of the touch of your chair, of a certain background taste, the subtle balancing of your body against gravity, a flow of conversation in the background, or the delicately guided eye fixations needed to see *this phrase*; nor are you now aware of the fleeting present of only a few seconds ago, of your feelings for a friend, and even some of your major life goals.

These unconscious elements are as important as the conscious ones. *They also give us natural comparison conditions for conscious contents.* For example, while you are conscious of words in your visual focus, you surely did not consciously label the word *focus* just now as a noun; yet this sentence would be incomprehensible if highly specialized language regions did not treat focus as a noun unconsciously. On reading the word *focus*, you were surely unaware of its nine alternative meanings, though in a different sentence you would instantly bring a different meaning to mind. What happened to the others? A body of evidence supports the notion that some of those meanings were active unconsciously for a few tenths of a second before your brain decided on the right one. Most words have multiple meanings, but in reading, only one at a time becomes conscious at any moment.

These examples illustrate the sense of the word 'consciousness' scientists aim to understand, i.e. focal consciousness of easily described events, like, 'I see a printed page', or 'He imagined his mother's face'. Conscious contents like this can be reported with good accuracy under the right conditions. These conditions include immediate report, freedom from distraction, and some way for the outside observer to verify the report. These are standard laboratory conditions that apply to many experiments in perception, memory, attention and mental imagery.

5.2 Unconscious comparisons

As we have learned more about unconscious processes, we have come to accept them as useful comparison conditions for conscious ones. For example, there is now good evidence that unconscious 'threat faces' can activate brain areas that are similar to those evoked by conscious threat expressions (de Gelder *et al.*, 2005). Whatever the brain difference is between conscious and unconscious threat faces may give us some hints about the brain basis of conscious experience. This approach has been highly productive in human and animal experiments, as we will see. Numerous experiments have compared seen versus unseen stimuli, novel versus habitual (automatic) skills, conscious and non-conscious processing of ambiguous stimuli, and much more (Kihlstrom, 1987; Baars *et al.*, 2003; Bargh *et al.*, 2006). The older idea that conscious cognition cannot be studied at all has simply faded (e.g. Baars, 1988, 2002b; Edelman, 1989; Crick and Koch, 1995; Edelman and Tononi, 2000).

Binocular rivalry and flash suppression

Binocular rivalry is often used to study conscious vision, by delivering two different images to the two eyes. Only one of two incompatible images can be conscious at any particular moment. Chapter 6 discussed some of the classic experiments on this topic, and we will develop them here. Figure 8.21 shows an example of binocular rivalry, viewed from the top of the head.

It is easy to demonstrate binocular rivalry simply by placing a small mirror in front of one eye, and slanting it so that what you see in the mirror is at the same distance

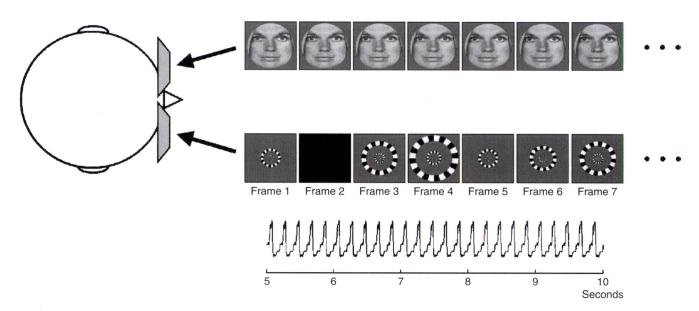

FIGURE 8.21 Binocular rivalry allows comparisons between a conscious and unconscious picture. A view from above of a subject receiving two separate streams of images in the two eyes, one with a woman's face and the other with expanding white circles. The subject is wearing prism goggles, so that each stream of pictures is directed to a different eye. These two inputs cannot be fused into a single visual experience. Notice, however, that even when people are conscious of the expanding circle pattern, their left eye still receives the face information just as before. The unconscious stimulus is processed into the visual cortex, but the subject can only report the conscious one (Sheinberg and Logothetis, 1997). This basic concept is used routinely in experiments on conscious vision. *Source*: Cosmelli *et al.*, 2004.

as the things you can see with the uncovered eye. Because the eyes tend to focus on objects at the same distance, this allows two equally distant objects to compete against each other. You will see the two visual scenes alternating, and also some islands of fusion between them.

To avoid fusion, binocular experiments use a technique called *flash suppression*, which drives the conscious input directly. A face may be shown to the left eye for two seconds, and one second afterwards a competing pattern is flashed to the right eye. Under those conditions the new stimulus becomes conscious, blocking the first one. Again, both eyes still receive the optical input. Flash suppression is useful for defining the onset times of the conscious and the unconscious stimuli, so that brain recordings can be examined for differences in the critical second or so when the new stimulus succeeds the old one.

Visual backward masking

Another method to study conscious vision is shown in Figure 8.22, using visual backward masking. Subjects are presented with two faces in quick succession. The smiling face is shown for only 20 ms, and it is immediately followed by the neutral face for 100 ms. In this case, subjects never experience the smiling face, because it is 'backward masked' by the second picture. Again, the brain appears to identify both stimuli, though only one becomes conscious and reportable. What is the difference in the brain?

Inattentional blindness

A third method used to study visual awareness is called *inattentional blindness* (Simons, 2000). The most famous example is shown in Figure 8.23. Here, subjects are asked to watch a basketball being tossed between one team (white-shirted) or the other (black-shirted). This is a demanding attentional task, and when someone dressed in a gorilla suit walks across the scene, most observers are not conscious of the gorilla – even when it stands still, faces the camera, and waves at the audience.

There are other ways to induce inattentional blindness, which add more flexibility to study specific materials. Thus, Rees *et al.* (1999) induced inattentional blindness simply by having subjects pay attention to a series of red line drawings of animals superimposed on blue line drawings of words. By showing the slide series quickly and having subjects monitor for targets in the red series, the blue words were simply not

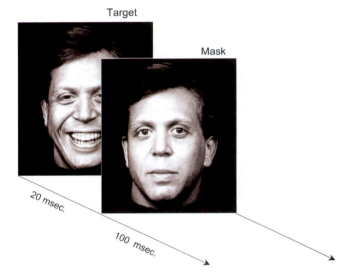

FIGURE 8.22 Backward masking to compare conscious and unconscious stimuli. Subjects do not perceive the smiling face in this backward masking design, but the unconscious face still primes behavior and brain activity. *Source*: Killgore and Yurgelun-Todd, 2004.

FIGURE 8.23 The invisible gorilla. Daniel Simons and coworkers have shown that watching a basketball tossed between several students can exclude other events from consciousness. Many subjects cannot see the person in the gorilla costume walking across the scene. This is an example of *inattentional blindness* – the fact that we are often unaware of visual events at the very center of visual gaze, if they are incompatible with the structure of the conscious event. Such experiments support William James notion that '*each of us chooses, by his ways of attending to things, what sort of universe he shall appear . . . to inhabit*'. *Source*: Simons, 2000.

reportable, even though they were presented at the center of visual fixation. Again, brain studies show that the unconscious stimulus may still be processed in the appropriate regions of the cortex.

The single most important point to remember is that the comparison conditions for selective attention and conscious perception are different. In selective attention, we study selection: the time to detect expected versus unexpected stimuli, for example. In the case of conscious cognition, however, we compare conscious and unconscious events, those that are reportable versus those that are not. Brain activity in these two conditions is strikingly different.

With that distinction clearly in mind, we will look at the empirical findings.

5.3 Binding features into conscious objects

How do we recognize the sight of a coffee cup or pencil? We know that visual cortex contains millions of feature-sensitive neurons, arrayed in hierarchical maps of the visual field. But the early visual maps seem to be sensitive to only one or a few features of the input – location, line orientation, light contrast, color, repeated patterns of light and dark (called spatial frequency), and the like. How and where are these features combined into conscious coffee cups and houses?

The cognitive psychologist, Anne Treisman, conducted a classic series of experiments on feature conjunction of colored lines (see Figure 8.9). Treisman suggested that one function of an attentional spotlight is to bind features into objects, as in Figure 8.24. An optical stimulus like the pink ball in the figure evokes light receptors in the retina. Using visual search experiments, Treisman and Gelade came to the conclusion that attention serves to bind features into objects, using a stored description of known objects in memory (Treisman and Gelade, 1980). An object buffer (a momentary holding store) allows different features to organize into an object, which subjects can report as conscious events.

Direct evidence for such feature integration in association with reportability was first found by Logothetis

---

BOX 8.2   Varieties of unconsciousness

Fifty years of study has yielded evidence that unconscious processes may represent functionally important knowledge. Kihlstrom (2004) lists five categories:

1. *Implicit memory* A classic example is amnesic patients like HM and Clive Wearing (see Chapters 2 and 9) who are given a word like 'assassin' to memorize, and who cannot recall it later. However, given a word fragment, such as '_ss_ss__' they are more likely to produce 'assassin' without remembering when they heard it. They have lost conscious access to the source memory, but the implicit retrieval is improved.
2. *Implicit learning*, typically applied to the way we learn the regularities of language. Young children do not learn language by grammatical rules, but by repeated exposure to sequences of conscious words. The rules and regularities of grammar are inferred unconsciously.
3. *Implicit perception* is often studied by means of subliminal or masked stimulation, as in the masked face experiment described above. Subliminal semantic priming is a reliable phenomenon, in which an unconscious word will increase the chances that a semantically related one will be detected a few seconds later. But it also includes what is widely thought to be non-conscious stimulus processing before a perceptual event comes to mind and can be reported (Cheeseman and Merikle, 1986; Draine and Greenwald, 1998). Unconscious perception also occurs when perceptual cortex is damaged, as in blindsight (damage to visual area V1; see Chapter 6), parietal neglect (inability to perceive the left half of visual space), face blindness, and other damage to visual cortex (Kihlstrom, 2004).

4. *Automaticity* Highly practiced and predictable skills become unconscious. Some processes are innately automatic, whereas others become automatized after extensive practice. In either case, execution of an automatic process consumes no attentional resources; nor does it interfere with other ongoing cognitive processes, or leave any trace of itself in memory. Experiments on social cognition and behavior indicate that complex cognitive activities can go on outside of conscious awareness as well (Bargh and Chartrand, 1999; Kihlstrom, 2004).
5. *Unconscious cognition*, such as priming of problem incubation – the unconscious period between thinking of a question and the realization of the answer, often called the 'Aha!' experience (Bowers *et al.*, 1990). We will see some of its brain correlates in Chapter 10 (Jung-Beemann *et al.*, 2004).
6. Finally, good evidence has been emerging about unconscious influences on *motivation and social cognition*. Bargh and Williams (2006) write that:

Much of social life is experienced through mental processes that are not intended and about which one is fairly oblivious. These processes are automatically triggered by features of the immediate social environment . . . Recent research has shown these non-conscious influences to extend beyond the perception and interpretation of the social world to the actual guidance, over an extended time period, of one's important goal pursuits and social interactions.

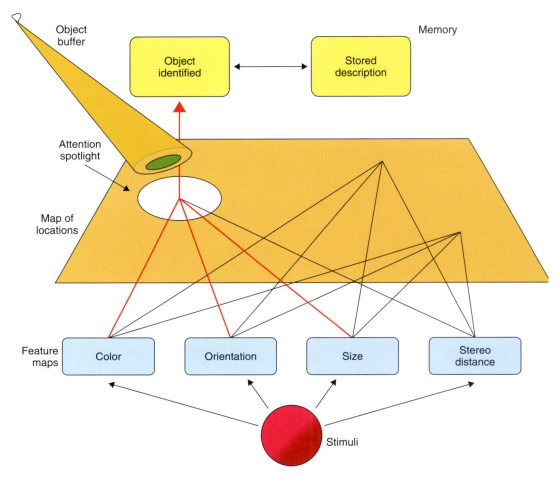

FIGURE 8.24 Treisman's spotlight for binding visual features. The concept of feature binding – combining color, location, shape, and the like into a single neuronal assembly – is often taken to be necessary for visual consciousness. Treisman suggested that an attentional spotlight (above) was required to combine different aspects of a stimulus into a reportable event. *Source*: Baars, modified from Posner and Raichle, 1994, based on Treisman and Gelade, 1980.

and colleagues, using single-cell experiments in the macaque monkey. Logothetis used binocular rivalry to study conscious versus unconscious input processing, as we see next.

5.4 Visual feature integration in the macaque

A classic series of experiments by Logothetis and colleagues in the macaque monkey helped establish scientific credibility for the effort to study conscious visual perception (Blake and Logothetis, 2002). There are many kinds of binocular rivalry. When two fields with different line orientations are presented to the two eyes, they will compete against each other (Figure 8.25). Different color patches will rival, and pictures of faces and objects. If objects in one eye field are moving in different directions than the ones in the other field, they will rival. As long as the input into the two eyes cannot be integrated

into a single, coherent visual event, they will compete against each other for conscious visual dominance. This fact is very useful experimentally, because we can devise rivaling stimuli that will evoke neuronal activity at different levels of the visual hierarchy.

In the case of the macaque, a matching task is used to determine what the monkey is seeing. The monkey is rewarded by correctly matching a rivaling display to a normal visual stimulus. Since the rivaling stimuli are perceived as one *or* the other, but not both, a well-trained monkey will presumably give accurate reports of its actual conscious percepts, just as humans do. As noted above, the 'flash suppression' method of binocular rivalry is often used to ensure maximal control over the timing of the conscious and unconscious stimuli.

It is worth noting in this connection that the macaque visual brain has been extensively studied, so that the most detailed hypotheses about the human visual brain

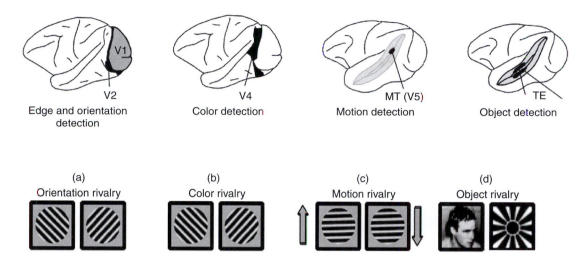

FIGURE 8.25 Binocular competition engages different visual areas. To study visual consciousness, a useful fact is that binocular stimuli can engage separate visual levels. Four pairs of visual stimuli are presented in the lower portion of the figure and the brain areas activated are show in the upper portion: (a) the orientation of the two visual inputs is different and are hard to fuse into a single, coherent visual image; (b) the color of the two visual inputs is different and are hard to fuse into a single, coherent visual image; (c) the flow of lines flows upward on the left and downward on the right; (d) a face competes against a sunburst icon. These four sets of stimuli are analyzed in different regions of visual cortex (see Chapter 6). For that reason, they are useful for probing the effects of conscious and unconscious visual stimulation to see whether different visual areas have different roles in constructing a conscious visual percept. *Source:* Revised from Logothetis, 1998.

are often derived from invasive studies of the macaque (e.g. Orban *et al.*, 2004). The similarities between the human and macaque visual brains are striking.

Logothetis and colleagues conducted an extensive series of experiments, using different kinds of binocular rivalry. In each experiment, the corresponding level of the visual cortex was studied using single cell recording in each visual area.

Figure 8.27 shows the result from the entire experimental series. The percentages of neurons firing to the conscious stimulus are indicated. In early visual regions (V1, V2, and V4) only 20 per cent of the neurons responded to the dominant percept, the one that the monkey reported. In these early regions about the same numbers of neurons fired to the non-dominant percept, the one that the macaques did not report. Somewhat higher in the visual cortex, the dominant percept for motion evoked activity in 40 per cent of the neurons sampled (areas MT and MTS). Thus, in the feature-sensitive layers of visual cortex, roughly equal numbers of neurons responded to the reportable, presumably conscious stimuli and non-reportable stimuli.

This pattern changed dramatically when the Logothetis team studied visual object regions of the macaque brain. Using face-versus-pattern rivalry, they recorded from some hundreds of cells in the temporal cortex (areas IT and STS). Here more than 90 per cent of

the neurons fired in response to the reported percept, and no cells were found for the non-reportable input. The clear implication is that monkeys became visually conscious of objects when the flow of input activity reached areas IT/STS, but not before.

Probably for the first time in modern history, the word 'subjective visual perception' was used in the title of the *Science* report of these results (Logothetis and Schall, 1989; Sheinberg and Logothetis, 1997). This reflects the fact that the Logothetis team isolated subjective visual perception from unconscious visual activity for the same stimuli in the same brain regions.

Other studies of perceptual consciousness have followed these pioneering efforts, using functional imaging in humans as well as other mammals. Many other experimental stimuli have been used, including ambiguous figures, visual backward masking, and hidden figures. Thus, there is evidence that visual objects are 'bound' into coherent units in visual object regions, which are found in the inferior temporal cortex in humans.

Do these results show us the 'necessary and sufficient' conditions for visual consciousness? One interpretation is that it does, that consciousness arises in visual regions. However, we will see that object integration may be only one ingredient. Feature binding may be necessary but is not sufficient.

FIGURE 8.26 Binocular rivalry in the macaque. A binocular flash suppression controls which of two competing stimuli to the eyes of the macaque monkey will be perceived at any moment. The monkey is trained to respond with a 'face' or 'starburst' movement of the lever. In this case, a human face in one eye competes against a sunburst symbol in the other eye. The viewing apparatus in front of the monkey's eyes shows two separate, competing images. *Source*: Logothetis, 1998.

5.5 Conscious events recruit widespread brain activation

A large amount of evidence suggests that conscious contents mobilize frontal and parietal brain regions, as shown at the beginning of this chapter (see Figures 8.3 and 8.4). Table 8.1 lists some examples out of dozens that have been published (reviewed in Baars, 2002b).

Dehaene *et al*. (2001) used visual backward masking, described in Figure 8.22. That is, they compared conscious words on a screen to the same words when they were masked by a pattern presented immediately afterwards. Masked words are unconscious, but they are not physically blocked from entering the eyes. They activate retinal receptors with exactly the same energy pattern as conscious words do, and evoke neuronal firing in the visual pathway well into cortex. Thus there is a close similarity between the two stimuli, and it makes sense to compare their brain responses. Dehaene *et al*. used both fMRI and simultaneous visual evoked potentials, to be able to localize 'hot spots' as well as the high temporal resolution of the averaged electrical signature (see Chapter 4). Figure 8.28 shows the results from the evoked potential. Beginning at the top, we see the evoked voltages over the occipital cortex, 156 ms after the words are presented on the screen. On the right hand side, for the unconscious words, we see much less activity, but still more over the occipital cortex than elsewhere, as we might expect. After 244 ms, the middle row of brain images shows high activity in frontoparietal regions on the left side, but markedly lower activity on the right side. And after almost half a second, at 476 ms, there is again high activity over the back half of the head, as if the visual words are being 'played back' for a moment, to see what they were. On the right side, the activity level is lower, but appears to be relatively higher over the top of the head, perhaps

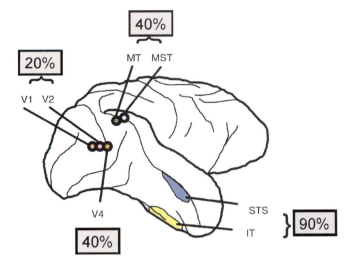

FIGURE 8.27 Visual percepts are integrated in the temporal lobe. Logothetis and colleagues recorded single-cell activity in response to different kinds of binocular rivalry from area V1/V2, MT/MST (motion), V4 (color), and finally IT/STS, the object perception region of the macaque temporal lobe. As the figure shows, only 20 to 40 per cent of neurons sampled in early visual regions responded to the reported (conscious) percept, with a roughly equal number responding to the unreported percept. However, in the temporal lobe, 90 per cent of the neurons responded only to the conscious percept (Sheinberg and Logothetis, 1997). Since object recognition combines many basic features like color, motion and location into a single percept, this region is a plausible place for conscious objects to arise. *Source*: Leopold and Logothetis, 1999.

reflecting activity in the cingulate cortex. (For the fMRI results, see Chapter 1, Figure 1.27.) fMRI analysis showed that conscious and unconscious words activated vision and word recognition areas, which analyze such things as stimulus location, shape, color, and word identity. The identical words, when conscious, triggered 12 times more activity in these regions. In addition, conscious words evoked a great deal of additional activity in parietal and frontal cortex. It seems as

TABLE 8.1   Studies showing widespread activation for conscious but not unconscious stimuli

Evidence for wider cortical processing of conscious versus non-conscious events

Source	Method	Results of non-conscious conditions (not reportable)	Results of conscious conditions (accurately reportable)
Sensory consciousness			
Logothetis *et al.* multiple studies (e.g. Sheinberg and Logothetis, 1997)	Binocular rivalry between diagonal contrast edges, color, motion, and objects. Multi-unit recording in visual cortex of the macaque.	In early visual cortex 12–20% of cells responded. In object recognition areas (IT/STS) no cells responded.	In early visual cortex 12–20% of cells responded. In object recognition areas(IT/STS) 90% of cells responded.
Tononi *et al.*, 1998	MEG of flickering input with binocular rivalry in humans, allowing tracing of input signal with high S/N ratio across large regions of cortex.	Widespread frequency-tagged activation in visual and non-visual cortex.	50–80% higher intensity in many channels throughout cortex.
Srinivasan *et al.*, 1999	As above.	Widespread frequency-tagged activation in visual and non-visual cortex.	Higher intensity and coherence in visual and non-visual cortex.
Dehaene *et al.*, 2001	fMRI of visual backward masked vs unmasked words in cortex.	Regional activation in early visual cortex only.	Higher intensity in visual cortex plus widespread activity in parietal and frontal cortex.
Rees *et al.*, 2001	fMRI of unattended and attended words and pictures.	Less activation in word/picture areas of visual cortex	More activation in word/picture areas of visual cortex.
Kjaer *et al.*, 2001	Subliminal vs supraliminal visual verbal stimuli using PET.	Activation in visual word areas only.	Activation in visual word areas plus parietal and prefrontal cortex.
Beck *et al.*, 2001	Change blindness vs change detection.	Activation of ventral visual regions including fusiform gyrus.	Enhanced activity in parietal and right dorsolateral prefrontal cortex as well as ventral visual regions
Vuilieurnler *et al.*, 2001	Seen and unseen faces in visuospatial neglect, using fMRI and ERPs.	Activation of ventral visual regions	Ventral visual activation plus parietal and prefrontal regions.
Driver and Vuilieumier, 2001	Extinguished vs conscious stimuli in unilateral neglect, fMRI and ERPs.	Activation in ventral visual regions including fusiform gyrus.	Activation also in parietal and frontal areas of the intact left hemisphere.
Learning and practice			
Haier *et al.*, 1992	PET before and after learning computer game Tatris.	Drastic drop in cortical metabolic activity.	Widespread, intense cortical metabolic activity.
Raichie *et al.*, 1994	Word association vs. simple noun repetition before and after training.	Trained word association indistinguishable from simple word repetition.	More intense activity in anterior cingulate, left prefrontal and left posterior temporal lobe and right cerebellar hemisphere.
Mental effort			
Duncan and Owan, 2001	Meta-analysis of 10 tasks comparing low and high mental effort (including perception, response selection, executive control, working memory, episodic memory and problem solving)	Low prefrontal activation.	High prefrontal activation, in mid-dorsolateral, mid-ventro lateral and dorsal interior cingulate cortex.
Waking vs general anesthesia			
John *et al.*, 2001	OEEG for anesthesia vs waking	Loss of gamma band activity, loss of coherence across major quadrants of cortex	Widespread gamma band coherence across and within hemispheres.

Source: Baars, 2002b.

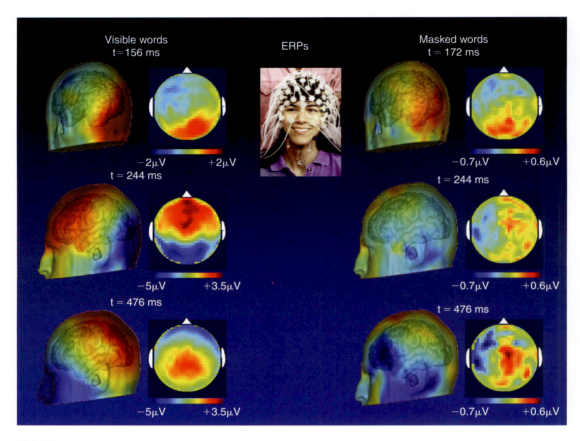

FIGURE 8.28 Evoked potentials to conscious and backward-masked visual words. Evoked potential results from Dehaene *et al.* (2001). (See Figure 8.4 for similar results from other laboratories.) Evoked potential has high temporal resolution, so that we can follow a wave of brain activity starting in the primary visual area V1, and sweeping forward by the 244 ms time point. Even at the long delay of 476 ms (almost one-half second), there is a rebound of activity roughly in the posterior half of the brain (bottom left). The computer-constructed brain images on the right hand side reflect the unconscious control condition, with lower activity at all three points in time. *Source*: Dehaene *et al.*, 2001.

if the stimulus-related activity in the conscious case is widely distributed from visual regions to other areas in the brain (Baars, 1988, 2002b). This pattern of results is shown from additional studies in Figure 8.4.

This is in fact predicted by several current theories (see section 6.0).

A recent study by Kreiman *et al.* (2002) adds to these results at the level of single neurons in the human brain. Using human patients with electrodes implanted deep in the temporal lobe, to find the source of epileptic seizures, they presented two images to the two eyes. Using binocular flash suppression, two-thirds of the deep temporal neurons sampled were found to follow the conscious stimulus; none responded to the unconscious one, even though we know from independent evidence that the unconscious image is represented in visual cortex (Dehaene *et al.*, 2001).

Now consider a very different example, the perception of pain from sensory neurons in the heart region of the body. Rosen *et al.* (1996) compared two kinds

of brain responses to reduced oxygen supply to the heart. In one group, patients reported intense conscious pain (called angina pectoris). The comparison group showed unconscious cardiac hypoxia (or silent ischemia). Again, conscious pain involves very wide activity spreading from the sensory regions to the rest of cortex. By comparison, unconscious 'pain' activity barely reached cortex. As before, similar sensory stimuli have very different effects in the brain depending whether they are consciously perceived or not. Table 8.1 cites additional studies that have shown a similar pattern of results.

Finally, sensorimotor tasks show the same pattern of results. When children learn to walk or ride a bicycle they must pay a lot of attention at first to the details of balance, going in one direction and not another, and not falling down. A few months later they are much less conscious of those details, and when they are well-practiced they hardly seem to be conscious of the action at all, unless some sudden change takes place.

Riding across an unexpected curb or a speed bump in the road will force us to pay attention again, so that we become conscious of the details of trying to stay upright. As a rule of thumb, when we learn a predictable skill, we begin with a lot of conscious access, we lose it when we become well-practiced, and find more conscious access again if something goes wrong or there is a change in the conditions of the task (Shiffrin and Schneider, 1977).

Haier *et al.* (1992) used the computer game Tetris to show widespread cortical PET activity when the game was being learned, and a marked drop four weeks later, when subjects were quite skilled and automatic. This is a reliable result (Schneider and Chein, 2003). It shows that more conscious involvement, and more cortical activity, do not necessarily go along with greater processing efficiency (Baars, 1988). On the contrary, when we become more skilled at a predictable task, cortical activity and conscious access both decline. There is evidence that subcortical brain regions take over in automatic tasks, particularly the basal ganglia and cerebellum.

The loss of unconscious processing in a simple task was studied by Stephan *et al.* (2002). They studied a very simple tapping task, in which subjects were told to follow a regular clicking sound from a metronome. Simple tasks like this can become automatic within minutes. After automaticity was established, the metronome rhythm was changed randomly by 3 per cent, 7 per cent, or 20 per cent. Thus, the predictability of the stimulus was disrupted. Figure 8.29 shows the results using fMRI.

The blue areas showed increased activity with 3 per cent rhythmic variability, a small effect. The green dots reflect 7 per cent variability, with some activity in brain regions involved in executive control (the anterior cingulate cortex (ACC) and dorsolateral regions of the prefrontal lobe (DL-PFC)). The most visible results occurred with 20 per cent random variability in the tapping task. At this point, the automatic skill of regular tapping no longer works at all, and cortex is required to track every tick from the metronome. The red color in the brain scans shows wide recruitment of frontal and parietal activity.

In sum, there are many sources of evidence suggesting that the more we are conscious of some event, from visual perception to motor control, the more cortical activity we are likely to find. Box 8.3 cites a number of researchers who suggest that conscious phenomena require widespread brain activity, when compared to similar unconscious ones.

Distinctive and widespread brain activity associated with consciousness has actually been known since 1929, when Hans Berger discovered that the entire brain's electrical activity changes visibly when we wake up.

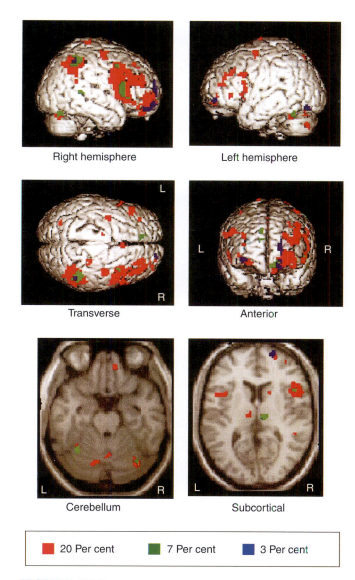

FIGURE 8.29 A sensorimotor task shows widespread activation in the more conscious condition. Stephan *et al.* (2002) asked subjects to tap along with the sound of a regular metronome. Once the task becomes habitual they varied the metronome rhythm randomly by 3, 7, and 20 per cent. Cortical activity increased dramatically as a function of the unpredictability of the tapping task. *Source*: Stephan *et al.*, 2002.

Waking activity reveals electrical voltages that are fast, irregular, and low in amplitude. Deep sleep – the least conscious state of the daily cycle – is marked by voltages that are slow, regular, and much higher in amplitude. Other kinds of unconscious states, such as general anesthesia, epileptic seizures and coma/vegetative states also show massive slow-wave, high-peak activity. Recent studies indicate that frontoparietal regions are markedly lower in metabolism during unconscious states than in waking control conditions (Baars *et al.*, 2003). Thus, there is also evidence from studies of

---

BOX 8.3   Conscious cognition as a brainwide phenomenon

Conscious access themes from the past 20 years

Presented here are some conscious access themes, from various authors. The frequency of such themes in the science and philosophy of consciousness has increased in recent years.

• **Baars, 1983** 'Conscious contents provide the nervous system with *coherent, global information.*' [a].
• **Edelman, 1989** 'Global mapping in a reentrant, selectionist model of consciousness in the brain.' [b].
• **Damasio, 1989** 'Meaning is reached by time-locked multiregional retroactivation of widespread fragment records. Only the latter records can become contents of consciousness.' [c].
• **Freeman, 1991** 'The activity patterns that are formed by the [sensory] dynamics *are spread out over large areas of cortex,* not concentrated at points. Motor outflow is likewise *globally distributed. . . . In other words, the pattern categorization does not correspond to the selection of a key on a computer keyboard but to an induction of a global activity pattern.' [Italics added] [d].*
• **Llinas et al., 1998** '. . . *the thalamus represents a hub from which any site in the cortex, can communicate with any other such site or sites. . . . temporal coincidence of specific and non-specific thalamic activity generates the functional states that characterize human cognition.' [e]*
• **Edelman and Tononi, 2000** 'When we become aware of something . . . it is as if, suddenly, many different parts of our brain were privy to information that was previously confined to some specialized subsystem . . . the wide distribution of information is guaranteed mechanistically by *thalamocortical and cortiocortical reentry,* which facilitates the interactions among distant regions of the brain.' [f] [pp. 148–149].
• **Dennett, 2001** 'Theorists are converging from quite different quarters on a version of the global neuronal workspace model of consciousness. On the eve of the Decade of the Brain, Baars [1988] had already described a "gathering consensus" in much the same terms. "Consciousness", he said, is accomplished by a "distributed society of specialists that is equipped with a working memory, called a global workspace, whose contents can be broadcast to the system as a whole'. [g] (p.42)
• **Kanwisher, 2001** '. . . in agreement with Baars [1989], it seems reasonable to hypothesize that *awareness of a particular element of perceptual information must entail not just a strong enough neural representation of information, but also access to that information by most of the rest of the mind/brain.' [h]*

• **Dehaene and Naccache, 2001** We then propose a theoretical framework that synthesizes those facts: the hypothesis of a global neuronal workspace. We postulate that this global availablity of information through the workspace is what we subjectively experience as the conscious state.'[j]
• **Rees, 2001** 'One possibility is that activity in such a distributed network might reflect stimulus representations gaining access to a 'global workspace' that constitutes consciousness.' [j] (p.679)
• **John, 2001** 'Evidence has been steadily accumulating that information about a stimulus complex is distributed to many neuronal populations dispersed throughout the brain.' [k]
• **Varela et al., 2001** '. . . the brain . . . transiently settling into a globally consistent state . . . [is] the basis for the unity of mind familiar from everyday experience.' [l]

References

a Baars, B.J. (1983) Conscious contents provide the nervous system with coherent, global information. In: Davidson, R.J. (ed) *Consciousness and Self-Regulation.* Plenum Press, New York.
b Edelman, G.M. (1989) *The Remembered Present: a biological theory of consciousness.* Basic Books Inc, New York.
c Damasio, A.R. (1989) Time-locked multiregional retroactivation: a systems-level proposal for the neural substrates of recall and recognition. *Cognition* 33, 25–32.
d Freeman, W.J. (1991) The physiology of perception. *Sci. Am.* 264, 78–85.
e Llinas, R., Ribary, U. (2001) Consciousness and the brain: the thalamocortical dialogue in health and disease. *Ann. N. Y. Acad. Sci.* **929**, 166–175.
f Edelman, G.M., Tononi, G. (1999) *A Universe of Consciousness: how matter becomes imagination.* Basic Books Inc, New York.
g Dennett, D. (2001) Are we explaining consciousness yet? *Cognition* 79, 221–237
h Kanwisher, N. (2001) Neural events and perceptual awareness. *Cognition* 79, 89–113.
i Dehaene, S., Naccache, L. (2001) Towards a cognitive neuroscience of consciousness: basic evidence and a workspace framework. *Cognition* 79, 1–37.
j Rees, G. (2001) Seeing is not perceiving. *Nat. Neurosci.* **4**, 678–680.
k John, E.R. *et al.* (2001) Invariant reversible qeeg effects of anesthetics. *Conscious. Cogn.* **10**, 165–183.
l Varela, F. *et al.* (2001) The brainweb: phase synchronization and large-scale integration. *Nat. Neurosci.* **2**, 229–239.

---

conscious and unconscious *states* that consciousness involves brainwide patterns of activity.

5.6 Fast cortical interactions may be needed for conscious events

In the last two sections we learned that visual feature integration may be a necessary condition for visual consciousness (5.4), and that conscious, but not unconscious conditions, evoked widespread frontal and parietal activity across a range of different tasks (5.5). Recent technical advances now make it possible also to record the *interactivity* of brain regions. If we consider a conscious task like pointing to a visual coffee cup, we notice that it involves a great many different cortical and subcortical regions. Here are some of the brain areas that might be involved just in pointing at a cup:

1 Visual cortex to detect the coffee cup, identify its color, size, location, and shape, and retrieve memory of the object, using temporal regions.

2 Prefrontal, premotor and motor regions to decide to point at the cup, generate the plan to move one's finger, and actually move the appropriate skeletal muscles.

3 A decision to execute the action, beginning perhaps in prefrontal regions, activating parietal spatial maps, and triggering subcortical motor control to perform the action.

4 Sensory feedback to check whether the action has been accomplished.

We believe that each of these steps requires hundreds of millions of neurons, firing in some coordinated pattern. How is this orchestra going to be conducted? A range of evidence and theory suggests that synchronous firing of large numbers of neurons plays a part. Gamma synchrony has been particularly implicated

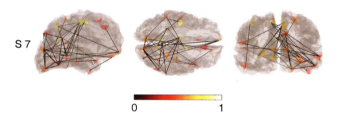

S 7

0   1

FIGURE 8.30 Visual flicker evokes widespread brain synchrony in conscious perception. A flickering visual stimulus evokes correlated synchronous firing between active brain regions. Spontaneous firing in the 40 Hz range has also been observed with conscious tasks. It is believed that rhythmic synchrony between different brain regions may signal cooperative and competitive interactions between neuronal populations needed to perform tasks, particularly those that are conscious and under voluntary control. *Source*: Cosmelli *et al.*, 2004.

in feature binding of visual objects that become conscious. However, coherent oscillatory firing of large populations of cells has been observed in other tasks as well, including theta activity in episodic retrieval from long-term memory (involving MTL and higher cortex). (Reminder: gamma activity is often taken to be 30–70 Hz, centered about 40 Hz; and theta rhythms are about 5–8 Hz.) Some authorities suggest that the slower electrical rhythms may group the faster ones, so these are not necessarily independent events (Steriade, 2006).

Figure 8.30 shows one study in which different regions seem to sing in unison around 40 Hz, recorded with MEG because of its high temporal and relatively good spatial resolution (Lutz *et al.*, 2002; Cosmelli *et al.*, 2004). Notice that not all the areas are firing in synchrony – if they did, the result might resemble an epileptic seizure, where one single rhythm takes over large regions of cortex. Rather, there seem to be rapid moments of synchrony between different brain regions that need to work together to accomplish the task of conscious perception. In deep sleep and other unconscious conditions, the individual firing rate of cortical neurons may not change, but rapid interactive rhythms like the ones in Figure 8.30 seem to be disrupted.

6.0 A SUMMARY AND SOME HYPOTHESES

We can summarize this chapter with two brain diagrams, one for selective attention, the second for conscious perception (Figure 8.31 from Figures 8.1 and 8.3).

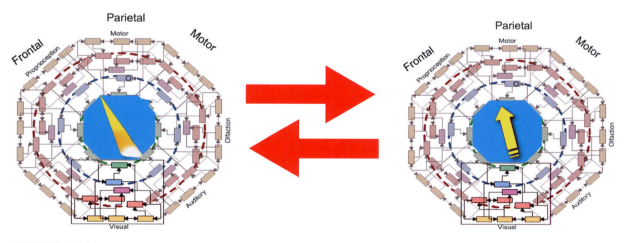

FIGURE 8.31 Attention and conscious perception: selection and integration. In sum, it may be that selective attention helps to bind visual percepts together, to allow consciously experienced objects to emerge from the visual object regions of the temporal lobe. Prior to that point, equal numbers of neurons may respond to both conscious and unconscious inputs, but the brain does not seem to prefer one over the other. Thus, binding of separate features into objects like coffee cups and pencils seems to be a requirement of visual object perception. (After Friston, 2003).

CHAPTER

9

Learning and memory

Morris Moscovitch, Jason M. Chein, Deborah Talmi, and Melanie Cohn

1.0 INTRODUCTION

Memory can be defined as a lasting representation that is reflected in thought, experience or behavior. Learning is the acquisition of such representations, which involve a wide range of brain areas and activities. Human memory has some surprising limits and some very impressive capacities. For example, most students would like

Cognition, Brain, and Consciousness, edited by B. J. Baars and N. M. Gage
ISBN: 978-0-12-373677-2

Copyright 2007, Elsevier Ltd. All rights reserved.

to have a 'better memory' – by which we mean a capacity deliberately to store and recall information, at will, easily and accurately. However, the human brain has not evolved for academic study and testing, which is a very recent cultural invention. Rather, it has evolved for the tasks of survival. Our best memory performance is not for the exact symbol sequences that conventional computers handle so well. Rather, our brains are exceptionally good in dealing with complex, ill-defined, and novel challenges, the kinds that people have to deal with in the real world.

Humans are exceptionally *flexible* in adapting to new conditions. Learning and memory provide the royal road to that flexibility. Our great capacity for learning allows us to use a brain adapted to a neolithic environment, and apply it with great success in a world of computers, brain science, and academic learning. There must be something special about our great ability to learn.

Memory storage is believed to involve very widespread synaptic alterations in many parts of cortex. This process is often taken to involve large-scale Hebbian learning, following the rule that 'neurons that fire together, wire together' (see Chapter 3 and Appendix A). Thus, correlated activity between neurons leads to strengthened connections between them, both excitatory and inhibitory. Temporary cell assemblies are thought

to maintain immediate memories, while long-term memories require more lasting strengthening of synaptic connections, both excitatory and inhibitory ones. While evidence has been found for these phenomena, we cannot yet observe changed long-term connectivity directly throughout the brain regions where it is thought to occur. Thus, the Hebbian memory trace itself remains an inferential concept.

In some views, all of the cortex may be able to learn by changing synaptic connectivities, from the posterior perceptual regions to the frontal executive and motor cortex (Fuster, 2004). Others focus more on the temporal lobe, which traditional neurology associates with memory functions. The most important brain structures we look at in this chapter are the *neocortex* – the visible outer brain – and the *medial temporal lobes* (MTL), which contain the two hippocampi and their surrounding tissues ((b) on p. 254, Figures 9.1 and 9.2). The MTL is spatially complex, and you should devote some time to the drawing exercises at the end of this chapter, to get an overall sense of its shape and location.

Until recently, the hippocampus was believed to be mainly responsible for transferring experiences into memory, but better methods now implicate the entire hippocampal neighborhood, the medial temporal lobes. The MTL overlap with the ancient mammalian smell cortex, which has fewer than the six layers. The

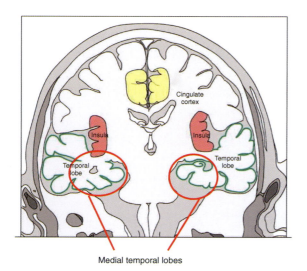
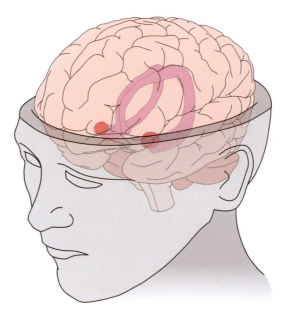

FIGURE 9.1 The medial temporal lobes and hippocampi. The memory regions are spatially complex and difficult to visualize. This collage shows two perspectives. The left panel shows a coronal cross-section of the brain, with the medial temporal lobes (MTL) circled in red. The right panel shows the hippocampi in both hemispheres, tipped by red structures, the amygdalae. Notice that the hippocampi are looped structures, nestled inside of each temporal lobe. The MTL includes the hippocampi and neighboring 'rhinal' structures (see Chapter 5). *Source*: Drawn by Shawn Fu.

neocortex, which is the 'new' cortex of modern mammals, consistently has six layers, one of its most distinctive features. The giant neocortex and the MTL are in constant dialogue with each other, as we store and retrieve the flow of our daily experiences.

Because of its ancient evolutionary lineage, the MTL has multiple functions. The hippocampus was first studied as a map for spatial localization in rats and other mammals. However, it also encodes olfaction, which is why parts of the MTL are called the 'rhinal', 'entorihinal', and 'perirhinal' cortex. ('Rhinos' means 'nose' in Greek, as in the word rhinoceros, 'nose horn' – Figure 9.3.)

MTL also interacts with visual area IT, the inferior temporal lobe (see Figure 9.2). You may remember that area IT has been shown to integrate high-level visual object information (see Chapter 8). Neurons firing in this region correlate with conscious visual perception (Sheinberg and Logothetis, 1997). Thus, the MTL is strategically located to take in high-level, presumably conscious visual information.

Just around the corner from the MTL is the auditory cortex, suggesting that auditory information can be fed to MTL as well (see Chapter 7), and the amygdalae reside near the tip of the hippocampi, a major hub of emotional information (Figure 9.3). Thus, MTL is a highly interactive crossroads, well-placed for integrating multiple brain inputs, and for coordinating learning and

retrieval in many parts of the neocortex. It is a 'hub of hubs'.

Most of human cortex is neocortex, which ballooned out from earlier regions over more than a hundred million years of mammalian evolution. As mentioned above, the neocortex is believed to encode long-term memories by altering synaptic connections between billions of neurons. There are literally trillions of such synapses in the cortex and its satellite organs, especially the thalamus (see Chapter 3). The hippocampus is ideally situated to combine information about the cognitive (neocortex) and emotional (limbic) areas, and bind that information into a memory trace that codes for all aspects of a consciously-experienced event (Moscovitch, 1995).

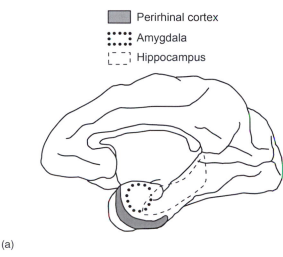

(a)

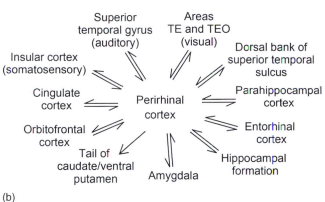

(b)

FIGURE 9.2 Memory areas receive visual object information. This midline view shows that the medial temporal lobe (MTL) is closely connected to area IT, the inferotemporal cortex. Area IT seems to support conscious visual object perception (see Chapter 8). MTL also includes the amygdala. Auditory cortex is located just around the corner, on the outside of the temporal lobe. *Source*: Vuilleumier, 2005.

FIGURE 9.3 The medial temporal lobe is a hub with widespread connections. The MTL, including the perirhinal cortex, has very wide connectivity to visual, auditory, somatosensory, emotional, motor, memory and executive regions. This makes the MTL an ideal place to receive, bind and distribute information for long-term memory. Notice that almost all connections run in both directions (double arrows). *Source*: Murray and Richmond, 2001.

1.1 A functional overview

Figure 9.4 suggests that the visual cortex (for example) first takes in the sight of a coffee cup on a table. Cortical activity corresponding to the perceived coffee cup then spreads to the MTL, which activates and 'binds' widespread memory traces in both the visual cortex and other regions. Some scientists believe that, for a brief period of time, a few tenths of a second, the visual input regions and other parts of the 'bound' neocortex resonate with each other, as shown in coordinated gamma electrical activity (often called the '40 Hertz hypothesis') (Llinas and Pare, 1991; Engel and Singer, 2001; Freeman *et al.*, 2003). Comprehending a visual stimulus like a coffee cup probably requires several hundred milliseconds. Thus, in less than a second, visual cortex has identified an object in front of our eyes, and triggered MTL to bind many regions of the neocortex to start making memory traces. However, as we will see, a permanent memory takes more time to consolidate.

Memory is for use in the real world, and retrieval is therefore as important as learning. When we encounter a reminder of a specific past experience of the coffee cup, the bound memory traces 'light up' the corresponding regions of cortex again. We thereby *reconstruct* some part of the original memory, again using the MTL to integrate memory traces into a coherent conscious experience. That experience – of imagining yesterday's coffee cup – makes use of visual cortex again. Because this is the central theme of this chapter, we begin with a cartoon version in Figure 9.4.

Learning is not limited to the neocortex. Other types of learning use other parts of the brain (see Section 8.0). However, in this chapter we will focus on learning and retrieving everyday memories.

1.2 Learning and memory in the functional framework

According to our functional framework, sensory input goes to 'working storage', which is part of *working memory* which, in turn, allows information to be actively maintained and manipulated (Figure 9.5; see Chapter 2). Working memory allows us temporarily to retain small

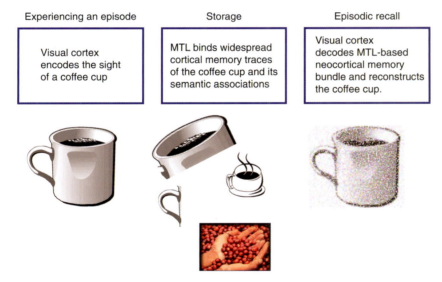

Experiencing an episode	Storage	Episodic recall
Visual cortex encodes the sight of a coffee cup	MTL binds widespread cortical memory traces of the coffee cup and its semantic associations	Visual cortex decodes MTL-based neocortical memory bundle and reconstructs the coffee cup.

FIGURE 9.4 How MTL is believed to help store and retrieve episodic memories. In the left panel, the sight of a coffee cup standing on a table activates visual cortex up to the level of object perception (see Chapter 6). In the middle panel, storage is achieved when MTL coordinates widespread memory traces (involving synaptic modification) throughout many parts of cortex. These include semantic associates of the coffee cup, such as the coffee beans in the picture below. Visual features of the cup, like the handle, are also part of the associative complex that becomes activated. When the *episodic memory* – the sight of the coffee cup – is cued the following day, maybe by someone asking, 'Did you like the way I made the coffee yesterday?', MTL is once again involved in retrieving and organizing widespread cortical memory traces. Visual cortex is therefore needed to reconstruct the sight of the coffee cup, which is never identical to the original cup, but rather a plausible recreation of a pattern of visual activation that overlaps with the first one. Notice that visual cortex is involved in perception, learning, and episodic recall.

amounts of information in an accessible form. Many everyday tasks call upon this working memory capacity, such as keeping a phone number in mind for the several seconds it takes to dial the number. Working memory also gives us a sense of continuity over time, by embedding our immediate conscious experiences into a longer psychological present. There is debate about the exact relationships between conscious events, working memory and selective attention. Some scientists believe that working memory (WM) gives rise to our conscious experiences; others suggest that working memory is itself coordinated by conscious cognition (Baars and Franklin, 2003). But there is good agreement that all three interact very closely. That is the most important point.

Two key properties of WM are its relatively small capacity and its limited duration. In his famous paper on the *span* of immediate memory, George Miller (1956) concluded that only seven (plus or minus two) items can be held in immediate memory at any one time. More recent work suggests that the true WM span may

be even smaller, closer to four items when rehearsal is prevented (Cowan, 2001; see Chapter 2). Likewise, the time an item is available is quite short, on the order of seconds.

Why have we evolved a memory system with these limits? The answer is not known. One possibility is that WM limits give special status to only the few pieces of information that are most relevant to our present goals, thus protecting them from interference from irrelevant information. It might also be adaptive for items in working memory to fade quickly. If material lingered beyond its period of relevance it might block out new information.

How we interpret and deal with material in working memory is determined by our current goals and concerns, as well as by our existing knowledge. Sensory and internal information may be brought to consciousness using attention. Once it becomes conscious, a number of theorists maintain that information is rapidly *encoded* into long-term memory (e.g. Moscovitch, 1990). There is also evidence for some unconscious learn-

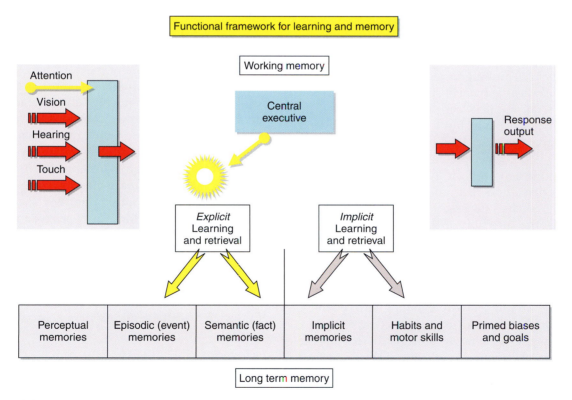

FIGURE 9.5 Explicit and implicit aspects of memory. A functional diagram for learning and memory. Working Memory (on top) can now be viewed as input to different types of long-term memory, divided into *Explicit and Implicit* ones. Explicit learning and retrieval involves conscious knowledge, both for facts and autobiographical experiences. Memory for facts is called *semantic* memory, while autobiographical memory is also called *episodic* because it reflects life episodes. Working Memory can manipulate explicit memories, like words, numbers, semantic facts and autobiographical episodes. Implicit learning and retrieval involves primed tasks, highly practiced habits and motor skills.

ing, but so far only unconscious fear conditioning has been shown to result in long-term memory (LeDoux, 1996). In general, conscious exposure correlates well with learning. While details of this broad picture continue to be debated, it is a useful outline to start with.

Figure 9.5 brings out several features of learning and memory. Notice that conscious cognition leads to *explicit* learning and memory retrieval in this figure. An obvious example is deliberately trying to memorize a technical term in cognitive neuroscience. What may not be so obvious, however, is that *implicit* learning also happens along with learning of conscious or explicit stimuli (Section 2.4).

Thus, Figure 9.5 shows both explicit or conscious *and* implicit or unconscious learning. Episodic memory is the storage of conscious episodes (also called autobiographical memory). Semantic memory, usually viewed as memory for facts, is also conscious, in the strict sense that people can accurately report the facts they believe. This is the standard operational definition of conscious brain events (see Chapter 8). Finally, perceptual memory capacities, such as our ability to 'learn to hear' music and art, also involve conscious, explicit kinds of memories.

On the right-hand side of Figure 9.5 we also see the learning of implicit memories. Infants may hear sequences of speech sounds, but they are not explicitly learning the rules and regularities of grammar. Those are apparently learned unconsciously, as we will see later. In general, implicit learning is often evoked by explicit, conscious events, but it often goes far beyond the events given in conscious experience (Banaji and Greenwald, 1995). Over-practiced habits and motor skills are also largely implicit. As we will see, priming effects are often implicit. Contextual phenomena are often implicit, such as the assumptions we make about visual space, the direction of the incoming light in a visual scene, the conceptual assumptions of a conversation, and so on. These are often hard to articulate, implicit, and to some degree unconscious (Baars, 1988).

As we will see, the 'Central Executive' of working memory plays an important role in long-term learning and retrieval. For example, if you are trying to learn a word, you might deliberately rehearse it to yourself, using your executive capacities to control inner rehearsal and to shut out distractions. When you are studying for a test, it is a good idea to monitor your own performance 'metacognitively' – i.e. to think about your own thinking process, and to see if your understanding of the material is good enough to pass the exam. All these are examples of executive processes (see Chapters 10, 11, and 12).

1.3 Implicit and explicit memory

Implicit memory is not accompanied by conscious awareness that one has a memory; the memory's existence is inferred only from the effects it has on behavior. Implicit memories may be retrieved without an intention to remember. Priming effects are used extensively to test for implicit memory.

Priming refers to the effect of a stimulus in creating readiness for a similar one. For example, showing a picture of a face will increase the processing efficiency of a following face, as measured by faster reaction time and greater accuracy. Priming can be either perceptual or conceptual.

Suppose you are asked to read a set of words and then your memory for them is tested a week later. We could test your memory directly by asking you to recall as many of the studied words as you can remember, or to recognize the words by picking them out from a list of old and new words. If the interval is long enough, you are likely to recall or recognize only a small subset of the items, and mistakenly classify old words that you studied as new ones that did not appear on the list.

However, if your memory is tested indirectly by asking you to read the words as quickly as you can, you will be able to say old words faster than new words. The old words are *primed*. On such an indirect test no mention is made of memory, and the subject is typically not even aware that memory is being tested. Yet by looking at how quickly subjects read a word we can tell whether the previous experience left a residue in memory. The same result can be seen in amnesic patients who cannot recall studying the words at all.

In the case of conceptual or semantic priming, words such as 'food' may increase the processing efficiency of words like 'water', even though they share little perceptual content. Priming can be viewed as a way of tapping into the general tendency of the brain to engage in predictive processing at every moment.

Perceptual priming is based on alterations of perceptual representation in posterior neocortex associated with perceptual processing. Conceptual priming is associated with alterations of conceptual systems in prefrontal cortex.

1.3.1 *Procedural memory*

Procedural memory refers to sensorimotor habits or automatic skills, which are largely unconscious. The structures implicated in these habits are the basal ganglia.

> Imagine you are riding a bicycle, and you start falling to the right. How would you avoid the impending crash?

Many cyclists say they would compensate by leaning towards the left, but that action would precipitate the fall. When responding to the same situation while actually riding a bicycle, these same cyclists would turn their handlebars in the direction of the fall. The example highlights the distinction between implicit and explicit knowledge. Implicit learning refers to the ability to learn complex information (e.g. skills such as bicycle riding) in the absence of explicit awareness. Anecdotes such as the bicycle example offer subjectively compelling demonstrations for the existence of implicit forms of knowledge that are distinct from (and possibly in conflict with) explicit knowledge . . . (Curran, 2001).

The basal ganglia-frontal networks are the mediators of different classes of sensorimotor learning (Yin and Knowlton, 2006).

2.0 AMNESIA

Chapter 2 touched on the case of Clive Wearing, who has lived with a dense amnesia since 1985, when a viral infection destroyed some brain areas for memory. Over a few days, Wearing was transformed from a rising young musician to a man for whom each waking moment feels like the first, with almost no recollection of the past, and no ability to learn for the future.

Little has changed for Wearing since 1985. While he cannot recall a single specific event, some aspects of his memory are spared. He can carry on a normal, intelligent conversation. Some short-term memory is spared, allowing him to stay with a topic over several seconds. His has retained general world knowledge, an extensive vocabulary, and a tacit understanding of social conventions. Wearing also remains a skilled musician, able to play complex piano pieces from sheet music. Though he cannot remember specific events, he does recall a limited number of general facts about his life. Among the few memories that have survived is the identity of his wife, Deborah. He greets her joyfully every time she comes into his room, as though they have not met for years.

However, just moments after she leaves, Wearing has forgotten that she was there at all. In a recent book, Deborah Wearing (2005) tells of coming home after visiting Clive at his care facility, and finding these messages on her answering machine:

Hello, love, 'tis me, Clive. It's five minutes past four, and I don't know what's going on here. I'm awake for the first time and I haven't spoken to anyone . . .

Darling? Hello, it's me, Clive. It's a quarter past four and I'm awake now for the first time. It all just happened a minute ago, and I want to see you. . . .

Darling? It's me, Clive, and it's 18 minutes past four and I'm awake. My eyes have just come on about a minute ago. I haven't spoken to anyone yet, I just want to speak to you.

Wearing's history suggests that amnesia is selective – certain kinds of memory may survive while others are lost. Skills like the ability to speak or play the piano are distinct from our memories of specific events. Thus, *memory is not unitary, but consists of different types*. Wearing's history also hints that different parts of the brain may be involved in different kinds of memory.

Figure 9.6 shows how specific Clive Wearing's memory loss is. Organic amnesia – the kind that is involves damage to both MTLs – interferes with episodic learning and recall. In addition, semantic learning is impaired, but not semantic retrieval. Clive Wearing still understands the world in much the way he understood it in 1985; his previous semantic knowledge is remarkably intact. But he cannot learn new ideas. And he can neither learn nor remember specific events. We will see later why this pattern of impairment makes sense.

Although all amnesic patients have memory loss, it varies in degree. Clive Wearing's amnesia resembles that of other patients, but he is unusual in his recurrent sense that he has just awoken from some unconscious state. He also 'perseverates' more than most amnesics, repeating the same thoughts and actions over and over again, as in the repetitive telephone messages he leaves for his wife. These symptoms may result from additional damage to prefrontal structures that allow us to monitor our own actions.

2.1 HM: the best-studied amnesia patient

We know a great deal about Clive Wearing's life from the extensive publicity about his case. However, another patient, known only as HM, is by far the best-studied victim of amnesia. In the case of HM we know exactly where the lesion occurred (Figures 9.7 and 9.8). This makes him very rare. Most brain injuries are very 'messy', can spread wider than the visible lesions, and may change over time. Clive Wearing's viral infection apparently destroyed hippocampal regions on both sides of the brain, but also some frontal lobe areas. Wearing may also have suffered brain damage that we simply do not know about. In the case of HM, however, because his lesion was carefully performed by a

Functional framework for learning and memory

Working memory

Attention

Vision

Hearing

Touch

Central executive

Conscious

Attention

Explicit Learning and retrieval

Implicit Learning and retrieval

Response output

Major losses in amnesia:

Perceptual memories	Episodic (event) memory	Semantic (fact) memory	Implicit memories	Habits and motor skills	Primed biases and goals

Long-term memory

FIGURE 9.6 Functional framework: the typical loss in organic amnesia. Amnesia due to bilateral damage to MTL is highly specific. It impairs recollection of episodic (autobiographical) memories and blocks episodic learning. It also makes it impossible to learn new facts and concepts (semantic learning). However, amnesics like HM and Clive Wearing can carry on a normal-seeming conversation because they can still *retrieve* semantic information that was learned before the injury. *Implicit* learning and retrieval also continue. Since the MTL and neocortex work together to enable episodic learning, damage to MTL on both sides of the brain seems to explain these specific deficits. (Notice that the terms 'explicit' and 'conscious' are essentially equivalent; both are indexed by accurate report, as discussed in Chapter 8. Similarly, 'implicit' and 'unconscious' are equivalent for our purposes).

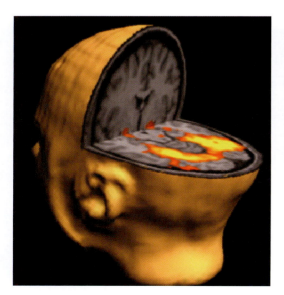
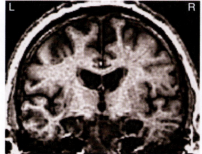
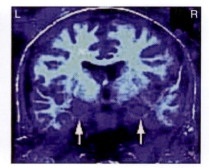

FIGURE 9.7 Bilateral hippocampal damage in the classic patient HM. The lesions in HM's temporal lobes are shown in the coronal brain scan in the left panel. On the right is a normal scan for comparison, with the white arrows pointing to the medial temporal lobes. Those regions are missing in HM. The cutout brain image on the left will help you to understand the location of the coronal sections. *Source*: *left*, Aminoff and Daroff, 2003; *right*, Corkin *et al.*, 1997.

surgeon, we know that both sides of the medial temporal lobe (MTL) were removed as accurately as was possible at the time. The extent of HM's brain damage and functional deficits have been verified with great care, in more than 100 published articles. This has made HM one of the most important patients in the history of brain science (Box 9.1).

Olfaction and taste – the chemical senses – are often thought to be the earliest sensory systems to emerge in evolution, simply because detecting nutrients and avoiding poisons is a fundamental requirement for life. Some scientists therefore believe that human senses like vision and speech audition built on an earlier foundation of the chemical senses. If that is true, it would explain

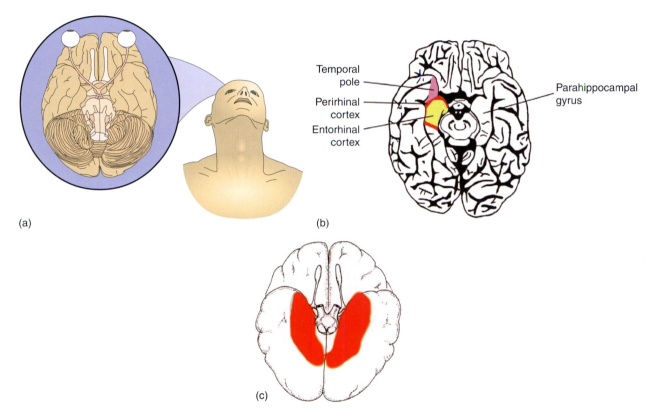

FIGURE 9.8   The medial temporal lobes and HM's lesions, seen from below. (a) The orientation of the head and brain; (b) the bottom of the MTL, with major subregions for memory labeled. Notice that the rhinal (smell) cortices indicate the ancient origin of this region. In all figures you can see the two olfactory bulbs pointing upward, an important landmark for orientation. (c) The surgical lesion in HM's brain. The surgeon at the time was unaware of the importance of this region for memory. *Source*: (b) Buckley and Gaffan, 2006; (c) Moscovitch, personal communication.

BOX 9.1   The case of HM

The cognitive neuroscience of memory arguably began with Herbert Scoville and Brenda Milner's (1957) report of a memory disorder in HM after bilateral removal of his medial temporal lobes to control severe epileptic seizures. As a result of a head injury from a bicycle collision when he was a young boy, HM was beset with epileptic fits that increased in frequency and severity into his late 20s. As a treatment of last resort, Scoville performed an operation in which he removed tissue in and around the hippocampus on both sides of HM's brain (see Figure 9.8). While the surgery reduced HM's seizures, it had a profound and unexpected impact on his memory. This result was unknown at

the time, and Scoville would undoubtedly have changed the procedure had he known about this harmful result. The report of HM's case by Scoville and Brenda Milner (1957) was the first to demonstrate directly the importance of the hippocampus and surrounding structures for memory.

As a result of the operation, HM could not remember any of the events of his life thereafter – the people he met, the things he did, events taking place in the world around him. Even today, he cannot keep track of his age, and can no longer recognize himself in the mirror because he is unfamiliar with his changed appearance. In addition to this *anterograde* (post-damage) memory deficit, HM also can't

(*Continued*)

remember events or experiences from the years immediately before the surgery, a *retrograde* amnesia. While his episodic (autobiographical) memory loss is acute, other cognitive functions seem to be intact. He can reason, solve problems, and carry on a normal conversation. His intelligence is normal, and he has retained his language abilities.

HM has intact short-term memory. He performs like healthy controls on tests of working memory, like the digit span task. HM had been under the care of doctors from a young age, and his intellectual abilities before surgery were well documented. The specific locus of damaged tissue is both limited and well characterized. In most amnesias, the damage is more widespread and difficult to identify. HM has been tested and imaged a number of times since his surgery, giving a very complete picture of his condition.

As you can tell from Figures 9.1 and 9.2, HM has an apparently intact neocortex – the outer structures in brain scan. Like Clive Wearing, HM can carry on a normal conversation. He can discuss the immediate present, using his general knowledge of the world. He is conscious, has normal voluntary control over his actions, and appears to be emotionally well adjusted. It is only when his episodic memory is tested that he reveals that he simply cannot remember the past, or learn new memories for the future.

It is useful for you to review some important regions of the cortex (Figures 9.3, 9.9; also see p. 254). You should recall the location of the prefrontal lobes particularly, in front of the motor and premotor cortex. All of the neocortex is important for memory (see p. 254), but the prefrontal lobes may be especially important.

why vision, for example, has some of its highest levels of analysis in the smell brain, particularly the entorhinal cortex (ento – inside; rhinal – nose or smell).

2.2 A summary of amnesia

HM represents the features of amnesia in a very 'pure' form. More generally, amnesia is any loss of memory for personal experiences and other information, despite otherwise normal cognitive functions. The cause can be organic, including infection, stroke, tumor, drugs, oxygen deprivation, epilepsy and degenerative diseases, such as Alzheimer's disease. Amnesia can also be *psychogenic*, resulting from trauma or suggestion (Nilsson and Markowitsch, 1999).

As we have seen, organic amnesia is caused by bilateral damage to the medial temporal lobes, which includes the hippocampal formation. It generally reveals:

1 *Impaired memory but preserved perception, cognition, intelligence and action.* Amnesic people perform normally on standard tests of intelligence, but are impaired on standard tests of memory. They can play chess, solve crossword and jigsaw puzzles, comprehend complex instructions, and reason logically.

2 *Impaired long-term but not working memory.* Amnesic people have a normal digit span. They are impaired, however, if they are distracted. The same holds for words, stories, visual patterns, faces, melodies, smells and touch.

3 *Impaired recent but not remote memories.* Memory loss is most noticeable for events learned *after* the onset of the disorder, as well as in the period immediately preceding it, but not for information acquired years before. That is, amnesia victims have an *anterograde amnesia* that extends into the future but a limited *retrograde amnesia*. The length and severity of retrograde amnesia varies.

4 *Impaired explicit but not implicit memory.* Anterograde (post-injury) memory loss applies only to information that can be remembered consciously or *explicitly*. Learning, retention and retrieval of memory without awareness or *implicitly* is normal.

2.3 Spared functions in amnesia: implicit and procedural memory

As mentioned above, implicit memory is commonly assessed by priming tasks. Perceptual priming is mediated by sensory cortex, and conceptual priming is believed to involve both the temporal and prefrontal regions. Amnesics do not lose their capacity to perform well on priming tasks, such as word-fragment completion. For example, subjects may study a list of words (such as *metal*) and are tested with fragments of the words they studied, to see if they can complete them (*met__*). The study phase increases the speed of completion. On such tasks, amnesic patients can perform as well as normals.

Functional neuroimaging studies confirm the perceptual locus of perceptual priming. Unlike tests of explicit memory, which are associated with *increased activation* during retrieval in regions that support memory performance, such as the MTL and prefrontal cortex, perceptual priming is associated with *decreased activation* on repeated presentations in regions believed to mediate perceptual representations. Thus, repeated presentation of faces and words leads to decreases in activation in inferior temporal and extra-striate cortex which mediate face and word perception (Wigg and Martin, 1998; Schacter *et al.*, 2004).

2.3.1 Conceptual priming

In conceptual priming the relationship between study and test items is meaning-based. Conceptual tasks include word association ('Tell me the first word that comes to mind for Elephant'), category exemplar generation ('Provide examples of animals') and general knowledge ('What animal is used to carry heavy loads in India?') (Moscovitch *et al.*, 1993; Roediger and McDermott, 1993). Conceptual priming occurs if studied words (e.g. elephant) are retrieved more frequently than unstudied ones. Because conceptual priming depends on meaning, a change in the physical form of stimuli has little influence on conceptual priming.

Conceptual priming is impaired in people with damage to regions of cortex mediating semantics. Thus, patients with semantic dementia whose degeneration affects lateral and anterior temporal lobes show an inability to recognize repeated objects which share a common meaning, for example, two different-looking telephones. But they have no difficulty recognizing the object if it is repeated in identical form (Graham *et al.*, 2000).

Likewise, patients with Alzheimer's disease show preserved perceptual priming but impaired conceptual priming. Functional neuroimaging studies of conceptual priming implicate semantic processing regions, such as prefrontal and lateral temporal areas. As in tests of perceptual priming, tests of conceptual priming lead to decreases in activation in those regions (Buckner *et al.*, 1998; Schacter *et al.*, 2004). Asking people repeatedly to generate examples of 'animals' results in *reduced* activation in the same regions.

Numerous studies have shown that priming on a variety of tests is normal in amnesic patients. This applies to most tests of perceptual and conceptual priming, indicating that the MTL does not contribute to them.

2.3.2 Spared procedural memory in amnesia

One of the earliest demonstrations of preserved memory in amnesia was on tests of learning perceptual motor skills called *procedural memory*. Corkin (1965) and Milner (1965) showed that HM was able to learn and retain a pursuit-rotor task, keeping a pointer on a moving target. HM showed improvement on these tasks even months later, though he could not recall

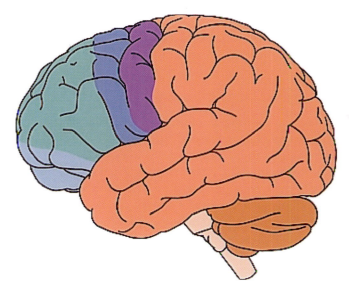

FIGURE 9.9 Neocortex: motor, premotor, and prefrontal regions. In this lateral view of the cortex, the motor strip is tinted purple, and just in front of it, the premotor area encodes the cognitive intention to move specific limbs. The true prefrontal cortex is in front of these motor regions (light green). The light blue area of the prefrontal lobe is sometimes called the orbitofrontal cortex, because it is located just above the orbital hollows of the two eyes. You are encouraged to review the other visible structures, including the major lobes, the Sylvian fissure and the central sulcus, which divides the posterior half of cortex from the frontal half. *Source*: Drawn by Shawn Fu.

doing it even minutes afterwards, if he was distracted. These findings have been repeated in other cases.

Procedural memory depends on perceptual-motor regions, like the basal ganglia, which interact with the neocortex, both the posterior and frontal (see Chapter 5). Patients with impaired basal ganglia due to Parkinson's or Huntington's disease show little or no improvement after practicing sensorimotor tasks (Kaszniak, 1990; Gabrieli *et al.*, 1994).

In the serial reaction time task (SRT), dots are presented on a computer screen in one of four locations, and participants are instructed to press a key corresponding to the location of the dots they see (Willingham *et al.*, 1989). Some of the sequences are repeated while others change randomly. Reaction time to the repeated sequences becomes faster with repetition, but remain the same for the random sequences, even though participants cannot consciously distinguish one from the other (Willingham, 1998). Amnesic patients perform normally on the implicit SRT task but poorly on the explicit version (Nissen and Bullemer, 1987; Reber and Squire, 1998). Again, patients with basal ganglia disorders like Parkinson's disease perform poorly on both SRT tasks (Knopman and Nissen, 1987; Vakil *et al.*, 2000).

Functional neuroimaging studies also show that learning on the implicit SRT task is associated with activity in the basal ganglia but not with MTL activity.

2.4 Spared implicit learning

Academic learning is often explicit: professors point out the things to be learned, and students try their best to memorize them. But most ordinary human learning is probably implicit. A hunter may teach young people how to track an animal, or how to kill and skin it. Most of the time such practical activities can be taught more easily by modeling than by explicit labeling. Many of the subtleties of hunting and gathering may not even have names. Experimentally, subjects who are given a set of stimuli generated by a simple set of rules, unconsciously infer the underlying regularities. Social habits are probably learned mostly implicitly. Children learning language surely don't label the words they hear as nouns or verbs. Rather, they pay attention to speech sounds and the underlying regularities are learned *implicitly*. We rarely become conscious of abstract patterns – the regularities of grammar, the harmonic progressions of a symphony, or the delicate brushwork of a work of art. Most knowledge is tacit knowledge; most learning is implicit.

Knowlton *et al.* (1994, 1996) used a probabilistic classification task to study implicit learning. Participants were shown sets of four cards that predicted the 'weather' with different probabilities (Figure 9.10). After each set of cards, participants were asked whether it predicted 'rain' or 'sunshine'. Some sets predicted 'rain' 20 per cent of the time, and others 80 per cent of the time. Learning this association takes about 50 trials in normal people, but it takes considerably longer for subjects to realize explicitly which card sequence predicted which kind of weather. That is, the weather prediction is learned *implicitly* before it can be stated *explicitly* (Knowlton *et al.*, 1994, 1996).

Amnesia patients performed as well as controls in the early trials, the implicit association, but not in the later trials when performance was based on explicit, declarative memory. However, patients with Parkinson's disease, a basal ganglia dysfunction, performed poorly during the early trials, but caught up during the later ones. Brain imaging showed activity in the basal ganglia throughout the task, but a shift in MTL activity as the task progressed (Poldrack *et al.*, 1998).

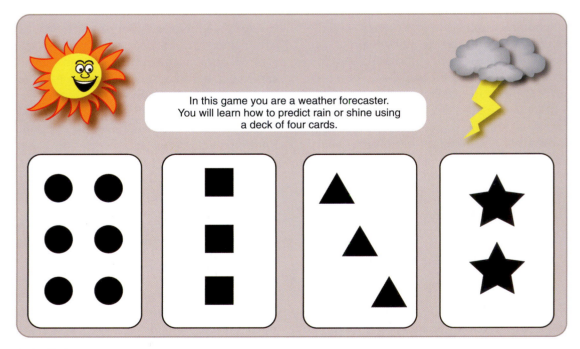

In this game you are a weather forecaster.
You will learn how to predict rain or shine using
a deck of four cards.

FIGURE 9.10 An implicit 'weather prediction' learning task. Knowlton *et al.* (1994) devised this 'weather prediction' task for four-card sequences. Participants learned to predict the probabilistic outcomes implicitly before they were able to state the pattern explicitly. Amnesic patients performed well during the implicit early part of the learning process, but did not learn to state the association between the cards and the 'weather' explicitly. *Source*: Knowlton *et al.*, 2003.

In summary, amnesia due to bilateral damage to MTL seems to be primarily a disorder of *episodic memory*, resulting from impaired transfer of information from working memory into long-term memory. Because memories acquired long before the onset of amnesia are relatively spared, it is believed that the hippocampus and related structures in the medial temporal lobe are needed only temporarily to hold information in memory until they are consolidated elsewhere in the brain, presumably in neocortex.

3.0 MEMORIES ARE MADE OF THIS

Traditionally, a memory is considered to be a stable record of an event, which can be recalled accurately in the same form it was learned. In this commonsense view, memories can be retrieved, examined, and played back like a high fidelity music recording. Memories can also be forgotten without affecting other cognitive systems.

There are reasons to question this common sense idea. One is that real memories of past events are rarely accurate. The *process view* considers memory to be a product of a dynamic process, a reconstruction of the past influenced by past and current conditions, anticipations of future outcomes, and by other cognitive processes. In the process view, memory is based on stored information, but is not equivalent to it. It is dynamic and mutable, and interacts with other processes. Thus, two people experiencing the same event may have different memories of it. It is not simply that one person is right and the other wrong, but that in retrieving the memory each person's outlook, knowledge, motivation, and retentive abilities may alter what is retrieved.

Everyone's memory changes with time. We forget most of what has happened within minutes or hours, and what remains is commonly reorganized and distorted by other knowledge or biases. We would not want computer files or books to be that way. We do not want files to decay over time, or to leak into neighboring files. Computers and libraries are designed to keep everything as distinct and stable as possible. Yet normal memories do fade, and are often confused with others.

Try to reconstruct in as much detail as possible all the things you did two weekends ago, in the exact order in which you did them. To do that, most of us have to search for cues, to determine exactly what we did. Having found a cue, there is a process of reconstruction, especially in trying to figure out the sequence

of events. Did I meet my friend before I spoke to my parents or afterwards? Did I go shopping, and what was the order of the stores I visited? In each store, in what order did I look at the merchandise and buy it? You can try this with a recent movie, and then see how accurate your memory is by checking it against a copy of the movie.

To answer these questions you must draw on a body of knowledge and inference that is unlike anything that is needed when you enter a file name to access a computer file, or use a call number to find a library book. You may confuse what you did two weekends ago with what happened another time. As we will see, some patients with brain damage have a disorder called *confabulation*, in which they make up false memories without any intention of lying, and without any awareness that their memories are incorrect.

Memories influence how other memories are formed and retrieved. They also shape our actions even when we are not conscious that they do so. Our memories and dispositions influence our thoughts and actions and, in turn, are influenced by them. In short, memory is needed to carry on the affairs of daily life and to plan for the future, and is, in turn influenced by the past, whether conscious or not, and by our thoughts about the future.

3.1 Electrically evoked autobiographical memories

For some fifty years, brain surgeons have reported that awake patients report vivid, specific conscious recollections during temporal lobe stimulation. Penfield and Roberts (1959) were among the first to use pinpoint electrical stimulation of cortex to map out functional regions. Their aim was to remove 'epileptic foci' in the cortex, regions of scarred tissue that can trigger the massive electrical storm of major seizures. In order to locate epileptic foci, and to avoid harming functionally important areas, the cortex of awake patients was mapped using low-voltage electrical stimulation in specific cortical locations.

This is only possible because the cortex itself has no pain receptors. As long as local anesthetic is used to block pain from the scalp incision, conscious patients can talk about their experiences without harm. Open-brain surgery provides a unique source of evidence for cognitive neuroscience.

Stimulation of the temporal lobe sometimes results in an unexpected flood of conscious memories. For example, a recent patient during brain stimulation

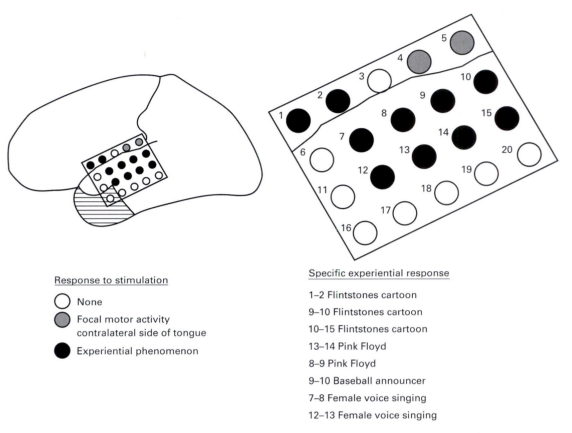

Response to stimulation

○ None

◐ Focal motor activity
contralateral side of tongue

● Experiential phenomenon

Specific experiential response

1–2 Flintstones cartoon

9–10 Flintstones cartoon

10–15 Flintstones cartoon

13–14 Pink Floyd

8–9 Pink Floyd

9–10 Baseball announcer

7–8 Female voice singing

12–13 Female voice singing

FIGURE 9.11 Autobiographical memories evoked by temporal lobe stimulation. Spontaneous reports of memory experiences by electrical brain stimulation in a patient with a surgical lesion in the left medial temporal lobe. Notice the electrode grid that was placed on the cortex as shown. Electrodes were places 1 cm apart. Different electrodes consistently evoked different memory episodes. Spontaneous reports of this kind are not unusual with temporal lobe stimulation, but are not routinely reported as a result of other locations of cortical stimulation. *Source*: Moriarty *et al.*, 2001.

gave the following reports of his experiences (Moriarty *et al.*, 2001):

1　At four electrode locations shown in Figure 9.11, re-experiencing Flinstones cartoons from childhood

2　At four different electrode locations, hearing the rock band Pink Floyd

3　At two other locations, a baseball announcer

4　At four more locations, an unknown female voice.

Notice that the open circles in the figure show electrode locations that led to no experiential memories at all. Some of the electrode sites are close to the auditory cortex of the upper temporal lobe, but some are not. And these auditory regions are not known to provide such rich memories of experiences that patients report having heard at specific points in their lives. However, this particular patient had a surgical lesion in the medial temporal lobe, and we must be careful about generalization to other cases.

The patient in this case is not told which electrode is currently stimulating the temporal lobe, so that it is not possible to fake this pattern of results. Scientists have been skeptical about these reports, since stimulation in one place might activate other regions as well. Epileptics have atypical brains, since cortex commonly changes in response to disorders. However, it is extremely unlikely that so many different patients would report a flow of conscious memories over fifty years of stimulation of the temporal lobe. After numerous animal experiments, careful studies of amnesic patients and brain imaging of memory tasks, there is little doubt today that there is something about the temporal lobe that is specific to long-term episodic memory. One reasonable hypothesis is that temporal lobe stimulation somehow activates specific memories by way of the MTL.

Figure 9.12 shows a possible explanation of this phenomenon. What we are seeing in the neurosurgical patient is an established memory pattern, which is

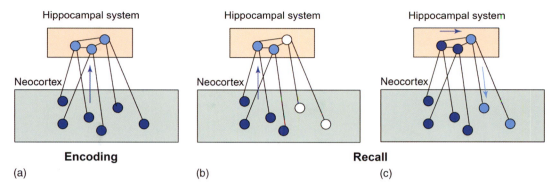

FIGURE 9.12   The hippocampal system (MTL) and neocortex in learning and recall. A neural net model of MTL (the hippocampal system) in interaction with neocortex. During the encoding or learning process, information from cortex is transferred to the hippocampal system. During recall, a neocortical event serves to evoke an overlapping pattern of neural activation in the MTL (the blue dots). The hippocampal system responds by activating neocortical regions that provide the experience of recall of some part of the original event. *Source*: Gluck *et al.*, 2003.

re-evoked by direct electrical stimulation to the temporal lobe. Thus, the flow of information is from the neocortex (temporal) to the hippocampal system (MTL), which causes the hippocampal system to resonate with the original neocortical memory traces to produce the original episodic experience, or something very much like it. However, this still leaves many questions unanswered, such as, what is the relationship between the electrical stimulus and the normal process of episodic memory retrieval? Why are such extremely specific memories evoked under these circumstances, among the many millions of episodes the average person has experienced? Is there perhaps a relationship between the electrical stimulus and the oscillatory EEG phenomena that are observed in connection with retrieval, like the theta rhythms that seem to coordinate MTL-neocortical retrieval (see below)? Episodic memories reported by patients in neurosurgery after electrical stimulation are fascinating, and appear to be robust and reliable phenomena. But we do not have a good specific explanation as yet.

3.2 Long-term potentiation and long-term depression: excitatory and inhibitory memory traces

Most synapses in cortex are excitatory, using the neurotransmitter *glutamate* (see Chapter 3). A very large minority use inhibitory neurotransmitters like *GABA* (gamma amino butyric acid). To encode long-term memory traces in changed synaptic efficiency, these excitatory and inhibitory connections must somehow

be made more permanent. These two processes are believed to occur in what is called long-term potentiation (LTP) for excitatory synapses and long-term depression (LTD) for inhibitory ones. These events, which have been observed in specific regions, are simply an increase and a decrease in the firing probability of a postsynaptic potential given a presynaptic spike.

LTP has been observed within the hippocampus itself, using single-cell recording in one of the neuronal layers of the hippocampus (Figure 9.13). Single cell recording has been extensively done in animals, but there are cases of such recordings in human epileptic patients as well (Kreiman *et al.*, 2002).

While we can observe LTP and LTD in specific locations like the hippocampus, the standard hypothesis about long-term memory involves billions of synapses in cortex and its satellites, amounting to literally trillions of synapses. We have no way of taking a census of all of the synapses in this system, or even a substantial fraction of them, at this time. Rather, we have a number of studies showing increased LTP and LTD in experiments like the one described in Figure 9.14, supplemented by studies of brain damage and of population activity among billions of neurons as measured by EEG, ERP, fMRI and so on. In addition, we have evidence from stimulation studies, like temporal lobe stimulation of awake patients during neurosurgery, and transcranial magnetic stimulation (TMS) in normal subjects. What we know about memory is therefore an inferential picture, in which many hundreds of studies have been performed. But we cannot yet come close to observing large numbers of changed synaptic connectivities directly at the submicroscopic level.

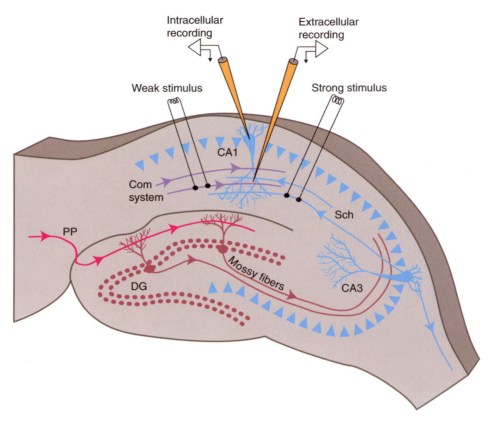

FIGURE 9.13　Single-cell recording in hippocampus. A schematic of single cell recording and stimulation either inside of hippocampal neurons, or outside. An electrode placed outside of a neuron can pick up electrical field potentials, which are similar to EEG but much more localized. Electrical field potentials often reflect the activity of small populations of neurons, as opposed to the axonal or dendritic potential of a single neuron. Notice that a very similar technique can be used to stimulate single cells, or small sets of cells, in the hippocampus. *Source*: Squire *et al.*, 2003.

With that caution in mind, there is good agreement today that the evidence is consistent with these propositions:

1. Episodic input is initially represented via neocortex.
2. It is integrated for memory purposes in the MTL (medial temporal lobes), containing the hippocampi and related structures, and perhaps also the thalamus and surrounding regions.
3. Consolidation: MTL and related regions then bind and integrate a number of neocortical regions, a process that transforms temporary synaptic connectivities into longer-lasting memory traces in both MTL and neocortex. The main mechanism for such changes is believed to be LTP and LTD.

We focus on the last point next.

3.3 Consolidation: from temporary to permanent storage

We can now add the final steps. Chapter 2 suggested a widely accepted hypothesis about the relationship between immediate memory and long-term memory called the *consolidation hypothesis*. Consolidation is generally defined as a progressive stabilization of long-term memory traces so that they are relatively resistant to decay or disruption. It is this process which is absent or severely disrupted in amnesic patients and accounts for their poor ability to transfer information from short- to long-term memory.

Figure 9.15 shows one version of learning with consolidation, in which input into the neocortex and the hippocampal regions (MTL) evoke an active state, with neuronal processes making new synaptic connections. As mentioned above, immediate memory is encoded in

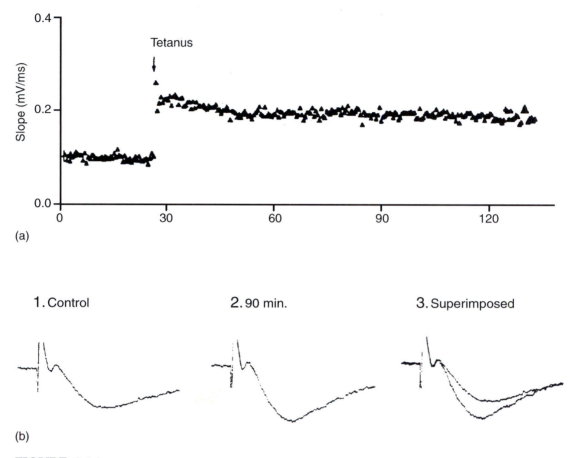

(a)

1. Control   2. 90 min.   3. Superimposed

(b)

FIGURE 9.14 Long-term potentiation in the hippocampus. Memory traces are believed to be encoded in changed synaptic efficiency among billions of neurons in the neocortex and MTL. These are called long-term potentiation (LTP), corresponding to a permanent increase in excitatory transmission, and long-term depression (LTD), a permanent increase in inhibitory neurotransmission. Direct evidence for LTP has been obtained in hippocampal single cell recordings, as shown above. The lower half of the diagram shows three cases of changed EPSP (excitatory postsynaptic potentials) after strong electrical stimulation presynaptically (called tetanus). Notice that after 90 minutes, the EPSP dips more deeply (remember that a more negative potential means more electrical spiking activity). The graph above shows a long-lasting change in the conductivity of the synapse, as measured by the slope of the EPSPs for two hours after the strong electrical stimulus (tetanus). *Source*: Byrne in Squire *et al.*, 2003.

improved synaptic connectivity between billions of neurons in the neocortex. Normal sleep, especially the slow-wave stage, is important to turn these temporary connectivities into long-lasting memory traces.

However, more permanent memories are believed to require protein synthesis – such as the growth of dendritic spikes, tiny stalks that grow on top of axons and dendrites, bearing new synaptic connections with neighboring neurons.

The idea that new learning takes some time to 'fix' is quite old. In 1904, Burnham wrote that:

The fixing of an impression depends on a physiological process. It takes time for an impression to become so fixed that it can be reproduced after a long interval; for

it to become part of the permanent store of memory considerable time may be necessary. This we may suppose is not merely a process of making a permanent impression upon the nerve cells, but also a process of association, of organization of the new impressions with the old ones (quoted by Moscovitch).

Figure 9.16 shows these two kinds of consolidation conceptually. The LTP-LTD process discussed above involves cellular consolidation, a local change of connective efficiency in trillions of synapses. However, there is also believed to be *systems consolidation*, in which large-scale reorganization of memories may occur. There is considerable evidence that different sleep stages may have different effects upon this systems consolidation

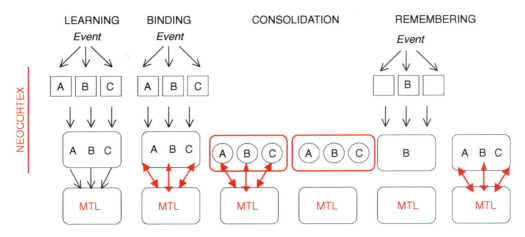

FIGURE 9.15 The steps of learning, binding, consolidation and remembering. In this summary, Step 1 is the learning of an event, consisting of three elements, A, B, and C. It is initially encoded by neocortex (such as the visual cortex) and sent to MTL. In Step 2, MTL and neocortex resonate with each other to begin establishing the memory trace. In Step 3, the stimulus event is no longer available, and the MTL-neocortical resonance is now independent of external support. Step 4 shows how consolidation leads to permanent, separate memory traces (synaptic changes) in both the MTL and neocortex, which now exist separately from each other, while other input is being processed. In Step 5, element B of the original event (A-B-C) is presented as a reminder or recall cue. In Step 6, the memory traces of A-B-C are activated by resonating activity between MTL and neocortex. At this point, the episodic memory has been retrieved in the absence of the original stimulus. *Source*: Moscovitch, modified with permission.

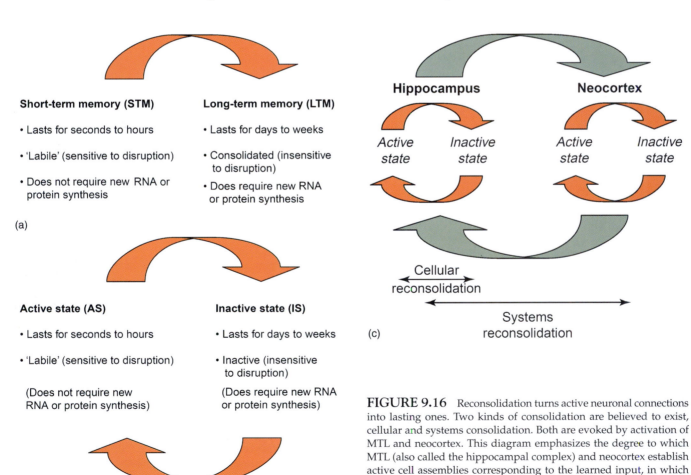

FIGURE 9.16 Reconsolidation turns active neuronal connections into lasting ones. Two kinds of consolidation are believed to exist, cellular and systems consolidation. Both are evoked by activation of MTL and neocortex. This diagram emphasizes the degree to which MTL (also called the hippocampal complex) and neocortex establish active cell assemblies corresponding to the learned input, in which neurons resonate with each other until more permanent connections are established. *Source*: Nader, 2003.

process. Notice that both types of consolidation are thought to involve an active dialogue between the MTL (hippocampus) and neocortex.

3.4 Rapid consolidation: synaptic mechanisms, gene transcription, and protein synthesis

Rapid or synaptic consolidation is accomplished within the first minutes to hours after learning occurs. Weiler and colleagues (Weiler *et al.*, 1995) showed that it correlates with morphological changes in the synapse itself. Stimulus presentation initiates a cascade of neurochemical events at the synaptic membrane and within the cell which increase the synaptic strength or efficiency with which neurons that form the memory trace can communicate with one another. The first of these processes involves local, transient molecular modifications that lead to an increase in neurotransmitter release at the affected synapse. If the stimulus is intense enough and/or repeated, additional processes are activated. These involve gene transcription and protein formation that lead to long-lasting cellular changes, including the creation of new synapses, that support the formation and maintenance of long-term memory. These processes may last from hours to days (Lees *et al.*, 2000; McGaugh, 2000; Dudai, 2004).

Though we are well on our way to understanding the basic cellular and molecular mechanisms of synaptic consolidation, we are far from understanding prolonged or system consolidation, which is being debated heatedly in the literature.

3.5 System consolidation: interaction between the medial temporal lobes and neocortex

System consolidation can take much longer to complete and may range from days to years or decades. Patients with MTL lesions show a retrograde memory loss that is temporally-graded, so that recent memory loss (before the amnesia) is greater than earlier memory loss. This temporal gradient is restricted to explicit memory, leaving implicit memory intact and stable over time (Scoville and Milner, 1957).

These observations suggest that the MTL forms a temporary memory trace needed for explicit memories until they are consolidated elsewhere in the brain, presumably in the neocortex (Squire, 1992; Squire and Alvarez, 1995). This standard model of consolidation makes no distinction between various types of explicit memory. For instance, it predicts a similar pattern for episodic and semantic memory.

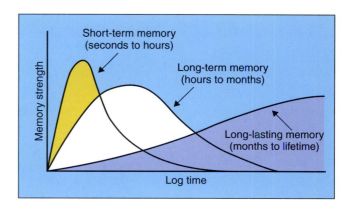

FIGURE 9.17 The time course of consolidation. McGaugh (2000) suggests that there are three overlapping time courses for consolidation. The fastest is referred to as 'short-term memory', from seconds to hours. Long-term memory consolidation takes place over hours to months. Finally, long-lasting memory is needed to account for certain facts, such as the retained long-term memory of early life events in amnesics, who do not have spared memory for some years before brain damage occurred, and none for the time afterwards. *Source*: McGaugh, 2000.

Nadel and Moscovitch concluded, contrary to the standard consolidation model, that MTL is needed to represent even old episodic memories for as long as the memory exists (Nadel and Moscovitch, 1997, 1998; Moscovitch and Nadel, 1998; Nadel *et al.*, 2000). Neocortex, on the other hand, is sufficient to represent *repeated* experiences with words, objects, people, and environments. MTL may aid in the initial formation of these neocortical traces, but once formed they can exist on their own. Thus, unique autobiographical memories are different from repeated memories, in that they continue to require MTL. Repeated experiences are proposed to create multiple traces, adding more traces each time the event is brought to mind.

Neuroimaging studies provide evidence for this interpretation (Box 9.2). These studies found that the hippocampus is activated equally during retrieval of recent and remote autobiographical memories (Conway *et al.*, 1999; Ryan *et al.*, 2000; Gilboa *et al.*, 2004; for review see Maguire, 2000; Moscovitch *et al.*, 2005, 2006). These questions continue to be debated at this time.

4.0 VARIETIES OF MEMORY

Memory is not unitary. Clive Wearing's memory for specific past events in his life is almost entirely destroyed, but he can maintain active knowledge of the immediate past for about 7 seconds (if he is not

BOX 9.2   Multiple trace theory versus traditional consolidation

Nadel and Moscovitch (1997) proposed a *multiple trace theory*, suggesting that the hippocampal complex rapidly encodes all information that becomes conscious. MTL binds the neocortical neurons that represent the conscious experience into a memory trace. MTL neurons act as a pointer, or *index*, to the neocortical ensemble of neurons that represent the experience (Teyler and DiScenna, 1986). A memory trace of an episode, therefore, consists of a bound ensemble of neocortical *and* MTL neurons. Formation of these traces is relatively rapid, lasting on the order of seconds or at most days (Moscovitch, 1995).

In this model, there is no prolonged consolidation process that slowly strengthens the neocortical memory trace. Instead, each time an old memory is retrieved, a new hippocampally-mediated trace is created, so that old memories are represented by more traces than new ones, and therefore are less susceptible to disruption. Because the memory trace is distributed in the MTL, the extent and severity of retrograde amnesia is related to the amount and location of damage to the MTL.

While each autobiographical memory trace is unique, the existence of many related traces facilitates retrieval. Episodic memories are integrated to form semantic memories. Thus, facts about people and events that are learned in specific episode become separated from their sources. This process may give the appearance of classical consolidation, but the brain mechanism is different from the classical view.

distracted). Clearly, some forms of memory have been targeted by his disorder and others not. This pattern is routine in amnesic patients, and suggests that different types of memory have different neural underpinnings. A standard view of the major long-term memory systems is shown in Figure 9.18. However, the exact relationship between memory types is still a matter of debate. For example, perceptual memory is classified under non-declarative memory, but this is rather arbitrary. Perceptual memory manifests in an improvement in sensory discrimination at the cortical level, often by reorganization of cortical receptive fields. The result is a change in conscious perception, as in learning to identify clearly the sound of a guitar in music. This has much in common with episodic memory, which can also be largely perceptual and which is generally believed to be conscious. Nevertheless, the memory classification shown in Figure 9.18 is widely used,

and is part of the vocabulary students of the field are expected to know.

4.1 Episodic and semantic memory: 'Remembering' versus 'knowing'

As Figure 9.18 shows, declarative memory can be divided into two types, *episodic* and *semantic* (Tulving, 1972). *Episodic memory* refers to memories that have a specific source in time, space and life circumstances. Episodic memories are often autobiographical in nature, in that we can travel mentally back in time to relive the experience. By contrast, *semantic memories* involve facts about the world, about ourselves, and about other knowledge that we share with a community. Semantic memories are independent of the spatial and temporal context in which they were acquired.

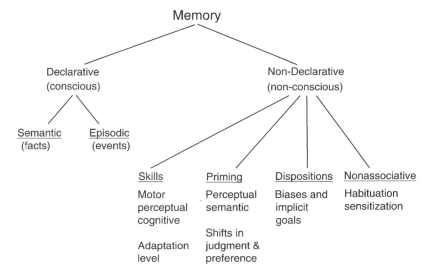

FIGURE 9.18 A classification of memory types. Schacter and Tulving proposed this classification of memory types. Declarative memories have been studied in great detail, and are believed to be explicit (conscious). Non-declarative memory types are said to be unconscious or implicit, but this claim is still debated. While the non-declarative memory types in this diagram undoubtedly have unconscious aspects, it is not yet clear that they can be learned without conscious input. *Source*: Adapted from Schacter and Tulving, 1994.

A semantic memory may refer to our knowledge of Paris as the capital of France, or Ottawa as the capital of Canada, or the knowledge that we attended a particular high school. By comparison, episodic memory may refer to an event that we experienced in Paris, Ottawa or in high school (Figure 9.19). We often have an auto-biographical *source memory* about a specific time, place, and set of circumstances when our episodic memory was acquired. The terms 'episodic' and 'autobiographical' memory are near synonyms.

Episodic memories typically:

1 have reference to oneself
2 are organized around a specific time period
3 are *remembered* consciously, in such as way that we seem to be able to re-experience them
4 are susceptible to forgetting
5 are context-dependent, with respect to time, space, relationships with others, and other circumstances.

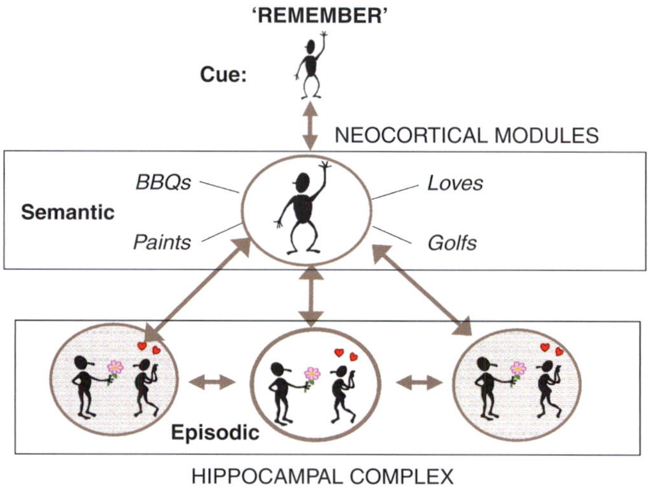

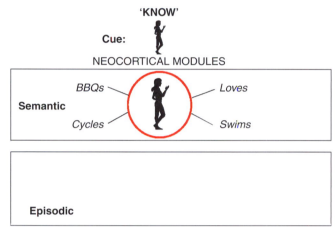

FIGURE 9.19 Remembering: autobiographical episodes. Remembering involves an active reconstruction of the original (conscious) episode. These conscious recollections seem to require hippocampal activity. *Source*: Moscovitch.

FIGURE 9.20 Knowing: semantic information. Semantic memories are assessed by feelings of knowing, which can be very accurate. However, they do not require active reconstruction of the original episode, and can apparently be accomplished by neocortex without the aid of the hippocampal complex. *Source*: Moscovitch.

BOX 9.3   False feelings of familiarity: AKP, a person with déjà vecu

People can falsely believe they have known something before when they have not. AKP was an 80-year-old Polish immigrant to Britain, a retired engineer who had a masters degree in his field. He presented to his family doctor with memory problems, and complaining of frequent sensations of what his wife described as déjà vu (actually, déjà vecu, the feeling of having lived through the same experience before). The sensation of déjà vecu was so strong that it influenced AKP's daily activities. He refused to read the newspaper or watch television because he said he had seen it before. The sensation of déjà vecu was extremely prominent when he went for a walk – AKP complained that it was the same bird in the same tree singing the same song, for instance. He also read car number plates and stated that the drivers must have very regular habits always passing by at the exact same time every day. When shopping, AKP would say that it was unnecessary to purchase certain items, because he had bought the item the day before. There

was also further evidence of confabulation, including the belief that he had been married three times to the same woman, with three different ceremonies around Europe.

On formal testing, AKP had an above average IQ, scoring above the 90th percentile on some of the subtests. He scored poorly on some, but not all, tests of frontal function. His scores on standardized memory tests, however, were impaired, as were his scores on laboratory tests. Consistent with his condition, he would mistake the lures for targets. As in real life, he not only found new events familiar, but actually believed that he experienced them before.

Structural neuroimaging revealed atrophy of the medial temporal lobes but frontal lobes that appeared normal. Metabolic measures also showed only medial temporal abnormality. This medial temporal abnormality may cause 'memory' signals to be emitted continuously which tag on-going perceptions as memories.

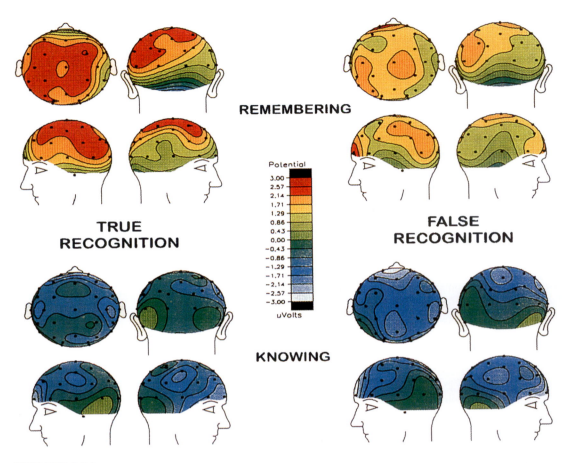

FIGURE 9.21 Even-related potentials for remembering versus knowing. The act of remembering (recollecting the original experience) results in much higher brain activation than the 'feeling of knowing', even for the same material. These brain images involve event-related potentials, scalp EEG traces averaged over trials. This is consistent with evidence discussed in Chapter 8 indicating that conscious stimuli evoked widespread forward activity, outside of sensory cortices, while unconscious stimuli evoke purely local activity. Recollecting original experiences may involve more consciously retrieved material, and it may also require more mental effort, which evokes high activity in prefrontal cortex (see Chapters 10, 11 and 12). *Source*: Duzel *et al.*, 1997.

In contrast, semantic memories generally:

1 have reference to shared knowledge with others
2 are not organized around a specific time period
3 give a *'feeling of knowing'* rather than a fully conscious recollection of the original event
4 are less susceptible to forgetting than specific episodes
5 are relatively independent of context.

To investigate the types of consciousness in memory tasks, Tulving (1985) introduced the remember/know procedure. This involves asking participants to introspect about their conscious experience when they recognize studied items. If they believe an item was studied before, they must decide whether they *remember* the item (i.e. they can re-experience episodic details about the event) or whether they *know* the item (it feels familiar). Local hippocampus seems to affect only 'remember' judgments. Memory based on feelings of knowing is spared (Moscovitch and McAndrews, 2002; Yonelinas, 2002). Similarly, in functional neuroimaging studies, hippocampal activation is associated more with remembering than familiarity (Eldridge *et al.*, 2002; Yonelinas *et al.*, 2005).

Thus, the hippocampally-mediated memory trace is suffused with the consciousness that accompanied the original experience, or what Tulving called *autonoetic consciousness*. This is contrasted with simply having a sense of familiarity about an event, which Tulving refers this as *noetic consciousness*. Noetic consciousness is associated with semantic memory.

4.2 Episodic memories may turn into semantic memories over time

In 1958, Penfield and Milner wrote that:

> The record of the stream of consciousness ... depends upon the integrity of the bilateral hippocampal structures. . . Later on, a person deals with what may be called generalizations, and he can summon them to his purposes. All events, even 'memorable' ones, slip away from the reach of voluntary recall unless he has talked about them or preserved them by reflective reconsideration. For example, one remembers a song or a poem that one has heard repeatedly, forgets each hearing or reading, but remembers the generalization. (p. 494)

Almost five decades later many memory scientists would agree. There is good evidence that semantic memories may be formed from repeated, similar episodes. Attending a high school is a long series of episodes. We may be able to recall dozens of those episodes, but much of the time they seem 'smeared' together in memory in the semantic belief that 'I attended such-and-such high school'.

Figure 9.22 shows how episodic and semantic memories may be related in the brain. Specific episodic memories are shown in the cartoon below: a man cooking on a barbecue grill, presenting flowers to a young lady, painting a picture, and playing golf. These are separate autobiographical memories, remembered as conscious events. Above, a small semantic network combines all these very specific and richly detailed episodes into a single figure: a semantic network of a man who BBQs, loves, paints and plays golf. The semantic network is more abstract and general than the episodes about particular events in the life of the person. Moscovitch (2004) claims that the bottom row of episodes depends upon the MTL, and the top figure depends upon neocortical modules.

We can summarize this concept in three steps:

1 Initially, memories are episodic and context-dependent
2 Over time, episodic memories are transformed into semantic memories
3 MTL is important for recovering episodic memories, which are linked to the specific autobiographical context in which they were acquired.

In this view, the hippocampal complex or MTL supports:

1 Storage and retrieval of detailed, remote autobiographical and spatial memories.

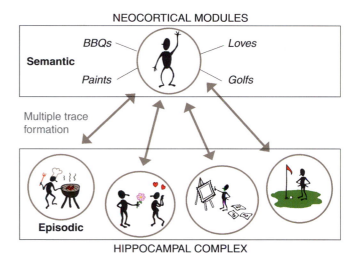

FIGURE 9.22 How semantic and episodic memories may be related: semantic memories may be the neocortical residue of many episodic memories. Thus one may have many experiences with the stick figure above, such as watching him or her cooking a barbecue, presenting flowers to a young lady, painting and playing golf. Over time, these episodes may be forgotten, and only the semantic knowledge remains, that this is the kind of person who does all those things. These are multiple traces, created each time there is another episodic experience with this person. Semantic memory may require only neocortex (particularly temporal and frontal lobes). Episodic information may require both neocortex and the hippocampal complex. *Source*: Moscovitch, 2004, modified with permission.

2 Formation and assimilation of semantic memory in neocortex.

4.3 Episodic and semantic memory are often combined

When you are asked if the face of a particular person is familiar to you, say the movie star Brad Pitt, on what basis are you making your judgment? Are you relying on your semantic memory, episodic memory, or both? Westmacott *et al.* (2004) have shown that *both* systems may contribute, because performance on semantic tests is better if the participant also has some episodic memory associated with the famous name.

Semantic dementia is diagnosed in a subset of Alzheimer's disease patients who show widespread deficits in understanding meaning, often with spared perceptual abilities. These patients, whose degeneration of anterior and lateral temporal lobes leads to semantic loss, can identify common objects only if they can make a personal association to them. For example, they can identify a vase if it belongs to them, but not any other vase (Snowden *et al.*, 1996; Graham *et al.*, 1999).

Remarkably, however, if MTL is injured very early in development, during infancy, semantic memory develops relatively normally in most cases (Vargha-Khadem and Mishkin, 1997). However, episodic memory still remains impaired without an MTL. What these findings suggest is that early in life, the semantic system has the capacity to acquire knowledge on its own, without the help of the episodic system (MTL).

5.0 MTL IN EXPLICIT LEARNING AND MEMORY

MTL is necessary for conscious recollection of long-term, episodic memories. We do not have a way voluntarily to 'switch on' our MTL. Rather, all we need to do is to pay attention to some material we want to memorize. As pointed out in Chapter 8, that means in most cases that we become conscious of the material, and an episodic memory is apparently established without doing anything more.

That is, conscious experiences, such as the sight of the coffee cup in Figure 9.4, appears to be necessary and sufficient to record a conscious experience, using MTL; assuming of course that we are dealing with an intact brain. The episodic memory trace consists of an ensemble of MTL and neocortical neurons, while the MTL acts as a pointer to the neural elements in neocortex for the event. Retrieval occurs when a conscious cue triggers the MTL, which in turn activates the entire neocortical ensemble associated with it. When we recover episodic memories, we recover conscience experiences (Moscovitch, 1995). The recovery of these consciously-experienced events, in rich detail, always depends on the hippocampus no matter how long ago the memory was acquired. As Moscovitch (1992) has argued, the hippocampal complex acts as a module whose domain is consciously apprehended information. Much of the evidence seemed consistent with that view.

Some recent studies, however, have questioned this hypothesis. Using fMRI, Henke and her collaborators (Henke et al., 2003; Degonda et al., 2005) showed that the hippocampus can be activated by subliminal presentation of faces and their associated professions. Moreover, these activations are correlated with performance on subsequent explicit tests of memory for faces-profession pairs. Likewise, Daselaar et al. (2006) found that the posterior medial temporal lobe was activated more by old, studied items at retrieval, even when the person was not aware that the item was old. Finally, Schedon et al. (2003) showed that the hippocampus was activated on the SRT task if the repeated sequences were of a higher-order of association.

There also have been similar reports from studies with amnesic patients. Ostergaard (1987) was the first to suggest that performance on some priming tests was related to the extent of medial temporal damage. More recently, Chun and Phelps (1999) showed that non-conscious context effects in visual search were not found in amnesic patients, suggesting that the MTL was needed for retaining contextual information of which the person was not aware. Likewise, Ryan and Cohen (Ryan et al., 2000) showed that amnesic people did not show the normal pattern of eye movements around the location where a change occurred in a studied picture, even though neither they nor the normal people were consciously aware of the change.

These are a handful of studies in an armful of older studies which claimed that the hippocampus is associated only with explicit memory. If the recent studies are replicated and not found wanting, then it would change our ideas about the relation of the hippocampus to consciousness and memory.

5.1 Divided attention interferes with learning

Learning works best when you pay attention. Trying to study in an environment where lots of other interesting things are happening is not likely to work. Psychologists have used this 'divided attention' or 'dual task' technique to understand the contribution of attention (or consciousness) to memory. In a typical study, participants are asked to process target material, such as words or pictures, while at the same time their attention is diverted with another task, such as tracking a dot on the screen, or deciding whether a running count of digits contains three successive odd numbers. Under such conditions, even if the participant is given a task that requires in-depth, meaningful analysis of the material, memory under divided attention is much worse than memory under full attention. Successful encoding requires a level of attention and presumably consciousness.

Exactly why that is the case is not well understood. One possibility is that deeper processing requires time to complete, and divided attention limits the time allotted to encoding. Another possibility is that consciousness or awareness is a necessary contributor to memory. If one is not fully conscious of the processed material, no matter how deeply it was processed, memory will suffer accordingly. A third possibility is that attention limits elaboration or organization, both of which contribute to good memory.

TABLE 9.1   Some types of learning and memory – explicit and implicit

Type	Learning	Retention	Retrieval
Episodic memory	Conscious or explicit	Unconscious	Conscious or explicit of the learning experience
Semantic memory	Conscious or explicit	Unconscious	Unconscious or implicit for the learning experience
Implicit learning	Conscious stimuli, but unconsciously learned regularities	Unconscious	Unconscious retrieval
Subliminal learning (rarely robust and long term)	Unconscious of target stimuli	Unconscious	Unconscious retrieval

Fletcher *et al.* (1995) found, in a PET study, that activation of the left inferior prefrontal region is reduced under divided attention. This finding was replicated by Anderson *et al.* (2000) in younger and older adults, with the additional observation that divided attention also reduced activity in the left medial temporal lobes, regions known to be important for verbal memory.

Memory and learning have both conscious and unconscious aspects. If we think about three phases – learning, retention and retrieval – we can lay out the possibilities in a 3×2 matrix (Table 9.1). Of the three, retention is generally viewed as unconscious, although it is shaped by conscious experiences. Learning is often thought to require consciousness and, intuitively, we certainly try to learn things by paying attention and becoming conscious of what we need to learn. That is perhaps the basic learning strategy we have as human beings.

However, there is some evidence for learning without consciousness, especially in the case of emotional stimuli. There is much stronger evidence for implicit learning, in which some inferential process takes conscious input and encodes unconscious results of conscious input. However, implicit learning tasks always ask subjects to pay attention and become conscious of a set of stimuli (Section 2.4). It is the rules and regularities that generate those stimuli that are learned without consciousness, just as we normally learn the rules of linguistic grammars without knowing those rules explicitly. But we must hear spoken words and word sequences consciously in order for implicit learning to occur.

The terms implicit and explicit memory are used in the context of remembering, i.e. retrieval of stored information. *Explicit memory* refers to memory with conscious awareness, namely, memory of which the individual is aware, can declare its existence, and comment on its content, either verbally or non-verbally (Schacter, 1987). For this reason, such memories also are known as *declarative memories* (Ryle, 1949; Cohen and Squire, 1980). They are the kind of memory to which we typically refer in everyday conversation when we ask 'Did you remember to call your aunt to thank her for the birthday present?' or, 'Do you remember who won the Academy Award for Best Actor or Actress?'

6.0 PREFRONTAL CORTEX, CONSCIOUSNESS AND WORKING MEMORY

The prefrontal cortex (PFC) plays a critical role in working memory. The prefrontal cortex is situated in front of the motor cortex in both humans and other primates (Figure 9.23). The macaque monkey has been the primary experimental animal in many studies of working memory. Obviously, humans have other abilities, like language, that are not directly paralleled in other species. But, in the case of working memory studies, the macaque has been a constantly important source of evidence.

Knowledge of a link between the PFC and short-term memory dates back to the 1930s, when it was first discovered that large bilateral lesions of the PFC in animals impaired performance on a delayed response task. In this task, a sample stimulus is presented (e.g. a color or location), and its identity must be maintained over a short delay period so that it can guide a later response (Figure 9.24). Using variants of this basic task with more recent neuroscientific techniques, modern research has firmly established the role of the PFC in active maintenance of WM information.

Much of the animal research has focused on a specific frontal region called the dorsolateral prefrontal cortex (DL-PFC, see Figure 9.23). (In the human cortex dorsal is 'upper' and lateral means 'to the side'.) One of the key early findings came from the laboratory of Joaquin Fuster (Fuster and Alexander, 1971). Fuster and his colleagues trained monkeys to perform a delayed-response task in which they had to remember a color over a brief delay, and then point to the correct color when later presented with two alternatives. Since no information about the

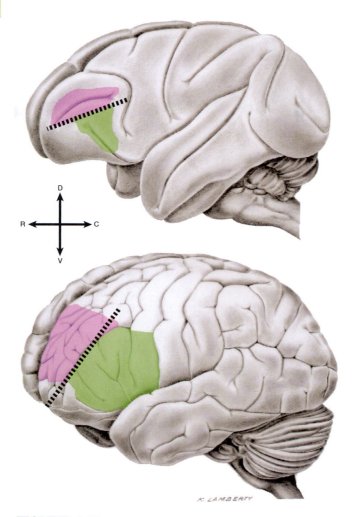

FIGURE 9.23 The prefrontal cortex in monkeys (top) and humans (bottom). The most common division is between upper and lower halves of the prefrontal cortex (PFC), called the dorsolateral prefrontal cortex (DL-PFC) for the light purple region, and the ventrolateral pfc (VL-PFC) for the light green area. Also notice the orientation cross, pointing to dorsal (upper), ventral (lower), rostral (toward the nose in humans), and caudal (toward the back of the head in humans). *Source*: Ranganath, 2006.

wide variety of tasks. For example, to confirm that PFC contributions are truly memory-related, and not simply a reflection of subtle preparatory motor gestures, Patricia Goldman-Rakic and her colleagues developed a version of the task in which monkeys see a target presented briefly at one of several possible locations on a display, and then after a delay, must shift their gaze to that location in order to receive a reward. Importantly, the monkey is required to look straight ahead until the end of the delay period, so neural activity during the delay cannot be simply a byproduct of moving the eye, but must instead reflect memory processes. Again, this paradigm produces sustained neuronal activity in the DL-PFC and, what's more, the *amount* of delay-period activity predicts whether or not items will be remembered; when DL-PFC delay-period activity is weak there is a greater likelihood of forgetting (Funahashi *et al.*, 1993).

There is debate whether PFC is subdivided according to the content of the information that is stored, or according to the function that each region carries out. According to the content approach, the DL-PFC seems to be particularly involved in holding onto information about spatial locations, whereas different parts of the ventral and lateral PFC have been implicated in storing non-spatial types of information (e.g. objects, faces, words, etc.). Alternatively, each of these regions may have different functions, with DL-PFC implicated in manipulation of information and VL-PFC in maintenance (ventro-lateral, downward and to the side). The term ventral refers to the down direction in cortex; literally, 'ventrum' means 'belly' in Latin.

Monkey brain lesion studies have further implicated the PFC, and the DL-PFC in particular, in working memory function. With very precise techniques for localizing experimentally induced lesions, it has been shown that damage isolated specifically to the DL-PFC is sufficient to impair performance on working memory tasks (Fuster, 1997). Such findings show a causal role for the PFC in working memory. Not only are cells in this region active during a delay, but their lesioning impairs working memory. This impairment gets worse as the length of the delay increases, suggesting that there is more rapid forgetting when the PFC is prevented from sustaining them.

Studies in humans using neuroimaging have corroborated many of the findings from the animal literature. Hundreds of imaging studies have shown PFC activity when participants are trying to maintain task-relevant information. Consistent with the animal work, fMRI studies in humans show that PFC activity persists during the delay period of a working memory task (see Chapters 4, 10 and 12; Appendix B).

correct color was offered after the initial presentation, its identity had to be retained in working memory. Using implanted electrodes to record neural activity during performance of the task (see Chapter 4), it was found that individual neurons in the monkey DL-PFC exhibited sustained and persistent activity across the delay period. That is, after the color had been removed from the visual display, neurons in the DL-PFC continued to fire at an increased rate, and this activity then subsided once the match/non-match response was made (Figure 9.24).

This pattern of sustained delay-period activity in the DL-PFC has been replicated many times since, and in a

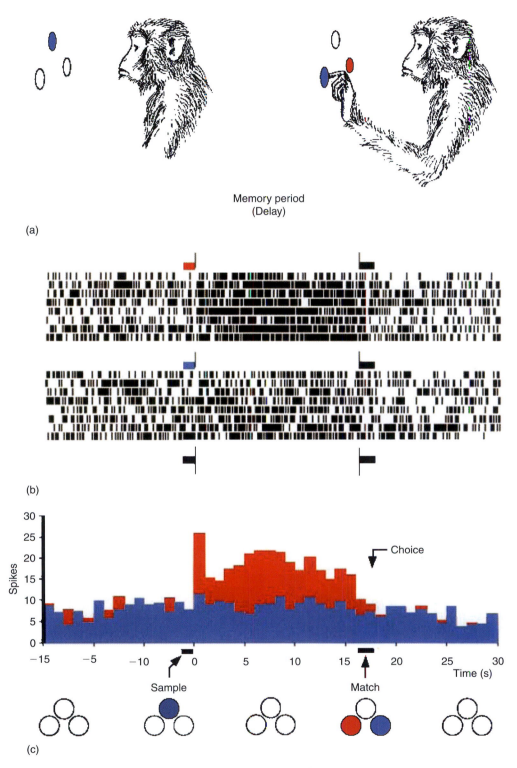

FIGURE 9.24 'Delayed match to sample' in the macaque. In a classic experiment, a macaque monkey is trained to delay responding to a stimulus, in this case the location of a red, white or blue light. The monkey shows recognition of the stimulus after delay by matching it in the display, in a task called 'delayed match to sample'. In effect, the monkey is communicating 'this is what I saw'. DMTS methods are widely used in animals, non-verbal babies, and other subjects. *Source*: Fuster, 1997.

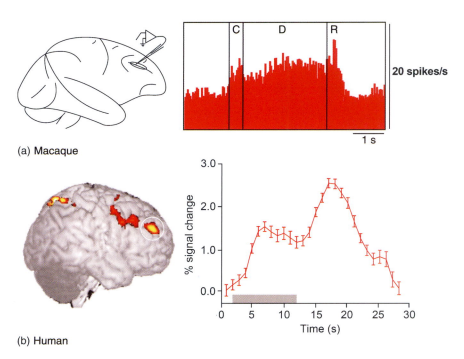

(a) Macaque

(b) Human

FIGURE 9.25 A delayed-response task to study working memory in monkeys and humans. It has been proposed that the PFC serves a specific role in the active *storage* of information in working memory (e.g. Goldman-Rakic, 1998). That is, sustained activity in prefrontal neurons reflects this region's role in maintaining specific representations of the items that must be kept in mind over the delay. This interpretation is supported by the finding that individual neurons in the PFC are selective for particular target stimuli. For example, a given cell may fire strongly over the delay period when the target is in the upper left portion of the display, but weakly when the target is elsewhere in the display. This pattern suggests direct involvement in the internal representation of target features. In this figure, neurons in prefrontal cortex respond during the delay period in a delayed-match-to-sample task. Results in macaques and humans are similar. *Source*: Curtis and D'Esposito, 2003.

Human neuroimaging studies have also varied *working memory load* – the number of items that must be held in immediate memory (Cohen *et al.*, 1997; Rypma *et al.*, 2002). In one study, memory load was varied between one and eight items, and subjects had to hold these items for a short delay. PFC activation was found to be positively correlated with the number of items in memory. Such 'load dependence' in the PFC supports the notion that this part of the brain is involved in working memory storage.

While PFC contributions to working memory have been clearly demonstrated, its specific contribution to working memory storage has been recently questioned. Several other cortical and subcortical areas exhibit similarly persistent stimulus-specific activity over short delays. It appears that PFC may be part of a more distributed brain network supporting working memory. Other data suggest that the PFC may not be involved in storage *per se*, but in providing top-down, or *executive*, support to other regions where information is actually stored.

6.1 Working with memory: the frontal lobe works purposefully *with* memory

According to this model, both encoding and retrieval of consciously-apprehended information via the hippocampus and related structures is obligatory and automatic, yet we know from experience and from experimental investigation that we have a measure of control over what we encode and what we retrieve from memory. Moreover, if encoding is automatic and obligatory, the information cannot be organized, yet memory appears to have some temporal and thematic organization. How can we reconcile this model of memory with other facts we know about how memory works? One solution is that other structures, particularly those in the frontal lobes, control the information delivered to the medial temporal system at encoding, initiate and guide retrieval, and monitor, and help interpret and organize the information that is retrieved. By operating on the medial temporal and diencephalic system, the frontal lobes act as *working-with-memory* structures that control the more automatic medial temporal system and confer a measure of intelligence and direction to it. Such a complementary system is needed if memory is to serve functions other than mere retention and retrieval of past experiences (Moscovitch, 1992).

6.2 Prefrontal cortex in explicit (conscious) and implicit (unconscious) learning and memory

Figure 9.5 pointed out that working memory may help us to learn both explicit (conscious) and implicit (unconscious) information. One of the functions often attributed to consciousness is the integration of information across domains. In a very illuminating study, McIntosh et al. (1998) had subjects perform in a trace conditioning task which requires the person to make an association between a color and a tone separated by a blank delay of about a second. Previous work had shown that such conditioning is dependent on the hippocampus. Moreover, Clark and Squire (1999) showed conscious awareness of the association was a prerequisite for this kind of learning.

Using PET, McIntosh showed that learning, and the conscious awareness that accompanied it, was associated both with frontal activation and with coherence of activation across many areas of cortex. McIntosh et al. speculated that consciousness is associated with activation in prefrontal cortex which, in turn, leads to a correlated pattern of activity across disparate regions of cortex. It remains to be seen, however, whether frontal activation preceded or followed conscious awareness of the association. To do so, it is necessary to have a clear understanding of the sequence of activation across regions of cortex, using techniques that have a higher temporal resolution than fMRI, such as ERP or MEG. As yet few, if any, studies have used ERP and MEG to address issues regarding the time course of consciousness as it relates to memory.

If the prefrontal cortex plays a pivotal role in consciousness, as many people have speculated, deficits on all memory tests dependent on consciousness should be observed in patients with frontal lesions. However, so far, the evidence indicates that the effects of frontal lesions are much more selective and not nearly as debilitating as lesions to MTL and related nuclei of the thalamus.

The prefrontal cortex contributes to performance on implicit learning and memory if it requires search, sequencing, organization and deliberate monitoring. Implicit learning of language is a good example (Box 9.4).

BOX 9.4 Implicit learning of language. While we are given the words and sequences of language, the rules and regularities of grammar and perhaps meaning are often inferred unconsciously, i.e. using implicit learning (Cleeremans et al., 1998)

Implicit learning and language acquisition

The past few years have witnessed the emergence of increasing connections between implicit learning and psycholinguistics. This is perhaps not so surprising, in that language acquisition, like implicit learning, involves incidental learning conditions. Further, cogent use of language likewise does not require explicit knowledge of grammar. Recently, several authors have begun to explore this connection empirically. For instance, Saffran et al.[a] showed how incidental exposure to artificial language-like auditory material (e.g. *bupadapatubitutibu . . .*) was sufficient to enable both children and adult subjects to segment the continuous sequence of sounds they had heard into the artificial words (e.g. *bupada*, *patubi*, etc.) that it contained, as evidenced by their above-chance performance in a subsequent recognition test. Based on these data, Saffran et al. suggested that the word segmentation abilities demonstrated by these subjects were due to the transitional probabilities of successive syllables are higher *within* words than *between* words. Saffran and colleagues interpreted their findings as representing a form of implicit learning. The connection is obvious when one recognizes that language acquisition, like implicit learning[b,c] is likely to involve, at least in part, incidental learning of complex information organized at differing levels. Part of the convergence between language acquisition and implicit

learning suggested by Saffran and colleagues can be attributed to the impact of computational modeling on the field of memory research. For instance, connectionist models such as the Simple Recurrent Network have been extensively used with significant success in both the language acquisition and implicit learning domains[d,e]. In effect, the problems faced in both domains are quite similar: how to best extract structure from a complex stimulus environment characterized by 'deep' systematic regularities when learning is incidental rather than intentional. The answer, in both domains, appears to be embodied by distributional approaches.

References

a Saffran, J.R. et al. (1997) Incidental language learning, listening (and learning) out of corner of your ear *Psychol. Sci.* 8, 101–105
b Berry, D.C. and Dienes, Z. (1993) *Implicit Learning: Theoretical and Empirical Issues*, Erlbaum
c Cleeremans, A. (1993) *Mechanisms of Implicit Learning: Connectionist Models of Sequence Learning*, MIT Press
d Christiansen, M.H., Allen, J. and Seidenberg, M.S. (1998) Learning to segment speech using multiple cues: a connectionist model *Lang. Cognit. Process.* 3, 221–268
e Redington, M. and Chater, N. (1997) Probabilistic and distributional approaches to language acquisition *Trends Cognit. Sci.* 1, 273–281

Even though we rarely try to make the rules of grammar conscious and explicit, we nevertheless need to direct our attention to the order of words in a sentence, for example, to learn a language implicitly. It is likely that unconscious inferences help us to discover rules or regularities, provided that we pay 'conscious attention' to a series of words, for example, from which we can discover the implicit regularities.

6.3 Different types of working memory

In proposing the concept of working memory, Baddeley and colleagues (2004) reasoned that subjects should have difficulty keeping items in memory if asked to perform other tasks simultaneously that disrupt specific components of the working memory system. Consistent with this view, Baddeley and others have shown that asking subjects to repeat aloud a simple utterance (like the word 'the') during retention can dramatically reduce short-term memory for verbal information, presumably because the repetitive speech task disrupts the rehearsal mechanism of the phonological loop. Importantly, the same repetitive speech task hasa much smaller effect on working memory for visuospatial information because holding such information does not make as much use of the phonological loop. Meanwhile, other tasks (e.g. visually tracking a moving object) have been found to disrupt visuospatial, but not verbal, maintenance.

We have already encountered examples of patients, like Clive Wearing and HM, who seem to have spared short-term memory but impaired long-term memory. Elizabeth Warrington and Tim Shallice (Shallice and Warrington, 1970) reported one of the earliest recognized cases of a patient, KF, with the opposite pattern of impairment – a severely impaired short-term memory but apparently intact long-term memory. For example, when asked to recall short lists of spoken digits, the *digit-span task*, KF could recall only one or two items reliably (as compared to a typical digit-span of around seven items). Still, KF had comparatively normal speech-production abilities, and could learn and transfer new information into long-term memory. The finding that a patient with severely impaired short-term memory could still transfer information into long-term memory presented a challenge to the standard hypothesis posited that a unitary short-term memory serves as the gateway into long-term memory. Baddeley's working memory model suggested that if verbal rehearsal is impaired, the visuospatial sketchpad might be used to compensate (see Figure 9.5).

Indeed, the short-term memory impairment in patient KF, and a number of similar patients reported since,

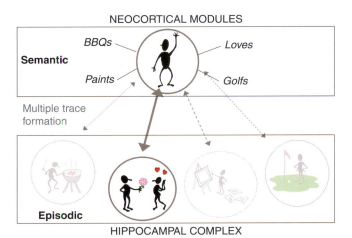

FIGURE 9.26 Damage in patients with this *auditory-verbal* working memory impairment is fairly consistently localized to a region near the left temporo-parietal junction, typically including the supramarginal gyrus of the parietal lobe. This region has accordingly been proposed as the site of the *phonological store*, the storage component of the verbal maintenance subsystem. In other patients this region is intact, but damage to more anterior areas in the VL-PFC and nearby cortex leads to working memory impairments consistent with disruption of the subvocal rehearsal process that supports verbal maintenance. (These areas are known to be involved in speech production, see Chapter 11). Still other patients have been identified with selective impairment of visuospatial memory, as evidenced for example by an inability to remember even a very small number of spatial locations presented sequentially. The selectivity of these deficits with damage to different parts of the cortex has been taken as strong support for the basic framework of the working memory model (Baddeley *et al.*, 2004). *Source*: Moscovitch, personal communication.

seems to be tied to particular types of information. For example, while these patients struggle to remember verbal items when presented auditorily, their performance is considerably improved when the items are presented visually. What might account for this pattern of findings? Baddeley's answer is that visually presented items can be coded directly into the visuospatial sketchpad, thus avoiding the damaged verbal rehearsal loop.

Neuroimaging has helped to clarify different kinds of memory. These include the distinction between verbal and visuospatial maintenance subsystems (e.g. Smith *et al.*, 1996), the dissociability of storage and rehearsal in verbal maintenance (Paulesu *et al.*, 1993; Awh *et al.*, 1996) and the assumption of a central executive processor that mediates the behavior of the subsidiary maintenance subsystems (e.g. Curtis and D'Esposito, 2003). In general, neuroimaging studies have tended to support the basic model (Smith and Jonides, 1998; Hartley and Speer, 2000; Henson, 2001).

Figure 9.27 illustrates the brain network implicated in neuroimaging studies of WM (Curtis and D'Esposito, 2003). The central executive corresponds to DL-PFC,

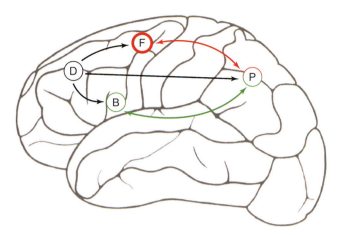

FIGURE 9.27 Brain areas believed to be involved in verbal and visual working memory. A simplified brain model of working memory (Figures 9.4 and 9.5). Abbreviations are D = dorsolateral prefrontal, B = Broca's area, also called the left inferior frontal gyrus (L-IFG), P = phonological loop for verbal rehearsal, also called the supramarginal gyrus; and F = frontal eye fields, believed to be involved in the visuospatial sketchpad of Baddeley's working memory model. *Source*: Curtis and D'Esposito, 2003.

the verbal maintenance subsystem in left lateralized regions of the temporo-parietal junction and VL-PFC, and the visuospatial maintenance subsystem in the superior parietal cortex, posterior PFC and frontal eye fields (FEF). However, we should be cautious in our acceptance of these findings as direct support for the framework, since few researchers have considered the applicability of these findings to alternative theories of working memory (Chein *et al.*, 2003; Ravizza *et al.*, 2005). In addition, the neuroimaging literature has at times challenged aspects of the standard working memory model. For example, neuroimaging evidence suggests that different types of visuospatial information may depend on different storage subsystems. For instance, there seem to be different neural substrates for the maintenance of *object* information as compared to the maintenance of *spatial* locations, a distinction that is not addressed by the traditional working memory model. (Recall that this 'what' versus 'where' dichotomy is important also in the visual processing pathways, see Chapter 6).

6.4 Prefrontal cortex – storage or process control?

In the beginning of this section on working memory, we reviewed several sources of evidence suggesting that the PFC is an important site for working memory function. According to one interpretation, this brain region participates directly in the storage of information. However, consideration of findings in the context of Baddeley's multiple-component model suggests an alternative account. Namely, that the PFC is more closely associated with control, or executive, aspects of working memory.

Specific evidence against a 'storage' interpretation of PFC function also comes from studies of humans. We discussed earlier a group of patients with left temporo-parietal damage who appear to have a storage deficit in working memory, and can't perform even simple maintenance tasks with auditory-verbal information. The findings from these patients can be contrasted with those from patients with damage to the PFC. In a review of published reports from patients with damage to large regions of the lateral PFC (D'Esposito and Postle, 1999), it was found that PFC patients showed little or no impairment on tasks that called for the passive maintenance of information over a delay (e.g. verbal and non-verbal memory span tasks). However, these patients were found to be substantially impaired at tasks that required information in working memory to be mentally *manipulated* or *acted upon*. This pattern of findings suggests that the PFC serves to support the mental 'work' performed on stored information, rather than as a site for storage itself. Few of the patients in this review had bilateral lesions, leaving open the possibility that storage and rehearsal are achieved via bilateral PFC representations and may thus allow functional compensation from the undamaged hemisphere (D'Esposito and Chen, 2006).

One possibility is that different parts of the PFC do different things. This proposal has generally focused on differences between dorsal (DL-PFC) and ventral (VL-PFC) areas. Advocates of this view have argued that the PFC is not organized by domain (e.g. spatial versus non-spatial), but by process, with ventral areas of the PFC supporting the passive storage and maintenance of items, while more dorsal areas are called upon when the task demands selection, monitoring, manipulation, or other 'mental work' to be performed on these items. This is the so-called 'maintenance' versus 'manipulation' processing distinction. While this view seems capable of explaining a wide range of findings, several studies have cast doubt on even the assumption that the VL-PFC contributes to storage in WM (e.g. Rushworth *et al.*, 1997).

More recently, it has been argued that *all* of the PFC has an executive function in working memory, but that different subdivisions of the PFC perform this function at different levels of analysis (Ranganath, 2006). This emerging view asserts that the primary function of the

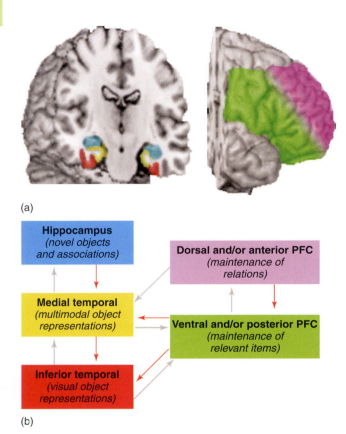

(a)

(b)

FIGURE 9.28   Combined brain regions work together for visual working memory. One view of visual working memory suggests that the hippocampus may encode WM items that are novel, the wider MTL may combine them with other modalities, and IT is involved in high-level visual object representation. The DL-PFCs and anterior PFC (purple) is involved with the short-term maintenance of relations, while the VL-PFC and posterior PFC is involved with maintenance of relevant items. As pointed out in the text, this is only one current hypothesis about the functions of these regions. However, it is widely believed that some network of functions like this may be needed to give a complete account of working memory. *Source*: Ranganath and D'Esposito, 2005.

PFC is to modulate the activity of other cortical areas where the items in memory are stored. Specifically, PFC representations enhance relevant information (or inhibit irrelevant information) represented in other parts of the cortex. When the information is specific to individual items in memory, more ventral PFC regions are engaged. When the information regards the integration of (or relations between) multiple items in memory, more dorsal PFC regions are engaged. Anterior regions of PFC, at the frontal pole, are implicated in coordinating and monitoring activity among different PFC regions to implement higher-order functions, such as planning. Accordingly, the primary role of the PFC is not in working memory, but in *working with memory* (Moscovitch, 1992; Moscovitch and Winocur, 1992).

6.5   Combining prefrontal and MTL regions for working memory

Working memory is usually believed to operate over a few dozen seconds or minutes. However, even within a few minutes' time, we can find differences between different kinds of memory. In particular, you may have seen the word 'combining' only a minute or two ago, and yet you may not be able consciously to recall it. We can therefore make a prediction, based on our previous understanding of the role of MTL in explicit memory: if you can recall seeing the word 'combining' a brief time ago, your MTL should show activity in an fMRI experiment in which you are asked to recall the first word of this section. On the other hand, if you do not have an explicit memory of it – even over a short time period – your MTL should show less activity. But perhaps you will still retain a semantic memory of the title of this section, based on your neocortical encoding of that word.

We can therefore even describe working memory in terms of MTL, prefrontal cortex, sensory cortex and the like. Figure 9.28 shows a model of how these brain areas may interact, based on a large number of studies of this kind (Ranganath and D'Esposito, 2005). Many of the specifics of this model are still debated, and we can expect new studies to cast some light on them. There seems to be an emerging consensus, however, that a complete explanation of working memory functions will require a multi-regional model of this kind.

7.0   RETRIEVAL AND METACOGNITION

Clive Wearing knows that something is terribly wrong, but he has no idea what it is. 'I've just woken up for the first time. I'm conscious for the first time' is his only way to express it. For more than twenty years he has expressed the most intense frustration with his condition. Wearing must therefore have some *metacognitive* conception of his own cognitive functioning, unlike patient HM, for example, who is spared the emotional pain of sensing what he is missing. Metacognition is defined as the ability to know our own cognitive functions, and to be able to use that knowledge. Many neurological patients who are severely impaired have no metacognitive insight that anything is wrong (Milner and Rugg, 1992).

For retrieval to be effective, information at retrieval must overlap with the information that was learned or encoded. In addition, the person must have the goal of

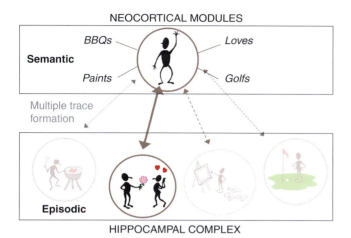

FIGURE 9.29 Retrieving semantic memories by using episodic cues and vice versa. We can often retrieve a semantic memory, like a fact about the world, by being cued with an episodic memory; the association can also go the other way. Thus episodic and semantic memory continue to be potentially connected, even if they exist relatively independently of each other in the hippocampal complex (MTL) and neocortex. Notice that most episodic memories for this semantic cluster of associations (on top) have faded. *Source*: Moscovitch, personal communication.

retrieving memories and paying attention to cues, as well as mentally searching for the desired memory. In all these processes, monitoring and verification are necessary, as is coordination of the various activities. Different regions of prefrontal cortex are implicated in many of these processes. The MTL is implicated most strongly with retrieval success for episodic memories. Automatic retrieval of a memory often occurs once the cue is found (Figure 9.29). Strategic or purposeful retrieval, however, is attention demanding and is impaired by any effortful competing task.

Metacognition is an important aspect of normal memory retrieval. A memory trace may be retrieved spontaneously, or more often by cues or reminders. A cue could be as simple as 'Recall the words you just studied' or as complex as 'Describe in detail what you did today'. The kind of self-monitoring we tend to do when we try to remember a missing word is a kind of metacognition that involves prefrontal cortex.

Schacter and colleagues (Schacter *et al.*, 1984) showed that memory for source in amnesic patients was related to the extent of their accompanying frontal deficits, rather than the severity of their amnesia. Extending these findings to older adults, Glisky (Glisky *et al.*, 1995) showed that those with poor frontal function were impaired on tests of source memory but performed normally on tests of item memory, whereas the reverse was true of those with poor medial temporal function.

Similarly, damage to prefrontal cortex leads to deficits in memory for frequency of occurrence (Smith and Milner, 1984) and temporal order (Milner, 1971; Shimamura, 1984) even when memory for the item itself is preserved.

The functional neuroimaging literature is consistent with the lesion literature. In comparison to tests of item memory, tests of source memory activate the DL-PFC and the frontal pole more strongly (Fletcher and Henson, 2001; Fletcher *et al.*, 2005), as do tests of temporal order (Nyberg *et al.*, 1996; Cabeza *et al.*, 1997).

The role of metacognition, using prefrontal cortex, is especially dramatic when it fails. This is the case when people cannot recognize their own mistakes, as we see next.

7.1 False retrieval

There are deficits of retrieval that are quite remarkable. The case of confabulation is particularly important, the inability of some brain damage patients to tell that the 'memories' they are retrieving are entirely imaginary. One such case is illustrated in Box 9.5.

7.2 Hemispheric lateralization in retrieval

In light of the left hemisphere preference for language production (Chapter 11), it is perhaps unsurprising that memory functions may also be lateralized according to the nature of the material being processed. In working memory, for example, maintenance of verbal materials activates left regions in the parietal cortex and VL-PFC, whereas maintenance of non-verbal materials tends to be right-sided. Regions in the VL-PFC are also implicated in encoding information into long-term memory, and seem to interact with areas of the MTL in serving this function. Accordingly, both the VL-PFC and MTL have been found to exhibit hemispheric asymmetries in long-term memory encoding (Kelley *et al.*, 1998).

Lateralization may depend upon the materials used (verbal, for example), and also upon the task and cognitive process. Endel Tulving and colleagues (Habib *et al.*, 2003) proposed that, in general, learning is associated with greater involvement of the left PFC, while retrieval shows greater involvement of the right PFC (Figure 9.30). This model has received substantiation from a large number of neuroimaging studies.

Some researchers have questioned, however, whether this encoding/retrieval asymmetry may arise simply due to a greater dependence on verbal processes during learning than retrieval. The hemispheric bias seems to hold for episodic memories, while for semantic

---

BOX 9.5   HW, a confabulating patient

HW is a 61-year-old man who was married to the same woman, Martha, for over thirty years and had four grown children, ranging in age from 32 to 22. He worked in a management position at a factory. He had an aneurysm of the anterior communicating artery, which feeds the medial frontal lobes and basal forebrain. Surgical clipping of the aneurysm was followed by widespread bilateral ischemia (loss of oxygen) and infarction. CAT scans confirmed widespread frontal damage, with sparing of the temporal lobes medially and laterally.

His brain damage led to memory problems exacerbated by confabulations and an unawareness of his memory deficits. His intelligence was normal, as measured by standard tests. HW's confabulations were spontaneous and, because he believed they were true memories, he attempted to act on them, making it difficult to let him live on his own. For example, there were times in the hospital that he believed he was at work, even though the hospital had beds, nurses, etc., and he wore hospital clothes. Many days at 5 pm he would prepare to go home and became frustrated and belligerent when he was told he had to stay.

Here is a part of an interview with HW:

Q: How long have you been married?
A: About 4 months.
Q: What's your wife's name?
A: Martha.
Q: How many children do you have?
A: Four. (He laughs). Not bad for four months.
Q: How old are your children?
A: The oldest is 32 . . . the youngest is 22. (He laughs again).
Q: How did you get these children in four months?
A: They're adopted.
Q: Who adopted them?
A: Martha and I. . . .
Q: Does it all sound a little strange to you?
A: (He laughs) I think it is a little strange.
Q: Your record says that you've been married for over 30 years. Does that sound more reasonable to you?
A: No.
Q: Do you really believe that you have been married for four months?
A: Yes.

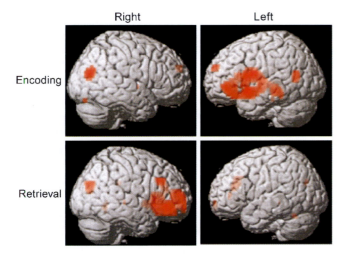

FIGURE 9.30 Left hemisphere for learning, right hemisphere for retrieval? Tulving and colleagues (Habib *et al.*, 2003) found that the left hemisphere shows greater activity in episodic learning (encoding), while the right side showed more activity in episodic retrieval. *Source*: Habib *et al.*, 2003.

memory, both learning and retrieval seem more dependent on left hemisphere mechanisms.

A recent study by Rossi and colleagues (Rossi *et al.*, 2006) using transcortical magnetic stimulation (TMS, see Chapter 4), a technique that allows temporary disruption to cortex in healthy subjects, supports the Tulving proposal. Their study showed that temporary disruption in the left PFC reduced learning efficiency, as measured by recognition accuracy. In contrast, TMS over the right PFC

reduced retrieval efficiency. Thus, there seems to be a relationship between hemispheric lateralization and the learning-retrieval distinction.

7.3 Theta rhythms may coordinate memory retrieval

A new literature shows that theta rhythms (5–8 Hz) appear in the frontal lobes during memory retrieval. Depth electrodes placed in the hippocampi show that the MTL and prefrontal regions may be coordinated during retrieval (Siapas *et al.*, 2005). Figure 9.31 summarizes these findings, which begin to show how the neural networks of prefrontal and hippocampal structures may cooperate to draw out and coordinate memory traces during retrieval.

8.0 OTHER KINDS OF LEARNING

We have only discussed some kinds of memory. We can only briefly mention some others, which make use of other brain structures. For example, the amygdala mediates fear conditioning (see Chapter 14). The cerebellum and basal ganglia are needed for habits and skills, as well as some kinds of conditioning. The thalamus is one of the great information hubs of the brain, constantly trading signals with cortex. It is therefore believed to be involved with cortical learning mechanisms.

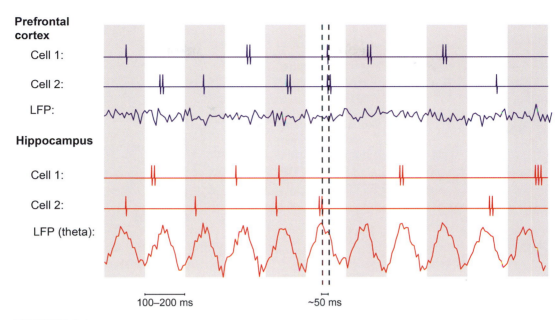

FIGURE 9.31   Theta oscillations may coordinate MTL and the prefrontal lobe during retrieval. Regular brain rhythms may serve to coordinate separate brain regions. Hippocampal theta is believed to reflect memory retrieval processes, and to coordinate prefrontal cortex with the MTL. *Source*: Jensen, 2005.

Perceptual and motor learning involve the dynamic organization and reorganization of cortical maps (Chapters 2 and 5). This is called *neural plasticity*. For example, losing a finger will change the motor map representing the finger in the macaque cortex. In humans, brain surgery can alter sensory body maps very quickly, even during the operation. Life development itself can be viewed as a process of learning, adaptation and memory formation (see Chapter 15). Finally, we now know that new neurons can be born throughout the lifetime, starting from stem cells (neural progenitor cells). The ongoing replacement of some neurons also involves a dynamic learning and adaptation process. There are many ways for the brain to learn. Though we have focused on more standard concepts of learning and memory, it is important to keep that in mind.

9.0 SUMMARY

The medial temporal lobes (MTL) are crucial to episodic memory in which we retain information about the conscious source of the memory. Amnesia patients with bilateral damage to the MTL are correspondingly unable to remember specific past episodes, or to learn new ones. However, implicit learning and memory may be spared in these patients. Patients suffering from semantic deficits typically have damage in the temporal lobe (especially the anterior and lateral parts) and prefrontal cortex. Such patients with semantic dementia, for example, may retain their episodic memory but are impaired on semantic tasks.

While explicit memory is assessed by accurate source memory reports, implicit methods like priming and sensorimotor performance may be needed to assess implicit memory types. Much of our learning is implicit, such as the learning of language. However, it is important to keep in mind that implicit learning requires conscious and attentive orienting to the stimuli to be learned. What is unconscious about implicit learning is not the original stimuli, but the inferential regularities that allow us to organize those stimuli. Sensorimotor skills are guided by the frontal cortex in collaboration with the basal ganglia and cerebellum. After overpracticing predictable tasks, such learned skills become less conscious and seem to rely only on subcortical structures like the basal ganglia.

Working memory can be decomposed into visual (the visuospatial sketchpad) and verbal (verbal rehearsal or the phonological loop). Further divisions are often possible, such as a separation between spatial and visual working memories.

A complete conception of human memory requires multiple brain regions: the MTL for explicit episodic memories, the prefrontal cortex for metacognition, maintenance, and use of memory, and sensory regions for perceptual and sensory memories. The cerebellum and basal ganglia are required for sensorimotor skill learning, in interaction with the frontal lobes. Further, sensory

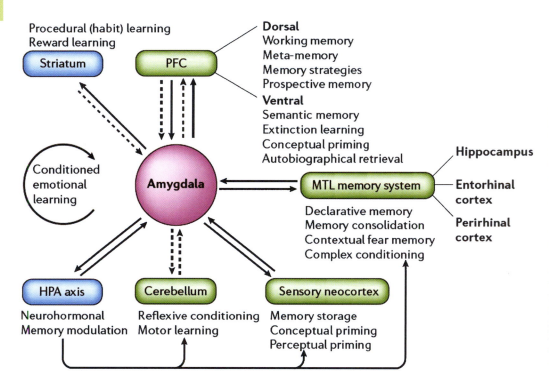

FIGURE 9.32 Different kinds of memory use different brain regions. An overview of multiple learning systems in the brain. The MTL system discussed in this chapter is involved in learning and recalling declarative, explicit memories; in memory consolidation; and the like. The PFC appears to be active in working memory tasks, metacognitive memory judgments, semantic memory, and conceptual priming. Perceptual priming involves sensory cortex, while motor learning and some kinds of classical conditioning seem to require the cerebellum. *Source*: Moscovitch.

and motor halves of the cortex are in constant dialogue with each other, as when we hear ourselves speak. Finally, the amygdala is deeply involved in emotional learning, along with associated regions in the limbic system.

A wide range of memory deficits can be used to separate different memory components from each other. You should know some examples of such dissociations.

10.0 DRAWINGS AND STUDY QUESTIONS

1 Fill in the missing labels in the functional diagram given in Figure 9.33. Define each of the terms.

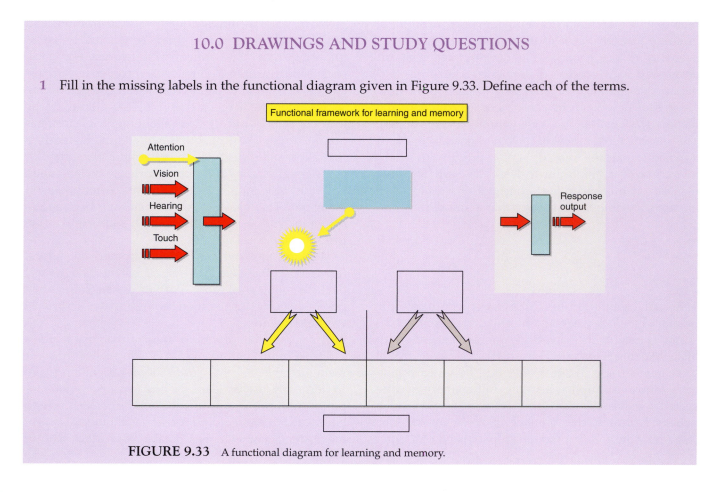

FIGURE 9.33 A functional diagram for learning and memory.

2 Label the regions and associated types of memory.

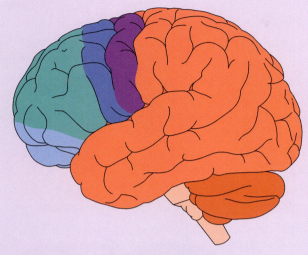

FIGURE 9.34 Relevant parts of the cortex.

3 Label the brain regions that are relevant to learning and memory in Figure 9.35.

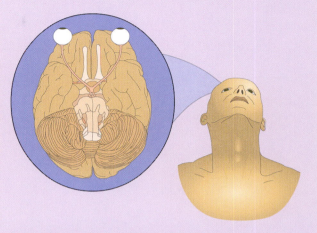

FIGURE 9.35 Location of some memory regions.

4 Label and describe:

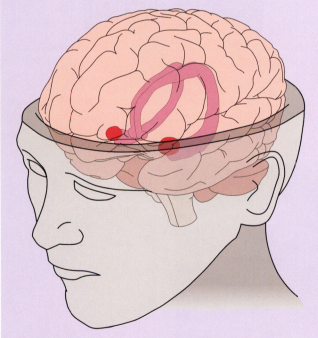

FIGURE 9.36 Location of some memory regions.

5 Label the abbreviations in Figure 9.37. What system does this describe?

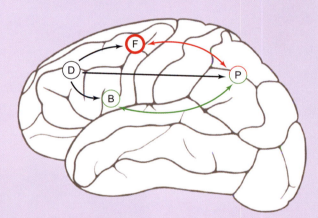

FIGURE 9.37

Recruitment of executive attention is normally associated to a subjective feeling of mental effort.

Lionel Naccache, Stanislas Dehaene, Laurent Cohen,
Marie-Odile Habert, Elodie Guichart-Gomez,
Damien Galanaud and Jean-Claude Willer,
2004

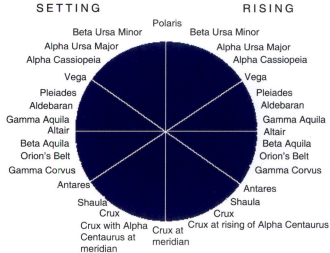

High level problem solving. Micronesian navigation is a highly complex and successful type of expertise. If it were not, island peoples of the Pacific Ocean could not navigate hundreds of miles in tiny craft to travel from island to island, surviving 'the stern test of landfall', as they have for thousands of years. The star compass on the upper right is an invention of Oceanic navigators, who keep track of their location by noting the angle of rising and setting stars at night with respect to the North Star. High level knowledge of navigation was developed, memorized and passed on by renowned experts, like the man in the lower figure. The outrigger sailing craft is a very efficient way to make the long journeys, but hardly without danger.

Thinking and problem-solving

Bernard J. Baars

Human problem-solving comes in two varieties, explicit and implicit. These two modes differ remarkably. Explicit thinking has clear, conscious goals and subgoals, and clearly defined steps for getting from a starting point to a solution. We can think of mental arithmetic as an everyday example. Explicit thinking involves greater executive control, higher mental workload, more frequent conscious access, and wider recruitment of cortical regions in pursuit of explicit goals.

In contrast, implicit problem-solving may be more common, since we learn and practice many kinds of skills from early on in life. These problem-solving skills become more proficient, implicit (unconscious) and automatic with practice. Understanding this sentence is an example, or completing a sentence that is predictable, so that we can tell what its last words are likely to be. Implicit problem-solving takes less executive control

than the explicit kind, less conscious access, less cognitive load, and less cortical involvement. It is much more dependent, on the other hand, on long-term memory and highly practiced routines. Very often, the unstated goal of learning is to turn explicit problem-solving into the implicit kind.

In the realm of thinking, the historic debate between local and distributed brain functioning continues. With neuroimaging methods we can see far more local regions and processes than ever before. We might imagine therefore that localist theories might finally be winning the day, but that has not (yet) happened. While ever smaller and more specific brain regions are being examined, the evidence for widely distributed processes is still compelling (see Chapter 9). A number of theorists are therefore developing models that embody both localized *and* widely distributed neural networks.

Cognition, Brain, and Consciousness, edited by B. J. Baars and N. M. Gage
ISBN: 978-0-12-373677-2

Copyright 2007, Elsevier Ltd. All rights reserved.

1.0 WORKING MEMORY

In a broad sense of the term, working memory is the domain of problem-solving, language and thought (Chapter 2). It is 'the set of mental processes holding limited information in a temporarily accessible state in service of cognition' (Cowan *et al.*, 2005). We need working memory to perform mental arithmetic, to carry on a conversation, or to solve a pathfinding problem – How do I walk home from here? You cannot understand the sentence you are reading now without keeping words, ideas and syntax in immediate memory. When we think about a problem, we constantly use inner speech and visuospatial thinking, directing attention to what is currently most important. As discussed in Chapter 8, attention leads us to become conscious of sensory events, of inner speech and action planning. Finally, whatever we are actively thinking about interacts with what we already know – our long-term store of memories, knowledge and skills. Every word in this sentence is also part of our long-term vocabulary. Every eye movement you make is based on long-practiced routines (see Chapter 9). Thus, all the components of Figure 10.1

come into play in the realm of thinking and problem-solving.

Surprisingly, much of this chapter is not about the colored boxes in the functional diagram, but about the

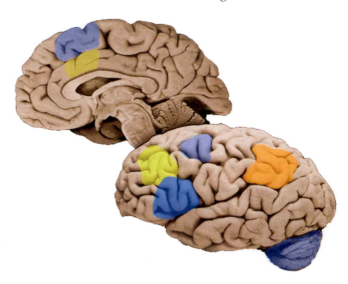

FIGURE 10.2 Proposed working memory regions. Common regions involved in working memory functions. *Source*: Schneider and Chein, 2003.

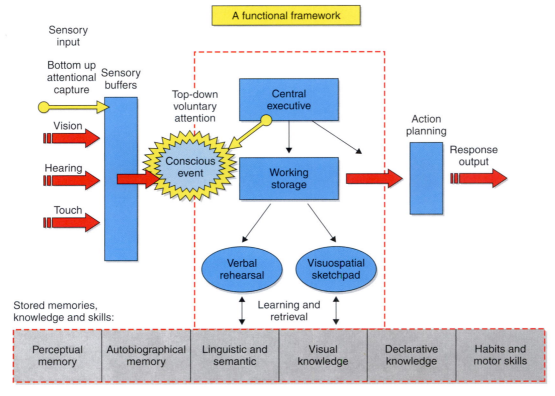

FIGURE 10.1 Problem-solving in the functional diagram. Working memory (WM) is constantly involved in problem-solving. However, WM functions also make use of stored information, such as the words and meanings of natural language, habits and motor skills, and various types of memory, shown in the gray boxes along the bottom of the diagram.

row of gray boxes along the bottom. The colored boxes refer to active processes, the ones that require neuronal firing and integration. But they constantly run along habitual pathways encoded by previous active processes, which have now formed permanent networks of connections. Such permanent stores may not show up directly in brain imaging studies because they are encoded in the connective strengths between neurons. Methods like functional magnetic resonance imaging (fMRI) activity may therefore under-represent the vast amount of long-term knowledge.

1.1 Working memory overlaps with attention, conscious events and episodic recall

Experiments generally aim to distinguish between working memory and related tasks. For example, in some working memory experiments, activity from single neurons in prefrontal cortex is recorded from cats or monkeys using a 'delayed match to sample' experiment in which the animal is given a stimulus, then must wait during a delay period after the stimulus disappears, and then point to the remembered stimulus among several others. Typical findings are that neurons keep firing during the delay portion, interpreted as an example of working memory function in which the animal must keep in mind the stimulus while waiting to perform a learned task (Goldman-Rakic, 1995, see Chapter 4). Selective attention presents people with two competing inputs. Conscious cognition compares conscious (reportable) to unconscious (unreportable) stimuli, using experimental methods like binocular rivalry (see Chapters 6 and 8). And episodic memory retrieval may involve asking people about their memory of yesterday's lunch. By using precise comparison conditions, we often find different parts of the brain 'lighting up'. New and reliable insights often come from these kinds of studies.

There is another side, shown in Figure 10.3, demonstrating widespread activation of frontal and parietal regions for four different brain activities that we often separate from each other: working memory, attention, episodic recall, and conscious perception. The overlap is enormous. That does not mean that they are identical theoretical constructs. They can be distinguished experimentally. But we cannot forget that the brain does whatever it does, not necessarily what we design our experiments to do. In this chapter, we will use the term 'working memory' to explore language and thought, but we might equally talk about it in terms of conscious and unconscious cognition, perception, and long-term

memory. The most active aspects of working memory tasks are conscious or voluntary. It has been suggested therefore that passive working memory functions may be controlled by conscious/voluntary features, like perceptual input, recall, rehearsal, action planning and response output (Baars and Franklin, 2003).

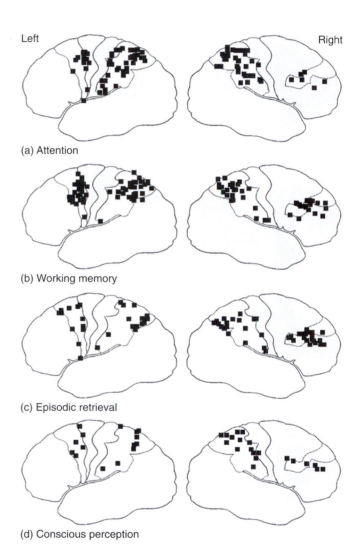

(a) Attention

(b) Working memory

(c) Episodic retrieval

(d) Conscious perception

FIGURE 10.3 Overlapping brain regions support working memory, selective attention, autobiographical retrieval and conscious perception. This figure shows schematically the widespread activation of frontal and parietal regions for four different brain activities that we often separate from each other: working memory, attention, episodic recall, and conscious perception. There is substantial overlap in these regions and it is not obvious that they can be separated. Attention = simultaneous selection, WM = delayed selection, conscious perception = comparing a seen target to the same unconscious target, episodic retrieval = becoming conscious of an autobiographical event retrieved from memory. While these four brain activities are typically separately tested in experiments, there are many overlapping features of those functions. *Source*: Naghavi and Nyberg, 2005.

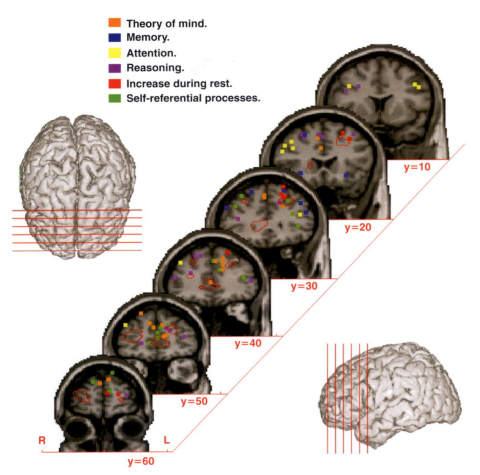

- ■ Theory of mind.
- ■ Memory.
- ■ Attention.
- ■ Reasoning.
- ■ Increase during rest.
- ■ Self-referential processes.

y=10

y=20

y=30

y=40

y=50

R   L

y=60

FIGURE 10.4 Some frontal capacities for high-level thinking. The frontal lobes are also needed for advanced skills, ranging from the ability to understand other people's intentions to reasoning, imagination and self-understanding. These frontal capacities constantly interact with posterior and subcortical brain regions. *Source*: Wicker *et al.*, 2003.

The limits of working memory must have posed difficult challenges for humans before the invention and spread of writing. Today we can scribble notes on a piece of paper, or look up information on the web. But over the neolithic period no one could write down their shopping list before going hunting and gathering. Perhaps for that reason, spoken language gives us many tricks and tools for chunking large amounts of information into smaller packages: sentences, words, phrases, sayings, narratives, personal names and pronouns, all serve as pointers and reminders. We also condense large amounts of knowledge by means of named abstractions and classification schemes (Box 10.1). Much of our large vocabulary consists of such labels. The vocabulary of natural language is a treasury of culturally compounded chunks of meaningful information (see Chapter 11).

Each chunk may point to a very large body of knowledge. In this book, the word 'brain' can be thought of as a link to everything you know about cognitive neuroscience. By pointing to knowledge via brief labels, we can optimize our cognitive bottlenecks.

2.0 EXPLICIT PROBLEM-SOLVING

Unterrainer and Owen (2006) described the basic conditions of explicit problem-solving:

> First, one needs to create a mental representation of both the current situation and the goal. Furthermore, these representations have to be linked by establishing which actions are needed to transform the current state into the goal state. Problems therefore have three general characteristics: (1) an initial state, or the state in which the problem solver sorts out the givens; (2) a goal state, or the solution state that the problem solver tries to achieve; and (3) the steps that the problem solver takes to transform the initial state into the goal state that initially may not be obvious. (Sternberg and Ben-Zeev, 2001).

Problem-solving can be thought of as finding a path through a maze of *choice-points* between possible *subgoals* toward a final goal. In the standard puzzle called the Towers of Hanoi, we are given a problem as in Figure 10.6. The goal is to end up with the three disks

BOX 10.1 How chess experts chunk known game positions

Expert memory for chess position

Much of what is known about expertise goes back to De Groot[a] and Chase and Simon[b]. One of De Groot's enduring contributions was to demonstrate the existence of clear differences between levels of player in a memory task, involving the brief presentation of a position taken from a tournament game. Typically, players at and above master levels recall the entire position almost perfectly, but weaker players perform poorly (see Figure 10.5).

However, Chase and Simon found no difference in recall of *random* positions between their three subjects: a master, a class A player, and a novice. This uniformly poor recall of random positions taken together with the superior performance of masters and grandmasters on game positions, presented such a vivid illustration of the principle that knowledge is the key to expertise that it has become a classic finding, widely cited in textbooks of cognitive psychology and in papers on expertise.

However, an earlier version of CHREST, a re-implementation and extension of MAPP[c], made contrary predictions about the recall of random positions. In the chess simulations, CHREST is trained from a database of master games, identifying patterns of pieces in these positions. As expected, the model's ability to remember game positions improved as the number and average size of its chunks increased. However, the model also showed a small, but robust increase in recall with random positions. The skill differences in recall were the result of an easily explained mechanism: simply by chance, a larger discrimination network is likely to include patterns found in random positions. A systematic review of experiments that asked chess players to recall random positions[d] yields 12 studies in which masters demonstrated some superiority, and only one, Chase and Simon's study[b], where the master actually did worse than novices. Although the skill differences were not significant in most studies because of lack of statistical power, the effect becomes clear when the various studies are pooled (see Figure 10.5(b)). The fact that perceptual chunking provides masters with an advantage even in random positions offers strong support for chunk-based theories, and is hard to explain for theories of expertise based upon high-level knowledge or schemata[a].

References

a De Groot, A.D. (1946) *Het Denken van den Schaker.* Noord Hollandsche.

b Simon, H.A. and Chase W.G. (1973) Skill in chess. *Am. Sci.* 61, 393–403.

c Simon, H.A. and Gilmartin, K.J. (1973) A simulation of memory for chess positions. *Cognit. Psychol.* 5, 29–46.

Source: Gobet *et al.*, 2001.

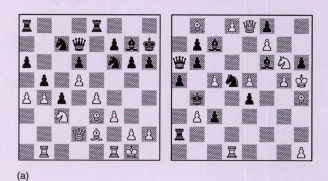

(a)

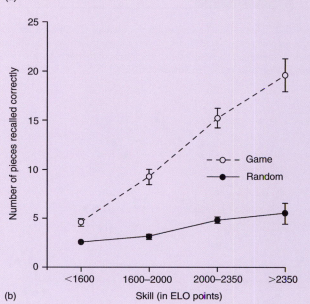

(b)

FIGURE 10.5 (a) Types of positions typically used in chess memory research. A game position taken from a masters' game (left), and a random position obtained by shuffling the piece locations of a game position (right). (b) Mean number (averaged over 13 studies) of pieces placed correctly as a function of position type (game or random) and skill level. Positions had 25 pieces on average, and the presentation time was ≤10 s. Error bars indicate standard errors of the means. (Adapted from Ref. d.)

d Gobet, F. and Simon, H.A. (1966) Recall of rapidly presented random chess positions is a function of skill. *Psychonomic Bull. Rev.* 3, 159–163.

e Gobet, F. (1998) Expert memory: a comparison of four theories. *Cognition* 66, 115–152.

on the rightmost rod in the same order they are shown at the beginning. This requires subgoal planning. The tree of choices is called a *problem space*, as in Figure 10.7. Some sequences of steps lead to a solutions while the others do not. Figure 10.8 shows brain regions active while solving Tower of Hanoi puzzles, notably the dorsolateral prefrontal cortex (DL-PFC).

Towers problems are puzzles rather than real-life problems. Real problems for human beings are such things as how to travel from one place to another across

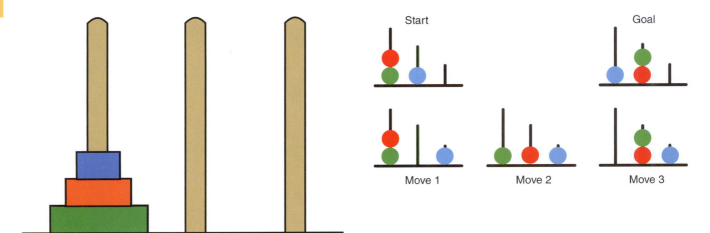

FIGURE 10.6 The Towers of Hanoi. Shallice (1982) used the puzzle called the Towers of London (also called Towers of Hanoi) to diagnose frontal impairments. The difficulty level of these puzzles can be adjusted, as in the figure on the right side. Tower problems have been standardized for clinical testing, and have led to a great deal of research. Instructions to plan improve performance for people with intact frontal lobe functioning. *Source*: Miller and Wallis, in Squire *et al.*, 2003.

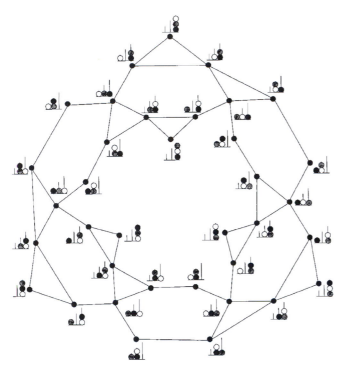

FIGURE 10.7 A problem space. The problem space for the towers puzzle shows all possible positions, choice-points, and pathways.

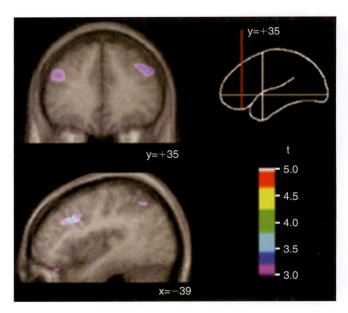

FIGURE 10.8 Dorsolateral prefrontal cortex in tower problems. Tower problems elicit brain activity in the middle part of the dorsolateral prefrontal cortex (DL-PFC), a crucial region for executive functions. *Source*: Unterrainer and Owen, 2006.

difficult and dangerous territory, how to find food and shelter, how to protect children and group members from dangers, how to maintain relationships, or how to prevail in a competitive situation. Life problems are rarely easily defined, and the stakes can be much higher. Nevertheless, even simple puzzles can represent important features of real problems. Ideas like goals and subgoals, of choice points in a problem space, and costs and benefits, show up in many kinds of ways.

While a complete problem space description is rarely available for more real-life problems, a useful strategy is to break down larger problem spaces into subgoals that can be described explicitly and completely.

2.1 Executive control in problem-solving

The cliché that 'generals tend to wage the previous war' applies to many kinds of problems. In science, for example, there is a tendency, even among the most celebrated scientists, to become focused on one major approach which may not always work. One famous case is Albert Einstein, who had an intense dislike of quantum mechanics, even though it made it possible to explain phenomena that could not be addressed any other way. Einstein was philosophically deeply opposed to the idea that physics could be statistical rather than deterministic, and tried for thirty years tried to find an alternative to quantum theory. Hundreds of other examples can be found in the history of science. 'Fixedness' appears to be a very widespread difficulty in human problem-solving.

It is easy to induce *functional fixedness* in problem-solving (Duncker, 1945). One only needs to encourage subjects to become accustomed to one way of reaching the goal, even when that way no longer works. Functional fixedness can be shown in a great range of tasks. In language there are 'garden-path sentences' that mislead readers into misunderstanding the syntax of a sentence. A famous example is the sentence, 'The horse raced past the barn fell'. This grammatically correct sentence can cause many minutes of puzzlement. The problem comes from the fact that there is an outer clause, 'The horse . . . fell' and an inner clause, 'raced past the barn'. The sentence can be rephrased as, 'The horse *which* raced past the barn fell'. However, in English the marker 'which' is optional for subordinate clauses.

The sentence therefore leads the reader down the wrong path, and we only discover at the end of the sentence that we are left with an extra verb, 'fell'. Such misleading sentences are far more common than we realize, simply because we normally interpret language based on contextual knowledge. For example, we might be watching horses racing around a stud farm, and know that one horse raced past the barn, while another one raced past the farm house.

Fixed and misleading mental sets are very common. Figure 10.9 shows the Wisconsin Card Sorting Task (WCST), which is designed to induce a misleading set in a simple card sorting task. Subjects are asked to guess which card is 'correct', using either color, number or shape. They are given feedback for each guess. Initially they are rewarded for one pattern, e.g. the rule that the color yellow is always correct. At some point the rule is changed without telling the subjects. The time and number of missed trials needed for subjects to shift set is taken as an index of their ability to test different hypotheses.

Patients with impaired frontal lobes often lack cognitive flexibility, and tend to score low on the WCST. *Perseveration* in unsuccessful strategies is a marker of disorders like Alzheimer's dementia (Ridderinkhof *et al.*, 2002). The WCST is especially useful when frontal lobe damage is too subtle to be detected by standard brain scans.

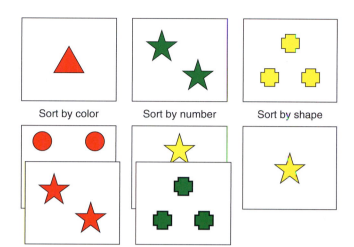

FIGURE 10.9 The Wisconsin Card Sorting Task. The WCST encourages subjects to adopt a certain rule like 'the yellow color predicts correct cards'. At some point a different rule comes into play, such as *number* or *shape* of items. This is a challenge to our ability to think of alternatives to the first rule, and people with frontal lobe impairments will typically perform poorly when the rule is shifted. *Source*: Psychological Assessment Resources, 2003.

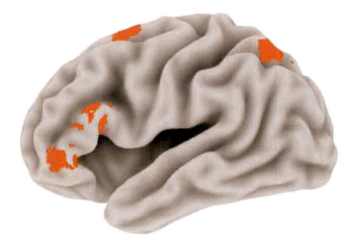

FIGURE 10.10 Task switching. Regions of high activity during task switching overlap with brain areas required in other executive tasks. Compare to Figure 10.17 (page 303). *Source*: Braver *et al.*, 2003.

Changing rules is difficult when we are mentally fatigued or drowsy, or otherwise impaired. Even switching from one task to another seems to require additional mental resources beyond those involved in routine and automatic actions. Thus, drivers who are sleepy might find it harder to make fast decisions in unpredictable traffic situations, presumably because their frontal lobe may be functioning below par. Workers on night shifts have been shown to be more error prone than daytime workers, and frontal lobe function may have something to do with that difference as well.

Figure 10.11 shows a model of executive functioning from Schneider and Chein (2003). We will use it to summarize our current knowledge about explicit problem-solving. The area marked DL-PFC (dorsolateral prefrontal cortex) is considered to be a goal processor. Thus, in the Towers of Hanoi, goals and subgoals would be represented in this region. The ACC (anterior cingulate cortex) monitors errors and conflicts between goals (see Chapter 8, 11 and 12). PPC (the posterior parietal cortex) is involved in attentional control (see Chapter 8), while the medial temporal cortex (MTL) is the gateway to episodic memory, the autobiographical store of past conscious experiences (Chapter 9). Finally, the thalamus (marked THAL) is considered to be a 'gating and reporting relay'. The last label may be controversial, and really stands for a broader thalamo-cortical gating and reporting system (see Chapters 5 and 8).

We have already seen the DL-PFC involved in the Towers of Hanoi problem, and in task shifting (above). Figure 10.12 shows how both the DL-PFC and ACC become involved in five different tasks requiring executive effort, including response conflict (as in the Stroop task), novelty, immediate memory loading, and even perceptual difficulty.

Figure 10.13 summarizes ACC activation across yet different executive tasks, including emotionally

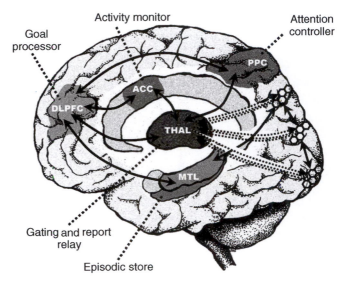

FIGURE 10.11 A proposed model. On the outer surface of each hemisphere, peak activity during problem-solving appears in the dorsolateral prefrontal cortex (DL-PFC). During task conflict or errors we find high activity in the forward part of the cingulate cortex (ACC). These two territories consistently show high activity when a cognitive task is difficult. *Source*: Schneider and Chein, 2003.

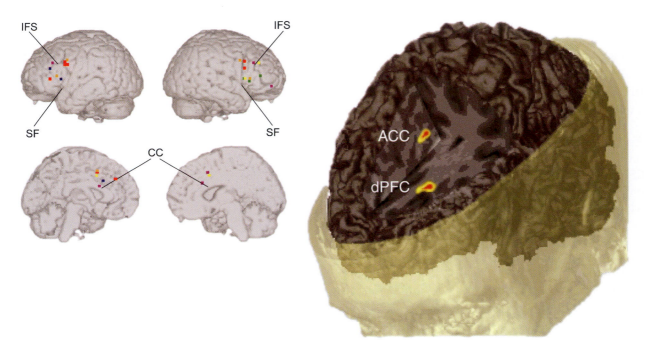

FIGURE 10.12 Mental effort activates executive regions. Duncan and Owen (2000) showed that five very different tasks that all involve mental effort activate lateral and medial sides of the frontal lobe. The five tasks shown are response conflict (green dots), task novelty (pink), the number of elements in working memory (yellow), the delay required in working memory (ref) and perceptual difficulty, such as visually obscured stimuli (blue). Abbreviations: CC: corpus callosum; IFS, inferior frontal sulcus; SF: Sylvian fissure. The image on the right shows a different perspective of the ACC (anterior cingulate cortex) and DL-PFC (dorsolateral prefrontal cortex) (MacLeod and MacDonald, 2003). *Source: left*, Duncan and Owen, 2000; *right*, MacLeod and MacDonald, 2003.

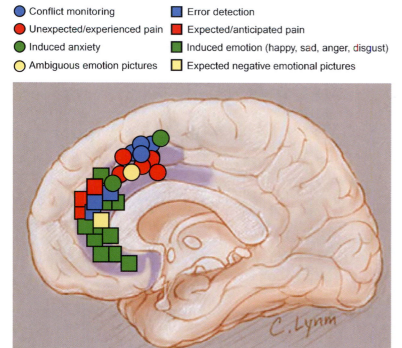

○ Conflict monitoring   ■ Error detection
● Unexpected/experienced pain ■ Expected/anticipated pain
● Induced anxiety   ■ Induced emotion (happy, sad, anger, disgust)
○ Ambiguous emotion pictures   ■ Expected negative emotional pictures

FIGURE 10.13 Error detection and resolution. As in Figure 10.10, this one shows a number of different tasks, all of which activate parts of the anterior cingulate cortex (ACC). Previous studies showed that conflict monitoring (as in the Stroop Effect) evoked ACC activity. However, tasks as different as ambiguous emotional pictures, induced anxiety, expected, unexpected and experienced pain, induced emotion and expected emotional pictures, all showed reliable ACC activation. Other studies locate the emotional aspects of ACC activation to the anterior tip of the ACC, and cognitive activation, as in error detection, to the upper part of the ACC. *Source*: Botvinick *et al.*, 2004.

demanding ones. As we might expect, executive regions become involved in a very wide range of conditions that require flexible decision-making. In contrast, as we will see, unconscious memory traces and skills do *not* recruit these executive regions. Instead, they are thought encoded in widespread traces in the temporal cortex and elsewhere in the brain (Moscovitch *et al.*, 2006).

This model therefore shows general-purpose functions, like:

1   sustained goal pursuit and deciding on subgoals
2   maintaining attentional focus on the task
3   inhibitory control over distracting thoughts and emotions
4   metacognitive monitoring of the quality of required sensory, motor, language, and immediate memory functions.

We will later see how executive processes also make constant use of stored information, including chunked information that is needed to circumvent capacity limits.

3.0 MENTAL WORKLOAD AND CORTICAL ACTIVITY

Effortful tasks show a wider spread of brain activity, even beyond the executive regions of the frontal cortex.

For example, in a classic study, Smith and Jonides (1998) found dramatically expanded cortical activity as a function of memory load. These authors used an 'n-back' technique (Figure 10.14). Subjects were shown a series of memory items. In the 1-back condition, they only had to recall the last item; in the 2-back case, the

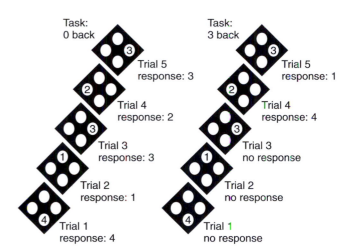

FIGURE 10.14 Loading working memory: the n-back task. In the 0-back case subjects only need to report what they see. As n goes from 0-back to 3-back, they must keep in mind more items, keep track of the order of each one, and at the same time notice each new slide to add to their mental stack. Task difficulty rises steeply with the number of items to be kept in running memory. *Source*: Smith and Jonides, 1998.

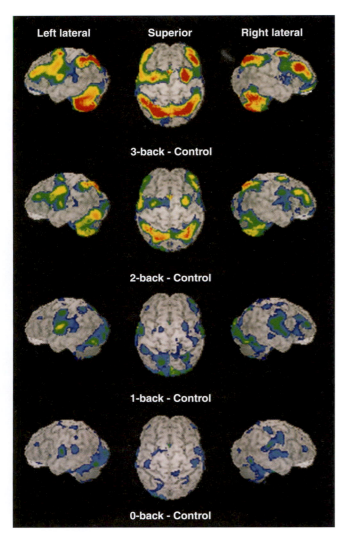

FIGURE 10.15 Effortful tasks recruit wider brain regions. Notice that increased working memory load recruits progressively wider regions, including parts of frontal and posterior cortex and cerebellum. Thalamus and basal ganglia are not shown, but are likely to be more mobilized as well. *Source*: Smith and Jonides, 1998.

item shown before the last one; in the 3-back case, the item shown 3 slides before. The n-back task is the human equivalent of a hamster's running wheel. One must keep constantly working to keep up with the flow of information. Difficulty level rises very quickly with the number of items to be kept in mind. Results from the Smith and Jonides (1998) study are presented in Figure 10.15.

What we cannot see yet, even with advanced brain recording methods, is the strength of connections between brain cells. Figure 10.16 indicates that mental effort also changes connection strengths, the neural signaling density between cortical locations.

Judging by brain activity, cognitive effort is one of the biggest factors in brain functioning. That may seem odd. After all, tasks that take mental effort are not usually the most complex or sophisticated ones we perform. The sentence you are reading right now is far more complex than the n-back memory task we just discussed. Why doesn't the sophisticated language processing use a great deal of brain activity? Figure 10.17 suggests an answer: the level of activity in cortex (at least) drops with practice and automaticity. While language analysis is extremely complex, it is also highly practiced over a period of years. Thus, neural firing or brain metabolism is not a direct measure of the complexity of some mental process. Rather, it seems to indicate the recruitment of neuronal resources that are needed to work together to perform a task that is new or unpredictable. Once even very complex processes are learned, they seem to require less cortical activity. Automaticity also involves a loss of conscious access and voluntary control, as assessed by behavioral measures (Schneider, 1995; Baars, 2002).

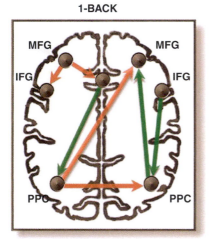

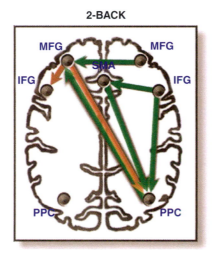

FIGURE 10.16 Connection strengths change with task difficulty. The colored lines in the two brain diagrams indicate connection strengths between executive and other regions of the brain. Connection patterns change with increase in memory workload. *Source*: Honey *et al.*, 2002.

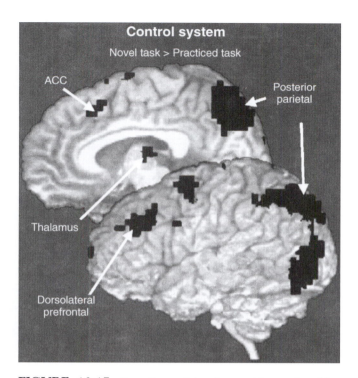

FIGURE 10.17 Executive activity drops with practice. After practice in predictable tasks, cortical activity is dramatically reduced. This summary image shows reductions in executive regions (compare to Figure 10.10). However, other active cortical regions also show decrements with increased practice and automaticity. It is believed that control over routine tasks is relegated to subcortical regions like the basal ganglia and cerebellum. However, intermittent cortical control may remain at unpredictable choice-points in the task. *Source*: Schneider and Chein, 2003.

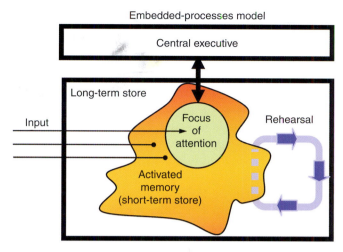

FIGURE 10.18 Working memory constantly activates long-term storage. Cowan (2001) suggests that working memory may be thought of as active and time-limited neuronal activity playing on long-term patterns of structural connectivity, i.e. long-term memory. Within working memory there is a limited capacity focus of attention, presumably corresponding to the current contents of conscious experience (personal communication). By analogy, the flow of traffic in a city is structured by the permanent 'memory' of streets and highways. *Source*: Chein, 2004.

4.0 USING EXISTING KNOWLEDGE

One theme of this chapter is how the human brain makes constant use of chunking strategies to solve problems within the capacity limits of immediate memory. How does the brain manage this?

One way to think about chunking is to reverse our usual concept of working memory and emphasize the degree to which mental operations make use of existing learning, encoded in forests of acquired synaptic connections (see Chapter 3). Working memory is crucially dependent upon stored long-term information. Your understanding of this sentence depends upon your memory for words, sentence structure and meaning. Cowan (2001) and others therefore suggest that we can flip the roles of working and long-term memory, and conceive of working memory (WM) as playing upon years of previous stored information (Figure 10.18).

Current brain imaging methods reveal active neuronal signaling, but not the synaptic connectivities that encode those years of learning. Brain recording is therefore much like watching the flow of traffic in a city from outer space. We might easily see car lights streaming back and forth each day. But with our current instruments it is harder to observe the slower process of building new roads, highways, and parking lots that make it possible for traffic to move. Yet the entire system depends upon the physical layout of streets and highways, a kind of permanent memory of the city. A space observer could learn a lot from traffic patterns – one neighborhood may be a financial center, another one might have an airport. But, on weekends, traffic flows might change. In bad weather more people may stay home. Depending upon unknown conditions traffic may flow along different routes, while still making use of the permanent connectivity of streets and highways. Just watching signal flow reveals only part of what makes the brain work.

Thus, knowing the connections and their strengths – the streets and highways – is an essential part of the puzzle that is still hard to study. Yet we know that long-term memory is crucial (look back at Box 10.1). We will take a look at evidence for long-term changes next.

4.1 Practice and training may change connectivities in the brain

As discussed previously, long-term memories are believed to be encoded in the connections between neurons. If memories are encoded in synaptic connections, they may not show up directly in brain measures like fMRI. Connections and active brain processes are not necessarily correlated; in fact, in the section above, we found evidence that more skilled and expert tasks might show less cortical activity. Thus, long-term stores may not be reflected in fMRI, magnetoencephalography (MEG), electroencephalography (EEG), and other standard measures.

Other measures are currently being developed to assess the efficiency of synaptic connections in the brain's neural networks. One possibility is shown in Figure 10.19, from a classic study by Maguire *et al.* (2000) on London taxi drivers, who must pass examinations about their knowledge of the complex street map of London. After years of experience in a real-world spatial task like this, would their brains show differences as a result?

4.2 Semantic memory

We have previously noticed the close connection between sensory and motor systems in the brain, and their use for endogenous or 'inner' cognitive functions. It seems that visual imagery makes use of visual cortex, that inner speech makes use of speech cortex. Figure 10.20 may take that rule of thumb a step further, in that semantic concepts seem associated with the temporal lobe (including the medial temporal region and the hippocampal neighborhood, not visible in the figure). More generic concepts are believed to be encoded posterior to unique concepts in the left lateral temporal lobe. Biological motion – the rather sinuous movements of animals – is located near area MT (the visual motion region), while human-made artifacts and instruments seem to activate a slightly different part of the occipital-temporal area. There is independent evidence that tools may also activate regions close to somatosensory and motor cortex. Hauk *et al.* (2004) recently found fMRI evidence that, 'action words referring to face, arm, or leg actions (e.g. to lick, pick, or kick) . . . differentially activated areas along the motor strip that either were directly adjacent to or overlapped with areas activated by actual movement of the tongue, fingers, or feet'. This supports the general theme of sophisticated and biologically recent semantic capacities making use of

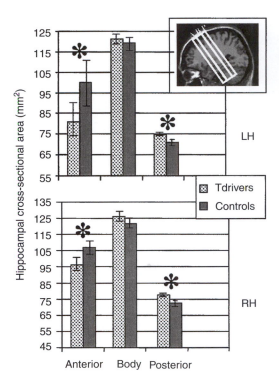

FIGURE 10.19 Long-term brain changes in experts. Maguire *et al.* (2000) found that London taxi drivers showed larger posterior hippocampal volume on the right side than controls, consistent with the known role of hippocampus in spatial processing. However, this methodology does not prove that the number of synaptic connections is greater as a result of expertise. The difference could be due to other factors, such as myelination, the number of support cells, and the size of neurons. However, the sheer size of relevant brain regions seems to relate to expertise in other studies as well. *Source*: Maguire *et al.*, 2000.

long-established brain regions adapted to dealing with the sensorimotor world.

In a recent review, Martin and Chao (2001) wrote:

Distributed networks of discrete cortical regions are active during object processing. The distribution of these regions varies as a function of semantic category. The same regions are active, at least in part, when objects from a category are recognized, named, imagined, and when reading and answering questions about them. . . .

Taken together, these data suggest that ventral occipitotemporal cortex may be best viewed not as a mosaic of discrete category-specific areas, but rather as a lumpy feature-space, representing stored information about features of object form shared by members of a category . . .

A feature-based model can accommodate the observation that an arbitrary category such as chairs elicited a pattern of neural activity distinct from other object

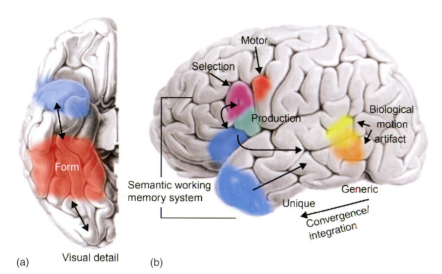

(a) Visual detail   (b)

FIGURE 10.20 Brain regions involved in semantic memory. A recent summary of semantic memory location in the left hemisphere (figure on the left) and the bottom of the temporal lobe, facing upward (on the right). The spatial location of the bottom of the temporal lobe may take some study to understand clear. The upper row of figures is for orientation. Notice that there are believed to be semantic *gradients* between specific visual object areas and more abstract visual forms. Semantic Working Memory involves constantly looping activity between temporal and frontal regions, which must make use of subcortical connections running between them. *Source*: Martin and Chao, 2001.

categories (i.e. faces and houses). Clearly, it would be difficult, as well as unwise, to argue that there is a 'chair area' in the brain. There are simply too many categories, and too little neural space to accommodate discrete, category-specific modules for every category. In fact, there is no limit on the number of object categories. Feature-based models can provide the flexibility needed to represent an infinite variety of objects.

In other words, the temporal-prefrontal system shown in Figure 10.20 is not likely to be a dictionary of all the semantic categories we know. There are too many of them. Rather, it may represent important features of major categories, which can index a number of categories represented in widely distributed cortical networks. We can find parts of this large region that respond more to houses than faces, or more to tools than houses or cars. The 'tool' biased regions might *index* a vast range of objects that can be used as tools – not just hammers and chisels, but perhaps computers and telephone companies. It would be very interesting to see whether one category (such as human faces) would show a 'tool use' bias if it were stated as a tool. For example, masks of human faces can be 'used as a tool' to scare people on Halloween. Such experiments might test the hypothesis that 'tool' regions might, in fact, represent a more abstract proposition such as 'can be used to accomplish a concrete goal'.

Neurologists have suggested that 'object concepts are defined by sensory and motor attributes and features acquired during experience'. This appears to be a powerful organizing principle for concepts in the brain.

Possible contradictory evidence has come from single cell studies in epileptic patients, with electrodes implanted in the temporal lobe. Some of these studies have shown very specific categorical responses, for example to very different photos of President Clinton (Kreiman *et al.*, 2002). Presumably, highly specific neuronal responding represents one node in a large network, or set of overlapping networks, having to do with political figures, or famous people. It is possible that, as we learn to sample more locally in the temporal lobe, such networks containing highly specific information may be observed.

As shown in Figure 10.20, prefrontal regions close to the classical Broca's area may support a 'semantic working memory system', somewhat separate from the phonological and visuspatial components of working memory.

4.3 Abstract concepts, prototypes, and networks

Intuitively, we tend to have some misleading ideas about human cognition. One is that we carry pictures in our heads that represent the perceptual world around us. The evidence suggests instead that we tend to use visual images that are *prototypical* reminders of categories in the world, rather than accurate images of categories like chairs and movie stars. We seem to have a network of perceptual, cognitive and motoric knowledge about chairs and their uses. Such networks can be accessed by prototypical pictures of chairs (Figure 10.21). Humans have a preference for such prototypical images, but they are not accurate depictions of all the chairs we have ever known (Rosch, 1975; Barsalou, 1999). Rather, they are special members of a category – of chairs or movie stars – which stand for the entire category. The wooden chair in

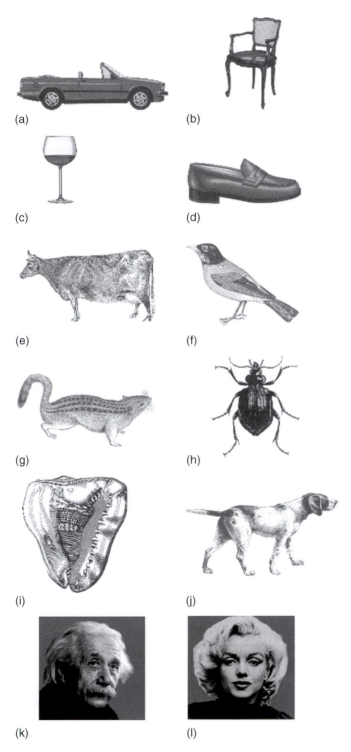

FIGURE 10.21 A set of visual prototypes tend to stand for more abstract categories. *Source*: Laeng *et al.*, 2003.

Figure 10.21 may not be the average chair you have seen and used. But for the tested group that kind of visual image would come to mind more easily than the plastic or metal chairs we tend to see more often.

Barsalou (1999, 2005) has suggested that humans have a strong perceptual bias, even in dealing with abstract categories. One reason is that we do not come into the world with an understanding of abstractions. The early years of childhood are devoted to sensory, motor and emotional exploration which, from an evolutionary point of view, are matters of survival. The developing brain may select early populations of neurons and connections before we learn adult concepts of the world.

The same point comes from studies by Barsalou and others on 'perceptual symbol systems'. Do we represent the car in Figure 10.22 the way an engineer might, as having a list of features like engines and wheels? The evidence appears to show instead that the abstract concept of a car is more dependent upon perceptual features of the appearance of the car, and a cognitive re-enactment of the actions of cars (Barsalou *et al.*, 2003).

4.4 Knowledge comes in networks

Another common intuition is that common words and concepts are simple because they often have simple names like 'car', '"brain', and 'person'. This intuition is also very misleading. Mental representations, including words, visual images and concepts, should be viewed in terms of elaborate networks of knowledge. The cognitive evidence for such networks was extensive even before the advent of brain imaging methods. It can indeed be found in the study of science in the mid-20th century (Kuhn, 1962). Naively, we tend to think of basic scientific ideas like 'gravity' and 'molecule' as single ideas. Some philosophers therefore proposed that there must be a one-to-one relationship between the Newtonian concept of force and the physical observations that gave rise to that concept. But others pointed out that there is no observable correlate of Newtonian force at all – we only measure mass and acceleration. 'Force' is a purely inferential concept in physics (see Chapter 1). Newtonian theory is not just a list of concepts, but a network of carefully defined ideas supported by standard experiments, by predictable observations, and tied into a web of mathematical inferences. Scientific theories are therefore semantic networks, not just labeled collections of observations. The same argument applies to the words of natural language.

These points are fundamental for understanding how the brain represents knowledge. In brain imaging we do not see abstract classes of objects. Rather, we see perceptual objects in sensory regions of the brain, which gradually shade into more abstract forms of representation (see Figure 10.19). Ideas appear to be represented in the cortex in terms of complex webs of learned connectivities,

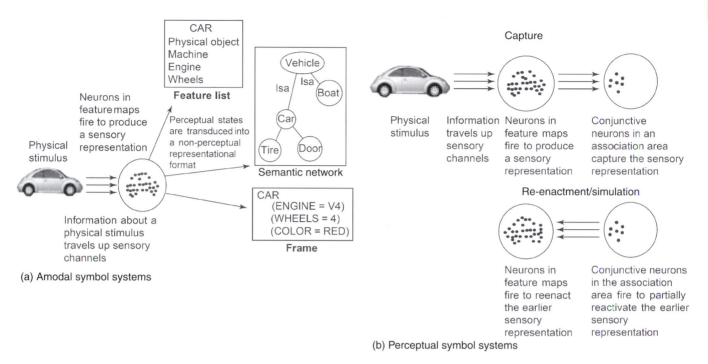

FIGURE 10.22   Amodal versus perceptual symbol systems. Barsalou (2003) has suggested that humans think by way of 'perceptual symbol systems' (a) rather than abstract categories with feature lists. (b) Such a proposal is consistent with the general tendency in the brain to build on what information it is given, especially early in life. *Source*: Barsalou, 2003.

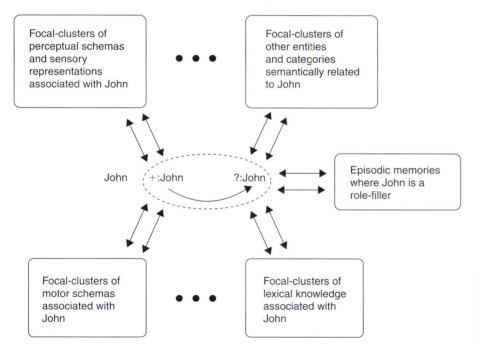

FIGURE 10.23   A proposed network for a single word. Each word in our lexicon refers to a *network* of related perceptual, semantic, motor, and lexical nodes. *Source*: Shastri, 2002.

rather than localized filing systems with neatly arranged conceptual categories. The brain is a very practical organ, always close to the sensorimotor and motivational world, rather than being an abstract logic machine. (The brain can do logic, of course, but most of the time it is focused on more down-to-earth processes.)

The need for semantic networks, not simple concept nodes, is important to understand when we look for the neural basis of cognitive units like words, ideas and images. For example, Figure 10.23 shows how a single personal name might be represented in a neural net.

Since related concepts often share features, the same line of reasoning suggests that feature-related neurons might participate in more than one concept network. Figure 10.24 illustrates this hypothesis for the concepts of 'tiger' and 'elephant'.

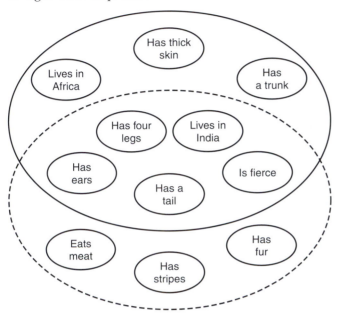

FIGURE 10.24 Overlapping semantic networks for two concepts. The brain may have feature-sensitive neurons that participate in more than one semantic network. *Source*: Hodges and Patterson, 1997.

It has been extremely difficult to discover specific cortical locations for specific concepts. Some of the exceptions are shown in Figure 10.25.

4.5 Conceptual deficits

In general, Martin and Chao (2001) report that:

> Patients with damage to the left prefrontal cortex (LPC) often have difficulty retrieving words in response to specific cues (e.g. words beginning with a specific letter, the names of objects belonging to a specific semantic category) . . . This suggests that the LPC plays a general, albeit crucial, role in retrieving lexical and semantic information. Patients with damage to the temporal lobes often have difficulty naming objects and retrieving information about object-specific characteristics . . . This suggests that object-specific information may be stored, at least in part, in the temporal lobes.

However, some language deficits seem to be very precise and limited. For example, in the bottom of the temporal lobe, neighboring regions seem to be devoted to somewhat different concepts, like chairs, faces, and houses. Tools, animals and vehicles have been reported to show peak activity in separate areas. That does not mean that specific regions are the only ones involved in a concept like 'hammer' versus 'bicycle'. Rather, we see

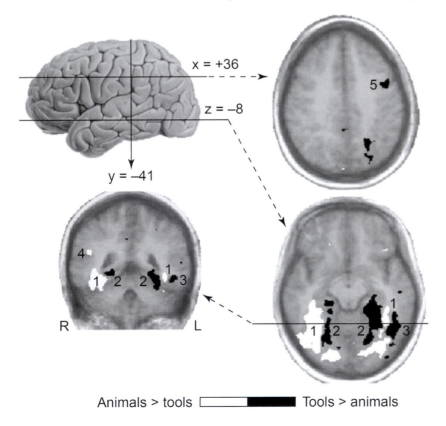

FIGURE 10.25 Areas of increased activity for animals, vehicles, tools and vegetables. Conceptual categories are hard to find in the brain. The exceptions are very broad categories like the ones shown in this figure. Like other brain images, we can only see activation differences, between animals and tools, for example. The areas that show differential conceptual activity are in the medial temporal region. Some scientists suggest that these specific categories may serve as general indices for retrieving larger and more specific networks related to elephants and apples, rather than showing us the specific neural code for the concepts. *Source*: Caramazza and Mahon, 2003.

peak activity in different parts of the temporal lobe, and there are cases of very local deficits as well.

Caramazza and co-workers have performed careful studies of a patient known as EW, who shows a deficit in naming animals (Caramazza and Mahon, 2003; Box 10.2). By presenting pictures with known frequency and familiarity ratings EW's knowledge of pictured categories could be tested in a controlled way. She had greater difficulty naming animals compared to other categories. EW also had difficulty simply recognizing animal pictures, but not other categories. Her deficit was not restricted to pictures, but also extended to spoken animal names. Yet the patient performed in the normal range on complex visual picture processing, such as face recognition and picture matching.

Finally, EW had trouble with major attributes of animals, but not attributes of other objects. Given questions like 'Does a whale fly?' and 'Does a cow have a mane?' she was incorrect about a third of the time. She performed better on other categories. While the idea of specific deficits is compelling, there are alternative interpretations of the evidence (Tyler and Moss, 2001).

4.6 Judgments of quantity and number

To the surprise of many, good evidence has emerged in recent years for a specific area of parietal cortex for number naming and judgments. Dehaene *et al.* (2004) suggest that the region shown in Figure 10.28 has a special affinity for quantitative judgments, though it may have other functions as well. When we perform mental arithmetic, however, as you might expect, inner speech areas are activated, presumably because we are mentally talking through the steps of subtraction or multiplication (Figure

---

BOX 10.2 Specific conceptual deficits in patient EW

An illustrative case of category-specific semantic deficit: Patient EW

To appreciate the remarkable nature of category-specific semantic deficits, consider the case of patient EW[a]. This patient presented with a disproportionate semantic impairment for the category 'animals' compared with other categories. Here we outline the empirical characteristics of EW's profile of impairment.

Picture naming

On subsets of the Snodgrass and Vanderwart[b] picture set matched jointly for familiarity and frequency, and for visual complexity and familiarity, EW was disproportionately impaired at naming animals compared with naming non-animals (Table I). This indicates that EW's category-specific deficit for picture naming cannot be attributed to uncontrolled stimulus variables (e.g. c, d).

EW's picture-naming performance was not only quantitatively different for animals and non-animals but was also qualitatively different. For animals, EW either named the picture incorrectly or did not recognize the picture, whereas for non-animals, EW recognized the picture but could not retrieve the name (Figure 10.26(a)).

TABLE I.   EW's picture-naming performance for matched sets of items[b]

	Matched familiarity and frequency		Matched visual complexity and familiarity	
	Animals	Non-animals	Animals	Non-animals
EW	12/22 (55%)	18/22 (82%)	7/17 (41%)	16/17 (94%)
Controls	11/11 (100%)	10.8 (98%)	16.6/17 (98%)	16/17 (94%)
Range	11	10–11	16–17	16–17

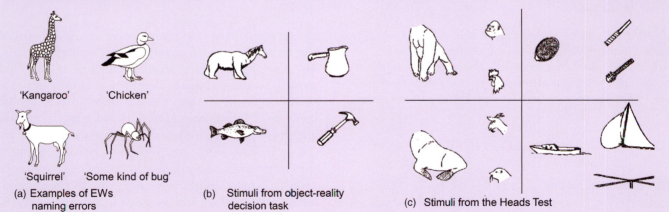

(a) Examples of EWs naming errors

(b) Stimuli from object-reality decision task

(c) Stimuli from the Heads Test

FIGURE 10.26   (a) Examples of EW's naming errors. (b) Examples of stimuli from the object-reality decision task. (c) Examples of objects from the 'Parts decision test' or 'Heads test'.

(Continued)

EW's naming deficity was restricted to the category 'animals' and did not extend to the other living things such as 'fruit/vegetables', for which performance was at ceiling.

Sound identification

EW was also impaired at naming animals compared with non-animals based on their characteristic sounds (8/32; 25% correct versus 20/32; 63% correct: z 3.06, $P < 0.05$), indicating that the naming impairment is not restricted to visual input.

Object decision

EW was asked to decide ('yes' or 'no') whether a depicted object was real (see Fig. lb for examples of stimuli). Performance on this task is interpreted as reflecting the integrity of the visual/structural description system (i.e. the modality-specific input system that stores representations corresponding to the form or shape of objects, and which is used to access conceptual information). EW performed significantly below the normal range for differentiating real from unreal animals (36/60: 60% correct; control mean: 54/60: 90%) but within the normal range for differentiating real from unreal non-animals (55/60: 92% correct; control mean: 50.5/60: 84% correct).

Parts decision

EW was asked to decide which of two heads (or parts) went with a headless body (or object missing a part) (see Fig. lc for examples of stimuli). EW was severely impaired on this task for animals (60% correct; normal mean = 100%) but performed within the normal range for artifacts (97% correct; normal mean = 97%).

Visual processing

EW performed within the normal range on complex visual processing tasks, such as visual matching and face recognition. These date indicate that EW does not have a general

Source: Caramazza and Mahon, 2003.

deficit for processing visually complex stimuli and suggest that the impairment for object reality decision for animals is categorically based.

Central-attribute judgments

EW was asked to decide whether a given attribute was true of a given item (see Table II for examples of stimuli). EW was severely impaired for attributes pertaining to animals (65% correct; control range 85–100%) but within the normal range for attributes pertaining to non-animals (95% correct; control range 86–100%). EW was equivalently impaired for both visual/perceptual and functional/associative knowledge of living things (65% correct for both types of knowledge) but within the normal range for both types of knowledge for non-animals (visual/perceptual: 93.5% correct; control range 86–100%; functional/associative: 98% correct; normal range 92–100%). EW's performance on answering central-attribute questions indicates that her deficit is not restricted to production.

TABLE II.   Examples of central-attribute questions

Visual/Perceptual	Functional/Associative
Does a cow have a mane?	Does a whale fly?
Does a whale have a large tail fin?	Does an eagle lay eggs?
Does a whale have eight legs?	Is a cow a farm animals?

References

a. Caramazza, A., Shelton, J.R. (1998) Domain-specific knowledge systems in the brain: the animate-inanimate distinction. *J Cogn. Neuro*, 10, 1-34.
b. Snodgrass, J., Vanderwart, M. (1992) A standardized set of 260 pictures: norms for name agreement, familiarity, and visual complexity. *J. Exp Psychol. [Hum. Learn.]* 6, 174-215.
c. Stewart, F. *et al*. (1992) Naming impairments following recovery from herpes simplex encephalitis. *Q. J. Exp. Psycho. A* 44, 261-284.
d. Funnel, E., Sheridan, J.S. (1992) Categories of knowledge? Unfamiliar aspects of living and nonliving things. *Cogn. Neuropsychol.* 9, 135-153.

10.29). It would be interesting to find subjects who are skilled in using visual arithmetic, such as users of an abacus. We would not expect the phonological region to become activated for arithmetic operations in such people, but rather regions of the occipital and parietal cortex.

5.0 IMPLICIT THINKING

The story is told that as a child, Wolfgang Amadeus Mozart would tease his father Leopold (who was also his music teacher) by playing a phrase on the harpsichord and deliberately leaving it unfinished. Western music almost always completes a series of notes or chords to end up where it started, at the tonic note of the scale. In

Mozart's time that rule could not be violated. Leopold Mozart would have to get out of bed, walk downstairs, and play the sequence of notes running in his mind before he could go back to sleep. It was simply intolerable to hear an incomplete melodic series. You can get the same effect by playing a favorite recorded song, and stopping it just before it comes to a conclusion.

Completion of expected sequences is one example of implicit problem-solving. We do not *tell* ourselves consciously to listen until the music comes to a resolution. But once started, we feel the need to do so. The goal is implicit or unconscious, like the rules of harmony and melody. Few people can explain those basic rules, but they have powerful effects nevertheless. If we compare listening to a song to solving the Tower of Hanoi puzzle

FIGURE 10.27 Visual agnosia. A patient with associative visual agnosia was able to copy the everyday pictures above, but not to name them (Rubens and Benson, 1971). *Source*: Squire *et al.*, 2003.

(above), music understanding is unconscious in almost all the ways the Tower problem is conscious.

Most human problem-solving is a mixture of explicit and implicit ingredients. We tend to underestimate the complexity of implicit cognition, precisely because it is unconscious. In fact, it is our highly expert, overlearned habits that may be the most efficient tools for solving problems. The explicit aspect of problem-solving may be better used for temporary executive functions in otherwise habitual tasks. For example, in driving a car we may be 'on automatic' much of the time, because of the routine and predictable nature of the task. But when traffic becomes dense and unpredictable, when the car tire springs a leak, or when someone is distracting us by talking, executive control of driving may be more needed. Thus, there may be a flexible tradeoff between more controlled and more automatic aspects of the act of driving. The same principles may apply to other kinds of problem-solving.

5.1 Feelings of knowing

Feelings of knowing and 'fringe' or 'vague' conscious events are believed to be very common (James, 1890). These include the well-studied 'tip of the tongue' feeling

---

BOX 10.3   Associative visual agnosia

Case study of associative visual agnosia

The subject was a 47-year-old man who had suffered an acute loss of blood pressure with resulting brain damage. His mental status and language abilities were normal, and his visual acuity was 20/30, with a right homonymous hemianopia (blindness in the right visual hemifield). His one severe impairment was an inability to recognize most visual stimuli. For the first 3 weeks in the hospital, the patient could not identify common objects presented visually and did not know what was on his plate until he tasted it. He identified objects immediately on touching them.

When shown a stethoscope, he described it as "a long cord with a round thing at the end" and asked if it could be a watch. He identified a can opener as a key. Asked to name a cigarette lighter, he said, "I don't know" but named it after the examiner lit it. He said he was "not sure" when shown a toothbrush. He was never able to describe or demonstrate the use of an object if he could not name it. If he misnamed an object, his demonstration of use would correspond to the mistaken identification. Identification improved very slightly when given the category of the object (e.g., something to eat) or when asked to point to a named object instead of being required to give the name. When told the correct name of an object, he usually responded with a quick nod and often said, "Yes, I see it now." Then, often he could

point out various parts of the previously unrecognized item as readily as a normal subject (e.g., the stem and bowl of a pipe and the laces, sole, and heel of a shoe). However, if asked by the examiner, "Suppose I told you that the last object was not really a pipe, what would you say?" He would reply, "I would take your word for it. Perhaps it's not a pipe." Similar vacillation never occurred with tactilely or aurally identified objects.

After he had spent 3 weeks on the ward, his object-naming ability improved so that he could name many common objects, but this was variable; he might correctly name an object at one time and misname it later. Performance deteriorated severely when any part of the object was covered by the examiner. He could match identical objects but could not group objects by categories (clothing, food). He could draw the outlines of objects (key, spoon, etc.) that he could not identify.

He was unable to recognize members of his family, the hospital staff, or even his own face in the mirror. Sometimes he had difficulty distinguishing a line drawing of an animal face from a man's face but always recognized it as a face. The ability to recognize pictures of objects was impaired greatly, and after repeated testing he could name only 1 or 2 of 10 line drawings. He was always able to name geometrical forms (circle, square, triangle, cube). Remarkably, he could make excellent copies of line drawings and still fail to

(Continued)

name the subject. He easily matched drawings of objects that he could not identify and had no difficulty discriminating between complex nonrepresentational patterns, differing from each other only subtly. He occasionally failed in discriminating because he included imperfections in the paper or in the printer's ink. He could never group drawings of objects by class unless he could first name the subject. Reading, both aloud and for comprehension, was limited greatly. He could read, hesitantly, most printed letters but often misread 'K' as 'R,' and 'L' as 'T' and vice versa. He was able to read words slowly by spelling them aloud.

Hillary R. Rodman, Luiz Pesson, and Leslie G. Ungerleider

Excerpted from Rubens and Benson, 1971.

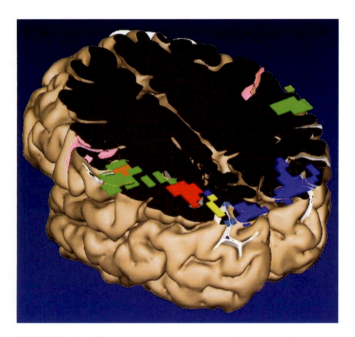

FIGURE 10.28 A network for number judgments? This parietal network was found to be involved in number and quantitative judgments, especially the intraparietal sulcus. *Source*: Dehaene *et al.*, 2004.

and 'feelings of knowing'. It is easy to induce a tip-of-the-tongue state. All we need to do is provide people with definitions of fairly rare but known words, and ask them if they feel they almost have the answer, but not quite. Effective questions might include 'what is the name of a vegetarian dinosaur?' or 'what are two words for the technology for making artificial limbs?'

Such subjectively vague but reportable events have been found to guide intuitive problem-solving, including verbal and pictorial problems (Bowers *et al.*, 1990), promote persistence in memory search during tip-of-the-tongue states (Brown and MacNeill, 1966), guide memory retrieval and persistence (Metcalfe, 1986), and influence judgment tasks and decision-making (Yzerbyt *et al.*, 1998). Only a few brain studies are available, but Maril *et al.* (2001) have shown that the tip-of-the-tongue state, which can be easily induced, showed high activity in prefontal regions, the same cortical areas that are associated with persistence in problem-solving (Duncan and Owen, 2000) (Figure 10.30).

There is good evidence that spontaneous thought is problem-oriented, even if the goal of the mental process is not explicit (Greenwald *et al.*, 2002). The contents of

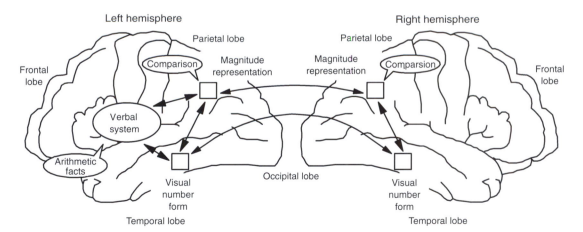

FIGURE 10.29 Mental arithmetic uses the phonological loop of inner speech. Notice the overlap in phonological tasks (such as mental rehearsal of a word list) and the subtraction task. Presumably inner speech is involved in subtraction, in this case. *Source*: Wynn in Ramachandran, 2002.

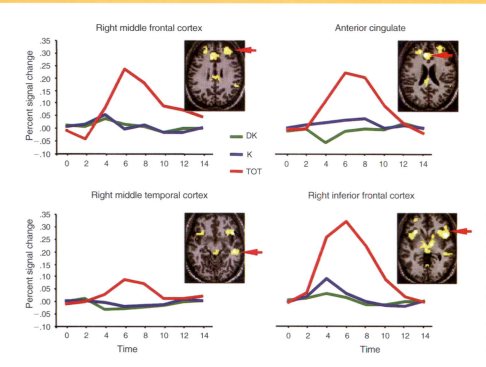

FIGURE 10.30 Effortful thought in word finding. These figures show both the location of the increased activity in the 'tip of the tongue' state, and their time course (using event-related potentials). Notice that the classical executive regions are again active. While these regions are not normally viewed as contributing to conscious experience, the fact that tip-of-the-tongue states can be reported in a verifiable manner suggests that they are at least 'fringe' conscious. *Source*: Maril *et al.*, 2001.

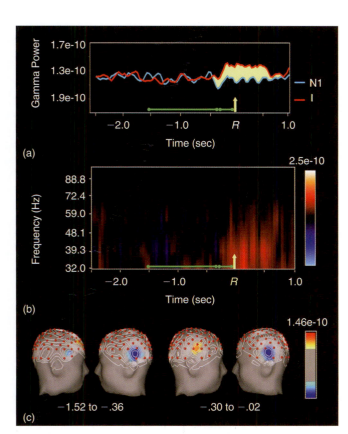

FIGURE 10.31 Sudden insight in problem-solving. Alpha and gamma density in decomposed EEG at the moment of insight in a word association task. Notice that just before a correct response, alpha density declines just as gamma density increases. Gamma activity is thought to be due to active and synchronized processing in a network of related regions needed to solve the problem. In (c), immediately before the solution (marked with minus values in seconds), there is an EEG shift to the left hemisphere. *Source*: Jung-Beeman *et al.*, 2004.

spontaneous thoughts are often described as one's 'current concerns'. Social psychology experiments have found that one can experimentally prime some current concern, such as relationship arguments, by showing videos that 'play out' those concerns. Thus, college students who rated their relationships with their parents as conflictual reported more common thoughts related to conflict when they were provoked by a video.

However, similar problem-solving patterns are found to be very common when careful studies have been performed on the routine 'stream of consciousness' (Singer, 1994). 'Jumps' in the flow of thought are apparently routine, and they can be elicited experimentally in tip-of-the-tongue experiments (see Figure 10.30) and the well-known Remote Associates Test (Kihlstrom, 1996).

6.0 SUMMARY AND CONCLUSIONS

Working memory is the domain of problem-solving. Completely explicit problem-solving is probably rare in the natural world. However, explicit puzzles like the 'tower problems' are quite sensitive to frontal lobe damage, and to other impairments of problem-solving capacities, like drowsiness, drug effects, boredom, cognitive overload or distraction. Thus, explicit problem-solving tasks are useful indices of brain functioning. In addition, tasks like the Wisconsin Card Sorting Test can be used to set up 'fixed' expectations about a puzzle, to allow testing of cognitive flexibility in the face of unexpected changes in tasks. Subjects with prefrontal impairments are again vulnerable to such task shifting.

Because of capacity limits of working memory, attention, conscious processes, and voluntary control, a major strategy in problem-solving is to use chunking or other long-term memory components to shift routine aspects of problem-solving to the large-capacity memory systems. Chess experts, for example, know a great many predictable chess positions from memory, freeing their working memory capacity to deal with novel and unpredictable aspects of a chess game. Long-term semantic memory is still rather mysterious in its details, but is known to use temporal and prefrontal regions, as well as the episodic learning capacities of the medial temporal lobe.

While implicit thinking is efficient, it is also vulnerable to rigidity and lack of flexible control. An optimal problem-solving strategy mixes explicit and implicit approaches. Fringe-conscious judgments are commonly encountered in tasks like 'feelings of knowing' and 'tip of the tongue'. These tasks may give us metacognitive knowledge of ongoing implicit problem-solving processes. They are now believed to activate the classical executive regions of the prefrontal cortex.

7.0 DRAWINGS AND STUDY QUESTIONS

1   Fill in the boxes in Figure 10.32. Notice that the boxes are paired. One of each pair refers to a brain region, and the other to a major possible function discussed in this chapter.

2   Do the same for Figure 10.33. What is the relationship between the two figures?

3   Give an example of 'chunking' in an expert task. Why is chunking necessary in the human brain?

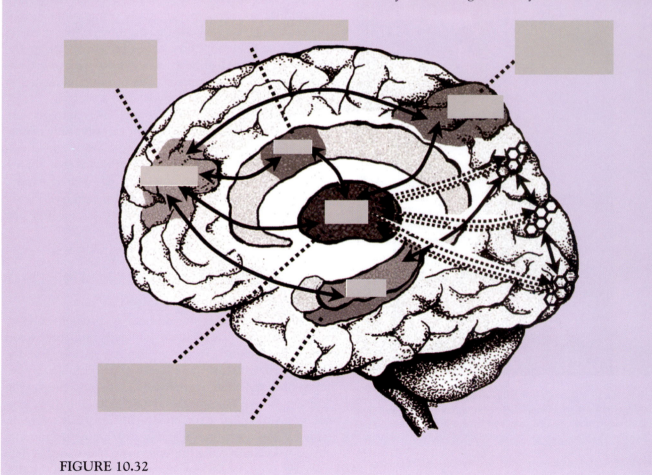

FIGURE 10.32

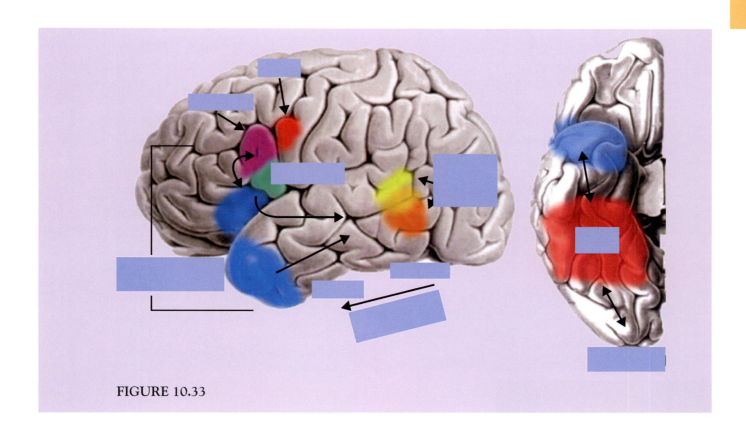

FIGURE 10.33

Mr Broca, on the occasion of this report, presented the brain of a fifty-one-year-old man who died in his care at Bicêtre hospital, and who had lost the use of speech . . . When the patient was admitted to Bicêtre, at the age of 21, he had lost, for some time, the use of speech; he could no longer pronounce more than a single syllable, which he ordinarily repeated twice at a time; whenever a question was asked of him, he would always reply tan, tan, *in conjunction with quite varied expressive gestures. For this reason, throughout the hospital, he was known only by the name of* Tan.

Pierre Paul Broca (1861) Loss of Speech, Chronic Softening and Partial Destruction of the Anterior Left Lobe of the Brain, First published in *Bulletin de la Société Anthropologique*, **2**, 235–238. Translation by Christopher D. Green. http://psychclassics.yorku.ca/Broca/perte-e.htm

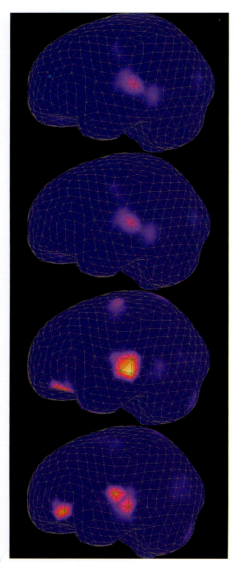

Brain activity to a single spoken word (starting with the first panel at the top). Notice the fast spread of activity beyond the auditory cortex. By the third image down, there is spread forward to the left inferior frontal gyrus (L-IFG), as well as central sulcus, parietal cortex and even the occipital pole. These MEG scans show mismatch negativity (MMN), a large wave of electro-magnetic activity in response to an unexpected stimulus. *Source*: Pulvermüller *et al.*, 2006.

Language

Bernard J. Baars

1.0 INTRODUCTION

Language is the foremost tool of human thought and culture. It is also one of the major landmarks of child development, with no close parallel in other species. Before our fourth birthday we have solved the problems of understanding our first phonology, our first basic lexicon and syntax. New words are acquired at a very fast pace during those years. While our understanding of syntax is still not fully settled, children acquire it with little visible difficulty. In addition, young children know how to use their emerging language skills to accomplish important goals (Figure 11.1). Even before they acquire language they have a good understanding of the world around them. These are achievements of brain development, enabled by good caregivers, helped by cognitive and emotional stimulation and experience, and of course by the cultural gift of a native language.

To illustrate the scientific questions posed by language, it is interesting to ask someone to repeat a sentence they have just heard. You may be surprised: people can rarely remember a sentence verbatim after only a few seconds. It's not that we have poor memories, but rather that we tend to *retain the meaning, not the words of what we hear* (Sachs, 1967). Most people can therefore give us a *paraphrase* of what they hear – a different sentence with a similar meaning – but not the

Cognition, Brain, and Consciousness, edited by B. J. Baars and N. M. Gage
ISBN: 978-0-12-373677-2

Copyright 2007, Elsevier Ltd. All rights reserved.

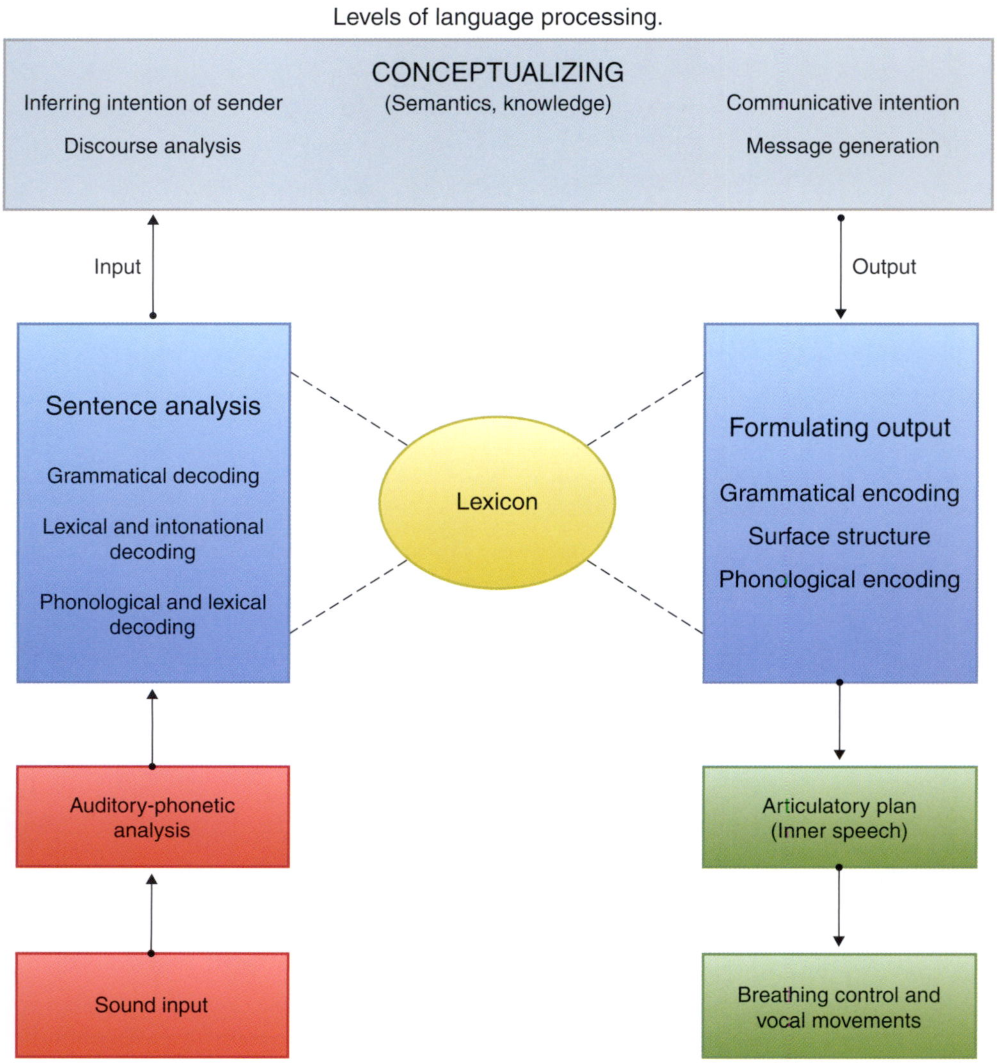

Levels of language processing.

FIGURE 11.1 Levels of language – analysis and production. A sketch of levels of language analysis and production. Each level is highly complex, but is processed by skilled speakers largely unconsciously and in seconds. *Source*: Baars, adapted from Miller, 1991.

original sentence. As soon as speech is understood, we tend to forget its 'outer form'. It has served its purpose.

Thus, within a few seconds, sound input seems to go through the following analyses:

- Acoustical analysis – turning sounds into linguistic elements such as phonemes; phoneme coding and serializing, to construct syllables and morphemes (meaningful units)
- Lexical identification – assigning words to the input, chosen from a vocabulary of tens of thousands of words
- Syntactic analysis – identifying nouns, verbs, and other grammatical categories, and constructing a syntactic frame

- Semantics – building the semantic network of the lexical and syntactic structure
- Discourse and conversational reference – how does the identified meaning relate to previous concepts in the conversation or discourse?
- Pragmatic and social inferences – what is the speaker's goal, and what does it mean for my goals? (Figure 11.1)

2.0 THE NATURE OF LANGUAGE

As Barrett *et al.* (2003) have put it, monkeys think 'what now?', but apes think 'what if?' That is, primates with larger frontal cortices can think about imagined events, not in the here-and-now, but in the there-and-then as well. It seems like a small difference, but language and a host of language-based cultural developments have turned it into moon landings and toothbrushes, and perhaps some developments that are not quite as pleasant. The evolutionary history of the human species is, in many ways, the history of the deployment of language in pursuit of personal and cultural ends.

BOX 11.1 Ambiguities exist at all levels of language

Figure 11.1 gives the impression that there is a point-to-point relationship between sound input and phonetic analysis, or between words and their meanings. This is an impression expert speakers tend to have, and it is wrong. Language is rife with ambiguities at every level of analysis, both in input and output. That is to say, there are *choice-points* in processing (see Chapter 10). For example, most common words have more than one meaning, so that the mapping between the lexicon and the conceptual representation at the top of Figure 11.1 always involves alternatives. There are also frequent ambiguities in acoustical analysis, and famous syntactic ambiguities, like the tree diagram of a surface structure ambiguity in Figure 11.2 (Chomsky, 1957).

A recent estimate of lexical ambiguity suggests an average of two high-frequency interpretations per word (Miller, 1991). More common words tend to have more meanings, so that the word 'set', for example, has more than two dozen senses according to the Oxford English Dictionary (Simpson and Weiner, 1989).

Choice-points also exist in the production of speech and language. We tend to become conscious of them in creative writing, when we perceive a choice between two words with slightly different meanings. Synonyms and para-phrases create choice-points in language production, while ambiguities at different levels of analysis create choice-points in language input.

Choice-points in the flow of processing require resolution, often using different levels of analysis. They turn a simple flow from one linguistic level to another into a maze, which tends to lead to a 'combinatorial explosion'. That is, for n binary choice points, the number of possible paths through the maze rises exponentially as 2^n. This number rises so quickly that computer-based speech and language interpretation has proven to be very difficult.

The general solution is called 'top down' or 'expectation-driven' processing. That is, when we encounter an ambiguous word like 'set' in 'Please set the table', we can tell from the semantic context that dishes are involved. In 'Please, set an example', something very different is intended. In these cases, semantic knowledge is needed to resolve the ambiguity. Thus, higher levels of analysis are needed to resolve choice-points at lower levels. The 'hierarchy' of language, like the processing hierarchy of vision (Chapter 3) requires flow of information in all directions. The flow of information might look something like Figure 11.3.

In general, as Mesalum (1990) has written:

> Cognitive problems are not resolved by a sequential and hierarchical progression toward predetermined goals but instead by a simultaneous and interactive consideration of multiple possibilities and constraints until a satisfactory fit is achieved. The resultant texture of mental activity is characterized by almost infinite richness and flexibility. According to this model, complex behavior is mapped at the level of multifocal neural systems rather than specific anatomical sites, giving rise to brain-behavior relationships that are both localized and distributed.

Top-down or expectation-driven processing appears to be a universal property of the cognitive brain.

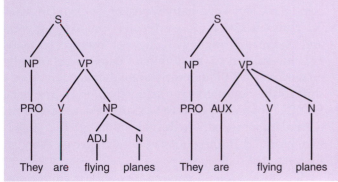

FIGURE 11.2 A syntactic ambiguity. There are two ways to understand the sentence, 'They are flying planes', either as 'The pilots are flying planes' or 'The planes are flying'. The assignment of the subject (they) is ambiguous, and as a result, the underlying structure is as well. Pronouns like 'they' are a rich source of ambiguity in language, since they take the referent for granted. Skilled speakers are rarely conscious of such ambiguities, but newcomers to any language community tend to misunderstand them. Syntactic ambiguities are just one kind of choice point in language analysis.

(Continued)

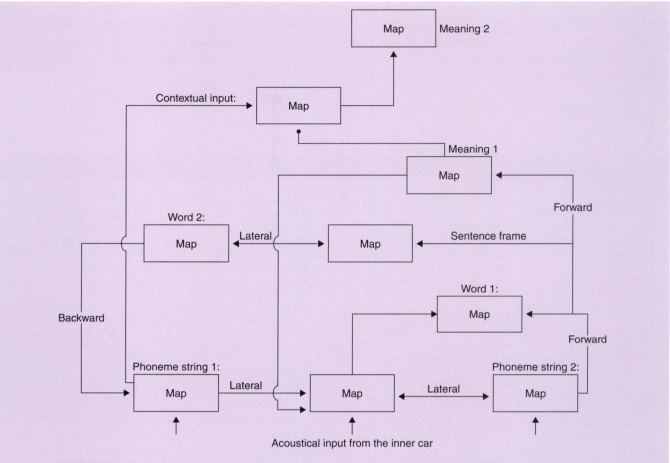

FIGURE 11.3 Information does not flow point-to-point in the language hierarchy. Like the visual processing hierarchy of Chapter 3, the physical speech signal presents the brain with a great many choice-points, both in input and output. In input processing there are numerous ambiguities of sound, word-meaning and syntax, that are believed to be resolved by expectations from other levels of analysis throughout the hierarchy. There is no strict bottom-up flow in language, just as there is no simple one-to-one mapping in vision. The same point applies to output processing. *Source*: Baars.

2.1 Biological aspects

Virtually all humans learn to speak in the first several years of life, and no other species does. There are interesting exceptions, like the chimps and gorillas, who are able to acquire Sign Language by observational learning and training early in life. But, as a species, other living primates do not acquire language, while humans do. This is not to minimize the special capacities of Bonobos and other primates, nor of other species, like the African Grey Parrots Alex and Arthur (Pepperberg, 2002), it is simply that language appears to be a human capacity for which we are biologically and culturally prepared. That is why we are good at it.

Children acquire language in predictable stages, and even develop their own 'creoles', true rule-governed languages, when they grow up in mixed-language communities without a single dominant language (see Box 11.2). After childhood it becomes more difficult to acquire the skills of a native speaker. Spoken language is a complex biological overlay over pre-existing vocal and auditory physiology. Language production tends to be lateralized to the dominant hemisphere (usually on the left side), though early brain damage can cause a shift to the non-dominant side (Chapter 1). The gene *FOXP2* apparently needs to be expressed accurately for normal human speech to develop, although that gene is widely found throughout vertebrate species (Vargha-Khadem *et al.*, 2005).

Repeating a sentence requires specific brain regions, assuming that the brain has developed normally. The best-known examples are Broca's and Wernicke's areas

(Chapter 1), but speech and language recruit much wider cortical and subcortical activity. The classic language regions have other functions. Broca's area, for example, also contains mirror neurons (Chapter 14), which are specialized for imitating the actions of others. 'Language cortex' has only become specialized for speech within hominid evolution, less than 3 million years out of the 200 million years of mammalian evolution. Prior to hominids, Broca's area may have been involved with vocal tract control for other purposes: it is located, after all, immediately adjacent to the mouth and tongue control areas of the motor homunculus. Many ingredients of spoken language, like hearing and vocal control, must have emerged very early. But there is speculation that the full panoply of language abilities may have become available in a much shorter time span than 3 million years, perhaps as short as 30–100 000 years. Certainly, the working vocabulary of living languages seems to have expanded considerably in recent history, although syntax may have become simpler.

All these points suggest that speech and language involve biological preparedness, in much the way that manual dexterity, vision, brain development and social relationships do. Like other genetic influences, this one is enormously interactive. Which language we acquire in childhood, how well we learn it, what vocabulary (and consequently conceptual system) we acquire, and many other variables depend upon our experiences. Nevertheless, the biological substrate of language is an important source of insight, as we will see. It does not reduce humans to some simpler living species, but rather should be taken to emphasize the enormous complexity and adaptive significance of language. Our cultural and personal accomplishments are heavily dependent upon the biological gifts of our species.

Chapter 1 touched on the discovery of the brain areas for speech production and perception in the 19th century, by Pierre-Paul Broca and Carl Wernicke, respectively. However, their findings with a small number of brain-damaged patients touched off more than a century of debate on the question of localization of language in the brain. That debate continues today, often involving neural net models of language functions,

for example, and sophisticated brain recording methods (Chapters 3 and 4).

Figure 11.4 shows the classical understanding of Broca's area (for speech production), and Wernicke's area for speech perception and comprehension. In addition, physicians in the 19th century discovered a number of other aphasias (language deficits). The best known of these is conduction aphasia, associated with a deficit of the arcuate fasciculus, the 'arched little bundle' running between Broca's and Wernicke's areas (Catani and ffytche, 2005). One of the most important developments today is the ability to study the large white matter tracts that run between cortical areas, and which fill by far the greatest amount of space in the hemispheres. Tractography (Chapter 4) and other methods for studying brain connectivity in the living brain should make it possible to learn much more about both cortical specializations and their connections in the next several years.

Wernicke's area abuts the auditory cortex in the Sylvian fissure and superior temporal gyrus (STG in Figure 11.4). Broca's area is immediately adjacent to the mouth and vocal tract regions of the motor cortex. Things have gotten a lot more complex in our understanding of these regions, but it is useful to realize that the location of these areas in those particular neighborhoods makes functional sense.

In 1861, when Broca discovered patients with damage to the left inferior frontal gyrus (L-IFG), which is now called Broca's area, a great debate broke out among neurologists who found it hard to find patients with exactly the same damage and the same symptoms. That debate lasted well into the next century. We might expect the debate to be resolved with the use of sophisticated brain imaging methods, or with direct cranial stimulation studies of hundreds of patients in open brain surgery (Penfield and Roberts, 1959; for a review, see Ojemann, 2003). Surprisingly, it has not. Debates about localization of function continue today.

That is not to say that nothing has been learned in more than a century of research. Most scientists believe that Broca's area is necessary for normal speech production. But a lot more is going on in this part of the brain than previously suspected, and there are cases of

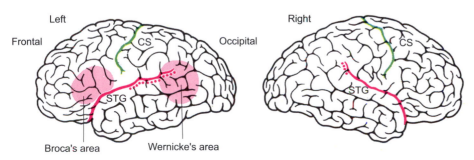

FIGURE 11.4 Classical language regions of cortex. The traditional location of Broca's and Wernicke's areas of the left hemisphere, based on neurological patients showing production and comprehension deficits. The right hemisphere has receptive language functions that are not shown here. (STG: superior temporal gyrus; CS: central sulcus.) *Source*: Standring, 2005.

damage to Broca's area that do not show the classic inability to speak. As improving neuroimaging methods are able to examine smaller and smaller regions of cortex, new subdivisions of the left inferior frontal gyrus (LIFG) are constantly being proposed.

The brain doesn't file its memory stores in neat, separate locations. However, there may be a general tendency for long-term functions to activate related sensory, motor, motivational and language regions. The cortex has numerous very local connections within single vertical columns and sets of columns; it has slightly more remote connections between neighboring regions of larger size; and it has a vast highway system of remote connections coursing from one end of the brain to the other, from the posterior to anterior poles, from right to left hemispheres, and flowing upward and downward into the sensory and motor apparatus of the cranial nerves and the spinal cord (see Chapter 5). This kind of highly interconnected system looks more like the world-wide web than like the organizational chart of a college campus.

Before we leap to the conclusion that language and thought are represented in easily identifiable locations in the brain, it is useful to look at a large-scale summary of the literature by Vigneau *et al.* (2006). Figure 11.5 shows the results of a major meta-analysis of more than 125 brain imaging experiments, resulting in more than 700 identified regions of peak activity in the left hemisphere. The different colors represent phonology, semantics (concept-related activity) and sentence or text processes. The degree of overlap is remarkable. This is not the kind of pattern we encounter in studying sensory regions like vision, where clearly defined visual maps like V1 can be shown to map topographically on to the retina.

These facts have a strong theoretical interpretation. They suggest that much of the brain works by way of *distributed networks* of language functions, like the world-wide web. An Internet chat group may work even if the participants come from different many parts of the world. The idea of distributed brain functioning seems to support the connectionist view of the brain, as discussed in Chapter 3 (see also Neural Darwinism, Chapter 3).

By performing a statistical cluster analysis of hundreds of data sets, Vigneau *et al.* were able to suggest more specific loci, interacting in classical working memory loops (Figure 11.6). The analysis suggests three separable working memory loops, for phonological, semantic and sentence processing. But now we are left with a puzzle that has occupied scientists at least since Pierre-Paul Broca: which figure tells us what's really happening? It is possible that the statistical analysis shows the 'true' nature of the regions in Figure 11.6. That would be a sensible interpretation if there were random jitter in the data for methodological or biological

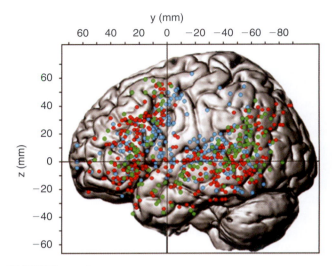

FIGURE 11.5 Widely distributed language networks may be compatible with regional specialization. A summary of more than 100 brain imaging experiments, reflecting some 730 activity peaks using fMRI and PET (Vigneau *et al.*, 2006). The blue points show peaks for phonology – the sounds of speech. Red regions show peak regions for semantics, the meanings of words and phrases and the green dots show the effects of sentences and text. The overlap and wide scatter of the three functions is striking. *Source*: Vigneau *et al.*, 2006.

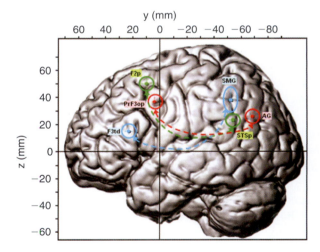

FIGURE 11.6 Working memory loops for phonology, semantics and sentences. The wide scatter of peak activations in Figure 11.6 can be simplified by a cluster analysis, resulting in plausible centers of speech-related activity in the left hemisphere. However, such an analysis must then explain why the wide distribution of phonology, semantics and sentence processing was found in the first place. The answers are not obvious at this time. (STSp: superior temporal sulcus, posterior; AG: angular gyrus; SMG: supramarginal gyrus; F2p: middle frontal gyrus, posterior; PrF3op: operculum of inferior frontal gyrus; F3td: inferior frontal gyrus). The word 'operculum' refers to a flap of cortical tissue that covers the hidden regions of the insula and Sylvian fissure. Frontal gyri are numbered downward (superior = F1, middle = F2, inferior = F3). *Source*: Vigneau *et al.*, 2006.

reasons. But each data point in Figure 11.5 represents the best efforts of each laboratory to ensure that there is no such random jitter. Thus we have a choice between accepting either a more localizationist account suggested by the cluster analysis, or the distributionist account suggested by Figure 11.6. It is not obvious which one is correct, and the debate continues.

Nevertheless, there is good agreement on some basic points. For example, both figures show constant interactive looping between the more sensory-related (posterior) and motor-related (anterior) parts of cortex. While the left hemisphere is usually studied because of the well-established left-side bias in most people, it is important to understand that language functions are *not* confined to the left hemisphere. There is good evidence for speech and language *input processing* on both sides – speech perception and comprehension. But for reasons that are not well understood, language *output*, the planning and controlled of speech, is weighted toward by the left hemisphere in more than 90 per cent of the population. As we will see later, the right hemisphere may even have its own way of understanding sophisticated communications like jokes, metaphors, and irony, while the left side may have a more humdrum preference for literal language (Zaidel *et al.*, 2000).

We will see these ideas again as we explore how the brain supports human language and thought. Various scientists have suggested somewhat different interpretations of the very large empirical literature. We have carefully collected evidence from studies of brain damage, single-neuron recording, positron emission tomography (PET), functional magnetic resonance imaging (fMRI), magnetoencephalography (MEG), electroencephalography (EEG), evoked potentials and the like. Not all the evidence is easily reconciled, but it is useful to take a broad organizing perspective.

For example, Hagoort (2005) suggests that we should take a larger view of what is classically called Broca's area. He proposes a division of labor as shown in Figure 11.7. Broca's area has now expanded forward to include the gray oval area, which is proposed to serve the function of *unifying* speech sounds, meaning, and syntactic relationships. This area is intended to include both memory areas of the temporal lobe, including the MTL (medial temporal lobe, which is hidden in the left viewpoint). Finally, an executive region includes the dorsolateral prefrontal cortex (DL-PFC).

As we know from the dramatic case of young children with left hemisphere surgeries, the left-side bias for language can switch to the other side if there is severe damage to the speaking hemisphere in early childhood (see Chapter 2). Lateralization of function is also found in some other species, but the reasons for it are still quite mysterious. For this topic, it is only important to understand that the wide distribution of language activity points is not limited to the left hemisphere.

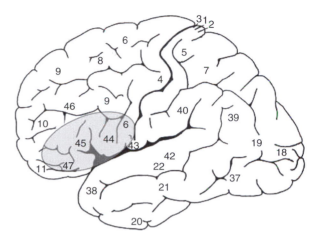

FIGURE 11.7   L-IFG: an expanded concept of Broca's area. The left inferior frontal gyrus (L-IFG) is a more accurate label for the broad area involved in speech planning and production. Hagoort (2005) also suggests that L-IFG is a 'convergence zone' for speech, i.e. it is a place where the different features of spoken language are unified into an integrated plan before being sent to the motor map. *Source*: Hagoort, 2005.

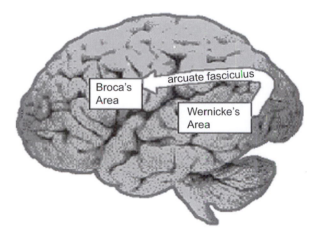

FIGURE 11.8   Wernicke-Geschwind model. The best-known neurologically based model of the language regions is due to Geschwind (1979). While the Wernicke-Geschwind model continues to be widely studied, the advent of neuroimaging methods has led to a wave of new evidence. *Source*: Weems and Reggia, 2006.

It expands like some vast metropolis into the non-speaking hemisphere. Anatomically, the great bridge between the hemispheres, the corpus callosum, fans out on both sides in a point-to-point fashion, so that neurons in the frontal cortex on one side sprout axons that spread across to the frontal cortex on the other side (see Chapter 5, Figure 5.23). For many functions the two hemispheres are thoroughly integrated.

It is still true that damage to Broca's area will tend to impair speech output, while damage to Wernicke's area and neighboring regions tends to degrade speech perception and comprehension (Figure 11.8).

Historically, Broca and Wernicke were not wrong on the evidence – they just didn't have the complete story.

In Figure 11.9, we present a model for auditory language in the cortex proposed by Hickok and Poeppel (2004). Notice that the upper regions of the temporal lobe, toward the back of the Sylvian fissure, contain audi-tory regions that are believed to represent phonemes or possibly the 'syllabary' mentioned above. These are the sound-based representations of speech (Figure 11.9). This is a plausible model, but as mentioned, we do not yet have the spatial resolution to know whether there is a more microscopic mosaic of feature-sensitive neurons, such as exist in visual cortex.

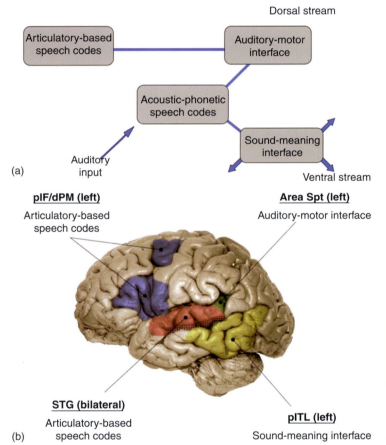

FIGURE 11.9 Hickok-Poeppel model of auditory language. Upper panel shows a schematic for the model of auditory language processing proposed by Hickok and Poeppel (2004). Lower panel shows brain regions proposed to reflect stages of the model. Note that early speech perceptual systems for mapping the acoustic-phonetic information in sounds onto meaning are proposed to be mediated bilaterally in left and right hemispheres while later processes are proposed to be mediated by left hemisphere regions. *Source*: Adapted with permission from Hickok and Poeppel, 2004.

BOX 11.2   Creole languages are produced by children in multilingual communities

Creoles are languages with simple syntactic structures that develop when speakers of several different languages are forced to communicate with one another. This can occur through immigration and invasion or when individuals are brought together from different cultures to work. The adults in such situations develop a crude pidgin, an impoverished communication system in which a limited number of nouns, verbs, and modifiers are combined with extensive gesturing. Children of the pidgin speakers learn their parents' language, but not the pidgin; instead, in addition to using their parents' language, they also create a creole for communication with one another that is based on the pidgin. All creoles share a set of common features, which can contrast with those in fully developed languages.

1 The grammar is based on word order; in contrast, most human languages rely largely on inflection (agreement and derivation – see earlier discussion).
2 There are seven parts of speech: nouns, pronouns, adjectives, verbs, adverbs, articles, and conjunctions; many human languages omit one or more of these categories or add new ones.
3 Nouns are distinguished as singular, plural, or indefinite in number, many languages lack the latter category.

4 There are three particles used as auxiliary verbs to indicate whether an action is successful, unsuccessful, or repeated; many languages lack these distinctions.

5 There is a single verb conjugation system; most languages have a general rule for most verbs, but special-case rules for most of the commonly used (irregular) verbs.

6 Questions are based on intonation rather than word order; many languages use both.

Bickerton points out that, in many cases, these universal features of creoles are not present in the languages spoken by the parents of the children who created the creole. Therefore, creoles are very likely to be related to innately specified features of language.

However, even creoles do not illustrate such features directly. If all the features of creoles just listed were innate, it would be impossible to explain how any languages have any other features. Innate properties of language must be more abstract than the features found in creoles and must allow all the different forms of language that are currently found to develop. Instead of thinking of creoles as demonstrating universal features of language directly, we might better think of them as showing us what features of language develop most easily. It is possible that these features characterized human languages at an early stage of their development.

From Squire *et al*. (2003).

2.2 Language origins

People have wondered about the origins of language for thousands of years. If children grew up without language, would they invent their own? In fact, nature provides experiments a little bit like that. In some isolated communities, like small islands, adult speakers of different languages may settle in the same place. Fluent adults rarely acquire the 'accent' (phonology) or grammar of languages they learn after puberty. Instead, they tend to speak a 'broken' version of the new language, one that is good enough to communicate with adults from other parts of the world, but generally without the fluency and expressive richness of their original languages. Children in such bicultural communities do a very interesting thing: they may develop a language of their own, now called a 'creole' because they were first studied in the Creole communities of the Caribbean Islands (Bickerton, 1984; 1990).

2.3 Speech versus language

Scholars often make a distinction between speech and language, in part because of the striking plasticity of the human brain in learning different input and output modalities. Right now you are using your eyes and perhaps your hands, to take notes. You have learned to read and write or type with quite remarkable facility. You could also learn sign language, Braille, and para-linguistic symbol systems like mathematics, logic and computer programming. Thus, the purely vocal and auditory nature of speech seems to be unnecessary.

However, a hard-and-fast distinction between speech and language is not justified. Human brains are pre-adapted to acquire auditory and vocal speech. The great majority of children learn spoken language in the first years of life, but reading and writing come later and have a lower rate of success. The fact that we can exercise remarkable linguistic flexibility, given the need and the opportunity, does not falsify the biological primacy of spoken language.

3.0 THE SOUNDS OF SPOKEN LANGUAGE

Chapter 7 discussed the auditory nature of speech, consisting of fast-expanding three-dimensional bubbles of high and low air pressure waves, which set the delicate membranes of the inner ear into vibrating motion. We can also look at speech from a vocal *output* point of view.

The human vocal tract is basically a tube, with two flexible flaps just above the lungs and its diaphragm muscles, which together create air pressure when we breathe out (Figure 11.10). The vocal tract is therefore much like a reed horn like a saxophone, with the reed vibrating at the top of the tube. The vocal flaps can vibrate faster or slower, producing higher or lower-pitched sounds. We produce consonants by closing the entire vocal tube at one of several places. In English we use the lips at the very front (/b//p//m/), the tongue against the palate in the back or middle (/g//k//ng//r/) and the teeth in the front (/th//the//s//z//v//w/). However, stopping the flow of air completely produces no sound at all, so that it is the fast *transitions* between closing and opening of the air flow that produces the so-called stop consonants (/b//p//t//d//k/g/). Other languages shape the air flow

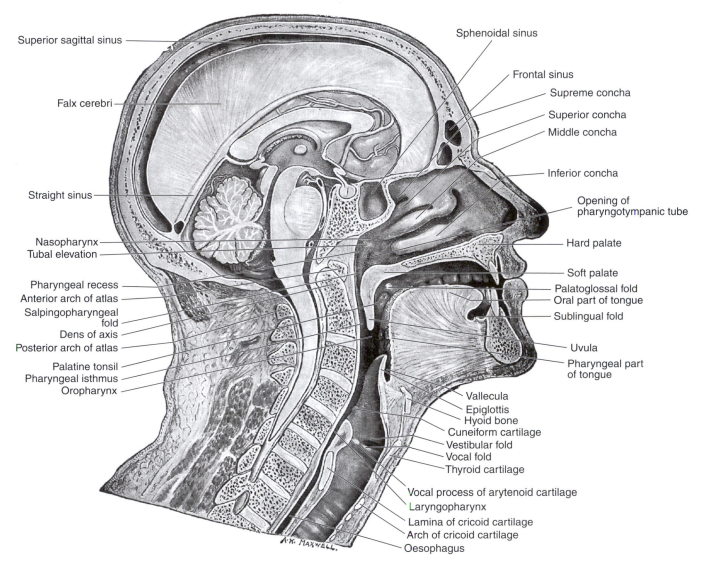

Superior sagittal sinus
Falx cerebri
Straight sinus
Nasopharynx
Tubal elevation
Pharyngeal recess
Anterior arch of atlas
Salpingopharyngeal fold
Dens of axis
Posterior arch of atlas
Palatine tonsil
Pharyngeal isthmus
Oropharynx

Sphenoidal sinus
Frontal sinus
Supreme concha
Superior concha
Middle concha
Inferior concha
Opening of pharyngotympanic tube
Hard palate
Soft palate
Palatoglossal fold
Oral part of tongue
Sublingual fold
Uvula
Pharyngeal part of tongue
Vallecula
Epiglottis
Hyoid bone
Cuneiform cartilage
Vestibular fold
Vocal fold
Thyroid cartilage
Vocal process of arytenoid cartilage
Laryngopharynx
Lamina of cricoid cartilage
Arch of cricoid cartilage
Oesophagus

A.K. MAXWELL.

FIGURE 11.10   The human vocal tract makes use of pre-existing mechanisms of breath control, mouth, tongue, glottis and larynx inherited from ancestral species. The vocal tract is a tube with a source of tuned vibrations in the vocal cords, two flaps of tissue in the larynx. The quality of vocal sounds results from vibratory resonance with the movable tissues and air pockets throughout the head and torso. While consonants involve restriction of closing of the air tube, vowels are mostly shaped by moving the tongue and lips to shape the oral cavity. This has the effect of changing the resonant frequencies or formants of the vocal tract. Thus vowels and consonant-vowel pairs are the minimal physical units of speech production (if one considers hissing sounds like /h/ /th/ /tha/ /s/ and so on to be vowel-like). *Source*: Standring, 2005.

in somewhat different ways, but the physical principles of sound production are the same.

Vocal vibrations echo through the head and body, triggering vibrations in all the cavities in our head and torso, so that by holding one's nose, for example, one can change the quality of the voice. Those vibrating air-filled body cavities also allow us to tell the difference between individual voices. Children's voices sound higher than adults' simply because they have smaller vibrating cavities.

Just as closing the vocal tube creates consonants, shaping the vocal cavity with the mouth open produces different vowels. Singing is closely related to speaking: it is just stretching the length of vowels and tuning them to a specific pitch using the vocal cords. But even ordinary speech has a kind of melodic phrasing called *intonation contours*. In English, a question intonation tends to raise the pitch of the last few syllables of a spoken phrase. A great range of emotional qualities is conveyed by the intonational melodies of speech.

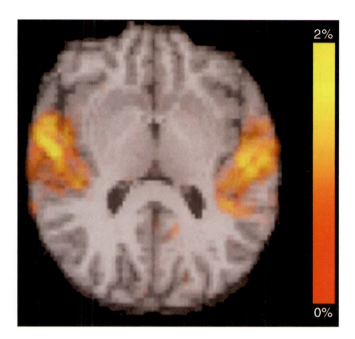

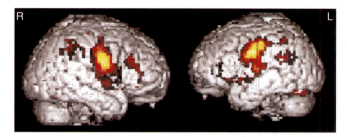

FIGURE 11.12 Extending the tongue without making a sound. Even without making a sound, horizontally extending the tongue shows marked activity in the 'language' regions of both hemispheres. As this shows, the tongue and mouth are very well represented in motor cortex, unlike, for example, regions of the back. Motor cortex over-represents more important regions of motor control, and under-represents less important ones. *Source*: Dogil *et al.*, 2002.

FIGURE 11.11 Auditory cortex shows local activity to different speech-like stimuli. Recent research shows finer parcellation of the auditory and speech perception regions. With the development of more refined imaging tools, it is possible that localized arrays of speech feature-sensitive neurons will be identified, much as has happened in the visual cortex. *Source*: Langers *et al.*, 2003.

Even the rhythm of music has a close analogue in vocal stress patterns, as used in poetry and rap music, for example. Thus, singing and speech intonation, rhythm, and vocal gestures can be viewed as using the same voice instrument in somewhat different ways.

In sum, humans can shape the vocal tract in a great variety of ways, a rare (but not unique) adaptation among animal species.

Until the invention of typewriting, speaking was the fastest-moving and most precise skill that most people ever acquired. As Chapter 7 points out, the difference between the syllable /pa/ and /ba/ involves only a few tens of milliseconds between the onset of vocal vibrations and the opening of the lips. In the case of /pa/ the lips open slightly before voicing begins, while for /ba/, voice onset starts just before the lips open up. Because we are skilled readers and writers, we tend to believe intuitively that language is made up of sequences of letters, but that is a misunderstanding. Spoken language involves a series of articulatory gestures, which shape the moment-to-moment frequency distribution of air vibrations emanating from our vocal tract. While we can *see* isolated visual letters (as on this page), there is no such thing as an isolated vocal consonant. We cannot

pronounce /k/ without making a following sound, even if it is just a long /hhhh/, simply because the tube needs both to *close and open* to produce any sound. For that reason, the physics of sound suggests that simple syllables (like /ba/ and /pa) and isolated vowels may be the simplest elements of speech. For that reason some theorists suggest that humans make use of a syllabary – not just an alphabet of phonemes, but a larger set of speech gestures of vowels and consonant-vowel combinations (Levelt and Wheeldon, 1994). A syllable alphabet would have to be larger than a set of phonemes, but it would reflect the way we produce speech sounds.

It follows from these points that the phonemes of human language are abstract percepts, much as visual objects are. Our eyes don't see trees – rather, they receive retinal projections of light and dark that are interpreted by the cortex as three-dimensional trees at a certain distance from the eyes. Similarly, phonemes are *abstract* categories of sounds, which are acoustically quite different depending upon their neighboring speech gestures. When speakers say /ba/ versus /bee/, the acoustical information for the lip-opening that produces the consonant /b/ is quite different in the two cases. In the case of /bee/ there is a fast-*rising* transition to signal the consonant, while for /ba/ there is a fast-*dropping* transition (see Chapter 7). Yet we perceive the consonant /b/ to be the same in both cases. This is typical for human languages, which tend to have about forty *abstract* phonemes, which stand for the much larger set of physical sounds that actually reach our ears. Abstract phoneme perception appears to be species-specific.

Are phonemes reflected in neat fields of feature-sensitive neurons in the cortex? We do not know the answer. In the case of vision, feature-sensitive cells that

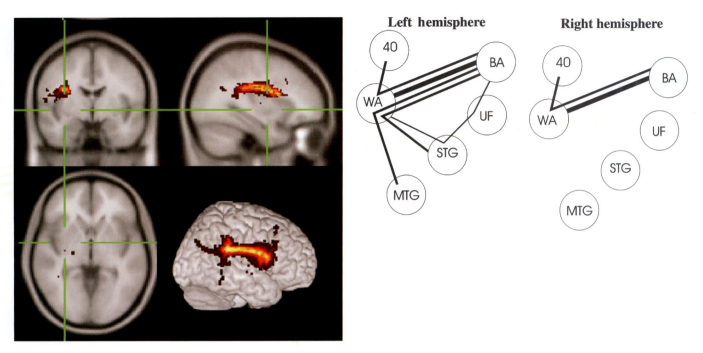

FIGURE 11.13 Pathways between speaking and hearing. The results of a tractography study of the connections between production and perception regions. The tractographic display (above) shows the classical arcuate fasciculus running between Broca's and Wernicke's areas, although an additional pathway has been reported as well. The lower two figures show mathematical connections weights for the left and right hemispheres respectively. (BA: Broca's area; WA: Wernicke's area; UF: uncinate fasciculus; STG: superior temporal gyrus; MTG: middle temporal gyrus.) *Source*: Parker *et al.*, 2005.

respond to color, line orientation and the like, were first discovered in the macaque monkey, using single-cell recording. Such experiments are not done on humans, and of course macaques are not biologically adapted for speech perception. For that reason the answers still await better brain imaging methods. Reports of high-resolution fMRI studies of auditory cortex in the macaque were published even as this book was going to press (Petkov *et al.*, 2006). In the next several years we may find out if there are feature-sensitive fields of auditory neurons in the cortex. Because the brain tends to do things similarly for similar functions in the cortex, it seems like a reasonable prediction. But direct evidence is simply not available.

4.0 PLANNING AND PRODUCING SPEECH

Output from the language areas of cortex is at least as complex and adaptive as speech perception and comprehension. Figure 11.14 shows a current model of the output flow, beginning with the conceptual level.

Grammatical encoding of sentences is believed to involve lemmas, much like formulas for translating semantics into the morphemes and phonemes that govern vocal movements. It is important to understand again that these linguistic units are abstract, in the sense that any given phoneme, for example, can be articulated in more than one way, depending upon the neighboring phonemes. The vocal tract is a physical system, and it takes considerable time for the tongue, for example, to travel between the teeth (for shaping the consonant /th/) and the soft palate at the back of the mouth to make a /g/ sound. As a result, there is a fair amount of 'sloppiness' in the acoustical signal that is produced, because of the smearing of speech gestures. In English, for example, the word 'tan' will foreshadow the final /n/ even during the time when the /ae/ is being pronounced. The /ae/ is therefore nasalized or 'co-articulated'. Thus, the actual sounds of speech changes, even though the abstract phoneme is believed to be represented the same way, whether we have the /ae/ in 'act' or in 'tan'. If you listen carefully, you will be able to hear the difference.

Notice that this situation parallels the case of vision. In the visual cortex, area V1 mirrors the output of the

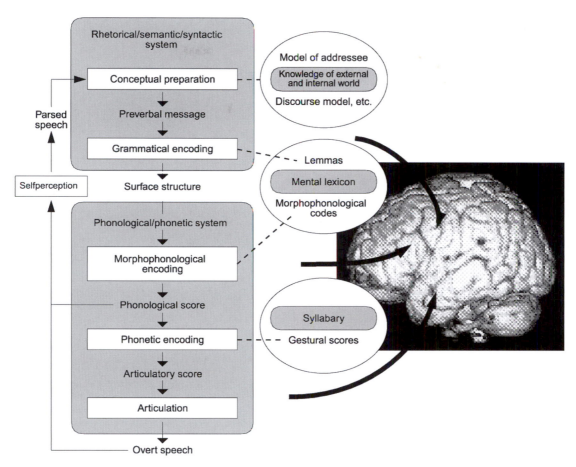

FIGURE 11.14 Producing speech: from meaning to movements. A model of the production of speech. Compare to Figure 11.1. *Source*: Dogil *et al.*, 2002.

retina. It is very detailed, with small receptive fields and very high optical resolution. Even though later visual areas are also visuotopic maps, they are much less detailed and much more abstract in representing features of the visual input like color, object identity and the like. The idea that the visual system becomes more abstract as we look upstream is therefore well justified by the evidence. Speech may be similar in that respect, although our brain evidence is far less complete.

Notice also that the cortex is not the only control region for speaking. Actions that are initiated voluntarily from frontal cortex also enlist regions of the basal ganglia and cerebellum. Traditionally, it has been believed that basal ganglia are involved in the automatic aspects of action control, such as the specific pronunciation of /r/ sounds compared to /l/ sounds, a distinction that is very difficult for native Japanese speakers, for example. English speakers have comparable difficulties in controlling the French sound /u/ versus /oo/. These highly overpracticed speech sounds are not completely controlled by the cortex. In addition, cerebellum is traditionally believed to be needed for fine motor control.

However, recent brain imaging evidence implicates both cerebellum and basal ganglia in purely cognitive aspects of brain activities, including working memory and some types of associative learning (Figure 11.15).

While language areas of the cortex have been known since the 19th century, even the exact functions of Broca's and Wernicke's area are still debated (see Chapter 1). It isn't that Broca and Wernicke were wrong in their proposals about speech production and comprehension. Rather, as our observations become more and more precise, we are finding more functions for the classical language regions of the left hemisphere, and speech related functions outside their traditional boundaries (see Chapter 14). Our understanding is constantly being revised. We are, in effect, exploring a new planet, and as our space probe comes closer and closer, we need to chart a much more detailed and surprising geography of this novel world.

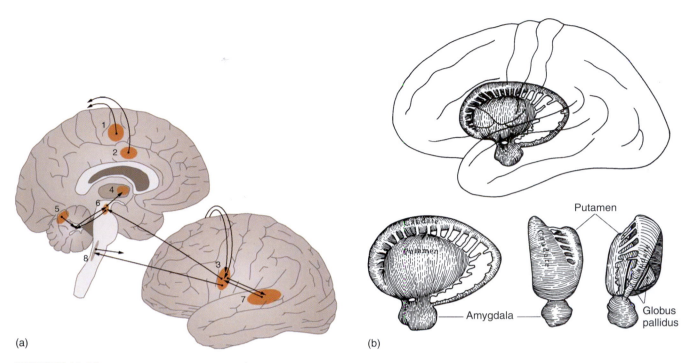

(a)   (b)

FIGURE 11.15 (a) A neural network for speech production: the supplementary motor area (1) and the cingulated motor area (2) are connected with the primary motor cortex (3) subcortical activation is in the thalamus (4), the basal ganglia (not shown), the red nucleus (6), and the cerebellum (5). Additionally, the posterior temporal gyrus in both hemispheres is activated in speech production (7). In the brainstem, areas such as the nucleus hypoglossus (8) are innervated during speech production. Cortical regions work with basal ganglia, thalamus and cerebellum in speech control. Subcortical satellite regions like the basal ganglia are involved in sequential behaviors like speaking. In addition, the cerebellum and thalamic nuclei (not shown) play an important role. *Sources: Left*, Soros *et al.*, 2006; *right*, Angerine, 2002.

5.0 EVOLUTIONARY ASPECTS OF SPEAKING AND LISTENING

Our highly specialized vocal apparatus is attuned to producing spoken language. It evolved from the non-linguistic vocal organs of ancestral species. These, in turn, built upon a breathing apparatus that we share with other land-dwelling creatures, as well as neuromuscular control of chewing and swallowing. For example, tree-dwelling young gibbons in the wild sound very much like human children at play. However, soon after birth human babies begin to babble, experimenting with syllables that are quite different from non-linguistic sounds (Schirmer and Kotz, 2006).

Anatomically, vocalization involves a dual-control system, like breathing and emotional facial expressions (Chapter 2). In socially provocative situations, vocal sounds can be produced with minimal executive control from the lateral prefrontal cortex, ranging from making cooing sounds to a baby, to crying out of sadness, shouting with anger, or groaning with distress. Figure 11.16 shows the dual-control of vocalization schematically. As

you can tell, it is not a simple system, having evolved over many millions of years.

In this chapter, we are concerned with the right side of the diagram, the cortical control of speech beginning with prefrontal cortex and Broca's area (broadly defined), while on the input side we are looking at speech perception and comprehension.

Cortical regions for speech are closely associated with audition (for sensory input) and with mouth and vocal tract representation (on the output side). The classical Broca's and Wernicke's areas are adjacent to cortical regions for vocal production and sound perception, respectively (Figure 11.17). Figure 11.18 show the mouth and vocal region of the motor homunculus, immediately adjacent to Broca's area. Direct stimulation of the motor map results in muscular movements, but stimulation of premotor regions such as BA6 results in reports of 'urges to move' the corresponding part of the body. Motor map stimulation is perceived as externally controlled by the physician, not by the patient. Broca's area may be considered premotor cortex for speech, i.e. a cortical region for the 'intention to speak'. When Broca's area is stimulated in a conscious

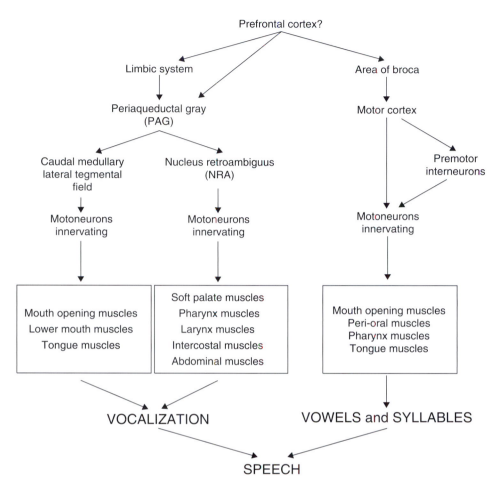

FIGURE 11.16 Speaking may have evolved from socially evoked sound production. Vocalization has a dual-control pathway, much like breathing, facial expressions, eye movements and other motor systems. The left branch is sometimes called the emotional motor path. Originating in prefrontal cortex, it follows a classic mammalian route for vocalization including the limbic system and peri-aqueductal gray (PAG). The PAG plays a major role in distress vocalizations when rat pups and mothers are separated. Like the emotional motor path, the right-hand branch begins in prefrontal cortex, and then follows the better-known steps from Broca's area to motor cortex and thence to the cranial nerves for vocal control. Both pathways also receive input from basal ganglia and cerebellum. The right-hand pathway is under greater voluntary control. *Source*: Holstege *et al*., 2004.

patient, it appears to block the intention to speak (Quinones-Hinojosa *et al*., 2003).

As more has been learned about the cortical aspects of speech and language, the production and perception regions have expanded and also become more finely fragmented into specialized areas. Additional functions have also been discovered for the classical Broca's and Wernicke's areas, as in the case of the 'mirror neurons' discussed in Chapter 14. Speech perception (but not production) also appears to recruit the non-speaking hemisphere (the right hemisphere in most people), even though speech planning and production is typically limited to the left side.

6.0 WORDS AND MEANINGS

English is a member of the Indo-European language family. This family includes Persian and a number of languages spoken on the Indian subcontinent. Other language families make quite different choices with respect to such basic-seeming units as words. Finnish and Turkic languages are called 'agglutinative', because they string morphemes into long utterances, like the unusually long English word 'antidisestablishmentarianism'. Such long strings of morphemes are normal in agglutinative languages. Tonal languages like Chinese and Tibetan take

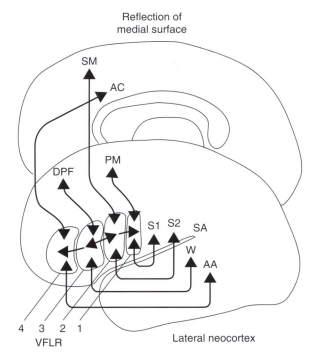

FIGURE 11.17 Speech production and perception loops constantly. Speech production and perception regions of the cortex are constantly exchanging information, both directly via subcortical connections, and indirectly, as we hear the sound of our own vocal apparatus. As pointed out in Chapter 2, there is good evidence that most people spend most of the day talking to themselves cortically. Indeed, studies of sleep stages seem to show that inner speech continues during sleep and dreaming. *Source*: Dogil *et al.*, 2002.

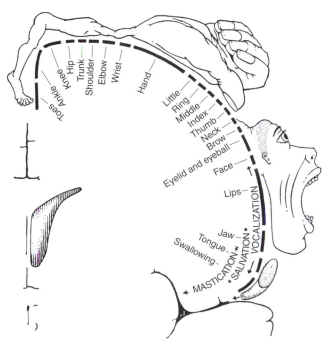

FIGURE 11.18 In the motor homunculus (BA5), muscular control of the mouth, jaw, tongue, vocal cords, as well as actions like chewing and swallowing reside next to Broca's area for the control of speaking (BA 6, 44 and 45). The 'motor homunculus', first discovered by Wilder Penfield using electrical stimulation of motor cortex in awake patients during exploratory neurosurgery (Penfield and Roberts, 1959). Notice that mastication, vocalization and swallowing are marked next to the mouth region of the homunculus. *Source*: Standring, 2005.

the opposite approach, compounding sentences from typically short words, modulated by a rich melodic shaping of each syllable, so that a word like 'Chang' can mean quite different things depending on its tonal contour. However, all languages have lexical units of some kind – utterances of one or more syllables that refer to meaning categories, or to relations between categories.

Figure 11.19 shows a current model of how the brain may translate different linguistics codes from one to the next. As Figure 11.1 showed, language may be viewed as a double hierarchy, going from sound to meaning on the input side, and from meaning to vocal gestures in output. But we can repeat a nonsense syllable like 'fronk' even though it has no particular meaning, and Figure 11.19 suggests that such recoding from sound to speaking may occur in the inferior parietal cortex. Broca's area was traditionally thought to serve the translation from thought to speech articulation, the current favored term is the left inferior frontal gyrus (L-IFG), because wider regions of the left hemisphere are thought to be involved. The older term 'Wernicke's

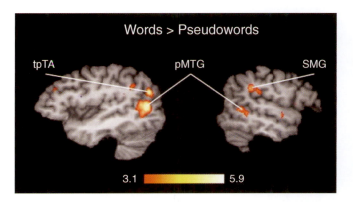

FIGURE 11.19 Brain activations for meaningful versus meaningless words. Words are not just sequences of phonemes. Although the brain basis of word meaning continues to be mysterious (presumably because word meanings are part of long-term memory, see Chapter 9), meaningful words activate distinct regions of language-related cortex, when compared to nonsense words. In this study, three areas appeared in the comparison, the temporoparietal transition area (tpTA), the posterior part of the medial temporal gyrus (pMTG), and the supramarginal gyrus (SMG). *Source*: Friederici and Kotz, 2003.

area' for speech comprehension is now called the TPO junction (for temporal-parietal-occipital). This location makes sense, because we know that the temporal lobe is involved in memory-based concepts, including those abstracted from visual objects, like the differences between animate and inanimate figures, for tools and instruments, and for parts of the body. As Chapters 9 and 10 pointed out, it may be that these very specific semantic regions serve to index larger classes of words and concept, rather than being a localized semantic field.

6.1 A cultural treasury of words and ideas

Language is used to communicate meanings. While phonemes are defined as minimal speech units that make a *difference* in meaning, words refer to things, which phonemes do not. Words are the basic building blocks of meaning. However, sentences, and particularly *propositions* built out of sentences can be taken as basic 'meaning formulae', analogous to mathematical formulae. We think and communicate in sentences. Many communications are of course elliptical, i.e. they abbreviate a whole thought into a few words. Nevertheless, they express a semantic proposition of some kind.

As Chapter 10 suggested, the words of natural language are an immense legacy of useful chunks of meaning, developed over centuries. Indeed, in many cases we can trace word origins over more than a thousand years. A particularly nice example is the word 'quality' derived from the Latin translation (by Cicero) of the ancient Greek expression 'po io tes', or 'what is-ness'. Cicero apparently encountered it in a Socratic dialogue. Before his invented word *qualitas* became popular, European languages had no way to refer to the 'what is it-ness' of a sound, of a taste, or any other class of events. We can always use longer phrases for the ideas for which we do not have single words, but single words allow us to treat concepts as single chunks in our very limited working memory space. Thus, inventing new and useful words is a real contribution to our capacity to understand the world.

Science is hard to imagine without a word like 'quality'. Yet it took a certain realization at a certain point in intellectual history, more than twenty centuries ago, to chunk the concept of 'quality' in a way that we can use as an abstract noun. Probably all modern languages have some term for 'quality' today, because we can no longer think easily without it. Since modern languages have tens of thousands of words, with more being produced every day, we must multiply Cicero's invention by tens of thousands of other invented words to get some sense of the body of knowledge that is passed down to each new native speaker.

Roget's Thesaurus, first compiled by Peter Mark Roget (1779–1869) is one historic effort to classify the words of a natural language into its semantic categories, so that one can find a word by starting with a concept. In a thesaurus, words with similar meanings are clustered together, giving us a kind of semantic treasury of standard ideas; indeed the word 'thesaurus' means 'treasure'. Modern efforts along those lines use computational methods, but characterizing our knowledge of basic concepts is still an awesome enterprise. George A. Miller's WordNet system at Princeton University is one effort along those lines (http://wordnet.princeton.edu/), an online lexical reference system. Over a period of years, it has classified more than 200 000 word-meaning pairs in English. Parallel efforts have been undertaken for other languages. By the WordNet count, English has some 128 000 single-meaning words, and about 80 000 words with multiple meanings. However, this estimate does not include words with multiple syntactic roles, like 'book', which is both a noun and a verb (as in 'booking the arrested person'). 'Book' also can be adjectival (as in book-learning, book-binding, a bookish person, a book-reader and so on.).

Thus, the words and meanings that we know as skilled speakers of human language are enormous. The Oxford English Dictionary (OED) is another massive effort along similar lines, tracing the history of standard English words to their written origins. Obviously, however, the real origins of words are lost in time, since language is basically a spoken medium, which only turned into a standardized printed body of knowledge long after the invention of writing, two or three millennia ago. Nevertheless, the OED gives us some sense of the sheer size of the human lexicon of words and concepts.

6.2 Recognizing synonyms

Gitelman *et al.* (2005) made a state-of-the-art effort to specify language areas using the identical cognitive task with the same group of subjects, looking at orthography (spelling), semantics and phonology in the same experimental session. (Syntax involves word sequencing, and is therefore left until later.) Subjects were shown word pairs as in Figure 11.20, and asked to respond either 'same' or 'different'. In the case of 'rain' versus 'reign', they were to say if the words were homophones (HOM), i.e. words with different spelling but the same pronunciation. In the case of 'boat' versus

	Phonologic (HOM)	Semantic (SYN)	Orthographic (ANA)	Control (C)
Match *(response)*	Rain Reign	Boat Ship	Aunt Tuna	Fplk Fplk
Non-Match *(no response)*	Axe Ask	Key Lock	Horse Short	Gkjs Gskt

FIGURE 11.20 Sample stimuli from the Gitelman *et al.* (2005) study. The experimental conditions are shown and include phonologic (homophone, HOM), semantic (synonym, SYN), and orthographic (anagram, ANA) contrasts in a match and a non-match condition. *Source*: Gitelman *et al.*, 2005.

'ship', they were to identify synonyms (SYN), different words with the same meaning. In the case of 'aunt' versus 'tuna', they were to identify anagrams (scrambled letters, ANA); and in the control condition they were simply identifying whether two sets of four consonants were the same or different. The control condition allows common activity due to reading, visual stimulation and the like, to be subtracted from the other conditions. fMRI was recorded during stimulus exposure in each same-different trial. Comparisons were made within individuals to minimize inter-individual differences. Word stimuli were carefully selected for equal numbers of nouns and verbs in comparison conditions, while other variables like word frequency were controlled statistically.

Figure 11.21 shows the results for the HOM and SYN condition.

6.3 Current evidence about words and their meanings is fragmentary

As Chapter 10 points out, we only know a few brain locations that are differentially sensitive to specific meanings, such as tools, animate versus inanimate objects, and the like. The function of those locations is still unclear. As Moscovitch (1992) has suggested, they could function as *indices* to a wide network of meaning-related connectivities in the neocortex. It is always possible that advances in brain recording methods will reveal a thesaurus-like array of neuronal patches, corresponding to semantic categories (see Chapter 10). But it seems equally likely that word meanings are simply highly distributed, that they are inherently networks, and must therefore mobilize widely distributed regions of cortex.

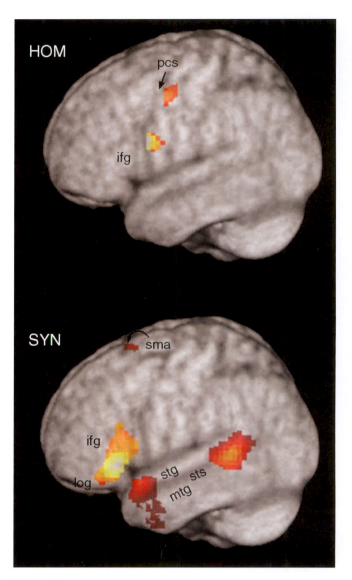

FIGURE 11.21 Word meaning activation in the left hemispheres. Above, fMRI activity for matching homonyms, words with different spelling but the same pronunciations, like 'rain' and 'reign'. Below, matching synonyms, like 'boat' and 'ship'. A control activation pattern elicited by meaningless consonant strings was subtracted from each of the fMRI activation patterns to eliminate brain activities related to reading and other common task features. Meaning-related activation (SYN, below) is far more widespread than homonym matching. Activity is prominent in the superior temporal gyrus and sulcus (STG and STS), and in the tip of the medial temporal gyrus (MTG). The inferior frontal gyrus (IFG) receives activation, as well the lateral orbitofrontal gyrus (LOG). Higher in the left hemisphere for the SYN condition, there is some activation in the supplementary motor area (SMA), a region that is associated with the intention to act. The homonym task (HOM) also shows some activity in the posterior central sulcus (PCS). *Source*: Gitelman *et al.*, 2005.

This is not to say that semantics lacks a specific brain basis. A number of recording methods show high sensitivity to distinctions between words that differ in meaning. So far, however, these methods show very widespread changes in cortex (and elsewhere), as on page 316.

7.0 SYNTAX, NESTING, AND SEQUENCING

Syntax is often said to be the most distinctive aspect of language. Figure 11.23 shows a syntactic tree structure with a subordinate clause. Tree structures can be considered to be recursive, i.e. they can embed sentences within sentences. Although for theoretical reasons it is often supposed that syntactic recursion can go to multiple levels, the human brain is limited to one or two self-embedded clauses. That is presumably because of the capacity limits of working memory. When we develop more elaborate plans, as in the Tower of Hanoi, in chess playing, or in other complex activities, we typically use other memory aids. Thus, the sentence structure in Figure 11.22 is about typical for a single sentence.

The tree structures of sentence syntax resemble the problem-solving spaces discussed in Chapter 10. That is not likely to be an accident. In many ways, syntax gives us a framework for planning the elements of a sentence in much the way we use goals and subgoals to plan a series of actions, like navigating from one place to another, or making moves in a chess game. Syntax can therefore be seen as a cognitive planning tool, but it appears to be something human beings are adapted

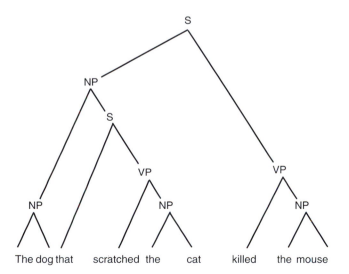

FIGURE 11.22 Syntactic tree structures allow nested propositions. A basic syntactic tree, containing an embedded clause. *Source*: Gitelman *et al.*, 2005.

for. For skilled speakers, the planning of speech is of course mostly implicit (see Chapter 10).

8.0 PROSODY AND MELODY

Speaking and singing are similar activities; physically, singing is just a lengthening and tuning of vowel sounds. If you stretch out the vowels of any word – like 'cognitive neuroscience' – you are already singing in a monotone. Vary the pitch of each syllable, and you have a little song. Like language, music and dance are species-specific capacities for humans. (The biological basis for that is puzzling: language has an obvious survival function, but why music?)

Some sort of musical scale is widely used among many different cultures. All divide up the octave. In Western music, major scales are commonly perceived to be happier than minor scales. Musical notes, like the vowels of language, are based on the physics of resonant tubes, like bamboo flutes, or the tension of a bow string. When the vibrating column of air in a flute is half as long, it sounds an octave higher. When a guitar string is twice as tight, it is also heard as the same note an octave up. Small animals make high-pitched sounds and big ones low ones because of the acoustics of resonant cavities. Thus, there is a physical basis for sound perception with biological implications. It makes more sense to run away if you hear the roar of a lion than the chirp of a cricket.

Human speech also conveys emotion via intonation and sound quality. Depressed people tend to show a declining intonation contour, perhaps reflecting a lower level of subglottal air pressure. Joy is often signalled with upward inflexions of sound. Emotional expression musical intervals. Dividing up the octave is universal, though different musical cultures do it differently. Emotional expression and signaling may precede and later co-evolve with denotative language. Different musical intervals – i.e. two-tone sequences – seem to have different emotional meanings.

Even rhythm is an aspect of normal speech, as we can see in the stress pattern of spoken sentences: 'The *rain*/ in *Spain*/ falls *mainly*/ in the *plain*/'. You can intuitively mark the stressed syllables in any sentence. Even languages that minimize syllable stress, like French, still give a melodic shape to phrases. Babies babble in singsong, and adults spontaneously speak to young children (and pets) using exaggerated intonation. While different cultures have different musical forms, it seems likely that there are some universal (probably biological) connections between language and music.

BOX 11.3   Some basics of syntax

Table 1

The building blocks of syntactic knowledge

Operation	Description	Examples

Basic relationships among words and phrases

Operation	Description	Examples
LEX	Lexical relations that have syntactic relevance. For example, an argument structure of a verb – the type and number of arguments that natural language predicates require.	1. argument: *He* ran/slept/died 2. arguments: *He* saw/hit/followed *Mary* 3. arguments: *He* gave/sent/mailed *Sue presents*
MERGE	A class of highly constrained structure-building operations, which analyze sentences into hierarchical structures. This example shows how syntactic *MERGE* rules build a sentence from the set of lexical categories ('numeration'). *MERGE* creates phrasal nodes (NP = noun phrase, VP = verb phrase, PP = prepositional phrase) out of merged categories (DETerminer, Noun, Verb, Preposition), which are in turn merged into a 'root', sentence node.	Numeration: (DET = *a, the*; N = *man, woman, tree*; V = *saw*; P = *near*) Result of Iterated MERGE:

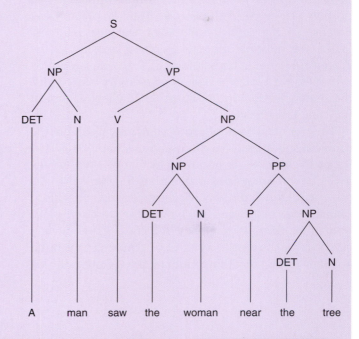

Dependency relations within a sentence

Operation	Description	Examples
MOVE$_{XP}$	A central syntactic operation on trees (created by *MERGE*). It links an audible phrase XP (=NP,VP,PP) to one or more silent, yet syntactically active, position(s) '■' in the representation of the same sentence.	Sam knows that the saw the ballet dancer on Monday ⇒ Which dancer does Sam know that he saw ■ on Monday?
MOVE$_V$	A movement relationship that links distinct positions a verb might occupy. Only one is audible; the rest are silent ('◆'). This relation is shown in English yes/no questions, and in German, in which the verb 'sah' (saw) and its participle 'gesehen' (seen) occupy different positions.	*English*: John is tall ⇒ Is John ◆ tall? *German*: Hans hat Maria gesehen ⇒ Hans sah Maria ◆ ⇒ Gestem Sah Hans ◆ Maria ◆
BIND	A relationship that determines how reflexives and pronouns link to other NPs, on which they depend for reference, in the same sentence.	John looked at himself Mary asked John to help her

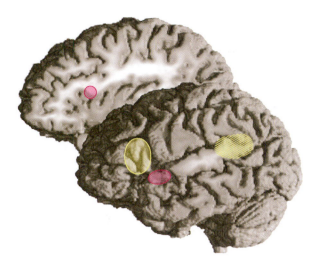

FIGURE 11.23 Syntax evokes distinctive brain regions. Grodzinsky and Friederici (2006) suggest that different cortical regions support different syntactic functions, as indicated in the figure. *Source*: Grodzinsky and Friederici, 2006.

9.0 MEANINGFUL STATEMENTS

We do not speak in single words, but in propositions – i.e. in semantically meaningful statements about the world. Syntax is tailored to enable such propositions, but even when syntax is impaired, as in some types of aphasia, people may still be able to think and express themselves propositionally. For example, aphasics may be able to point to desired food, to express discomfort or pleasure, or express any number of 'paralinguistic' statements about themselves and the world. Shastri (2002) has proposed a model of meaningful propositions encoded in a simulated neural network, based on hippocampal and cortical neurons. Figure 11.24 gives an idea of how different neurons might express different parts of a proposition. By coordinating the firing of these neurons (for example, by way of gamma synchrony), one can suggest how full propositions might be expressed in the brain.

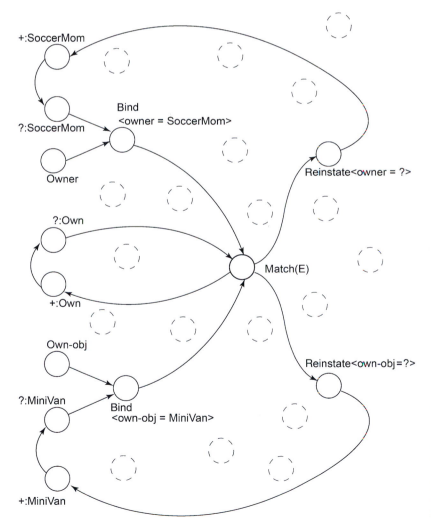

FIGURE 11.24 A proposition may involve a distributed brain network. At the level of neural networks, the proposition, 'Soccer moms are likely to own minivans' may be represented by a collection of neural populations corresponding to the main elements of the proposition: minivans, moms, soccer, relationships like 'owner-of', and the like. Such propositional networks have not been observed in the brain. The model simply suggests neural nets as we understand them. *Source*: Shastri, 2002.

10.0 UNIFIED REPRESENTATIONS OF LANGUAGE

In the 19th century, the psychologist Wilhelm Wundt suggested that language production begins with a *Gesamtvorstellung*, a unified mental representation of a sentence one was about to utter (Blumenthal, 1979). This unified representation would need many different levels of description: semantic, syntactic, phonemic, perhaps vocal, pragmatic (i.e. involving one's goals), and more. Once this many-layered tower of brain activations was ready, it would begin issuing vocal commands to move the parallel structure of the unified representation into a long series of vocal gestures. Figure 11.25 shows a contemporary example of the same basic idea. Notice that there are many simultaneous or overlapping levels of description and control, each presumably reflected in something like a set of neural arrays. In this case, each level is associated with a distinctive signal in the evoked potential (Friederici, 2002). For example, semantic information is known to evoke a large negative wave 400 ms after the onset of a stimulus (called N400).

If that seems awesomely complex, that is probably accurate. It is always useful to remember that language as we know it appears to be a distinctively human achievement. The human lineage separated from other hominids some three million years ago, and it is often suggested that the basic elements of human intelligence, such as language, persistence in problem-solving, cooperative and competitive behavior, and the like, may have emerged on the order of 100 000 years ago. While our vocabulary, for example, is the result of centuries of cultural development, the biological preparedness of our brains and bodies for such developments has many evolutionary layers, some shared with other mammals, others with land-dwelling vertebrates. The kind of complexity we see displayed in Figure 11.25 evolved over many generations.

Chapters 3 and 6 showed that the visual system appears to have at least one region of integration 'where

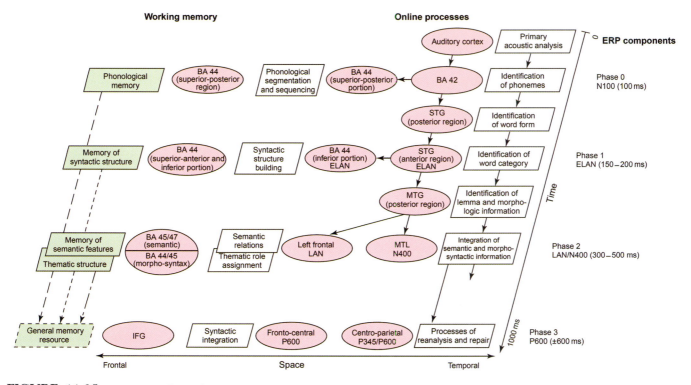

FIGURE 11.25 Putting it all together. A neurocognitive model of auditory sentence processing. The boxes represent the functional processes, the ellipses the underlying neural correlate identified either by fMRI, PET, or ERPs. The neuroanatomical specification (indicated by text in parentheses) is based on either fMRI or PET data. The ERP components specified in their temporal structure (left-hand side) are assigned to their neural correlation by the function rather than the localization of their generator. Abbreviations: BA, Brodmann's area; ELAN, early left-anterior negativity; ERP, event-related brain potential; fMRI, functional magnetic resonance imaging; IFG, inferior frontal gyrus; MTG, middle temporal gyrus; MTL, middle temporal lobe; PET, positron imaging tomography; STG, superior temporal gyrus. *Source*: Friederici, 2002.

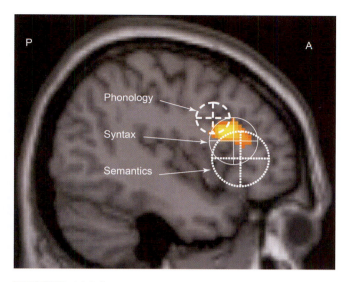

FIGURE 11.26 An area of integration? Hagoort (2005) points out that Broca's area has multiple functions which go beyond the control of speech. Nevertheless, he suggests that an expanded version of Broca's area may be considered an area for unification of speech and semantic information. To avoid confusion with the traditional concept of Broca's area, this part of cortex is referred to by its location as the left inferior frontal gyrus (L-IFG). *Source*: Hagoort, 2005.

everything comes together', that is the inferotemporal cortex (area IT) (Sheinberg and Logothetis, 1997). In that area, neurons respond not to single retinal stimuli, nor to separate features like colors or light edges, but rather to entire visual objects. It is at least possible that language may have a similar region of integration (Figure 11.26).

The notion of a place 'where everything comes together' for some brain function is attractive and can be modeled in neural networks (e.g. McClelland, 1986; Shanahan, 2005) as well as in symbolic models of cognition (Baars and Franklin, 2003). It is an ancient idea, going back at least to Aristotle, who proposed that human cognition must have a way to combine information from the special senses like vision and hearing into single multimodel objects in the world – the guitar that you can see, touch, and listen to (Baars, 1988). Aristotle suggested that there must be a 'common sense' – some central sensory modality that combines all the special senses into a single medium. That is indeed one plausible account of multimodal regions of the parietal and frontal lobes. However, many brain regions show hub-like neuronal connections, ranging from the brainstem reticular formation to the amygdala, entorhinal cortex, prefrontal lobes, and thalamus. Some theorists suggest that the entire cortex, or the thalamo-cortical system, should be viewed as massive networks for integrating, differentiating, and distributing

signals (e.g. Edelman, 1989; Edelman and Tononi, 2000; Freeman, 2004). One can imagine a brain consisting of hubs of hubs, consistent with some of the concepts of consciousness discussed in Chapter 8. Hagoort's notion of the left IFG as one anatomical hub for integrating language and meaning appears to be one version of this general idea. However, as pointed out above, attractive and plausible ideas do not constitute proof, and this hypothesis requires additional evidence.

11.0 SUMMARY

Language is a distinctive human capacity, one that makes it possible to transmit culture across time and space. The brain bases of language are still being clarified, but the discoveries of 19th century neurology continue to be important starting points. Broca's area for speaking and Wernicke's for speech comprehension are only part of large cortical regions involved. Current work has expanded and fractionated the traditional language areas, so that the left inferior frontal gyrus (L-IFG) is a more appropriate term for Broca's area, and posterior auditory and speech regions of the parietal and temporal cortex are more accurate than the term 'Wernicke's area'. However, there is constant interplay between frontal and posterior language areas, and a hard-and-fast division is to some extent artificial. In addition, the evidence is strong that the right hemisphere has its own role to play in language perception.

Each level of linguistic description has neuroimaging evidence in its favor (see Figure 11.1). Nonetheless, we do not have the kind of detailed knowledge of language cortex that we have for vision. One major reason is the absence of an appropriate animal model, like the macaque monkey for vision. However, recent techniques that are appropriate for humans are beginning to approach the right level of detail, and we may soon find such things as speech feature sensitive arrays of neurons, for both speech input and output.

So much of speech and language is dependent on long-term memory, however, that many scientists believe that we must ultimately look for highly distributed cortical networks to account for the vocabulary, syntax and semantics of language. These networks are believed to depend upon the synaptic connectivities of very large numbers of neurons. Current techniques are just beginning to be able to assess such web-like patterns of distributed neurons.

12.0 PRACTICE DRAWINGS AND STUDY QUESTIONS

1. Fill in the labels in Figure 11.27 of processing hierarchies of language.
2. Give examples of the need for 'top-down' or 'expectation-driven' processing in the input flow of speech. What about the output flow?
3. What evidence is there for biological preparedness of human language capacity?
4. In what respects does the human vocal apparatus resemble a musical instrument?

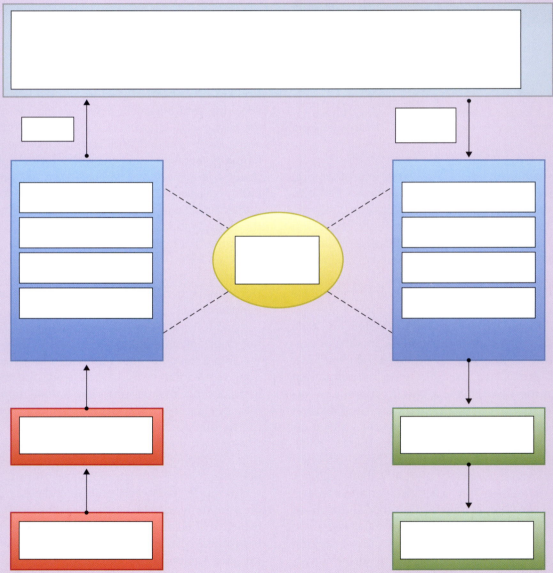

Levels of language processing.

FIGURE 11.27 Linguistic processing hierarchy.

5. In Figure 11.28, show the following:
   a A cortical region likely to be involved in speech perception.
   b One for speech planning.
   c One for motor control of the vocal tract, such as the tongue.
   d One for coordinating perception and production (you may have to draw it in).

6. What role, if any, does the right hemisphere play in language?

7. What is the approximate size of the lexicon (vocabulary of natural language)? What do we know about the organization of this number of words and meanings?

8. Explain a syntactic ambiguity. What do ambiguities imply about the nature of language processing?

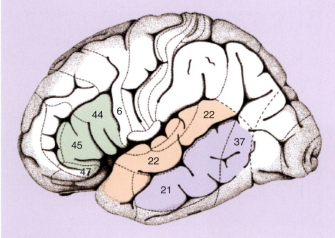

FIGURE 11.28

He is fitful, irreverent, indulging at times in the grossest profanity (which was not previously his custom), manifesting but little deference for his fellows, impatient of restraint or advice when it conflicts with his desires. . . A child in his intellectual capacity and manifestations, he has the animal passions of a strong man. . . His mind was radically changed, so decidedly that his friends and acquaintances said he was 'no longer Gage'.

Harlow JM. Recovery from the passage of an iron bar through the head.
Publ Mass Med Soc 1868; 2: 327–347. Quoted in: *BMJ* 1998; 317: 1673–1674 (19 December)
'No longer Gage': an iron bar through the head.

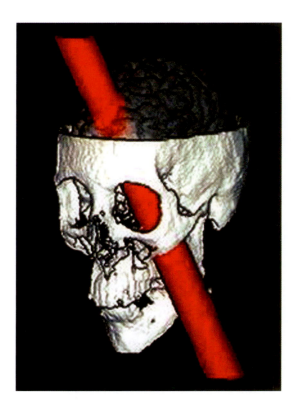

A reconstruction of the injury to Phineas Gage. A reconstruction of Phineas Gage's railroad accident in 1848, when he was 25 years old. Notice likely damage to orbitofrontal and medial frontal regions as well. Injuries like this create damage from swellings, bleeding, heat, infection, inflammation and physical twisting of tissues that extend far beyond the immediate region of impact. Thus, we do not really know the extent of brain damage in this classic neurological patient. *Source*: Squire *et al.*, 2003.

C H A P T E R

12

Goals, executive control, and action

Elkhonon Goldberg and Dmitri Bougakov

1.0 INTRODUCTION

Frontal lobes and executive control: the concept of executive functions or executive control is intimately linked to the function of the frontal lobes. Therefore, the term *(pre)frontal lobe functions* and *executive functions* are often used interchangeably. Nonetheless, not all functions of the frontal lobes fall under the domain of executive control and not all of executive control components are subserved by the frontal lobes *per se*.

From the silent lobes to the organ of civilization: it took scientists many years to begin to appreciate the importance of the frontal lobes for cognition. But when this finally happened, a picture of particular complexity and elegance emerged. For the most part, this chapter will focus on the prefrontal cortex, the most anterior part of the frontal lobes, in front of the motor areas (Figure 12.1).

Prefrontal cortex is located in front of the primary motor cortex, sometimes called the motor strip. The frontal lobes used to be known as 'the silent lobes' because they are not easily linked to any single, easily defined function. Over the last decades, however, new imaging techniques are suggesting more specialized regions within the prefrontal cortex for functions like executive control, conflict monitoring, emotion, and working memory. There is still considerable debate about these issues, however.

Cognition, Brain, and Consciousness, edited by B. J. Baars and N. M. Gage
ISBN: 978-0-12-373677-2

Copyright 2007, Elsevier Ltd. All rights reserved.

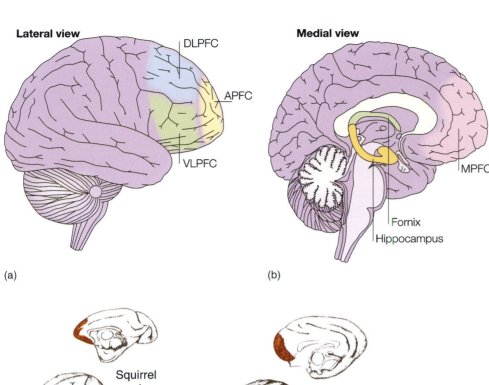

FIGURE 12.1 The major divisions of the prefrontal cortex. Prefrontal cortex can be divided into lateral (side), medial (midline), ventral (bottom) and frontal regions. The lateral division divides into upper (dorsal) and lower (ventral) halves, separated by a major horizontal fold, the inferior lateral sulcus. *Source*: Simon and Spiers, 2003.

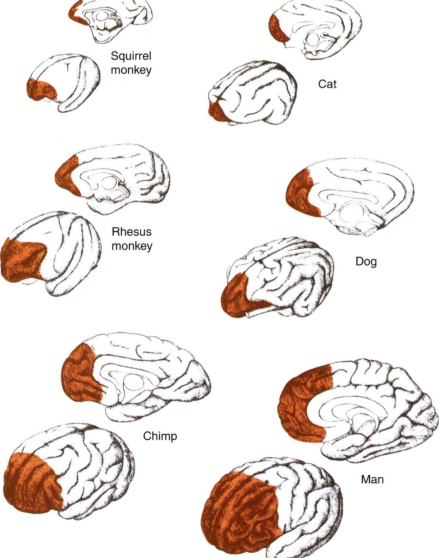

FIGURE 12.2 The prefrontal cortex expands over mammalian and primate evolution. A greatly enlarged prefrontal cortex is a distinctively human and primate feature. Other large-brained mammals like whales and dolphins have expanded parietal rather than prefrontal regions. Bottom right, a human brain, with a chimp brain on the bottom left. *Source*: Squire *et al.*, 2003.

2.0 PHYLOGENY AND ONTOGENY

In evolution, the frontal lobes accelerated in size only with the great apes. These regions of cortex underwent an explosive expansion at the late stage of evolution. According to Brodmann (1909), the prefrontal cortex or its analogs account for 29 per cent of the total cortex in humans, 17 per cent in the chimpanzee, 11.5 per cent in the gibbon and the macaque, 8.5 per cent in the lemur, 7 per cent in the dog and 3.5 per cent in the cat (Figure 12.2). While whales and dolphins have large brains, it is the parietal rather than frontal cortex that has expanded in these aquatic mammals.

As the 'seat' of goals, foresight, and planning, the frontal lobes are perhaps the most uniquely 'human' of all the components of the human brain. In 1928, the neurologist Tilney suggested that all human evolution should be considered the 'age of the frontal lobe', but scientific interest in the prefrontal cortex was late in coming. Only gradually did it begin to reveal its secrets to the great scientists and clinicians like Hughlings Jackson (1884), and Alexander Luria (1966), and in the last few decades to researchers like Antonio Damasio (1993), Joaquin Fuster (1997), Patricia Goldman-Rakic (1987), Donald Stuss and Frank Benson (1986), and others.

3.0 FUNCTION OVERVIEW

The functions of the frontal lobes defy a simple definition. They are not invested with any single, ready-to-label function. A patient with frontal-lobe damage will typically retain the ability to move around, use language, recognize objects, and even memorize information. However, prefrontal cortex plays the central role in forming goals and objectives and then in devising plans of action required to attain these goals. It selects the cognitive skills needed to implement the plans, coordinates these skills, and applies them in a correct order. Finally, the prefrontal cortex is responsible for evaluating our actions as success or failure relative to our intentions (Table 12.1).

Human cognition is forward-looking, *proactive* rather than *reactive*. It is driven by goals, plans, hopes, ambitions and dreams, all of which pertain to the future and not to the past. These cognitive powers depend on the frontal lobes and evolve with them. The frontal lobes endow the organism with the ability to create neural models as a prerequisite for making things happen, models of something that, as of yet, does not exist but

TABLE 12.1 Some common prefrontal functions

1	Planning, setting goals, and initiating action
2	Monitoring outcomes and adapting to errors
3	Mental effort in pursuing difficult goals
4	Interacting with other regions in pursuit of goals (basal ganglia, thalamic nuclei, cerebellum, motor cortex)
5	Having motivation, being willing to engage in action
6	Initiating speech and visual imagery
7	Recognizing others people's goals, engaging in social cooperation and competition
8	Regulating emotional impulses
9	Feeling emotions
10	Storing and updating working memory
11	Active thinking
12	Enabling conscious experiences (Deheane, 2001)
13	Sustained attention in the face of distraction
14	Decision-making, switching attention and changing strategies
15	Planning and sequencing actions
16	Unifying the sound, syntax and meaning of language
17	Resolving competition between plans

Source: Moss *et al.*, 2005

which you *want* to bring into existence. To makes plans of the future, the brain must have an ability to take certain elements of prior experiences and reconfigure them in a way that does not copy any actual past experience or present reality exactly. To accomplish that, the organism must go beyond the mere ability to *form* internal representations, the models of the world outside. It must acquire the ability to *manipulate and transform* these models. One can argue that tool-making, one of the fundamental distinguishing features of primate cognition, depends on this ability, since a tool does not exist in a ready-made form in the natural environment and has to be *imagined* in order to be made. The neural machinery for creating and holding 'images of the future' was a *necessary prerequisite* for tool-making, and thus for launching human civilization.

One can also argue that the generative power of language to create new ideas depends on this ability as well. The ability to manipulate and recombine internal representations depends critically on the prefrontal cortex, which probably made it critical for the development of language.

Goal formation is about 'I need' and not about 'it is'. Therefore, the ability to formulate goals must have been inexorably linked to the emergence of the mental representation of self. It should come as no surprise that *self-awareness* is also intricately linked to the frontal lobes.

All these functions can be thought of as metacognitive rather than cognitive, since they do not refer to any particular mental skill, but provide an overarching organization for all of them. For this reason, some authors refer to the functions of the frontal lobes as *executive functions*, by analogy with a governmental or corporate executive.

4.0 CLOSER LOOK AT FRONTAL LOBES

4.1 Gross anatomy and connections

On the surface of cerebral cortex the following boundaries are used to delimit the frontal lobes: on the

dorsolateral surface of the brain they lie just in front of the demarcation line formed by the *lateral* (or *Sylvian*) *fissure* and the *central sulcus*; medially, the boundaries are roughly formed by the continuation of the central sulcus to the mediodorsal surface of the brain, and by an imaginary line corresponding to a projection of the lateral fissure to the medioventral surface of the brain (Carpenter and Parent, 1995).

The prefrontal cortex is directly connected with every distinct functional unit of the brain (Nauta, 1972). It is connected to the highest levels of perceptual integration,

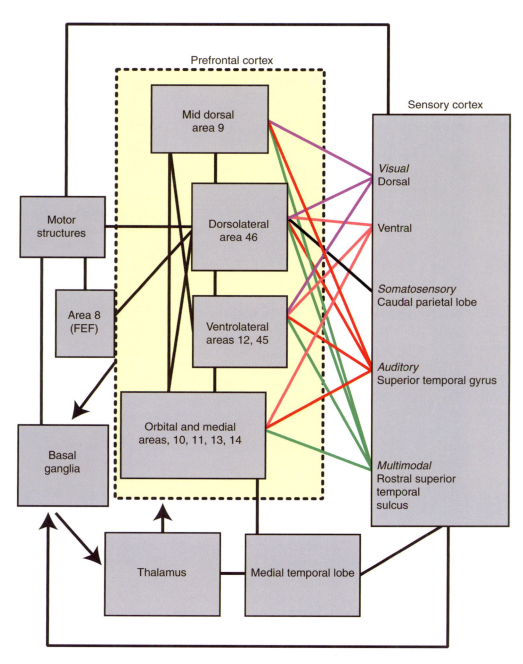

FIGURE 12.3 The major connections of the frontal lobes. The prefrontal lobes (inside the yellow box) and its prolific connections. Among its many functions we focus mainly on the executive ones. *Source*: Squire *et al.*, 2003.

and also with the *premotor cortex*, *basal ganglia* and the *cerebellum*, all involved in aspects of motor control and movements. Prefrontal cortex is also connected with the *dorsomedial thalamic nucleus*, often considered to be the highest level of integration within the thalamus; with the *hippocampi* and *medial temporal structures*, known to be critical for memory; and with the *cingulate cortex*, believed to be critical for emotion and dealing with uncertainty. In addition, prefrontal cortex connects with the *amygdala*, which regulates most emotions and social cognition, and with the *hypothalamus*, in charge of control over the vital homeostatic functions of the body. Finally, prefrontal cortex is also well-connected with the *brainstem* nuclei involved in wakefulness, arousal, and overall alertness, regulation of sleep and REM dreams. A schematic (and by no means exhaustive) representation of this complex connectivity is depicted in Figure 12.3.

This unique connectivity makes the frontal lobes singularly suited for coordinating and integrating the work of other brain structures (Figure 12.4). This extreme connectivity also puts the frontal lobes at a particular risk for disease. Some scientists believe that the prefrontal cortex contains a map of the whole cortex, an assertion first made by Hughlings Jackson (1884) at the end of the 19th century. This hypothesis asserts that prefrontal regions are needed for normal consciousness. Since any aspect of our mental world may, in principle, be the focus of our consciousness, it stands to reason that an area of convergence of all its neural substrates must exist. This leads to the provocative proposition that the evolution of consciousness, the highest expression of the developed brain, parallels the evolution of the prefrontal cortex.

4.2 How prefrontal cortex is defined

A more precise definition of prefrontal cortex can be accomplished by using *Brodmann area* maps (Brodmann, 1909). Brodmann areas are based on the types of neurons and connections that are typically found there within. According to this definition, the prefrontal cortex consists of Brodmann areas 8, 9, 10, 11, 12, 13, 44, 45, 46 and 47 (Fuster, 1997) (Figure 12.5). These areas are characterized by the predominance of the so-called 'granular' neural cells found mostly in layer IV (Campbell, 1905, in Fuster, 1997).

Another method of outlining the prefrontal cortex is through its subcortical projections. The dorsomedial thalamic nucleus is, in a sense, the point of convergence, the 'summit' of the integration occurring within the specific thalamic nuclei (Figure 12.6). Prefrontal cortex is then defined as the area receiving projections from the dorsomedial thalamic nucleus.

Finally, the prefrontal cortex is sometimes delineated through its biochemical pathways. According to that definition, the prefrontal cortex is defined as the area receiving projections from the mesocortical dopamine system. The various methods of delineating the prefrontal cortex outline roughly similar territories.

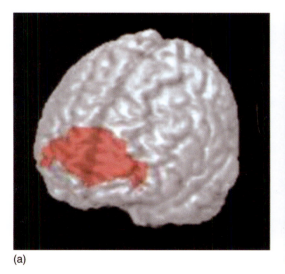
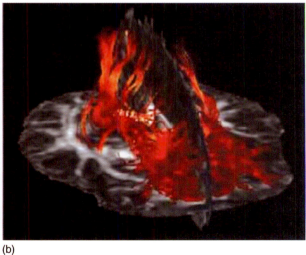

(a)   (b)

FIGURE 12.4 Some detailed connectivity of the anterior frontal lobe. The massive connectivity of the frontal lobes is suggested by this tractograph of the fiber tracts to Brodmann 10 (a). The red and dark vertical fibers show only the ipsilateral (same side) connections. In addition, there are connections between the two sides, traveling across the corpus callosum, and many local loops. *Source*: Thottakkara *et al.*, 2006.

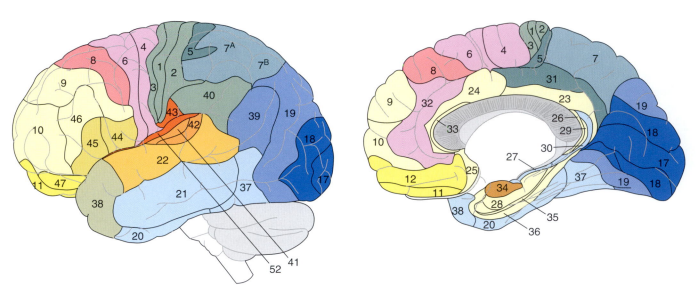

FIGURE 12.5 Brodmann areas in the frontal lobes. Areas forward of motor cortex are considered to be prefrontal. (Brodmann areas 4 and 6 are motor and premotor regions.) However, the boundary is not rigid. It is often useful to think of a gradual transition between more 'cognitive' areas and primary motor cortex (BA 4), which directly controls voluntary muscles. *Source:* Drawn by Shawn, Fu, after M. Dubin, with permission.

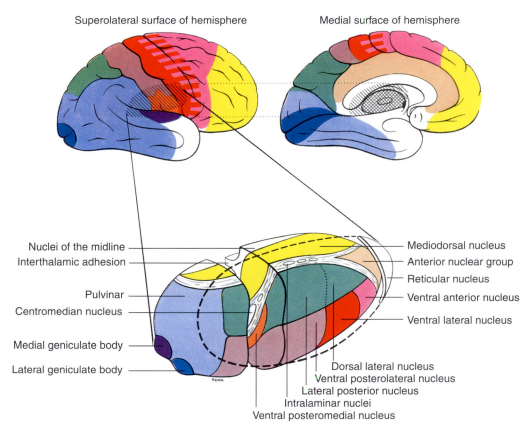

FIGURE 12.6 Prefrontal cortex is also defined by major thalamic connections. The yellow cortical areas are considered to be prefrontal because of their connections with mediodorsal nucleus of the thalamus. Many scientists believe that the connections between cortex and thalamus are so close and intimate that thalamic nuclei can be considered to be additional layers of cortex. Thus, we are looking at a thalamo-cortical system. *Source*: Standring, 2005.

5.0 A CLOSER LOOK AT FRONTAL LOBE FUNCTION

5.1 Traditional perspective on frontal lobe function: motor functions, actions and plans

As mentioned earlier, currently, the concept of executive functions is inextricably linked to the function of the frontal lobes. The groundwork for defining the executive functions system was laid by Alexander Luria as early as 1966 (Luria, 1966). At the time, Luria proposed the existence of a system in charge of intentionality, the formulation of goals, the plans of action subordinate to the goals, the identification of goal-appropriate cognitive routines, the sequential access to these routines, the temporally ordered transition from one routine to another, and the editorial evaluation of the outcome of our actions (Figure 12.7).

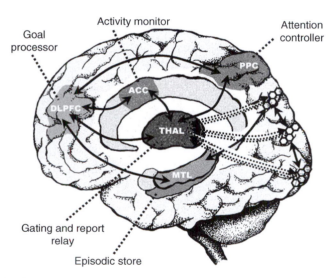

FIGURE 12.7 Prefrontal lobes coordinates goals and actions. An integrated model of goal processing in the prefronal cortex (the dorsolateral part), connecting to the anterior cingulate to resolve conflicts. Memory is involved in retrieving stored action plans and contextual information (temporal lobe and MTL), and the posterior parietal cortex is considered as a control of spatial attention, needed for actions. The thalamus serves as a hub for multiple functions. *Source*: Schneider and Chein, 2003.

Subsequently, two broad types of cognitive operations linked to the executive system figured most prominently in the literature:

1 an organism's ability to guide its behavior by internal representations (Goldman-Rakic, 1987) – the formulation of plans and then guiding behavior according to these plans

2 an organism's ability not only to guide its behavior by internal representations, but also the capacity of 'switching gears' when something unexpected happens (Milner, 1982).

To deal effectively with such transitions, a particular ability is needed – *mental flexibility* – that is the capacity to respond rapidly to unanticipated environmental contingencies (Figure 12.8). Sometimes this is referred to as an ability to shift *cognitive set*. Additionally, the executive system is critical for planning and the generative processes (Goldberg, 2001).

Fuster (1997) enlarged on the premise originally developed by Luria by suggesting that the so-called 'executive systems' can be considered functionally 'homogeneous' in the sense that they are in charge of actions, both external and internal (such as logical

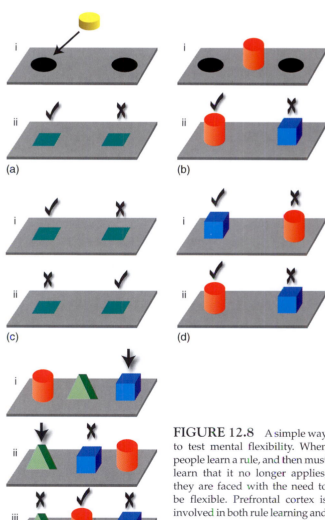

FIGURE 12.8 A simple way to test mental flexibility. When people learn a rule, and then must learn that it no longer applies, they are faced with the need to be flexible. Prefrontal cortex is involved in both rule learning and unlearning. Patients with prefrontal damage have difficulties changing their minds. *Source*: Miller and Wallis, 2003.

reasoning). In general, the executive functions are not unique to humans. However, the uniqueness of the human executive functions is in the *extent* to which they are capable of integrating such factors as time, informational novelty, and complexity, and possibly ambiguity.

Currently, an ever-increasing body of research is being dedicated to the study of executive functions, particularly to the investigation of one aspect of executive functions, *working memory*. In the study of working memory, two main lines of scientific inquiry can be clearly discerned: one guided by a premise of *domain specificity* and the other guided by the premise of *process specificity*. According to the domain specificity theory, different regions of prefrontal cortex process different types of information, for instance, spatial information versus object information (Goldman-Rakic, 1987, 1998). This theory is an extension of the object versus spatial ('what' versus 'where') visual processing streams found in posterior cortices (Mishkin *et al.*, 1983). According to the process specificity theory, which draws on earlier human lesion studies (Petrides and Milner, 1982), different regions of the brain are responsible for maintenance and manipulation of information (Petrides, 1994, 1995).

6.0 MEMORIES OF THE FUTURE

David Ingvar (1985) coined a phrase: 'Memory of the future'. Ingvar was referring to one of the most important functions of advanced organisms: making plans and then following the plans to guide behavior. Unlike primitive organisms, humans are active, rather than reactive, beings. The transition from mostly reactive to mostly proactive behavior is among the central themes of the evolution of the nervous system. We are able to form goals, our visions of the future. Then we act according to our goals. But, in order to guide our behavior in a sustained fashion, these mental images of the future must become the content of our memory; thus the 'memories of the future' are formed.

We anticipate the future based on our past experiences and act according to our anticipations. The ability to organize behavior in time and to extrapolate in time is also the responsibility of the frontal lobes. Patients with frontal-lobe damage are notorious for their inability to plan and to anticipate the consequences of their actions. Damage to other parts of the brain does not seem to affect these abilities. A subtle impairment of planning and foresight is often among the first signs of dementia.

BOX 12.1   Current debates about the specificity of working memory in prefrontal cortex

Prefrontal cortex is believed to be needed for working memory – but which aspects? Are specific prefrontal regions responsible for specific functions? Figure 12.9 shows one set of viable hypotheses (Rees *et al.*, 2002).

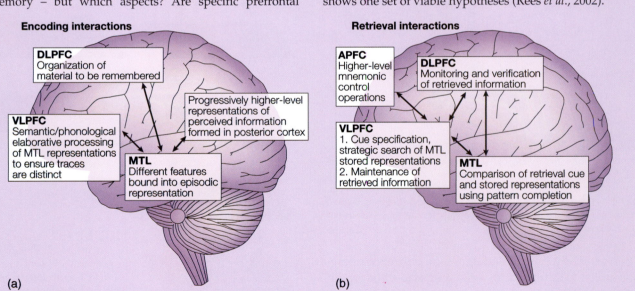

FIGURE 12.9   Rees *et al.* (2002) distinguish between three parts of the prefrontal cortex (PFC), ventrolateral (lower side) or VL, dorsolateral (upper side) or DL, and anterior (front) PFC. A number of scientists believe these regions have distinct functions, although debate continues about the degree of specificity. In addition, the MTL (medial temporal lobe) plays a central role in episodic or autobiographical memory (see Chapter 9). The figure suggests how these four brain territories might work together. *Source*: Simon and Spiers, 2003.

It is often present in other conditions, usually reflecting frontal lobe dysfunction.

7.0 NOVELTY AND ROUTINE

Another function that is currently being linked to the prefrontal cortex is an ability to deal with *cognitive novelty* (Goldberg *et al.*, 1994). Positron emission tomography (PET) experiments by Raichle and his colleagues highlight the relationship between the frontal lobes and novelty very dramatically (Raichle *et al.*, 1994). When the task in the experiment was first introduced, the blood flow in the frontal lobes reached its highest level. As the subjects' familiarization with the task increased, frontal-lobe involvement all but disappeared (Figure 12.10). When a new task was introduced, generally resembling the first task but not exactly like it, frontal blood flow increased somewhat but did not quite reach its initial level. To the extent that blood flow levels are correlated with neural activity (which most scientists believe to be the case), these experiments provide strong and direct evidence about the role of the frontal lobes in dealing with cognitive novelty.

A more general theory links cognitive novelty with the right hemisphere (Goldberg and Costa, 1981). According to this theory, the special role played by the frontal lobes and the right hemisphere in dealing with novelty and by the left hemisphere in implementing routines suggests that the dynamic changes associated with learning are at least twofold. With learning, the locus of cognitive control shifts from the right hemisphere to the left hemisphere, and from the frontal to the posterior parts of the cortex.

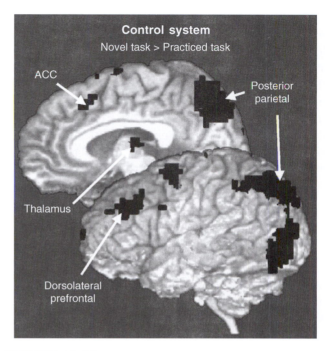

FIGURE 12.10 Novelty and automaticity. The dark areas in this composite brain image show regions that control novel actions, but which lose activity when the identical action becomes automatic with practice. When the task is changed again to become new, these areas tend to 'light up' again, confirming that they are involved in explicit control of actions. *Source*: Schneider and Chein, 2003.

This dual phenomenon was dramatically demonstrated in several functional neuroimaging studies (Gold *et al.*, 1996; Kamiya *et al.*, 2002). A compelling demonstration of this phenomenon provided in a study by Kamiya *et al.* (2002) is schematically depicted in Figure 12.11.

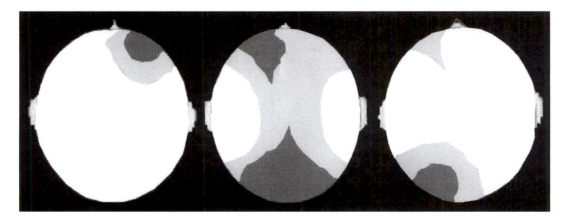

FIGURE 12.11 Prefrontal cortex and novelty. With task familiarity, cognitive control shifts from the right hemisphere to the left side, and from the frontal to the posterior cortex. *Source*: Goldberg and Bougakov, 2000.

In the old literature, the right hemisphere was referred to as the 'minor hemisphere' and the frontal lobes as the 'silent lobes'. Today, we know that these structures are neither minor nor silent. The functions of the right hemisphere are less transparent than the functions of the left hemisphere, and the functions of the frontal lobes are less transparent than the functions of the posterior cortex precisely because they deal with situations defying easy codification and reduction to an algorithm.

8.0 AMBIGUITY AND ACTOR-CENTERED COGNITION

In our everyday life, we encounter two types of situations that require two different ways to address them. Situations like balancing a checkbook, remembering a phone number or a name are *deterministic*. Each of them has a single correct solution intrinsic in the situation, all the other responses being false. By finding the correct solution, we engage in *veridical decision-making*.Situations like deciding what to wear, which movie to see or which career path to choose are *ambiguous*. They do not have an intrinsically correct solution. By making our choice, we engage in *adaptive* (or *actor-centered*) *decision-making*.

In school, we are given a problem and must find the correct answer. Only one correct answer usually exists. But aside from high school exams, college tests, and factual and computational trivia, most decisions we make in our everyday lives do not have intrinsically correct solutions. The choices we make are not inherent in the situations at hand. They are a complex interplay between the properties of the situations and our own properties, our aspirations, our doubts, and our histories. The prefrontal cortex is central to such decision-making. Finding solutions for deterministic situations is often accomplished algorithmically. It is increasingly delegated to various devices: calculators, computers, directories of all kinds, but making choices in the absence of inherently correct solutions remains, at least for now, a uniquely human territory. In a sense, the freedom of choice is possible only when ambiguity is present.

Resolving ambiguity often means choosing the question first, i.e. reducing the situation to a question which does have a single correct answer. Precisely how we disambiguate the situation depends on our priorities at the moment, which themselves may change depending on the context. An inability to reduce ambiguity leads to vacillating, uncertain, inconsistent behavior.

At the same time, an individual must have the flexibility to adopt different perspectives on the same situation at different times. The organism must be able to disambiguate the same situation in a multiple of different ways and to have the capacity to switch between them at will. Dealing with inherent ambiguity is among the foremost functions of the frontal lobes. Studies have shown that patients with frontal-lobe damage approach inherently ambiguous situations differently from the way healthy people do. The loss of the ability to make decisions is among the most common signs of early dementia. Damage to other parts of the brain does not seem to affect these processes.

In summary, veridical decisions deal with 'finding the truth', and adaptive, actor-centered decisions deal with choosing 'what is good for me'. The cognitive processes involved in resolving ambiguous situations through priorities are very different from those involved in solving strictly deterministic situations. Ironically, cognitive ambiguity and priority-based decision-making was, until recently, ignored in cognitive neuropsychology. Only relatively recently have a number of experimental paradigms been developed to study non-veridical cognition. One of the procedures designed to tap adaptive decision-making is called *the Cognitive Bias Task* (CBT) (Goldberg *et al.*, 1994) (Figure 12.12). It is a response selection task based on preference rather than correctness. This 'cognitive projective' paradigm proves to be very informative.

In one experiment, healthy individuals and patients with various types of brain damage were tested. Damage to the frontal lobes dramatically changed the nature of responses. Damage to other parts of the brain had very little or no effect. Then the experiment was repeated in a disambiguated form. Instead of instructing the subjects to 'Make the choice you like the best', they were asked to 'Make the choice most similar to the target', and then to do it again, this time making the choice 'most different from the target'. In disambiguated conditions, the effects of frontal lesions disappeared and the subjects with a frontal brain lesion could perform the task as well as the healthy controls!

This experiment shows that the frontal lobes are critical in a free-choice situation, *when it is up to the subject to decide how to interpret an ambiguous situation*. Once the situation has been disambiguated for the subject and the task has been reduced to the computation of the only correct response possible, the input of the frontal lobes is no longer critical, even though all the other aspects of the task remain the same.

Of all the aspects of the human mind none are more intriguing than *intentionality*, and *volition*. But these

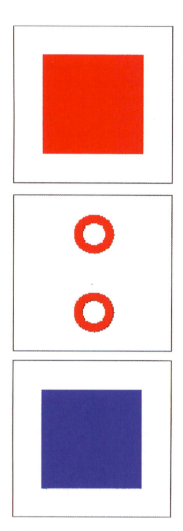

FIGURE 12.12 The Cognitive Bias Task is designed to reflect everyday preference judgments, which are complex, context-sensitive and mostly implicit. The CBT may be more sensitive to prefrontal damage than simpler decision tasks. *Source*: E. Goldberg.

attributes of human mind are fully at play only in situations affording multiple choices. Numerous assertions have been made by philosophers and scientists that volition and intentionality are uniquely human traits. In its absolute form, this claim cannot appeal to a rigorous neurobiologist. It is more likely that these properties of the mind have developed gradually through evolution, possibly following an exponential course. An argument can be made that this process paralleled the development of the frontal lobes.

Adaptive decision-making declines before veridical decision-making at early stages of dementia (Goldberg *et al.*, 1997). When the Cognitive Bias Task and its disambiguated, veridical analog is administered to patients

at different stages of Alzheimer's type dementia, performance on the actor-centered, preference-based version of the task shows decline much earlier in the disease process than the performance on the veridical, 'match to similarity' version.

9.0 WORKING MEMORY AND WORKING *WITH* MEMORY

In a typical memory study, a subject is asked to memorize a list of words, a series of pictures of faces, and then to recall or recognize the material under various conditions. The subject memorizes certain information because the examiner instructs him to – what to recall is up to the examiner and not the subject.

However, in most real-life situations we store and recall information, not for the sake of recall itself, but as a prerequisite for solving a problem at hand. Furthermore, certain memories are accessed and retrieved not in response to an external command coming from someone else, but in response to an internally generated need. Instead of being told what to recall, we have to decide for ourselves which information is useful in the context of our ongoing activities at the moment. In other words, in real life memory usually involves *selection*.

Therein lies a crucial difference between a typical memory experiment and the way memory is used in real life. In real life, we are to make the decision what to remember. In a typical memory experiment, the decision is made for us by the examiner. By shifting the decision-making process from the individual to the examiner, to a large extent, we remove the role of the frontal lobes. Most real life acts of recall involve working memory and the frontal lobes, but most procedures used in memory research and to examine patients with memory disorders do not.

The disparity between the way memory functions and the way it is studied helps explain the confusion about the role of the frontal lobes in memory. An inconclusive debate on the subject has been going on for years, since the subject was first raised by C. F. Jacobsen at an international conference in 1935 and Luria (1966). In large measure due to the work of the neuroscientists Patricia Goldman-Rakic (1987) and Joaquin Fuster (1997), the role of the frontal lobes in memory has been reasserted and the concept of 'working memory' gained prominence. Working memory is closely linked to the critical role the frontal lobes play in the temporal organization of behavior and controlling the proper sequence

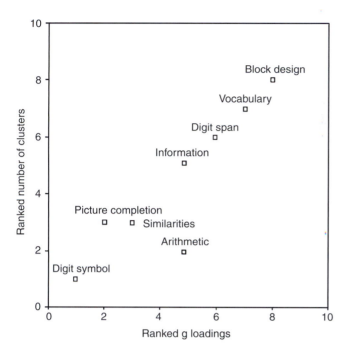

FIGURE 12.13 Mental effort, gray matter and general intelligence. Mental effort is involved in general intelligence, sometimes called the 'g-factor' because it involves a common factor loading between different measures of general intelligence. Executive effort or persistence in problem-solving may be a brain correlate of g (Duncan and Owen, 2000). However, Colom et al. (2006) argue that general intelligence also correlates with the amount of cortical gray matter. This is presumably a measure of the number of cells in the cortex. Thus, general intelligence may involve both executive control and the processing capacity provided by many cortical neurons. *Source*: Colom *et al.*, 2006.

frequently deal with several problems in parallel. This highlights a very peculiar feature of working memory: its constantly and rapidly changing content.

The paradox of working memory is that even though the frontal lobes are critical for accessing and activating task-relevant information, they do not themselves contain this information – other parts of the brain do. To demonstrate this relationship, Patricia Goldman-Rakic and her colleagues studied delayed responses in the monkey (Funahashi *et al.*, 1989). They recorded neurons in the monkey frontal lobes, which fire as long as a memory trace must be 'held on' to, but stop firing once the response has been initiated. These neurons are involved in keeping a memory trace 'on line', but not in the storage of the memory itself.

Different parts of the prefrontal cortex are involved in different aspects of working memory, and a peculiar parallelism exists between the functional organization of the frontal lobes and the posterior cortical regions. Apparently, different aspects of working memory are under the control of different regions within the frontal lobes. Nonetheless, the area around the *frontal poles*, the furthermost forward extension of the frontal lobe, Brodmann area 10, has so far eluded most attempts to characterize its function in specific terms. It is possible that the areas immediately surrounding the frontal poles serve a particularly synthetic function and superimpose an additional level of neural hierarchy over the dorso-lateral and orbitofrontal cortical regions.

in which various mental operations are enacted to meet the organism's objective (Fuster, 1985).

Since the selection of the information required to solve the problem at hand is made in the frontal lobes, they must 'know', at least roughly, where in the brain this information is stored. This suggests that all the cortical regions are somehow represented in the frontal lobes, an assertion first made by Hughlings Jackson (1884). Such representation is probably coarse, rather than specific, enabling the frontal lobes to know what type of information is stored where, but not the specific information itself. The frontal lobes then contact the appropriate parts of the brain and bring the memory trace 'on-line', by activating the circuitry that embodies it.

Since different stages of solving a problem may require different types of information, the frontal lobes must constantly, and rapidly, bring new engrams on-line, while letting go of the old ones. Furthermore, we must often make rapid transitions from one cognitive task to another, and to make things even more challenging, we

10.0 THEORY OF MIND AND INTELLIGENCE

What do we mean by the terms 'intelligent' and 'obtuse'? And what are the brain structures whose individual variations determine these global traits?

Many scientists suggest there may be multiple intelligences, ranging from social to verbal and spatial. However, these capacities may share a single common factor of executive intelligence that we intuitively recognize as 'being smart'. The 'executive talent' shapes our perception of a person as a human being, not just as a carrier of a certain cognitive trait (Shaw *et al.*, 2006). Executive intelligence may also allow us to have insight into, and to anticipate the behavior, motives and intentions of other people. Given the social nature of human beings, this ability is of great importance.

In the earlier description of the essential executive functions, we emphasized their sequential, planning, and temporal ordering aspects. Now imagine that you have to plan and sequentially organize *your* actions in coordination with a group of other individuals and institutions engaged in the planning and sequential organization of *their* actions. To succeed in this interaction, you must not only be able to have an action plan of your own, but you must also have an insight into the nature of the other fellow's plan. You must not only be able to foresee the consequences of your own actions, but you must also foresee the consequences of the other fellow's actions. To do that, you must have the capacity to form an internal representation of the other person's mental life or to use the high language of cognitive neuropsychology to form the *theory of mind* of the other person (see Chapter 13). Your own actions will then be chosen under the influence of your theory of the next person's mind formulated in your own mind. And other group members presumably will have a theory of *your* mind formulated in *their* heads. The relative success of each of you will largely depend of the accuracy and degree of precision of your abilities to form the internal representation of the other. This makes the executive processes required for success in an interactive environment much more complex than the executive processes required in a solitary situation, for example while solving a puzzle. This is true for competition, cooperation and mixed situations.

When, in a number of studies, normal subjects were asked to imagine the mental states of other people while their brains were being scanned with PET or fMRI, invariably, particular activation was found in the medial and lateral inferior prefrontal cortex (Frith and Frith, 1999).

11.0 FRONTAL LOBE PATHOLOGY, EXECUTIVE IMPAIRMENT, AND SOCIAL IMPLICATIONS OF FRONTAL LOBE DYSFUNCTION

11.1 The fragile frontal lobes

Frontal lobe dysfunction often reflects more than direct damage to the frontal lobes (Goldberg, 1992). The frontal lobes seem to be the bottleneck, the point of convergence of the effects of damage virtually anywhere in the brain. There is a reciprocal relationship between frontal and other brain injuries. Damage to the frontal lobes produces wide ripple effects through the whole brain. At the same time, damage anywhere in the brain sets off ripple effects interfering with frontal lobe function. This unique feature of the frontal lobes reflects its role as the 'traffic hub' of the nervous system, with a singularly rich set of connections to and from other brain structures. This makes frontal lobe dysfunction the most common and least specific finding among neurological, psychiatric, and neurodevelopmental conditions (Goldberg, 1992).

The frontal lobes' exceptionally low 'functional breakdown threshold' is consistent with Hughlings Jackson's concept of 'evolution and dissolution' (1884). According to Jackson's proposal, the phylogenetically youngest brain structures are the first to succumb to brain disease. The frontal lobes' unique vulnerability is probably the flip side of the exceptional richness of their connections. A frontal lobe dysfunction does not always signify a direct frontal lobe *lesion*. Instead, it may be a remote effect of a diffuse, distributed or distant lesion.

11.2 Frontal lobe syndromes

The importance of executive functions can be best appreciated through the analysis of their disintegration following brain damage. A patient with damaged frontal lobes retains, at least to a certain degree, the ability to exercise most cognitive skills in isolation (Luria, 1966). Basic abilities such as reading, writing, simple computations, verbal expression, and movements, may remain largely unimpaired. Deceptively, the patient will perform well on the psychological tests measuring these functions in isolation. However, any synthetic activity requiring the coordination of many cognitive skills into a coherent, goal-directed process will become severely impaired.

Damage to different parts of the frontal lobes produces distinct, clinically different syndromes. The most common among them are the *dorsolateral* and *orbitofrontal syndromes* (Goldberg and Costa, 1985).

Most common symptoms of dorsolateral frontal syndrome are *perseverative behavior* and *field-dependent behavior*. Clinically, a patient with dorsolateral frontal syndrome will be characterized by impaired ability to initiate behaviors. He or she tends to show 'flat affect' – i.e. monotonous speech and sense of indifference. The patient is neither sad nor happy; in a sense, he has no mood. This state of indifference persists no matter what happens to the patient, good things or bad. However, the most conspicuous feature of a patient with dorsolateral syndrome is a drastically impaired ability to initiate behaviors. Once started in a behavior, however, the patient is equally unable to terminate or change it on his/her own. Such combined 'inertia of initiation and termination' is seen in various disorders affecting the frontal lobes, including chronic schizophrenia.

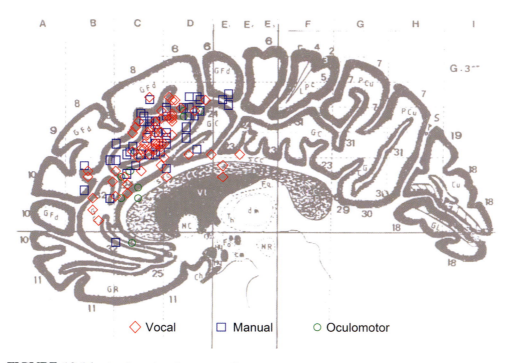

◇ Vocal   □ Manual   ○ Oculomotor

FIGURE 12.14 Conflictual and emotion affect anterior cingulate cortex. Just above the white loop of the corpus callosum is the cingulate cortex. The figure summarizes a number of studies showing how the forward half of the cingulate becomes active in a variety of conflict tasks. The ACC (anterior cingulate cortex) may be involved in conflict monitoring and detection, and perhaps in the integration of non-conflicting inputs. Conflicting input or output signals are a common feature of the human cognitive architecture, which excels in resolving ambiguities and making decisions between alternative courses of action. *Source*: Botrinick *et al.*, 2004.

Following even relatively mild head trauma, it is common for patients to become indifferent and devoid of initiative and drive. The change may be subtle, and it is not always apparent to family members or even physicians that the change is neurological in nature, that it is a mild form of the frontal lobe syndrome. These symptoms are often called 'personality change', but 'personality' is determined to a large extent by neurobiology. The frontal lobes have more to do with our 'personalities' than any other part of the brain, and frontal lobe damage can produce profound personality change.

11.2.1 Utilization syndrome – losing autonomy from environmental stimuli

Another common symptom of the dorsolateral prefrontal syndrome is that the patient is at the mercy of incidental distractions and thus is unable to follow internally generated plans. In extreme cases it may take the form of 'field-dependent behavior'. A frontal lobe patient will drink from an empty cup, put on a jacket belonging to someone else, or scribble with a pencil on the table surface, merely because the cup, the jacket and the pencil are there, even though these actions make no sense. This phenomenon was studied extensively by the French neurologist Francois Lhermitte, who called it *utilization behavior* (Lhermitte, 1983). In the most extreme cases, field-dependent behavior takes the form of direct imitation, called *echolalia* (imitation of speech) or *echopraxia* (imitation of action).

Such patients will perform particularly poorly (Stuss *et al.*, 2001) on the *Stroop Test* (Stroop, 1935). What makes the Stroop Test so interesting? It requires that we go against our immediate impulse. The impulse is to read the words; this is the natural tendency of every literate person when you see written material. But the task is to name the colors. To complete the task successfully, we must follow the internal plan, the task, *against our natural, entrenched tendency* (see also Chapters 2 and 8).

When neurological illness affects the frontal lobes, the ability to 'stay on track' often becomes lost, and the

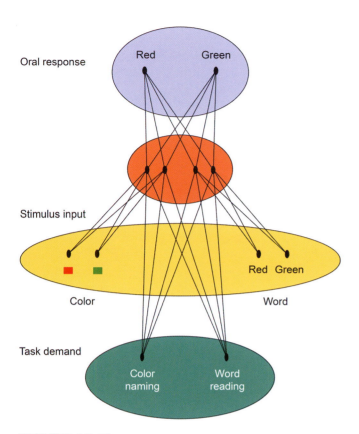

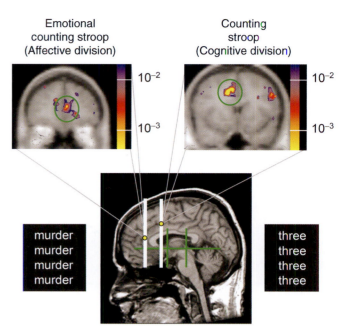

FIGURE 12.16 The emotional counting Stroop. The Stroop color-naming task can be adapted to study emotion, as shown here. Stimulus conflict with emotional content evokes activity in front of the anterior cingulate cortex, with non-emotional control condition evoking activity just behind it. *Source*: Bush *et al.*, 2000.

FIGURE 12.15 A neural net model of the Stroop task. The model shows competing populations of neurons sensitive to color and to color names, shaped by task demands in the lower green oval. At the top, the oral response, such as saying 'red' or 'green' is determined by a network that detects, integrates and resolves conflicting input (orange oval). The human anterior cingulate cortex is believed to serve this function. (After Cohen *et al.*, 1990.) *Source*: MacLeod and MacDonald, 2000.

patient is often at the mercy of incidental environmental stimuli and tangential internal associations. Easy distractibility is a feature of many neurological and psychiatric disorders, and it is usually associated with frontal lobe dysfunction. For example, *attention deficit hyperactivity disorder (ADHD)*, with its extreme distractibility, is usually linked to frontal lobe dysfunction (Barkley, 1997). The relationship between the frontal lobes' role in guiding behavior by internal representation during performance on Stroop Test, ADHD, and emotional valence of a task was elucidated in a combined analysis of multiple studies (Figure 12.17).

11.2.2 Mental rigidity

Our ability to maintain mental stability has to be balanced by *mental flexibility*. No matter how focused we are on an activity or a thought, there comes a time when the situation calls for doing something else. Being able to change one's mindset is as important as staying mentally on track. The capacity to switch with ease from one activity or idea to another is so natural and automatic, that we take it for granted. In fact, it requires complex neural machinery, which also depends on the frontal lobes. Mental flexibility, the ability to see things in a new light, creativity and originality all depend on the frontal lobes. More profound forms of mental rigidity produce *obsessive-compulsive disorder* (OCD), in which dysfunction of the caudate nuclei closely linked to the frontal lobes has been implicated (Rauch *et al.*, 1994).

Frontal lobe damage often produces extreme mental rigidity, which may severely undermine the patient's cognition. Quite often a closer look at a frontal patient's performance on a number of tasks shows that complete transition from one task to another is impossible, and fragments of a previous task attach themselves to the new one. This phenomenon is called *perseveration*.

A seemingly simple neuropsychological test is quite sensitive to subtle impairment of mental flexibility. The test, known as the Wisconsin Card Sorting Test (Grant

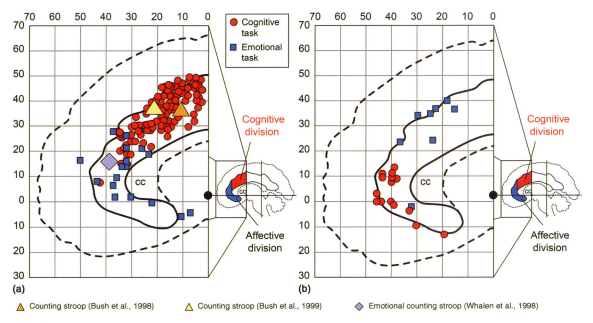

FIGURE 12.17 Confirming separate cognitive and emotional conflict regions. A summary of many studies of the anterior cingulate cortex, showing different cognitive and emotional regions. *Source*: Bush *et al.*, 2000.

and Berg, 1948), requires the subject to sort cards with simple geometric forms into three categories according to a simple principle. The classification principle is not revealed in advance and the subject must establish it through trial and error. But when the principle has finally been mastered it abruptly changes unbeknownst to the subject. Once the subject catches up with the new principle, the principle is changed without forewarning again, and again, and again. The task requires planning, guidance by internal representation, mental flexibility, and working memory – in short all the aspects of frontal lobe function that we discussed before.

11.2.3 Orbitofrontal syndrome and self-control

The *orbitofrontal syndrome* is, in many ways, the opposite of the dorsolateral syndrome. The patients are behaviorally and emotionally *disinhibited*. Their affect is rarely neutral, constantly oscillating between euphoria and rage, with impulse control ranging from poor to non-existent. Their ability to inhibit the urge for instant gratification is severely impaired. They do what they feel like doing, when they feel like doing it, without any concern for social taboos and legal prohibitions. They have no foresight of the consequences of their actions. A patient afflicted with the orbitofrontal syndrome (due to head injury, cerebrovascular illness, or dementia) may engage in shoplifting, sexually aggressive behavior, reckless driving or other actions commonly perceived as antisocial. These patients are known to be 'selfish', boastful, puerile, profane and sexually explicit. Their humor is off-color and their jocularity, known as *Witzelsucht*, resembles that of a drunken adolescent (Oppenheim, 1889). If the dorsolateral patients are in a sense devoid of personality, then orbitofrontal patients are conspicuous for their 'immature' personality.

11.2.4 Reticulofrontal disconnection syndrome

In cases when the frontal lobes themselves are structurally intact but the patient presents with 'frontal lobe' symptoms, the problem may lie with the pathways connecting frontal lobes to some other structures. Damage to these pathways may result in a condition known as the *reticulofrontal disconnection syndrome* (Goldberg *et al.*, 1989).

The brainstem contains the nuclei thought to be responsible for the arousal and activation of the rest of the brain. A complex relationship exists between the frontal lobes and the brainstem reticular nuclei, which

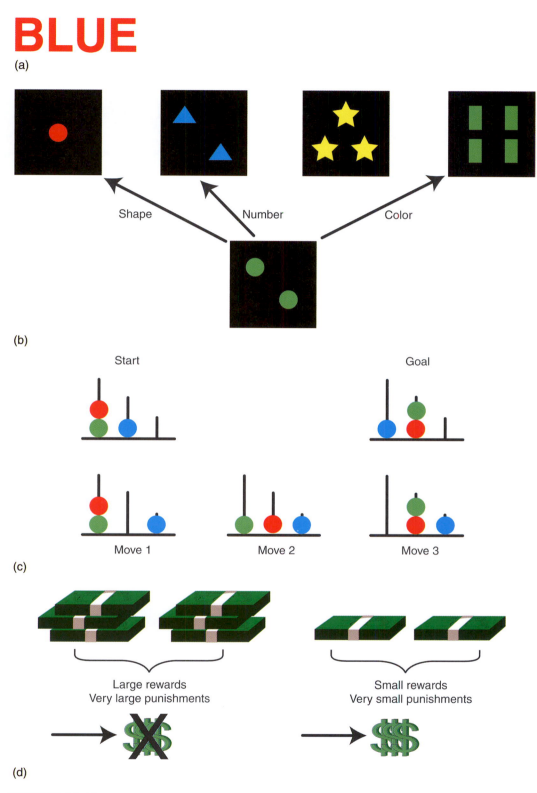

FIGURE 12.18   Four tasks are sensitive to frontal lobe damage. Frontal lobe patients tend to underperform on the Stroop color-naming task (a), on a change of rule in the Wisconsin Card Sorting Test (b), on relatively simple puzzles like the Tower of Hanoi (c), and on tasks involving small monetary losses and gains (d). *Source*: Squire *et al.*, 2003.

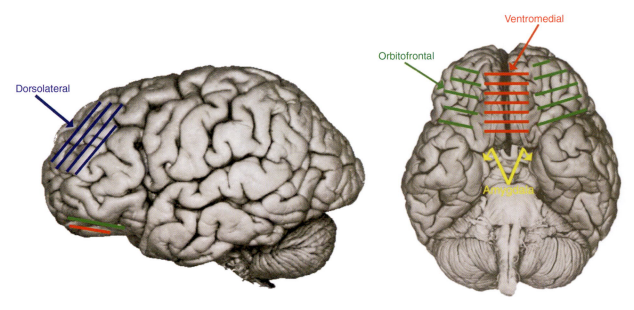

FIGURE 12.19 The orbitofrontal region is just above the orbits of the eyes. The orbitofrontal cortex (green stripes) can be distinguished in the ventral prefrontal lobe. Orbitofrontal cortex is involved in understanding future rewards, changes in reward contingencies, and goal selection. Damage to the orbitofrontal region may lead to a loss of behavioral inhibition. *Source*: Davidson and Irwin, 1999.

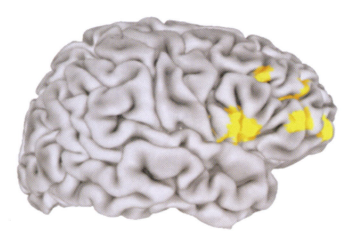

FIGURE 12.20 Dopamine modulates prefrontal functioning. The yellow areas indicate fMRI changes due to the midbrain dopamine projections to the frontal lobes. Dopamine secretion in this area is under the control of COMT gene expression. Dopamine may have different effects depending upon the receptors it engages in different parts of the brain. In the frontal lobes, dopamine is associated with working memory and reward. *Source*: National Institutes of Mental Health, Clinical Disorders Branch.

are in charge of activation and arousal. The relationship is best described as a loop. On the one hand, the arousal of the frontal lobes depends on the ascending pathways from the brainstem. These pathways are complex, but one of its components is thought to be particularly important for the proper function of the frontal lobes. This component is called the mesocortical dopamine system; it originates in the ventral tegmental area (VTA) of the brainstem and projects into the frontal lobes. If the frontal lobes are the decision-making center of the brain, then the ventral tegmental area is its energy source, the battery, and the ascending mesocortical dopamine pathway is the connecting cable (see Chapter 14).

On the other hand, there are pathways projecting from the frontal lobes to the reticular nuclei of the ventral brainstem. Through these pathways the frontal lobes exert their control over the diverse brain structures by modulating their arousal level. If the frontal lobes are the decision-making device, then the brainstem structures in question are an amplifier helping communicate these decisions to the rest of the brain in a loud and clear voice. The descending pathways are the cables through which the instructions flow from the frontal lobes to the critical ventral brainstem nuclei.

One can easily see how damage to the pathways between the brainstem and the frontal lobes may disable executive functions without actually damaging the frontal lobes *per se*.

11.3 Other clinical conditions associated with frontal lobe damage

Prefrontal cortex is afflicted in a wide range of conditions (Goldberg, 1992; Goldberg and Bougakov, 2000) and it is not necessary to have a focal frontal lesion to have prefrontal dysfunction. The frontal lobes are particularly vulnerable in numerous non-focal conditions. Such disorders as schizophrenia (Ingvar and Franzen, 1974; Franzen and Ingvar, 1975), traumatic brain injury (TBI) (Deutsch and Eisenberg, 1987), Tourette's syndrome (Tourette, 1885; Shapiro and Shapiro, 1974; Sacks, 1992) and attention deficit (hyperactivity) disorder (AD(H)D) (Barkley, 1997) are known to involve frontal lobe dysfunction. In TBI, for instance, the frontal lobe dysfunction can be caused by either direct frontal injury, or by injury disrupting the brainstem-frontal connection (Goldberg et al., 1989). Executive functions are also compromised in dementia and in depression.

It appears that it is not necessary to have a frontal lobe lesion to have a 'frontal lobe syndrome'. There are many conditions where, based on functional neuroimaging and neuropsychological studies, frontal lobe dysfunction is present, but there is no evidence of structural morphological damage to the frontal lobes.

11.3.1 ADHD

The prefrontal cortex and its connections to the ventral brainstem play a particularly important role in the mechanisms of attention. When we talk about the attention deficit (hyperactivity) disorder (AD(H)D), we usually implicate these systems. The exact causes of damage to these systems vary. They may be inherited or acquired early in life. They may be biochemical or structural. As we already know, frontal lobes are particularly vulnerable in a very broad range of disorders, hence the very high rate of frontal lobe dysfunction. The way the diagnosis of AD(H)D is commonly made, it refers to any condition characterized by mild dysfunction of the frontal lobes and related pathways in the absence of any other, comparably severe dysfunction. Given the high rate of frontal lobe dysfunction due to a variety of causes, the prevalence of genuine AD(H)D should be expected to be very high.

BOX 12.2   Attention deficit hyperactivity disorder

Do you pay attention to captivating yet irrelevant stimuli? Do you have trouble acting appropriately, fidgeting while listening to a lecture? Do you have difficulty planning and pursuing long-term goals? Do distractions knock you "off task"? When these not uncommon difficulties occur to a severe degree, they are symptoms of attention deficit hyperactivity disorder (ADHD), a disorder seen in children and adults. It is estimated that 3–5% of children have this disorder, with about half retaining problems into adulthood. The symptoms of ADHD involve dysfunction of the prefrontal cortex (PFC) and its cortical and subcortical connections.

Criteria for the diagnosis of ADHD include symptoms of "inattention" and "hyperactivity/impulsivity." Patients can have either the combined type, or predominantly "inattentive" or predominantly "hyperactive/impulsive" types. Many of the symptoms for "inattention" used to diagnose ADHD relate to attentional abilities of the PFC: e.g., difficulty sustaining attention or organizing, easily distracted, and, forgetful. Similarly, many of the symptoms of "hyperactivity/impulsivity" describe PFC deficits: e.g. difficulty awaiting turn. The PFC controls attention via its projections to the parietal and temporal cortices (see Chapter 8), while it controls motor responses via its projections to the motor cortices and striatum. These circuits appear to be impaired in patients with ADHD. ADHD symptoms are especially evident in "boring" settings that require endogenous rather than exogenous regulation of behavior. For example, ADHD children can sit still and play video games for hours, but have trouble attending in school. ADHD patients have difficulty sustaining a behavior or thought over a delay. As described in this chapter, PFC cells exhibit sustained firing over a delay that regulates thought and behavioral output.

Structural and functional imaging studies show consistent alterations in PFC-striatal-cerebellar circuits in ADHD patients. Volumetric measures have detected smaller right-sided PFC regions (the right side is most associated with attention; see Chapter 8). Changes in the size of the striatum also have been reported, and functional imaging studies have shown abnormal activity of both the PFC and the striatum in ADHD patients performing tasks that require PFC inhibitory or attentional functions. Structural imaging studies have also shown consistent decreases in the size of the cerebellar vermis, a region that may exert regulatory influences on noradrenergic (NE) cells of the locus coeruleus (LC) and dopaminergic (DA) cells of the ventral tegmental area. These NE and DA cells in turn have profound influences on PFC-striatal circuitry (see later). Thus, a smaller vermis in ADHD patients may lead to impaired catecholamine inputs to PFC and striatum. Some evidence supports this idea: a neuroreceptor imaging study suggests that there are reduced numbers of catecholamine terminals in the PFC of adults with ADHD.

(Continued)

NE and DA have a critical influence of PFC-striatal circuits, and thus changes in these inputs can have tremendous impact on PFC cognitive functions. This chapter describes how DA has an important effect of PFC function, and the same is true for NE. NE cells fire when a stimulus is of interest to the animal, releasing NE in the PFC. NE stimulates postsynaptic α_{2A}-adrenoceptors, enhancing delay-related firing and strengthening regulation of behavior and attention. However, very high levels of NE and DA, such as are released during stressful conditions, can impair PFC function via a_1-adrenoceptors and D1 receptors, respectively. Thus, the PFC has to have just the right neurochemical conditions to function optimally.

What causes ADHD? ADHD appears to be at least partially inherited, and one can imagine that genetic alterations that interfere with NE or DA signaling could have large effects on PFC function. Several studies indicate that two DA genes, the DA transporter and the DA D4 receptor, may be associated with susceptibility to ADHD. (The D4 receptor also has very high affinity for NE.) Environmental factors may also lead to the disruption of

Source: Squire *et al.*, 2003.

PFC-striatal circuits. For example, some kinds of infection may lead to autoantibodies that attack PFC-striatal circuits.

Medications for ADHD likely reduce symptoms of inattention and impulsivity by optimizing the neurochemical environment in the PFC and in the striatum. All effective treatments for ADHD interact with catecholamines: Stimulants such as Ritalin (methylphenidate) and Adderall (a mixture of amphetamines) increase NE and DA release and/or block catecholamine reuptake. Research in rats suggests that low doses of these compounds preferentially increase the release of NE. Consistent with these data, NE reuptake blockers are also used to treat ADHD (e.g., desipramine), including highly selective NE agents (atomoxetine). Drugs that mimic NE at α_{2A}-adrenoceptors (guanfacine and clonidine) are effective, especially in decreasing impulsivity. Wellbutrin (also known as Zyban or bupropion) is a DA reuptake blocker that is used to treat ADHD. How do these medications actually work to ameliorate ADHD symptoms?

To understand better the proposed mechanism of AD(H)D one needs to understand the nature of another aspect of executive control – selective attention. The goal of action must be identified and it must effectively guide behavior for a period of time. We already know that goal-setting and goal-maintenance are provided by the *prefrontal cortex*. The prefrontal cortex exerts its influence on the posterior aspects of the cortical hemispheres. These are the structures most directly involved in processing the incoming information. Depending on the goal at hand, distinct, particular parts of the posterior cortex must be brought into the state of optimal activation. The selection of these areas is accomplished by the prefrontal cortex. The prefrontal cortex exerts its influence through the nuclei of the *ventral brainstem*, which can selectively activate vast cortical regions through their ascending projections. The prefrontal cortex guides the influence of these nuclei on the posterior cortices through its own descending pathways into the ventral brainstem. Finally, the prefrontal cortex *modifies* its control over brainstem nuclei, based on the *feedback* it receives from the posterior cortex.

In sum, attention can be best described as a loop-like process involving complex interactions between the *prefrontal cortex, ventral brainstem* (and possibly also *non-specific midline thalamic nuclei*), and *posterior cortex* (Figure 12.21). Breakdown anywhere along this loop may interfere with attention, thus producing a form of attention deficit disorder. Therefore, any damage to the

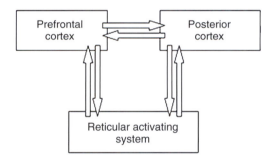

FIGURE 12.21 An attentional loop combining frontal, brainstem, and posterior cortex. Goldberg (2001) proposed that attentional functions may be influenced not just by the frontal lobes, but by a causal loop extending downward into the reticular formation of the brainstem, going upward to posterior cortex. This view is consistent with evidence regarding the brainstem arousal system. *Source*: E. Goldberg, with permission.

prefrontal cortex or its pathways may result in attentional impairment.

12.0 EXECUTIVE CONTROL AND SOCIAL MATURITY

The capacity for volitional control over one's actions is not innate, but it emerges gradually through development and is an important, perhaps central, ingredient of *social maturity*.

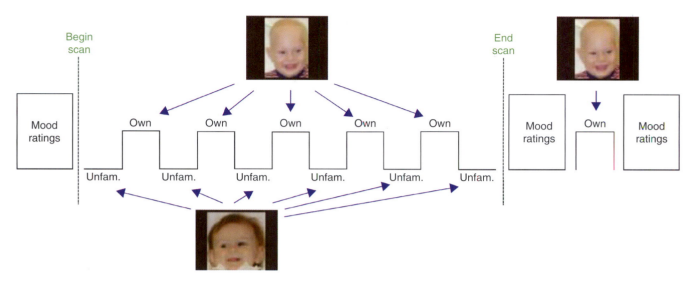

FIGURE 12.22 Mothers looking at their own babies. When mothers look at their own baby versus another baby, regions of the medial prefrontal cortex show higher activation. *Source*: Nitschke *et al.*, 2004.

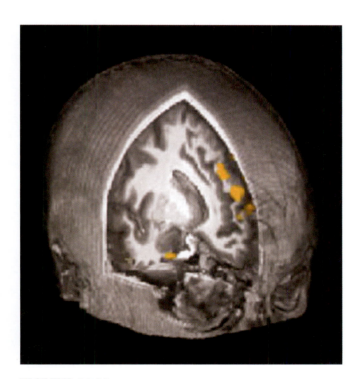

FIGURE 12.23 Moral guilt also evokes activity in the medial prefrontal lobe. In a remarkable finding, the medial frontal regions show increased activity related to moral guilt. *Source*: Harenski and Hamann, 2006.

Allan Schore (1999) believes that early mother-infant interaction is important for the normal development of the orbitofrontal cortex during the first months of life. By contrast, early-life stressful experiences permanently damage the orbitofrontal cortex, predisposing the individual to later-life psychiatric diseases. This implies that early social interactions help shape the brain. Scientists have known for years that early sensory stimulation promotes the development of visual cortex in the occipital lobes, and early-life sensory deprivation retards its development. It is possible that social stimulation is to the development of the frontal cortex what visual stimulation is to the development of the occipital cortex.

Furthermore, following this logic, is it possible that moral development involves the frontal cortex, just as visual development involves occipital cortex and language development involves temporal cortex? The prefrontal cortex is the association cortex of the frontal lobes, the 'action lobes'. The posterior association cortex encodes generic information about the outside world. It contains the taxonomy of the various things known to exist and helps recognize a particular exemplar as a member of a known category. By analogy, the prefrontal cortex may contain the taxonomy of all the *sanctioned, moral actions and behaviors*? And could it be that, just as damage or maldevelopment of the posterior association cortex *produces object agnosias*, so does damage or maldevelopment of the prefrontal cortex produce, in some sense, *moral agnosia*?

A report by Damasio and colleagues lends some support to this idea (Anderson *et al.*, 1999). Damasio studied two young adults, a man and a woman, who suffered damage to the frontal lobes very early in life. Both engaged in antisocial behaviors: lying, petty thievery, truancy. Damasio claims that not only did these

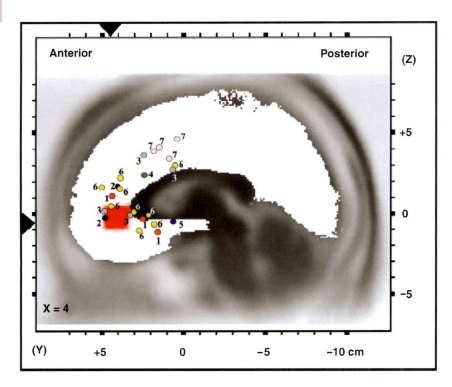

FIGURE 12.24 Medial prefrontal activity in depression. Depressed subjects show increased activity in the frontal half of the cingulate cortex. By itself this experiment does not show whether these are direct effects of negative mood, or indirect conflict signals related to depression. *Source*: Frackowiak *et al.*, 2004.

patients fail to act according to the proper, socially sanctioned moral precepts, but they even failed to recognize them as morally wrong.

The orbitofrontal cortex is not the only part of the frontal lobes linked to socially mature behavior. The *anterior cingulate cortex* occupies a mid-frontal position and is closely linked to the prefrontal cortex. The anterior cingulate cortex has been traditionally linked to emotion. According to Michael Posner, it also plays a role in social development by regulating distress (Posner and Rothbart, 1998).

The implicit definition of social maturity changes throughout the history of society, and so does the time of 'coming of age'. In modern Western societies, the age of 18 (or thereabout) has been codified in the law as the age of social maturity. This is the age when a person can vote and is held responsible for his or her actions as an adult. The age of 18 is also the age when the maturation of the frontal lobes is relatively complete. Various estimates can be used to measure the course of maturation of various brain structures. Among the most commonly used such measures is pathway myelinization (Yakolev and Lecours, 1967). The frontal lobes cannot fully assume this role until the pathways connecting the frontal lobes with the far-flung structures of the brain are fully myelinated.

The agreement between the age of relatively complete maturation of the frontal lobes and the age of social

maturity is probably more than coincidental. Without the explicit benefit of neuroscience, but through cumulative everyday common sense, society recognizes that an individual assumes adequate control over his or her impulses, drives, and desires only by a certain age. Until that age, an individual cannot be held fully responsible for his actions in either a legal or moral sense. This ability appears to depend critically on the maturity and functional integrity of the frontal lobes.

The relationship between frontal lobe damage and asocial behavior is particularly intriguing and complex. It has been suggested, based on several published studies, that the prevalence of head injury is much higher among criminals than in the general population, and in violent criminals than in non-violent criminals (Volavka *et al.*, 1995; Raine *et al.*, 1997). For reasons of brain and skull anatomy, closed head injury is particularly likely to affect the frontal lobes directly, especially the orbitofrontal cortex. Furthermore, damage to the upper brainstem is extremely common in closed head injury, even in seemingly 'mild' cases, and it is likely to produce frontal lobe dysfunction even in the absence of direct damage to the frontal lobes by producing the 'reticulofrontal disconnection syndrome' (Goldberg *et al.*, 1989).

Adrian Raine and his colleagues (Raine *et al.*, 1997) studied the brains of convicted murderers with PET scans and found abnormalities in the prefrontal cortex.

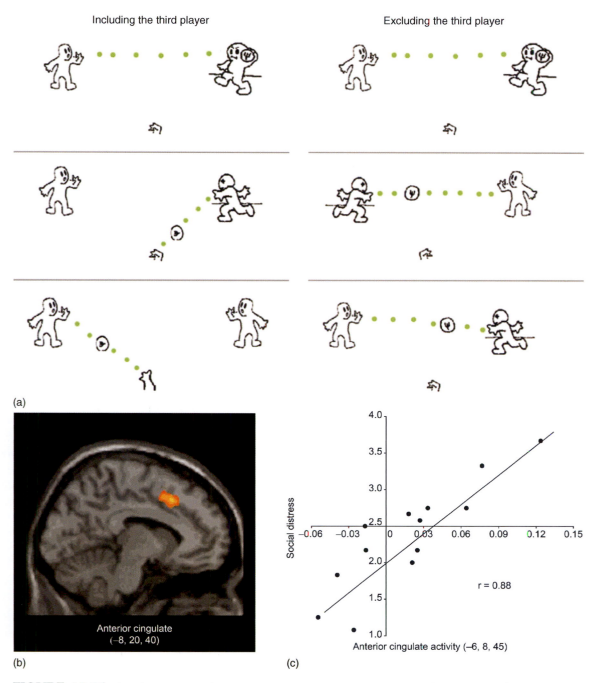

(a)

Anterior cingulate
(−8, 20, 40)

(b)

(c)

FIGURE 12.25 Social rejection and pain perception. In a task designed to evoke the sense of social rejection (as felt by a child in a ball game), the frontal part of the cingulate cortex again 'lights up'. *Source*: Eisenberger and Lieberman, 2004.

Raine and colleagues (2000) also studied the brains of men with antisocial personality disorder and found an 11 per cent reduction in the gray matter of their frontal lobes. The cause of this reduction is uncertain, but Raine believes that this reduction is at least in part congenital, as opposed to caused by environmental factors such as abuse or bad parenting. The link between frontal lobe dysfunction and asocial behavior raises an important set of social, moral and legal issues far beyond the scope of this chapter.

13.0 TOWARDS A UNIFIED THEORY OF EXECUTIVE CONTROL: A CONCLUSION

To summarize, after having been overlooked for many decades, executive functions have become the focus of an ever-increasing body of research. Unfortunately, the main character of many such investigations continues to be reductionistic in nature, which leads to a paradoxical situation. Numerous attempts have been made to fractionate executive functions along the familiar lines of sensory modalities, linguistic versus non-linguistic, object versus spatial ('what' versus 'where'), etc. distinctions. While such claims make executive functions appear to be more tangible, at least on the surface, they do not always lead to better understanding of the nature of executive control as a whole. Furthermore, the introduction and rapid refinement of various functional powerful neuroimaging techniques has invited numerous attempts to 'localize' various specific cognitive functions within the prefrontal cortex.

A very different approach traces its lineage to the work by the great Russian neuropsychologist Alexander Luria (1966). A continuation and extension of Luria's original theory can be seen in the relatively recent trend toward the refutation of the modular view of functional neocortical organization in favor of the distributed-emergent principle of functional cortical organization (Goldberg *et al.*, 1989; Goldberg, 1992; Fuster, 2003). According to Goldberg's gradiental theory, the functional organization of heteromodal association cortices (such as prefrontal cortices) is interactive and distributed. The heteromodal association cortex develops along the continuous distributions. In these distributions (called 'gradients') functionally close aspects of cognition are represented in anatomically close areas of the association neocortex.

Yet another theory of cortical representation elaborating on Luria's functional systems theory was put forth by Joaquin Fuster (2003). Fuster maintains that cognitive functions do not have discrete cortical representation. In his theory, he introduces a re-entrant unit, called *cognit*, which he proposes as a generic term for any representation of knowledge in the cerebral cortex. Cognits are dynamic structures which, in neural terms, roughly coincide with neuronal assemblies and the connections between the neurons. According to Fuster, cognitive functions are represented by information exchange within and between cognits and different cognitive functions draw upon many overlapping cognits. The crucial tenet of Fuster's theory is that different cognits (neural networks) have identifiable cortical distribution but cognitive functions that use them do not, since different functions may rely on same or similar circuits.

According to these theories the nature of cortical representation of executive control is distributed as well as localized. Executive control can be considered unitary in the sense that it is in charge of actions, both external and internal, and works to integrate such factors as time, novelty, complexity, and possibly ambiguity.

14.0 DRAWING EXERCISES AND STUDY QUESTIONS

1 What are some of the functions attributed to the prefrontal lobe?
2 Discuss a current debate about the specificity of prefrontal functions.
3 In the outline brain in Figure 12.26:
   a Color the major lobes
   b Label major landmarks, like the central sulcus and Sylvian fissure
   c Label the major gyri (green lines) and sulci (dotted red lines).
4 In the brain image in Figure 12.27, show the prefrontal and cingulate cortex from the medial point of view. What are two major functions attributed to this part of the brain?

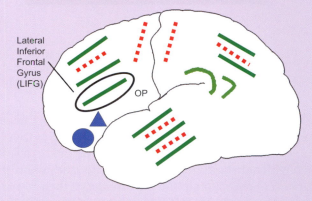

FIGURE 12.26

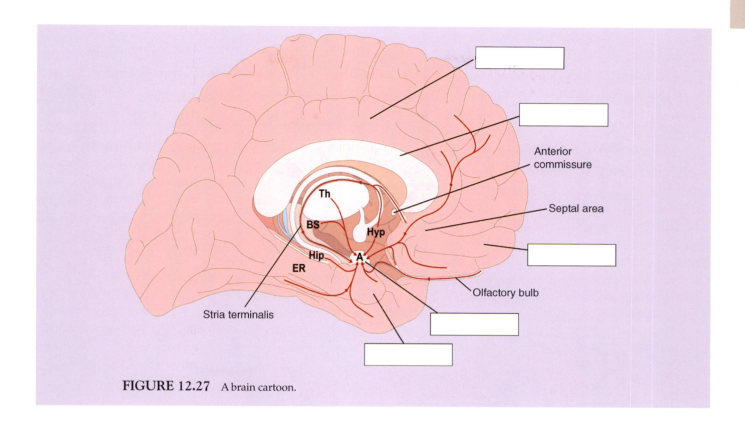

FIGURE 12.27   A brain cartoon.

For Charles Darwin, it was obvious beyond any need for argument that non-human animals are sentient '. . . the lower animals, like man', he wrote in 1871, 'manifestly feel pleasure and pain, happiness and misery' (p. 39). 'The fact that the lower animals are excited by the same emotions as ourselves is so well established that it will not be necessary to weary the reader by many details' (However,) . . . in the belief that identifying problems and finding ways to answer them is a way to move forwards, I shall first emphasize why sentience is still a profound problem, despite the ease with which Darwin spoke about the mental experiences of animals.

Marian Stamp Dawkins (2006) Through animal eyes: What behaviour tells us.
Applied Animal Behaviour Science, 100, 4–10

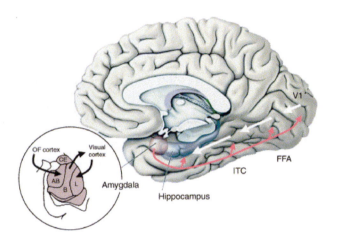
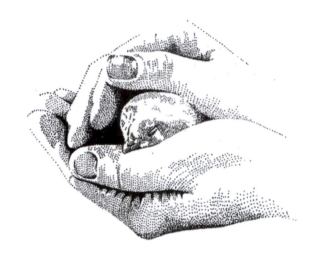

The basic emotional brain is highly conserved among mammals, and possibly even more widely. Upper left, a human brain seen from the midline (medially), showing how information can flow from visual cortex (V1) to the amygdala, an emotional "hub" for neuronal traffic from many different sources. Snakes appear to be a biological stimulus for fear for both humans and other mammals. On the opposite pole, cradling young birds and other newborns seems to evoke a soothing and calming effect. Obviously humans have a giant neocortex, which modifies basic mammalian emotional systems centered in the limbic (core) brain.

C H A P T E R

13

Emotion

Katharine McGovern

1.0 INTRODUCTION

Do you remember where you were on the morning of September 11th, 2001? You likely do recall that day, and you probably do not have a strong memory for, say, September 9th of that year. Why is this? The events of September 11th are firmly etched in our brains because of the highly charged emotions that are entwined with the memory of the occurrences of that day. In previous chapters, we have discussed higher cognitive brain functions such as memory, executive functions, and language. Our emotions are strongly coupled with the brain systems underlying these cognitive functions. In this chapter, we will explore the emotion systems of the brain and their interactions with cognitive processing. The term 'affective neuroscience' was coined in the late 1990s to denote a new area of study: the neuroscience of emotion. While a great deal is now known about emotion in the brain, we will focus here on how emotion systems shape and influence cognitive processes.

Cognition, Brain, and Consciousness, edited by B. J. Baars and N. M. Gage
ISBN: 978-0-12-373677-2

Copyright 2007, Elsevier Ltd. All rights reserved.

1.1 The triune brain

Paul MacLean introduced the 'triune brain' concept in 1990 to describe the functionally distinct layers of the mammalian brain. It has become a widely used way of thinking about the overall functional organization of the brain. In MacLean's view, the brain developed over the course of vertebrate evolution into a three-layered organ, where these layers retain some of the separateness of their different evolutionary origins despite being highly interconnected. We can see the effects of each of the layers in human behavior, especially in the relationship of cognition and emotion.

The oldest layer of the brain is called the *reptilian brain*. It is composed of the brainstem (medulla, pons, cerebellum, midbrain, globus pallidus, and olfactory bulbs) – the structures that dominate in the brains of snakes and lizards. This brain layer does not learn very well from experience but is inclined to repeat instinctual behaviors over and over in a fixed way. In humans, this part of the brain controls survival activities like breathing, heart rate, and balance. We will not have much to say about the reptilian brain in this chapter.

The *mammalian brain* is layered over the reptilian brain (Figure 13.1). It consists primarily of a system of brain parts called the *limbic system*. The word 'limbic' comes from the Latin word *limbus* and means 'border, edge, or hem' – it refers to the location inside the cerebral hemispheres around the edge of the lateral ventricles (fluid filled spaces). The limbic system was first recognized in the late 1800s, but an understanding of its function in emotion did not develop until the work of neuroanatomist Papez was published in 1937. Another older name for the limbic system is the Papez circuit.

The list of component parts of the limbic system varies depending on the researcher that we consult – there seems to be no universal agreement about what the limbic system actually consists of! Some neuroscientists think that we should no longer speak of a limbic system at all. We will retain the term as a useful organizing concept for a set of related subcortical brain parts that support our emotional life. Commonly cited constituents are the amygdala, hippocampus, parahippocampal cortex, cingulate gyrus, hypothalamus, and ventral striatum/nucleus accumbens.

The limbic system has a major role in human emotion. We see the effects of the limbic system in our conscious experience in the added valence (positive or negative value or feeling) and salience ('noticeableness') of particular images and thoughts. We share this part of our brain with other mammals. Prototypic mammalian emotional responses are easily recognizable in our pet dogs and cats.

In terms of the adaptive role of the limbic system, we can say that the limbic system contains several distinct systems evolved to respond to mammalian evolutionary pressures such as danger, reproductive and nurturance needs, and acquisition of food. For example, the amygdala and hypothalamus cooperate in an *early warning system* for danger, initiating survival maneuvers automatically when confronted with stimuli similar to those encountered in past dangerous situations. However, the amygdala's stimulus processing has low resolution of details compared to that of the sensory areas of the cerebral cortices. Stimulus recognition in the limbic system follows a 'close enough is good enough' rule, so we sometimes find ourselves jumping at the site of a long, dark coil in the grass, only to find that it is a garden hose and not a snake. Following the conditioning of evolutionary history, the limbic system would 'rather be safe than sorry'. In our conscious experience, we find ourselves acting without voluntary initiation under the influence of the amygdala. Moments later, our rational selves feel embarrassment at our apparently silly behavior. We can easily find other examples of the interplay of the limbic system and the cortical system in our everyday behavior. We will look more closely at this shortly.

The limbic system is densely interconnected with the cortex, particularly through the orbital gyri of the VM-PFC (ventromedial prefrontal cortex) and also the

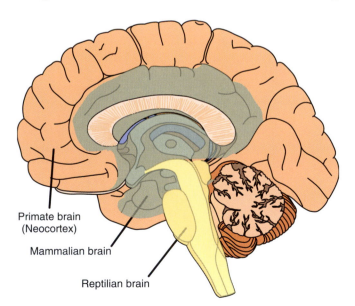

Primate brain
(Neocortex)

Mammalian brain

Reptilian brain

FIGURE 13.1 The triune brain: orange represents neocortex, green is the mammalian brain, and yellow is the reptilian brain.

insular cortex. The dense connections with the VM-PFC have led to its nickname as the *feeling part of the thinking brain*. VM-PFC is a gateway between limbic system and neocortex.

The *neocortex* or *primate brain* is the most recent addition to our brains. It consists of the wrinkled covering of the cerebral hemispheres (as well as some subcortical nuclei, such as the basal ganglia), which has mushroomed in primates and humans compared to other mammals. The neocortex is the home of our complex cognitive, linguistic, motor, sensory, and social abilities. The neocortex gives us considerable flexibility and creativity in adapting to a changeable environment. Cortex functions to socialize and control expression of emotions that originate in the limbic system; cortical appraisal of situations is also necessary for a more nuanced emotional repertoire than is possible based on the functioning of the limbic system alone.

1.2 Basic emotions and the role of reflective consciousness

Emotional responsiveness is governed by:

1 *classically conditioned responses* to stimuli that previously brought pleasure or created pain mediated by subcortical systems and
2 *cognitive appraisals* of stimuli in context mediated by neocortex.

Neuroscientists have given most attention to the classical conditioning studies conducted with animal models. Almost no attention has been given to the possibility of multiple emotional systems in the brain. To date, the origins of fear in the amygdala have received attention as the dopamine-based 'reward system'. But interest in the explanation of neural bases of the wide variety of distinctly felt emotional experiences is lacking. With the advent of increasingly fine-grained brain imaging methods, this may change.

While classical conditioning remains an important explanation of learned emotional associations, affective neuroscientists have begun to think of mammalian emotion as arising from *several separate genetically-determined networks* of brain areas, each serving a particular adaptive function, each giving rise to a unique motor routine when activated, each having a unique 'calling condition' or evoking stimulus, and each being the neural substrate of distinct conscious emotional feelings. A psycho-ethological perspective allows us to see emotional functioning in an adaptive context.

2.0 PANKSEPP'S EMOTIONAL BRAIN SYSTEMS

Jaak Panksepp (1998) offered a functional definition of an emotional system in the brain (illustrated in Figure 13.2):

1 The underlying circuits are genetically predetermined to respond unconditionally to stimuli representing evolutionary pressures faced by the species
2 The circuits organize motor programs and autonomic and hormonal changes to respond to the environmental challenge or opportunity at hand
3 The circuits tune sensitivities of sensory systems to be responsive to stimuli relevant to the emotion evoked
4 The positive feedback of neural activity means emotional arousal outlasts the precipitating circumstances
5 Emotional circuits can come under cognitive control
6 Emotional circuits reciprocally influence higher decision-making and appraisal systems and consciousness
7 The circuit is capable of elaborating distinctly difference subjective feelings (not shown in Figure 13.2).

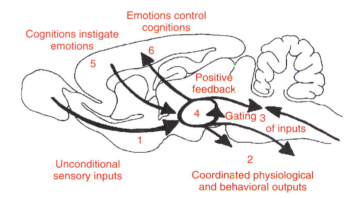

FIGURE 13.2 The functions of emotional systems: (1) unconditioned sensory inputs, (2) coordinated physiological and behavioral outputs, (3) gating of inputs, (4) positive feedback, (5) cognitions instigating emotions, and (6) emotional control over cognitions. *Source*: Panksepp, 2006.

Panksepp (1998) described a small set of 'hard-wired' emotion systems found in mammalian brains. (We will follow Panksepp's convention of identifying the systems by capitalized labels; the capital letters remind us that we are speaking of systems of emotion and not simply the conscious feelings associated with the systems or single brain locations.) The first four emotion systems appear shortly after birth in all mammals:

• SEEKING: the appetitive system that makes mammals curious about their world and promotes

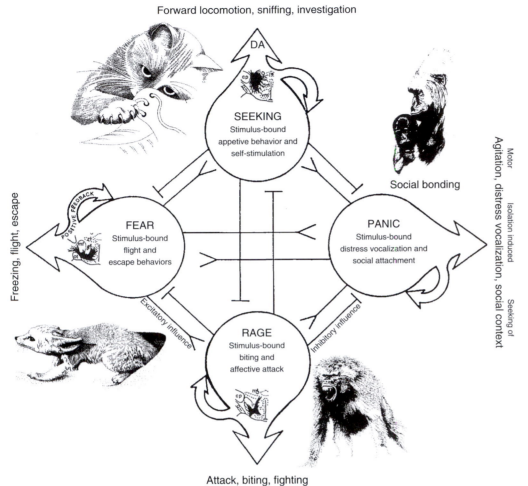

FIGURE 13.3 Four funda-
mental mammalian emotional
systems, shown with prototypical behaviors. *Source*: Panksepp,
1998.

goal-directed behavior toward a variety of goal objects, such as food, shelter, sex
- FEAR: the system which responds to pain and threat of destruction and leads to the well-known flight, fight, or freeze behavior
- RAGE: this system mediates anger and is aroused by frustration, bodily irritation, or restraint of free movement
- PANIC: the system that responds to separation of young animals from their caregiver by activating crying and separation calls.

These four emotional systems and their mutually inhibitory or excitatory relationships with each other are illustrated in Figure 13.3.

In addition to the four fundamental emotion systems, three other special-purpose systems come on-line at different stages of mammalian development. They are:

- LUST: the system that coordinates sexual behavior and feelings

- CARE: the care-giving system that is the adult counterpart of the infant PANIC system; CARE operates in both mothers and fathers and promotes social bonding and care-giving behaviors
- PLAY: the neural system that organizes rough-and-tumble play which occurs spontaneously in mammalian young; this system supports laughter and may be the neural substrate of joy.

Since each of these emotional systems has its own 'wiring diagram', understanding emotion in the brain can become quite complex!

Much of what we know about the mammalian emotional systems (shown in Table 13.1) comes from studies of non-human mammals. Studies of emotion in human participants are limited by ethical constraints on use of invasive techniques and on the kinds and intensities of emotional stimuli that can be used to evoke emotional responses. Laboratory studies of human emotion rely on behavioral observation and neural imaging following

TABLE 13.1 Basic emotional systems in the brain and associated brain areas (adapted from Panksepp, 2006)

Basic emotional system	Associated mammalian brain areas	Associated emotional feelings
FEAR/anxiety	Central and lateral amygdala to medial hypothalamus and dorsal PAG	Fear, anxiety
SEEKING/expectancy	Mesolimbic outputs of the VTA to the nucleus accumbens; mesocortical VTA outputs to orbitofrontal cortex; lateral hypothalamus to PAG	Interest, curiosity
RAGE/anger	Medial amygdala to bed nucleus of the stria terminalis (BNST); medial and perifornical hypothalamic to PAG	Anger, contempt
PANIC/separation distress	Anterior cingulate, BNST and preoptic area; dorsomedial thalamus, PAG	Sadness, shyness, guilt/shame
LUST/sexuality	Cortico-medial amygdala, BNST; preoptic area, VTA, PAG	Erotic feeling, jealousy
CARE/nurturance	Anterior cingulate, BNST; preoptic area, VTA, PAG	Love
PLAY/joy	Dorsomedial hypothalamus; parafascicular area, PAG	Joy, happiness

PAG = periaqueductal gray matter is located in the interior of the mid-brain, surrounding the cerebral aqueduct, running from the posterior commissure rostrally to the locus coeruleus caudally. BNTS = bed nucleus of the stria terminalis is a cluster of subcortical nuclei medial to the basal ganglia and above the hypothalamus. VTA = ventral tegmental area which is located in the midbrain.

relatively *mild* emotion-evoking tasks such as direct sensory stimulation and conditioning, observation of images of emotional events involving others, and emotion-generation through recall and mental imagery of emotion laden memories. Additional evidence comes from examination of neurological patients who have suffered lesions in various brain areas.

2.1 Feelings of emotion

Feelings of emotion cannot be studied in non-human mammals, though we can make some guesses about the felt experiences of other mammals by observing their behavioral reactions. There is currently considerable debate about whether any evidence justifies speaking of 'feelings' in non-human mammals. It appears that there is growing sentiment in favor of this position based on commonality of neuroanatomy of emotion and of the systems underlying conscious experience.

Damasio *et al.* (2000) studied the neural substrates of emotional feelings in humans. They looked for brain areas active during different emotional states when participants were asked to recall and re-experience emotion-laden personal memories. Using positron emission tomography (PET) imaging, the researchers located significantly different neural maps for fear, happiness, sadness, and anger (Figure 13.4). They noted different patterns of activation and deactivation in cortical and subcortical areas related to the representation and regulation of emotion as well as bodily homeostasis, including insular cortex, secondary somatosensory areas (SII), cingulate cortex, and nuclei in the brainstem and hypothalamus.

Since these emotional experiences were internally generated and did not require either perception of external stimuli or facial or motor expression, Damasio and his colleagues argued that the resulting neural maps represent the neural correlates of the different *feelings* of emotion, and conclude:

> The neural patterns depicted in all of these structures constitute multidimensional maps of the organism's internal state, and we believe that they form the basis for an important aspect of mental states known as feelings.

3.0 THE FEAR SYSTEM

We will take a closer look at the FEAR system and the SEEKING system, two emotional systems that have been studied in great detail and that have well-known influences on cognition.

The FEAR system is a neural system for avoiding pain or injury. It is based primarily in the central and lateral nuclei of the amygdala with connections to the medial hypothalamus and dorsal periaqueductal gray matter (PAG) of the midbrain. This system responds to both unconditioned stimuli (loud sounds, looming and sudden movements, painful stimuli, fearful faces) and conditioned stimuli (classically-conditioned danger signals, memories, images) arriving from the thalamus and sensory and association cortices (Figure 13.5). Reciprocal efferent pathways return feedback signals to these thalamic and cortical sites to tune sensory processing in emotion-specific ways (Figure 13.6). It is clear that the efferent (outgoing) pathways *from* the amygdala to cortex are as complex and rich as the afferent (incoming) pathways from cortex *to* the amygdala.

Afferent signals to the amygdala arrive via four pathways. *Olfactory information*, important for mammals, arrives directly at the amygdala from the olfactory

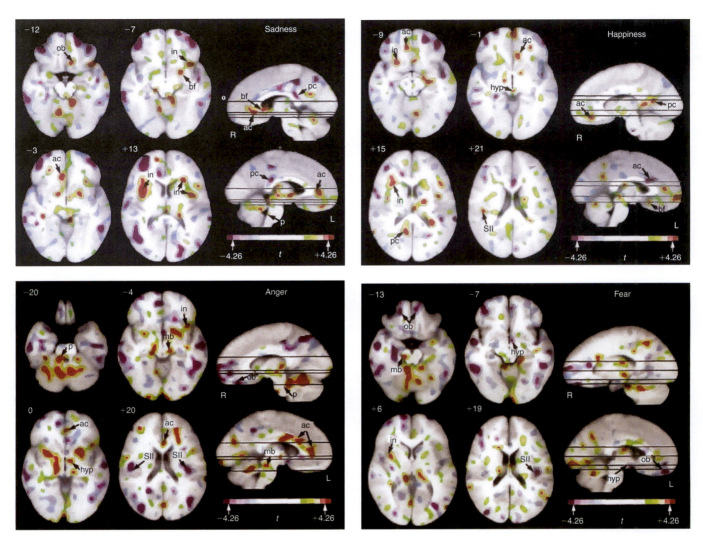

FIGURE 13.4 PET imagery results of participants' self-generated happiness and sadness (top row) and fear and anger (bottom row). Red and yellow indicate areas of increased metabolic activity; purple and blue indicate areas of decreased metabolic activity. Ob = orbitofrontal cortex; in = insula; bf = basal forebrain; ac = anterior cingulate; p = pons; hyp = hypothalamus; pc = posterior cingulate; SII = secondary somatosensory cortex; mb = midbrain. *Source*: Damasio *et al.*, 2000.

cortex without preprocessing in the thalamus; this may account for the profound ability that odors have to evoke emotional memories. *Visceral information* reaches the amygdala from the hypothalamus and septal area through the stria terminalis. *Affect-relevant information about internal states* also arrives from the hypothalamus, thalamus, and brainstem as well as the orbital cortex and anterior cingulate cortex via the ventral pathway. Finally, sensory information arrives directly from *temporal lobe structures* such as the primary auditory cortex and the hippocampus.

The amygdala itself is a collection of nuclei and internal pathways that serve different functions in emotional processes: the *basolateral complex*, the *centromedial nucleus* and the *cortical nucleus*. The basolateral complex can be further subdivided into lateral, basal, and accessory-basal nuclei. The lateral amygdala, which is afferent to the rest of the basolateral complex as well as the centromedial nucleus, receives input from sensory systems. The centromedial nucleus is the main output for the basolateral complex, and is involved in emotional arousal in mammals. The cortical nucleus is involved in smell and pheromone processing; it receives input from the olfactory bulb (Figure 13.7).

Efferent pathways from the amygdala mirror afferent pathways, returning signals to subcortical locations and to the brainstem. Of significance for our study of cognition-emotion interactions is the direct efferent pathway from the amygdala to entorhinal cortex, inferior temporal lobe cortex, and finally to visual cortex

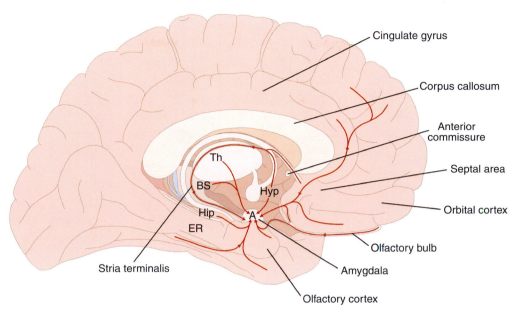

FIGURE 13.5   Afferent pathways to the amygdala. Hip= hippocampus; BS = brainstem; Th = thalamus; Hyp = hypothalamus; A = amygdala.

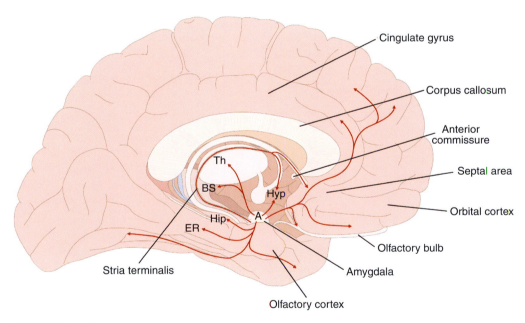

FIGURE 13.6   Efferent pathways from the amygdala. Hip= hippocampus; BS = brainstem; Th = thalamus; Hyp = hypothalamus; Am = amygdala.

including the fusiform face area (Figure 13.7). There are *top-down* and *bottom-up relationships* between amygdala and cortex as they work together to tune the brain for adaptive responses to significant environmental threats.

While most of the research on the neuropsychological function of the amygdala and its functioning has been done on rat and other mammalian models, accumulating evidence from human studies has yielded mostly consistent results. Subcortical emotional systems of the brain are thought to be *conserved* across mammalian groups; the same brain structures operate in the same ways in diverse animals. Most researchers believe that findings from rats and other mammals will apply to human neuropsychology. However, research is ongoing to confirm this hypothesis. Among early human studies confirming the role of the amygdala in fear

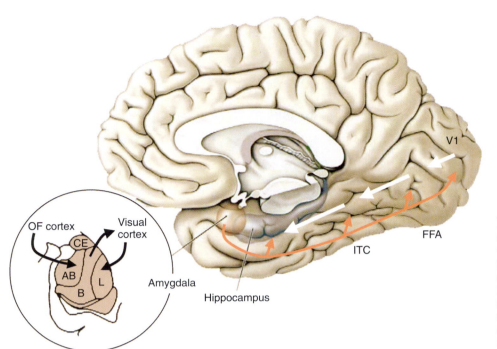

FIGURE 13.7 The nuclei of the amygdala and their efferent connections with sensory cortex. CE = centromedial, L = lateral, B = basal, and AB = accessory-basal nuclei of the amygdala. ITC = inferior temporal cortex; FFA = fusiform face area; V1 = primary visual cortex. Remember that there is an amygdala in each hemisphere of the brain. *Source:* Vuilleumier, 2005.

learning, LaBar *et al.* (1998) found that fear conditioning in humans resulted in an increased blood-oxygen-level-dependent (BOLD) signal in the amygdala as assessed with functional magnetic resonance imaging (fMRI) and that the magnitude of this BOLD response was predictive of the strength of the conditioned response.

3.1 Conscious and unconscious fear processing: LeDoux's high road and low road

LeDoux (1996) labeled the two sensory input pathways to the amygdala for perception of fearful stimuli the 'low road' and the 'high road'. The 'low road' is a fast pathway from sensory receptor to sensory thalamus to the amygdala that bypasses the cerebral cortex (Figure 13.8). As we discussed at the beginning of the chapter, the direct thalamo-amygdala (low road) processing is only capable of low spatial resolution of stimuli and thus can respond only to simple stimuli or to the gross characteristics of complex stimuli. This 'quick and dirty' processing enables automatic, unconscious reactions to the broad outlines of potentially dangerous stimuli before we have to time to think about our responses.

The longer thalamo-cortico-amygdala pathway (high road) takes somewhat longer to traverse but allows complex, contextualized processing of stimuli followed by conscious, deliberate responding. The high road represents the pathway that is more influenced by social and personal decision-making processes and thus can reflect culture-specific emotional responses.

3.2 Fear without awareness

Support for the hypothesis that emotional stimuli can be processed via alternate conscious and non-conscious pathways comes from research from a number of studies. We will look at one conducted by Vuilleumeir and his colleagues (2002). They looked for differential neural responses to fearful and neutral stimuli when processed with and without conscious awareness in a patient with right parietal neglect and visual extinction due to damage in his right inferior parietal cortex (Figure 13.9).

Parietal neglect is a deficit in body perception and visuospatial processing in individuals who have lesions in their parietal cortex. Patients with right parietal damage may have difficulty perceiving stimuli shown to them in the part of their visual field contralateral (on the opposite side) to the lesioned area – in the left visual field. In the laboratory, when shown single stimuli in the right or left visual fields, neglect patients have no difficulties with perception. However, when shown two different, simultaneously presented stimuli in the right and left visual fields, patients with right parietal neglect will frequently report not being able to see the stimulus presented to their left visual field. This phenomenon is called *extinction*. It provides researchers with an opportunity to study stimulus processing with and without conscious perception of the stimulus.

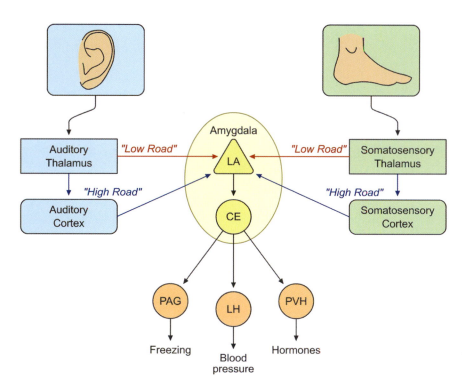

FIGURE 13.8 Two pathways to fear: the low road and the high road.

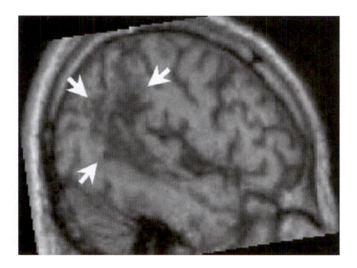

FIGURE 13.9 Damaged right inferior parietal cortex in Vuilleumeir *et al.* (2002) participant. *Source*: Vuilleumeir *et al.*, 2002.

Vuilleumeir *et al.* (2002) showed their participant pictures of fearful faces, neutral faces, or a house, individually or together as shown in Figures 13.10 and 13.11. The important results involved spared processing of faces in the right hemisphere despite parietal damage and participant's self-reported inability to see the stimuli.

Vuilleumier and his colleagues found that:

1   Fearful faces (but not neutral faces) activated the left amygdala, extrastriate (visual) cortex, bilateral orbitofrontal cortex, and right and left fusiform gyri *when seen and when extinguished*.

2   There was no difference in processing of the fearful faces in the amygdala whether seen or extinguished. Fearful faces can be processed without awareness despite the damaged parietal areas.

3   Conscious perception increased activity in the left fusiform, parietal, and prefrontal cortices of the left hemisphere compared with processing during extinction trials. Consciousness alters cortical processing.

Separate results from non-lesioned participants confirm that *attention to stimuli* (for both task-relevant and non-task-relevant stimuli) and the *emotional significance* of stimuli (fearful or neutral) make independent contributions to visual perception (Vuilleumier *et al.*, 2001). Activity in the fusiform gyrus of the ventral temporal lobe is greater for attended stimuli than for non-attended stimuli; fusiform activation is greater for fear faces regardless of attentional level (Figure 13.12).

The findings support the idea that there are independent *conscious* and *unconscious pathways* to the fear processing system of the amygdala.

3.3   Affective blindsight

We have known for some time (Weiskrantz, 1986) that patients with lesions in their visual cortex have a preserved ability to respond to the visual features of objects

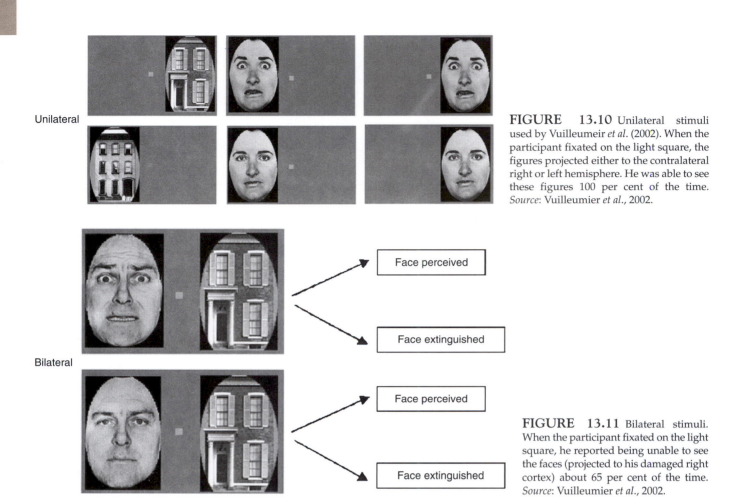

Unilateral

FIGURE 13.10 Unilateral stimuli used by Vuilleumeir *et al.* (2002). When the participant fixated on the light square, the figures projected either to the contralateral right or left hemisphere. He was able to see these figures 100 per cent of the time. *Source*: Vuilleumier *et al.*, 2002.

Bilateral

Face perceived

Face extinguished

Face perceived

Face extinguished

FIGURE 13.11 Bilateral stimuli. When the participant fixated on the light square, he reported being unable to see the faces (projected to his damaged right cortex) about 65 per cent of the time. *Source*: Vuilleumier *et al.*, 2002.

presented in the corresponding blind visual field. Even though such patients have no awareness of the stimuli and cannot describe them, they can, nevertheless, react in behaviorally appropriate ways to specific objects, i.e. they can make appropriate grasping movements with their hands, they can 'guess' at above chance levels the direction of movement, orientation, and color of objects. This ability has been called *blindsight*. Recently, researchers have begun to simulate blindsight in the laboratory by using transcranial magnetic stimulation (TMS) temporarily to interrupt processing in the visual cortex (Ro *et al.*, 2004). This research seems to confirm the long-held belief that such non-conscious visual processing depends on sensory abilities of the evolutionarily ancient superior colliculus.

The term *affective blindsight* has been coined to refer to the preserved ability of patients with visual cortical lesions to respond to the *affective qualities* of stimuli shown to them in their blind visual field (de Gelder *et al.*, 2000; Heywood and Kentridge, 2000).

de Gelder *et al.* (2005) were able to study the interaction of conscious and unconscious emotional processing

in a participant with extensive left visual cortex lesions by presenting facial expressions simultaneously to the intact and blind visual fields. By examining the participant's report of consciously experienced stimuli, the researchers could look for effects of the non-conscious stimuli on conscious reports. When the conscious and non-conscious fear stimuli were congruent (fear seen face with a fear unseen face), correct identification of facial expression was high. However, for incongruent faces (happy seen face paired with fear unseen face or vice versa), the correct identification dropped off to chance level. In congruent fear face trials, there was increased activity in the left amygdala, leading researchers to conclude that unconscious processing of unseen fear faces influenced conscious processing and that this effect was mediated by the amygdala and superior colliculus. In an additional experiment, the researchers looked at the influence of seen and unseen faces on perception of an emotional voice (happy or fearful). For congruent fear face and fear voice, perception of the voice was much more accurate than when the face and voice were incongruent – irrespective of whether the face was consciously

We will look at paradigmatic studies involving human participants.

3.5 Implicit emotional learning and memory

Implicit memory has been discussed in an earlier chapter. It is a kind of learning that is demonstrable in behavioral indicators but which cannot be recollected or consciously reported. It includes various kinds of procedural knowledge, grammars of languages, and classically conditioned associations. Implicit emotional memory involves retention of classically conditioned emotional relationships that cannot be voluntarily recollected or reported. One kind of evidence comes from patients with various kinds of neurological damage.

Patients with damaged amygdalas but spared hippocampi fail to show the physiological indicators of fear conditioning (heart rate increases, electrodermal responses, etc.) but they can recollect and report episodic memories of the circumstances around the fear conditioning. Conversely, patients with lesions in the hippocampus where the amygdalas are spared are unable consciously to report the events surrounding the fear conditionally but show normal fear conditioning measured physiologically (Bechara *et al.*, 1995). This dissociation between the physiological expression of fear conditioning (amygdala-dependent) and the episodic reporting of events surrounding conditioning (hippocampus-dependent) suggest that there are multiple systems supporting emotional memories.

Clinical psychologists who work with victims of traumatic events (accidents, abuse, combat) also have an interest in implicit emotional memory.

3.6 Emotional modulation of explicit memory

Psychological evidence has been available for some time indicating that moderate levels of emotional arousal (most often fear-based arousal) at the time of an event lead to better retention of explicit memories. For example, frightening films are better remembered than neutral films, with a linear relationship between degree of emotional arousal in the film (measured by self-report and by PET activity in the amygdala) and level of free recall (Cahill *et al.*, 1996). The familiar inverted U-shaped function is in operation in predicting the interaction of emotion and memory consolidation. Too much activation in the amygdala leads to loss of explicit memories for emotional events (Cahill and McGaugh, 1998).

Pathways to consolidation of explicit memories seem to depend on reception of emotional stimuli by the amygdala, followed by activation of the hypothalamus

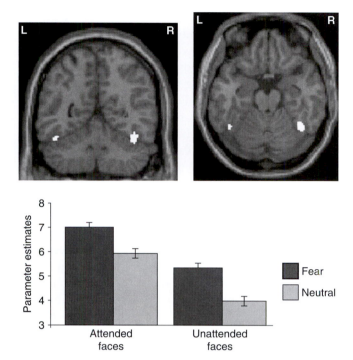

FIGURE 13.12 Activity in the fusiform face area of the temporal lobe: contributions of attention and emotion. Top left: coronal section showing fusiform activity. Top right: horizontal section showing fusiform activity. Bottom: effects of attention and emotion on level of fusiform activation. *Source*: Adapted from Vuilleumier *et al.*, 2001.

or non-consciously processed. Unseen happy faces and emotional pictures other than faces did not have similar enhancing effects. Overall, the researchers concluded that recognition of fear is mandatory and independent of awareness. There are separable cortical and subcortical pathways for perception of fearful stimuli.

3.4 Cognition-emotion interactions: FEAR

Now that we understand the basic wiring diagram of the amygdala's inputs and outputs, we can begin to examine cognition-emotion interactions that depend on the amygdala and its associated areas.

A recent review of the role of the amygdala in emotional processing (Phelps and LeDoux, 2005) identified five areas in which there is converging evidence from animal and human studies of cognition-emotion interactions involving the amygdala:

1 implicit emotional learning and memory
2 emotional modulation of memory
3 emotional influences on perception and attention
4 emotion and social behavior
5 emotion inhibition and regulation.

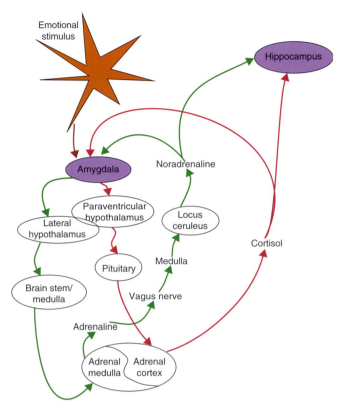

FIGURE 13.13 Stress hormones and explicit memory consolidation. Adrenaline pathway: green. Cortisol pathway: red. Notice that both pathways begin in the amygdala, circulate to the adrenal gland, and feedback to the amygdala and hippocampus after passing throughout the body.

and pituitary gland, resulting in release of the adrenomedullary hormone adrenaline and subsequently the adrenocortical hormone cortisol. Both adrenaline and cortisol (often called stress hormones) appear to influence the hippocampus-dependent formation of explicit memories (Figure 13.13). Improved memory for emotional stimuli is absent in patients with bilateral amygdala lesions (Cahill *et al.*, 1995). The arousal effect due to stress hormone release can also be eliminated by administering β-adrenergic antagonists ('beta blockers' such as propanolol) that block adrenaline receptors (Cahill *et al.*, 1994). The hyper-responsivity of post-traumatic stress disorder (PTSD) patients can be ameliorated by administration of propanolol in the emergency room soon after traumatic events (Pitman *et al.*, 2002).

3.7 Emotional influences on perception and attention

One of the defining features on emotional systems, according to Panksepp's criteria (presented at the beginning of the chapter), is that emotional circuits can influence higher level processing. Evidence for such influence has been obtained in non-human mammals where fear conditioning was found to alter the neural representation of the conditioned stimulus (CS) in the auditory cortex. Studying the guinea pig, Bakin *et al.* (1996) found that classical conditioning of tones shifts the tuning frequency of individual cortical neurons toward the frequency of the CS. The researchers report that such receptive field plasticity is associative, highly specific, rapidly acquired, and indefinitely retained.

Parallel but more limited findings have been obtained for human participants. As we have seen above, the amygdala has direct and indirect connections to sensory cortices that are possible pathways for positive feedback to perceptual processes. Imaging studies using visual masking methods and subliminal fear conditioning (Morris *et al.*, 2001) have shown that human participants who are subliminally exposed to face stimuli as CS for an aversive loud noise (UCS) show an increased responsiveness in the amygdala and visual cortex over trials to the CS. The researchers concluded that 'the parallel learning-related responses observed in ventral amygdala and visual cortex are consistent with a proposal, therefore, that "feed-back" efferents from basal amygdala nuclei mediate emotion-dependent modulation of visual processing'.

The amygdala appears to play a role in determining how unattended but significant stimuli gain access to consciousness by temporary feedback to cortical areas involved in receiving sensory input. The action of the amygdala can make the cortical areas momentarily more receptive to certain adaptively important stimuli.

An example of this greater receptivity to significant stimuli can be found in the Stroop test (Box 13.1) when personally emotion evoking words are compared with other positive, negative, and neutral words. The result has been obtained with Vietnam veterans (McNally *et al.*, 1990) as well as civilian trauma survivors (Taylor *et al.*, 2006). Words that have personal significance for participants (body bags, 'Nam, Medevac for the Vietnam veterans versus revolver, incest, 9/11, or fire for civilian victims) are repeatedly found to gain access to awareness more readily than neutral words and, consequently, cause greater delay in naming the color of the ink in which the words are printed. However, patients who have suffered bilateral damage to the amygdala fail to show the expected facilitation of attention for emotional words that is found in normal participants. Though participants with amygdala lesions comprehend the meaning of the words, they do not display selectively enhanced perception of verbal stimuli with aversive content (Anderson and Phelps, 2001).

BOX 13.1

Emotional Stroop test – a version of the emotional Stroop test that influenced responding by Vietnam veterans (adapted from McNally *et al.*, 1990)

Controls	War-related	Negative	Neutral	Positive
OOOOOOO	firefight	germs	mix	loyal
OOOOOOO	Medevac	filth	millionaire	pleasant
OOOOOOO	Nam	dirty	concrete	happy
OOOOOOO	bodybag	urine	input	friendship

3.8 Emotion and social behavior

Bilateral damage to the amygdala in monkeys causes dramatic changes in their behavior, including lack of fear for dangerous stimuli, eating inedible objects, and atypical sexual behavior (Kluver-Bucy syndrome). However, parallel behavioral changes have not been noted in human patients with lesions of the amygdala, presumably because humans have extensive neocortical social control and inhibition systems not available to other primates. There is, however, some evidence that more subtle deficits exist in patients with amygdala damage, for example, in processing of emotional facial expressions.

As we noted at the beginning of the chapter, the amygdala responds to simple aspects of complex stimuli, specifically to low spatial frequency aspects of faces (Vuilleumeir *et al.*, 2003). Consistent with this general rule, evidence shows that the amygdala responds to the wide-open eyes of fearful and surprised expressions. In a recent refinement, Whalen and his colleagues (Whalen *et al.*, 2004) found that the amygdala responded selectively to subliminally presented *whites* of fearful eyes compared to the whites of happy eyes (Figure 13.14).

Finally, Adolphs *et al.* (2005) found that patients with bilateral amygdala damage fail to look at the eyes when judging facial expression. This deficit may account for observed difficulties in interpretation of others' emotion among such patients. Patients with amygdala lesions underestimate emotional intensity and overestimate trustworthiness and approachableness of others compared to non-lesioned participants.

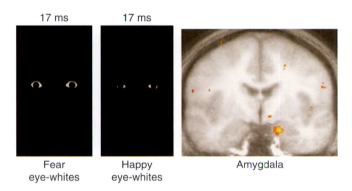

FIGURE 13.14 Amygdala responds to the whites of fearful eyes more strongly that to happy eyes. On the right, the BOLD response of the left ventral amygdala to fearful whites. *Source*: Whalen *et al.*, 2004, as adapted in Phelps and LeDoux, 2005.

3.9 Emotion inhibition and regulation

Fear learning is a long lasting and stable kind of learning that is remarkably resistant to change and voluntary control. It is very difficult to think one's self out of a fearful response. While fear learning is adaptive in that it allows us to avoid predictable dangers in the environment, it can become disabling if it is misplaced or exaggerated. Research on modification or elimination of emotional associations by extinction or reversal, reconsolidation, and emotion regulation is of considerable importance.

Extinction is a method of Pavlovian conditioning where a conditioned stimulus (CS) that was previously linked to an aversive unconditioned stimulus (UCS) is presented alone for a number of trials. The participant learns that the CS is no longer a signal for the aversive event in that context. The CS will continue to evoke the fear response after the passage of time, in other locations, with re-exposure to the UCS. This shows that the learned fear response has been retained in memory and that extinction learning operates by inhibiting the fear response.

The neuroscience of extinction is well studied. It depends critically on the activity of NMDA receptors in the amygdala. When NMDA receptors are blocked in rats, extinction learning is disrupted. When activity at NMDA receptors is enhanced, extinction is augmented. Recently, researchers (Ressler *et al.*, 2004) used NMDA agonists for the first time to improve extinction learning in human agoraphobic patients. They found that two doses of d-cycloserine significantly reduced agoraphobia in conjunction with exposure therapy compared to therapy with a placebo, assessed by self-report and by electrodermal responses to the UCS. The improvements were maintained at three months post-treatment. These results suggest possibilities for future treatments of negative emotion that rely on the neuroscience of fear in the amygdala.

Reversal conditioning is similar to extinction learning in that it modifies the contingencies between conditioned stimuli and responses. In this paradigm, participants are first conditioned to fear one stimulus (CS+) which is reliably followed by a fear-inducing stimulus (UCS), such as a loud noise, and not to fear another stimulus (CS−) which is never followed by the UCS. In the next phase, the contingencies are reversed so that the previously neutral stimulus is now paired with the UCS.

Morris and Dolan (2004) used reversal conditioning to explore the role of the amygdala and the orbitofrontal cortex in fear conditioning. They used a neutral facial expression as CS+ with a loud noise as UCS. They found that during initial conditioning, strong bilateral activation in the amygdala developed to the CS+. After reversal, the new face CS elicited enhanced responses in the orbitofrontal cortex while the old CS continued to evoke increased responses in the right ventral amygdala. While the orbitofrontal cortex is capable of rapid reversal of fear responses, the amygdala showed a persistent, non-reversing response to previous fear-related stimuli. Cortex and limbic system seem to follow different programs – cortex is rapidly responsive to new contingencies while limbic system is more conservative and retains old triggers.

This finding speaks to the neurological basis of the experience of 'being of a divided mind' where part of us knows that the danger no longer exists and part of us still responds to old cues. Those who live with post-traumatic stress disorder (PTSD) are quite familiar with this non-voluntary kind of responding despite changed circumstances.

Memories, including fear memories, become permanent through a process of protein synthesis called consolidation. When retrieved, the memory again becomes labile and is susceptible to further manipulation and alteration prior to *reconsolidation*. Evidence shows that reconsolidation of fear memories in rats involves additional protein synthesis in the amygdala (Nader *et al.*, 2000). Infusion of an antibiotic that interrupts protein synthesis eliminates the conditioned response at test the next day. To date, no direct studies of protein synthesis and reconsolidation involving human participants have been published. It is a promising line of future research with potential to alleviate PSTD symptoms.

Finally, emotional responsiveness can be regulated to some extent by top-down influences from cortex to amygdala. *Reappraisal and reinterpretation* of events are primary coping strategies for human beings. We can reappraise circumstances and attempt to see them in a different way with different meanings and implications for us. For example, we can reinterpret taking a wrong turn from an inconvenience and time-waster to an opportunity to explore new territory. We thereby change our emotion from frustration to curiosity. Reappraisal can lead to both down-regulation as well as up-regulation of affect. Such reappraisal alters our subjective experience as well as our physiological responses. In general, reappraisal strategies activate prefrontal and anterior cingulate cortex involved in cognitive control and the amygdala increasing or increasing activation in parallel with emotional arousal.

Ochsner and his colleagues (Ochsner *et al.*, 2004) looked for fMRI correlates of reappraisal of pictured negative events. They looked for areas of brain activation when participants up-regulated or down-regulated negative affect related to pictured negative events, such as a sick person in the hospital. Participants were assigned one of two kinds of appraisal strategies. In the *self-focus group*, they were asked to focus internally on the meaning of the negative event – either *up-regulating* the negative affect by imagining themselves or someone they love as the person in the picture or *down-regulating* by increasing personal distance from the event by seeing it from a detached objective perspective. In the *situational focus group*, participants were asked to consider aspects

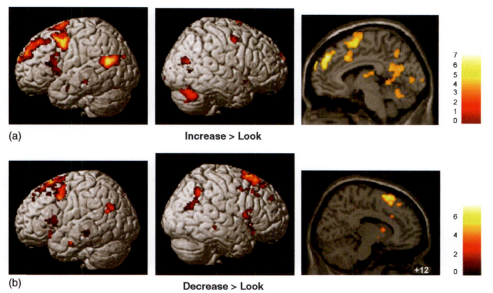

(a) Increase > Look

(b) Decrease > Look

FIGURE 13.15 Up and down regulation. Activations for appraisal strategies compared to looking at pictures without appraisal. (a) Activation related to up-regulation of negative affect. Lateral views are shown on the left and center; medial views on right. Note left dorsal lateral and medial prefrontal as well as anterior cingulate cortical activation. (b) Views for down-regulation. Note bilateral activation of lateral and medial prefrontal cortex, including many left-sided regions similar to those used when increasing affect. *Source*: From Ochsner *et al.*, 2004.

of the situation either imagining that things would get better (down-regulating negative affect) or imagining that things would get worse (up-regulating negative affect).

Both up- and down-regulating negative emotion recruited prefrontal and anterior cingulate regions commonly implicated in cognitive control. Amygdala activation was modulated up or down in accord with appraisal strategies used. Up-regulation uniquely recruited regions of left rostromedial PFC implicated in the retrieval of emotion knowledge, whereas down-regulation uniquely recruited regions of right lateral and orbital PFC implicated in behavioral inhibition (Figure 13.15).

Results also indicated that self-focused regulation recruited medial prefrontal regions (BA 32) implicated in internally processing and self-referential judgments. Situation-focused regulation recruited lateral prefrontal regions (BA46) implicated in maintenance and manipulation of information about the external world via working memory (Figure 13.16).

These data suggest that both common and distinct neural systems support various forms of reappraisal. Particular prefrontal systems modulate the amygdala in different ways depending on the regulatory goal and strategy employed.

We can see that the FEAR system that gives rise to negative emotion has numerous interactions with cognitive systems in the cortex. We turn now to the SEEKING system, another highly studied emotional system in the brain. We will look at a few examples of cognition-emotion interactions involving the SEEKNG system.

4.0 THE SEEKING SYSTEM

To review, Panksepp (1998) described the SEEKING system as the appetitive system that makes mammals curious about their world and promotes goal-directed behavior toward a variety of goal objects, such as food, shelter, sex. This concept of the SEEKING system includes classical *reward pathways* in the brainstem as well as other subcortical areas. In contrast with the FEAR system which gives rise to freezing, hiding, or flight in service of self-protection when activated, the SEEKING system is a positively-valenced, energizing system that moves animals out into their environment to forage and explore.

In 1954, Olds and Milner discovered that rats would learn to work for electrical stimulation of the subcortical areas including areas around the lateral hypothalamus. Subsequent studies have shown this electrical self-stimulation (ESS) is highly reinforcing. Rats will self-stimulate areas in the lateral hypothalamus up to 2000 times an hour and choose ESS over food to the point of starvation. Development of microelectrodes in the 1970s allowed increasingly fine-grained studies of brain locations involved in reward.

The primary reward pathways in mammals include the:

1 mesolimbic dopamine pathway: dopaminergic neurons that originate in the ventral tegmental area (VTA) of the brainstem terminate at the nucleus accumbens in the forebrain and

2 mesocortical dopamine pathway: dopaminergic neurons project from VTA to orbitofrontal cortex

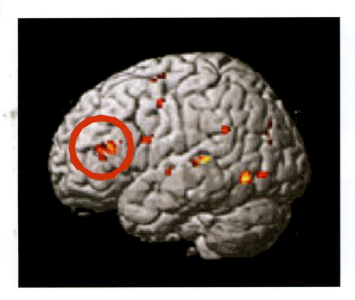

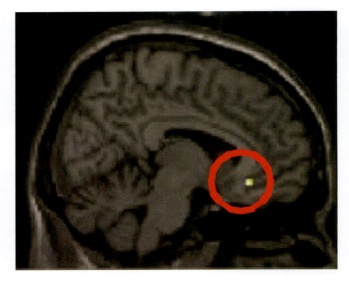

FIGURE 13.16 Situation-focused regulation. Activations unique to appraisal strategies when down-regulating affect. Situation focus on left: notice activity in BA 46 (circled). Self-focus on right: note activity in BA32 (circled). *Source*: Ochsner *et al.*, 2004.

(Figure 13.17). VTA is located inside the pons in the midbrain, surrounded by other midbrain nuclei and pathways. Nucleus accumbens is located near and anterior to the amygdala and below the striatum (basal ganglia) in each hemisphere.

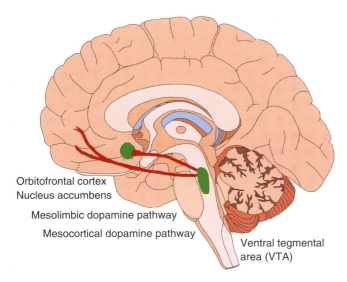

FIGURE 13.17 Dopamine reward pathways including the meso-cortical dopamine and mesolimbic dopamine pathways.

4.1 Re-interpreting 'reward': from reward to reward prediction to reward prediction error

Understanding of the reward concept and the role of midbrain dopamine pathways have evolved. For a long time, the dopamine system was thought to respond at *receipt* of rewarding stimuli, such as ESS, intracranial drug injections, food, or sweet water or to conditioned stimuli that predicted the reward. Subsequent research has shown that neurons in this system are more responsive to *anticipation of reward* than to receipt of reward (Schultz, 1998, 2002). Evidence in support of this hypothesis shows that dopamine neurons:

1. fire selectively in response to unexpected rewards and novel, attention-grabbing events, followed by a rapid decrease in responding with repeated arrival of reward as expected
2. stop responding to predictable rewards, as they gradually become responsive to conditioned stimuli that *predict* rewarding events
3. are inhibited by the omission of expected rewards.

The reward system begins with unconditioned responses to sensory aspects of rewarding objects: unconditioned stimuli (UCS) such as sweet tastes, musky smells, etc. Since the primary reinforcing event is actually the arrival of dopamine at the nucleus accumbens, the UCSs are not the rewards. They are proximal cues of upcoming internal events. With experience, more distal, environmental signals such as landmarks and sounds (conditioned stimuli, CS) come to predict the availability of taste and smell-carrying objects. Now these new cues come to evoke dopaminergic responses in the midbrain. Over time, it is the acquired reward stimuli that seem to produce the greatest pleasure. In our own lives, we are more excited about the prospect of a pay raise or a hot date than we are at 'receipt' of these desired events (Wise, 2002). Sadly, at least from the point of view of the dopamine system, there seems to be something to the idea that the desired object, once attained, is no longer as desirable.

The simple reward prediction view has been revised in light of evidence suggesting that dopaminergic neurons respond specifically to *errors in prediction of rewards*. For example, over time, activation disappears to CSs that reliably predict reward. The loss of response is not due to a generalized loss of response to the reward itself, since the dopaminergic system responds to the rewards outside the test situation. Also, response of dopaminergic neurons is depressed when rewards are withheld or delayed when CSs indicate that they should arrive. Since there are no other novel stimuli present at the time when rewards are expected, the depressed response cannot be interpreted as a response to another stimulus. The depressed dopaminergic response when rewards are withheld is seen as a reaction to the failed arrival of a predicted event.

The evidence suggests that dopamine neurons shift responsiveness toward situations where rewards are highly unpredictable. In fact, CSs cannot be conditioned to rewards that are already reliably predicted. The long-standing empirical test for this hypothesis is the blocking paradigm. In the blocking paradigm, it can be demonstrated that a new stimulus will not become associated with a reinforcer when it is presented in a circumstance where the reinforcer is already predicted 100 per cent of the time. Direct empirical evidence that the dopaminergic system is involved in mediating this behavioral learning has been obtained in monkeys where microelectrodes record responses of individual dopaminergic neurons.

A study by Tobler *et al.* (2003), reviewed by Ungless (2004), showed that dopamine neurons are not activated by all salient stimuli. They trained monkeys by rewarding them every time a light was turned on. Then the light came on and a tone was simultaneously sounded, no reward was delivered (see Figure 13.18), thus the tone predicted the omission of a reward. When the tone was presented alone, the dopamine neuron was inhibited. Ungless (2004) suggested that these findings indicate that dopamine neurons are not activated in a non-specific manner when salient stimuli are presented: it is stimuli's predictive powers and not just the presence of a reward that modulates dopamine neuron activity. The conclusion is that associative learning depends on increased predictive power of new stimuli, which selectively activate the mesolimbic dopamine system. The conclusion is that associative

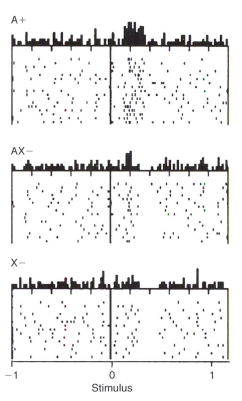

FIGURE 13.18 An example of an individual dopamine neuron that is inhibited by a stimulus predicting reward omission. At the top of each panel is a cumulative histogram of action potential number across time (each bar is 10 ms) for repeated presentations of the stimuli; below each histogram, the dashes represent individual action potentials occurring in each trial. Stimulus 'A' is paired with reward (A+) and excites the dopamine neuron. When 'A' is presented with 'X' no reward occurs (AX−), and therefore 'X' predicts reward omission. When 'X' is presented alone, the dopamine neuron is inhibited (X−). Other control stimuli were also presented but are not shown here. *Source:* From Ungless, 2004; this figure was reproduced from Tobler *et al.*, 2003, with permission.

learning depends on increased predictive power of new stimuli, which selectively activate the mesolimbic dopamine system.

Currently, reward prediction error theory is the most widely accepted understanding of the dopaminergic reward system.

4.2 Reward is more than learning

The reward prediction error theory of reward focuses heavily on the learned aspects of rewards. Quoting Thorndike's early view, Schultz (2002) emphasized the function of rewarding events in 'stamping in' associations between conditioned stimuli and their consequences. In response, it has been noted by other researchers

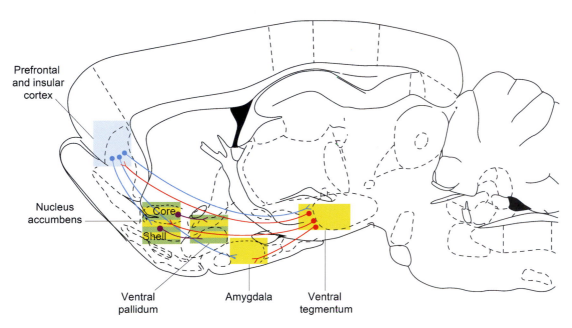

FIGURE 13.19 Simplified view of subcortical liking and wanting pathways, shown in a rat brain. 'Liking' pathways are shown in green; 'wanting' pathways in yellow; cognitive processing of cues is shown in blue. *Source*: Berridge and Robinson, 2003.

(Berridge and Robinson, 1998, 2003; Panksepp, 2005) that reward prediction theory leaves out important hedonic and motivational components of rewarding events that should not be ignored.

The hedonic feeling of 'liking' has been shown to have reliable facial characteristics across different mammals (Figure 13.19) and to be dissociable from the dopamine system. 'Liking' reactions are neurally modulated by a distributed brain network that includes the *shell of the nucleus accumbens, ventral pallidum,* and *brainstem parabrachial nucleus* (Berridge and Robinson, 2003). Liking reactions to sweet water in rats are not affected by activation or suppression of the mesolimbic dopamine systems but are increased by injections of opioid- or GABA-agonist microinjections. Lesions that eliminate dopamine in the nucleus accumbens and produce a profound aphagia (disinclination to eat) fail to disrupt taste 'liking'(Wyvell and Berridge, 2000). Dopamine receptor antagonists often fail to suppress subjective pleasure ratings of amphetamines and cigarettes in humans. Finally, activation of the human dopamine system by amphetamine correlates better with subjective ratings of wanting for drug or food than with subjective ratings of pleasure (Leyton *et al.*, 2002). In subjective terms, the dopamine system makes food and drugs more desired and sought out but does not make them palatable, tasty, or enjoyable once acquired. Likeability apparently depends on

a separate system involving the shell of the nucleus accumbens.

It makes some sense in light of this evidence to separate the *learning* aspects of reward, i.e. the ability of rewarded behaviors to be retained, from the hedonic *liking* aspects. Homologies in behavioral responses to tastes give us indicators of the hedonic impact of stimuli (Berridge, 2000). Homologous indicators of 'liking' across species of mammals include tongue protrusion for tastes such as sweet water. Conversely, disliking reactions include open-mouthed gapes to bitter tastes like quinine (Figure 13.20).

A third component of the reward architecture is the element of *wanting* or incentive salience (Berridge and Robinson, 1998). Wanting is separable from liking and learning subjectively and neurologically. We can want things, such as drugs of abuse or cigarettes, even when we don't like them. Learning may be motivated by wanting but can take place without wanting. Likewise, learning can take place without subjective 'liking' as when receiving intracranial drug injections for learning lever pressing responses without an accompanying sensory experience of a reinforcer. Wanting 'transforms mere sensory information about rewards and their cues (sights, sounds, and smells) into attractive, desired, and riveting incentives' (p. 510). In contrast to the liking component of reward, wanting, or in humans craving,

'Liking' expression – sweet

'Disliking' expression – bitter

FIGURE 13.20 Liking reactions: objective indices of hedonic aspects of emotion. Homologous affective facial expressions by infant human, juvenile orang-utan and adult rat to 'liked' sucrose (top) versus 'disliked' quinine (bottom). *Source*: Berridge and Robinson, 2003.

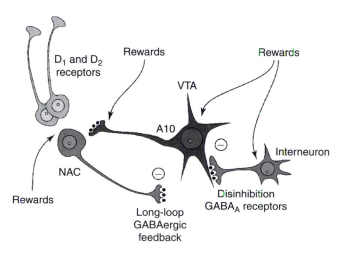

FIGURE 13.21 Drugs and their effects on the 'wanting' system. Direct and indirect activation of VTA dopaminergic activity by natural rewards and drugs in the mesolimbic dopamine system. A10 dopaminergic neurons originate in the VTA and project to the shell of the nucleus accumbens (NAC). GABA-ergic interneurons within the VTA and long-loop GABA-ergic feedback from the NAC provide inhibitory control (minus signs) of the A10 neurons. Different dopamine receptors in the NAC (D_1 and D_2) mediate reward effects. *Source*: Spanagel and Weiss, 1999.

is highly dependent on the mesolimbic dopamine pathway.

4.3 'Reward pathway' and drug use

All drugs of abuse have their effects on the 'wanting' system via the dopamine pathways and their connections in the midbrain (Figure 13.21). Animals will learn to press a lever to receive intracranial microinjections and acquire conditioned place preferences for locations where they receive such microinjection of drugs. The behavior of these animals has helped to isolate brain areas involved in the rewarding effects of cocaine, amphetamine, nicotine, alcohol, and opiates (Spanagel and Weiss, 1999; Ikemoto and Wise, 2004). In addition, drug effects in humans have been studied by investigating the effect of drug agonists and antagonists on the experience of drugs of abuse by drug-using individuals.

Natural rewards and drugs of abuse act in different ways on the mesolimbic dopamine system. Food, as well as opioids, indirectly affect the reward system by decreasing the action of inhibitory interneurons that normally inhibit the dopaminergic neurons of the VTA; the result is increased activity in the dopaminergic neurons of the VTA. In contrast, cocaine and amphetamine act directly in the nucleus accumbens to

maintain high levels of dopamine at synapses of dopaminergic neurons; cocaine inhibits reuptake while amphetamine apparently increases dopamine release. The specific modes of action of various drugs are still being investigated. However, it is clear that the agents outlined in Table 13.2 affect behavior and subjective experience through their effects on the mesolimbic dopamine system (Spanagel and Weiss, 1999; Ikemoto and Wise, 2004).

4.4 Reward cues influence attention

Consistent with the reward prediction error view, cues that predict availability of drugs of abuse quickly become conditioned stimuli and powerful evokers of craving in humans. Drug-related cues not only activate the dopaminergic system and create the subjective experience of craving but they also influence cognitive activities. Use of drugs shifts attention toward drug-related cues at the expense of other stimuli. Numerous studies using the Stroop paradigm (discussed earlier) have shown that drug-related cues (pictures and words) divert attention from the color naming task in drug using participants but not in non-using participants (Hester *et al.*, 2006). Corresponding brain imaging studies have shown that smokers have significantly greater responses to smoking-related picture cues in the

TABLE 13.2 Agents and their effects on behavior: sites implicated in the rewarding effects of natural rewards and drugs of abuse

Agent	Effective site
Food, liquids, sex	Cause dopamine release in VTA through inhibition of GABA-ergic interneurons that normally inhibit the dopaminergic neurons
Mu and delta opioids	Opioids act indirectly through inhibition of GABA-ergic neurons in VTA and NAC that normally inhibit the dopaminergic neurons
Amphetamine	Acts directly to release dopamine in the nucleus accumbens
Cocaine	Acts directly to block the dopamine transporter system/reuptake in the shell of the nucleus accumbens
Phencyclidine (PCP)	Acts directly in the shell of the nucleus accumbens through blockade NMDA receptors
Cannabis	Acts in the posterior VTA and shell of the nucleus accumbens
Ethanol	Acts indirectly through posterior VTA through inhibition of the GABA-ergic interneurons
Nicotine	Nucleus accumbens/ventral striatum

nucleus accumbens and neighboring ventral striatum than non-smokers (David *et al.*, 2005), though there is no difference between the groups' imaging responses to neutral images.

5.0 CONCLUSION

Mammals have separate emotional systems in the brain, each with patterned, innate responses to stimuli in the expected environment of the species related to survival. Systems such as the FEAR system and SEEKING system have been shown to have both unconditioned and conditioned responses to significant 'calling conditions' supported by separate neural networks, FEAR relying on the amygdala and its connections, SEEKING relying heavily on the mesolimbic and mesocortical pathways of the VTA. Each of these systems can come under cognitive control and also reciprocally influence higher decision-making, appraisal systems, and consciousness. Each system is capable of elaborating distinctly different subjective feelings.

6.0 CHAPTER REVIEW

6.1 Study questions

1 What are the key differences between the reptilian and the mammalian brain?
2 What are examples of 'hard-wired' emotions as described by Panksepp?
3 Why has the fear system been more studied than other emotion systems?
4 What do the terms 'high road' and 'low road' refer to in terms of fear processing?
5 In what ways has the study of affective blindsight informed us about emotion processing?
6 What factors distinguish 'reward' from 'learning' in the study of SEEKING.

6.2 Drawing exercises

1 Label the regions of the triune brain.

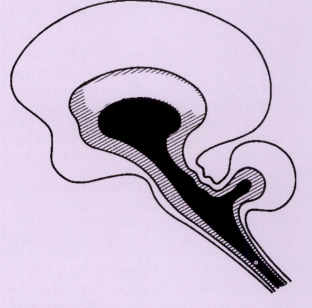

FIGURE 13.22

2   Label the afferent connections to the amygdala.

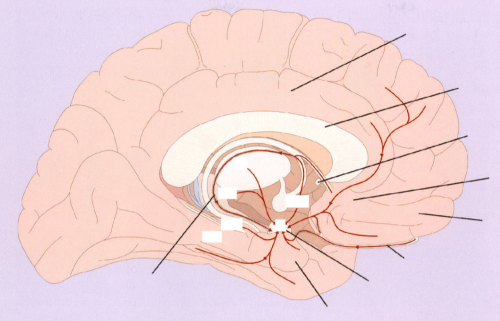

FIGURE 13.23

3   Label the efferent connections from the amygdala.

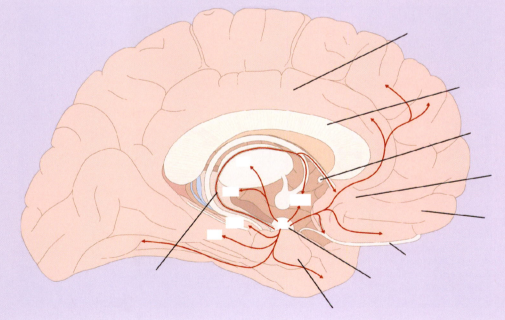

FIGURE 13.24

Man is a social animal.
Attributed to Aristotle

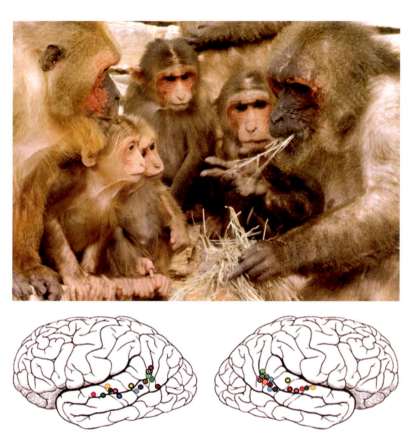

If this looks like a scene we could imagine with humans, it is because our social brains have large areas of overlap and similarity with the brains of other primates. The two cortical hemispheres shown below show how social cognition often activates the superior temporal sulcus (STS) in the human brain. *Source: top*, de Waal, 2004; *bottom*, Allison *et al.*, 2000.

Social cognition: Perceiving the mental states of others

Katharine McGovern

1.0 OVERVIEW

In this chapter, we will examine one aspect of human cognition that makes us unique among our mammalian relatives – our ability to understand each other as conscious beings with internal mental states. Other mammals have partial abilities to tune into the psychological states of members of their own species, their conspecifics. They can perceive aspects of posture, vocalization and facial expression as signs and take action based on those signs. Some primates have 'mirror neurons'

that appear to allow them to register the commonality between actions of other monkeys and their own actions. However, no other animal has been shown to understand, to make use of, or to depend on the *subjectivity* of other members of its species. It is a peculiarly human ability.

The 'question of other minds' is an old one among philosophers. However, psychological and neuroscientific study of how we understand the mental states of others is more recent. As yet, psychologists and neuroscientists have not agreed on common definitions of the terms that are used to describe and explain social

Cognition, Brain, and Consciousness, edited by B. J. Baars and N. M. Gage
ISBN: 978-0-12-373677-2

Copyright 2007, Elsevier Ltd. All rights reserved.

TABLE 14.1   Perspective in social cognition and in science

	First-person perspective	Second-person perspective	Third-person perspective
Data type	Phenomenological data	Empathic understandings	Ordinary empirical data; sense data
Methods of data gathering	Controlled introspection on internal states; traditional psychophysics	Reflection on empathic attunement; internal scanning of emotional and cognitive responses in the presence on another	Objective observation of external objects
Linguistic markers	*I feel, I know*	*You* seem, *You* look	*It is, S/he is*

cognition. So a few brief definitions are in order before we begin our study of social cognition.

1.1 Terms that are used to refer to social cognition

In the research literature, terms that refer to aspects of social cognition are often used interchangeably and in different ways by different researchers.

Empathy carries the sense of feeling the feelings of others. In Latin, the word means 'feeling inside' or 'feeling with'. On the other hand, *theory of mind* (TOM, see Section 1.3) is often used to highlight the idea that we normally have complex metacognitive understandings of our own minds as well as the minds of others – including cognitive and affective aspects. Similarly, Frith and Frith (1999) introduced the term *mentalizing* to capture the idea that, when we have a well-developed theory of mind, we understand ourselves and others not just as sensory objects but also as subjective beings with mental states. We understand others as having mental states that we can anticipate and make use of to guide our own behaviors. *Mind-reading*, like mentalizing, identifies our ability to attune our own behaviors to the minds and anticipated actions of others.

One of the most difficult aspects of understanding the concept of theory of mind is understanding the difference between seeing others as sensory objects versus seeing others as subjective beings with minds and mental states. Having a complete TOM gives us the ability to go beyond the sensory into the mental. We can do things that those with deficient TOMs cannot do. Once we have a TOM we can pretend, lie, deceive, guess, play hide-and-seek, predict and understand the full range of human emotion. People who have deficits in TOM (people with autism, for example) have limited abilities to do these things, as we will see.

Philosophers use the term *intentionality* when they want to speak about how minds and mental states are always 'about something else' in a way that other physical objects, i.e. body parts, are not. Our thoughts always

have an object. For example, we think 'about' the chair, the book, or the idea in a way that our stomach, arm, or tooth are not about anything other than themselves. Minds have mental states; minds *represent* objects and events outside themselves. It is not clear that other species comprehend the intentional nature of minds in their conspecifics. Humans seem to have an implicit understanding of the contents of others' minds.

A separate concept is the psychological term 'intention', our ability to form an image of a goal state and to organize action in pursuit of that goal state. Be careful not to confuse these two very similar terms! Theory of mind abilities allow us to read the intentions of others and to share attention with others about a common focus.

Finally, the term *intersubjectivity* emphasizes our ability to coordinate mutual interactions in light of our perception of the subjectivity and intentionality of others. When this ability is absent, we readily recognize the deficiency in the social exchanges of others. Examples are found in autistic spectrum disorders, in the sometimes deficient emotion recognition of schizophrenia and in the empathic failures of psychopathic and borderline personalities.

1.2 The importance of perspective: the first, second, and third person

Science usually works from a *third person perspective*. This means that researchers adopt an objective point of view, seeing all evidence as a physical object. Even human beings are seen as objects, as sensory surfaces. The mental 'insides' of human beings are also viewed through objective means such as behavioral observation or brain imagery. Recently, scientists interested in consciousness have begun arguing for an additional way of conducting science that appreciates and accepts data gathered from a *first person perspective*, i.e. using phenomenological data from introspection or self-report. To a certain extent, self-report under controlled circumstances is a well-established scientific method, for example, in psychophysics and the study of perception.

BOX 14.1   In 1923, philosopher Martin Buber wrote about the second person perspective in his classic book *I and Thou.*

FIGURE 14.1 Martin Buber (1878–1965).

move easily between these two ways of perceiving others. As we adopt one or the other stance, our own internal states change. Within the past decade, these internal states have been assessed via brain imaging techniques.

Buber wrote:

Primary words are spoken from the being.

If Thou is said, the I of the combination I-Thou is said along with it.

If It is said, the I of the combination I-It is said along with it. . . .

There is no I taken in itself, but only the I of the primary word I-Thou and the I of the primary word I-It. . .

When Thou is spoken, the speaker has no thing for his object. For where there is a thing there is another thing. Every It is bounded by others; It exists only through being bounded by others. But when Thou is spoken, there is no thing. Thou has no bounds.

Buber identified two fundamentally different ways of being in relation to other people and objects, I-It and I-thou. I-It involves perceiving others as objects; I-Thou involves an empathic perceiving of others as subjects. Ordinarily we can

What about the *second person perspective*? In this stance, the other person is viewed as a *subject* rather than an object, as someone who has mental states. This perspective is less well established in psychological science and neuroscience, though it is well known in philosophy and in clinical psychology. Contemporary social cognition research comes close to examining the second person perspective. To be exact, we are adopting a third person perspective (objective view) on other people as *they* engage in a second person activity.

1.3 Approaches to perceiving others' minds

Once past our fourth birthday (whether we are normally developing or developmentally delayed), we human beings give indications of understanding other minds – 'mentalizing' as Chris Frith has called it. We can recognize and respond to the invisible, internal subjective regularities that account for the behaviors of others. We will call the full-fledged ability to understand and predict our own and others' minds *theory of mind* (TOM). TOM has been explained by three kinds of theories: module theories, theory theories, and simulation theories.

According to *module theories*, such as that of Simon Baron-Cohen, human beings develop a theory of mind module (TOMM) that is separate from but builds on other mental abilities that may be shared with non-human primates and other mammals; only

humans are presumed to have a complete TOMM. This kind of theory fits well with findings from the study of autism.

Theory theories suppose that TOM capabilities develop as a primitive, implicit theory over the course of development, much like Piaget's conservation theories. Such implicit theories predict abrupt changes in behavior as new knowledge is added, as is seen in the abrupt change in children's understanding of their own minds between ages three and four.

Simulation theories suppose that we understand other minds by internally simulating or 'running off line' the mental states of others in each situation. The dual responsiveness of mirror neurons to self- and other-generated action could be taken as support for simulation theory.

It seems very likely that all three kinds of theory are needed to account for human 'mentalizing' abilities. As we will see, there are separable skills that develop in mammals and humans that operate much like *modules*; we can lose one module but still have the other. The system that allows us to imitate others seems to operate through *internal simulation* of the actions of others. Finally, adult human beings have sophisticated social perception abilities that allow us to reason about other people's internal states; we act as if we have a complex set of rules about our own and others' mental states that could be called an *implicit theory.*

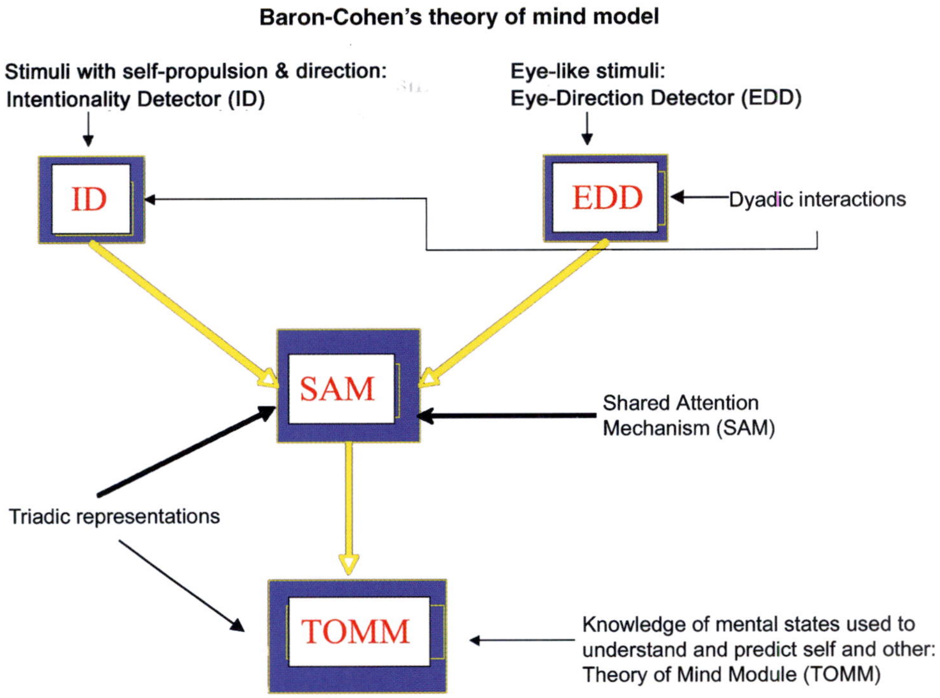

Baron-Cohen's theory of mind model

FIGURE 14.2 A schematic diagram of Baron-Cohen's Theory of Mind Model with the eye-direction detector (EDD), shown on the upper right, sending inputs to the intentionality detector (ID), upper left, and to the shared attention mechanism (SAM), shown in the center of the diagram. The SAM also receives inputs from the ID and interacts with the Theory of Mind Module (TOMM). *Source*: adapted from Baron-Cohen, 1995.

2.0 AN ORGANIZING FRAMEWORK FOR SOCIAL COGNITION

Simon Baron-Cohen (1995) hypothesized that a fully developed theory of mind is composed of four kinds of skills that develop independently. These skills are *detection of intentions of others, detection of eye-direction, shared attention*, and a complex repertoire of implicit knowledge about others, which he called the *theory of mind module*. Some of these skills are observed in mammals and non-human primates as well as in humans. However, only the theory of mind module appears in normally developing human beings. We will first introduce Baron-Cohen's model (summarized in Figure 14.2) and then use it as a way to organize the larger body of social cognition research.

2.1 Intention

The first component of Baron-Cohen's TOM is called the *intentionality detector* (ID). This is the ability to perceive intention or purposeful action in many forms of biological and non-biological movement. For example, when we watch leaves swirling in a parking lot, we have a tendency to see the leaves as 'wanting to go together'. We ascribe common purpose to the pile of leaves. Or, when we watch pieces of modeling clay being moved around an artificial landscape in clay-mation films, we readily attribute intentions and other mental states to the pieces of clay. Likewise, when we watch people and animals engaged in behaviors, we seem to understand their goals and the desired outcomes of their actions. We interpret *action* as intention.

2.2 Eye detection

The second component of the model is the *eye direction detector* (EDD), the skill to detect eyes and eye-like stimuli and to determine the direction of gaze. Many mammals seem to have the ability to notice and use information about eye direction. Cats, for example, use eye direction as part of their social dominance behavior with other cats; the non-dominant cats must avert their eyes in the face of the dominant cat. Humans, from the first hours of life, search for and focus on the eyes of their caregivers. We also have a strong tendency to see non-living stimuli as eye-like; hence, we see the 'man in the moon' and faces on automobiles, gnarled trees, and mountains. The 'language of the eyes' seems to be a fundamental means of communicating mental states among humans.

Both the intentionality detector and the eye direction detector involve *dyadic* (two-way) interactions. That is, there is *one perceiver* and *one object of perception*. As yet, no sharing of mental states is necessarily involved. Both EDD and ID are found in non-humans as part of their social perception abilities. It is the third module of TOM that is unique to human social cognition.

2.3 Shared attention

The *shared attention mechanism* (SAM) is the ability we have, by the end of our first year of life, to understand that when someone else shifts the direction of their gaze they are 'looking at' something. We seem to learn that looking leads to seeing – an advance over the simpler signal of eye direction. We realize that we can look too and see the same thing. Gaze shifting and social pointing of fingers are ways we learn to direct the attention of a companion.

Infants before one year of age, most other primates, and other mammals do not have a shared attention ability. We can see this in our much loved companion animals. While our family dog may chase a ball and bring it back, he will not follow our gaze if we look toward a ball lying in the grass. He will not follow our pointing finger when we try to direct his gaze toward the ball. The dog has considerable intelligence but does not have shared attention. Similarly, an infant at 6 months does not turn his head to follow the caregiver's gaze; a one year old does. Shared attention abilities mark the human species.

2.4 Higher-order theory of mind

The final component of full-fledged theory of mind is what Baron-Cohen has called the *theory of mind module* (TOMM), a complex knowledge base containing rules of social cognition that develops by the time we reach our fourth birthday. TOMM tells us that:

- Appearance and reality are not necessarily the same – a rock can look like an egg but not be an egg; I can pretend to be a dog but not be a dog
- A person who is sitting still in a chair may be 'doing something', i.e. thinking, imagining, or remembering (young children do not appreciate this)
- Other people can have mental states as well as physical states
- Other people can know things that I don't know; I can be fooled or deceived, I can detect deception
- I can know things that other people don't know: I can fool or deceive others, I understand the point of games like hide-and-seek
- My mental state in the past was different from how it is now
- Facial expressions are indicators of mental states as much as they are indicators of physical states; I can distinguish a surprised face from a yawning one.

TOM is not the same as intelligence or IQ. Developmentally delayed children and adults display complete TOM abilities despite low IQs, while people living with autistic spectrum disorders (ASD) may have high IQs but markedly deficient TOM abilities.

We can now use Baron-Cohen's four TOM skills as a way to organize and guide our study of social cognition.

3.0 MIRROR NEURONS AND INTENTION DETECTION

Where is social cognition located in the brain? Some recent investigations of mirror neuron systems have brought to light some dramatic findings regarding where social and intentionality systems may be processed in the brain.

3.1 From action to intention

The *mirror neuron system* (MNS) is a collection of cortical neurons that allow humans to understand the intentions of others from observation of their actions. Mirror neurons were first discovered in the frontal cortex of macaque monkeys and shortly thereafter in their parietal cortex. These cortical neurons have the remarkable property that the individual mirror neuron fires not only when a particular action is perceived but also when the observer performs the same action. Immediately, researchers grasped the possibility that mirror neurons might be a means of comparing one's own actions with those of others. In addition, mirror neurons are being examined as a basis for inferring the goals and intentions of others through internal matching of action representations of others' actions with action representations in one's own action repertoire.

The original work on mirror neurons was conducted by Rizzolatti *et al.* at the University of Parma in Italy in the early 1990s. They found mirror neurons in the frontal motor area of monkey cortex in an area labeled F5. Using single cell recordings of macaque cortical neurons, they found that such neurons would respond when the experimenter grasped peanuts placed on a board as well as when the monkey grasped the peanuts; the neuron did not respond when the peanut was observed alone on the board or when the experimenter grasped the peanut with a tool. Clearly, the act of grasping food with one's hand was the act that the neuron was 'tuned' to. Figure 14.3 illustrates a monkey with a microelectrode apparatus affixed to his head; he is sitting in a functional magnetic resonance imaging (fMRI) recording apparatus. Figure 14.4 shows the experimental arrangement for assessing responses of single mirror

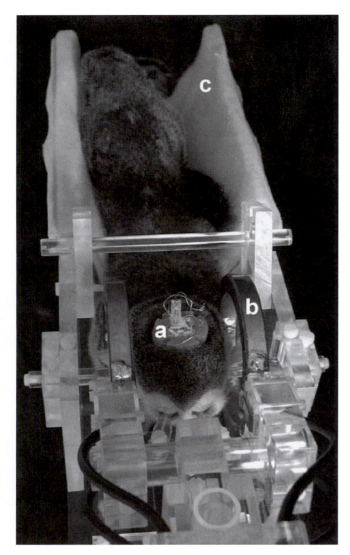

FIGURE 14.3 Monkey with a microelectrode attached to his head, performing inside an fMRI apparatus. a, microelectrode; b, fMRI coil; c, cradle. *Source*: Tammer *et al.*, 2006.

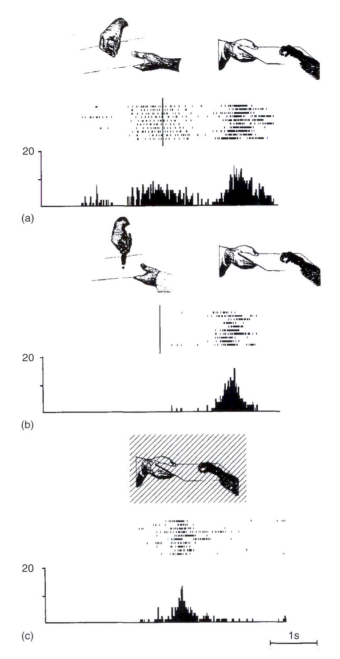

FIGURE 14.4 The observed acts and single cell responses of mirror neurons. (a) The experimenter places a piece of food on the board, moves it toward the monkey, and the monkey grasps the food. The figure at the top of the panel illustrates the acts. Individual responses of the neuron over time are presented in the middle of the panel. At the bottom is a histogram representing the total responses in each 20-millisecond time segment over time. Notice the numerous responses when the experimenter grasps the food, the lack of responses while the board is moved and the numerous responses again when the monkey grasps the food. (b) The experimenter grasps the food with a tool, moves the food toward the monkey, and the monkey grasps the food with its hand. Notice here that responses occur only when the monkey's hand grasps the food. (c) The monkey grasps the piece of food in the dark. Notice the numerous responses to the grasping act even when it is conducted in the dark. *Source*: Rizzolatti *et al.*, 1996.

neurons in different conditions used by Rizzolatti and his colleagues.

To insure that the single-cell recordings were not an artifact of monkey-experimenter interaction or food expectancy, the researchers also recorded from the monkey while it observed nearby food grasping actions between the experimenter and a second monkey. The mirror neuron responded as before, i.e. it responded when the observed monkey grasped the food, not when the food was moved, but again when the observed monkey grasped the food (Figure 14.5).

Research with macaque monkeys has been done with single cell recording of individual prefrontal neurons. The existence of mirror neurons in macaques is well

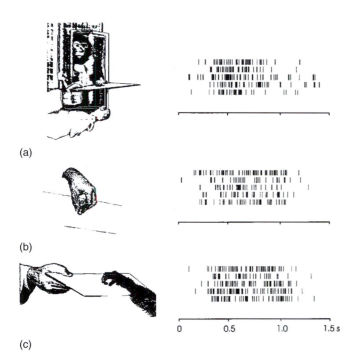

(a)

(b)

(c)

FIGURE 14.5 Observed acts of another monkey can evoke mirror neuron responses. The mirror neuron responds to observed action of another monkey (a), of the experimenter (b), and of the recorded monkey itself (c). *Source*: Rizzolatti *et al.*, 1996.

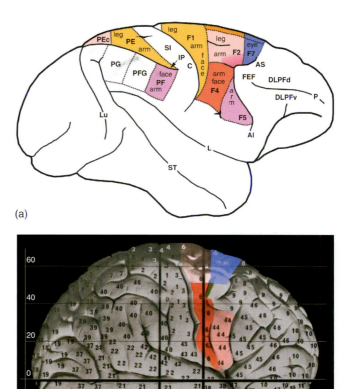

(a)

(b)

FIGURE 14.6 Monkey to human homologies in mirror neuron locations and functions. (a) A lateral view of the macaque right cortex. (b) A lateral view of the human right cortex. *Source*: Rizzolatti *et al.*, 2002.

established. Similar single cell recordings of neurons have not been conducted in humans; evidence for the human mirror neuron system (MNS) comes from imaging data that aggregates the activity of many neurons. Thus, individual human mirror neurons have not been studied to date. Nevertheless, there are marked similarities between mirror neuron systems studied in monkeys using single unit recordings and in human using neuroimaging of population-level neuronal responses. Rizzolatti *et al.* (2002) have summarized the monkey to human homologies in Figure 14.6.

Area F5 in the macaque (purple in Figure 14.6) and Brodmann area 44 in humans (pink) seem to code for hand actions, such as those studied in the original mirror neuron research. Area F4 in the macaque and the ventral premotor cortex (vPM or lower Brodmann area 6 in humans (colored red in Figure 14.6) both respond to arm and wrist movement. Individual frontal neurons in the macaque and prefrontal areas in humans are tuned to arm and wrist movements toward particular locations in the space around the individual. This implies that mirror neurons in these areas are not simply representing general movements of the arm and wrist, but rather they are responding to acts connected to particular goals, i.e. reaching locations in space.

Note: you may remember that Brodmann area 44 in the left hemisphere has been called *Broca's area*. It has traditionally been seen as the cortical speech area. Recent studies of imitation in humans have shown that Brodmann area 44 has mirror neuron capabilities, involving representation of actions with the hand and arm (Iacoboni, 2005). Thus, Broca's area has mixed abilities.

A long-standing challenge in the study of mirror neurons has been distinguishing between simple *action recognition* (is that grasping, reaching, or holding?) and *intention detection* (where an agent has a goal which is accomplished by the action: drinking tea versus cleaning up after tea). The final piece of evidence linking mirror neurons to intention detection comes from studies of human acts carried out in different contexts. A central question in these studies is: does the MNS respond to the act regardless of context or does it respond to acts in particular contexts? The first alternative implies that mirror neurons do action recognition. The second

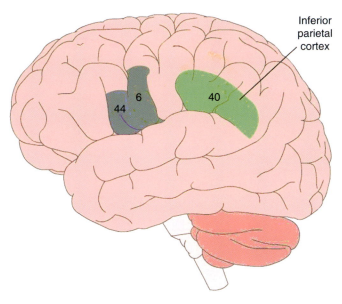

FIGURE 14.7 A simplified view of the left hemisphere with locations of the frontal mirror neuron system highlighted. (Note: inferior parietal cortex = supramarginal gyrus = BA 40; ventral premotor cortex = lower Brodmann area 6; posterior inferior frontal gyrus = Pars opercularis of IFG = Brodmann area 44.)

FIGURE 14.8 Two different contexts, acts and intentions used in Iacoboni *et al.* (2005): Drinking tea versus cleaning up after tea. Left panel shows the stimuli in the Context condition, center panel shows the Action condition and right panel shows the Intention condition. *Source:* Iacoboni *et al.*, 2005.

allows us to extend the inference: MNS is for intention detection.

Marco Iacoboni and his colleagues have obtained evidence supporting the argument that the MNS responds to intentions rather than particular actions by examining fMRI images as participants observe acts with and without context. They found that actions embedded in contexts (Intention in Figure 14.8), compared with the other two conditions (Context only or Action), yielded a significant fMRI increase in the posterior part of the

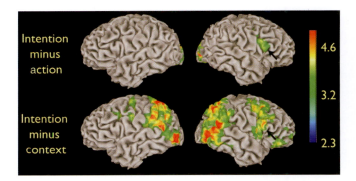

FIGURE 14.9 fMRI results from Iacoboni *et al.* (2005). Upper panel shows response in the Intention minus Action conditions; lower panel shows Intention minus Context conditions. *Source:* Iacoboni *et al.*, 2005.

inferior frontal gyrus and the adjacent sector of the ventral premotor cortex where hand actions are represented. In order to demonstrate that intention could be assessed separately from action, the researchers compared fMRI images from the two intention and action conditions. These comparisons are shown in Figure 14.9. Notice particularly the significant difference between the top pair of images (black arrow). Intention detection is different from action recognition in the right inferior frontal gyrus, an area associated with the MNS. Iacoboni and colleagues summarize their findings in this way:

> Thus, premotor mirror neuron area – areas active during the execution and the observation of an action – previously thought to be involved only in action recognition are actually also involved in understanding the intentions of others. To ascribe an intention is to infer a forthcoming new goal, and this is an operation that the motor system does automatically (Iacoboni *et al.*, (2005), p. 0529).

3.1.1 Automaticity of intention detection

A final piece of the puzzle from the Iacoboni study was evidence related to the automaticity of intention detection by the MNS. Iacoboni *et al.* (2005) wanted to find out whether the *conscious goal to infer intention* mattered to the activity of the MNS. They asked half of their participants (Explicit group) to watch the drinking tea and cleaning up video clips with explicit instructions to focus on the dishes in the context clips, on the hands' grip in the action clips, and to infer the intention of the action in the intention clips. The other half of the participants simply watched the videos without instruction (Implicit group). The results? While there was increased activity in the anterior cingulate gyrus for the Explicit group – reflecting greater mental effort – there was no difference between the groups in activity in the inferior frontal gyrus. The researchers concluded that the MNS could operate automatically.

3.2 Finding posterior mirror neuron

The frontal mirror neuron system was discovered first in the early 1990s. A key question in this line of research was whether mirror neuron systems were localized to the frontal regions. This proved not to be the case, however. Within a decade, mirror neuron properties were discovered in the inferior parietal cortex. Fogassi *et al.* (2005) reported results of microelectrode studies in the inferior parietal cortex of macaque monkeys that parallel those found earlier in the frontal lobe. Like frontal mirror neurons, the parietal mirror neurons respond to particular acts in particular contexts. Fogassi and his colleagues see these findings as support for the notion that the mirror neuron system reads intentions.

Corresponding research in human participants also developed. Decety *et al.* (2002) found that when we imitate actions that we observe in others, the left inferior parietal cortex (IPC) becomes active; when we observe others imitating us, the right IPC has significant activation. There seems to be some consensus that there are two centers of mirror neuron activity in humans – frontal and parietal. Together they can be referred to as the frontoparietal mirror neuron system.

3.2.1 Two roles for the mirror neuron system: imitation learning and social mirroring

Based on recent evidence, Iacoboni (2005) has argued that the frontal and parietal mirror neuron system plus the superior temporal sulcus (STS) constitute a *core social imitation system*. The known connections among these areas suggest that:

1 STS creates a higher-order visual representation of the observed action
2 which is then fed forward to the frontoparietal MNS where the goal of the action as well as the motor specification for the action is coded, and
3 finally, copies of the motor representation are returned to the STS where matching between the expected sensory consequences of the action and the visually observed action takes place.

The core social imitation system recruits other brain areas in order to accomplish imitative learning and social mirroring.

Imitative learning occurs when we observe others performing an action and then recreate that action

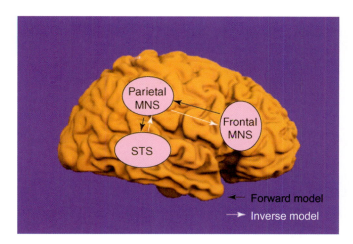

FIGURE 14.10   The core social imitation system, showing frontal mirror neuron systems (MNS) interacting with parietal MNS, which in turn interact with both frontal and superior temporal regions. *Source:* Iacoboni, 2005.

ourselves. Buccino and colleagues (2004) looked at the role of the MNS in the context of imitative learning of hand actions, in this case, learning the hand position of a guitar cord. Using the head of a guitar, Buccino had participants:

1 observe the fingering of a guitar cord when a guitarist did the action
2 pause
3 imitate the fingering and
4 rest.

The researchers found that, compared to simply observing the fingering or observing and then engaging in some other action with the guitar neck, those participants who imitated the fingering action showed a unique pattern of cortical activity during the observation and pause phases. Observing the fingering when one knows that imitation will be called upon gives rise to strong activation of the rostral part of the inferior parietal lobule (supramarginal gyrus) and the ventral premotor cortex plus the posterior part (or pars opercularis) of the inferior frontal gyrus. These are the same areas previously identified as constituting the frontoparietal MNS. Buccino goes on to note that during the pause there are marked differences between participants who will go on to imitate and those who merely observe or who will perform non-imitative acts. The imitation groups shows marked frontal activity while the other groups show cortical patterns more akin to rest. This seems to indicate that preparatory representation of actions is going on just prior to imitation. Finally, during the executive phase, the core imitation circuit recruits significantly more activity in areas associated with motor preparation

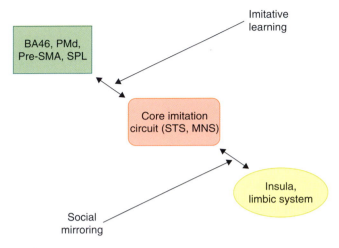

FIGURE 14.11 The core mirror neuron system supports two forms of imitation (from Iacoboni, 2005). BA46 = dorsolateral prefrontal cortex; PMd = dorsal premotor cortex; pre-SMA = pre-supplementary motor area (anterior paracingulate gyrus); SPL = superior parietal lobe; STS = superior temporal sulcus; MNS = frontoparietal mirror neuron system. *Source*: Iacoboni, 2005.

and execution including the dorsolateral prefrontal cortex (BA 46), dorsal premotor cortex (PMd), paracingulate gyrus (pre-SMA), and superior parietal lobule (SPL). Involvement of BA 46 has been interpreted as reflecting selection of motor acts appropriate to the task. Paracingulate activation is interpreted as reflecting internal effort, in this case, involving inhibition of the selected action until its execution is needed.

Other researchers have looked at imitation of emotion in others. Wicker *et al.* (2003a) found that participants who experience the emotion of disgust show brain activation in areas similar to those that they have when they watch another person experiencing disgust: the insula and the anterior cingulate cortex (part of the limbic system) become active. Here the imitation is a mirroring of the emotion involved rather than recreation of an observed goal and action. Iacoboi calls this *social mirroring* to distinguish it from *imitative learning*. Iacoboni's summary of recent work leads to the diagram of these two kinds of imitation shown in Figure 14.11. A schematic of brain areas that correspond to Iacoboni's diagram is presented in Figure 14.12.

3.3 Eye detection and gaze perception

Perception of eyes in conspecifics and guiding of social behavior in light of that perception occurs in many classes of animals from reptiles to humans. A clear understanding of the role of the eyes in social cognition requires that we understand the various kinds of eye and gaze processing that have been studied. In a review of literature including numerous animal classes, Emery (2000) showed an evolutionary trend in complexity of gaze processing. Table 14.2 summarizes Emery's findings.

While fish, reptiles, birds and other mammals have some ability to process eye-like stimuli (horizontal pair

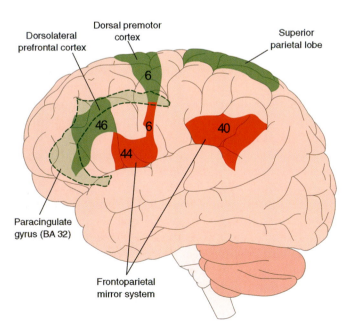

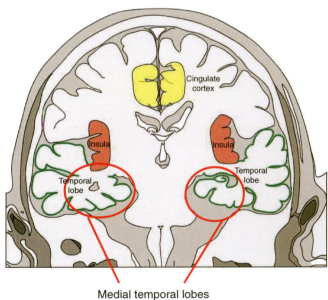

FIGURE 14.12 The mirror neuron system (red areas on left) with other brain areas that support imitation learning (green on left) and social mirroring (insula and anterior cingulate on right, shown in a coronal section). *Source*: As proposed by Iacoboni, 2005; figure by Fu and Baars.

TABLE 14.2   Ethological review of eye/gaze processing across classes of animals (from Emery, 2000)

Subject Group	Eye presence	Simple Gaze	Gaze Following	Joint Attention	Mental Attribution
Fish	✔	?	?	?	?
Reptiles	✔	✔	?	?	?
Birds	✔	✔	?	✔ (?)	?
Rodents	✔	?	?	?	?
Dogs (domestic)	?	✔	✔	?	?
Prosimians	?	✔	X	?	?
Monkeys	✔	✔	✔	✔	X
Great Apes	✔	✔	✔	✔	X (?)
Human					
– 3 months	✔	X	X	X	X
– 9 months	✔	✔	X	X	X
– 12 months	✔	✔	X	✔	X
– 18 months	✔	✔	✔	✔	X
– 24 months	✔	✔	✔	✔	X
– 48 months	✔	✔	✔	✔	✔
– Autism	✔ (?)	✔	?	X	X
– Down syndrome	✔	✔	✔	✔	✔
– Schizophrenia	✔	✔	?	?	?
– Amygdala damage	✔ (?)	X	X (?)	?	X (?)

✔ = positive evidence; X = no evidence; ? = not tested or controversial evidence

of dark circles) and perceive gaze direction, only great apes (gorillas, chimpanzees, bonobos and orang-utans) and humans have shared attention and can use the 'language of the eyes' to understand mental states of others (Figure 14.13).

Several types of eye and gaze processes are shown in Figure 14.13. Where do these processes take place in the brain? The superior temporal sulcus registers eyes and eye-like stimuli. The more complex levels of gaze processing (gaze direction and detection of gaze aversion) involve connections between STS and areas in the parietal lobe, particularly the intraparietal sulcus (IPG; Haxby *et al.* 2000) (Figure 14.14). In addition, connections of STS and IPG with subcortical structures, such as the amygdala, allow us to register the social and emotional significances of gaze, including threat.

Social information from eyes and gaze direction come from the *changeable aspects of the human face*. We can also use visual information to detect the *invariant aspects of individual faces*, such as identity. These aspects of face perception occur in a separate area of the temporal cortex discussed in a section later in this chapter.

Finally, attribution of mental states involves connections of the STS to the MNS and to medial frontal cortical areas (Iacoboni, 2005). We will discuss attribution of mental states in greater detail shortly.

3.4 Shared attention

Shared attention seems to be a social skill that is unique to great apes and humans. Remember shared attention

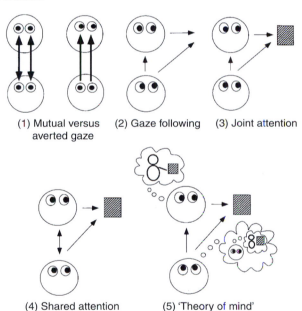

(1) Mutual versus averted gaze   (2) Gaze following   (3) Joint attention

(4) Shared attention   (5) 'Theory of mind'

FIGURE 14.13 Eye and gaze processing. (1) Mutual gaze is where the attention of individuals A and B is directed to one another. Averted gaze is when individual A is looking at B, but the focus of B's attention is elsewhere. (2) Gaze following is where individual A detects that B's gaze is not directed toward them and follows the light of sight of B to a point in space. (3) Joint attention is the same as gaze following except that there is a focus of attention (an object) so that individuals A and B are looking at the same object. (4) Shared attention is a combination of mutual attention and joint attention, where the focus of attention of A and B is on an object of joint focus and on each other ('I know you're looking at X and you know that I'm looking at X'). (5) Theory of Mind relies on 1–4 as well as higher order social knowledge that allows individuals to know that the other is attending to an object because they intend to do something with the object. *Source*: Emery, 2000.

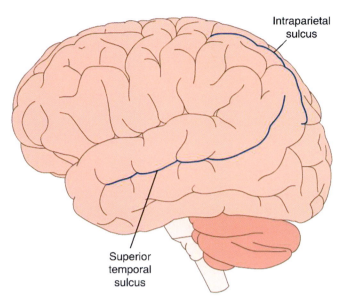

FIGURE 14.14 Superior temporal sulcus and intraparietal sulcus: eye and gaze detection areas.

is more than simply looking at the same thing that another person is looking at. Shared attention involves the additional qualification that the two observers not only observe the same object but also know that the other is looking at the object. It is a triadic (three-way) activity. Shared attention allows us implicitly to recognize that: '*I* know that *you* are looking at *that*'. Apes and humans seem to know that when conspecifics are gazing at something, they are also internally representing it. Looking leads to seeing. If I want to see what you see, I can follow your gaze.

How do these shared processes get set up in humans? Brooks and Meltzoff (2003) have shown that human infants begin to follow the direction in which an adult turns his/her head by the age of 9 months; however, at 9 months, the infant follows head direction whether the model's eyes are open or closed. By 12 months of age, the infant will follow gaze more often when the model's eyes are open that when they are shut. The infant follows gaze rather than head direction now. Shared attention has developed. The infant seems to know implicitly that open eyes allow looking; looking leads to seeing (Figure 14.15).

What areas of the brain support shared attention? We know that STS supports eye detection. In order to move from simple detection to shared attention, areas in the prefrontal cortex become involved. Williams and colleagues (2005) studied adults when they were experiencing shared attention compared to a control condition (Figure 14.16).

BOX 14.2   Gaze-following experiment

Try this experiment with shared attention:
When you are in a gathering of friends or classmates, shift your gaze to the corner of the room without saying anything. See whether others follow your gaze. Ask them why they did what they did.

FIGURE 14.15 An 18-month old pointing. Pointing is a sign of triadic interaction. *Source*: Brooks and Meltzoff, 2003.

Images from fMRI analyses show that shared attention recruits frontal areas including the ventromedial prefrontal cortex (VM-PFC), the left superior frontal gyrus (BA 10), cingulate gyrus and caudate nucleus. The VM-PDF is associated with registering the mental state of the other as we will discuss next. Williams and colleagues speculate that BA 10 is responsible for matching perception and action (Figure 14.17).

3.5 Higher-order TOM abilities

3.5.1 Attribution of mental states to ourselves and others

In the previous sections, we found that the paracingulate is involved in imitation learning and that the ventromedial prefrontal cortex (VM-PFC) is involved in shared attention. In this section, we will examine the role that the medial wall of the PFC plays in attribution of mental states to others, or, as Chris Frith calls it, 'mentalizing'.

The medial wall of prefrontal cortex can be divided into three segments from top to bottom: dorsomedial prefrontal cortex (DM-PFC), medial prefrontal cortex

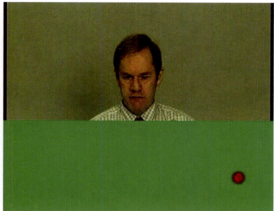

FIGURE 14.16 Stimuli used to create joint attention. When we look at the red dot on the left, we have the sense that the man is looking at the same object as we are; looking at the red dot on the right does not lead to the same sense of shared attention. *Source*: Williams *et al.*, 2005.

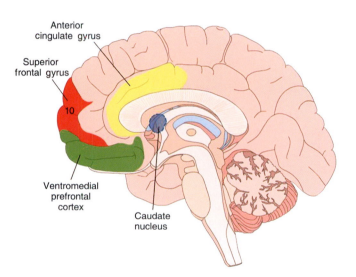

FIGURE 14.17 Networks for shared attention.

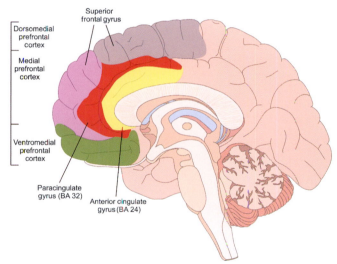

FIGURE 14.18 Divisions of prefrontal cortex: DM-PFC, M-PFC, and VM-PFC. Superior frontal gyrus, cingulate (BA 24), and paracingulate (BA 32) are areas shown to be important in attribution of mental states.

(M-PFC), and ventromedial prefrontal cortex (VM-PFC). (They are divided by convention according to their Talairach coordinates in three-dimensional space, which we will not worry about here.) DM-PFC includes the cortex at the top of the medial wall of the prefrontal cortex. M-PFC is the middle section of the medial wall of PFC. VM-PFC is composed of the bottom of the prefrontal lobe and the lower inside wall of the prefrontal cortex (Figure 14.18).

The cingulate and paracingulate gyri, which are sometimes spoken of collectively as the anterior cingulate cortex (ACC), form a belt (*cingulum* in Latin) around the corpus callosum. In addition, depending on how the gyri of individual brains are folded, the paracingulate gyrus may be folded into a sulcus. Figure 14.19 helps us see the anatomy of the cingulate and paracingulate

gyri. Figure 14.20 depicts brain areas active for perspective taking and intentional stance.

3.5.2 Perspective-taking and intentional stance

Perspective-taking is a social skill that is fundamental to human empathy. It allows us to understand how another person thinks and feels about a painful situation. For example, when people are asked to imagine the pain that they or another person would feel (compared to how an artificial limb would feel) when their fingers are pinched in a car door, the medial prefrontal cortex is significantly activated as well as other cortical areas

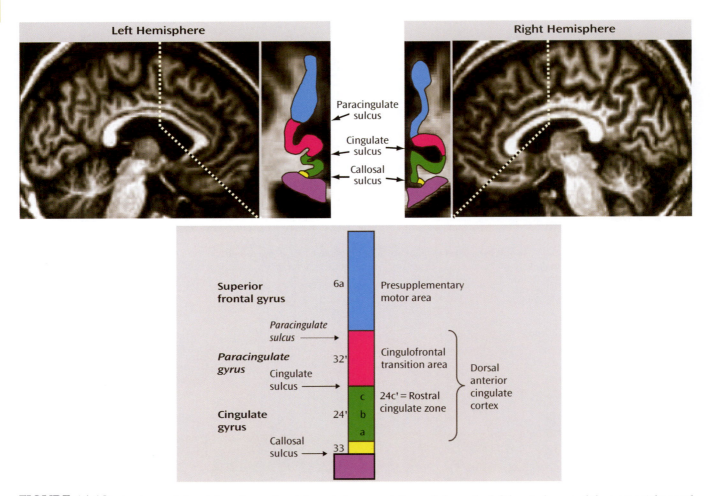

FIGURE 14.19 Anatomy of cingulate and paracingulate gyri: the upper left panel shows the left hemisphere, and the upper right panel shows the right hemisphere. The paracingulate sulcus is shown in blue, the cingulate sulcus is shown in pink, and the callosal sulcus is shown in purple. Lower panel shows these regions in more detail, including the rostral portion of the cingulate zone. *Source*: Heckers *et al.*, 2004.

associated with pain perception (Jackson *et al.*, 2006). Specifically, the paracingulate (BA 32) cortex of the M-PFC is significantly activated in both perspectives; it registers imagined self and other pain. In addition, when participants were imagining their own pain, the cingulate cortex (BA 24) was also active. This difference reflects our ability to empathize with the pain of others but also to distinguish our own pain from theirs.

Or consider playing a game with another: gamers and athletes speak of 'psyching out' their opponent. A lot of what they mean is that they read the other person's mind. To do this, we put ourselves in the other person's shoes or, to say it another way, we use empathy. When we play the game 'Rock, scissors, paper' against an unseen person (compared to an unseen computer), we adopt an intentional stance – we act as if the opponent is another subjective being. And, we can see a difference in the metabolic activity of the brain that coincides with our adoption of an intentional stance. In Figure 14.21, we can see that the anterior paracingulate cortex (BA 32) is

activated – that part of the medial prefrontal cortex implicated in perception of mental states in ourselves and others (Gallagher *et al.*, 2002).

We are sometimes asked to make decisions for others, keeping in mind what they would want. In a study where medical students were asked to adopt the perspective of a patient in order to make putative health care decisions for them, PET scans again reveal unique medial frontal activity, in this case, in the medial superior frontal gyrus (Figure 14.22) (Ruby and Decety, 2003).

PET activation appears in the dorsomedial prefrontal cortex (DM-PFC) and medial parietal (precuneus) when study participants watch a film of two people engaged in social interaction (Figure 14.23) (Iacoboni *et al.*, 2004). The same areas are not active when participants watch a single person engaged in solitary activity. The red areas in the figure show activity present during social interaction but not solitary action. The blues areas show activity that was present while participants watched social interaction compared to resting state.

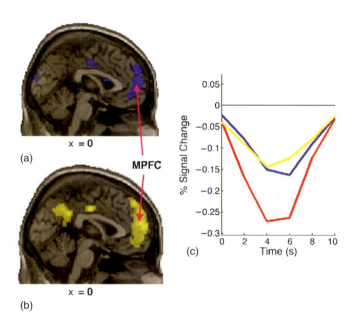

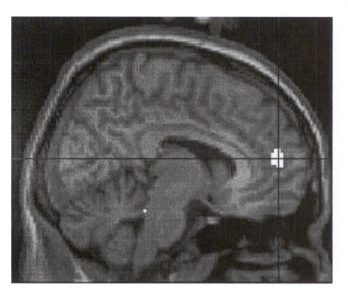

FIGURE 14.21   Activation in anterior paracingulate cortex when we mentalize about our opponent. *Source*: Gallagher *et al.*, 2002.

FIGURE 14.20   Perspective-taking and intentional stance. (a) Significant medial prefrontal activation for self versus artificial pain. (b) Significant M-PFC activation for other versus artificial pain. (c) Change in regional blood flow in the PET procedure in M-PFC; self = blue line; other = yellow; artificial limb = red. *Source*: Jackson *et al.*, 2006.

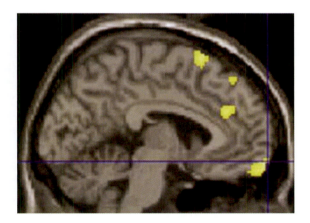

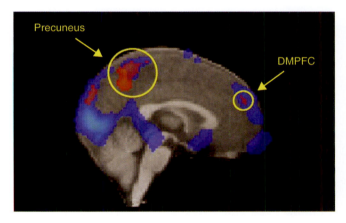

FIGURE 14.22   Adopting the perspective of another to make health care decisions for them. Medial PFC activation appears in yellow toward the right. *Source*: Ruby and Decety, 2003.

FIGURE 14.23   Thinking about social relationships. Dorsomedial prefrontal cortex and medial parietal cortex system for thinking about social relationships. *Source*: Iacoboni *et al.*, 2004.

Iacoboni and his colleagues (2004) suggest that:

The dorsomedial prefrontal cortex and medial parietal cortex system for thinking about social relationships is apparently part of the brain's default state circuitry; it may continuously, often without effort or intention, assess and analyze past, present, or possible future social relationships whenever non-social tasks do not demand full attention (p. 1171).

3.6   Social cognition of others like and unlike us: I-It in the brain?

Of significance for social psychology is the question of how the brain is involved when we perceive others who are like us versus others who are unlike us. When other people are not perceived as belonging to our social in-group, we may feel justified in treating them differently. Among other things, we may deny that they experience higher mental states and feelings. In

Ventral mPFC

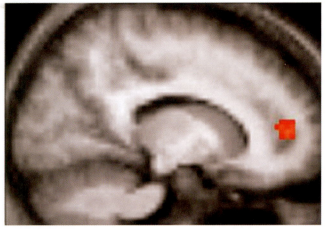

(a)

Dorsal mPFC

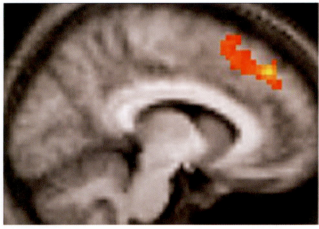

(b)

FIGURE 14.24 Understanding similar and dissimilar others. (a) Ventromedial PFC activation in judgements of similar others. (b) Dorsomedial PFC activation in judgements of dissimilar others. *Source*: Mitchell *et al.*, 2006.

addition, dissimilar 'others' are more likely to be treated as objects in Buber's sense of I-It (see Box 14.1). It appears that we are close to being able to see brain activity that corresponds to Buber's distinction.

Research by Mitchell *et al.* (2006) reveals distinct activation differences in the medial prefrontal cortex of participants who are asked to make inferences about the preferences of other people who are like them (similar) or not like them (dissimilar) politically. They found that areas in the ventromedial prefrontal cortex (VM-PFC) are active during judgments about similar people, whereas areas in the dorsomedial PFC were active in judgments about dissimilar individuals (Figure 14.24).

Mitchell and his colleagues conclude that, based on their results, we may actively deploy a different set of social cognition strategies in perceiving dissimilar others. Using less of the VM-PFC's perception of dissimilar others implies attributing less feeling and emotion to them. The next section addresses the issue of different strategies for perception of others.

3.6.1 Cognitive versus affective empathy?

Psychologists sometimes make a distinction between cognitive empathy and affective empathy. They point out a difference between theory of mind skills that draw on understanding of others' *beliefs* and empathic skills that help us understand how another person *feels*.

Shamay-Tsoory *et al.* (2005) found differences reflecting this when they tested adults with ventromedial PFC lesions on different kinds of social inference tasks. The researchers asked their participants to answer questions about three kinds of stories, those involving (1) second order false beliefs, (2) social *faux pas*, and (3) detection of irony. Box 14.3 summarizes the stories and questions that they used. The researchers believed that understanding social *faux pas* and irony involve greater dependence on emotional processing, while second order false belief tasks rely more heavily on cognitive processing.

Shamay-Tsoory and his colleagues found that patients who had ventromedial prefrontal lesions performed like the healthy control participants and patients with posterior lesions on the second order false belief task – they all performed at ceiling. However, the VM-PFC patients did very poorly on the irony and social *faux pas* tasks in comparison with other participants. The researchers interpreted these findings to mean that VM-PFC is essential to affective empathy but not to cognitive empathic skills.

It appears that empathic abilities follow the general rule that applies to other cognitive skills: facts about the world, beliefs and sensory representations are processed by the dorsal and lateral cortices. Feelings, emotional values and social significances depend on ventral and medial cortices that are closely interconnected with the subcortical limbic system.

3.7 Face perception

Perception of the unchanging aspects of the human face occurs in the fusiform face area (FFA), which is part of the inferior temporal lobe (Figure 14.25).

As an example of how the FFA looks in a brain image, we can look at the PET/MRI image from Caldara and colleagues (2006) (Figure 14.26). These researchers compared cortical activation when participants observed objects versus human faces. In the image, we are looking

BOX 14.3   Stories testing three kinds of social inference (from Shamay-Tsoory *et al.*, 2005)

Second-order false belief

Hana and Benny are sitting in the office talking about their meeting with their boss. Benny is putting an open bottle of ink on his desk. As he is doing so, some ink spills, so he leaves the office to look for a towel to clean up the spilled ink. While Benny is out of the office, Hana moves the ink bottle to the cabinet. While Benny is outside the office, he looks back through the keyhole and sees Hana moving the ink bottle. Benny enters the office.

Following the story, four questions were asked:

Belief question: Where will Hana think that Benny thinks the ink bottle is?
Reality question (assessing story comprehension): Where, actually, is the ink bottle?
Memory question: Where did Benny put the ink bottle?
Inference question: Where would there be an ink stain?

Irony

A sarcastic version item: Joe came to work and, instead of beginning to work, he sat down to rest. His boss noticed his behavior and said: 'Joe, don't work too hard!'

A neutral version item: Joe came to work and immediately began to work. His boss noticed his behavior, and said: 'Joe, don't work too hard!'

Following each story, two questions were asked:
Factual question (assessing story comprehension): Did Joe work hard?
Attitude question (assessing comprehension of the true meaning of the speaker): Did the manager believe Joe worked hard?

Recognition of social *faux pas*

Mike, a 9-year-old boy, just started at a new school. He was in one of the cubicles in the bathroom at school. Joe and Peter, two other boys at school, came in and were standing at the sinks talking.

Joe said, 'You know that new guy in the class? His name's Mike. Doesn't he look weird? And he's so short!' Mike came out of the cubicle, and Joe and Peter saw him. Peter said, 'Oh, hi, Mike! Are you going out to play soccer now?'

The participant is then asked the following questions:

Detection of the faux pas *question:*
Did anyone say anything they shouldn't have said?
Who said something they shouldn't have said?
Why shouldn't they have said it?
Why did they say it?

Control question (assessing story comprehension):

In the story, where was Mike while Joe and Peter were talking?

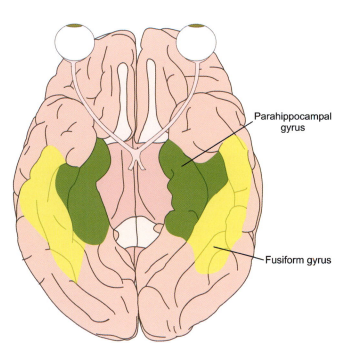

FIGURE 14.25 View from the underside of the theme brain, showing the fusiform face area (FFA).

Parahippocampal gyrus

Fusiform gyrus

at the bottom of the brain. The temporal lobes take up most of the outside areas of the image. The right and left FFAs are clearly marked in red, showing face receptive areas. Next to the FFAs are other parts of the inferior temporal lobe, the right and left parahippocampal gryi (PHG) that respond to inanimate objects, such as houses or shoes.

Haxby and his colleagues (2002) put the results of numerous studies together to create a model of face perception areas in the brain (Figure 14.27). They proposed a hierarchical system of interconnected brain areas to account for both the changeable and invariant aspects of face perception that have been discussed in this chapter.

In this model, early visual analysis of facial features occurs in the visual cortex (IOG). The IOG sends information to the superior temporal sulcus (STS) where changeable aspect of faces, such as eyes, are processed; from there information about eyes is joined with spatial information in the intraparietal sulcus (IPS) to generate gaze direction information. Information from STS can also be sent to the amygdala where social and affective meanings are attached and to the auditory cortex where

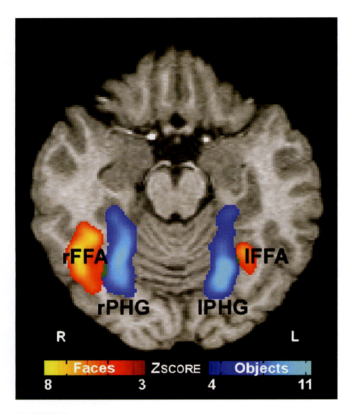

FIGURE 14.26 A view of the underside of the brain with fusiform face areas (FFA) shown in red and parahippocampal gyri (PHG) shown in blue. *Source*: Caldara *et al.*, 2006.

lip movements are registered. Invariant aspects of faces such as personal identity are processed in the lateral fusiform gyrus (the fusiform face area, FFA) that is interconnected with the temporal lobe where specific information about name and biographical data are retrieved.

3.8 Disordered social cognition in autism

One of the ways that clinicians diagnose autistic spectrum disorders (ASD) in children is to engage them in a false belief 'game' much like the Hana and Benny story in Box 14.3, often using puppets or dolls to make the game more accessible. Children are asked to mentalize about the beliefs of the characters in the story. Those children who cannot read the characters' minds may be further assessed for autism. Deficits in theory of mind skills have long been diagnostic of ASDs (Baron-Cohen, 1995).

Since the discovery of the mirror neuron system in humans, researchers have turned to studying neural processes in individuals with autism to see where deficits lie. Dapretto *et al.* (2006) obtained evidence suggesting that functional deficits in the frontal mirror neuron system are present in children with autism. Their participants were high functioning children with ASD and matched typically developing children who were asked to imitate pictured facial expressions of anger,

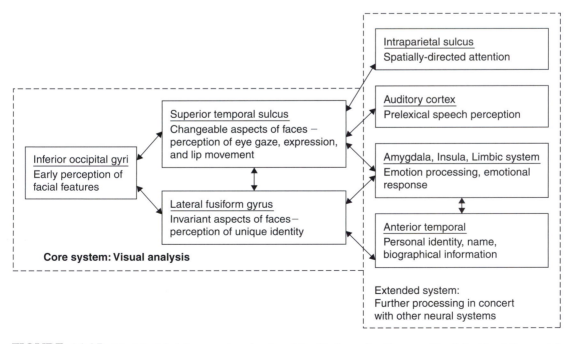

FIGURE 14.27 Model of facial perception developed by Haxby and colleagues. The left side of the model shows early visual regions for face perception, the center shows brain regions for changing and non-changing features in faces, and the right side shows further processing of facial features. *Source*: Haxby *et al.*, 2002.

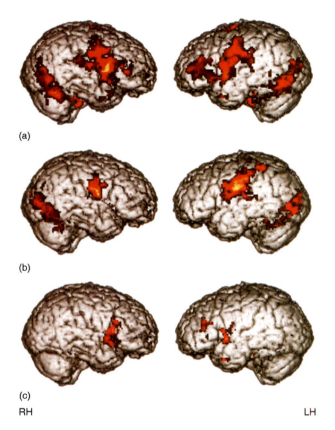

(a)

(b)

(c)

RH   LH

FIGURE 14.28 Disordered social cognition in autism. Reliable activity during imitation of emotional expression in mirror neuron system areas. (a) Activity in normally developing children. (b) Lower levels of activity in children diagnosed with autism. (c) Significant differences between the two groups of children in the pars opercularis, BA 44. *Source*: Dapretto *et al.*, 2006.

happiness, fear, sadness, or neutrality. Typically developing children showed strong bilateral activation of the pars opercularis of the inferior frontal lobe (BA 44) as well as neighboring BA 45, areas that we have described as the frontal portion of the mirror neuron system (Figure 14.28). Children with autism were able to perform the facial imitation task; activation in their fusiform gyri indicate that they perceived the pictured faces. However, they showed no significant activation as a group in the pars opercularis, even when the fMRI data were examined at liberal thresholds. Further, the researchers found that activation in the mirror neuron area correlated negatively with the severity of the children's autistic symptoms, as assessed by the Autism Diagnostic Observation Schedule.

4.0 SUMMARY

Social cognition abilities in human beings are complex and multifaceted. They are supported by multiple systems of interconnected cortical and subcortical areas. During evolution, the simpler valuation and behavioral system of the limbic brain was overlaid by the growing cerebral cortices that make complex cognition possible. It is very likely that our large and complex cerebral cortices evolved in part due to selective pressures brought to bear by the increasing complexity of human society and the demands of social cognition. Increasing social and cognitive complexity in the environment go hand in hand with increasing complexity in the correlated brain systems.

5.0 CHAPTER REVIEW

5.1 Study questions

1 Briefly describe what is meant by a Theory of Mind.
2 According to Frith, what is mentalizing?
3 Why are shared attention mechanisms important for human development? When do they develop?
4 How do mirror neuron systems differ from other neuron systems? What is their role in social cognition?
5 What role does context play in understanding intention?
6 Why is perspective-taking a key social skill?

5.2 Drawing exercises

1 Label the key brain regions (shown in shades of red and pink in Figure 14.29) of the frontal mirror neuron system.

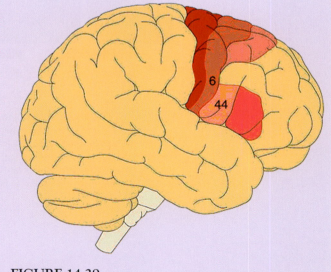

FIGURE 14.29

Life is a flame that is always burning itself out, but it catches fire again every time a child is born.

George Bernard Shaw

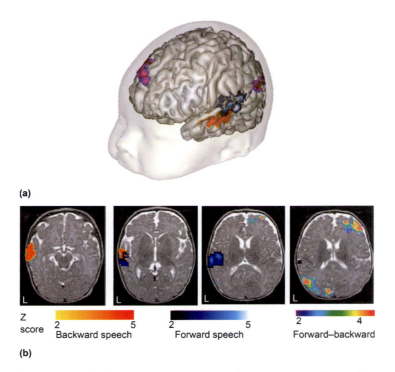

(a)

(b)

fMRI study of infants' speech processing. fMRI activation obtained in awake 3-month-old infants listening to blocks of normal (forward speech, shown in blue shading), reversed (backward speech, shown in yellow-red shading) relative to activity during silence. Activation to forward speech (blue scale) occurred in superior temporal regions of the brain that are superior and posterior to areas activated by backward speech. *Source*: Dehaene-Lambertz *et al.*, 2006.

C H A P T E R

15

Development

Nicole M. Gage and Mark H. Johnson

1.0 INTRODUCTION

In this chapter, we provide an overview of how humans grow and develop across multiple stages of life: from prenatal to infancy, from child to adolescent. Much of our focus will be on early stages of brain and cognitive development because the first years of human life represent a dramatic explosion of neurodevelopmental change as babies learn about their world. We will explore the roles of nature and nurture in the development of the brain and mind, discovering the intricacies of the complex interactions between genetics and experience.

The field of developmental cognitive neuroscience – i.e. the investigation of the maturing brain and the correspondence to human cognition – is a relatively young one. The advent of new non-invasive ways to measure brain function in infants and children have literally revolutionized the study of what infants and young children understand about the world surrounding them. A central focus of the study of the development of

Cognition, Brain, and Consciousness, edited by B. J. Baars and N. M. Gage
ISBN: 978-0-12-373677-2

Copyright 2007, Elsevier Ltd. All rights reserved.

the brain and its relation to behavior relies on the combination of multiple techniques and experimental approaches in order to elucidate the complexities of the mind-brain.

In this chapter, we will briefly discuss the emerging techniques for investigating infant and child development. Next, we will trace the anatomical development of the brain from prenatal to postnatal stages of life. We then focus on brain and cognitive development in the first year of life: an explosive time of large-scale changes both in brain and in cognition. Next, we track mind-brain development through childhood and adolescence. We end the chapter looking at the long-term effects of early perinatal brain damage with a discussion of brain plasticity in childhood. Throughout the chapter, we highlight recent empirical investigations of the development of the brain and its correspondence to cognition, however, we add a caveat as this field of study is relatively new and

we are only beginning to understand the relationship between brain and human behavior.

1.1 New techniques for investigating the developing brain

The emergence of new ways to investigate the human brain has been discussed in Chapter 4. Two techniques that have been employed in studies of infants and young children are electroencephalography/event-related potentials (EEG/ERPs) and functional magnetic resonance imaging (fMRI) (Figure 15.1). While these techniques have revolutionized the young field of cognitive neuroscience, nowhere is the effect felt as strongly as in the study of the unfolding of human brain development and the correspondence to behavior. Studies of adult behavior and brain function have informed us about how

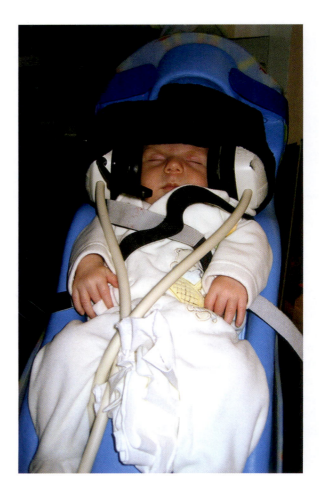

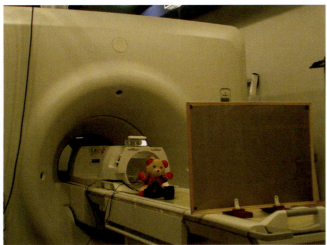

FIGURE 15.1 Techniques for studying brain function in infants and children: left panel shows an EEG electrode array, center panel shows an MRI set up for scanning infants and children, right panel shows a specialized infant seat for us in MRI scanning. *Source*: Ghislaine Dehaene-Lambertz, with permission.

the typically developing brain functions across domains such as language, emotion, and memory. They also inform us about the effects of brain damage or disease. However, the pattern of deficit found in adults following brain damage differs sharply from the effects when brain damage occurs early in life. Therefore, the advent of neuroimaging techniques allows us to understand the brain regions and cognitive capabilities across cognitive domains while it is unfolding in development.

New and sophisticated methods to investigate anatomical developmental changes throughout life have also increased our ability to understand the complex patterns of brain development (Figure 15.2). These methods allow us to track the development of gray matter across brain regions as well as to assess connectivity patterns across and between the cerebral hemispheres.

1.2 The mystery of the developing brain: old questions and new

In this chapter, we address some brain questions that have been asked for many years. A central question in human development is the trading roles of nature and nurture. A related issue is to what extent the brain is flexible in adapting to new situations in its environment and to recover from damage. Some new questions can be posed that we were previously unable to address due to the limitation of our experimental approaches or techniques, such as what does a baby know before birth? What are the long-standing effects of very early brain damage? How do dynamic processes in brain development differ across brain regions and hemispheres? We will discuss advances in our knowledge about the developmental pathways of three main areas of cognition that have been a focus in the field: language, executive function and social cognition.

2.0 PRENATAL DEVELOPMENT: FROM BLASTOCYST TO BABY

Much of this chapter will be devoted to a discussion of brain development and its correspondence to cognition during infancy and childhood. Before we begin that

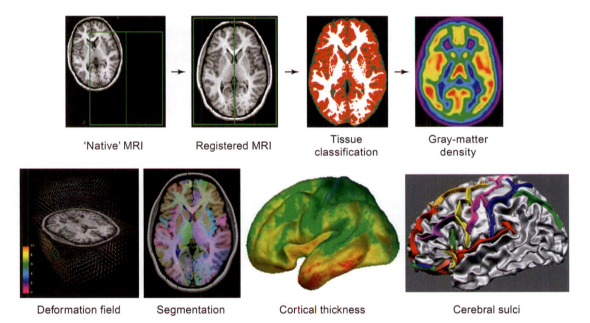

'Native' MRI   Registered MRI   Tissue classification   Gray-matter density

Deformation field   Segmentation   Cortical thickness   Cerebral sulci

FIGURE 15.2 Image-processing pipeline. Top row: a typical image-processing pipeline begins with a transformation of a magnetic-resonance (MR) image from the acquisition ('native') to standardized stereotaxic space; this process generates an image that is 'registered' with the template brain. The next step involves voxel-wise classification of brain tissue into three main classes: gray matter (in red), white matter (in white) and cerebrospinal fluid (in green). Each of these binary images (0, tissue absent; 1, tissue present) is then filtered (or smoothed) to generate 'density' images; the image of gray-matter (GM) density shown here indicates, at each voxel, the local concentration of GM on a continuous scale from 0 to 1 (the 'hotter' the colour, from blue to red, the higher the value of WM density). Bottom row: non-linear registration of the sample image to the template brain allows one to characterize local shape differences; the deformation field quantifies such sample-template differences throughout the brain. By combing non-linear registration with tissue classification, one can segment automatically various brain structures, such as the frontal lobe or the amygdala. Other techniques produce maps of cortical thickness or identify sulci in the subject's cerebral cortex. *Source*: Paus, 2005.

discussion, we provide a brief description of the processes that occur before birth, during prenatal development. While little is known about the sensory, perceptual, or cognitive processes of a fetus *in utero*, recent investigations have focused on what a baby experiences before birth. These pre-birth experiences can be critical for later development. And whether they are positive – hearing a mother's voice or her heartbeat – or negative – experiencing the effects of maternal alcohol abuse – these prenatal experiences can have long-standing effects on later cognitive and social development. Let's begin our prenatal section with a discussion of gene expression and the role of the environment.

2.1 Epigenesis

A central debate in the field of human development is the influence of nature versus nurture. Does our genetic makeup predetermine who we will become? Or does our experience shape who we are? Clearly, both genes and the environment have an impact on the developing human. Does gene expression unfold, followed by the development of brain structures and functions that later are affected by experience? Or does experience – the local environment, whether within a cell, a system, or the brain *in toto* – have an affect on gene expression? The interplay between genes and the environment is a complex one, with these interactive processes occurring long before birth. Here, we begin the topic of the cognitive neuroscience of human development with a discussion of the nature of epigenesis.

Epigenesis, the unfolding of genetic information within a specific context, is key to modern ideas about development. Different viewpoints on epigenesis underlie different perspectives on developmental cognitive neuroscience. Gottlieb and Halpern (2002) have drawn a useful distinction between 'predetermined epigenesis' and 'probabilistic epigenesis'. *Predetermined epigenesis* assumes that there is a unidirectional causal pathway from genes to brain anatomy to changes in brain and cognitive function (Figure 15.3). A hypothetical example of this would be if the endogenous expression of a gene in the brain generated more of a certain neurochemical. Higher levels of this neurochemical might make a particular neural circuit active in the brain, and this additional neural activity allows for more complex computations than were previously possible. This increased cognitive ability will be evident in behavior as the child being able to pass a task that they failed at young ages. In contrast, *probabilistic epigenesis* views the interactions between genes, structural brain changes, and function

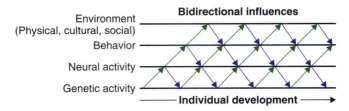

FIGURE 15.3   A systems view of psychobiological development. *Source*: Adapted from Gottlieb and Halpern, 2002.

as bidirectional (Figure 15.3). Bidirectional interactions mean that not only can genes trigger a behavioral change, but also that sensory input to the child can change patterns of gene expression. For example, we will hear later that newborn infants have primitive brain circuits that bias them to look toward the faces of other humans (Johnson, 1991). This early attention to faces results in some of the neural circuits involved in the visual pathways of the baby becoming shaped or tuned to process faces. The neuroanatomical changes that underlie this shaping process are due to differential gene expression.

2.2 The anatomy of brain development

Much of early brain development occurs in the first weeks following fertilization and we will focus on those processes here. Shortly after conception, a fertilized cell undergoes a rapid process of cell division, resulting in a cluster of proliferating cells (called the *blastocyst*) that resembles a tiny bunch of grapes (Figure 15.4). After a few days, the blastocyst differentiates into a three-layered structure (the embryonic disk). Each of these layers will subsequently differentiate into a major organic system, with the *endoderm* (inner layer) becoming internal organs (digestive, respiratory, etc.), the *mesoderm* (middle layer) becoming skeletal and muscular structures, and the *ectoderm* (outer layer) developing into the skin surface and the nervous system (including the perceptual organs).

The nervous system itself begins with a process known as *neurulation*. A portion of the ectoderm begins to fold in on itself to form a hollow cylinder called the *neural tube* (Figure 15.5).

The neural tube differentiates along three dimensions: length, circumference and radius. The length dimension differentiates into components of the central nervous system, with the forebrain and midbrain arising at one end and the spinal cord at the other (Figure 15.6). The end of the tube that will become the spinal cord differentiates into a series of repeated units or segments,

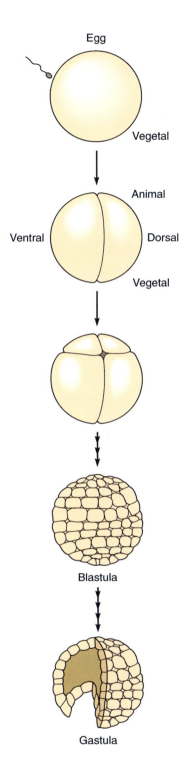

FIGURE 15.4 Blastocyst development. The early processes of animal development follow a conserved pattern; after fertilization, a series of cleavage divisions divide the egg into a multicellular blastula. The animal and vegetal poles represent an initial asymmetry in the oocyte, and the second axis, dorsal-ventral in this example, is established after fertilization. The process of gastrulation brings some of the cells from the surface of the embryo to the inside and generates the three-layered structure common to most multicellular animals. *Source*: Sanes *et al.*, 2006.

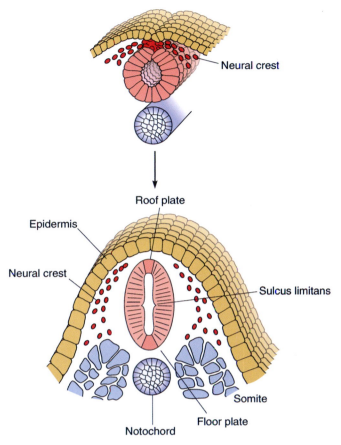

FIGURE 15.5 The neural tube. The overall organization of the neural tube emerges soon after closure. The most ventral part of the neural tube becomes flattened into a distinct 'floorplate'. The most dorsal aspect of the neural tube develops into a tissue known as the roof plate. A distinct fissure, the *sulcus limitans*, forms between the dorsal and ventral parts of the neural tube along most of its length. *Source*: Sanes *et al.*, 2006.

while the other end of the neural tube organizes and forms a series of bulges and convolutions. Five weeks after conception these bulges become protoforms for parts of the brain. One bulge gives rise to the cortex, a second becomes the thalamus and hypothalamus, a third turns into the midbrain and others to the cerebellum and medulla.

The distinction between sensory and motor systems develops along the axis tangential to the surface of the neural tube with the dorsal (top-side) becoming mainly sensory cortex, and the ventral (bottom-side) developing into motor cortex. The various association cortices and 'higher' sensory and motor cortices tend to arise from the tissue between.

The radial dimension of the tube differentiates into some of the layering patterns in the adult brain. Across the radial dimension of the neural tube the

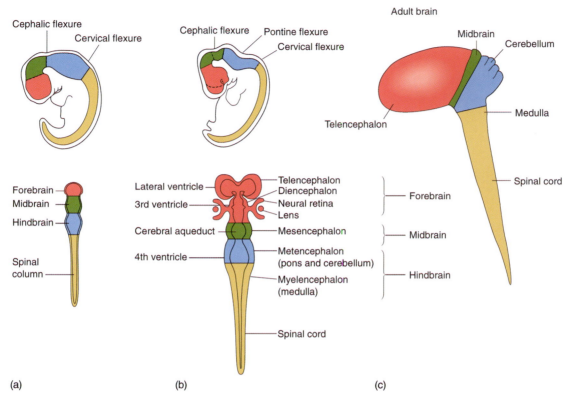

FIGURE 15.6 The vertebrate brain and spinal cord develop from the neural tube. Shown here as lateral views (upper) and dorsal views (lower) of human embryos at successively older stages of embryonic development (a,b,c). The primary three divisions of the brain (a) occur as three brain vesicles or swellings of the neural tube, known as the forebrain (prosencephalon), midbrain (mesencephalon), and hindbrain (rhombencephalon). The next stage of brain development (b) results in further subdivisions, with the forebrain vesicle becoming subdivided into the paired telencephalic vesicles and the diencephalon, and the rhombencephalon becoming subdivided into the metencephalon and the myelencephalon. These basic brain divisions can be related to the overall anatomical organization of the mature brain (c). *Source*: Sanes *et al.*, 2006.

bulges grow larger and become more distinctive. Within these bulges cells *proliferate* (are born), *migrate* (travel), and *differentiate* into particular types. The vast majority of the cells that will compose the brain are born in *proliferative zones* (Figure 15.7). These zones are close to the hollow centre portion of the tube (that itself later becomes the ventricles of the brain). One of these proliferation sites, the *ventricular zone*, may be phylogenetically older (Nowakowski, 1987). Another, the *subventricular zone*, only contributes significantly to phylogenetically recent brain structures such as the neocortex (i.e. 'new' cortex since its only found in mammals). These two zones yield separate glial (support and supply cells) and neuron cell lines and give rise to different forms of migration.

Neurons and *glial cells* are produced by the division of cells within the proliferative zone to produce *clones* (a clone is a group of cells which are produced by division of a single precursor cell – such a precursor cell is said to give rise to a lineage) (Figure 15.8). *Neuroblasts* produce neurons, with each giving birth to a definite and limited number of neurons. In some cases neuroblasts give rise to particular types of neuron. For example, less than a dozen proliferating cells produce all the Purkinje cells of the cerebellar cortex, with each producing about 10 000 cells (Nowakowski, 1987).

2.3 Neural migration

After young neurons are born, they have to *migrate* from the proliferative zone to the particular region where they will be employed in the mature brain. The most common type of migration involves *passive cell displacement*. In this case young cells are simply pushed further away from the proliferative zone by more recently born cells. This gives rise to an outside-to-inside pattern, resulting in the oldest cells ending up toward the surface of the brain, while the youngest cells are toward the inside. This type of migration gives rise to brain structures such as the thalamus and many regions of the brainstem.

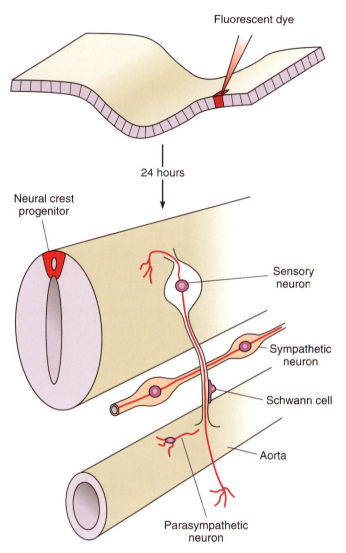

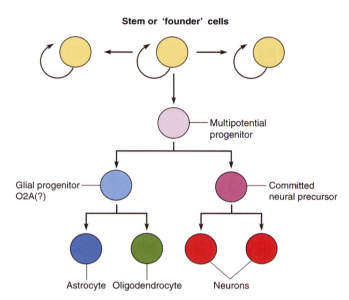

FIGURE 15.8 Basic lineage relationships among the cell types of the central nervous system of vertebrates. Through a variety of cell cultures and *in vivo* studies, the relationships among the various cell classes within the nervous system have been established. The early cells of the neural tube have the potential to generate an enormous number of progeny and, as a result, are sometimes called founder cells or stem cells, which undergo symmetric cell divisions to produce additional founder cells as well as progenitor cells. (The term stem cells is also used to describe the persistent progenitors found in adult animals.) It is thought that the early founder cells also generate progenitor cells that are capable of a more limited number of cell divisions, and this is the reason that clones of progenitor cells labeled late in embryogenesis have fewer progeny. Nevertheless, the late progenitor cells are capable of generating both neurons and all macroglia, the oligodendrocytes and the astrocytes. Although *in vitro* studies of certain regions of the nervous system, particularly the optic nerve, have shown that the lineages of astrocytes and oligodendrocytes share a common progenitor, known as the O2A glial progenitor, in the spinal cord, motoneurons and oligodendrocytes share a common progenitor. Thus, the lineage relationships shown may vary depending on the region of the CNS. *Source*: Sanes *et al.*, 2006.

FIGURE 15.7 Fates and migration of neural crest cells. A single progenitor cell is injected with a lineage tracer, and its progeny are followed as they migrate out of the neural tube. Some may become sensory neurons, while others become Schwann cells or neurons of the autonomic nervous system. Environments these cells pass through on their migration routes influence their fate choice. *Source*: After Bronner-Fraser and Fraser, 1991; Sanes *et al.*, 2006.

The second form of migration is more active and involves the young cell moving past previously generated cells to create an *'inside-out' pattern* (Figure 15.9). This pattern is found in the cerebral cortex and in some subcortical areas that have a laminar structure (divided into parallel layers) (Figure 15.10).

The best-studied example of active migration comes from the prenatal development of cerebral cortex and the *radial unit model* proposed by Pasko Rakic (1988).

As mentioned earlier, most cortical neurons in humans are generated outside the cortex itself in a region just underneath what becomes the cortex, the 'proliferative

zone'. Recall that the cerebral cortex is much more extensive in humans than in most other species. This means that these cells must migrate to take up their final locations within the cortex. Rakic proposed a *'radial unit model'* of neocortical differentiation that gives an account of how *both* the regional and the layered structure of the mammalian cerebral cortex arise (Rakic, 1988). According to his model, the laminar organization of the cerebral cortex is determined by the fact that each relevant proliferative unit gives rise to about one hundred neurons. The progeny from each of these proliferative units all migrate up the same radial glial fibre, with the latest to be born travelling past their older relatives. A radial glial fibre is a long process that stretches from top to bottom of the cortex and originates from a glial cell.

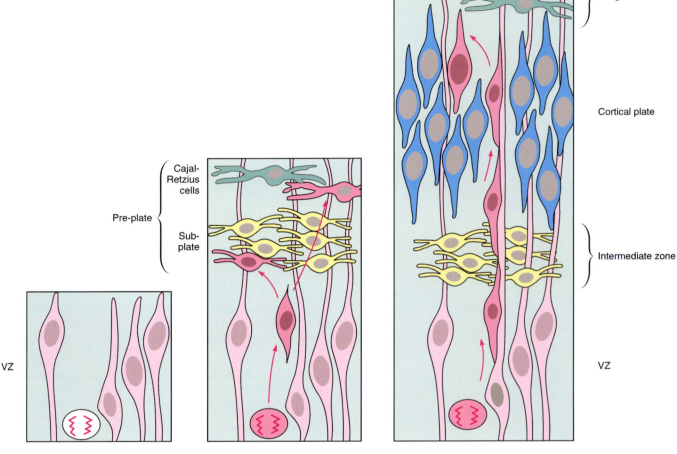

FIGURE 15.9 Histogenesis in the cerebral cortex proceeds through three stages. In the first stage of histogenesis, the wall of the cerebral cortex is made up of the progenitor cells, which occupy the ventricular zone (VZ). In the next stage of development, the first neurons exit the cell cycle (red) and accumulate in the preplate, adjacent to the pial surface. The neurons of the preplate can be divided into the more superficial Cajal-Retzius cells and the subplate cells. In the next stage of cortical histogenesis, newly generated neurons (red) migrate along radial glial fibers to form a layer between the Cajal-Retzius cells and the subplate. This layer is called the cortical plate, and the majority of the neurons in the cerebral cortex accumulate in this layer. *Source*: Sanes *et al.*, 2006.

Radial glial fibres effectively act like a climbing rope to ensure that neurons produced by one proliferative unit all contribute to one radial column within the cortex (Figure 15.11).

There are some interesting consequences of the radial unit model for species differences in the cerebral cortex. Rakic (1988) points out that greater cell division at the proliferative unit formation stage would increase the number of cortical columns and hence the total area of cortex that results. In contrast, an additional single round of division at a later stage, from the proliferative zone, would only increase the size of a column by one cell (about 1 per cent). This corresponds well with the fact that there is very little variation between mammalian species in the general layered structure of the cortex, while the total surface area of the cortex can vary by a factor of 100 or more between different species of mammal. It seems likely, therefore, that species differences originate (at least in part) in the number of 'rounds' of cell division that are allowed to take place within and across regions of the proliferative zone.

Thus, in the early weeks of gestation, the embryo undergoes complex processes that form the basis for the central nervous system. It is important to note that prenatal brain development is not a passive process involving the unfolding of genetic instructions. Rather, from an early stage *interactions* between cells are critical, including the transmission of electrical signals between neurons. In one example, patterns of spontaneous firing of cells in the eyes (before they have

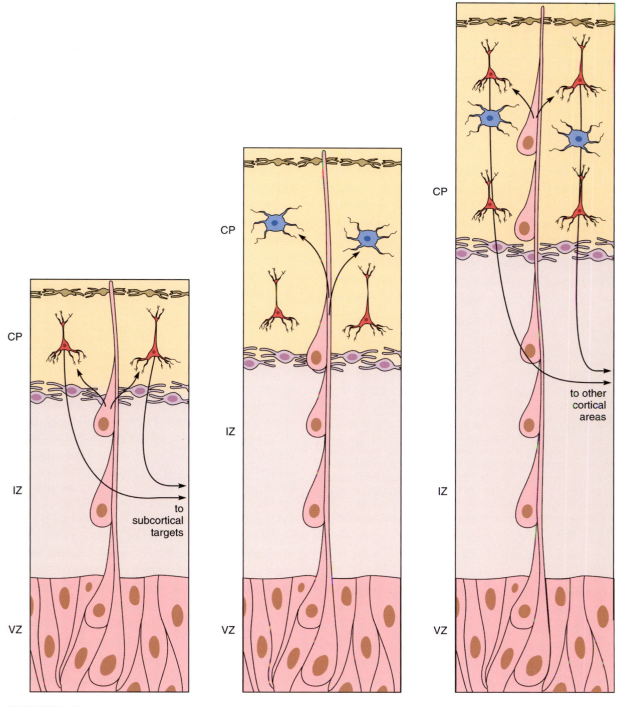

FIGURE 15.10 Histogenesis of pyramidal neurons of the deep layers, V and VI. (a) After the birth and migration of the Cajal Retzius cells and the subplate cells, the next neurons to be generated in the cortex are the pyramidal neurons of the deep layers, V and VI, whose axons project to subcortical targets. (b) The next neurons to be born are the local interneurons in layer IV of the cortex. (c) Finally, the pyramidal cells of the upper layers, II and III, are generated. They send axons to other cortical areas. *Source*: Sanes *et al.*, 2006.

opened in development) transmit signals that appear to specify the layered structure of the visual thalamus, the lateral geniculate nucleus (LGN) (see Shatz, 2002; O'Leary and Nakagawa, 2002). Thus, waves of firing intrinsic to the developing organism may play an important role in specifying aspects of brain structure long before sensory inputs from the external world have any effect.

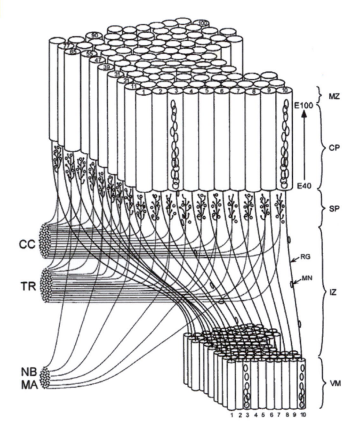

FIGURE 15.11 The radial unit model of Rakic (1988). Radial glial fibers span from the ventricular zone (VZ) to the cortical plate (CP) via a number of regions: the intermediate zone (IZ) and the subplate zone (SP). RG indicates a radial glial fiber, and MN a migrating neuron. Each MN traverses the IZ and SP zones that contain waiting terminals from the thalamic radiation (TR) and cortico cortico afferents (CC). As described in the text, after entering the cortical plate, the neurons migrate past their predecessors to the marginal zone (MZ). *Source*: Rakic, 2005.

2.4 Nature and nurture revisited

As we mentioned at the beginning of this section, the role of the prenatal environment in the unfolding of genetic instructions and brain development can have long-lasting effects, both good and bad. The developing infant is susceptible to events occurring within this environment. One such event is the incursion of a *teratogen*. A teratogen is defined as any environmental agent that causes damage during the prenatal period. Examples of teratogens are: prescription and even non-prescription drugs, caffeine found in coffee and soft drinks, illegal drugs such as cocaine and heroin, tobacco and marijuana products, and alcohol. The effects of the teratogen(s) can be complex depending on the dosage level, the time it occurs during prenatal development, and the genetic makeup of the mother, since some individuals are more susceptible than

others. Prenatal counseling for mothers-to-be providing education regarding potential sources of terotogens has helped to reduce the occurrences of brain damage due to teratogens.

The prenatal brain is particularly susceptible to the effects of alcohol. Alcohol abuse by the mother during pregnancy results in long-term deficits in cognition, language, and social development called *fetal alcohol syndrome* (FAS) (Jones and Smith, 1973; Jones, 1975). A recent brain mapping study of children, teenagers, and young adults with severe FAS showed gray-matter density differences in FAS individuals as compared to age and gender matched controls. Specific findings were reduced gray-matter density in frontal and parietal areas and increased density in temporal and inferior parietal lobe regions (Figure 15.12). As we will see in later sections of this chapter, these brain areas mature throughout childhood and into late adolescence, therefore these gray-matter density differences in FAS individuals indicate that prenatal exposure to alcohol has a resounding and long-lasting impact on brain development and cognitive development throughout the lifespan.

Longitudinal studies assessing the long-term effects of smoking cigarettes or marijuana during pregnancy have provided new evidence about their impact on a child's cognitive development. Fried and colleagues (Fried *et al.*, 2003) have followed a cohort of children in Canada from birth through young adulthood. Using neuropsychological test batteries to assess cognitive functions like verbal intelligence, visual spatial processing, language abilities, attentional function, Fried and colleagues found that there are early-occurring (by age 3) and long-lasting cognitive impairments caused by smoking either tobacco or marijuana. The specific effects of prenatal exposure to cigarette smoke differ sharply from exposure to marijuana, although both cause harm. Exposure to cigarette smoke resulted in lower general intelligence in the children coupled with deficits in auditory function and verbal working memory that continued from early childhood (age 3) through adolescence (age 16) (Fried *et al.*, 2003). Exposure to marijuana smoke resulted in no general intelligence deficit, however, executive functions, such as attention and working memory, were impaired in these children and, in particular, visual processes such as visual integration, analysis and reasoning. Again, these impairments were observed early (age 3) and continued through teenage years.

The cognitive impairments reflected by the neuropsychological test batteries implicated specific brain regions for further study of the effects of prenatal exposure to cigarette and marijuana smoke. Visuospatial integrative processes tap frontal lobe regions in adults

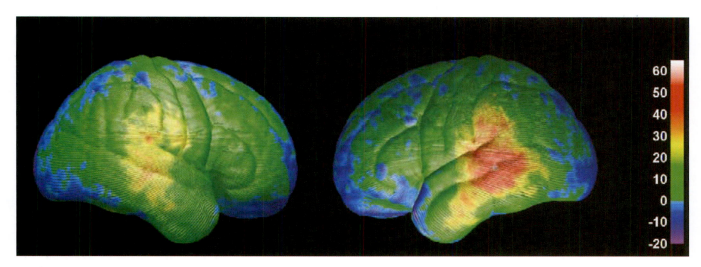

FIGURE 15.12 Differences in gray-matter density between subjects with fetal alcohol syndrome (FAS). Warmer colors represent positive differences, indicating an increase in the patient group (arbitrarily coded as 1) relative to the control group (arbitrarily coded as 0), with red representing the largest group difference. Note that the maximum value varies on the three color bars, depending on the maximum group difference from each comparison. (Adapted, with permission, from Sowell *et al.*, 2002.) *Source*: Toga *et al.*, 2006.

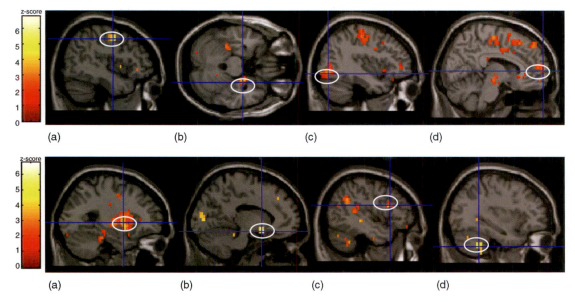

FIGURE 15.13 Effects of prenatal use of marijuana smoke on young adults (18–22 years) measured using fMRI. Frontal lobe circuits engaged in a task tapping visuospatial working memory systems, with reduced right hemisphere activity and increased left hemisphere activity as compared to an age matched control group. *Source*: Smith *et al.*, 2006.

(see Chapter 6). Fried and colleagues (Smith *et al.*, 2006) continued their investigation into the long-term effects of prenatal exposure to marijuana using a neuroimaging technique, fMRI, with a sample of young adults (18–22 years) from the Canadian cohort with prenatal exposure to marihuana smoke. Results of the study revealed a differing pattern of neural activity in frontal lobe regions that are engaged in a visuospatial task.

Specific findings were reduced activity in right hemisphere regions (Figure 15.13, upper panel) and increased activity in left hemisphere regions (Figure 15.13, lower panel). The authors interpreted these findings as indicating that right hemisphere neural circuitry engaged in tasks that tap visuospatial short-term memory are less active in children with prenatal marijuana smoke exposure. While it is difficult to know at this stage of the research just why left hemisphere activity was increased, it could be that left hemisphere regions were recruited as a compensatory mechanism due to the decreased neural activation in the right hemisphere. More research is clearly need in order fully to understand the effects of prenatal cigarette and marijuana smoke exposure, however, the work of Fried and colleagues provide compelling evidence that the damage appears early in a child's cognitive development and is very long lasting. The clear message from these studies is that early insult caused by a teratogen, such as cigarette or marijuana smoke, can produce lifelong cognitive impairment and may correspond to differing patterns in cortical development.

2.5 Prenatal hearing experience: voice and music perception before birth

What do babies know before they are born? Is it important for a mother-to-be to talk to her unborn baby? Read to her baby? Sing to her baby? Is there an impact on later language, music, and cognitive function? In other words, what are the perceptual abilities of an unborn child and how do they relate to later cognitive development? This question has intrigued developmental psychologists for at least a hundred years (see Kisilevsky and Low, 1998 for a review), however, systematic investigations of fetal perception did not get underway until the 1980s. How do you measure a fetal response to sounds? Usually, the investigators measure heart rate changes and sometimes body movements in response to differing types of sounds. These early studies provided evidence that by approximately 30 weeks gestational age, a fetus hears and responds to simple sounds such as bursts of white noise. By 37–42 weeks, a fetus can discriminate between types of speech sounds (such as vowels, consonant-vowel syllables) (Lecanuet et al., 1987; Groome et al., 1999).

The finding that a fetus can both hear and discriminate between sounds before birth has led to investigations of what a fetus knows about specific sounds, namely his/her own mother's voice. DeCasper and colleagues studied the listening preferences of newborn infants in a series of investigations in the 1980s. They found that newborns prefer their mother's voice to that of a female stranger (DeCasper and Fifer, 1980). These results led to a debate regarding the bases of speech perception: does a newborn's preference for his/her own mother's voice reflect a genetically pre-wired disposition for human language? Or does the newborn's preference reflect prenatal experience? A recent work

by Kisilevsky and colleagues (Kisilevsky et al., 2003) advanced the results provided by DeCasper with more specific evidence that a late-term fetus recognizes the voice of his/her mother over the voice of a female stranger. They reported that the fetal heart rate *increases* when listening to the mother's voice and *decreases* when listening to a stranger's voice. While the findings of Kisilevsky and colleagues (Kisilevsky et al., 2003) do not resolve the nature versus nurture debate regarding the genetic or experience basis of a newborn's speech perceptual acuity, they provide intriguing evidence that a fetus can not only discern between familiar and unfamiliar voices, but suggests that before birth, there is a specific preference for the mother's voice.

There has recently been an increased focus on the effects of prenatal exposure to music. This focus is largely due to claims that prenatal exposure to music produces increases in intelligence or cognitive function as the baby develops. These claims are based on anecdotal information, however, with no rigorous scientific basis. Let's examine the evidence of what we do know about music perception at or near birth: there have been many infant studies investigating music perception abilities in the first months of life. Trehub and colleagues report that infants as young as 2 months old perceive rhythmic patterns in music. Further, Trehub reports that there are many parallels between early infant musical knowledge and adult patterns that appear to support some notion of an innate or at least a biological bias for music perception (see Trehub and Hannon, 2005, for a review).

Little is known about musical perception before birth, however, the work of Kisilevsky and colleagues (Kisilevsky et al., 2004) have reported that late-term (33–37 weeks gestational age) fetuses can discriminate between changes in tempo in musical sequences. Importantly, earlier term fetuses (28 weeks) did not show this effect, leading Kisilevsky to conclude that there are developmental changes *in utero* in music perception, with later term fetuses discriminating features in music that earlier term fetuses did not discriminate. Cumulatively, the research carried out by Kisilevsky and colleagues (2003) provides evidence that some higher order auditory perception for maternal voice and for music is not only occurring before birth, but is changing, maturing in its nature.

Does evidence that a fetus perceives human voice and music before birth rule out the idea of a genetic predisposition for language and music? Not really. The elucidation of the complex interactions between genetic expression and experience that underlie human speech and music perception are still being elucidated in the field of developmental cognitive neuroscience.

New techniques and experimental designs are being developed in order to address this very important question about human development.

3.0 THE DEVELOPING BRAIN: A LIFE-TIME OF CHANGE

3.1 The rise and fall of postnatal brain development

While the overall appearance of the newborn human brain is rather similar to that in adults, and most neurons have already reached their final locations, a number of substantive *additive* changes occur during postnatal development of the brain. Specifically, brain volume quadruples between birth and adulthood, an increase that comes from a number of sources, but generally not from additional neurons. The generation and migration of neurons takes place almost entirely within the period of prenatal development in the human. Although there may be some addition of neurons in the hippocampus and elsewhere, the vast majority are present by around the seventh month of gestation (Rakic, 1995).

Perhaps the most obvious change during postnatal neural development is the increase in size and complexity of the *dendritic trees* of most neurons. An example of the dramatic increase in dendritic tree extent during human postnatal development is shown in Figure 15.14. While the extent and reach of a cell's dendritic arbor may increase dramatically, it also often becomes more specific and specialized.

In addition to the more extensive processes involved in the inputs and outputs of cells, there is a steady increase in the density of synapses in most regions of the cerebral cortex in humans (Huttenlocher *et al.*, 1982; Huttenlocher, 1990, 1994). The process of creating new synapses, *synaptogenesis*, begins approximately around the time of birth for all cortical areas studied to date, with the most increases, and the final peak density, occurring at different ages in different areas. For example, in the visual cortex there is rapid synaptogenesis at 3 to 4 months, and the maximum density of around 150 per cent of that seen in adult humans is reached between 4 and 12 months. In contrast, while synaptogenesis starts at the same time in a region of the prefrontal cortex, density increases much more slowly and does not reach its peak until well after the first year.

Another additive process is *myelination*. Myelination refers to an increase in the fatty sheath that surrounds neuronal processes and fibers, and that increases the efficiency of electrical transmission. Because myelination continues in cortical areas for many years after birth, there has been speculation about its role in behavioral development (Yakovlev and Lecours, 1967; Parmelee and Sigman, 1983; Volpe, 1987). Owing to the increased lipid content of the brain caused by myelination of fibres, structural MRI images can reveal a clear gray-white matter contrast and this allows quantitative volume measurements to be made during development (see Sampaio and Truwit 2001). While some controversy remains about the interpretation of images from infants under 6 months, there is consensus that the appearance of brain structures is similar to that of adults by 2 years of age, and that all major fiber tracts can be observed by 3 years of age (Huttenlocher and Dabholkar, 1997; Bourgeois, 2001). Changes in the extent of white matter are of interest since they presumably reflect inter-regional communication in the developing brain. While increases in white matter extend through adolescence into adulthood, particularly in frontal brain regions (Huttenlocher *et al.*, 1982), the most rapid changes occur during the first 2 years. Myelination appears to begin at birth in the pons and cerebellar peduncles and, by 3 months, has extended to the optic radiation and splenium of the corpus callosum. Around 8–12 months the white matter associated with the frontal, parietal, and occipital lobes becomes apparent.

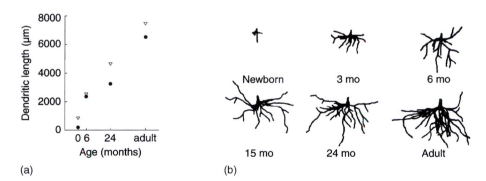

(a)   (b)

FIGURE 15.14 Dendritic arborisation. A drawing of the cellular structure of the human visual cortex based on Golgi stain preparations from Conel (1939–1967). *Source*: Quartz, 1999, from Conel, 1953, *New England J of Medicine*.

Surprisingly, human postnatal brain development also involves some significant *regressive events*. One quantitative neuroanatomical measure of a regressive event is the density of synapses, where there is a period of synaptic loss or *pruning* (Huttenlocher, 1990, 1994). Like the timing of bursts of synaptogenesis, and the subsequent peaks of density, the timing of the reduction in synaptic density appears to vary between cortical regions, at least in humans. For example, synaptic density in the visual cortex begins to returns to adult levels after about 2 years, while the same point is not reached until teenage age for regions of the prefrontal cortex. Huttenlocher (1990, 1994) suggests that this initial overproduction of synapses may have an important role in the apparent plasticity of the young brain.

Thus, the *rise and fall* developmental sequence is seen in a number of different measures of neuroanatomical and physiological development in the human cortex. However, we need to bear in mind that not all measures show this pattern (e.g. myelinization) and that measures of synaptic density are static snapshots of a dynamic process in which both additive and regressive processes are continually in progress.

While most of this section has focused on the cerebral neocortex, other brain structures, such as the hippocampus and cerebellum, also show some postnatal development. Indeed, the postnatal development of some subcortical structures (such as the hippocampus, cerebellum and thalamus) poses something of a paradox; on the one hand there is much behavioral and neural evidence to indicate that these structures are functioning at birth, while on the other they all show some evidence of postnatal development and/or functional re-organization. One resolution of this puzzle is that as the cerebral cortex develops postnatally, its interactions with subcortical regions undergo certain changes. Thus, while some subcortical structures are capable of functioning relatively independently of the cortex early in life, the increasing development of the cortex requires some structural and functional adjustment.

3.2 Regional differences in brain development

As compared to other species, humans take a very long time to develop into independent creatures. Human postnatal cortical development, for example, is extended roughly four times as long as non-human primates. The 'down' side of this slow development is that there are many years during which a child is highly dependent on the care provided by family members. The 'up' side of this protracted developmental timetable is that the human brain has far more opportunity for experience, and interactions with others, to shape and mould its development.

As suggested above, the 'rise and fall' pattern of additive and regressive events occurs at different timeframes in regions and lobes in the human brain. These events are heavily experience driven and reflect synapse formation and dendritic arborization that are due to cognitive and sensory development, learning and integrative processes that occur throughout infancy and childhood and continue through the teen years. A timecourse of brain development from conception to late teenage is presented in Figure 15.15 (Casey *et al.*, 2005). Prenatal changes are shown on the left side of the figure and largely reflect neurulation, cell proliferation and migration processes. Postnatal changes reflect developmental processes such as synaptogenesis and dendritic arborization. Sensory areas for processing visual and auditory information, for example, develop earlier than frontal lobe regions such as the prefrontal cortex for processing executive functions (Casey *et al.*, 2005).

How can we objectively measure brain development over the lifespan? One way in which to track developmental changes in the brain is to measure gray-matter density across regions in the cortex. A large cross-sectional study of 176 subjects ranging in age from 7 to 87 years provided evidence for different patterns of gray-matter density decrease across the lifespan (Toga *et al.*, 2006). In the superior frontal sulcus, gray-matter density decreases rapidly beginning in adolescence, however, in the superior temporal sulcus, gray-matter density decreases more gradually through life (Figure 15.16).

While we are beginning to map out the developmental patterns for brain regions across the lifespan, a key issue that is being addressed is the notion of individual differences in how the brain matures and the correspondence to cognitive development. In other words, what is the relationship between brain and behavior? Do differing patterns of brain development reflect different levels of intellectual ability? These questions were addressed in a recent neuroimaging investigation of gray-matter density in a large sample of more than 300 children and adolescents (Shaw *et al.*, 2006). The sample was *a priori* divided into three groups based on their performance on an IQ battery of tests: 'Superior' with IQ ranging from 121 to 149; 'High' with IQ ranging from 109 to 120; and 'Average' with IQ ranging from 83 to 108. The results indicated that there are, indeed, differing patterns of

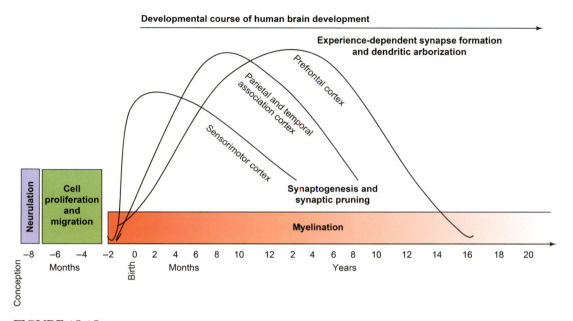

FIGURE 15.15 Developmental course of human brain development. The human brain undergoes dramatic changes in both its structural architecture and functional organization that reflect a dynamic interplay of simultaneously occurring progressive and regressive events. Although the total brain size is about 90 per cent of adult size by age 6 years, the brain continues to undergo dynamic changes throughout adolescence and well into adulthood. Figure 15.15 illustrates some of these developmental changes, including proliferation and migration of cells mostly during fetal development, regional changes in synaptic density during postnatal development, and protracted development well into adulthood. Current non-invasive neuroimaging methods do not have the resolution to delineate which of these processes underlies observed developmental changes beyond gray and white matter subcomponents. (Adapted from Thompson and Nelson, 2001.) *Source*: Casey *et al.*, 2005.

brain change corresponding to overall level of intelligence (Figure 15.17). The notable finding was that high IQ was associated with thinner cortex, especially in frontal and temporal lobe areas, in early childhood. By late childhood, the opposite pattern was found, with high IQ associated with thicker cortex.

The important finding of this study was that there was a differing pattern of cortical development in frontal lobe regions for children in the 'Superior' group as compared to either of the other groups. Specifically, there were differences in the dynamic rate of cortical thickening and thinning throughout early childhood and into adolescence and early adulthood. The authors concluded that differences in gray-matter density in and of itself did not lead to children with superior intellectual abilities, rather they suggested that the dynamic properties of development of the cortex corresponded to level of intelligence, perhaps enabling the child to extract more information from his environment. Open issues raised by this study are: are dynamic changes in brain growth patterns due to genetic predispositions in the 'Superior' group? Or do they reflect differences in the environment? Or do they reflect a combination of both genetic influences and experience?

These findings from recent studies of brain development throughout the lifespan are helping us prepare new models for human cognitive growth and the correspondence to cognition. These studies are still very early work in an ongoing series of investigations of complex brain developmental processes. Although this investigation is still in its early stages, results to date provide evidence that the brain is changing in dynamic ways throughout early childhood and into adulthood.

4.0 DEVELOPING MIND AND BRAIN

We have seen that the brain undergoes significant developmental changes throughout childhood. An important question to address in the field of developmental cognitive neuroscience is how these brain changes reflect development of cognitive processes. New techniques are allowing us to begin to map brain development and the correspondence to cognition. The emergence of longitudinal multidisciplinary studies combining neuroimaging studies of cortical change and behavioral studies of

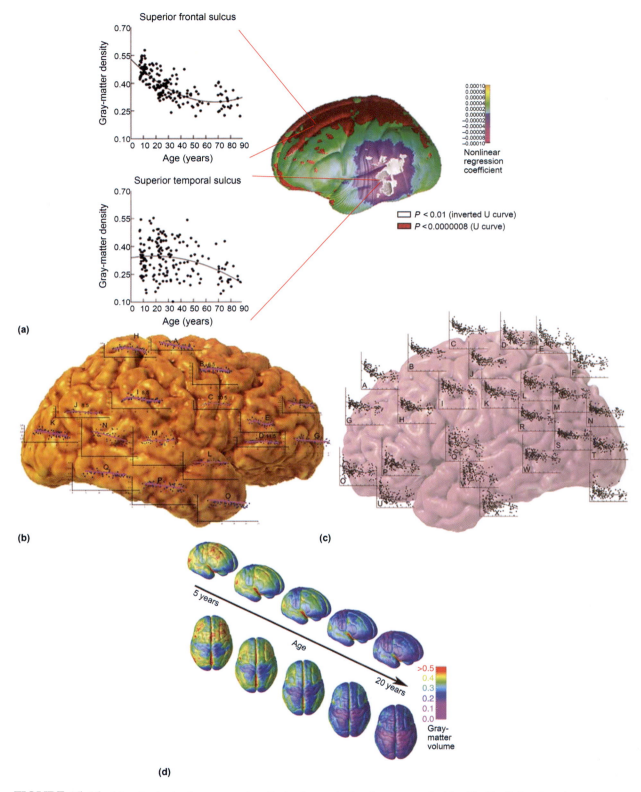

FIGURE 15.16 Mapping brain change over time. Brain changes in development can be identified by fitting time-dependent statistical models to data collected from subjects cross-sectionally (i.e. across a group of subjects at a particular time), longitudinally (i.e. following individual subjects as they aged), or both. Measurements such as cortical thickness are then plotted onto the cortex using a color code. (a, b) Trajectory of gray-matter loss over the human lifespan, based on a cohort of 176 subjects aged 7 to 87 years (Sowell et al., 2003). Plots superimposed on the brain in (b) show how gray–matter density decreases for particular regions; (a) highlights example regions in which the gray-matter density decreases rapidly during adolescence (the superior frontal sulcus) or follows a more steadily declining time-course during lifespan (the superior temporal sulcus) (c,d). *Source*: Toga *et al.*, 2006.

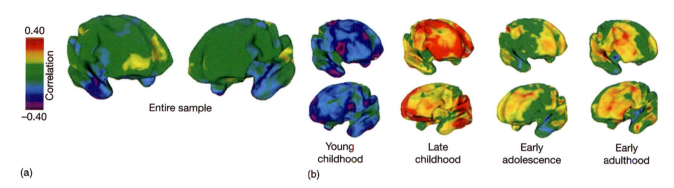

FIGURE 15.17 Correlations between IQ and cortical thickness. (a) Pearson's correlations for all 307 subjects were generally positive and modest ($p > 0.05$), with r between 0 and .10 (green/yellow), except in the anterior temporal cortex (which showed a negative correlation, with r between 0 and -1; blue/purple). (b) Correlations in different age groups showed that negative correlations were present in the youngest group, indicating that higher IQ was associated with a thinner cortex particularly in frontal and temporal regions. The relationship reverses in late childhood with most of the cerebral cortex correlating positively with IQ. *Source:* Shaw *et al.*, 2006.

performance on cognitive tasks will provide us with better ways to asses the relationship between brain development and cognition. In this section, we will discuss what we know at present about the relation between brain development and child developmental processes. While we highlight some recent studies, it is important to note that the field of developmental cognitive neuroscience is a very young one. The first fMRI studies of children were published in 1995 by Casey and colleagues (Casey *et al.*, 1995). Thus, while the findings we present here are informative, the answer to our questions regarding the neural bases of language acquisition, cognitive control processes, and social cognition are still being discovered in laboratories throughout the world.

We have discussed a functional framework for understanding the processes of cognition. Developmental cognitive neuroscientists are seeking to understand how these systems and processes that are observed in healthy adults (Figure 15.18) are developed and formed in infancy, childhood and through adolescence. Once again, the question of the role of nature versus nurture is debated in the field. Is the human brain pre-wired for language? Face perception? Or are these processes based on experience throughout life? Since these topics are of central interest in the study of human development, we will focus on three general areas of developmental cognitive neuroscience investigations that may shed light on these issues: the emergence of language; the development of cognitive control mechanisms; and the development of social cognition, with a specific focus on face perception. In the following section, we provide a brief summary of research to date on these topics in infants during the first year of life. Next, we present findings on these topics for older children and adolescents. Last, we review the effects of early (perinatal) brain damage on these systems.

4.1 The first year of life: an explosion of growth and development

The human brain increases fourfold in size from newborn to adult. Many of the dynamic changes that occur in development happen during the first year of life. During this 12-month span, an infant develops from a tiny creature with few voluntary movements to a busy toddler smiling, reaching for attractive objects, producing many speech sounds, crawling and even walking as he or she explores the world around.

4.1.1 Developing the linguistic brain: infant language capabilities

Remember the studies showing that babies can hear and discriminate their mother's voice before birth? Studies like these have provided compelling evidence that a newborn infant already has experience with human language. We have discussed the nature versus nurture debate regarding the genetic predisposition for language versus the role of experience. This debate has been influential in the field of developmental cognitive neuroscience, with many studies investigating just what an infant knows about language. Most studies of young infants (less than 12 months old) focus on the classes and categories of speech sounds: phonology. Studies with older infants and children also investigate semantic (meaning-based) and syntactic (grammar-based) knowledge.

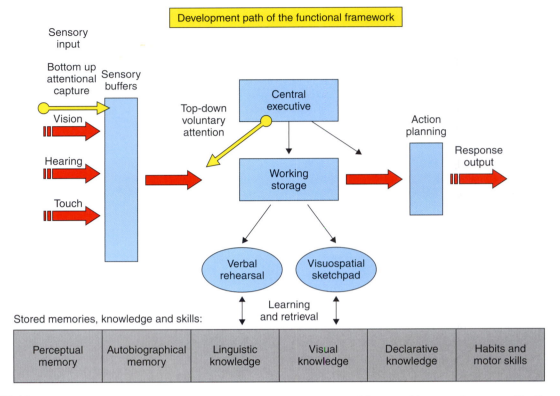

FIGURE 15.18   A functional framework for development, adapted from the general functional framework presented in Chapter 2.

Is language 'biologically special'? One way to begin to address this question is to see whether young babies are specifically sensitive to human speech. If there are specific neural correlates of speech processing observable very early in life, this may indicate language-related neural processing prior to significant experience.

One example of this approach concerns the ability to discriminate speech relevant sounds such as *phonemes* (see Chapter 7). Each human language has a set of sounds that map onto individual phonemes, which typically are conscripted within slashes: /p/ for example to reflect the sounds (phones) that map onto the phoneme /p/. Recall the 'lack of invariance' problem discussed in Chapter 7: the differing phonemes that are articulated before and after the articulation of /p/ affect its acoustic features. Thus, there is not a single invariant physical property that uniquely defines /p/. Rather, the representation of the phoneme /p/ must rely on some abstract (not just physical) features. This aspect of human speech has been exploited in speech perception studies where phonemes that differ in a single feature are prepared using speech synthesizing software to create a series of sounds that differ in graded steps between, for example, the phonemes /b/ and /p/ which differ only in their initial voicing (vocal chord vibration).

As English-speaking adults, if we were to listen to a graded phonetic transition from speech sounds 'ba' to 'pa', we would perceive the intermediates between /ba/ and /pa/ as being either one, or the other. In other words, we show a categorical boundary between the two. Behavioral experiments have revealed that young babies also show enhanced (categorical) discrimination at phonetic boundaries used in speech such as /ba/ /pa/. That is, a graded phonetic transition from /ba/ to /pa/ is also perceived as a sudden categorical shift by infants. These observations initially caused excitement as evidence for a human speech perception specific detection mechanism in humans. However, recent research has shown that other species, such as chinchillas, show similar acoustical discrimination abilities. This indicates that this ability may merely reflect general characteristics of the mammalian auditory processing system and not an initial spoken language specific mechanism (see Werker and Vouloumanos, 2001).

Intriguingly, and unlike us adults, young human infants can initially discriminate a very wide range of phonetic constructs, including those not found in the native language. For example, Japanese infants, but not Japanese adults, can discriminate between 'r' and 'l' sounds. However, this ability becomes restricted to the phonetic constructs found in the native language by around 10 months of age. These findings might reflect early speech perceptual processes that take into account the physical or acoustic features in all speech sounds in early infancy, developing later into mechanisms with less reliance on the physical aspects and more on the abstract representations of phonemes in their native language. In this way, the role of experience has a strong hand in shaping an infant's language knowledge.

If brain correlates of this process could be identified, it may be possible to study the mechanisms underlying this speech specific selective decrease of sensitivity. Event-related potentials (ERPs) have been used to investigate this question. When components of ERP differ in both latency (following the event) and spatial resolution, we may be confident that different neural circuitry is being activated in the brain. Dehaene-Lambertz and Dehaene (1994) presented babies with trials in which a series of four identical syllables (the standard) was followed by a fifth that was either identical or phonetically different (deviant). They time-locked the ERP to the onset of the syllable and observed two peaks with different locations on the scalp. The first peak occurred around 220 s after stimulus onset and did not habituate to repeated presentations (except after the first presentation) or dishabituate to the novel syllable. Thus, the brain generators of this peak, probably primary and secondary auditory areas in the temporal lobe, did not appear to be sensitive to the subtle acoustical differences that encoded phonetic information.

The second peak reached its maximum around 390 ms after stimulus onset and again did not habituate to repetitions of the same syllable, except after the first presentation. However, when the deviant syllable was introduced, the peak recovered to at least its original level. Thus, the neural generators of the second peak, also in the temporal lobe, but in a distinct and more posterior location, are sensitive to phonetic information. Further studies need to be carried out to ascertain whether the recovery of the second peak is due to the categorical perception of phonemes, or whether it would be elicited by any change in sound.

Further investigations by Dehaene-Lambertz and colleagues used two imaging methods with better spatial resolution to investigate early correlates of speech perception. For example, Dehaene-Lambertz et al. (2002) measured brain activation with fMRI in awake and sleeping healthy 3 months old while they listened to forwards and backwards speech in their native tongue (French). The authors assumed that forward speech would elicit stronger activation than backward speech in areas related to the higher-order processing of language, while both

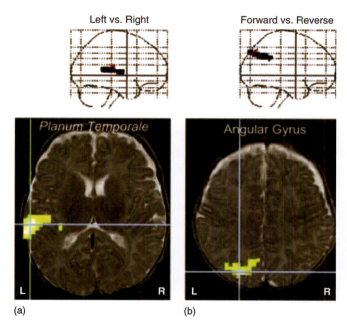

FIGURE 15.19 Speech activation of the human infant brain. fMRI images were obtained from 2- to 3-month-old infants during presentation of native speech. (a) A transparent brain view (top) and an axial section (bottom) map the relative sound-evoked activity for left versus right temporal cortex. The activation was significantly greater on the left side. (b) An activation map showing the relative sound-evoked activity in response to forwards speech versus reverse speech. While there was no difference in the temporal cortex, there was an asymmetry within the angular gyrus. (From Dehaene-Lambertz et al., 2002.) *Source*: Sanes et al., 2006.

stimuli would activate mechanisms for processing fast temporal auditory transitions. Compared to silence, both forwards and backwards speech activated widespread areas of the left temporal lobe, which was greater than the equivalent activation on the right for some areas (such as the planum temporale, see Figure 15.19, left panel). This activation pattern is consistent with the ERP experiment described above. However, forwards speech activated some areas that backwards speech did not, including the angular gyrus (see Figure 15.19, right panel) and mesial parietal lobe (precuneus) in the left hemisphere. These findings demonstrate an early functional asymmetry between the two hemispheres. However, the results cannot discriminate between an early bias for speech perception, or a greater responsivity of the left temporal lobe for processing features contained within speech sounds, such as rapid temporal changes.

The general conclusions from the above studies are reinforced by converging results from a new methodology – near infra-red spectroscopy (NIRS). In one experiment, Mehler and colleagues (Pena et al., 2003) played normal infant directed speech or the same utterances played in reverse while they measured changes in the concentration of total hemoglobin within parts of the right and left hemisphere. They observed that left temporal areas showed significantly more activation when infants were exposed to normal speech than to backwards speech or silence, leading them to conclude that neonates are born with a left hemisphere already biased for speech processing.

Language acquisition and speech perception have been some of the most active areas of developmental cognitive neuroscience. The use of converging methodologies, and frequent comparisons between typical and atypical trajectories of development, make it the domain most likely to see major breakthroughs over the next decade (see Gage et al., 2003a,b for a discussion of auditory mechanisms underlying speech development in children with autism disorder).

4.1.2 Developing the executive brain: what do babies know?

A critical aspect of an infant's cognitive growth during the first year of life is the ability to learn about his or her environment. New items will attract the attention of a young infant and he or she will gaze at these items for longer durations than for items that are accustomed to being seen. While it is important for an infant to gaze at a new item, it is also important for an infant to orient to other aspects of their environment. The trading effects of looking at new items and shifting attention to other elements in the world about them provides infants both with learning opportunities for understanding features in new items and a wide range of such experiences by changing the focus of their attention, both of which are critical to cognitive development.

The executive control for directing attention to new items, orienting, maintaining goals and control over reaching movements are thought to require the most anterior portion of the brain, the prefrontal cortex (PFC) (see Chapter 12). As discussed earlier, the frontal cortex shows the most prolonged period of postnatal development of any region of the human brain, with neuroanatomical changes evident even into the teenage years (Huttenlocher, 1990; Giedd et al., 1999). For this reason, it has been the part of the brain most commonly associated with developments in cognitive abilities during childhood.

One of the most comprehensive attempts to relate a cognitive change to underlying brain developments has concerned the emergence of object permanence in infants. Object permanence is the ability to retain an object in mind after it has been hidden by another object or a cover

(Figure 15.20). Specifically, Piaget observed that infants younger than around 7 months fail accurately to retrieve a hidden object after a short delay period if the object's location is changed from one where it was previously and successfully retrieved. In particular, infants at this age make a particular perserverative error in which they persistently reach to the hiding location where the object was found on the immediately preceding trial. This characteristic pattern of error, called 'A not B', was cited by Piaget (1954) as evidence for the failure of infants to understand that objects retain their existence or permanence when moved from view. Beyond about 7 months infants begin to succeed in the task at successively longer delays of 1 to 5 seconds (Diamond, 1985, 2001).

Diamond and Goldman-Rakic (1989) found that infant monkeys also make errors in an adapted version of Piaget's object permanence task. Similar errors were also seen in adult monkeys with damage to dorsolateral prefrontal cortex (DL-PFC). Damage to other parts of cortex did not have the same effects, indicating a specific role for DL-PFC in this task.

Evidence linking this change in behavior to brain development also comes from EEG studies with human infants (Fox and Bell, 1990; Bell, 1992a, b; Bell and Fox, 1992). In these studies, increases in frontal EEG responses correlate with the ability to respond successfully over longer delays in delayed response tasks. Most recently, an optical imaging study with infants has revealed a correlation between behavioral success at the AB task and blood oxygenation in prefrontal cortex (Baird et al., 2002).

Converging evidence for the importance of frontal cortex development comes from studies on children with an atypical neurochemical balance in the prefrontal cortex resulting from phenylketonuria (PKU) (Welsh et al., 1990; Diamond 2001). Even when treated, this metabolic disorder can have the specific consequence of reducing the levels of a neurotransmitter, dopamine, in the dorsolateral prefrontal cortex. These reductions in dopamine levels in the dorsolateral prefrontal cortex result in these infants and children being impaired on tasks thought to involve prefrontal cortex such as the object permanence task, and having typical performance in tasks thought to be dependent on other regions of cortex, such as delayed non-matching to sample (Welsh et al., 1990; Diamond 2001).

Thus, converging evidence from several sources supports the view that development of DL-PFC allows infants to succeed in the object permanence task. According to Diamond (1991), the critical features of the task carried out by DL-PFC is the ability to retain information over spatial delays and to inhibit prepotent (previously reinforced) responses. However, two recent

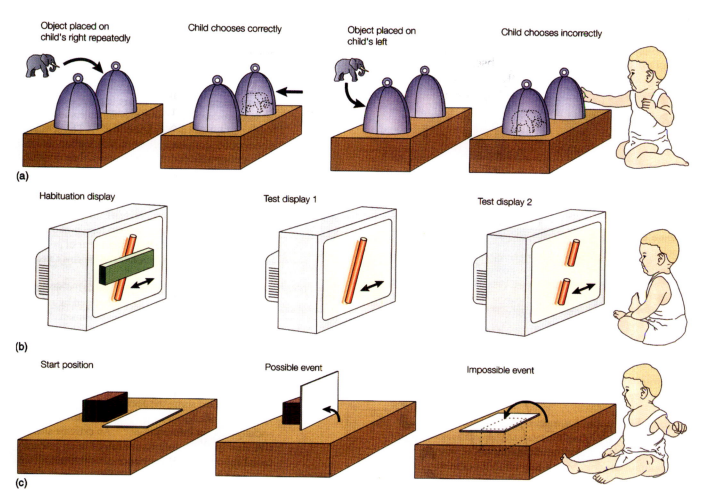

FIGURE 15.20 Behavioral testing in infants. (a) An object retrieval task that infants fail up to 9 months of age. In full view of the infant, the experimenter hides the object in one location and the infant reaches for it successfully. After a few such trials, the experimenter hides the object in a second place but the infant searches again at the original location (Piaget, 1954). (b) A visual habituation technique can be used to show that infants from as young as 4 months perceive the left-hand figure as a continuous rod moving behind an occluder. Infants dishabituated (found novel) the test display with two short rods, indicating that they perceptually 'filled in' the occluded area in the habituation display. Infants under 4 months are only partially successful in such tasks, depending on the complexity of the display. (c) The infant views two event sequences, one possible and one impossible, in which a flap is rotated towards a solid cube. In the 'possible' case the flap stops when it comes into contact with the object. In the impossible case the flap rotates through the object. Infants as young as 4 months appear surprised (look longer) when viewing the impossible event, showing that they appreciate that objects are solid and (usually) non-compressible. *Source*: Johnson, 2001.

lines of evidence suggest that the DL-PFC development hypothesis is not the whole story and that some modification or elaboration of the original account may be required. The first of these lines of evidence comes from another task thought to require DL-PFC: the oculomotor delayed response task (Figure 15.21). Gilmore and Johnson (1995) found that infants can succeed on this task at a much younger age than is indicated by the object retrieval tasks, even though it also requires the infant to maintain spatial information over a delay and needs to inhibit a prepotent response.

One explanation of the discrepancy between performance in Piaget's object permanence task and the results of

Gilmore and Johnson (1995) is that tasks in which the response is an eye movement (looking) are easier since eye movement planning develops more rapidly than other forms of motor output such as reaching. This proposal is consistent with several studies showing that infants can perform successfully in analogous object permanence tasks as young as 4 or 5 months of age if looking rather than reaching performance is measured (Lecuyer *et al.*, 1992).

In order to explain the difference between results obtained with eye movements as the measure and those with the manual reaching measures, it has been argued that infants do not yet have the necessary action planning

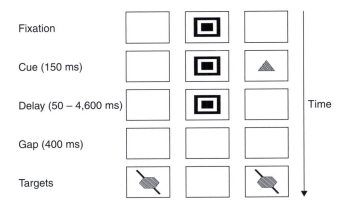

Fixation

Cue (150 ms)

Delay (50 – 4,600 ms)   Time

Gap (400 ms)

Targets

FIGURE 15.21 The oculomotor delayed response task as designed for use with infants. Infant subjects face three computer screens on which brightly colored moving stimuli appear. At the start of each trial a fixation stimulus appears on the central screen. Once the infant is looking at this stimulus, a cue is briefly flashed up on one of the two side screens. Following the briefly flashed cue, the central stimulus stays on for between 1 and 5 seconds, before presentation of two targets on the side screens. By measuring delayed looks to the cued location prior to the target onset, Gilmore and Johnson (1995) established that infants can retain information about the cued location for several seconds. *Source*: Gilmore and Johnson, 1995.

skills to coordinate the sequence of motor behaviors to retrieve a hidden object (Diamond, 1991; Baillargeon, 1993). To test this idea, Munakata *et al.* (1994) trained 7 months old to retrieve objects placed at a distance from them by means of pulling on a towel or pressing a button. Infants retrieved objects when a transparent screen was interposed between them and the toy, but not if the screen was sufficiently opaque to make the object invisible. Since the same means-ends planning is required whether the screen is transparent or opaque, it was concluded that this cannot account for the discrepancy between the looking and the reaching tasks. Munakata *et al.* (1994) proposed an alternative 'graded' view of the discrepancy implemented as a neural network model. This model illustrates how weak internal representations of a stimulus can be sufficient to drive a simple output, such as an eye movement, but may be insufficient to initiate a more complex motor output, such as reaching.

An alternative approach to understanding the role of the prefrontal cortex in cognitive development has been advanced by several authors who have suggested that the region plays a critical role in the *acquisition* of new information and tasks. From this perspective, the challenge to the infant brain in, for example, learning to reach for an object, is equivalent in some respects to that of the adult brain when facing complex motor skills like learning to drive a car. Three predictions from this view are that: (i) the cortical regions crucial for a particular task

will change with the stage of acquisition; (ii) the prefrontal cortex plays a role in organizing or allocating information to other regions of cortex; and (iii) that development involves the establishment of hierarchical control structures, with frontal cortex maintaining the currently highest level of control. Recent evidence showing PFC activation early in infancy has given further credence to this view. The limited number of fMRI and PET studies that have been done with infants have often surprisingly revealed functional activation in PFC, even when this would not be predicted from adult studies. For example, in an fMRI study of speech perception in 3 month olds, Dehaene-Lambertz and colleagues (Dehaene-Lambertz *et al.*, 2002) observed a right dorsolateral prefrontal cortex activation that discriminated (forwards) speech in awake, but not sleeping, infants (Figure 15.22). Similar activation of DL-PFC was found in response to faces at the same age (Tzourio-Mazoyer *et al.*, 2002). While this is evidence for activation of at least some of the PFC in the first few months, it remains possible that this activation is passive as it does not play any role in directing the behavior of the infant.

Developmental ERP studies have often recorded activity changes over frontal leads in infants and some recent experiments suggest that this activity has important consequences for behavioral output. These experiments involve examining patterns of activation that precede the onset of a saccade. In one example, Csibra and colleagues (Csibra *et al.*, 1998, 2001) observed that pre-saccadic potentials that are usually recorded over more posterior scalp sites in adults, are observed in frontal channels in 6-months old infants. Since these potentials are time-locked to the onset of an action, it is reasonable to infer that they are the consequence of computations necessary for the planning or execution of the action.

Further evidence for the developmental importance of the PFC from early infancy comes from studies of the long-term and widespread effects of perinatal damage to PFC. Selective perinatal damage to the relevant regions activated in adults often has, at worst, mild effects on infants with subsequently nearly complete recovery of function. In contrast, perinatal damage to frontal and PFC regions often results in both immediate and long-term difficulties. This generalization from several domains suggests that PFC could play an important structuring or enabling role from very early in postnatal development.

The issue raised at the beginning of this section concerned how to reconcile evidence for continuing neuroanatomical development in the frontal cortex until the teenage years on the one hand, and evidence for some functioning in the region as early as the first few

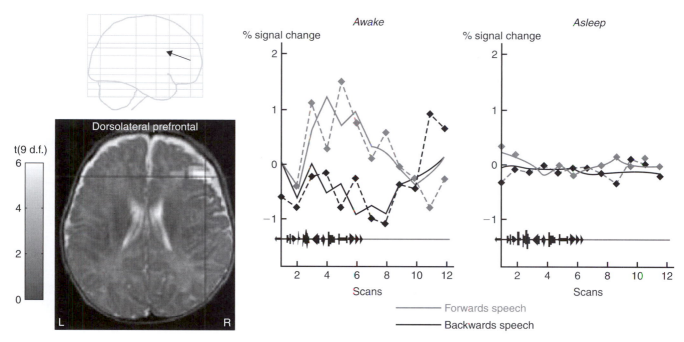

FIGURE 15.22 Speech perception in infants. Interaction between wakefulness and the linguistic nature of the stimuli. This comparison isolated a right dorsolateral prefrontal region that showed greater activation by forwards speech than by backwards speech in awake infants, but not in sleeping infants. *Source*: Dehaene-Lambertz *et al.*, 2002.

months of age on the other. One possible resolution to this issue is that representations that emerge within this region of cortex are initially weak and sufficient only to control some types of output, such as saccades, but not others, such as reaching (Munakata *et al.*, 1994). Other plausible resolutions of this issue come from Diamond's (1991) proposal that different regions of frontal cortex are differentially delayed in their development, and Thatcher's (1992) suggestion that prefrontal regions may have a continuing role in the cyclical reorganization of the rest of cortex.

Whether these hypotheses work out or not, there is good reason why some degree of PFC functioning is vital from the first weeks of postnatal life, or even earlier (Fulford *et al.*, 2003). The ability to form and retain goals, albeit for short periods, is essential for generating efforts to perform actions such as reaching for objects. Early and often initially unsuccessful attempts to perform motor actions provide the essential experience necessary for subsequent development.

4.1.3 Developing the social brain: faces and places

As described in Chapter 14, one of the major characteristics of the human brain is its social nature. A variety of cortical areas have been implicated in the 'social brain' including the superior temporal sulcus (STS), the fusiform 'face area' (FFA) and orbitofrontal cortex. One of the major debates in cognitive neuroscience concerns the origins of the 'social brain' in humans and theoretical arguments abound about the extent to which this is acquired through experience.

One aspect of social brain function in humans that has been the topic of many investigations is the perception and processing of faces. There is a long history of research on the development of face recognition in young infants extending back to the studies of Fantz more than 40 years ago (e.g. Fantz, 1964). Over the past decade, numerous papers have addressed cortical basis of face processing in adults, including identifying areas that may be specifically dedicated to this purpose (see Chapter 6). Despite these bodies of data, surprisingly little remains known about the developmental cognitive neuroscience of face processing.

In a review of the available literature in the late 1980s, Johnson and Morton (1991) revealed two apparently contradictory bodies of evidence: while the prevailing view, and most of the evidence, supported the idea that infants gradually learn about the arrangement of features that compose a face over the first few months of life, the results from at least one study indicated that newborn infants, as young as 10 minutes old, will track a face-like pattern further than various 'scrambled' face patterns (Goren *et al.*, 1975). Evidence that newborns showed a preferential response to faces was used by some to bolster nativist views of infant cognition. In contrast, the

BOX 15.1   Face preferences in newborns

Over the last decade more than a dozen papers have been published on the face-related looking preferences of newborn infants. Most of these papers concluded that newborns are biased to attend to stimuli that possess certain characteristics of faces, but two alternative views have been expressed.

The first of these views (the 'sensory hypothesis') is that all newborn visual preferences, including those for face-related stimuli, can be accounted for simply in terms of the relative visibility of the stimuli. The newborn visual system is restricted to the lower part of the range of spatial frequencies that is visible to adults. It has been proposed that newborns prefer to look at faces merely because the amplitude at different frequencies of these stimuli happen to best match the sensitivity of the newborn visual system. The sensory hypothesis has fallen out of favor because, even when amplitude is controlled, phase information (configuration) still influences the newborn preference towards faces. In addition, attempts to simulate newborn preferences with neural network models based on the sensory

hypothesis are unlikely to account for other experiments involving realistic faces within the complex visual scenes to which newborns are exposed.

The second alternative view is that we have complex face processing abilities from birth. The findings used to support this claim include a preference for images of attractive faces, data indicating that newborns are sensitive to the presence of eyes in a face and evidence that they prefer to look at faces that engage them in eye contact. In addition to the immaturity of the cortex at birth, all of these results could be accounted for by a low spatial frequency face configuration detector. For example, older infants prefer more attractive faces because these faces are closer to an average or prototypical face. Inspection of realistic face images through the appropriate spatial frequency filters for newborns reveals that a mechanism that is sensitive to the configuration of a face could be preferentially activated by (i) the most prototypical face configuration presented, (ii) the presence (or absence) of open eyes and (iii) direct versus averted gaze (see Figure 15.23).

BOX 15.2   Why does the fusiform develop a face area?

A central debate in cognitive neuroscience concerns the origin and specificity of the fusiform face area (FFA) and other face-sensitive regions of cortex. One view is that the FFA is selectively activated by faces owing to genetically-specified and domain-specific computational properties of that region. In contrast, others have proposed that the region is involved in processing visual stimuli in domains of perceptual expertise and most human adults become experts in face processing. From the developmental perspective taken in this chapter, an alternative 'middle way' account of FFA emerges. By this account, parts of the fusiform cortex become specialized for processing faces as a result of several constraining factors. First, the subcortical route described in this chapter ensures that newborns preferentially orient to faces and therefore foveate them, thus providing input to cortical visual pathways. Second, the cortical projection patterns of the subcortical route

may enhance activation of specific areas, including the fusiform cortex, when faces are within the visual field of the young infant. Third, the parts of the fusiform cortex that become face sensitive receive foveal cortical visual input and are at the 'object-level' of visual stimulus processing in the ventral pathway. Thus, information from both face routes may converge in the FFA. These and other possible constraints, such as multi-modal inputs and general biases in gene expression levels between the right and left cerebral cortex, combine to ensure that certain developing cortical circuits become specialized for face-related stimuli. By this developmental account it is inevitable, barring some disruption to the normal constraints, that parts of the fusiform cortex will specialize for faces. However, this inevitable outcome is achieved without genetically specified domain-specific patterns of connectivity with the FFA.

evidence for the graded development of face processing abilities over several months tended to be cited by theorists who believed that such skills need to be learned, and result from experience of the world.

Although detailed issues remain, the finding that newborns preferentially respond to patterns that correspond to faces remains valid (see Johnson, 2005b for review) (Figure 15.23). Recent evidence from a variety of sources indicates that there may be a subcortical route for face processing involving the superior colliculus, pulvinar, and amygdala (Johnson, 2005b). While this route is only evident in adults with functional imaging, or after acquired brain damage, it may be the main influence

over the behavior of the newborn in which cortical routes for visual processing are relatively immature.

How may we investigate face perception in infants? Several laboratories have examined changes in event-related potentials (ERPs) as adults view faces. In particular, interest has focused on an ERP component termed the 'N170' (because it is a negative-going deflection that occurs after around 170 ms) that has been strongly associated with face processing in a number of studies on adults. Specifically, the timing and size of this component vary according to whether or not faces are present in the visual field of the adult volunteer under study. An important aspect of the N170 in adults is that its response is

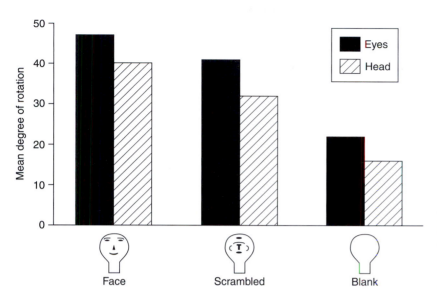

FIGURE 15.23 Face perception in newborns. Data showing the extent of newborns' head and eye turns in following a schematic face, a scrambled face and a blank (unpatterned) stimulus. The infant tracked the face significantly further than the other stimuli. *Source*: Johnson *et al.*, 1991.

highly selective. For example, the N170 shows a different response to human upright faces than to very closely related stimuli such as inverted human faces and upright monkey faces. While the exact underlying neural generators of the N170 are currently still debated, the specificity of response of the N170 can be taken as an index of the degree of specialization of cortical processing for human upright faces. For this reason de Haan, Johnson and colleagues (2002) undertook a series of studies on the development of the N170 over the first weeks and months of postnatal life (Figure 15.24).

The first issue addressed in these developmental ERP studies is when does the face-sensitive N170 emerge? In a series of experiments, a component was identified in the infant ERP that has many of the properties associated with the adult N170, but that is of a slightly longer latency (240–290 ms). In studying the response properties of this potential at 3, 6 and 12 months of age it was discovered that: (1) the component is present from at least 3 months of age (although its development continues into middle childhood), and (2) the component becomes more specifically tuned to human upright faces with increasing age. To expand on the second point, it was found that while 12 months old and adults showed different ERP responses to upright and inverted faces, 3 and 6 months old do not. Thus, the study of this face-sensitive ERP component is consistent with the idea of increased specialization of cortical processing with age, a result also consistent with some behavioral results (see below).

While we still await definitive functional imaging studies on face processing in infants and young children, a recent PET study conducted on 2-month-old infants reported neural activity for face processing that was in similar regions as found for adults, however, with

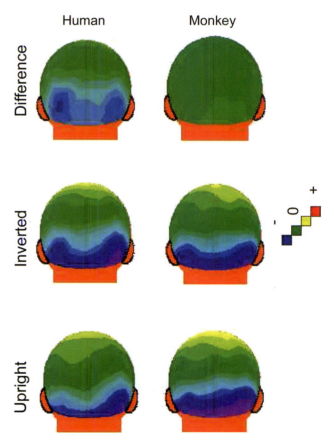

FIGURE 15.24 An EEG electrode net for recording ERPs in infants. *Source*: Ghislaine Dehaene-Lambertz, with permission.

relatively larger, more diffuse activations in infants than the focal activation found in adults. Specifically, a large network of cortical areas was activated when infants viewed faces as compared to a moving dot array.

This study involved the 'subtraction' of the activation resulting from a complex dynamic stimulus from that elicited by photographs of a female face. The resulting areas of activation corresponded to those regions activated by face processing in adults. Namely, bilateral activation of the superior and middle temporal gyrus (though the regions activated in infants may be more anterior than those in adults). Despite a low baseline of overall metabolic activity in the frontal lobes, there was a significant increase in activity in left orbitofrontal cortex and Broca's area in the face condition.

Converging evidence about the increasing specialization of face processing during development comes from a behavioral study that set out to test the intriguing idea that, as processing 'narrows' to human faces, infants will lose their ability to discriminate non-human faces. Pascalis and colleagues (Pascalis *et al.*, 2002) demonstrated that while 6 months old could discriminate between individual monkey faces as well as human faces, 9 months old and adults could only discriminate the human faces. These results are particularly compelling since they demonstrate a predicted competence in young infants that is not evident in adults.

Moving beyond the relatively simple perception of faces, a more complex attribute of the adult social brain is processing information about the eyes of other humans. There are two important aspects of processing information about the eyes. The first of these is being able to detect the direction of another's gaze in order to direct your own attention to the same object or spatial location. Perception of averted gaze can elicit an automatic shift of attention in the same direction in adults, allowing the establishment of 'joint attention'. Joint attention to objects is thought to be crucial for a number of aspects of cognitive and social development, including word learning. The second critical aspect of gaze perception is the detection of direct gaze, enabling mutual gaze with the viewer. Mutual gaze (eye contact) provides the main mode of establishing a communicative context between humans and is believed to be important for normal social development. It is commonly agreed that eye gaze perception is important for mother–infant interaction and that it provides a vital foundation for social development.

In a series of experiments with 4-month-old infants using a simple eye gaze cueing paradigm, Farroni and colleagues (Farroni *et al.*, 2000) have established that it is only following a period of mutual gaze with an upright face that cueing effects are observed. In other words, mutual gaze with an upright face may engage mechanisms of attention such that the viewing infant is more likely to be cued by subsequent motion. In summary, the critical features for eye gaze cueing in young infants are

(1) lateral motion of elements and (2) a brief preceding period of eye contact with an upright face.

Following the surprising observation that a period of direct gaze is required before cueing can be effective in infants, the earliest developmental roots of eye contact detection have been investigated. It is already known that human newborns have a bias to orient toward face-like stimuli (see earlier), prefer faces with eyes opened and tend to imitate certain facial gestures. Preferential attention to faces with direct gaze would provide the most compelling evidence to date that human newborns are born prepared to detect socially relevant information. For this reason we investigated eye gaze detection in humans from birth. Farroni and colleagues tested healthy human newborn infants by presenting them with a pair of stimuli, one a face with eye gaze directed straight at the newborns, and the other with averted gaze. Results showed that the fixation times were significantly longer for the face with the direct gaze. Further, the number of orientations was higher with the straight gaze than with the averted gaze.

In a second experiment, converging evidence for the differential processing of direct gaze in infants was obtained by recording event-related potentials (ERPs) from the scalp as infants viewed faces. Farroni and colleagues studied 4-month-old babies with the same stimuli as those used in the previous experiment with newborns and found a difference between the two gaze directions at the time and scalp location at the previously identified face-sensitive component of the infant ERP discussed earlier. The conclusion from these studies is that direct eye contact enhances the perceptual processing of faces even in infants as young as 4 months.

Beyond face processing and eye gaze detection, there are many more complex aspects of the social brain, such as the coherent perception of human action and the appropriate attribution of intentions and goals to conspecifics. Investigating the cognitive neuroscience of these abilities in infants and children will be a challenge for the next decade. One way in which these issues have been addressed is through studying genetic developmental disorders in which aspects of social cognition are either apparently selectively impaired (autism) or, selectively intact amidst otherwise impaired cognition (Williams syndrome).

The first year of life brings dynamic changes in both behavior and the brain. While we provided separate discussions of the emergence of language, executive functions and social cognition in this busy first year of life, these three domains of human cognition have complex interactions throughout development. An infant's interest in faces, for example, will help him or her to understand speech. The ability to focus on new objects aids the infant in developing knowledge about the world around him or her. While we do not fully understand the explosive growth of brain processes and their relation to behavior in infants, studies such as the ones we presented here are helping to map the complex correspondence between mind and brain.

4.2 Childhood and adolescence: dynamic and staged growth

While the first year of life represents an unparalleled stage in dynamic human development, many aspects of brain and cognitive growth take years to mature. As we mentioned earlier, the field of developmental cognitive neuroscience is a young one. In this section, we will present results from some studies investigating the development of brain areas subserving language, executive functions and social cognition in children and adolescents and the relation to behavior. While these studies are informative, it is important to bear in mind that relating complex brain activation to performance on cognitive tasks is a highly complex process. For example, it may well be the case that the brain activity that we observe in adults – once a cognitive process has been developed – may tap differing brain regions while it is being acquired. Thus, simply comparing regions of interest in neuroimaging experiments across groups of children versus adults may not provide us with the level of sensitivity that we require in order to formulate inferences about brain and behavior. Similarly, differing cognitive strategies or coping mechanisms in childhood versus adulthood may also impact the network of brain areas tapped in certain task paradigms.

With those caveats in mind, let's review the evidence regarding the development of neural systems for language, executive control and social cognition.

4.2.1 The linguistic brain: language acquisition

Language is not a unitary system: in order to express our ideas verbally, we need to progress through stages of formulating the concepts, mapping them onto words in our mental lexicon, accessing our mental grammar to form sentences and mapping this information onto sound-based representations of the articulation of the ideas we want to express. Thus, the language system has multiple stages of computation across many categories or aspects of language. It makes intuitive sense that, early in life, infants develop their knowledge about language based largely on the sounds of language that

they hear in their environment. Thus, it is not surprising that studies with young infants (less than 12 months) typically focus on the phonology of human language. With older infants, children and adolescents, studies typically test other aspects of language such as lexical-semantic (meaning based) and syntactic (grammar based) knowledge.

Do all aspects of language develop in similar ways, with similar brain developmental processes underlying them? This is a question that has been addressed by developmental cognitive neuroscientists investigating the neural substrates of human language. Here is a brief summary of what we have learned so far.

We have previously discussed the use of event-related potentials (ERPs) for measuring the time course of human brain response for stimulus events. Several ERP components have been used to investigate language emergence in infants and young children and we describe them here:

- The mismatch negativity (MMN) component: this component shows a negativity at 100–250 ms which reflects the ability for the brain to discriminate between acoustic/phonetic features in sounds
- The N400, a negativity at ~400ms which has source generators in Centro-parietal regions. The N400 is thought to reflect lexical-semantic processes in word and sentence congrehension
- A left anterior negativity (E/LAN) which occurs, ~150–350 ms and reflects online syntactic processes
- The P600, a positive deflection at ~600 ms with a centro-parietal distribution of sources. The P600 reflects processes engaged in syntactic revision and reanalyses.

Friederici (2005) describes the time course of language development in infants and children in a recent review of the child language literature (Figure 15.25). According to this review, phonological and intonational processes develop relatively early (birth to 9 months) while lexical, semantic and syntactic processes develop somewhat later (1–3 years) as infants and young children acquire information at word and sentence levels.

During the first 2 years of life, there is an explosion of language knowledge and abilities as the infant begins to babble, produce simple sounds ('mama'), words ('dog') and two to third word utterances ('want juice'). By age 2, a child can typically produce many words. But, what does a 2 year old understand about the meaning of words? Are they simply mimicking words/sounds they have heard? Or do they have knowledge beyond simple repetition of sound? Researchers have devised clever experimental procedures to investigate the semantic knowledge of infants and young children.

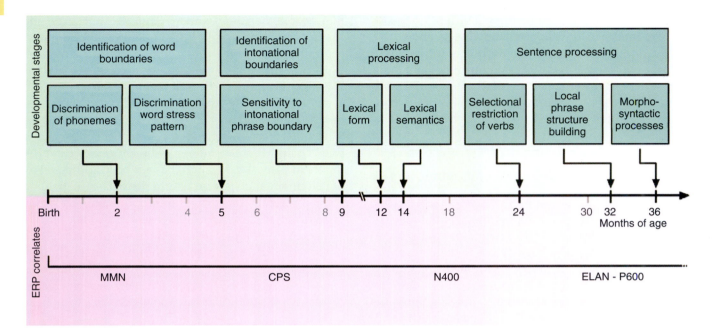

FIGURE 15.25 A schematic overview of the developmental stages of auditory language perception and the ERP correlates that provide the possibility to investigate phonological, semantic and syntactic processes. The developmental stages can be viewed as interrelated steps during which novel information is extracted and processed on the basis of previously acquired knowledge. Once the basic phonological processes are established, phonemic knowledge is used to identify and represent the first lexical forms and create a larger lexical semantic knowledge base, which is then used to process meaning in sentential context. The depicted time course of the different developmental stage is an approximation and is based on the ERP studies available in the literature. This also holds for the relation between the developmental age and the ERP components reported in the different studies discussed in the text. *Source*: Friederici, 2005.

One method is to present a picture of an object that the child is familiar with, for example, a duck, following by the word 'duck' (congruous condition) or a word that does not match the picture ('cat', incongruous condition). These careful testing procedures have enabled language researchers to test very young children in order to elucidate their level of semantic knowledge. Results of one such study are presented in Figure 15.26, providing evidence that infants as young as 14 months have semantic contextual knowledge, reflected in N400 responses for congruous and incongruous events (Friederici, 2005).

What do 2 years old know about the grammatical rules of their language? Sentence level processing was investigated in a sample of 2 years old and adults by contrasting sentences that were grammatically well formed ('The lion roars') to sentences that were not grammatical ('The lion in the roars'). The 2-years old were able to discriminate between well-formed and ill-formed sentences, as indexed by the E/LAN and P600 components (Figure 15.27).

How do these ERP studies inform us about brain processes for language acquisition in childhood? While these types of studies are in their early stages, these investigations reflect developments in ERP recording techniques and experimental designs that are effective at providing sensitive measures of early language knowledge. While more work is needed to understand fully the complexities of human language acquisition, these studies provide important new data about language knowledge in very young children.

Cortical brain areas develop throughout childhood and adolescence, as mentioned in earlier sections of this chapter. How do brain regions for speech perception and production develop and mature in childhood? Classical brain areas for language include a frontal lobe region (functionally identified as Broca's area) and a temporal lobe region (functionally known as Wernicke's area) that subserve speech production and perceptual processes. Throughout childhood, these regions become connected through the experiences of producing and perceiving auditory language. A study by Paus and colleagues (Paus *et al.*, 1999) used fMRI to investigate the development of connects between Broca's area and Wernicke's area using white matter density measures in a large sample (N = 111) of children in the age range 4–11 years. Their results show age-related changes in the internal capsule (Figure 15.28, left panel) and the left arcuate fasciculus, the fiber tract thought to connect Broca's and

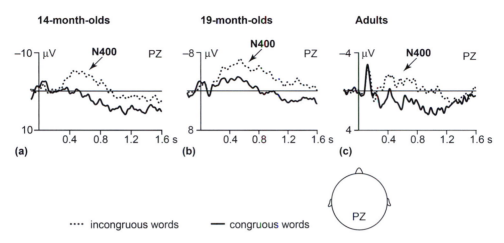

FIGURE 15.26 Semantic processing to congruous and incongruous words. The brain response of (a) 14 months old, (b) 19 months old and (c) adults in a picture priming paradigm. A picture was presented for 4 s on a screen and 900 ms after the picture onset an indefinite article was acoustically presented, followed 1 s later by a word that was either congruous with the picture (e.g. a picture of a duck followed by the word 'duck') or not (a picture of a duck followed by the word 'cat'). The solid line represents the ERP to the congruous word condition and the broken line to the incongruous word condition. ERPs shown for one selected electrode (Z) – a negativity starting around 400 ms (N400) is observable in all age groups. ((a) Adapted with permission from Friedrich and Friederici, 2005. (b,c) adapted from Friedrich and Friederici, 2005). *Source*: Friederici, 2005.

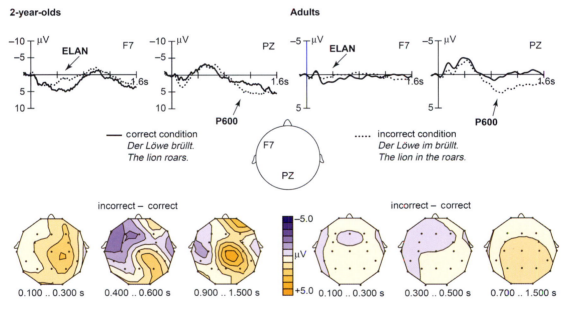

FIGURE 15.27 Syntactic processes in 2 year olds. (a) Brain responses of 2-year-old children and adults to phrase structure violations in simple active sentences. ERPs are shown for the critical last word in the syntactically correct condition (solid line) and the syntactically incorrect condition (broken line), from the word onset for two selected electrodes (F7, PZ). An early left anterior negativity (ELAN) and a late positivity (P600), both known to be elicited in adults in response to phrase structure errors, were also observed for 2-year-old children. (b) Topographic maps showing the difference in brain activation when the correct condition is subtracted from the incorrect condition, indicating the topographical distribution of the effects in 2 year olds (left) and adults (right). (Adapted from Oberecker *et al.*, 2005). *Source*: Friederici, 2005.

Wernicke's areas in the left hemisphere (Figure 15.28, right panel).

Recall that measures of cortical thickness have been used to investigate patterns of development in cortex. Are there specific changes in anatomical brain regions that support language function? Toga and colleagues

(Toga *et al.*, 2005) investigated this using a longitudinal approach in a sample of 45 typically developing children studied between the ages of 5 and 11 years. Cortical thickening increases of ~0.10–0.15 mm/year were found in brain regions corresponding to Broca's and Wernicke's areas (Figure 15.29).

Does this evidence for cortical thickening in brain regions subserving language reflect the ongoing and dynamic changes in child language? It is likely the case, however, more studies relating these anatomical changes to language ability must occur before we fully understand the mind-brain correspondence in the development of language.

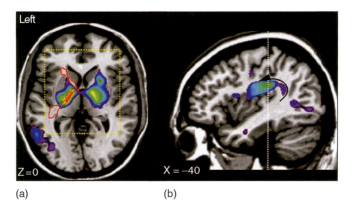

(a)   (b)

FIGURE 15.28   Age related changes in white-matter density in (a) the internal capsule and (b) the left arcuate fasciculus. Thresholded maps of t-statistic values are superimposed on axial (capsule) and sagittal (arcuate) sections through the MR image of a single subject. The images depict the exact brain locations that showed statistically significant (t > 4.0) correlations between white-matter density and the subject's age (n = 111; age 4–17 years). (Reprinted with permission from Paus et al., 1999.) Source: Paus et al., 2005.

In this section, we have highlighted evidence that very young children have sophisticated knowledge about semantic and syntactic information in spoken language. We have also shown that language regions in the brain continue to develop throughout childhood and into adolescence. However, there are many questions that remain unanswered regarding language acquisition. A central issue that remains unresolved is the trading relationship between nature (genetic predisposition for language) and nurture (the role of experience). Other aspects of language acquisition that are currently under investigation are the development of language systems in children who are bi-lingual or multi-lingual.

4.2.2   The executive brain: taking cognitive control

Even young infants must learn what information in their world is important and what is unimportant or irrelevant. These learning mechanisms fall under the general category of 'cognitive control' and have been the focus of much study in infant and child development. Recall that, in infants, the A not B task has been used to investigate the ability to ignore or inhibit irrelevant information and to inhibit prepotent response (Piaget, 1937, 1954; Diamond, 1985). These capabilities become more and more important throughout childhood as a child's environment becomes increasingly complex. Consider a 6-year-old child in a first grade classroom: this child must be able to attend to the teacher or to a task at hand

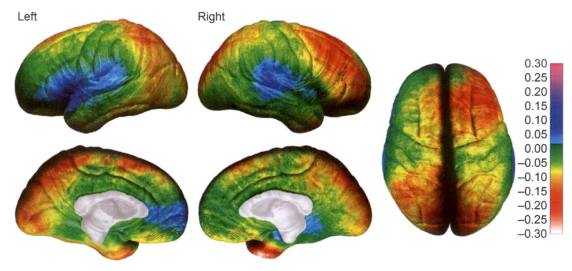

FIGURE 15.29   Annualized rate of change in cortical thickness. The average rate of change in cortical thickness is shown in millimeters according to the color bar on the right (maximum gray-matter loss is shown in shades of red and maximum gray-matter gain is shown in shades of blue). Forty-five children were studied twice (two-year scan interval) between 5 and 11 years of age. Source: Toga et al., 2005, from Sowell et al., 2004, with permission.

despite the many distractions that surround him, such as children talking, books dropping, chairs scraping. The trading of attentional resources towards relevant aspects of the environment and away from less important aspects, is a vital element in development.

In adults, the dorsal lateral prefrontal cortex (DL-PFC) is implicated as an important cortical region in tasks that tap cognitive control functions. We know from histological and neuroanatomical studies of developing children that the PFC has a prolonged developmental path, not reaching mature, adult-like stages until mid to late adolescence. Behavioral studies of cognitive control function in children and adolescents have provided evidence for a similar time course in the development of cognitive control abilities. An open question in the field of developmental cognitive neuroscience is that, is there correspondence between these late-to-mature brain regions and the late developing cognitive control abilities?

Studies of the neural substrates of cognitive control have only recently been undertaken with children. Casey and colleagues (see Casey *et al.*, 2005, for a review) have conducted seminal studies of cognitive control using a combination of fMRI and behavioral methods in order to investigate the neural patterns of brain activation measured while children perform tasks likely to engage PFC regions. In one experiment, they used event-related fMRI while children and adults were engaged in a 'go-no go' task (Durston *et al.*, 2002). In this task, participants had to suppress their response when presented with a particular visual item within an ongoing sequence of stimulus presentations (e.g. one Pokemon character within a sequence of other Pokemon characters). The difficulty of the task was increased by increasing the number of 'go' items that preceded the 'no go' character. Successful response inhibition was associated with stronger activation of prefrontal regions for children than for adults. Also, while in adults the activation of some prefrontal regions increased with increasing numbers of preceding 'go' trials (consistent with increasing need for inhibition), in children the circuit appeared to be maximally active for all trial types. Along with the poorer behavioral performance of children in this and other inhibitory tasks, these findings suggest that the functional development of some PFC regions is important for the mature ability to inhibit prepotent tendencies.

A general finding of Casey and colleagues has been that younger children exhibit broader, more diffuse brain activation for cognitive control tasks as compared to adults. During development, these brain areas mature and the brain activity that correlates to task performance abilities (such as reaction time and accuracy) become

more focal and fine-tuned. In Figure 15.30, we present a figure from a recent article by Casey and colleagues (Casey *et al.*, 2005) reviewing the literature of developmental cognitive control investigations. The general notion of brain activation becoming more focal and defined as a function of a child's age is shown with references to those studies showing increased activation with age and those showing decreased activation with age.

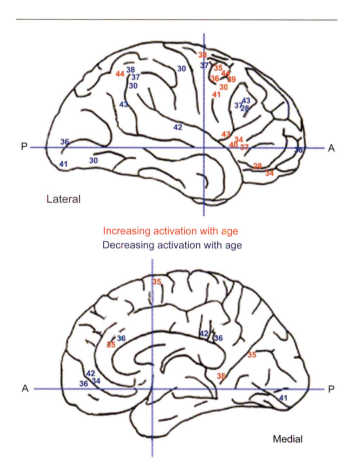

FIGURE 15.30 The development of human cortical function, as measured by contemporary imaging methods, reflects fine-tuning of a diffuse network of neuroanatomical regions. Collectively, developmental neuroimaging studies of cognitive control processes suggest a general pattern of increased recruitment of slow maturing prefrontal cortex (references depicted here in red), especially dorsolateral prefrontal cortex and ventral prefrontal cortex and decreased recruitment of lower level sensory regions (references in blue), including extrastriate and fusiform cortex and also posterior parietal areas. Importantly, specific activations vary with task demands, so working memory and Stroop tasks recruit different regions from response inhibition tasks. This pattern of activity, which has been observed across a variety of paradigms, suggests that higher cognitive abilities supported by association cortex become more focal or fine-tuned with development, whereas other regions not specifically correlated with that specific cognitive ability become attenuated. A = anterior; P = posterior. *Source*: Casey *et al.*, 2005.

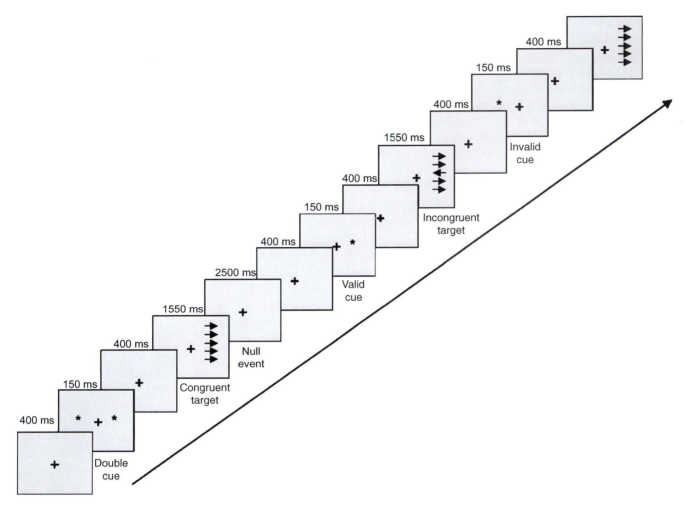

FIGURE 15.31 Experimental paradigm: modified version of the Attentional Network Task (Fan *et al.*, 2002). This figure illustrates the time course of the four different cue and the two target conditions. *Source*: Konrad *et al.*, 2005.

Another approach to elucidate the role of frontal circuits in tasks that tap cognitive control functions was provided in a recent fMRI study of children aged 8–12 years (Konrad *et al.*, 2005). Konrad and colleagues utilized a well-accepted model for adult attentional processes (Posner and Petersen, 1990) and combined it with a task that has been well described in how it engages attentional processes, the Attention Network Task (ANT) (Fan *et al.*, 2002) (Figure 15.31).

The attention model proposed by Posner and colleagues describes differing (separable but highly overlapping) neural networks for:

1   alerting to new and relevant information
2   orienting and reorienting to relevant information or stimuli, and

3   executive control of attentional processes (Posner and Peterson, 1990).

For example, consider the 6-year-old child in a first grade classroom. In order to cope with the complex environment with many sensory inputs competing for his attention, he must first be ready and in an alert state. Next, he must be flexible in changing his attentional focus to orient to new sensory inputs, for example, or to reorient to relevant information when required. Last, he must have a means for controlling these attentional resources.

These processes have been the focus of much study in adults. In adults, brain areas for alerting processes are located in frontal and parietal regions in the right hemisphere (Witte and Marrocco, 1997). Brain areas for orienting are located in the right hemisphere temporo-parietal

Alerting

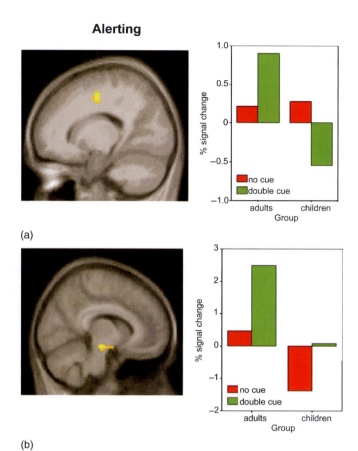

(a)

(b)

FIGURE 15.32 Alerting results. Differential activation of adults and children as identified in a two-sample test for the alerting condition (thresholded at $P_{svc} < 0.05$, extend threshold 5 voxel, shown on averaged group T1 image). (a) Increased activation in the right cingulated gyrus in adults compared to children. (b) Increased brainstem activity in adults compared to children. Plots of the per cent BOLD signal change are shown separately for both groups as a function of trial type (pooled over congruent and incongruent targets) for the respective activation maximum. *Source*: Konrad *et al.*, 2005.

junction and the inferior frontal gyrus (Corbetta *et al.*, 2000). Brain areas for executive control include the anterior cingulate and lateral prefrontal cortex (Marrocco and Davidson, 1998). Konrad and colleagues (Konrad *et al.*, 2005) used these brain areas that have been demonstrated to be active in adults during performance of the ANT as regions of interest in an fMRI study of 16 boys, aged 8–12 years, and 16 male adults.

Results for the alerting portion of the protocol are presented in Figure 15.32. Children did not show adult-like activation patterns in the predefined regions of interest. The key activation differences between adults and children were in right frontal cingulate gyrus (Figure 15.32, upper panel) and the midbrain (Figure 15.32, lower panel). The authors suggested that these differing patterns of activation are due to modulation by 'top down'

mechanisms used in the task by the adults that may not be fully established in children in the age range of 8–12 years.

Results for the reorienting portion of the protocol showed a typical pattern of right hemisphere activation for the adults, while the children showed a more diffuse and broader distribution of activation during reorienting. These differences can be summarized as increased activation in the right side temporo-parietal junction in adults versus children (Figure 15.33a); stronger activation in the putamen and insula in children versus adults (Figure 15.33b); and increased activation in the superior frontal gyrus in children versus adults (Figure 15.33c). These findings may represent the recruitment of brain regions for performing the tasks due to immature cognitive control mechanisms in young children.

The results of the executive attention portion of the protocol showed increased activation in the superior parietal cortex and inferior frontal gyrus in adults versus children (Figure 15.34a,b), and increased activation in the superior temporal gyrus and superior frontal gyrus in children versus adults (Figure 15.34c,d).

Cumulatively the results of the study by Konrad and colleagues show a strikingly differing pattern of brain activation for children versus adults when performing attentional tasks. While these results must be treated with caution until more studies can be completed using similar tasks and brain measures, the results of Konrad and colleagues provide evidence for immature frontal-parietal networks in cognitive control tasks, a finding similar to the results reported by Casey and colleagues (reviewed in Casey *et al.*, 2005).

A general conclusion from these fMRI studies of cognitive control in children provides evidence for attentional systems that are functional but immature in children as compared to adults. Children show a pattern of activation that is more diffuse and encompasses a wider area of brain regions than those active in adults. These findings may reflect the immature nature of the systems during childhood, which may become more focal and specialized with development and experience.

Future work in the investigation of cognitive control and development of PFC in children will need to take into account many other aspects of the prolonged developmental path of the frontal regions and the correspondence to behavior. Some areas of future research may include investigating gender differences in cognitive control functions and related brain activation patterns. You may have noticed that most of the tasks detailed in this section included visual presentation of task items. More work is needed to evaluate the

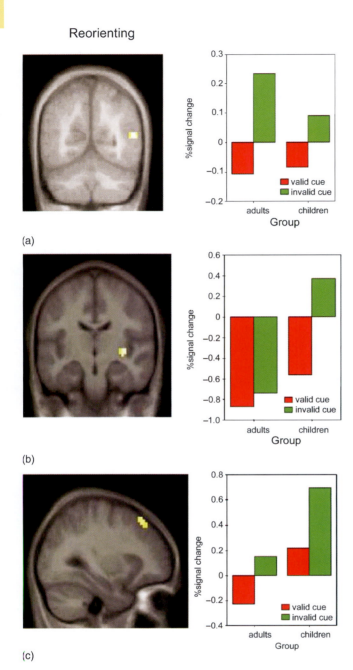

Reorienting

(a)

(b)

(c)

FIGURE 15.33 Differential activation of adults and children as identified in a two-sample test for the reorienting condition (thresholded at $P_{svc} < 0.05$ or $P < 0.1$ corrected for multiple comparisons for whole-brain analyses, extend threshold 5 voxel, shown on averaged group T1 image). (a) Increased activation in the right-sided temporoparietal junction in adults compared to children. (b) Stronger activation in the putamen and insula in children compared to adults. (c) Increased activation in the superior frontal gyrus in children compared to adults. Plots of the per cent BOLD signal change are shown separately for both groups as a function of trial type (pooled over congruent and incongruent targets) for the activation maximum. *Source*: Konrad *et al.*, 2005.

frontal lobe networks that mediate auditory attentional control as well as those that subserve tasks that require integration of multimodal (e.g. visual + auditory) information in tasks performance.

4.2.3 The social brain: face perception in childhood

Human face perception has been the focus of many neuroimaging and behavioral investigations in adults, in infants, and throughout childhood and adolescence. Why is this area of research important to the field of cognitive neuroscience? Investigating brain regions that may be specialized for perception of our species-specific faces may shed light on the nature versus nurture debate. Are we predisposed to attend to, focus on and interpret cues in faces? Or does our vast experience with faces provide the information processing abilities that are not specific to faces, but rather utilizes visual object perception networks? Studying face processing during development may help us determine how genetic predisposition interacts with experience.

Recall that, in infants, investigations of face processing used ERP measures and, in particular, evaluated the modulation of the N170 component in response to faces as compared to other visual objects. Results from these studies as well as studies using other imaging techniques (MEG, fMRI) provide converging evidence that face processing is less specialized in young children (5–10 years) as compared to older children (11–14 years), with more diffuse and less focal brain activity for faces (Gathers *et al.*, 2004; Aylward *et al.*, 2005; Kyllainen *et al.*, 2006). Also, older children show more bilateral fusiform face area activation for faces as compared to houses than younger children, and the pattern of activation correlates with age (Aylward *et al.*, 2005). Nevertheless, these studies indicate that, while older children show more focal activation than younger children, they do not show adult-like patterns of response, indicating that face perception is a slow-to-mature process.

Most of these studies use faces with neutral or happy expressions, however, they leave open the question of how children perceive emotional information in faces. Understanding emotional cues in facial expressions is a vital aspect of social cognition in humans. The study of face processing of emotional cues is complex, however, and not well understood in adults let alone in developing children. Here, we highlight two recent studies of emotional cues in faces with children: one study uses fMRI to elucidate brain regions employed in decoding emotional face cues and the second utilizes the EEG N170 component to investigate the time course of emotional cues in face processing. It

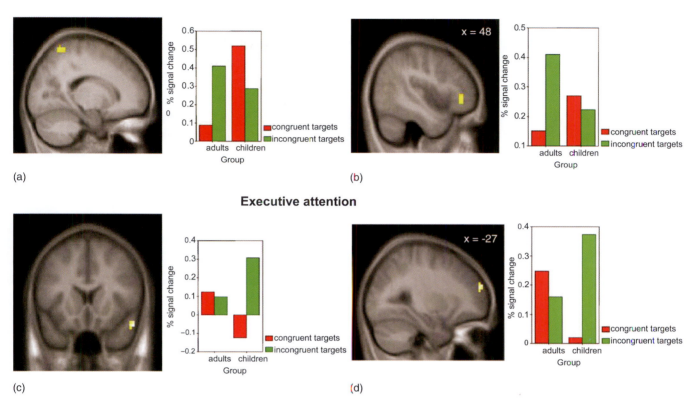

Executive attention

FIGURE 15.34 Differential activation of adults and children as identified in a two-sample test for the executive control condition (thresholded at Psvc < 0.05 or P < 0.1 corrected for multiple comparisons for whole-brain analyses, extend threshold 5 voxel, shown on averaged group T1 image). (a) Increased activation in the superior parietal cortex and (b) inferior frontal gyrus in adults compared to children. (c) Increased activation in the superior temporal gyrus and (d) superior frontal gyrus in children compared to adults. Plots of the per cent BOLD signal change are shown separately for both groups as a function of target type (pooled over cueing conditions) for the activation maximum. *Source*: Konrad et al., 2005.

is important to note that the study of the developmental path of emotional cues in face processing is in its early stages: while these studies provide some useful early data for understanding how these processes develop and mature, much more work is needed before we can claim to understand fully the intricacies of human face perception.

Batty and Taylor (2006) investigated the N170 response for faces showing six different emotions (happiness, surprise, sadness, fear, anger and disgust) as well as a neutral face in a large sample (82) of children between the ages of 4 and 15 years. Batty and Taylor reported that only the oldest group of children (14–15 years) showed N170 patterns of response that were similar to adults. And, even in this group, the N170 response did not appear to be adult-like in discriminating between emotional cues. They suggested that interpreting complex emotional information in human faces was a slow-to-mature process that was not fully realized even in middle teenage years.

A related study was conducted by Lobaugh and colleague (Lobaugh et al., 2006) using fMRI and the same eight emotional categories. In this study, the children were 10–12 years old. Lobaugh and colleagues used a gender decision task for investigating emotional cues in faces: the children were asked to decide if the face was male or female. In this way, Lobaugh and colleagues attempted to understand the neural substrates of implicit recognition of emotional cues during face processing. First, Lobaugh and colleagues evaluated brain areas that were differentially responsive to faces versus a looking condition. These are shown in Figure 15.35. These areas were right fusiform/parahippocampal gyrus, which were more active in the face task, and bilateral superior temporal gyrus and posterior temporal gyrus, which showed decreased activity in the face task.

A second key finding was that brain activation to negative emotions (disgust, fear) was stronger than responses to positive (happiness) or neutral emotions

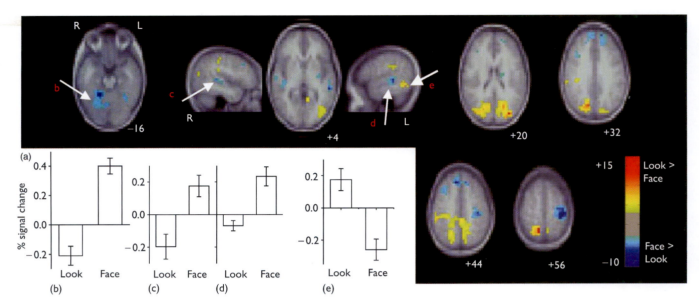

FIGURE 15.35   Face versus look results. (a) Regions in blue showed more activity on face trials than look trials. The response was reversed for regions in yellow/red. Arrows (b–e) highlight peak clusters. Mean percentage change (±SEM) in peak voxel response across the block is shown for the selected clusters. (b) A large expanse of right fusiform/parahippocampal gyrus (20/ 40/ 16) was more active in the face task. (c and d) Bilateral superior temporal gyrus (c: 48/32/ +4, d: +44/ 32/ +8). (e) Posterior temporal gyrus (44/ 52/ 4) showed decreased activity to faces. *Source*: Lobaugh *et al.*, 2006.

(Figure 15.36). The strongest responses were to faces with expressions of fear. The authors interpreted these findings to indicate that functional emotional networks are established by age 10.

What do the findings of the work of Batty and Taylor and Lobaugh and colleagues tell us about how children understand complex emotional cues in faces? It is important to note that the brain measures used by the two studies (ERP study of the latency and amplitude of the N170 component versus fMRI study of hemodynamic changes) are quite different in just what brain responses they are able to measure. Next, one study (Batty and Taylor, 2006) had a large sample (82) of children across a wide range of ages (4–15 years), while the other had a small sample (10) of children in a narrow age range (10–12 years). The differing tasks and techniques used in these studies make an interpretation of the findings problematic in spite of the fact that the two studies investigated very similar processes, emotional cues in faces.

The investigations presented here provide early evidence for differing patterns of brain response in childhood when processing emotional cues in faces. Many more studies are needed in order to for us to understand fully the brain area and developmental path of emotional cue processing in face perception. Some important aspects of the future studies may entail determining if boys and girls process emotional cues in a similar way and assessing if children pay more attention to certain aspects of faces (such as eyes) as compared to adults.

What have we learned about the development of language, executive function and social cognition in childhood and adolescence? One central finding from a variety of data sources (histological, pathological, neuroimaging) is that the cortical regions subserving these high order cognitive functions have a prolonged developmental path extending to mid to late adolescence. We have a wealth of behavioral data showing a similar pattern in tasks that tap more complex and higher order aspects of these cognitive functions, with task performance not reaching adult-like levels until late adolescence. Putting these two bodies of information together in order to map brain development onto cognitive function remains a challenge for the developmental cognitive neuroscientist.

While we have made significant headway, as data presented in this chapter demonstrate, there are many complexities in each of these areas of cognition that remain undiscovered. While we have a general notion of how language emerges in young children, the cortical mapping of complex language systems is still being worked out in adults, with less known about the patterns of emergent language. Similarly, the field continues to discover how PFC subserves aspects of tasks tapping attentional, planning and working memory systems. The relation of these networks with ability or

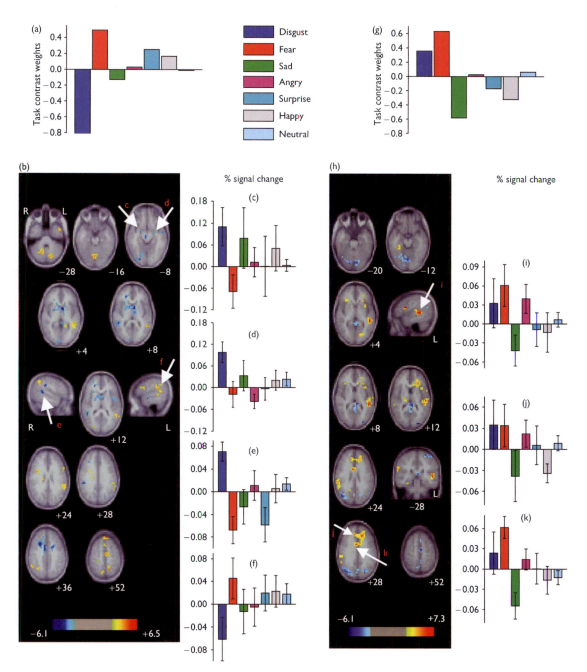

FIGURE 15.36 Emotional faces results. (a) Task contrasts for the first latent variable. The first pattern most strongly distinguished disgust (blue, negative task weight) from fear (red, positive task weight) and, to a smaller extent, from surprise (cyan) and happiness (gray). (b) Brain regions whose activity differentiated fear and disgust. Yellow/red: regions where the response to fear was greater than that to disgust; blue: regions where the response to disgust was larger than that to fear. (c– f) Location and mean percentage change (7 SEM) in peak voxels for selected clusters (mean of 8 TRs after trial onset). (c and d) Bilateral amygdala (c: +20/ 4/ 8; d: 24/ 4/ 8). (e) Right superior temporal gyrus (+48/ 40/+8). (f) Left superior temporal gyrus/inferior supramarginal gyrus (48/ 40/+20). (g) Task contrasts for the second latent variable. This pattern most strongly distinguished disgust and fear (blue and red, positive task weights) from sadness (green, negative task weight). Surprise (cyan) and happiness (gray) also differed from disgust and fear. (h) Brain regions whose activity most strongly differentiated fear and disgust from sadness. Yellow/red: regions where the response to disgust and fear was greater than that to sadness; blue: regions where the response to sad faces was larger than that to disgust and fear. (i–k) Mean percentage change in peak voxels (7 SEM) for selected clusters. (i) Left superior temporal gyrus (44/ 28/+8). (j and k) Anterior cingulate (j: +12/ +36/ +24, BA32; k: +8/+8/+28, BA 24). Color bars indicate the magnitude of the voxel stability. Left is on the right of the image. *Source*: Lobaugh *et al.*, 2006.

specific task demands is still unresolved in adults and remains to be elucidated in children. Face perception and the integration of emotional, linguistic and pragmatic cues faces into social cognition knowledge is also an ongoing field of investigation in adults, with less known about the emergent patterns and trading relations among these many factors in understanding human social behavior.

An important direction in the field of developmental cognitive neuroscience is to combine methodologies – for example, fMRI with EEG – with behavioral measures in order to provide converging evidence across methodologies and measures regarding aspects of higher order cognitive function. Combining fMRI with EEG, for example, can provide high resolution spatial information regarding brain activations coupled with high resolution of the time course of that activation. Another important direction in the field is to conduct longitudinal studies in order to track the development over time of individual children. In this way, early 'baseline' measures can be taken and then the development and change in these measures may be assessed at specific intervals. Finally, new experimental design approaches with young infants are demonstrating that babies know and understand a lot more about the world around them than we previously thought. New advances in measuring infant cognition and mapping the relevant brain activity will provide important insights into the developmental changes occurring in the first year of life.

5.0 EARLY BRAIN DAMAGE AND DEVELOPMENTAL PLASTICITY

We mentioned, above, the importance of longitudinal studies for tracking individual progress and outcomes throughout development. This type of study is especially important when assessing the long-term outcome of early (perinatal) brain injury. We have seen in earlier chapters that, in adults, brain damage due to stroke, disease, or traumatic accident, typically leads to deficits in aspects of cognition that are fairly severe, with complete recovery of function unlikely. What happens when brain damage occurs near birth? This question has an important bearing on the nature versus nurture debate. Consider the hypothesis that some brain systems, such as language, have a strong genetic predisposition for their development in specified regions of the brain. If there is early insult to those pre-specified regions, will the infant develop language in a typical fashion? Or will language develop in an aberrant fashion due to the early

and unrecoverable damage to those brain regions? Alternatively, if experience plays the dominant role in the development of brain regions that become tuned for language function, will the infant develop language in a typical fashion in spite of the early brain damage?

The effects of perinatal brain damage have been extensively investigated in animal studies in the field of neurobiology. The effects of early brain damage and the impact on later cognitive development have been far less studied in humans. One reason for this is that a single, unilateral (in one hemisphere only) pre- or perinatal brain insult is relatively rare. Typically, instances of early brain insult are more global in nature and combine with other neurological complications (Figure 15.37, left panel). In these cases of larger scale damage coupled with other traumatic events, it is difficult to compare cognitive development to children without this early damage and trauma. In cases where the perinatal damage is limited to a circumscribed region (Figure 15.37, center and right panels), the long-term effects are typically milder. These are the types of cases that we will focus on in this section: early, focal, unilateral brain insult.

While we are just beginning to understand the complexities of early insult on later cognitive growth in humans, a series of longitudinal studies by Stiles and colleagues (2005) shed some light on the long-term effects of perinatal insult and we highlight some results here (for a review, see Stiles *et al.*, 2005). The San Diego Longitudinal Project (Stiles *et al.*, 2002) is the largest USA investigation of the long-term effects of perinatal brain damage. Stiles and colleagues have followed the cognitive development of several hundred children with perinatal brain damage for the past 20 years.

Much of the focus of the investigations by Stiles and colleagues in the San Diego Longitudinal Project has been on language development in children with

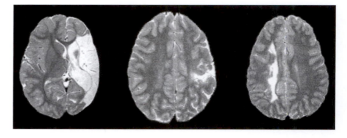

FIGURE 15.37 Large scale and smaller scale perinatal brain damage. Structural MRI scans in the axial plane from three children with perinatal brain damage, illustrating different patterns of injury. (Left) A large unilateral lesion involving most of one cerebral hemisphere. (Middle) A small lesion confined to one cerebral lobe. (Right) A deep lesion involving subcortical regions. *Source*: Stiles *et al.*, 2005.

perinatal brain damage. One key finding is that, while in adults, focal brain damage (typically through lesions due to stroke) in language centers results long-lasting deficits, this pattern is quite different with infants who suffer perinatal brain damage. While there is typically delay in early linguistic milestones, such as onset of word comprehension at 9–12 months and word production at 12–15 months, by the age of 5 years, however, these children have largely 'caught up' in linguistic abilities. The important finding, however, is that when tested carefully there remain some underlying deficits even at the age of 5, especially in complex sentence structures (Reilly *et al.*, 2004). These children with early brain damage do ultimately achieve language competence, however, the evidence provided by the longitudinal studies by Stiles and colleagues (reviewed in Stiles *et al.*, 2005) indicate that their language proficiency is in the lower than normal range. Thus, while the children do acquire many skills and proficiencies with respect to language, there remains throughout childhood, adolescence and presumably adulthood, some key deficits due to the very early damage to important brain regions for language acquisition and processing.

Another aspect of cognition that has been the focus of study by the San Diego Longitudinal Project has been spatial cognition. Spatial cognition and the effects produced by adult acquired brain damage have been the target of many neuropsychological and neuroimaging investigations. The central findings have been that there is a hemisphere asymmetry in the decoding of visual patterns, with the left hemisphere biased for extracting feature (local) information and the right hemisphere biased for extracting configuration (global) information (Figure 15.38).

Functional MRI studies of typically developing adolescents show that they demonstrate a similar hemisphere asymmetry, with greater right hemisphere occipital-temporal activation for global processing and greater left hemisphere occipital-temporal activation for local processing (Figure 15.39). In stark contrast, a 15-year-old adolescent who had suffered right hemisphere perinatal brain damage showed stronger activation for both global and local processing in the left (undamaged) hemisphere (Figure 15.39) and a 13-year-old adolescent who had suffered left hemisphere perinatal brain damage showed stronger activation for both global and local processing in the right (undamaged) hemisphere (Figure 15.39). Thus, the fMRI data for the two adolescents who suffered perinatal brain damage provide evidence for long-lasting damage to spatial cognition mechanisms, however, they also provide intriguing evidence for a brain system that is highly flexible, with

recruitment of neural territory in the undamaged hemisphere for spatial cognition functions.

What have we learned about the long-term effects of early brain damage in the longitudinal studies of Stiles and colleagues? And how do they inform us about the complex and highly interactive roles of nature and nurture in human development? While these efforts are still in early stages, results to date indicate that early brain damage results in long-term, though typically somewhat subtle, deficits. A second important finding is that despite the early insults and the delays that they typically produce in cognitive development, the children mature and acquire higher cognitive function, although sometimes at the lower than normal level. Cumulatively, these findings provide evidence that there are some brain systems that have long-term impairments when damaged, even when the damage occurs at or near birth. This provides some support that some systems have a level of genetic predisposition and can suffer long-term harm when disrupted. On a brighter note, these findings provide evidence for significant amounts of early brain plasticity so that the cognitive functions that suffer early damage develop in an alternative manner.

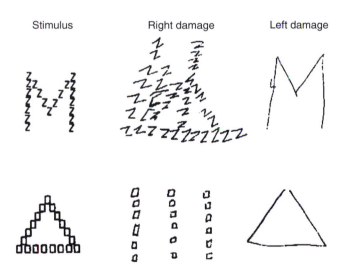

FIGURE 15.38 Global versus local: examples of visuospatial deficits. Examples of memory reproductions of hierarchical form stimuli by adult stroke patients with either right or left hemisphere injury. (Adapted, with permission, from Delis *et al.*, 1986.) The sample stimulus to be copied is shown on the left side of the figure. Center of the figure: patients with right hemisphere damage typically produce the local (detailed) aspects of the stimulus but omit the global (overall) aspects of the stimulus: in this case, the 'M' or triangle shape of the stimulus. Right side of the figure: patients with left hemisphere damage typically produce the global aspects of the stimulus but omit the local aspects of the stimulus. *Source*: Stiles *et al.*, 2005.

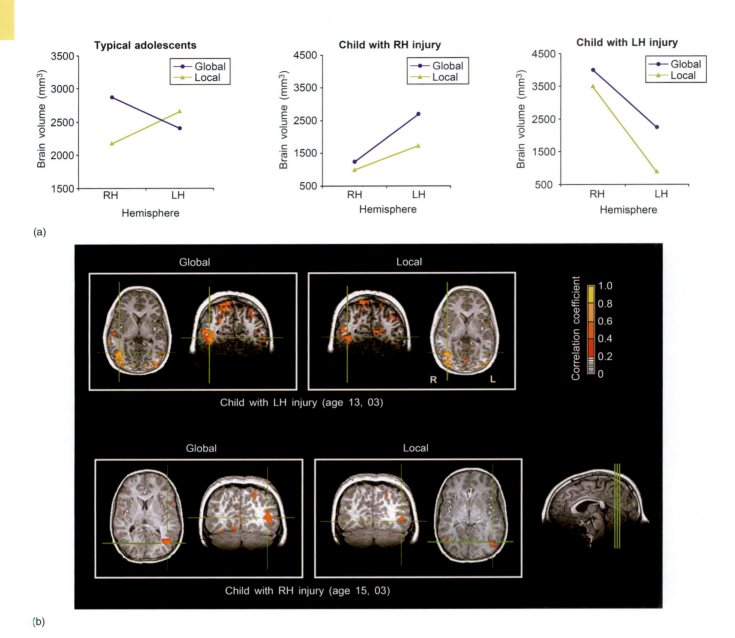

(a)

(b)

FIGURE 15.39 Global and local processing in the brain. Functional MRI activation data from two teenagers with prenatal focal brain injury on a hierarchical form-processing task, compared with data from typical adolescents. Each child participated in separate imaging runs, where they were asked to attend to either the global or the local level of the stimulus pattern. Unlike typical controls, who show different patterns of lateralization for global and local processing, the two children with lesions showed activation largely confined to the uninjured hemisphere. Activation images for the two children with PL are shown. *Source*: Adapted from, Stiles *et al.*, 2005 with permission.

6.0 CHAPTER SUMMARY

In this chapter, we have tracked the stages of human development from early embryo to infant to adolescent. While the field of developmental cognitive neuroscience is still a very young one, nevertheless, the findings presented in this chapter demonstrate the answers to important questions about human brain development and the correspondence to cognition. An overarching topic of much debate in the field of human development is the role of nature versus nurture. From the data presented here, you see that at each stage of human development there are important genetic effects and biological constraints at work in the unfolding of the human brain and mind. Similarly, at each state there are critical effects of the surrounding environment, whether at the level of the cell, the system, or the brain.

The advent of new techniques for non-invasively studying human development has provided the means to address new questions about cognitive development, such as what does a baby know before birth? Does an infant understand the grammar of language? How does the sense of self develop in an infant, a child? What are the long-term effects of focal brain damage? These and other questions will be addressed in future studies investigating the unfolding complex pattern of human brain development and its relation to cognition.

7.0 CHAPTER REVIEW

7.1 Study questions

1 In what ways have neuroimaging techniques changed the way infant and child development is investigated?

2 What does the term 'bidirectional influences' refer to in human development? Why is it an important concept?

3 Provide an example of a nature and nurture interaction that occurs before birth (prenatally).

4 What are some effects of maternal use of alcohol, tobacco and marijuana on her unborn child?

5 What brain regions develop and mature early in childhood? What regions develop later in childhood?

6 The development of object permanence in infants has been the focus of much study. Describe an experiment for investigating object permanence and possible results for:

a a 6-month old

b a 12-month old.

Appendix A

Neural models: A route to cognitive brain theory

Igor Aleksander

Cognition, Brain, and Consciousness, edited by B. J. Baars and N. M. Gage
ISBN: 978-0-12-373677-2

Copyright 2007, Elsevier Ltd. All rights reserved.

PART 1: TRADITIONAL NEURAL MODELS

1.0 WHY TWO PARTS?

There are two specific aims of this appendix. Part 1 tries to describe the excitement felt by a large group of model-builders who have made contributions to our understanding of the fine neural structure of the brain and our cognitive abilities. Beginning in the early 1940s, this movement was concerned with the learning abilities of a neuron and how this contributes to the behavior of neural networks. The history of such models has seen ups and downs, with a decrease of interest in the 1970s but a revival in the 1980s, leading to well-established paradigms at the present time. Although this is largely a mathematical enterprise, the details have been left in the background. In this way, the reader will get a grasp of the main intentions of the modelers, without requiring a detailed knowledge of math.

In Part 2, called *Seeing Is Believing*, the reader is given close access to artificial neural networks, ranging from single neurons to networks and cognitive architectures. For this purpose a simulation system called the *neural representation modeler* is made available.

2.0 WHAT IS A NEURAL MODEL?

The aim of neural modeling is to determine how neurons interact in intricate ensembles, forming specialized modules and ultimately an architecture that operates on those modules. How does this ensemble stand a chance of producing the activity we call thought? That is, how does one go from the operation of neurons to cognitive neuroscience?

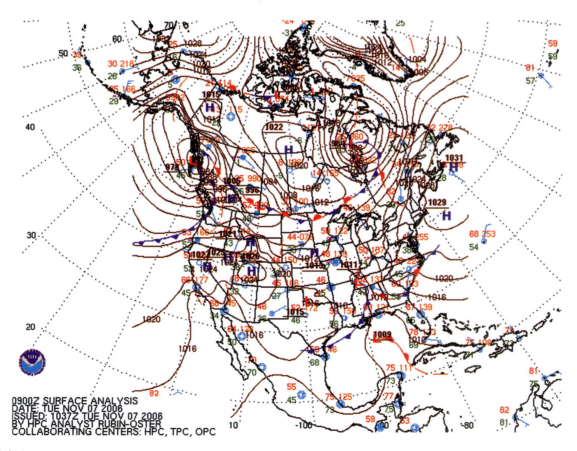

FIGURE A.1   Using data from satellites the computer plots the features of the weather on a map, using a model of atmospheric dynamics. In this case, the path of a hurricane is being predicted. Neural network models describe and predict cognitive events. *Source*: National Oceanic and Atmospheric Administration, USA.

Let's begin with a few definitions. A *model* is a physical or an informational structure (a *program*) that embodies the functional characteristics of what is being modeled (the *target domain*). The model must be usable, so that testing it provides results that are akin to what one might find in the target domain. A model may embody testable hypotheses about target systems.

For example, models of the atmosphere are built to predict the weather. If the model makes accurate predictions, that suggests that the nature and parameters involved in the weather have been understood. In addition, a model allows 'what if' manipulations and could predict, for example, the effect of increasing carbon gases without having to wait for that to happen in nature.

What is meant by differing levels of detail or granularity? As already suggested, the smallest 'grain' is the *neuron*. We shall look at ways of modeling a neuron from a mathematical expression to a simple digital program. These models have two properties in common with the living neuron: they can 'learn' a response for a given set of inputs and they must be able to respond not only to the patterns, but also to patterns that are similar to the learned ones. This is called the 'generalization' of a neuron.

At the next level, there are *single* or *multiple layers* of neurons. A single layer learns to map input patterns into output patterns, with restrictions on what can be done. Multiple layers are used to lift the restrictions on such mappings. Typically, a few hundred neurons have been simulated at this level.

The next level is a *network*, in which the output pattern of some neurons goes to the input of other neurons. This is known as a *recursive* or *dynamic* network. This level is capable of sustaining learned patterns of firing, even in the absence of input. This is considered to be the basis of memory, as defined by neural network modeling. We shall see examples of tens of thousands neurons operating at this level.

Finally, there is the level of the *architecture*, and here we shall see tens of the above dynamic modules interacting with one another. At this level our models begin to perform cognitive tasks.

3.0 THE NEURON

Chapter 3 gave a basic introduction to neurons. Here we ask: 'what does a neuron do and how could this be modelled?' An anatomical picture of a neuron is given in Figure A.2.

On the output side, neuronal axons fire spikes or impulses. The body of the neuron integrates the incoming activity of the input synapses at all the dendrites. (The biochemistry of neurons is covered elsewhere, e.g. Kandel, 2000.) This is called an *activation*, 'presynaptic' on the output side of the axon and 'postsynaptic' on the input side. This labeling is therefore focused on synapses, the connections between neurons. High postsynaptic activation on the input side causes the firing of the neuronal axon. The synapses have a controlling effect on each button: some enhance postsynaptic activation positively and others decrease it. It is here that the ability of a neuron to change is thought to reside. Finally, changes of synaptic strength are thought to be the key electrochemical feature that enables learning and memory in the brain.

To understand this, it is worth looking at the earliest known and most influential neural model, by Warren McCulloch and Walter Pitts (1943) (Figure A.3).

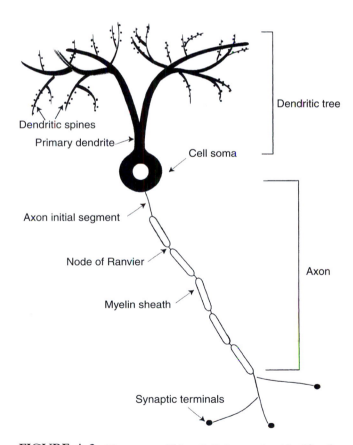

FIGURE A.2 The neuron. This artist's impression identifies the *axon*, which is the transmission line that links the electrical pulsing or 'firing' of the body (*soma*) of the neuron and passes it on via *boutons* to the *dendrites* of other neurons. The contact between a bouton and a dendrite is called a *synapse*. The *myelin sheath* supports the propagation of the axonal spike.

FIGURE A.3 Pioneers of neural modeling at MIT, Warren McCulloch (left) and Walter Pitts (right) wrote the seminal paper in 1943: 'A logical calculus of the ideas immanent in nervous activity'. McCulloch was a physician and Pitts a self-taught logician.

4.0 THE BASIC ARTIFICIAL NEURON (McCULLOCH AND PITTS, 1943)

The basic neuron model is shown in Figure A.4. It assumes that a neuron either fires or does not. That is, the input X and the output F have two possible values: 1 (firing) and 0 (not firing). The weights W represent either an excitatory effect or an inhibitory effect on the postsynaptic activation A. Such weights are often given values between 0 and $+1$ for excitation and between 0 and -1 for inhibition. n stands for the number of inputs.

If the actual activation level A exceeds the threshold Θ, the neuron fires and $F = 1$. Otherwise, the neuron does not fire and $F = 0$. The value of the threshold Θ needs to be between the minimum and maximum activation A for n inputs.

(The maximum of Θ occurs for n inputs with Xs all at the maximum level of 1 and their weights set to their maximum value of 1. The minimum level of Θ is an activation level A of $-n$, which occurs when the Xs are all 1, but the weights are set to their minimum value of -1.)

It's time for a little example. Say that the neuron has only two input values, X_1 and X_2 with respective connection weights W_1 and W_2.

The mathematical function of the whole neuron may then be written as:

$$F = 1 \text{ if and only if,} \qquad X_1 W_1 + X_2 W_2 \geqslant \Theta \qquad \textbf{A.1}$$

And $F = 0$ otherwise.

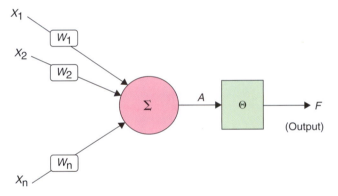

FIGURE A.4 The basic artificial neuron defined by McCulloch and Pitts. The Xs represent the firing of incoming neurons. The Ws are 'weights' that represent the synaptic effect. Σ is the effect of the neuron body, which sums all the incoming activity. Θ represents a threshold that has to be overcome for the neuron to fire an output spike.

That is, the value of each input X is multiplied by its W value, corresponding to the activity of an incoming neuron being multiplied by its connection weight to the neuron we are trying to describe. You can think of this as multiplying a percentage of the maximum firing rate (from zero to 100 per cent) of the previous neuron by the probability of the connection (which also ranges from zero to 100 per cent).

Say that W_1 is 0.5, W_2 is -0.6 and $\Theta = -0.2$. We can now work out what this neuron will do for all possible combinations of X_1 and X_2 as follows.

TABLE A.1   Truth table for a neuron with $W_1 = 0.5$, $W_2 = -0.6$ and $\Theta = -0.2$

X_1	X_2	A	F
0	0	0	1
0	1	−0.6	0
1	0	+0.5	1
1	1	−0.1	1

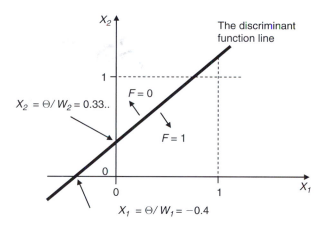

FIGURE A.5   The discriminant function for a neuron with $W_1 = 0.5$, $W_2 = -0.6$ and $\Theta = -0.2$. Everything *above* the line represents inputs that do *not* fire (only $X_1, X_2 = 0,1$) with the neuron firing for all other combinations of the inputs.

For example, assume that X_1 is 1, X_2 is 0

Then, the left hand side of **A.1** becomes $1 \times 0.5 + 0 \times (-0.6) = 0.5$.

As this is greater than Θ, the neuron will fire ($F = 1$).

In this way the complete set of input-output values, called the Truth Table (Table A.1) of the neuron can be calculated.

At this point we note a very important fact. Despite the graded numerical values of the weights, summation and threshold, the overall character of the neuron is that of a binary logic system. In fact, the *function* of the neuron could be described using logical terminology:

$$F = (not \ X_2) \ or \ (X_1) \qquad \text{[think about it!]} \qquad \textbf{A.2}$$

However, the whole point about a neuron is that it *learns* to perform one of many possible functions. The function can be changed by changing the weights and the threshold. To clarify this we continue with the basic neuron with two synaptic inputs.

Equation **A.1** is a linear equation which could be rewritten to indicate the condition under which the neuron changes from firing to non-firing. This so-called *discriminant function* is where the activation A equals the threshold Θ.

That is,

$$X_1 W_1 + X_2 W_2 = \Theta$$

We can plot this equation on a graph of X_2 versus X_1 as shown in Figure A.5.

There are several remarkable things about this way of looking at the function of the neuron.

First, choosing values for W_1, W_2 and Θ positions the discriminant function line to map the input values in different ways.

Second, the graph tells us something about the logical functions that a single neuron can and cannot achieve. It can achieve anything that can be achieved by repositioning the discriminant line. But this indicates a particular couple of functions that the neuron *cannot* achieve. These are the so-called 'exclusive-or' and 'equivalence' functions.

The exclusive-or function is:

$$F = 1 \text{ for } X_1, X_2 = (0,1) \text{ and } (1,0) \text{ and } F = 0 \text{ for} \\ X_1, X_2 = (0,0) \text{ and } (1,1);$$

The equivalence function is:

$$F = 0 \text{ for } X_1, X_2 = (0,1) \text{ and } (1,0) \text{ and } F = 1 \text{ for} \\ X_1, X_2 = (0,0) \text{ and } (1,1);$$

From the graph in Figure A.5, it is clear that no single line will provide the separations required by these two functions. There are a total of 2^4, that is, 16 functions of two binary inputs of which two cannot be achieved.

Not bad, one might think. But this is much worse for larger neurons. However, 'Worse', this low density of achievable functions has its uses when the neuron has to *learn* the values of its synaptic weights and thresholds.

We cannot delay in looking at this vital topic: *learning*.

5.0 LEARNING IN A NEURON – SOME BASIC NOTIONS

The way neurons are made to learn is a major topic that has excited experts in artificial neural networks as far back as the McCulloch and Pitts model of 1943. In recent years, it is still a major bullet point at neural network conferences. Here, we present some very basic ideas and then briefly mention some of its many variants. It's best first to look back to Figure A.4. We recognize that for the neuron to change its function, some means must be provided to change the weights between presynaptic and postsynaptic activation.

But what could drive this change? The answer is an *error* or *deviation* in the performance of the neuron from some set goal. Somehow, the system must correct the behaviour of a neuron if it is not at the goal.

Early in the history of artificial neural networks learning, algorithms were based on measuring the error at A from a target value and distributing the duty for removing the error by an incremental adjustment of the weights.

Again, an example will serve us best here. Let us say that the weights are currently adjusted as in the above example, giving the logic function in **A.2**. But let us say that the desired function is:

$$F = (not\ X_1)\ and\ (not\ X_2)$$

That is, F should be 1 if and only if both X_1 and X_2 are 0. We want the neuron to learn this input-output behavior. So we need to apply some inputs to the neuron to correct its error. The reader should check this possibility with the aid of a small spreadsheet.

Say that the order of the steps is (X_1, X_2): $(0,0) \rightarrow (0,1) \rightarrow (1,1) \rightarrow (1,0)$, and repeat these steps if necessary.

(X_1, X_2): (0,0) then A is 0 and F is 1, so no adjustment needs to be made.
(0,1) then A is -0.6 and F is 0, so no adjustment needs to be made.
(1,1) then A is -0.1 and F is 1, which needs correcting.

For the last case, A is greater than Θ by 0.1, when it should be less to obtain the desired result. We distribute the duty of getting rid of this error between W_1, W_2 and Θ equally, by step sizes of 0.04, as follows:

W_1 needs to be *decreased* by 0.04 to 0.46,
W_2 needs to be *decreased* by 0.04 to -0.64 and
Θ needs to be *increased* 0.04 to -0.16.

So, for the (1,1) input above, $A = 0.46 - 0.64 = -0.18$ which now does not exceed Θ and makes $F = 0$ as required.

We now test (1,0) which gives us an A of 0.46 and an F of 1 which needs correction of a total error of A being 0.62 too high. We now only have Θ and W_1 to adjust, by more than 0.31 each, say 0.32.

While this process corrects the current output, as changes have to be made, this process has to be repeated. It has been shown that a process such as this converges to a stable answer after some iterations. A solution

found for the desired function has been $W_1 = -0.02$, $W_2 = -0.64$ and $\Theta = -0.01$. There are many such solutions. The reader is encouraged to try the self-test puzzles 1.1 and 1.2 at the end of this Appendix.

We have seen that *learning in a neuron is the positioning of the discriminant line to satisfy a progressive set of training examples for which the desired output of the neuron is known.*

It's worth noting that not all possible inputs need be given. Looking at Figure A.5 for example, if (X_1, X_2): (1,1) is given as 0, (1,0) as 1 and (0,1) as 1 there is only one place to put the discriminant line *which fixes* (0,0) at 1.

But what of neurons with more than two inputs, say n? We now no longer have a nice 2-dimensional graph as in Figure A.5. For $n = 3$ we do have a cube with vertices that represent the values of (X_1, X_2, X_3) as shown in Figure A.6. However, in the general case of the McCulloch and Pitts formulation for n-input neurons, the neuron only performs functions determined by an $(n - 1)$-dimensional plane. It is said to perform only *linearly discriminant functions*.

In later years, more flexible schemes were sought. We shall look at some of these briefly in the next few sections.

In summary, the legacy left by McCulloch and Pitts is the notion that a neuron is the basic building brick of the brain and cognition. How it links to cognition remains to be seen in the rest of this Appendix. But, for

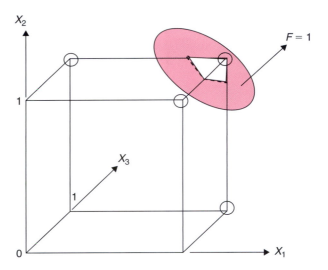

FIGURE A.6 A 3-dimensional graph for a 3-input neuron. The discriminant line from Figure A.5 has now become a discriminant plane. In this case, the discriminant plane has formed a three-input 'and gate'. Only four points (marked with small circles) are needed to fix this plane. This means that the neuron has learned *not* to fire if there is at east one zero in the input pattern. But this pattern is *generalized* to stop the neuron from firing if there are any more than one zeroes in the input pattern, even if such patterns have not been included in the training examples.

now, we merely need to think of it as a device that is capable of adjusting its function to classify patterns of input firing signals at its synaptic contacts into 'firing' or 'not firing' at its axonal output. A 'training' set of input-output pairs is involved in the process. However, it cannot be guaranteed that the neuron can find weights that satisfy the whole training set, as there are some mappings it cannot achieve (such as the 'exclusive-or' mentioned earlier). But, when a training set is learned, many other inputs patterns that were not in the training set will be made to fire in ways similar to those in the training set (see the caption to Figure A.6).

This capacity for *generalization* is crucial when the neuron is considered in the context of a network of neurons.

6.0 OTHER TOPICS IN NEURON MODELING

6.1 Hebbian learning

Another influential principle of learning is due to Donald Hebb (Figure A.7), who suggested that the connection weights for a neuron would grow when the input of

FIGURE A.7 Donald Hebb, Canadian psychologist who, in 1949, published the enormously influential *The Organisation of Behaviour: A Neuropsychological Theory* (Wiley). This not only proposed a way in which neurons learn useful features of their input, but also that they can sustain an activity in 'reverberating assemblies' (see later in this Appendix). *Source*: http://www.williamcalvin.com/bk9/bk9inter.htm

the neuron fired at the same time as it did. Hebb's principle is that 'neurons that fire together, wire together'.

To accomplish this, a Hebbian learning rule finds inputs that cause a neuron to fire. Here is an example.

Say that a three-input neuron receives binary numbers $(000 = 0, 001 = 1, 010 = 2, \ldots 111 = 7)$. Say that it is required to fire only for odd numbers. Say that it has a rule that makes the connection weight grow whenever the input correlates with the output. The full truth table is:

Inputs	Output
000	0
001	1
010	0
.	
.	
111	1

Notice that the third Input column correlates with the Output.

Now assume that the activation threshold is low and the connection weights all start off at 0. The weight associated with the least significant digit in the third column will grow. A Hebbian rule could take a random selection of output pairs to make the weight of the third input grow consistently and not the others, so the neuron will learn to pick out odd digits and suppress firing for even ones. This rule will generalize even if all the possible inputs have not been seen in training.

6.2 Activation functions

In the basic neural model, the total activation is submitted to a threshold function so that sharp decisions can be made. This is called an *activation function*. However, not all neural models have a threshold activation function. S-shaped functions (called *sigmoid* or *tanh*), are often used, particularly for the recursive networks that are discussed below. Another class of neuron that has come into use is the *radial basis function* neuron, which has a transfer function in the shape of a hill. That is, it responds most strongly for a range of activations and does not respond if the activation is too low or too high. However, these topics are beyond the scope of this discussion.

7.0 MORE THAN ONE NEURON

Even the early research in artificial neural networks concerned itself with what could be done with neurons when they act together in networks. After all, it is unlikely that any cognitive processes in the brain can be found in single neurons. Here we look at three historical events in the development of *layers* of artificial neurons and their processing properties.

7.1 The perceptron

An early example of a neural network is due to Frank Rosenblatt (1958). There were several variants of what Rosenblatt called a 'perceptron'. A version of this is shown in Figure A.8.

This network is intended to recognize patterns in a matrix of high dimension by means of a low dimensional code at its outputs. Often this code is simply a 1 among all zeros. So, if the network were to recognize printed letters of the alphabet in the input matrix, each McCulloch and Pitts neuron could be taught (by weight adjustment) to specialize in one of the 26 letters: a 1 on the first response unit and a 0 on all the others could indicate an 'A' , a 1 on the second, a 'B' and so on.

(It should be noted that the Association units are there to help reduce the dimensionality and hence cost of the response units. That is, they have just a linear activation function that is applied to randomly chosen points in the input matrix. So the Association units produce a number that tells the response units how many inputs of the Association unit are activated. The task for the response units is then to adjust the weights to distinguish these number vectors. We leave the reader to work through example 1.3 at the end of the Appendix to work out exactly how the perceptron works.)

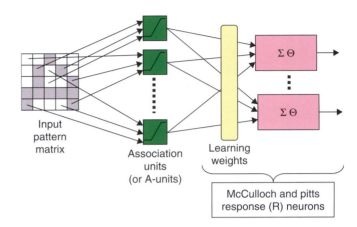

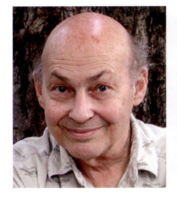

FIGURE A.8 The perceptron. A perceptron learns to classify patterns in a binary input matrix by a response vector at the output of the network.

FIGURE A.9 Marvin Minsky and Seymour Papert. In 1969, they dealt a severe blow to the use of perceptrons for pattern recognition, by showing that there were vast classes of patterns that could not be distinguished by this methodology. *Sources*: *left*, http://en. wikipedia.org/wiki/Marvin_Minsky; *right*, http://web.media.mit. edu/~paper

7.2 Limitations of the perceptron

In 1962, Frank Rosenblatt published an optimistic set of results about the way perceptrons can distinguish between classes of patterns, in his book entitled *Principles of Neurodynamics*. But this optimism was crushed by Marvin Minsky and Seymour Papert of MIT who, in 1969, published an analysis of the perceptron which showed that certain patterns cannot be distinguished by these systems (Figure A.9).

In a typical problem that limited the perceptron, the machine has to distinguish whether two regions of an input pattern are connected or not. Another difficulty was making a distinction between odd and even numbers of blobs in an image. Minsky and Papert pointed out that these tasks are easily solved by an appropriate symbolic algorithm. From a cognitive point

of view, a human being solves the problem by counting and eye movement. Some examples are difficult for humans but easy enough for conventional computer programs (Figure A.10). It seemed that symbolic computer programs could do many things that perceptrons could not.

The problem with perceptrons is that, because of the 'linear separability' nature of the McCulloch and Pitts neuron, they are insensitive to number or, indeed, the odd/even divide. This can be seen in Figure A.5, where the two input patterns (0,0), (1,1) cannot give a response which is the same for both, but different from a single-input response.

This simple deficit seriously arrested work in the USA on perceptron-like systems from the late 1960s to the early 1980s. And then a simple solution was found.

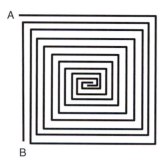

FIGURE A.10 The Minsky and Papert spiral. If the black lines form the walls of a maze, are the paths entered from A and from B connected or disconnected? Note that a computer program could easily follow the paths to answer the question.

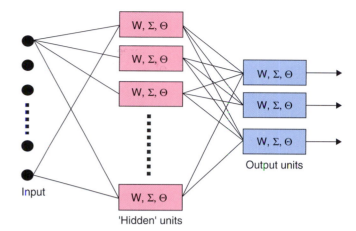

FIGURE A.11 The multilayer perceptron. The hidden layer provides auxiliary functions to 'sort out' the difficulties found in single-layer perceptrons.

7.3 The multilayer perceptron

If a single layer of response units cannot compute a particular transfer function, such as the parity property that caused trouble as seen above, it occurred to several theoreticians that adding a 'sorting-out' layer between the input pattern and the output response unit will solve the problem (Figure A.11). In fact, it is possible to prove that whatever the desired classification between inputs and outputs, there exists a structure of 'hidden' units that will allow that function to be achieved.

Two problems arise: how does one train the *hidden layer*? How does one design the structure of the hidden layer? The solution to the first problem was found from a known way of adjusting the parameters of a layered control system used by Paul Werbos in 1974. But, in 1986, in a celebrated pair of books called *Parallel Distributed Processing*, Rumelhart, Hinton and Williams showed that there was a way of *propagating errors backwards* from the output layer and adjusting the weights to remove errors. (The term 'error' refers to any deviation from a desired input-output function.) Without going into detail, this procedure requires that the threshold activation functions be replaced by smooth S-shaped ones, so that gradients of change in the outputs of the neurons can be calculated. This gives a gradual approach to the removal of errors, i.e. less weight change is required as the activation curve levels out.

In general, the weights of a unit are adjusted according to the known error of that unit and an expectation of how much the input to a weight is responsible for that error. But, for a multilayer network, the error at the output of a hidden unit is not known. It was proven that, if it is assumed that the error of a particular hidden unit is proportional to the sum of all the units to which that unit is connected, weight adjustment procedures converge to a stable input-output function. Therefore,

the training of a multilayer perceptron has two phases. One for the propagation of errors to the output layer and the second for a computation of errors of hidden units by the propagation *backwards* of the measured output errors, to compute the required sum of all the errors caused by a single hidden unit. It works!

The choice of numbers of neurons in the hidden layer became an empirical procedure, where failures to achieve a classification were usually met by increasing the size of this layer. In theory, if there are n binary input nodes, the upper limit to the size of the hidden layer is 2^n because then each unit can detect one combination of inputs and the output units simply piece together those combinations that require a response from the output unit. This is a costly solution and most problems can be solved with a smaller number of hidden units.

7.4 Cognition and perceptrons?

The publication of the properties of multilayer perceptrons and ways of training them had the effect of removing the stigma against neural networks introduced by Minsky and Papert. So, in the late 1980s, a vast number of laboratories around the world began developing neural networks, mainly for solving practical problems. But, in this volume, we are mainly concerned with theory which underpins our cognitive life. In the brain there certainly is a great deal of multilayering, but whether error back-propagation has an explanatory role to play in real neurons remains an open question.

However, another line of work in artificial neural networks took place at the same time: the consideration of networks where neurons form closed informational loops – the recursive or dynamic network.

8.0 RECURSIVE OR DYNAMIC NETWORKS

This was a revival of an idea enunciated by Donald Hebb. Neurons are capable of forming closed loops which, in Hebb's terms, are capable of 'reverberating', or in more current terms, are capable of sustaining internal states. Largely initiated by two influential papers by John Hopfield, the work of Stephen Grossberg and Teuvo Kohonen explained memory storage and recall as important cognitive properties that could be handled by neural models.

In order to set the scene, we shall work through a very simple example.

8.1 A simple example of a recursive net

Consider the network shown in Figure A.12.

Assume that the three neurons all perform the same 'or' function: the output becomes 1 if one or both inputs are 1. Say that the state (P,Q,R) and the input (A,B,C) are both $(0,0,0)$. Then (P,Q,R) remains $(0,0,0)$ with the passage of time. Now imagine that A goes to 1. Then (P,Q,R) will become $(1,0,0)$, but now the second neuron becomes activated, so the sequence of states will continue $(1,1,0) \rightarrow (1,1,1)$. If A is now returned to 0, this will not cause the state to change from $(1,1,1)$ – the state is *self-sustaining*. So, with an input of $(0,0,0)$ we note that there are two stable states $(0,0,0)$ and $(1,1,1)$ for this simple network, given the same input. The second stable state can be triggered from the first by any of the inputs going to 1, but the first can never be triggered from the first.

Achieving stable states in complex networks is fundamentally important. All biological organisms maintain homeostasis – keeping blood pressure within limits, or body temperature, or oxygen consumption. Any major departure from stability in these vital functions threatens survival. In the case of the brain, where tens of billions of neurons have very dense connectivity, loops can naturally occur that would make the system run out of control. Epileptic seizures are often viewed in that way. Therefore, for any important neural function to be accomplished, such as learning, pattern recognition, or pursuit of a goal, a stable neural system is essential.

Larger networks can have many such stable states or even cycles of recurring states. Such internal occurrences can, therefore, be thought of as contributing to the inner or 'mental' states of a neural network – say the brain? These results therefore relate to Donald Hebb's notion of a 'reverberation' of a physical loop of neurons. Any

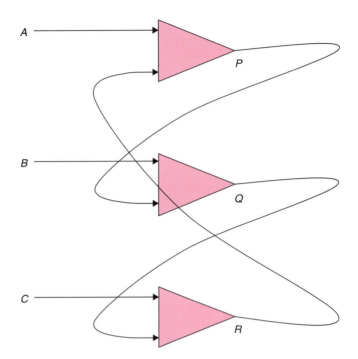

FIGURE A.12 A three-neuron network. This 3-neuron network has the particular property of neurons not only being connected to some external (binary) interface at A, B, or C. But neurons also receive inputs from other neurons. This creates a 'state' for the system at P, Q and R.

stable state or cycle requires the presence of physical loops.

8.2 Hopfield nets and Boltzmann machines

Several elegant analyses of recursive nets emerged in the 1970s and 1980s. Here we describe a particularly influential scheme, the net described by John Hopfield, then of Cal Tech (Figure A.13).

In an early version of Hopfield's theory (1982), he used McCulloch and Pitts binary neurons in configurations where every neuron receives inputs from every other neuron except from itself. Also, if neuron A connects to neuron B through weight w_{AB}, then the return connection is the same ($w_{AB} = w_{BA}$). Assuming that in the system only one neuron can do its computation at one time, Hopfield was able to prove that each such computation may be associated with a reduction in an overall *energy level* of the network. The upshot of this is that the net settles in a minimum energy 'hole', with the state of the network resembling a ball that can fall into this state. This is important, because such low energy states may be created purely by solving equations for the weights. From a cognitive point of view, *these low energy stable states can be seen as the knowledge repository*

FIGURE A.13 John Hopfield: he showed that an energy could be associated with a recursive net. That is, a stable state that cannot easily be disturbed is at a low energy, like a ball in a hole. *Source*: http://www.cs.princeto.edu/~dpd/sabbat/2004/12.08-2104people/IMG_0467.jpg. Courtesy of David Dobkin, Princeton.

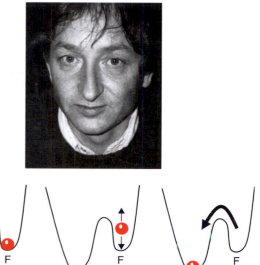

FIGURE A.14 Geoffrey Hinton and the Noisy Recursive Net: the diagram shows a system with a meaningful low energy state **M** and a 'false' energy minimum **F** in which the net is stuck. Introducing noise is like causing the ball to start bouncing around, eventually allowing it to fall into the required meaningful state.

Photograph source: http://www.cs.toronto.edu/~hinton/Geoff4.jpg

of a neural net. We shall see that they can actually have the form of a perceived input pattern. They could therefore be used to model visual memory and mental imagery.

However, at first sight, it might appear that the brain might constantly be blundering into some irrelevant low energy inner state. The reason this does not happen is that a closed net that may be a little like the Hopfield model, is constantly bombarded by input from other nets or from the senses. As we shall see later, when we do some serious modeling, adding input connections to the Hopfield net changes the 'landscape' of low energy states.

This can be seen in the example of Figure A.12. If the input is 000, there are two stable states, 000 or 111. But, if the input is 001, then there is only one, that is, 111. Here is another useful metaphor that applies to these recursive or dynamic nets. In Figure A.12, the 000 state is more precarious than 111. That is, a brief moment of one of the inputs or outputs going to 1 and the system will fall into 111, from which it cannot be extracted. In Hopfield's terms, this is not an energy hole, but an energy hill! This is generally known as a meta-stable state.

Another snag with recursive networks is that, having created important knowledge-bearing low-energy holes, the ball may never fall into them because it could get trapped in some local holes or 'false minima' as they are called. This problem was tackled by Geoffrey Hinton, then at Carnegie Mellon University, working with colleagues Dana Ballard and Terry Sejnowski (in

Rumelhart and McClelland, 1986). They suggested that in order to reach meaningful low energy states, an amount of noise could be introduced into the system (Figure A.14).

This system was dubbed 'The Boltzmann Machine' after Ludwig Boltzmann who, at the end of the 19th century, discovered that the random motion of the molecules of a gas was directly related to the temperature of the gas.

Why is all this important in cognitive neuroscience? As mentioned above, meaningful minima can represent memories. Neural modeling provides a new language with which to talk about the brain. For example, recall of a well-known image, given only a snippet of the image, can be talked of falling into a network minimum that represents the image. Seeing a corner of the image is like being in an energy landscape, in the vicinity of the complete image minimum. Not being quite able to recall the image is like falling into a false minimum or just wandering around the landscape.

8.3 Other recursive systems

In addition to the work reviewed above, the end of the 1970s and through the 1980s was a very exciting period for innovative thought on recursive neural networks

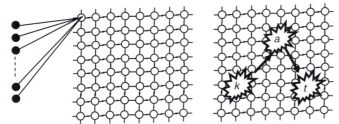

FIGURE A.15 Teuvo Kohonen and a version of the Self-Organising Feature Map: the nodes of the network form a 2-dimensional grid (left), each node receiving inputs from a feature vector of the data to be recognized. Lateral inhibition in the net causes local areas to become specialized in combinations of features. So a phonetic net may represent the word 'cat' as a trajectory of firing intensity in localized areas of the net. *Photograph source*: http://www.cis.hut.fi/people_photos_new/large/teuvo.jpg.

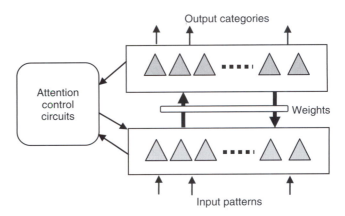

FIGURE A.16 Stephen Grossberg and the ART structure which he developed with Gail Carpenter. The input layer operates at the pattern level, while the output layer determines categories. There are circuits for short-term memory (not shown) and attentional gain control (shown). *Photograph source*: http://www.bu.edu/bridge/archive/2001/03–16/cns.html, Kalman Zabarsky.

and their relationship to what may be going on in the brain. Hopfield also developed a continuous (non-binary) model of a recursive net, which has been used for optimization problem. Also important for cognition is Teuvo Kohonen's self-organizing feature map network (SOFMN) (1982). Kohonen (Figure A.15), showed that matrix-like neural networks could create localized areas of firing for similar sensory features. Such networks would have neurons connected to neighbours and sensory input and would find a localized center of firing for a particular feature of the input. Other features would find physically disconnected areas, building a feature map according to the similarity of the features.

So, for example, given a speech input, a network might find a center of firing for all sounds with similar sounds in the neighbourhood. A speech utterance could thus be recognized by *where* it stimulates the neural network. Such mechanisms are known to occur in the brain, where different frequencies of a sound become localized in the cochlea and the auditory regions of the brain (see Chapter 7).

About the same time, Stephen Grossberg developed his Adaptive Resonance Theory (ART) Networks. This has its roots in Grossberg's early neural network research of the late 1960s and early 1970s, developing into the ART style co-researched with Gail Carpenter throughout the 1980s (Carpenter and Grossberg, 1991). ART networks were a progressing series of systems that respected the biological theory that explains the interplay between image and category level representations (Figure A.16). From a biocognitive point of view this is a very important model and the reader is encouraged to follow the vast output of work produced by these authors. This covers various aspects of vision, speech categorization, temporal sequence recognition, chemical transmitter control, sensory motor control and much else.

9.0 LOOKING BACK ON PART 1

A number of excellent scientists have contributed to our current knowledge of what may be going on in the neural 'soup' we call the brain. This Appendix has certainly not done full justice to them all and there are some major omissions. The reader who wishes to deepen her or his knowledge should also look at the comprehensive corpus of work generated by Shun-Ichi Amari (analysis), Kunihiko Fukushima (the Neocognitron), John Taylor (probabilistic neural nets, among others), J A Anderson (cognitive neural models), Jeffrey Elman (recurrent networks), Bart Kosko (bidirectional networks) and Bernie Widrow (a pioneer of the 1960s who studied a system of McCulloch and Pitts neurons called the 'Adaline').

PART 2: SEEING IS BELIEVING

10.0 WHAT IS TO BE SEEN?

The title of this part indicates that what follows is a simulation that outputs a visible result. In addition, most of the examples relate to vision. This results from simulation software called the Neural Representation Modeller (NRM), which was designed by Barry Dunmall in the author's laboratory at Imperial College, London, to study neural *architectures*, i.e. systems in which the components are neural networks. The NRM approach allows us to ask how important cognitive properties arise in a brain-like system. We can ask questions about the generic neural mechanisms that are needed for cognitive properties like attention, memory, imagination, emotion, planning and consciousness.

11.0 THE NRM NEURON

This is shown in Figure A.17.

The basic NRM neuron has been designed to allow experiments with color vision. Its inputs consist of groups of 8 which can be made to sample an input pattern of 8-value colors. As shown, each training pattern is stored together with its desired output color. For a neuron with n groups of color inputs, an *image* of $(8 \times n)$ picture points can be fully covered, or a larger image can be sparsely covered. For each training pattern a vector of $(8 \times n) + 3$ bits is demanded from the com-

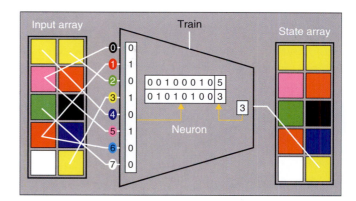

FIGURE A.17 The NRM basic digital neuron (BDN). A neuron with eight inputs and one output is shown. Color coding indicates that the 8 input lines each 'filter' one color. These input lines sample an 8 color input pattern and produce a vector consisting of 0s and 1s, depending on whether the filter matches the color of the input line. Training consists in storing the input pattern as a binary vector and assigning to it an output color which is also stored as being associated with the input. Admissible colors are black, white, red, pink, yellow, green, cyan and blue.

puter: this accommodates the stored input vector and the assigned output. Training proceeds as indicated in Figure A.17. In addition to this there is a check that the same input has not been entered twice with different classifications. Should this happen, a special 'contradicted' symbol will be associated with the input, causing the neuron to generate a color at random.

11.1 The activation and output computation algorithm

To qualify as a neuron, the basic digital neuron (BDN) needs not only to store the training data, but to react appropriately to unknown inputs. The activation algorithm goes as follows:

1. Create the filtered binary vector as in the training scheme.
2. Compare it with all the non-contradicted stored training vectors (say, set V).
3. Create M, a subset of V, which represents those elements of V that have the same number of maximum number of matches m, whether they be 0 or 1.
4. If all the vectors in M have the same associated output color c, produce the output c as the result of the activation algorithm.
5. If there are different associated output colors in M $(8 \times n)$. If m is less than some pre-defined generalization percentage, g, also output a randomly chosen color.

To put it simply, an unknown input is compared to inputs that occurred during training. The 'nearest neighbour' to the unknown is found and classified as learned. In this way, the BDN has all the necessary properties of a neuron. Learning happens in a 'one-shot' fashion as a simple memory loading operation without requiring many cycles of repetition, as in a model that requires iterative weight adjustment. It is also noted that the model does not suffer from having 'impossible' functions – it will always respond accurately to the training set assuming that there are no contradictions. Generalization (insensitivity to small differences from the training patterns) is ensured by the 'nearest neighbor' action. Interestingly, even large differences are tolerated as long as there is a clearest nearest neighbor. Of course, the generalization parameter g is used to control this property. (As an aside, biological neurons are unlikely always to have the same generalization, because they could be affected by neurochemical events in the brain.) This property is hard to model in conventional weight-changing models.

NRM is optimized so as to obtain good performance even with large simulations. A net with 8-input sets (64 binary inputs) per neuron, 100 000 neurons and, say 100 training patterns will occupy 80 megabytes of fast computer memory. This can be updated (teaching or behaving) in about 200 milliseconds. If more memory is required, NRM switches into virtual-memory mode using the hard disk. Some of the largest neural architectures in artificial neural networks have been achieved using this technology. This is important, because the brain is not just a neural network, but a massive combination of networks, an architectural system. Yet such large systems have been difficult to simulate.

11.2 An experiment with a single basic digital neuron

Here we introduce the NRM screen (Figure A.18).

To indicate the activity of the neuron, only the content of the input window is shown together with the state of the output. A time varying output is shown as a sequence of states. For example the action of a totally untrained neuron is shown in Figure A.19.

(Note: at this point we will introduce a 'stop and think' symbol☺, at which the reader should try to work out what results to expect before reading the author's explanation at the foot of the page.)

What activity could be expected from an untrained neuron positioned over the blue mouse?

FIGURE A.18 The NRM screen with a single neuron. The upper window is that of a 2-D 'world' that exists as a bit-map in a computer. Over the blue mouse there is a window which is the input to the neuron. In the current example it samples 98 × 98, 8-color dots. It can either be moved over the world the by 'clicking and dragging' the window, or under program control. The neuron is shown as Neuron A and its current (Sta)te is a blue output. In the top bar are dropdowns that control the process and the bar below contains buttons for direct action on the simulation.

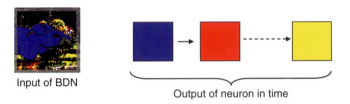

Input of BDN   Output of neuron in time

FIGURE A.19   The random output of an untrained neuron.

When an input does not find any near neighbors, the activation algorithm can find no associated response: it then produces outputs at random.

Say that the input is fully sampled by about (98 × 98/8) or roughly 1200, 8-color bundles that form the neuron input. Hence the vector for each training pattern consists of a string of 1200 8-bit vectors. We now train the neuron as follows. Back at Figure A.18, we position the window over a full color square. Say this is blue. The system allows us to select a desired color which is to be associated with the input. We choose the same color (blue) as that in the window and press a 'T' button to associate the color with the input vector. We repeat this for a second color, say red. Obviously, if the neuron is activated by the color patterns on which it was trained it will respond with the correct color. But what if it was to be activated by say a completely white

Training patterns

Test patterns

FIGURE A.20 Training and test patterns. 3904 neurons arranged as a 122 × 32 output array in which only black/white outputs are used to label the input patterns. The neurons are connected at random to the 98 × 98 input window, with each neuron sampling the window with 32 8-bit inputs.

input?☺ Or what if the input of the blue mouse is the one shown in Figure A.19?

The result of the training is that the neuron has learned to recognize the major color, in this case red or blue. In general, it can become a detector of any color. Indeed, eight arbitrary input patterns and their small variants can be recognized by causing them to output the eight colours, one for each class.

11.3 An experiment with a layer of basic digital neuron

BDNs can be used as single layer perceptrons, but without the Minsky and Papert disadvantages discussed before. That is, BDNs are not limited in the transfer functions they can compute.

In the next experiment, we set up a net in which a single layer of neurons is organized as a black/white matrix on which a description of the object has been written. In Figure A.20, the net has been trained to respond with the words 'blue mouse' and 'red cat' when the appropriate patterns are sampled at the input. We test the system with displaced versions of the trained input patterns and note that there are enough neurons whose inputs are similar to the training ones. The 'noise' that enters in the response is due to neurons that

FIGURE A.21 Recognition result with one 8-bit bundle per neuron.

are either classifying their inputs wrongly or have become noisy. Careful measurement shows that the noise in the output is less than the change in the input image, as the majority of the inputs of a neuron would have to be disrupted to produce the wrong response.

What would happen if the input size of the neuron were to be greatly reduced? A simple prediction is that it would be more likely for a neuron input to be compromised by a change from the training set and Figure A.21 shows the effect of reducing the number of inputs per neuron to just one bundle of 8.

Notice that far more errors occur in the response. In other words, the greater the sample by the neuron input, the more likely it is that the activation will be representative of the training set, if similarities exist.

12.0 THE NRM DYNAMIC NEURAL NET

12.1 The state as a label of the input

As suggested earlier, cognitive properties such as sensory memories result from networks that include *feedback* among the neurons. In NRM, this is organized by having a net with the output neurons connecting to some of the inputs of the same neurons through a clocking gate. That is, the output of a network becomes a 'state' of the network, which together with the input activates the inputs to the neuron. At the arrival of a clock pulse the state is updated.

For training to take place, the state to be learned is loaded into the state box. With this arrangement, the system can only be trained to sustain a state related to the input in the state box. Other possibilities will be seen later. Consider Figure A.22.

Here the training of the state box has been completed for the two animals and then with the input window blacked out for both the M(ouse) and the (C)at states. Without feedback this would cause great contradictions in the training of the neurons, as the same input cannot

---

☺ For each color, the stored vector string consists of identical 8-bit vectors with the same bit set for one color (say 01000000,01000000,01000000 . . .), and another bit for the string for the other color (say 00001000,00001000,00001000 . . .). Then the code for white (say 10000000,10000000,10000000 . . .) is easily seen to be equally distant from either of the training patterns, causing it to output a random color sequence.

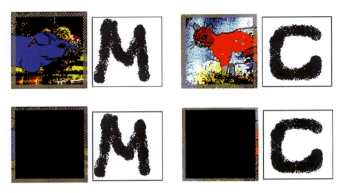

FIGURE A.22   A complete training set. In this experiment, the output box has the same dimensions as the input box. So there are 98 × 98 (i.e. 9604) neurons here in black/white output mode. Their inputs have 64 8-bit bundles, half sampling the input and the other half sampling the output (now, called the state box). The complete training set is shown.

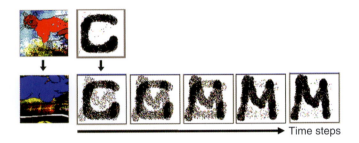

FIGURE A.23   Step-by-step state changes. The input recalls C when seeing the training cat. As the input switches to a mouse different from the training mouse, notice that the state changes step-by-step from C to M – a good labeling state for the mouse.

lead to two outputs. But as a result of the feedback, the overall input of the neurons is not the same in the two cases. But what do we now expect to happen when this system is tested?☺

To demonstrate the dynamic behaviour resulting from the training shown above, consider Figure A.23.

The role of the feedback is to create a stable inner state which may be triggered by input. In this case, the inner state is a label for an input, M or C. But the system is very flexible. We will demonstrate this next.

12.2   The state as an inner image (icon) of the input

The inner state of a dynamic neural net (DNN) can be an iconic state, a pictorial representation of vision-like input. We believe DNNs can be models of mental

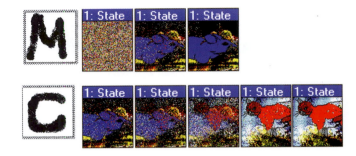

FIGURE A.24   The iconically trained system starts in a randomly selected state. Given the input symbol image M, it rapidly finds the stable state of the mouse image. Starting with the mouse image, the input symbol image is changed to a C. The mouse state is then no longer stable and the net finds the cat state, which is stable.

imagery. The training is like that of Figure A.22, with the letters replaced by the appropriate animal image in its central position. In addition, the training can be extended to recognizing the letter at the input leading to the picture as the state. We can now demonstrate the results of iconic training.

Figure A.24 is probably the most important figure of this Appendix, because it forms the basis of the way that inner mental states may either have an autonomous existence of their own or be controlled by sensory input. I introduce some notions from automata theory (analysis of digital systems) and chaos theory (analysis of systems whose properties emerge from the interaction of components).

We have already accepted the notion that a dynamic net has an inner state. When a net is trained in the manner that has been described, the trained state is described as a *stable* state because, on the whole, it remains constant in time. (There could be the odd twinkle from the odd neuron due to it being contradicted during training, but this is relatively minimal in a net with sufficient feedback.) Chaos researchers call this state an *attractor*, because, when started in some other state, the state neurons become stable in time. It is as if the operation of the net is attracted to the stable state. Automata researchers call it a *re-entrant* state with states leading to it being called *transients*. This is the same as the notion of balls falling into holes (above), except that the mathematics of continuous systems cannot be applied to this digital DNN model.

Now for a simple bit of automata theory. Each neuron has an output dependent on the input and the state of all the neurons. This means that the next state of the

---

☺ There are two stable states, M and C. Either should be sustainable with a black input, but it is switched to the appropriate label when an animal is presented to the input.

system is dependent on the previous state and the input. When the state settles into an attractor, i.e. if it remains constant in time, it is still dependent on the input. However, in Figure A.24 we suddenly change the input from M to C while the inner state is that of the mouse. Now, the combination of an input from C and a mouse state is not what most neurons 'know' how to respond to. So many neurons will be contradicted and output random colours, that is noise. The system fails to find a single stable output. This destabilizes the net as shown in Figure A.24. However, due to the constant input C, the net favours outputs that come from the cat image. This too is like falling down a hole, until the cat image is reached. In other words, in this case, the 'landscape' of hills and holes depends entirely on the input. In this example, it seems as if only one attractor exists for each of the input symbol images.

However, this cannot be guaranteed and tends to be less true when one attempts to create a large number of attractors. But what does 'large' mean? As a rule of thumb, the state space starts getting crowded when the number of attractors approaches 2^i, where i is the number of input bundles per neuron. In this case, this is 2^{32} which is roughly 10 billion!

The *cognitive* implication of what we have explained above is that we have identified a mechanism for *visualizing* the image associated with a symbol. In a sense, the iconically trained net 'knows' what things related to a name look like.

12.3 The inner state as a repository of sensory memories

We recall that the network has not only been trained to sustain the animal images for appropriate symbol image inputs, but it has also been trained to sustain the animal images for a black or meaningless input. The result of doing this is shown in Figure A.25.

In *cognitive* terms, this network may be said to be able to remember one of its only two experienced visual inputs. There is a process of *competition* at work that determines which attractor is entered. The important fact here is that this experiment illustrates the way in which memory of sensory information exists in a dynamic neural net. Usually, in automata theory, one talks of the 'state space' of a dynamic system as a definitive statement of the 'mental' or internal properties of the network.

12.4 The state space of the memory network

Figure A.26 shows the 'state space' diagram for the above network and its implications. This figure shows states or sets of states as circles, transitions as lines or dotted lines, and the image content of states as images. Input images that determine the transitions between states are shown as little pictures.

In this diagram, all the 'meaningless' states or random states have been lumped together as one because their effects are very much the same. This set is astronomically large, since it contains all the possible color combinations of 98×98 8-colour pixels (8^{9604}). More usefully, two attractors are shown as re-entrant states – they attract any state trajectory with the appropriate letter image or visual image that is related to the attractor. There are many more entries than shown. Fragments of input images will fall into attractors representing the whole image, an important property for simulating human recognition memory. Iconic training creates inner states that resemble prototypical 'mental' states. These may show the representational capacities of a neural system. This result allows us to suggest that this is what neurons may be doing in the brain.

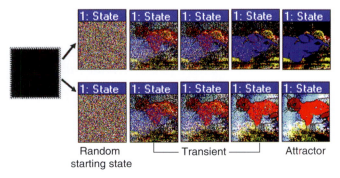

Random
starting state — Transient — Attractor

FIGURE A.25 The system has a black, meaningless input and starting in a random state, can either end up in the cat or the mouse attractor.

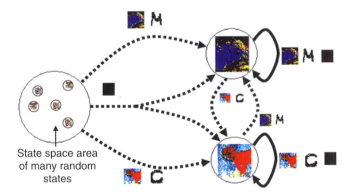

FIGURE A.26 The state space diagram of the dynamic net trained as a memory. Dotted lines indicate transitions that could involve more than one clock step, while solid ones involve a single clock step change. The small symbol images indicate inputs. These inputs act to control the state trajectories in the network.

13.0 A COMPLEX COGNITIVE SYSTEM IN NRM

Cognition is much more complex than the action of a single element. We will therefore look at a more comprehensive system that has been studied using NRM. This model is intended to show how eye movements may be used to create a reconstruction of a world scene which is being attended only by a foveal window, aided by perifoveal signals (perifoveal means near the fovea). The scheme includes selective attention to scene features, recall of reconstructed scenes, interplay between reconstruction and memory, sleep, dreaming, the self, auditory input and output.

The model's screen image is shown in Figure A.27.

In this system, each window represents the state of a neural network. Such networks are inspired by the visual regions of cortex (Chapter 6) to produce an 'awareness' of both the reality and the imagination of the world.[1]

1 *The world and the retinal image.* This is marked 'Input 1' on the screen. It is an area in which 400×400 8-color pixel images can be loaded. This is the visual world of the system. Projected onto this world are two concentric square windows. The inner one is a model of a *fovea* – i.e. the highest-density receptor array in the retina, surrounded by a *perifoveal*, a lower-resolution ring of receptors surrounding the fovea. The fovea is a 48×48 window, while the rest is represented by a 17×17 window.

2 *The primary visual cortex (V1).* Areas 1, 5 and 13 are a direct projection of the foveal and perifoveal windows: area 5 has no color information, whereas area 1 does. In the real eye, the fovea contains most color receptors.

3 *Eye movement generation.* This (nets 6 to 11) represents the function of the *superior colliculus* which, in the brain, builds a non-cortical map of the visual field. It is responsible for pre-conscious eye saccades that ensure that the fovea moves to salient parts of the visual scene. This eye movement map is shown in 6 forming a target that has to be found by the fovea, while 9 indicates how much of this target has been found by an eye movement. Net 9 selects a position in the target that has, as yet, not been analyzed and generates signals for a 'motor neuron' 12. This is a special neuron that has the power to move the window on the world (as in 1 above). Nets 7 and

10 keep track of how much of the target has been covered.[2] Defined function neurons are found in neurons 6–12. 8 and 11 are control neurons that notice changes in the input image, which might require a resetting of the eye movement mechanism.

4 *Depiction – the key to visual awareness.* Network 14 is probably the most important area of this system. It corresponds to what brain scientists call the 'extra-triate' parts of the visual cortex, i.e. the areas outside of the primary projection area V1. According to Crick and Koch (2003), extrastriate visual cortex generates a representation of vision that compensates for the movement of the eyes, head and body. In this model, only the movement of the eyes themselves is taken into account. Network 14 receives inputs from the foveal area (recorded in 13) and from 3 and 18, which measure the movement of the eye as discussed in 3 above. 14 then positions and copies the 48×48 foveal area into a world-related position in a field of 144×144, 8-color neurons. This visual area has short-term memory so as to make this construction of the visual world continuous.

5 *Memory and imagination.* Another key network is 16, which is a classical attractor net (144×144, 8-color neurons). It has an *iconic* relationship with network 14 – i.e. it learns attractors that represent the content of 14. It also can receive input from another classical attractor net, 15, which contains word images related to the attractors of 16.

6 *A hypothesis about awareness.* Our notion of awareness suggests that neural areas contribute to visual consciousness only if they are depictive. A depictive neuron is one whose state is related to a minimal event in the outside world. Therefore, 14 and 16 together are the awareness areas of the system.

But how does one represent a 'sensation' of visual awareness? In the brain, a visual event in the world, like a little colored bug landing on a white wall, causes neural changes in many areas of the visual cortex specialized in color, shape and motion. Nevertheless, the conscious sensation is experienced as integrated. In the model, depiction indexes neural activity to the position in the world of an elemental event. Even if different features of the stimulus are represented in different brain areas, depiction carries indexing information of the location of the event in the world, which integrates the disparate neural feature maps. In this view, the sensation of the event is an overlap of the activity in all the areas that depict it.

---

[1] The description in this part of the Appendix is brief and functional. The reader can explore the model through software provided with this book.
[2] NRM supports a large number of different neuron types. Some are called defined function neurons (DFNs), which serve different functions that are beyond our current scope.

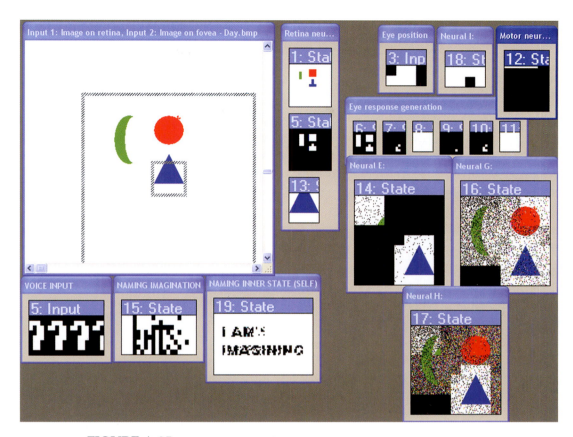

FIGURE A.27   An NRM system of visual awareness. See description in the text.

In network 17, we have created a non-biological model that integrates the content of the only two depictive areas in the system: 14 and 16. There may be no such network in the brain, as the depictive representations may be sufficient to indicate a sensation. Network 17 only displays the depictive overlap on the screen and allows us to make judgments about the accuracy of the integrated visual representation produced by the model.

7   *The self.* The concept of 'self' refers to the translation of depictive states into language. Without an attempt at serious biological plausibility, we show a network (19) that can translate the depictive areas and the state of the auditory input (5) into statements such as 'I am seeing' or 'I am imagining'.

13.1   What does the model currently tell us?

In Figure A.27, the eye is fixating its fovea on part of a blue triangle. This input is transmitted to the primary, non-depictive area 13. The perifoveal image is transmitted to primary areas 1 and 5 in very low

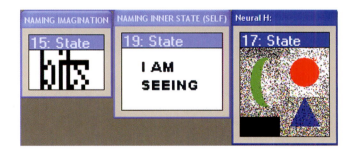

FIGURE A.28   State of awareness 10 steps after Figure A.27. The system is aware of the sensory input without requiring too much imagination and is therefore more confident that it is seeing the 'bits' image and not imagining it.

resolution. Areas 6–11 represent the action of the superior colliculus, creating in area 12 the planned move for the next fixation point of the fovea. Areas 3 and 8 indicate the position of the fovea, which is used in positioning the content of 13 in the depictive 'perceptual' area 14. 14 also shows other previous foveal fixations that are just beginning to fade (to black). This partial perception provides sufficient input to the memory module 16 to anticipate a complete depiction of what the system is 'seeing.' Because the system has seen the input before, it has learned a preparatory activation pattern to see it again.

The system is therefore 'aware' of the fact it is looking at the input pattern 'bits' shown in 17. According to 19, it is also aware of relying on imagination while attempting to describe the scene in 15. With time, the awareness becomes clearer, as seen in Figure A.28.

6 steps after change

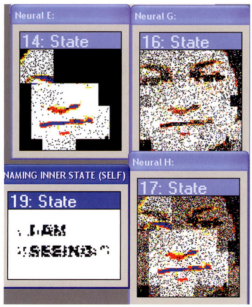

12 steps after change

FIGURE A.29 Noticing change in the system. This figure shows the way in which memory of one input lingers while another is being reconstructed and how the 'self' model notices the change.

13.2 Response to input changes

It is interesting to change the input image and observe the dynamic changes in the system (Figure A.29).

In many cognitive experiments what is felt when input stimuli are changing is of major interest. The NRM system above suggests how the influence of one area of awareness on another may be tracked and how this might affect the verbal expression of what is sensed.

13.3 Response to simulated voice input

The current model resembles an act of visualizing an image in a totally dark room or with one's eyes closed. Suppose that a name of a known person is called and one is asked to recall what that person looks like. Figure A.30 shows how a voice-like input may appear in the imagination module. The result of inputting the

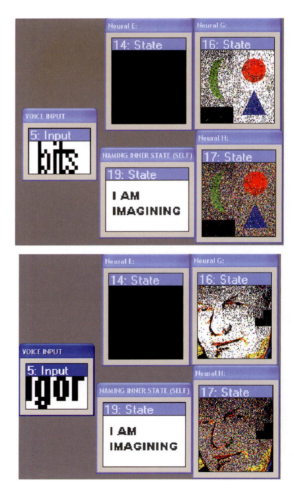

FIGURE A.30 Response of the system to images that represent voice inputs. The memory/imagination module falls into a state which matches the 'voice input'.

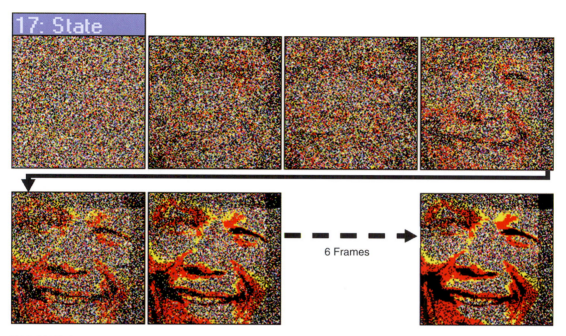

FIGURE A.31 NRM of Nelson Mandela. The first frame of state 17 is with the feedback loops of layer 13 'anesthetized' while the next frame is with the loops allowed to operate. An imagination of Nelson Mandela appears (learned during the author's visit to South Africa).

pattern 'bits,' the name of the picture of colored shapes and the author's name 'Igor' is shown in Figure A.30. Of course, the system is familiar with this information, as the voice input was present during the learned perception of Igor's face.

13.4 Recall in the absence of stimulus

The word 'imagination' has a variety of meanings, but one is the following. Say you stay with your eyes closed and just relax. It is almost impossible to prevent the awake brain from 'thinking'.

This can occur in connection with a subject that has not been noticeably triggered by input, as a direct result of the property we have seen in Figure A.25, but now within the framework of a more elaborate model of awareness. We can cause the model to enter a kind of 'anesthesia'[3] of layer 16 and then release it from this condition. When anesthetized, the system loses its attractors through the fact that transitions to any state become feasible and such a state is likely to be random. The number of random states is astronomically vast. But as the 'anesthesia' is removed, the learned state structure returns and what follows is shown in Figure A.31. In simple terms, layer 16 follows a trajectory determined

by the similarity of the starting random state to one of the learned attractors in the network.

13.5 Summary of NRM work

Why is modeling useful? In our laboratory, we have found that NRM acts as a place-holder for possible large-scale brain functions that are too complex to understand simply by inspection. A system like NRM should be large enough to capture the emergence of cognitive phenomena and yet manageable enough to work on state-of-the-art computers. Shanahan (2005) has applied some aspects of Baars' Global Workspace theory using NRM for these reasons.

13.6 Neural models of cognition: conclusion

It is clear that the drive to build neural networks, which dates back to the mid-1940s, includes the desire to capture the cognitive properties of the brain in an artificial domain. But it is clearly not enough just to create large neural networks with their emergent processing of pattern labeling in feed-forward schemes and memory in dynamic schemes. The ability of the brain to lay down memory, often unaided and deploy it not only to drive

---

[3]Technically, 'anesthesia' is achieved by reducing the 'generalization' of the neurons down to zero (see section 11.1).

a panoply of actions but also internal deliberations, remained a challenge. As the century changed so did attitudes to this kind of neural modeling. It became clear that neural networks are formidable components of complex architectures within which one begins to see cognitive representations that resonate with our own inner sensation of cognition.

The important realization is that the brain is anything but a vast neural network. It is a beautiful, intricate interaction of areas with complex properties that will require research for many years to come. What I have just written does not come as a surprise to neurophysiologists (who have no illusions about the complexity of the brain), but it does give cognitive scientists pause for thought. Whereas tradition in cognitive science is to model a process by creating an ensemble of well-framed understandable rules, it seems like a break in this tradition to base a neural modeling technique on complex components in which useful properties emerge, sometimes not in an entirely analytic way. Then to use these elements in architectures where further dynamic process is required to begin to see cognitively useful representations seems contrary to the needs of a good understanding.

In these pages, I have argued the opposite: it is possible to design neural models that capture the two levels of complexity – the element and the architecture. This allows the modeler to study complex phenomena in the functional framework in which they may occur in the brain. The understanding comes from the modeling itself and the observation of changes of behavior that result from what-if hypotheses in model changes. In other words, this is the same activity as is normally exercised in science. It is reminiscent of the modeling with which the greatest leaps in science were made, for example, Crick and Watson's double helix model of the basis of life. The NRM methodology described in some detail offers the opportunity for such experimentation.

14.0 SELF-TEST PUZZLES AND SOME SOLUTIONS

Q1 For the 2-input neuron in Figure A.4, find a set of weights and a threshold that creates an 'and gate' starting with all weights and the threshold set to 0.5.

Q2 Try to do this by inspection of Figure A.4 (a possible answer is $W_1 = -0.4$, $W_2 = -0.4$ and $\Theta = -0.1$).

In Figure A.32, show that for the given connections, both weights at unity and the R-unit threshold at 3, the system differentiates between the two patterns shown. Give examples of patterns that are classified equally with T and H and comment on your results.

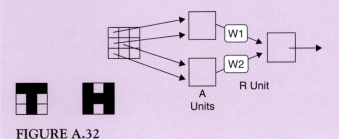

FIGURE A.32

14.1 Exercises with NRM

1 Simple experiments on neurons and a homogeneous net

Open the Simple Experiments folder.

Look at the active NRM User Manual just to familiarize yourself with the basics. Don't try to absorb it – use it as a reference when needed. You will almost certainly run into problems in attempting to solve the experiments below. The Manual can also be reached by clicking on 'help' on the toolbar.

Click on NRM Birm 1 then click OK on the window that appears. Maximize the NRM window.

Click on Configuration.

2 Single neuron experiment

Open HK1, click on the green B symbol on the toolbar to build the neuron, then click on the yellow C symbol to hide the circuit.

Clicking on the yellow symbol of two arrows causes the system to run. Try it. You can move the neuron input by putting the cursor onto it, then clicking and dragging in the usual way.

What's the neuron (Neural A) window doing? Why?

Stop the system from running by clicking on the yellow arrows again.

To notice a difference, train the neuron by putting the window on (say) a red patch, clicking on the Neural A window, then clicking on the blue R (randomizing) button until the neuron output goes red. Then click (once) on the pink T button. T means 'Train selected neurons'. Repeat with (for example) the blue patch and training on blue. Then run the system and observe the way that the neuron responds to different inputs which can be created by moving the input window to different parts of the scene.

3 Single layer net

This is found in HK2. This time the input window is connected to a 122×32 network of neurons that spell out the names of the animals in the scene. First run the system before training to see how this window reacts to input. The way that a name is forced onto the output window (Neural A) is by first clicking on the output window and then clicking on the blue Up or Down arrows on the toolbar.

To train the system to, for example, recognize the blue mouse, position the window on the head of the blue mouse, then click on the output window and adjust the blue arrows until it displays 'blue mouse'. Then train the system by clicking on the pink T. Repeat for all the animals. Then run the system and test it to see how the net responds. What causes the 'noise' in response?

4 Feedback net

This is HK3. Notice that the output is now of the same dimensions as the input window and that it feeds back to the input of the neurons. To create an 'attractor,' position the window (for example) on the head of the blue mouse. Then click in the blue C (for Copy) on the toolbar. Click on the output window then on the blue P (Paste), which will force the input image on the feedback loops. Clicking on the pink T button creates the attractor. You need at least two attractors to do anything interesting – so create a

second one with another animal. Test the system with other inputs. (At times if the state of the output does not change, click on the blue R button on the toolbar, which randomizes the state.)

For more advanced work, find out from the Users Manual how one changes the number of connections in the circuit, and explore what happens if the 'feedback to input' ratio of connections is altered or if localized feedback connections are used. In the above experiment the ratio is 1:1.

14.2 Looking at a more complex system (visual awareness)

1 *Object of the experiment: to gain a passing acquaintance with a more complex digital neuromodel*

Open the 'VIS AW' (visual awareness) folder and load 'nrmp6' version of NRM. Load the A RI FINAL.cfg configuration.

This is a complex system that has many specialized neurons that you don't know much about. So just play with the system as a working machine. To clear the model, click on Build it (Green B) and remove the circuit diagram (Yellow C).

Load some previous training by dropping the 'Network' menu from the toolbar, selecting 'Training' and clicking on 'Load Training'. This opens a menu from which you should open 'RIfinal.ntr'.

Identify the important windows: a foveal/perifoveal input window currently on a black background. A large (Neural H) 'awareness' area; a 'voice' input; a 'naming imagination window' and a 'naming inner state window'.

The system starts off with black input (as if its eyes are closed) and the voice input with white question marks (meaning no voice input). The model 'knows' three images: MOY, BITS and IGOR. Run the model (yellow arrows) and observe what happens in the awareness window. The model will imagine one of its known images.

You can force the model to discover another image by shouting at it – that is clicking on the voice window and selecting a state for it with the blue arrows on the toolbar.

While the model is imagining something, return the voice input to the question marks and click in

(*Continued*)

the input window, and then on the blue L on the toolbar. Select one of the two images that the model is currently *not* imagining. Note how the awareness input reconstructs the image, and how the imagination suddenly switches to anticipate the observed input.

At all times note how the 'naming inner state' window assesses the overall state of the system.

To learn a little more about this system grab and drag down the 'awareness' Neural H window to reveal constituent parts. Repeat the above tests, and observe what the constituent parts are doing. If desired, take a look at the system diagram by clicking on C.

If the complex detail of the system defeats you, don't worry. Only a passing acquaintance with the system is required. Good luck!

14.3 Beyond the call of duty: stacking and self

Object of the experiment: to gain a passing acquaintance with a toy demonstration of all five axioms. Also this uses a 'run script' and it is possible to investigate what it does

Load the 'Stacking and Self' folder from the disk.

Open 'NRM Well' from it.

Load the 'A RI plus one.cfg' configuration. Build the system and Clear the diagram.

Under Network → Training → Load Training . . . open 'Final + 1.ntr'

Under Network → Run/Train Executive → Load/Run open 'Run RI inc 5 + 1.

Now identify the following windows:

WORLD STATE Input: here appears the state of the stack of colored cylinders (driven by the program).

TARGET Input: here appears the desired stacking of the cylinders.

INTERNAL STATE: is a neural module that perceives and also imagines earlier experience.

VISCERAL EMOTION: learned non-depictive states that become active if the target becomes different from the 'internal state'.

EMOTION INTERPRETATION: taught decoder for the visceral emotion.

NEURAL D: the hand – becomes active when the world can be changed to restack the blocks. (The hand cannot act on the world, this is FAKED by the program.)

STATE OF THE SELF: monitors the state of the entire system and has been taught to express it in words.

It is worth spending a bit of time studying how the thing is connected (Yellow C).

With the diagram out of the way, click the yellow R button (run program once) to see what the system does. Repeat as many times as you like. Work out where the axioms come in.

Then take a look at the program which is a notepad file (Run RI inc 5 + 1). This will only make sense if you are familiar with programming. The details of the language are found in the User Manual for NRM.

For more exercises, and to try the software yourself, refer to this book's website at http://textbooks.elsevier.com.

Appendix B

Methods for observing the living brain

Thomas Ramsøy, Daniela Balslev, and Olaf Paulson

1.0 HISTORICAL BACKGROUND

1.1 Correlating brain and mind

Understanding the complex functions of the brain, including sensation, motor function, consciousness and thoughts, has always triggered our curiosity. The brain is activated when we are engaged in solving a task, such as thinking, speaking, or purposeful movements. The activation is accompanied by local changes in the cerebral blood flow in the activated, i.e. involved, brain regions and this forms the basis for functional brain mapping studies. In the following, we provide a brief overview of some of the milestones in this field.

It was recognized early that a hemispheric lesion led to contralateral palsy, a loss of the ability to move a body part. If the lesion was on the left side, language disturbances could occur. In the 19th and the beginning of the 20th century, the functional organization of the brain was investigated through clinical-pathological correlations. Detailed descriptions of symptoms were subsequently (after the patient's death) related to autopsy findings, enabling the localization of specific functions in the brain. The main limitation of this method is that human brain lesions are accidental and thus unspecific in terms of localization because the damage is diffuse and often extends to regions without relevance for the neurological deficit in question. Moreover, adaptive brain responses may modify the neurological deficits over time. With the clinical-pathological correlation we learn about deficits that occur if a given brain region is injured, i.e. for which functions a given brain region is essential. For example, it was lesion studies that taught us that Wernicke's and Broca's areas are both essential for normal language function.

Cognition, Brain, and Consciousness, edited by B. J. Baars and N. M. Gage
ISBN: 978-0-12-373677-2

Copyright 2007, Elsevier Ltd. All rights reserved.

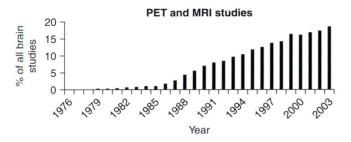

FIGURE B.1 The dramatic increase of neuroimaging in brain science. In 2005, every fifth published brain study was indexed by PubMed under the keywords PET or MRI. *Source*: Ramsøy *et al.*, 2005.

These limitations have provided the incentive for parallel development of other methods that allow a systematic study of the relation between brain and behavior in humans. The new neuroimaging techniques introduced towards the end of the 20th century measure changes in brain activity that correlate with a change in behavior. Current neuroimaging equipment can measure the changes in activity of brain volumes smaller than 1 mm^3 and as fast as tens of milliseconds. The popularity of these new imaging methods is illustrated by the continuous increase in the percentage of studies that use them. For example, in 2005 every fifth published brain study was indexed by PubMed under the keywords PET (positron emission tomography) or MRI (magnetic resonance imaging) (Figure B.1).

The clinical-pathological correlation and the newer brain imaging methods both tell us about the functional organization of the brain, but fundamental differences separate these methods. Thus, with the clinical-pathological correlation, we learn what deficits occur if a given brain region is *injured*, i.e. for which functions a given brain region is essential. On the contrary, with PET and fMRI (functional MRI) we observe which regions are *activated* in a given task as compared with a control condition. Thus, from the clinical-pathological correlation, we know that Wernicke's and Broca's areas are essential for normal language function, but in any speech task, however, both sensory and motor areas involved in articulation will also be activated. For these reasons, sophisticated design of paradigms becomes essential in modern brain mapping. The task and control condition should, in principle, be identical except for the single psychological function whose location we want to map. It is practically very difficult, if not impossible, to control perfectly all behavioral parameters. For instance, in a paradigm designed to identify the neural correlate of spatial attention by presenting visual stimuli at either a cued or an un-cued location, a change in activity in a brain area may as well reflect involuntary eye movements or the subject's effort to prevent a saccade towards the stimulus.

1.2 Recording brain activation

The brain is activated when we are engaged in solving a task, thinking, speaking, purposeful movements, etc. Such activation is accompanied by changes in the hemodynamics in the activated brain regions. This forms the basis for several functional brain mapping studies including the now dominating fMRI methods. In the following, a brief overview of some of the milestones in this field will be given.

Changes in hemodynamics during sensory, motor and cognitive processes were observed about 120 years ago by Mosso in Italy (Mosso, 1881). He had a patient with a skull defect allowing him to make external recordings of the 'brain pulse'. He saw changes in the brain pulse, not only when the church bells were ringing, but also when the man said a prayer even if he did it silently without words. About 10 years later, Roy and Sherrington (1890) proposed that there was a relation between the brain's function and its perfusion (blood flow). This theory had indeed shown to be valid and has formed the basis for extensive research.

In the late 1920s Fulton (1928) observed a patient with an *intracranial arteriovenous malformation*, a condition where lesions of the cerebral vasculature develop such that blood flows directly from the arterial system to the venous system without passing through a capillary system. The patient complained of an abnormal sound (bruit) in the head, which was louder during reading. The bruit and its aggravation could be recorded, demonstrating that some kind of cerebral hemodynamic changes had to occur during reading (at least in this patient). In the late 1950s, it was demonstrated that stimulation of the brainstem resulted in activation in the EEG (electroencephalograph) as well as in cerebral blood flow increase (Ingvar and Söderberg, 1956, 1958).

In the mid-1960s, Cooper (Cooper *et al.*, 1966) observed an increase of the oxygen tension locally in the brain during activation in patients undergoing surgery. This study further strengthened the fact that hemodynamic changes had to occur during cerebral activation. Moreover, this was the first study illustrating a change in the coupling between flow and metabolism during activation.

A milestone in investigation of regional cerebral function was achieved in the early 1960s when Lassen and Ingvar introduced the intra-arterial injection method using radiolabeled inert gases. In their first studies, they measured the clearance of the beta-imaging isotope [85]crypton from the exposed surface of the brain in experimental animals (Lassen and Ingvar, 1961). Soon the method was adapted for investigation in humans using the gamma-emitting isotope [133]xenon, which could be detected through the intact skull. Using multiple external scintillation detectors (sensors measuring ionizing radiation), it became possible to measure blood flow from as many as 250 regions. The method was used in the 1970s abundantly for functional localization in the brain and was, indeed, the first method used for functional brain mapping (Lassen *et al.*, 1978). One drawback of this method was that the tracer had to be injected directly into the internal carotid artery, limiting studies to patients who were undergoing angiograms for diagnostic purposes.

In the 1970s, Sokoloff (Sokoloff *et al.*, 1977) introduced the ^{14}C-deoxyglucose method for measurement of the metabolism of glucose in regions of experimental animals' brains. Soon the method was further developed for PET studies in humans with fluorinated deoxyglucose (FDG) labeled with the positron emitter [18]F. It is known that changes in blood flow and in glucose metabolism are coupled. Although measurement of a regional cerebral glucose metabolism in many aspects represents a milestone, it has not turned out to be very useful for measurement of the functional cerebral activation due to the limited time resolution (15–45 minutes) as compared to flow measurement with PET and fMRI to be discussed later in this chapter.

The establishment of PET in the 1980s and of fMRI in the 1990s provided new non-invasive methods suitable for studies of regional changes in the brain's hemodynamics as an expression of changes in regional cerebral activity. The non-traumatic nature of these methods has allowed investigation of not only patients but also normal subjects and thereby expanded research in functional cerebral activation.

2.0 COUPLING BRAIN ACTIVITY TO BLOOD FLOW AND METABOLISM

2.1 The physiological basis of functional brain mapping using PET and fMRI

The physiological basis of the neuroimaging signal is the coupling between regional cerebral activation and blood flow and, further, the uncoupling between flow and oxygen consumption during activation. Put simply, an increase in activity in the cerebral tissue leads to a blood flow increase that can be measured with PET. The increase in flow markedly exceeds the increase in oxygen consumption so that the concentration of deoxyhemoglobin decreases. This local decrease in deoxyhemoglobin gives rise to the fMRI signal.

The epileptic seizure can be considered as an extreme non-physiological activation where all neurons fire at maximal rate. In this condition, blood flow is markedly increased and oxygen consumption is also increased but much less so, resulting in an increase in oxygen content in the cerebral venous blood (Brodersen *et al.*, 1973). This corresponds to the observation by Cooper and co-workers, described earlier, of an increased *oxygen tension* in cerebral tissue. Raichle and Fox, in an elegant PET study, demonstrated that during normal physiological activation of the brain blood flow, as measured by $^{15}O_2$, and glucose phosphorylation, as measured by the ^{18}F-FDG, increase in parallel, whereas oxygen consumption only increases to a minor extent (Fox and Raichle, 1986; Fox *et al.*, 1988).

Theoretical calculations suggest that a large share of the metabolic energy is spent on action potential propagation along axon collaterals (Attwell and Laughlin, 2001). However, empirical studies using simultaneous electrophysiological and hemodynamic recordings by Lauritzen and co-workers (Lauritzen, 2001) and by Logothetis and co-workers (Logothetis *et al.*, 2001) have demonstrated that the increase in flow and BOLD (blood oxygenation-level-dependent) signal reflects the increased synaptic activity and local field potentials in the dendrites, rather than a higher firing activity in the postsynaptic neurons. Thus, a release of stimulating as well as of inhibiting neurotransmitters will result in an increased metabolic turnover that increases blood flow and the BOLD signal.

3.0 METHODS

Positron emission tomography (PET) and functional magnetic resonance imaging (fMRI) are today the dominant methods for investigation of functional cerebral activation. Single photon emission computer tomography (SPECT) has features similar to PET, but has a lower resolution and is therefore less suitable for studies of functional activation. Other methods use the electrical and magnetic signal from the working brain produced by the activity in the neurons. These methods

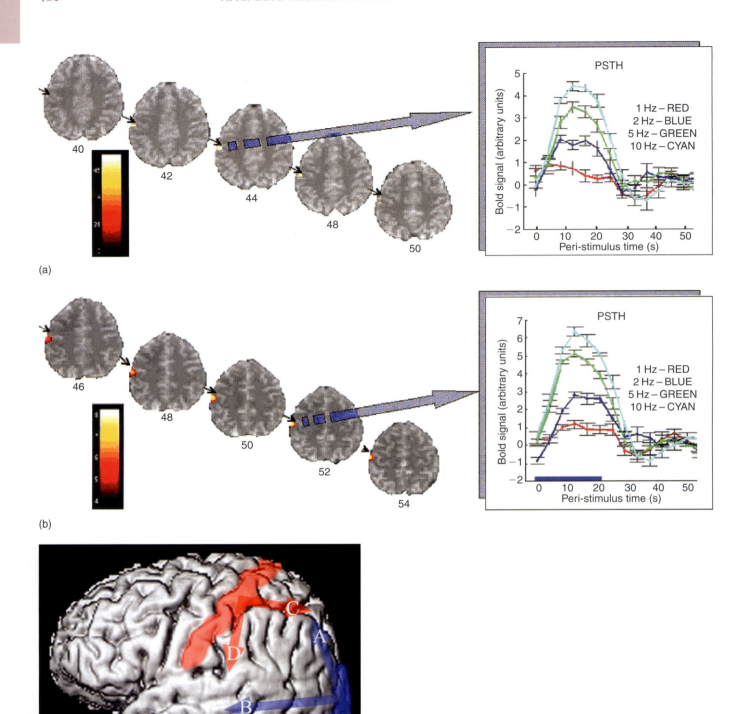

FIGURE B.2 The BOLD signal to finger stimulation. When the right finger is stimulated with a mild electrical shock, the change in blood flow can be picked up on the left hemisphere in the somatosensory body map. This is the blood oxygen-level dependent or BOLD response of fMRI. Top: Averaging brain slices. Bottom: the blood oxygenated-level dependent signal change (hemodynamic response) after the neural activation. *Source*: McConigle in Frackowiak *et al.*, 2004.

are electroencephalography (EEG) and magnetoencephalography (MEG) and feature an excellent time resolution of about 10 milliseconds at the cost of limited localizing ability. Research using EEG has gained new interest when combined with fMRI, because it takes advantage of both the spatial resolution of fMRI and the temporal resolution of EEG. MEG is a research field which is currently expanding.

All these methods manipulate behavior and measure a change in brain activity. A complementary category of methods, including lesion studies or transcranial magnetic stimulation (TMS), allows manipulation of the brain in order to measure the effect on behavior. TMS induces an electric current in the brain whose effect is either stimulatory or inhibitory for the neuronal activity, depending on the parameters of the current induced. Using such a 'virtual lesion' mode, this method can reduce the excitability of a brain area with effects that mimic a brain lesion. TMS is a promising tool for confirming brain-behavior links identified with functional imaging. If an activated brain area is indeed essential for task performance, then its inactivation should change the subject's behavior during the task.

3.1 Designing experiments

In order to understand more fully the complex interactions between brain regions, intelligent designing of activation paradigms is essential. For identification of the localization of a specific function, the task and control conditions should be matched so that the differences in brain activation patterns only reflect that specific function. At times it is very difficult, if not impossible, to control perfectly for all behavioral parameters. For instance, in a paradigm designed to identify the neural correlate of spatial attention by presenting visual stimuli at either a cued or an un-cued location, a change in activity in a brain area may as well reflect involuntary eye movements or the subject's effort to prevent a saccade towards the stimulus.

3.2 Electroencephalography (EEG)

Electroencephalography is a neurophysiological measurement of electrical activity in the brain. This recording is performed by placing electrodes either on the scalp or directly on the cortex. The resulting brainwave output is referred to as an *electroencephalogram* (EEG), originally named by the German psychiatrist Hans Berger (Berger and Gloor, 1969). Work on EEG techniques had already been performed by Richard Caton (Caton, 1875) and Vladimir Vladimirovich Pravdich-Neminsky (Pravdich-Neminsky, 1913). EEG is today used in clinical settings to assess brain damage, epilepsy and other brain disorders. In many jurisdictions around the world it is used to assess brain death. It is also a cognitive neuroscience research tool due to its superior temporal resolution and its results are often compared to other brain recording techniques.

The EEG ranges from several to about $75\,\mu V$ in the awake and healthy individual. The EEG signal as such is mostly attributable to graded postsynaptic potentials occurring in the cell body and large dendrites. The pyramidal cells of layers 3 to 5 are the major contributing units to the signal and these neurons are synchronized by rhythmic discharges from thalamic nuclei. The degree of synchronization of the underlying cortical activity is reflected in the amplitude of the EEG. Not surprisingly, most of the signal recorded in the EEG stems from the outer cortical layers near the electrode and the folded organization of the cortex in humans contributes to the electrical summation of neuronal signals rather than mutual cancellation.

The EEG recorded at the scalp represents a passive conduction of currents produced by summating activity over large neuronal aggregates. Regional desynchronization of the EEG reflects increased mutual interaction of a subset of the population engaging in 'cooperative activity' and is associated with decreases in amplitude. Thus, from the raw EEG alone it is possible – even for the untrained eye – to determine the level of synchrony. To the trained eye, it is also possible to see pathological patterns following states such as epilepsy. As can be seen in Figure B.3, it is possible to make out some basic differences in healthy and pathological brain activation.

In general, we can think of the EEG as two kinds of measures. First, *spontaneous activity* is the activity that goes on continuously in the living individual, as measured on the scalp or directly on the cortex. The measurement of this signal is what we call the encephalogram, which can be thought of as a measurement of electrical signals within a time window, but with no additional time factors. The amplitude of the EEG is about $100\,\mu V$ when measured on the scalp and about $1–2\,mV$ when measured on the surface of the brain (intracranial recording). The bandwidth of this signal is from under $1\,Hz$ to about $50\,Hz$. Figure B.3 displays different kinds of spontaneous EEG activity. Today, the EEG is used extensively for clinical purposes, especially in testing for epilepsy, but recently, the combination with imaging methods with high spatial resolution, such as fMRI, has led to renewed interest in the EEG.

The second kind of EEG measure, *evoked potentials* (EP) and *event-related potentials* (ERP) are components of the EEG that arise in response to a stimulus (e.g. auditory, somatosensory or visual input). Such signals are usually below the noise level and not normally possible to distinguish in the raw EEG output. In order to see the effects of the stimulus, one must apply a train of

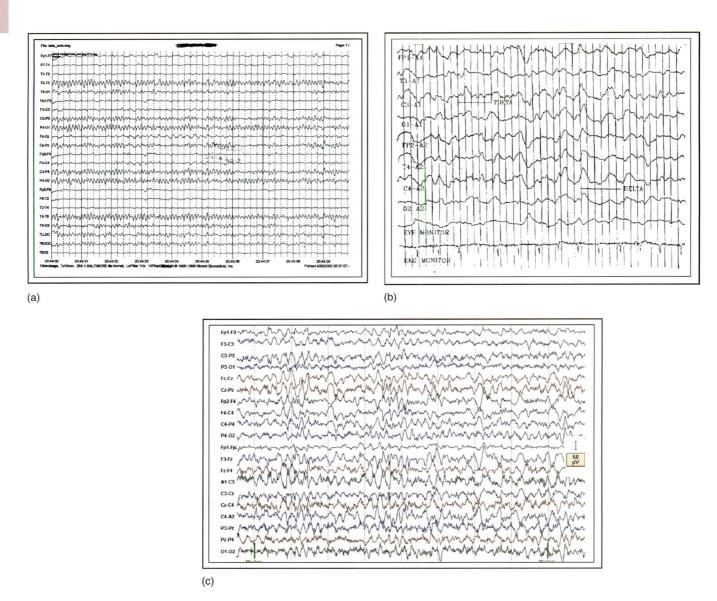

(a)

(b)

(c)

FIGURE B.3 The raw EEG in different states. (a) The record of a healthy and awake individual shows different low-amplitude and high-frequency bands of activation, indicative of rapid communication between ensembles of neurons. (b) When going to sleep the brain can operate at several different levels of sleep, ranging from rapid eye movement (REM) sleep to stages of deep sleep. Deep sleep stages display high-amplitude and low-frequency patterns, which indicate lower cooperation between and within brain areas. (c) Finally, epileptic seizures show up clearly on the EEG as both high-amplitude and relatively high-frequency patterns on all recorded channels. This demonstrates that most parts of brain are affected by the seizure. This pattern of activity is indicative of areas that get into a mutual loop of activation, eventually leading to chaos and non-information processing in the brain. *Source*: Thomas Ramsøy, Daniela Balsler, and Olaf Paulson, with permission.

similar stimuli and then average the signal for all these epochs. In this way, the signals recorded at the time of a stimulus are grouped into one category. Averaging the signal for a time frame cancels out any spontaneous fluctuation in the EEG and it is therefore possible to make out and display the signal intensity within a time frame common to all stimulus epochs. So, for a visual stimulus, such as a word, we get different waves of increase and decrease in signal intensity (Figure B.4).

Each of these components is today identified as relevant indicators of cognitive processing states. For example, EEG recordings of a subject reading a word show early increases or decreases indicative of early visual processing and the drawing of attention to the stimulus and later we find a significant peak after approximately 400 milliseconds thought to indicate semantic processing. This component is called the P400, where P = a positive signal change.

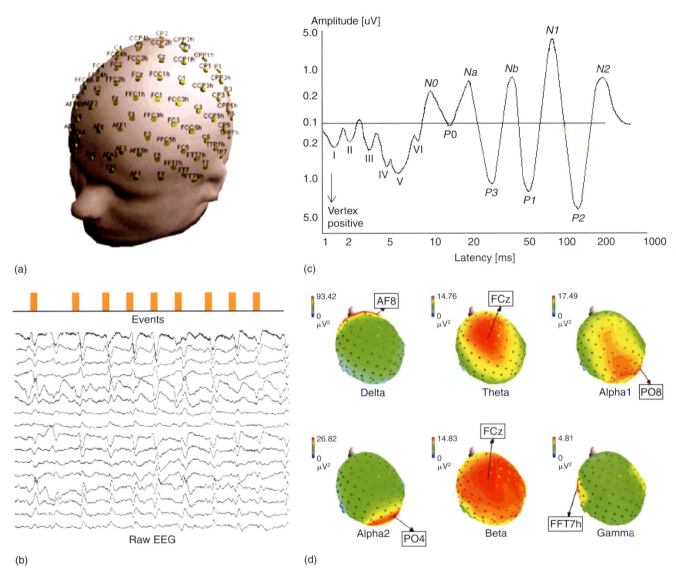

(a)

(b)

(c)

(d)

FIGURE B.4 The raw electroencephalogram and two ways to analyze it. (a) A number of electrodes are placed on specific places around the scalp according to a prespecified system. (b) The readouts from each of these electrodes, or channels, can be plotted as separate curves over time and make up the raw encephalogram. Events such as sound stimuli can be plotted on the same time curve, both to give an idea of trends in the raw EEG, but also to be used in the later averaging of the data. The events are shown for illustrative purposes. (c) The event-related analysis of the raw EEG is made by averaging the EEG signal changes at the time interval around each stimulus event. By averaging the signal spontaneous activation is cancelled out, while the signal change common to all stimulus events will be visible. In this way, several components have been determined. These include early positive or negative peaks thought to involve subcortical activations (e.g. from the brainstem) and later onsets thought to involve more elaborate, cognitive processes. An example is the P400 component (P400 = positive peak around 400 milliseconds after stimulus onset, not shown here), which is thought to be an indicator of semantic processing. Finally, more recent developments have made it possible to analyze the data both in terms of the EEG bandwidths during a period and the relative spatial localization of these. (d) The EEG power spectrum topography shows the average bandwidths at rest. As can be seen, delta activity is focal at the prefrontal site and maximal at the AF8 electrode site. Theta activity is found at the frontal midline area, maximal at the FCz electrode site. Alpha-1 activity was centered on the parietal-occipital midline area and maximal at the PO8 electrode site. Alpha-2 activity was focal at the occipital area and maximal at the PO4 electrode site. Beta activity was highly diffused across the scalp and a maximal site at the FCz electrode site was selected. Gamma activity was focal at bilateral temporal areas and maximal at FFT7h electrode site. *Source*: (a) & (d) Andrew *et al.*, 2006; (b) & (c) chapter authors, with permission.

BOX B.1   The electromagnetism of meditation

A very interesting study by Lutz *et al.* (2004), using EEG, focused on the brain activity of experienced Buddhist meditators. In this study, EEG signals were recorded in expert meditators and meditation-naïve control subjects during normal resting phases and during different stages of meditation. Three task stages were used: baseline rest, meditative state and a pause stage between meditative states. Lutz *et al.* found that, during meditation, the group of experienced meditators had a dramatically higher level of gamma-band oscillations. The researchers also found a long-distance phase synchrony between frontal and parietal areas in the brain. From these results, Lutz *et al.* speculate that meditative training enhances the integration of distant brain areas. Interestingly, the results also showed that the brain activation even at rest before meditation practice differed between the expert and naïve groups. This indicates that substantial meditative experience can alter the workings of the brain, although at present we can only speculate at the precise cause and effect relationships.

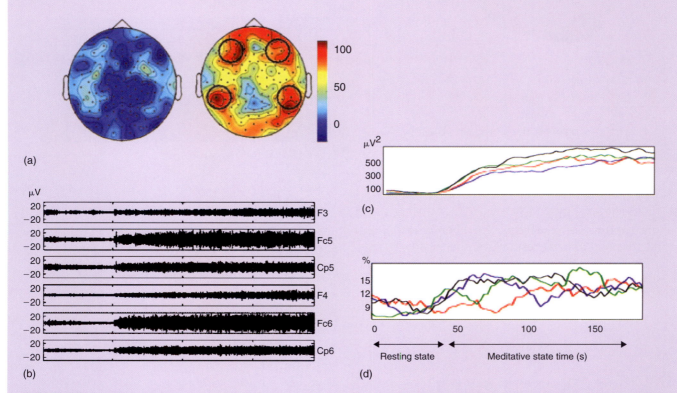

FIGURE B.5   Measuring the brain effects of meditation: the study of Lutz *et al.* (2004) shows that the absolute gamma power during mental training is much higher in practicing meditators (right) as compared to non-meditating controls (left). The color scale indicates the percentage of subjects in each group that had an increase of gamma activity during the mental training. *Source*: Lutz *et al.*, 2004.

The ERP shows how it is possible to identify specific activation patterns within the brain according to the changes in signal intensities across time. Although EEG is traditionally thought of as superior in temporal resolution but with poor spatial resolution, continuous technical developments have improved the spatial resolution dramatically. Today, EEG is performed by applying hundreds of electrodes on the scalp, typically by using a head cap with predefined positions. As a research tool, EP/ERP can thus provide valuable information about both the precise timing and now also the gross cortical distribution of the activity generated during mental activity.

3.2.1 Intracranial EEG and deep electrodes

Not all EEG recordings are done from the outside of the skull. In some cases, it is also possible to record the electrical properties directly from the brain itself. There are, in general, two ways of doing this: by laying an intracranial grid of electrodes on the surface of a part of the brain; or by using deep electrodes directly into the brain. Both methods are invasive and are only applied in humans as part of a clinical evaluation, typically in the search for epileptic foci for surgical planning. In this clinical procedure, the surgeons need to know not only where the epileptic seizure initiates, but also where other important cognitive functions are located. If possible, surgeons avoid ablating brain tissue that is involved in a cognitive function such as memory or language. Therefore, the patient needs to be awake during the test, both in order to respond to the set of cognitive tasks that are applied and, in order to report any changes occurring during the test. While the electrodes are implanted, researchers are sometimes allowed a limited time to do scientific testing on these patients.

In a study of intracranial deep electrodes in humans, Quiroga and colleagues (Quiroga *et al.*, 2005) recorded the response of single neurons in the medial temporal lobe when subjects saw images of faces and objects. Remarkably, a subset of the neurons responded selectively to strikingly different pictures of specific famous people, landmarks or objects. In other words, they found that one neuron responded specifically to pictures of actress Jennifer Aniston, another neuron responded significantly more to pictures of actress Halle Berry and yet another neuron responded most to the Sydney Opera House (Figure B.6). This finding demonstrates an invariant, sparse and explicit neural code that may be important in turning visual percepts into memories.

While deep electrodes are implanted in the brain, it is possible to reverse the electrical current and stimulate the same area of the brain. In this way, one may grossly activate a highly specific region of the brain. By using this method, Barbeau and colleagues (Barbeau *et al.*, 2005) found a difference in the subjective reports of subjects when stimulating the hippocampus or the adjacent perirhinal cortex, both areas within the medial temporal lobe. When stimulating the hippocampus, their patient reported full-blown episodic memories in rich detail and with scenic and episodic content. When stimulating the perirhinal cortex (Figure B.7), the patient reported recollection of a specific object that later developed into a full-blown episodic memory. While this study is limited by only using a few experimental stimulations and therefore should be interpreted with caution, the results indicate that areas within the medial temporal lobe play different roles in memory and recall. It seems that the hippocampus is involved in the recall of full episodic memories, while the perirhinal cortex is more involved in specific object memory.

Intracranial imaging is also done on non-human primates such as the macaque monkey. This animal 'model' of the human cognitive system allows scientists to further their exploration of the neural correlates of cognitive functions. Important discoveries have been made using this approach, such as the findings of mirror neurons made by Gallese and colleagues (Gallese *et al.*, 1996).

Together, EEG presents a whole range of different recording (and stimulation) approaches that each makes significant contribution to the study of brain-mind relationships. With its superior temporal resolution, the EEG provides valuable information to combine with other imaging techniques that have a high spatial resolution. We will return to the combination of such data at the end of this Appendix.

3.3 Magnetoencephalography (MEG)

Magnetoencephalography (MEG) is the measurement of the magnetic fields produced by electrical activity in the brain, usually recorded from outside the skull. It is a highly interesting tool for investigation of functional activation of and connectivity in the brain. The spatial resolution with the most advanced instruments comes down to a few millimeters and the temporal resolution is, as with EEG, down to milliseconds. This allows us to record how activation spreads from one region to another.

3.3.1 The principles of MEG

The physical principles of MEG are based on the old observation from H.C. Ørsted from 1820, that an electrical current in a wire will generate a surrounding circular magnetic field. Since impulses propagating in the brain are generated by electrical currents, an abundant amount of small local magnetic fields will be generated. The magnetic field from a single neuron is far below detection level; however, the combined fields from a region of about 50 000 active neurons can give rise to a net magnetic field that is measurable.

Let us for simplicity consider a single electrical wire which will be surrounded by a circular magnetic field

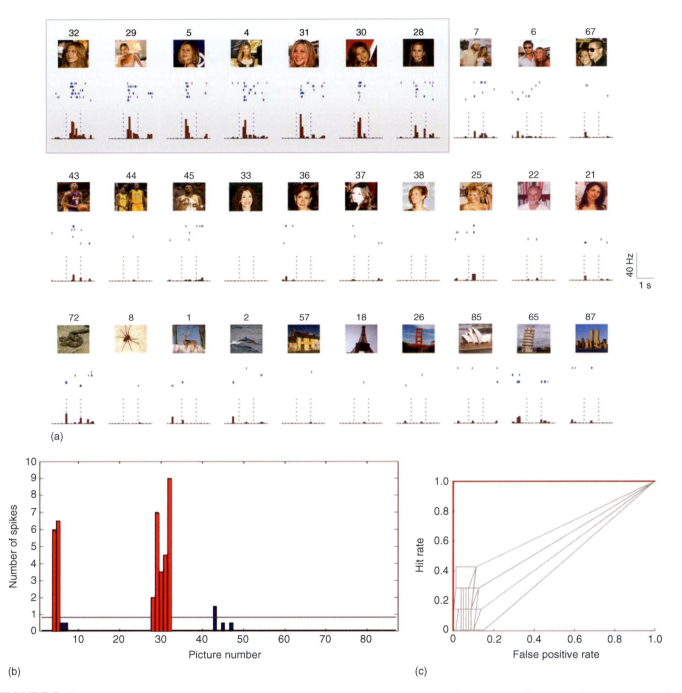

FIGURE B.6 Quiroga and colleagues (Quiroga *et al.*, 2005) found a neuron in the left posterior hippocampus that selectively responded to different views of the actress Jennifer Aniston. Responses in 30 of a total of 87 images are shown (inset: the responses to images of Jennifer Aniston). Numbers indicate the image number; graph indicates number of neural spikes recorded. Similar findings were made in other neurons for other stimuli, including the actress Hale Berry and the Sidney Opera House. *Source*: Quiroga *et al.*, 2005.

orthogonal to the electrical current. If it corresponds to an electrical current in the brain, an electrical dipole, parallel to the surface of the skull, then the magnetic field will exit the skull on one side of the current and re-enter the skull on the other side. Changes in the electrical current in the brain and in the magnetic field will induce an electrical current in a circular lead placed parallel to the surface of the skull. The induced

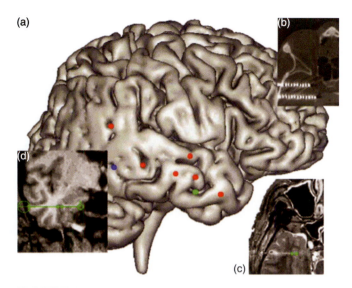

FIGURE B.7 The stimulation of perirhinal cortex in object memory. (a) Image reconstruction of the patient's brain with the site of implantation of each electrode. The green line shows the implantation site of the electrode running through the perirhinal region. Red and blue dots indicate other electrode implantation points in the same brain. (b) A CT-scan showing contact location of the electrodes (white dotted lines). (c) Axial MRI structural scan showing the thin trace left by the electrode (white line). (d) Coronal MRI scan showing the stimulation site (green dots) in the depth of the occipitotemporal sulcus of the right temporal lobe, an area that corresponds to the perirhinal region (see text for discussion). *Source*: Barbeau *et al.*, 2005.

current will change direction if the lead is moved from one side to the other of the current in the brain (Figure B.8). If, by contrast, an electrical current in the brain is perpendicular to the surface of the skull, then no magnetic gradients are produced outside the skull and an external lead will remain silent.

The electromagnetic signals in the brain derive from the net effect of ionic currents in the dendrites of neurons and in the extracellular space as return currents during impulse propagation and synaptic transmission. Action potentials do not produce significant fields as the currents associated with action potentials flow in opposite directions canceling out the magnetic fields.

From the above considerations on the direction of the electrical dipoles and generated magnetic fields, it appears that it is the neurons located in the wall of the sulci of the cortex with orientations parallel to the surface of the head that project measurable portions of their magnetic fields outside of the head. Thus, neurons

on the top and in the bottom of the sulci will have an orientation which yields magnetic fields with minimal gradients outside the skull and will not be recordable. Still, deviation of the radial direction of the convex source by only 10 to 20 degrees can be enough to give a detectable signal. Therefore, it seems likely that especially the convex sources near the skull and thus near the recording apparatus contribute significantly to the MEG signals.

3.3.2 MEG recording

The magnetic signal emitted from the working brain is extremely small, of a few femtoteslas ($1\,\text{fT} = 10^{-15}\,\text{T}$[1]). Therefore, extremely sensitive and expensive devices such as the Superconducting Quantum Interference Device (SQUID) are used. The SQUID is an ultrasensitive detector of magnetic flux. It acts as a current-to-voltage converter that provides the system with sufficient sensitivity to detect neuromagnetic signals. In order to record these weak magnetic fields, shielding from external magnetic signals, including the Earth's magnetic field, is necessary. An appropriate magnetically shielded room can be constructed from mu-metal, which is effective at reducing high-frequency noise, while noise cancellation algorithms reduce low-frequency common mode signals. With proper shielding, the SQUID acts as a low-noise, high-gain current-to-voltage converter that provides the system with sufficient sensitivity to detect neuromagnetic signals of only a few femto Tesla in magnitude.

The first detection of magnetic rhythm from the brain dates back nearly 40 years and used an induction coil magnetometer in a magnetically shielded room (Cohen, 1968). Modern systems have now up to about 300 SQUID channels placed around the head and have a noise level of around 5 to 7 femtoteslas. This has to be compared to an overall magnetic field of the brain of around 100 to 1000 femtoteslas.

3.3.3 Data analysis

The primary technical difficulty with MEG is that the problem of inferring changes in the brain from magnetic measurements outside the head (the 'inverse problem') does not, in general, have a unique solution.

---

[1] The tesla is the value of the total magnetic flux (a magnet's 'power') divided by area. Hence, reducing the affected area will generally increase the magnetic flux density. The tesla is a unit to define the intensity (density) of a magnetic field. The Earth's magnetic field at latitude 50° is 58 μT ($5.8 \times 10^{-5}\,\text{T}$) and on the equator at a latitude of 0° is 31 μT ($3.1 \times 10^{-5}\,\text{T}$).

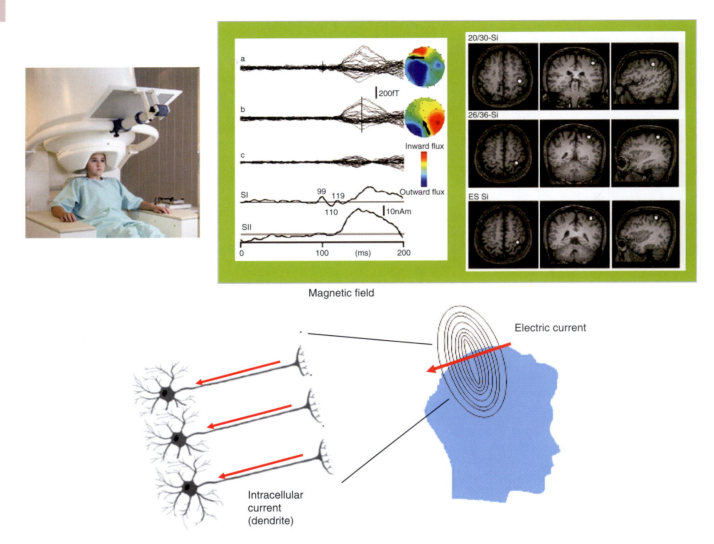

FIGURE B.8 Magnetoencephalography and its analyses. The subject is placed in the scanner that has a large set of shielded sensors. The signals themselves derive from the net effect of ionic currents flowing in the dendrites of neurons during synaptic transmission and in the extracellular medium as return currents (bottom). Action potentials do not produce an observable field because the currents associated with action potentials flow in opposite directions and the magnetic fields cancel out. Inset left: magnetic fields following painful (epidermal) stimulation where (a) shows the recorded data; (b) and (c) displays residual magnetic fields obtained after filtering the somatosensory processing signals from the recorded data. The bottom two lines show the time course of the source strengths during the painful stimulation. Inset right: source locations of the MEG data overlaid on MR images. *Source*: 4D Neuroimaging, San Diego, with permission.

The problem of finding the best solution is itself the subject of intensive research today. Adequate solutions can be derived using models involving prior knowledge of brain activity and the characteristics of the head, as well as localization algorithms. It is believed by some researchers in the field that more complex but realistic source and head models increase the quality of a solution. However, this also increases the opportunity for local minima and potentially makes the numeric conditioning of the system worse, thus increasing the effects of model errors. Many experiments use simple models, reducing possible sources of error and decreasing the computation time to find a solution. Localization algorithms make use of the given source and head models to find a likely location for an underlying focal field generator. An alternative methodology involves performing an independent component analysis first, in order to sort out the individual sources, and then localizing the separated sources individually. This method has been shown to

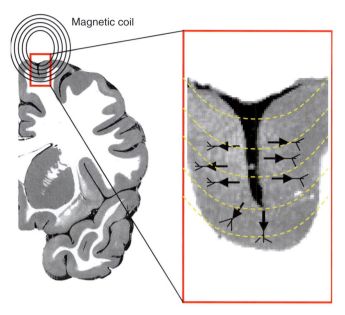

Magnetic coil

FIGURE B.9 The magnetic gradient of the neurons at the top and bottom of a sulcus do not have an orientation that maximizes their contribution to the MEG recording. The magnetic changes occurring in neurons on the sulci walls are better measurable by the MEG apparatus. Source: Adams *et al.*, 2004.

improve the signal-to-noise ratio of the data by correctly separating non-neuronal noise sources from neuronal sources, and has shown promise in segregating focal neuronal sources.

Generally, localization algorithms operate by successive refinement. The system is initialized with a first guess. Then a loop is entered, in which a forward model is used to generate the magnetic field that would result from the current guess and the guess then adjusted to reduce the difference between this estimated field and the measured field. This process is repeated until a convergence between estimated and measured field is reached.

Another approach is to ignore the inverse problem and use an estimation algorithm to localize sources. One such approach is the second-order technique known as *synthetic aperture magnetometry* (SAM), which uses a linear weighting of the sensor channels to focus the array on a given target location. This approach, also known as 'beamforming', has an advantage over more traditional source localization techniques because most sources in the brain are distributed and cannot be well described with a point source such as a current dipole.

A solution can then be combined with MRI images to create *magnetic source images* (MSI). The two sets of

data are combined by measuring the location of a common set of fiducial points marked during MRI with lipid markers and marked during MEG with electrified coils of wire that give off magnetic fields. The locations of the fiducial points in each data set are then used to define a common coordinate system so that superimposing ('co-registering') the functional MEG data onto the structural MRI data is possible.

A criticism of the use of this technique in clinical practice is that it produces colored areas with definite boundaries superimposed upon an MRI scan: the untrained viewer may not realize that the colors do not represent a physiological certainty, because of the relatively low spatial resolution of MEG, but rather a probability cloud derived from statistical processes. However, when the magnetic source image corroborates other data, it can be of clinical utility.

3.3.4 Relation to other recording modalities

MEG has been in development since the 1970s but has been greatly aided by recent advances in computing algorithms and hardware and promises good spatial resolution and extremely high temporal resolution (better than 1 ms). Since MEG takes its measurements directly from the activity of the neurons themselves, its temporal resolution is comparable with that of intracranial electrodes. MEG's strengths complement those of other brain activity measurement techniques such as EEG, PET and fMRI whose strengths, in turn, complement MEG. Other important strengths to note about MEG are that the biosignals it measures are not distorted by the skull, as in EEG (unless magnetic metal implants are present) and that it is completely noninvasive, as opposed to PET.

In research, the primary use of MEG is the measurement of time courses of activity as these courses cannot be measured using fMRI. Due to various technical and methodological difficulties in localization of sources using MEG, its use in creating functional maps of human cortex plays a secondary role, as verification of any proposed maps would require verification using other techniques before they would be widely accepted in the brain mapping community.

The clinical uses of MEG have until now essentially been limited to investigation of special cases for detecting and localizing seizure activity in patients with epilepsy and in localizing cortical pathology for surgical planning in patients with brain tumors or intractable epilepsy.

BOX B.2   Phantom limb sensation and brain plasticity

A good example of the application of MEG to study psychological or perceptual issues is a study done by Yang *et al.* (Yang *et al.*, 1994) (see also Ramachandran and Hirstein 1998; Ramachandran and Rogers-Ramachandran 2000). These researchers studied the plastic changes that occur in the brain after amputation of a limb. Phantom limb sensations occur in almost all people who have a limb amputated. What this means is that people who lose their arm are still experiencing sensations from that arm, although it is not there! This phenomenon has been known throughout history – e.g. by Lord Nelson, whose phantom arm led him and others to think that the phantom was proof that the immaterial soul could exist without the physical body. Today, we are able to measure changes occurring in the brain of those unfortunate people.

It is possible to produce phantom limb sensations in these patients. For example, in an arm amputee, one may produce a phantom arm sensation by tickling the chin or jaw on the face on the same side as the amputation. By doing this, Yang *et al.* found that those areas that would normally be activated by stimuli to an intact arm now became activated by stimuli to either the face or the amputation stump on the patient. These findings demonstrate that amputation leads to a remapping of the primary somatosensory cortex and that one brain area can alter its functional connections, even in adults. Today, it is believed that amputation leads to three steps of change in the somatosensory cortex. First, amputation leads to a loss of input from the original sensory area. This then leads to functional changes in already existing connections within the somatosensory cortex. Finally, as these functional changes continue, they will eventually lead to changes in the physical connectivity between neurons.

Normally, adjacent areas that represent different body parts – e.g. face and hand areas – have tight interconnections. This facilitates the representations to be specific, in saying both 'this is input from the hand' and 'this is *not* input from the face'. When an arm is amputated (or even disabled for a prolonged time), it leads to such a remapping of the somatosensory cortex. This was clearly demonstrated by Yang *et al.*'s MEG study.

In the study by Yang and colleagues, stimulation of the face led to phantom sensations and was correlated to co-activation of both the face and hand representation areas in the somatosensory cortex. A nice feature in this study is that the non-affected hemisphere serves as a control condition. That is, in addition to looking at other, non-amputated subjects, we can also compare the activation between the hemispheres. The study by Yang *et al.* is today considered to be among the very first studies to demonstrate plastic changes in the human brain.

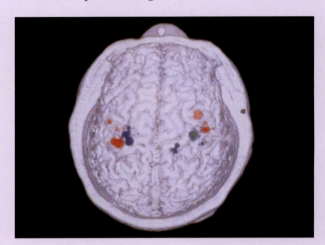

FIGURE B.10   Normally, adjacent areas that represent different body parts, for example the face and hand areas, are tightly interconnected. This helps make the representations highly specific, in saying both, 'this is input from the hand' and 'this is *not* input from the face'. When an arm is amputated (or even disabled for a long time), it leads to such a remapping of the somatosensory cortex. This was clearly demonstrated by Yang *et al.*'s 1994 MEG study, where they reported that stimulation of the face led to phantom sensations in the missing (amputated) hand, which correlated to co-activation of both the face and hand representation areas in the somatosensory cortex. Clearly, a remapping had occurred in this patient. *Source*: Yang *et al.*, 1994.

3.4 Single photon emission computed tomography (SPECT)

Single photon emission tomography (SPECT) is an emission tomographic method that builds on the detection of gamma rays emitted from radiolabeled compounds. A *collimator* is a physical filter that permits only gamma rays of a specific spatial trajectory to reach the detector. Most commonly, a collimator is a lead structure that is interposed between the subject and the detector. The collimator contains many holes of sufficiently long and narrow dimensions so that only photons of a parallel trajectory are allowed through. Collimation is less

efficient than coincidence detection because many potentially informative photons are lost. However, the sensitivity of SPECT has been largely enhanced by advances in collimator design and an increase in the number of detectors.

Most SPECT systems available in clinical practice are of the type known as rotating gamma cameras. These are well suited for clinical nuclear medicine uses in the body as a whole, but their limited resolution, which also depends on the distance from the detector, precludes their wide use in brain research. 'Head-dedicated' scanners have a circular array of detectors with focused collimators; alternatively, mobile 3-headed detector blocks can rotate around the head as closely as possible. These can give high-resolution images, with spatial resolutions approaching those with PET (see next section).

The radioisotopes that are most frequently used for measurement of cerebral blood flow include ^{99}Tc-HMPAO, ^{99}Tc-ECD and ^{123}IMP. These radioisotopes have, due to their long half-lives[2] (^{99}Tc: 6 hours, ^{123}I: 13 hours) limited values in terms of identifying activated brain regions. There are, however, a few situations where SPECT is superior to PET, for instance when immediate imaging is needed. The trace ^{133}Xe, or xenon, for blood flow recording should also be mentioned as it was more frequently used in previous years. Xenon is an inert gas which, to some extent, is soluble in tissue and which is highly diffusible. It can thus be applied with the inspiratory air and will be taken up by and cleared from the organs in proportion to the blood flow. ^{133}Xe has a physical half-life of 5 days but, as most of it is cleared from the organism when the blood passes through the lungs, the biological half-life will be much shorter and allow repeated measurements after only 15 minutes.

A basic difference between SPECT and PET is that, in the former method, the isotopes used for radiolabeling emit single photons. This means that when calculating the source, the localization of the source of each detected photon must take into account both the energy and the trajectory of individual photons. Collimators mean that SPECT can have good spatial resolution but at the expense of sensitivity, i.e. the fraction of all photon emissions which result in a recorded event. Estimates of the effect of attenuation by intervening tissues are done mathematically (attenuation correction). With PET, absolute quantification of regional cerebral blood flow (rCBF) can be made if arterial concentrations of radiotracer are measured or otherwise known. With most SPECT flow tracers, except for ^{133}Xe, measures are given in terms of relative rCBF, in which the region of interest is compared with some reference area, assumed to be unaltered (most often cerebellum) or to the mean of the whole-brain rCBF value.

Whereas the ^{133}Xe inhalation technique yields quantitatively correct images of rCBF, image resolution with ^{133}Xe is relatively poor as the dynamic rapid uptake and clearance from the organs only allows for shorter recording time. Appropriate radiolabeled molecules must, in order to reflect CBF, cross the blood–brain barrier quickly and their uptake must be in proportion to CBF. Currently used tracers include ^{99}technetium-hexamethylpro-pyleneaminoxime (^{99}Tc-HMPAO) and ^{123}I-iodoamphetamine. About 60 per cent of HMPAO crosses the blood–brain barrier by its first passage (Strauss *et al.*, 1999) and is trapped within the brain cells where it remains for several hours. This allows for rCBF imaging to be 'taken' at the time of injection (or rather, within 3–4 minutes after intravenous injection) and can subsequently be 'stored' and recorded up to several hours later.

3.5 Positron emission tomography (PET)

A modern PET scanner has more than 10 000 scintillation detectors registering the decay of positron emitting isotopes. When these isotopes decay, the emitted positron will immediately meet a normal electron which merges and forms two gamma rays with energy of 511 keV[3] and an angle of precisely 180° relative to each other. When two detectors in the scanner register a photon of 511 keV exactly simultaneously then a decay must have occurred on the line connecting these two detectors. At normal counting rates, the chance that two detectors simultaneously record two photons originating from two different positron decays is unlikely. Thus, it becomes possible to reconstruct a three-dimensional picture of the distribution of the isotope in the field of view of the PET camera.

The most used isotope compound for PET measurement of functional brain activation is $H_2^{15}O$. ^{15}O is a positron emitting isotope with a half-life of only 2 minutes. For that reason, the isotope has to be produced in a cyclotron in the immediate vicinity of the PET camera. $H_2^{15}O$ is injected intravenously and will reach the brain regions in proportion to the blood supply. Although not completely diffusible, water is highly diffusible across the blood–brain barrier and most of the water arriving at the vascular bed in the brain will diffuse into the tissue. Later washout of the radiolabeled water from the brain will take place, also in proportion to the perfusion. Thereby it becomes possible to calculate cerebral blood flow. A quantitative calculation is possible; however, in many studies of functional activation only relative changes are recorded. Due to the fast decay of ^{15}O, the radiation dose to the subject investigated is rather low, especially when using a PET scanner in 3D mode (three

---

[2]The half-life of a quantity subject to exponential decay is the time required for the quantity to fall to half of its initial value. The concept originated in the study of radioactive decay, but it now also occurs in many other fields.

[3]An electronvolt (eV) is the amount of kinetic energy gained by a single unbound electron when it passes through an electrostatic potential difference of one volt, in vacuum. The kilo-electronvolt (keV) is 1000 eV.

dimensional recording with high counting efficiency). It is possible to make about 24 activation studies with a radiation exposure of only approximately two times the yearly background radiation. Since PET relies on radioactive compounds, there are specific ethical limitations to how high a dose a subject can be given within a given period of time. As a result, weight is put on the radioactive property when choosing between compounds in a study.

Another positron emitting isotope which has been used for functional activation studies is ^{10}C in the form of ^{10}C carbon dioxide (Law *et al.*, 2001). The half-life of ^{10}C is only 19 seconds yielding a very low exposure for radiation and thus allowing for up to 64 PET scans with the same radiation exposure as for 12 scans using $H_2^{15}O$. The short half-life of ^{10}C also allows repeated measurements with shorter intervals or following the activation during continuous infusion at the tracer. $^{10}CO_2$ has only gained limited use, probably because an even higher time resolution without exposure to radioactivity can be obtained with fMRI. Still, the $^{10}CO_2$ method might have special interest in areas where fMRI is hampered with susceptibility artifacts, as for instance close to the nasal sinuses, such as the orbitofrontal cortex.

More recently, advances have been made toward functional imaging of neurotransmission; exciting prospects have recently emerged for *in vivo* monitoring of the brain's own signaling in terms of neurotransmitter release. A prime example is the PET demonstration of competition effects between endogenous dopamine and the radiolabeled dopamine D2 receptor antagonist ^{11}C-raclopride or the SPECT tracer ^{123}I-IBZM (see Figure B.12). Striatal radioligand binding decreased as the dopamine level increased under a successful video game session (Koepp *et al.*, 1998). So far, the concept has primarily been used in conjunction with D2 receptor imaging and, in spite of attempts to identify PET tracers sensitive to, e.g. serotonin release (Pinborg *et al.*, 2004), a well-suited tracer still needs to be identified.

3.5.1 Image analysis

An image analysis approach frequently used to compare groups is the 'region of interest' (ROI) technique. In this, each subject's image is shown on a visual display unit and a tracker ball or pen is used to outline regions of interest. The mean activity for each region for the experimental subjects would then be compared with that of the controls. The main drawback with this technique is that it takes no account of structural brain differences

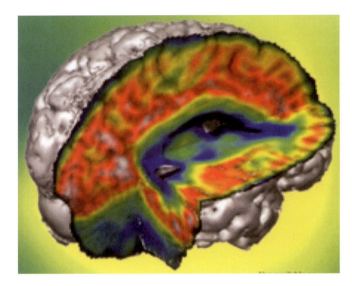

FIGURE B.11   5-HT2A receptor binding as measured with PET and co-registered to a structural MRI image. *Source*: Adams *et al.*, 2004.

which might exist between subjects. Using a human operator to decide the boundaries of regions of interest on the functional image requires the assumption that the operator knows where to place the boundaries. On a functional image, the inference that structural boundaries can be identified is obviously a circular one. There are two solutions to this problem. The first is to obtain structural imaging data as well as functional imaging data for each subject. Then, data-processing techniques can be used to 'co-register' the imaging data on a voxel-by-voxel basis, such that a superimposed map for each subject is obtained. The PET image in Figure B.11 shows a 3D rendered image of a co-registered PET and MRI image.

3.6 Magnetic resonance imaging (MRI)

MRI is an imaging technique used primarily in medical settings to produce high quality images of the inside of the human body. It is based on the principles of nuclear magnetic resonance, which is a spectroscopic technique used by scientists to obtain information about the chemical and physical properties of molecules. As such, MRI started out as a tomographic imaging technique – a method for obtaining pictures of the interior of the body. Today, MRI has advanced far beyond this and now represents a battery of different approaches that can measure the structure, function, connectivity and chemistry of any part of the body.

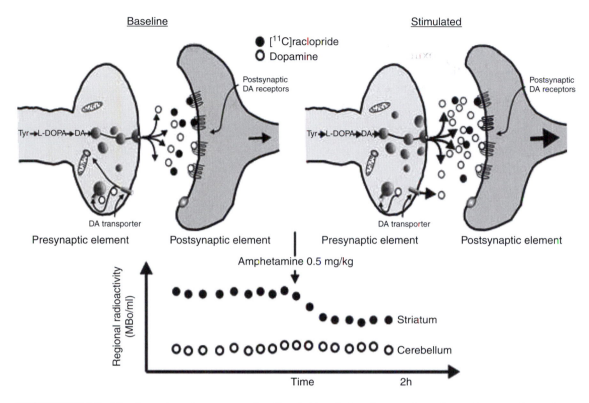

FIGURE B.12 The dopaminergic synapse at baseline (left) and after pharmacological stimulation with amphetamine. Bottom panel shows 11C-raclopride binding levels (in a steady-state approach) as dopamine levels increase. *Source*: Laruelle, 2000.

MRI is based on the absorption and emission of energy in the radio frequency range of the electromagnetic spectrum. The human body is mostly made of fat and water – body tissues that have many hydrogen atoms. As such, the human body consists of about 65 per cent hydrogen atoms. These hydrogen nuclei form the very basis for the signal in MRI. A voxel is a volume element that represents a value in 3D space. This is analogous to a pixel, which represents 2D image data. Voxels are frequently used in the visualization and analysis of medical and scientific data. In brain imaging, the brain is divided into a number of voxels and within each voxel one can do different kinds of statistical testing. Each voxel (Figure B.14) in the human body contains one or more tissues. Zooming in on the voxel reveals cells and within each cell there are water molecules. Each water molecule consists of one oxygen atom and two hydrogen atoms. If we zoom into one of the hydrogen atoms past the electron cloud we see a nucleus comprised of a single proton.

In a magnetic field, such as the MR scanner, the magnetic orientation of each hydrogen atom is aligned to the magnetic field and spins around this orientation (Figure B.15b and c). If a brief electromagnetic (radiofrequency) pulse is applied, it temporarily distorts the atom's alignment to the magnetic field (Figure B.15d). When the radiofrequency pulse ends, the atoms start to realign to the magnetic field, a process called *relaxation* (Figure B.15e). It is during this phase that the atom loses its own energy by emitting its own energy, providing information about the environment. The relaxation occurs in two dimensions: Time-1 and Time-2. The realignment with the magnetic field is termed *longitudinal relaxation* and the time in milliseconds required for a certain percentage of the tissue nuclei to realign is termed 'Time 1' or T1. This is the basis of T1-weighted imaging, which produces the most well-known structural images in MRI. T2-weighted imaging relies upon local dephasing of spins following the application of a transverse energy pulse; this *transverse relaxation time* is termed 'Time 2' or T2.

The T1 and T2 constants provide the basis for most medical imaging. In different parts of the body, such as the brain, different tissues alter the speed in which T1

BOX B.3   Altered neurochemistry in psychiatric disease

In a study by Adams *et al.* (2005) patients suffering from obsessive-compulsive disorder (OCD) were scanned for the binding of serotonin in the brain (using the [^{18}H]altanserin binding to 5-HT$_{2A}$ receptors). OCD is a psychiatric condition affecting 2–3 per cent of the population worldwide and it is classified as an anxiety disorder. The symptoms include recurrent, unwanted thoughts (obsessions) and conscious, ritualized acts (compulsions), usually attempting to deal with the apprehension generated by the obsessions. OCD is often treated with a selective serotonin reuptake inhibitor (SSRI), a chemical compound that makes serotonin available in the synapse for a longer time.

When comparing a group of OCD patients to an age- and gender-matched control group, Adams and her colleagues found an increased [^{18}H]altanserin binding in the caudate nuclei. This indicates that there are more active 5-HT$_{2A}$ receptors in the OCD brain than in healthy controls. Such an up-regulation of serotonin receptors is suggested to be a compensatory mechanism due to lack of serotonin in OCD patients. The serotonin network being affected includes structures such as the orbitofrontal prefrontal cortex, thalamus, caudate nucleus and the globus pallidus.

The researchers then rescanned the patients after administering SSRI for at least 12 weeks, a treatment that would increase the amount of serotonin available in the OCD brain. The results now showed no difference between the control group and the patient group in the serotonin binding. In other words, there were not more active 5-HT$_{2A}$ receptors in the OCD groups after treatment than in the control group.

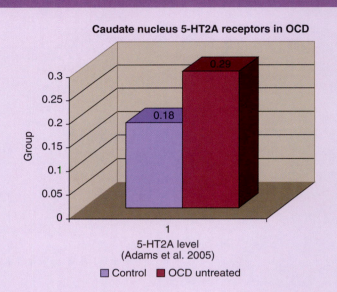

Caudate nucleus 5-HT2A receptors in OCD

5-HT2A level
(Adams et al. 2005)

□ Control   ■ OCD untreated

FIGURE B.13   5-HT$_{2A}$ receptor activation level in untreated OCD and healthy controls.

PET studies like these provide important information about the neurochemistry of psychiatric disease and they have extended this understanding by providing new evidence about the neurochemical workings of psychiatric drugs such as SSRI.

---

and T2 relaxation occurs. The three most typical tissues of the brain are gray matter (GM), white matter (WM) and cerebrospinal fluid (CSF). The influence of these tissues produces different signal intensities – contrast – that make it easy to distinguish between them. By varying different parameters during scanning, such as the rate and amplitude of the radiofrequency pulse, or the time from excitation to recording, it is possible to highlight different properties of the tissues and their differences.

This can clearly be seen in images that display the difference between T1 and T2 weighted images (Figure B.16). As the images show, a brain tumor that can be hard to see on a T1-weighted image is clearly visible on the T2-weighted image. This is due to the fact that tumors contain more water and hence give rise to a larger signal using T2-weighted imaging due to the slower longitudinal relaxation time. Since the longitudinal relaxation is fast in water, the extra water in the tumor produces no extra signal in T1-weighted imaging.

Structural scanning techniques are obvious choices when studying alterations in the brain due to aging, brain injury or degenerative disorders such as Alzheimer's disease. Based on such imaging of brain morphology (structure), it is also possible to ask questions about how the brain changes structurally as a result of development, aging and degenerative diseases. For example, Jernigan *et al.* (2001) demonstrated age-related changes in different parts of the cortex and cerebellum. By using the structural MRI images and drawing in the anatomical regions, the researchers were able to compare the relative size of these structures across the age range. As Figure B.17 illustrates, there are profound changes occurring in the brain as we age. Furthermore, there is a non-linear relationship between age and brain volume, something that contradicted the earlier views about the aging brain. Finally, a significant finding in this literature has been that there are regional differences in how the brain ages.

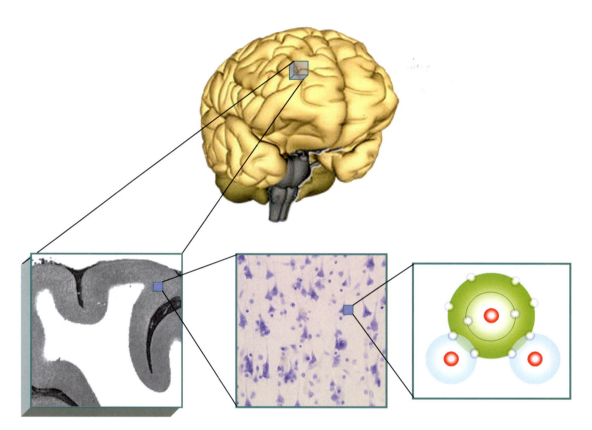

FIGURE B.14 Voxels as minimum boxes of brain space. A voxel of the brain. The voxel is a representation of a volume in three-dimensional space. In the brain, the resolution of the scanner determines how small the voxels can be. Parameters such as higher scanner field strengths increase the spatial resolution and hence the ability to represent separate structures in the brain. The brain voxel extracts the signal from one part of the brain, where the local molecular environment influences the magnetic response. The voxel chosen here is much larger than usual for MRI scans, for illustrative purposes. Source: Jones *et al.*, 2002.

3.6.1 Functional MRI

While T1- and T2-weighted images are superior at imaging the structure of the brain, MRI also offers ways to measure different functions of the brain. In general, there are two main approaches: BOLD fMRI and perfusion MRI. While the BOLD approach relies on a complex series of events that couple brain activation to vascular changes and the relative level of regional oxygenated blood, perfusion MRI measures the cerebral blood flow (CBF) or cerebral blood volume (CBV).

Blood oxygen level dependent (BOLD) fMRI is the most used and well-known way to assess brain activation with MRI. Brain activation changes the relative concentration of oxygenated and deoxygenated hemoglobin – blood with or without oxygen, respectively – in the local blood supply. While oxygenated blood is *diamagnetic* and does not change the MRI signal,

deoxygenated blood is *paramagnetic* and leads to a drop in the MRI signal. If there is more deoxygenated blood in a region it therefore leads to a drop in the BOLD signal and more oxygenated blood in the region leads to a higher signal. The BOLD response can be thought of as the combination of four processes (Figure B.18):

1 *An initial decrease* (dip) in signal caused by a combination of a negative metabolic and non-metabolic BOLD effect. In other words, when groups of neurons fire they consume more oxygen. When this happens, the local level of oxygenated blood drops and there is relatively more deoxygenated blood in that area. In addition, there is also a dilation of the blood vessels, which further increases the negative BOLD effect.

2 *A sustained signal increase* or positive BOLD effect due to an increased blood flow and a corresponding shift in the deoxy/oxyhemoglobin ratio. When the

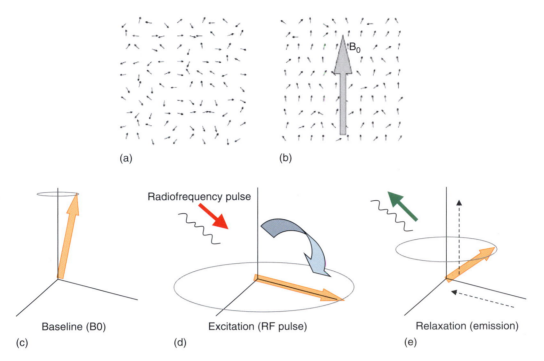

(a)   (b)

Baseline (B0)   Excitation (RF pulse)   Relaxation (emission)

(c)   (d)   (e)

FIGURE B.15   The signal that makes up the MRI. (a) Outside the scanner the atoms are oriented at random in the brain. (b) When a subject is put into the scanner, the atoms align to the magnetic field of the scanner (B_0). However, the alignment is not perfect, since neighboring atoms influence each other. (c) At such baseline, the atom spins along the y axis, i.e. the B_0 field. (d) When a radiofrequency (RF) pulse is applied the spin of the atoms is influenced and 'pushed' down. This is a state of disequilibrium and during equilibration towards the B_0 field the atom releases energy that it received from the RF pulse. (e) The local milieu of the atom, i.e. whether it is in gray matter, white matter, bone or cerebrospinal fluid, determines the speed of this *relaxation*. This is the basis of contrast in the MR image and thus what makes it possible to visualize the different tissues of the body.

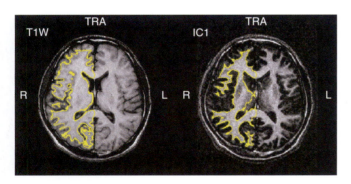

FIGURE B.16   T1 and T2 weighted images. Note that the brain tumor can be hard to see on a T1-weighted image, while it is easy to see on the T2 weighted image – it is the round dark spot on the left of the brain image on the right. *Source*: Nakai *et al.*, 2004.

neurons go back to a lower level of activation, their increased consumption of oxygenated blood drops. At the same time, influx of new oxygenated blood is increased due to the previous demand. As the blood oxygenation level increases, the signal continues to increase. This drop in demand of oxygenated blood, combined with a delayed supply of oxygenated

blood, leads to a dramatic 'overshoot' of the relative amount of oxygenated blood. This abundance leads to the main effect of the BOLD signal.

3 *A sustained signal decrease* which is induced by the return to normal flow and normal deoxy/oxy hemoglobin ratios.

4 *A post-stimulus undershoot* caused by a slow recovery in cerebral blood volume.

The 'initial dip' is thought to be the measure most closely related to the neural activation, since it relates to the first drop in signal intensity due to consumption of oxygenated blood. However, the signal changes at this stage are so small that they are mostly detectable by the use of extra strong MRI scanners, which are both expensive and not yet generally approved for human testing. It is therefore the second phase – the sustained signal increase – that is used in most BOLD fMRI studies. This signal is an indirect measure of neural activation, as it is the result of a delayed vascular overshoot of oxygenated blood, as a response of demand for oxygenated blood in a region. Although the BOLD response is an indirect and delayed measure of neural

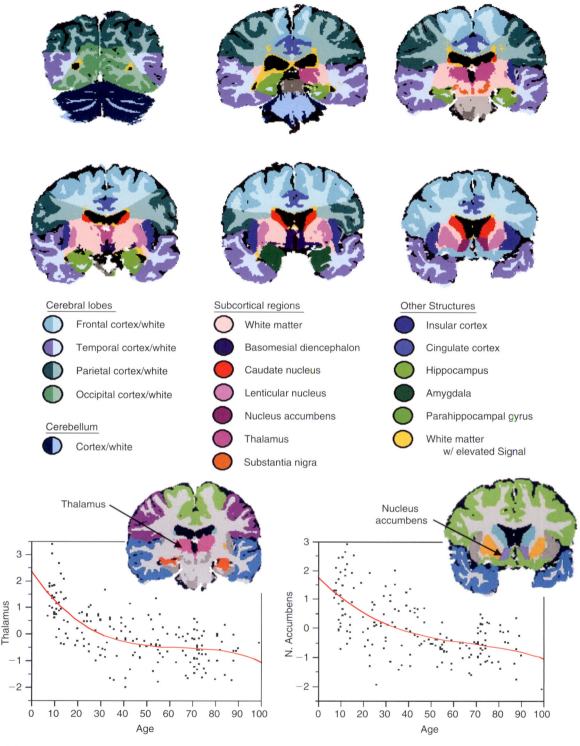

Cerebral lobes
- Frontal cortex/white
- Temporal cortex/white
- Parietal cortex/white
- Occipital cortex/white

Cerebellum
- Cortex/white

Subcortical regions
- White matter
- Basomesial diencephalon
- Caudate nucleus
- Lenticular nucleus
- Nucleus accumbens
- Thalamus
- Substantia nigra

Other Structures
- Insular cortex
- Cingulate cortex
- Hippocampus
- Amygdala
- Parahippocampal gyrus
- White matter w/ elevated Signal

FIGURE B.17 The brain ages differently in different brain regions. Top: example of structural boundaries of the brain drawn as Regions of Interest. Note that the slices consist of both gray and white matter separately; white matter is presented with a lighter color. All white matter voxels that show elevated signal in a group of elderly relative to younger adults are shown in yellow. Bottom: age-related changes in two regions of the brain in the age range 10–100 years, the thalamus and nucleus accumbens (indicated by arrow). Two major effects can be seen. First, both structures seem to have three time-related phases: (1) a precipitant loss of volume in both structures during adolescence and into young adulthood; (2) a flat-tening out and relatively stable state until late adulthood; (3) a late adulthood loss of volume. Second, the two structures show different trajectories in loss of volume. *Sources*: *top*, Jernigan *et al.*, 2001; *bottom*, Jernigan, with permission.

activation, it has been shown to have a time resolution at the millisecond scale. In addition, the method has a very high spatial resolution at below 1 mm resolution. With recent technical advances, the resolution has become even smaller than this, bringing MRI to the sub-millimeter scale.

There are different ways in which a study can be conducted using fMRI. In general, there are two main design categories – block designs and event-related designs. Following PET studies, the *block design* was the most used design in the earliest days of fMRI. Typically, a block design consists of a presentation of stimuli as blocks containing many stimuli of the same type. For example, a blocked design may be used for a sustained attention task, where the subject is instructed to press the button every time he or she sees an X on the screen among other letters. Typically, blocks are separated by equally long periods of rest, although one may design blocked experiments without rest. A block design could be used if we were interested in seeing

the difference between encoding of the identity versus the position of objects (Figure B.19).

In an *event-related design*, stimuli are presented in a random or pseudo-randomized order. Here, individual stimuli of various condition types are presented in randomized order, with variable stimulus onsets. This approach provides a means to look at different trial-relevant changes such as correct versus error responses. An event-related paradigm therefore lies closer to a traditional psychological experiment and it allows *post-hoc* analyses with trial sorting (accuracy, performance, response time etc.). This design is more efficient, because the built-in randomization ensures that preparatory or anticipatory effects (which are common in blocks designs) do not confound event-related responses. An example of an event-related paradigm can be seen in Figure B.20.

When do you choose to use either a blocked or event-related design? In general, one can say that if you want to study state-related processes (as in 'encoding state'

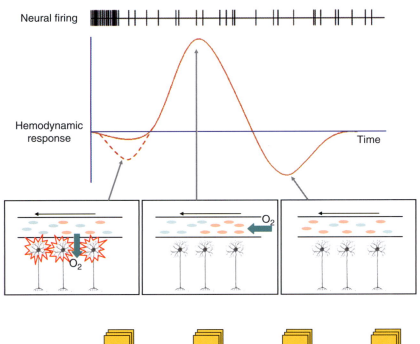

FIGURE B.18 The blood oxygenated-level dependent signal simplified in four steps. Step 1: increased neural activation leads to an increase in the consumption of oxygen from the blood, leading to a lower level of oxygenated blood and more deoxygenated blood, leading to a drop in the BOLD signal. Step 2: the vascular response to the increase in oxygen consumption leads to a dramatic increase in new, oxygenated blood at the same time as the oxygen consumption drops due to decreased levels of neuronal activation. Step 3: a normalizing of flow and deoxy/oxyhemoglobin levels (not shown). Step 4: a post-stimulus undershoot caused by the slow recovery of blood volume.

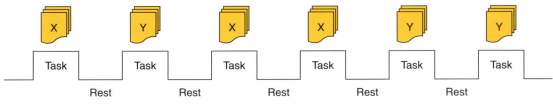

FIGURE B.19 The block design. Intervals of separate trials (X and Y) are separated by periods of rest. Note that the order of X and Y trials are random. In such a design, X trials could be 'reading letters' while Y trials could be 'reading numbers'.

versus 'retrieval state'), then a block-design would be the best choice. However, if you want to study item-related processes (as in correct versus incorrect responses), an event-related design is optimal. In certain experimental setups, it is possible to combine block and event-related designs, making it possible both to track overall differences in cognitive states, as well as being sensitive to differences from instance to instance.

When considering the experiment design, another important issue concerns the states that are compared. There are several different contrasts one can choose to make. In some cases, especially in older neuroimaging studies, a comparison is made between a specific task

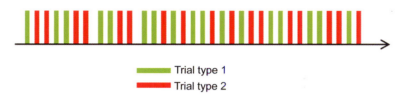

Trial type 1
Trial type 2

FIGURE B.20 The event-related design. Unlike the block design the event-related design focuses on individual trials. Hence, the order of stimuli is much more random and is good for use in psychological designs where we do not want the subject to be able to predict the order of stimuli. An example paradigm could be to present stimuli at very brief durations and ask for each stimulus presentation whether the subject has seen the stimulus. Responses will vary according to the duration of the stimulus, as well as endogenous processes (e.g. inattention). The subjects are not able to predict their next response (or stimulus experience).

BOX B.4   The BOLD nature of conscious perception

What is the neural fate of stimuli that are consciously perceived? How do these processes compare to stimuli that are processed but not experienced? Are there situations where we get vague impressions that something was presented yet we are unable to describe it? If so, how does the brain work under such perception?

The neural correlates of consciousness have been studied for well over a decade using neuroimaging tools. Such findings converge on the idea that conscious perception – as opposed to unconscious perception – involves a widespread network of areas in the brain (Baars, 2002b). This network is comprised of prefrontal and parietal cortices and very often temporal areas. It is also speculated that the spreading of information within this network occurs through cortico-thalamo-cortical loops, i.e. signals initiating in the cortex spread to widespread connections through the thalamic nuclei.

Recently, behavioral studies have documented that the usual distinction between conscious and unconscious perception has to be reconsidered (Ramsøy and Overgaard, 2004). If subjects are allowed to make use of more elaborate responses about their experiences, they consistently acknowledge that some of their experiences can best be described as vague. This condition can be thought of as the detection of something being presented without the ability to identify what it was. One question thus becomes: how does this experience relate to conscious and unconscious perception? Just as important, one may ask if there is a different neural substrate for such experiences.

In a study by Christensen *et al.* (2006), this question was examined by presenting backward masked visual stimuli at different durations while scanning subjects with fMRI. This paradigm leads to different levels of experience of the stimuli and, from the experience of previous behavioral studies (Ramsøy and Overgaard, 2004), subjects were allowed to use a non-dichotomous rating scale to report experiences as not seen, vague and clear experiences. Simple visual objects were presented for brief durations up to about 100 milliseconds. For each stimulus the subjects rated how clearly they had seen the object. This made it possible to compare unique activations for neural processes underlying clear and vague experiences.

First, the comparison between reports of *clear and no experience,* i.e. the traditional difference between conscious and unconscious perception, led to the previously seen widespread network of brain areas. This included the parietal and prefrontal cortices, the temporal lobe (fusiform gyrus), well-known for its role in object perception (Figure B.21a). Conscious perception was also shown to involve large amounts of the thalami in both hemispheres. As such this finding supports a 'globalist' account of consciousness in the brain, stating that conscious perception requires a widespread network of brain areas.

What, then, about vague experiences? When comparing reports of vague and no experience the researchers found activation in much of the same network only not as widespread, as they had found in conscious perception (Figure B.21b). By comparing states of clear experience to vague experiences, it was possible to identify the areas that are involved in turning detection into identification (Figure B.21b). From this, it seems that when we detect something, or have a vague feeling of seeing something, we use a widespread network of brain areas, with special activity found in the prefrontal cortices. If this vague perception changes into a fully conscious perception of a stimulus, the activity in the network increases dramatically both in spread and amplitude. As such, this study by Christensen *et al.* has provided novel and important new data to our understanding of conscious and unconscious perception.

(Continued)

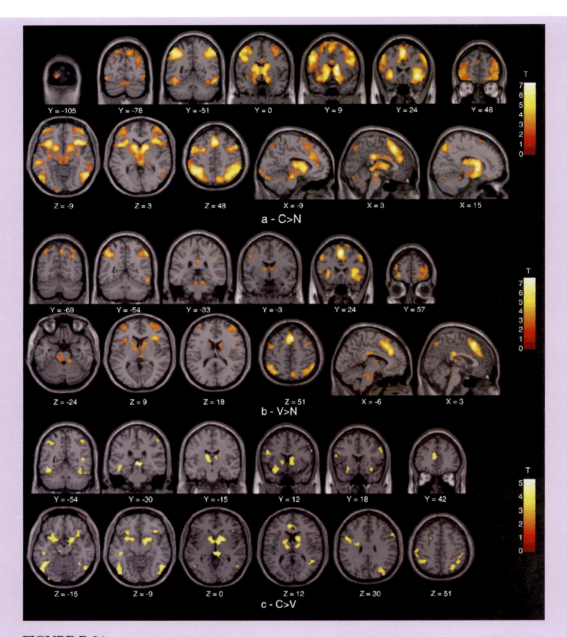

FIGURE B.21   An fMRI study by Ramsøy and colleaugues (Christensen *et al.*, 2006) shows differing networks of activation for visual stimuli that are clearly perceived versus vaguely perceived. Top two rows (a) show the significant activity for clear perception (CP) compared to no perceptual experience of the stimulus (NP). Next two rows (b) show the activity for vague or glimpse-like (VP) perceptual experience compared to NP. *Source:* Christensen *et al.*, 2006.

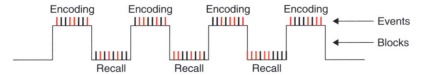

FIGURE B.22   Combining blocked and event-related designs is possible under certain circumstances. Here, analysis can focus either on the block level, e.g. comparing encoding and recall activation, or it can use the behavioral data from a recall phase to look at the neuronal activation within the encoding blocks for the instances of successful encoding only (i.e. ignoring data for stimuli that were later forgotten).

TABLE B1   Different designs for neuroimaging studies

Within-subject designs	*Examples*
Different processing states	Reading words aloud versus self-generation of words
Compare effects of contents during same state	Encoding of faces versus houses
Longitudinal study	Test-retest of the same cognitive function
	• Learning effects
	• Aging effects
	• Disease effects (only for diseases that changes over time)

Between-subject designs	*Examples*
Manipulation effects	Attention processing in ecstasy abusers versus non-users
Training effects	Effect of juggling training on motor cortex activation
Patients and controls	Working memory function in schizophrenic patients versus healthy controls
Different groups of patients	Encoding in patients with Alzheimer's disease versus patients with semantic dementia

and a rest period (see Figure B.19). Today, it is more usual to compare two or more active states. In general, we can distinguish between within-subject comparisons and between-subject comparisons. In *within-subject designs*, a comparison can be made between two different processing states, between different contents during a given state, or as effects of time. *Between-subjects designs* allow for studying group effects in a number of ways, including comparison of patients and healthy subjects, between different groups of patients, or between two groups who have been manipulated (e.g. trained) differently. A list of some possible designs is presented in Table B.1. In this way, it is imperative to pay attention to what comparisons are being made in a given experiment.

When studying the effects of one condition, one must always contrast that to some other condition to achieve any meaningful data. Let us demonstrate this with a study on the perception of facial expressions. In a standard emotion task in neuroimaging (Del Ben *et al.*, 2005), subjects are asked to look at images of different faces. Half of the faces are female and the subject's task is to report whether the face is a male or a female. At the same time, the faces also vary according to what kind of emotion is expressed. The faces can either be neutral or aversive (e.g. sad or frightened). During the experiment, our main focus is on the difference between seeing aversive and neutral faces. During the analysis of the data, we first determine when the aversive and the neutral faces were shown. We then determine the signal intensities for each of these periods and look at the mean signal intensity for neutral and aversive faces, respectively. The mean signal and distribution in the brain for each condition are shown in Figure B.23. If we are interested in identifying areas that are involved in the processing of aversive faces, we take the mean activity during aversive

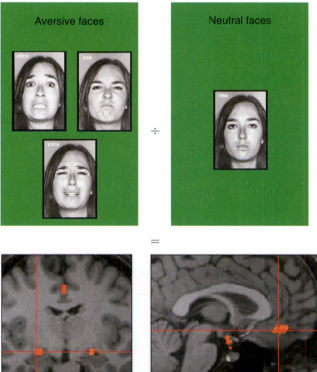

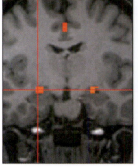
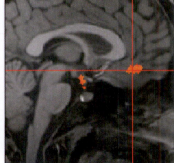

FIGURE B.23 fMRI for aversive emotional faces. Looking at aversive faces activates emotion areas of the brain. In a series of different face stimuli, some faces are aversive (e.g. frightened, sad and showing repulsion) and others are neutral. If we subtract the activity associated with neutral faces from aversive faces, we get neural signal that is selective for looking at aversive faces. Here, bilateral amygdala and orbitofrontal activation can be seen in an individual subject using this contrast. *Source*: Del Ben *et al.*, 2005.

BOX B.5   ASL of Alzheimer's disease and mild cognitive impairment

Although significant cognitive changes can be detected at an early stage of Alzheimer's disease (AD), including memory deficits, more physiological changes also occur in the brain. By studying the perfusion of blood in these patients, it is possible to see what areas show a general lower metabolism or flow of blood. In such a study, Johnson *et al.* (2005) used arterial spin labeling to compare the perfusion levels in a group of AD patients to that of healthy old subjects and subjects suffering from mild cognitive impairment, a pre-diagnostic syndrome where at least a subgroup show a high conversion rate to AD.

The researchers found a significant decrease in perfusion in the AD group, compared to the control group, in a number of regions in the parietal cortex, posterior cingulate cortex and frontal cortex. At a lower statistical threshold, the MCI group demonstrated a lower perfusion in the right inferior parietal lobe, the same place where the largest effect was seen in the AD group. This study demonstrates that perfusion scanning using ASL can be used to detect differences between groups at different stages in Alzheimer's disease.

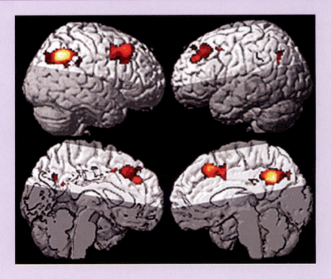

FIGURE B.24   ASL in Alzheimer's disease. (Johnson *et al.*, 2005.)
Source: Johnson *et al.*, 2005.

stimuli and subtract the mean activity of all neutral stimuli. In this way, all activations that are common for both conditions, including primary visual processing and rudimentary face perception are cancelled out. What we end up is where in the brain we see specific rise (or fall) in activation when the subjects see aversive faces.

BOLD fMRI is probably the most used measure of brain activation today. It has demonstrated its utility in every aspect of cognitive neuroscience and is continuously being developed as a research tool. With increasing technological advances the method will lead to a better understanding of the temporal and spatial workings of the mind and brain.

3.6.2 Arterial spin labeling (ASL)

By altering the magnetic properties of the blood flooding into the brain, an MRI measurement can also be made sensitive to the blood perfusion in the brain. A technique called *arterial spin labeling* uses this idea by 'labeling' the blood in the carotid artery by applying a brief radiofrequency pulse. This alters the magnetic properties of this part of the blood. As this blood continues to flood into the brain, it makes it possible to measure the relative change in magnetic susceptibility of a region of the brain, or the entire brain. A perfusion weighted image can be performed by subtracting a baseline brain image with no magnetized blood from a brain image with magnetized blood. In this way, one can measure the blood perfusion in a region of the brain and it is also possible to compare perfusion images between groups, see Box B.5.

3.6.3 Other specialized MRI sequences

Diffusion tensor imaging (DTI) and tractography
MRI can also be used to measure the movement of water molecules over time. In a free and unconstrained (isotropic) environment, water will diffuse equally in all directions, also known as Brownian movement. If you measure the diffusion in this medium, the resulting image will be a sphere. If water is put into a more constrained (anisotropic) environment, however, it cannot diffuse freely but can only move along the structures that it is physically limited by. For example, in a glass of water, the water in the middle can move freely in all directions. The movement potential of one water molecule is equal in all directions. However, if you put a drinking straw into the water, the movement potential of the water molecules within that tube is dramatically limited. If you now measure the water diffusion within this tube, it is no longer circular or equipotent, but an oblong sphere (Figure B.25).

In biological matter such as the brain, the water diffusion is significantly limited. However, there is a systematic difference between gray and white matter. While gray matter has little inner structure in the sense of limiting water diffusion, white matter consists of

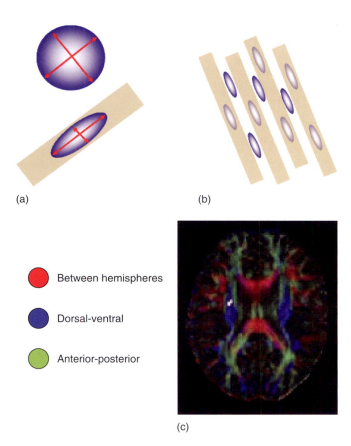

(a)   (b)

🔴 Between hemispheres

🔵 Dorsal-ventral

🟢 Anterior-posterior

(c)

FIGURE B.25 Diffusion of water depends on the local environment. (a) In the free and unrestricted medium (i.e. a glass of water) water can diffuse freely. The diffusion is *isotropic*; it has the potential to move in all directions. If the water molecule is physically restricted it can no longer move freely in any direction. This diffusion is *anisotropic*; it cannot move in any direction. In a medium of fibers such as the brain's white matter (schematically shown in (b)) water molecules are highly restricted by the axonal fibers. In this way, it is possible to visualize the fiber tracts of the brain and furthermore to estimate the integrity (homogeneity) of white matter in a given region. (c) Such visualization produces the typical colored DTI brain image that displays different trajectory trends in regional white matter.

fibers that constrain the diffusion in some directions more than others. Just like putting one or more straws into the glass of water hinders water from moving through the straw walls, neuronal fibers constrain water diffusion across, but not along, the fiber direction (see Figure B.25b). Connections between brain areas occur as bundles of fibers (axons). By using diffusion tensor imaging, it is possible to measure the relative direction and coherence of these white matter tracts. Thus, DTI can be used to measure white matter changes in neurological disease, but it is also possible to determine how a selected area is connected to other brain areas by following the fibers from the selected region, a method called *fiber tracking*. The use of DTI in a healthy brain can be seen in Box B.6.

MR spectroscopy

Magnetic resonance spectroscopy (MRS) is closely related to magnetic resonance imaging. Both techniques use the magnetic properties of atomic nuclei to get information about a biological sample. However, there is a crucial difference: while MRI measures the spatial distribution of magnetization, MRS measures the amount of signal from each chemical environment (chemical or molecular distribution). In other words, MRI allows one to study a particular region within an organism or sample, but gives relatively little information about the chemical or physical nature of that region. MR spectroscopy, which is an NMR method, provides a wealth of chemical information about the same region. The frequency distribution is called a spectrum and is analogous to the optical spectra of substances which are responsible for their visible colors. In this way, MRS can measure the chemical composition in a given region of the brain. MRI and MRS can be combined to provide the spatial distribution of chemical compounds as shown in Figure B.27. This figure shows the spectrum from a region of the brain and the corresponding chemical distribution of this region. If you compare this healthy area with an area from a diseased brain region, you can see some dramatic changes. First, from the healthy hemisphere it is possible to see that the N-acetylaspartate (NAA) signal is the highest of all molecular compounds. The NAA is a marker of mature axonal white matter in the living brain (Bjartmar *et al.*, 2002). By contrast, this is precisely the same signal that drops dramatically if we measure the same area in the lesioned hemisphere. Even without such dramatic effects, MRS can be used to study degeneration of brain tissue in diseases such as multiple sclerosis (De Stefano *et al.*, 2005), stroke (Saunders, 2000) and Alzheimer's disease (Falini *et al.*, 2005), but also the effects of substance abuse (Magalhaes 2005; Reneman *et al.*, 2006).

3.7 MRI – a tool for the future

With its superior spatial resolution and multiple uses, the MR scanner is an indispensable tool in cognitive neurosciences. The advances in MRI come from many directions but, in general, we can speak of two categories of advancements: *technical* and *analytical* tools. *Technical advances* include the production of scanners operating at higher field strengths. Increased field strengths enhance the scanner's ability to record signals. So, by exchanging a 1.5 Tesla (1.5 T) scanner with a 3 T scanner, we get a higher spatial resolution in both the structural images as well as the functional images.

BOX B.6   Reading ability and brain connectivity

Reading is a complex cognitive skill that is the result of coordination between many different brain regions. In order for such a communication between brain regions to occur, there must be physical contacts between these areas. This can be either through direct connections between two or more areas, or indirect connections through one or more additional areas. Although many studies using functional imaging address the cooperation between such areas, they do not provide direct evidence about the structural connections that are present in the brain to support this cooperation.

In a study by Beaulieu and colleagues (Beaulieu *et al.*, 2005), this was addressed by studying the brain connectivity in children with diverse reading abilities. By comparing white matter connectivity and integrity changes and reading ability in children, Beaulieu discovered five white matter areas that were good indicators of the children's reading ability.

The researchers went on by looking at the different connectivities in these areas. By using each white matter area as a 'seed point', the researchers could detect and visualize the connectivity of each cluster. These were generally ordered in three groups: one going between the front (anterior) and back (posterior) ends of the brain; one group of left-right orientated fibers; and one traveling from the upper (superior) to the lower (inferior) parts of the brain.

In this way, Beaulieu and colleagues were able to determine both the white matter regions that are important in reading skills in children and, at the same time, say which pathways these areas represented. Following these discoveries, it is now possible to generate more specific hypotheses about the neural substrate for reading skill acquisition, how these areas could be functionally connected and to test them using other methods, e.g. fMRI.

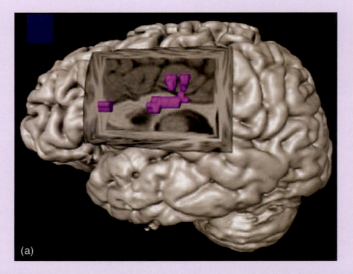

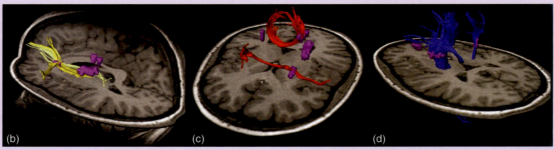

FIGURE B.26   Connectivity patterns in the brain were investigated by Beaulieu and colleagues (2005) using DTI. (a) Shows the brain areas (in purple) selected for investigation. Four were in the left hemisphere and one in the right. (b) Shows white matter tracts (in yellow) for the pre-selected regions that have an anterior-posterior (front to back of the brain) orientation. (c) Shows white matter tracts (in red) for the pre-selected regions that have a left-right orientation. (d) Shows white matter tracts (in blue) for the pre-selected regions that have a superior-inferior (top to bottom of the brain) orientation. *Source*: Beaulieu *et al.*, 2005.

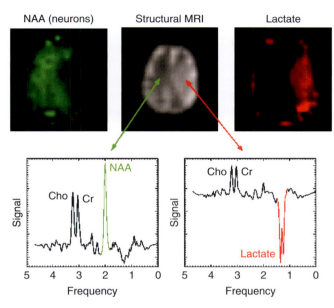

FIGURE B.27 Spectroscopic MRI detects chemical differences in brain pathology. Left: (green), the healthy part of the brain shows normal NAA levels (green peak), while on the left hand side this NAA level has diminished, while lactate has a significantly altered (red drop).

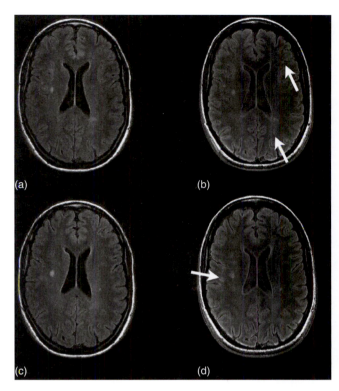

FIGURE B.28 Increased field strength leads to higher resolution images. By comparing the image of the same subject on both a 1.5T and a 3T scanner it is possible to see the resolution increase. Here, the pathological changes occurring in sclerosis are best seen using 3T (b and d) while several lesions are not even detected at 1.5T (a and c, see arrow in d). All image acquisitions were done with the injection of a contrast agent, gadolinium. *Source*: Nielsen *et al.*, 2006.

While 3T or 4T is the current high-field standard in scanning subjects and patients, scanners are already available at higher field strengths such as 7T and 11T. Scanning the cortex at 7T or higher field strengths has now demonstrated the possibility to make out the different layers of the cortex (Fatterpekar *et al.*, 2002; Zhao *et al.*, 2006). This is important not only because we get a higher resolution for studies already performed, but it will also generate whole new ways to study the brain, and our ideas about its workings.

Advances in field strengths are complemented by other areas such as improvements in the apparatus that generate the magnetic pulse, or the receiver that records the signal. Such ongoing improvements are likely to make significant contributions to the possibility of scanning the brain with increasingly higher resolution and sometimes invent novel ways to acquire the data. While these advances promise a better resolution, they are also associated with specific problems. For example, the higher field strength that produces better signal to noise ratio in most parts of the brain, leads to greater loss of signal in other areas. Since the BOLD signal (see previously) relies on the relative amount of oxygenated blood in an area, areas with oxygen that are not part of the brain influence the signal in that area. The medial temporal lobe and ventral prefrontal cortex both lie close to the nasal air cavities. As a result the BOLD signal in these brain regions is corrupted by the non-brain areas filled with oxygen. When moving from field strengths of 1.5T to 3T, this became a problem that needed to be addressed. Acquiring fMRI activation data from the hippocampus, amygdala and orbitofrontal cortex were distorted by a loss of signal at 3T. To overcome this problem, studies now use specialized sequences that minimize the artifacts in these areas. However, when moving from the standard 3T or 4T to 7T or higher field strengths, these problems re-emerge. Only new advancements in noise reduction methods can solve these problems.

The other general area of advance is *software improvements*. In a few years, the field of neuroimaging has seen a significant expansion in the number of ways to analyze data. Many of these improvements are not isolated to MRI alone, but are relevant to most or all neuroimaging approaches. While the early days of fMRI neuroimaging analyzed trial blocks, later advances, such as the event-related paradigm, has led to new analytical tools. One such is the dynamic causal modeling (DCM) analysis of neural activation patterns. In general, DCM is a way to analyze how activations across the brain occur at the same time or are caused. There are two main ways to analyze such data. An analysis of the *functional connectivity* focuses on correlations between brain areas. For example, one can ask whether there is a contingent relationship between activation in the hippocampus and the dorsolateral prefrontal cortex (DL-PFC) during an encoding task. Here, one can get an estimate of how correlated two (or more) areas of the brain are, in other words the relative activation strength between two or more areas. The second kind of analysis is to look at the *effective connectivity* between areas. Here, one tries to move beyond mere correlation and estimate the relative cause and effect relationship between areas. In our example of hippocampus and DL-PFC, we move beyond asking how correlated the regions are and now how one area is causing the other to activate. Today, both approaches are being developed continuously and are increasingly being used in the analysis of neuroimaging data. However, since they rely on specific experimental design and data sampling, only paradigms specifically tailored to the analysis can be used.

3.8 Optical imaging

Optical imaging is a quite recent addition to the brain imaging toolbox. A laser source of near-infrared light is positioned on the scalp. A bundle of optical fibers is used as detectors and placed a few centimeters away from the light source. The detectors record how the path of light from the laser source is altered, either through absorption or scattering, as it traverses brain tissue. This information is used in two ways. First, it can measure the concentration of chemicals in the brain by measuring the absorption of light in an area. Second, it can provide information about more physiological properties of the brain that are associated to the level of neuronal firing. This is done by measuring the scattering of light, which is an indicator of swelling of glia cells and neurons. In this way, optical imaging provides a simultaneous measure of both the source and time course of neural activation within an area of the brain.

In a study using optical imaging, Sato and colleagues (Sato *et al.*, 2005) studied the activity of somatosensory cortex in the pre-surgical planning stage of patients with brain tumors or epilepsy. As with previous findings in the human and non-human animal literature, Sato *et al.* found that the organization of the somatosensory cortex consisted of neighboring response areas, for example the fingers, and that the areas demonstrated a certain amount of functional overlap. This is illustrated in Figure B.29. It is also noteworthy to consider the relation between these findings and the study of brain plasticity in phantom limb sensation presented in Box B.2. This study also demonstrates that optical imaging has a potential use in pre-surgical planning.

4.0 MULTIMODAL BRAIN IMAGING

Neuroscience today rests on a number of different imaging techniques (modalities) and we have only mentioned the most prominent here. Each approach continues to provide novel findings that contribute to our understanding of the brain and our cognitive apparatus. But, as Figure B.30 demonstrates, each imaging technique has its strengths and weaknesses, especially in terms of their relative spatial and temporal resolution. An obvious solution is therefore to compare findings from studies using these different imaging approaches. However, since each method is different from the rest, we will never get identical results. Instead, what we get is added information about our area of interest. For example, if our study focuses on subjects reading a text aloud, we can compare the results from EEG and fMRI. In this way, we can get a better understanding of both the localization of areas that are responsible for text reading (fMRI) and, at the same time, get results about the millisecond to millisecond changes in activation levels during the task (EEG).

Imaging modalities can be compared in many ways. In addition to the comparison of the results in different studies, an often-used approach is to combine imaging techniques more directly. A PET study will most often co-register its findings to a standard MRI or CT structural brain. The same is actually done with fMRI images: the activation images are co-registered to the structural scans. This process gives us the opportunity to have a better ability to see where in the brain our changes are found. The activation images in themselves bear too little information about the localization of the activations to be meaningful.

4.1 Simultaneous imaging from different sources

While most comparisons are done on images that have been recorded separately, for example the PET scan and the structural MRI scan, it is also possible to record and co-register results from recordings that have been done simultaneously. For example, Dang-Vu and colleagues (Dang-Vu *et al.*, 2005) used combined EEG and PET to study the contributions of brain areas in different levels of sleep. The EEG and PET recordings were done simultaneously while the subjects were sleeping. The researchers then identified the unique stages of sleep from the EEG patterns and focused on delta activation during non-REM (NREM) sleep and compared this to REM sleep and normal wakefulness (see Figure B.31). The researchers found a negative correlation between delta power and

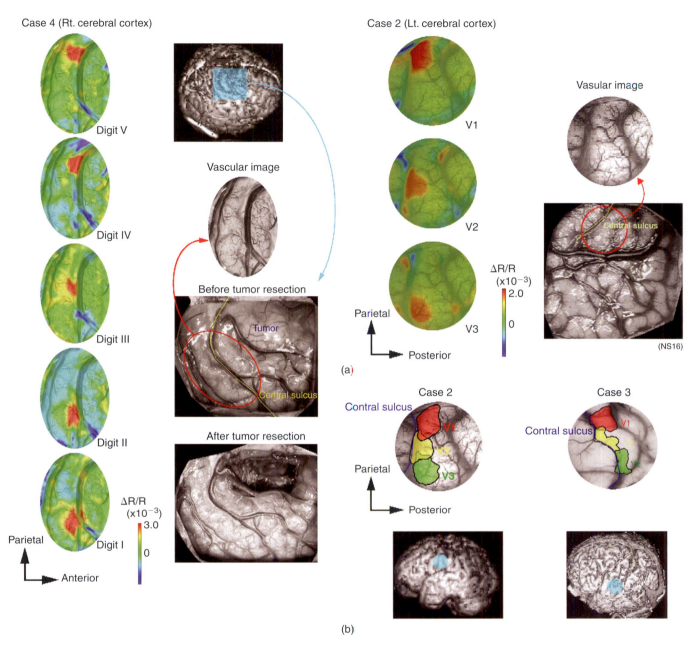

FIGURE B.29 Optical imaging: The cortex responds visibly to stimulation. Intrinsic optical responses to stimulation of the digits from the left somatosensory cortex of a 47-year old patient. The detected optical responses are illustrated in added color superimposed on a vascular image. *Source*: Adapted from Sato *et al.*, 2005.

regional cerebral blood flow in the ventromedial prefrontal cortex, the basal forebrain, the striatum, the anterior insular and the precuneus. These findings thus hint about areas that vary in delta activation according to our level of awareness.

Similarly, Laufs and colleagues (Laufs *et al.*, 2003) combined EEG and fMRI measurements in the study of subjects at rest. The study of 'resting state' must be seen as controversial, due to the fact that neither the mind nor the brain can be seen as being at 'rest' at any time. Laufs *et al.* assessed the different patterns of activity occurring within phases in which subjects were 'at rest' and found that the resting phase consisted of 'intertwined yet dissociable dynamic brain processes' (p. 11056) in the EEG. In other words, the neuroimaging studies imply that the brains of subjects at rest are doing different things at different times within the rest period. Furthermore, the researchers were able to make out separate neural networks underlying EEG bands, such as the alpha and beta band activity.

It should be noted that there is a substantive difference between combining EEG with PET and with fMRI.

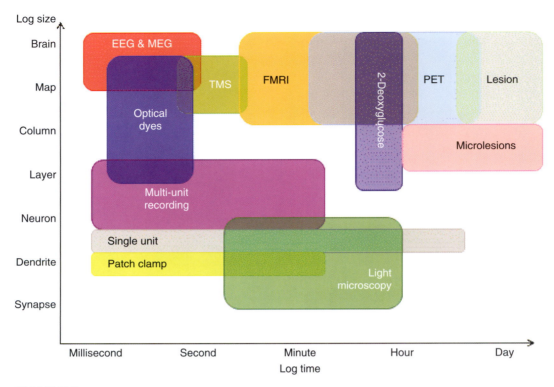

FIGURE B.30 Pros and cons of imaging techniques. Different imaging modalities have different resolution. While some approaches have a very high temporal resolution but a low spatial resolution, other modalities have an opposite relation.

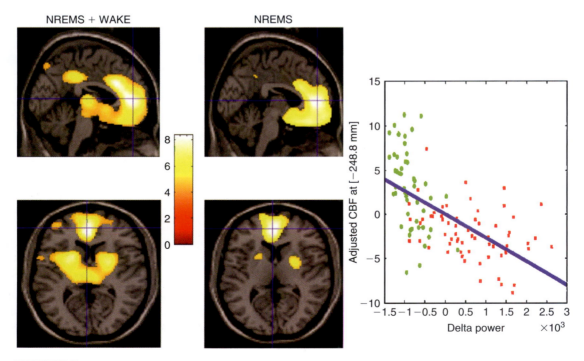

FIGURE B.31 The brain substrate for delta power during non-REM sleep. The image shows regional changes in the cerebral blood flow as a function of delta power during non-REM sleep. The activations are shown on a mid-sagittal slice (left) and different axial slices (right). *Source*: Dang-Vu, 2005.

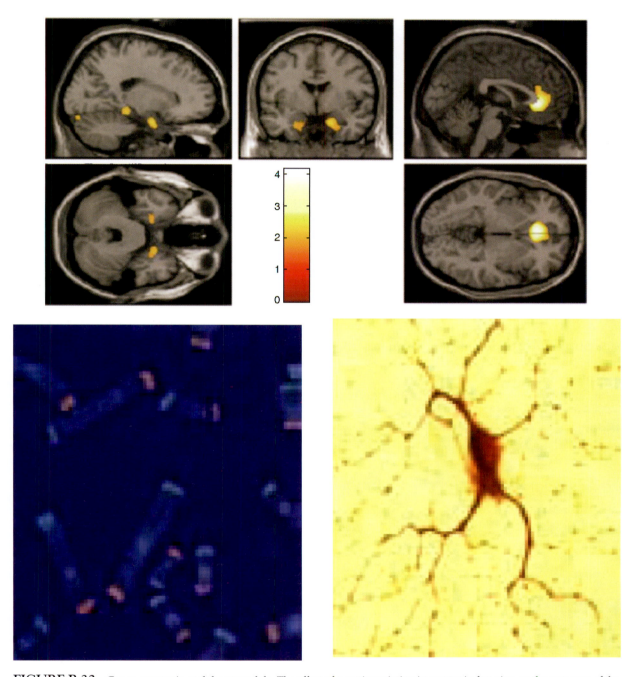

FIGURE B.32 Genes, serotonin and the amygdala. The effect of genetic variation in serotonin function on the response of the human amygdala. Using BOLD fMRI, Hariri *et al.* (2002) demonstrated that short allele carriers of the serotonin transporter gene exhibited greater activation of the amygdala to threatening stimuli than long allele carriers. This is indicative of the short allelic carriers having greater synaptic serotonin levels and it might contribute to an increased fear and anxiety in this group. *Source*: Hariri *et al.*, 2002.

While the PET scanner does not induce artifacts that are insurmountable for the EEG, the MR scanner produces artifacts in the EEG so substantial that attempts until only recently have been unsuccessful at such a combination. One approach has been to read the EEG from people between fMRI runs and, in this way, assess the state of awareness, e.g. whether they are sleeping or awake.

Through proper noise filtering it has now become possible to filter out the scanner artifacts and make the EEG data useable even from within the fMRI scanner. In this way, it has become possible to combine the high temporal resolution from the EEG with the high spatial resolution in the MRI. Still, the filtering of artifacts is seen as problematic – we may see a significant loss of true signal, while some residual artifacts (even from the filter applied) can occur. Combined measures such as the EEG/fMRI must therefore still be interpreted with caution.

4.2 Imaging genetics

Within the area of multimodal brain imaging, new important steps are taken to combine our understanding of how genes make up your mind. Genes act at the molecular level in the body and thus act as the very building blocks of neurons. In this way, individual differences in the genetic makeup can influence the workings of the brain in significant ways.

A natural variation in the promoter region of the serotonin transporter gene (called 5-HTTLPR) has been linked to alterations in serotonin transcription as well as serotonin uptake. Individuals who have two copies of the long (l) variant have a higher concentration of the serotonin transporter mRNA and therefore have greater serotonin uptake in comparison to individuals who have two versions of the short (s) variant. These subjects have a relatively lower concentration of the transporter and, as an effect, relatively greater synaptic serotonin levels. Hence, the genetic makeup you might have in this area influences how much or little serotonin you have available in the brain. Just looking at your genetic

makeup with respect to the serotonin transporter gene, it is now possible to predict the level of active serotonin in any given person.

By applying such a combination of neuroimaging and genotyping, Hariri and colleagues (Hariri *et al.*, 2002) demonstrated that the type of genetic makeup had implications for the response of the amygdala to pictures of facial expressions (Figure B.32). Subjects with the short genetic version demonstrated elevated levels of amygdala activation, presumably caused by a higher concentration of serotonin in these subjects. This genetically driven difference in amygdala excitability might contribute to the increased fear and anxiety typically associated with the short genetic version. As such, the study by Hariri and colleagues is a powerful demonstration about what can drive the individual differences in how the brain works (Figure B.33). Today, many researchers hold the view that this area of 'imaging genetics' holds the promise to give significant new insights into the workings of the brain and mind.

5.0 CONCLUDING REMARKS

Neuroimaging has grown into one of the most important approaches to our increased understanding of

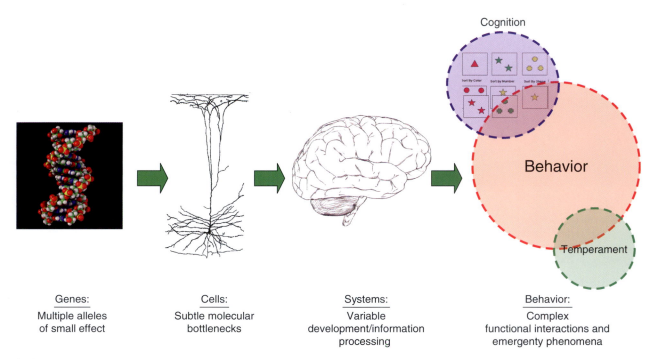

Genes:	Cells:	Systems:	Behavior:
Multiple alleles of small effect	Subtle molecular bottlenecks	Variable development/information processing	Complex functional interactions and emergenty phenomena

FIGURE B.33 Multileveled understanding of brain and mind. Four levels of understanding the mind and its brain. Imaging genetics allows for the estimation of genetic effects at the level of brain information processing, which represents a more proximate biological link to genes as well as an obligatory intermediate of behavior. Adapted from Hariri *et al.*, 2006.)

the human brain and mind. Advances within each modality – be it optical imaging, EEG or fMRI – rapidly change ways in which data can be analyzed and even the way we are posing our questions. Continuing innovations, both within hardware and software, make any prediction of the future of neuroimaging hazardous. However, some trends are very likely to continue, including the continuing increase in higher resolution in all modalities and new ways of combining data from different modalities.

We must keep in mind what we are really studying. The study of the human mind and its brain is founded on the very building biological blocks of our body: our genes. Our genes determine how and when our brain develops and it is thus the recipe for our mind that we should seek to understand. In order to do this we need to understand the levels at which we are working to understand ourselves. Here, let us distinguish between four levels. The first level is the genetic and how we understand how genes make up the recipe for cellular components such as proteins and transmitters. Secondly, we must understand how single neurons work and how they collaborate in networks. Thirdly, we can study the brain to see morphological and functional factors influencing thought. Finally, we can study how effects at any of the previous levels have an effect on our thought, behavior and even personality.

References

Abraham, W. C., Robins, A. (2005). Memory retention – the synaptic stability versus plasticity dilemma. *Trends Neurosci,* **28**(2), 73–78.

Adams, K. H., Hansen, E. S., Pinborg, L. H. *et al.* (2005). Patients with obsessive-compulsive disorder have increased 5-HT2a receptor binding in the caudate nuclei. *Int J Neuropsychopharmacol,* **8**(3), 391–401.

Adams, K. H., Pinborg, L. H., Svarer, C. *et al.* (2004). A database of [(18)f]-altanserin binding to 5-ht(2a) receptors in normal volunteers: normative data and relationship to physiological and demographic variables. *Neuroimage,* **21**(3), 1105–1113.

Adelman, G., Smith, B.H. (2004). *Encyclopedia of neuroscience,* 3rd edn. Elsevier, Amsterdam.

Adolphs, R., Gosselin, F., Buchanan, T. W., Tranel, D., Schyns, P., Damasio, A. R. (2005). A mechanism for impaired fear recognition after amygdala damage. *Nature,* **433**(7021), 68–72.

Ahissar, M., Hochstein, S. (2004). The reverse hierarchy theory of visual perceptual learning. *Trends Cogn Sci,* **8**(10), 457–464.

Albright, T. D. (1984). Direction and orientation selectivity of neurons in visual area MT of the macaque. *J Neurophysiol,* **52**(6), 1106–1130.

Albright, T. D. (1992). Form-cue invariant motion processing in primate visual cortex. *Science,* **255**(5048), 1141–1143.

Aleksander, I. (2005). The world in my mind, my mind in the world.

Aleksander, I., Browne, C., Dunmall, B., Wright, T. (1998). Towards visual awareness in a neural system. In Kasabov, S.I. (ed.), *Brain-like computing and intelligent information systems,* pp. 513–533. Springer, Berlin.

Alitto, H. J., Ursey, W. M. (2003). Corticothalamic feedback and sensory processing. *Curr Opin Neurobiol,* **13**(4), 440–445.

Alle, H., Geiger, J. R. (2006). Combined analog and action potential coding in hippocampal mossy fibers. *Science,* **311**(5765), 1290–1293.

Allison, T., Puce, A., McCarthy, G. (2000). Social perception from visual cues: role of the STS region. *Trends Cogn Sci,* **4**(7), 267–278.

Aminoff, M., Daroff, R. (eds) (2003). *Encyclopedia of the neurological sciences.* Academic Press, San Diego.

Anderson, A. K., Phelps, E. A. (2001). Lesions of the human amygdala impair enhanced perception of emotionally salient events. *Nature,* **411**(6835), 305–309.

Anderson, N. D., Iidaka, T., Cabeza, R., Kapur, S., McIntosh, A. R., Craik, F. I. (2000). The effects of divided attention on encoding- and retrieval-related brain activity: a PET study of younger and older adults. *J Cogn Neurosci,* **12**(5), 775–792.

Anderson, S. W., Bechara, A., Damasio, H., Tranel, D., Damasio, A. R. (1999). Impairment of social and moral behavior related to early damage in human prefrontal cortex. *Nat Neurosci,* **2**(11), 1032–1037.

Andoh, J., Artiges, E., Pallier, C. *et al.* (2006). Modulation of language areas with functional MR image-guided magnetic stimulation. *Neuroimage,* **29**(2), 619–627.

Andrew, C. N. Chen, F-J, Wang, L, Arendt-Nielsen, L. (2006). Mode and site of acupuncture modulation in the human brain: 3d (124-ch) EEG power spectrum mapping and source imaging. *Neuroimage,* **29**(4), 1080–1091.

Angecine, J. B. Jr. in Ramachandran (2002). *Encyclopedia of the human brain.* Elsevier, San Diego.

Arthurs, O. J., Boniface, S. (2002). How well do we understand the neural origins of the fMRI bold signal? *Trends Neurosci,* **25**(1), 27–31.

Atkinson, R. C., Shiffrin, R. M. (1968). Human memory: a proposed system and its control processes. In *The psychology of learning and motivation: II.* Academic Press, Oxford.

Attwell, D., Laughlin, S. B. (2001). An energy budget for signaling in the grey matter of the brain. *J Cereb Blood Flow Metab,* **21**(10), 1133–1145.

Awh, E., Jonides, J., Smith, E. E., Schumacher, E. H., Koeppe, R. A., Katz, S. (1996). Dissociation of storage and rehearsal in verbal working memory: evidence from positron emission tomography. *Psychol Sci,* **7**(1), 25–31.

Awh, E., Armstrong, K. M., Moore, T. (2006). Visual and oculomotor selection: links, causes and implications for spatial attention. *Trends Cogn Sci*, **10**(3), 124–130.

Aylward, E. H., Park, J. E., Field, K. M. *et al.* (2005). Brain activation during face perception: evidence of a developmental change. *J Cogn Neurosci*, **17**(2), 308–319.

Baars, B. J. (1983). Conscious concepts provide the nervous system with coherent, global information. In Davidson, R. J. (ed.), *Consciousness and self-regulation*. Plenum Press, New York.

Baars, B. J. (1986). What is a theory of consciousness a theory of? The search for criterial constraints on theory. *Imaginat Cogn Personality*, **6**(1), 3.

Baars, B. J. (1988). *A cognitive theory of consciousness*. Cambridge University Press, New York.

Baars, B. J. (2002). The conscious access hypothesis: origins and recent evidence. *Trend Cogn Sci*, **6**(1), 47–52.

Baars, B. J., Banks, W. P., Newman, J. B. (2003a). *Essential sources in the scientific study of consciousness*. MIT Press, Cambridge.

Baars, B. J., Franklin, S. (2003). How conscious experience and working memory interact. *Trends Cogn Sci*, **7**(4), 166–172.

Baars, B. J., Ramsoy, T. Z., Laureys, S. (2003b). Brain, conscious experience and the observing self. *Trends Neurosci*, **26**(12), 671–675.

Baddeley, A. (2000). The episodic buffer: a new component of working memory? *Trend Cogn Sci*, **4**(11), 417–423.

Baddeley, A. (2003). Working memory: looking back and looking forward. *Nat Rev Neurosci*, **4**(10), 829–839.

Baddeley, A. D. (2002). Is working memory still working? *Eur Psychol*, **7**(2), 85.

Baddeley, A. D., Hitch, G. J. (1974). Working memory. In Bower, G. A. (ed.), *Recent advances in learning and motivation*, Vol. 8, pp. 47–90. Academic Press, New York.

Baddeley, T. C., Davidson, I. G., Glidewell, C., Low, J. N., Skakle, J. M., Wardell, J. L. (2004). Supramolecular structures of substituted alpha, alpha'-trehalose derivatives. *Acta Crystallogr B*, **60**(Pt 4), 461–471.

Baillargeon, R. (1993). The object concept revisited: new directions in the investigation of infant's physical knowledge. In Granrud, C. E. (ed.), *Visual perception and cognition in infancy*, pp. 265–315. Lawrence Erlbaum Associates, Hillsdale.

Baird, A. A., Kagan, J., Gaudette, T., Walz, K. A., Hershlag, N., Boas, D. A. (2002). Frontal lobe activation during object permanence: data from near-infrared spectroscopy. *Neuroimage*, **16**(4), 1120–1125.

Bakin, J. S., South, D. A., Weinberger, N. M. (1996). Induction of receptive field plasticity in the auditory cortex of the guinea pig during instrumental avoidance conditioning. *Behav Neurosci*, **110**(5), 905–913.

Banaji, M. R., Greenwald, A. G. (1995). Implicit gender stereotyping in judgments of fame. *J Pers Soc Psychol*, **68**(2), 181–198.

Bar, M., Tootell, R. B., Schacter, D. L. *et al.* (2001). Cortical mechanisms specific to explicit visual object recognition. *Neuron*, **29**(2), 529–535.

Barbeau, E., Wendling, F., Regis, J. *et al.* (2005). Recollection of vivid memories after perirhinal region stimulations: synchronization in the theta range of spatially distributed brain areas. *Neuropsychologia*, **43**(9), 1329–1337.

Bargh, J. A. (2006). What have we been priming all these years? On the development, mechanisms, and ecology of nonconscious social behavior. *Eur J Social Psychol*,

Bargh, J. A., Chartrand, T. L. (1999). The unbearable automaticity of being. *Am Psychol*, **54**(7), 462.

Bargh, J. A., Williams, E. L. (2006). The automaticity of social life. *Curr Directions Psychol Sci*, **15**, 1–4.

Barkley, R. A. (1997). *ADHD and the nature of self-control*. The Guilford Press, New York.

Barlow, H. B., Blakemore, C., Pettigrew, J. D. (1967). The neural mechanism of binocular depth discrimination. *J Physiol*, **193**(2), 327–342.

Baron-Cohen, S. (1995). *Mindblindness: an essay on autism and theory of mind*. MIT Press/Bradford Books, Boston.

Barrett, N. A., Large, M. M., Smith, G. L. *et al.* (2003). Human brain regions required for the dividing and switching of attention between two features of a single object. *Brain Res Cogn Brain Res*, **17**(1), 1–13.

Barsalou, L. W. (1999). Perceptual symbol systems. *Behav Brain Sci*, **22**(4), 577–609; discussion 610–660.

Barsalou, L. W. (2005). Continuity of the conceptual system across species. *Trends Cogn Sci*, **9**(7), 309–311.

Barsalou, L. W., Kyle Simmons, W., Barbey, A. K., Wilson, C. D. (2003). Grounding conceptual knowledge in modality-specific systems. *Trends Cogn Sci*, **7**(2), 84–91.

Bartels, A., Zeki, S. (2005). Brain dynamics during natural viewing conditions – a new guide for mapping connectivity in vivo. *Neuroimage*, **24**(2), 339–349.

Batty, M., Taylor, M. J. (2006). The development of emotional face processing during childhood. *Dev Sci*, **9**(2), 207–220.

Beauchamp, M. S. (2005). See me, hear me, touch me: multisensory integration in lateral occipital-temporal cortex. *Curr Opin Neurobiol*, **15**(2), 145–153.

Beaulieu, C., Plewes, C., Paulson, L. A. *et al.* (2005). Imaging brain connectivity in children with diverse reading ability. *Neuroimage*, **25**(4), 1266–1271.

Bechara, A., Tranel, D., Damasio, H., Adolphs, R., Rockland, C., Damasio, A. R. (1995). Double dissociation of conditioning and declarative knowledge relative to the amygdala and hippocampus in humans. *Science*, **269**(5227), 1115–1118.

Beck, D. M., Rees, G., Frith, C. D., Lavie, N. (2001). Neural correlates of change detection and change blindness. *Nat Neurosci*, **4**(6), 645–650.

Bell, M. A. (1992a). Electrophysiological correlates of object search performance during infancy. *Proceedings of the VIIth International Conference on Infant Studies*. Miami Beach.

Bell, M. A. (1992b). A not B task performance is related to frontal EEG asymmetry regardless of locomotor experience. *Proceedings of the VIIIth International Conference on Infant Studies*. Miami Beach.

Bell, M. A., Fox, N. A. (1992). The relations between frontal brain electrical activity and cognitive development during infancy. *Child Dev*, **63**(5), 1142–1163.

Bennett, M. R. (1999). The early history of the synapse: from Plato to Sherrington. *Brain Res Bull*, **50**(2), 95–118.

Berger, H., Gloor, P. (1969). *Hans Berger on the electroencephalogram of man: the fourteen original reports on the human electroencephalogram*. Elsevier, Amsterdam.

Berridge, K. C. (2000). Measuring hedonic impact in animals and infants: microstructure of affective taste reactivity patterns. *Neurosci Biobehav Rev*, **24**(2), 173–198.

Berridge, K. C., Robinson, T. E. (1998). What is the role of dopamine in reward: hedonic impact, reward learning, or incentive salience? *Brain Res Brain Res Rev*, **28**(3), 309–369.

Berridge, K. C., Robinson, T. E. (2003). Parsing reward. *Trends Neurosci*, **26**(9), 507–513.

Berry, D. C., Dienes, Z. (1993). *Implicit learning: theoretical and empirical issues*, Erlbaum.

Bickerton, D. (1984). The language bioprogram hypothesis. *Behav Brain Sci*, **7**(2), 212–218.

Bickerton, D. (1990). *Language and species*. University of Chicago Press, Chicago.

Binder, J. (1997). Functional magnetic resonance imaging. Language mapping. *Neurosurg Clin N Am*, **8**(3), 383–392.

Binder, J. R., Frost, J. A., Hammeke, T. A. *et al.* (2000). Human temporal lobe activation by speech and nonspeech sounds. *Cereb Cortex*, **10**(5), 512–528.

Bjartmar, C., Battistuta, J., Terada, N., Dupree, E., Trapp, B. D. (2002). N-acetylaspartate is an axon-specific marker of mature white matter in vivo: a biochemical and immunohistochemical study on the rat optic nerve. *Ann Neurol*, **51**(1), 51–58.

Blake, R., Logothetis, N. K. (2002). Visual competition. *Nat Rev Neurosci*, **3**(1), 13–21.

Blanke, O., Ortigue, S., Landis, T., Seeck, M. (2002). Stimulating illusory own-body perceptions. *Nature*, **419**(6904), 269–270.

Blumenthal, J. L., Elman, J. L. (1979). Wilhelm Wundt, the founding father we never knew. *Contemp Psychol*, **24**(7), 547–550.

Blumstein, S. E. (1997). A perspective on the neurobiology of language. *Brain Lang*, **60**(3), 335–46.

Boatman, D. F. (2006). Cortical auditory systems: speech and other complex sounds. *Epilepsy Behav*, **8**(3), 494–503.

Bodamer, J. L. (1947). Die prosop-agnosie. *Eur Arch Psychiatr Clin Neurosci*, **179**(1), 6–53.

Borgstein, J., Grootendorst, C. (2002). Half a brain. *Lancet*, **359**(9305): 473–475.

Botvinick, M. M., Cohen, J. D., Carter, C. S. (2004). Conflict monitoring and anterior cingulate cortex: an update. *Trends Cogn Sci*, **8**(12), 539–546.

Bourgeois, J. P. (2001). Synaptogenesis in the neocortex of the newborn: the ultimate frontier for individuation? In *The handbook of developmental cognitive neuroscience*, pp. 23–34. MIT Press, Cambridge.

Bouvier, S. E., Engel, S. A. (2006). Behavioral deficits and cortical damage loci in cerebral achromatopsia. *Cereb Cortex*, **16**(2), 183–191.

Bowers, K. S., Regehr, G., Balthazard, C., Parker, K. (1990). Intuition in the context of discovery. *Cogn Psychol*, **22**(1), 72–110.

Braver, T. S., Reynolds, J. R., Donaldson, D. I. (2003). Neural mechanisms of transient and sustained cognitive control during task switching. *Neuron*, **39**(4), 713–726.

Bregman, A. S. (1990). *Auditory scene analysis: the perceptual organization of sound*. MIT Press, Cambridge.

Broadbent, D. E. (1957). A mechanical model for human attention and immediate memory. *Psychol Rev*, **64**(3), 205–215.

Broadbent, D. E. (1982). Task combination and selective intake of information. *Acta Psychol (amst)*, **50**(3), 253–290.

Broca, P. (1861a). Pert de la parole, ramollissement chronique et destruction partielle du lobe antérieur gauche eu cerveau. *Bull Soc Anthropol*, **2**, 235–238.

Broca, P. (1861b). Remarques sur le siège de la faculté du langage articulé, suives d'une observation d'aphémie (pert de la parole). *Bull Soc Anat*, **6**, 330–357, 398–407.

Brodersen, P., Paulson, O. B., Bolwig, T. G., Rogon, Z. E., Rafaelsen, O. J., Lassen, N. A. (1973). Cerebral hyperemia in electrically induced epileptic seizures. *Arch Neurol*, **28**(5), 334–338.

Brodman, K. (1909). *Vergleichende lakalisationslehre der grosshirnrinde: In ihren prinzipien dargestellt anf grund des zellenbaues*. Verlag von Johann Ambrosius Barth, Leipzig.

Brooks, R., Meltzoff, A. (2002). The importance of eyes: how infants interpret adult looking behavior. *Devel Psychol*, **38**(6), 958–966.

Brooks, R., Meltzoff, A. (2003). Gaze following at 9 and 12 months: a developmental shift from global head direction to gaze. Poster presented at SRCD conference. Society for Research in Child Development, Tampa.

Brown, M. C. (2003). Audition. In Squire, L. R., Bloom, F. E., McConnell, S. K., Roberts, J. L., Spitzer, N. C., Zigmond, M. J. (eds), *Fundamental neuroscience*, 2nd edn. Elsevier, San Diego.

Brown, R., McNeill, D. (1966). The 'tip of the tongue' phenomenon. *J Verbal Learn Verbal Behav*, **5**(4), 325.

Brown, R. E., Milner, P. M. (2003). The legacy of Donald O. Hebb: more than the Hebb synapse. *Nat Rev Neurosci*, **4**(12), 1013–1019.

Brugge, J. F., Howard, M. A. (2003). Hearing. In Squire, L. R., Bloom, F. E., McConnell, S. K., Roberts, J. L., Spitzer, N. C., Zigmond, M. J. (eds), *Fundamental neuroscience*, 2nd edn. Elsevier, San Diego.

Brugge, J. F., Merzenich, M. M. (1973). Responses of neurons in auditory cortex of the macaque monkey to monaural and binaural stimulation. *J Neurophysiol*, **36**(6), 1138–1158.

Buccino, G., Vogt, S., Ritzi, A., Fink, G., Zilles, K. (2004). Neural circuits underlying imitation learning of hand actions: an event-related fMRI study. *Neuron*, **42**, 323–334.

Buckley, M. J., Gaffan, D. (2006). Perirhinal cortical contributions to object perception. *Trends Cogn Sci*, **10**(3), 100–107.

Buckner, R. L., Goodman, J., Burock, M. *et al.* (1998). Functional-anatomic correlates of object priming in humans revealed by rapid presentation event-related fMRI. *Neuron*, **20**(2), 285–296.

Bullier, J. (2001). Feedback connections and conscious vision. *Trends Cogn Sci*, **5**(9), 369–370.

Bunzeck, N., Wuestenberg, T., Lutz, K., Heinze, H. J., Jancke, L. (2005). Scanning silence: mental imagery of complex sounds. *Neuroimage*, **26**(4), 1119–1127.

Burgess, N., Hitch, G. (2005). Computational models of working memory: putting long-term memory into context. *Trends Cogn Sci*, **9**(11), 535–541.

Burgess, N., Hitch, G. J. (1999). Memory for serial order: a network model of the phonological loop and its timing. *Psychol Rev*, **106**(3), 551–581.

Bush, G., Luu, P., Posner, M. I. (2000). Cognitive and emotional influences in anterior cingulate cortex. *Trends Cogn Sci*, **4**(6), 215–222.

Byrne, J. H., Roberts, J. L. (2004). *From molecules to networks: an introduction to cellular and molecular neuroscience*: Elsevier Academic Press.

Cabeza, R., Mangels, J., Nyberg, L. *et al.* (1997). Brain regions differentially involved in remembering what and when: a PET study. *Neuron*, **19**(4), 863–870.

Cahill, L., Babinsky, R., Markowitsch, H. J., McGaugh, J. L. (1995). The amygdala and emotional memory. *Nature*, **377**(6547), 295–296.

Cahill, L., Haier, R. J., Fallon, J. *et al.* (1996). Amygdala activity at encoding correlated with long-term, free recall of emotional information. *Proc Natl Acad Sci USA*, **93**(15), 8016–8021.

Cahill, L., McGaugh, J. L. (1998). Mechanisms of emotional arousal and lasting declarative memory. *Trends Neurosci*, **21**(7), 294–299.

Cahill, L., Prins, B., Weber, M., McGaugh, J. L. (1994). Beta-adrenergic activation and memory for emotional events. *Nature*, **371**(6499), 702–704.

Caldara, R., Segher, M., Rossion, B., Lazeyras, F., Michel, C., Hauert, C. (2006). The fusiform face area is tuned for curvilinear patterns with more high-contrasted elements in the upper part. *NeuroImage*, **31**, 313–319.

Caplan, D. N., Gould, J. L. (2003). Language and communication. In L. R. Squire, F. E. Bloom, S. K. McConnell, J. L. Roberts, N. C. Spitzer & M. J. Zigmond (Eds.), *Fundamental neuroscience* (Second ed.). San Diego: Elsevier.

Caramazza, A., Mahon, B. Z. (2003). The organization of conceptual knowledge: the evidence from category-specific semantic deficits. *Trends Cogn Sci*, **7**(8), 354–361.

Caramazza, A., Shelton, J. R. (1998). Domain-specific knowledge systems in the brain the animate-inanimate distinction. *J Cogn Neurosci*, **10**(1), 1–34.

Carpenter, G. A., Grossberg, S. (1991). *Pattern recognition by self-organizing neural networks*. MIT Press, Cambridge.

Carpenter, M. B., Parent, A. (1995). *Carpenter's human neuroanatomy* (9th edn). Lippincot, Williams & Wilkins, Baltimore.

Casey, B. J., Cohen, J. D., Jezzard, P. *et al.* (1995). Activation of prefrontal cortex in children during a nonspatial working memory task with functional MRI. *Neuroimage*, **2**(3), 221–229.

Casey, B. J., Tottenham, N., Liston, C., Durston, S. (2005). Imaging the developing brain: what have we learned about cognitive development? *Trends Cogn Sci*, **9**(3), 104–110.

Catani, M., ffytche, D. H. (2005). The rises and falls of disconnection syndromes. *Brain*, **128**(Pt 10), 2224–2239.

Caton, R. (1875). The electric currents of the brain. *Br Med J*, **2**(1), 278.

Cattell, J. M. (1886). The time it takes to see and name objects. *Mind*, **11**, 63–65.

Chartrand, T. L., Bargh, J. A. (1999). The chameleon effect: the perception-behavior link and social interaction. *J Pers Soc Psychol*, **76**(6), 893–910.

Cheeseman, J., Merikle, P. M. (1984). Priming with and without awareness. *Percept Psychophys*, **36**(4), 387–395.

Cheeseman, J., Merikle, P. M. (1986). Distinguishing conscious from unconscious perceptual processes. *Can J Psychol*, **40**(4), 343–367.

Chein, J. M. (2004). *Evaluating models of working memory: fMRI and behavioral evidence on the effects of concurrent irrelevant information*. Dissertation, University of Pittsburgh, USA.

Chein, J. M., Schneider, W. (2005). Neuroimaging studies of practice-related change: fMRI and meta-analytic evidence of a domain-general control network for learning. *Brain Res Cogn Brain Res*, **25**(3), 607–623.

Chein, J. M., Ravizza, S. M., Fiez, J. A. (2003). Using neuroimaging to evaluate models of working memory and their implications for language processing. *J Neurolinguist*, **16**(4), 315–339.

Cherry, E. C. (1953). Some experiments on the recognition of speech, with one and with two ears. *J Acoustic Soc Am*, **25**, 975.

Chomsky, N. (1957). *Syntactic structures*. Mouton, The Hague.

Christensen, M. S., Ramsøy, T. Z., Lund, T. E. Madsen, K. H., Rowe, J. B. (2006). An fMRI study of the neural correlates of graded visual perception. *Neuroimage*, **31**(4), 1711–1725.

Christiansen, M. H., Allen, J., Seidenberg, M. S. (1998). Learning to segment speech using multiple cues: A connectionist model. *Language and Cognitive Processes*, **13**(2/3), 221–268.

Chun, M. M., Phelps, E. A. (1999). Memory deficits for implicit contextual information in amnesic subjects with hippocampal damage. *Nat Neurosci*, **2**(9), 844–847.

Clark, R. E., Squire, L. R (1999). Human eyeblink classical conditioning: effects of manipulating awareness of the stimulus contingencies. *Psychol Sci*, **10**(1), 14–18.

Clarke, S., Bellmann Thiran, A., Maeder, P. *et al.* (2002). What and where in human audition: selective deficits following focal hemispheric lesions. *Exp Brain Res*, **147**(1), 8–15.

Cleeremans, A. (1993). *Mechanisms of implicit learning: Connectionist models of sequence learning*. MIT Press.

Cleeremans, A., Destrebecqz, A., Boyer, M. (1998). Implicit learning: news from the front. *Trends Cogn Sci*, **2**(10), 406–415.

Cohen, D. (1968). Magnetoencephalography: evidence of magnetic fields produced by alpha-rhythm currents. *Science*, **161**(843), 784–786.

Cohen, J., Perlstein, W., Braver, T. *et al.* (1997). Temporal dynamics of brain activation during a working memory task. *Nature*, **386**(6625), 604–608.

Cohen, J. D. *et al.* (1990). On the control of automatic processes: a parallel distributed processing account of the Stroop effect. *Psychol Rev*, **97**, 332–361.

Cohen, N. J., Squire, L. R. (1980). Preserved learning and retention of pattern-analyzing skill in amnesia: dissociation of knowing how and knowing that. *Science*, **210**(4466), 207–210.

Colom, R., Jung, R. E., Haier, R. J. (2006). Distributed brain sites for the g-factor of intelligence. *Neuroimage*, **31**(3), 1359–1365.

Computerised Wisconsin card sort task. (2003). Version 4 ed., Vol. (WCST): Psychological Assessment Resources.

Conway, A. R., Cowan, N., Bunting, M. F. (2001). The cocktail party phenomenon revisited: the importance of working memory capacity. *Psychon Bull Rev*, **8**(2), 331–335.

Conway, M. A., Turk, D. J., Miller, S. L. *et al.* (1999). A positron emission tomography (PET) study of autobiographical memory retrieval. *Memory*, **7**(5–6), 679–702.

Cooper, R., Crow, H. J., Walter, W. G., Winter, A. L. (1966). Regional control of cerebral vascular reactivity and oxygen supply in man. *Brain Res*, **3**(2), 174–191.

Corbetta, M., Akbudak, E., Conturo, T. E. *et al.* (1998). A common network of functional areas for attention and eye movements. *Neuron*, **21**(4), 761–773.

Corbetta, M., Kincade, J. M., Ollinger, J. M., McAvoy, M. P., Shulman, G. L. (2000). Voluntary orienting is dissociated from target detection in human posterior parietal cortex. *Nat Neurosci*, **3**(3), 292–297.

Corbetta, M., Kincade, J. M., Shulman, G. L. (2002). Neural systems for visual orienting and their relationships to spatial working memory. *J Cogn Neurosci*, **14**(3), 508–523.

Corbetta, M., Shulman, G. L. (2002). Control of goal-directed and stimulus-driven attention in the brain. *Nat Rev Neurosci*, **3**(3), 201–215.

Corkin, S. (1965). Tactually-guided maze learning in man: effects of unilateral cortical excisions and bilateral hippocampal lesions. *Neuropsychologia*, **3**, 339–351.

Corkin, S., Amaral, D. G., Gonzalez, R. G., Johnson, K. A., Hyman, B. T. (1997). H.M.'s medial temporal lobe lesion: Findings from magnetic resonance imaging. *J Neurosci*, **17**(10), 3964–3979.

Cosmelli, D., David, O., Lachaux, J. P. *et al.* (2004). Waves of consciousness: ongoing cortical patterns during binocular rivalry. *Neuroimage*, **23**(1), 128–140.

Cowan, N. (2001). The magical number 4 in short-term memory: A reconsideration of mental storage capacity. *Behav Brain Sci*, **24**(1), 87–114; discussion 114–185.

Cowan, N., Izawa, C., Ohta, N. (2005). Working-memory capacity limits in a theoretical context. In *Human learning and memory: advances in theory and application. The 4th Tsukuba International Conference on Memory*, pp. 155. Lawrence Erlbaum Associates, Publishers, Mahwah.

Cowey, A., Stoerig, P. (1995). Blindsight in monkeys. *Nature*, **373**(6511), 247–249.

Cowey, A., Walsh, V. (2000). Magnetically induced phosphenes in sighted, blind and blindsighted observers. *Neuroreport*, **11**(14), 3269–3273.

Cowey, A., Walsh, V. (2001). Tickling the brain: studying visual sensation, perception and cognition by transcranial magnetic stimulation. *Prog Brain Res*, **134**, 411–425.

Craig, A. D. (2005). Forebrain emotional asymmetry: a neuroanatomical basis? *Trends Cogn Sci*, **9**(12), 566–571.

Crick, F., Koch, C. (1995). Are we aware of neural activity in primary visual cortex? *Nature*, **375**(6527), 121–123.

Crick, F., Koch, C. (2003). A framework for consciousness. *Nat Neurosci*, **6**(2), 119–126.

Csibra, G., Tucker, L. A., Johnson, M. H. (1998). Neural correlates of saccade planning in infants: a high-density ERP study. *Int J Psychophysiol*, **29**(2), 201–215.

Csibra, G., Tucker, L. A., Johnson, M. H. (2001). Differential frontal cortex activation before anticipatory and reactive saccades in infants. *Infancy*, **2**(2), 159–174.

Cumming, B. G. (2002). An unexpected specialization for horizontal disparity in primate primary visual cortex. *Nature*, **418**(6898), 633–636.

Curran, T. (2001). Implicit learning revealed by the method of opposition. *Trends Cogn Sci*, **5**(12), 503–504.

Curtis, C. E., D'Esposito, M. (2003). Persistent activity in the prefrontal cortex during working memory. *Trends Cogn Sci*, **7**(9), 415–423.

Cusack, R. (2005). The intraparietal sulcus and perceptual organization. *J Cogn Neurosci*, **17**(4), 641–651.

D'Esposito, M., Chen, A. J. (2006). Neural mechanisms of prefrontal cortical function: implications for cognitive rehabilitation. *Prog Brain Res*, **157**, 123–139.

D'Esposito, M., Postle, B. R. (1999). The dependence of span and delayed-response performance on prefrontal cortex. *Neuropsychologia*, **37**(11), 1303–1315.

D'Haenen, H., Boer, J. A., Willner, P. (2002). *Biological psychiatry*: John Wiley & Sons.

Dalrymple-Alford, E. C., Budayr, B. (1966). Examination of some aspects of the Stroop color-word test. *Percept Mot Skills*, **23**, 1211–1214.

Damasio, A. R. (1989). Time-locked multiregional retroactivation: a systems level proposal for the neural substrates of recall and recognition. *Cognition*, **33**, 25–32.

Damasio, A. R., Grabowski, T. J., Bechara, A. *et al.* (2000). Subcortical and cortical brain activity during the feeling of self-generated emotions. *Nat Neurosci*, **3**(10), 1049–1056.

Damasio, H., Grabowski, T., Frank, R., Galaburda, A. M., Damasio, A. R. (1994). The return of Phineas Gage: clues about the brain from the skull of a famous patient. *Science*, **264**(5162), 1102–1105.

Dang-Vu, T. T., Desseilles, M., Laureys, S. *et al.* (2005). Cerebral correlates of delta waves during non-REM sleep revisited. *Neuroimage*, **28**(1), 14–21.

Dapretto, M., Davies, M. S., Pfeifer, J. H. *et al.* (2006). Understanding emotions in others: mirror neuron dysfunction in children with autism spectrum disorders. *Nat Neurosci*, **9**(1), 28–30.

Daselaar, S. M., Fleck, M. S., Prince, S. E., Cabeza, R. (2006). The medial temporal lobe distinguishes old from new independently of consciousness. *J Neurosci*, **26**(21), 5835–5839.

Darwin, C. (1872). *The expression of the emotions in man and animals.* John Murray, London.

Davatzikos, C., Ruparel, K., Fan, Y. *et al.* (2005). Classifying spatial patterns of brain activity with machine learning methods: application to lie detection. *Neuroimage*, **28**(3), 663–668.

David, S. P., Munafo, M. R., Johansen-Berg, H. *et al.* (2005). Ventral striatum/nucleus accumbens activation to smoking-related pictorial cues in smokers and nonsmokers: a functional magnetic resonance imaging study. *Biol Psychiatr*, **58**(6), 488–494.

Davidson, R. J., Irwin, W. (1999). The functional neuroanatomy of emotion and affective style. *Trends Cogn Sci*, **3**(1), 11–21.

de Gelder, B., Morris, J. S., Dolan, R. J. (2005). Unconscious fear influences emotional awareness of faces and voices. *Proc Natl Acad Sci USA*, **102**(51), 18682–18687.

de Gelder, B., Vroomen, J., Pourtois, G., Weiskrantz, L. (2000). Affective blindsight: are we blindly led by emotions?

Response to Heywood and Kentridge (2000). *Trends Cogn Sci*, **4**(4), 126–127.

De Groot, A. D. (1946). *Het denken van den schaker*. Noord Hollandsche, Amsterdam.

de Haan, M., Pascalis, O., Johnson, M. H. (2002). Specialization of neural mechanisms underlying face recognition in human infants. *J Cogn Neurosci*, **14**(2), 199–209.

De Stefano, N., Bartolozzi, M. L., Guidi, L., Stromillo, M. L., Federico, A. (2005). Magnetic resonance spectroscopy as a measure of brain damage in multiple sclerosis. *J Neurol Sci*, **233**(1–2), 203–208.

De Waal, F. B. (2004). Peace lessons from an unlikely source. *PloS Biol*, **2**(4), E106.

DeCasper, A. J., Fifer, W. P. (1980). Of human bonding: new-borns prefer their mothers' voices. *Science*, **208**(4448), 1174–1176.

Decety, J., Chaminade, T., Gre'zes, J., Meltzoff, A. (2002). A PET exploration of the neural mechanisms involved in reciprocal imitation. *NeuroImage*, **15**, 265–272.

DeFelipe, J. (2002). Sesquicentenary of the birthday of Santiago Ramon y Cajal, the father of modern neuroscience. *Trends Neurosci*, **25**(9), 481–484.

Degonda, N., Mondadori, C. R., Bosshardt, S. *et al.* (2005). Implici associative learning engages the hippocampus and interacts with explicit associative learning. *Neuron*, **46**(3), 505–520.

Dehaene, S. (2001). Calculating creative connections. *Trends Cogn Sci*, **5**(8), 364.

Dehaene, S., Naccache, L. (2001). Towards a cognitive permanence of consciousness: basic evidence and a workspace framework. *Cognition*, **79**, 1–37.

Dehaene, S., Molko, N., Cohen, L., Wilson, A. J. (2004). Arithmetic and the brain. *Curr Opin Neurobiol*, **14**(2), 218–224.

Dehaene, S., Naccache, L., Cohen, L. *et al.* (2001). Cerebral mechanisms of word masking and unconscious repetition priming. *Nat Neurosci*, **4**(7), 752–758.

Dehaene-Lambertz, G., Dehaene, S. (1994). Speed and cerebral correlates of syllable discrimination in infants. *Nature*, **370**(6487), 292–295.

Dehaene-Lambertz, G., Dehaene, S., Hertz-Pannier, L. (2002). Functional neuroimaging of speech perception in infants. *Science*, **298**(5600), 2013–2015.

Dehaene-Lambertz, G., Hertz-Pannier, L., Dubois, J. (2006). Nature and nurture in language acquisition: anatomical and functional brain-imaging studies in infants. *Trends Neurosci*, **29**(7), 367–373.

Del-Ben, C. M., Deakin, J. F., McKie, S. *et al.* (2005). The effect of citalopram pretreatment on neuronal responses to neuropsychological tasks in normal volunteers: an fMRI study. *Neuropsychopharmacology*, **30**(9), 1724–1734.

Delaney, P. F., Ericsson, K. A., Knowles, M. E. (2004). Immediate and sustained effects of planning in a problem-solving task. *J Exp Psychol Learn Mem Cogn*, **30**(6), 1219–1234.

Dell, G. S., Sullivan, J. M. (2004). Speech errors and language production: neuropsychological and connectionist perspectives. In Ross, B. H. (ed.), *The psychology of learning and motivation*, pp. 63–108. Elsevier, San Diego.

Dennett, D. (2001). Are we explaining consciousness yet? *Cognition*, **79**(1–2), 221–237.

Desimone, R., Albright, T. D., Gross, C. G., Bruce, C. (1984). Stimulus-selective properties of inferior temporal neurons in the macaque. *J Neurosci*, **4**(8), 2051–2062.

Deutsch, G., Eisenberg, H. M. (1987). Frontal blood flow changes in recovery from coma. *J Cereb Blood Flow Metab*, **7**(1), 29–34.

Diamond, A. (1985). Development of the ability to use recall to guide action, as indicated by infants' performance on AB. *Child Dev*, **56**(4), 868–883.

Diamond, A. (1991). Neuropsychological insights into the meaning of object concept development. In Carey, S. G. R. (ed.), *The epigenesis of mind: essays on biology and cognition*, pp. 67–110. Lawrence Erlbaum Associates, Hillsdale.

Diamond, A. (2001). A model system for studying the role of dopamine in the prefrontal cortex during early development in humans: early and continuously treated phenylketonuria. In Nelson, C. A. L. (ed.), *Handbook of developmental cognitive neuroscience*, pp. 433–472. MIT Press, Cambridge.

Diamond, A., Goldman-Rakic, P. S. (1989). Comparison of human infants and rhesus monkeys on Piaget's AB task: evidence for dependence on dorsolateral prefrontal cortex. *Exp Brain Res*, **74**(1), 24–40.

Dietl, T., Trautner, P., Staedtgen, M. *et al.* (2005). Processing of famous faces and medial temporal lobe event-related potentials: a depth electrode study. *Neuroimage*, **25**(2), 401–407.

Dietrich, V., Nieschalk, M., Stoll, W., Rajan, R., Pantev, C. (2001). Cortical reorganization in patients with high frequency cochlear hearing loss. *Hear Res*, **158**(1–2), 95–101.

Dixon, N. F. (1971). *Subliminal perception: the nature of a controversy*. McGraw-Hill.

Dogil, G., Ackermann, W., Grodd, W. *et al.* (2002). The speaking brain: a tutorial introduction to fMRI experiments in the production of speech, prosody, and syntax. *J Neurolinguist*, **15**(1), 59–90.

Dolan, R. J., Fink, G. R., Rolls, E. *et al.* (1997). How the brain learns to see objects and faces in an impoverished context. *Nature*, **389**(6651), 596–599.

Doniger, G. M., Foxe, J. J., Schroeder, C. E., Murray, M. M., Higgins, B. A., Javitt, D. C. (2001). Visual perceptual learning in human object recognition areas: a repetition priming study using high-density electrical mapping. *Neuroimage*, **13**(2), 305–313.

Downing, P. E., Bray, D., Rogers, J., Childs, C. (2004). Bodies capture attention when nothing is expected. *Cognition*, **93**(1), B27–38.

Draine, S. C., Greenwald, A. G. (1998). Replicable unconscious semantic priming. *J Exp Psychol Gen*, **127**(3), 286–303.

Drake, R., Vogl, W., Mitchell, A. (Eds.). (2005). *Gray's anatomy for students*: Churchill Livingston, Edinburgh.

Driver, J., Mattingley, J. B. (1998). Parietal neglect and visual awareness. *Nat Neurosci*, **1**(1), 17–22.

Driver, J., Vuilleumier, P. (2001). Perceptual awareness and its loss in unilateral neglect and extinction. *Cognition*, **79**(1–2), 39–88.

Dronkers, N. F., Ogar, J. (2003). Aphasia. In Aminoff, M., Daroff, R. (eds), *Encyclopedia of the neurological sciences*. Academic Press, San Diego.

Dudai, Y. (2004). The neurobiology of consolidations, or, how stable is the engram? *Annu Rev Psychol*, **55**, 51–86.

Dudley, H. (1939). The automatic synthesis of speech. *Proc Natl Acad Sci USA*, **25**(7), 377–383.

Duncan, J., Owen, A. M. (2000). Common regions of the human frontal lobe recruited by diverse cognitive demands. *Trend Neurosci*, **23**(10), 475–483.

Duncker, K. (1945). On problem-solving. *Psychological Monographs*, **58**(5).

Durston, S., Thomas, K. M., Worden, M. S., Yang, Y., Casey, B. J. (2002). The effect of preceding context on inhibition: an event-related fMRI study. *Neuroimage*, **16**(2), 449–453.

Duzel, E., Yonelinas, A. P., Mangun, G. R., Heinze, H. J., Tulving, E. (1997). Event-related brain potential correlates of two states of conscious awareness in memory. *Proc Natl Acad Sci USA*, **94**(11), 5973–5978.

Eagleman, D. M. (2001). Visual illusions and neurobiology. *Nat Rev Neurosci*, **2**(12), 920–926.

Edelman, G. M. (1989). *The remembered present: a biological theory of consciousness*. Basic Books Inc, New York.

Edelman, G. M., Mountcastle, V. B. (1978). *The mindful brain: cortical organization and the group-selective theory of higher brain function*. Massachusetts Institute of Technology Press, Oxford.

Edelman, G. M., Tononi, G. (2000). *A universe of consciousness: how matter becomes imagination*. Basic Books Inc, New York.

Eisenberger, N. I., Lieberman, M. D. (2004). Why rejection hurts: a common neural alarm system for physical and social pain. *Trends Cogn Sci*, **8**(7), 294–300.

Ekman, P. (2003). Emotions inside out. 130 years after Darwin's 'the expression of the emotions in man and animal'. *Ann NY Acad Sci*, **1000**, 1–6.

Eldridge, L. L., Sarfatti, S., Knowlton, B. J. (2002). The effect of testing procedure on remember-know judgments. *Psychon Bull Rev*, **9**(1), 139–145.

Emery, N. J. (2000). The eyes have it: the neuroethology, function and evolution of social gaze. *Neurosci Biobehav Rev*, **24**(6), 581–604.

Engel, A. K., Singer, W. (2001). Temporal binding and the neural correlates of sensory awareness. *Trends Cogn Sci*, **5**(1), 16–25.

Epstein, R., Kanwisher, N. (1998). A cortical representation of the local visual environment. *Nature*, **392**(6676), 598–601.

Falini, A., Bozzali, M., Magnani, G. *et al.* (2005). A whole brain MR spectroscopy study from patients with Alzheimer's disease and mild cognitive impairment. *Neuroimage*, **26**(4), 1159–1163.

Fan, J., McCandliss, B. D., Fossella, J., Flombaum, J. I., Posner, M. I. (2005). The activation of attentional networks. *Neuroimage*, **26**(2), 471–479.

Fan, J., McCandliss, B. D., Sommer, T., Raz, A., Posner, M. I. (2002). Testing the efficiency and independence of attentional networks. *J Cogn Neurosci*, **14**(3), 340–347.

Fantz, R. L. (1964). Visual experience in infants: decreased attention to familiar patterns relative to novel ones. *Science*, **146**, 668–670.

Farah, M. J., Tanaka, J. W., Drain, H. M. (1995). What causes the face inversion effect? *J Exp Psychol Hum Percept Perform*, **21**(3), 628–634.

Farroni, T., Johnson, M. H., Brockbank, M., Simion, F. (2000). Infants' use of gaze direction to cue attention: the importance of perceived motion. *Visual Cognition*, **7**(6), 705–718.

Fatterpekar, G. M., Naidich, T. P., Delman, B. N. *et al.* (2002). Cytoarchitecture of the human cerebral cortex: MR microscopy of excised specimens at 9.4 tesla. *Am J Neuroradiol*, **23**(8), 1313–1321.

Faubert, J., Diaconu, V., Pitto, M., Pitto, A. (2002). Residual vision in the blind field of hemidecorticated humans predicted by a diffusion scatter model and selective spectral absorption of the human eye. *Vision Res*, **39**(10), 149–157.

Feldman, J. (2003). What is a visual object? *Trends Cogn Sci*, **7**(6), 252–256.

Felleman, D. J., Van Essen, D. C. (1991). Distributed hierarchical processing in the primate cerebral cortex. *Cereb Cortex*, **1**(1), 1–47.

Filley, C. M. (2002). Neuroanatomy. In Ramachandran, V. S. (ed.), *Encyclopedia of the human brain*. Academic Press, San Diego.

Finkelstein, G. (2000). Why Darwin was English. *Endeavour*, **24**(2), 76–78.

Fishman, Y. I., Reser, D. H., Arezzo, J. C., Steinschneider, M. (2001). Neural correlates of auditory stream segregation in primary auditory cortex of the awake monkey. *Hear Res*, **151**(1–2), 167–187.

Fletcher, P. C., Frith, C. D., Grasby, P. M., Shallice, T., Frackowiak, R. S., Dolan, R. J. (1995). Brain systems for encoding and retrieval of auditory-verbal memory. An in vivo study in humans. *Brain*, **118**(Pt 2), 401–416.

Fletcher, P. C., Henson, R. N. (2001). Frontal lobes and human memory: insights from functional neuroimaging. *Brain*, **124**(Pt 5), 849–881.

Fletcher, P. C., Zafiris, O., Frith, C. D. *et al.* (2005). On the benefits of not trying: brain activity and connectivity reflecting the interactions of explicit and implicit sequence learning. *Cereb Cortex*, **15**(7), 1002–1015.

Fogassi, L., Ferrari, P. F., Gesierich, B., Rozzi, S., Chersi, F., Rizzolatti, G. (2005). Parietal lobe: from action organization to intention understanding. *Science*, **308**(5722), 662–667.

Fourier, J. (1822). *The analytical theory of heat* (English transl Freeman, 1878). Republished 1955. Dover, New York.

Fox, M. D., Snyder, A. Z., Vincent, J. L., Corbetta, M., Van Essen, D. C., Raichle, M. E. (2005). The human brain is intrinsically organized into dynamic, anticorrelated functional networks. *Proc Natl Acad Sci USA*, **102**(27), 9673–9678.

Fox, N. A., Bell, M. A. (1990). Electrophysiological indices of frontal lobe development. In Diamond, A. (ed.), *The development and neural bases of higher cognitive functions*, Vol. 608, pp. 677–698. New York Academy of Sciences, New York.

Fox, P. T., Raichle, M. E. (1986). Focal physiological uncoupling of cerebral blood flow and oxidative metabolism during somatosensory stimulation in human subjects. *Proc Natl Acad Sci USA*, **83**(4), 1140–1144.

Fox, P. T., Raichle, M. E., Mintun, M. A., Dence, C. (1988). Nonoxidative glucose consumption during focal physiologic neural activity. *Science*, **241**(4864), 462–464.

Frackowiak, R. S. J. (Ed.). (2004). *Human brain function*, 2nd edn. Vol. xvi. Elsevier Academic Press, Boston.

Fraisse, P. (1969). Why is naming longer than reading? *Acta Psychol*, **30**, 96–103.

Franzen, G., Ingvar, D. H. (1975). Abnormal distribution of cerebral activity in chronic schizophrenia. *J Psychiatr Res*, **12**(3), 199–214.

Freeman, W. J. (1991). The physiology of perception. *Sci Am*, **284**, 78–85.

Freeman, W. J. (2004). Origin, structure, and role of background EEG activity. Part 1 Analytic amplitude. *Clin Neurophysiol*, **115**(9), 2077–2088.

Freeman, W. J., Burke, B. C., Holmes, M. D. (2003). Aperiodic phase re-setting in scalp EEG of beta-gamma oscillations by state transitions at alpha-theta rates. *Hum Brain Mapp*, **19**(4), 248–272.

Fried, P. A., Watkinson, B., Gray, R. (2003). Differential effects on cognitive functioning in 13- to 16-year-olds prenatally exposed to cigarettes and marihuana. *Neurotoxicol Teratol*, **25**(4), 427–436.

Friederici, A. D. (2002). Towards a neural basis of auditory sentence processing. *Trends Cogn Sci*, **6**(2), 78–84.

Friederici, A. D. (2005). Neurophysiological markers of early language acquisition: from syllables to sentences. *Trends Cogn Sci*, **9**(10), 481–488.

Friederici, A. D., Kotz, S. A. (2003). The brain basis of syntactic processes: functional imaging and lesion studies. *Neuroimage*, **20** Suppl 1, S8–17.

Fries, P. (2005). A mechanism for cognitive dynamics: neuronal communication through neuronal coherence. *Trends Cogn Sci*, **9**(10), 474–480.

Fries, P., Fernandez, G., Jensen, O. (2003). When neurons form memories. *Trends Neurosci*, **26**(3), 123–124.

Fries, P., Schroder, J. H., Roelfsema, P. R., Singer, W., Engel, A. K. (2002). Oscillatory neuronal synchronization in primary visual cortex as a correlate of stimulus selection. *J Neurosci*, **22**(9), 3739–3754.

Friston, K. (2003). Learning and inference in the brain. *Neural Netw*, **16**(9), 1325–1352.

Frith, C. D., Frith, U. (1999). Interacting minds – a biological basis. *Science*, **286**(5445), 1692–1695.

Fulford, J., Vadeyar, S. H., Dodampahala, S. H. *et al.* (2003). Fetal brain activity in response to a visual stimulus. *Hum Brain Mapp*, **20**(4), 239–245.

Fulton, J. F. (1928). Observations upon the vascularity of the human occipital lobe during visual activity. *Brain*, **51**, 310–320.

Funahashi, S., Bruce, C. J., Goldman-Rakic, P. S. (1989). Mnemonic coding of visual space in the monkey's dorsolateral prefrontal cortex. *J Neurophysiol*, **61**(2), 331–349.

Funahashi, S., Bruce, C. J., Goldman-Rakic, P. S. (1993). Dorsolateral prefrontal lesions and oculomotor delayed-response performance: evidence for mnemonic 'scotomas'. *J Neurosci*, **13**(4), 1479–1497.

Funnel, E., Sheridan, J. S. (1992). Categories of knowledge? Unfamiliar aspects of living and nonliving things. *Cognit Neuropsychol*, **9**, 135–153.

Fuster, J. M. (1985). Temporal organization of behavior. *Hum Neurobiol*, **4**(2), 57–60.

Fuster, J. M. (1997). Network memory. *Trends Neurosci*, **20**(10), 451–459.

Fuster, J. M. (2003). *Cortex and mind: unifying cognition*. Oxford University Press, New York.

Fuster, J. M. (2004). Upper processing stages of the perception-action cycle. *Trends Cogn Sci*, **8**(4), 143–145.

Fuster, J. M. and Alexander, G. E. (1971). Neuron activity related to short-term memory. *Science*, **173**(997), 652–6654.

Gabrieli, J. D., Keane, M. M., Stanger, B. Z., Kjelgaard, M. M., Corkin, S., Growdon, J. H. (1994). Dissociations among structural-perceptual, lexical-semantic, and event-fact memory systems in Alzheimer, amnesic, and normal subjects. *Cortex*, **30**(1), 75–103.

Gage, N., Poeppel, D., Roberts, T. P., Hickok, G. (1998). Auditory evoked m100 reflects onset acoustics of speech sounds. *Brain Res*, **814**(1–2), 236–239.

Gage, N., Roberts, T. P., Hickok, G. (2006). Temporal resolution properties of human auditory cortex: reflections in the neuromagnetic auditory evoked m100 component. *Brain Res*, **1069**(1), 166–171.

Gage, N. M., Roberts, T. P. (2000). Temporal integration: reflections in the m100 of the auditory evoked field. *Neuroreport*, **11**(12), 2723–2726.

Gage, N. M., Roberts, T. P., Hickok, G. (2002). Hemispheric asymmetries in auditory evoked neuromagnetic fields in response to place of articulation contrasts. *Brain Res Cogn Brain Res*, **14**(2), 303–306.

Gage, N. M., Siegel, B., Callen, M., Roberts, T. P. (2003a). Cortical sound processing in children with autism disorder: An MEG investigation. *Neuroreport*, **14**(16), 2047–2051.

Gage, N. M., Siegel, B., Roberts, T. P. (2003b). Cortical auditory system maturational abnormalities in children with autism disorder: An MEG investigation. *Brain Res Dev Brain Res*, **144**(2), 201–209.

Galaburda, A. M., Pandya, D. N. (1983). The intrinsic architectonic and connectional organization of the superior temporal region of the rhesus monkey. *J Comp Neurol*, **221**(2), 169–184.

Gallagher, H., Jack, A., Roepstorff, A., Frith, C. (2002). Imaging the intentional stance in a competitive game. *NeuroImage*, **16**, 814–821.

Gallese, V., Fadiga, L., Fogassi, L., Rizzolatti, G. (1996). Action recognition in the premotor cortex. *Brain*, **119**(Pt 2), 593–609.

Ganis, G., Thompson, W. L., Kosslyn, S. M. (2004). Brain areas underlying visual mental imagery and visual perception: an fMRI study. *Brain Res Cogn Brain Res*, **20**(2), 226–241.

Gastaut, D. (1958). The role of the reticular system in establishing conditioned reactions. In Jasper, H. M., Proctor, L. D., Knighton, R. S., Noshay, W. C., Costello, R. T. (eds), *The reticular formation of the brain*. Little, Brown, Boston.

Gathers, A. D., Bhatt, R., Corbly, C. R., Farley, A. B., Joseph, J. E. (2004). Developmental shifts in cortical loci for face and object recognition. *Neuroreport*, **15**(10), 1549–1553.

Gauthier, I., Skudlarski, P., Gore, J. C., Anderson, A. W. (2000). Expertise for cars and birds recruits brain areas involved in face recognition. *Nat Neurosci*, **3**(2), 191–197.

Geschwind, N. (1979a). Anatomical and functional specialization of the cerebral hemispheres in the human. *Bull Mem Acad R Med Belg*, **134**(6), 286–297.

Geschwind, N. (1979b). Specializations of the human brain. *Sci Am*, **241**(3), 180–199.

Geschwind, N., Levitsky, W. (1968). Human brain: left-right asymmetries in temporal speech region. *Science*, **161**(837), 186–187.

Geschwind, N., Galaburda, A. M. (1985a). Cerebral lateralization. Biological mechanisms, associations, and pathology. I. A hypothesis and a program for research. *Arch Neurol*, **42**(6), 428–459.

Geschwind, N., Galaburda, A. M. (1985b). Cerebral lateralization. Biological mechanisms, associations, and pathology. II. A hypothesis and a program for research. *Arch Neurol*, **42**(6), 521–552.

Geschwind, N., Galaburda, A. M. (1985c). Cerebral lateralization. Biological mechanisms, associations, and pathology. III. A hypothesis and a program for research. *Arch Neurol*, **42**(6), 634–654.

Gevins, A., Leong, H., Smith, M. E., Le, J., Du, R. (1995). Mapping cognitive brain function with modern high-resolution electroencephalography. *Trends Neurosci*, **18**(10), 429–436.

Gibbs, S. E., D'Esposito, M. (2006). A functional magnetic resonance imaging study of the effects of pergolide, a dopamine receptor agonist, on component processes of working memory. *Neuroscience*, **139**(1), 359–371.

Giedd, J. N., Blumenthal, J., Jeffries, N. O. *et al.* (1999). Brain development during childhood and adolescence: a longitudinal MRI study. *Nat Neurosci*, **2**(10), 861–863.

Gilboa, A., Winocur, G., Grady, C. L., Hevenor, S. J., Mscovitch, M. (2004). Remembering our past: functional neuroanatomy of recent and very remote personal events. *Cereb Cortex*, **14**(11), 1214–1225.

Gilmore, R. O., Johnson, M. H. (1995). Working memory in infancy: six-month-olds' performance on two versions of the oculomotor delayed response task. *J Exp Child Psychol*, **59**(3), 397–418.

Girard, P., Salin, P. A., Bullier, J. (1991). Visual activity in areas V3a and V3 during reversible inactivation of area V1 in the macaque monkey. *J Neurophysiol*, **66**(5), 1493–1503.

Gitelman, D. R., Nobre, A. C., Sonty, S., Parrish, T. B., Mesulam, M. M. (2005). Language network specializations: an analysis with parallel task designs and functional magnetic resonance imaging. *Neuroimage*, **26**(4), 975–985.

Glisky, E. L., Polster, M. R., Routhieaux, B. C. (1995). Double dissociation between item and source memory. *Neuropsychology*, **9**(2), 229–235.

Gluck, M. A., Meeter, M., Myers, C. E. (2003). Computational models of the hippocampal region: linking incremental learning and episodic memory. *Trends Cogn Sci*, **7**(6), 269–276.

Gobet, F. (1998). Expert memory: a comparison of four theories. *Cognition*, **66**, 115–152.

Gobet, F., Simon, H. A. (1996). Recall of rapidly presented random chess positions. *Psychonomic Bull Rev*, **3**, 159–163.

Goebel, R., Muckli, L., Zanella, F. E., Singer, W., Stoerig, P. (2001). Sustained extrastriate cortical activation without visual awareness revealed by fMRI studies of hemianopic patients. *Vision Res*, **41**(10–11), 1459–1474.

Gold, J. M., Berman, K. F., Randolph, C., Goldberg, T. E., Weinberger, D. R. (1996). PET validation of a novel prefrontal task: delayed response alternation. *Neuropsychology*, **10**(1), 3–10.

Goldberg, E. (1992). Introduction: the frontal lobes in neurological and psychiatric conditions. *Neuropsychol Neuropsychiatr Behav Neurol*, **5**(4), 231–232.

Goldberg, E. (2001a). *The executive brain*: Oxford University Press, New York.

Goldberg, E. (2001b). *The executive brain: frontal lobes and the civilized mind* (Vol. xix). Oxford University Press, New York.

Goldberg, E., Bilder, R. M., Hughes, J. E., Antin, S. P., Mattis, S. (1989). A reticulo-frontal disconnection syndrome. *Cortex*, **25**(4), 687–695.

Goldberg, E., Bougakov, D. (2000). Novel approaches to the diagnosis and treatment of frontal lobe dysfunction. *International handbook of neuropsychological rehabilitation. Critical issues in neuropsychology*, 93–112.

Goldberg, E., Costa, L. D. (1981). Hemisphere differences in the acquisition and use of descriptive systems. *Brain Lang*, **14**(1), 144–173.

Goldberg, E., Costa, L. D. (1985). Qualitative indices in neuropsychological assessment: an extension of Luria's approach to executive deficit following prefrontal lesion. In Grant, I., Adams, K. M. (eds), *Neuropsychological assessment of neuropsychiatric disorders*, pp. 48–64. Oxford University Press, New York.

Goldberg, E., Bilder, R. M., Hughes, J. E., Antin, S. P., Mattis, S. (1989). A reticulo-frintal disconnection syndrome. *Cortex*, **25**(4), 687–695.

Goldberg, E., Harner, R., Lovell, M., Podell, K., Riggio, S. (1994). Cognitive bias, functional cortical geometry, and the frontal lobes: laterality, sex, and handedness. *J Cogn Neurosci*, **6**(3), 276–293.

Goldberg, E., Kluger, A., Griesing, T., Malta, L., Shapiro, M., Ferris, S. (1997). *Early diagnosis of frontal-lobe dementias.* Paper presented at the Eighth Congress of International Psychogeriatric Association, Jerusalem, Israel, August 17–22.

Goldman-Rakic, P. S. (1987). Circuitry of primate prefrontal cortex and regulation of behavior by representational memory. *Handbook Physiol*, **5**, 373–417.

Goldman-Rakic, P. S. (1995). Cellular basis of working memory. *Neuron*, **14**(3), 477–485.

Goldman-Rakic, P. S. (1998). The prefrontal landscape: implications of functional architecture for understanding human mentation and the central executive. In Roberts, A. C., Robbins, T. W., Weiskrantz, L. (eds), *The prefrontal cortex: executive and cognitive functions* (pp. 87–102). Oxford University Press, Oxford.

Goodale, M. A., Humphrey, G. K. (1998). The objects of action and perception. *Cognition*, **67**(1–2), 181–207.

Goodale, M. A., Milner, A. D. (1992). Separate visual pathways for perception and action. *Trends Neurosci*, **15**(1), 20–25.

Goodale, M. A., Milner, A. D., Jakobson, L. S., Carey, D. P. (1991). A neurological dissociation between perceiving objects and grasping them. *Nature*, **349**(6305), 154–156.

Gore, A.C., Roberts, J. L. in Squire, L. R., Bloom, F. E., McConnell, S. K., Roberts, J. L., Spitzer, N. C., Zigmond, M. J. (Eds.). (2003). *Fundamental neuroscience*, 2nd edn. San Diego: Elsevier Academic Press.

Goren, C. C., Sarty, M., Wu, P. Y. (1975). Visual following and pattern discrimination of face-like stimuli by newborn infants. *Pediatrics*, **56**(4), 544–549.

Gottesmann, C. (1999). Neurophysiological support of consciousness during waking and sleep. *Prog Neurobiol*, **59**(5), 469–508.

Gottlieb, G., Halpern, C. T. (2002). A relational view of causality in normal and abnormal development. *Dev Psychopathol*, **14**(3), 421–435.

Graham, K. S., Murre, J. M., Hodges, J. R. (1999). Episodic memory in semantic dementia: a computational approach based on tracelink. *Prog Brain Res*, **121**, 47–65.

Graham, N. L., Patterson, K., Hodges, J. R. (2000). The impact of semantic memory impairment on spelling: evidence from semantic dementia. *Neuropsychologia*, **38**(2), 143–163.

Grant, D. A., Berg, E. A. (1948). A behavioral analysis of degree of reinforcement and ease of shifting to new responses in a Weigl-type card-sorting problem. *J Exp Psychol*, **38**, 404–411.

Greenwald, A. G., Banaji, M. R., Rudman, L. A., Farnham, S. D., Nosek, B. A., Mellott, D. S. (2002). A unified theory of implicit attitudes, stereotypes, self-esteem, and self-concept. *Psychol Rev*, **109**(1), 3–25.

Griffiths, T. D., Warren, J. D. (2002). The plenum temporale as a computational hub. *Trends Neurosci*, **25**(7), 348–353.

Grill-Spector, K., Kushnir, T., Edelman, S., Avidan, G., Itzchak, Y., Malach, R. (1999). Differential processing of objects under various viewing conditions in the human lateral occipital complex. *Neuron*, **24**(1), 187–203.

Grill-Spector, K., Kushnir, T., Hendler, T., Malach, R. (2000). The dynamics of object-selective activation correlate with recognition performance in humans. *Nat Neurosci*, **3**(8), 837–843.

Grodzinsky, Y., Friedrici, A. D. (2006). Neuroimaging of syntax and syntactic processing. *Curr Opin Neurobiol*, **16**(2), 240–246.

Groome, L. J., Mooney, D. M., Holland, S. B., Smith, L. A., Atterbury, J. L., Dykman, R. A. (1999). Behavioral state affects heart rate response to low-intensity sound in human fetuses. *Early Hum Dev*, **54**(1), 39–54.

Gross, C. G. (1992). Representation of visual stimuli in inferior temporal cortex. *Philos Trans R Soc Lond B Biol Sci*, **335**(1273), 3–10.

Habib, R., Nyberg, L., Tulving, E. (2003). Hemispheric asymmetries of memory: the Hera model revisited. *Trends Cogn Sci*, **7**(6), 241–245.

Hagoort, P. (2005). On Broca, brain, and binding: a new framework. *Trends Cogn Sci*, **9**(9), 416–423.

Hahn, S., Carlson, C., Singer, S., Gronlund, S. D. (2006). Aging and visual search: automatic and controlled attentional bias to threat faces. *Acta Psychol (Amst)*.

Haier, R. J., Siegel, B. V. Jr, MacLachlan, A., Soderling, E., Lottenberg, S., Buchsbaum, M. S. (1992). Regional glucose metabolic changes after learning a complex visuospatial/motor task: a positron emission tomographic study. *Brain Res*, **570**(1–2), 134–143.

Handy, T. C., Gazzaniga, M. S., Ivry, R. B. (2003). Cortical and subcortical contributions to the representation of temporal information. *Neuropsychologia*, **41**(11), 1461–1473.

Hanon, E. E., Trehub, S. E. (2005). Tuning in to musical rhythms: infants learn more readily than adults. *Proc Natl Acad Sci USA*, **102**(35), 12639–12643.

Harenski, C. L., Hamann, S. (2006). Neural correlates of regulating negative emotions related to moral violations. *Neuroimage*, **30**(1), 313–324.

Hariri, A. R., Brown, S. M., Williamson, D. E., Flory, J. D., de Wit, H., Manuck, S. B. (2006). Preference for immediate over delayed rewards is associated with magnitude of ventral striatal activity. *J Neurosci*, **26**(51), 13213–13217.

Hariri, A. R., Mattay, V. S., Tessitore, A. *et al.* (2002). Serotonin transporter genetic variation and the response of the human amygdala. *Science*, **297**(5580), 400–403.

Hartley, A. A., Speer, N. K. (2000). Locating and fractionating working memory using functional neuroimaging: storage, maintenance, and executive functions. *Microsc Res Tech*, **51**(1), 45–53.

Hauk, O., Johnsrude, I., Pulvermuller, F. (2004). Somatotopic representation of action words in human motor and premotor cortex. *Neuron*, **41**(2), 301–307.

Haxby, J., Hoffman, E., Gobbini, M. (2002). Human neural systems for face recognition and social communication. *Biol Psychiat*, **51**, 59–67.

Haxby, J., Hoffman, E. A., Gobbini, M. I. (2000). The distributed human neural system for face perception. *Trends Cogn Sci*, **4**(6), 223–233.

Haxby, J. V., Gobbini, M. I., Furey, M. L., Ishai, A., Schouten, J. L., Pietrini, P. (2001). Distributed and overlapping representations of faces and objects in ventral temporal cortex. *Science*, **293**(5539), 2425–2430.

Hayhoe, M., Ballard, D. (2005). Eye movements in natural behavior. *Trends Cogn Sci*, **9**(4), 188–194.

Haynes, J. D., Deichmann, R., Rees, G. (2005). Eye-specific effects of binocular rivalry in the human lateral geniculate nucleus. *Nature*, **438**(7067), 496–499.

Hebb, D. O. (1949). *The organization of behavior: a neuropsychological theory*. Wiley, Oxford.

Heckers, S., Weis, A., Deckersbach, T., Goff, D., Mrecraft, R., Bush, G. (2004). Anterior cingulate cortex activation during cognitive interference in schizophrenia. *Am J Psychiatr*, **161**, 707–715.

Heimer, L., Van Hoesen, G. W. (2006). The limbic lobe and its output channels: implications for emotional functions and adaptive behavior. *Neurosci Biobehav Rev*, **30**(2), 126–147.

Hendry, S. H. *et al.*, in Squire, L. R., Bloom, F. E., McConnell, S. K., Roberts, J. L., Spitzer, N. C., Zigmond, M. J. (Eds.). (2003). *Fundamental neuroscience*, 2nd edn. San Diego: Elsevier Academic Press.

Henke, K., Mondadori, C. R., Treyer, V., Nitsch, R. M., Buck, A., Hock, C. (2003). Nonconscious formation and reactivation of semantic associations by way of the medial temporal lobe. *Neuropsychologia*, **41**(8), 863–876.

Henson, R. N. (2001). Repetition effects for words and nonwords as indexed by event-related fMRI: a preliminary study. *Scand J Psychol*, **42**(3), 179–186.

Hermann, L. (1870). Eine Erscheinung simultanen Contrastes. *Pflügers Arch Physiol*, **3**, 13–15.

Hesslow, G. (2002). Conscious thought as simulation of behaviour and perception. *Trend Cogn Sci*, **6**(6), 242–247.

Hester, R., Dixon, V., Garavan, H. (2006). A consistent attentional bias for drug-related material in active cocaine users across word and picture versions of the emotional stroop task. *Drug Alcohol Depend*, **81**(3), 251–257.

Heywood, C. A., Kentridge, R. W. (2000). Affective blindsight? *Trends Cogn Sci*, **4**(4), 125–126.

Hickok, G., Poeppel, D. (2004). Dorsal and ventral streams: a framework for understanding aspects of the functional anatomy of language. *Cognition*, **92**, 67–99.

Hillyard, S. A., Hink, R. F., Schwent, V. L., Picton, T. W. (1973). Electrical signs of selective attention in the human brain. *Science*, **182**(108), 177–180.

Hobson, J. A., Stickgold, R. (1995). Sleep. Sleep the beloved teacher? *Curr Biol*, **5**(1), 35–36.

Hodges, J. R., Graham, K. S. (2001). Episodic memory: Insights from semantic dementia. *Philos Trans R Soc Lond B Biol Sci*, **356**(1413), 1423–1434.

Hodges, J. R., Patterson, K. (1997). Semantic memory disorders. *Trends Cogn Sci*, **1**(2), 68–72.

Hodgkin, A. L., Huxley, A. F. (1952). Currents carried by sodium and potassium ions through the membrane of the giant axon of loligo. *J Physiol*, **116**(4), 449–472.

Hofer S., Frahm J. (2006). Topography of the human corpus callosum revisited – comprehensive fiber tractography using magnetic resonance diffusion tensor imaging. *NeuroImage*, **32**, 989–994.

Holmes, G. (1918). Disturbances of vision by cerebral lesions. *Br J Ophthalmol*, **2**, 353–384.

Holstege, G., J., M. L., Gerrits, N. M. (2004). Chapter 36. In Paxinos, G. (ed.), *The human nervous system*. Academic Press, San Diego.

Honey, G. D., Fu, C. H., Kim, J. *et al.* (2002). Effects of verbal working memory load on corticocortical connectivity modeled by path analysis of functional magnetic resonance imaging data. *Neuroimage*, **17**(2), 573–582.

Hopfield, J. J. (1982). Neural networks and physical systems with emergent collective computational abilities. *Proc Natl Acad Sci USA*, **79**(8), 2554–2558.

Huang, H., Zhang, J., Jiang, H. *et al.* (2005). DTI tractography based parcellation of white matter: application to the midsagittal morphology of corpus callosum. *Neuroimage*, **26**(1), 195–205.

Hubel, D. H., Wiesel, T. N. (1962). Receptive fields, binocular interaction and functional architecture in the cat's visual cortex. *J Physiol*, **160**, 106–154.

Hubel, D. H., Wiesel, T. N. (1968). Receptive fields and functional architecture of monkey striate cortex. *J Physiol*, **195**(1), 215–243.

Hubel, D. H., Wiesel, T. N. (1998). Early exploration of the visual cortex. *Neuron*, **20**(3), 401–412.

Hudspeth, A. J., Logothetis, N. K. (2000). Sensory systems. *Curr Opin Neurobiol*, **10**(5), 631–641.

Hulsmann, E., Erb, M., Grodd, W. (2003). From will to action: sequential cerebellar contributions to voluntary movement. *Neuroimage*, **20**(3), 1485–1492.

Humphrey, N. K. (1974). Vision in a monkey without striate cortex: a case study. *Perception*, **3**(3), 241–255.

Humphrey, N. K., Weiskrantz, L. (1967). Vision in monkeys after removal of the striate cortex. *Nature*, **215**(101), 595–597.

Huttenlocher, P. R. (1990). Morphometric study of human cerebral cortex development. *Neuropsychologia*, **28**(6), 517–527.

Huttenlocher, P. R. (1994). Synaptogenesis, synapse elimination, and neural plasticity in human cerebral cortex: Threats to optimal development. In Nelson, C. A. (ed.), *The Minnesota symposia on child psychology*, Vol. 27, pp. 35–54. Lawrence Erlbaum Associates, Hillsdale.

Huttenlocher, P. R., Dabholkar, A. S. (1997). Regional differences in synaptogenesis in human cerebral cortex. *J Comp Neurol*, **387**(2), 167–178.

Huttenlocher, P. R., De Courten, C., Garey, L. J., Van der Loos, H. (1982). Synaptic development in human cerebral cortex. *Int J Neurol*, **16–17**, 144–154.

Iacoboni, M. (2005). Neural mechanisms of imitation. *Curr Opin Neurobiol*, **15**, 632–637.

Iacoboni, M., Lieberman, M., Knowlton, B. *et al.* (2004). Watching social interactions produces dorsomedial prefrontal and medial parietal bold fMRI signal increases compared to a resting baseline. *NeuroImage*, **21**, 1167–1173.

Iacoboni, M., Molnar-Szakacs, I., Gallese, V. *et al.* (2005). Grasping the intentions of others with one's own mirror neuron system. *PLoS Biol*, **3**(3), 0529–0535.

Ikemoto, S., Wise, R. A. (2004). Mapping of chemical trigger zones for reward. *Neuropharmacology*, **47** Suppl 1, 190–201.

Ingvar, D. H. (1985). 'Memory of the future': an essay on the temporal organization of conscious awareness. *Hum Neurobiol*, **4**(3), 127–136.

Ingvar, D. H., Franzen, G. (1974). Abnormalities of cerebral blood flow distribution in patients with chronic schizophrenia. *Acta Psychiatr Scand*, **50**(4), 425–462.

Ingvar, D. H., Söderberg, U. (1956). A new method for measuring cerebral blood flow in relation to the electroencephalogram. *Electroencephalogr Clin Neurophysiol Suppl*, **8**(3), 403–412.

Ingvar, D. H., Söderberg, U. (1958). Cortical blood flow related to EEG patterns evoked by stimulation of the brain stem. *Acta Physiol Scand*, **42**, 130–143.

Inouye, T. (1909). *Die Sehstörungen bei Schussverletzungen der Kortikalen Sehsphäre, nach Beobachtungen an Verwundeten der Letzten Japanischen Kriege*. Wilhelm Engelmann, Leipzig.

Itti, L., Rees, G., Tsotsos, J. K. (2005). *Neurobiology of attention*. Academic Press, San Diego.

Iverson, L. (2004). Neurotransmitter transporters and their impact on the development of psychopharmacology. *Br J Pharmacol*, **147**, 582–588.

Jackson, H. (1884). Evolution and dissolution of the nervous system, *Croonian Lecture*: Selected Papers.

Jackson, P., Brunet, E., Meltzoff, A., Decety, J. (2006). Empathy examined through the neural mechanisms involved in imagining how I feel versus how you feel pain. *Neuropsychologia*, **44**(5), 752–761.

James, T. W., Culham, J., Humphrey, G. K., Milner, A. D., Goodale, M. A. (2003). Ventral occipital lesions impair object recognition but not object-directed grasping: An fMRI study. *Brain*, **126**(Pt 11), 2463–2475.

James, W. (1890). *The principles of psychology* (Vol. I). Henry Holt and Co, Inc., New York.

Jancke, D., Chavane, F., Naaman, S., Grinvald, A. (2004). Imaging cortical correlates of illusion in early visual cortex. *Nature*, **428**(6981), 423–426.

Javel, E. (2003). Auditory periphery. In Aminoff, M., Daroff, R. (eds), *Encyclopedia of the neurological sciences*. Academic Press, San Diego.

Jensen, O. (2005). Reading the hippocampal code by theta phase-locking. *Trends Cogn Sci*, **9**(12), 551–553.

Jernigan, T. L., Archibald, S. L., Fennema-Notestine, C. *et al.* (2001). Effects of age on tissues and regions of the cerebrum and cerebellum. *Neurobiol Aging*, **22**(4), 581–594.

John, K. R. (2001). Invariant reversible effects of anaesthesia. *Conscious Cogn*, **10**, 165–183.

John, M. S., Brown, D. K., Muir, P. J., Picton, T. W. (2004). Recording auditory steady-state responses in young infants. *Ear Hear*, **25**(6), 539–553.

Johnson, M. H. (2001). Functional brain development in humans. *Nat Rev Neurosci*, **2**(7), 475–483.

Johnson, M. H. (2005a). *Developmental cognitive neuroscience*, 2nd edn. Blackwell Publishing, Oxford.

Johnson, M. H. (2005b). Subcortical face processing. *Nat Rev Neurosci*, **6**(10), 766–774.

Johnson, M. H., Dziurawiec, S., Ellis, H., Morton, J. (1991). Newborns' preferential tracking of face-like stimuli and its subsequent decline. *Cognition*, **40**(1–2), 1–19.

Johnson, M. H. (1991). *Biology and cognitive development: the case of face recognition*. Blackwell, Oxford.

Johnson, N. A., Jahng, G. H., Weiner, M. W. *et al.* (2005). Pattern of cerebral hypoperfusion in Alzheimer disease and mild cognitive impairment measured with arterial spin-labeling MR imaging: initial experience. *Radiology*, **234**(3), 851–859.

Jones, K. L. (1975). The fetal alcohol syndrome. *Addict Dis*, **2**(1–2), 79–88.

Jones, K. L., Smith, D. W. (1973). Recognition of the fetal alcohol syndrome in early infancy. *Lancet*, **2**(7836), 999–1001.

Jones, L. B., Johnson, N., Byne, W. (2002). Alterations in MAP2 immunocytochemistry in areas 9 and 32 of schizophrenic prefrontal cortex. *Psychiatry Res*, **114**(3), 137–148.

Jousmaki, V. (2000). Tracking functions of cortical networks on a millisecond timescale. *Neural Netw*, **13**(8–9), 883–889.

Jung-Beeman, M., Bowden, E. M., Haberman, J. *et al.* (2004). Neural activity when people solve verbal problems with insight. *PLoS Biol*, **2**(4), E97.

Kaas, J. H., Hackett, T. A., Tramo, M. J. (1999). Auditory processing in primate cerebral cortex. *Curr Opin Neurobiol*, **9**(2), 164–170.

Kamitani, Y., Shimojo, S. (1999). Manifestation of scotomas created by transcranial magnetic stimulation of human visual cortex. *Nat Neurosci*, **2**(8), 767–771.

Kamiya, Y., Aihara, M., Osada, M. *et al.* (2002). Electrophysiological study of lateralization in the frontal lobes. *Jap J Cogn Neurosci*, **3**(1), 88–191.

Kandel, E. R. (2000). *Principles of neural science*, 4th edn. McGraw-Hill, New York.

Kandel, E. R. (2004). The molecular biology of memory storage: a dialog between genes and synapses. *Biosci Rep*, **24**(4–5), 475–522.

Kanwisher, N. (2001). Neural events and perceptual awareness. *Cognition*, **79**, 221–237.

Kanwisher, N., McDermott, J., Chun, M. M. (1997). The fusiform face area: a module in human extrastriate cortex specialized for face perception. *J Neurosci*, **17**(11), 4302–4311.

Kastner, S., Ungerleider, L. G. (2000). Mechanisms of visual attention in the human cortex. *Annu Rev Neurosci*, **23**, 315–341.

Kastner, S., Ungerleider, L. G. (2001). The neural basis of biased competition in human visual cortex. *Neuropsychologia*, **39**(12), 1263–1276.

Kaszniak, A. W. (1990). Psychological assessment of the aging individual. In Birren, J. E., Schaie, K. W. (eds), *Handbook of the psychology of aging*, 3rd edn, Vol xvii, pp 427–445. Academic Press, San Diego.

Kelley, W. M., Miezin, F. M., McDermott, K. B. *et al.* (1998). Hemispheric specialization in human dorsal frontal cortex and medial temporal lobe for verbal and nonverbal memory encoding. *Neuron*, **20**(5), 927–936.

Kelly, O. E., Johnson, D. H., Delgutte, B., Cariani, P. (1996). Fractal noise strength in auditory-nerve fiber recordings. *J Acoust Soc Am*, **99**(4Pt 1), 2210–2220.

Kemp, A. H., Gray, M. A., Silberstein, R. B., Armstron, S. M., Nathan, P. J. (2004). Augmentation of serotonin enhances pleasant and suppresses unpleasant cortical electrophysiological responses to visual emotional stimuli in humans. *Neuroimage*, **22**(3), 1084–1096.

Kihlstrom, J. F. (1987). The cognitive unconscious. *Science*, **237**(4821), 1445–1452.

Kihlstrom, J. F. (2004). Availability, accessibility, and subliminal perception. *Conscious Cogn*, **13**(1), 92–100.

Kihlstrom, J. F., Shames, V. A., Dorfman, J. (1996). Intimations of memory and thought. In Reder, L. (ed.), *Implicit memory and metacognition*, pp 1–23. Erlbaum, Mahwah.

Killgore, W. D., Yurgelun-Todd, D. A. (2004). Activation of the amygdala and anterior cingulate during nonconscious processing of sad versus happy faces. *Neuroimage*, **21**(4), 1215–1223.

Kim, C. Y., Blake, R. (2005). Psychophysical magic: Rendering the visible 'invisible'. *Trends Cogn Sci*, **9**(8), 381–388.

Kisilevsky, B. S., Hains, S. M., Lee, K. *et al.* (2003). Effects of experience on fetal voice recognition. *Psychol Sci*, **14**(3), 220–224.

Kisilevsky, B. S., Low, J.A. (1998). Human fetal behavior: 100 years of study. *Develop Rev*, **18**, 1–29.

Kisilevsky, S., Hains, S. M., Jacquet, A. Y., Granier-Deferre, C., Lecanuet, J. P. (2004). Maturation of fetal responses to music. *Dev Sci*, **7**(5), 550–559.

Kjaer, T. W., Nowak, M., Kjaer, K. W., Lou, A. R., Lou, H. C. (2001). Precuneus-prefrontal activity during awareness of visual verbal stimuli. *Conscious Cogn*, **10**(3), 356–365.

Knowlton, B. J., Squire, L. R., Gluck, M. A. (1994). Probabilistic classification learning in amnesia. *Learn Mem*, **1**(2), 106–120.

Knowlton, B. J., Mangels, J. A., Squire, L. R. (1996). A neostriatal habit learning system in humans. *Science*, **273**(5280), 1399–1402.

Knopman, D. S., Nissen, M. J. (1987). Implicit learning in patients with probable Alzheimer's disease. *Neurology*, **37**(5), 784–788.

Koch, C. (1996). A neuronal correlate of consciousness? *Curr Biol*, **6**(5), 492.

Koehler, P. (2003). Carl Wernicke. In Aminoff, M., Daroff, R. (eds), *Encyclopedia of the neurological sciences*. Academic Press, San Diego.

Koelsch, S. (2005). Neural substrates of processing syntax and semantics in music. *Curr Opin Neurobiol*, **15**(2), 207–212.

Koelsch, S., Siebel, W. A. (2005). Towards a neural basis of music perception. *Trends Cogn Sci*, **9**(12), 578–584.

Koepp, M. J., Gunn, R. N., Lawrence, A. D. *et al.* (1998). Evidence for striatal dopamine release during a video game. *Nature*, **393**(6682), 266–268.

Koffka, K. (1935). *Principles of gestalt psychology*. Harcourt, Brace and World, Jovanovic.

Kohonen, T. (1982). A simple paradigm for the self-organisation of structured feature maps, competition and cooperation in neural nets. *Lecture Notes Biomath*, **45**, 248–266.

Konrad, K., Neufang, S., Thiel, C. M. *et al.* (2005). Development of attentional networks: an fMRI study with children and adults. *Neuroimage*, **28**(2), 429–439.

Kosslyn, S. M. (1994). *Image and brain: the resolution of the imagery debate*. The MIT Press, Cambridge.

Kourtzi, Z., Kanwisher, N. (2001). Representation of perceived object shape by the human lateral occipital complex. *Science*, **293**(5534), 1506–1509.

Kozhevnikov, M., Kosslyn, S., Shephard, J. (2005). Spatial versus object visualizers: a new characterization of visual cognitive style. *Mem Cognit*, **33**(4), 710–726.

Kreiman, G., Fried, I., Koch, C. (2002). Single-neuron correlates of subjective vision in the human medial temporal lobe. *Proc Natl Acad Sci USA*, **99**(12), 8378–8383.

Kuffler, S. W. (1953). Discharge patterns and functional organization of mammalian retina. *J Neurophysiol*, **16**(1), 37–68.

Kuhn, T. S. (1962). *The structure of scientific revolutions*. The University of Chicago Press, Chicago.

Kylliainen, A., Braeutigam, S., Hietanen, J. K., Swithenby, S. J., Bailey, A. J. (2006). Face and gaze processing in normally developing children: a magnetoencephalographic study. *Eur J Neurosci*, **23**(3), 801–810.

LaBar, K. S., Gatenby, J. C., Gore, J. C., LeDoux, J. E., Phelps, E. A. (1998). Human amygdala activation during conditioned fear acquisition and extinction: a mixed-trial fMRI study. *Neuron*, **20**(5), 937–945.

Laeng, B., Zarrinpar, A., Kosslyn, S. M. (2003). Do separate processes identify objects as exemplars versus members of basic-level categories? Evidence from hemispheric specialization. *Brain Cogn*, **53**(1), 15–27.

Lamme, V. A., Roelfsema, P. R. (2000). The distinct modes of vision offered by feedforward and recurrent processing. *Trends Neurosci*, **23**(11), 571–579.

Landauer, T. K. (1986). How much do people remember? Some estimates of the quantity of learned information in long-term memory. *Cogn Sci*, **10**(4), 477.

Langer, E. J., Imber, L. G. (1979). When practice makes imperfect: debilitating effects of overlearning. *J Pers Soc Psychol*, **37**(11), 2014–2024.

Langers, D. R., Backes, W. H., van Dijk, P. (2003). Spectrotemporal features of the auditory cortex: the activation in response to dynamic ripples. *Neuroimage*, **20**(1), 265–275.

Laruelle, M. (2000). Imaging synaptic neurotransmission with in vivo binding competition techniques: a critical review. *J Cereb Blood Flow Metab*, **20**(3), 423–451.

Lassen, N. A., Ingvar, D. H. (1961). The blood flow of the cerebral cortex determined by radioactive krypton. *Experientia*, **17**, 42–43.

Lassen, N. A., Ingvar, D. H., Skinhoj, E. (1978). Brain function and blood flow. *Sci Am*, **239**(4), 62–71.

Lau, H. C., Rogers, R. D., Haggard, P., Passingham, R. E. (2004a). Attention to intention. *Science*, **303**(5661), 1208–1210.

Lau, H. C., Rogers, R. D., Ramnani, N., Passingham, R. E. (2004b). Willed action and attention to the selection of action. *Neuroimage*, **21**(4), 1407–1415.

Laufs, H., Krakow, K., Sterzer, P. *et al.* (2003). Electroencephalographic signatures of attentional and cognitive default modes in spontaneous brain activity fluctuations at rest. *Proc Natl Acad Sci USA*, **100**(19), 11053–11058.

Laureys, S., Goldman, S., Peigneux, P. (2002). Brain imaging. In D'Haene, H., den Boer, J. A., Wilner, P. (eds), *Biological Psychology*. John Wiley & Sons, New York.

Lauritzen, M. (2001). Relationship of spikes, synaptic activity, and local changes of cerebral blood flow. *J Cereb Blood Flow Metab*, **21**(12), 1367–1383.

Lavie, N. (2005). Distracted and confused? Selective attention under load. *Trends Cogn Sci*, **9**(2), 75–82.

Law, I., Jensen, M., Holm, S., Nickles, R. J., Paulson, O. B. (2001). Using (10)CO2 for single subject characterization of the stimulus frequency dependence in visual cortex: a novel positron emission tomography tracer for human brain mapping. *J Cereb Blood Flow Metab*, **21**(8), 1003–1012.

Lecanuet, J. P., Granier-Deferre, C., DeCasper, A. J., Maugeais, R., Andrieu, A. J., Busnel, M. C. (1987). [fetal perception and discrimination of speech stimuli; demonstration by cardiac reactivity; preliminary results]. *C R Acad Sci III*, **305**(5), 161–164.

Lecuyer, R., Abgueguen, I., Lemarie, C. (1992). 9-and-5 month olds do not make the AB error if not required to manipulate objects. *Proceedings of the VIIth International Conference on Infant Studies*. Miami.

LeDoux, J. E. (1996). *The emotional brain*. Simon & Schuster, New York.

Lees, G. V., Jones, E. G., Kandel, E. R. (2000). Expressive genes record memories. *Neurobiol Dis*, **7**(5), 533–536

Leopold, D. A., Logothetis, N. K. (1996). Activity changes in early visual cortex reflect monkeys' percepts during binocular rivalry. *Nature*, **379**(6565), 549–553.

Leopold, D. A., Logothetis, N. K. (1999). Multistable phenomena: Changing views in perception. *Trends Cogn Sci*, **3**(7), 254–264.

Levelt, W. J., Wheeldon, L. (1994). Do speakers have access to a mental syllabary? *Cognition*, **50**(1–3), 239–269.

Lewis, J. W., Wightman, F. L., Brefczynski, J. A., Phinney, R. E., Binder, J. R., DeYoe, E. A. (2004). Human brain regions involved in recognizing environmental sounds. *Cereb Cortex*, **14**(9), 1008–1021.

Leyton, M., Boileau, I., Benkelfat, C., Diksic, M., Baker, G., Dagher, A. (2002). Amphetamine-induced increases in extracellular dopamine, drug wanting, and novelty seeking: a PET/[11c]raclopride study in healthy men. *Neuropsychopharmacology*, **27**(6), 1027–1035.

Lhermitte, F. (1983). 'Utilization behaviour' and its relation to lesions of the frontal lobes. *Brain*, **106** *(Pt 2)*, 237–255.

Liberman, A. M., Cooper, F. S., Shankweiler, D. P., Studdert-Kennedy, M. (1967). Perception of the speech code. *Psychol Rev*, **74**(6), 431–461.

Liberman, A. M., Mattingly, I. G. (1985). The motor theory of speech perception revised. *Cognition*, **21**(1), 1–36.

Llinas, R, Bihary, U. (2001). Consciousness and the brain: the thalamocortical dialogue in health and disease. *Ann NY acad Sci*, **226**, 166–175.

Llinas, R. R., Pare, D. (1991). Of dreaming and wakefulness. *Neuroscience*, **44**(3), 521–535.

Lobaugh, N. J., Gibson, E., Taylor, M. J. (2006). Children recruit distinct neural systems for implicit emotional face processing. *Neuroreport*, **17**(2), 215–219.

Logothetis, N. K. (1998). Single units and conscious vision. *Philos Trans R Soc Lond B Biol Sci*, **353**(1377), 1801–1818.

Logothetis, N. K., Pauls, J., Augath, M., Trinath, T., Oeltermann, A. (2001). Neurophysiological investigation of the basis of the fMRI signal. *Nature*, **412**(6843), 150–157.

Logothetis, N. K., Pauls, J., Poggio, T. (1995). Shape representation in the inferior temporal cortex of monkeys. *Curr Biol*, **5**(5), 552–563.

Logothetis, N. K., Schall, J. D. (1989). Neuronal correlates of subjective visual perception. *Science*, **245**(4919), 761–763.

Lotze, M., Erb, M., Flor, H., Huelsmann, E., Godde, B., Grodd, W. (2000). fMRI evaluation of somatotopic representation in human primary motor cortex. *Neuroimage*, **11**(5 Pt 1), 473–481.

Luckman, A. J., Allinson, N. M., Ellis, A. W., Flude, B. M. (1995). Familiar face recognition: a comparative study of a connectionist model and human performance. *Neurocomputing*, **7**(1), 3–27.

Luria, A. R. (1966). *Higher cortical functions in man* (Haigh, B. trans.). Tavistock, London.

Luria, A. R. (1976). *The neuropsychology of memory* (translated by Haigh). V. H. Winston & Sons, Oxford.

Lutz, A., Greischar, L. L., Rawlings, N. B., Ricard, M., Davidson, R. J. (2004). Long-term meditators self-induce high-amplitude gamma synchrony during mental practice. *Proc Natl Acad Sci USA*, **101**(46), 16369–16373.

Lutz, A., Lachaux, J. P., Martinerie, J., Varela, F. J. (2002). Guiding the study of brain dynamics by using first-person data: synchrony patterns correlate with ongoing conscious states during a simple visual task. *Proc Natl Acad Sci USA*, **99**(3), 1586–1591.

Mack, A., Pappas, Z., Silverman, M., Gay, R. (2002). What we see: inattention and the capture of attention by meaning. *Conscious Cogn*, **11**(4), 488–506.

Mackworth, N. H., Bruner, J. S. (1970). How adults and children search and recognize pictures. *Hum Dev*, **13**(3), 149–177.

MacLean, P. D. (1967). The brain in relation to empathy and medical education. *J Nerv Ment Dis*, **144**(5), 374–382.

MacLeod, C. M., MacDonald, P. A. (2000). Interdimensional interference in the Stroop effect: uncovering the cognitive

and neural anatomy of attention. *Trends Cogn Sci*, **4**(10), 383–391.

Magalhaes, A. C. (2005). Functional magnetic resonance and spectroscopy in drug and substance abuse. *Top Magn Reson Imaging*, **16**(3), 247–251.

Maguire, E. A., Gadian, D. G., Johnsrude, I. S. *et al.* (2000). Navigation-related structural change in the hippocampi of taxi drivers. *Proc Natl Acad Sci USA*, **97**(8), 4398–4403.

Maia, T. V., Cleeremans, A. (2005). Consciousness: converging insights from connectionist modeling and neuroscience. *Trends Cogn Sci*, **9**(8), 397–404.

Malach, R., Reppas, J. B., Benson, R. R. *et al.* (1995). Object-related activity revealed by functional magnetic resonance imaging in human occipital cortex. *Proc Natl Acad Sci USA*, **92**(18), 8135–8139.

Mandler, G. (2003). Consciousness: respectable, useful, and probably necessary. In Baars, B. J., Banks, W. P. Newman, J. (eds), *Essential sources in the scientific study of consciousness* (Vol. xiii). MIT Presss, Cambridge.

Maril, A., Wagner, A. D., Schacter, D. L. (2001). On the tip of the tongue: an event-related fMRI study of semantic retrieval failure and cognitive conflict. *Neuron*, **31**(4), 653–660.

Marrocco, R. T., Davidson, M. C. (1998). Neurochemistry of attention. In Parasuraman, R. (ed.), *The attentive brain* (pp. 35–50). MIT Press, Cambridge.

Martin, A., Chao, L. L. (2001). Semantic memory and the brain: structure and processes. *Curr Opin Neurobiol*, **11**(2), 194–201.

Masquelet, A. C., Valenti, P., Nordin, J. Y. (1986). Osteoid osteoma of the coronoid process of the elbow: Surgical excision by a posteromedial approach. *J Hand Surg (Am)*, **11**(5), 733–735.

Mateer, C. A., Sira, C. S., O'Connell, M. E. (2005). Putting Humpty Dumpty together again: the importance of integrating cognitive and emotional interventions. *J Head Trauma Rehabil*, **20**(1), 62–75.

Matthews, S. C., Paulus, M. P., Simmons, A. N., Nelesen, R. A., Dimsdale, J. E. (2004). Functional subdivisions within anterior cingulate cortex and their relationship to autonomic nervous system function. *Neuroimage*, **22**(3), 1151–1156.

Mazoyer, B., Zago, L., Mellet, E. *et al.* (2001). Cortical networks for working memory and executive functions sustain the conscious resting state in man. *Brain Res Bull*, **54**(3), 287–298.

McCarthy, G., Puce, A., Gore, J. C., Allison, T. (1997). Face-specific processing in the human fusiform gyrus. *J Cogn Neurosci*, **9**(5), 605–610.

McClelland, J. L., Elman, J. L. (1986). The trace model of speech perception. *Cognit Psychol*, **18**(1), 1–86.

McClelland, J. L., Rogers, T. T. (2003). The parallel distributed processing approach to semantic cognition. *Nat Rev Neurosci*, **4**(4), 310–322.

McConigle, D. in Frackowiak, R. S. J. (Ed.). (2004). *Human brain function*, 2nd edn, vol. xvi. Boston: Elsevier Academic Press.

McCulloch, W. S., Pitts, W. (1943). A logical calculus of the ideas immanent in nervous activity. *Bull Math Biophys*, **5**, 115–133.

McGaugh, J. L. (2000). Memory – a century of consolidation. *Science*, **287**(5451), 248–251.

McGuire, E. A., Gadian, D. G., Johnsrude, I. *et al.* (2000). Navigation-related structural change in the hippocampi of taxi drivers. *Proc Natl Acad Sci USA*, **97**(8), 4398–4403.

McGurk, H., MacDonald, J. (1976). Hearing lips and seeing voices. *Nature*, **264**(5588), 746–748.

McIntosh, A. R., Lobaught, N. J., Cabeza, R., Bookstein, F. L., Houle, S. (1998). Convergence of neural systems processing stimulus associations and coordinating motor responses. *Cereb Cortex*, **8**(7), 648–659.

McKeeff, T. J., Tong, F. (2006). The timing of perceptual decisions for ambiguous face stimuli in the human ventral visual cortex. *Cereb Cortex*,

McNally, R. J., Kaspi, S. P., Riemann, B. C., Zeitlin, S. B. (1990). Selective processing of threat cues in posttraumatic stress disorder. *J Abnorm Psychol*, **99**(4), 398–402.

McNeil, J. E., Warrington, E. K. (1993). Prosopagnosia: a face-specific disorder. *Q J Exp Psychol A*, **46**(1), 1–10.

Meadows, J. C. (1974a). Disturbed perception of colours associated with localized cerebral lesions. *Brain*, **97**(4), 615–632.

Meadows, J. C. (1974b). The anatomical basis of prosopagnosia. *J Neurol Neurosurg Psychiatry*, **37**(5), 489–501.

Meng, M., Remus, D. A., Tong, F. (2005). Filling-in of visual phantoms in the human brain. *Nat Neurosci*, **8**(9), 1248–1254.

Mesulam, M. M. (1990). Large-scale neurocognitive networks and distributed processing for attention, language, and memory. *Ann Neurol*, **28**(5), 597–613.

Metcalfe, J. (1986). Feeling of knowing in memory and problem solving. *J Exp Psychol Learn Memory Cogn*, **12**(2), 288–294.

Miller, E. K., Wallis, J. D. (2003). Prefrontal cortex and executive brain function. In Squire, L. R., Bloom, F. E., McConnell, S. K., Roberts, J. L., Spitzer, N. C., Zigmond, M. J. (eds), *Fundamental neuroscience*, 2nd edn. Elsevier, San Diego.

Miller, G. A. (1956). The magical number seven plus or minus two: Some limits on our capacity for processing information. *Psychol Rev*, **63**(2), 81–97.

Miller, G. A. (1962). *Psychology: the science of mental life*. Harper and Row, New York.

Miller, G. A. (1991). *The science of words*. New York: Scientific American Library.

Milner, A. D., Rugg, M. D. (1992). *The neuropsychology of consciousness*. Academic Press, San Diego.

Milner, B. (1971). Interhemispheric differences in the localization of psychological processes in man. *Br Med Bull*, **27**, 272–277.

Milner, B. (1982). Some cognitive effects of frontal-lobe lesions in man. *Philos Trans R Soc Lond B Biol Sci*, **298**(1089), 211–226.

Minsky, M., Pappert, S. (1969). *Perceptrons: an introduction to computational geometry*. MIT Press, Cambridge.

Mishkin, M., Ungerleider, L. G., Macko, K. A. (1983). Object vision and spatial vision: two cortical pathways. *Trends Neurosci*, **6**(4), 14–14.

Mitchell, J. P., Macrae, C. N., Banaji, M. R. (2006). Dissociable medial prefrontal contributions to judgments of similar and dissimilar others. *Neuron*, **50**(4), 655–663.

Mizrahi, A., Katz, L. C. (2003). Dendritic stability in the adult olfactory bulb. *Nat Neurosci*, **6**(11), 1201–1207.

Moore, B. C. J. (1995). *Hearing*. Academic Press, San Diego.

Moray, N. (1959). Attention in dichotic listening: affective cues and the influence of instructions. *Q J Exp Psychol*, **11**, 56.

Moriarity, J. L., Boatman, D., Krauss, G. L., Storm, P. B., Lenz, F. A. (2001). Human 'memories' can be evoked by stimulation of the lateral temporal cortex after ipsilateral medial temporal lobe resection. *J Neurol Neurosurg Psychiatr*, **71**(4), 549–551.

Morin, A. (1993). Self-talk and self-awareness: on the nature of the relation. *J Mind Behav*, **14**, 223–234.

Morris, J. S., Buchel, C., Dolan, R. J. (2001). Parallel neural responses in amygdala subregions and sensory cortex during implicit fear conditioning. *Neuroimage*, **13**(6 Pt 1), 1044–1052.

Morris, J. S., Dolan, R. J. (2004). Dissociable amygdala and orbitofrontal responses during reversal fear conditioning. *Neuroimage*, **22**(1), 372–380.

Moscovitch, M. (1992). Memory and working-with-memory: a component process model based on modules and central systems. *J Cogn Neurosci*, **4**(3), 257–267.

Moscovitch, M. (1995). Recovered consciousness: a hypothesis concerning modularity and episodic memory. *J Clin Exp Neuropsychol*, **17**(2), 276–290.

Moscovitch, M., McAndrews, M. P. (2002). Material-specific deficits in 'remembering' in patients with unilateral temporal lobe epilepsy and excisions. *Neuropsychologia*, **40**(8), 1335–1342.

Moscovitch, M., Nadel, L. (1998). Consolidation and the hippocampal complex revisited: in defense of the multiple-trace model. *Curr Opin Neurobiol*, **8**(2), 297–300.

Moscovitch, M., Winocur, G. (1992). The neuropsychology of memory and aging. *Handbook Aging Cogn*, 315–372.

Moscovitch, M., Nadel, L., Winocur, G., Gilboa, A., Rosenbaum, R. S. (2006). The cognitive neuroscience of remote episodic, semantic and spatial memory. *Curr Opin Neurobiol*, **16**(2), 179–190.

Moscovitch, M., Rosenbaum, R. S., Gilboa, A. *et al.* (2005). Functional neuroanatomy of remote episodic, semantic and spatial memory: a unified account based on multiple trace theory. *J Anat*, **207**(1), 35–66.

Moscovitch, M., Winocur, G., Behrmann, M. (1997). What is special about face recognition? Nineteen experiments on a person with visual object agnosia and dyslexia but normal face recognition. *J Cogn Neurosci*, **9**(5), 555–604.

Moss, H. E., Rodd, J. M., Stamatakis, E. A., Bright, P., Tyler, L. K. (2005). Anteromedial temporal cortex supports fine-grained differentiation among objects. *Cereb Cortex*, **15**(5), 616–627.

Mosso, A. A. (1881). *Ueber den Kreislauf des Blutes im Menschlichen Gehirn*. Viet, Leipzig.

Mountcastle, V. B. (1978). Brain mechanisms for directed attention. *J R Soc Med*, **71**(1), 14–28.

Moutoussis, K., Zeki, S. (2002). The relationship between cortical activation and perception investigated with invisible stimuli. *Proc Natl Acad Sci USA*, **99**(14), 9527–9532.

Moutoussis, K., Zeki, S. (2006). Seeing invisible motion: a human fMRI study. *Curr Biol*, **16**(6), 574–579.

Muckli, L., Kohler, A., Kriegeskorte, N., Singer, W. (2005). Primary visual cortex activity along the apparent-motion trace reflects illusory perception. *PLoS Biol*, **3**(8), e265.

Muller, H. M., Kutas, M. (1996). What's in a name? Electrophysiological differences between spoken nouns, proper names and one's own name. *Neuroreport*, **8**(1), 221–225.

Munte, T. F., Kohlmetz, C., Nager, W., Altenmuller, E. (2001). Neuroperception. Superior auditory spatial tuning in conductors. *Nature*, **409**(6820), 580.

Muraven, M., Baumeister, R. F. (2000). Self-regulation and depletion of limited resources: does self-control resemble a muscle? *Psychol Bull*, **126**(2), 247–259.

Murray, E. A., Richmond, B. J. (2001). Role of perirhinal cortex in object perception, memory, and associations. *Curr Opin Neurobiol*, **11**(2), 188–193.

Nadel, L., Moscovitch, M. (1997). Memory consolidation, retrograde amnesia and the hippocampal complex. *Curr Opin Neurobiol*, **7**(2), 217–227.

Nadel, L., Moscovitch, M. (1998). Hippocampal contributions to cortical plasticity. *Neuropharmacology*, **37**(4–5), 431–439.

Nadel, L., Samsonovich, A., Ryan, L., Moscovitch, M. (2000). Multiple trace theory of human memory: computational, neuroimaging, and neuropsychological results. *Hippocampus*, **10**(4), 352–368.

Nader, K. (2003). Memory traces unbound. *Trends Neurosci*, **26**(2), 65–72.

Nader, K., Schafe, G. E., Le Doux, J. E. (2000). Fear memories require protein synthesis in the amygdala for reconsolidation after retrieval. *Nature*, **406**(6797), 722–726.

Naghavi, H. R., Nyberg, L. (2005). Common fronto-parietal activity in attention, memory, and consciousness: shared demands on integration? *Conscious Cogn*, **14**(2), 390–425.

Nakai, T., Muraki, S., Bagarinao, E. *et al.* (2004). Application of independent component analysis to magnetic resonance imaging for enhancing the contrast of gray and white matter. *Neuroimage*, **21**(1), 251–260.

Nauta, W. J. (1972). Neural associations of the frontal cortex. *Acta Neurobiol Exp (Wars)*, **32**(2), 125–140.

Navalpakkam, V., Itti, L. (2005). Modeling the influence of task on attention. *Vision Res*, **45**(2), 205–231.

Neisser, U., Becklen, R. (1975). Selective looking: attending to visually specified events. *Cogn Psychol*, **7**(4), 480–494.

Nielsen, K., Rostrup, E., Frederiksen, J. L. *et al.* (2006). Magnetic resonance imaging at 3.0 tesla detects more lesions in acute optic neuritis than at 1.5 tesla. *Invest Radiol*, **41**(2), 76–82.

Nieto-Castanon, A., Ghosh, S. S., Tourville, J. A., Guenther, F. H. (2003). Region of interest based analysis of functional imaging data. *Neuroimage*, **19**(4), 1303–1316.

Nilsson, L. G., Markowitsch, H. J. (1999). *Cognitive neuroscience of memory*. Hogrefe & Huber, Seattle.

Nissen, M. J., Bullemer, P. (1987). Attention requirements of learning: evidence from performance measurements. *Cogn Psychol*, **19**(1), 1–32.

Nitschke, J. B., Nelson, E. E., Rusch, B. D., Fox, A. S., Oakes, T. R., Davidson, R. J. (2004). Orbitofrontal cortex tracks positive mood in mothers viewing pictures of their newborn infants. *Neuroimage*, **21**(2), 583–592.

Nowakowski, R. S. (1987). Basic concepts of CNS development. *Child Dev*, **58**(3), 568–595.

Nyberg, G., Andersson, J., Antoni, G. *et al.* (1996). Activation PET scanning in pretreatment evaluation of patients with

cerebral tumours or vascular lesions in or close to the sensorimotor cortex. *Acta Neurochir (Wien)*, **138**(6), 684–694.

Ochsner, K. N., Ray, R. D., Cooper, J. C. *et al.* (2004). For better or for worse: neural systems supporting the cognitive down- and up-regulation of negative emotion. *Neuroimage*, **23**(2), 483–499.

O'Craven, K. M., Kanwisher, N. (2000). Mental imagery of faces and places activates corresponding stiimulus-specific brain regions. *J Cogn Neurosci*, **12**(6), 1013–1023.

Ohye, C. (2002). Thalamus and thalamic damage. In Ramachandran, V. S. (ed.), *Encyclopedia of the human brain*. Academic Press, San Diego.

Ojemann, G. A. (2003). The neurobiology of language and verbal memory: observations from awake neurosurgery. *Int J Psychophysiol*, **48**(2), 141–146.

O'Leary, D. D., Nakagawa, Y. (2002). Patterning centers, regulatory genes and extrinsic mechanisms controlling arealization of the neocortex. *Curr Opin Neurobiol*, **12**(1), 14–25.

Olds, J., Milner, P. (1954). Positive reinforcement produced by electrical stimulation of septal area and other regions of rat brain. *J Comp Phsiol Psychol*, **47**(6), 419–427.

Oppenheim, H. (1889). Zur pathologie der grossenhirngeschwuelste. *Arch Psychiatr*, **21**, 560.

Orban, G. A., Van Essen, D., Vanduffel, W. (2004). Comparative mapping of higher visual areas in monkeys and humans. *Trends Cogn Sci*, **8**(7), 315–324.

O'Shea, R. P. (1991). Thumb's rule tested: visual angle of thumb's width is about 2 deg. *Perception*, **20**(3), 415–418.

Ostergaard, A. L. (1987). Episodic, semantic and procedural memory in a case of amnesia at an early age. *Neuropsychologia*, **25**(2), 341–357.

Overgaard, M., Nielsen, J. F., Fuglsang-Frederiksen, A. (2004). A TMS study of the ventral projections from V1 with implications for the finding of neural correlates of consciousness. *Brain Cogn*, **54**(1), 58–64.

Palmer, S. E. (1999). Color, consciousness, and the isomorphism contraint. *Behav Brain Sci*, **22**(6), 923–943; discussion 944–989.

Palmer-Brown, D., Tepper, J. A., Powell, H. M. (2002). Connectionist natural language parsing. *Trends Cogn Sci*, **6**(10), 437–442.

Panksepp, J. (1998). *Affective neuroscience: the foundations of human and animal emotions*: Oxford University Press, New York.

Panksepp, J. (2005). Affective consciousness: core emotional feelings in animals and humans. *Conscious Cogn*, **14**(1), 30–80.

Panksepp, J. (2006). Emotional endophenotypes in evolutionary psychiatry. *Prog Neuropsychopharmacol Biol Psychiatr*, **30**(5), 774–784.

Papez, J. W. (1937). A proposed mechanism of emotion. *Arch Neurol Psychiatr*, **79**, 217–224.

Parker, G. J., Luzzi, S., Alexander, D. C., Wheeler-Kingshott, C. A., Ciccarelli, O., Lambon Ralph, M. A. (2005). Lateralization of ventral and dorsal auditory-language pathways in the human brain. *Neuroimage*, **24**(3), 656–666.

Parmelee, A. H., Sigman, M.D. (1983). Perinatal brain development and behavior. In Haith, M. M. C. (ed.), *Infancy and biological development*, Vol. II, pp. 95–155. Wiley, New York.

Pascalis, O., de Haan, M., Nelson, C. A. (2002). Is face processing species-specific during the first year of life? *Science*, **296**(5571), 1321–1323.

Pascual-Leone, A., Walsh, V. (2001). Fast backprojections from the motion to the primary visual area necessary for visual awareness. *Science*, **292**(5516), 510–512.

Pashler, H. (1989). Dissociations and dependencies between speed and accuracy: evidence for a two-component theory of divided attention in simple tasks. *Cogn Psychol*, **21**(4), 469.

Pasley, B. N., Mayes, L. C., Schultz, R. T. (2004). Subcortical discrimination of unperceived objects during binocular rivalry. *Neuron*, **42**(1), 163–172.

Pasternak, T., Merigan, W. H. (1994). Motion perception following lesions of the superior temporal sulcus in the monkey. *Cereb Cortex*, **4**(3), 247–259.

Pasupathy, A., Connor, C. E. (2002). Population coding of shape in area V4. *Nat Neurosci*, **5**(12), 1332–1338.

Paulesu, E., Frith, C. D., Frackowiak, R. S. (1993). The neural correlates of the verbal component of working memory. *Nature*, **362**(6418), 342–345.

Paus, T. (2005). Mapping brain maturation and cognitive development during adolescence. *Trends Cogn Sci*, **9**(2), 60–68.

Paus, T., Jech, R., Thompson, C. J., Comeau, R., Peters, T., Evans, A. C. (1997) Transcranial magnetic stimulation during positron emission tomography: a new method for studying connectivity of the human cerebral cortex. *Journal of Neuroscience*, **17**(9), 3178–3184

Paus, T., Zijdenbos, A., Worsley, K. *et al.* (1999). Structural maturation of neural pathways in children and adolescents: in vivo study. *Science*, **283**(5409), 1908–1911.

Paxinos, G., Mai, J. (eds) (2004). *The human nervous system*, 2nd edn. Academic Press, San Diego.

Pena, M., Maki, A., Kovacic, D. *et al.* (2003). Sounds and silence: an optical topography study of language recognition at birth. *Proc Natl Acad Sci USA*, **100**(20), 11702–11705.

Penfield, W., Milner, B. (1958). Memory deficit produced by bilateral lesions in the hippocampal zone. *AMA Arch Neurol Psychiatry*, **79**(5), 475–497.

Penfield, W., Roberts, L. (1959). *Speech and brain mechanisms*. Princeton University Press, Princeton (URL:http://pup.princeton.edu)

Pepperberg, I. M. (2002). In search of King Solomon's Ring: cognitive and communicative studies of grey parrots (*Psittacus erithacus*). *Brain Behav Evol*, **59**(1–2), 54–67.

Peretz, I., Zatorre, R. J. (2005). Brain organization for music processing. *Annu Rev Psychol*, **56**, 89–114.

Perky, C. W. (1910). An experimental study of imagination. *Am J Psychol*, **21**(3), 422.

Pessoa, L., Kastner, S., Ungerleider, L. G. (2003). Neuroimaging studies of attention: from modulation of sensory processing to top-down control. *J Neurosci*, **23**(10), 3990–3998.

Petkov, C. I., Kayser, C., Augath, M., Logothetis, N. K. (2006). Functional imaging reveals numerous fields in the monkey auditory cortex. *PLoS Biol*, **4**(7), e215.

Petrides, M. (1994). Frontal lobes and working memory: evidence from investigations of the effects of cortical excisions in nonhuman primates. *Handbook Neuropsychol*, **9**, 59–82.

Petrides, M. (1995). Impairments on nonspatial self-ordered and externally ordered working memory tasks after lesions of the mid-dorsal part of the lateral frontal cortex in the monkey. *J Neurosci*, **15**(1 Pt 1), 359–375.

Petrides, M., Milner, B. (1982). Deficits on subject-ordered tasks after frontal- and temporal-lobe lesions in man. *Neuropsychologia*, **20**(3), 249–262.

Phelps, E. A., LeDoux, J. E. (2005). Contributions of the amygdala to emotion processing: from animal models to human behavior. *Neuron*, **48**(2), 175–187.

Piaget, J. (1937/1964). *The construction of reality in the child*. Basic Books New York.

Piaget, J. (1954). *The construction of reality in the child* (Cook, M. trans.). Basic Books, New York.

Piazza, M., Izard, V., Pinel, P., Le Bihan, D., Dehaene, S. (2004). Tuning curves for approximate numerosity in the human intraparietal sulcus. *Neuron*, **44**(3), 547–555.

Pinborg, L. H., Adams, K. H., Yndgaard, S. *et al.* (2004). [18f]altanserin binding to human 5HT2a receptors is unaltered after citalopram and pindolol challenge. *J Cereb Blood Flow Metab*, **24**(9), 1037–1045.

Pitman, R. K., Sanders, K. M., Zusman, R. M. *et al.* (2002). Pilot study of secondary prevention of posttraumatic stress disorder with propranolol. *Biol Psychiatr*, **51**(2), 189–192.

Plant, G. T., Laxer, K. D., Barbaro, N. M., Schiffman, J. S., Nakayama, K. (1993). Impaired visual motion perception in the contralateral hemifield following unilateral posterior cerebral lesions in humans. *Brain*, **116**(Pt 6), 1303–1335.

Plourde, G., Belin, P., Chartrand, D. *et al.* (2006). Cortical processing of complex auditory stimuli during alterations of consciousness with the general anesthetic propofol. *Anesthesiology*, **104**(3), 448–457.

Poeppel, D. (2001). Pure word deafness and the bilateral processing of speech code. *Cogn Sci*, **25**, 679–693.

Poldrack, R. A., Desmond, J. E., Glover, G. H., Gabrieli, J. D. (1998). The neural basis of visual skill learning: an fMRI study of mirror reading. *Cereb Cortex*, **8**(1), 1–10.

Pollen, D. A. (1999). On the neural correlates of visual perception. *Cereb Cortex*, **9**(1), 4–19.

Polonsky, A., Blake, R., Braun, J., Heeger, D. J. (2000). Neuronal activity in human primary visual cortex correlates with perception during binocular rivalry. *Nat Neurosci*, **3**(11), 1153–1159.

Ponton, C. W., Don, M., Eggermont, J. J., Waring, M. D., Kwong, B., Masuda, A. (1996a). Auditory system plasticity in children after long periods of complete deafness. *Neuroreport*, **8**(1), 61–65.

Ponton, C. W., Don, M., Eggermont, J. J., Waring, M. D., Masuda, A. (1996b). Maturation of human cortical auditory function: differences between normal-hearing children and children with cochlear implants. *Ear Hear*, **17**(5), 430–437.

Portas, C. M., Krakow, K., Allen, P., Josephs, O., Armony, J. L., Frith, C. D. (2000). Auditory processing across the sleep-wake cycle: simultaneous EEG and fMRI monitoring in humans. *Neuron*, **28**(3), 991–999.

Posner, M. I. (1980). Orienting of attention. *Q J Exp Psychol*, **32**(1), 3–25.

Posner, M. I. (2003). Attentional mechanisms. In Aminoff, M., Daroff, R. (eds), *Encyclopedia of the neurological sciences*. Academic Press, San Diego.

Posner, M. I., Cohen, Y., Rafal, R. D. (1982). Neural systems control of spatial orienting. *Philos Trans R Soc Lond B Biol Sci*, **298**(1089), 187–198.

Posner, M. I., Desimone, R. (1998). Beyond images. *Curr Opin Neurobiol*, **8**(2), 175–177.

Posner, M. I., Petersen, S. E. (1990). The attention system of the human brain. *Annu Rev Neurosci*, **13**, 25–42.

Posner, M. I., Raichle, M. E. (1997). *Images of mind*. Scientific American Library/Scientific American Books, New York.

Posner, M. I., Rothbart, M. K. (1998). Attention, self-regulation and consciousness. *Philos Trans R Soc Lond B Biol Sci*, **353**(1377), 1915–1927.

Posner, M. I., Rothbart, M. K. (2005). Influencing brain networks: implications for education. *Trends Cogn Sci*, **9**(3), 99–103.

Posner, M. I., Walker, J. A., Friedrich, F. J., Rafal, R. D. (1984). Effects of parietal injury on covert orienting of attention. *J Neurosci*, **4**(7), 1863–1874.

Potter, R., Kopp, G., Green, H. (1947). *Visible speech*. Van Nostrand Reinhold, New York.

Pravdich-Neminsky, V. V. (1913). Ein versuch der Registrierung der Elektrischen Gehirnerscheinungen. *Zbl Physiol*, **27**, 951–960.

Pulvermuller, F., Shtyrov, Y., Ilmoniemi, R. J., Marslen-Wilson, W. D. (2006). Tracking speech comprehension in space and time. *Neuroimage*, **31**(3), 1297–1305.

Quartz, S. R. (1999). The constructivist brain. *Trends Cogn Sci*, **3**(2), 48–57.

Quinones-Hinojosa, A., Ojemann, S. G., Sanai, N., Dillon, W. P., Berger, M. S. (2003). Preoperative correlation of intraoperative cortical mapping with magnetic resonance imaging landmarks to predict localization of the Broca area. *J Neurosurg*, **99**(2), 311–318.

Quiroga, R. Q., Reddy, L., Kreiman, G., Koch, C., Fried, I. (2005). Invariant visual representation by single neurons in the human brain. *Nature*, **435**(7045), 1102–1107.

Raaijmakers, J. G., Shiffrin, R. M. (1992). Models for recall and recognition. *Annu Rev Psychol*, **43**, 205–234.

Raichle, M. E., Fiez, J. A., Videen, T. O. *et al.* (1994). Practice-related changes in human brain functional anatomy during nonmotor learning. *Cereb Cortex*, **4**(1), 8–26.

Raine, A., Buchsbaum, M., LaCasse, L. (1997). Brain abnormalities in murderers indicated by positron emission tomography. *Biol Psychiatr*, **42**(6), 495–508.

Raine, A., Lencz, T., Bihrle, S., LaCasse, L., Colletti, P. (2000). Reduced prefrontal gray matter volume and reduced autonomic activity in antisocial personality disorder. *Arch Gen Psychiatr*, **57**(2), 119–127; discussion 128–129.

Rajan, R., Irvine, D. R., Wise, L. Z., Heil, P. (1993). Effect of unilateral partial cochlear lesions in adult cats on the representation of lesioned and unlesioned cochleas in primary auditory cortex. *J Comp Neurol*, **338**(1), 17–49.

Rakic, P. (1988). Specification of cerebral cortical areas. *Science*, **241**(4862), 170–176.

Rakic, P. (1995). Corticogenesis in human and nonhuman primates. In Gazzaniga, M. S. (ed.), *The cognitive neurosciences*. MIT Press, Cambridge.

Rakic, P. (2005). Less is more: Progenitor death and cortical size. *Nat Neurosci*, **8**(8), 981–982.

Ramachandran, V. S. (2002). *Encyclopedia of the human brain*. Academic Press, San Diego.

Ramachandran, V. S., Hirstein, W. (1998). The perception of phantom limbs. The D. O. Hebb lecture. *Brain*, **121**(Pt 9), 1603–1630.

Ramachandran, V. S., Rogers-Ramachandran, D. (2000). Phantom limbs and neural plasticity. *Arch Neurol*, **57**(3), 317–320.

Ramsøy, T. Z., Overgaard, M. (2004). Introspection and subliminal perception. *Phenomenol Cogn Sci*, **3**(1), 1–23.

Ranganath, C. (2006). Working memory for visual objects: complementary roles of inferior temporal, medial temporal, and prefrontal cortex. *Neuroscience*, **139**(1), 277–289.

Ranganath, C., D'Esposito, M. (2005). Directing the mind's eye: prefrontal, inferior and medial temporal mechanisms for visual working memory. *Curr Opin Neurobiol*, **15**(2), 175–182.

Rauch, S. L., Jenike, M. A., Alpert, N. M. *et al.* (1994). Regional cerebral blood flow measured during symptom provocation in obsessive-compulsive disorder using oxygen 15-labeled carbon dioxide and positron emission tomography. *Arch Gen Psychiatr*, **51**(1), 62–70.

Ravizza, S. M., Behrmann, M., Fiez, J. A. (2005). Right parietal contributions to verbal working memory: spatial or executive? *Neuropsychologia*, **43**(14), 2057–2067.

Reber, P. J., Squire, L. R. (1998). Encapsulation of implicit and explicit memory in sequence learning. *J Cogn Neurosci*, **10**(2), 248–263.

Redington, M., Chater, N. (1997). Probabilistic and distributional approaches to language acquisition. *Trends Cogn Sci*, **1**(7), 273–281.

Rees, G. (2001). Seeing is not perceiving. *Nat Neurosci*, **4**, 678–680.

Rees, G., Lavie, N. (2001). What can functional imaging reveal about the role of attention in visual awareness? *Neuropsychologia*, **39**(12), 1343–1353.

Rees, G., Kreiman, G., Koch, C. (2002). Neural correlates of consciousness in humans. *Nat Rev Neurosci*, **3**(4), 261–270.

Rees, G., Russell, C., Frith, C. D., Driver, J. (1999). Inattentional blindness versus inattentional amnesia for fixated but ignored words. *Science*, **286**(5449), 2504–2507.

Reid, R. C. (2003). Vision. In Squire, L. R., Bloom, F. E., McConnell, S. K., Roberts, J. L., Spitzer, N. C., Zigmond, M. J. (eds), *Fundamental neuroscience*, 2nd edn. Elsevier, San Diego.

Reilly, J., Losh, M., Bellugi, U. Wulfeck, B. (2004). 'Frog, where are you?' narratives in children with specific language impairment, early focal brain injury, and Williams syndrome. *Brain Lang*, **88**(2), 229–247.

Reneman, L., de Win, M. M., van den Brink, W., Booij, J., den Heeten, G. J. (2006). Neuroimaging findings with MDMA/ecstasy: technical aspects, conceptual issues and future prospects. *J Psychopharmacol*, **20**(2), 164–175.

Ress, D., Heeger, D. J. (2003). Neuronal correlates of perception in early visual cortex. *Nat Neurosci*, **6**(4), 414–420.

Ressler, K. J., Rothbaum, B. O., Tannenbaum, L. *et al.* (2004). Cognitive enhancers as adjuncts to psychotherapy: use of d-cycloserine in phobic individuals to facilitate extinction of fear. *Arch Gen Psychiatr*, **61**(11), 1136–1144.

Reynolds, J. H., Desimone, R. (2003). Interacting roles of attention and visual salience in V4. *Neuron*, **37**(5), 853–863.

Reynolds, J. H., Gottlieb, J. P., Kastner, S. (2003). Attention. In Squire, L. R., Bloom, F. E., McConnell, S. K., Roberts, J. L., Spitzer, N. C., Zigmond, M. J. (eds), *Fundamental neuroscience*, 2nd edn. Elsevier, San Diego.

Ribeiro, S., Gervasoni, D., Soares, *et al.* (2004). Long-lasting novelty-induced neuronal reverberation during slow-wave sleep in multiple forebrain areas. *PLoS Biol* **2**(1).

Ridderinkhof, K. R., Span, M. M., van der Molen, M. W. (2002). Perseverative behavior and adaptive control in older adults: performance monitoring, rule induction, and set shifting. *Brain Cogn*, **49**(3), 382–401.

Rizzolatti, G., Fadiga, L., Gallese, V., Fogassi, L. (1996). Premotor cortex and the recognition of motor actions. *Cogn Brain Res*, **3**, 131–141.

Rizzolatti, G., Fogassi, L., Gallese, V. (2002). Motor and cognitive functions of the ventral premotor cortex. *Curr Opin Neurobiol*, **12**, 149–154.

Ro, T., Shelton, D., Lee, O. L., Chang, E. (2004). Extrageniculate mediation of unconscious vision in transcranial magnetic stimulation-induced blindsight. *Proc Natl Acad Sci USA*, **101**(26), 9933–9935.

Robinson, R. (2004). fMRI beyond the clinic: will it ever be ready for prime time? *PLoS Biol*, **2**(6), e150.

Rodman, H. R., Gross, C. G., Albright, T. D. (1989). Afferent basis of visual response properties in area MT of the macaque. I. Effects of striate cortex removal. *J Neurosci*, **9**(6), 2033–2050.

Rodman, H. R., Pessoa, L., Ungerleider, L. (2003). Visual perception of objects. In Squire, L. R., Bloom, F. E., McConnell, S. K., Roberts, J. L., Spitzer, N. C., Zigmond, M. J. (eds), *Fundamental neuroscience*, 2nd edn. Elsevier, San Diego.

Roediger, H. L., McDermott, K. B. (1993). Implicit memory in normal human subjects. *Handbook Neuropsychol*, **8**, 63–131.

Rosch, E. (1975). Cognitive representations of semantic categories. *J Exp Psychol: General*, **104**(3), 192–233.

Rosen, S. D., Paulesu, E., Nihoyannopoulos, P. *et al.* (1996). Silent ischemia as a central problem: regional brain activation compared in silent and painful myocardial ischemia. *Ann Intern Med*, **124**(11), 939–949.

Rosenblatt, F. (1958). The perception: a probabilistic model for information storage and organization in the brain. *Psychol Rev*, **65**(6), 386–408.

Rosenblatt, F. (1962). *Principles of neurodynamics: perceptrons and the theory of brain mechanisms*. Spartan, Washington, DC.

Rossi, S., Pasqualetti, P., Zito, G. *et al.* (2006). Prefrontal and parietal cortex in human episodic memory: an interference study by repetitive transcranial magnetic stimulation. *Eur J Neurosci*, **23**(3), 793–800.

Roy, C. S., Sherrington, C. S. (1890). On the regulation of the blood supply of the brain. *J Physiol*, **11**, 85–108.

Rozin, P. (1976). The evolution of intelligence and access to the cognitive unconscious. *Prog Psychobiol Physiol Psychol*, **6**, 245–280.

Rubens, A. B., Benson, D. F. (1971). Associative visual agnosia. *Arch Neurol*, **24**(4), 305–316.

Ruby, P., Decety, J. (2003). What you believe versus what you think they believe: a neuroimaging study of conceptual perspective-taking. *Eur J Neurosci*, **17**, 2475.

Rumelhart, D. E., Hinton, G. E., Williams, R. J. (1986). Learning internal representations by error propagation. In Rumelhart, D. E., McClelland, J. L. (ed.), *Parallel distributed processing: explorations in the microstructure of cognition*, vol. 1: Foundations. MIT Press, Cambridge.

Rumelhart, D. E., McClelland, J. L. (eds) (1986a). *Parallel distributed processing: explorations in the microstructure of cognition* (Vol. 2). MIT Press, Cambridge.

Rumelhart, D. E., McClelland, J. L. (eds) (1986b). *Parallel distributed processing: foundations* (Vol. 1: Foundations). MIT Press, Cambridge.

Rushworth, M. F., Nixon, P. D., Eacott, M. J., Passingham, R. E. (1997). Ventral prefrontal cortex is not essential for working memory. *J Neurosci*, **17**(12), 4829–4838.

Rutkowski, R. G., Weinberger, N. M. (2005). Encoding of learned importance of sound by magnitude of representational area in primary auditory cortex. *Proc Natl Acad Sci USA*, **102**(38), 13664–13669.

Ryan, J. D., Althoff, R. R., Whitlow, S., Cohen, N. J. (2000). Amnesia is a deficit in relational memory. *Psychol Sci*, **11**(6), 454–461.

Ryle, G. (1949). *The concept of mind*. Hutchinson, London.

Rypma, B., Berger, J. S., D'Esposito, M. (2002). The influence of working-memory demand and subject performance on prefrontal cortical activity. *J Cogn Sci*, **14**(5), 721–731.

Sachs, J. D. S. (1967). Recognition memory for syntactic and semantic aspects of connected discourse. *Perception Psychophys*, **2**(9), 437–442.

Sacks, O. (1984). *A leg to stand on*. Simon & Schuster, New York.

Sacks, O. (1985). *The man who mistook his wife for a hat: and other clinical tales*. Simon & Schuster, New York.

Sacks, O. (1992). Tourette's syndrome and creativity. *Br Med J*, **305**(6868), 1515–1151.

Saffran, J. R., Newport, E. L., Aslin, R. N., Tunick, R. A., Barrueco, S. (1997). Incidental language learning: Listening (and learning) out of the corner of your ear. *Psychological Science*, **8**(2), 101–105.

Salzman, C. D., Britten, K. H., Newsome, W. T. (1990). Cortical microstimulation influences perceptual judgements of motion direction. *Nature*, **346**(6280), 174–177.

Sampaio, R. C., Truwit, C. L. (2001). Myelination in the developing brain. In Nelson, C. A. L., (ed.), *The handbook of developmental cognitive neuroscience*, pp. 35–45. MIT Press, Cambridge.

Sanes, D. H., Reh, T. A., Harris, W. A. (2006). *Development of the nervous system*, 2nd edn. Elsevier Academic Press, Amsterdam, Boston.

Sasaki, Y., Watanabe, T. (2004). The primary visual cortex fills in color. *Proc Natl Acad Sci USA*, **101**(52), 18251–18256.

Sato, K., Nariai, T., Tanaka, Y. *et al.* (2005). Functional representation of the finger and face in the human somatosensory cortex: intraoperative intrinsic optical imaging. *Neuroimage*, **25**(4), 1292–1301.

Saunders, D. E. (2000). MR spectroscopy in stroke. *Br Med Bull*, **56**(2), 334–345.

Schacter, D. L. (1987). Implicit expressions of memory in organic amnesia: learning of new facts and associations. *Hum Neurobiol*, **6**(2), 107–118.

Schacter, D. L., Tulving, E. (1994). *Memory systems*. MIT Press, Cambridge.

Schacter, D. L., Dobbins, I. G., Schnyer, D. M. (2004). Specificity of priming: a cognitive neuroscience perspective. *Nat Rev Neursci*, **5**(11), 853–862.

Schacter, D. L., Harbluk, J. L., McLachlan, D. R. (1984). Retrieval without recollection: an experimental analysis of source amnesia. *J Verbal Learn Verbal Behav*, **23**, 593–611.

Scheibel, M. E., Scheibel, A. B. (1965). Activity cycles in neurons of the reticular formation. *Recent Adv Biol Psychiatr*, **8**, 283–293.

Schirmer, A., Kotz, S. A. (2006). Beyond the right hemisphere: brain mechanisms mediating vocal emotional processing. *Trends Cign Sci*, **10**(1), 24–30.

Schneider, P., Scherg, M., Dosch, H. G., Specht, H. J., Gutschalk, A., Rupp, A. (2002). Morphology of Heschl's gyrus reflects enhanced activation in the auditory cortex of musicians. *Nat Neurosci*, **5**(7), 688–694.

Schneider, W., Chein, J. M. (2003). Controlled and automatic processing: behavior, theory, and biological mechanisms. *Cogn Sci*, **27**, 525–559.

Schneider, W. X. (1995). Vam: a neuro-cognitive model for visual attention control of segmentation, object recognition and space-based motor action. *Visual Cogn*, **2**, 331.

Schore, A. (1999). *Affect regulation and the origin of the self: The neurobiology of emotional development*. Lawrence Erlbaum Associates, Hillsdale.

Schultz, W. (1998). Predictive reward signal of dopamine neurons. *J Neurophysiol*, **80**(1), 1–27.

Schultz, W. (2002). Getting formal with dopamine and reward. *Neuron*, **36**(2), 241–263.

Schwarzlose, R. F., Baker, C. I., Kanwisher, N. (2005). Separate face and body selectivity on the fusiform gyrus. *J Neurosci*, **25**(47), 11055–11059.

Scott, S. K. (2005). Auditory processing – speech, space and auditory objects. *Curr Opin Neurobiol*, **15**(2), 197–201.

Scott, S. K., Wise, R. J. (2004). The functional neuroanatomy of prelexical processing in speech perception. *Cognition*, **92**(1–2), 13–45.

Scoville, W. B., Milner, B. (1957). Loss of recent memory after bilateral hippocampal lesions. *J Neurol Neurosurg Psychiatr*, **20**(1), 11–21.

Serences, J. T., Yantis, S. (2006). Selective visual attention and perceptual coherence. *Trends Cogn Sci*, **10**(1), 38–45.

Shallice, T. (1982). Specific impairments of planning. *Philos Trans R Soc Lond B Biol Sci*, **298**(1089), 199–209.

Shallice, T., Warrington, E. K. (1970). Independent functioning of verbal memory stores: a neuropsychological study. *Q J Exp Psychol*, **22**(2), 261–273.

Shamay-Tsoory, S., Tomer, R., Berger, B., Goldsher, D., Aharon-Peresztz, J. (2005). Impaired 'affective theory of mind' is associated with right ventromedial prefrontal damage. *Cogn Behav Neurol*, **18**, 55–67.

Shanahan, M. P. (2005). Consciousness, emotion, and imagination: a brain-inspired architecture for cognitive robotics.

Proceedings AISB 2005 Symposium on Next Generation Approaches to Machine Consciousness, 26–35.

Shannon, R. V., Zeng, F. G., Wygonski, J. (1998). Speech recognition with altered spectral distribution of envelope cues. *J Acoust Soc Am*, **104**(4), 2467–2476.

Shapiro, A. K., Shapiro, E. (1974). Gilles de la Tourette's syndrome. *Am Fam Physician*, **9**(6), 94–96.

Sharma, R., Sharma, A. (2004). Physiological basis and image processing in functional magnetic resonance imaging: neuronal and motor activity in brain. *Biomed Eng Online*, **3**(1), 13.

Shastri, L. (2002). Episodic memory and cortico-hippocampal interactions. *Trends Cogn Sci*, **6**(4), 162–168.

Shatz, C. J. (2002). Emergence of order in visual system development. In Johnson, M. H., Munakata, Y., Gilmore, R.O. (eds), *Brain development and cognition: a reader*, 2nd edn, pp.231–244. Blackwell, Oxford.

Shaw, P., Greenstein, D., Lerch, J. *et al.* (2006). Intellectual ability and cortical development in children and adolescents. *Nature*, **440**(7084), 676–679.

Sheinberg, D. L., Logothetis, N. K. (1997). The role of temporal cortical areas in perceptual organization. *Proc Natl Acad Sci USA*, **94**(7), 3408–3413.

Shepard, R. C., Cooper, L. (1982). *Mental images and their transformations*. MIT Press, Cambridge.

Shepherd, ? ? (2004). In Paxinos, G. (ed.), *The human nervous system*, 2nd edn. Academic Press, San Diego.

Sherrington, C. S. (1947). *The integrative action of the nervous system*. Cambridge University Press, Cambridge. Quoted by Joseph Bogen http://www.its.caltech.edu/~jbogen/text/mentali.htm

Shevrin, H., Dickman, S. (1980). The psychological unconscious: a necessary assumption for all psychological theory. *Am Psychol*, **35**(5), 421–434.

Shiffrin, R. M., Schneider, W. (1977). Controlled and automatic human information processing: II. Perceptual learning, automatic attending and a general theory. *Psychol Rev*, **84**(2), 127.

Shiffrin, R. M., Huber, D. E., Marinelli, K. (1995). Effects of category length and strength on familiarity in recognition. *J Exp Psychol Learn Mem Cogn*, **21**(2), 267–287.

Shimamura, A. P., Squire, L. R. (1984). Paired-associate learning and priming effects in amnesia: a neuropsychological study. *J Exp Psychol Gen*, **113**(4), 556–570.

Siapas, A. G., Lubenov, E. V., Wilson, M. A. (2005). Prefrontal phase locking to hippocampal theta oscillations. *Neuron*, **46**(1), 141–151.

Silver, M. A., Ress, D., Heeger, D. J. (2005). Topographic maps of visual spatial attention in human parietal cortex. *J Neurophysiol*, **94**(2), 1358–1371.

Simon, H. A., Chase, W. G. (1973). Skill in chess. *Am Sci*, **61**, 393–403.

Simon, H. A., Gilmartin, K. J. (1973). A simulation of memory for chess positions. *Cognit Psychol*, **5**, 29–46.

Simons, D. J. (2000). Attentional capture and inattentional blindness. *Trends Cogn Sci*, **4**(4), 147–155.

Simons, J. S., Spiers, H. J. (2003). Prefrontal and medial temporal lobe interactions in long-term memory. *Nat Rev Neurosci*, **4**(8), 637–648.

Singer, J. L. (1993). Experimental studies of ongoing conscious experience. *Ciba Found Symp*, **174**, 100–116; discussion 116–122.

Singer, W. (1994). A new job for the thalamus. *Nature*, **369**, 444–445.

Singh, K. D., Smith, A.T., Greenless, M. W. (2000). Spatiotemporal frequency and direction of sensitivities of human visual areas measured using fMRI. *NeuroImage*, **12**(5), 550–564.

Simpson, J. A., Weiner, E. S. C. (1989). *The Oxford English Dictionary*, 2nd edn. Oxford University Press/Clarendon Press, Oxford, New York.

Smith, A. M., Fried, P. A., Hogan, M. J., Cameron, I. (2006). Effects of prenatal marijuana on visuospatial working memory: an fMRI study in young adults. *Neurotoxicol Teratol*, **28**(2), 286–295.

Smith, E. E., Jonides, J. (1997). Working memory: A view from neuroimaging. *Cognit Psychol*, **33**(1), 5–42.

Smith, E. E., Jonides, J. (1998). Neuroimaging analysis of human working memory. *Proc Natl Acad Sci USA*, **95**(20), 12061–12068.

Smith, E. E., Jonides, J., Koeppe, R. A. (1996). Dissociating verbal and spatial working memory using PET. *Cereb Cortex*, **6**(1), 11–20.

Smith, M. L., Milner, B. (1984). Differential effects of frontal-lobe lesions on cognitive estimation and spatial memory. *Neuropsychologia*, **22**(6), 697–705.

Snodgrass, J. G., Vanderwart, M. (1980). A standardized set of 260 pictures: Norms for name agreement, image agreement, familiarity, and visual complexity. *J Exp Psychol [Hum Learn]*, **6**(2), 174–215.

Snowden, J. S., Griffiths, H. L., Neary, D. (1996). Semantic-episodic memory interactions in semantic dementia: implications for retrograde memory function. *Cogn Neuropsychol*, **13**(8), 1101–1139.

Sokoloff, L., Reivich, M., Kennedy, C. *et al.* (1977). The [14C]deoxyglucose method for the measurement of local cerebral glucose utilization: theory, procedure, and normal values in the conscious and anesthetized albino rat. *J Neurochem*, **28**(5), 897–916.

Sowell, E. R., Thompson, P. M., Peterson, B. S. *et al.* (2002). Mapping cortical gray matter asymmetry patterns in adolescents with heavy prenatal alcohol exposure. *Neuroimage*, **17**(4), 1807–1819.

Sowell, E. R., Peterson, B. S., Thompson, P. M., Welcome, S. E., Henkenius, A. L., Toga, A. W. (2003). Mapping cortical change across the human life span. *Nat Neurosci*, **6**(3), 309–315.

Spanagel, R., Weiss, F. (1999). The dopamine hypothesis of reward: past and current status. *Trends Neurosci*, **22**(11), 521–527.

Squire, L. R. (1992). Declarative and nondeclarative memory: multiple brain systems supporting learning and memory. *J Cogn Neurosci*, **4**(3), 232–243.

Squire, L. R., Alvarez, P. (1995). Retrograde amnesia and memory consolidation: a neurobiological perspective. *Curr Opin Neurobiol*, **5**(2), 169–177.

Squire, L. R., Bloom, F. E., McConnell, S. K., Roberts, J. L., Spitzer, N. C., Zigmond, M. J. (eds). (2003). *Fundamental neuroscience*, 2nd edn. San Diego: Elsevier Academic Press.

Srinivasan, R., Russell, D. P., Edelman, G. M., Tononi, G. (1999). Increased synchronization of neuromagnetic responses during conscious perception. *J Neurosci*, **19**(13), 5435–5448.

Stahnisch, F. W., Nitsch, R. (2002). Santiago Ramon y Cajal's concept of neuronal plasticity: the ambiguity lives on. *Trends Neurosci*, **25**(11), 589–591.

Standring, S. (ed.) (2005). *Gray's anatomy: the anatomical basis of clinical practice*, 39th edn. Churchill Livingstone, Edinburgh.

Stephan, K. M., Thaut, M. H., Wunderlich, G. *et al.* (2002). Conscious and subconscious sensorimotor synchronization – prefrontal cortex and the influence of awareness. *Neuroimage*, **15**(2), 345–352.

Steriade, M. (2006). Grouping of brain rhythms in cortico-thalamic systems. *Neuroscience*, **137**(4), 1087–1106.

Sternberg, R. J., Ben-Zeev, T. (2001). *Complex cognition: the psychology of human thought*. Oxford University Press, Oxford.

Stewart, F., Parkin, A. J., Hunkin, N. M. (1992). Naming impairments following recovery from herpes simplex encephalitis: Category-specific? *Q J Exp Psychol A*, **44**(2), 261–284.

Stickgold, R., Hobson, J. A., Fosse, R., Fosse, M. (2001). Sleep, learning, and dreams: off-line memory reprocessing. *Science*, **294**(5544), 1052–1057.

Stiles, J., Bates, E. A., Thal, D., Trauner, D.A., Reilly, J. (2002). Linguistic and spatial cognitive development in children with pre- and perinatal focal brain injury: a ten-year overview from the San Diego Longitudinal Project. In Johnson, M. H., Munakata, Y., Gilmore, R.O. (eds), *Brain development and cognition: a reader*, 2nd edn, pp. 272–291. Blackwell Publishing, Oxford.

Stiles, J., Reilly, J., Paul, B., Moses, P. (2005). Cognitive development following early brain injury: evidence for neural adaptation. *Trends Cogn Sci*, **9**(3), 136–143.

Stoerig, P., Zontanou, A., Cowey, A. (2002). Aware or unaware: assessment of cortical blindness in four men and a monkey. *Cereb Cortex*, **12**(6), 565–574.

Strauss, G. I., Hogh, P., Moller, K., Knudsen, G. M., Hansen, B. A., Larsen, F. S. (1999). Regional cerebral blood flow during mechanical hyperventilation in patients with fulminant hepatic failure. *Hepatology*, **30**(6), 1368–1373.

Stroop, J. R. (1935). Studies of interference in serial verbal reactions. *J Exp Psychol*, **18**, 643–662.

Stuss, D. T., Floden, D., Alexander, M. P., Levine, B., Katz, D. (2001). Stroop performance in focal lesion patients: dissociation of processes and frontal lobe lesion location. *Neuropsychologia*, **39**(8), 771–786.

Sussman, E. S. (2005). Integration and segregation in auditory scene analysis. *J Acoust Soc Am*, **117**(3 Pt 1), 1285–1298.

Sutherland, G. R., McNaughton, B. (2000). Memory trace reactivation in hippocampal and neocortical neuronal ensembles. *Curr Opin Neurobiol*, **10**(2), 180–186.

Talairach, J., Tournoux, P. (1988). *Co-planar stereotaxic atlas of the human brain: 3-dimensional proportional system: an approach to cerebral imaging*: Thieme Medical Publishers, Stuttgart.

Tallal, P. (2004). Improving language and literacy is a matter of time. *Nat Rev Neurosci*, **5**(9), 721–728.

Tammer, R., Ehrenreich, L., Boretius, S., Watanabe, T., Frahm, J., Michaelis, T. (2006). Compatibility of glass-guided recording microelectrodes in the brain stem of squirrel monkeys with high-resolution 3D MRI. *J Neurosci Meth*, **153**(2), 221–229.

Tanaka, K. (1996). Inferotemporal cortex and object vision. *Annu Rev Neurosci*, **19**, 109–139.

Taylor, F. B., Lowe, K., Thompson, C. *et al.* (2006). Daytime prazosin reduces psychological distress to trauma specific cues in civilian trauma posttraumatic stress disorder. *Biol Psychiatr*, **59**(7), 577–581.

Teyler, T. J., DiScenna, P. (1986). The hippocampal memory indexing theory. *Behav Neurosci*, **100**(2), 147–154.

Thatcher, R. W. (1992). Cyclic cortical reorganization during early childhood. *Brain Cogn*, **20**(1), 24–50.

Thottakara, P., Lazar, M., Johnson, S. C., Alexander, A. L. (2006). Application of Brodmann's area templates for ROI selection in white matter tractography studies. *Neuroimage*, **29**(3), 868–878.

Tiitinen, H., Salminen, N. H., Palomaki, K. J., Makinen, V. T., Alku, P., May, P. J. (2006). Neuromagnetic recordings reveal the temporal dynamics of auditory spatial processing in the human cortex. *Neurosci Lett*, **396**(1), 17–22.

Toga, A. W., Thompson, P. M., Sowell, E. R. (2006). Mapping brain maturation. *Trends Neurosci*, **29**(3), 148–159.

Tong, F. (2003). Primary visual cortex and visual awareness. *Nat Rev Neurosci*, **4**(3), 219–229.

Tong, F., Engel, S. A. (2001). Interocular rivalry revealed in the human cortical blind-spot representation. *Nature*, **411**(6834), 195–199.

Tong, F., Nakayama, K., Moscovitch, M., Weinrib, O., Kanwisher, N. (2000). Response properties of the human fusiform face area. *Cogn Neuropsychol*, **17**, 257–279.

Tong, F., Nakayama, K., Vaughan, J. T., Kanwisher, N. (1998). Binocular rivalry and visual awareness in human extrastriate cortex. *Neuron*, **21**(4), 753–759.

Tononi, G., Srinivasan, R., Russell, D. P., Edelman, G. M. (1998). Investigating neural correlates of conscious perception by frequency-tagged neuromagnetic responses. *Proc Natl Acad Sci U S A*, **95**(6), 3198–3203.

Tootell, R. B., Dale, A. M., Sereno, M. I., Malach, R. (1996). New images from human visual cortex. *Trends Neurosci*, **19**(11), 481–489.

Tourette, G. (1885). Etude sur une affection nerveuse caractérisée par de l'incorrdination motrice accompagné d'echolalie et de copralalie. *Arch Neurol*, **9**, 158–200.

Treisman, A. M., Gelade, G. (1980). A feature-integration theory of attention. *Cognit Psychol*, **12**(1), 97–136.

Tsao, D. Y., Freiwald, W. A., Tootell, R. B., Livingstone, M. S. (2006). A cortical region consisting entirely of face-selective cells. *Science*, **311**(5761), 670–674.

Tulving, E. (1972). Episodic and semantic memory. In Tulving, E., Donaldson, W., Bower, G. H. (eds), *Organization of memory*, pp 381–403. Academic Press, New York.

Tulving, E. (1985). How many memory systems are there. *Am Psychol*, **40**(4), 385–398.

Tulving, E. (2002). Episodic memory: from mind to brain. *Annu Rev Psychol*, **53**, 1–25.

Tyler, L. K., Moss, H. E. (2001). Towards a distributed account of conceptual knowledge. *Trends Cogn Sci*, **5**(6), 244–252.

Tzourio, N., Massioui, F. E., Crivello, F., Joliot, M., Renault, B., Mazoyer, B. (1997). Functional anatomy of human auditory attention studied with pet. *Neuroimage*, **5**(1), 63–77.

Tzourio-Mazoyer, N., De Schonen, S., Crivello, F., Reutter, B., Aujard, Y., Mazoyer, B. (2002). Neural correlates of woman face processing by 2-month-old infants. *Neuroimage*, **15**(2), 454–461.

Ungerleider, L. G., Mishkin, M. (1982). Two cortical visual systems. In Ingle, M. A., Goodale, M.A., Mansfield, J.W. (eds), *Analysis of visual behavior*. The MIT Press, Cambridge.

Ungless, M. A. (2004). Dopamine: The salient issue. *Trends Neurosci*, **27**(12), 702–706.

Unterrainer, J. M., Owen, A. M. (2006). Planning and problem solving: from neuropsychology to functional neuroimaging. *J Physiol Paris*, **99**(4–6), 308–317.

Vakil, E., Kahan, S., Huberman, M., Osman, A. (2000). Motor and non-motor sequence learning in patients with basal ganglia lesions: the case of serial reaction time (SRT). *Neuropsychologia*, **38**(1), 1–10.

Valet, M., Sprenger T., Boeck H., *et al.* (2004). Distraction modulates connectivity of the cingulo-frontal cortex and the midbrain during pain—an fMRI analysis, *Pain*, **109**, 399–408.

Van Essen, D. C. (2005). A population-average, landmark- and surface-based (PALS) atlas of human cerebral cortex. *Neuroimage*, **28**(3), 635–662.

Varela, F. *et al.* (2001). The brainwave: phase synchronization and large-scale integration. *Nat Neurosci*, **2**, 229–238.

Vargha-Khadem, F., Mishkin, M. (1997). Speech and language outcome after hemispherectomy in childhood. *Paediatr Epilepsy Syn Surg Treat*, 774–784.

Vargha-Khadem, F., Gadian, D. G., Copp, A., Mishkin, M. (2005). Foxp2 and the neuroanatomy of speech and language. *Nat Rev Neurosci*, **6**(2), 131–138.

Vigneau, M., Beaucousin, V., Herve, P. Y. *et al.* (2006). Meta-analyzing left hemisphere language areas: phonology, semantics, and sentence processing. *Neuroimage*, **30**(4), 1414–1432.

Vogeley, K., Kurthen, M., Falkai, P., Maier, W. (1999). Essential functions of the human self model are implemented in the prefrontal cortex. *Conscious Cogn*, **8**(3), 343–363.

Volavka, J., Mohammad, Y., Vitrai, J., Connolly, M., Stefanovic, M., Ford, M. (1995). Characteristics of state hospital patients arrested offenses committed during hospitalization. *Psychiatr Serv*, **46**(8), 796–800.

Volpe, J. J. (1987). Brain death determination in the newborn. *Pediatrics*, **80**(2), 293–297.

Vuilleumier, P. (2005). How brains beware: neural mechanisms of emotional attention. *Trends Cogn Sci*, **9**(12), 585–594.

Vuilleumier, P., Armony, J. L., Clarke, K., Husain, M., Driver, J., Dolan, R. J. (2002). Neural response to emotional faces with and without awareness: event-related fMRI in a parietal patient with visual extinction and spatial neglect. *Neuropsychologia*, **40**(12), 2156–2166.

Vuilleumier, P., Armony, J. L., Driver, J., Dolan, R. J. (2001). Effects of attention and emotion on face processing in the human brain: an event-related fmri study. *Neuron*, **30**(3), 829–841.

Vuilleumier, P., Armony, J. L., Driver, J., Dolan, R. J. (2003). Distinct spatial frequency sensitivities for processing faces and emotional expressions. *Nat Neurosci*, **6**(6), 624–631.

Walsh, V., Cowey, A. (2000). Transcranial magnetic stimulation and cognitive neuroscience. *Nat Rev Neurosci*, **1**(1), 73–79.

Ward L. M. (2003) Synchronous neural oscillations and cognitive processes. *Trends in Cognitive Sciences*, **7**(12), 553–559.

Wearing, D. (2005). *Forever today: a true story of lost memory and never-ending love*. Corgi Books, London.

Weems, S. A., Reggia, J. A. (2006). Simulating single word processing in the classic aphasia syndromes based on the Wemicke-Lichtheim-Geschwind theory. *Brain and Language*, **98**(3), 291–309.

Weiler, I. J., Hawrylak, N., Greenough, W. T. (1995). Morphogenesis in memory formation: synaptic and cellular mechanisms. *Behav Brain Res*, **66**(1–2), 1–6.

Weiskrantz, L. (1986). *Blindsight: a case study and implications*. Oxford University Press, Oxford.

Weiskrantz, L., Warrington, E. K., Sanders, M. D., Marshall, J. (1974). Visual capacity in the hemianopic field following a restricted occipital ablation. *Brain*, **97**(4), 709–728.

Welsh, M. C., Pennington, B. F., Ozonoff, S., Rouse, B., McCabe, E. R. (1990). Neuropsychology of early-treated phenylketonuria: specific executive function deficits. *Child Dev*, **61**(6), 1697–1713.

Werbos, P. (1974). *Beyond regression: new tools for prediction and analysis in the behavioral sciences*. Harvard University, Cambridge.

Werker, J. F., Vouloumanos, A. (2001). Speech and language processing in infancy: a neurocognitive approach. In Nelson, C. A. L. (ed.), *Handbook of developmental cognitive neuroscience*, 2nd edn, pp. 269–280. MIT Press, Cambridge.

Wernicke, C. (1874). *Der Aphasische Symptomencomplex: eine Psychologische Studie auf Anatomischer Basis*. Cohn and Weigert, Breslau.

Wertheimer, M. (1912). Experimentelle Studien über Sehen von Bewegung. *Zeits Psychol*, **61**, 161–265.

Wessinger, C. M., VanMeter, J., Tian, B., Van Lare, J., Pekar, J., Rauschecker, J. P. (2001). Hierarchical organization of the human auditory cortex revealed by functional magnetic resonance imaging. *J Cogn Neurosci*, **13**(1), 1–7.

Westmacott, R., Black, S. E., Freedman, M., Moscovitch, M. (2004). The contribution of autobiographical significance to semantic memory: evidence from Alzheimer's disease, semantic dementia, and amnesia. *Neuropsychologia*, **42**(1), 25–48.

Wexler, M. (2001). Two new face illusions. *Trends Cogn Sci*, **5**(4), 137.

Whalen, P. J., Kagan, J., Cook, R. G. *et al.* (2004). Human amygdala responsivity to masked fearful eye whites. *Science*, **306**(5704), 2061.

Wheeler M. E., Buckner R. L. (2004). Functional-anatomic correlates of remembering and knowing. *NeuroImage*, 21:1337–1349.

White, J. A. (2002). Action potentials. In Ramachandran, V. S. (ed.), *Encyclopedia of the human brain*. Academic Press, San Diego.

Wicker, B., Keysers, C., Plailly, J., Royet, J., Gallese, V., and Rizzolatti, G. (2003a). Both of us disgusted in my insula, the common neural basis of seeing and feeling disgust. *Neuron*, **40**(3), 655–664.

Wicker, B., Ruby, P., Royet, J. P., Fonlupt, P. (2003b). A relation between rest and the self in the brain? *Brain Res Brain Res Rev*, **43**(2), 224–230.

Wigg, C. L., Martin, A. (1998). Properties and mechanisms of perceptual priming. *Curr Opin Neurobiol*, **8**, 227–233.

Williams, J., Waiter, G., Perra, O., Perrett, D., Whiten, A. (2005). An fMRI study of joint attention experience. *NeuroImage*, **25**, 133–140.

Willingham, D. B. (1998). A neuropsychological theory of motor skill learning. *Psychol Rev*, **105**(3), 558–584.

Willingham, D. B., Nissen, M. J., Bullemer, P. (1989). On the development of procedural knowledge. *J Exp Psychol Learn Mem Cogn*, **15**(6), 1047–1060.

Wilson, B. A., Baddeley, A. D., Kapur, N. (1995). Dense amnesia in a professional musician following herpes simplex virus encephalitis. *J Clin Exp Neuropsychol*, **17**(5), 668–681.

Wise, R. A. (2002). Brain reward circuitry: insights from unsensed incentives. *Neuron*, **36**(2), 229–240.

Witte, E. A., Marrocco, R. T. (1997). Alteration of brain noradrenergic activity in rhesus monkeys affects the alerting component of covert orienting. *Psychopharmacology (Berl)*, **132**(4), 315–323.

Woldorff, M. G., Tempelmann, C., Fell, J. *et al.* (1999). Lateralized auditory spatial perception and the contralaterality of cortical processing as studied with functional magnetic resonance imaging and magnetoencephalography. *Hum Brain Mapp*, **7**(1), 49–66.

Wolfe, J. M. (2003). Moving towards solutions to some enduring controversies in visual search. *Trends Cogn Sci*, **7**(2), 70–76.

Wunderlich, K., Schneider, K. A., Kastner, S. (2005). Neural correlates of binocular rivalry in the human lateral geniculate nucleus. *Nat Neurosci*, **8**(11), 1595–1602.

Wyvell, C. L., Berridge, K. C. (2000). Intra-accumbens amphetamine increases the conditioned incentive salience of sucrose reward: enhancement of reward 'wanting' without enhanced 'liking' or response reinforcement. *J Neurosci*, **20**(21), 8122–8130.

Yakovlev, P. I., Lecours, A. R. (1967). The myelogenetic cycles of regional maturation of the brain. In Minokowski, A. (ed.), *Regional development of the brain in early life*, pp 3–70. Davis, Philadelphia.

Yang, T. T., Gallen, C. C., Ramachandran, V. S., Cobb, S., Schwartz, B. J., Bloom, F. E. (1994). Noninvasive detection of cerebral plasticity in adult human somatosensory cortex. *Neuroreport*, **5**(6), 701–704.

Yarbus, A. F. (1967). *Eye movements and vision*. Plenum Press, New York.

Yin, H. H., Knowlton, B. J. (2006). The role of the basal ganglia in habit formation. *Nat Rev Neurosci*, **7**(6), 464–476.

Yonelinas, A. P. (2002). The nature of recollection and familiarity: a review of 30 years of research. *J Mem Lang*, **46**(3), 441–517.

Yonelinas, A. P., Otten, L. J., Shaw, K. N., Rugg, M. D. (2005). Separating the brain regions involved in recollection and familiarity in recognition memory. *J Neurosci*, **25**(11), 3002–3008.

Yzerbyt, V. Y., Lories, G., Dardenne, B. (eds). (1998). *Metacognition: Cognitive and Social Dimensions*. Sage Publications, Thousand Oaks.

Zaidel, E., Kasher, A., Soroker, N., Batori, G., Giora, R., Graves, D. (2000). Hemispheric contributions to pragmatics. *Brain Cogn*, **43**(1–3), 438–443.

Zaidel, E., Zaidel, D. W., Bogen, J. E. (2002). The split brain. In Ramachandran, V. S. (ed.), *Encyclopedia of the human brain*. Academic Press, San Diego.

Zatorre, R. J. (2002). Auditory cortex. In Ramachandran V. S. (ed.), *Encyclopedia of the human brain*. Academic Press, San Diego.

Zatorre, R. J., & Halpern, A. R. (2005). Mental concerts: Musical imagery and auditory cortex. *Neuron*, **47**(1), 9–12.

Zeki, S. (2003). Improbable areas in the visual brain. *Trends Neurosci*, **26**(1), 23–26.

Zeki, S. M. (1974). Functional organization of a visual area in the posterior bank of the superior temporal sulcus of the rhesus monkey. *J Physiol*, **236**(3), 549–573.

Zeki, S. M. (1977). Colour coding in the superior temporal sulcus of rhesus monkey visual cortex. *Proc R Soc Lond B Biol Sci*, **197**(1127), 195–223.

Zhao, F., Wang, P., Hendrich, K., Ugurbil, K., Kim, S. G. (2006). Cortical layer-dependent BOLD and CBV responses measured by spin-echo and gradient-echo fMRI: insights into hemodynamic regulation. *Neuroimage*, **30**(4), 1149–1160.

Zheng, X., Rajapakse, J. C. (2006). Learning functional structure from FMR images. *Neuroimage*, **31**(4), 1601–1613.

Index